W9-BBX-522

How will you **benefit** from using the S.O.S. Edition tools?

✓ **Reinforces** textbook concepts.

✓ Provides **feedback** on your learning progress.

✓ Helps you **maximize** your study time.

✓ Adds **variety** to your study routine.

✓ **Supports** you with live tutors who can answer your questions and help you master the text.

✓ Gives you more **control** over your grade!

" The students benefit from the individualized study plan that identifies their weak and strong areas. It saves them time because they are more aware of what they need to study. Taking the pre- and post-tests enhances their test-taking skills, and ultimately helps them earn better grades on their chapter exams. "

— **Professor Teresa R. Stalvey,
North Florida Community College***

A better grade is right here at your fingertips!

WWW.SOSEDITION.COM

What's the best way to **review** concepts and **practice** for exams?

It's built right into your textbook!

Printed Practice Tests with Answers

Practice makes perfect when you have the right tools. What better way to review textbook concepts than with tools built in to the back of your textbook. Master the text material by utilizing the Practice Tests at the end of your S.O.S. Edition. You'll find multiple-choice and fill-in-the-blank questions for every chapter, organized by the major text sections to help you quickly connect the concepts. Answers are included for all questions to help you measure your performance. What's more, all Practice Tests are perforated so you can remove them and take them with you!

> " I recommend that students take the Practice Test after they have read each chapter. The students that use them do better on my exams. "
>
> — **Professor Jarvis Gamble,**
> **Owens Community College**

For demonstration purposes, samples shown are from one of our Allyn & Bacon / Longman S.O.S. Editions.

How well do **you** want to do in this course?

A better grade starts here.

Register today for your S.O.S. Edition's online grade-boosting tools.

(Your registration code is included at the back of this textbook.)

A L L Y N & B A C O N

Introducing the **S.O.S. Edition** for
Psychology: The Brain, The Person, The World...

Get ready to Study... Organize... and _Succeed_!

We give you the tools to take control and succeed in your course!

✓ Practice Tests
✓ TestXL – Online Test Prep
✓ Tutor Center – Live Tutor Support

Want help mastering the course?
Looking to change that B to an A?

Our S.O.S Edition for *Psychology: The Brain, The Person, The World* offers a personalized study and review system that helps you master psychological concepts, save time studying, and perform better on exams.

With the purchase of this textbook, you get a powerful combination of tools that includes Practice Tests with Answers, live tutoring assistance from our Tutor Center, and access to our TestXL online diagnostic testing and review system. With the S.O.S. Edition tools, you can test with confidence and complete your course with greater comprehension and higher grades!

Read on to find out how...

you go out and buy a magnet to help you with a repetitive-stress injury caused by typing too many term papers!

WHAT DO WE MEAN BY ABNORMAL BEHAVIOR?

This is an easy question to ask but a surprisingly difficult one to answer. Is talking to yourself abnormal? What about feeling depressed for weeks and weeks after a break-up? Or drinking a bottle of vodka with friends on the weekend? Drawing the line between what is abnormal and what is just human behavior can be difficult sometimes. No two of us are alike, and although some of us can exhibit behaviors that are considered quirky, indulgent, or experimental, others with similar behavior may be considered mentally ill, afflicted, or addicted.

It may come as a surprise to you that there is still no universal agreement about what we mean by *abnormality* or *disorder*. This is not to say we do not have definitions.

The S.O.S. Edition Practice Tests (right) include questions for every major section of the textbook (above), providing you with a thorough review of the material.

PRACTICE TESTS

CHAPTER 1 Abnormal Psychology: An Overview

What Do We Mean by Abnormal Behavior?

1. Which of the following statements about the terms "abnormality" and "disorder" is true?
   a. Universally agreed upon definitions exist for each of these terms.
   b. While there is cross-cultural agreement on how to define "abnormality," there is still much debate as to how to define "disorder."
   c. While there is no consensus on how to define these terms, there is much agreement about which conditions are disorders and which are not.
   d. In order for "abnormality" to be viewed as a "disorder," it must have an identified physiological basis.

2. Why is it important to have a classification system for mental disorders?
   a. Classification systems allow for information about disorders to be structured in a useful manner.
   b. Research advances can only be made when we know what we should be studying.
   c. Classifying conditions as mental disorders establishes the range of problems that mental health professional can address.
   d. All of the above are true.

3. Which of the following is a disadvantage of establishing a classification scheme for mental disorders?
   a. Classification leads to a loss of information.
   b. Physiological causes for abnormal behavior are ignored once a condition is determined to be a mental disorder.
   c. Psychotherapy is less likely to be used once a disorder has been labeled.
   d. Classification schemes are inherently an impediment to research advances.

4. Which of the following is *not* an element of the DSM-IV-TR definition of mental disorders?
   a. Disorders are associated with distress, disability, or an increased risk of other serious consequences (such as death or loss of freedom).
   b. A disorder is not a culturally accepted and expected response to a particular life event.
   c. Disorders have identifiable causes.
   d. Deviant behavior is not a sign of a mental disorder unless specifically defined as a symptom of dysfunction.

5. Clinically significant depression
   a. is only seen in Western cultures.
   b. is probably experienced in all cultures.
   c. must not exist in some cultures as there is no word in the language equivalent to the word "depressed" in English.
   d. can only be identified when there are obvious signs of emotional pain.

6. Which of the following is an example of a culture-specific disorder?
   a. Depression
   b. Schizophrenia
   c. Kana
   d. Koro

7. Which of the following is almost universally considered to be the product of a mental disorder?
   a. Hearing the voice of a dead relative
   b. Believing a number to be unlucky
   c. Engaging in deviant behaviors
   d. Believing things that no one else believes

How Common Are Mental Disorders?

8. _____ is the study of the distribution of diseases or disorders in a given population.
   a. Epidemiology
   b. Prevalence
   c. Distribution
   d. Incidence

9. "There were 30 new cases of disease Z identified during the last month." This statement describes the _____ of disease Z.
   a. lifetime prevalence
   b. point prevalence
   c. 1-month prevalence
   d. incidence

10. Which of the following frequency measures includes those who have recovered from the disorder in question?
   a. Lifetime prevalence
   b. Point prevalence.
   c. 1-month prevalence
   d. Incidence

11. Which of the following types of disorders has the highest 1-year prevalence?
   a. Any mood disorder
   b. Any anxiety disorder
   c. Any substance-use disorder
   d. Schizophrenia

PT-1

For demonstration purposes, samples shown are from one of our Allyn & Bacon / Longman S.O.S. Editions.

A better grade is right here at your fingertips!

WWW.SOSEDITION.COM

Jump-start your grade with our **TestXL** online test prep system!

Who doesn't want better grades?

About **TestXL**

Designed specifically to help enhance your performance, this S.O.S. Edition's online test preparation system gauges your prior knowledge of content and creates a unique Individualized Study Plan to help you pinpoint exactly where additional study and review is needed. You can follow the plan as a guide to focus your efforts and improve upon areas of weakness with one-on-one assistance from our qualified tutors and/or by utilizing the printed Practice Tests in the back of the textbook. Additional testing features in this program help you assess your progress with the textbook material to reach your ultimate goal of success in the course.

> **❝** I like the fact that I can take a pre-test before I study the course material to test how much I know, and then I can take the post-test to see my improvement. **❞**
> — *Natalie Ricks, student**

Knowing what to study is key to your success.

TestXL Pre-Test

Why waste time studying what you already know? TestXL's Pre-Test helps you measure your level of understanding of the material in each chapter. After logging in to the S.O.S. Edition online program, you'll find the Table of Contents for your textbook, with links to Pre-Test, Post-Test, and Study Plan. Choose your chapter of interest and select Pre-Test to assess your existing knowledge about the subject matter.

You'll be prompted with multiple questions per major topic area in each chapter. Complete all of the questions, submit the test, and TestXL will produce your Individualized Study Plan (see next page) based on the results to help you focus your study efforts where they're needed most.

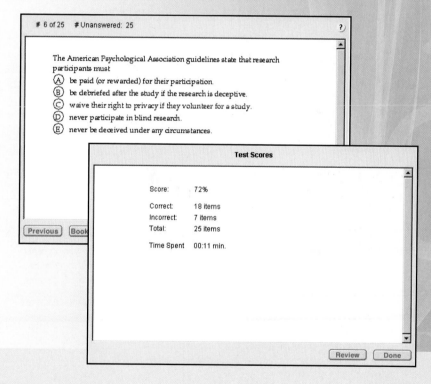

With the Pre-Tests, I feel like I'm learning more by being directed to specific text pages for additional study.

— **Bridget San Angelo, student***

TestXL Post-Test

Measure your progress with Post-Tests for each chapter. Organized exactly like the Pre-Tests, with multiple questions per major topic area, the Post-Tests show you how much you've improved, or where you need continued help. Continue to take the Post-Tests as often as you like, revisiting your progress in the Study Plan, which is updated every time a test is taken.

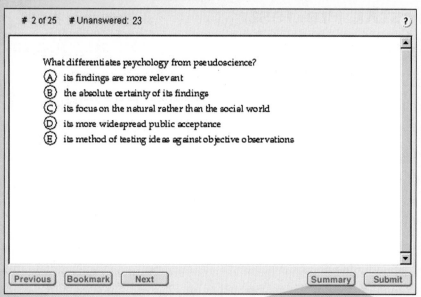

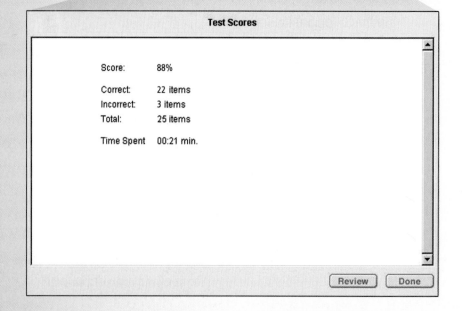

> **Each time I take a post-test, I see an improvement in my test score. It challenges me to see if I can better my score until it's perfect.**
>
> — *Tammi Smith, student**

TestXL Individualized Study Plan

Maximize your study time by reviewing and following your very own Study Plan created from the results of your Pre- and Post-Tests. The Study Plan quickly identifies your areas of weakness and strength in a clear outline, directing you back to specific areas in your textbook (section heads) for further study. The Study Plan helps you immediately pinpoint where additional time is needed, so you can feel confident about where you're saving time! Use this customized guide to re-study material as necessary for mastery of the material and success on your tests and in your course.

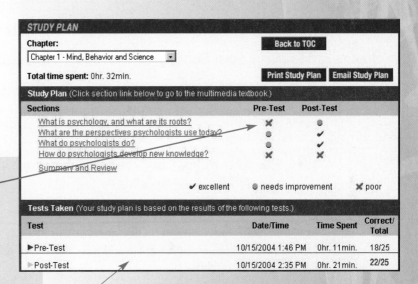

For each major topic in the chapter (shown in blue), the Study Plan "grades" your understanding based on your Pre-Test results. Ratings of "Excellent," "Needs Improvement," and "Poor" are used to identify areas of strength and weakness.

Post-Test results are included after you participate in this next stage (see opposite page). Note how most areas have improved after the Post-Test.

The Study Plan keeps a log of your Pre- and Post-Test activity, noting time spent as well as score summaries. Additional Post-Test results will appear here. You can take the Post-Tests as many times as you like, until you're comfortable with your level of mastery of the material.

> " The Individualized Study Plans help me study at a faster pace by focusing on my underscored areas. "
> — *Kim Skains, student**

Need additional assistance studying or completing assignments?

One-on-One Tutoring!

The Tutor Center

www.ablongman.com/tutorcenter

Our Tutor Center from Addison-Wesley Higher Education provides one-on-one tutoring to registered students. Our tutors are qualified college instructors who assist students with both questions and concepts from the textbook as well as any publisher-authored technology used in the course. The center is open during peak student studying hours from **Sunday to Thursday, 5PM to midnight EST,** when professors are usually unavailable. Students are offered multiple channels for tutor contact — toll-free phone, email, fax, and interactive web — affording various learning opportunities, both auditory and visual, to get through even the most difficult concepts. **Be sure to visit our website for more details!**

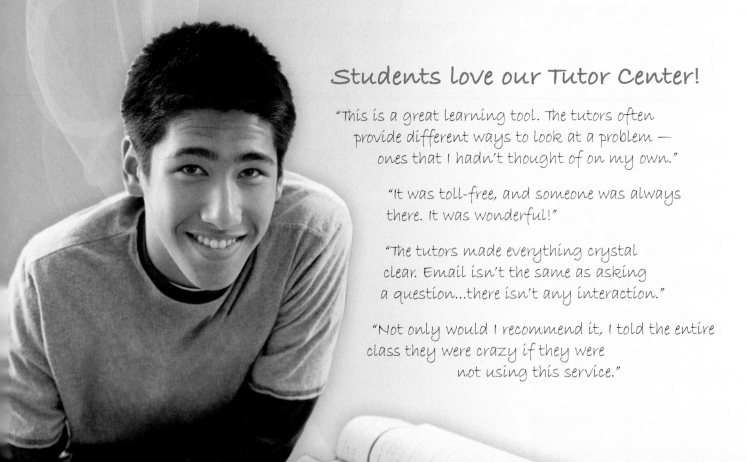

Students love our Tutor Center!

"This is a great learning tool. The tutors often provide different ways to look at a problem — ones that I hadn't thought of on my own."

"It was toll-free, and someone was always there. It was wonderful!"

"The tutors made everything crystal clear. Email isn't the same as asking a question...there isn't any interaction."

"Not only would I recommend it, I told the entire class they were crazy if they were not using this service."

A support service that's available when your instructor isn't! Our qualified tutors are on hand to assist you during key studying hours – from Sunday to Thursday, 5PM to midnight EST, during the school term.

The Tutor Center

Addison-Wesley • Allyn & Bacon • Benjamin Cummings • Longman

❝What I benefited from the most was the Tutor Center. I am a working mother, and to have the opportunity to come home late at night and still be able to have someone to help me is a true blessing. ❞

— *Jennifer Kelly, student*

A better grade is right here at your fingertips!

WWW.SOSEDITION.COM

Getting started on the path to success is **quick** and **easy!**

✓ **Take advantage of the Practice Tests**

At any point in your studies, you can use these tests to quiz yourself, prepare for exams, or simply gain understanding of the most important concepts in each chapter of this textbook.

✓ **Access your online resources**

The Student Starter Kit packaged with this textbook gives you a **FREE 6-month subscription** to the S.O.S. Edition's TestXL program and Tutor Center resources. You'll find your access code under the tear-off tab in the back of your book. **Follow these quick and easy steps...**

1 **GET YOUR CODE.**

Open your S.O.S. Edition to the inside back cover to find your code.

2 **LOG ON TO www.sosedition.com** and **CHOOSE YOUR TEXTBOOK.**

3 CLICK "REGISTER" AND ENTER YOUR ACCESS CODE.

4 THAT'S IT!

You'll find the table of contents for your book with links to Pre-Test, Post-Test, and Study Plan to get started.

A better grade is right here at your fingertips!

WWW.SOSEDITION.COM

Bring more balance to your life.

If you're like most other students, you need every minute
of your studying to count and you want better grades.
Take advantage of the complete suite of tools in the S.O.S. Edition
to maximize your valuable study time and succeed in your course.
From our Practice Tests to our Tutor Center and TestXL program,
everything you need to master your course
is right here at your fingertips.

Register today for your S.O.S. Edition's
online grade-boosting tools.
www.sosedition.com

PEARSON

Allyn & Bacon

* (about TestXL used in our MyPsychLab product)

Psychology
The Brain, the Person, the World

S.O.S. Edition

Stephen M. Kosslyn
Harvard University

Robin S. Rosenberg
Adjunct Faculty
Lesley University

PEARSON

Boston   New York   San Francisco
Mexico City   Montreal   Toronto   London   Madrid   Munich   Paris
Hong Kong   Singapore   Tokyo   Cape Town   Sydney

Associate Developmental Editor, Practice Tests: Jennifer Trebby
Editorial Production Service and Electronic Composition: Omegatype Typography, Inc.
Composition and Prepress Buyer: Linda Cox
Manufacturing Buyer: Megan Cochran
Cover Designer, S.O.S Edition: Rubin Pfeffer

Copyright © 2005   Pearson Education, Inc.

All rights reserved. No part of the material protected by this copyright notice may be
reproduced or utilized in any form or by any means, electronic or mechanical, including
photocopying, recording, or by any information storage and retrieval system, without
written permission from the copyright owner.

To obtain permission(s) to use material from this work, please submit a written request to
Allyn and Bacon, Permissions Department, 75 Arlington Street, Boston, MA 02116 or
fax your request to 617-848-7320.

ISBN   0-205-45588-3

Printed in the United States of America

10   9   8   7   6   5   4   3   2   1   VHP   09   08   07   06   05   04

secondedition

Psychology

The Brain, the Person, the World

Stephen M. Kosslyn

Harvard University

Robin S. Rosenberg

Adjunct Faculty
Lesley University

PEARSON

Boston   New York   San Francisco
Mexico City   Montreal   Toronto   London   Madrid   Munich   Paris
Hong Kong   Singapore   Tokyo   Cape Town   Sydney

To Nathaniel, David, and Justin,
for showing us how psychology really works

Executive Editor: Carolyn Merrill
Series Editorial Assistant: Carolyn Mullroy
Senior Development Editor: Lisa McLellan
Senior Marketing Manager: Wendy Gordon
Production Editor: Michael Granger
Editorial Production Service: Andrea Cava
Composition Buyer: Linda Cox
Manufacturing Buyer: Megan Cochran
Cover Administrator: Linda Knowles
Electronic Composition: Omegatype Typography, Inc.
Photo Research: Sarah Evertson, Image Quest
Fine Art Research: Helane M. Prottas
Text Design: Carol Somberg

For related titles and support materials, visit our online catalog at www.ablongman.com.

Copyright © 2004, 2001 Pearson Education, Inc.

All rights reserved. No part of the material protected by this copyright notice may be reproduced or utilized in any form or by any means, electronic or mechanical, including photocopying, recording, or by any information storage and retrieval system, without written permission from the copyright owner.

To obtain permission(s) to use material from this work, please submit a written request to Allyn and Bacon, Permissions Department, 75 Arlington Street, Boston, MA 02116 or fax your request to 617-848-7320.

Between the time Website information is gathered and then published, some sites may have closed. Also, the transcription of URLs can result in typographical errors. The publisher would appreciate notification where these errors occur so that they may be corrected in subsequent editions.

Library of Congress Cataloging-in-Publication Data
Kosslyn, Stephen Michael, 1948–
    Psychology: the brain, the person, the world / Stephen M. Kosslyn. — 2nd ed.
        p. cm.
    Includes bibliographical references and index.
    ISBN 0-205-37609-6 (alk. paper)
    1. Psychology. I. Title.
BF121 .K59 2004
150—dc21

                                                    2003043710

Credits appear on pages C-1–C-2, which should be considered an extension of the copyright page.

Printed in the United States of America

10   9   8   7   6   5   4   3   VHP   08   07   06   05   04

Brief Contents

Contents

chapter 1

Psychology: *Yesterday and Today* 2

chapter 2

The Research Process: *How We Find Things Out* 32

---

chapter 3

The Biology of Mind and Behavior   70

chapter 6

Learning   *210*

chapter 9

Types of Intelligence: *What Does It Mean to Be Smart?* 346

chapter 12

Psychology Over the Life Span: *Growing Up, Growing Older, Growing Wiser* 480

chapter **15**

Treatment 622

Preface

How can we write a book that engages students and provides them with an *integrated* introduction to the field of psychology? That is what we asked each other as we began writing this textbook. One of us is a cognitive neuroscientist and the other a clinical psychologist. In writing collaboratively, we began to see how our different areas of psychology were dovetailing. Our teaching experiences convinced us that the different areas of psychology really do reflect different facets of the same whole—and we are inspired to try to bring this view to a larger audience. We also wanted to show students how to apply the results of psychological research to make learning and remembering easier—not just for this course, but for any course, from economics to art history, and for the demands of life in general.

Our Vision: Brain, Person, World

Our vision is a textbook that better integrates the field of psychology. We do this by exploring how psychology can be viewed from the levels of the brain, the person, and the world. This theme is reflected in the overall organization of the text and its individual chapters.

The key to this book is the idea that psychology can best be understood in terms of events that occur at different *levels of analysis*: the brain (biological factors), the person (beliefs, desires, and feelings), and the world or group (social, cultural, and environmental factors). We stress that none of these events occur in isolation. Not only do all of these events occur in the world, where we are bathed with specific stimuli and behave in accordance with certain goals, but also these events are constantly interacting. For example, our brains are affected by our beliefs (just think of how worrying can make our bodies become tense), and our social interactions both shape and are affected by our beliefs. In fact, as we discuss in this book, social interactions can actually cause the genes in our brains to operate differently. All psychological events, from group interactions to psychological disorders to memory and creativity can best be understood by considering events at all three levels and

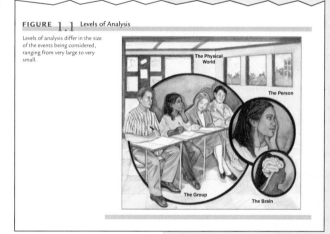

FIGURE 1.1 Levels of Analysis

Levels of analysis differ in the size of the events being considered, ranging from very large to very small.

The Physical World

The Person

The Group

The Brain

how they interact, both with the world and with each other. This view of psychology is exciting because it offers a way to organize a diverse range of theories and discoveries. Different fields of psychology are interconnected, although they are not often presented this way in textbooks. We wrote this book because no other textbook, in our opinion, was able to successfully connect the diverse fields of psychology.

Greater Emphasis on the *Science* of Psychology

In this edition, we have added a chapter on research methods (Chapter 2). Given our emphasis on the science of psychology, we decided that students really need to see this material in one place. This chapter describes the scientific method, types of studies that psychologists typically conduct, and fundamental concepts of statistics. In addition, we describe a novel way to conceptualize and analyze research. This method relies on clearly understanding the Question that is asked, the Alternative answers that are considered, and the Logic of the study, as well as the Method, Results, and Inferences you can draw from the results. In Chapter 2, we use this method to take a detailed look at a specific study, and we continue to use it in each subsequent chapter to examine one study in detail, in a new feature called "Understanding Research."

Text Organization

Most psychology textbooks have anywhere from 16 to 22 chapters; ours has 16. Market research has shown that when using textbooks with more chapters, introductory psychology instructors often end up skipping parts in the interest of time, or requiring students to read multiple chapters per week. Neither option is ideal, and both are likely to result in only a superficial grasp of the field as a whole. Because introductory psychology is intended to be a survey of the entire field, we believe that a book with fewer chapters would allow students to sample all the areas of psychology. We have carefully chosen core and cutting-edge concepts, theories, and findings, to give students a deeper understanding of the field.

We have combined several topics that are best covered in a more integrated manner. For example, Chapter 4 covers both sensation and perception. These two topics are strongly related, and recent brain research suggests that the same brain systems underlie both types of phenomena. Combining the two topics in one chapter makes it easier for students to see how sensation and perception work to achieve the same ends, specifically, the identification of stimuli and the representation of spatial relations.

Similarly, Chapter 10 discusses the essentials of emotion and motivation in one chapter. The reason for including the two topics in one chapter is straightforward: Emotion is a major factor that motivates us. By beginning the chapter with emotion, we are able to show how dramatic breakthroughs in the study of emotion (which have occurred, in part, because of discoveries about the brain) can illuminate aspects of human motivation.

We also include a single chapter on social psychology, Chapter 16. This chapter is further divided into two sections: social cognition and social behavior, the traditional domains of the field. Again, by including both topics in a single chapter, we are better able to show how they are related. Students learn how cognition about other people's beliefs, desires, and feelings plays a key role in our social interactions.

Pedagogical Features

Chapter Story

We begin each chapter with a different story about a person or group. The story is then elaborated throughout the chapter, providing a framework for the chapter's discussion of relevant psychological theories and research. These stories serve several purposes. They allow students to see how the psychological material covered in the chapter might apply to people outside of a psychological laboratory. This also makes the material more interesting and applicable to their lives, thus facilitating learning and remembering. In addition, the story integrates the various topics addressed within a chapter, creating a coherent, thematic whole to further enhance student understanding. Finally, the story itself provides retrieval cues to help students remember the material. In the second edition, we have introduced new stories in Chapters 2 (Research Methods), 4 (Sensation and Perception),

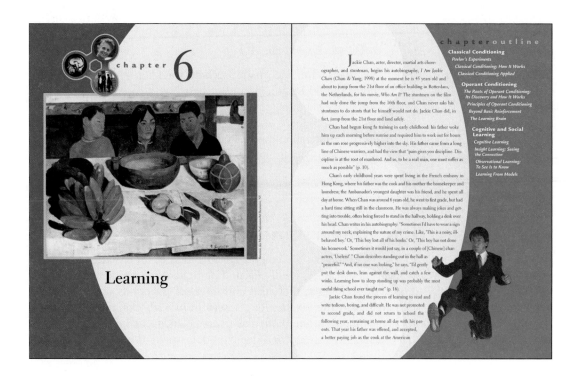

6 (Learning), 7 (Memory), and 8 (Language and Thinking). For instance, Chapter 6, the chapter on learning principles, discusses martial arts film director, actor, and choreographer Jackie Chan. As readers learn more about Chan's life over the course of the chapter, they also learn more about learning principles and their applications. Because readers are likely to remember his biographical information, they will also remember a lot about learning principles.

The chapter story is continued at the beginning of each section. This fosters integration with the rest of the chapter and introduces each section's topic in an applied context.

Looking at Levels

At the end of each section, we take some aspect of that section's content—a theory, a research study, the application of a psychological phenomenon—and consider it from three levels of analysis: the brain, the person, and the group, as well as interactions among events at each level. For instance, the section on sleep in Chapter 5 examines jet lag from the point of view of the brain (what happens at the biological level), the person (how jet lag affects the person's beliefs, desires, and feelings), and the group (how it affects interactions with others). We then show how events at the three levels affect one another. The events in the brain, for instance, clearly affect social interactions—if you're jet lagged, you will be slower and possibly more irritable in your interactions with others.

The information in the "Looking at Levels" feature serves to integrate knowledge about the brain; personal beliefs, desires, and feelings; and group interactions. We integrate these diverse types of knowledge within each chapter, rather than relegating such information to only one or two chapters. This feature also forges bridges that reach across chapters, leading to more effective learning and remembering.

Test Yourself!

At the end of each major section, we ask general questions that students should be able to answer based on a careful reading of the material. We encourage students to answer these questions *before* they go to the website (www.ablongman/kosslyn2e) to see our answers. These questions should help students identify which concepts they've mastered, and which topics will need more of their attention before moving on.

Understanding Research

Certain basic elements are included in all research reports. In this new feature, we discuss and illustrate these elements, which will help students as they read and interpret published research studies and also write up their own research. In each chapter, we walk students through one particular research study so they can understand the content in greater depth and learn to think critically about research.

Hands On!

In most chapters we have included at least one Hands On! feature, which is a demonstration of psychological phenomena for students to try alone or with others. The brief exercises will (1) provide students with another way to learn about the phenomenon—experiencing, not merely reading about it; (2) make the material more vivid, thereby enhancing students' attention and memory; and (3) put psychological principles into a concrete context, showing students that the principles really can affect how we think, feel, and behave.

The minidemonstrations include:

Introspection (p. 11)
Simulated participation in a research study (pp. 45–46)
Measured neural conduction time (p. 76)
Transduction in the retina (p. 128)
Finding your blind spot (p. 129)
Dark adaptation (p. 129)
Seeing afterimages (p. 131)
Ambiguous figures (p. 136)
Motion cues (p. 139)
Recognition and identification (pp. 141–142)
Pop-out (p. 146)
The Stroop Effect (p. 148)
Kinesthetic sense (p. 163)
Meditation (pp. 195–196)
Mental image and classical conditioning (p. 221)
Chunking (p. 257)

Modality-specific memory (p. 259)
Lincoln's head on a penny (p. 269)
False memory (pp. 281, 283)
Interactive images (p. 290)
Method of loci (pp. 290–291)
Pegword systems (p. 291)
Rhyming words (p. 291)
Building mnemonics (p. 292)
Memory enhancing techniques (pp. 293–294)
Discovering syntax (p. 303)
Mental imagery (pp. 320–322)
Prototypes (pp. 325–326)
The hiking monk problem (p. 329)
The candle problem (p. 329)
Wason and Johnson-Laird's card task (p. 338)

Mental models (p. 338)
Representativeness (p. 340)
"Fake" personality readings (p. 439)
Prochaska self-test (p. 550)
Suicide misconceptions self-test (pp. 583, 584)
Progressive muscle relaxation (p. 626)
Cognitive dissonance (p. 678)
Asch experiment (pp. 704–705)

Consolidate!

We've included several features at the end of the chapter to help students further consolidate what they have learned and provide an opportunity for additional learning by applying the material to new situations.

Summary. At the close of each chapter is a section-by-section review of the material. These summaries highlight key points that students should know after a thorough reading of the material. This feature helps consolidate the core material even further in memory.

Think It Through. Critical thinking questions called "Think It Through" are provided for each section of the chapter. These questions ask students to apply the material to real-world settings and the opening story, and require them to think deeply about the material. Such active processing enhances memory.

Key Terms. We provide a list of key terms, including page references, to aid in student mastery of key vocabulary.

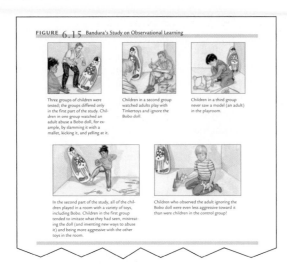

FIGURE 6.15 Bandura's Study on Observational Learning

Three groups of children were tested; the groups differed only in the first part of the study. Children in one group watched an adult abuse a Bobo doll, for example, by slamming it with a mallet, kicking it, and yelling at it.

Children in a second group watched adults play with Tinkertoys and ignore the Bobo doll.

Children in a third group never saw a model (an adult) in the playroom.

In the second part of the study, all of the children played in a room with a variety of toys, including Bobo. Children in the first group tended to imitate what they had seen, mistreating the doll (and inventing new ways to abuse it) and being more aggressive with the other toys in the room.

Children who observed the adult ignoring the Bobo doll were even less aggressive toward it than were children in the control group!

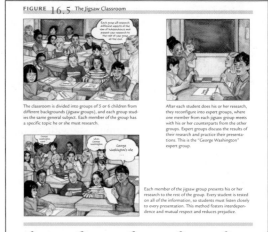

FIGURE 16.5 The Jigsaw Classroom

The classroom is divided into groups of 5 or 6 children from different backgrounds (jigsaw groups), and each group studies the same general subject. Each member of the group has a specific topic he or she must research.

After each student does his or her research, they reconfigure into expert groups, where one member from each jigsaw group meets with his or her counterparts from the other groups. Expert groups discuss the results of their research and practice their presentations. This is the "George Washington" expert group.

Each member of the jigsaw group presents his or her research to the rest of the group. Every student is tested on all of the information, so students must listen closely to every presentation. This method fosters interdependence and mutual respect and reduces prejudice.

Illustration Program: Visualizing Information

The second edition includes two major refinements of the art. First, we adopted a clearer style of drawings. Many of the most important studies are not only described in the text but are also visually demonstrated in step-by-step illustrations. These multimodal presentations enhance learning in several ways. (1) The panel illustrations walk students through each study, allowing them to understand its details more fully. (2) The clear, uncomplicated illustrations use perceptual principles to convey information effectively (these principles are described in detail in Kosslyn, 1994b). (3) This dual-mode format allows for both visual and verbal learning; students can recall either the words in the text *or* the illustrations when remembering the study. (4) Working through these displays leads to active processing—and better remembering. Examples include a study on alcohol and sexual aggression (p. 202), Watson's famous experiment with Little Albert (p. 217), Garcia's taste aversion (p. 224), the training of dolphins at Sea World (p. 237), Bandura's Bobo doll experiment (p. 247), and systematic desensitization (p. 627). Second, we've continued to make good use of photos. We now use photos to illustrate a particularly important or interesting fact. The captions of photos convey information pertinent to the section, and the photos themselves are used as hooks to allow students to better understand this material.

What's New in the Second Edition?

Every chapter is brimming with new research and cutting-edge coverage. Some of the key changes in the second edition are listed below, by chapter.

Chapter 1: Psychology: Yesterday and Today

- A shorter, more focused introduction to the field and the book (Methodology has been moved into the new Chapter 2)
- Updated opening story and expanded treatment of "Levels of Analysis"—which is now the *only* central theme of the book (in the interest of simplicity and clarity, "Using Psychology to Learn Psychology" has been eliminated as a theme, although the approach is still used in the actual treatment of material)

- Expanded, reorganized, and revised History of Psychology, which preserves the "story" told in the previous edition and continues to draw on Tiger Woods to illustrate key concepts
- New "Looking at Levels" section, "Sex and Emotional Involvement" (expanding coverage of Evolutionary Psychology)
- New photos to illustrate the central concepts (such as "what is psychology"), to underline the role of women in the history of psychology, and to make the summary of history come alive
- 2 new references, 1 from the year 2000 or later

Chapter 2: The Research Process: How We Find Things Out

- New chapter, which focuses on research methods
- Opening story that focuses on the International Space Station and the psychology that needs to be understood to make the space station work
- Expanded treatment of the scientific method
- Expanded and revised treatment of research concepts used in psychology (such as the new table on four types of validity)
- Expanded and revised treatment of research methods used in psychology
- Introduction of the QALMRI method (question/alternatives/logic/method/results/inferences), which is used in all subsequent "Understanding Research" sections
- Introduction of the "Understanding Research" feature, with the first one, "When Does Mental Practice Improve Later Performance?"
- New "Looking at Levels" sections on sleep disturbances and cognitive function, leadership, graph design for the eye and mind, and imitation
- 24 new references, 10 from the year 2000 or later

Chapter 3: The Biology of Mind and Behavior

- Expanded treatment of glial cells, processes in axons, and neurotransmitters (including a new table summarizing major neurotransmitter substances)
- New section on endogenous cannabinoids and their role in memory and attention
- New figure showing action at the synapse
- New "Understanding Research" section, "The Hemispheric Interpreter"
- Additional discussion of key brain areas, such as the nucleus accumbens
- New "Looking at Levels" section, "Brain Damage on the Roller Coaster"
- Expanded discussion of fMRI brain scanning, and discussion of optical brain imaging
- Expanded discussion of transcranial brain stimulation (TMS)
- Reorganized discussion of brain stimulation
- Greatly expanded and reorganized discussion of genetics
- New figure illustrating homozygous and heterozygous genotypes
- Discussion of knockin and knockout mice
- Discussion of brain plasticity
- 42 new references, 36 from the year 2000 or later

Chapter 4: Sensation and Perception: How the World Enters the Mind

- New opening story, based on the Mexican artist Frida Kahlo
- New organization, in terms of the traditional distinction between sensation and perception

- Psychophysics addressed at the beginning, before the nature of visual sensation
- Expanded coverage of the new type of photodetector discovered in the retina
- New material on the differences between mixing colored lights versus paints
- Additional genetic research on sex differences in color perception
- Additional discussion of neural processes of perception, including that of Hubel and Weisel
- Expanded discussion of perceptual learning, including that which is used in "chicken sexing"
- Expanded discussion of cross-cultural differences in drawing
- New section on motion perception
- New figure illustrating signal detection outcomes
- New figure illustrating the phi phenomenon
- New figure showing two visual pathways (the "what" and "where" pathways)
- New "Understanding Research" section, "Two Ways to Specify Spatial Relations" (a study that involves using barbiturates to "put to sleep" temporarily only a single cerebral hemisphere)
- Expanded and reorganized section on attention, integrated into perception
- Expanded treatment of hearing
- Expanded treatment of smell (including effects of female hormones on sensitivity) and female pheromones (including those that sexually attract males)
- Expanded treatment of taste, pain, and magnetic sense
- 64 new references, 43 from the year 2000 or later

Chapter 5: Consciousness

- Expanded section on the nature of consciousness
- New section on the function of sleep (restorative and evolutionary theories)
- Expanded section on narcolepsy—a discussion of the role of orexin
- Expanded section on sleep apnea—the role of heart rate and the nervous system
- New "Understanding Research" section on hypnosis and memory
- Added coverage of cannabinoids (particularly anandamide)
- 41 new references, 28 from the year 2000 or later

Chapter 6: Learning

- New chapter opening story, based on the life of Jackie Chan
- Addition of the topic of habituation
- Forward, delayed, trace, higher order, and evaluative conditioning added
- Simultaneous and backward pairing labeled
- New "Understanding Research" section on taste aversion
- Expanded section on escape conditioning and avoidance learning
- Positive and negative punishment added (versus simply "punishment")
- Update of the effects of TV on aggression
- New figure illustrating variations of the classical conditioning procedure
- New figure illustrating higher order conditioning
- New panel illustration depicting positive and negative reinforcement and punishment
- 16 new references, 13 from the year 2000 or later

Chapter 7: Memory: Living With Yesterday

- New opening story, focusing on the memory expert "S."
- Expanded discussion of the Atkinson and Shiffrin model (plus new figure illustrating the three-stage model of memory)

- Expanded discussion of working memory
- New minidemonstration on chunking
- New section on the formation of neural connections, with an expanded discussion of knockout and knockin mice and the genetics of memory
- New figure illustrating the structure of semantic memory networks
- New discussion of cultural differences in memory
- New "Understanding Research" section, "A Better Police Lineup"
- Expanded discussion of false memories
- 50 new references, 38 from the year 2000 or later

Chapter 8: Language and Thinking

- New opening story, focusing on Albert Einstein's language and thought
- Expanded treatment of language comprehension versus production
- Expanded treatment of "pragmatics" in language
- New illustration of a "tree structure" showing syntactic analysis of a sentence
- New "Understanding Research" section, "Untangling Ambiguity During Comprehension"
- Expanded discussion of child speech and the development of language ability
- New table summarizing key milestones in language acquisition
- New section on gesture
- Expanded discussion of second language learning
- Revised discussion of concepts
- New figure containing a mental rotation exercise
- Expanded discussion of heuristics
- New "Looking at Levels" section, "Cognitive Engineering at Home and at the Nuclear Power Plant"
- New panel illustration showing three different problem-solving techniques
- New figure on mental models
- New section on framing decisions
- New "Looking at Levels" section, "Judging Pain"
- 87 new references, 52 from the year 2000 or later

Chapter 9: Types of Intelligence: What Does It Mean to Be Smart?

- Additional headings to indicate structure
- Reorganized section, "Is There More Than One Way to Be Smart?," which now includes the section, "Boosting IQ"
- New "Diversity in Intelligence" section that combines discussions of mental retardation, the gifted, and creativity
- Revised section on the genetics of intelligence, including recent brain-neuroimaging results
- New material on the relation between testosterone levels in IQ
- Revised treatment of creativity
- New section on enhancing creativity
- New "Understanding Research" section, "Constrained Creativity"
- 61 new references, 54 from the year 2000 or later

Chapter 10: Emotion and Motivation: Feeling and Striving

- New research on "basic emotions" added
- Expanded coverage of the biological basis of emotions

- Added coverage of the neural bases of reward
- New section on controlling emotions
- Expanded coverage of the biological basis for appetite
- Updated coverage of the concept of a "set point" for body weight
- New section on mating preferences
- New research on visual sexual stimuli
- Updated coverage on sexual orientation
- 73 new references, 67 from the year 2000 or later

Chapter 11: Personality: Vive la Différence!

- Gordon Allport's notion of central traits added
- Added information about specific tests, such as the Cattell 16PF, MMPI-2, and NEO-PI-R
- More coverage of projective tests
- Updated coverage of the behavioral genetics of personality
- New "Understanding Research" section, "The Minnesota Study of Twins Reared Apart"
- New "Looking at Levels" section, "The Cyberstudent Personality" (how traits affect Web-based learning)
- Added discussion of Bandura's concept of self-reflectiveness
- Updated coverage of individualism versus collectivism
- 55 new references, 36 from the year 2000 or later

Chapter 12: Psychology Over the Life Span: Growing Up, Growing Older, Growing Wiser

- Revised section on teratogens
- New "Understanding Research" section, "Stimulating the Unborn"
- New "Looking at Levels" section, "Cued Emotions" (how mothers shape their infants' emotional responses)
- Revised section on motor development, exploring the relation between SIDS and infant sleeping positions
- Revised section on infant perception
- New material on Siegler's "wave model" of cognitive development
- New material on memory development
- Revised section on effects of daycare on behavior
- Revised section on gender identity
- Additional material on "the secular trend" and factors affecting the age of menarche
- Revised sections on adolescent reasoning and egocentrism
- New section on evolving peer relationships during adolescence
- Revised section on moral development
- New material on the "cerebral reserve hypothesis" regarding cognitive aging
- Revised section on the effects of aging on personality
- New section on emotion in the elderly
- New section on adult relationships
- Completely revised section on death and dying
- 87 new references, 64 from the year 2000 or later

Chapter 13: Stress, Health, and Coping

- Update on Selye's work, including Taylor's notion of "tend-and-befriend"
- Work-related factors expanded to include economic factors and Karasek's demand-control model
- Psychoneuorimmunology added (moved from another chapter)

- Reorganized section on health-impairing behaviors—why we engage in them as well as how to change them
- Update on humor in the section on coping
- New "Understanding Research" section, "Emotional Disclosure and Health"
- Expanded section on placebos
- 39 new references, 31 from the year 2000 or later

Chapter 14: Psychological Disorders

- Reorganized and expanded section, "Identifying Psychological Disorders: What's Abnormal?"
- More cross-cultural material
- New "Understanding Research" section, "Symptoms of Depression in China and the United States"
- Discussion of general anxiety disorder added
- New "Looking at Levels" section, "Individual Differences in Responses to Trauma"
- New figure on Beck's "Negative Triad"
- Expanded coverage of DID
- New figure on "Body Image Distortion"
- 58 new references, 48 from the year 2000 or later

Chapter 15: Treatment

- Separate section on biomedical treatment
- New "Looking at Levels" section on depression and the placebo effect
- Revised section on prevention
- Addition of antidepressant/placebo effect information
- Additional information on exposure
- New "Understanding Research" section, "For OCD: CBT Plus Medication, Without Exclusion"
- Expanded coverage of cybertherapy
- New table on the effects of medication
- 47 new references; 40 from the year 2000 or later

Chapter 16: Social Psychology: Meeting of the Minds

- New section on "thin slices" work (Ambady)
- New section on the primacy effect and self-fulfilling prophecy
- New section on implicit attitudes
- New section on social cognitive neuroscience
- New "Understanding Research" section, "How Stereotypes Can Prime Behavior"
- New figure on the self-fulfilling prophecy
- New figure on the "Implicit Attitudes Test"
- Addition of the elaboration likelihood model
- Expanded coverage of cognition and prejudice (e.g., Payne's study on priming of racial stereotypes)
- New discussion of the jigsaw classroom technique (Aronson)
- New figure, "The Jigsaw Classroom"
- New discussion of informational and normative social influence in conformity section
- New figure on the choice points of bystander behavior
- Groupthink moved to this chapter
- 47 new references, 36 from the year 2000 or later

Instructor and Student Resources

Psychology: The Brain, the Person, the World, Second Edition, is accompanied by the following teaching and learning aids.

Instructor's Supplements

Test Bank (0-205-39295-4). Prepared by Eric Miller at Kent State University and accuracy checked by Stephen Kosslyn and one of his graduate students, the test bank contains over 175 items per chapter, in essay, short-answer, multiple-choice, and true/false format. Page references to in-text material, answer justification, and a difficulty rating scale allow you to customize the assessment materials to best fit your needs. An appendix includes a sample open-book quiz.

Instructor's Manual (0-205-39366-7). Prepared by Marcia J. McKinley at Mount St. Mary's College, the IM contains additional material to enrich your class presentations. For each chapter, the IM provides a Chapter-at-a-Glance grid; detailed lecture outlines; demonstrations and activities for classroom use; updated video, media, and Web resources; and other detailed pedagogical information. In addition, this manual includes a preface and a sample syllabus, and the appendix includes a comprehensive list of student handouts.

Computerized Test Bank (0-205-38896-5). This computerized version of the test bank is available with Tamarack's easy-to-use TestGenEQ software, which lets you prepare printed, network, and online tests. It includes full-edition capability for Windows and Macintosh. This supplement is available upon adoption of the textbook from your local Allyn and Bacon sales representative.

Powerpoint Presentation CD-ROM (0-205-39570-8). Prepared by Daniel Horn at the University of Michigan, this multimedia resource contains textbook images with demonstrations, key points for lectures, and the full *Instructor's Resource Manual* in digitized form.

Allyn & Bacon Transparencies for Introductory Psychology, 2004. *New publication!* Over 200 full-color transparencies taken from the text and other sources are referenced in the *Instructor's Manual* for the most appropriate use in your classroom presentations.

Insights to Psychology: Volumes I and II (Part I: 0-205-39477-9; Part II: 0-205-39478-7). *New publication!* These interactive videos illustrate the many theories and concepts surrounding 16 areas of psychology. The Interactive Video contains 2–3 video clips per topic, followed by critical thinking questions that challenge students. A Video Guide provides further exploration questions and Internet resources for more information. These videos are also available on DVD from your Allyn and Bacon sales representative.

The Allyn & Bacon Digital Media Archive for Psychology, 4.0 (0-205-39537-6). *New publication!* This collection of media products—charts, graphs, tables, figures, and audio and video clips—enlivens your classroom with resources that can be easily integrated into your lectures. Now, the video clips include classic psychology experiments footage.

Course Management. Use our pre-loaded, customizable content and assessment items to teach your online courses. Available in CourseCompass, Blackboard, and WebCT formats.

Student Supplements

Companion Website. This unique resource for connecting the textbook to the Internet can be accessed at www.ablongman.com/kosslyn2e. Each chapter includes learning objectives, chapter summaries, updated and annotated Web links for additional sources of information, flash card glossary terms, and online practice tests.

Grade Aid Study Guide **(0-205-39538-4).** Developed by Marcia J. McKinley at Mount St. Mary's College, this is a comprehensive and interactive study guide. Each chapter includes "Before You Read," with a brief chapter summary and chapter learning objectives; "As You Read," a collection of demonstrations, activities, and exercises; "After You Read," containing three short-practice quizzes and one comprehensive practice test; and "When You Have Finished," with Web links for further information and crossword puzzles using key terms from the text. An appendix includes answers to all practice tests and crossword puzzles.

MyPsychLab: Where Learning Comes to Life! **(0-205-39770-0).** *MyPsychLab* is an exciting new learning and teaching tool designed to increase student success in the classroom and provide instructors with every resource needed to teach and administer an introductory psychology course. Designed to be used as a supplement to a traditional lecture course or for complete administration of an online course, *MyPsychLab* features a text-specific e-book—matching the exact layout of the printed textbook—with multimedia and assessment icons in the margins. These icons launch to exciting resources—stimulating animations, video clips, audio explanations, activities, controlled assessments, and profiles of prominent psychologists—to expand upon the key topics students encounter as they read the text.

With *MyPsychLab*, instructors can quickly and easily manage class information and provide students with extra resources to help improve their success rate. *MyPsychLab* includes access to Research Navigator, Allyn & Bacon's online journal database program, and to the Tutor Center, which directs students to free tutoring from qualified college psychology instructors on all material in the text. Tutors are available via phone, fax, e-mail, or the Internet during the Tutor Center hours of 5 P.M.–12 A.M. EST, Sunday through Thursday.

Research Navigator Guide for Psychology **(0-205-37640-1).** This easy-to-read guide helps point students in the right direction as they explore the tremendous array of information on psychology on the Internet. In addition, the guide provides a wide range of additional annotated Web links for further exploration.

This guide also contains an access code to Research Navigator, Allyn and Bacon's online collection of academic and popular journals. Research Navigator offers students three exclusive databases (Ebsco's ContentSelect, *The New York Times* on the Web, and Link Library) of credible and reliable source content to help students focus their research efforts and get the research process started.

Mind Matters II CD-ROM **(0-205-38881-7).** *New publication!* The Allyn and Bacon *Mind Matters II CD-ROM* makes psychology more engaging, interactive, informative, and fun! *Mind Matters II* covers the core concepts of psychology through a combination of text, graphics, simulations, video clips of historic experiments, and activities. Assessments test comprehension at both the topic and unit levels. New to *Mind Matters II*—innovative modules on Personality, Developmental Psychology, and Social Psychology.

Acknowledgments

We want to give a heartfelt thanks to the many reviewers who read earlier versions of one or more chapters, sometimes the entire book. This is by far a better book for their efforts.

Second Edition Reviewers

Joel Alexander, Western Oregon University
Mark Bardgett, Northern Kentucky University
Mark Baxter, Harvard University
Marlene Behrmann, Carnegie Mellon University
Joseph Bilotta, Western Kentucky University
Sarah Bing, University of Maryland Eastern Shore
Galen Bodenhausen, Northwestern University
Douglas Cody Brooks, Denison University
Greg Buchanan, Beloit College
Michelle Butler, U.S. Air Force Academy
Laura Carstensen, Stanford University
Patrick Cavanagh, Harvard University
Paul Costa, National Institute of Aging, NIH
Joseph Davis, San Diego State University
Perri Druen, York College
Lorin Elias, University of Saskatchewan
Delbert Ellsworth, Elizabethtown College
Merrill Garrett, University of Arizona
Michael Garza, Brookhaven College

Peter Gerhardstein, State University of New York–Binghamton
Harvey Ginsburg, Southwest Texas State University
Jordan Grafman, National Institute of Neurological Disorders and Strokes
Dana Gross, St. Olaf College
Larry Hawk, State University of New York–Buffalo
Julie Hoigaard, University of California–Irvine
Dan Horn, University of Michigan
Stephen Hoyer, Pittsburgh State University
Kathy Immel, University of Wisconsin–Fox Valley
Alan Kazdin, Yale University
Melvyn King, State University of New York–Cortland
Joseph Le Doux, New York University
Matthew Lieberman, University of California, Los Angeles
Sherry Loch, Paradise Valley Community College
Linda Lockwood, Metropolitan State College
Eric Loken, University of Pittsburgh
Michael Markham, Florida International University

Bruce McEwen, Rockefeller University
Marcia McKinley, Mount St. Mary's College
Marisa McLeod, Santa Fe Community College
Richard McNally, Harvard University
Todd D. Nelson, California State University
Jacqueline Pope-Tarrence, Western Kentucky University
Beth Post, University of California, Davis
Celia Reaves, Monroe Community College
Gregory Robinson-Riegler, University of St. Thomas
Bennett Schwartz, Florida International University
Alan Searleman, St. Lawrence University
Paul Shinkman, University of North Carolina–Chapel Hill
Larry Squire, Veterans Affairs Medical Center, San Diego
Robert Stickgold, Harvard Medical School
Irene Vlachos-Weber, Indiana University
John Wiebe, University of Texas, El Paso

First Edition Reviewers

Sharon Akimoto, Carleton College
Jeff Anastasi, Francis Marion University
Joe Bean, Shorter College
James Benedict, James Madison University
James F. Calhoun, University of Georgia
Brad Carothers, Evergreen Valley College
James Carroll, Central Michigan University

M. B. Casey, St. Mary's College of Maryland
Dave Christian, University of Idaho
George A. Cicala, University of Delaware
Gerald S. Clack, Loyola University of New Orleans
Verne C. Cox, University of Texas, Arlington
Nancy Dickson, Tennessee Technical College

William O. Dwyer, University of Memphis
Valeri Farmer-Dougan, Illinois State University
William Ford, Bucks County Community College
Mary Gauvain, University of California, Riverside
Dan Gilbert, Harvard University
Peter Graf, University of British Columbia

Peter Gram, Pensacola Junior College

Karl Haberlandt, Trinity College

Richard Hackman, Harvard University

Richard Haier, University of California, Irvine

Marjorie Hardy, Eckerd College

Bruce Henderson, Western Carolina University

James Hilton, University of Michigan

Rich Ingram, San Diego State University

John H. Krantz, Hanover College

Richard Lippa, California State University, Fresno

Walter J. Lonner, Western Washington University

Michael Markham, Florida International University

Pam McAuslan, University of Michigan, Dearborn

David G. McDonald, University of Missouri

Rafael Mendez, Bronx Community College

Sarah Murray, Kwantlen University College

Paul Ngo, Saint Norbert College

Thomas R. Oswald, Northern Iowa Area Community College

Carol Pandey, Los Angeles Pierce College

Robert J. Pellegrini, San Jose State University

Dorothy C. Piontkowski, San Francisco State University

Brad Redburn, Johnson County Community College

Cheryl Rickabaugh, University of Redlands

Alan Salo, University of Maine, Presque Isle

Jim Schirillo, Wake Forest University

Michael Scoles, University of Central Arkansas

Michael Shaughnessy, Eastern New Mexico University

Nancy Simpson, Trident Technical College

Linda J. Skinner, Middle Tennessee State University

Michael Spiegler, Providence College

Don Stanley, North Harris College

Bruce B. Svare, State University of New York at Albany

Thomas Thielan, College of St. Catherine

Paul E. Turner, Lipscomb University

Lori Van Wallendael, University of North Carolina, Charlotte

Frank J. Vattano, Colorado State University

Rich Velayo, Pace University

Rich Wesp, East Stroudsburg University

We also profited enormously from conversations with our friends and colleagues, particularly Nalini Ambady, Mahzarin Banaji, Mark Baxter, Alain Berthoz, John Cacioppo, David Caplan, Alfonso Caramazza, Patrick Cavanagh, Verne Caviness, Christopher Chabris, Jonathan Cohen, Suzanne Corkin, Francis Crick, Richard Davidson, Susan Edbril, Jeffrey Epstein, Michael Friedman, Giorgio Gain, Al Galaburda, Jeremy Gray, Anne Harrington, Marc Hauser, Kenneth Hugdahl, Steven Hyman, Jerome Kagan, Julian Keenan, Denis Le Bihan, Fred Mast, Richard McNally, Merrill Mead-Fox, Ken Nakayama, Kevin O'Regan, Alvaro Pascual-Leone, Steven Pinker, Scott Rauch, Melissa Robbins, Robert Rose, Steven Rosenberg, Daniel Schacter, Jeanne Serafin, Lisa Shin, Dan Simons, Edward E. Smith, Elizabeth Spelke, David Spiegel, Larry Squire, Eve van Cauter, Laura Weisberg, and Edgar Zurif. We thank Maya and Alain Berthoz, Maryvonne Carafatan and Michel Denis, Josette and Jacques Lautrey, Christiane and Denis Le Bihan, Bernard Mazoyer, and Nathalie Tzurio-Mazoyer for their hospitality during our year in France, which made it possible and enjoyable to work productively there. We also thank the staff at the Collège de France for their help, in too many ways to list. And to our parents (Bunny, Stanley, Rhoda, and the late Duke), and our children (Nathaniel, David, and Justin), a huge thanks for your patience with our work-filled weekends and evenings, and for your love, support, and good humor. You have sustained us.

Other people have been instrumental in making this book a reality. These include Andrea Volfova (for her good-humored assistance and incisive comments), Jennifer Shephard, Bill Thompson, David Hurvitz, Steve Stose, Cinthia Guzman, Nicole Rosenberg, Marie Burrage, and Deborah Bell for their patience and willingness to help us dig out references and check facts, especially via long-distance communication during the year we were in France. The idea for the book developed over years of working with the Sophomore Tutors and Assistant to the Head Tutor, Shawn Harriman, at Harvard University, and we want to thank them all; helping them grapple with the concepts of levels of analysis led us to make this book clearer. We are particularly indebted to two of the tutors, Laurie Santos and Jason Mitchell, who read an early draft of the book and offered copious and wise comments. Finally, we wish to thank

Christopher Brunt, an undergraduate who used the first edition of the book and spotted an ambiguity in one of the figures; we fixed the figure, and appreciate his feedback. We welcome with open arms feedback from all students who read this book and have ideas about how to improve it.

Last, but definitely not least, we want to thank the crew at Allyn and Bacon—for their vision, support, good humor, and patience. We are glad you are on our team! Many special thanks to Carolyn Merrill, Executive Psychology Editor, who challenged us to make this edition even better; Wendy Gordon, Senior Marketing Manager, whose enthusiasm for the book and its message buoyed us all; Michael Granger, Production Manager, whose diligence and great eye made the book look good; Andrea Cava, of Editorial Production Services, for her amazing ability to keep thousands of details in her mind at one time; Nancy Forsyth, President, for her interest and good cheer; Sandi Kirshner, President of Addison Wesley Higher Education, and Bill Barke, CEO of Addison Wesley Higher Education, for their continuing support and participation in the project; Marcie Mealia, Sales Specialist extraordinaire, whose gift with people is truly inspiring; and most important, to Lisa McLellan, Senior Development Editor, without whom this edition would not exist. Lisa—thanks for the months of long days, hard work, and gusto that you brought to each chapter.

I nterest in gender and cultural diversity issues remains an important theme in modern psychology. These topics are treated throughout the text in an integrated fashion.

Integrated Coverage of Gender Issues

Integrated Coverage of Cross-Cultural Issues

About the Authors

Stephen M. Kosslyn

Stephen M. Kosslyn is John Lindsley Professor of Psychology in Memory of William James at Harvard University and Associate Psychologist in the Department of Neurology at Massachusetts General Hospital. He received his B.A. from UCLA and his Ph.D. from Stanford University, both in psychology. His first academic position was at Johns Hopkins University, where he was appointed Assistant Professor. He joined the Harvard faculty in 1977 as Associate Professor, and left in 1980 to take a Research Career Development Award. After a brief stay at Brandeis University and a visit to Johns Hopkins in 1983, Kosslyn returned to Harvard as a Full Professor. His research has focused primarily on the nature of visual mental imagery and visual communication, and he has published 5 books and over 200 papers on these topics. Kosslyn has received numerous honors, including the National Academy of Sciences Initiatives in Research Award, the Prix Jean-Louis Signoret, and election to the American Academy of Arts and Sciences and the Society of Experimental Psychologists. He is currently "head tutor," supervising graduate students who teach a year-long introductory psychology course using levels of analysis, and chairs the Committee on Undergraduate Instruction at Harvard. He is currently on the editorial boards of many professional journals; is a Fellow of the American Psychological Association, American Psychological Society, and American Association for the Advancement of Science; and has served on several national Research Council committees to advise the government on new technologies. Kosslyn has been a guest on local National Public Radio stations, CBS radio, CNN news, and *Nova*, and has been quoted in many newspapers and magazines.

Robin S. Rosenberg

Robin Rosenberg is a clinical psychologist in private practice and has taught introductory psychology at Lesley University. She is certified in clinical hypnosis and is a member of the Academy for Eating Disorders. She received her B.A. in psychology from New York University, and her M.A. and Ph.D. in clinical psychology from the University of Maryland, College Park. She did her clinical internship at Massachusetts Mental Health Center and had a postdoctoral fellowship at Harvard Community Health Plan before joining the staff at Newton-Wellesley Hospital's Outpatient Services, where she worked for a number of years before leaving to expand her private practice. She specializes in treating people with eating disorders, depression, and anxiety and is interested in the integration of different therapy approaches. She was the founder and coordinator of the New England Society for Psychotherapy Integration and has given numerous professional talks on various topics related to the treatment of people with eating disorders, as well as popular talks on relapse prevention and on developing a healthy relationship with food, and with one's body.

Psychology
The Brain, the Person, the World

Faith Ringgold © 1991

Psychology
Yesterday and Today

On a balmy April day in 2002, a young man was playing golf. Nothing unusual about that. But when this young man sank his final putt, the watching crowd let out a roar, and he looked for his parents and embraced them, fighting back tears. The occasion was the PGA Masters Tournament, and the young man was Tiger Woods.

Think of the magnitude of his victory: At 26, Woods was the youngest three-time winner of the Masters. And golf's reigning champion, in a sport that had long been effectively closed to all but whites, was of Asian, black, white, and Native American ancestry. If you could discern and explain the events that led up to this dramatic moment, you would be a very insightful psychologist.

But where would you begin? You could look at Tiger Woods's hand-eye coordination, his concentration and focus, his ability to judge distances and calculate factors of wind, temperature, and humidity.

You could look at his personality—his reaction to racist hate mail (as a college student at Stanford University, he even kept one particularly vile letter taped to his wall), his religious beliefs (he was raised in his mother's faith, Buddhism), his demeanor during play, and his discipline in training.

You could look at his relationships with the social world around him—his family, his competitors, his fans.

Is this psychology? Indeed it is. Psychology asks and, in scientific ways, attempts to answer questions about why and how people think, feel, and behave as they do. Because we are all human and so have much in common,

Psychology is about mental processes and behavior, both exceptional and ordinary.

sometimes the answers are universal. But we are also, like snowflakes, all different, and psychology helps to explain our uniqueness. Psychology is about mental processes and behavior, both exceptional and ordinary. In this chapter, we show you how to look at and answer such questions by methods used in current research and (because the inquiry into what makes us tick has a history) how psychologists over the past century have approached them.

The Science of Psychology: Getting to Know You

Virtually everything any of us does, thinks, or feels falls within the sphere of psychology. You may observe psychology in action when you watch people interacting in a classroom or at a party, or notice that a friend is in a really terrible mood. Psychology is at work when you daydream as you watch the clouds drift by, when you have trouble recalling someone's name, even when you're asleep.

What Is Psychology?

Although it may seem complex and wide-ranging, the field you are studying in this textbook can be defined in one simple sentence: *Psychology is the science of mental processes and behavior.* Let's look at the key words in this definition.

First, *science:* From the Latin *scire,* "to know," science avoids mere opinions, intuitions, and guesses, and strives to nail down facts—to *know* them—by using objective evidence to answer questions such as, What makes the sun shine? Why does garlic make your breath smell strong? How is Tiger Woods able to direct his swings so superbly? Science uses logic to reason about the possible causes of a phenomenon and then tests the resulting ideas by collecting additional facts, which will either support the ideas or refute them, and thus nudge the scientist further along the road to the answer.

Second, *mental processes:* **Mental processes** are what your brain is doing not only when you engage in "thinking" activities such as storing memories, recognizing objects, and using language, but also when you feel depressed, jump for joy, or savor the experience of being in love. How can we find objective facts about mental processes, which are hidden and internal? One way, which has a long history in psychology, is to work backward, observing what people do and inferring from outward signs what is going on "inside." Another, as new as the latest technological advances in neuroscience, is to use brain-scanning techniques to take pictures of the living brain that show its physical changes as it works.

Third, *behavior:* By **behavior** we mean the outwardly observable acts of a person, either alone or in a group. Behavior consists of physical movements, voluntary or involuntary, of the limbs, facial muscles, or other parts of the body. A

● **Psychology:** The science of mental processes and behavior.

● **Mental processes:** What the brain does when a person stores, recalls, or uses information, or has specific feelings.

● **Behavior:** The outwardly observable acts of an individual, alone or in a group.

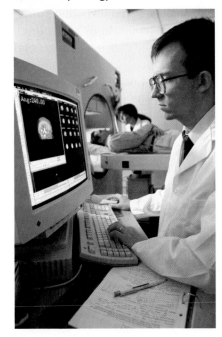
Science

Mental Processes

Behavior

particular behavior is often preceded by mental processes such as a perception of the current situation (how far the golf ball must travel) and a decision about what to do next (how forcefully to swing the club). A behavior may also be governed by the relationship between the individual and a group. Tiger Woods might not have performed the way he did in 2002 had he been playing in 1920, when many in the crowd would not have wanted a nonwhite person to win. So there are layers upon layers: An individual's mental processes affect his or her behavior, and these processes are affected by the surrounding group (the members of which, in turn, have their own individual mental processes and behaviors).

The goals of psychology are not simply to *describe* and *explain* mental processes and behavior, but also to *predict* and *control* them. As an individual, you'd probably like to be able to predict what kind of person would make a good spouse for you, or which politician would make sound decisions in crisis situations. As a society, we all would greatly benefit by knowing how people learn most effectively, how to control addictive and destructive behaviors, and how to cure mental illness.

Levels of Analysis: The Complete Psychology

The areas you might explore to answer questions about Tiger Woods's success—his coordination and focus, his beliefs and attitudes, his relationships with his parents and his audience—occur at three levels of scale, each of which provides a field for analysis. First, at the level of the *brain,* we can ask questions about his visualization techniques, hand–eye coordination, and concentration. Second, at the level of the whole *person,* we can ask how his beliefs and goals may have motivated him. And third, at the level of the *group,* we can investigate the roles of his parents and the reactions of crowds. At any moment in Tiger Woods's day, or yours, events are happening at all three levels: brain, person, and group. Of course, a

person is not just a larger-scale brain, and a group is not a larger-scale person. But looking at the individual at a microlevel (the brain) and a macrolevel (in relation to a group) reveals much that would be hidden were we to look at only one level. The concept of levels of analysis has long held a central role in science in general (Anderson, 1998; Nagel, 1979; Schaffner, 1967) and in the field of psychology in particular (Fodor, 1968, 1983; Kosslyn & Koenig, 1995; Looren de Jong, 1996; Marr, 1982; Putnam, 1973), and for good reason: This view of psychology not only allows you to see how different types of theories and discoveries illuminate the same phenomena, but it also lets you see how these theories and discoveries are interconnected—and thus how the field of psychology as a whole emerges from them. The concept of levels of analysis is a thread that ties together the topics in this book, and it is so important that it warrants a closer look now.

Events Large and Small

Imagine that it's the first day of class. You are standing at the front of the room, gazing over the lecture hall full of students (see Figure 1.1). Focus on a single student sitting near the middle of the room. Like a camera lens, zoom in so that the student's head fills your field of view. Zoom in even closer, to a small spot on the forehead, and shift an inch forward and zoom closer yet, to visualize the inside of the brain. As you continue to zoom in, magnification increases, and groups of brain cells appear. Finally, you home in on a single brain cell (which you will examine close up in Chapter 3).

FIGURE 1.1 Levels of Analysis

Levels of analysis differ in the size of the events being considered, ranging from very large to very small.

Now, reverse the journey: Zoom back until you see the entire person, whose psychology you would describe in terms of his or her beliefs, desires, and feelings, not just as a container of brain cells. Continue zooming back, to the point where you can take in the entire view, the full lecture hall. Now you see the world surrounding that particular student—the 20 or 30 other students, the color of the walls, the height and width of the room, the arrangement of chairs into rows, the sunlight streaming in.

At the **level of the brain,** psychologists focus on relatively small things. At this level we consider not only the activity of the brain but also the structure and properties of the organ itself—brain cells and their connections, the chemical soup in which they exist (including the hormones that alter the way the brain operates) and the genes that give rise to them. At the level of the brain, you are able to hear and understand a lecture because the appropriate cells are firing and making various connections. At the level of the brain, a psychologist might want to design an experiment to study how Tiger Woods can focus his attention so exquisitely well when preparing to swing.

The brain is only part of the story, though. As we've said, brains are not people. People have beliefs (such as ideas, explanations, expectations), desires (such as hopes, goals, needs), and feelings (such as fears, guilts, attractions). The brain is in many ways a canvas on which life's experiences are painted. To talk about the picture itself, we must shift to another level of analysis. At the **level of the person,** psychologists focus on a larger unit, the person as a whole and his or her beliefs, desires, and feelings. At this level we consider the *content* of mental processes, not just their internal mechanics. At the level of the person, you are in a psychology class because you hope it will be interesting, because you want to learn about people, and perhaps because you know that the course is a graduation requirement. At the level of the person, a psychologist might want to investigate the factors— among them, possibly, Tiger Woods's Buddhist faith—behind the strong sense of inner calm he displays under pressure.

"No man is an island," the poet John Donne wrote. We all live in *social environments* that vary over time and space and that are populated by our friends and professors, our parents, the other viewers in a movie theater, the other drivers on a busy highway. Our lives are intertwined with other people's lives, and from birth to old age, we take our cues from other people around us. The relationships that arise within groups make them more than simply a collection of individuals. Mental processes and behavior characterize groups as well as individuals. Street gangs and political parties both have distinct identities based on shared beliefs and practices that are passed on to succeeding generations of members as *culture*, which has been defined as the "language, beliefs, values, norms, behaviors, and even material objects that are passed from one generation to the next" (Henslin, 1999). Thus, at the **level of the group,** psychologists focus on units even larger than the brain or the person, looking at the ways collections of people (as few as one other person, as many as a society) shape individual mental processes and behavior. As you shift in your seat in the lecture hall, you are not alone: Other students' reactions, their questions, their irritating habits or encouraging comments, affect the way you experience the course. At the level of the group, a psychologist might want to examine the role of a supportive and enthusiastic audience in helping Tiger Woods birdie instead of bogey.

Events that occur at every level of analysis—brain, person, and group—are intimately tied to conditions in the physical world. All our mental processes and

● **Level of the brain:** Events that involve the structure and properties of the organ itself— brain cells and their connections, the chemical soup in which they exist, and the genes.

● **Level of the person:** Events that involve the nature of beliefs, desires, and feelings—the *content* of the mind, not just its internal mechanics.

● **Level of the group:** Events that involve relationships between people (e.g., love, competition, cooperation), relationships among groups, and culture. Events at the level of the group are one aspect of the environment; the other aspect is the physical environment itself (the time, temperature, and other physical stimuli).

behaviors take place within and are influenced by a specific *physical environment.* A windy day at the golf course changes the way Tiger Woods plays a shot; if the classroom is too hot, you may have trouble focusing on the lecture. The group is only part of the world; to understand the events at each level of analysis, we must always relate them to the physical world that surrounds us.

All Together Now

Events at the different levels not only occur at the same time, they are constantly interacting. As you sit in the lecture hall, the signals among your brain cells that enable you to understand the lecture, and the new connections among your brain cells that enable you to remember it, are happening because your desire to pass the course has put you in the room: That is, events at the level of the person are affecting events at the level of the brain. But, as you listen to the lecture, your neighbor's knuckle cracking is really getting to you, and you're finding it hard to concentrate: Events at the level of the group are affecting events at the level of the brain. Because you really want to hear this stuff, you're wondering how to get your neighbor to cut it out, and you decide to shoot a few dirty looks his way: Events at the level of the person are affecting events at the level of the group (which, as we've seen, affect events at the level of the brain). And all of this is going on within the physical environment of the room, where the sunlight that had seemed warm and welcoming is now pretty hot, and you're getting drowsy, and you're *really* irritated, and you finally change your seat. . . . And round and round. Events at the three levels of analysis, in a specific physical context, are constantly changing and influencing one another. To understand fully what's going on in life situations, you need to look at all three.

Looking *at* Levels

Drought Among the Maasai

The Maasai, a native people of Kenya and Tanzania, keep herds of cattle, following them as they graze across the plains of East Africa. Rather than feeding their infants on a fixed schedule, Maasai mothers feed them whenever they cry or otherwise make their need known. At the height of a 10-year drought in the early 1970s, many cattle died; some families lost 98% of their cattle. With cow's milk scarce, the infants were more dependent on their mothers' milk. Psychiatrist Marten deVries (1984), who was studying the Maasai children when the drought began, had been following the development of a group of 48 infants. He had focused on 20 of them, characterizing half as "easy" and half as "difficult"; easy babies were calm and cooperative, difficult ones testy and demanding. As the drought intensified, deVries tried to track down these 20 babies, now 6 to 8 months old. He expected that the "difficult" babies would stress their caregivers even more than usual and hence these babies would suffer behavioral impairments and ill health. To his surprise, he found the opposite: More of the easy babies had died (five of the seven he could find, compared to only one of the six difficult babies). Despite the small number of cases, the results were highly suggestive. Apparently, the difficult babies demanded to be fed more often, boosting their mothers' milk supply (frequent breast-feeding stimulates milk production), even though the mothers were malnourished. The less demanding, easy babies died when their mothers' milk supplies dwindled.

The deaths of the easy babies illustrate the crucial role played by events at each of the three levels of analysis and their interactions within a physical context. Temperament is at least in part biologically determined, a topic we explore in Chapters 11 and 12. The child's temperament *(level of the brain)* regulated the mother's behavior; her behavior, based on her belief that she should feed her child only when it fussed *(level of the person)*, in turn affected how her body functioned. Finally, in the Maasai culture *(level of the group)*, babies are cared for by an extended family, and thus the stress presented by difficult babies does not fall on the mother only, as is common in our society. Thus, a difficult baby was not as stressful as he or she would be for a single caretaker. Moreover, because the Maasai are nomads *(level of the group)*, they were dependent on the naturally available supplies of water (they didn't farm or irrigate). As a result, the physical environment—that is, the drought—was disastrous for them.

Note that we cannot understand what happened to the babies by considering only the physical environment. Although the drought set the stage for the psychological drama that followed, it did not determine the outcome. Nor can we understand what happened if we consider events only at a single level. To under-

Interactions among events at the different levels of analysis can explain why, during a drought, "easy" babies died but "difficult" babies survived.

stand fully why more difficult babies than easy babies survived the drought, we must consider how events at all three levels interacted. Only by investigating the interactions among the babies' temperaments, the mothers' beliefs about feeding, and the Maasai's culture can we understand the psychological factors that led to the deaths of the easy children.

TEST YOURSELF!

1. Psychology can illuminate all aspects of a person's life, but what is psychology?
2. What is the concept of "levels of analysis," and how can you use it to understand psychology?

Psychology Then and Now: The Evolution of a Science

How do you think psychologists 50 or 100 years ago might have interpreted Tiger Woods's performance? Would they have focused on the same things that psychologists do today? One hallmark of the sciences is that rather than casting aside earlier findings, researchers use them as stepping stones to the next set of discoveries. Reviewing how psychology has developed over time will help us understand where we are today. In the century or so during which psychology has taken shape as a formal discipline, the issues under investigation have changed, the emphasis has shifted from one level of analysis to another, and events at each level have often been viewed as operating separately or occurring in isolation.

Margaret Floy Washburn was not only Edward Titchener's first graduate student to receive a Ph.D., but was also the first woman Ph.D. in psychology (1894, Cornell).

In one form or another, psychology has probably always been with us. People have apparently always been curious about why they and others think, feel, and behave the way they do. In contrast, the history of psychology as a scientific field is relatively brief, spanning little more than a century. The roots of psychology lie in philosophy (the use of logic and speculation to understand the nature of reality, experience, and values) on the one hand and physiology (the study of the biological workings of the body, including the brain) on the other. From philosophy, psychology borrowed theories of the nature of mental processes and behavior. For example, the 17th-century French philosopher Renés Descartes focused attention on the distinction between mind and body and the relation between the two (a topic still of considerable debate). John Locke, a 17th-century English philosopher (and friend of Sir Isaac Newton) stressed that all human knowledge arises from experience of the world and from reflection about it. Locke argued that we only know about the world via how it is represented in the mind. From physiology, psychologists learned to recognize the role of the brain in giving rise to mental processes and behavior and acquired tools to investigate these processes. These twin influences of philosophy and physiology remain in force today, shaped and sharpened by developments over time.

Early Days: Beginning to Map the Mind

The earliest scientific psychologists were not much interested in why we behave as we do. Instead, these pioneers focused their efforts on understanding the operation of perception (the ways in which we sense the world), memory, and problem solving—events at what we now think of as the level of the brain.

Structuralism

Wilhelm Wundt (1832–1920), usually considered the founder of scientific psychology, set up the first psychology laboratory in 1879 in Leipzig, Germany. The work of Wundt and his colleagues led to structuralism, the first formal movement in psychology. The structuralists sought to identify the "building blocks" of consciousness. Part of Wundt's research led him to characterize two types of elements of consciousness. The first comprised sensations, which arise from the eyes, ears, and other sense organs; the second consisted of feelings, such as fear, anger, and love. The goal of **structuralism** was to describe the rules that determine how particular sensations or feelings may occur at the same time or in sequence, combining in various ways into mental *structures*. Edward Titchener (1867–1927), an American student of Wundt, broadened the structuralist approach to apply it to the nature of concepts and thinking in general.

The structuralists developed and tested their theories partly with objective techniques, such as measures of the time it takes to respond to different sensations.

● **Structuralism:** The school of psychology that sought to identify the basic elements of experience and to describe the rules and circumstances under which these elements combine to form mental *structures*.

Wilhelm Wundt (the man standing, with the long gray beard) in his laboratory.

Their primary research tool, however, was **introspection,** which means literally "looking within." Here is an example of introspection: Try to recall how many windows and doors are in your parents' living room. Are you aware of "seeing" the room in a mental image, of scanning along the walls and counting the windows and doors? Introspection is the technique of noticing your mental processes as, or immediately after, they occur.

Had the structuralists been asked to analyze Tiger Woods's golf success—how, for example, he perceives distances, fairway terrain, and wind direction—they probably would have trained him to use introspection to describe his mental processes. By 1913, however, another German scientist, Oswald Külpe, had discovered that not all mental processes are accompanied by mental imagery. In fact, if you asked Tiger Woods how he manages to swing a golf club so well, he probably wouldn't be able to tell you. Contemporary researchers have discovered that as our expertise in a skill increases, we are correspondingly less able to use introspection to describe it, an apparent paradox that reflects the use of "implicit memories" (see Chapter 7).

Let's say that although you are able to use introspection as a tool to recall the numbers of windows and doors in your parents' living room, your best friend doesn't seem to be able to do the same. How could you prove that mental images actually exist and objects can indeed be visualized? For the early psychologists, this was the core of the problem. Barring the ability to read minds, there was no way to resolve disagreements about the nature of introspection. If the only way you can gather evidence is through a process that cannot be verified, you cannot establish the evidence it yields as fact. This is precisely what happened when the structuralists tried to use introspection as a scientific tool. Their observations could not be objectively repeated with the same results, and thus their theorizing based on introspective reports fell apart.

HANDS ON

● **Introspection:** The process of "looking within."

Functionalism

Rather than trying to chart the elements of mental processes, the adherents of **functionalism** sought to understand how our minds help us to adapt to the world around us—in short, how to *function* in it. As psychology historian Edwin G. Boring (1950) put it, the structuralists were interested in "the psychology of the *Is*," whereas the functionalists were interested in the "*Is-for*." Whereas the structuralists asked *what* are mental processes and *how* do they operate, the functionalists wanted to know *why* humans think, feel, and behave as we do. The functionalists, many of whom were Americans, shared the urge to gather knowledge that could be put to immediate use. Sitting in a room introspecting simply didn't seem worthwhile to them. The functionalists' interest lay in the methods by which people learn and in how goals and beliefs are shaped by environment. As such, their interests spanned the levels of the person and the group.

The functionalists sought to apply knowledge of psychology, and helped to improve education in the United States.

The functionalists were strongly influenced by Charles Darwin (1809–1882), whose theory of evolution by natural selection stressed that some individual organisms in every species, from ants to oaks, possess characteristics that enable them to survive and reproduce more fruitfully than others. The phrase "survival of the fittest," often quoted in relation to natural selection, doesn't quite capture the key idea. (For one thing, these days "the fittest" implies the muscle-bound star of the health club rather than its older meaning of something "fit for" or "suited to" its situation.) The idea of natural selection is that certain inborn characteristics make particular individuals more fit for their environments, enabling them to have more offspring that survive, and they in turn have more offspring, and so on, until the characteristics that led them to flourish are spread through the whole population. Darwin called the inborn characteristics that help an organism survive and produce many offspring *adaptations*. (Chapter 3 covers Darwin's theory more fully.)

The functionalists applied Darwin's theory to mental characteristics. For example, William James (1842–1910), who set up the first psychology laboratory in the United States at Harvard University, studied the ways in which consciousness helps an individual survive and adapt to an environment. The functionalists likely would have tried to discover how Tiger Woods's goals and beliefs enable him to press on in the face of adversity, such as losing an important match or receiving hate mail.

The functionalists made several enduring contributions to psychology. Their emphasis on Darwin's theory of natural selection and its link between human and nonhuman animals led them to theorize that human psychology is related to the psychology of animals. This insight meant that the observation of animals could provide clues to human behavior. The functionalist focus on issues of society, such as improving methods of education, also spawned research that continues today.

Gestalt Psychology

Although their work began in earnest nearly 50 years later, the Gestalt psychologists, like the structuralists, were interested in consciousness, particularly as it arises

● **Functionalism:** The school of psychology that sought to understand the ways that the mind helps individuals *function*, or adapt to the world.

We do not see isolated individual musicians, but a marching band. In the words of the Gestalt psychologists, "the whole is more than the sum of its parts."

during perception (and thus also focused on events at the level of the brain). But instead of trying to dissect the elements of experience, **Gestalt psychology**—taking its name from the German word *Gestalt*, which means "whole"—emphasized the overall patterns of thoughts or experience. Based in Germany, scientists such as Max Wertheimer (1880–1943) and his colleagues noted that much of the content of our thoughts comes from what we perceive and, further, from inborn tendencies to structure what we see in certain ways.

Have you ever glanced up to see a flight of birds heading south for the winter? If so, you probably didn't pay attention to each individual bird but instead focused on the flock. In Gestalt terms, the flock was a *perceptual unit*, a whole formed from individual parts. The Gestalt psychologists developed over 100 perceptual laws, or principles, that describe how our eyes and brains organize the world. For example, both because the birds are near one another (the law of proximity) and because they are moving in the same direction (the law of common fate), we perceive them as a single unit. Gestaltists believed that these principles are a result of the most basic workings of the brain and that they affect how we all think. Most of these principles illustrate the dictum that "the whole is more than the sum of its parts." When you see the birds in flight, the flock has a size and shape that cannot be predicted from the size and shape of the birds viewed one at a time. To Gestalt psychologists, just as the flock is an entity that is more than a collection of individual birds, our patterns of thought are more than the simple sum of individual images or ideas. Gestaltists would want to know how Tiger Woods can take in the overall layout of each hole, or even an 18-hole course, and plan his strategy accordingly.

Today the study of perception has grown beyond the province of Gestalt psychology alone and is now a central focus of psychology, as well it should be. Perception is, after all, our gateway to the world; if our perceptions are not accurate, our corresponding thoughts and feelings will be based on a distorted view of reality.

● **Gestalt psychology:** An approach to understanding mental processes that focuses on the idea that the whole is more than the sum of its parts.

The research of the Gestaltists addressed how the brain works, and today Gestaltism has become integrated into studies of the brain itself.

Psychodynamic Theory: More Than Meets the Eye

Sigmund Freud (1856–1939), a Viennese physician specializing in neurology (the study and treatment of diseases of the brain and nervous system), developed a detailed and subtle theory of how thoughts and feelings affect our actions. This theory addresses mental processes and behavior less at the level of the brain and more at the level of the person (and, to some extent, the level of the group). We consider Freud and theorists who followed in his footsteps in Chapter 11; here we touch briefly on key points of his theory.

Sigmund Freud, the father of psychodynamic theory.

Freud stressed the notion that the mind is not a single thing, but in fact has separate components. Moreover, some of these mental processes are **unconscious,** that is, they are outside our conscious awareness and beyond our ability to bring to awareness at will. Freud believed that we have many unconscious sexual, and sometimes aggressive, urges. On a conscious level, Freud argued, we often find these urges unacceptable and so banish them to the unconscious. According to Freud, unconscious thoughts and feelings build up until, eventually and inevitably, they demand release as thoughts, feelings, or actions.

Freud developed what has since been called a **psychodynamic theory.** From the Greek words *psyche,* or "mind," and *dynamo,* meaning "power," the term refers to the continual push-and-pull interaction among conscious and unconscious forces. Freud believed that it was these interactions that produced abnormal behaviors, such as obsessively washing one's hands until they crack and bleed. According to Freud, such hand-washing might be traced to unacceptable unconscious sexual or aggressive impulses bubbling up to consciousness (the "dirt" perceived on the hands) and that washing symbolically serves to remove the "dirt." What would followers of psychodynamic theory say about Tiger Woods? A Freudian would probably ask Woods about his earliest memories and experiences and try with him to analyze the unconscious urges that led to his intense interest in golf.

Others modified Freud's theory in various ways, for example, by de-emphasizing sex in favor of other sources of unconscious conflicts; Alfred Adler (1870–1937), for instance, stressed the role of feelings of inferiority. Psychodynamic theories have attracted many passionate followers. Rather than deriving from objective scientific studies, however, their guiding principles rest primarily on subjective interpretations of what patients say and do. Moreover, psychodynamic theory became so intricate and complicated that it could usually explain any given observation or research result as easily as the opposite result, and thus became impossible to test—obviously a serious drawback.

Nevertheless, the key idea of psychodynamic theory—that behavior is driven by a collection of mental processes—had a crucial influence on later theories. In addition, the idea that some mental processes are hidden from conscious awareness has proven invaluable, as has the focus on the level of the person. Furthermore, these theorists focused attention on novel kinds of observations, such as

● **Unconscious:** Outside conscious awareness and not able to be brought to consciousness at will.

● **Psychodynamic theory:** A theory of how thoughts and feelings affect behavior; refers to the continual push-and-pull interaction among conscious and unconscious forces.

slips-of-the-tongue and the analysis of dreams. These observations sparked much subsequent research. Psychodynamic theory led to entirely new approaches to treating psychological problems, which have since been modified and refined (see Chapter 14). For instance, Freud's theory led to psychoanalysis, in which a therapist listens to a patient talk about his or her childhood, relationships, and dreams, and attempts to help the patient understand the unconscious basis of his or her thoughts, feelings, and behavior.

Behaviorism: The Power of the Environment

By the early part of the 20th century, a new generation of psychologists calling themselves behaviorists began to question a key assumption shared by their predecessors, that psychologists should study hidden mental processes. Because they found the theories of mental processes so difficult to pin down, American psychologists such as Edward Lee Thorndike (1874–1949), John B. Watson (1878–1958), and Clark L. Hull (1884–1952) rejected the idea that psychology should focus on these unseen phenomena. Instead, these followers of **behaviorism** concluded that psychology should concentrate on understanding directly observable behavior.

Some behaviorists were willing to talk about internal stimuli such as motivation, but only those stimuli that were directly reflected in behavior (such as running quickly to catch a bus). Later behaviorists, among them B. F. Skinner (1904–1990), urged that psychology move away from the study of internal processes altogether, arguing that they played no role at all in causing behavior. Skinner and his followers went so far as to argue that there is no such thing as mental processes, that people don't really have "thoughts." For instance, rather than saying that someone treats dogs well because she "likes" them ("liking" being an unobservable mental process), these behaviorists would say that she approaches dogs, protects them from harm, pets them, and otherwise treats them well because such responses have come to be associated with the stimulus of perceiving a dog. Behaviorists thus cut out the middleman of mental processes: The behaviors that are generally regarded as reflections of the internal state of "liking" can instead be viewed as direct responses to particular stimuli. Because of their concern with the content of the stimulus–response associations, the behaviorists focused on events at the level of the person.

The behaviorists had many important insights, among them the fact that responses usually produce consequences, either negative or positive, which in turn affect how the organism responds the next time it encounters the same stimulus. Say you put money in a vending machine (a response to the stimulus of seeing the

THE FAR SIDE° BY GARY LARSON

"Stimulus, response! Stimulus, response! Don't you ever *think*?"

● **Behaviorism:** The school of psychology that focuses on how a specific stimulus (object, person, or event) evokes a specific response (behavior in reaction to the stimulus).

machine) and the machine dispenses a tasty candy bar; chances are good that you will repeat the behavior in the future. If, on the other hand, the machine serves up a stale candy bar with a torn wrapper, you will be less inclined to use this or another machine like it again (see Chapter 6 for a detailed discussion of how consequences affect learning).

How might the behaviorists explain Tiger Woods's success? A key idea in behaviorism is *reinforcement*, the strengthening or supporting consequences that result from a given behavior. A reward, such as payment for a job, is a common type of reinforcement. If the consequences of a behavior are reinforcing, we are likely to repeat the behavior. Conversely, if a behavior produces an undesirable outcome ("punishment"), we are less likely to do it again. From his earliest days, Tiger Woods received an extraordinary amount of reinforcement for playing well, at first from his father and then from an increasingly larger affirming public. It was this reinforcement, the behaviorists would argue, that spurred him to repeat those acts that brought desirable consequences, while shunning behaviors (including ineffective golfing techniques) that did not help him play well.

The behaviorists developed many principles that describe the conditions in which specific stimuli lead to specific responses, many of which have stood up well in later investigations (as you will see in Chapter 6). For example, they found that individuals respond more frequently when the desirable outcomes are intermittent than when those "rewards" occur every time. Thus, if Tiger were hitting golf balls one after the other onto a putting green, he would be more likely to play longer and hit more balls if he had sunk only some of them than if he had sunk every shot. Contemporary behaviorists often develop theories (sometimes derived from economics) to describe how humans and other animals choose which responses to make to sets of competing stimuli (Grafen, 2002; Herrnstein, 1990).

The behaviorists' emphasis on controlled, objective observation has had a deep and lasting impact on psychology. Today, even studies of mental processes must conform to the level of rigor established by the behaviorists. Behaviorist insights also have improved psychotherapy and education. On the other hand, as you will see, many of the behaviorists' objections to the study of mental processes have been refuted by subsequent research.

Humanistic Psychology

Partly as a reaction to the mechanistic theories of the Freudians and behaviorists, which viewed people as driven either by the content of their mental processes or by external stimuli, in the late 1950s and early 1960s a new psychology emerged. According to **humanistic psychology,** people have positive values, free will, and a deep inner creativity, which in combination allow us to choose life-fulfilling paths to personal growth. The humanistic approach (focused on the level of the person) rests on the ideas that the "client" (no longer the "patient") must be respected as equal to the therapist and that each person has dignity and self-worth.

Psychologists such as Carl Rogers (1902–1987) and Abraham Maslow (1908–1970) developed therapies based on these theories. Rogers's *client-centered therapy* incorporated Maslow's theory that people have an urge to *self-actualize*— that is, to develop to their fullest potentials—and that given the right environment this development will in time occur. Rather than serving as an expert in a position of authority, the client-centered therapist provides a "mirror" in the form of an

● **Humanistic psychology:** The school of psychology that assumes people have positive values, free will, and deep inner creativity, the combination of which leads them to choose life-fulfilling paths to personal growth.

unconditionally supportive and positive environment. How might humanistic psychologists explain Tiger Woods's psychology? No doubt they would point to him as someone who is striving to reach his full potential. They might question, however, whether in the long run his intense focus on golf will prove entirely satisfying, especially if he ignores other aspects of life.

Humanistic psychology continues to attract followers today, but it is no longer a major force in the field. Nevertheless, many of the therapies now in use reflect the influence of humanistic thinking (as we discuss in Chapter 15).

The Cognitive Revolution

The tension between psychological approaches—on the one hand, structuralism, functionalism, and psychodynamic psychology, which studied unobservable mental processes, and on the other hand, behaviorism, which addressed only directly observable behavior—was resolved by an unlikely source, the computer. The computer led to the *cognitive revolution* of the late 1950s and early 1960s; its proponents looked to the computer as a model for the way human mental processes work. This movement came into full flower in the mid-1970s, led by, among others, psychologist/computer scientists Herbert A. Simon and Alan Newell (Simon went on to win a Nobel Prize, in part for this work) and linguist Noam Chomsky. (Gardner [1985] provides a detailed history of the cognitive revolution.)

Computers provided a new way to conceptualize mental processes and to develop detailed theories about them.

The cognitive revolution produced a new way to conceive of mental events, giving birth to **cognitive psychology**, which attempts to characterize the nature of human *information processing*, that is, the way information is stored and operated on internally (Neisser, 1967). In this view, mental processes are like computer software (programs), and the brain is like the hardware (the machine itself). Cognitive psychologists believe that just as different types of software can be discussed without ever considering how the hardware works, mental processes can be discussed without regard to the structure of the brain.

Computers showed, once and for all, why it is important that there be a science of the unobservable events that take place in the head, not just a science of directly observable behavior. Consider, for example, how you might react if your word-processing program produced *italics* whenever you entered the command for **boldface**. Noticing the software's "behavior" is only the first step in fixing this error: You need to dig deeper in order to find out where the program has gone wrong. This would involve seeing what internal events are triggered by the command and how those events affect what the program does. So, too, for people. If somebody is acting odd, we must go beyond the essential step of noticing the unusual behavior; we also need to think about what is happening inside and consider what is causing the problem. Indeed, the cognitive revolution led to new ways of conceptualizing and treating mental disorders, such as depression. For example, Albert Ellis (b. 1913) and Aaron Beck (b. 1921) claimed that people's distressing

● **Cognitive psychology:** The approach in psychology that attempts to characterize how information is stored and operated on internally.

feelings or symptoms are caused by irrational and distorted ways of thinking about their interactions with others, themselves, and their surroundings. Beck showed that symptoms such as anxiety and depression could be addressed by attacking the problems in thinking.

Cognitive psychology defined many of the questions that are still being pursued in psychology, such as how information is stored when we perform a given task, and it continues to develop subtle experimental methods to study hidden mental processes. Principles of cognitive psychology have been used to compare abilities across cultures, in part to sort out which aspects of our psychologies arise from inherent properties of the brain (common to all people) and which are a product of our particular social experiences (Cole, 1996; Cole et al., 1997).

The theories and research methods developed by cognitive psychologists have also proven crucial in the recent development of **cognitive neuroscience,** which blends cognitive psychology and neuroscience (the study of the brain). Cognitive neuroscientists argue that "the mind is what the brain does" (Kosslyn & Koenig, 1995) and hope to discover the nature, organization, and operation of mental processes by studying the brain. This is one of the most exciting areas of psychology today, in part because new brain-scanning technologies have allowed us, for the first time in history, to observe human brains at work.

The cognitive neuroscience approach considers events at the three levels of analysis, but with a primary focus on the brain. Cognitive neuroscientists seeking to explain Tiger Woods's golfing achievements would likely investigate how different parts of his brain function while he plays golf, looking to discover the way his brain processes information. For example, how does the visual input he receives standing at the tee allow him to judge distance to the pin? They would also compare Woods's brain function with that of less accomplished golfers and would even program computers to mimic the way his brain works during play.

Evolutionary Psychology

One of the most recent developments in the field, evolutionary psychology, first made its appearance in the late 1980s. This school of thought has a heritage—with a twist—in the work of the functionalists and their emphasis on Darwin's theory of natural selection. Central to the **evolutionary psychology** approach is the idea that certain cognitive strategies and goals are so important that natural selection has built them into our brains. But instead of proposing that evolution has selected specific behaviors per se (as earlier evolutionary theorists, including Charles Darwin himself, believed), these theorists believe that general cognitive strategies (such as using deception to achieve one's goals) and certain goals (such as finding attractive mates) are inborn. This approach is currently being developed by researchers such as Lida Cosmides and John Tooby (1996), David Buss (1994, 1999), and Steven Pinker (1994, 1997, as reviewed by Barkow et al., 1992; Plotkin, 1994, 1997). For example, these theorists claim that we have the ability to lie because our ancestors who could lie had an advantage: They could trick their naïve companions into giving up resources. These more devious ancestors had more children who survived than did their nonlying contemporaries, and their lying children had more children, and so on, until the ability to lie was inborn in all members of our species. Notice that lying is not a specific behavior; it is a strategy that can be expressed by many behaviors, all of them deceitful.

● **Cognitive neuroscience:** A blending of cognitive psychology and neuroscience (the study of the brain) that aims to specify how the brain stores and processes information.

● **Evolutionary psychology:** The approach in psychology that assumes that certain cognitive strategies and goals are so important that natural selection has built them into our brains.

Probably the best source of evidence for theories in evolutionary psychology is *cultural universals,* instances of the same practices occurring in all cultures.

How can you test a theory about the history of human psychology? Fossils will tell you little. Instead, some researchers seek evidence for evolutionary developments in contemporary humans. Probably the best source of evidence for theories in evolutionary psychology is *cultural universality,* instances of the same practice occurring in all cultures. If people even in remote areas with very different cultures show the same tendencies, it is likely that the tendencies are not the result of learning. In fact, people in all cultures have been found to share certain concepts and practices, including lying, telling stories, gossiping, using proper names, expressing emotions with facial expressions, fearing snakes, dancing, making music, giving gifts, making medicines; the list goes on and on (Brown, 1991). Being human is more than having a certain type of body; it is also having a certain type of brain and mind that works in certain ways.

Evolutionary psychologists also compare human abilities with those of animals, particularly nonhuman primates (Hauser, 1996). For example, by studying the way animals communicate, researchers try to infer which abilities formed the basis of human language. By studying animals, researchers hope to discover the abilities of our common ancestors and, from those data, develop theories about the way they may have been refined over the course of evolution. When asked about what might underlie Tiger Woods's achievements, an evolutionary psychologist might note that although our species did not evolve to play golf, the abilities that arose via natural selection for hunting game and avoiding predators could also be used in other ways, including sports.

But evidence of universality or shared abilities in nonhuman animals and humans does not tell us *why* those characteristics are present. Are they really adaptations? Evolutionary theories are notoriously difficult to test because we don't know what our ancestors were like and how they evolved. Just because we are born with certain tendencies and characteristics does not mean that these are evolutionarily selected adaptations. As Stephen Jay Gould and Richard Lewontin (1979) point out, at least some of our modern characteristics are simply by-products of other characteristics that were in fact selected. Your nose evolved to warm air and direct scents; and once you have a nose, you can use it to hold up your eyeglasses. But just as nobody would claim that the nose evolved to hold up glasses, nobody should claim that all the current functions of the brain resulted from natural selection. The various schools of psychological thought are summarized in Table 1.1 on page 20.

TABLE 1.1 Schools of Psychological Thought

Name	Landmark Events	Key Ideas
Structuralism	Wundt founds first psychology laboratory, 1879.	Use introspection to discover the elements of mental processes and rules for combining them.
Functionalism	James's *Principles of Psychology,* published 1890.	Study why thoughts, feelings, and behavior occur, how they are adaptive.
Gestalt psychology	Wertheimer's paper on perceived movement, 1912.	Focus on overall patterns of thoughts or experience; "the whole is more than the sum of its parts."
Psychodynamic theory	Freud publishes *The Ego and the Id,* 1927.	Conflicts among conscious and unconscious forces underlie many thoughts, feelings, and behaviors.
Behaviorism	Watson's paper *Psychology as the Behaviorist Views It,* 1913; Skinner's *The Behavior of Organisms,* 1938.	Behavior is the appropriate focus of psychology, and it can be understood by studying stimuli, responses, and the consequences of responses.
Humanistic psychology	Maslow publishes *Motivation and Personality,* 1954.	Nonscientific approach; belief that people have positive values, free will, and deep inner creativity.
Cognitive psychology	Neisser's book *Cognitive Psychology* gives the "school" its name, 1967.	Mental processes are like information processing in a computer.
Cognitive neuroscience	First issue of the *Journal of Cognitive Neuroscience* appears, 1989.	"The mind is what the brain does."
Evolutionary psychology	Barkow, Cosmides, and Tooby edit *The Adapted Mind,* 1992.	Mental strategies and goals are often inborn, the result of natural selection.

Dates prior to Maslow based on Boring (1950).

Looking *at* Levels

Sex and Emotional Involvement

Evolution is particularly sensitive to characteristics of organisms that are involved in reproduction and the survival of offspring. However, even these sorts of characteristics are not entirely predetermined by built-in mechanisms. For example, Buunk and colleagues (1996) asked German, Dutch, and American men and women whether they would be more upset if their mates had sex with someone else or if their mates became emotionally involved with another person. These researchers found that men claimed that they would be more upset if their mates had sex with someone else, but women tended to have the opposite response. However, this difference was larger in the United States than it was in European countries, suggesting that culture can play a role in modulating or modifying evolutionarily relevant behaviors.

At the level of the brain, the genes may affect whether men are more interested, in general, in having sex with attractive mates (which would allow them to distribute their genes widely) or in having stable, long-term relationships. In contrast, the genes may affect whether women are more interested, in general, in having a mate who will devote himself to her children (which would increase the likelihood that they will survive) than in having sex with attractive men. These factors, in turn, can be modulated by personal beliefs and desires. For example, members of certain religious orders have sworn off having sex altogether, in spite of what their genes may have to say. Events at the level of the group can also modulate the differences between men and women, as evidenced by the differences between countries. Moreover, events at the different levels of analysis clearly interact: Religions are passed down through generations at the level of the group, and these ideas shape the personal beliefs of individuals, which in turn modulate how people respond to genetically programmed predispositions. In addition, our built-in impulses and desires have shaped our cultures; for example, the laws and mores of our societies are designed in part to help us manage our sexual relationships, both for the good of ourselves and the good of our society. Clearly, events at the different levels interact in many subtle and intricate ways.

TEST YOURSELF!

1. What were the key ideas in each of the earliest schools of psychology: structuralism, functionalism, Gestalt psychology?
2. How are these ideas different from the psychodynamic theory, behaviorism, and humanistic psychology approaches?
3. Cognitive psychology, cognitive neuroscience, and evolutionary psychology are the most recent developments in psychology. How do these approaches build on what came before?

The Psychological Way: What Today's Psychologists Do

If you read that Tiger Woods had seen a psychologist, would you think that he had a personal problem, or that he was suffering from too much stress? Neither guess is necessarily true; psychologists do much more than help people cope with their problems. As the field of psychology developed, different schools of thought focused on different aspects of mental processes and behavior; their varying influences are felt in what today's psychologists do. And just what is that?

Here we consider three major types of psychologists: those who help people deal with personal problems or stress, those who study mental processes and behavior scientifically, and those who seek to solve specific practical problems, such as helping athletes perform better.

Mary Whiton Calkins, the first woman president of the American Psychological Association (1905). As of 1997, fully two thirds of all Ph.D.'s in psychology were earned by women (American Psychological Association, http://www.apa.org/pi/wpo/wapa/final.html).

Clinical and Counseling Psychology: A Healing Profession

Andrea is a **clinical psychologist** who specializes in treating people with eating disorders. Many of Andrea's clients have a disorder called *anorexia nervosa*, characterized by refusal to maintain a healthy weight. Others, who have a disorder called *bulimia nervosa*, eat and then force themselves to vomit or take laxatives immediately afterward. Andrea sees such patients once or twice a week, for 50 minutes per session. During these sessions, Andrea's job is usually to discover why behaviors that are so destructive in the long run seem so desirable to the patient in the short run. She then helps her patients phase out the destructive behaviors and replace them with more adaptive behaviors—for instance, responding to anxiety

● **Clinical psychologist:** The type of psychologist who provides psychotherapy and is trained to administer and interpret psychological tests.

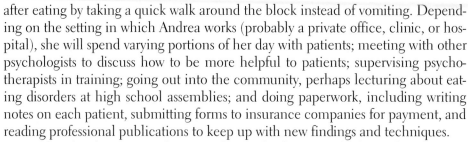

- **Psychotherapy:** The process of helping clients learn to change so they can cope with troublesome thoughts, feelings, and behaviors.

- **Counseling psychologist:** The type of psychologist who is trained to help people with issues that naturally arise during the course of life.

- **Psychiatrist:** A physician who focuses on mental disorders; unlike psychologists, psychiatrists can prescribe drugs, but they are not trained to administer and interpret psychological tests, nor are they trained to interpret and understand psychological research.

There are many kinds of psychotherapy, and different training prepares therapists in different ways. Psychiatrists, for example, typically would not treat families, but clinical psychologists and social workers—as well as other mental health professionals—might.

after eating by taking a quick walk around the block instead of vomiting. Depending on the setting in which Andrea works (probably a private office, clinic, or hospital), she will spend varying portions of her day with patients; meeting with other psychologists to discuss how to be more helpful to patients; supervising psychotherapists in training; going out into the community, perhaps lecturing about eating disorders at high school assemblies; and doing paperwork, including writing notes on each patient, submitting forms to insurance companies for payment, and reading professional publications to keep up with new findings and techniques.

Andrea has been trained to provide **psychotherapy,** which involves helping clients learn to change so they can cope with troublesome thoughts, feelings, and behaviors. She also administers and interprets psychological tests, which can help in diagnosis and planning the appropriate treatment. *Clinical neuropsychologists* are clinical psychologists who work specifically with tests designed to diagnose the effects of brain damage on thoughts, feelings, and behavior and to indicate which parts of the brain are impaired following trauma. Other clinical psychologists work with organizations, such as corporations, to help company groups function more effectively; for example, a psychologist might advise a company about reducing stress among workers in a particular unit, or teach relaxation techniques to all employees. Some clinical psychologists have a Ph.D. (doctor of philosophy) degree, awarded by a university psychology department; these graduate programs teach students not only how to do psychotherapy and psychological testing, but also how to conduct and interpret psychological research. A clinical psychologist may also have a Psy.D. (doctor of psychology), a graduate degree from a program with less emphasis on research. In some states, clinical psychologists can obtain additional training and be granted the right to prescribe drugs (the first state to grant this privilege was New Mexico, in 2002).

If Andrea had been trained as a **counseling psychologist,** she would have learned to help people deal with issues we all face, such as choosing a career, marrying, raising a family, and performing at work. Counseling psychologists often provide career counseling and vocational testing to help people decide which occupations best suit their interests and abilities. They sometimes provide psychotherapy, but these professionals may have a more limited knowledge of therapeutic techniques than do clinical psychologists. They may have a Ph.D. (often from a program that specifically trains them in this area) or often an Ed.D. (doctor of education) degree granted by a school of education.

Andrea could also have become a **psychiatrist.** If she had gone this route, her training and competence would have differed from that of the other mental health professionals. First, as a physician with an M.D. (doctor of medicine) degree, a psychiatrist has extensive medical training and can prescribe drugs whereas, in general, psychologists cannot. Second, a medical doctor, unlike a clinical psychologist, has typically not been trained to interpret and understand psychological research or psychological testing.

There are two other types of clinical mental health practitioners who are not psychologists. Her interest in clinical work might have led Andrea to choose either of those professions: social work or psychiatric nursing. If she had earned an M.S.W. (master of social work) degree, as a **social worker** she would typically focus on using psychotherapy to help families and individuals, and she also would teach clients how to use the social service systems in their communities. A **psychiatric nurse** holds a master's degree in nursing (M.S.N., master of science in nursing) as well as a certificate of clinical specialization (C.S.) in psychiatric nursing. A psychiatric nurse provides psychotherapy, usually in a hospital or clinic, or in private practice, and works closely with medical doctors to monitor and administer medications; in some cases, a psychiatric nurse can prescribe medications.

Academic Psychology: Teaching and Research

James is a professor of psychology at a large state university. Most mornings he prepares lectures, which he delivers three times a week. He also has morning office hours, when students can come by to ask questions about their program of courses in the department or their progress in one of James's classes. Once a week at noon he has a committee meeting; this week the committee on computer technology is discussing how best to structure the department computer network. His afternoons are taken up mostly with research. (If he worked at a smaller college, he might spend more time teaching and less time on research; alternatively, if he worked at a hospital, he might spend the lion's share of his time doing research and very little time teaching.) James's specialty is *developmental psychology*, the study of how thinking, feeling, and behaving develop with age and experience. Today his research work takes place at a laboratory preschool at the university, where he and his assistants are testing the ways children become attached to objects such as dolls and blankets. James also must find time to write papers for publication in professional journals, and he regularly writes grant proposals requesting funding for his research, so that he can pay students to help him test the children in his studies. He also writes letters of recommendation, grades papers and tests, and reads journal articles to keep up with current research in his and related fields. James tries to eat lunch with colleagues at least twice a week to keep up-to-date on departmental events and the work going on at the university in other areas of psychology.

Developmental psychologists often take special care to prevent their presence from affecting the child's behavior in any way.

Although the activities of most **academic psychologists** are similar in that they all teach and conduct research, the kinds of research vary widely. Different types of psychologists focus on different types of questions. For example, if James had become a *cognitive psychologist* (one who studies thinking, memory, and related topics), he might ask, "How was Tiger Woods able to hit the ball with the appropriate force in the correct direction?" but not "What was the role of the audience, and would it have been different if the tournament had been held 50 years ago?" If he had become a *social psychologist* (one who studies how people think and feel about themselves and other people, and how groups function), he might ask the second question, but not the first. And in neither case would he ask, "What aspects of Tiger Woods's character help him deal with the extreme stress he faces?" That question would interest a *personality psychologist* (one who studies individual differences in preferences and inclinations).

● **Social worker:** A mental health professional who helps families (and individuals) with psychotherapy and helps clients use the social service systems in their communities.

● **Psychiatric nurse:** A nurse who holds a master's degree in nursing as well as a certificate of clinical specialization in psychiatric nursing (M.S.N., C.S.), and who provides psychotherapy and works with medical doctors to monitor and administer medications.

● **Academic psychologist:** The type of psychologist who focuses on conducting research and teaching.

Because psychology is a science, it rests on objective tests of its theories and ideas. It is through research that we learn how to diagnose people's problems and how to cure them; it is through research that we determine what kind of career will make good use of a particular person's talents; it is through research that we understand how to present material so that students can understand and remember it most effectively. Theories about such issues can come from anywhere, but there is no way to know whether an idea is right or wrong except by testing it scientifically, through research.

There are at least as many different types of academic psychologists as there are separate sections in this book. In fact, this book represents a harvest of their research. Thousands of researchers are working on the topics covered in each chapter, and it is through their efforts that we have learned enough to be able to write a book like this one.

Applied Psychology: Better Living Through Psychology

Maria works in the software development department of a high-tech company; she is a *human factors psychologist*, a professional who works to improve products so that people can use them more intuitively and effectively. Maria begins her day by testing several versions of menus to be used with a computer program under development. She wants to know which commands the software users will expect to find listed under the headings on the menu bar at the top of the screen. She has designed a study in which she asks people to find specific commands and records by computer where they look for the commands and how long it takes to find them. Maria often has lunch in the company cafeteria, but today she is eating at her desk, studying the results from the morning's testing session. Puzzled by what she sees, Maria suddenly realizes that the way she has labeled the commands is affecting how people think of them. She quickly begins to set up another series of tests on the computer. After lunch, she attends a talk by a visiting scientist about his new research, some of which may prove useful in her project:

The subject is the nature of memory, and she takes careful notes. Afterward, she has a weekly meeting of the project team. Today the person who is designing the screen icons reports that he has run into difficulty; he describes the problem to the team, and various members ask questions and make suggestions. After this meeting, Maria goes to her office and works for an hour on a written progress report, then spends another hour on an article she is writing for a technical journal.

Applied psychologists use the principles and theories of psychology in practical areas such as education, industry, and marketing. An applied psychologist may hold a Ph.D. or, sometimes, only a master's degree in an area of psychology (in North America a master's degree typically requires two years of postgraduate study instead of the four to six for a Ph.D.). Applied psychologists not only work on improving products and procedures but also conduct research aimed at solving specific practical problems. Working in applied psychology, a *developmental psychologist* may be employed by or consult with the product development department of a toy company. Using her knowledge of children, she can help design toys that would be appropriate for particular age levels; she would then bring children to a playroom at the company to

Applied psychologists have many roles, one of which is to help attorneys decide which potential jurors are likely to be sympathetic or hostile to the defendant.

● **Applied psychologist:** The type of psychologist who studies how to improve products and procedures and conducts research to help solve specific practical problems.

see how they play with new toys. A *physiological psychologist* studies the brain and brain/body interactions and may work at a company that makes drugs or brain-scanning machines. A *social psychologist* may help lawyers decide which possible jurors should be rejected. A *personality psychologist* may design a new test to help select suitable personnel for a job. An *industrial/organizational (I/O) psychologist* focuses on using psychology in the workplace; he or she might help an employer create a more comfortable and effective work environment so as to increase worker productivity, or might redesign work spaces to promote more effective employee communication. A *sport psychologist* works with athletes to help them improve their performances, by helping them learn to concentrate better, deal with stress, and practice more efficiently (Tiger Woods works with a sport psychologist). An *educational* or *school psychologist* works with educators (and sometimes families), devising ways to improve the cognitive, emotional, and social development of children at school.

The relative numbers of the various types of psychologists are illustrated in Figure 1.2, and their occupations are summarized in Table 1.2.

FIGURE 1.2 Percentages of Psychologists Working in Different Specialty Areas

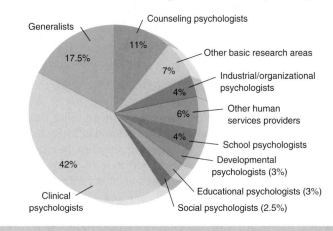

TABLE 1.2 What Psychologists Do

Clinical psychologist	Administers and interprets psychological tests; provides psychotherapy.
Clinical neuropsychologist	Diagnoses effects of brain damage on thoughts, feelings, and behavior, and diagnoses the locus of damage.
Counseling psychologist	Helps people with issues that arise during everyday life (career, marriage, family, work).
Developmental psychologist	Researches and teaches the development of mental processes and behavior with age and experience.
Cognitive psychologist	Researches and teaches the nature of thinking, memory, and related aspects of mental processes.
Social psychologist	Researches and teaches how people think and feel about themselves and other people, and how groups function.
Personality psychologist	Researches and teaches individual differences in preferences and inclinations.
Physiological psychologist	Researches and teaches the nature of the brain and brain/body interactions.
Human factors psychologist	Applies psychology to improve products.
Industrial/organizational psychologist	Applies psychology in the workplace.
Sport psychologist	Applies psychology to improve athletic performance.
Educational or School psychologist	Applies psychology to improve cognitive, emotional, and social development of schoolchildren.

Looking *at* Levels

A Science of the Obvious?

Science is an attempt to cajole Mother Nature into giving up her secrets. Over the years, the science of psychology has made many such attempts at unveiling the secrets of mental processes and behavior by means of the various approaches just reviewed. In the process, research psychologists of various persuasions are sometimes accused of merely demonstrating the obvious.

For example, the old saw that familiarity breeds contempt states the obvious—or does it? Let's see how a social psychologist would approach testing the obvious in this case. Robert Zajonc (1968, 1970) was interested in the factors that lead us to like something or someone. He found, repeatedly, that people like previously seen things *better* than unfamiliar ones; research shows that familiarity breeds not contempt but affinity (Bornstein, 1989). This is called the *mere-exposure effect*. At the level of the brain, the repeated presentation of a picture allows it to be taken in with less effort, which at the level of the person leads to positive feelings and preferences (Bornstein & D'Agostino, 1994). These effects can in turn alter behavior, including behavior toward other people (the level of the group).

In another study, Leone and Galley (described by Bornstein et al., 1987) demonstrated that the mere-exposure effect is not just a laboratory curiosity. They showed participants photographs of one of two faces, flashing them so briefly that the faces could not be identified. Following this, the participant met with the person in the photograph and another person, ostensibly to decide whether the author of some poems was a man or a woman. As arranged beforehand, the two other people disagreed, and the participant had to be the tie-breaker. The participants tended to side with the person whose face they had seen in the photograph, even though they were unaware they had seen it. The mere-exposure effect was at work here across levels, an event in the brain affecting a preference (level of the person) that in turn affected a social interaction (level of the group).

So, not all results from psychological research are obvious and, in fact, you will see many such examples of discoveries that are not obvious as you continue in this book. Chapter 2 explores in more detail just how studies can be conducted to discover new and sometimes surprising facts about mental processes and behavior.

TEST YOURSELF!

1. What do clinical and counseling psychologists do?
2. What do academic psychologists do?
3. What do applied psychologists do?

Ethics: Doing It Right

Let's say that Tiger Woods wants to learn how to overcome pain so that he can practice hard even when he is hurt, but that practicing when injured might cause long-term damage to his body. Would it be ethical for a sport psychologist to teach Tiger—or anyone else—techniques for continuing to work out even in the presence of damaging pain? Or, what if Tiger developed a "block" that impaired his playing? Would it be ethical for a therapist to treat him with new, unproven techniques?

Ethics in Research

Following World War II, people were horrified to learn that the Nazis had performed ghastly experiments on human beings. The war trials in Nuremberg led directly to the first set of rules, subscribed to by many nations, outlawing these sorts of experiments (in the next chapter, we will consider in detail the kinds of research methods psychologists use).

Sometimes the actions of psychologists also call for a set of rules, especially when participants' rights conflict with a research method or clinical treatment.

Certain methods are obviously unethical; everybody knows not to cause people in experiments to become addicted to drugs to see how easily they can overcome the addiction, and not to beat people to help them overcome a psychological problem. But most situations are not so clear-cut.

Research With People: Human Guinea Pigs?

In 1996, some New York psychiatrists were tapping the spines of severely depressed teenagers at regular intervals in order to see whether the presence of certain chemicals in the spinal fluid could predict which particular teens would attempt suicide. As required by law, the youths' parents had given permission for the researchers to draw the fluids. However, this study was one of at least ten that a court in New York brought to a screeching halt on December 5, 1996 (*New York Times*, page A1). The New York State Appeals Court found that the existing rules for the treatment of children and the mentally ill were unconstitutional because they did not properly protect these participants from abuse by researchers. However, the researchers claimed that without these studies they would never be able to develop the most effective drugs for treating serious impairments, some of which might lead to suicide. Do the potential benefits of such studies outweigh the pain they cause?

New York was more lax in its policies than many other states. California, Connecticut, Massachusetts, and Illinois do not allow researchers to conduct experiments in which the gain is not outweighed by the pain, or that have risks but do not benefit a participant directly, unless the participants themselves (not someone else for them) provide **informed consent.** Informed consent means that before agreeing to take part, potential participants in a study must be told what they will be asked to do and must be advised of the possible risks and benefits of the procedure. They are also told that they can withdraw from the study at any time without being penalized. Only after an individual clearly understands this information and gives consent by signature can he or she take part in a study.

Any study that uses funds from the U.S. government or from most private funding sources must be approved by an Institutional Review Board (IRB) at the university, hospital, or other institution that sponsors or hosts the study. The IRB monitors all research projects at that institution, not just those of psychologists. An IRB usually includes not only scientists but also physicians, clergy, and representatives from the local community. The IRB considers the potential risks and benefits of each research proposal and decides whether the study can be performed. In many universities and hospitals, researchers are asked to discuss their projects with the board, to explain in more detail what they are doing and why.

Concerns about the ethical treatment of human participants lead most IRBs to insist that participants be **debriefed,** that is, interviewed after the study about their experience. The purpose of debriefing is to ensure that they are having no negative reactions as a result of their participation and that they have understood the purposes of the study. Deceiving participants with false or misleading information is frowned on and approved only when the participants will not be harmed and the knowledge gained clearly outweighs the use of dishonesty.

Research With Animals

Animals are studied in some types of psychological research, particularly studies that focus on understanding the brain. Animals, of course, can't give informed consent, don't volunteer, and can't decide to withdraw from the study if they get nervous or uncomfortable. But this doesn't mean animals are not protected. Animal studies, like human ones, must have the stamp of approval of an IRB. The IRB makes sure

● **Informed consent:** The requirement that a potential participant in a study be told what he or she will be asked to do and possible risks and benefits of the study before agreeing to take part.

● **Debriefing:** An interview after a study to ensure that the participant has no negative reactions as a result of participation and understands why the study was conducted.

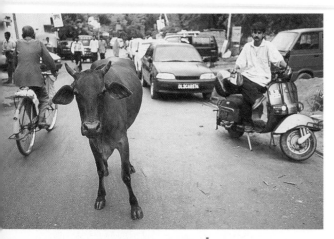

In large parts of India, animals are not eaten (some are even considered sacred). Many in that culture may believe that animal research is not appropriate.

the animals are housed properly (in cages that are large enough and cleaned often enough) and that they are not mistreated. Researchers are not allowed to cause animals pain unless that is explicitly what is being studied—and even then, they must justify in detail the potential benefits to humans (and possibly to animals, by advancing veterinary medicine) of inflicting pain.

Is it ethical to test animals at all? This is not an easy question to answer. Researchers who study animals argue that their research is ethical. They point out that although there are substitutes for eating meat and wearing leather, there is no substitute for the use of animals in certain kinds of research. So, if the culture allows the use of animals for food and clothing, it is not clear why animals should not be studied in laboratories if the animals do not suffer and the findings produce important knowledge. This is not a cut-and-dried issue, however, and thoughtful people disagree. As the new brain-scanning technologies improve (see Chapter 3), the need for some types of animal studies may diminish.

Ethics in Clinical Practice

Imagine a Dr. Smith who has developed a new type of therapy that she claims is particularly effective for patients who are afraid of some social situations, such as public speaking or meeting strangers. You are a therapist who has a patient struggling with such difficulties and not responding to conventional therapy. You haven't been trained in Smith therapy, but you want to help your patient. Should you try Smith therapy? According to the American Psychological Association guidelines (see Table 1.3), the answer is clear: No. If you have not been trained appropriately or are not learning the therapy under supervision, you have no business delivering it.

This sort of ethical decision is relatively straightforward. But the process of psychotherapy sometimes requires careful stepping through emotional and ethical minefields. Psychologists are bound by their states' laws of confidentiality and may not communicate about a patient without specific permission from the patient, except in certain extreme cases, as when a life or (in some states) property is at stake. Therapists have gone to jail rather than reveal personal information about their patients. Indeed, difficult cases sometimes cause new laws to be written. A patient at the University of California told a psychologist at the student health center that he wanted to kill someone and named the person. The campus police were told; they interviewed the patient and let him go. The patient then killed his targeted victim. The dead woman's parents sued the university for "failure to warn." The case eventually wound its way to California's highest court. One issue was whether the therapist had the right to divulge confidential information from therapy sessions. The court ruled that a therapist is obligated to use reasonable care to protect a potential victim. More specifically, in California (and in most other states now), if a patient has told his or her psychologist that he or she plans to harm a specific other person, and the psychologist has reason to believe the patient can and will follow through with that plan, the psychologist must take steps to protect the target person from harm, even though doing so may violate the patient's confidentiality. Similar guidelines apply to cases of potential suicide.

Further, a therapist cannot engage in sexual relations with a patient or mistreat a patient physically or emotionally. The American Psychological Association has developed many detailed ethical guidelines based on the principles listed in Table 1.3.

TABLE 1.3   General Ethical Principles and Code of Conduct for Psychologists

Principle A: Beneficence and Nonmaleficence
"Psychologists strive to benefit those with whom they work and take care to do no harm. . . . Because psychologists' scientific and professional judgments and actions may affect the lives of others, they are alert to and guard against personal, financial, social, organizational, or political factors that might lead to misuse of their influence."

Principle B: Fidelity and Responsibility
"Psychologists uphold professional standards of conduct, clarify their professional roles and obligations, accept appropriate responsibility for their behavior, and seek to manage conflicts of interest that could lead to exploitation or harm."

Principle C: Integrity
"Psychologists seek to promote accuracy, honesty, and truthfulness in the science, teaching, and practice of psychology. In these activities psychologists do not steal, cheat, or engage in fraud, subterfuge, or intentional misrepresentation of fact. Psychologists strive to keep their promises and to avoid unwise or unclear commitments."

Principle D: Justice
"Psychologists recognize that fairness and justice entitle all persons to access to and benefit from the contributions of psychology and to equal quality in the processes, procedures, and services being conducted by psychologists."

Principle E: Respect for People's Rights and Dignity
"Psychologists respect the dignity and worth of all people, and the rights of individuals to privacy, confidentiality, and self-determination. . . . Psychologists are aware of and respect cultural, individual, and role differences, including those based on age, gender, gender identity, race, ethnicity, culture, national origin, religion, sexual orientation, disability, language, and socioeconomic status and consider these factors when working with members of such groups."

Source: APA (2002), direct quotes with portions abridged; a complete description can be found at http://www.apa.org/ethics/code.html.

Looking *at* Levels

Gambling With a Mind

Schizophrenia is a devastating brain disease that often cripples a person's ability to function in the world. Research has found that its victims benefit greatly if medicated as soon as possible after the onset of the disease (DeQuardo, 1998; Johnstone, 1998; Wyatt et al., 1998). Given this finding, we have an ethical dilemma: When new treatments are created, how can we justify trying *them* when we know that delaying the treatments already known to be effective can cause long-term negative effects for the patient?

You've seen earlier how the levels approach helps us to understand psychological events, and now you can see that it also guides us in asking appropriate questions. Focusing on the level of the brain, you would consider how likely it is that a new drug or treatment will be better than available treatments. If a well-supported theory of brain functioning leads you to be confident that a new drug will be better than those available, it would

be easier to justify trying it. At the level of the person, you must consider whether delaying effective treatment will change how the person can function in everyday life. If the possible changes would be drastic (for example, leading the person to lose a job), a strong note of caution should temper your deliberations. At the level of the group, you might ask how the new drug might affect the person's family. Would it make him or her more irritable? less responsive? And of course, you must think about how events at the different levels could interact: If the treatment makes the patient more irritable, how will the reactions of the family affect the sufferer? Considering such concerns, what is *your* view on this dilemma?

TEST YOURSELF!

1. What are proper ethics in research with humans and animals?
2. What are proper ethics in clinical practice?

CONSOLIDATE!

The Science of Psychology: Getting to Know You

- Psychology is the science of mental processes and behavior.

- The goals of psychology are to describe, explain, predict, and control mental processes and behavior.

- Psychology can best be understood by studying events at different levels of analysis: the levels of the brain, person, and group.

- The level of the brain is where we examine the activity of certain brain systems, structural differences in people's brains, and effects of various genes and chemicals (such as hormones) on mental processes and behavior.

- The level of the person is where we study the contents of mental processes, not just the mechanisms that give rise to them. The contents of our memories, beliefs, goals, feelings, and the like are part and parcel of who we are.

- The level of the group includes both our previous and our present social interactions.

- Events at the different levels are interdependent and are always interacting.

THINK IT THROUGH   If you look at your own life, can you identify instances where events at the different levels of analysis were clearly at work?

Can you think of any dangers inherent in adopting a scientific understanding of psychology? Think about criminals. How would you react if it could be shown conclusively that all criminals have an abnormal structure in a certain part of their brains? If this were true, what should we do with this knowledge? Or, what if it could be shown that criminals have perfectly normal brains, but they all had weak parents who didn't give them enough discipline when they were children? Neither of these single-perspective views is likely to be correct, but what if one level of analysis turns out to be more important than the others?

Psychology Then and Now: The Evolution of a Science

- Psychology began as the study of mental processes, such as those that underlie perception, memory, and reasoning.

- The structuralists tried to understand such processes; their goal was to identify the elements of consciousness and the rules by which these elements are combined into mental structures. One of the primary methods of the structuralists was introspection ("looking within"), which turned out to be unreliable and not always valid.

- The functionalists rejected the goal of identifying mental processes and how they operated in favor of seeking explanations for thoughts, feelings, and behavior. The functionalists were interested in how mental processes adapt to help people survive in the natural world.

- In contrast, the Gestalt psychologists also reacted against the structuralists, but they were more disturbed by the emphasis on breaking mental processes into distinct elements. The Gestaltists studied the way the brain organizes material into overall patterns, both in perception and in thinking.

- Freud and his colleagues shifted focus to events at the level of the person (and, to some extent, the level of the group). Psychodynamic theories of the mind are concerned largely with the operation of unconscious mental processes and primitive impulses (often related to sex) in dictating what we think, feel, and do.

- The behaviorists rejected the assumption that psychology should focus on mental processes; they urged us to stick with what we could see—stimuli, responses, and the consequences of responses.

- The humanists, in part reacting against Freud's theory, were interested in developing treatments of psychological problems that relied on respect for individuals and their potentials.

- Elements of the various strands came together in the cognitive revolution, which began by thinking of the mind by analogy to a computer program; in this view, mental processing is information processing.

- Cognitive neuroscientists study the relation between events at all three levels of analysis, with an emphasis on how the brain gives rise to thoughts, feelings, and behavior.

- Evolutionary psychology treats many goals and cognitive strategies as adaptations that are the results of natural selection.

THINK IT THROUGH   If Tiger Woods were being studied by adherents of a single psychological "school," which would be least likely to produce useful insights? Most likely? When asked to account for his remarkable skill, Tiger Woods professes to have no conscious knowledge about how he plays so well. How would this report affect the approaches taken by the different schools?

Which "school" of psychology is most interesting to you? Can you think of any ways in which combining ideas or approaches from the different schools might be helpful?

The Psychological Way: What Today's Psychologists Do

- The three types of psychologists are distinguished by their training, work settings, and types of work.
- Clinical and counseling psychologists administer and interpret psychological tests, provide psychotherapy, offer career and vocational counseling, and help people with specific psychological problems.
- Academic psychologists teach and do research, in addition to helping to run their universities, colleges, or institutions.
- Applied psychologists use the findings and theories of psychology to solve practical problems.

THINK IT THROUGH If you were an athlete who began to freeze up whenever you played, what kind of psychologist would you seek? Would your choice be different if you already had a clear understanding of why you "choked"?

Would the President be more effective if he had a chief psychologist? If so, which sort of psychologist would be most helpful? (Don't assume it would necessarily be a clinical psychologist.) Why?

Ethics: Doing It Right

- Research with humans or nonhuman animals at universities, hospitals, and most industrial settings requires approval from an Institutional Review Board (IRB).
- For research with humans, the IRB will insist that the study include informed consent, which is information in advance about the possible risks and benefits of participation.
- The IRB will also require debriefing, which is an interview after the study to ensure that the participant had no negative reactions and did, in fact, understand the purpose of the study.
- The IRB will also prevent deception, unless the deception is harmless and absolutely necessary.
- For research with animals, the IRB requires that the animals be treated well (for example, housed in clean cages)

and that pain be inflicted only if that is what is studied and is justified by the benefits from the research.

- In clinical practice, psychotherapists have clear ethical guidelines to follow, which include maintaining confidentiality unless a specific other person (or, in some states, property) is clearly in danger, or suicide is an imminent genuine concern.
- In addition, therapists cannot use techniques that they have not been trained to use or engage in inappropriate personal behavior with patients.

THINK IT THROUGH Would it be ethical to study Tiger Woods as if he were some kind of guinea pig? How about to ask him to try out a new way to relieve stress, which you are convinced is better than anything else available but for which you have no evidence to back up your intuitions?

Imagine you are an academic psychologist doing research on whether sugar makes chimps more active and less able to concentrate on tasks. So far, your student who is carrying out the research has found that sugar clearly leads to increased activity and difficulty on cognitive tasks requiring concentration. A new student joins the project to help with the research, and she tells you that the animals appear to be agitated, have difficulty sleeping and, at times, appear to be in pain. The study is otherwise going well. What should you do? When you write up the study for publication, how will you address this issue?

Key Terms

academic psychologist, p. 23	introspection, p. 11
applied psychologist, p. 24	level of the brain, p. 7
behavior, p. 5	level of the group, p. 7
behaviorism, p. 15	level of the person, p. 7
clinical psychologist, p. 21	mental processes, p. 4
cognitive neuroscience, p. 18	psychiatric nurse, p. 23
cognitive psychology, p. 17	psychiatrist, p. 22
counseling psychologist, p. 22	psychodynamic theory, p. 14
debriefing, p. 27	psychology, p. 4
evolutionary psychology, p. 18	psychotherapy, p. 22
functionalism, p. 12	social worker, p. 23
Gestalt psychology, p. 13	structuralism, p. 10
humanistic psychology, p. 16	unconscious, p. 14
informed consent, p. 27	

chapter **2**

Smithsonian American Art Museum, Washington, DC/Art Resource, NY

The Research Process: *How We Find Things Out*

In 1984, President Ronald Reagan gave his official blessing to a daring project, building a permanent inhabited space station. A key part of President Reagan's vision was that the space station should be built and staffed by people from many different countries. His vision came to pass, and the International Space Station (ISS) is now being constructed some 250 miles above earth. The ISS is a mammoth project, comparable in size and scope to the pyramids of ancient Egypt. The station will span a distance greater than a football field and will weigh over 1 million pounds. Its solar panels will spread over almost an acre, and it will cost at least $90 billion.

The ISS is not just a technological marvel, it is also a testament to our very human ability to cooperate and interact effectively. The project is particularly impressive because it is being built by 16 countries—including former enemies, notably the United States and Russia.

In the first phase of the program (which began in 1995), American and Russian astronauts lived and worked together on the Russian *Mir* space station. These experiences taught astronauts and earth-bound scientists about living and working in space and, equally important, they also built cooperation and trust between the astronauts themselves and the respective organizations back on earth.

The ISS will be used not only to observe the earth, but also to experiment with new ways to manufacture materials, to make drugs, and to study diseases ranging from osteoporosis to cancer. But

> The ISS is not just a technological marvel, it is also a testament to our very human ability to cooperate and interact effectively.

more than that, the science of psychology will play a key role in discovering the best ways for people to live and function in space. The ISS will allow us to understand new facets of human mental processes and behavior, both when people are alone and when they are part of a group. How can we learn such things from the ISS, or from events in any other context? Through science. In this chapter, we see how the science of psychology can be used to learn about the brain, the person, and the group.

The Scientific Method: Designed to Be Valid

On November 2, 2000, the first astronauts moved into the ISS. They moved into just one small part of this work-in-progress, which provided the bare minimum in basic facilities. Among these basic essentials were a treadmill and an exercise bike. These pieces of equipment are not luxury items, but absolute necessities: Astronauts must exercise to retain their bone density and muscles. The trouble is (as too many of we earth-bound couch potatoes know only too well) that the benefits of exercising occur later, whereas the benefits of coping with the press of immediate events occurs right now—and thus it's sometimes difficult to be motivated to exercise. A substitute has been proposed: Simply vibrating the bones appears to prevent calcium loss. But could this procedure also disrupt the astronauts' concentration? Perhaps make it difficult for them to sleep?

How could we find out whether the new vibration treatment would have unintended consequences, for example by affecting the quality of sleep (either as the procedure was conducted, or afterward)? Psychology is a science because it relies on a specific type of method of inquiry, and this method, in principle, allows us to discover characteristics that predict human behavior.

The **scientific method** is a way to gather facts that will lead to the formulation and validation of a theory. It involves *specifying a problem; systematically observing events; forming a hypothesis of the relation between variables; collecting new observations to test the hypothesis; using such evidence to formulate and support a theory; and finally, testing the theory.* Let's take a closer look at the scientific method, one step at a time.

● **Scientific method:** The scientific method involves specifying a problem, systematically observing events, forming a hypothesis of the relation between variables, collecting new observations to test the hypothesis, using such evidence to formulate and support a theory, and finally testing the theory.

Step 1: Specifying a Problem

What do we mean by "specifying a problem"? Science tries to answer questions, any one of which may be rephrased as a "problem." Despite the way the word is often used in ordinary conversation, a problem is not necessarily bad: It is simply a question you want to answer, or a puzzle you want to solve. A scientist might notice what seems to be a consistent pattern, for example, and wonder if it reflects a connection or a coincidence. A scientist might notice that many cultures have an afternoon siesta or "tea time" and wonder whether humans have a biological rhythm that makes us sluggish at that time of day—and might then ask how living in weightlessness affects such biological rhythms. Speaking metaphorically, a scientist might notice a nail sticking above the boards and ask why it is different from other nails. Selecting astronauts is an example. We ask *what* personal characteristics will lead someone to be effective in this job, *why* those characteristics will lead them to behave in certain ways in specific circumstances, and *how* those characteristics were acquired and can be further developed.

Step 2: Observing Events

Consider the idea of "systematically observing events." Scientists are not content to rely on impressions or interpretations. They want to know the facts, as free from any particular notions of their significance as possible. Facts are established by collecting **data,** which are numerical measurements or careful observations of a phenomenon. Properly collected data can be **replicated,** that is, collected again by the original investigator or someone else. Scientists often prefer quantitative data (numerical measurements), such as how quickly a person can respond to an unexpected event or how accurately a person can establish up versus down in weightlessness. In addition to collecting numerical data, scientists rely on systematic observations, which simply document that a certain event occurs. But unless the data include numbers, it is often difficult to sort the observation from the interpretation. The data are just the facts, ma'am, nothing but the facts—when data are collected the interpretation must be set aside, saved for later.

What do we mean by "events"? An event in the scientific sense is the occurrence of a particular phenomenon. Scientists study two kinds of events: those that are themselves directly observable (such as how many times in an hour a mother strokes her infant) and those that, like thoughts, motivations, or emotions, can only be inferred. For example, when people smile without really meaning it (as many people do when posing for photographs), the muscles used are not the same ones that produce a sincere smile (Ekman, 1985). It is possible to observe directly which set of muscles is in use, and the recorded data would distinguish between the two kinds of contractions. But the researcher's interest goes beyond the directly observable muscle contractions to the link with inner (and invisible) thoughts and feelings. By studying what's observable (the muscles), researchers can learn about the unobservable (the mental state of the smiler).

Step 3: Forming a Hypothesis

What about "forming a hypothesis of the relation between variables"? First, by the term **variable,** researchers mean an aspect of a situation that is liable to change (or, in other words, that can vary); more precisely, a variable is a characteristic of a substance, quantity, or entity that is measurable. A **hypothesis** is a tentative idea that might explain a set of observations. For example, the ISS does not have normal patterns of "day" and "night," and thus astronauts do not sleep when it gets dark outside. Rather, they may get wrapped up in what they are doing and forget how much time has passed since they last slept. Could losing sleep interfere with learning? For

● **Data:** Objective observations.

● **Replication:** Collecting the same observations or measurements and finding the same results as were found previously.

● **Variable:** An aspect of a situation that can vary, or change—specifically, a characteristic of a substance, quantity, or entity that is measurable.

● **Hypothesis:** A tentative idea that might explain a set of observations.

optimal performance on the ISS, it's important to know whether lack of sleep impairs learning and later memory; memory lapses that would lead to harmless mishaps on earth could lead to disaster in space. This hypothesis comes down to the assertion that there's a connection between two variables—not sleeping and learning. However, before you urge the ISS astronauts to force themselves to sleep 8 hours in 24, you ought to test the hypothesis to find out whether it's correct.

Step 4: Testing the Hypothesis

Thus, you must go about "collecting new observations to test the hypothesis." The first thing you need to do is create operational definitions of the key concepts, which makes them concrete enough to test. An **operational definition** specifies a variable by indicating how it is measured or manipulated. In this example, "not sleeping" might be defined as having stayed continuously awake for 24 hours, and learning might be defined as retaining memory for material that was studied earlier in the day. Are there rigorous studies that bear on memory following a sleepless night? Yes, and researchers have found that staying up all night does disrupt memory for information learned that day (Graves et al., 2001; Stickgold et al., 2000). In fact, memory for verbal material is impaired even if people sleep, when their sleep patterns are disrupted because they've had to wake up intermittently (Ficca et al., 2000). A typical study has two groups: In one, participants learn some information, such as a list of words. These people then sleep normally, and their memory is tested the next day. Participants in a second group learn the same material (and learn it as well) as the participants in the first group, but stay up all night and are tested the next day. The hypothesis is that the participants will have better memory if they were allowed to sleep.

Step 5: Formulating a Theory

Now consider "using such evidence to formulate and support a theory." A **theory** consists of an interlocking set of concepts or principles that explains a set of observations. Unlike a hypothesis, a theory is not a tentative idea and doesn't focus on possible relationships among variables. Instead, theories are rooted in an established web of facts and concepts and focus on the *reasons* for established relationships among variables. In our example, the notion that people will fail to store information in memory if they don't sleep is a hypothesis, not a theory. A theory might explain that sleep is necessary for learning because: (1) Specific brain areas are activated when we learn during the day; and (2) Those areas must continue to operate for a specific period of time while we sleep in order to store the information acquired during the day. Hypotheses and theories both produce **predictions,** expectations about specific events that should occur in particular circumstances if the hypothesis or theory is correct.

Step 6: Testing a Theory

Finally, what do we mean by "testing the theory"? The history of science is littered with theories that turned out to be wrong. Researchers evaluate a theory by testing its predictions. For example, in one study researchers scanned the brains of people as they learned sequences of responses, and then scanned their brains again while they slept that night. Brain areas that were active during learning continued to be active during sleep. Moreover, these areas were more active during sleep for the people who had learned the task that day than for others who had not learned it (Maquet et al., 2000).

● **Operational definition:** A definition of a variable that specifies how it is measured or manipulated.

● **Theory:** An interlocking set of concepts or principles that explain a set of observations.

● **Prediction:** An expectation about specific events that should occur in particular circumstances if the theory or hypothesis is correct.

Each time a theory makes a correct prediction, the theory is supported, and each time it fails to make a correct prediction, the theory is weakened. If enough of its predictions are unsupported, the theory must be rejected and the data explained in some other way. A good theory is *falsifiable*; that is, it makes predictions it cannot "squirm out of." A falsifiable theory can be rejected if the predictions are not confirmed.

Looking *at* Levels

Sleep Disturbances and Cognitive Function

Sleep apnea ("apnea" in Greek means "without breath") is a disorder in which people stop breathing while they sleep. When the blood oxygen level falls low enough, brain circuits are activated to wake the person and to restart breathing. About 12 million Americans have this problem (American Sleep Apnea Association, 2002, *http://www.sleepapnea.org/index2.html*); some victims suffer hundreds of episodes a night. In most cases, the problem is caused by an obstruction in the throat, which also leads the person to snore while sleeping. Researchers hypothesized that because sleep apnea disrupts sleep, it should also impair memory and other cognitive abilities. To test this hypothesis, they studied the effects that surgically removing the obstruction had on learning, memory, and decision-making in 53 people who had this disorder. They administered tests of cognitive abilities before surgery and 6 months after surgery. Happily, surgery did lead to better learning, memory, and decision-making abilities. Moreover, the researchers found that the more effective the treatment was in eliminating the apnea, the larger the improvement in these abilities (Dahloef et al., 2002).

Consider this finding from the perspective of levels of analysis. First, brain processes monitor oxygen levels in the blood and wake the person. If sleep is disrupted, so is the ability to retain information acquired during the day. Second, at the level of the person, people with apnea typically feel drowsy during the day. They find it difficult to sustain interest and motivation. Third, at the level of the group, they under-perform at work, and are not as helpful to co-workers as they could be. In addition, these people typically snore as they sleep, which can disrupt the sleep patterns of their partners—impairing their partners' cognitive abilities the next day. (Even though sleep apnea is not contagious, its effects may be!) The events at the three levels of analysis interact. Indeed, relationships can be strained if one partner snores, and that strain can itself contribute to sleep problems, which in turn could make the cognitive deficits even worse. And consider the role of the surgeon: The social interactions between patient and surgeon, which culminate in the patient's deciding to have surgery, can have dramatically positive effects—vastly improving the quality of life of the sufferer.

TEST YOURSELF!

1. What are the steps of the scientific method?

The Psychologist's Toolbox: Techniques of Scientific Research

Life on the ISS is not like life on earth. The beginning of the day isn't signaled by the dawn's early light, and your morning shower is more likely to be a sponge bath. Drinking from a glass is a challenge; a wrong nudge, and a glob of liquid floats up into your face—or, worse yet, escapes and drifts toward sensitive equipment mounted on a nearby wall or ceiling. And forget about sleeping in a bed. Instead, you crawl into a special sleeping bag that is anchored to a wall, and tie your arms

- **Independent variable:** The aspect of the situation that is intentionally varied while another aspect is measured.

- **Dependent variable:** The aspect of the situation that is measured as an independent variable is changed. The value of the dependent variable *depends* on the independent variable.

down before nodding off. But perhaps the most striking differences from life as we usually experience it are social. The ISS will only house 7 people. How will they get along as time goes on? How should living quarters be designed to ensure enough privacy, to "give them some space"—but at the same time promote social support? How should daily wake/sleep schedules be synchronized for the different crew members? And how many of the crew should be men, how many women? Would it be best if most of the crew were married couples?

The questions go on and on. How can we answer them? Although all sound psychological investigations rely on the scientific method, the different areas of psychology often pose and answer questions differently. Psychologists use a variety of research tools, each with its own advantages and disadvantages.

Experimental Research

Much psychological research relies on conducting experiments, controlled situations in which variables are manipulated.

Independent and Dependent Variables

The variables in a situation—for example, "amount of sleep" and "memory performance"—are the aspects of a situation that can vary. The experimenter deliberately alters one aspect of a situation, which is called the **independent variable**, and measures another, called the **dependent variable.** In other words, the value of the dependent variable depends on the value of the independent variable. In our sleeplessness and memory example in the previous section, whether or not participants slept was the independent variable (it was deliberately varied), and memory performance was the dependent variable (it was measured; see Figure 2.1). By examining

FIGURE 2.1 Relationship Between Independent and Dependent Variables

The independent variable is what is manipulated—whether or not participants slept. In this example, the dependent variable, what is measured, is memory performance the next day.

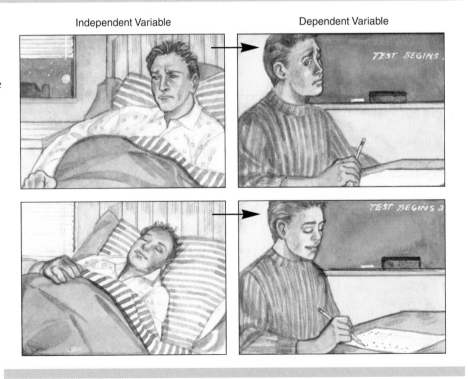

Independent Variable   Dependent Variable

the link between independent and dependent variables, a researcher hopes to discover exactly which factor is causing an **effect,** which is the difference in the dependent variable that results from a change in the independent variable. In our sleeplessness and memory example, the effect is the degree to which memory is better following sleep than it is following a sleepless night.

Once researchers have found a relation between two variables, they need to test that relation to rule out other possible explanations for it; only by eliminating other accounts can we know whether a hypothesized relation is correct. Say we had tested only one group, the one that was kept awake. The fact that these students failed to recall many words would not necessarily show that sleep is critical for learning. Why? Perhaps the test was too difficult and, even in the best of circumstances, the participants wouldn't have been able to remember much. Or perhaps the testing situation created a lot of anxiety, and that's what interfered with learning. A **confound,** or *confounding variable,* is another possible aspect of the situation (such as the anxiety that accompanies a test) that has become entangled with the aspects that you have chosen to vary. Confounds thus lead to results that are ambiguous, that do not have a clear-cut interpretation (see Figure 2.2).

Experimental and Control Conditions

One way to disentangle confounds is to use a control group. A **control group** is treated identically to the experimental group except with regard to the one variable you want to study; a good control group holds constant—or controls—all of the variables in the experimental group except the one of interest. In experiments on the role of sleep in learning, the experimental group doesn't sleep; the control group does. If the kinds of people assigned to the two groups differ markedly, say, in age, gender, or learning ability (or any combination of the three), those factors could be confounds that would mask a clear reading of the experiment's results; any difference in the groups' performance could have been caused by any of those elements. For instance, if the sleepless group happened to include more people

- **Effect:** The difference in the dependent variable that is due to the changes in the independent variable.

- **Confound** (or *confounding variable*): An independent variable that varies along with the ones of interest, and could be the actual basis for what you are measuring.

- **Control group:** A group that is treated exactly the same way as the experimental group, except for the one aspect of the situation being studied—the independent variable. The control group holds constant—"controls"—all of the variables in the experimental group except the one of interest.

FIGURE 2.2 Confounding Variable in Everyday Life

A particularly dramatic example of a confounding variable in everyday life was present during the Victorian age. At this time in history, women often were considered frail and delicate creatures, at least partly because they seemed prone to fainting spells. Did they faint because of their "inner natures" or for some other reason? Consider the fact that many of these women wore extremely tight corsets to give them tiny waists. In fact, the corsets were so tight that women could only take shallow breaths—if they took a deep breath, they ran the risk of being stabbed by the whalebone "stays" in the corset. These stays were thin and very sharp, and not only could they cause a bloody wound, but they could also puncture a lung! One consequence of continued shallow breathing is dizziness—hence the fainting spells common among stylish Victorian women. Can you think of an experiment to show conclusively that the corsets were to blame? How do you think views of women would have been different if men had worn tight corsets too?

who were elderly than the control group, the researchers should not conclude that sleeplessness led the experimental group to forget—perhaps these people simply learned less effectively in general. In a properly conducted experiment, therefore, the researchers rely on **random assignment**: participants are assigned randomly, that is, by chance, to the experimental and the control groups, so that no confounds can sneak into the composition of the groups.

Similarly, you can use a **control condition,** either for a group of people or a single person. Instead of testing a separate control group, you test the same group another time, keeping everything the same as in the experimental condition except for the single independent variable of interest. For example, you could test the same people twice, once when they were allowed to sleep normally after studying the words and once when they were kept awake. (Indeed, you can test them four times, twice while on earth and then twice while on the ISS; this experiment would allow you to discover whether sleep has the same effects on memory in weightlessness as it does normally.) To avoid confounding the order of testing with the condition (experimental versus control), you would test half the participants in the control condition before testing them in the experimental condition and would test the other half of the participants in the experimental condition before testing them in the control condition.

Quasi-Experimental Design

One element of a true experiment is that the participants are assigned randomly to the different groups. But in the real world, it is not always possible or desirable to achieve randomness, and so sometimes research designs must be *quasi-experimental* (quasi means "as if" in Latin). For instance, let's say that you want to discover whether the effects of sleep on learning are different for people of different ages, so you decide to test four groups of people: teenagers, college students, middle-aged people, and the elderly. Obviously you cannot assign people to the different age groups randomly. You should control for as many variables—such as health and education level—as you can in order to make the groups as similar as possible. Similarly, if you want to track changes over time (for example, in astronauts' memory abilities after they return from a stint in the ISS), it is not possible to assign people randomly to the groups as time goes by because you are taking measurements only from people you have measured before. In these examples, participants are not assigned randomly to groups, and such quasi-experiments rely on comparing multiple groups or multiple sets of measurements, attempting to eliminate potential confounds as much as possible. Unfortunately, because the groups can never be perfectly equated on all characteristics, you can never be certain exactly what differences among groups are responsible for the observed results. The conclusions you draw from quasi-experiments cannot be as strong as those from genuine experiments.

Correlational Research

Sometimes it is not possible to do an experiment or even a quasi-experiment, particularly if you are interested in studying large groups or if it is difficult (or unethical) to manipulate the variables. Let's say you want to answer this question: Do people who need minimal sleep make better astronauts? Not only is there a problem in randomly assigning participants to the long-sleep and minimal-sleep groups, but you also can't simply declare that someone is an astronaut. For a question like this, not even a quasi-experiment can be performed.

● **Random assignment:** Participants are assigned randomly, that is, by chance, to the experimental and the control groups, so that no biases can sneak into the composition of the groups.

● **Control condition:** Like a control group, but administered to the same participants who receive the experimental condition.

FIGURE 2.3   Strength of Correlation

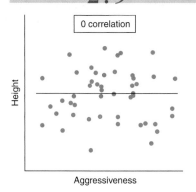

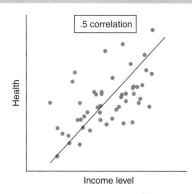

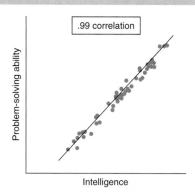

Tall people are as likely to be aggressive or gentle as short people, which is indicated by the 0 correlation between the two variables.

The more tightly the dots cluster around the line, the higher the correlation; the higher the correlation, the more accurately the value on one dimension predicts the value on the other. Here we see that knowing someone's income level predicts something about how healthy they are likely to be, but not very much.

We would expect smarter people to be better at solving problems, as reflected in this very high correlation. Although these are fictional data, why might you make these predictions?

From *Introduction to the Practice of Statistics* by David S. Moore and George P. McCabe. © 1989, 1993, 1999 by W. H. Freeman and Company. Used with permission.

In such situations, researchers use another method to study the relations among variables, a method that relies on the idea of correlation. **Correlation** is a relationship in which changes in the measurements of one variable are accompanied by changes in the measurements of another variable. A *correlation coefficient* (often simply called a *correlation*) is an index of how closely related two measured variables are. Figure 2.3 illustrates three predicted correlations between variables. A positive relationship (in which increases in one variable are accompanied by increases in another) is indicated by a correlation value that falls between zero and 1.0; a negative relationship (in which increases in one variable are accompanied by decreases in another) is indicated by a correlation that is between zero and –1.0. If we had plotted "sickness" instead of "health" in the middle panel, the line would have gone down—and the correlation we plotted would have been –.5 instead of +.5. A zero correlation indicates no relationship between the two variables; they do not vary together. The closer the correlation is to 1.0 or –1.0, the stronger the relationship; visually, the more tightly the numbers cluster around the line, the higher the correlation.

Correlational research involves measuring at least two things about each of a set of individuals or groups (or measuring the same individuals or groups at a number of different times), and looking at the way one set of measurements goes up or down in tandem with another set of measurements; correlations always compare one pair of measurements at a time. The main advantage of correlational research is that it allows researchers to compare variables that cannot be manipulated directly. The main disadvantage is that correlations indicate only that two variables tend to vary together, not that one *causes* the other. For example, evidence suggests a small correlation between poor eyesight and intelligence (Belkin & Rosner,

● **Correlation:** An index of how closely interrelated two sets of measured variables are, which ranges from –1 to +1. The higher the correlation (in either direction), the better you can predict the value of one type of measurement when given the value of the other.

1987; Miller, 1992; Williams et al., 1988), but poor eyesight doesn't cause someone to be smarter! Similarly, researchers have found that weightlessness disrupts spatial orientation (such as awareness of the position of your body) and that these effects may be related to space motion sickness (Young et al., 1993). Does motion sickness disrupt spatial orientation, or does impaired spatial orientation produce motion sickness? Or, does some other variable—such as abnormal head movements—produce both effects? Just given the correlation between problems in spatial orientation and the occurrence of motion sickness, you can't say. Remember: *Correlation does not imply causation.* In contrast, in an experiment, you can manipulate the independent variable and hold everything else constant, and thereby show that changes in the independent variable cause changes in the dependent variable.

Researchers have found that the lower the level of a chemical called monoamine oxidase (MAO) in the blood, the more the person will tend to seek out thrilling activities (such as sky diving and bungee jumping; Zuckerman, 1995). Thus there is a negative correlation between the two measures: as MAO levels go down, thrill seeking goes up. But we don't know whether MAO level causes the behavior or vice versa—or whether some other chemical, personality trait, or social factor causes the levels of both MAO and thrill seeking to vary together.

Descriptive Research

Although the scientific method is always described in terms of testing hypotheses, this isn't quite the whole story. Not all research is sparked by specific hypotheses. Some research is devoted simply to describing "things as they are." Theorizing without facts is a little like cooking without ingredients.

Naturalistic Observation

For the scientist, "facts" are not intuitions, impressions, or anecdotes. Essential to the scientific method is careful, systematic, and unbiased observation that can be repeated by others, and some researchers specialize in collecting such data from real-world settings. For example, some researchers observed caregivers interacting with young children, and noted that the caregivers changed their language and speech patterns, using short

sentences and speaking in a high pitch. This speech modification, originally dubbed *motherese*, is now often called *child-directed speech* (Morgan & Demuth, 1996; Snow, 1991, 1999).

Some scientists observe animals in the wilds of Africa; others observe sea life in the depths of the ocean; and others observe humans in their natural habitats.

Although naturalistic observation is an essential part of science, it is only the first step. You cannot control for confounding variables, and you cannot change the variables to see what the critical factor in a particular mental process or behavior might be. The discovery of motherese does not tell us whether caregivers use it in order to help children understand them, or to entertain them, or simply to imitate other caregivers they have heard. In science, observing an event is only the first step.

Case Studies

Sometimes nature or human affairs lead to unique situations, which change an independent variable in a novel way. A **case study** focuses on a single instance of a situation, examining it in detail. For example, a researcher might study a single astronaut, looking closely at her life and circumstances in an effort to formulate hypotheses about the psychological underpinnings that lead someone to succeed in this profession. Many neuropsychologists study individual brain-damaged patients in depth to discover which abilities are "knocked out" following certain types of damage (in Chapter 3 you will read about a young soldier who, after suffering brain injury, had bizarre visual impairments). A psychologist who studies abnormal behavior might study a reported case of multiple personalities to discover whether there's anything to the idea (books such as *Sybil* and *The Three Faces of Eve* describe such cases in great detail), a cognitive psychologist may investigate how an unusually gifted memory expert is able to retain huge amounts of information almost perfectly, and a personality psychologist might study in detail how astronauts remain motivated through years and years of hard work with no guarantee that they will ever fly into space.

Unlike naturalistic observation, case studies are not necessarily limited simply to describing values of variables and relations among them. Rather, in some situations you can actually perform experiments with only a single case (such as testing the ability of a memory expert to recall lists of familiar versus unfamiliar things, or to remember words versus pictures), and such studies can help us understand the particular situation in detail. Nevertheless, we must always be cautious about generalizing from a single case; that is, we must be careful in assuming that the findings in the case study extend to all other similar cases. Any particular person may be unusual for many reasons and so may not be at all representative of people in general.

Surveys

A **survey** is a set of questions put to the participants about their beliefs, attitudes, preferences, or activities. Surveys are a relatively inexpensive way to collect a lot of data fairly quickly, and they are popular among psychologists who study personality and social interactions. Surveys provide data that can be used to formulate or test a hypothesis. However, the value of surveys is limited by what people are capable of reporting accurately. You could ask people how they feel about the government's using tax dollars to build the ISS, but would not use a survey to ask people how their brains work, or to report subtle behaviors, such as body language,

Brain damage following an accident can cause someone to fail to name fruits and vegetables while still able to name other objects (Hart et al., 1985). A case study would examine such a person in detail, documenting precisely what sorts of things could and could not be named.

● **Case study:** A scientific study that focuses on a single instance of a situation, examining it in detail.

● **Survey:** A set of questions, typically about beliefs, attitudes, preferences, or activities.

that they may engage in unconsciously. Moreover, even if they are capable of answering, people may not always respond honestly; as we note in Chapter 11, this is especially a problem when the survey touches on sensitive personal issues, such as sex. And even if people do respond honestly, what they say does not always reflect what they do. We cite a classic example in Chapter 16, reported in 1934 by La Piere, in which restaurant managers were asked whether they would serve Chinese people; although most said they would not, when Chinese people actually came to their restaurants, virtually all served them without question. Finally, not everyone who is asked to respond does, in fact, fill in the survey. Because a particular factor (such as income or age) may incline some people, but not others, to respond, it is difficult to know whether you are justified in generalizing from the respondents to the rest of the group of interest.

Survey questions have to be carefully worded so that they don't lead the respondent to answer in a certain way and yet still get at the data of interest. In the survey mentioned in Chapter 1, in which the respondents had to decide which was worse, a mate's having sex with or becoming emotionally involved with someone else, people who disliked both possibilities equally had no way to say so, and the forced choice would not reflect their true position (which may be a serious problem with this study; DeSteno & Solvey, 1996; Harris, 2002). Similarly, the nature of the response scale (for example, the range of values presented) affects what people say, as does the order in which questions are asked (Schwarz, 1999). Table 2.1 summarizes the basic research methods used in psychology.

TABLE 2.1 Summary of Research Methods

Experimental design	Participants are assigned randomly to groups, and the effects of manipulating one or more independent variables on a dependent variable are studied.
Quasi-experimental design	Similar to experiments but participants are not assigned to groups randomly.
Correlational research	Relations among different variables are documented, but causation cannot be inferred.
Naturalistic observation	Observed events are carefully documented.
Case study	A single instance of a situation is analyzed in depth.
Survey	Investigation requires participants to answer specific questions.

Be a Critical Consumer of Psychology

No technique is always used perfectly, so you must be a critical consumer of all science, including the science of psychology. Metaphorically speaking, there are no good psychologists on salt-free diets—we take everything with at least a grain of salt! But this doesn't mean that you should be cynical, doubting everything you hear or read. Rather, whenever you read a report of a psychological finding in a newspaper, a journal article, or a book (including this one), look for aspects of the study that could lead to alternative explanations. You already know about the possibility of confounds; here are a few other issues that can cloud the interpretation of studies.

Reliability: Count on It!

Not all data are created equal; some are better than others. One way to evaluate data is in terms of reliability. **Reliability** means consistency. A reliable car is one you can count on to behave consistently, starting even on cold mornings and not dropping random parts on the highway. A reliable study is one that can be replicated, that is, repeated with the same results. When you read about the results of a study, find out if they have been replicated; if so, then you can have greater confidence that the results are reliable.

Validity: What Does It Really Mean?

Something is said to be valid if it is what it claims to be; a valid driver's license, for example, is one that was, in fact, issued by the state and has not expired (and thus does confer the right to drive). In science, **validity** means that a method provides a true measure of what it is supposed to measure. A study may be reliable but not valid, or vice versa. Table 2.2 lists four of the major types of validity (Carmines & Zeller, 1979).

- **Reliability:** Data are reliable if the same results are obtained when the measurements are repeated.

- **Validity:** A measure is valid if it does in fact measure what it is supposed to measure.

TABLE 2.2 Four Major Types of Validity

Type	Description	Example
Face validity	Design and procedure appear to assess the variables of interest.	Sample essay as part of an entrance exam for journalism school.
Content validity	Measures assess all aspects of phenomenon of interest.	Test of knowledge of research methods that covers all methods.
Criterion validity	A measure or procedure is comparable to a different, valid measure or procedure.	A paper-and-pencil test of leadership ability correlates highly with poll results of leadership of actual leaders.
Construct validity	Measures assess variables specified by a theory.	A theory defines "fatigue" in terms of lack of alertness, and the measure assesses this lack.

HANDS ON

To understand the concept of validity, let's see what it's like to be a participant in a study. So, before reading further, try this exercise. Table 2.3 (p. 46) contains a list of words. Decide whether the first word names a living object or a nonliving one (circle the word "living" at the right if it is living; otherwise move to the next word); then decide whether the second word begins with the letter t (circle the words "begins with t" if it does; otherwise move to the next word); then decide whether the third word names a living or a nonliving object, whether the fourth word begins with the letter t, and so on, alternating judgments as you go down the list. Please do this now.

TABLE 2.3 What's in a Word?

Circle the word on the right if the word on the left has the named property; otherwise, move on to the next word. After you finish the list, read on.

salmon	living		trout	living
tortoise	begins with *t*		donkey	begins with *t*
airplane	living		teapot	living
toad	begins with *t*		house	begins with *t*
guitar	living		table	living
goat	begins with *t*		terrain	begins with *t*
truck	living		tiger	living
automobile	begins with *t*		rosebush	begins with *t*
snake	living		bacteria	living
tent	begins with *t*		carpet	begins with *t*
toast	living		staple	living
television	begins with *t*		tricycle	begins with *t*
wagon	living		lawn	living
tarantula	begins with *t*		ocean	begins with *t*
toadstool	living		tuna	living
elephant	begins with *t*		terrier	begins with *t*

When you have finished marking the list, take out a piece of paper and (without looking!) write down as many of the words as you can. How many words from the list were you able to remember?

The standard result from this kind of study is that people will remember more words after making a living/nonliving judgment than after making a t/non-t judgment (for example, see Craik & Tulving, 1975). This result is usually interpreted to mean that the more we think about (or "process") the material, as we must in order to make the living/nonliving decision, the better we remember it; for the t words, we only need to look at the first letter, not think about the named object at all. In fact, if we are forced to think about something in detail but don't consciously try to learn it, we end up remembering it about as well as if we did try to learn it (we discuss this curiosity more in Chapter 7).

Does this demonstration of differences in memory following differences in judgment really bear out this interpretation? What if you remembered the words you judged as living/nonliving better because you had to read the whole word to make the required judgment, but you only looked at the first letter of the other words to decide whether they began with t? If this were the case, your better memory of words in the living/nonliving category would have nothing to do with "think-

A study of mind-reading can be highly reliable (repeatable), but not valid if the mind-reader has figured out a way to cheat; and a study that uses facial expression to determine what someone is feeling can be valid but not reliable (because a given expression may be difficult to discriminate from other expressions).

ing about it more." Therefore, the experiment would not be valid—it would not be measuring what the investigator designed it to measure.

When you read a result, always try to think of as many interpretations for it as you can; you may be surprised at how easy this can be. And, if you can think of an alternative interpretation, see whether you can think of a control group or condition that would allow you to tell who was right, you or the authors of the study.

Bias: Playing With Loaded Dice

Sometimes beliefs, expectations, or habits alter how participants in a study respond or affect how a researcher sets up or conducts a study, thereby influencing its outcome. This leaning toward a particular result, whether conscious or unconscious, is called **bias**, and it can take many forms. One form of bias is **response bias**, in which people have a tendency to respond in a particular way regardless of their actual knowledge or beliefs. For example, many people tend to say yes more than no, particularly in some Asian cultures (such as that of Japan). This sort of bias toward responding in "acceptable" ways is a devilish problem for survey research. For example, when asked whether you support research on the ISS that could produce a cure for cancer, you would be hard-pressed to say "no." Another form of bias is **sampling bias,** which occurs when the participants or items are not chosen at random but instead are selected so that an attribute is over- or underrepresented— which leads to a confound. For example, say you wanted to know the average heights of male and females, and you went to shopping malls to measure people. What if you measured the males outside a toy store (and so were likely to be measuring little boys), but measured the women outside a fashion outlet for tall people (and so were likely to find especially tall women)? Or, what if the words in the living/nonliving group in Table 2.3 were interesting words such as centipede and boomerang, and the words in the t/non-t group were bland words such as toe and broom? Or, perhaps the living/nonliving words were more emotionally charged than the t/non-t words, or were more familiar. What if only language majors were

● **Bias:** An investigator's previous beliefs or expectations alter how a study is set up or conducted, leading it to come out a certain way.

● **Response bias:** A tendency to respond in a particular way regardless of respondents' actual knowledge or beliefs.

● **Sampling bias:** A bias that occurs when the participants or items are not chosen at random, but instead are chosen so that one attribute is over- or underrepresented.

tested, or only people who read a lot and have terrific vocabularies? Could we assume that all people would respond the same way? Take another look at Table 2.3; can you spot any potential sampling bias?

Sampling bias isn't just something that sometimes spoils otherwise good studies. Do you remember the U.S. Presidential election of 2000? Albert Gore and George W. Bush were in a dead heat, and the election came down to the tally in a few counties in Florida. Based on surveys of voters exiting their polling places, the TV commentators predicted that Gore would be the winner. What led them astray? Sampling bias. The news organizations that conducted the surveys did not ask absentee voters how they cast their ballots. In such a close election, this was an important factor because the absentee voters included many members of the armed services, who tend to be Republicans. Thus, sampling only from those who voted on election day produced a biased view of how the entire population voted—and the TV commentators had to eat their words.

Experimenter Expectancy Effects: Making It Happen

Clever Hans, a horse that lived in Germany in the early 1890s, apparently could add (Rosenthal, 1976). When a questioner (one of several) called out two numbers to add, for example, "6 plus 4," Hans would tap out the correct answer with his hoof. Was Hans a genius horse? Was he psychic? No. Despite appearances, Hans wasn't really adding. He seemed to be able to add, and even to spell out words (with one tap for "a" and an additional tap for each letter in the alphabet), but he responded only if his questioner stood in his line of sight and knew the answer. The questioner, who expected Hans to begin tapping, always looked at Hans's feet right after asking the question—thereby cuing Hans to start tapping. When Hans had tapped out the right number, the questioner always looked up—cuing Hans to stop tapping. Although, in fact, Hans could neither add nor spell, he was a pretty bright horse: He was not trained to do this; he "figured it out" on his own.

The cues offered by Hans's questioners were completely unintentional; they had no wish to mislead (and, in fact, some of them were probably doubters). But unintentional cues such as these lead to **experimenter expectancy effects,** which occur when an investigator's expectations lead him or her (consciously or unconsciously) to treat participants in a way that encourages them to produce the expected results. Such effects can occur in all types of research, from experiments to surveys—in all cases, the investigator can provide cues that influence how participants behave.

At least for experiments, it's clear how to guarantee that experimenter expectancy effects won't occur: In a **double-blind design** not only is the participant "blind" to (unaware of) the predictions of the study and hence unable consciously or unconsciously to serve up the expected results, but also the experimenter is "blind" to the condition assigned to the participant and thus unable to induce the expected results. What would have happened if a questioner of Clever Hans had not known the answer to the question?

Psychology and Pseudopsychology: What's Flaky and What Isn't?

Are you a fire sign? Do you believe that your Zodiac sign matters? So many people apparently do that the home page for the *Yahoo!* site on the World Wide Web will automatically provide your daily horoscope. But astrology—along with palm reading and tea-leaf reading, and all their relatives—is not a branch of psychology; it is pseudopsychology. **Pseudopsychology** is superstition or unsupported

● **Experimenter expectancy effects:** Effects that occur when an investigator's expectations lead him or her (consciously or unconsciously) to treat participants in a way that encourages them to produce the expected results.

● **Double-blind design:** The participant is "blind" to (unaware of) the predictions of the study (and so cannot consciously or unconsciously produce the predicted results), and the experimenter is "blind" to the condition assigned to the participant (and so experimenter expectancy effects cannot produce the predicted results).

● **Pseudopsychology:** Theories or statements that at first glance look like psychology, but are in fact superstition or unsupported opinion pretending to be science.

Dogbert (Dilbert's dog) is thinking scientifically about astrology. He proposes a relationship among seasonal differences in diet, sunlight, and other factors and personality characteristics. These variables can be quantified and their relationships tested. If these hypotheses are not supported by the data but Dogbert believes in astrology nevertheless, he's crossed the line into pseudopsychology.

opinion pretending to be science. Pseudopsychology is not just "bad psychology," which rests on poorly documented observations or badly designed studies and, therefore, has questionable foundations. Pseudopsychology is not psychology at all. It may look and sound like psychology, but it is not science.

Appearances can be misleading. Consider extrasensory perception (ESP). Is this pseudopsychology? ESP refers to a collection of mental abilities that do not rely on the ordinary senses or abilities. Telepathy, for instance, is the ability to read minds. This sounds not only wonderful but magical. No wonder people are fascinated by the possibility that they, too, may have latent, untapped, extraordinary abilities. The evidence that such abilities really exist is shaky, as discussed in Chapter 4. But the mere fact that many experiments on ESP have come up empty does not mean that the experiments themselves are bad or "unscientific." One can conduct a perfectly good experiment, guarding against confounds, bias, and expectancy effects, even on ESP. Such research is not necessarily pseudopsychology.

Let's say you want to study telepathy. You might arrange to test pairs of participants, with one member of each pair acting as "sender" and the other as "receiver." Both the sender and receiver would look at hands of playing cards that contained the same four cards. The sender would focus on one card (say, an ace), and would "send" the receiver a mental image of the chosen card. The receiver's job would be to guess which card the sender is seeing. By chance alone, with only four cards to choose from, the receiver would guess right about 25% of the time. So the question is, can the receiver do better than mere guesswork? In this study, you would measure the percentage of times the receiver picks the right card, and compare this to what you would expect from guessing alone.

But wait! What if the sender, like the questioners of Clever Hans, provided visible cues (accidentally or on purpose) that have nothing to do with ESP, perhaps smiling when "sending" an ace, grimacing when "sending" a two. A better experiment would have sender and receiver in different rooms (or better yet, have one on the ISS and another here on earth), thus controlling for such possible confounds. Furthermore, what if people have an unconscious bias to prefer red over black cards, which leads both sender and receiver to select them more often than would be dictated by chance? This difficulty can be countered by including a control condition, in which a receiver guesses cards when the sender is not actually sending. Such guesses will reveal response biases (such as a preference for red cards), which exist independently of messages sent via ESP.

Whether ESP can be considered a valid, reliable phenomenon will depend on the results of such studies. If they conclusively show that there is nothing to it, then people who claim to have ESP or to understand it will be trying to sell a bill of goods—and will be engaging in pseudopsychology. But as long as proper studies are under way, we cannot dismiss them as pseudopsychology.

Looking *at* Levels

Who Will Be a Good Leader?

The ISS will be under the command of a single person, who will have to manage people from various nationalities with different backgrounds and skills. Can psychology offer any insights into the characteristics of a good leader? To answer this question, Simon Taggar, Rick Hackett, and Sudhir Saha (1999) studied 94 teams (each with 5 or 6 undergraduates, who had been together for 13 weeks). They asked the students to complete personality tests and to rate each other for leadership ability. The researchers also obtained a measure of general intelligence. The various test scores were analyzed using a type of correlation, seeing which were most strongly related to the leadership ratings. The most important predictor of who would emerge as a leader turned out to be the level of intelligence, the more the better. But this was not the sole contributor; those perceived to be high in "leadership" were also more likely to be conscientious, extraverted, and emotionally stable. Moreover, the most effective teams were those in which more of the members scored high on such "leadership" characteristics. An effective leader has good followers.

Consider this finding from the levels of analysis perspective. First, the best teams were not simply those that had good leaders. They also needed team members who shared the characteristics of good leaders (level of the group). Second, the characteristics of good leaders included personality characteristics such as being conscientious and extraverted (level of the person). And third, intelligence, which depends on memory and brain processing speed (level of the brain), also proved important for good leaders. As usual, events at the different levels interacted: Good teamwork (level of the group) emerged when team members shared personality characteristics (level of the person) and had higher intelligence (level of the brain).

TEST YOURSELF!

1. What are the key ingredients of experimental research?
2. What is correlational research?
3. What types of descriptive studies do psychologists conduct?
4. Which methodological aspects of studies should you always critically evaluate?

Statistics: Measuring Reality

Like Rome or the pyramids, the ISS won't be built in a day. This goes not only for the physical structure, but also for how its members will function as a team. Only over time, largely by evaluating current practices and trying to improve them, will researchers discover how best to help astronauts work together smoothly. Over time, researchers will collect various measures of mental processes and performance, such as the rate of human error when operating machines, levels of stress, sleep quality, and memory ability. **Statistics** are numbers that summarize or indicate differences or patterns of differences in measurements. Statistics from the crew of the ISS will be used to guide planners of future missions to outer space, such as the manned mission to Mars.

Mark Twain, borrowing a line from Benjamin Disraeli (Best, 2001), once said that there are three kinds of lies: "Lies, damn lies, and statistics." The point is that statistics can be used to obscure the facts as easily as to illuminate them. For instance, although the divorce rate in the United States is about 50%, this does not necessarily mean that out of 10 couples only 5 will stay married. If 3 of those 10

● **Statistics:** Numbers that summarize or indicate differences or patterns of differences in measurements.

In trying to assess the success of his company's new ad campaign, Dilbert is searching for statistical evidence of success, rather than relying on people's intuitions.

couples divorce and remarry, and all 3 of those second marriages end in divorce, that makes 6 divorces out of 13 marriages; and if one of those ex-partners remarries a third time and divorces again, we now have 14 marriages and 7 divorces: this is a 50% divorce rate, even though 7 of the original 10 couples stayed married from the start. To understand and evaluate reports of psychological research, be they surveys in newspapers or television or formal research reports in scientific publications, you need to know a few basics about statistics.

Descriptive Statistics

There are two major types of statistics: One type describes or summarizes data, whereas the other indicates which differences or patterns in the data are worthy of attention. This is the distinction between descriptive statistics and inferential statistics. **Descriptive statistics** are concise ways of summarizing properties of sets of numbers. You're already familiar with such statistics: They are what you see plotted in bar graphs and pie charts, and presented in tables. But descriptive statistics are not limited to figures and tables. For example, in financial news, the Dow Jones Industrial Average is a descriptive statistic, as is the unemployment rate.

You already know a lot about descriptive statistics, but you may not be aware you know it—and you may not be familiar with the technical vocabulary scientists use to discuss such statistics. This section provides a review of the essential points of descriptive statistics.

Data

As we noted earlier, data are numerical measurements or careful observations of a phenomenon. In other words, in an experiment or quasi-experiment, data are the values of the dependent variable as it varies. Examples of dependent variables used in psychological research are response time (how fast it takes to press a button after perceiving a stimulus), scores on an intelligence test, and ratings of fatigue or the severity of depression.

To understand properties of data, let's consider an example. Astronauts face long hours and grueling work as a normal part of their job and might put to good use a safe medication that could boost memory (particularly if it countered the effects of losing sleep). But before we would recommend taking such a drug, we would want to know whether it really is more effective than a **placebo,** a medically inactive substance, such as a sugar pill. If the drug works as promised, it would be

- **Descriptive statistics:** Concise ways of summarizing properties of sets of numbers.

- **Placebo:** A medically inactive substance that is presented as though it has medicinal effects.

TABLE 2.4 Fictional Participant Data From Drug and Placebo Conditions

Number of Words Remembered	
Placebo	**Memory drug**
15	27
12	34
18	21
21	17
22	31
38	47
28	31
15	23
14	40
17	19

● **Raw data:** Individual measurements, taken directly from the phenomenon.

● **Central tendency:** The clustering of the most characteristic values, or scores, for a particular group.

● **Mean:** The arithmetic average.

● **Median:** The score that is the midpoint of the values for the group; half the values fall above the median, and half fall below the median.

● **Mode:** The value that appears most frequently in the set of data.

● **Normal distribution:** The familiar bell-shaped curve, in which most values fall in the midrange of the scale and scores are increasingly less frequent as they taper off symmetrically toward the extremes.

in great demand—for instance, by language-learning schools, Wall Street firms, and countless students. To test whether the drug is effective, you ask people to learn a set of words either after taking the drug or, on another day, after taking a placebo. You are interested in whether the participants can later recall more words if they've taken your drug than if they've taken the placebo; the condition, drug versus placebo, is the independent variable, and the number of words recalled is the dependent variable. Half of the participants get the drug first, and half get an identical-looking and -tasting placebo first. You've put the pills in coded envelopes so that your assistant doesn't know when she's giving the drug versus the placebo (nor do the participants because you've used a double-blind procedure). The comparison would be expressed as the number of words remembered following the drug minus the number following the placebo. The data (scores) from 10 participants are shown in Table 2.4.

Frequency Distributions

Frequency distributions indicate the number of each type of case that was observed in a set of data. For example, one frequency distribution would indicate how many participants recalled 0 words, 1 word, 2 words, and so on, up to the total of 20 possible words, after taking the drug versus after taking the placebo. Another example of a frequency distribution would be one that indicated the number of men versus women in each state who favor building the ISS. If you worked for a company that manufactured key components of the ISS (earning a hefty portion of that estimated $90 billion price tag), you could use such data to decide how to spend your advertising budget to promote the ISS: You could target the regions of the country where people were skeptical about the project, or you could write your ads to appeal to men or to women (or both, as the polling data indicated).

Measures of Central Tendency

When individual measurements are directly presented, they are considered **raw data**; Table 2.4 presents raw data. Descriptive statistics are used to summarize characteristics of a set of such data. Transforming raw data into statistical terms makes the data useful, allowing you to discover and illustrate the relationships among the values or scores. One important type of descriptive statistic is the **central tendency** of the data: the clustering of the most characteristic values, or scores, for a particular group. Central tendency can be expressed three ways. The most common, and probably the one with which you are most familiar, is the arithmetic average, or **mean**, of the scores or values. You calculate a mean by adding up the values in the set of measurements, then dividing that sum by the total number of entries you summed. In Table 2.4, the mean for the placebo condition is 20 words remembered, and the mean for the drug condition is 29 words remembered.

A second way to specify central tendency is the **median**, which is the score that is the midpoint of the values for the group; half the values fall above the median, and half fall below the median. It is easier to find the median if the data are arranged in order, as shown in Table 2.5. The median in the placebo condition is 17.5, halfway between 17 and 18, the fifth and sixth ordered scores. In the drug condition, the median is 29.0, halfway between the fifth and sixth ordered scores of 27 and 31.

A third measure of central tendency is the **mode**, the value that appears most frequently in the set of measurements. The mode can be any value, from the highest to the lowest. The mode in Table 2.5 is 15 for the placebo condition and 31 for the drug condition.

The mean is the measure of central tendency that is most sensitive to extreme values or scores; if you have a few values at the extreme end of the scale, the mean would change much more than would the median (which often will not change at all). The mode does not generally change in response to an extreme score. For example, if you changed the last score in Table 2.5 in the placebo condition from 38 to 100, the mean would change from 20 to 26.2, but the median and mode would remain the same. When a set of data has many scores near one extreme value and away from the center, it is said to have a *skewed distribution*. When a set of data has a skewed distribution, the median is often a more appropriate measure of central tendency than the mean.

However, the three measures of central tendency generally yield similar results; this is especially likely as the number of observations (data points) becomes larger and the data follow a normal distribution. The **normal distribution** is the familiar bell-shaped curve, in which most values fall in the midrange of the scale, and scores are increasingly less frequent as they taper off symmetrically toward the extremes (see Figure 2.4). Normal distributions occur many places in nature. For example, look at stone stairs in a very old building: You can usually see that they are worn more deeply in the center, and then less so as you move toward the sides. (If the building isn't old enough, you will see the beginnings of a normal curve,

TABLE 2.5 Fictional Data From Drug and Placebo Conditions, Arranged in Order

Number of Words Remembered	
Placebo condition	**Memory drug condition**
12	17
14	19
15	21
15	23
17	27
– – – – Median 17.5	– – – – Median 29.0
18	31
21	31
22	34
28	40
38	47
Mean* = 20	Mean* = 29
Mode† = 15	Mode† = 31

*Mean = The arithmetic average.
†Mode = The value that appears most frequently.

If you look at the feet of everyone you know, you'll notice a few very small or very large feet, but most will be an intermediate size. The same is true for many psychological qualities, such as scores on intelligence or personality tests.

which over the generations will become deeper in the center until it resembles the shape of the bell curve in Figure 2.4 upside down.)

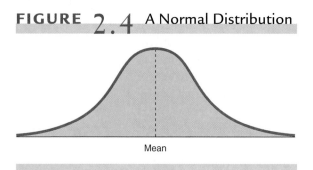

FIGURE 2.4 A Normal Distribution

Mean

You've probably heard a news announcer say that "Exit polling indicates that it's a dead heat! Smith has 51% and Jones has 49%, with a margin of error of 4%." The margin of error—usually called a *confidence interval*—specifies the range of values within which the mean is likely to fall. The confidence interval is calculated like the standard deviation.

● **Range:** The difference obtained when you subtract the smallest score from the largest, the simplest measure of variability.

● **Standard deviation:** A kind of "average variability" in a set of measurements, based on squaring differences of each score and the mean and then taking the mean of those squared differences.

Measures of Variability

Whereas measures of central tendency convey information about the most common values or scores, measures of variability convey information about the spread of the scores. The **range** is the difference obtained when you subtract the smallest score from the largest, the simplest measure of variability. For the data in Table 2.5, for example, the range of scores in the placebo condition is 38 – 12, or 26. The range of scores for the drug condition is 47 – 17, or 30. But the range does not tell you how variable the scores are in general.

Another method of assessing variability is the **standard deviation,** which is a kind of "average variability" in a set of measurements. In Chapter 9, you will see how important the standard deviation is for understanding intelligence. Here is the key idea: If you take the mean for one group, say the placebo group, and then subtract each of the individual observations (data points) from this mean, you will see how much each score deviates from the mean. These differences are *deviation scores.* But how should you take the average of these scores? Because you've subtracted each observation from the mean, the deviation scores above the mean will equal those below the mean. So, if you took the average of the deviation scores, you would get zero; the positive deviation scores would cancel out the negative scores. To get around this problem, you simply square each deviation score (which gets rid of the signs), and then take the mean of these scores (which, as you see in Table 2.6, is 55.6 for the placebo condition). Finally, you need to "unsquare" this mean, by taking its square root. This number is the standard deviation (7.46 for the placebo condition).

For values that are normally distributed, the standard deviation will tell you the percentage of values that fall at different points on the distribution. For instance, about 68% of values fall between one standard deviation below the mean and one standard deviation above the mean. And about 95% of the values fall between two standard deviations below the mean and two standard deviations above the mean.

TABLE 2.6 Computing the Standard Deviation From the Placebo Condition Data in Table 2.5

Step 1:

(Number of words remembered – Mean)^2 = Deviation score^2

$(12 - 20)^2 = -8^2 = 64$	$(18 - 20)^2 = -2^2 = 4$
$(14 - 20)^2 = -6^2 = 36$	$(21 - 20)^2 = 1^2 = 1$
$(15 - 20)^2 = -5^2 = 25$	$(22 - 20)^2 = 2^2 = 4$
$(15 - 20)^2 = -5^2 = 25$	$(28 - 20)^2 = 8^2 = 64$
$(17 - 20)^2 = -3^2 = 9$	$(38 - 20)^2 = 18^2 = 324$

Step 2: Sum of squares (SS) = Sum of squared deviation scores = 556

Step 3: Variance = SS ÷ Number of deviation scores = 556 ÷ 10 = 55.6

Step 4: Standard deviation = Square root of the variance = $\sqrt{55.6}$ = 7.46

For example, if the placebo condition had a standard deviation of 7.46 words (for simplicity's sake, we'll round this down to 7 words) and a mean of 20 words, then roughly 68% of the participants in this condition will remember somewhere between 13 and 27 words (20 – 7 to 20 + 7). At two standard deviations from the mean, roughly 95% of participants will remember between about 6 and 34 words.

Relative Standing

Sometimes you want to know where a particular score stands relative to other scores. For example, college admissions officers want to know how an applicant's SAT scores stand relative to other applicants' scores. One way to convey this information is in terms of measures of variability. You could specify how many standard deviations a score is from the mean. However, this isn't very useful if you are interested in the specific number or percentage of other cases that fall above or below a particular one. Another way of conveying information about a value relative to other values in a set of measurements is to use a **percentile rank**: the percentage of data that have values at or below a particular value. A value converted to a percentile rank of 50, for example, instantly tells you that 50% of the values fall at or below that particular score; the median is a percentile rank of 50. Quartiles are percentile ranks that divide the group into fourths (25th, 50th, 75th, and 100th percentiles); a score that is at the third quartile signifies that 75% of the group falls at or below that score. Deciles are percentile ranks that divide the group into tenths; a score at the sixth decile indicates that 60% of the scores fall at or below that value.

Inferential Statistics

Inferential statistics are the results of tests that reveal whether differences or patterns in measurements reflect true differences or just chance variations. For instance, if you toss a coin 10 times and it lands heads up 7 times, instead of the 5 you would expect purely by chance, does this mean that it is a "trick coin" or an

● **Percentile rank:** The percentage of data that have values at or below a particular value.

● **Inferential statistics:** The results of tests that reveal whether differences or patterns in measurements reflect true differences or patterns versus just chance variations.

edge is worn away, or could this outcome also arise from just chance? Inferential statistics seek to address this question of whether patterns in a set of data are random, or whether they reflect a true underlying phenomenon. A correlation is an example of inferential statistics; if the correlation is high enough (we will discuss what "high enough" means later), it tells you that the scores on one variable do in fact vary systematically with the scores on another variable.

Correlation: The Relationship Between Two Variables

We've seen that a correlation is not about the central tendency and variability of a set of scores, but instead indicates whether two variables are related to each other. Is a change in one variable accompanied by a change in another? To think about how the correlation value is calculated, go back to the idea of a standard deviation. But now, instead of computing the deviations relative to the mean of all the numbers, imagine that you have a line fitting through the data (see Figure 2.3). The closer the data points hug the line, the higher the absolute value of correlation (that is, the higher the number—ignoring whether it is positive or negative). The *method of least squares* is a way to fit a line through a cloud of points. Again, squared numbers are used to eliminate the signs of the difference values. This method positions the line to minimize the square of the vertical distance of each point from the line.

Correlations and other types of inferential statistics may or may not be **statistically significant.** What does "significant" mean? In statistics, it does not mean "important." Rather, it means that the measured relationship is not simply due to chance. If you correlate any two randomly selected sets of measurements, it is likely that the correlation will not be precisely zero. Say you correlated visual acuity with height and found a correlation of –.12. Should you pay attention to this correlation, developing a grand theory to explain it? The size of a correlation needed for statistical significance—to be taken as more than just chance variation—depends on the number of pairs of values analyzed (each represented by a point in Figure 2.3). As a general rule, the more observations considered when computing the correlation, the smaller the correlation value needs to be to achieve statistical significance. Why? Imagine that you were randomly throwing darts into a rectangular corkboard on the wall. It is possible that the first few on the left would be lower than those on the right. But as you tossed more and more darts, those initial quirks would be balanced out by quirks later in the process—so after 100 darts, there would no longer be any discernible pattern. In addition, the more observations you have, the less influence extreme values will have.

Statistical significance is expressed in terms of the probability (p) that a value (such as the size of a correlation) could be due to chance. For example, $p < .05$ means that the probability that the result was simply due to chance is less than 5 in 100; $p < .001$ means that the probability that it was due to chance is less than 1 in 1,000. Usually, any value with $p < .05$ or smaller is considered statistically significant—not likely to be a result simply of chance variation in the data. You can look up a correlation value in a table to determine its significance, but most computer programs that compute correlation do this for you automatically.

Samples and Populations

Back to the memory-enhancing drug study. Did the drug work? If you had measured every person on the planet, all you would need to do is look at the descriptive statistics. Either the drug resulted in more learning than the placebo, or it didn't. But such all-inclusive testing just isn't practical. Virtually all research in

● **Statistical significance:** The measured relationship is not simply due to chance.

psychology relies on studying data from a **sample**—a group drawn from the population at large—and the goal is to generalize from the findings with the sample to the larger **population,** the group from which the sample is drawn. Inferential statistics let you infer that the difference found between your samples does in fact reflect a difference in the corresponding populations.

Here's a simple example: You are impressed by astronaut Sally Ride's memory, and want to know whether astronauts in general tend to have better memories than the population as a whole (you theorize that to be a successful astronaut you need to remember many facts and procedures). To find out, you send memory tests to current and former astronauts all over the world and include stamped, self-addressed return envelopes. No luck—these people are very busy and don't have time to take your test. So you travel to Houston and get permission to visit the astronauts at NASA headquarters. By some miracle, you are actually able to induce 10 astronauts to take your test. You will next need to compare them with 10 non-astronauts selected to be as similar as possible to your sample—same ages, education levels, gender, and even the same level of fitness. If you then compare the two groups, you will probably find a difference in memory performance. But now consider this: If you had data from 20 astronauts and *randomly* assigned them to two groups of 10, you probably would also find a difference in the mean memory scores for these arbitrarily formed groups! This difference would arise because of how you happened to assign the people to groups. No matter how you did it, the groups would probably have different average memory performance. Only if you had a large number of people would assigning them randomly to two equal-sized groups be likely to result in groups that had nearly identical scores. When you have enough data, people who happen to have unusually good or poor memories will be assigned equally often to each group, on average, and thus their disproportionate contributions will cancel out.

When you compare astronauts and non-astronauts, the problem is to know for sure whether any difference between them is "real"—reflecting actual differences between the two classes in general—or is due to sampling error. **Sampling error** produces differences that arise from the luck of the draw, not because two samples are in fact representative of different populations. In this example, if differences in memory scores between astronauts and non-astronauts are due to sampling error, this means that the two groups are not actually different. (There are statistical tests that can indicate whether a difference between two groups is due to sampling error or reflects a real difference, but details about such inferential tests are beyond the scope of this introduction.)

Meta-Analysis

Science is a community effort. Usually many people are studying the same phenomenon, each one painting additional strokes onto an emerging picture. **Meta-analysis** is a technique that allows researchers to combine results from different studies. This is particularly useful when results have been mixed, with some studies showing an effect and some not. Meta-analysis can determine whether a relationship exists among variables that transcends any one study, a strand that cuts across the entire set of findings.

Sometimes results that are not evident in any individual study become obvious in a meta-analysis. Why? Studies almost always involve observing or testing a sample from the population; if a sample is relatively small, the luck of the draw could obscure an overall difference that actually exists in the population. For example,

- **Sample:** A group from which one obtains measures or observations that is drawn from a larger population.

- **Population:** The entire set of relevant people or animals.

- **Sampling error:** Non-random sampling from a population, which produces differences that arise from the luck of the draw, not because two samples are in fact representative of different populations.

- **Meta-analysis:** A statistical technique that allows researchers to combine results from different studies, which can determine whether a relationship exists among variables that transcends any one study.

if you stopped the first two males and first two females you saw on the street and measured their heights, the females might actually be taller than the males. The problem of variation in samples is particularly severe when the difference of interest—the effect—is not great. If men averaged 8 feet tall and women 4 feet tall, small samples would not be a problem; you would quickly figure out the usual height difference between men and women. But if men averaged 5 feet 10 inches and women averaged 5 feet 9 inches (and the standard deviation was a few inches), you would need to measure many men and women before you were assured of finding the difference. Meta-analysis is a way of combining the samples from many studies, giving you the ability to detect even subtle differences or relations among variables (Rosenthal, 1991).

Lying With Statistics

Statistics can be used or misused. In a famous book entitled *How to Lie with Statistics*, Derrell Huff (1954) demonstrated many ways that people use statistics to distort the pattern of results. Joel Best (2001) has followed in this tradition. Such books play a valuable role in inoculating people against deceptive techniques, and some of their key points are summarized here. Be on the lookout for these manipulations whenever you see statistics.

Selective Reporting

Because different types of statistics convey different information, the same data can be manipulated to "say" different things. Look at Figure 2.5 and Table 2.7, which present fictitious data for the results of a new type of therapy for people with acrophobia—a fear of heights (obviously a crucial problem to overcome for aspiring astronauts). Before the therapy, participants reported, on average, 9 symptoms of acrophobia; that is, before treatment, the mean number of symptoms was 9. After the therapy, the mean number of symptoms was 4.85, the median was 3.5, and the mode was 10. Proponents of the new therapy make the following claims: On average, symptoms decreased by almost half (based on the mean), and more than 50% of participants had substantial symptom reduction (based on the median). Opponents, however, convey the data differently. A spokeswoman from the pharmaceutical company that manufactures a medication to treat acrophobia makes several counterclaims when she promotes the superiority of her company's medication: The number of symptoms most frequently reported was 10, which shows that the therapy actually made people more symptomatic (based on the mode). Also, the therapy achieved mixed results, as indicated by the fact that the number of symptoms after treatment ranged from 1 to 10.

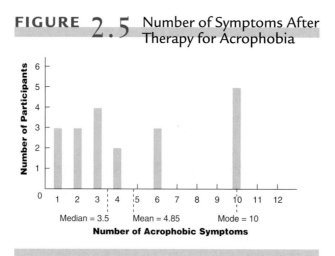

FIGURE 2.5 Number of Symptoms After Therapy for Acrophobia

As you can see, both supporters and detractors of the new treatment are correct. They are just presenting different aspects of the data. Thus, when hearing or reading about research or survey results, you should ask several questions before taking the results too seriously.

1. What is the distribution of the results? If they are normally distributed, the measures of central tendency will be similar to each other. If they are skewed, the measures of central tendency will convey different information, and the one presented will be the one that conveys the information the reporter wants you to know about. Do the other measures of central tendency paint a different picture of the results?

2. How variable are the data? What does it mean if the results vary a lot rather than a little?

Lying With Graphs

Many results are presented in graph form. Graphs work largely because of a single principle: *More is more* (Kosslyn, 1994a). Larger bars, higher lines, or bigger wedges all stand for greater amounts than do smaller bars, lines, or wedges. Our tendency to see more on the page as standing for more of a substance can lead us astray if graphs are constructed to deceive. Be alert to the following tricks.

Shortening the *Y* (Vertical) Axis to Exaggerate a Difference. As you can see in Figure 2.6, starting the Y axis at a high value and devoting the Y axis to a small part of the scale, as in the right half of Figure 2.6, makes what is in fact a small difference look like a large one. If a difference is statistically significant, it should look that way (and thus shortening the axis may be appropriate). But if it's not, then shortening the axis to exaggerate the difference is deception.

TABLE 2.7 Fictional Results of Therapy for Acrophobia

Mean number of symptoms after therapy for acrophobia

= Total number of symptoms ÷ Total number of participants

= 1 + 1 + 1 + 2 + 2 + 2 + 3 + 3 + 3 + 3 + 4 + 4 + 6 + 6 + 6 + 10 + 10 + 10 + 10 + 10

= 97 ÷ 20 = 4.85

Median = 3.5

Mode = 10

FIGURE 2.6 Shortening the *Y* Axis Can Mislead

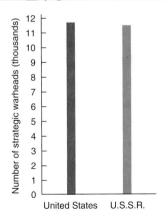
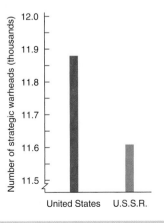

The left panel presents the actual numbers in a neutral way; the right panel exaggerates the difference.

From Kosslyn, 1994a, pp. 209 and 211. Data for illustration on left from Natural Resources Defense Council.

Using an Inappropriately Large Range of Values to Minimize a Difference. The flip side of the coin is illustrated in Figure 2.7, in which a difference is made to appear smaller by using a large range in values on the Y axis.

FIGURE 2.7 Lengthening the *Y* Axis Can Mislead

The left panel presents the actual numbers in a neutral way; the right panel minimizes the difference.

From Kosslyn, 1994a, pp. 209 and 211. Data for illustration on left from Natural Resources Defense Council.

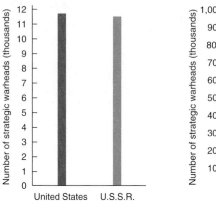
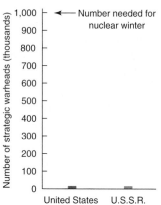

Using Three-Dimensional Graphics to Exaggerate Size. As shown in Figure 2.8, a designer can take advantage of our tendency to impose size constancy (see Chapter 4), so that a bar that is farther away will be seen as much larger than a same-size bar that is closer. Even if an actual difference exists, this technique can exaggerate its magnitude.

FIGURE 2.8 Size Constancy Can Exaggerate 3-D Bar Size

Size constancy leads us to see the bars that are farther away as larger than they are, thereby exaggerating a difference.

From Kosslyn, 1994a, p. 227. Data from Hacker, 1992, p. 98, cited in *Newsweek*, 23 March 1992, p. 61.

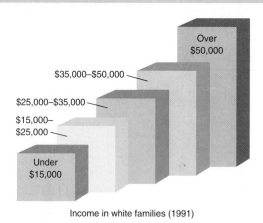

Income in white families (1991)

Transforming the Data Before Plotting. Compare the two panels of Figure 2.9. The first shows the size of the stock market in three countries over 3 years, the second the percentage increase over two 5-year periods. If you saw only

FIGURE 2.9 Transforming Data Can Distort the Conclusions

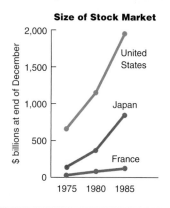

Size of Stock Market

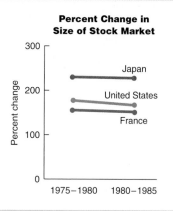

Percent Change in Size of Stock Market

The left panel shows the actual dollar figures, and the right shows the percentage change. Clearly, the message conveyed by the two displays is different. Which one is "more honest" depends on the purpose for which the graph is used.

From Kosslyn, 1994a, p. 219. Data from Morgan Stanley Capital International, cited in *The Economist World Atlas and Almanac*, 1989, p. 90.

the second, you wouldn't realize that the increases in the U.S. stock market were actually much greater than those in Japan. If the user is trying to sell Japanese stocks, you can guess which display will be preferred.

Changing Width Along With Height. As shown in Figure 2.10, our visual system does not register height and width separately, but rather we see them simultaneously, as specifying area. So changing the width along with the height gives a much larger impression of amount than is conveyed by changing height alone.

In short, you can see that there is nothing magical or mysterious about statistics or how they are represented visually. Whenever you see a graph in the newspaper, you are seeing statistics; when you hear that a poll is accurate to "plus or minus 3 points," that's the spread within which the mean is likely to occur if you look at other samples. The crucial ideas are that there are measures of central tendency (mean, median, and mode), measures of variability (such as the range and standard deviation), and statistical tests that tell you the likelihood that a measured difference is due to chance alone. What you've learned here is enough to enable you to read and understand many reports of original research in psychology.

FIGURE 2.10 Changing Width With Height Exaggerates Size

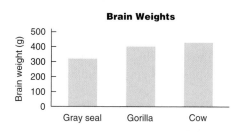

Brain Weights

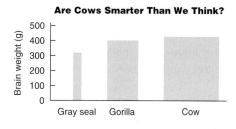

Are Cows Smarter Than We Think?

Expanding the bar width conveys the impression that more quantity is being presented than increasing the height alone signals.

From Kosslyn, 1994a, p. 225. Data from Weisberg, 1980, cited in Chambers et al., 1983, p. 371.

Looking *at* Levels

Graph Design for the Eye and Mind

Astronauts on the ISS will have to monitor many sources of data, both for the experiments they conduct and to ensure that the space station functions effectively. Graphs are a way to convey a lot of information without overwhelming the user. But what kind of graph should be used? It depends on what message needs to be conveyed. For example, Jeffrey Zacks and Barbara Tversky (1999) found that bar graphs are better than line graphs when you need to make or illustrate comparisons between discrete data points (such as specific numbers of Democratic versus Republican voters who support the space program), whereas line graphs are better when you need to understand or illustrate trends (such as changes in the numbers of Democratic and Republican supporters in different parts of the United States over time). Bars end at discrete locations, and thus it's easy to compare data points simply by comparing the heights of the bars. In contrast, bars are not as useful for conveying trends because the reader needs mentally to connect the tops of bars, creating a line in order to determine visually whether there is a trend. Hence, if that's what you want to convey, it's better to give the reader the line in the first place. But if the reader needs to compare discrete data points, a line isn't so good: Now the reader must "mentally break down" the line into specific points, which requires effort (Kosslyn, 1994a).

Think about this finding from the levels perspective: When designing a graph, you should create one that most effectively communicates to other people (level of the group). To do so, you need to respect the way the human perceptual and conceptual systems work (level of the brain). And you need to keep in mind that the best graph type minimizes the effort required of the reader; people will be more likely to understand a graph if they aren't forced to work hard (level of the person). And, of course, events at the different levels interact: If the graph is so hard to read (level of the brain) that people aren't motivated to decipher it (level of the person), it won't end up communicating anything (level of the group).

TEST YOURSELF!

1. What are descriptive statistics?
2. What are inferential statistics? How do they differ from descriptive statistics?
3. How can people (intentionally or not) lie with statistics?

How to Think About Research Studies

Large amounts of research have been reported from studies of human performance in space. Unfortunately, many reports of this important research are not as easy to understand as they should be. If a piece of research is going to have an impact (for example, on the design of a future space station or expedition to another planet), it must be read and understood. We have found it useful to approach reading—and writing—research reports armed with what we call the *QALMRI method*. This method is a vehicle for understanding the meaning of a research study in the literature—and for reporting your own research. This method will help you become clear about what question is being asked, how the researchers have tried to answer it, and whether the results really do support the preferred answer (the hypothesis).

Reading Research Reports: The QALMRI Method

When you read a research report, try to identify the following components.

Q Stands for the Question

All research begins with a question, and the point of the research is to answer it.

The first few paragraphs of the General Introduction should tell the reader what question the article is addressing. In addition, the context provided by the General Introduction's review of previous studies should explain why the question is important, why anybody should care about answering it. In some cases, the question is important for practical reasons, whereas in others it is important as a way to test a theory (and, in some cases, it is important for both practical and theoretical reasons, as in our example with placebo). The General Introduction should provide the general context, explaining the reasons why the question is worthy of consideration.

A Stands for Alternatives

A good report describes at least two possible answers to the question and explains why both are plausible. After describing the question that is being addressed, the General Introduction should explain what alternatives are being considered. When reading the General Introduction, identify the question and then the alternative answers that will be addressed by the study. If the alternatives are not spelled out, try to figure out for yourself what they might be; if the study is simply seeking to confirm a theory's prediction, try to get a sense of whether other theories (or just common sense) would make the same prediction. If all of the theories make the same prediction, it probably isn't worth testing.

L Stands for the Logic of the Study

The goal of the study is to discriminate among the alternatives, and the logic is the general idea behind the study—the way the study will distinguish among the alternatives. The logic is typically explained toward the end of a study introduction and has the following structure: *If* alternative 1 (and not the other alternatives) is correct, *then* when a particular variable is manipulated, the participant's behavior should change in a specific way. For example, the logic of the memory-enhancing study described earlier was: "If the drug enhances memory (and the placebo doesn't), then people should recall more test words after taking the drug than after taking a placebo."

M Stands for the Method

The details of what the researcher did are found in the Method section. The Method section has the following parts:

Participants: Look to see how the participants were selected. Are they a representative sample of the population of interest? If a study was conducted to make a recommendation for a particular type of people (such as men and women in their early 20's), then the participants should be as similar to that group as possible. If no particular population is specified, then the sample should be representative of the population in general. If the study involves more than one group, they should be equivalent on important variables, such as age and education. Depending on the study, variables such as the level of depression, experience with medicine, or experience in large, noisy brain-scanning machines can be relevant. Try to think of all possible confounds that could make the groups different in ways that might affect the study's outcome.

Materials: If questionnaires are used in the study, they should have been shown to be valid (that is, they should measure what they are supposed to measure). And they should be reliable (that is, they should produce consistent results). In addition, materials used in different parts of the study should not differ except as required to answer the research question.

Apparatus: The apparatus delivers stimuli or defines the experimental situation. If a computer is used, the authors should describe exactly how it presented the stimuli. They also should describe in detail all other physical props they used. Think about how the apparatus looked to the participants and whether it could have distracted them or allowed them to pick up inappropriate cues.

Procedure: The procedure is the step-by-step process of what happens in a study. Try to picture yourself in the study. A good procedure should be described so well that you could replicate the study, doing exactly the same thing as the original investigators. Were participants given appropriate instructions (clear, but not leading them on)? Was it clear that the participants did in fact understand the instructions? Could the investigator have unintentionally treated participants in different groups differently?

R Stands for the Results

The outcome of the study is described in detail in the Results section. What happened? First, look for measures of central tendency (means, medians, modes) and some measure of the sampling variability (commonly, standard deviations). The actual results—what the researchers found—are descriptive, and often are presented in a graph or table. Second, not all differences and patterns in the results should be taken seriously; some differences are simply quirks due to chance. Inferential statistics should be reported to indicate which patterns of variation are unlikely to have arisen due to chance. Look for the "p values" that document differences; if the p value is .05 or less, you can be reasonably certain that the difference found in the sample reflects an actual difference in the population as a whole.

I Stands for Inferences

The payoff of a study is the inferences that can be drawn about the alternative answers to the question being asked, given the results that were obtained. Look to see whether the researchers convincingly answered the question they posed at the outset. The Discussion section usually contains the inferences the authors want to draw from their results. If the study was well designed (the logic sound and the method rigorous), the results should allow you to eliminate at least one of the alternatives, and ideally should be most consistent with only one of the alternatives. At this point, take a step back and think about potential confounds that could have led to the results. Were any alternative explanations not ruled out? For example, perhaps participants in different groups were treated differently by the investigators, or perhaps they were tested at different times of day or at different periods in the semester (closer or farther from anxiety-inducing exams). And consider any loose ends—what else would you want to know about the phenomena?

In sum, the QALMRI method helps you focus on the "big picture": What a study is about, why it's important, and what the results actually mean. When you read a study, figure out exactly what question the authors wanted to answer and what alternative answers they've considered. Can you think of others? Always be on the lookout for potential alternative explanations, and look for features of the study that limit how well its results can be generalized; for example, can you assume that the results necessarily apply to other ages, races, or cultures? Be sure to read the footnotes. The single most important advice we can give about reading a study is to be an active reader: Think about what the authors are claiming, and think about whether it makes sense.

Writing Your Own Research Papers

The same principles apply to writing your own research papers. Write the Introduction so that the reader clearly understands the question you are addressing and why it is important. Your question can be important because it is an extension of previous research (which you summarize in the Introduction), or because you've spotted a hole in the literature and aim to fill it by supplying new information, or because you've identified a variable that might invalidate a previous study (and want to find out whether those researchers did in fact overlook something crucial). When you review previous studies and theories in the published literature, only review those that help you explain why your question is worth considering, that put it in context. Abraham Lincoln was once asked how long a man's legs should be, and replied, "Long enough to reach the ground." The same principle applies to Introductions: Don't include any more or less material than you need to put your question in context.

The Introduction should also explain the alternative possible answers you will consider—including, in most cases, your "favorite" one, which is called "the hypothesis." You need to explain why each alternative is plausible, usually by referring to previously published findings and theories. Finally, the Introduction should end with a clear statement of the logic of your study, the basic idea underlying what you did.

In the Method section, be sure to include enough detail to allow another researcher to repeat exactly what you did. Explain what sort of participants were tested, and how you ensured that participants in different groups were comparable in terms of important variables. In addition, you need to describe the materials in detail, and you also need to describe precisely the apparatus and the procedure.

In the Results section, first present results that bear directly on the question and alternative answers. The results that address the question being asked are most important—even if they are not as striking as some of the other findings. If your Introduction is clear, the reader is focused like a laser beam on the question you are asking and is waiting to find out which alternative answer is supported by the results. Don't keep the reader in suspense; present the results that speak to the question at the outset of the Results section. These results should be measures of central tendency and variability, which are often best presented in a graph; you should also present inferential statistics along with the results, so the reader will know which differences to take seriously. After you present these results, present everything else that you may have found.

Finally, in the Discussion section, return to the question and alternative answers, and discuss exactly what you can infer from your results. Have you shown that some of the alternatives must be discarded? Is only one viable? What should future research focus on to propel the field even further ahead?

When writing a research report, always put yourself in the place of the intelligent reader. If a report has been written clearly, the reader will glide through it effortlessly, understanding what the author intended to convey, why the research was conducted in a particular way, what the discoveries were, and why the report is interesting and important.

When Does Mental Practice Improve Later Performance?

In each chapter, we will examine one study in detail, using the QALMRI method. In this chapter, let's look at *mental practice*, the ability to rehearse an activity mentally, without actually making any movements. Mental practice is particularly interesting in the context of the ISS. Mission planners intend to give astronauts "leisure time," and on earth most astronauts would use at least some of this time to play tennis, golf, or some other sport. Unfortunately, few of these sports can be played on the ISS—balls don't bounce properly in weightless environments, and there really isn't room to run around (which would jeopardize delicate equipment, even if there were room). Does this mean that the astronauts must resign themselves to getting rusty at their favorite sports? Perhaps not. Perhaps they can practice mentally, which would preserve—or even improve—their game. For example, many golfers claim that when they are off the course, they can practice by imagining themselves whacking the ball straight down the fairway or out of the sand trap. Players regularly claim that the mental practice improves their game. Well, maybe. The only way we can find out whether mental practice really works is by conducting a scientific study, and many such studies have been reported. Let's now consider one of them.

QUESTION: Can mental practice change subsequent golf putting? Woolfolk, Parrish, and Murphy (1985) asked whether mentally rehearsing golf putts can help as well as hurt subsequent performance.

ALTERNATIVES: (1) Mental practice improves putting when participants imagine successfully tapping the ball into the hole, but it actually hurts performance when they imagine tapping the ball so that it misses the hole; (2) Mental practice might always improve putting; (3) It might not have any effect at all.

LOGIC: If Alternative 1 is correct and the other alternatives are not, then when people imagine rehearsing the right kind of movements for a successful putt, their performance should later improve—but if they imagine rehearsing the wrong kinds of movements, their performance should actually get worse.

METHOD: The researchers first asked 30 college students to putt golf balls into a hole and assessed how well they could do so. After performing 20 putts (from 8.5 feet away), equal numbers of students of comparable skill were randomly assigned to each group. The researchers then gave each group different instructions for mental rehearsal. They asked students in the *positive imagery group* to imagine making a "gentle but firm backswing," and seeing the ball "rolling, rolling, right into the cup" (p. 338). Students in the *negative imagery group* received the identical instructions but were told to imagine the ball "rolling, rolling, toward the cup, but at the last second narrowly missing." Finally, they asked students in the *control group* to imagine putting, with no specific instructions about how to imagine the ball. The students then imagined practicing, following the instructions given to their group. After this, the researchers again asked the students actually to putt and again assessed how well they could do.

RESULTS: Students in the positive imagery group performed 30.4% better after mental practice than they had when tested initially. In contrast, students in the negative imagery group actually got worse, scoring 21.2% poorer than they had earlier. Finally, students in the control group improved a bit (9.9%).

INFERENCES: The authors conclude that mental practice depends on the specific movements you imagine. If the movements are appropriate, mental practice will help later performance—but if the movements are not appropriate, mental practice will actually hurt later performance. The students in the control group apparently often imagined putting correctly, but not as often (or as effectively) as the students in the positive imagery group. Many other studies have found that mental practice improves subsequent performance (Doheny, 1993; Driskell et al., 1994; Druckman & Swets, 1988; Prather, 1973; Vieilledent et al., in press; White & Hardy, 1995), and the present results begin to suggest why it might work.

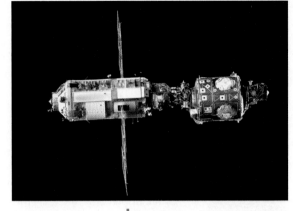

One glance of the International Space Station from the outside makes it clear why astronauts would get a lot out of mentally practicing sports—there just isn't much room on board for the real thing.

You might wonder, however, whether the results occurred not because of differences in the images, but because the students in the positive imagery group were more relaxed than those in the negative imagery group. Or perhaps the students in the negative group found it frustrating to keep missing the hole, and thus stopped practicing altogether. Or perhaps at the time of the second actual testing, students in the negative imagery group thought the experimenter expected poorer performance, and so "threw the game" and performed more poorly than they could have. Each of these alternative explanations can be tested.

Looking *at* Levels

Imitation Is the Sincerest Form of Flattery

Imagine what life would be like if every astronaut had to learn the job solely by trial-and-error. Fortunately, we can often learn by observing and imitating others. In fact, mental practice appears to rely on many of the same neural mechanisms as does imitation—you are mentally imitating what you "see" in a mental image. This idea is plausible because many researchers have found that a set of the same brain areas is activated when people perform an action, watch somebody else perform an action, or simply imagine performing the action (e.g., Decety, 2001; Grèzes & Decety, 2001). Decety and colleagues (2002), reflecting on such findings, raise a conundrum: If the same brain areas are used in these different cases, how do we know when we've performed an action versus only watched someone else perform it? Their hypothesis was that certain brain areas keep track of exactly this distinction, whether you or someone else has performed the action. To test this hypothesis, researchers monitored participants' brain activation while they either imitated the experimenter's hand movements as he manipulated small objects, or themselves made such movements and watched the experimenter imitate them (the participants also took part in three other conditions that did not involve imitation, which allowed the researchers to zero in on which brain areas are involved in imitation per se). The important finding was that the left portion of one brain region (the bottom part of the parietal lobe, as is explained in the following chapter) was more active when the participants imitated the experimenter, but the right portion of this same region was more active when the participants watched the experimenter imitate their actions. This area of the brain seems to play a critical role in distinguishing whether you produce an action or somebody else does.

Consider this finding from the levels of analysis perspective. First, imitation is by definition a social affair: You

LOOKING *at* LEVELS (continued)

need somebody else to imitate, or to imitate you (level of the group). Second, the brain registers what other people do similarly to what you yourself do—which allows others' actions to guide you in the future (level of the brain). However, the brain does not respond identically in the two conditions; rather, subtle differences distinguish between your making actions versus your watching actions that someone else makes. Third, you need to be motivated to watch someone else, or you won't learn by imitation (level of the person). Events at the three levels interact: If nobody was available to show you how to perform an action (such as operate a space shuttle or play golf) then, even if you were

motivated to learn, you wouldn't have the chance—and your brain would not have the opportunity to respond in a certain way. But once your brain has had such good fortune, this opens up more opportunities for choosing actions (level of the person), which in turn will affect others (perhaps providing them with the opportunity to learn from you).

TEST YOURSELF!

1. What does QALMRI stand for? How can you use the QALMRI method when you read research reports?
2. How can you use the QALMRI method when you write your own research papers?

CONSOLIDATE!

The Scientific Method: Designed to Be Valid

- The science of psychology relies on the scientific method, which involves specifying a problem, systematically observing events, forming a hypothesis of the relation between variables, collecting new observations to test the hypothesis, using such data to formulate and support a theory, and testing the theory.

THINK IT THROUGH Think of 5 questions about the way being cooped up with 7 other people for months on end could change relationships (imagine that there are 4 men and 3 women in total). Can each one of your questions be answered using the scientific method? Why or why not? What are the limits of the scientific method for studying psychology? Are there any? If you think there are such limits, what other methods could you use to study such aspects of mental processes and behavior?

The Psychologist's Toolbox: Techniques of Scientific Research

- Psychologists test hypotheses and look for relations among variables using a variety of tools, including experiments, quasi-experiments, correlational studies, naturalistic observation, case studies, and surveys.

- In an experiment, the effect of manipulating one or more independent variables on the value of a dependent variable is measured, and participants are assigned randomly to groups.

- Quasi-experiments are like experiments but participants are not assigned to groups randomly.

- In correlational studies, the relationship between the values of pairs of variables is assessed, showing how the values of one go up or down as the values of the other increase (but not showing that changes in the values of one variable *cause* changes in the other).

- Naturalistic observation involves careful observation and documentation of events.

- Case studies are detailed investigations of a single instance of a situation (the detailed exploration of an astronaut's training would be a case study).

- In surveys participants are asked to answer sets of specific questions.

- When reading reports of studies, you should be alert for the following: (1) evidence that the data are reliable, (2) evidence that the data are valid, (3) possible contamination from confounding variables, (4) biases, including the tendency to respond in particular ways to everything (response bias) and the nonrandom selection of participants or experimental materials (sampling bias), and (5) experimenter expectancy effects

- Pseudopsychology differs from psychology not necessarily in its content, but in how it is supported by data.

THINK IT THROUGH
If you wanted to know whether Sally Ride's upbringing played a crucial role in leading her to become an astronaut, how would you go about studying this? Don't assume that it has to be a case study. Which specific questions would you ask? What are the best methods for answering them?

What characteristics and qualities do you think an astronaut should have? Do you think psychologists should prevent anyone from entering astronaut training who does not have these characteristics and qualities? Why and why not?

Statistics: Measuring Reality

- Descriptive statistics characterize observations by specifying measures of central tendency and variability.

- Measures of central tendency include the mean (which is the arithmetic average), median (which is the numbers for which half the other numbers are higher and half are lower), and mode (which is the value at which the most observations occur).

- Measures of variability include the range (which is the difference between the highest and lowest score) and standard deviation (which is a measure of "average spread" from the mean).

- Different descriptive statistics indicate the frequency of different scores and the standing of any one score relative to the others (for example, in terms of quartiles or deciles).

- Inferential statistics tell you which differences among values or patterns (such as increasing or decreasing trends) in the data should be taken seriously. Inferential statistics rely on assigning a probability that a difference or pattern could have arisen purely due to chance. Generally speaking, if that probability is less than 5 times in 100, the result is considered "statistically significant."

- A correlation indicates whether one set of measurements tends to vary along with another set.

- A meta-analysis identifies trends or patterns that are present across many studies.

- Inferential statistics can be used deceptively, largely because of selective reporting.

- Graphs can be constructed to bias the interpretation of the reader, either appropriately emphasizing the actual results (statistically significant differences or patterns in the data) or inappropriately emphasizing non-significant results.

THINK IT THROUGH
Aspiring astronauts take a variety of psychological tests. If the values of the mean, median, and mode are not the same, which one should you take most seriously? To what extent does this depend on the purposes to which you will put these data, and to what extent should your confidence reflect properties of the measures themselves? Would it matter how many observations you have?

People sometimes argue that "garbage in, garbage out": If the data you begin with are no good, you won't be able to use them to draw inferences. This observation is sometimes applied to meta-analyses, which often include studies that have flaws. To what extent do you think it applies? Should all meta-analyses only include "perfect" studies? What if the flawed studies are flawed in different ways, so that the flaws are not correlated with the outcomes?

How to Think About Research Studies

One way to think about the relation between theory and data relies on the QALMRI method.

- *Q* stands for the **question,** what the study is about and why it is important.
- *A* stands for **alternative** answers to that question, which the study is designed to discriminate among.
- *L* stands for the **logic** of the study, the basic idea that will allow the researchers to discriminate among the alternatives.
- *M* stands for the **method,** the details of exactly what was done in the study.
- *R* stands for the **results,** which include both descriptive and inferential statistics.
- *I* stands for **inferences** that can be drawn from the results, indicating which alternatives can be eliminated and which receive support.

THINK IT THROUGH
Pick your favorite hobby and design an experiment to discover whether mental practice could improve your performance. Use the QALMRI framework to describe the study.

Key Terms

bias, p. 47
case study, p. 43
central tendency, p. 52
confound, p. 39
control condition, p. 40
control group, p. 39
correlation, p. 41
data, p. 35
dependent variable, p. 38
descriptive statistics, p. 51
double-blind design, p. 48
effect, p. 39
experimenter expectancy
   effects, p. 48
hypothesis, p. 35
independent variable, p. 38
inferential statistics, p. 55
mean, p. 52
median, p. 52
meta-analysis, p. 57
mode, p. 52
normal distribution, p. 52
operational definition, p. 36

percentile rank, p. 55
placebo, p. 51
population, p. 57
prediction, p. 36
pseudopsychology, p. 48
random assignment, p. 40
range, p. 54
raw data, p. 52
reliability, p. 45
replication, p. 35
response bias, p. 47
sample, p. 57
sampling bias, p. 47
sampling error, p. 57
scientific method, p. 34
standard deviation, p. 54
statistical significance, p. 56
statistics, p. 50
survey, p. 43
theory, p. 36
validity, p. 45
variable, p. 35

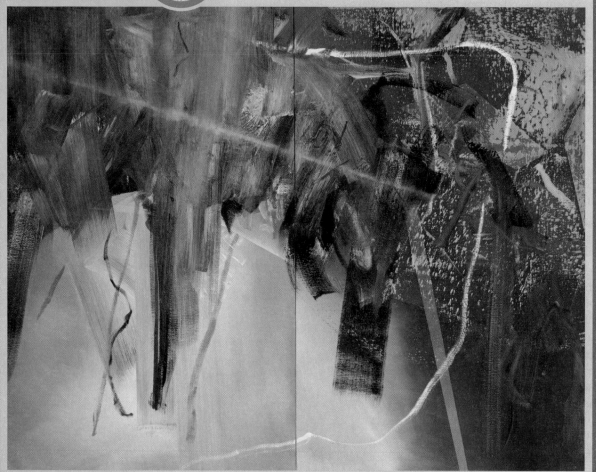

chapter 3

Digital Image © The Museum of Modern Art/Licensed by SCALA/Art Resource, NY

The Biology of Mind and Behavior

As the hard jets of water massaged the 25-year-old soldier while he showered, colorless and odorless fumes of carbon monoxide, which are known to cause brain damage, slowly seeped into the stall. Unaware that he was gradually being poisoned, the soldier continued his routine until he eventually passed out.

After the soldier was discovered and revived, doctors examined him. The young man could get around with ease, but he presented a host of bizarre symptoms. He was unable to name objects by sight, but as soon as he touched them, he could say what they were. He could identify things by smell and sound, he could name colors or identify them by pointing to a color named by someone else, and he had no difficulty recognizing familiar people when they spoke. But he couldn't identify these same people by sight alone. In fact, when he looked at his own face in the mirror, he thought he was looking at his doctor. When he was shown a rubber eraser, he identified it as "a small ball"; when shown a safety pin, he said it was "like a watch or nail clipper." When the doctors asked the soldier to inspect a picture of a nude woman and show where her eyes were, he pointed to her breasts (Benson & Greenberg, 1969).

Clearly, something was wrong with the young soldier's vision, but the problem had nothing to do with his eyes; it had to do with his brain. He couldn't get knowledge by way of his sense of sight. Why? Though he retained some aspects of his vision, he had lost others—he seemed unable to recognize what he clearly could see. The fumes the soldier had inhaled had affected his brain, but how? What, exactly, had gone wrong? To consider these questions, you need to understand essential facts about how the brain works.

As you have seen, events at the level of the brain can influence many aspects of behavior, in ways not immediately apparent. If you should break your hand, you will have trouble holding a pencil: The effect of the accident is direct and mechanical. If you were in any doubt before your mishap about the role of muscle and bone in grasping and holding, you're in no doubt now, when those abilities are distinctly impaired because muscles are torn and bones fractured. But, although it is

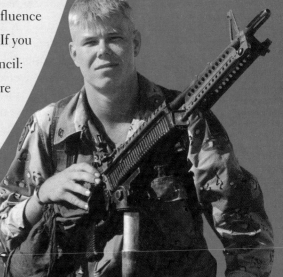

a physical organ like muscle and bone, the brain is unique: It is also a *psychological* organ, ultimately responsible for our moods of despair and elation, our sense of well-being and our sense that something's wrong, our perception of the outside world and our awareness of its meaning. The effects of an accident in the brain are no less real than a broken hand, but the path to them is less obvious (and, indeed, until recently was invisible). It is this path, through a thicket of sometimes difficult names and processes, that we must trace if we are to gain a meaningful understanding of who we are and why we behave as we do.

So, how does it work, this mysterious brain? What is it made up of; what are its building blocks? Can we ever see the brain at work? How could we find out exactly which parts of the soldier's brain were damaged? Do all of our brains respond the same way to the same environmental influences? Or, do different people, with different genetic makeups and life experiences, respond differently? Let's start finding out.

> **Clearly, something was wrong with the young soldier's vision, but the problem had nothing to do with his eyes; it had to do with his brain.**

Brain Circuits: Making Connections

The carbon monoxide fumes that the soldier breathed interfered with his brain's ability to use oxygen, causing him to pass out. Unfortunately, he inhaled enough of these fumes that some brain cells probably died; ordinarily, brain cells begin to succumb after a few minutes without oxygen. But just saying that brain cells "died" isn't much of an explanation—that would be a little like saying that a building fell down because its molecules were rearranged. Why did the death of these cells have the effects it did?

The Neuron: A Powerful Computer

The brain is "the psychological organ"; it gives rise to the mind in both senses of the term (see Chapter 1), mental processes (such as perception, memory, and language) and mental experiences. The brain is arguably the most complex object in the known universe and, to begin to grasp its general outlines, we start small (with brain cells) and then move to large (brain structures). We could easily write a book about each of these topics; we present here just what you will need to know to understand material in the remainder of this book (for example, the actions of drugs that treat psychological disorders).

All brain activity hinges on the workings of brain cells, or **neurons.** There are three types of neurons. Some, the **sensory neurons,** respond to input from the

- **Neuron:** A cell that receives signals from other neurons or sense organs, processes these signals, and sends the signals to other neurons, muscles, or bodily organs; the basic unit of the nervous system.

- **Sensory neuron:** A neuron that responds to input from sense organs.

FIGURE 3.1 Examples of Types of Neurons

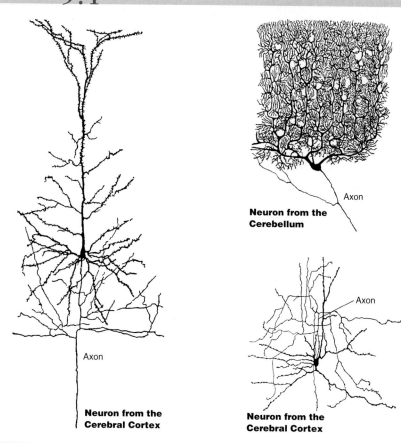

Neurons come in many shapes and sizes. Researchers are still discovering the ways in which the differences among cells affect their functioning. From Dowling, 1992.

Neuron from the Cerebellum

Axon

Neuron from the Cerebral Cortex

Axon

Neuron from the Cerebral Cortex

Axon

senses; others, the **motor neurons**, send signals to muscles to control movement; finally, **interneurons** stand between the neurons that register what's out there and those that control movement (or, they stand between other interneurons). Most of the neurons in the brain are interneurons.

Neurons differ in their size, shape, and function. Some typically excite other neurons to send signals; others typically inhibit them. Some major types of neurons are shown in Figure 3.1. Just as you can use stone to build either a hut or a palace, the same neural building blocks can build very different brains. For example, most mammals, from horses to humans, largely share the same types of neurons.

The average human brain contains about 100 billion neurons, plus ten times as many **glial cells** (the name comes from the Greek word for "glue"), which fill the gaps between neurons. Glial cells are crucial for the formation of the connections among neurons (Ullian et al., 2001), and also facilitate the communication between neurons, clean up the remains of dead neurons, and generally help in the care and feeding of neurons.

Neurons would not be much good if they did not affect other neurons or the rest of the body—how useful would the internet be if only one computer were connected to it? **Brain circuits** are sets of neurons that affect one another. When one neuron in a circuit is triggered by another neuron, it in turn triggers others, and so on, causing a chain reaction. Neurons often receive and put together many inputs at the same time. The result can be the awareness that a sumptuous dessert is on the table, a command to the muscles to turn up the volume of a stereo, a sudden

● **Motor neuron:** A neuron that sends signals to muscles to control movement.

● **Interneuron:** A neuron that is connected to other neurons, not to sense organs or muscles.

● **Glial cell:** A cell that fills the gaps between neurons, influences the communication among them, and generally helps in the care and feeding of neurons.

● **Brain circuit:** A set of neurons that affect one another.

memory of an assignment due yesterday, a flash of feeling for an attractive class-mate—anything we perceive, think, feel, or do.

Structure of a Neuron: The Ins and Outs

To understand psychological events, you need to know a few facts about the structure of the neuron. As you can see in Figure 3.2, each neuron has a receiving end, a sending end, and a part in the middle.

FIGURE 3.2 Major Parts of a Neuron

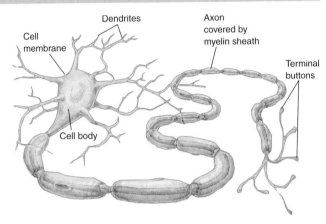

A neuron has many parts. The major ones are labeled here, but much of the action occurs internally where a complex dance of chemicals occurs.

Dendrites

Cell membrane

Axon covered by myelin sheath

Terminal buttons

Cell body

The part in the middle is called the **cell body.** Like all cells, it has a nucleus, which regulates the cell's functions, and a **cell membrane,** which is the skin of the cell. The sending end of the neuron is the **axon,** the long, cablelike structure extending from the cell body, along which signals travel to other neurons, muscles, or bodily organs. Although each neuron has only a single axon, most axons divide into many branches, called terminals, so that a neuron can send a message to more than one place at a time. At the end of each terminal are **terminal buttons,** little knoblike structures that release chemicals into the space between neurons when the neuron has been triggered. Most neurons communicate this way, releasing chemicals that affect other neurons, usually at their receiving end. (A few neurons, such as some of those in the eye, communicate via electrical impulses, but this electrical communication is rare.)

Each neuron has only one sending end—that is, only one axon—but a neuron may have many receiving ends. These are the **dendrites;** their name is derived from the Greek word *dendron,* meaning "tree," which makes sense when you look at their shape, in Figure 3.2. The dendrites receive messages from the axons of other neurons. Although axons sometimes connect directly to the cell body of another neuron, the connection is usually made from axon to dendrite.

Neural Impulses: The Brain in Action

Neurons are not always firing. When at rest, they maintain a negative charge within; this negative charge is called the **resting potential.** This potential arises in part because more sodium **ions** are outside the neuron than inside it, and more potassium ions are inside the neuron than are in the surrounding fluid (ions are

- **Cell body:** The middle part of a cell, which contains the nucleus.

- **Cell membrane:** The skin of a cell.

- **Axon:** The sending end of the neuron; the long cable extending from the cell body.

- **Terminal button:** A structure at the end of axons that, when the neuron is triggered, releases chemicals into the space between neurons.

- **Dendrite:** The twiggy part of a neuron that receives messages from the axons of other neurons.

- **Resting potential:** The negative charge within a neuron when it is at rest.

- **Ion:** An atom that has a positive or negative charge.

FIGURE 3.3 Ion Flow That Produces an Action Potential

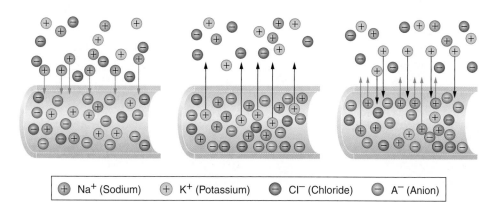

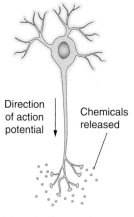

⊕ Na⁺ (Sodium) ⊕ K⁺ (Potassium) ⊖ Cl⁻ (Chloride) ⊖ A⁻ (Anion)

Na+ channels open after the neuron is stimulated, and Na+ ions rush into the cell; the inside of the cell then becomes positively charged. (Note: Ions are not drawn to scale, but relative proportions are correct.)

The Na+ channels close, K+ channels briefly open, and K+ goes outside the cell. (The K+ is pushed out be-cause of the addition of the positively charged Na+ ions.)

After this, "Na+ pumps" actively push Na+ back outside, and K+ is drawn inside, until the inside/outside concentrations are returned to their original levels.

When the ion exchanges reach the end of the axon, they cause chemicals to be released from the terminal buttons.

atoms that are positively or negatively charged). The membrane covering the axon has very small holes, or pores, called *channels*. The channels open and close: When particular channels are open, particular ions either flow into the cell from the surrounding fluid or flow from inside the cell to the surrounding fluid. When a neuron receives enough stimulation from other neurons (so that a *threshold* is exceeded), some of the channels in the cell membrane open, allowing a complex exchange of ions that changes the charge in the axon. This exchange works its way down to the end of the axon, finally causing the terminal buttons to open, releasing chemicals that will affect other neurons. When this occurs, the neuron is said to "fire." The shifting change in charge that moves down the axon is known as an **action potential**. This process, the basis of the neural communication that permits us to live in the world and respond to it, is illustrated in Figure 3.3.

Notice that the action potential obeys an **all-or-none law**. If enough stimulation reaches the neuron, it fires. In other words, the sequence of shifting charges sends the action potential all the way down the axon, releasing chemicals from the terminal buttons. Either the action potential occurs or it doesn't. Many neurons can fire hundreds of times a second because chemical reactions reset the neuron so it can fire again if it receives adequate stimulation.

Nevertheless, neurons require a measurable amount of time to work; to convince yourself that this is so, try the simple exercise described in Figure 3.4 (p. 76) together with some friends (developed by Rozin & Jonides, 1977).

Neurons would operate substantially more slowly were it not for the fact that most axons are covered with **myelin**, a fatty substance that helps impulses travel down the axon more efficiently. Myelin is a bit like the insulation around copper wires, which allows them to transmit current more effectively. Multiple sclerosis (MS) is one of

● **Action potential:** The shifting change in charge that moves down the axon.

● **All-or-none law:** States that if the neuron is sufficiently stimulated, it fires, sending the action potential all the way down the axon and releasing chemicals from the terminal buttons; either the action potential occurs or it doesn't.

● **Myelin:** A fatty substance that helps impulses travel down the axon more efficiently.

FIGURE 3.4   Measuring Neural Conduction Time

In the fastest neurons, impulses travel only about 120 meters per second, compared with 300,000,000 meters per second for the speed of light. Even compared with the impulses traveling in a computer, our neurons are extremely slow. You can actually measure the speed of neural processing. Here's how.

Sit in a row with some friends, with each person using his or her left arm to grasp the ankle of the person on his or her left. The person at the head of the line, the leader, says "Go" and starts a stopwatch at the same time he or she squeezes the ankle of the person to his or her left; as soon as that person feels the squeeze, he or she squeezes the ankle of the next person to the left; and so on. When the last person feels the squeeze, he or she says "Done." The leader records the time.

Now repeat the exercise, but each of you should grasp not the ankle but the shoulder of the person to your left. Less time is required for the squeezes to make their way down the row when shoulders are squeezed than when ankles are squeezed. Why? Because the impulses have farther to travel when the ankle is squeezed. By subtracting the difference in times and estimating the average distance from ankle to shoulder for each person you can actually estimate neural transmission time! This exercise should be done several times, first ankle, then shoulder, then shoulder, and then ankle; this procedure helps to control for the effects of practice in general.

HANDS ON

several disorders that illustrates the importance of myelin. In MS, the myelin has deteriorated, which makes impulses stumble as they move down the axon. People with MS experience impaired sensation in their limbs, loss of vision, and paralysis. Could myelin loss have caused the young soldier's problem? Probably not: His visual problem was selective, whereas myelin loss creates overall problems in seeing.

Neurotransmitters and Neuromodulators: Bridging the Gap

When just one neuron in your brain fires, it might be sending a chemical message to thousands of other neurons. Each neuron is typically connected to about 10,000 others (and some neurons are connected to up to 100,000 others; Shepherd, 1999). The number of possible connections among neurons is shockingly large. In fact, Thompson (1993) has estimated that the number of possible connections in your brain is greater than the number of atoms in the universe! There are about 100,000,000,000 neurons in the brain, and if each could be connected to an average of even 10,000 others (varying which ones are connected in all combinations), the numbers of ways your brain can be "connected up" becomes . . . well, astronomical!

How do neurons actually communicate? What are the connections between them like? The site where communication between neurons occurs is the **synapse,** where an axon of one neuron sends a signal to the membrane of another neuron. In most cases, the sending and receiving neurons are not hooked up physically but are separated by a gap called the **synaptic cleft,** shown in Figure 3.5.

FIGURE 3.5 The Synapse

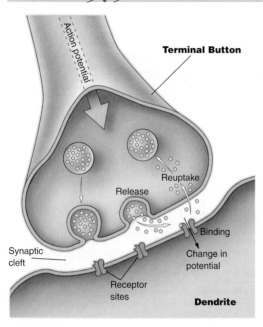

Impulses cross between neurons at the synapse. Chemicals released at the terminal buttons cross the synaptic cleft, where they bind to receptors and trigger events in the receiving neuron.

Chemical Messages: Signals and Modulators

As their name suggests, the chemicals that send signals, crossing from the terminal buttons across the synaptic clefts, are the **neurotransmitters.** The **neuromodulators** are chemicals that modulate, or alter, the effects of the neurotransmitters.

Imagine that you are using a pair of tin cans with a string between them as a walkie-talkie. When you speak into one can and your friend holds the other up to her ear, sound waves transmit the message. The gap from your mouth to one of the cans, and from the other can to her ear, is crossed by these waves, which carry the message. Neurotransmitters play the same role as the sound waves, allowing the message to cross the gap.

In contrast to the neurotransmitters, neuromodulators would produce the effect of tightening or loosening the string connecting the cans. When the string is drawn tight, the message is transmitted more effectively from one can to the other; when it is slackened, the sound must be louder to be heard. Other substances (which are not, strictly speaking, called neuromodulators) can affect what happens at the gap itself, for example, by affecting how quickly the neurotransmitters are removed from the synaptic cleft. Imagine that the room holding the linked tin cans has very thin air, with fewer molecules to vibrate. In this case, a louder sound would be needed to cause the bottoms of the tin cans to vibrate. On the other hand, if the air pressure were greater, a softer sound could convey the signal. Researchers have discovered many substances that act as neurotransmitters or neuromodulators in the brain, including some unexpected ones such as nitric oxide and carbon monoxide

● **Synapse:** The place where an axon of one neuron meets the membrane (on a dendrite or cell body) of another neuron.

● **Synaptic cleft:** The gap between the axon of one neuron and the membrane of another, across which communication occurs.

● **Neurotransmitter:** A chemical that sends signals from the terminal buttons on one neuron to the dendrites or cell body of another.

● **Neuromodulator:** A chemical that alters the effects of neurotransmitters.

(Barañano et al., 2001). Table 3.1 summarizes key properties of the major neurotransmitter substances.

Glial cells, the cells that fill the gaps between neurons, also influence what goes on at the synaptic cleft. These cells control the amount of neurotransmitters that can

TABLE 3.1 Major Neurotransmitter Substances

Summary of the most important neurotransmitters and neuromodulators, distinguishing features, major associated disorders, and typical drugs that modulate their effects. The disorders are discussed in later chapters of this book. A question mark indicates that the substance may be involved in the disorder, but conclusive evidence has yet to be obtained.

Name	Distinguishing Features	Related Disorders and Symptoms	Drugs That Alter
Acetylcholine (ACh)	Transmitter at the neuromuscular junction (causes muscles to contract), memory, used in autonomic nervous system	Alzheimer's disease, delusions (shortage); convulsions, spasms, tremors (excess)	Physostigmine (increases; used to treat Alzheimer's disease); scopolamine (blocks)
Dopamine (DA)	Motivation, reward, movement, thought	Parkinson's disease, depression (shortage); aggression, schizophrenia (excess)	Amphetamine, cocaine (causes release); chlorpromazine (blocks at receptors)
Noradrenaline (NA) (Norpinepherine, NE)	Dreaming, locomotion	Depression, fatigue (shortage); anxiety, headache, schizophrenia (excess)	Tricyclic antidepressants (such as Elavil) keep more available at the synapse
Adrenaline (Epinephrine)	Orientation towards stimuli	Depression, Alzheimer's disease (?) (shortage); arousal or apprehension (excess)	Amphetamine, cocaine (mimic effects)
Serotonin (5-Hydroxytryptamine; 5HT)	Primary inhibitory neurotransmitter regulating mood; sleep	Obsessive Compulsive Disorder, insomnia, depression (shortage); sleepiness, lack of motivation (excess)	Fluoxetine (Prozac), tricyclic anti-depressants (keeps more present at the synapse)
Glutamate	Most widely used fast excitatory neurotransmitter; memory formation; pain	Amyotrophic lateral sclerosis (ALS—Lou Gehrig's disease), (shortage); neurodegeneration, stroke, interferes with learning (excess)	Phencyclidine (PCP), dextromethorphan (blocks glutamate)
GABA (Gamma-Amino Butyric Acid)	Inhibits "sending" neuron	Anxiety, panic (?), epilepsy, Huntington's disease (shortage); sluggish, unmotivated (excess)	Sedatives (such as Phenobarbital), alcohol, benzodiazepines (such as Valium, Halcion) mimic effects
Beta-Endorphin	Inhibits acetylcholine and glutamate at the receiving neuron; blocks pain, alters mood	Pain sensitivity, immune problems (shortage); numb to pain (excess)	Naxalone (blocks the effects of); opiates (mimic effects)
Endogenous cannabinoids	Memory, attention, emotion, movement control, appetite	Chronic pain (shortage); memory and attention problems, eating disorders, schizophrenia (?) (excess)	SR141716A (blocks the effects of); THC (mimic effects)

reach a neuron. Some of them apparently produce substances that increase or decrease a neuron's sensitivity to inputs from other neurons (Newman & Zahs, 1998).

Not all neuromodulators are released at terminal buttons. Notably, **endogenous cannabinoids** are chemicals released by the *receiving* neuron that then influence the activity of the *sending* neuron (Wilson & Nicoll, 2002). This signaling system is one of the most important in the brain; cannabinoids affect precise locations on neurons, which allows them to fine-tune activity underlying learning, memory, pain perception, and attention (Katona et al., 2000; Kreitzer & Regehr, 2001b; Sanudo-Pena et al., 2000). Endogenous cannabinoids work by subtly dampening down both inhibitory sending neurons (especially those in the hippocampus, amygdala, and cerebellum; Katona et al., 2001; Kreitzer et al., 2002; Manning et al., 2001; Wilson & Nicoll, 2001; Wilson et al., 2001) and excitatory sending neurons (Kreitzer & Regehr, 2001a). Marijuana contains cannabinoids, but it affects neurons indiscriminately and promiscuously and thereby overwhelms this exquisitely tuned system—which in turn disrupts memory and attention, as well as other cognitive functions (Ashton, 2001; Schneider & Koch, 2002). As Barinaga (2001) put it, the chemicals introduced by marijuana eliminate the fine-tuned "local activity patterns . . . just as spilling a bottle of ink across a page obliterates any words written there" (p. 2531).

Receptors: On the Receiving End

What do the neurotransmitters do once they cross the gap? That depends. Each neuron has **receptors,** specialized sites on the dendrites or cell bodies that respond to specific neurotransmitters or neuromodulators. The receptor sites are the places where "messenger molecules" of the released chemicals—neurotransmitters or neuromodulators—attach themselves. A good analogy here is an ordinary lock set: The lock is the receptor, which is opened by the keylike action of a particular neurotransmitter or neuromodulator.

When neurotransmitters or neuromodulators become attached to receptors, they are said to *bind* (see Figure 3.6, p. 80). After binding, they can have one of two general types of effects. They can be *excitatory*, making the receiving neuron more likely to fire an action potential, or they can be *inhibitory*, making the receiving neuron less easily triggered. Because the typical axon divides into many branches and each neuron has many dendrites, there are many binding sites, so the neuron can receive thousands of different inputs from different sending neurons at the same time. The exciting and inhibiting inputs to each receiving neuron add up or cancel one another out, and their sum determines whether and when the neuron fires an action potential down its axon.

Each particular neuron produces a small number of transmitters or modulators, and each neuron can have many types of receptors. The same neurotransmitter or neuromodulator can have very different effects, depending on which receptors are present. In fact, the same neurotransmitter can have opposite effects on a neuron depending on which type of receptor accepts it, and the same chemical that can act as a neurotransmitter (sending a signal) in one context can act as a neuromodulator (altering a signal) in another (Dowling, 1992). For example, acetylcholine (ACh) can act as a neurotransmitter to slow down the heart, and can also function as a neuromodulator to help us store new memories. We will return to these substances repeatedly throughout the book, particularly when we consider the factors contributing to mental illness.

Not all of a given neurotransmitter released by the terminal buttons is taken up by receptors; some of it remains in the gap. Special chemical reactions are

● **Endogenous cannabinoids:** Neuromodulators released by the receiving neuron that then influence the activity of the sending neuron; the cannabinoid receptors are also activated by chemicals in marijuana.

● **Receptor:** A site on the dendrite or cell body where a messenger molecule attaches itself; like a lock that is opened by one key, a receptor receives only one type of neurotransmitter or neuromodulator.

FIGURE 3.6 Neurotransmitters

The terminal buttons release molecules that act as neurotransmitters. These molecules have their effect by binding to specific receptors. The molecules are often likened to keys, the receptors to locks. When transmitter molecules bind to receptors, as in the orange shaded circle, the receiving neuron is stimulated.

Adapted from *Psychology: Themes and Variations* (with Infotrac), 5th edition, by Weiten. © 2001. Reprinted with permission from Wadsworth, a division of Thomson Learning: www.thomsonrights.com Fax: 800-730-2215.

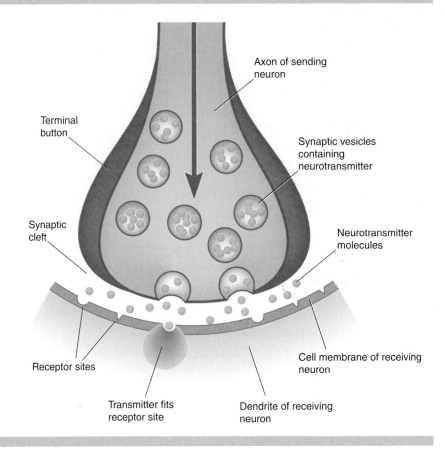

Axon of sending neuron

Terminal button

Synaptic vesicles containing neurotransmitter

Synaptic cleft

Neurotransmitter molecules

Receptor sites

Cell membrane of receiving neuron

Transmitter fits receptor site

Dendrite of receiving neuron

required to reabsorb—or **reuptake**—the excess neurotransmitter back into the *vesicles* (which store a neurotransmitter) of the sending neuron.

Unbalanced Brain: Coping With Bad Chemicals

By piecing together the story of how neurons communicate, scientists are not only developing a clear picture of how the brain works but also are learning how its functioning can go awry and how they can use drugs to repair it. Drugs that affect the way the brain works either increase or decrease the effectiveness of neural activity. Some of these drugs are **agonists,** which mimic the effects of a neurotransmitter or neuromodulator by activating a particular type of receptor. Other drugs may actually increase the amount of a neurotransmitter, sometimes by slowing down its reuptake. Depression, for example, is currently treated by several types of drugs that affect neurotransmitters and neuromodulators, including **selective serotonin-reuptake inhibitors (SSRIs),** which block the reuptake of the neurotransmitter serotonin. (Prozac, Zoloft, and Paxil are all SSRIs.) Still other drugs interfere with the effect of a neurotransmitter or neuromodulator. Some of these drugs are **antagonists,** which block a particular receptor. (As a memory aid, think of an "antagonist" at a party who is "blocking you" from meeting a charmer across the room.)

Could the young soldier whose vision was so strangely disrupted have had malfunctioning neurotransmitters or neuromodulators? Could such a disturbance have produced the highly selective impairments he experienced after inhaling the carbon monoxide fumes? It's possible, if just the right combinations of chemicals were disrupted. However, this scenario is unlikely. Because most neurotransmitters

● **Reuptake:** The process by which surplus neurotransmitter is reabsorbed back into the sending neuron so that the neuron can effectively fire again.

● **Agonist:** A chemical that mimics the effects of a neurotransmitter (sometimes by preventing reuptake).

● **Selective serotonin-reuptake inhibiter (SSRI):** A chemical that blocks the reuptake of the neurotransmitter serotonin.

● **Antagonist:** A chemical that blocks the effect of a neurotransmitter (sometimes by blocking a receptor or enhancing the reuptake mechanism).

and neuromodulators are used widely throughout the brain, not solely in the parts of the brain involved in visual perception, we would expect their disruption to create more widespread difficulties, such as in hearing, understanding language, walking, and other functions.

Now that you know the essentials of how neurons work, and how they affect each other via neurotransmitters and neuromodulators, you are ready to examine how neurons work within different brain structures and how their functioning can break down. First, however, let's pause to review how the effects of neurotransmitter and neuromodulator activity can ripple outward from the brain and body to profoundly change a person's life.

Parkinson's Disease apparently can strike anyone, and can interfere with a wide variety of careers. However, as actor Michael J. Fox showed, at least in some cases, surgery can help keep symptoms in check.

Looking *at* Levels

Parkinson's Disease

The connection between brain and behavior is seen in the devastating effects of *Parkinson's disease*, a classic brain disorder. Named after the British physician James Parkinson, who first described the disorder in 1817, Parkinson's afflicts about half a million Americans. The hands of people with Parkinson's disease shake; they may move sluggishly, with a stooped posture and shuffling walk; their limbs often seem frozen in position and resist attempts to bend them.

A piano tuner named John had to stop working because he developed Parkinson's disease. He had difficulty controlling his movements, and his behavior changed as well. He became so listless that he rarely left his house. He missed meals. And he started to contract various minor illnesses, which worsened his other symptoms.

All of these changes, physical and behavioral, were caused directly or indirectly by the death of particular neurons in John's brain. In the brains of people with Parkinson's disease, cells that produce the neurotransmitter *dopamine* have died. Dopamine plays a key role in the areas of the brain that are involved in planning movements. When patients take a drug that helps produce dopamine, L-Dopa, symptoms decrease, often for a long period of time.

When John's neurons no longer produced enough dopamine, the working of his brain was affected, and his muscle control was impaired. Events at the level of the brain interacted with events at the level of the person: Shaky hands made it almost impossible for him to tune pianos, so John had to retire. After he gave up the work he loved, he became depressed. He began to think of himself as diseased, and he began interpreting all of his behaviors in terms of his disease and predicting his future behaviors in that light. As a consequence, he lost interest in going out. Now events at the level of the person affected events at the level of the group: He stopped seeing many people, who in turn stopped seeing, and helping, him. The events in his brain influenced his feelings about himself and his relationships with other people.

Events at the different levels interact in both directions: The brain-based symptoms of shaking hands and shuffling gait became worse when John was ill from other causes, which occurred more often than before because he stopped taking care of himself; and the lack of social interactions led to his physical health deteriorating even further, making him more depressed and less likely to seek out the company of others.

TEST YOURSELF!

1. How do neurons work? What could cause neurons to die?
2. How do chemicals allow neurons to communicate? What happens if healthy neurons can no longer communicate?

The Nervous System: An Orchestra With Many Members

Consider some additional problems experienced by the young soldier who was poisoned while taking a shower. When researchers showed him a blue page on which white letters were printed, he thought he was looking at a "beach scene"—the blue was water and the white letters were "people seen on the beach from an airplane." He could visually pick out similar objects when they were placed in front of him, but only if they were of a similar color and size. His doctors found that he could be trained to name a few everyday objects by sight as children are taught to recognize sight words on *Sesame Street* without actually reading them, but this training broke down when the color or size of the objects changed. The young man learned to name a red toothbrush as "toothbrush," but he couldn't properly name a green toothbrush, and when he was shown a red pencil, he called it "my toothbrush."

The results of the entire series of tests made it clear that the soldier could see and understand color and size, but not shape. He had *some* sense of shape, though; he didn't call the pencil a "shoe" or a "basketball" but a "toothbrush." To understand what had gone wrong in the soldier's brain, you need to know what the different parts of the nervous system do.

Overview

A brain living in a vat wouldn't be of much use to anyone—it would be like a computer with no keyboard or monitor. To do its job, the brain needs both to receive input from the body and the outside world and to be able to act on these inputs. To understand the brain's job, then, you must see what it receives and what it sends out.

The Cranial Nerves: Cables to Command Central

The brain sends and receives information from the 12 cranial nerves, so named because they connect to the brain through holes in the cranium, the part of the skull that encloses the brain. These nerves control specific muscles, and also receive information from sense organs. Damage to a cranial nerve can cut off key inputs or outputs from the brain. If you weren't wearing a seat belt in an automobile accident, for example, your head might slam into the steering wheel. This could cause your brain to slosh forward and scrape along the underside of your skull. The scraping could disrupt the functioning of your olfactory nerves, and thus impair your ability to smell. This may not sound like a severe problem, but as you will see in the following chapter, smell plays a major role in taste—and food would never taste the same again.

The Central Nervous System: Reflex and Reflection

The largest conduit for information going to and from the brain is the **spinal cord,** the flexible rope of nerves that runs inside the backbone, or *spinal column.* In fact, so intimately connected is the spinal cord to the brain that the two together are called the **central nervous system (CNS).** At each of 31 places, spinal nerves emerge from the spinal cord in pairs, one on the left and one on the right. Through these nerves the spinal cord plays a key role in sending the brain's commands to the body (along the front side of the cord) and, in turn, allowing the brain to

● **Spinal cord:** The flexible rope of nerves that runs inside the backbone, or spinal column.

● **Central nervous system (CNS):** The spinal cord and the brain.

register information about the state of the body (along the rear side of the cord). The spinal cord also allows us, through our sense of touch, to gain information about the world.

The spinal cord isn't simply a set of cables that relays commands and information between brain and body. The spinal cord itself can initiate some aspects of our behavior, such as reflexes. A **reflex** is an automatic response to an event, an action that does not require thought. Even a simple reflex requires hundreds of neurons. How do reflexes work? When sensory neurons in the skin detect a sharp thorn, for example, they send signals that stimulate sensory neurons in the spinal cord. These neurons in turn are connected to interneurons in the spinal cord, as shown in Figure 3.7. When you jerk away from something that pricks you, interneurons have sent signals to motor neurons, which then cause the muscles to jerk, pulling your finger away from the source of pain. This arrangement allows you to respond immediately, bypassing the brain—it wouldn't pay to have to think through what to do every time you encountered a noxious stimulus.

FIGURE 3.7 Reflexes

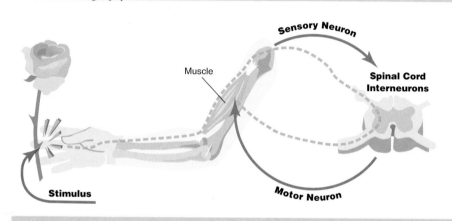

A simple reflex circuit allows the spinal cord to produce reflexive behavior without involving the brain. However, in some circumstances the brain can inhibit reflexes by stimulating an interneuron.

If the point of reflexes is to get things done in a hurry, why aren't the sensory neurons directly connected to motor neurons? Why the intermediary? Because interneurons provide a particular benefit: They allow the brain to send signals to *prevent* a reflex response. Perhaps you are handing a beautiful red rose to a good friend as a gift and accidentally prick your finger. Instead of flinging the rose away, you grit your teeth and continue to hold it. You are able to do this because the part of your brain that is involved in formulating goals and intentions knows not to flub this gesture and sends a signal to the interneurons to stop the motor neurons from firing.

The Peripheral Nervous System: A Moving Story

As shown in Figure 3.8 (p. 84), the CNS (which consists of the brain and the spinal cord) hooks into the **peripheral nervous system (PNS)**. The PNS links the central nervous system to the organs of the body. The PNS has two parts: the autonomic nervous system and the skeletal (or somatic) system. The **autonomic nervous system (ANS)** controls the smooth muscles in the body and some glandular functions. Smooth muscles, so called because they look smooth under a microscope, are found in the heart, blood vessels, stomach lining, and intestines. Many

● **Reflex:** An automatic response to an event.

● **Peripheral nervous system (PNS):** The autonomic nervous system and the skeletal system.

● **Autonomic nervous system (ANS):** Controls the smooth muscles in the body, some glandular functions, and many of the body's "self-regulating" activities, such as digestion and circulation.

FIGURE 3.8 Major Parts of the Nervous System

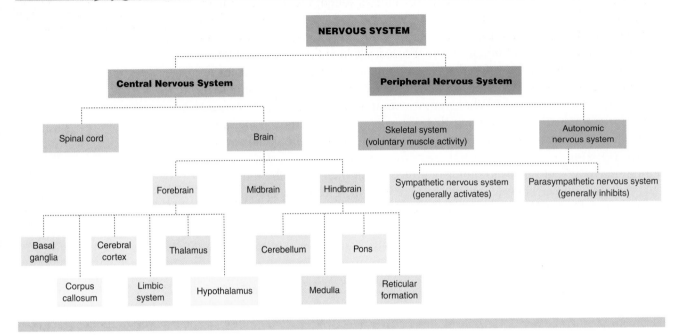

of the activities that the ANS controls, such as digestion and circulation, are self-regulating and are usually not under conscious control. In contrast, the **skeletal system** consists of nerves that are attached to voluntary muscles; these muscles are also known as striated muscles because under a microscope they appear "striated," or striped. If you clench your fist and "make a muscle," you are using this system.

The ANS itself has two major divisions. The **sympathetic nervous system** readies an animal (including you and the authors) to cope with an emergency. This system usually comes into play in response to a threat in the environment, perhaps a near-accident when you are driving in heavy traffic. As Figure 3.9 shows, the sympathetic system speeds up the heart, increases the breathing rate to provide more oxygen, dilates the pupils for greater light sensitivity and thus sharper vision, produces sweat slightly (giving your hand a better grip), decreases salivation, inhibits stomach activity, and relaxes the bladder. If your heart is pounding, your palms are sweaty, but your mouth is dry, it's a good bet that your sympathetic system has kicked in. The overall effect of these changes is to prepare your body to react—to fight or to flee. More oxygen flows into your muscles, your vision is improved, and the rest of your body is ready to support physical exertion.

Fight-or-flight situations are not the only conditions that activate the sympathetic nervous system. This system also operates in circumstances that may be less extreme but nonetheless threatening, such as getting ready to give an important speech, having a conversation with an irritable authority figure, or rushing to avoid being late for an important meeting. People prone to excessive amounts of anxiety tend to have sympathetic nervous systems that overshoot the mark and get the body too revved up. They might hyperventilate (that is, breathe in too much oxygen), sweat profusely, or experience a pounding heart when there is no apparent threat. These and other unpleasant physical symptoms of anxiety occur whenever the sympathetic nervous system responds too strongly.

● **Skeletal system:** Consists of nerves that are attached to striated muscles and bones.

● **Sympathetic nervous system:** Part of the ANS that readies an animal to fight or to flee by speeding up the heart, increasing breathing rate to deliver more oxygen, dilating the pupils, producing sweat, increasing salivation, inhibiting activity in the stomach, and relaxing the bladder.

The **parasympathetic nervous system** lies, figuratively, "next to" the sympathetic system (*para* is Greek for "next to" or "alongside") and tends to counteract its effects (see Figure 3.9). The sympathetic system speeds things up, and the parasympathetic system slows them down. Heart rate slows, pupils contract, salivation increases massively, digestion is stimulated, the bladder contracts. Whereas the sympathetic system tends to affect all the organs at the same time and can be thought of as increasing arousal in general, the parasympathetic system tends to affect organs one at a time or in small groups. The sympathetic and parasympathetic systems don't always work against each other. For example, an erection is caused by the parasympathetic system, but the sympathetic system controls ejaculation.

● **Parasympathetic nervous system:** Part of the ANS that is "next to" the sympathetic system and that tends to counteract its effects.

FIGURE 3.9 The Sympathetic and Parasympathetic Nervous Systems' Effects on the Body

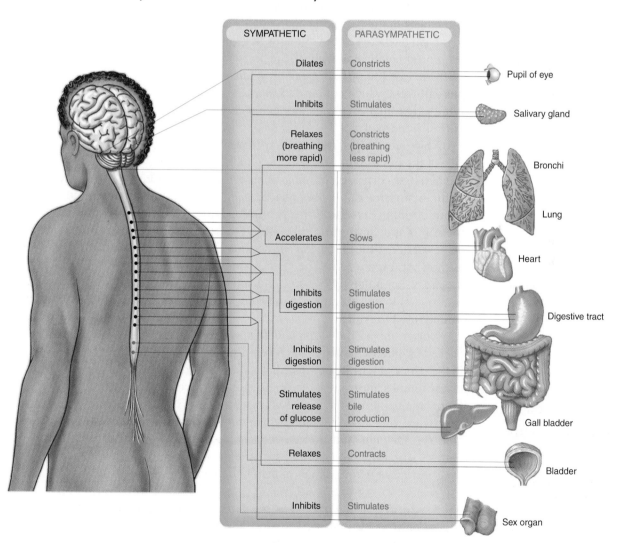

The two major branches of the ANS are the sympathetic and parasympathetic nervous systems. In general, the sympathetic nervous system prepares the body to fight or flee, and the parasympathetic dampens down the sympathetic nervous system.

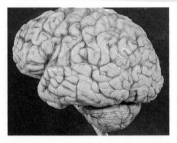

Most of your brain is water; the average brain weighs about 3 pounds, but if the water were removed, it would weigh only 10 ounces; this extra material (which includes proteins and fats, as well as various types of ions) are the parts of the neurons, glial cells, and everything else that gives the brain a structure.

● **Meninges:** The covering of the brain.

● **Cerebral hemisphere:** A left or right half-brain, roughly half a sphere in shape.

● **Lobes:** The four major parts of each cerebral hemisphere—occipital, temporal, parietal, and frontal.

● **Corpus callosum:** The huge band of nerve fibers that connects the two halves of the brain.

● **Cerebral cortex:** The convoluted pinkish-gray surface of the brain, where most mental processes take place.

● **Sulcus:** A crease in the cerebral cortex.

● **Gyrus:** A bulge between sulci in the cerebral cortex.

● **Ventricle:** A hollow area in the center of the brain that stores fluid.

● **Subcortical structure:** An organ that contains gray matter, located under the cerebral cortex.

The Visible Brain: Lobes and Landmarks

To understand the range of human abilities, you need to turn to the other part of the central nervous system, the brain itself. Imagine that you could see through someone's hair and scalp, even through the skull itself. The first thing you would see under the skull are the **meninges,** three protective layered membranes that cover the brain (*meningitis* is an infection of these membranes). Under this lies a network of blood vessels on the surface of the brain itself. Viewing the brain from above—looking down through the top of the head—you can see that the brain is divided into two halves, left and right, separated by a deep fissure down the middle. Each half-brain is called a **cerebral hemisphere** (*cerebrum* is Latin for "brain") because each is shaped roughly like half a sphere. Curiously, each hemisphere receives information from, and controls the muscles of, the opposite side of the body. For example, if you are right-handed, your left hemisphere controls your hand as you write.

Each hemisphere is divided into four major parts, or **lobes:** the *occipital* lobe, at the back of the brain; the *temporal* lobe, which lies below the temples, in front of the ears, where sideburns begin to grow down; the *parietal* lobe, in the upper rear portion of the brain, above the occipital lobe; and the *frontal* lobe, behind the forehead (see Figure 3.10). The two halves of the brain are connected by the **corpus callosum,** which contains somewhere between 250 to 300 million nerve fibers (some other smaller connections exist between the two halves of the brain, but they are less important).

Now, peer deeper. Immediately under the network of blood vessels on the surface of the brain is the convoluted, pinkish-gray surface of the brain itself: This is the **cerebral cortex** (*cortex* means "rind" or "shell" in Latin). This is where most of the brain's mental processes take place. Although the cerebral cortex is only about 2 millimeters thick, it is brimming with the cell bodies of neurons, giving the cortex its characteristic color and its nickname, "gray matter." Looking directly at the surface of the brain, you can see that the cortex has many creases and bulges, as shown in Figure 3.10. The creases are called **sulci** (the singular is sulcus), and the areas that bulge up between the sulci are the **gyri** (singular, gyrus). The cortex, so vital to our functioning, is crumpled up this way so that more of it can be stuffed into the skull.

Now peel back the cortex and look beneath it. Here you see lots of white fibers packed together. This material is actually myelinated axons, mostly from the neurons in the cortex; it is white because that is the color of the fatty white myelin insulation that surrounds the axons and, not surprisingly, these fibers are called "white matter." Below the white matter, in the very center of the brain, are hollow areas, called **ventricles,** where fluid is stored (the same fluid that fills the core of the spinal column). On either side and beneath the ventricles are the **subcortical** ("under the cortex") **structures** of the inner brain; these contain gray matter and are very similar to the organs of many animals that are much simpler than humans.

Structure and Function: No Dotted Lines

So far we've focused on the structure, or physical makeup, of the brain. But what do the various parts of the brain do? Consider a bike: You can point to its parts and discuss their physical structures (for example, a chain connects a metal gear to the back wheel), and you can discuss how the parts work (what the chain does). So too with the brain: You can point to the brain and discuss its physical parts, and you can describe how parts of the brain function—both individually and working together.

FIGURE 3.10   The Lobes of the Brain

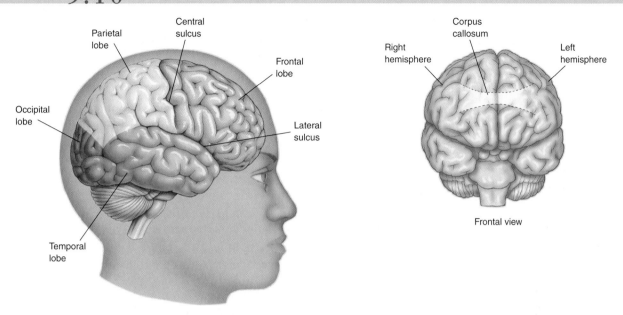

The brain is divided into four major lobes—occipital, temporal, parietal, and frontal. These lobes are named after the bones that cover them. The same major sulci (creases) and gyri (bulges) are evident on most brains.

Already, though, there is a problem. When it comes to its functioning, the brain isn't like the diagram of a cow in a butcher's shop; there are no dotted lines to show the different cuts of beef, the distinct regions that do different things. But in spite of the missing dotted lines, there are physical hints we can use to identify the brain's functional parts. Think of two stone walls; from a distance they may look the same—the same height, same color. But as you move up close, you can see that they are different, both because they are made up of different kinds of stones and because the stones are arranged differently. Similarly, under the microscope, parts of the brain appear to be different because they contain different types of neurons and these cells are organized differently. Brain areas that differ in terms of the arrangement of their neurons have often turned out to have distinct functions.

In addition, normal human brains do have certain major physical landmarks that help us to recognize parts that carry out different functions. Particular sulci and gyri, the creases and bulges in the cerebral cortex, for example, often consist of groups of neurons with well-defined functions. Unlike the creases and bulges that occur randomly when you crumple up a sheet of paper, some sulci and gyri occur for a reason. There are major connections between areas that tend to work together, and as the brain develops and the cortex expands, these firm connections force the cortex to fold in certain ways (Van Essen, 1997).

Let's focus more closely on some of these regions of the human brain.

The Cerebral Cortex: The Seat of the Mind

The four lobes have different functions, but always remember that the lobes do not function in isolation; they usually work in concert with one another.

Occipital Lobes: Looking Good

The **occipital lobes** are concerned entirely with different aspects of vision, and most of the fibers from the eyes lead to these lobes. If somebody were to hit you in the back of the head with a brick (an experiment we do not recommend), the "stars" you are likely to see appear because of the impact on this area. The occipital lobes contain many separate areas that work together to specify visual properties such as shape, color, and motion. Damage to these lobes results in partial or complete blindness. Because each half of the brain receives sensory information from the opposite side, if a surgeon has to remove the left occipital lobe (perhaps to take out a brain tumor), the patient will not be able to see things to his or her right side when looking ahead.

Because of the way the major arteries feed blood to the back of the brain, poisoning by carbon monoxide (which displaces oxygen) often leads to scattered cell death in the occipital lobe. Our young soldier probably suffered damage to the occipital lobes, perhaps in addition to injury to other parts of the brain. Such damage often affects visual perception, making the entire world seem fuzzy and making it difficult to organize information. Still, this probably does not sufficiently explain all of the soldier's vision problems; if this were all there was to it, why would he confuse white letters with sunbathers on the beach?

Temporal Lobes: Up to Their Ears in Work

The **temporal lobes,** which lie in front of the ears and roughly where sideburns start, play a key role in processing sound, entering new information into memory, storing visual memories, and comprehending language. The soldier may have had damage in either one or both temporal lobes, or in the connections from the occipital lobes to the temporal lobes. If the connections were damaged, only a small amount of information might now reach the part of the temporal lobes where visual memories of shapes are stored and compared to input (allowing you to recognize the stimulus). This diagnosis would go a long way toward explaining his problem. For example, in order to see a letter, he would have to look at one segment at a time (a vertical line, then a curved line, and so on), which isn't good enough to recognize the shape of a letter as whole. The world might look to the soldier like the images in Figure 3.11.

- **Occipital lobe:** The brain lobe at the back of the head; concerned entirely with different aspects of vision.

- **Temporal lobe:** The brain lobe under the temples, in front of the ears, where sideburns begin to grow down; among its many functions are visual memory and hearing.

- **Parietal lobe:** The brain lobe at the top, center/rear of the head, involved in registering spatial location, attention, and motor control.

- **Somatosensory strip:** The gyrus, located immediately behind the central sulcus, that registers sensation on the body and is organized by body part.

FIGURE 3.11 Shattered Vision

Some forms of brain damage may lead the victims to be aware of only small fragments of objects at a time, as shown here. Note how hard it is to recognize these common objects when all you have to go on are individual parts.

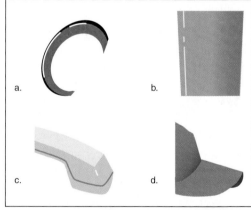

a. Scissors handle; b. table leg; c. telephone receiver; d. baseball hat

FIGURE 3.12 The Organization of the Somatosensory Strip

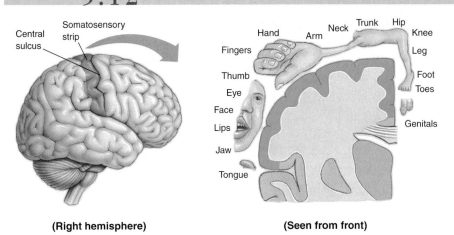

(Right hemisphere)

(Seen from front)

The somatosensory strip is organized so that different parts of the body are registered by adjacent portions of cortex; the size of the picture indicates the amount of brain tissue dedicated to that part of the body.

Parietal Lobes: Inner Space

When you recall where you left your keys, how to drive to a friend's house, or what's over your left shoulder, your **parietal lobes** (see Figure 3.10) are at work. Right now, your parietal lobes are playing a role in allowing you to define the distance between your face and the book and to shift attention to each of these words; they are even helping control your eye movements. The parietal lobes are also involved when you do arithmetic. Albert Einstein (1945) claimed that he reasoned by imagining objects in space, which is interesting in light of the fact that his parietal lobes were found to be about 15% larger than normal (Witelson et al., 1999). His unusual parietal lobes may have contributed to his genius.

Part of each parietal lobe, right behind the central sulcus (see Figure 3.12), is the **somatosensory strip.** This area registers sensation on your body. In fact, sensations from each part of your body are registered in a specific section of this strip of cortex. Tickling your toes, for example, activates neurons in the cortex next to the area devoted to stimulation from your ankle, as you can see in Figure 3.12. Larger areas of the cortex correspond to areas of the body that are more sensitive (notice the amount of space devoted to lips and hands).

The parietal lobes also play a role in consciousness, a topic explored in depth in Chapter 5. Patients who suffer damage to a parietal lobe may exhibit a curious deficit known as *unilateral visual neglect*. They aren't blind, but they typically ignore (that is, they "neglect") everything on the side opposite that of the damage—if the damage is in the right parietal lobe, they ignore everything on their left sides (see Figure 3.13). When they shave, for instance, they shave only half the face; when they dress, they put clothes on only half the body (pulling their shirt over only one arm,

FIGURE 3.13 Unilateral Visual Neglect

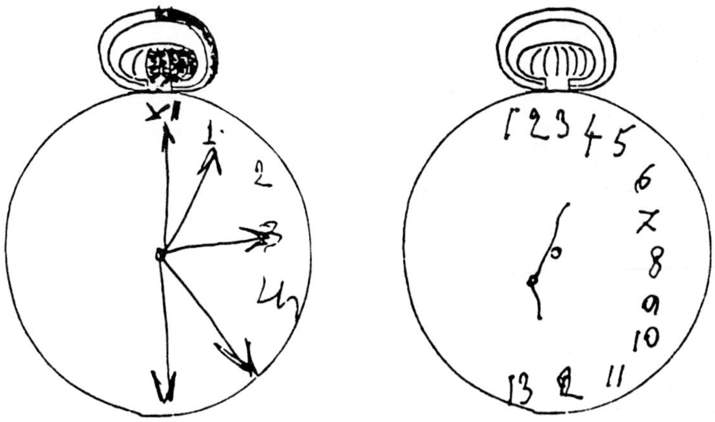

When patients who suffered from left-sided unilateral visual neglect are asked to draw a clock, they ignore the left side and try to cram all the numbers into the side to which they pay attention. Here are drawings from two such patients.

From Bisiach et al., 1981.

pants over only one leg). Many of these patients also have *anosognosia*, a lack of awareness that anything is wrong. Indeed, in one case a doctor showed such a patient her neglected arm and asked her what it was. The patient replied that the doctor had a third arm; she thought that her own arm was part of the doctor's body (Gerstmann, 1942, p. 892); similar cases are not uncommon (Aglioti et al., 1996; Yamadori, 1997).

Frontal Lobes: Leaders of the Pack

Probably the most dramatic difference between the appearance of a human brain and a monkey brain is how much the human brain bulges out in front. The size and development of the **frontal lobes** in conjunction with their rich connection to other areas, are features of the brain that make us uniquely human. The frontal lobes are critically involved in speech, the search for specific memories, reasoning (including the use of memory in reasoning), and emotions. These crucial lobes also contain the **motor strip** (also called the *primary motor cortex*), which is located in the gyrus immediately in front of the central sulcus. The motor strip controls fine movements and, as with the somatosensory strip, is organized in terms of parts of the body. Relatively large areas of this strip of cortex are dedicated to those parts of the body that we control with precision, such as the hands and mouth.

Hints about the functions of the frontal lobes, like other parts of the brain, have emerged from studies of patients with brain damage. Phineas Gage, the foreman of a gang of workers building a railroad in Vermont late in the 19th century, is perhaps the most famous case of a patient with damage to the frontal lobes. Gage's unfortunate loss was psychology's gain, as researchers were able to observe the consequences of damage to this vital area of the brain. The story began when Gage became distracted as he was packing blasting powder into a hole in a rock. When the metal bar he was using to pack in the powder accidentally hit the rock, it created a spark, which set off the powder. The metal bar, like a spear shot from a cannon, went right through the front part of his head, flew high in the air, and landed about 30 meters behind him. Miraculously, Gage lived, but he was a changed man. Previously, he had been responsible and organized; he now led a disorderly life. He couldn't stick to any decision, had little self-control, and his formerly decent language was now laced with profanity (Macmillan, 1986, 1992). Like Phineas Gage, other people with damage to the frontal regions of the brain have difficulty reasoning, may have trouble controlling their emotions and may have changed personalities.

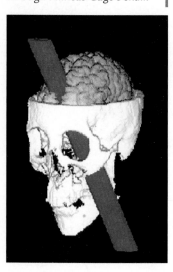

A computer-reconstructed picture of the path taken by the metal bar as it passed through Phineas Gage's skull.

● **Frontal lobe:** The brain lobe located behind the forehead; the seat of planning, memory search, motor control, and reasoning, as well as numerous other functions.

● **Motor strip:** The gyrus, located immediately in front of the central sulcus, that controls fine movements and is organized by body part; also called *primary motor cortex*.

The Dual Brain: Thinking With Both Barrels

The cortices of the two cerebral hemispheres, left and right, play distinct roles in cognition. What do the hemispheres do differently?

Split-Brain Research: A Deep Disconnect

The most compelling evidence to date that the two half-brains perform distinct functions has come from looking at the effects of severing the connection between the two hemispheres. When this is done, neuronal impulses no longer pass from one hemisphere to the other. Patients who have undergone this surgery are called **split-brain patients.** Why would such drastic surgery be performed? This procedure has been used to help patients with severe, otherwise untreatable epilepsy. *Epilepsy* is a disease that causes massive uncontrolled neuronal firing in parts of the brain, leading to bodily convulsions; in severe form, it prevents sufferers from leading a normal life. When the epilepsy engages the entire brain and is so severe that drugs cannot control it, surgeons may cut the corpus callosum. This operation prevents the spasm that originates in one hemisphere from reaching the other hemisphere, and thus the whole brain does not become involved in the convulsions—and their severity is thereby lessened.

Although it is easy to see how cutting the corpus callosum would decrease the severity of epileptic convulsion, the full effects of this procedure on mental processes cannot be understood without discussing vision. As shown in Figure 3.14, the left half of each eye is connected directly to the left hemisphere, but not to the right hemisphere; similarly, the right half of each eye is connected directly, and only, to the right hemisphere. (Note, it's not that the left eye is connected only to the left hemisphere, and the right only to the right.) Thus, if you stare straight ahead, objects to the left are seen first by the right brain, and those to the right are seen first by the left brain. If the corpus callosum is cut, the input stays in the hemisphere that receives the information; in normal people, it also crosses over to the other side.

FIGURE 3.14 The Eyes, Optic Nerves, and Cerebral Hemispheres

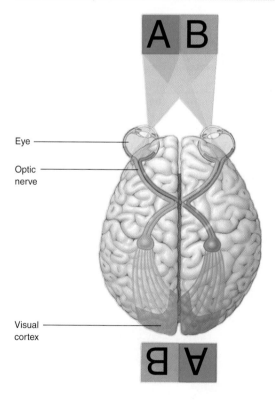

Eye

Optic nerve

Visual cortex

The backs of the eyes are actually parts of the brain pushed forward during development; the left half of each eye is connected only to the left cerebral hemisphere, whereas the right half of each eye is connected only to the right cerebral hemisphere.

● **Split-brain patient:** A person whose corpus callosum has been severed for medical reasons, so that neuronal impulses no longer pass from one hemisphere to the other.

The Hemispheric Interpreter

What are the practical effects of the division of the brain into two hemispheres? Gazzaniga and LeDoux (1979) reported a classic study of a split-brain patient, illustrated in Figure 3.15.

QUESTION: Does the left hemisphere construct stories to "fill in gaps" in its knowledge?

ALTERNATIVES: (1) The left hemisphere constructs stories to fill in the gaps in its knowledge; (2) the left hemisphere does not construct stories to fill in the gaps in its knowledge.

LOGIC: If the left hemisphere, which usually controls speech, makes up stories, then when a split-brain patient is asked about choices made by the right hemisphere (to which the left hemisphere is not privy because the hemispheres have been surgically disconnected), the patient should try to incorporate these choices into an interpretation consistent with what the left hemisphere knows.

METHOD: When researchers ask someone to stare directly ahead, and then present pictures or words to the left or right side (fast enough so that the participant can't move his or her eyes to look directly at them), the stimulus will be directed into a single cerebral hemisphere. Gazzaniga and LeDoux presented a picture of a snow scene to the right hemisphere and, at the same time, a picture of a chicken's claw to the left hemisphere. The patient was then shown several other pictures and asked to choose which of them was implied by the stimulus. The patient used his right hand (controlled by the left hemisphere) to select a picture of a chicken, and

FIGURE 3.15 Gazzaniga and LeDoux Experiment

The right hemisphere of split-brain patients is capable of understanding and responding to simple stimuli, but not speaking about them. Thus, the left hemisphere will sometimes make up stories to explain actions controlled by the right hemisphere.

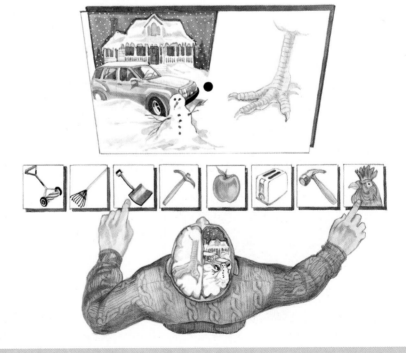

his left hand (controlled by the right hemisphere) to select a picture of a shovel. The investigators then asked the patient what he had seen and why he had made the selections.

RESULTS: The patient reported: "I saw a claw and I picked a chicken." Because the left hemisphere controls almost all of speech, it described what the left hemisphere saw. The patient continued: "And you have to clean out the chicken shed with a shovel." The left hemisphere did not actually know that the right hemisphere had seen a snow scene, so it made up a story.

INFERENCES: The left hemisphere, in right-handed people (and in most left-handed people), not only controls most aspects of language but also plays a crucial role in interpreting the world, in making up stories, and in many forms of reasoning (Gazzaniga, 1995; LeDoux et al., 1977).

Hemispheric Specialization: Not Just for the Deeply Disconnected

The methods used to study split-brain patients can also be used to study brain function in normal people. Because the corpus callosum is intact in normal people, information sent first to one hemisphere moves quickly to the other—but this takes a measurable amount of time, and it is possible that the information is of slightly poorer quality after it has crossed to the other hemisphere (Springer & Deutsch, 1994). Normal participants will make a judgment faster if information is delivered initially to the hemisphere that is better at making that kind of judgment (Hellige, 1993; Hellige & Sergent, 1986; Sergent & Hellige, 1986).

It's often said that the left brain is analytical and verbal, whereas the right brain is intuitive and perceptual. In fact, these generalizations must be made with caution. For example, the left brain is actually better than the right at some types of perception (such as determining whether one object is above or below another; Hellige & Michimata, 1989; Kosslyn et al., 1989), and the right brain is better than the left at some aspects of language (such as making the pitch of the voice rise at the end of a question or understanding humor; Bihrle et al., 1986; Brownell et al., 1984; Ellis & Young, 1987). Moreover, the abilities of the two hemispheres often differ only in degree, not in kind (Hellige, 1993). A major exception to this generalization is language. As you will see in Chapter 8, many aspects of language are carried out by a single hemisphere, usually the left.

The young soldier with difficulties in visual recognition could have suffered a functional deficit in his right hemisphere that prevented him from being able to see the overall shapes of objects. The right temporal lobe, in particular, appears to play a key role in recognizing overall shapes (Ivry & Robertson, 1998). After such damage, he would have had to rely on his left hemisphere, which tends to register details only, not overall shape.

Beneath the Cortex: The Inner Brain

The *subcortical* parts of the brain, situated deep beneath the cortex, often carry out crucial tasks that affect every moment of our lives. For example, although the examiners of the young soldier did not mention it, the soldier probably became lethargic after his accident—as is typical of people who have suffered brain damage. But why would brain damage cause someone to be less vigorous? The answer lies in the connections between the cortex and inner parts of the brain that are concerned with motivation and emotion. The most important of these subcortical areas are illustrated in Figure 3.16. Together with the cortex, most of these structures are considered to be part of the **forebrain** (so called because in a four-legged, horizontal animal such as a rat, these areas are at the front); but given their great variety of function, this traditional category is not very useful.

FIGURE 3.16 Key Subcortical Brain Areas

Many of the parts of the brain needed for day-to-day living are located beneath the cortex, such as those illustrated here.

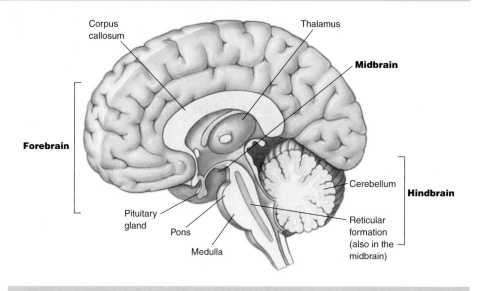

Thalamus: Crossroads of the Brain

The **thalamus** is often compared with a switching center but could also be likened to an airline hub where planes converge and then take off for far-flung destinations. The sensory systems, such as vision and hearing, and the motor systems that control muscles send fibers to the thalamus, which routes their signals to other parts of the brain. The intricate connections of the thalamus appear to explain a puzzling phenomenon reported by patients who have had a limb amputated. These people sometimes have the sensation that the limb is still there; they feel a *phantom limb*. Davis and her colleagues (1998) studied the thalamus in such patients and found that mild electrical stimulation of the thalamus produced sensations that seemed to come from the missing limb. Moreover, phantom limb sensations can be painful, and mild electrical stimulation of the thalamus has been found to relieve the pain.

The thalamus is also involved in attention; as a matter of fact, at this very second your thalamus is allowing you to fix your attention on each word you read. The thalamus is also involved in sleep control. The thalamus plays such a critical role in daily life that if it is badly damaged, the patient will die, even if the cortex remains untouched. If the young soldier's thalamus had been partially damaged, he might have exhibited some of the symptoms the doctors observed.

● **Forebrain:** The cortex, thalamus, limbic system, and basal ganglia.

● **Thalamus:** A subcortical region that receives inputs from sensory and motor systems and plays a crucial role in attention; often thought of as a switching center.

Hypothalamus: Thermostat and More

The **hypothalamus** sits under the thalamus, as illustrated in Figure 3.17. The small size of this structure shouldn't fool you: It is absolutely critical for controlling many bodily functions, such as eating and drinking; keeping body temperature, blood pressure, and heart rate within the proper limits; and governing sexual behavior. The hypothalamus also regulates hormones, such as those that prepare an animal to fight or to flee when confronted by danger. If visual recognition is impaired, as in the case of our young soldier, this organ would not receive the information it needs to function properly. If confronted by an enemy in the field, the soldier would not be able to register the information required to cause the right chemicals to flow into his bloodstream to marshal the body's resources for fight or flight.

Like the thalamus, the hypothalamus consists of clusters of neurons. Some of these can produce pain if stimulated by electrical current; others produce hunger or thirst; still others produce pleasure. In a now-famous experiment with rats, James Olds and his student Peter Milner (1954) electrically stimulated part of a rat's hypothalamus whenever it pressed a bar. The rodent found the electrical reward of pressing the bar so enticing that it continued to press it for hours. Stimulated this way, rats would press the bar thousands of times an hour; if given a choice of two bars to press—one producing food and the other, electrical stimulation—the rats consistently "chose" to press the bar for electrical stimulation (Valenstein, 1973). As a result of this well-documented finding (German & Bowden; 1974; Koob, 1999; Robbins & Everitt, 1999), this hypothalamic area has sometimes been called the "pleasure center."

Just how accurate the term "pleasure center" is has been brought into question, however. Noting the apparent gratification rats get when the appropriate part of the hypothalamus is stimulated, researchers turned their attention to humans. Experiments with humans about to have brain surgery have yielded no evidence

FIGURE 3.17 The Limbic System

These are the key structures that make up the limbic system, which plays a role in emotions and other psychological events.

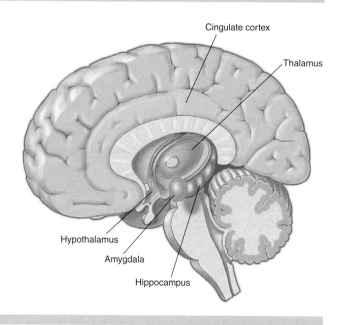

Cingulate cortex

Thalamus

Hypothalamus

Amygdala

Hippocampus

● **Hypothalamus:** A brain structure that sits under the thalamus and plays a central role in controlling eating and drinking, and in regulating the body's temperature, blood pressure, and heart rate.

suggesting that stimulating the hypothalamus produces such pure pleasure (LeDoux, 1996). At least at present, it is premature to think of any part of the hypothalamus as a "pleasure center" in the brain.

Hippocampus: Remember It

The **hippocampus** is a structure that looks something like a seahorse (at least to some people), and hence its name, from the Greek *hippokampos*, a mythological "seahorse" monster. This structure plays a key role in allowing us to enter new information into the brain's memory banks. The role of the hippocampus was vividly illustrated by the case of patient H.M., who had his hippocampus (and nearby brain structures) removed in an effort to control his epilepsy. After the operation, his doctors noticed something unexpected: H.M. could no longer learn new facts (Milner et al., 1968). His memory for events that occurred a year or so before the operation seemed normal, but he was stuck at that stage of his life. Each day began truly anew, with no memory of what had occurred earlier—in fact, he could not even remember what had happened a few minutes ago, let alone hours or days. Later, more careful study revealed that, in fact, he also could not remember events that had occurred within the year or so before the operation (Squire, 1987). H.M. does not seem particularly aware of his deficit, and when one of us interviewed him years after the operation, he was in good spirits and remarkably comfortable with himself. When asked about the meanings of words that were coined after his operation, he gamely offered definitions, suggesting, for example, that a jacuzzi is a "new kind of dance." He didn't seem to notice what was missing in his life. (Perhaps this is a case of the left hemisphere telling stories to fill in gaps, as Gazzaniga and LeDoux noted in their study of a split-brain patient.)

Patients such as H.M. led researchers eventually to discover that although the hippocampus itself does not contain stored memories, it triggers processes that store new information elsewhere in the brain. If the young soldier had damage to the occipital or temporal systems that register visual input, these areas would not feed the proper information to the hippocampus—and thus he would not be able to store in memory the stimuli he saw.

Amygdala: Inner Feelings

The **amygdala** is an almond-shaped structure (its name means "almond" in ancient Greek) near the hippocampus. The amygdala plays a special role in emotions such as fear and anger and even affects whether one can read emotions in facial expressions (Adolphs et al., 1996). The hypothalamus and amygdala play crucial roles as bridges between the CNS and the PNS. Indeed, both are key components of the **limbic system,** shown in Figure 3.17. The limbic system has long been thought of as being involved in the basics of emotion and motivation: fighting, fleeing, feeding, and sex. But each of the structures in this "system" is now known to have distinct roles that do not involve these functions (for example, the hippocampus is crucially important in storing new memories); further, other brain structures, outside this set, also play a role in emotion. For these reasons, some researchers regard the very concept of a "limbic system" as out of date (LeDoux, 1996).

Basal Ganglia: More Than Habit-Forming

The **basal ganglia,** positioned to the outer sides of the thalami, are involved in planning and producing movement (Iansek & Porter, 1980). People with Parkinson's disease often have abnormal basal ganglia; the functioning of this structure depends crucially on dopamine.

● **Hippocampus:** A subcortical structure that plays a key role in allowing new information to be stored in the brain's memory banks.

● **Amygdala:** A subcortical structure that plays a special role in fear and is involved in other sorts of emotions, such as anger.

● **Limbic system:** A set of brain areas, including the hippocampus, amygdala, and other areas, that have long been thought of as being involved in fighting, fleeing, feeding, and sex.

● **Basal ganglia:** Subcortical structures that play a role in planning and producing movement.

The basal ganglia also play a critical role in a particular type of learning: forming a habit. When you learn to put your foot on the brake automatically at a red light, the basal ganglia are busy connecting the stimulus (the light) with your response (moving your foot). As discussed in Chapters 6 and 7, this system is distinct from the one used to learn facts (the one, that, presumably, is at work right now, as you read this page). In addition, the nucleus accumbens, which is sometimes considered part of the basal ganglia, plays a crucial role in the brain's response to reward (Hall et al., 2001; Tzschentke & Schmidt, 2000) and its anticipation of reward (Knutson et al., 2001; Pagnoni et al., 2002). Indeed, drugs such as cocaine, amphetamines, and alcohol have their effects in part because they engage the nucleus accumbens (Dackis & O'Brien, 2001; Robbins & Everitt, 1999; Vinar, 2001). The neurotransmitter dopamine is central to the operation of this structure.

Brainstem: The Brain's Wakeup Call

As illustrated in Figure 3.16, at the base of the brain are structures that feed into, and receive information from, the spinal cord. These structures are often collectively called the **brainstem.** The **medulla,** at the lowest part of the lower brainstem (see Figure 3.16), is important in the automatic control of breathing, swallowing, and blood circulation. The brainstem also contains a number of small structures, together called the **reticular formation,** which has two main parts. The "ascending" part, the *reticular activating system (RAS)*, plays a key role in keeping you awake and making you perk up when something interesting happens. The RAS produces neuromodulators (as do several other specialized structures deep in the brain) that affect the operation of many other parts of the brain. Neurons of the RAS have long axons that reach up to other parts of the brain and alter the functioning of distant neurons. The soldier would have been sluggish following damage to these structures. The "descending" part of the reticular formation receives input from the hypothalamus and is important in producing autonomic nervous system reactions. It is also involved in connecting impulses from muscles not under voluntary control to those under voluntary control (such as those used in swallowing and speech).

The **pons** is a bridge (*pons* is Latin for "bridge") connecting the brainstem and the cerebellum; it is involved with a variety of functions, ranging from sleep to control of muscles used to form facial expressions.

Cerebellum: Walking Tall

The **cerebellum** is concerned in part with physical coordination. If your cerebellum were damaged, you might walk oddly and have trouble standing normally and keeping an upright posture. If you ever see an aging prizefighter, look at his walk: too many blows to the head may have damaged his cerebellum, leading to a condition aptly described as being punch-drunk. In addition, however, damage to some parts of the cerebellum might disrupt your ability to estimate time or to pay attention properly. The surface area of the cerebellum is nearly the same as that of the entire cerebral cortex, and hence it will not be surprising if this structure turns out to be involved in many cognitive functions. The medulla, pons, and cerebellum are often grouped together as the **hindbrain** because they lie at the rear end of the brain of a horizontal animal such as a rat; the other brainstem structures form the **midbrain,** which lies between the hindbrain and forebrain.

● **Brainstem:** The set of neural structures at the base of the brain, including the medulla and pons.

● **Medulla:** The lowest part of the lower brainstem, which plays a central role in automatic control of breathing, swallowing, and blood circulation.

● **Reticular formation:** Two-part structure in the brainstem; the "ascending" part plays a key role in keeping a person awake and alert; the "descending" part is important in producing autonomic nervous system reactions.

● **Pons:** A bridge between the brainstem and the cerebellum that plays a role in functions ranging from sleep to control of facial muscles.

● **Cerebellum:** A large structure at the base of the brain that is concerned in part with physical coordination, estimating time, and paying attention.

● **Hindbrain:** The medulla, pons, cerebellum, and parts of the reticular formation.

● **Midbrain:** Brainstem structures that connect the forebrain and hindbrain, including parts of the reticular formation.

- **Hormone:** A chemical produced by glands that can act as a neuromodulator.

- **Neuroendocrine system:** The system, regulated by the CNS, that makes hormones that affect many bodily functions; also provides the CNS with information.

- **Testosterone:** The hormone that causes males to develop facial hair and other sex characteristics and to build up muscle volume.

- **Estrogen:** The hormone that causes breasts to develop and is involved in the menstrual cycle.

- **Cortisol:** A hormone produced by the outer layer of the adrenal glands that helps the body cope with the extra energy demands of stress by breaking down and converting protein and fat to sugar.

- **Pituitary gland:** The master gland that regulates other glands but is itself controlled by the brain, primarily via connections from the hypothalamus.

The Neuroendocrine System: It's Hormonal

You now know that the central nervous system can affect the body not only by moving muscles voluntarily, but also by moving muscles automatically and by influencing the autonomic nervous system. In addition, some structures in the brain affect the body by producing (or causing to be produced) certain chemicals. For example, something happens during puberty that changes a child's body into an adult's and changes the child's behavior as well. Charming boys and sweet girls may become sullen and rebellious, moody and impulsive. That "something" is hormones. **Hormones** are chemicals that are produced by glands and can act as neuromodulators. The CNS hooks into the **neuroendocrine system,** which makes hormones that affect many functions. The CNS not only regulates this system, but also receives information from it—which in turn alters the way the CNS operates.

Figure 3.18 shows the locations of the major *endocrine glands;* endocrine glands secrete substances into the bloodstream, as opposed to other glands, such as sweat glands, that excrete substances outside the body. Some hormones affect sexual development and functioning. Among these, **testosterone** causes boys to develop facial hair and other external sexual characteristics, as well as to build up muscle, and **estrogen** causes girls to develop breasts and is involved in the menstrual cycle. Some hormones affect the levels of salt and sugar in the blood, and others help the body cope with stressful situations. The outer layer of the adrenal glands produces **cortisol,** which helps the body cope with the extra energy demands of stress by breaking down protein and fat and converting them to sugar; the sugar provides energy to the body, increases blood flow, and allows you to respond more vigorously and for a longer period of time. This system is engaged even by the sight of angry faces (van Honk et al., 2000).

A part of the brain called the **pituitary gland** is particularly interesting because its hormones actually control the other glands; for this reason it has sometimes been

FIGURE 3.18 The Major Endocrine Glands

The locations of major glands in the body.

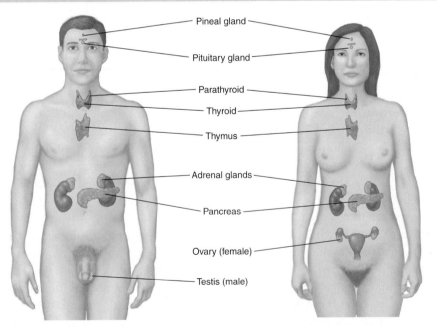

- Pineal gland
- Pituitary gland
- Parathyroid
- Thyroid
- Thymus
- Adrenal glands
- Pancreas
- Ovary (female)
- Testis (male)

called the "master gland." But, master or not, this gland is still controlled by the brain, primarily via connections from the hypothalamus. If information from the world isn't interpreted properly by the young soldier's cortex, it won't have the normal effect on the hypothalamus, which in turn will not produce the normal hormonal response.

Looking *at* Levels

Brain Damage on the Roller Coaster

At this point, it should be clear that damage to various parts of the brain can have far-reaching effects on the victim's life. Nobody wants brain damage. But some of us may unwittingly be putting ourselves at risk: It turns out that some attractions in amusement parks can cause brain damage, in particular the new breed of roller coaster. For example, after riding on the aptly named "Mind Eraser" at Six Flags Elitch Gardens in Denver, Colorado, Ms. Deborah Lee Benagh felt dazed and unsteady. Shortly afterwards, her left eye filled with blood. She had trouble remembering things she had just heard, could no longer see clearly, and she even blacked out sporadically. She saw a neurologist, who diagnosed her problem—she was suffering from brain damage. Ms. Benagh sued Six Flags, and eventually they settled out of court (Gilbert, 2002). Ms. Benagh is not alone (Braksiek & Roberts, 2002). Congressman Edward Markey (2002) held hearings in the U.S. Congress, and learned that such brain damage has been reported in 58 people who had ridden roller coasters—and eight of these people died! The most frightening fact is that these rides were operating normally; they didn't malfunction. In fact, almost 20 roller coasters in the U.S. exert more than 4 G's (4 times the force of gravity), which is potentially dangerous. One ride exerted more than 6 G's, which is what fighter pilots experience—but they are wearing special suits to help them cope with this stress. The operators of amusement parks have acknowledged the potential problem, and are setting voluntary G-force limits.

Think about this from the levels perspective. First, why did Ms. Benagh (or would you) get on the ride? In her case, the answer is clear: social pressure. Her sons chided her and convinced her to do so.

Why did the ride even exist? The owners thought they could make money from it, and thus created it in hopes that people would pay to ride it (level of the group). But such parks face stiff competition from other amusement parks, so the ride needs to be special. One way to make it special is to make it faster and more frightening. Second, at the level of the person, people don't believe that riding a roller coaster will cause brain damage. To counter this misconception, amusement park operators may soon post warning signs at the entrances to their roller coasters, warning smokers, pregnant women, the elderly, and people with arthritis that they are in danger. Do you think this would deter everyone in these categories? Some people with "macho" attitudes may be motivated to show how courageous they are in the face of such warnings, and thus the warnings may backfire. Third, the brains of some people may be particularly vulnerable to damage. For example, they may be born with vessels with thin walls that might burst when blood pressure increases. And events at the different levels interact. If the brain is damaged, this will not only affect daily life (as we've seen with our young soldier) but may also result in a lawsuit—which in turn may change the behavior of the operators of the ride (level of the group). Indeed, these operators may try to change the motivations and beliefs of potential riders (level of the person), if only to protect themselves against further lawsuits.

TEST YOURSELF!

1. What are the major parts of the nervous system that can sustain damage?
2. What is the cerebral cortex? What are the major cortical structures and what do they do?
3. How do the functions of the two sides of the brain differ?
4. What parts of the brain lie under the cerebral cortex? What do these subcortical structures do?

Probing the Brain

Having toured the major parts of the brain and noted their major functions, you can make a pretty good guess about what areas of the brain were damaged when the soldier suffered carbon monoxide poisoning. We cannot know for sure, given the limitations of the tests available at the time of his accident, in 1966. Today, however, doctors can obtain impressive high-quality images of a living brain. These images can show damage to particular brain structures and can record brain activity, or the disruption of it, in specific areas.

The Damaged Brain: What's Missing?

The first evidence that different parts of the brain do different things came from *natural experiments*, accidents in which people suffered damage to the brain. Such damage typically produces a region of impaired tissue, called a **lesion.** The most frequent source of damage is a **stroke,** which occurs when blood, with its life-sustaining nutrients and oxygen, fails to reach part of the brain (usually because a clot clogs up a crucial blood vessel) causing neurons in the affected area to die. In such cases, researchers study the patients, seeking to learn which specific abilities are disrupted independently of others when particular brain structures are damaged.

Although natural experiments can offer important clues about brain functioning, they have several serious limitations. Most important, natural experiments are rarely very neat. The damage caused by a stroke, for example, can extend over a large part of the brain, affecting more than one area and disrupting more than one function. This can make it difficult to relate the disruption in a particular function to the operation of a specific part of the brain. Also, stroke victims are usually older people, and often they have not led healthy lives (they've smoked, eaten high-cholesterol foods, not exercised); thus, they are not a representative sample of the population as a whole.

Such drawbacks have led some researchers to turn to *lesioning studies*. In these experiments, researchers remove specific parts of the brains of animals and observe the consequences on behavior. But, because animals are not people, we must be cautious in generalizing from animal brains to human brains.

Recording Techniques: The Music of the Cells

Rather than having to rely on the indirect evidence supplied by damaged brains, researchers can now make use of several methods to record the activity of normal brains. Neurons are never totally "off" (they maintain a baseline level of firing even when you sleep or are resting), but their rate of firing depends on what the brain is doing. Neurons that are used in a given task fire more frequently than those not involved in its performance, and this activity can be recorded.

To some extent, brain activity can be measured by making an electromagnetic recording. In one version of this technique, an **electroencephalograph (EEG)** machine records electrical current produced by the brain, as shown in Figure 3.19. When neurons fire, they produce electrical fields. When many neurons are firing together, these fields can be detected by electrodes (small metal disks that pick up electrical activity) placed on the scalp. Researchers can record electrical activity in response to a particular stimulus, or can record the activity over time; the result is a tracing of these "brain waves" of electrical fluctuation called an

● **Lesion:** A region of impaired tissue.

● **Stroke:** A result of the failure of blood (with its life-giving nutrients and oxygen) to reach part of the brain, causing neurons in that area to die.

● **Electroencephalograph (EEG):** A machine that records electrical current produced by the brain.

FIGURE 3.19 The Electroencephalograph

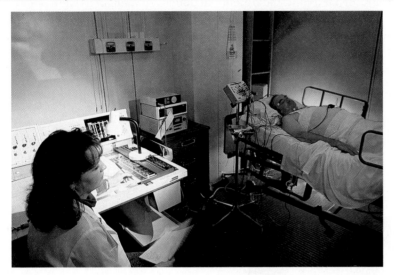

Relaxed/rest

Task performance

The top image shows an EEG during relaxed rest, whereas the bottom image shows an EEG during performance of a task; clearly, the brain is more active when an individual is performing a task than when he or she is relaxed.

This equipment allows researchers to record electrical activity on the scalp, which reflects electrical activity in the brain.

electroencephalogram (see Figure 3.19). Psychologists have used this technique to learn much about the brain. It is through EEGs, for example, that they learned that people go through distinct stages of sleep marked by different types of brain activity (see Chapter 5 for a detailed discussion of these stages).

Although EEGs have shed light on brain activity, particularly the time course of changes, the technique poses a major problem: The electrodes placed on the scalp cannot detect the precise locations of the electrical currents in the brain. The electrical current is distorted when it passes through the skull and current travels across the surface of the brain and the scalp.

Researchers can monitor activity in specific locations by recording neural activity directly. In this technique, called *single-cell recording*, tiny probes called **microelectrodes** can be placed in individual cells in the brain and used to record the firing rates of neurons. A typical microelectrode is at most only 1/10 as wide as a human hair (and some are only 1/100 as wide!). Usually researchers hook up the wires from microelectrodes to amplifiers and speakers rather than to a screen, so they can hear neuronal activity (as clicking sounds) rather than watch a monitor; their eyes are then free to guide the placement of the electrodes. Microelectrodes are sometimes put in human brains before brain surgery in order to find out what a part of the brain does before it is cut. Studies with microelectrodes have yielded some fascinating results. For example, when people look at words, some neurons respond to specific words but not others (Heit et al., 1988). However, single-cell recording also has its limitations. In some ways it is like looking at a picture though a pinhole in a piece of paper that covers it. This technique fails to indicate how large collections of neurons in the brain work together.

Neuroimaging: Picturing the Living Brain

Today, if you had an emergency like the young soldier's, you would probably be rushed to a hospital and immediately have your brain scanned. Your doctors

● **Electroencephalogram:** A recording from the scalp of electrical activity over time, which produces a tracing of pulses at different frequencies.

● **Microelectrode:** A tiny probe inserted into the brain to record the electrical activity of individual cells.

would order the procedure to determine both the structural damage (which areas were physically affected) and the functional deficits (which areas were performing below par). Because they yield an actual picture of neuronal structure and function, scanning techniques are referred to as **neuroimaging.** It is fair to say that neuroimaging techniques have transformed psychology, allowing researchers to answer questions that were hopelessly out of reach before the mid-1980s (Cabeza & Nyberg, 2000; Posner & Raichle, 1994).

Visualizing Brain Structure

The oldest neuroimaging techniques involve taking pictures of brain structures using X rays. The invention of the computer allowed scientists to construct machines for **computer-assisted tomography (CT,** formerly **CAT).** In this technique, a series of X rays builds up a three-dimensional image, slice by slice ("tomography" comes from a Greek word meaning "section"). More recently, **magnetic resonance imaging (MRI)** makes use of the magnetic properties of different atoms to take even sharper pictures of the structure of the brain. To understand how MRI works, consider how an opera singer can hit a note that will break a glass. This happens because the glass resonates with the sound waves so that it shakes at the same frequency as the note—shakes so hard that it shatters. Different materials resonate to different frequencies; the note that cracks a thin glass may not be the same as one that cracks a thicker, leaded glass. Similarly, different atoms in the brain resonate to different frequencies of magnetic fields. In MRI, a background magnetic field lines up all the atoms in the brain (or whatever organ is being scanned). A second magnetic field, oriented differently from the background field, is turned on and off many times a second; at certain pulse rates, particular atoms resonate and line up with this second field. When the second field is turned off, the atoms that were lined up with it swing back to align with the background field. As they swing back, they create a signal that can be picked up and converted into an image. The image shows the presence or absence of the substance of interest; in the brain, MRI often assesses the density of water in a region, which differs for gray versus white matter.

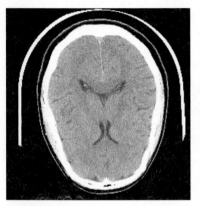 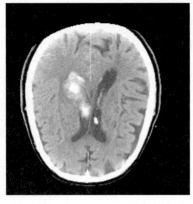

On the left, a computer-assisted tomography (CT) scan, and on the right, a magnetic resonance imaging (MRI) scan. The invention of MRI has provided much higher resolution images of structures of the brain.

● **Neuroimaging:** Brain scanning techniques that produce a picture of the structure or functioning of neurons.

● **Computer-assisted tomography (CT,** formerly **CAT):** A neuroimaging technique that produces a three-dimensional image of brain structure using X rays.

● **Magnetic resonance imaging (MRI):** A technique that uses magnetic properties of atoms to take sharp pictures of the structure of the brain.

Visualizing Brain Function

CT scans and MRIs give amazing views of the physical structure of the living brain; but for images that reflect the brain in action, researchers need other types of brain scans, those that track the amount of blood, oxygen, or nutrients moving to particular parts of the brain. When you take a shower or wash a load of laundry, water is drawn into the plumbing pipes from the water main. Similarly, when a part of the brain is working, it draws more blood. This fact was dramatically demonstrated by the case of Walter K (as described by Posner & Raichle, 1994). After a brain operation accidentally altered the shape of the bone over the back of his head, he noticed an odd humming noise coming from inside his head, which he thought became louder when he was using his eyes. His physician, John Fulton, took Walter's report seriously. He listened carefully to the back of Walter K's head

A positron emission tomography (PET) machine.

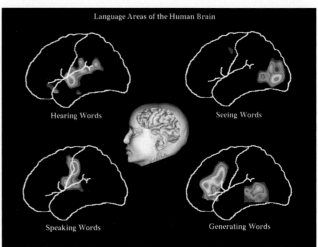

Language Areas of the Human Brain

Hearing Words

Seeing Words

Speaking Words

Generating Words

Brighter colors indicate regions of greater blood flow in the brain while the participant performed a particular task (from Posner & Raichle, 1994).

when his eyes were opened and when they were closed. Fulton too heard the sound, which became louder when Walter was looking carefully at something; the noise did not occur when Walter was listening carefully, or when he was smelling tobacco or vanilla. Fulton measured the sound coming from his patient's head and demonstrated conclusively that when Walter was looking carefully at something (for example, when he was reading a newspaper), the noise level increased. Why? Because the back of the brain is used in vision, and the noise, audible after the bone structure at the back of Walter's head changed, was the sound of the blood moving into the occipital lobe whenever it was needed for visual tasks.

One of the most important techniques for measuring blood flow or energy consumption in the brain is **positron emission tomography (PET).** Small amounts of radiation are introduced into the blood, which is then taken up into different brain areas in proportion to how hard the neurons are working. The amount of radiation emitted at different parts of the head is recorded, and a computer uses this information to build three-dimensional images of the brain. The main drawbacks with this technique are that it requires radiation, it takes at least 40 seconds or so of brain activity to collect enough data to build up an image, and it can cost as much as $2,000 to test a single person.

Probably the most popular type of neuroimaging today is **functional magnetic resonance imaging (fMRI).** The most common sort of fMRI reveals function by detecting the amount of oxygen that is being brought to a particular place in the brain. When a part of the brain is working hard, the blood that is drawn in brings with it more oxygen than can be used right away; so oxygen in that area piles up. The iron in the red blood cells carrying oxygen affects the surrounding water differently than the iron in the red blood cells that no longer have oxygen. The most common form of fMRI uses this difference to detect the regions where oxygen is piling up, which indicates where more brain activity is occurring. Unlike PET, fMRI does not require the introduction of radioactivity into the brain. Moreover, it is possible to build an image of events that occur in only a few seconds. However, this technique is not as simple to use as it may seem. For one thing, the brain is never completely "off," and thus you can't just see what brain areas are active while someone performs a task (such as looking at faces or solving problems). Instead, fMRI

● **Positron emission tomography (PET):** A neuroimaging technique that uses small amounts of radiation to track blood or energy consumption in the brain.

● **Functional magnetic resonance imaging (fMRI):** A type of MRI that usually detects the amount of oxygen being brought to a particular place in the brain.

studies must compare how performing one task alters brain processing *relative* to what happens during some other task. In many fMRI studies, the comparison is between a test task and rest. One problem here is that researchers really don't know what's going on in the brain during rest. For example, what if both men and women tend to daydream during rest, but daydream about different things (for instance, the men often think about sports, the women about their friends)—and the content of their thoughts alters brain processing? If so, then comparing brain activity that arises during another task (for example, looking at faces) to that during rest might suggest that the task is performed differently by men and women. But men and women could have the identical brain responses to the task, and it's the comparison state—rest—that's different. A major challenge in contemporary fMRI studies is to devise proper comparison tasks. Additional drawbacks of this technique are that the MRI machines are noisy and require the participant to lie very still within a narrow tube, a situation some people find uncomfortable.

Perhaps the most recent technique for visualizing brain activity relies on shining lasers through the skull. These lasers are very weak, but use frequencies of light (near infrared) to which the skull is transparent. It turns out that blood with oxygen in it absorbs different frequencies of light than does blood in which the oxygen has been consumed. Thus, by observing how much light of different frequencies is reflected back from the brain, researchers can track blood flow (Hochman, 2000; Hoshi et al., 2000; Villringer & Chance, 1997). This technique is called Near Infrared Spectroscopy (NIRS) or, when a map of activation is created, Diffuse Optical Tomography (DOT). A variant of this technique, called the Event-Related Optical Signal (EROS), observes how light is scattered following cellular changes that arise when neurons fire (Gratton & Fabiani, 2001a, b). Because only extremely weak lasers are employed, these techniques can be used to study even young infants. These techniques are inexpensive and relatively portable; they are also silent and safe. The major drawbacks at present are that the spatial resolution typically is poor, and only the cortex can be imaged—and not in its entirety.

Stimulation: Tickling the Neurons

To come closer to detecting just what neurons do, researchers can also stimulate them and observe the results. Two kinds of stimulation studies have been used to find out what parts of the human brain do.

In one technique, mild electricity is delivered to parts of the participant's brain, and the person is then asked to report what he or she experiences. Wilder Penfield and his colleagues (Penfield & Perot, 1963; Penfield & Rasmussen, 1950) pioneered this method with patients who were about to undergo brain operations. Penfield reported that people experience different images, memories, and feelings depending on the area in the brain that is stimulated. A problem with this method, however, is that researchers cannot be sure whether actual memories are activated or whether the participants are making up stories. In other stimulation studies, instead of asking for reports, researchers observe which activities are disrupted when current is applied (Ojemann, 1983; Ojemann et al., 1989). However, even this method is limited because stimulating particular neurons can lead to the activation of remote neurons, and these other neurons could produce the observed effects.

In a second, recently developed method, **transcranial magnetic stimulation (TMS)**, researchers stimulate the brain by putting a wire coil on a person's head and discharging a large current through the coil, thus creating a magnetic field. This magnetic field is so strong that it causes a large cluster of neurons under it to

● **Transcranial magnetic stimulation (TMS):** A technique where the brain is stimulated from outside by putting a wire coil on a person's head and delivering a magnetic pulse. The magnetic fields are so strong that they make neurons under the coil fire.

fire. Using this technique, researchers can make a person's fingers move by shifting the coil over the parts of the brain that control the fingers (in the motor strip) and producing on/off magnetic pulses (Pascual-Leone et al., 1997; Pascual-Leone et al., 1998; Walsh & Pascual-Leone, 2003). Similarly, if such pulses are directed to the occipital lobe, both visual perception and visual mental imagery can be temporarily impaired (Kosslyn et al., 1999). This technique can show that a brain area plays a causal role in allowing us to perform a particular task, as opposed to merely being stimulated by some other area that is actually doing the work. However, it is not always clear exactly which neurons have been affected by TMS.

Looking *at* Levels

The Musical Brain

Because even medium-sized hospitals have MRI machines for medical diagnosis, many researchers have been able to use these machines to explore all manner of human abilities. Part of the motor strip in the right half of the brain controls the fingers of the left hand. MRI has shown that this part of the brain is larger in orchestra members who play stringed instruments than in nonmusicians (Elber et al., 1995; Münte et al., 2002; Schlaug et al., 1995). Apparently brain areas that are used often actually grow larger, probably because of the formation of additional connections among neurons. Consider this finding from the levels perspective: the size of brain areas—the physical structure of your brain—depends in part on what you do! If you have musical talent and interest (characteristics at the level of the person) and have the opportunity to develop musical ability, your brain can be altered by the experience. If your playing is smiled upon by others (the level of the group), you will be even more motivated to continue practicing—and changing your brain. And, once your brain is altered, your playing may improve—leading to more praise from others. Even the structure of your brain can be fully understood only from the levels perspective. Lest you think that these findings apply only to musicians, consider the fact that taxi drivers have been found to have unusually large hippocampi (a brain structure that plays a special role in spatial memory)—and the longer a driver has worked, the larger they are (Maguire et al., 2000).

TEST YOURSELF!

1. What can researchers learn about the brain's function by studying behavior following brain damage?
2. What techniques allow us to record the activity of neurons in the brain as they function?
3. What is neuroimaging?
4. How can different parts of the brain be stimulated to see whether they are working properly?

Genes, Brain, and Environment: The Brain in the World

Why was the brain of the young soldier vulnerable to such damage from carbon monoxide fumes? Could he have done anything in advance to prepare his brain to survive such an event? Could he have done anything after the accident to speed his recovery? Let's consider the factors of environment and heredity that shape our brains so that they operate in particular ways and not in others, and the degree to which parts of the brain can change their functions if need be.

- **Mendelian inheritance:** The transmission of characteristics by individual elements of inheritance (genes), each acting separately.

- **Deoxyribonucleic acid,** or **DNA:** The molecule that contains genes.

Genes as Blueprints: Born to Be Wild?

Genes affect us from the instant of conception and continue to affect us at every phase of our lives. The story of genetics begins in 1866, when Gregor Mendel, an Augustinian monk living in what is now the Czech Republic, wrote one of the fundamental papers in all science. In it he formulated the core ideas of what is now known as **Mendelian inheritance,** the transmission of characteristics by individual elements of inheritance, each acting separately. Two ideas are key: (1) For each trait, an offspring inherits an "element" from each parent; and (2) In some cases, one of the elements dominates the other, and that is the one whose effect is apparent. If an element is not dominant, it is recessive: The effect of a recessive element is evident only when the offspring receives two copies of it, one from each parent. Mendel, through careful experimentation and record-keeping, traced these patterns of inheritance for a number of organisms (such as pea plants), but he never knew their mechanism. That great biochemical discovery, that the mysterious "elements" are genes, was not made until the early part of the 20th century. Figure 3.20 illustrates the **deoxyribonucleic acid,** or **DNA,** molecule that

FIGURE 3.20 The Secret of DNA

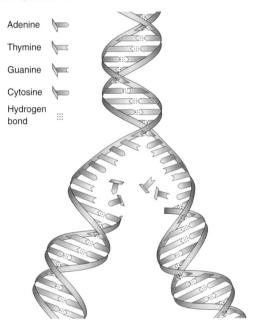

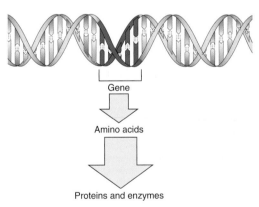

What, exactly, is a gene? Let's begin with a chromosome, which is a long, twisted molecule of deoxyribonucleic acid, or DNA, contained in the nucleus of all cells. Every cell of the human body (except for sex cells) has 23 pairs of chromosomes. The two strands in the DNA molecule are separated by pairs of four types of bases. The base adenine (A) always hooks up with thymine (T), and guanine (G) always hooks up with cytosine (C). Thus, if the helix is unzipped down the middle, extra bases floating about will hook up correctly to form two complete copies of the original molecule. This is how this amazing molecule is able to reproduce itself.

The particular ordering of pairs of bases codes genes; a gene is a segment along the strand of DNA that produces amino acids, which in turn are converted into proteins and enzymes. Everything else in our bodies (including our brains) is built of these molecules.

FIGURE 3.21 Homozygous and Heterozygous Genotypes

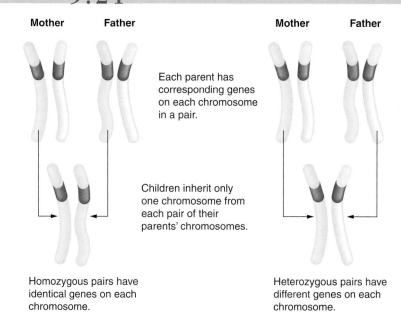

Mother **Father**

Each parent has corresponding genes on each chromosome in a pair.

Children inherit only one chromosome from each pair of their parents' chromosomes.

Homozygous pairs have identical genes on each chromosome.

Mother **Father**

Heterozygous pairs have different genes on each chromosome.

For all but the sex chromosomes, for each gene on one chromosome there is a corresponding gene on the other member of the pair. Homozygous genes are the same on both chromosomes of the pair; heterozygous genes are different.

Adapted from *Introduction to Psychology*, 3rd edition, by Kalat. © 1993. Reprinted with permission from Wadsworth, a division of Thomson Learning: www.thomsonrights.com Fax: 800-730-2215.

contains our genes. A **gene** is a stretch of DNA that produces a specific protein (including enzymes). Figure 3.21 illustrates cases where the corresponding genes in a pair of chromosomes are the same (*homozygous*) and where they are different (*heterozygous*).

In his pea plants, Mendel studied traits, such as skin texture and color; each trait, he observed, could appear in different "flavors," such as smooth or wrinkled, yellow or green. Thus, a gene for a trait can have different forms, called *alleles*. To inherit attached ear lobes or flat feet, for example, you need to receive the appropriate recessive allele from each of your parents. The sum total of your particular set of genes is your **genotype.** In contrast, the **phenotype** is the observable structure or behavior of an organism.

Many genes express their effects only in combination with other genes. When this occurs, we see quantitative variations in characteristics, such as differences in height, size, or intelligence, not qualitative variations, such as attached versus unattached ear lobes. In general, when a characteristic varies continuously, it reflects **complex inheritance,** the joint action of combinations of genes working together, rather than Mendelian inheritance, which describes the effects of individual elements of inheritance (Plomin & DeFries, 1998).

Genetic Programs: The Genes Matter

Did you ever wonder which came first, the chicken or the egg? The answer is now clear: The egg. A mutation modified the genes of an ancestor of the chicken, and these genes produced a novel egg—which, when hatched, developed into a novel bird, the chicken we all know and love. Genes affect not only obvious traits—such as eye color, height, and other physical features—but also, by affecting our brains, affect our behavior. That this is so is clear if you think about other animals. Consider dogs, for example. According to Plomin and his colleagues (1997), historically many dogs were genetically bred to behave in certain ways.

- **Gene:** A stretch of DNA that produces a specific protein, which in turn forms the building blocks of our bodies (including our brains) or drives the processes that allow us to live.

- **Genotype:** The genetic code carried by the organism.

- **Phenotype:** The observable structure or behavior of an organism.

- **Complex inheritance:** The joint action of combinations of genes working together.

Terriers were bred to crawl down holes and flush out small animals, Labrador retrievers to carry game such as ducks in their mouths, and so on. It is apparent that breeds of dogs differ in their intelligence and temperament, and yet all are members of the same species; they can interbreed. The variations among the different breeds are due to their genes.

In some organisms, such as yeast, researchers have *mapped* the genes in exquisite detail. To "map" a gene is to discover the particular base pairs along the DNA molecule that constitute the gene. In June 2000, The Human Genome Project announced a "rough draft" of such a map for humans, but it is only a rough draft—huge portions of the chromosomes remain uncharted territory. (Moreover, this project did not specify the range of alleles that can occur, nor how they are related to disorders.) In the single-celled organism paramecium (that wiggly oblong creature you may have labored to get into focus under a microscope in high school biology class), at least 20 genes are known to affect one aspect of its behavior—withdrawal. Scientists have found that **mutations,** or physical changes, of various genes produce different behaviors. The mutations are often given amusing names, which makes them easy to remember (we talk about such memory aids in Chapter 7). For example, "pawn" mutant paramecia can only swim forward, like a chess pawn; "paranoiac" mutants tend to swim backward (apparently wary of everything in front of them); and "sluggish" mutants are, well, sluggish.

It is staggering to discover the degree of understanding scientists have achieved over the way genes affect behavior. Consider a startling result reported in late 1996 by Ryner and her colleagues. These researchers identified a single gene that can change the sexual behavior of fruit flies. Usually, fruit flies engage in a "courtship dance" before they mate. The male follows the female, uses his forelegs to tap her body, produces a "song" by vibrating his wings, then licks her genitals, curls his abdomen, and tries to mate with her (Ferveur et al., 1995; Hall, 1994 [cited in Ryner et al., 1996]). By altering one gene, scientists produced male fruit flies that performed this courtship dance for other males. In fact, when a group of males with this gene were together, they lined up in a long chain, each male both being courted by and courting other males. The gene that produced this behavior affects only about 500 of the 100,000 neurons in the insect's head. A small genetic change, affecting a relatively small number of neurons, had a big effect. The affected neurons apparently coordinate many other neurons, which in turn produce the behavior.

Similar studies have been done with mice. Today it is commonplace for researchers to create new strains of mice by altering their genes. One such alteration involves removing a particular gene, creating **knockout mice.** Genes are knocked out when a part of the genetic code has been snipped away, deleting all (or crucial parts) of the gene so that it is disabled. The basic idea is that if a gene is used in a particular function, then knocking out the gene should create a deficit in that function. For example, Lijam and colleagues (1997) deleted a single gene in mice, which corresponded to one in fruit flies that has been dubbed "disheveled." In fruit flies, eliminating this gene causes the larvae to develop oddly along the head-to-tail axis, which makes them look disheveled. To the researchers' surprise, mice without this gene looked perfectly normal, but their social behavior was not at all normal. When normal mice are housed in the same cage, the dominant mouse usually trims away the whiskers and facial hair of the others—but the mutant mice don't follow this practice. Normal mice tend to sleep congenially in a huddled mass, but the mutants were scattered about the cage. And the mutants also had

● **Mutation:** A physical change of a gene.

● **Knockout mice:** Mice in which part of the genetic code has been snipped away, deleting all (or crucial parts) of a gene so that it is disabled.

trouble building the normal kind of nests for sleeping. In addition, the mutants had trouble with *sensorimotor gating*, which is the ability to focus on some stimuli while ignoring others. Of great interest is the fact that certain disorders in humans, such as autism, have similar symptoms. Thus, researchers are exploring the possibility that a similar gene plays a role in this (and other) disorders.

Researchers also use another technique to study the role of genes in affecting the brain and behavior. This one relies on creating **knockin mice,** where a gene is added or substituted for one already there. (The gene is introduced in the embryo.) The new gene expresses (produces) a different substance, or results in different amounts of the same substance. For example, in one study mice were given a gene that made their hippocampus vulnerable to *excitotoxic injury* (Zhu et al., 1999). Such injury occurs when too much glutamate is present. (Curiously, glutamate is not only the most common neurotransmitter in the brain, but it is also toxic to neurons if too much of it is present.) The gene the mice were given has been linked to Alzheimer's disease, which causes memory problems. Thus, the researchers were interested in the effects of this gene on the hippocampus (part of the brain critical for memory). And, in fact, this gene caused damage to neurons in the hippocampus. However, the study had an interesting twist. The researchers knew that putting mice on a diet could extend their life spans and protect them from various disorders (Sohal & Weindruch, 1996); could it also mitigate the effects of the new gene? When mice were fed only every other day, the bad effects of the gene were counteracted. This study suggests that food intake could play a role in regulating Alzheimer's disease.

Studies of humans have provided additional evidence that genes can make us vulnerable to certain diseases. For example, researchers in Iceland have discovered an allele for a certain gene that makes a person vulnerable to having a stroke. People who have this gene are 5 times more likely than normal to have a stroke—which means that having this gene is a bigger risk factor than are having high cholesterol, smoking, or having high blood pressure (Wade, 2002).

The far-reaching power of relatively small genetic changes can be seen dramatically by comparing chimpanzees with humans: About 99% of the genetic material in both species is identical (Wildman et al., 2002).

Tuning Genetic Programs: The Environment Matters

When it comes to physical, mental, and behavioral characteristics, what you see is not necessarily what you get in the genes: The phenotype may not simply be a read-out of the underlying genotype. There can be no question that genes play a major role in shaping our abilities, but it is critical to point out that genes *cannot* program the structure of the brain entirely in advance. Your brain contained far more connections at birth than it does now. As you interacted with the environment, certain neural connections were used over and over again, while others were used hardly at all. Connections between neurons in parts of the brain that are used frequently are retained, while others, which are not used frequently, are pruned away (Huttenlocher, 2002). **Pruning** is a process whereby certain neural connections are eliminated (Cowan et al., 1984; Huttenlocher, 2002): As the saying goes, "Use it or lose it." The genes define the possibilities for brain circuits, but interactions with the environment lead some connections to persist and others to disappear.

Pruning is only one of the ways in which your brain changes as you experience the world. Such changes are part and parcel of the brain's **plasticity,** its ability to change with experience. (Like plastic, the brain can be molded by external forces.)

● **Knockin mice:** Mice in which a new sequence of genetic code is added or is substituted for one already there.

● **Pruning:** A process whereby certain connections among neurons are eliminated.

● **Plasticity:** The brain's ability to be molded by experience.

Connections are also added. In fact, researchers have found that if rats are raised in enriched environments, with lots of toys and things to do, their brains actually become heavier than those of rats raised in average environments. The additional weight comes about in part because more blood flows to the cortex (Jones & Greenough, 1996), and in part because new connections are formed (Black et al., 1998; Comery et al., 1995; Diamond et al., 1972; Greenough & Chang, 1985; Greenough et al., 1987; Nelson, 1999; Turner & Greenough, 1985). The environment not only helps to select among connections established by the genes; it can also cause new connections to form.

In fact, even adult brains are capable of dramatic reorganization. If a finger is lost or immobilized, the part of the brain that used to register its input is soon taken over by inputs from other fingers (Merzenich et al., 1983; additional evidence is provided by Ramachandran, 1993; Ramachandran et al., 1992; Xerri et al., 1999). Moreover, if two fingers are surgically connected, the brain regions that register them start to function as a unit, but this unit splits up if the fingers are then surgically separated (Clark et al., 1988; Das & Gilbert, 1995; Kaas, 1995; Mogilner et al., 1993; Wang et al., 1995). We also now know that adult brains can create new neurons, at least in some regions (Gould et al., 1999).

Plasticity is most evident in four circumstances: (1) During infancy and childhood, when the brain is being shaped by interactions with the environment; (2) When the body changes, so that the sensory input changes; (3) When we learn something new, or store new information; and (4) As compensation after brain damage—even healthy portions of the young soldier's brain probably changed after his injury but, unfortunately, not as much as they probably would have if he were still a child (Payne & Lomber, 2001).

Thus, genes are not destiny; they don't fix our characteristics forevermore. The genes determine the range of what is possible (humans can't grow wings), but within those limits interactions with the environment can alter both the structure and the function of the brain.

Genes and Environment: A Single System

How do interactions with the environment alter the brain? Some people think of genes as blueprints for the body, providing the instructions on how to build organs, but this notion captures only part of the gene story. For one thing, rather than being filed away in a dusty drawer once their instructions have been followed, many genes keep working throughout your life. They are the reason some people go bald, others develop high cholesterol, and still others get varicose veins. Even more important, genes are not simply time bombs that are set at birth and ready to explode at the proper hour. Many genes change their operation constantly, sometimes producing proteins and sometimes not. Psychiatrist Steven Hyman suggested to one of us the following illuminating example: Say you want bigger biceps, so you go to the gym and start lifting weights. After the first week, all you have to show for your time and sweat is aching arms. But, after a few weeks, the muscles begin to firm up and soon may even begin to bulge. What has happened? When you first lifted weights, you actually damaged the muscles, and the damage caused the release of certain chemicals. Those chemicals then—and this is the important part—*turned on* genes in the muscle cells. By "turn on" we mean that the proteins coded

Some songbirds learn the songs of their particular species only by hearing other birds sing them. Mello and colleagues (1992) showed that the process of learning a song begins when certain genes are turned on as the bird first hears the song, which in turn regulates the effects of other genes that actually produce the learning.

by the genes were produced. These proteins were used to build up the damaged muscles. If the damage stops, so do the chemicals that signal the genes to turn on, and the genes will no longer produce those extra proteins. So, you need to lift increasingly heavier weights to keep building more muscle. No pain, no gain.

The important point to remember is that many genes are constantly being turned on and off, as needed, to produce new substances. As you read this, for example, terminal buttons are releasing neurotransmitters that enable you to understand the printed words. Genes are turned on to replenish the buttons' supply of neurotransmitters. Similarly, genes regulate the flow of neuromodulators, and it is the genes that lead to new connections among cells during learning of new material.

Just as interacting with the environment (such as lifting weights) can lead to bulging muscles, interacting with the environment can set your brain to operate more or less efficiently. And depending on how your brain is working, you behave differently. By regulating the brain, genes affect behavior.

It is commonplace today for scientists to stress that both genes and environment are important. This is true but, simply stated, it misses the mark. Genes and environment cannot really be considered as separate factors; they are instead *different aspects of a single system*. In much the same way as you can focus separately on the brushstrokes, texture, composition, and color of a painting, you can discuss genes and the environment as discrete entities. But, as with a painting, to appreciate the "whole picture," you must consider genes and environment together (Gottlieb, 1998).

Environment and Genes: A Two-Way Street

Genes can affect the environment, and the environment can regulate the genes. Remember, we are talking about a single system here. Plomin and colleagues (1997), Scarr and McCartney (1983), and others distinguish three ways that the genes and environment interact. First, **passive interaction** occurs when genetically shaped tendencies of parents or siblings produce an environment that is passively received by the child. An example: Parents with higher intelligence tend to read more, and thus have more books in the house. Given that parents with higher intelligence tend to have children with higher intelligence, this means that children with higher intelligence will tend to be born into environments with more books (Plomin, 1995). Second, **evocative** (or **reactive**) **interaction** occurs when our genetically influenced characteristics draw out behaviors from other people. We might call this the "blondes have more fun" effect. As it happens, responses to this stereotype vary, at least in U.S. culture. Some people react to blondes more positively than they do to brunettes. Others, however, may think blondes are less substantial people than are brunettes. Third, genes and environment interact when people deliberately choose to put themselves in specific situations and aggressively avoid others. Such **active interaction** involves constructing situations or shaping and modifying existing ones in ways that are comfortable for

Exercise does more than build muscles; it also turns on genes in the brain that build better neurons. Neeper and colleagues (1995, 1996) showed that exercise turns on genes that produce a chemical called brain-derived neurotrophic factor (BDNF). BDNF protects neurons and helps them continue to function properly.

● **Passive interaction:** Occurs when genetically shaped tendencies of parents or siblings produce an environment that is passively received by the child.

● **Evocative (or reactive) interaction:** Occurs when genetically influenced characteristics draw out behaviors from other people.

● **Active interaction:** Occurs when people choose, partly based on genetic tendencies, to put themselves in specific situations and to avoid others.

● **Behavioral genetics:** The field in which researchers attempt to determine how much of the differences among people are due to their genes and how much to the environment.

● **Heritability:** The degree to which variability in a characteristic is due to genetics.

existing genetic tendencies. A timid person, for instance, may avoid loud parties and amusement parks, instead seeking out peaceful settings and quiet pastimes.

Behavioral Genetics

Researchers in the field of **behavioral genetics** try to determine how much of the differences among people's abilities are due to their different genetic makeups and how much to differences in their environments. The environment varies at different times and places, so this is a difficult question indeed. Throughout this book, we talk about the relative contributions of genes and the environment to differences in mental processes or behavior. Here we need to stress a crucial point: Any conclusions about the relative contributions of genes and environment can apply only to the specific circumstances in which they were measured. You've just seen that genes are turned on in different circumstances and, depending on which genes are turned on in a given environment, the brain will work more or less effectively. Statements about relative contributions of genes and environments, therefore, apply only to the situation at hand and have no bearing on different circumstances.

Heritability, Not Inheritability

Researchers in behavioral genetics focus on estimating the "heritability" of various characteristics, ranging from intelligence to personality, as they occur in specific environments. **Heritability** is perhaps an unfortunate term. It does not indicate the amount of a characteristic or trait that is inherited, but rather how much of the *variability* in that characteristic in a population is due to genetics. Height in Western countries is about 90% heritable. This statement means that 90% of the variability among the heights of these people is genetically determined, not that *your* height was determined 90% by your genes and 10% by your

About 90 percent of the *variation* in height is controlled by the genes, and thus height is about 90% heritable. Heritability estimates assume that the environment is constant; if the environment varies (perhaps by providing a better or poorer diet), environmental factors can overshadow even very high heritability.

www.ablongman.com/kosslyn2e

environment. In fact, the possible differences in height owing to diet may actually be greater than the differences owing to genes; but *in a specific environment* (for example, one in which diet is constant), heritability indicates the contribution of the genes to variations. If the environment were different, the heritability might be different too.

Twin Studies: Only Shared Genes?

At first glance, the simplest way to study whether variability in a characteristic is inherited might seem to involve comparing the characteristics of parents and their children. But this method doesn't sort out the effects of genes and the environment. On the one hand, the parents and kids share a common household, which could *increase* the correlation. But factors such as different ages and occupations, and the likelihood that parents and children spend much of their days in different environments, could *decrease* the correlation. Because of these confounding variables, we can gain greater insight by studying brothers and sisters who are about the same age. But, because even small age differences can make a big difference in certain environments (such as school), it is best to study twins, people who are exactly the same age.

Twin studies compare the two types of twins, identical and fraternal. Identical twins start life when a single fertilized egg divides in two; these twins are **monozygotic** (like many scientific terms, this comes from Greek: *monos*, meaning "single" and *zygotos*, meaning "yoked," as occurs when a sperm and egg are joined). Monozygotic twins have identical genes. In contrast, fraternal twins grow from two separate eggs that are fertilized by two different sperm; these twins are **dizygotic**. Fraternal twins share only as many genes as any other pair of brothers or sisters—on average, half. By comparing identical twins and fraternal twins, we get a good idea of the contribution of the genes, if we assume that the environment is the same for members of both sets of twins. Such studies have shown that the amount of gray matter of the brain (where neural cell bodies exist) is very similar in identical twins, which suggests that the amount of gray matter is, in part, under genetic control (Thompson et al., 2001; summarized and commented on by Plomin & Kosslyn, 2001). This similarity was particularly pronounced in the frontal lobes and in Wernicke's area. So what? Well, the amount of such gray matter is correlated with scores on intelligence tests—and (as we see in Chapter 9), identical twins tend to have similar levels of intelligence, perhaps for this reason.

An even better way to gather evidence for the relative contributions of genes and environment is to study either related children who were separated at birth and raised in different households or unrelated children who were raised in the same versus different households. Called an **adoption study**, this type of investigation is particularly powerful when twins who have been separated at birth, or shortly thereafter, grow up in different environments. Even in these cases, however, it is difficult to separate genetic from environmental influences. If the twins are cute, for instance, caregivers in both households will treat them differently than if they look tough and fearless; if they are smart and curious, both sets of parents may be inclined to buy books and read to them. So findings from studies of twins separated at birth are fascinating, but even they don't allow us to separate genes from environment with confidence. The best we can say is that genes contribute a certain amount to differences among people in particular environments, and that environments contribute a certain amount to such differences when people have particular genes.

● **Twin study:** A study that compares identical and fraternal twins to determine the relative contribution of genes to variability in a behavior or characteristic.

● **Monozygotic:** From the same egg and having identical genes.

● **Dizygotic:** From different eggs and sharing only as many genes as any pair of brothers or sisters—on average, half.

● **Adoption study:** A study in which characteristics of children adopted at birth are compared to those of their adoptive parents or siblings versus their biological parents or siblings (often twins). These studies often focus on comparisons of twins who were raised in the same versus different households.

Evolution and the Brain: The Best of All Possible Brains?

The loss of consciousness and brain damage suffered by the young soldier occurred because he breathed toxic fumes and was deprived of oxygen. Not all species would react the way this member of our human species did, though, if faced with this situation. Sperm whales, for instance, do just fine if they take a breath every 75 minutes or so. Why don't our brains give us this extra protection? This question leads to thoughts about **evolution,** the gene-based changes in the characteristics of members of a species over successive generations.

Natural Selection: Reproduction of the Fittest

A major driving force of evolution is **natural selection,** which was first described in detail in 1858 by Charles Darwin and, independently, by Alfred Russel Wallace. Inherited characteristics that contribute to survival in an environment are those that will come to be widespread in a population. Why? Because the individuals with those characteristics are the ones that live long enough to have many offspring. In turn, those offspring, equipped with the favorable characteristics inherited from their parents, will survive to have more offspring. In this way, the "selection" of the survivors is made by "nature." An inherited characteristic that contributes to such selection is called an **adaptation.** The term "survival of the fittest," coined by Darwin, is perhaps unfortunate; the key point is that some characteristics lead some organisms to have more offspring, who in turn have more offspring, and so on—until their inheritable characteristics are spread throughout the population. Plomin and colleagues (1997) point out that the principle might better have been termed "reproduction of the fittest."

Darwin saw this pattern in a brilliant insight; but where are the genes in the story? Nowhere. Genes were not discovered until the early part of the 20th century, and not discovered to correspond to DNA until 1953. Darwin never knew that the mechanism for the transmission of traits from one generation to the next is the gene. Today, we would say that natural selection depends on the fact that there is variation in the genes carried by members of a population, and if a gene allows an organism to have more offspring that survive (and they have more offspring, and so on), eventually more of that particular gene will be present in the population.

Evolution via natural selection tends to mold the characteristics of a group of organisms to the requirements of its environment. If a certain animal lives at the North Pole, those individuals with warm fur will tend to have more babies that survive, and those individuals that are white (and thus harder for predators to spot in the snow) will tend to have more babies that survive. If these characteristics are useful enough in that environment, eventually the species as a whole will have warm white fur.

Here's a contemporary analogy of the way natural selection works. There were two Chinese brothers; one settled in Louisiana and the other in Ohio. They both opened Chinese restaurants and began with identical menus. After the first month, the brother in Louisiana noticed that his blander dishes were not selling well, so he dropped them from the menu; in Ohio, they were doing fine, so they remained. In Louisiana, the chef one day accidentally knocked a jar of chili powder into a pot of chicken he was simmering. He found he liked the taste, so this new dish became the special of the day. It sold so well that it became a standard on the menu. Hearing the tale, the brother up north in Ohio tried the chili dish, but it didn't sell well.

● **Evolution:** Gene-based changes in the characteristics of members of a species over successive generations.

● **Natural selection:** Changes in the frequency of genes in a population that arise because genes allow an organism to have more offspring that survive.

● **Adaptation:** A characteristic that increases "fitness" for an environment.

Menus of Chinese restaurants in different locales undergo evolution. Even if they start the same, the chefs will vary the menu from time to time. Depending on the diners' tastes, "natural selection" will eventually produce different menus in the different locales.

This chef bought a lot of corn, which was on sale. He tried adding it to a traditional dish and called it the special of the day. The Ohio chef wasn't trying to achieve a particular taste, he was just experimenting. That corn dish did not sell well, and so was dropped. But when he added corn to another recipe, the result was an instant hit. Both chefs continued with new elements in their cooking, with varying degrees of success on different occasions. After two years, the brothers' menus had little in common.

Two important principles of evolution are illustrated here. First, the "environment"—the hungry restaurant patrons—"selected" different aspects of the menus: The southerners, for example, apparently liked spicy food better than did the patrons in Ohio. Second, variation is at the heart of the process. Without the accidents and substitutions, the process would not have worked—the menus would not have evolved over time. Natural selection in the evolution of the two menus depended on random variation, which provided the "options" that proved more or less adaptive.

The same is true in the evolution of species, but in this case the "menu" is the set of genes different organisms possess. Genes that lead an organism to have offspring who have still more offspring stay on the menu, and those that do not lead to this result eventually get dropped.

So, back to the question of the sperm whale and breathing. If our ancestors had had to go for long periods without breathing in order to survive, then only those who could do so would have survived and had offspring—and we lucky descendants would have inherited this ability. And the story of our young soldier might have had a happier ending.

Not Just Natural Selection: Accidents Do Happen

A word of warning: Always exercise caution when trying to use the idea of natural selection to explain our present-day characteristics. Just because a characteristic exists doesn't mean that it is an adaptation to the environment or that it is the result of natural selection. Natural selection may or may not be the reason, for example, why some people are more prone than others to alcoholism. For one thing, as human brains and bodies evolved, the environment also changed: People created not only furniture, houses, and cities, but also automobiles, guns, computers, and candy. Our brains may not be ideally suited for what they are doing now.

Furthermore, natural selection is not the only way that evolution works. Accidents can happen. Sometimes characteristics piggyback on other characteristics. For example, sickle-cell anemia, a blood disease that is common among African Americans, is an unfortunate side-effect of protection from malaria. (The gene that causes the anemia codes for a protein that destroys cells infected with the malaria-causing parasite, which is useful in the parts of Africa where malaria is common.) And sometimes characteristics appear because the original adaptation can be put to good use in a new role that has nothing to do with the original adaptation; the nose originally evolved to warm air and direct scents, but once you have one, you can use it to hold up your glasses (Gould & Lewontin, 1979). For example, once we have the brain machinery to see lines and edges, abilities that probably helped our ancestors to discern prey, the brain can allow us to learn to read.

In short, some of our abilities, personality types, social styles, and so forth may have arisen from natural selection because they are useful, and others may have been accidental. It is not easy to sort out which is which, and we should not assume that there is a sound evolutionary reason for everything people do.

Looking *at* Levels

Alcoholism, Muslims, and Mormons

As we've seen from our discussion of the interaction between genes and the environment, only rarely do genes determine completely whether you will have a specific characteristic. For example, men with a particular gene (for which they can be tested) are likely to become alcoholics if they drink at all (Goedde & Agarwal, 1987). Having this gene presents no downside, however, for men who obey the norms of a strict Muslim or Mormon culture, in which alcohol is forbidden. And why do people adhere to certain rules and norms? At least in part, because of their beliefs. Thus, the adherence to group norms leads to behavior that regulates the genes. If a man knows he has this gene, this knowledge might even serve to support his beliefs and his group affiliation. Genes are merely one element in a larger system, which necessarily includes interactions among events at the different levels of analysis.

TEST YOURSELF!

1. Can "bad genes" make you more vulnerable to the environment? How do genes and the environment interact as the brain develops and functions?
2. What does *heritability* mean?
3. How has evolution shaped the functions of the brain?

CONSOLIDATE!

You've seen ample evidence that the fumes damaged the soldier's brain—but exactly how? We could narrow down our explanation for his problems to the following three aspects of brain function: First, many—but not all—neurons in the occipital lobes died because of a lack of oxygen and nutrients. This damage caused him to have fuzzy vision. Second, the parietal lobes, thalamus, or some other area used in attention was also damaged so that he had a narrow range of attention and thus could not perceive the context in which a shape appears. Hence, he only saw small details. Third, alternatively, or perhaps additionally, he saw small details because the temporal lobe in his right hemisphere was damaged, an area that typically registers overall shapes; or, possibly, the connections to the right temporal lobe from the occipital lobes were damaged. But his left hemisphere, particularly his left frontal lobe, apparently was intact enough to allow him to make up a story based on what he saw, allowing him to try to make sense of the stimulus. Thus he saw details in isolation and tried to think what they might be.

Brain Circuits: Making Connections

- The neuron is the key building block of the brain. The cell body receives inputs from the dendrites (or, sometimes, directly from axons of other neurons) and sends its output via the axon (which is connected to the dendrites of other neurons or, in some cases, their cell bodies).

- The axon is covered with myelin, a fatty insulating material, that makes neural transmission more efficient. The axon branches into separate terminals. The terminal buttons at the end of the terminals contain chemical substances that are released by an action potential. These substances are either neurotransmitters or neuromodulators.

- Neurotransmitters cross the synaptic cleft (the gap between the end of the axon and the receiving neuron) to affect another neuron. Neuromodulators can be released into this space, or can be distributed more diffusely in the fluid surrounding neurons. Both neurotransmitters and neuromodulators affect receptors, which are like locks that are opened by the right key. Once opened, the receptor causes a chain of events inside the neuron.

- Glial cells not only control the creation of synapses and support neurons, but they also help to regulate neurotransmitters and can affect neurons directly.

- When the total input to a neuron is sufficiently excitatory, the neuron "fires"—that is, chemical reactions work their way down the axon. After a neuron has fired, surplus neurotransmitter is reabsorbed back into the cells. Some drugs block this reuptake mechanism.

- Some neuromodulators are not released from terminal buttons. Endogenous cannabinoids, for example, are released by the receiving neuron and inhibit sending neurons.

THINK IT THROUGH Say you are a health-care provider who specializes in helping patients who have suffered brain damage. What would you try to do to help the young soldier? Are there any special strategies that you could teach him that might help him? Can you think of jobs that he could be trained to do in spite of his damage?

Imagine that you had invented a new drug that protected one particular cognitive ability from being disrupted by brain damage. If you could choose, which ability do you think is most important to protect? Why?

The Nervous System: An Orchestra With Many Members

- The nervous system has two major parts, the central nervous system (CNS) and the peripheral nervous system (PNS).

- The CNS consists of the spinal cord and the brain itself. In addition to sending commands from the brain to the body and passing along sensory input to the brain, the spinal cord also underlies some reflexes. Reflexes depend on the action of interneurons, neurons that hook up to other neurons.

- The brain itself is organized into lobes, and is covered by the cortex, a thin layer of neurons. The cortex contains many bulges (gyri) and creases (sulci), which allows a lot of cortex to be crammed into a relatively small space.

- The four major lobes in each hemisphere are the occipital, temporal, parietal, and frontal. The occipital lobe processes visual input. The temporal lobe is the seat of visual memories and is also involved in language comprehension, hearing, storing new memories, and some aspects of consciousness. The parietal lobe registers size, three-dimensionality, and location in space, and is also involved in attention, arithmetic, motor control, and consciousness; it includes the somatosensory strip, which registers sensation from parts of the body. The frontal lobe is involved in speech production, searching for memories, reasoning (and using memory to help in reasoning), fine motor control (governed by the motor strip), and making decisions.

- Each lobe is duplicated, one on the left and one on the right. The left hemisphere, which plays a larger role in language, appears to play a critical role in inventing stories to make sense of the world. The right hemisphere plays a larger role than the left in recognizing overall shapes and some nonverbal functions.

- Under the cortex, many subcortical areas play crucial roles in the brain's mission. The thalamus manages connections to and from distinct parts of the brain; the hypothalamus plays a crucial role in regulating hormones, which is important for its role in controlling bodily functions such as eating, drinking, and sex; the hippocampus is involved in the storage of new memories; and the amygdala plays a role in fear and other emotions.

- The hippocampus, amygdala, and other structures constitute the limbic system, which is involved in fighting, fleeing, feeding, and sex.

- The basal ganglia are used in planning and producing movements, as well as in learning new habits. The brainstem contains structures involved in alertness, sleep, and arousal; and the cerebellum is involved in motor control, timing, and attention.

- The PNS, engaged in part via the amygdala and hypothalamus, consists of the autonomic nervous system (ANS) and the skeletal system. The ANS is in turn divided into the sympathetic and parasympathetic systems, which are critically involved in the "fight or flight" response.

- The neuroendocrine system produces hormones, which not only affect the body but also affect the brain itself (as by, for example, altering moods).

THINK IT THROUGH Clearly, the organization of the brain has a lot to do with why brain damage produces one disorder and not another. It is possible that some parts of the brain receive information that is not available to the parts that control language. If so, can you think of types of behaviors that might reveal that the information was "in there"?

Can you think of a way by which you could have tried to find out whether the soldier had a problem with attention, or whether his paying attention to a small area was just a strategy? That is, perhaps he believed that by focusing on details he would see better, and did so even though he was in fact able to pay attention to overall shapes. What difference, if any, would it make whether his problem was due to a faulty strategy or a problem that was not under his control?

More careful examination of the soldier might have suggested that his problem was not confined to visual processing. What would you think if it could be shown that his personality was particularly unemotional? What if he had little interest in eating or sex?

Probing the Brain

- The earliest method used to discover what the various parts of the brain do involved observing the effects of brain damage on behavior. Such "natural experiments" led scientists to investigate the effects of lesioning parts of animal brains.

- Scientists can record electrical activity produced by neural firings while people and animals perform specific tasks, either from the scalp or from tiny electrodes placed in neurons; they find more vigorous activity in areas involved in the task than in those that are not being relied upon. Neurons can be electrically or magnetically stimulated to fire and the effects on behavior observed.

- Various neuroimaging techniques include the following: computer-assisted tomography (CT), which uses X rays to obtain images of the structure of the brain; magnetic resonance imaging (MRI), which makes use of magnetic fields to produce very sharp pictures of the brain; positron emission tomography (PET), which relies on small amounts of radioactivity to track blood flow or energy consumption in the brain; functional magnetic resonance imaging (fMRI), which uses changes in the magnetic properties of blood when oxygen is bound to red blood cells to track blood in the brain as a person performs a task; and optical imaging, which uses changes in how much light of different frequencies is absorbed or reflected by the brain while a person performs a task.

THINK IT THROUGH Dr. Scannering has invented an improved form of brain scan, which shines very dim lasers through your head and projects an image of brain activity as it is happening. This machine will be sold for less than the price of a personal computer, is very portable, and easy to use. What would you do with such a machine? What uses can you think of for education or psychotherapy? What sort of education would you need to make the best use of this technological breakthrough?

Genes, Brain, and Environment: The Brain in the World

- Individual genes can affect the brain and behavior (via Mendelian inheritance), or sets of genes working can have these effects (via complex inheritance). Genes cannot be considered in isolation. The genes lay down the basic structure of the brain, but the environment can mold both its structure and its function.

- Genes influence how resistant people are to drugs and other environmental effects. The effects of genes can be studied with knockout mice (which have a gene removed) or knockin mice (which have a gene replaced or a new one added).

- During brain development, the environment affects brain structure and function by pruning connections that are not working well, and also causes the brain to form new connections in response to increased activity.

- The genes place limits on what is possible (for example, people can't grow wings), and even small genetic changes can sometimes exert significant effects on cognition and behavior.

- However, many of your genes are under the control of the environment, and are turned on and off depending on what you are doing; specific genes can cause the manufacture of new neurotransmitters or neuromodulators at the terminal buttons, and can even cause neurons to hook up in new ways.

- Behavioral genetics attempts to discover how much of the variability in an ability is due to the genes versus the environment, but such estimates apply only to the environments in which the ability is measured.

- We have our present sets of genes because of evolution, which is partly a consequence of natural selection (genes are retained in the population when they produce characteristics that lead to more surviving offspring who in turn have surviving offspring), and is partly a consequence of accidents.

- Our brains and bodies were not designed for all that we use them for today, and hence it is not surprising that in some cases we are vulnerable to properties of the environment (such as sweets, drugs, and the opportunity to drive too fast).

THINK IT THROUGH Did natural selection design the brain so that it is vulnerable to damage such as the soldier's brain sustained? Is there reason to think that natural selection formed the brain so that vision is carried out by separate areas from hearing and language? Which parts of the brain would you expect to be shared by other animals, and why?

Can you think of any human abilities that you would bet are "adaptations"? How about abilities that could be accidents? How could you tell whether a characteristic is present because of natural selection?

Key Terms

action potential, p. 75
active interaction, p. 111
adaptation, p. 114
adoption study, p. 113
agonist, p. 80
all-or-none law, p. 75
amygdala, p. 96
antagonist, p. 80
autonomic nervous system (ANS), p. 83
axon, p. 74
basal ganglia, p. 96
behavioral genetics, p. 112
brain circuit, p. 73
brainstem, p. 97
cell body, p. 74
cell membrane, p. 74
central nervous system (CNS), p. 82
cerebellum, p. 97
cerebral cortex, p. 86
cerebral hemisphere, p. 86
complex inheritance, p. 107
computer-assisted tomography (CT, formerly CAT), p. 102
corpus callosum, p. 86
cortisol, p. 98
dendrite, p. 74
deoxyribonucleic acid, DNA, p. 106
dizygotic, p. 113
electroencephalogram, p. 101
electroencephalograph (EEG), p. 100
endogenous cannabinoids, p. 79
estrogen, p. 98
evocative (or reactive) interaction, p. 111
evolution, p. 114
forebrain, p. 94
frontal lobe, p. 90
functional magnetic resonance imaging (fMRI), p. 103
gene, p. 107
genotype, p. 107
glial cell, p. 73
gyrus, p. 86
heritability, p. 112
hindbrain, p. 97
hippocampus, p. 96
hormone, p. 98
hypothalamus, p. 95
interneuron, p. 73
ion, p. 74
knockin mice, p. 109
knockout mice, p. 108
lesion, p. 100
limbic system, p. 96
lobes, p. 86
magnetic resonance imaging (MRI), p. 102
medulla, p. 97
Mendelian inheritance, p. 106
meninges, p. 86
microelectrode, p. 101
midbrain, p. 97
monozygotic, p. 113
motor neuron, p. 73
motor strip, p. 90
mutation, p. 108
myelin, p. 75
natural selection, p. 114
neuroendocrine system, p. 98
neuroimaging, p. 102
neuromodulator, p. 77
neuron, p. 72
neurotransmitter, p. 77
occipital lobe, p. 88
parasympathetic nervous system, p. 85
parietal lobe, p. 88
passive interaction, p. 111
peripheral nervous system (PNS), p. 83
phenotype, p. 107
pituitary gland, p. 98
plasticity, p. 109
pons, p. 97
positron emission tomography (PET), p. 103
pruning, p. 109
receptor, p. 79
reflex, p. 83
resting potential, p. 74
reticular formation, p. 97
reuptake, p. 80
selective serotonin-reuptake inhibiter (SSRI), p. 80
sensory neuron, p. 72
skeletal system, p. 84
somatosensory strip, p. 88
spinal cord, p. 82
split-brain patient, p. 91
stroke, p. 100
subcortical structure, p. 86
sulcus, p. 86
sympathetic nervous system, p. 84
synapse, p. 77
synaptic cleft, p. 77
temporal lobe, p. 88
terminal button, p. 74
testosterone, p. 98
thalamus, p. 94
transcranial magnetic stimulation (TMS), p. 104
twin study, p. 113
ventricle, p. 86

chapter 4

Erich Lessing/Art Resource, NY

Sensation and Perception
*How the World
Enters the Mind*

The Mexican painter Frida Kahlo (1907–1954) did not simply paint what she saw—she painted what she felt and understood. Kahlo's style of painting is classified as *surrealist* because she took liberties in portraying what her eyes registered, distorting objects in order to reveal the feelings, desires, and longings that welled within her as she perceived the world (Lowe, 1995). Kahlo's painting *The Two Fridas* (p. 108) is an example of surrealism. This painting uses an X ray view to show her broken heart, which of course cannot literally be seen. Kahlo often injected her physical and emotional pain into her paintings.

As an adult, Kahlo was an old hand at managing pain. She contracted polio at the age of 6, which left her right leg thin and weak. During childhood, Kahlo embarked on an intensive program of exercise and athletics to help that leg recover its strength. When she was 18 years old, she was in a horrendous bus accident. She spent a month in a cast in the hospital, and most of the next year in bed. Kahlo's mother had a special easel made so that Kahlo could while away the hours in bed painting (a mirror was rigged up to the ceiling of her four-poster bed so that she could be her own model). Thus began Kahlo's painting career; about one third of her paintings are self-portraits.

Four years after the accident, Kahlo married the famed Mexican mural painter Diego Rivera. They shared passions for politics, art, music, Mexican culture, and food. Kahlo took great pleasure in learning to cook Rivera's favorite dishes. Their relationship gave her great joy, but also great pain; Diego was often unfaithful to her. They divorced, and then remarried each other about a year later. Shortly after divorce proceedings began, Frida painted her first large painting, *The Two Fridas*, which shows the "Frida" that Rivera loved (on the right) and the one that he no longer loved (this is the Frida with a broken heart, losing blood through a ruptured artery). Kahlo's artistic triumphs included exhibitions of her work in galleries in New York City and Paris. Her work has become even more popular now than it was during her lifetime.

Frida Kahlo was a person who delighted in her senses: She loved watching Rivera paint his giant murals; she enjoyed hearing the songs of street musicians in the local plaza; she reveled in the smells and tastes of Mexican food; she took pleasure

chapteroutline

Vision

Visual Sensation: More Than Meets the Eye

First Steps of Visual Perception: Organizing the World

Visual Perception: Recognition and Identification

Hearing

Auditory Sensation: If a Tree Falls but Nobody Hears It, Is There a Sound?

First Steps of Auditory Perception: Organizing the Auditory World

Auditory Perception: Recognition and Identification

Sensing and Perceiving in Other Ways

Smell: A Nose for News?

Taste: The Mouth Has It

Somasthetic Senses: Not Just Skin Deep

Other Senses

Kahlo's label as a surrealist painter comes, in part, from her use of "X ray" images, allowing the viewer to see what cannot normally be perceived. This painting, *The Two Fridas,* was painted in 1939 as Kahlo was getting divorced from Diego Rivera; the Frida on the left is, literally, heartbroken.

Frida Kahlo was a person who delighted in her senses: She loved watching Rivera paint his giant murals; she enjoyed hearing the songs of street musicians in the local plaza; she reveled in the smells and tastes of Mexican food; she took pleasure in her husband's caresses.

in her husband's caresses. The act of sensing and perceiving stimuli of any kind, whether a song, a color-soaked canvas, or a soft caress, encompasses a remarkable series of events at the levels of the brain, the person, and the social group, all happening within the context of the physical world. The processes of sensation and perception lie at the root of our experience of being alive, serving as the foundation for most of what we know and do. If we cannot sense the world, then for all practical purposes it does not exist for us; if we sense it incorrectly, our world will be bent and distorted. To understand mental processes and behavior, therefore, we must understand how our senses allow us to make contact with the world.

Despite Kahlo's medical problems, her fundamental ability to receive and interpret the array of colors, shapes, sounds, and other sensations that whirled around her remained intact. How do our brains register that something is "out there"? And what of the other senses through which we register this amazing world—how do we smell, and hear, and taste; how are we able to be aware of our bodies? And, is there a perception beyond these—a perception that is literally "extrasensory"—that some, if not all, of us possess? To a psychologist, the investigation of these questions provides fruitful clues in our discovery of ourselves.

Vision

Frida Kahlo learned new ways to see the world from her father, Guillermo Kahlo, who was a photographer. Frida worked as his assistant, retouching, developing, and coloring his photographs (Zamora, 1990). In her youth, Kahlo accompanied her father (who was the first official photographer of Mexico's architectural heritage) on a trip around Mexico, photographing local architecture. Her father worked carefully when choosing camera angles and tried to take best advantage of lighting effects (Herrera, 1983). Moreover, her father was an amateur painter. Kahlo's experiences watching her father both as photographer and painter no doubt led her to develop skills that would later serve her in good stead, when she herself took up the brush to become a professional painter. As a young adult, Frida worked for a colleague of her father who was a commercial printer; when he asked her to draw copies of impressionist prints, he saw that she had "enormous talent" (Herrera, 1983). Could such experiences literally have changed the way Kahlo saw?

Visual perception is not accomplished in one fell swoop, but in two broad phases. First, you register visual sensations. Psychologists define **sensation** as the awareness of properties of an object or event that occurs when a type of receptor (such as those at the back of the eye, in the ear, on the skin) is stimulated. Sensations arise when enough physical energy strikes a sense organ, so that receptor cells send neural impulses to the brain. As discussed in Chapter 3, receptors in general are like locks, which are opened by the appropriate key; for these sensory receptors, the appropriate physical energy serves as the key. The entire cell that responds to physical stimulation is called a receptor, not just the key parts that register the input. It is the signals sent by these receptors that cause you to become aware of the outside world. Visual sensation arises in the eye and in the first parts of the brain that register visual input.

Second, you actually perceive the stimulus; **perception** occurs when you've organized and interpreted the sensory input as signaling a particular object or event. Perception itself relies on two types of processing (Marr, 1982; Nakayama et al., 1995): (1) You don't see isolated blobs and lines, you see surfaces and objects. At the outset, you must organize patches of color, texture, edges, and other basic visual elements into coherent units, which usually correspond to surfaces and objects, such as the haystacks in a Monet painting. As part of this process, you need to specify the sizes and locations of objects. (2) But these surfaces and objects don't have meaning; they are just surfaces and forms. The processes that organize the input are a prelude to the final task of perception, which is to recognize and identify what you see, to realize you are seeing a haystack and not a honeycomb.

Visual Sensation: More Than Meets the Eye

In everyday experience, you may think you have direct contact with the world—but you don't. You know the world only as it is filtered through your senses, and your senses are not always accurate. Your senses are your windows on the world,

The impressionists tried to present the changing effects of light and color in nature. Rather than competing with the realism of the camera, they sought to evoke the visual sensations leading to perception. To accomplish this, impressionist artists used qualities inherent in color itself and took advantage of the way the human visual system works. The 19th-century French impressionist Claude Monet produced a series of paintings of haystacks in a field as day wore on to evening, and from season to season. Through his use of color, and the merging of subject (the "figure") and background (the "ground"), Monet tried to paint in a way that would replicate the process by which people actually see.

● **Sensation:** The awareness of properties of an object or event that occurs when a type of receptor (such as those at the back of the eye, in the ear, on the skin) is stimulated.

● **Perception:** The act of organizing and interpreting sensory input as signaling a particular object or event.

FIGURE 4.1 Visual Illusions

Visual systems are not like cameras that accurately capture the world, as illustrated by these visual illusions. In these examples, the two lines with the arrow heads are in fact the same length; the diagonal line that cuts across the vertical path is straight, not jagged; and the circles in the center of the two displays are actually the same size.

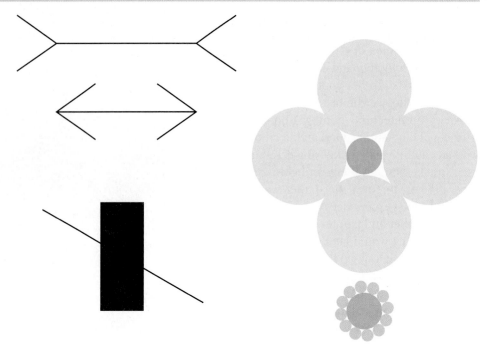

but sometimes the glass is not entirely transparent. The examples in Figure 4.1 show how far off base your perception can be.

Scientists have developed careful methods for discovering the relation between what's actually out there and what we sense and perceive; this field is known as psychophysics, and we explore its concepts and methods in the following section.

Psychophysics: A World of Experience

Well over a hundred years ago, scientists began trying to discover the relation between the properties of events in the world and people's sensations and perceptions of them. German scientist Gustav Theodor Fechner (1801–1887) founded the field of **psychophysics,** which studies the relation between physical events and the corresponding experience of those events. Researchers in psychophysics made a series of discoveries, which apply to all the senses.

Thresholds: "Over the Top."
Have you ever wondered how far away something can be and still be seen, or how low you can turn down the sound before it becomes inaudible? Much as you cross a doorway when going from one room to the next, stimuli cross a **threshold** when a physical event becomes strong enough to be noticed. An **absolute threshold** is the smallest amount of a stimulus needed in order to notice that the stimulus is present at all. The absolute threshold is defined as the magnitude of the stimulus needed to make it noticeable to the observer half the time. In establishing absolute thresholds, you are distinguishing between the background and the stimulus, and the stimulus must have enough of its defining quality that you are, in fact, able to notice it. If a warning light isn't bright enough, you won't notice that it's on—which could be a serious deficiency if the light is meant to indicate that your car's radiator is about to boil over.

● **Psychophysics:** The study of the relation between physical events and the corresponding experience of those events.

● **Threshold:** The point at which stimulation is strong enough to be noticed.

● **Absolute threshold:** The smallest amount of a stimulus needed in order to detect that the stimulus is present.

Sometimes you don't simply need to detect the presence of a stimulus, but rather to distinguish among stimuli. For example, suppose Kahlo were painting while the sun was setting; at what point would she notice that it had gotten darker in the room, and she should either adjust the way she was painting patterns of light or call it quits for the day? A **just-noticeable difference (JND)** is the size of the difference in a stimulus property (such as the brightness of light) needed for the observer to notice a difference. A JND is a kind of threshold. The change in light level might be so slight that sometimes you notice it, and sometimes you don't. This change would be defined as a JND if you noticed the difference half the time.

The size of a JND depends on the overall magnitude of the stimulus. If you are a thin person, a weight gain of 5 pounds is often noticeable at a glance, but if you are on the hefty side, a 5-pound gain might not be detected by anyone but you. Similarly, turning up the light the same amount is much more noticeable when the dimmer starts at a low setting than when it starts at a high setting. Why is this? Psychophysicists have an answer. **Weber's law** (named after another German researcher, Ernst Weber) states that a constant percentage of a magnitude change is necessary to detect a difference. So, the greater the magnitude of the light (or the thickness of the waist, or the volume of the sound), the greater the extra amount must be to be noticed. Weber's law is remarkably accurate except for very large or very small magnitudes of stimuli.

Detecting Signals: Noticing Needles in Haystacks. In World War II, radar operators sometimes "saw" airplanes that did not exist and sometimes missed airplanes that did. The simple fact that people make these kinds of errors led to a new way of thinking about thresholds. **Signal detection theory** seeks to explain why people detect signals in some situations but miss them in others. The key idea is that signals are always embedded in noise, and thus the challenge is to distinguish signal from noise. Noise, in this case, refers to other events that could be mistaken for the stimulus. Two key concepts explain how signals are detected or missed: sensitivity and bias. Greater **sensitivity** means a lower threshold for distinguishing between a stimulus (the "signal") and the background (the "noise"). For example, on a radar screen, the signal dots indicating enemy aircraft would not need to be very large or bright compared with the noise composed of random-appearing specks. **Bias** is the willingness to report noticing a stimulus (such as the willingness of a radar operator to risk identifying random specks as aircraft). You change your bias by adjusting your *criterion*—how strong the signal needs to be before you say you've detected it. Sensitivity and bias can be assessed by comparing the occasions when people *say* a stimulus is or is not present with the occasions when the stimulus is *in fact* present or not (Figure 4.2; Green & Swets, 1966; McNicol, 1972).

Let There Be Light

What is the bridge from objects in the world to the mind (the connection between the "psycho" and

- **Just-noticeable difference (JND):** The size of the difference in a stimulus property needed for the observer to notice that a change has occurred.

- **Weber's law:** The rule that a constant percentage of a magnitude change is necessary to detect a difference.

- **Signal detection theory:** A theory explaining why people detect signals, which are always embedded in noise, in some situations but not in others.

- **Sensitivity:** In signal detection theory, the threshold level for distinguishing between a stimulus and noise; the lower the threshold, the greater the sensitivity.

- **Bias:** In signal detection theory, a person's willingness to report noticing a stimulus.

FIGURE 4.2 Signal Detection Outcomes

Four types of responses are possible when a person is asked to report whether a signal was present. Signal detection theory uses the relative frequencies of these reports to compute a measure of how sensitive an observer is to a signal and a measure of how willing the observer is to report the signal.

Christopher Columbus had an intuitive grasp of signal detection theory. He offered a reward to the first sailor to spot land, but then sailors started mistaking low clouds for land. The reward not only increased sensitivity, but lowered the criterion. To adjust the criterion, Columbus announced that sailors who made false sightings would forfeit the reward. Columbus applied this higher criterion to himself, and didn't wake the crew on the night he first saw a glimmer of light on a distant island.

- **Amplitude:** The height of the peaks in a light wave.

- **Frequency:** The rate at which light waves move past a given point.

- **Wavelength:** The time between the arrival of peaks of a light wave; shorter wavelengths correspond to higher frequencies.

- **Transduction:** The process whereby physical energy is converted by a sensory neuron into neural impulses.

- **Pupil:** The opening in the eye through which light passes.

- **Iris:** The circular muscle that adjusts the size of the pupil.

- **Cornea:** The transparent covering over the eye, which serves partly to focus the light onto the back of the eye.

- **Accommodation:** Occurs when muscles adjust the shape of the lens so that it focuses light on the retina from objects at different distances.

- **Retina:** A sheet of tissue at the back of the eye containing cells that convert light to neural impulses.

- **Fovea:** The small, central region of the retina with the highest density of cones and the highest resolution.

"physics" of visual psychophysics)? The Greek philosopher Plato, who some 2,400 years ago theorized about many aspects of existence, psychological and otherwise, offered an interesting explanation of how humans see. Plato believed that the eyes produce rays that illuminate objects and that these rays are the basis of sight. Plato was no fool, and was reasoning based on what he perceived. He isn't the only intelligent person to come to the wrong conclusions based on observable facts: Surveys of college students reveal that a surprisingly high proportion of them—fully one third—believe the same thing! The percentage of students accepting this explanation actually doubled (to 67%) when participants were shown a computer-graphic illustration of the concept (Winer et al., 1996; Winer & Cottrell, 1996). Furthermore, two thirds of the college students who believe in such rays also believe that a person whose rays fail will go blind (Winer et al., 1996). These misconceptions are remarkably difficult to change (Gregg et al., 2001; Winer et al., 2002).

To set the record straight, there are no rays that shine from your eyes; in fact, essentially the process works the other way. Rather than producing rays, the eye registers light that is reflected from, or is produced by, objects in the line of sight. Similarly, the ear registers vibrations of air, and the skin responds to an object when pressure from it stimulates nerves.

Light is a form of electromagnetic radiation. All of us swim in a sea of electromagnetic radiation. This sea has waves: some large, some small, some that come in rapid succession, some spaced far apart. The height of a wave is its **amplitude,** and the rate at which the peaks of the waves move past a given point is its **frequency.** With higher frequency, the peaks of the waves arrive more often—and thus the length of time between peaks is shorter. When the length of time between arrivals of the peaks is shorter, the light is said to have a shorter **wavelength.** In the electromagnetic spectrum, which ranges from the terrifically long alternating currents and radio waves to the very short gamma rays and X rays, there is a narrow band of radiation perceived as visible light. An almost uncountable number of colors are conveyed in this light; the traditional seven we readily distinguish are red, orange, yellow, green, blue, indigo, and violet. The lower frequencies (and longer wavelengths—larger nanometers) are toward the red end of the spectrum; the higher frequencies (and shorter wavelengths) are toward the violet end, as illustrated in Figure 4.3.

FIGURE 4.3 The Range of Electromagnetic Radiation

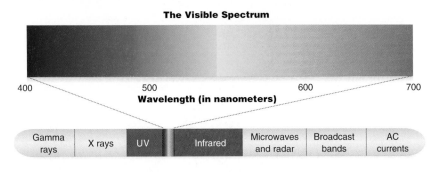

The Visible Spectrum

Wavelength (in nanometers)

| Gamma rays | X rays | UV | | Infrared | Microwaves and radar | Broadcast bands | AC currents |

Notice that only a small portion of the range gives rise to visible light. Also notice that the hue depends on the particular wavelength.

The Brain's Eye: More Than a Camera

The eye converts the electromagnetic energy that is light into nerve impulses; this conversion process is called **transduction**. As illustrated in Figure 4.4, light enters the eye through an opening called the **pupil.** Surrounding the pupil is a circular muscle called the iris. The **iris** changes the size of the pupil to let in more or less light. The light is focused mostly by the **cornea,** the transparent covering over the eye, and then focused even more by the lens. Unlike a camera lens, the lens in a human eye flexes. In fact, muscles can adjust the lens into a more or less round shape to focus light from objects that are different distances away. **Accommodation,** the automatic adjustment of the eye for seeing at different distances, occurs when muscles change the shape of the lens so that it focuses light on the retina from near or far away objects. The world appears sharp and clear because we are constantly moving our eyes, and what we choose to look at can quickly be moved into focus. With age, the lens thickens and becomes less flexible (Fatt & Weissman, 1992), often causing older people to have trouble seeing nearer objects, such as reading material.

FIGURE 4.4 Anatomy of the Eye

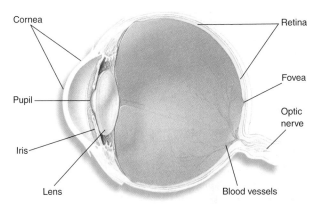

The many parts of the eye either focus an image on the retina or convert light into neural impulses that are sent to the brain.

Transduction: From Photons to Neurons.

The critical step in the transduction process occurs at the **retina,** a sheet of tissue at the back of the eye that is about as thick as a piece of paper. The central part of the retina contains densely packed cells that transform light to nerve impulses, and this region—called the **fovea**—gives us the sharpest images. We are not usually aware of how fuzzy our world looks. Most of the time we notice only the images that strike the fovea, which are sharp and clear, but much of what we see is in fact not very sharply focused. Take a moment to look up and focus on a single

When it comes to foveas, some animals have it all over us humans; some types of birds, for example, have two foveas. Next time you are annoyed at a noisy pigeon, appreciate the fact that it can focus to the side and ahead at the same time.

FIGURE 4.5 Rods and Cones

Two types of cells in the retina convert light into neural responses that produce visual sensations. The rods allow us to see with less light, but not in color; the cones allow us to see in color but are not as light-sensitive as the rods.

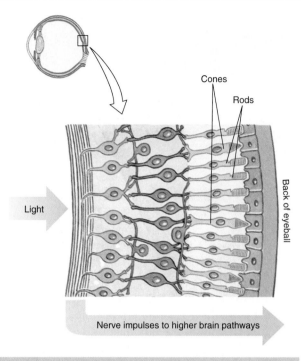

Cones

Rods

Light

Back of eyeball

Nerve impulses to higher brain pathways

HANDS ON

spot on the other side of the room; don't move your eyes, and notice how blurry things look even a short distance to the side of that spot.

Two kinds of cells in the retina are particularly important for converting light to nerve impulses: rods and cones. Oddly, as shown in Figure 4.5, these cells are at the very back of the eye, which requires light to pass through various other types of cells to reach them. **Rods** (which actually look like little rods) are extraordinarily sensitive to light, but they register only shades of gray. Each eye contains between 100 million and 120 million rods. The **cones** (which look like, yes, cones) are not as sensitive to light as are the rods, but they respond most vigorously to particular wavelengths of light, allowing us to see color. Each eye contains between 5 million and 6 million cones (Beatty, 1995; Dowling, 1992). The cones are densest near the fovea, and the rods are everywhere within the retina except in the fovea. At night, there isn't enough light for the less light-sensitive cones to work, so night vision is based on the firing of the rods alone. That is why a red apple looks black and an orange cat looks gray under a moonlit night sky.

The axons from retinal cells in each eye are gathered into a single large cord called the **optic nerve,** which is about as thick as your little finger. There are no rods or cones at the place where the optic nerve exits the retina, which causes a "blind spot" in what you can see laid out in front of you. Because the brain completes patterns that fall across this blind spot, you are not aware of it as you look around every day. Look at Figure 4.6, though, and you can "see" where your blind spot is.

HANDS ON

Dark Adaptation. When you first enter a darkened theater, you can't see a thing. You may have noticed, though, that the risk of tripping or bumping into

● **Rods:** Retinal cells that are very sensitive to light but register only shades of gray.

● **Cones:** Retinal cells that respond most strongly to one of three wavelengths and that play a key role in producing color vision.

● **Optic nerve:** The large bundle of nerve fibers carrying impulses from the retina into the brain.

FIGURE 4.6 Finding Your Blind Spot

X

Cover your left eye and stare at the X with your right eye. Now slowly bring the book closer to you, continuing to focus on the X. When the picture on the right disappears, you have found your right eye's blind spot.

someone is a lot less if you wait even a brief time because you soon can see much better. In fact, after about 30 minutes in the dark, you are about 100,000 times more sensitive to light than you are during full daylight. In ideal conditions, the rods can respond when they receive a single photon, the smallest unit of light. This process of acclimatization is called **dark adaptation.** Part of the increased sensitivity to what light there is arises because your pupil enlarges when you are in darkness; in fact, it can expand to let in about 16 times as much light as enters in full daylight. In addition, the rods actually become more sensitive as your eyes remain in the dark because your genes cause the production of a crucial chemical, called *rhodopsin*, that responds to light. Here's a hint: Because of the way the rods are arranged on the retina, if you want to see best at night, look slightly to the side of what you want to examine.

HANDS ON

More Than Rods and Cones. Researchers have known about rods and cones for well over 100 years, but only recently have they discovered evidence for a third kind of receptor in the eye that also registers light. Freedman and her colleagues (1999) observed that even mice whose eyes had no rods or cones still shifted their *circadian* behavior when light was shined on them. Circadian behavior is behavior that follows the daily pattern of light, such as waking and sleeping; in this case, the behavior was running, which in these mice varies depending on the time of day. But when the eyes were removed, the mice no longer adjusted their "running schedule" to the amount of light. Thus, the third kind of light-sensitive receptor must be in the eyes. Lucas and his colleagues (1999) investigated the decrease in production of a hormone called melatonin in the presence of light (melatonin is the hormone that some people use to overcome jet lag). Even mice without rods or cones showed a normal decrease in melatonin production when placed in light. Clearly, light affects the brain even when there are no rod or cone sensory cells. And, in fact, Berson et al. (2002) found that certain *ganglion cells* (usually treated as a kind of gathering station for input from rods and cones) in the retina respond to illumination in just the right ways to explain the observed effects of light on behavior. Thus, rods and cones are not the whole story: We have not two, but three kinds of cells that transduce light into neural impulses.

Color Vision: Mixing and Matching

How can you tell whether an apple is ripe? One way is to look at its color. Color also plays a key role in our appreciation of beauty in art, nature, and people. Kahlo associated certain colors with objects or feelings; for instance, she associated yellow with madness, sickness, and fear, and a reddish purple with liveliness (Herrera, 1983).

● **Dark adaptation:** The process whereby exposure to darkness causes the eyes to become more sensitive, allowing for better vision in the dark.

Vision | **129**

One of the remarkable aspects of human vision, which makes painting and appreciation of painting such rich experiences, is the huge range of colors that people can use and see. Indeed, colors vary in three separate ways. First, as noted earlier when we considered the electromagnetic spectrum, different wavelengths of light produce the sensation of different colors. This aspect of color—whether it looks red, blue, and so on—is called *hue*. Second, the purity of the input (the amount of white that's mixed in with the color) produces the perception of *saturation*, that is, how deep the color appears. And third, the amplitude of the light waves produces the perception of *lightness* or (if the object, such as a television screen, produces light) *brightness*—how much light is present. Different combinations of values on these three dimensions produce the incredibly rich palette of human color vision, which is more varied than that used by any painter.

Given the large number of ways that color can vary, you might think that complicated processes underlie our ability to see these visual properties—and you would be right. Color arises through the operation of two distinct types of processes.

Color Mixing. At one point in the study of color vision, there was a debate about how humans can see such a large range of colors. One camp took its lead from observations reported by Thomas Young and Hermann von Helmholtz in the 19th century. This approach focused on phenomena such as the mixing of colors to produce new colors (for example, mixing yellow and blue paint produces green). These researchers, arguing by analogy, believed that the brain registers color by combining responses to separate wavelengths. In particular, they argued that the eye contains three kinds of color sensors, each most sensitive to a particular range of wavelengths: long, medium, and short. This view was therefore called the **trichromatic theory of color vision.**

This theory turns out to be essentially correct, but it describes processing at only some places in the eye and brain. Consistent with trichromatic theory, our perception of hue arises because most of us possess three different types of cones. One type of cone is most responsive to light in the wavelength seen as a shade of yellow, another to light in the wavelength seen as green, and another in the wavelength seen as violet (Reid, 1999; note: at one point these colors were characterized as red, green and blue—but more careful testing has shown that this earlier characterization was close, but not quite right). The trick is that at least two of the three types of cones usually respond to any wavelength of visible light, but to different degrees (De Valois & De Valois, 1975, 1993). And here's the important part: The *mixture* of the three types of response signals is different for each of a huge range of wavelengths, and it is this mixture that is the crucial signal to the brain. The brain responds to the mixture, not the outputs from individual cones. Color television operates on this principle. Stare very closely at a color TV screen, and you will see little bubbles of three colors (red, green, and blue). Stand back, and a wide range of colors appears. Why? Because your eyes and your brain respond differently, depending on the mixture of wavelengths produced by clusters of these bubbles.

As if this weren't complicated enough, there's one more twist we must discuss, which is raised by the difference between what you see on a TV screen versus what you see when you mix paints. On the one hand, when you see a TV screen, each of the different wavelengths directly affects your cones. Thus, if red, green, and blue are mixed in an image, stimulating all your cones, you will see white. On the other hand, when you see paints, you see the light that is *reflected* from the

● **Trichromatic theory of color vision:** The theory that color vision arises from the combinations of neural impulses from three different kinds of sensors, each of which responds maximally to a different wavelength.

● **Opponent process theory of color vision:** The theory that if a color is present, it causes cells that register it to inhibit the perception of the complementary color (such as red versus green).

● **Afterimage:** The image left behind by a previous perception.

● **Opponent cells:** Cells that pit the colors in a pair, most notably blue/yellow or red/green, against each other.

paints—and not all the light may be reflected. What you see is what is not *absorbed* by the paints; a yellow paint, for example, absorbs all wavelengths except that underlying our perception of yellow. This wavelength is reflected, not absorbed, and so it reaches your eyes. When you mix paints, the wavelengths absorbed by each type of paint contribute to what is absorbed by the mixture. So if you mixed red, green, and blue you would see black: The combination of paints absorbs all the wavelengths that give rise to the perception of hue.

Recent genetic research has shown that some women possess not three, but four types of cones. As you might expect, these women see color differently from the rest of us. For example, they see more bands in a rainbow than people who have only three sorts of cones (Jameson et al., 2001). These differences arise from the same sort of mixing that underlies trichromatic theory, and thus the key ideas of that theory are correct even if—for some people—outputs from an additional type of cone are thrown into the mix.

A Color Tug-of-War? The other camp in the debate about how we see hue followed the lead of German physician Ewald Hering, who worked at the end of the 19th century and the beginning of the 20th. Hering noticed that some colors cannot be mixed: You can't make reddish-green or yellowish-blue. (As any preschooler would be happy to demonstrate, you can of course mix the colors—but yellow and blue produce green, not yellowish-blue, and red and green produce the color of mud.) This and similar observations led Hering to develop the **opponent process theory of color vision,** which states that the presence of one color of a pair (red/green, yellow/blue, and black/white) inhibits the perception of the other color.

And, in fact, researchers discovered that the mixtures of responses of the cones is not the whole story of color vision. If this were all there were to it, we should be able to see all mixtures of colors—but, as Hering originally observed, we can't. As the opponent process theory predicts, there's another factor, too, which will become apparent when you take a look at the strangely colored flag in Figure 4.7. Stare at the flag, and then look at the space to its right; you should see an **afterimage,** an image left behind by a previous perception.

FIGURE 4.7 Seeing Afterimages

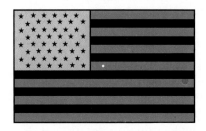 

Does this flag look strange to you? Stare at the dot in the center for about 60 seconds in a bright light, and then look at the blank space. You should see a brilliant afterimage of Old Glory, with red and white stripes and a blue field.

HANDS ON

Furthermore, the flag should look normal in the afterimage, not strangely colored as it is actually printed. Why are the colors of afterimages different from those of the object? You need to understand more about color vision to answer that question. A key fact is that the cones feed into special types of cells in the retina and the lateral geniculate nucleus of the brain (part of the thalamus): red/green, yellow/blue, and black/white **opponent cells.** These cells are set up to pit the colors in each pair against each other, with exactly the effect Hering predicted. For example, when wavelengths that produce blue are registered by these cells, they inhibit the perception of wavelengths that produce yellow, and vice versa (Hurvich & Jameson, 1957). This process helps you to distinguish among colors that have

- **Color blindness:** An inability, either acquired (by brain damage) or inherited, to perceive hue.

similar wavelengths, such as green and yellow (Reid, 1999, discusses the role of the cortex in such processing, as do Livingstone & Hubel, 1984). This is why you can't see greenish-red or yellowish-blue: Seeing one member of a pair inhibits seeing the other. It also explains why you see afterimages like the one illustrated by staring at Figure 4.7. An afterimage occurs when one member of a pair of opponent cells inhibits the other (for example, green inhibits red), and then releases it. In the process, the previously inhibited hue (red) temporarily overshoots the mark, creating an afterimage.

Color Blindness. People who have **color blindness** are either unable to distinguish one hue from another or, in more serious cases, are unable to see hue at all. Most color blindness is present from birth. Depending on the specific group, as many as 8% of European men but less than 0.5% of European women are born color-blind (Reid, 1999). Rather than being completely insensitive to hue, most color-blind people are unable to distinguish red from green. Researchers have found that people with the most common type of color blindness possess genes that produce similar pigments in their cones (Neitz et al., 1996), and thus the cones do not respond to wavelengths as they should. A small number of people (roughly 2% of males, and a very small number of females) are actually missing a type of cone. Even more severe deficits occur when more than one type of cone is affected (Reid, 1999).

Some people only become color blind after a particular part of their brains is damaged. In monkeys, visual area 4 (or V4) plays a major role in processing color (Zeki, 1993); similarly, a "color area" lights up in human brains when color is perceived. If this area is damaged, the ability to see hue is lost. This acquired color blindness is called *acquired achromotopsia* (Damasio, 1985). In Oliver Sacks's book *An Anthropologist on Mars* (1995), a color-blind artist describes how hard it is for him to eat food, particularly red food (such as apples and tomatoes), which appears to him to be a repulsive deep black.

Visual Problems: Distorted Windows on the World

Precisely because the visual system is so complicated, it does not always work perfectly. It is estimated that fewer than a third of the world's population has perfect vision (Seuling, 1986). These problems affect both absolute and relative thresholds, and also can distort the stimulus. People with *myopia*, or nearsightedness, have difficulty focusing on distant objects. As shown in Figure 4.8, myopia is usually caused by an eyeball that is too long to focus the image on the retina properly. This

People with normal color vision would see the crayons as shown on the left. People with the most common form of color blindness—inability to distinguish red from green—would see the crayons as shown on the right. Before traffic lights were arranged with red always on the top, not being able to see colors made driving hazardous for people with red/green color blindness. In what other ways would such a disorder affect your life?

FIGURE 4.8 Sources of Vision Difficulties

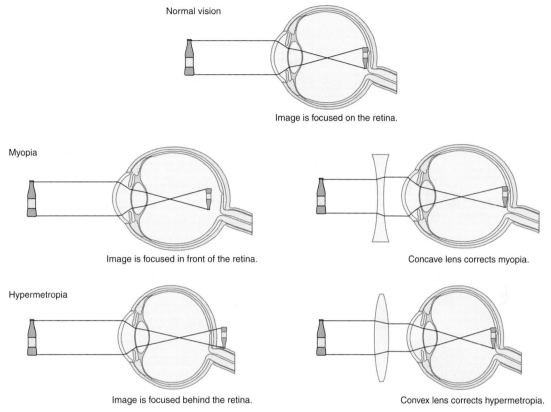

Normal vision

Image is focused on the retina.

Myopia

Image is focused in front of the retina.

Concave lens corrects myopia.

Hypermetropia

Image is focused behind the retina.

Convex lens corrects hypermetropia.

In normal vision, an image is focused on the retina. Depending on how the lens of the eye focuses light onto the retina, the image can be distorted in different ways. External lenses can bend the light in a way that compensates for the distortions in the lens of the eye, allowing light to be focused properly on the retina.

problem, which in the United States affects about one in five people, can be corrected by external lenses, either eyeglasses or contact lenses, that focus the image correctly on the retina. Moreover, laser surgery often can correct the lens of the eye itself. Time spent reading is correlated with myopia (see Young, 1981), but remember, correlation does not imply causation!

In contrast to nearsightedness, which involves problems with distance vision, people with *hypermetropia* have difficulty focusing on near objects. Such farsightedness usually results from an eyeball that is too short, or a lens that is too thin, to allow the image on the retina to focus properly. By the way, it is possible to be nearsighted in one eye and farsighted in the other, as was the case with President James Buchanan. This condition purportedly led him to tilt his head so he could see better when he was talking to someone (Seuling, 1978).

Astigmatism is a defect in the curvature of the cornea or lens, causing blurriness. Astigmatism, like nearsightedness and farsightedness, can be corrected with eyeglasses (and sometimes with contact lenses).

Of more serious concern, a *cataract* is a cloudy part of the lens of the eye, which can cause blurred vision, distorted images, and sensitivity to light and glare. About 70% of Americans over age 75 have (or have had) a cataract. Cataracts are responsible for at least half of all incidents of blindness (Riordan-Eva, 1992). Surgery can correct cataracts by removing the lens and replacing it with a substitute lens.

First Steps of Visual Perception: Organizing the World

Can you see which animals are present? The coloring of the horses blends nicely with the background. Why might animals look like their surroundings?

Although it seems that we perceive what we see in, literally, the blink of an eye, a large number of mental steps actually occur between the moment a pattern of light strikes your eyes and the time you recognize and identify an object. At each step, different areas of the brain are crucial (Grill-Spector et al., 1998). Once a stimulus has been sensed, the first task of visual perception is to organize the input into shapes that correspond to surfaces and objects and to specify their sizes and locations (Marr, 1982; Nakayama et al., 1995). A crucial goal of this phase of processing is to separate figure from ground. The **figure** is a set of characteristics (such as shape, color, texture) that corresponds to an object, whereas the **ground** is the background, which must be distinguished in order to pick out figures. When figure and ground are similar, the figure is said to be *camouflaged*. Armies the world over have long taken advantage of this property of the perceptual system.

- **Figure:** In perception, a set of characteristics (such as shape, color, texture) that corresponds to an object.

- **Ground:** In perception, the background, which must be distinguished in order to pick out figures.

- **Gestalt laws of organization:** A set of rules describing the circumstances under which marks will be grouped into perceptual units, such as proximity, good continuation, similarity, closure, and good form.

Perceptual Organization: Seeing the Forest Through the Trees

Separating figure from ground involves organizing regions into shapes that are likely to correspond to objects or their parts. A critical part of this process is finding edges. David H. Hubel and Torsten N. Wiesel received the Nobel Prize in 1981 for discovering that neurons in the first part of the cortex to process visual input (the *primary visual cortex*, in the occipital lobe) are arranged into columns, and the neurons in each column fire selectively to edges that have a specific orientation. These columns are in turn arranged into sets that are driven by input from either the left eye or the right eye, and these sets are arranged into a *hypercolumn*. The neurons in each hypercolumn respond to input from a single spot on the retina (Hubel & Wiesel, 1962, 1974). In addition, hypercolumns in the visual areas of the occipital lobe are *topographically organized*—that is, the pattern falling on the retina is spatially laid out on the cortex (Engel et al., 1997; Tootell et al., 1982). This arrangement helps the brain to delineate the edges of objects.

We often view objects when they are partly covered by other objects. (Look around the room right now: What do you actually see?) Nevertheless, even when you view an object behind a bush, you don't see isolated lines, dots, and so on, but rather overall patterns. How are edges and other visual features (such as patches of color) forged into patterns? Gestalt psychologists, who were introduced briefly in Chapter 1, discovered a set of laws that describe how the brain organizes the input from the eyes (Koffka, 1935; Wertheimer, 1923). The most important of these **Gestalt laws of organization** follow:

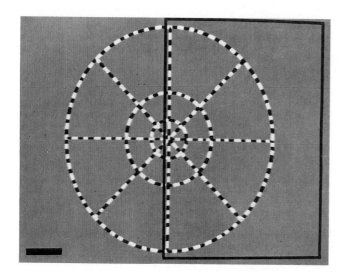

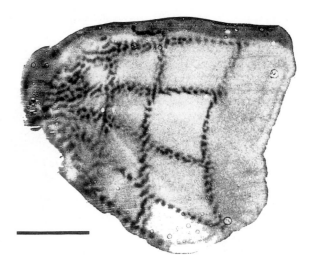

Proximity: Marks that are near one another tend to be grouped together. So, for example, we see XXX XXX as two groups, and XX XX XX as three groups, even though they have the same total number of X marks.

Continuity (also called *good continuation*): Marks that tend to fall along a smooth curve or a straight line tend to be grouped together. So, for example, we see _ _ _ _ as a single line, not four separate dashes; and we see _ _ _ _ _ _ _ _ as two separate lines because all eight of the dashes do not fall on the same plane.

Similarity: Marks that look alike tend to be grouped together. So, for example, we see XXXxxx as two groups. Whether the elements are the same or different colors also affects similarity, another reason color vision is so important.

Closure: We tend to close any gaps in a figure, so a circle with a small section missing will still be seen as a circle.

Good Form: Marks that form a single shape tend to be grouped together. So, for example, we see [ ] as a single shape, but not [_.

Tootell and colleagues (1982) produced this remarkable illustration of topographic organization in the monkey brain. The animal looked at the figure on the left while radioactive sugar was being ingested by the brain cells. The dark lines on the right show which brain cells in the primary visual cortex were working hardest when the animal viewed the figure (shown here is the left-hemisphere area, which processed the right side of the display). The spatial structure of the figure is evident on the surface of the brain.

Additional laws have been added since the time of the Gestalt psychologists (who began work in 1912). For example, Palmer (1992b) has shown that marks occurring in a common region tend to be grouped together. The details of how the brain actually works to organize the world in these ways are just now being discovered (Grossberg et al., 1997; Kovacs, 1996; Kovacs & Julesz, 1993; von der Heydt & Peterhans, 1989; von der Heydt et al., 1984).

You can see the middle part of this picture as a set of birds or a set of fish, which illustrates how the figure can serve as the ground or vice versa. Such artwork demonstrates the roles of figure and ground, and your participation in interpreting which is which.

FIGURE 4.9 Ambiguous Figures

In the left panel, you can see either two silhouetted faces or a vase, depending on what you pay attention to as the figure; in the right panel, you can see an old or a young woman, again depending on how you organize the figure.

HANDS ON

Sometimes a figure can be organized and perceived in more than one way. Figure 4.9 shows some of the classic *ambiguous figure-ground relationships.* Certain artists—for instance, Dutch illustrator Maurits Escher and Belgian surrealist René Magritte—were intrigued by how the mind actively organizes the visual world. As Figure 4.9 shows, sometimes you can voluntarily organize patterns in different ways. But, even when you organize visual patterns automatically, you organize them not only on the basis of their physical properties but also as a result of learning. For example, have you ever thought about becoming a professional "chicken sexer"? Before you dismiss this possible career path out of hand, consider the fact that even during the Great Depression members of this profession prospered. Why? Chicken farmers didn't want to send female chickens to be cooked in someone's pot—they were for laying eggs. It was the males who were sent to market. However, just looking at the pattern of bumps and indentations on a baby chick's bottom, it's very difficult to distinguish a male from a female. Traditionally, experts required years of practice before they could make this distinction accurately. Biederman and Shiffrar (1987) analyzed the problem and were able to teach people to make the discrimination by observing whether a particular part of the chick's bottom was convex versus concave or flat. However, even after training, these participants were not the same as the experts. The participants in the study had to look carefully, and knew exactly what they were trying to do. Experts can make this judgment with extraordinary accuracy after glancing at a chick for half a second, without even being aware of what they are doing. After extensive practice, the visual system becomes tuned so that you can automatically organize what you see in a new way (Crist et al., 2001; Olson & Chun, 2002; Vuilleumier & Sagiv, 2001).

Perceptual Constancies: Stabilizing the World

Imagine strapping a camera onto your head and making a videotape as you walk. What do you think the pictures would look like? The images striking your eyes change wildly depending on your viewpoint, but the objective world you relate to seems stable. Objects in the world appear to keep their shapes, their sizes, their colors, and so on, even when you view them in very different positions or circumstances. **Perceptual constancy** is the perception of the characteristics of

● **Perceptual constancy:** The perception of characteristics that occurs when an object or quality (such as shape or color) looks the same even though the sensory information striking the eyes changes.

objects (such as their shapes and colors) as the same even though the sensory information striking the eyes changes. For example, **size constancy** occurs when you see an object (such as a car) as the same actual size even when it is at different distances, so that its image (as in a photograph) is at different sizes. Because Kahlo did not strive to paint things as they actually appear, she did not always try to convey size constancy. For example, in *Self-Portrait with Cropped Hair*, Kahlo's long strands of hair do not get smaller and thinner as they recede in the distance, as they should be painted to suggest size constancy. Because their length and thickness stay constant, the viewer probably sees some of the strands as floating in the air rather than being farther in the distance (Herrera, 1983). Similarly, **shape constancy** occurs when you see an object as the same shape, even when you view it from different angles (again, so that its image in a photograph would be different). This stabilization occurs not in the eyes, but in the brain, and is fundamental to the ability to recognize objects and know how to interact with them.

Finally, consider **color constancy**. When Kahlo painted in her studio or bedroom, the lighting conditions were different than they are in a gallery (perhaps the light bounced off green foliage in one setting but not the other). Nevertheless, the painting will appear to have the same colors in the different conditions. Our ability to see colors as constant (green as green, red as red, and so on) even when the lighting changes may arise because we see the lightest thing in a scene as white and everything else relative to that color (Land, 1959, 1977, 1983).

Knowing the Distance

Because the world is three-dimensional, we need to register distances; this is necessary to appreciate how parts of an object are arranged, as well as to reach and navigate properly. This requirement poses an interesting problem: Our eyes project images onto the two-dimensional surface of our retinas, but we need to see objects in three dimensions. Given that our eyes capture images in only two dimensions, how is it that we see in three? Once again, the answer lies with the brain, which uses different types of cues to derive three dimensions from the two-dimensional images on the retinas of the eyes.

Static Cues. Static ("unmoving") information plays a large role in allowing us to determine how far away something is. **Binocular cues** arise from both eyes working together. Your brain uses slight differences in the images striking each of your eyes to assess the distance of an object. Because your eyes are separated, you need to cross them in order to focus on an object (so that the same image appears on the central, high-resolution fovea in each eye). When you do this, however, the images of other objects—those in front of or behind the one you are focused on—fall on slightly different parts of the retinas of the two eyes. This difference between the images on the two eyes is called **retinal disparity** (also called *binocular disparity*), and the brain uses the amount of disparity to determine which objects are in front of and which are behind others (Pinker, 1997, pp. 220–233). The process of figuring out depth from retinal disparity is called **stereopsis** (Anderson & Nakayama, 1994). Some neurons in the visual areas of the brain have been found to respond best with relatively little retinal disparity, whereas others fire more vigorously when lots of retinal disparity is present (Ohzawa et al., 1990; Patterson & Martin, 1992). Thus, neurons register the information the brain needs to figure out distance from the objects in view. Stereopsis works only for objects up to about 10 feet away—at distances greater than that, the eyes don't need to cross in order to focus, and thus there is no retinal disparity.

● **Size constancy:** Seeing an object as being the same size when viewed at different distances.

● **Shape constancy:** Seeing objects as having the same shape even when the image on the retina changes.

● **Color constancy:** Seeing objects as having the same color in different viewing situations.

● **Binocular cues:** Cues to the distance of an object that arise from both eyes working together.

● **Retinal disparity** (also called *binocular disparity*): The difference between the images striking the retinas of the two eyes.

● **Stereopsis:** The process that registers depth on the basis of retinal disparity.

Notice the relative sizes and spacing of the bricks in this example of a texture gradient, one cue that the street is receding into the distance.

Monocular (or "one-eyed") **static cues** for distance can be picked up with one eye, and operate even for far distances. Monocular static cues are used effectively by artists (even surrealists such as Frida Kahlo) to create the illusion of distance. One of these cues is the **texture gradient,** a progressive change in the texture of an object. Gibson (1966) described the way texture gradients signal distance. Look at the brick street in the photograph (or, for that matter, in life). The bricks that are closer to you, the observer, give rise to larger images (they are larger in the photograph) and you use this cue to determine distance.

In drawing pictures, artists also use *linear perspective,* or *foreshortening,* making the parts of objects that are farther away from the viewer actually smaller on the page. You also infer distance if one object partially covers another, indicating that the obscured object is behind the other and thus farther away; this relation is called an *occlusion cue.* And if the base of an object appears higher on the horizon than the base of another object, you take that as a cue that the higher one is farther away. Figure 4.10 provides good examples of the power of these monocular cues.

However, the way such cues are depicted in drawings sometimes relies on cultural conventions, which must be learned (Leibowitz, 1971). For instance, in some rural parts of Africa, children's books are very rare, and thus it is not surprising that these children may not initially understand all depth and perspective cues in drawings (Liddell, 1997). Young children in rural Africa sometimes describe shading cues on faces as blemishes, and may say that trees are on top of a house when the trees are drawn off in the distance, behind the house (Liddell, 1997). The actual drawing cues are ambiguous, and only after learning the conventions can you know what they are supposed to convey. Such problems in interpretation disappear with age, education, and experience. A number of cross-cultural studies have shown that people must learn how to interpret some cues in

● **Monocular static cues:** Information that specifies the distance of an object that can be picked up with one eye without movement of the object or eye.

● **Texture gradients:** Progressive changes in texture that signal distance.

● **Motion cues:** Information that specifies the distance of an object on the basis of its movement.

FIGURE 4.10 A Monocular Depth Cue

Even though you know that the two white bars on the rails are in fact the same size, the one that appears farther away also appears larger. Because you see the top one as farther away, the fact that it is the same size on the page signals that it is larger. Painters use depth cues like these to fool the eye.

drawings (Crago & Crago, 1983; Duncan et al., 1973; Liddell, 1997; Nodelmann, 1988).

Motion Cues. **Motion cues** specify the distance of an object on the basis of its movement, and these cues work as well with one eye as with two. In fact, motion cues are so effective that Wesley Walker, blind in one eye from birth, could catch a football well enough to be the star wide receiver for the New York Jets football team (in fact, he played for them for 13 years). To notice a motion cue, try this: Hold up this book and move your head back and forth as you look at it. Note how the images of objects behind the book seem to shift. As you shift your head to the left, the distant objects seem to move to the left; as you shift to the right, they shift to the right. Now focus on the background, still holding the book, and move your head back and forth; note how the image of the book seems to shift. This time the object you aren't focusing on, the book, seems to shift in the opposite direction to the way you move your head! Objects closer than the one on which you are fixated on seem to move in the opposite direction to your movements, whereas those farther away than the fixation point seem to move in the same direction. And, depending on the distance, the objects will seem to shift at different speeds. This difference in shifting provides information about relative distance, a cue called *motion parallax*. Figure 4.11 summarizes monocular and binocular depth cues.

Detecting Movement: Changing Places. Motion not only helps you perceive depth, but also signals that an object is changing position relative to you—

HANDS ON

The woman on the left is actually taller than the boy on the right. How is this possible? The woman is farther away, but this special Ames room has been constructed to eliminate the usual monocular depth cues.

FIGURE 4.11 Depth Cues

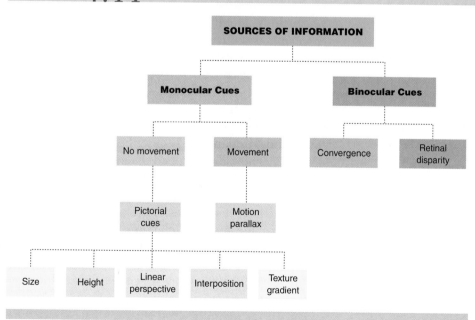

Depth perception depends on both binocular and monocular cues.

FIGURE 4.12 Phi Phenomenon

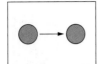

Movies are produced by a series of still photos, presented very rapidly in sequence. Why do we see movement, when there really isn't any? This sort of *apparent motion* arises from the *phi phenomenon,* a particular kind of illusion. When a stimulus appears in one location (such as in the left panel), disappears, and then appears in another location (as in the center panel), we will see it as having moved if the timing is just right (the farther the distance between locations, the greater the amount of time between removing the first stimulus and presenting the second). The phi phenomenon can produce the appearance of motion that is indistinguishable from real motion (Shioiri et al., 2000).

and as any driver or pedestrian will tell you, perceiving an object's movements is important in its own right. You use several types of cues to perceive movement. For example, if you are moving directly toward an object, it seems to expand symmetrically around its center and thus loom closer. Likewise, if you are moving toward its right side, that side will loom closer than the other. When silent movies were first shown to the public, the movement of an on-screen train rushing toward viewers was so startling that many moviegoers panicked and fled the theaters (Seuling, 1976). Only after they had experienced watching moving objects on a screen could they distinguish between the usual motion cues and the bogus cues in films (which are a kind of illusion called the *phi phenomenon,* Figure 4.12), and be able to relax and enjoy the show. Such learning was necessary because these cues are ordinarily so important. In fact, neuroimaging research with humans has revealed that special areas in the brain detect this kind of motion (Tootell et al., 1997; Zeki, 1978, 1993). Also, studies of brain-damaged patients have documented the role of particular brain areas for processing motion. For example, one patient could not pour tea into a cup: She would see the tea suddenly appear, not continuously flow; instead of motion, she saw a series of static images (Zihl et al., 1983).

Visual Perception: Recognition and Identification

Vision is more than organizing the world into shapes and knowing where they are, of course. If that were all, how would you know if something was good to approach (such as a useful tool or a tasty sweet) or necessary to avoid (such as a dangerous animal or an angry boss)? The processes of visual perception accomplish two major goals: They allow you to assign meaning to the shapes you see, and they allow you to map space so that you can guide your movements according to your goals (Goodale & Milner, 1992; Kosslyn, 1994b; Milner & Goodale, 1995; Ullman, 1996). These tasks are handled by separate mechanisms in the brain. From the results of experiments conducted with monkeys, Ungerleider and Mishkin (1982) described two major neural pathways, which they dubbed the *what* and *where pathways* (Figure 4.13). Further evidence for the existence of these distinct mechanisms comes from studies of humans who have had strokes. A stroke that affects the bottom parts of the temporal lobes impairs the patient's ability to recognize objects by sight, and a stroke that affects the back parts of the parietal lobes impairs the patient's ability to register locations (Levine, 1982). Moreover, these separate brain areas have been found to be activated during neuroimaging studies in which normal

FIGURE 4.13 Two Visual Pathways

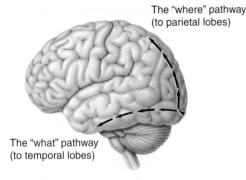

The "where" pathway (to parietal lobes)

The "what" pathway (to temporal lobes)

Visual input flows along two major pathways in the brain. The "where" pathway going up to the parietal lobes is concerned with spatial properties (such as an object's location) whereas the "what" pathway going down to the temporal lobes is concerned with properties of objects (such as their shape and color).

people are asked to distinguish shapes or locations (Bar et al., 2001; Bly & Kosslyn, 1997; Haxby et al., 1991, 1994, 2001; Kohler et al., 1995; Ungerleider & Haxby, 1994). The two pathways come together in the frontal lobes, where information about an object's identity and location is used to make decisions (Rao et al., 1997). Before reading on, take a moment to pick a card from Figure 4.14; we will return to these cards shortly.

FIGURE 4.14 Pick a Card, Any Card

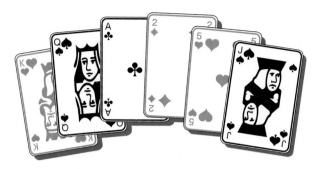

Look at this display and pick out a card. Then turn the page, look at Figure 4.15, and read that caption.

Knowing More Than You Can See

When you see an apple, the processes that underlie visual sensation respond to basic characteristics of the input, such as its wavelength and contours. The outputs from these processes are then organized in the first phases of perceptual processing to indicate a red, shiny object of a certain shape and size that is at a certain distance. But nothing in this information tells you that inside this object are

HANDS ON

seeds and, maybe, a worm. For you to know these things, the final phases of perceptual processing must occur, which allow the visual input to activate information you've stored in memory from your prior experience. To interpret what you see, you need to compare the input to stored information. If the input matches something you've stored in memory, that information can be applied to the present case (and that's how you know that an apple *may* have a worm inside, even if you can't see one *this time*). If the object is *recognized*, it seems familiar; if it is *identified*, you know additional facts about it.

Objects are sometimes recognized as collections of parts. Irving Biederman and his colleagues (Biederman, 1987; Hummel & Biederman, 1992) have suggested that objects are represented in the brain as collections of simple shapes, with each shape representing a part of the object, such as the head, neck, body, and legs of a dog. It is clear that we can see parts of objects individually (Hoffman & Richards, 1984). But take a look at the two photographs of Britney Spears, and then turn the book around so you can see the figure rightside up. It should also be clear that we do not always recognize or identify objects in terms of their

Look at these faces, and then turn the book and look at them rightside up. One explanation for the peculiar lapse in noticing the parts is that when you view the entire face, you are attending to a single pattern—but to see the parts in detail, you need to attend to smaller pieces of the whole. Notice that if you focus on each part, you can see that some are upside down. But when you focus on the entire face, you see the overall pattern, not a collection of parts.

FIGURE 4.15 Is Only Your Card Missing?

Look at this display only after you have picked out a card in the display on the previous page. After you have picked out a card, look for it here. Did we remove the card you were thinking of? At first glance, it probably appears that we have removed only that card and left the others alone. Magic? No. Your brain coded the suits and values of the cards separately, and you only see them combined properly when you pay attention to them (Arguin et al., 1994; Treisman & Schmidt, 1982). Thus, if you only paid attention to one particular card, you will notice its absence. As for the other cards, you will notice only the values and suits, not their combinations. Fortunately, some basic features, such as color and orientation, are automatically bound together when they are superimposed (Holcombe & Cavanagh, 2001).

individual parts. If that were the case, we wouldn't need to turn the book over to see how weird one of the versions is. Rather, we usually focus on the overall views of shapes, and look for details only if we need them (Cave & Kosslyn, 1993). When we do look at individual features, however, they may not always be properly combined, as demonstrated in Figure 4.15.

Informed Perception: The Active Viewer

As with a painting or a piece of music, in which form and color, harmony and rhythm, are at work simultaneously, so too with perceptual processing. The progression from sensation, to organization, to recognition and identification may seem to indicate a simple sequential process, but more is happening. Processing may be **bottom up,** initiated by the stimulus, or **top down,** guided by knowledge, expectation, or belief. And the two sorts of processes may be in play at the same time (Corbetta & Shulman, 2002; Humphreys et al., 1997; Kosslyn & Koenig, 1995). Here's how it works.

If you turn on the TV to a random channel, you will be able to understand what appears on the screen even if it's a complete surprise: the processing is bottom up, from the stimulus alone, unaided by any expectation you might have. Your eyes and ears register what's there, and your brain processes the resulting signals. Bottom-up processing operates like a row of standing dominoes: When the neural equivalent of the first domino is tripped by the light impulses reaching your eye and the sound vibrations reaching your ear, other neural signals are successively tripped, like falling dominoes, until you've understood what you're seeing and hearing. As shown in Figure 4.16, bottom-up processing can sometimes trigger additional sensory experiences, as well as comprehension.

Back to the couch, watching TV. After the first few moments of watching this randomly selected channel, even if you are the very picture of a vegetating couch

FIGURE 4.16 Synesthesia

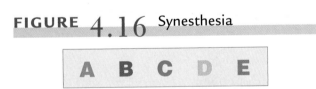

Bottom-up processing can sometimes produce remarkably complex experiences. For example, perhaps as many as 1 in 2,000 people experience *synesthesia,* where they simultaneously experience more than one perception when given certain stimuli (the term is from the Greek *syn,* which means "union," and *aisthises,* which means "of the senses"). Many of these people see letters, digits, and words as having consistent colors—even though they are printed in black. The neural bases of this phenomenon are just now coming to be understood (Rich & Mattingley, 2002).

potato, you are in fact actively anticipating what will appear next and using this information to help you see. Now you are engaging in top-down processing, which occurs when you use your knowledge of what to expect to help you look for specific characteristics and fill in missing parts of the stimulus. You can watch top-down processing at work if the TV image is really blurry and you use the sound track to provide clues to what's in the picture. For example, if the sound track makes it clear that two people are about to kiss, you will be able to make out the outlines of the faces more easily.

Top-down processing can alter the mechanisms used in bottom-up processing (Corbetta & Shulman, 2002; Humphreys et al., 1997; Kosslyn, 1994b). In a study by Delk and Fillenbaum (1965), for example, participants were shown stimuli that were all cut from the same orangish-red cardboard, including objects that are normally red (an apple and a valentine heart) and objects that are not normally red (a mushroom and a bell). The participants were to adjust the color of a display until they thought it matched the color of the cutouts. Apparently, the knowledge of the usual color of the objects affected how participants saw the actual color; when asked to match the color of the normally red objects, they consistently selected a redder color than the one they chose to match the color of the mushroom and the bell.

Your **perceptual set** is the sum of your assumptions and beliefs that lead you to expect to perceive certain objects or characteristics in particular contexts. For example, when the bottom light on a stoplight is illuminated, you will see it as green even if it is in fact a bluish green. People often use context to form such *perceptual expectancies*, perceptions dependent on their previous experience. Loftus (1972) showed that people require more time to identify an object when it is in an unusual context. When asked if an octopus is present in a picture display, for instance, people require more time to answer if the setting is unlikely—a barnyard, for instance—than if the setting is an underwater scene (Palmer, 1992a, reports similar findings). Cues in the current context are often used to guide top-down processing during perception (Chun, 2000).

Coding Space in the Brain: More Than One Way to Know "Where"

We have so far been focusing on the "what" pathway, but researchers have also studied the final phases of perceptual processing in the "where" pathway. The goal of this processing is to use the sum total of the distance cues (discussed earlier) to identify the distance and direction of objects, either relative to yourself or to other objects. Kosslyn (1987) proposed that the brain uses two different ways to code space. First, *categorical spatial relations* code positions with categories such as "above" or "left of" or "inside." Like all categories, these group together a set of specific examples. For instance, when giving you directions on how to find her apartment, a friend can tell you that her door is "next to" a trashcan on the sidewalk—it doesn't matter how far away that landmark is, nor would it matter if the trashcan's exact position is shifted from time to time. "Next to" specifies a general category, which includes many specific positions; for many purposes, we don't want to pay attention to the specifics, only to the general position (Laeng et al., 1999).

Second, categorical spatial relations are useless for the other main tasks of vision: navigation and reaching. Knowing that a table is "in front" of you (a categorical spatial relation) won't help you walk around it, or reach to the edge of it to pick up a pen. For these tasks, you need precise information about the distance and

- **Bottom-up processing:** Processing that is initiated by stimulus input.

- **Top-down processing:** Processing that is guided by knowledge, expectation, or belief.

- **Perceptual set:** The sum of your assumptions and beliefs that lead you to expect to perceive certain objects or characteristics in particular contexts.

direction of objects. *Coordinate spatial relations* specify continuous distance from your body or another object that serves as an "origin" of a coordinate space.

How can we tell whether the brain does in fact use these two different ways to specify spatial relations? Kosslyn (1987) proposed that the left cerebral hemisphere may be better at specifying categorical spatial relations, which are easily named by a word or two (and thus are compatible with the left hemisphere's facility at labeling). In contrast, the right hemisphere may be better at specifying coordinate spatial relations, which are essential for navigation (and the right hemisphere typically is better at this ability; De Renzi, 1982). Although much research has examined this hypothesis (for example, Banich & Federmeier, 1999; Chabris & Kosslyn, 1998; Christman, 2002; Hellige & Michimata, 1989; Kosslyn et al., 1989; Okubo & Michimata, 2002), a particularly strong test was reported by Slotnick and his colleagues (2001).

UNDERSTANDING RESEARCH
Two Ways to Specify Spatial Relations

QUESTION: Do the cerebral hemispheres differ in their abilities to specify categorical versus coordinate spatial relations?

ALTERNATIVES: (1) Yes, the left hemisphere is better at specifying categorical spatial relations than the right hemisphere, but the right hemisphere is better at specifying coordinate spatial relations than the left; (2) Yes, the right hemisphere is better at specifying categorical spatial relations than the left hemisphere, but the left hemisphere is better at specifying coordinate spatial relations than the right; (3) No, the left hemisphere is, in general, better at specifying all types of spatial relations; (4) No, the right hemisphere is, in general, better at specifying all types of spatial relations; (5) No, the hemispheres are equally good at specifying all types of spatial relations.

LOGIC: If the left hemisphere is better at specifying categorical spatial relations than is the right, then when the left hemisphere is temporarily deactivated (for medical reasons), the patient should be impaired while evaluating categorical spatial relations more than when the right hemisphere is deactivated. In contrast, if the right hemisphere is better at specifying coordinate spatial relations than is the left, then the opposite result should occur when each hemisphere is temporarily deactivated.

METHOD: The researchers took advantage of a technique that allowed them temporarily to anesthetize one hemisphere at a time. They tested 134 participants who were about to have brain surgery (and thus it was important to know in advance which mental processes were carried out by specific brain regions). The researchers injected sodium amobarbital into the major artery (the carotid) that provides blood to one or the other of the cerebral hemispheres, which temporarily anesthetizes it. They then presented two categorical tasks and three coordinate tasks. For example, one categorical task required participants to decide whether a dot was on or off a line drawing of a blob, and one coordinate task required participants to decide whether a plus and minus sign were less than 2 inches apart. The researchers recorded the number of errors.

RESULTS: Deactivating the left hemisphere caused patients to make more errors in the categorical tasks than did deactivating the right hemisphere. In contrast, for a difficult coordinate task, deactivating the right hemisphere caused patients to make more errors than deactivating the left hemisphere. However, for easy coordinate tasks (where the differences in the to-be-discriminated distances were very distinct), the participants made comparable numbers of errors when either hemisphere was deactivated.

INFERENCES: When the task was challenging, the left hemisphere was better at specifying categorical spatial relations whereas the right was better at specifying coordinate spatial relations. The fact that the hemispheres differed in this way is important because if there were only a single way to code spatial relations, either one hemisphere would always be better than the other or there would be no difference between them. The observed differences between the hemispheres shows that the brain can in fact code spatial relations in at least two ways. But why did this difference only emerge when the participants had to make difficult discriminations? One possibility is that when a metric discrimination is easy enough, you can quickly form a category to capture it (such as "1 versus 2 inches")—and thus either type of spatial relation can be used, and either hemisphere can perform the task.

Attention: The Gateway to Awareness

Let's say you are watching TV and waiting for the first appearance of your favorite actress. Do you think you would be more sensitive to this event if you were on the lookout for her? Research has shown that paying attention increases sensitivity to the attended events (Nakayama & Mackeben, 1989; Yeshurun & Carrasco, 1998, 1999). **Attention** is the act of focusing on particular information, which allows that information to be processed more fully than information that is not attended to. **Selective attention** allows you to pick out a particular characteristic, object, or event. We are aware only of what we pay attention to. Attention operates in virtually all domains of human thought and feeling, not only in visual perception; you can pay attention to a particular instrument in a band, a nuance of a word, a feeling, a taste, a particular place, or the feeling of a ladybug walking over the back of your hand. We pay attention to something for one of two reasons.

What Grabs Attention? One reason we pay attention is that something about an event grabs us, such as a sudden change in illumination or movement. Certain qualities or features of displays, such as advertisements, automatically (via bottom-up processes) leap out—a phenomenon psychologists refer to as **pop-out.** For example, look at the left panel of Figure 4.17 (p. 146). Is a red dot present? The red dot appears to pop out; it is immediately evident without your having to search for it. Attention is immediately drawn to this "odd man out." In general, pop-out occurs when objects differ in their fundamental qualities, such as size in vision or frequency in hearing (you immediately hear a high-pitched flute in a band if all the other instruments are playing low notes).

Not Just What Grabs Attention. The other reason we pay attention is that we are actively searching for a particular characteristic, object, or event (via top-down processes). Have you ever wondered whether you have actually glimpsed a friend in a crowd, or heard a familiar voice in an unexpected context? In many

● **Attention:** The act of focusing on particular information, which allows it to be processed more fully than what is not attended to.

● **Selective attention:** The process of picking out a particular quality, object, or event for relatively detailed analysis.

● **Pop-out:** Occurs when a stimulus is sufficiently different from the ones around it that it is immediately evident.

FIGURE 4.17 Pop-Out Versus Search

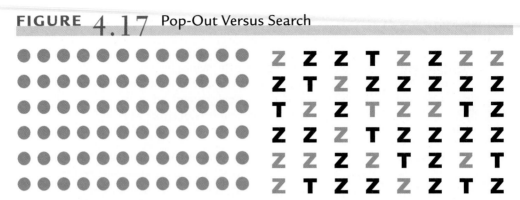

As shown in the left panel, basic features, such as color, are registered without the need for an item-by-item search. Is there a red T in the right panel? To find a combination of features, such as the arrangements of segments or a shape with a particular color, you must search the items one at a time.

situations, your initial perception of an event may not be very clear, and you need a "second look" or "second hear." In these cases, your first suspicions of what you might have perceived guide top-down processes to collect more information in a very efficient way: You search for distinctive characteristics, such as the shape of a particular haircut, or the pitch of a certain voice. Or, have you ever waited for a friend and anticipated her appearance with every passing stranger? *Vigilance* occurs when you are anticipating a particular event and thus maintain attention as you wait for it, which also relies on your ability to focus your attention voluntarily.

This voluntary type of attention is distinct from the sort that arises when a particular characteristic of a stimulus grabs your attention. We know this is so in part because the two types of attention are accomplished by different parts of the brain. In the case of a sudden change in the environment, such as a bright light or a quick movement, the superior colliculus (a small subcortical structure) acts like a reflex, shifting attention automatically to that event. Moreover, a brain region standing between the right temporal and parietal lobe and another region in the lower right frontal lobe are used in bottom-up processing (Corbetta & Shulman, 2002). In contrast, none of these areas underlie the voluntary shifts of attention that occur while you are searching for something or someone (or remaining vigilant); instead, the frontal eye fields (in the frontal lobes; Corbetta & Shulman, 2002; Kosslyn & Koenig, 1995; Paus, 1996) and regions of the parietal lobes are active (Hopf & Mangun, 2000; Intriligator & Cavanagh, 2001; Rosen et al., 1999; Synder et al., 2000).

In addition, the two types of attention operate differently. In contrast to pop-out, when you are searching for an object that is not distinct from the others around it, you must look at each possible candidate one at a time. Treisman and her colleagues (Treisman & Gormican, 1988; Treisman & Souther, 1985) demonstrated how this works in an experiment like the one illustrated in Figure 4.17. The more letters there are in a display like the one in the right panel, the longer it takes to find a target. With enough letters, people end up searching the display one item at a time. Pop-out and searching are distinct activities that arise from distinct areas of the brain. Using magnetic pulses to disrupt the parietal lobe, researchers found that while the ability to search for arrangements of features was impaired, the ability to experience pop-out was not (Ashbridge et al., 1997).

Attention is not a product of the brain alone but, like all other psychological events, it arises from the joint action of events at the different levels of analysis. What determines whether or not you will take that second look? That decision is influenced by what you believe (level of the person), which in part depends on your previous interactions with other people and your knowledge of the surrounding culture (level of the group). If you thought you saw a good friend, your attention would be engaged more fully than if you thought you saw a casual acquaintance. Similarly, if you are walking down the street and catch a glimpse of a dollar bill on the sidewalk, it will engage your attention differently than will a scrap of paper; but a young child, who doesn't know about the value of money, may react to the two stimuli the same way. Because of her experience with pain, Kahlo might have noticed a guest grimacing in pain, whereas Rivera might have "seen" the same thing but not paid attention to it. Prior experiences can govern how attention works.

Limits of Attention. Consider three limits on attention. First, we cannot pay attention to more than one task at the same instant in time. If we must perform two tasks that require attention, such as talking on a cell phone and driving during a hailstorm, we must divide attention. **Divided attention** occurs when you shift back and forth between different stimuli or tasks. Divided attention usually has a cost: You will perform one—or both—of the tasks more poorly than you would if you concentrated on one task alone (Han & Humphreys, 2002; Rodriguez et al., 2002). This problem may arise either because additional processes in the frontal lobes must be brought to bear when you shift attention back and forth (Nagahama et al., 2001), or because the same mechanisms are being used in competing tasks.

However, if the tasks are different enough, so that they can be accomplished by different mechanisms, they won't interfere as much with each other (Bonnel et al., 2001). Moreover, if the tasks or signals don't compete with each other, but instead lead to the same response, you might actually do better when you have to pay attention to two tasks or two signals at once (Beilock et al., 2002). For example, the *redundant signal effect* occurs when you are asked to respond as soon as you perceive a signal: If you are given two signals at once instead of one, you will respond more quickly. This effect occurs even if one member of the pair of visual signals is so dim you are not consciously aware of seeing it (Savazzi & Marzi, 2002).

Second, we can focus our attention only within a limited region of space and—if objects are moving—only when they move below a certain speed (Verstraten et al., 2000). For example, Intriligator and Cavanagh (2001) found that humans can focus on a particular item when 60 or fewer filled circles are placed within the central 30 degree region of the visual field (in vision research, the size of a region of space is specified in degrees; if you hold your thumb out at arm's length and look at it with one eye, it spans about 2 degrees); any more than that, and the participants could not focus on an individual item. Your ability to select one thing to pay attention to is much coarser than your ability to discriminate among fine visual details.

Third, attention is also limited in its ability to filter out information. Figure 4.18 (p. 148) illustrates a classic example of such a limit of attention: the Stroop effect. If you are asked to pay attention only to the color of the ink (and not the word itself), and say this color aloud, you will nevertheless have trouble if the word names another color; if the meaning of the word is different from the color of the ink, you experience interference when you try to name the color of the ink. Bottom-up processes lead you to read the meaning of the word, and attention cannot simply turn off such processes (do you think it would be a good idea to be able to do so?).

HANDS ON

● **Divided attention:** The process of shifting focus back and forth between different stimuli or tasks.

FIGURE 4.18 The Stroop Effect

In 1935, John Ridley Stroop published a classic paper describing what is now known as the Stroop effect. Name the color of the ink used to print each word in the left column (not the color named by the word); then do the same for the words in the right column. Which is easier? You cannot help both seeing the color and reading the word and, when the meaning of the word is different from the color of the ink, you experience interference.

From *Psychology* by Peter Gray. © 1991, 1994, 2002 by Worth Publishers. Used with permission.

GREEN	RED
RED	BLUE
BLUE	GREEN
BLACK	BLACK
BLUE	GREEN
RED	BLUE
GREEN	BLACK
BLACK	RED
RED	BLUE
BLUE	GREEN

Seeing Without Awareness

Some people who suffer strokes that leave them blind can nevertheless report accurately when spots of light are presented, and will even know where they are. These people have no awareness of seeing the dots but rather simply "know" when they are present. Similarly, animals with damage to the visual cortex in the occipital lobe may appear to be blind at all other times, but when they are lowered onto a surface, they stick out their legs to support themselves at just the right point; some of these animals can avoid obstacles when walking, even though the primary visual cortex has been removed (Cowey & Stoerig, 1995). Such behavior has been called *blindsight* (Weiskrantz, 1986). Multiple pathways from the eye lead to many places in the brain (Felleman & Van Essen, 1991; Zeki, 1978, 1993), and some of these pathways can function even though they do not pass through brain areas that give rise to conscious experience. Thus, even when the areas crucial for consciousness, or connections from these areas, are damaged, some visual function persists.

Our brains can respond when we see an object even if we are not aware of seeing it. Marcel (1983) took advantage of the discovery that presenting a word makes it easier for people to read a subsequent word that has a related meaning; this kind of carryover effect is one type of *priming*. Marcel and his collaborators found that priming occurs even when the first word is presented so quickly that people are not aware of having seen it (see Figure 4.19; Bar & Biederman, 1998, confirm these results). Perception of events outside awareness is called *subliminal perception*. After many years of unreliable findings, researchers have not only documented that subliminal perception exists, but they are even tracking down the brain events responsible for this effect (Kolb & Braun, 1995; Luck et al., 1996).

However, let's not overstate the case. More often than not, instead of perceiving more than you are aware of, you are actually perceiving less than you think. A classic real-world illustration of this situation occurred in 1878 when Eadweard Muybridge took a series of stop-action photographs of a running horse. These photos clearly showed that a running horse always has one foot on the ground, never all four in the air at once. So strong were people's beliefs about what they thought they saw when watching a horse gallop that they rejected Muybridge's first set of photographs, and he had to restage the event with witnesses from the press on hand to verify that the cameras were working properly (Sullivan, 1999). A large body of research shows that people can perceive with high accuracy only those stimuli to which they pay attention. Conversely, people are remarkably bad at noticing even

FIGURE 4.19 One Demonstration of Subliminal Perception

A word can be presented so briefly that the viewer has no awareness of having seen it.

After the initial word, a second word is presented, long enough to be seen clearly. The word is either related to the first one, such as "Doctor," or unrelated, such as "Denver." If the two words are related, participants can read the second one more easily.

large changes in stimuli if they are not paying attention to the relevant parts (O'Regan, 1992; Simons, 2000; Simons & Levin, 1997).

A bird in the hand is worth two in the the bush. Did you notice anything odd about the sentence you just read? Many people miss the repeated "the" and, in fact,

The two versions of these scenes were alternated every 640 milliseconds. In the pair of photos on the left, the railing changes, which is not of central interest. People had a difficult time noticing this change, requiring 16.2 alternations on average to spot it. In the pair of photos on the right, the location of the helicopter changes, which is of central interest. People noticed this change after only 4.0 alternations, on average (from Rensink et al., 1997).

● Repetition blindness: The inability to see the second occurrence of a stimulus that appears twice in succession.

● Attentional blink: A rebound period in which a person cannot pay attention to one thing after having just paid attention to another.

this is said to be the hardest error for a proofreader to catch. Kanwisher (1987, 1991) has dubbed this effect **repetition blindness** and has shown that people will fail to see a second example of an object if it occurs soon after the first instance. A related phenomenon is the **attentional blink,** in which attention is lost for a certain time immediately following a stimulus to which attention was paid. In contrast to repetition blindness, the attentional blink can occur for a different stimulus, not necessarily a second instance of the same or a closely related one, and the effect may actually be larger for stimuli that occur a few items after the one attended to (Arnell & Jolicoeur, 1999; Chun, 1997; Jolicoeur, 1998; Luck et al., 1996; Raymond et al., 1992). Proofreaders and copyeditors experience this unfortunate phenomenon all the time, missing obvious errors that happen to fall in the wake of a large error or a string of errors. Repetition blindness appears to result because the stimuli are not registered as individual events, but simply as a "type" of event (Kanwisher, 1987), whereas the attentional blink may occur because the act of registering information in detail may "lock up" certain neural processes for a brief period, during which attention cannot easily be reengaged (Fell et al., 2002).

Looking *at* Levels

The Importance of Body Parts in Physical Beauty

As any painter can tell you, vision is used for more than identifying objects and registering their locations. Through the visual system we also perceive what we call "beauty," including physical attractiveness. David Perrett and his collaborators (1998) asked Asian people (Japanese in Japan) and Caucasians (Scots in Scotland) to choose the most attractive faces from a set of photographs, some of which had been altered to emphasize features that reflect high levels of male or female hormones. The researchers found that both national groups preferred women's faces with a female "hormone enhanced" look to average faces. However, the effect was larger for faces within each participant's own population, a finding that was interpreted as indicating that this is a learned preference. In addition, both groups also found *male* faces more attractive if they showed effects of *female* hormones. Faces that showed effects of high levels of male hormones were rated as having high "perceived dominance," as being older, and as having less warmth, emotionality, honesty, and cooperativeness (as well as

other attributes). Apparently, the effects of female hormones not only made faces look younger but also softened these negative perceptions.

However, when it comes to bodies, the story is not so consistent. For example, Ford and Beach (1951) considered what people in over 200 cultures looked at when evaluating attractiveness and found that different cultures focused on different parts and characteristics of the body (such as the size of the pelvis, pudginess, and height). How can there be such differences in what is thought of as "beautiful" if everyone has the same visual equipment? Several reasons become apparent when we use the levels of analysis approach. First, at the level of the group, values and tastes develop and are taught, either explicitly (via instruction) or implicitly (via example) to the individual members of the group. These standards may evolve for different reasons. For example, before the spread of AIDS, gay men were often very thin; after AIDS, having a little extra weight was perceived as a sign of health and thus became attractive. Second, at the level of the person, these standards produce values and beliefs. These values and beliefs, in turn, affect top-down processing, leading people to look for certain body parts or attributes. And, at the level of the brain, the mechanisms of attention are at work when

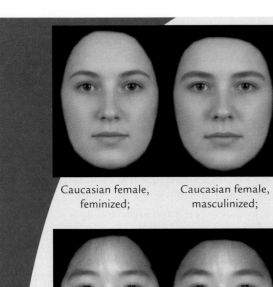
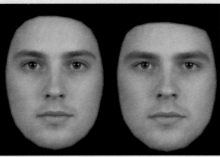

Caucasian female, feminized;

Caucasian female, masculinized;

Caucasian male, feminized;

Caucasian male, masculinized;

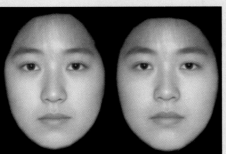
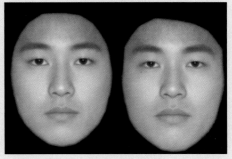

Japanese female, feminized;

Japanese female, masculinized;

Japanese male, feminized;

Japanese male, masculinized.

Facial images of Caucasian and Japanese females and males were "feminized" and "masculinized" 50% in shape. Which face do you prefer? In general, faces that reveal effects of female sex hormones are seen as more attractive.

people fixate on a salient part, registering it in detail. Once you evaluate someone as beautiful, various expectations and beliefs come to mind. Just as once you've identified an object as an apple, you know it has seeds inside, once you classify a person as attractive, you believe that he or she is likely to be kind, nurturing, and sensitive, and to have other positive attributes as well (Dion et al., 1972).

TEST YOURSELF!

1. What is "sensation," and how does it differ from "perception"?
2. What is the nature of light, and how do we see color, shape, and motion?
3. How are we able to separate figure from ground and see the world as a stable collection of objects?
4. How do we make sense of what we see?

Hearing

According to Diego Rivera's daughter, Kahlo loved whistles. They were sold in stands in the market: "They came in various sizes and made different sounds. She used them to call for [the different house staff], and she created quite a stir when she did" (Rivera & Colle, 1994, p. 100). How is it that Kahlo (and everyone else nearby whose hearing was intact) could *hear* the sounds of the whistles? And how could she (and we) notice that different whistles made different sounds?

Auditory Sensation: If a Tree Falls but Nobody Hears It, Is There a Sound?

We know that rays don't emanate from our eyes when we see. Now for a trick question: Do you think that sound waves emanate from our ears when we hear? In

1978, researchers found that when a click is presented to someone, the ear soon produces an echo (Kemp, 1978). Not long after this discovery, researchers (Kemp, 1979; Zurek, 1981, 1985; Zwicker & Schloth, 1984) found that even when a person isn't hearing a particular stimulus, the ear sometimes actually makes a sound. In fact, about 40% of normal people emit a detectable soft humming sound from their ears, of which they are unaware. In some cases, the humming is loud enough that other people can hear it. These sounds are not like the natural sonar used by whales, sound waves bouncing off objects and returning to the ear. These sounds play no role in hearing. They are probably caused by feedback from the brain to the ear; feedback (not the sounds produced by it) helps us hear slight differences in sounds (Pickles, 1988; Zurek, 1985). As in vision, there are many feedback connections between areas of the brain that process sound, and between these areas and the ear (Felleman & Van Essen, 1991). This is not the only similarity between hearing and seeing.

Sound Waves: Being Pressured

Like vision, auditory processing occurs in two major phases, sensation and perception. And, like vision, perception itself can be divided into processes used at the beginning and at the end. Hearing begins with the sensation of sound. Sound usually arises when something vibrates, creating waves of moving air that enter our ears. Sound can arise when any type of molecules—gas, liquid, or solid—move and create pressure waves. Thus we can hear when we are surrounded by either air or water or when we put an ear to the ground, to a wall, or to another solid object. An old (but true) cliché of Western movies is listening with an ear pressed to a rail to hear whether a train is approaching. But movies sometimes get it wrong. In outer space—where there are no molecules to be moved—we could not hear anything; the loud explosion of the demolished Death Star in the original *Star Wars* movie would in fact have been silent as the grave.

These pressure waves go up, and then down, repeatedly; each complete up-and-down movement is called a *cycle*. As with light waves for vision, sound waves have both frequency and amplitude. We usually hear variations in frequency as differences in **pitch**—how high or low the sound seems—and we hear variations in amplitude as differences in **loudness.** (It probably is no coincidence that people are most sensitive to the frequencies of a baby's cry, around 2,000–5,000 Hertz; a Hertz, or Hz, is the number of cycles per second.) The same psychophysical concepts that apply to vision, such as thresholds, JNDs, and so on, also apply to hearing and are measured in comparable ways.

A question often asked in beginning philosophy classes is this: If a tree falls in the forest but nobody hears it, is there a sound? The answer is now clear: No. Sound is *caused* by waves of molecules (a physical event), but the waves themselves are not sound. Sound is a psychological event and hence depends on a nervous system to transduce the physical energy of the vibrations to nerve energy. Without a brain to register the physical energy, there can be no sound. The situation is exactly analogous to the relationships of wavelength to hue and of amplitude to lightness. Physical properties *lead* to psychological events, but they are not the events themselves. The discipline of psychophysics charts the relationship between physical events and our experience of them.

- **Pitch:** How high or low a sound seems; higher frequencies of pressure waves produce the experience of higher pitches.

- **Loudness:** The strength of a sound; pressure waves with greater amplitude produce the experience of louder sound.

The Brain's Ear: More Than a Microphone

The anatomy of the ear is illustrated in Figure 4.20. The ear has three parts: the outer ear, middle ear, and inner ear. The eardrum (the *tympanic membrane*)

FIGURE 4.20 Anatomy of the Ear

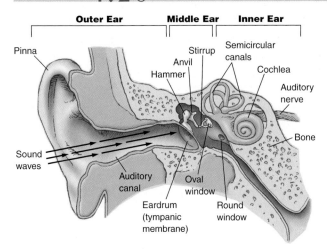

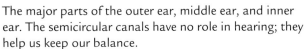

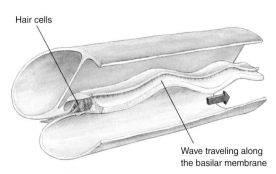

The major parts of the outer ear, middle ear, and inner ear. The semicircular canals have no role in hearing; they help us keep our balance.

If you unwound the cochlea and looked into it, you would see the basilar membrane with its hair cells.

stretches across the inside end of the auditory canal, and everything between the eardrum and the auditory nerve is designed to convert movements of the eardrum to nerve impulses that are sent to the brain. Specifically, waves move the eardrum, which in turn moves three bones in the middle ear (the hammer, anvil, and stirrup; incidentally, these are the smallest bones in the human body). If you hear a loud sound, the muscles in the ear reflexively tighten, which protects against damage (Borg & Counter, 1989). These muscles also contract when you talk, which protects you from hurting your own ears. Such protection is necessary because the ear is amazingly sensitive: We can hear a sound when the eardrum is moved less than one billionth of an inch (Green, 1976). The three bones of the middle ear not only transfer but also amplify the vibration and cause the *basilar membrane* (which is inside the cochlea, as shown in Figure 4.20) to vibrate. The basilar membrane is where different frequencies of sound are coded into different nerve impulses. Hairs sticking up from cells lining the basilar membrane in turn trigger nerve impulses, which are then sent to the brain. These **hair cells** function in hearing the same way rods and cones do in vision; they produce the initial nerve impulses.

There are two main theories about the way the basilar membrane converts pressure waves to perceived sound. **Frequency theory** holds that higher frequencies produce greater neural firing. This theory cannot explain the full extent of our ability to hear: Neurons can fire only about 1,000 times a second at most, so how is it that we can hear sounds produced by much higher frequencies (Gelfand, 1981)? According to **place theory**, different frequencies activate different places along the basilar membrane, as shown in Figure 4.21 (p. 154). This theory appears to be correct, at least for most frequencies; it is possible, however, that the rate of vibration does help us hear relatively low tones.

As in vision, a number of brain areas working together allow us to sense sound. The first part of the cortex to receive auditory information, the *primary auditory cortex*, is spatially organized. Researchers have shown that as the pitch changes,

● **Hair cells:** The cells with stiff hairs along the basilar membrane of the inner ear that, when moved, produce nerve impulses that are sent to the brain; these cells are the auditory equivalent of rods and cones.

● **Frequency theory:** The theory that higher frequencies produce higher rates of neural firing.

● **Place theory:** The theory that different frequencies activate different places along the basilar membrane.

Hearing | 153

FIGURE 4.21   Place Coding of Sound Frequency

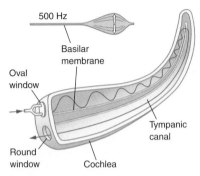

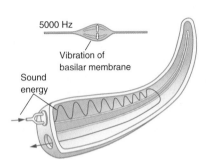

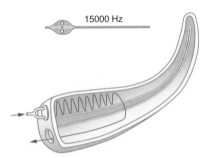

Low frequencies cause maximal vibration of the basilar membrane near one end.

Medium frequencies cause maximal vibration of the basilar membrane near the middle.

High frequencies cause maximal vibration of the basilar membrane near the other end.

activity shifts to different locations along this structure. Again, just as in vision, in which the pattern of activation on the eye is in turn laid out on the brain (see p. 135), the spatial arrangement of vibration on the basilar membrane is mimicked in the brain. This sort of spatial arrangement is called **tonotopic organization** (Clarey et al., 1992; Romani et al., 1982).

Deafness: Hear Today, Gone Tomorrow

More than 28 million Americans have some sort of difficulty in hearing (Soli, 1994). Over 30 genes have now been linked to deafness (Lynch et al., 1997), and thus we shouldn't be surprised to find that there are different forms of deafness, and that some forms of deafness are inherited. Lynch and colleagues studied the deaf descendants of a deaf man who was born in 1713 and found that they inherited a particular mutated gene. This gene plays a crucial role in stiffening the hairs in the inner ear and, because of the mutation, the hair cells fail to function properly. Not all forms of deafness are genetic, however. One of the most serious is **nerve deafness,** which typically occurs when the hair cells are destroyed by loud sounds. A rock band heard at close range can produce sounds loud enough to cause this sort of damage. Nerve deafness may affect only certain frequencies; in those instances, a hearing aid can amplify the remaining frequencies, and hearing can be improved. Many researchers believe that surgery will soon allow doctors to make an end run around a damaged ear and allow auditory input to stimulate the auditory cortex directly (Ubell, 1995).

Another form of hearing impairment, **tinnitus,** is signaled by a constant ringing or noise in the ears (McFadden, 1982). And some drugs, including aspirin, can dull a person's hearing (McFadden & Plattsmier, 1983). Fortunately, the dulling effects of aspirin are only temporary. **Conduction deafness** can result from any accident or other

One study found that almost a third of a group of college students who went regularly to a dance club featuring loud music exhibited permanent hearing loss for high-frequency sounds (Hartman, 1982).

cause that impairs the functioning of the external ear or middle ear. A broken eardrum, for example, can cause conduction deafness.

It is worth noting that if someone becomes deaf as a child, other senses can eventually compensate. Catalan-Ahumeda and colleagues (1993), Neville and colleagues (1983), Wolf and Thatcher (1990), and others have found increased activation in the visual cortex of deaf people, and by adolescence the deaf can focus visual attention in many tasks better than can hearing people (particularly when they have to attend to something not currently being focused on; Loke & Song, 1991; Neville, 1988, 1990; Neville & Lawson, 1987; Proksch & Bavelier, 2002). This is another example of the brain's plasticity (see Chapter 3; Bavelier & Neville, 2002).

First Steps of Auditory Perception: Organizing the Auditory World

In the last year of Kahlo's life, a Mexican gallery had the first-ever one-woman show of her work. The organizers scheduled a grand party on the show's opening night. Everyone wondered whether Kahlo would appear, but doubted it because she had been bedridden for some time. Friends, patrons, and well-wishers crowded into the gallery, waiting to see whether she would arrive. In the distance they heard a siren, which got louder and louder, and finally an ambulance pulled up in front of the gallery. The ambulance staff carried Kahlo, and the four poster bed on which she lay, out of the ambulance and into the gallery where everyone was waiting. On any other opening night, the patrons probably would not have paid much attention to the sound of a siren, but on this night they waited eagerly as they heard the sound growing louder. The processes engaged during the first phases of auditory perception allow us to organize sounds as coming from distinct objects and to locate the sources of sounds.

Sorting Out Sounds: From One, Many

In daily life, a single complex jumble of many sounds usually assaults our ears, not individual sounds one at a time. To make sense of what we hear, we first need to sort out individual sounds. As in vision, we need to distinguish figure from ground. Bregman (1990, 1993) calls this process *auditory scene analysis*, which relies on organization very much like what occurs in vision. Indeed, the Gestalt laws help us here, too. For example, people organize sounds partly based on similarity (for example, grouping sounds with the same pitch) and good continuation (grouping the same pitch continued over time). Recognizing and identifying speech relies crucially on auditory scene analysis because the actual stimulus is continuous, with no indication of breaks to delineate the beginnings and endings of words, and yet to communicate, people must identify individual words. This problem is the **speech segmentation problem.** By analogy, *thisproblemisliketheoneyouarenowsolving* in vision.

In vision, we see continuous variations in the frequency of light not as continuous variations in hue, but rather as a set of distinct colors. Similarly, we hear speech sounds as distinct categories. This **categorical perception** produces categories with remarkably sharp boundaries. For example, if a computer is programmed to vary the time between the start of a syllable (the consonant being pronounced, such as b) and the "voiced" part of the syllable (the sound of the vowel being pronounced, such as a), we will hear "ba" if the voice starts from 0 to around 25 thousandths of a second after the consonant starts; but if the voice starts after a longer interval, we will hear "pa." There is very little intermediate ground;

- **Tonotopic organization:** The use of distance along a strip of cortex to represent differences in pitch.

- **Nerve deafness:** A type of deafness that typically occurs when the hair cells are destroyed by loud sounds.

- **Tinnitus:** A form of hearing impairment signaled by a constant ringing or noise in the ears.

- **Conduction deafness:** A type of deafness caused by a physical impairment of the external or middle ear.

- **Speech segmentation problem:** The problem of organizing a continuous stream of speech into separate parts that correspond to individual words.

- **Categorical perception:** Identifying sounds as belonging to distinct categories that correspond to the basic units of speech.

we hear one or the other (Eimas & Corbit, 1973). Infants (Dehaene-Lambertz & Pena, 2001), as well as monkeys, chinchillas, and various other animals, also show categorical perception (Kuhl, 1989; Moody et al., 1990), which suggests that the perceptual system itself does this work—not the language systems of our various cultures. Indeed, the common ancestor of monkeys and humans may have evolved many of the "building blocks" that were later incorporated into speech.

Locating Sounds: Why Two Ears Are Better Than One

In vision, our brains use slight differences in the images striking the two eyes to assess the distance of an object. Similarly, hearing makes use of differences in the stimuli reaching the two ears to assess the distance of a sound source (Yost & Dye, 1991). Three kinds of differences are particularly important. First, sound waves reach the two ears at slightly different phases, that is, at slightly different points in the wave cycle. The *difference in phase* reaching the two ears is particularly useful for detecting the source of relatively low-frequency sounds, which arise from longer waves (Gulick et al., 1989). Second, a *difference in loudness* at the two ears is used as a cue. In addition to all of their other functions, our heads are useful because they block sound, and thus the amplitude of sound waves is smaller when it reaches the ear on the side of the head away from the sound source. This cue is particularly effective for high-frequency sounds. Third, the sound wave will reach the two ears at slightly different times; this *onset difference* is tiny, but the brain uses it effectively.

As in vision, we use many different cues to assess where an object is. Some cues depend on only one ear, not two. Consider three such cues. First, the simple loudness of a sound: Especially for familiar objects, we can use volume as an indicator of distance. If an ambulance is approaching, we can get a good sense of how far away it is from its sound. Second, the way our external ears are crinkled bends sound waves in different ways; these variations help us detect the location of the sound source (Moore, 1982). Third, by moving our heads and bodies, we can compare the relative volume of a sound from different vantage points, which helps us locate its source.

Bats and barn owls are adept at using sound to localize objects (Konishi, 1993; Suga, 1990). The structure of the barn owl's face has developed in a way to direct sound to its ears; this maximizes location cues. Bats produce sounds, and then listen for the echoes coming back. The echoes are precise enough for the bat to discern the shapes of even small objects (Simmons & Chen, 1989).

Auditory Perception: Recognition and Identification

We use sound in many ways. In addition to interpreting speech and music, we also recognize that the snap of a green bean indicates freshness, that a knock on a door means someone wants to come in, that a cat's mewing may mean she wants to be fed. As in vision, sounds become meaningful when they are matched to information already stored in memory, which is the job of auditory perceptual processing.

More Than Meets the Ear

Kahlo's biography recounts an incident when Kahlo and Rivera were to meet outside a movie theatre, but crowds prevented them from seeing each other. In trying to find each other, "Diego whistled the first bar of the *Internationale*. From somewhere in the crowd came the second; it was unmistakably Frida. After this, the task no doubt seemed easier, and the whistling continued until the couple found each other" (Herrera, 1983, p. 308). Why would hearing the whistle over the noise of the crowd seem easier once they knew to listen for their whistled tune? Just as in vision, you can adjust your criterion for "detecting a signal" and this adjustment would be based on what you expect to hear. But also, as in vision, what you expect to hear actually influences what you do hear. A demonstration of such an effect was reported by Warren and Warren (1970), who asked people to listen to a tape-recorded sentence after part of a word had been replaced with the sound of a cough. Although part of the word was actually missing, all the participants claimed that they actually heard the entire word and denied that the cough covered part of it. In fact, the listeners were not exactly sure at what point the cough occurred. This effect, more obvious for words in sentences than for words standing alone, is called the *phonemic restoration effect* (a phoneme is the smallest segment of spoken speech, such as "ba" or "da"). This filling-in effect occurs not only with speech sounds but also with musical instruments. In fact, if you see someone bowing the strings of a cello at the same time you hear the strings being plucked, the sight is enough to distort the sound you hear (Saldana & Rosenblum, 1993).

Hearing Without Awareness

As happens in vision, we pick up some auditory information without being aware of it. Perhaps the most common experience of perception without awareness is the **cocktail party phenomenon.** At an event like a party, you may not be aware of other people's conversation until someone mentions your name—which you hear immediately (Cherry, 1953; Conway et al., 2001). But in order to become aware of the sound of your name, you must have been tracking the conversation all along (using bottom-up processing); you simply were not aware of the conversation until that important word was spoken. In experiments she performed as an undergraduate, Treisman (1964a, 1964b) showed that when people listen to stimuli presented separately to the two ears (through headphones) and are instructed to listen to only one ear, a procedure known as **dichotic listening** (Hugdahl, 2001), they still register some information—such as whether the voice is male or female—from the ignored ear. To ensure that participants listen to only one voice, they often are asked to repeat it aloud—a practice known as *shadowing.*

This discovery spawned an industry that proclaimed people can learn in their sleep, simply by playing tapes (purchased at low, low discount prices). Unfortunately, it turns out that unless a person is paying attention, not much gets through. And even when information does get through, it is retained very briefly; when tested hours later, people remember virtually none of the information presented outside awareness (Greenwald et al., 1991).

Music: Cultural Creations?

Music is a part of virtually all cultures; in some, its importance is so great that governments have occasionally regulated what constitutes music itself. In the former Soviet Union, for example, some chords were labeled decadent and were actually outlawed. Closer to home, in North Carolina, singing out of tune was at one time a prosecutable offense (Seuling, 1975). Aside from these cultural curiosities, however, the existence of music depends on the fact that the brain registers sounds relative to one another, not in isolation (Krumhansl, 2000). For example, when you double a frequency, you hear the same note but an *octave* higher (an octave in Western music is 8 consecutive notes). The continuous variation in frequency

● **Cocktail party phenomenon:** The effect of not being aware of other people's conversations until your name is mentioned, and then suddenly hearing it.

● **Dichotic listening:** A procedure in which participants hear stimuli presented separately to the two ears (through headphones) and are instructed to listen only to sounds presented to one ear.

● **Absolute pitch:** The ability to identify a particular note by itself, not simply in relation to other notes.

between octaves is divided into distinct intervals, which form a *scale*. The nature of scales varies in different cultures. The Western scale relies on 12 half-steps for each octave, compared with more than 50 in Indian music. Nevertheless, all humans hear notes an octave apart as more similar than consecutive notes. This is another example of the way in which the physical nature of a stimulus differs from its psychological experience. Indeed, we can hear two different sequences of notes (which have different physical frequencies) as the same, provided that the notes are separated by the same intervals. However, not all people can recognize or remember musical steps equally well. Interestingly, identical twins have very similar abilities to recognize incorrect notes in familiar popular tunes, which (when compared with the less similar abilities of fraternal twins) led researchers to conclude that genetic differences are responsible for at least 70 percent of the variation in this ability (Drayna et al., 2001).

Within a given culture, the ease of identifying the notes in a scale depends partly on whether a person has **absolute pitch,** the striking ability to identify a particular note by itself, not simply in relation to other notes (Krumhansl, 1991, 2000). Studies have shown that Americans with absolute pitch identify the intervals between notes from a standard Western scale better if an instrument is "in tune" (that is, the notes are set to the correct absolute frequencies) than if it is a bit out of tune; people without absolute pitch do not show such a difference (Miyazaki, 1993). Many people with absolute pitch developed the ability during childhood (Krumhansl, 1991, 2000; Takeuchi & Hulse, 1993). People with absolute pitch have an unusually large planum temporale, a part of the auditory cortex that lies on the top part of the temporal lobe, near the back (Schlaug et al., 1995)—but research has yet to establish whether this is a cause or an effect of having this ability.

Looking *at* Levels

Beethoven, the Deaf Composer

Beethoven was stone deaf when he wrote much of his greatest music. How is this possible? The levels of analysis approach will help us understand his remarkable achievement. First, at the level of the brain, auditory mental imagery allowed him to hear music with his "mind's ear" as he was composing it. Auditory imagery arises when brain areas that are used in hearing are activated from stored memories (Halpern, 1988; Zatorre & Halpern, 1993). Right now, decide whether the first three notes of "Three Blind Mice" go up or down; to do this, you probably "heard" the tune in your head—you evoked auditory imagery. Imagery can occur even when the sense organs are damaged (for example, if the hair cells die). What Beethoven heard in his mind's ear would probably have been very similar to what he would have heard carried by sound waves had he not been deaf. Second, consider the level of the person. We can only speculate, but being forced to practice by his tyrannical father may have had at least two consequences for the young composer. Not only did he become a superb pianist and music theorist, but he also may have come to use his music as a refuge from his father. Third, at the level of the group, his playing may have been a way to appease his father and win his approval. Also, Beethoven lived in a society that appreciated music, and thus he was able to raise financial support for his work, despite the fact that he was deaf. (Beethoven was the first composer to "freelance" for a living.) And music itself is a cultural invention, as are the various detailed systems of notation that different human societies use to write it down. Finally, events at the different levels interacted: His culture allowed his brain to develop in certain ways, which in turn affected his social interactions—and these interactions affected his beliefs (for example, about how best to cope with his father).

TEST YOURSELF!

1. How do the ears register auditory sensation?
2. What auditory cues allow us to organize sounds into coherent units and locate their sources?
3. How do we make meaning out of sound?

Sensing and Perceiving in Other Ways

Left to his own devices, Rivera did not bathe frequently—and Kahlo was not fond of his body odor. She bought him bath toys in hopes that they would motivate him to bathe more often (apparently she was successful). Kahlo's sense of smell wasn't the only other sense of which she was keenly aware; she was very aware of tastes. During several lengthy visits to the United States, Kahlo consistently complained about the blandness of American food (although she did like applesauce and American cheese). Kahlo was also aware of the senses in her body; unfortunately, she experienced much pain, and gangrene in her right foot led to its eventual amputation. What have researchers discovered about these and other senses?

Smell: A Nose for News?

Smell and taste are often grouped together as the **chemical senses** because both, unlike the other senses, rely on registering the presence of specific chemicals. People differ widely in their sense of smell, or *olfaction*. Some people are 20 times more sensitive to odors than are other people (Rabin & Cain, 1986); Kahlo may simply have had a better sense of smell than Rivera, and hence was more sensitive to the odor when he hadn't bathed. Most people are remarkably poor at identifying odors, even though they often think they are good at it (de Wijk et al., 1995). Cain (1979) found that people could correctly identify only about half of 80 common scents; although we may know that an odor is familiar—that is, we recognize it—we may be unable to identify it. In general, women are better than men at detecting many types of odors (Cain, 1982). Women are particularly sensitive to smell when they are ovulating—unless they take birth control pills, in which case their abilities do not fluctuate over the course of the month (Caruso et al., 2001; Grillo et al., 2001). In addition, younger adults are better at detecting odors than either children (up to 14 years old) or middle-aged adults (between 40 and 50 years old) (Cain & Gent, 1991; de Wijk & Cain, 1994; Murphy, 1986). For many of the years of her marriage, Kahlo was probably at the peak of her olfactory sensitivity.

Distinguishing Odors: Lock and Key

The best theory of odor detection can be described using the lock and key metaphor. Molecules have different shapes, and the olfactory receptors are built so that only molecules with particular shapes will fit in particular places. The molecules are like keys, and the receptors like locks. When the right-shaped molecule

● **Chemical senses:** Taste and smell, which rely on sensing the presence of specific chemicals.

FIGURE 4.22 The Olfactory System

Depending on which olfactory receptor cells are stimulated, different messages are sent to the olfactory bulb, the first part of the brain to process such signals.

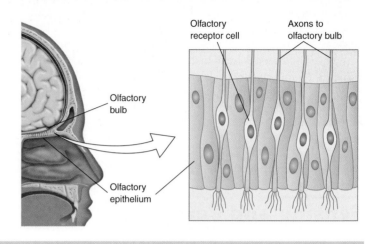

arrives at a particular receptor, it sends a signal to the brain, and we sense the odor. Just as there is not a single type of cone for each color we can see, there is not a single receptor for each odor we can smell (see Figure 4.22); rather, the overall pattern of activity signals a particular odor (Freeman, 1991).

Two major neural tracks send signals about odor into the brain. One, passing through the thalamus, is particularly involved in memory; the other, connected to the limbic system, is particularly involved in emotions. These connections explain why odors often tap emotionally charged memories—remember the way you felt when you unexpectedly smelled an old girlfriend's perfume or a boyfriend's aftershave?

Olfaction Gone Awry: Is It Safe to Cook Without Smell?

Have you ever wished you could not smell? Maybe that would be a relief once in a while, but losing your sense of smell completely is not a good idea. Smell serves to signal the presence of noxious substances; our brains are wired so that odors can quickly activate the "fight-or-flight" system. It would not be wise to ask a friend who has no sense of smell to cook dinner on a regular basis: Smell is often the only signal that meat or other food is spoiled. Relatively few people have no olfactory sense, a deficit that can arise from brain damage or a virus (Doty et al., 1991).

Pheromones: Another Kind of Scents?

Airborne chemicals released by female animals in heat arouse the male of the species. These are an example of **pheromones,** chemical substances that serve as a means of communication. Like hormones, they modulate the functions of various organs, including the brain. Unlike hormones, pheromones are released *outside* the body, in urine and sweat. The most famous example of effects of pheromones in humans was discovered by Martha McClintock (1971). She originally found that female roommates tend to synchronize their menstrual cycles and, along with Kathleen Stern (Stern & McClintock, 1998), has since found that this effect depends on certain pheromones reaching the nose (Russell et al., 1980, report consistent results). The receptors that are triggered by pheromones are accessed via the nose, and odors sometimes accompany these chemicals.

● **Pheromones:** Chemicals that function like hormones but are released outside the body (in urine and sweat).

Much to the delight of perfume manufacturers over the world, studies have now shown that female pheromones can attract men. In one study (McCoy & Pitino, 2002), university women began by recording seven social/sexual behaviors for two weeks (the baseline period), and then mixed a substance into their perfume and continued to record those behaviors; the substance was either a clear, odorless pheromone or an identically appearing but medically inactive substance (a placebo, for the control group). The study used a double-blind design; neither the investigator nor the participant knew whether a given participant received the pheromone or placebo. Participants who wore perfume with the pheromone reported having more petting (which included affectionate behavior in general), sexual intercourse, sleeping next to a partner, and formal dates—but did not report that more men had approached them or that they had more informal dates or an increase in masturbation. Fully 74% of the group receiving the pheromone reported increases in three or more of the four events that were affected, compared to only 23% of the group that got the placebo. All four of the affected types of events require intimate interaction with someone else, whereas none of the other three do. If this result holds up with repeated testing, do you think that women who wear pheromones should warn their dates?

Taste: The Mouth Has It

When scientists discuss taste, they are talking about sensing via receptors located solely in the mouth. **Taste buds** (see Figure 4.23) are microscopic structures mounted on the sides of the little bumps you can see on your tongue in a mirror. You have taste buds in other places in your mouth as well, such as the back of the throat and cheeks (Smith & Frank, 1993). Your taste buds die and are replaced, on average, every 10 days (McLaughlin & Margolskee, 1994). Humans have more taste buds than some species, such as chickens, but fewer than others; some fish have taste buds spread all over their skin (Pfaffmann, 1978). Children have more sensitive taste buds than adults, and thus flavors are presumably stronger for them than for adults—which may account for children's notoriously strong likes and dislikes of foods. Nevertheless, even adults can be remarkably sensitive to slight

FIGURE 4.23 Taste Buds on the Tongue

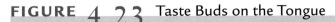

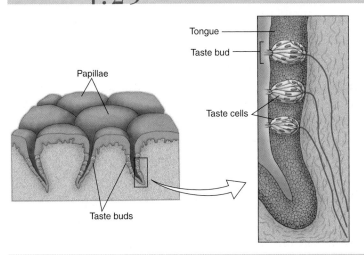

The taste buds on the tongue line the *papillae,* the visible bumps.

Tongue

Taste bud

Taste cells

Papillae

Taste buds

● **Taste buds:** Microscopic structures on the bumps on the tongue surface, at the back of the throat, and inside the cheeks; the four types of taste buds are sensitive to sweet, sour, salty, and bitter tastes.

differences in taste. When wine tasters speak of wine as having a flavor of mushrooms or cloves, they may not be speaking metaphorically. Depending on the composition of the soil in which the vines grow, grapes acquire different tastes.

Sweet, Sour, Salty, Bitter

You've seen how a wide range of colors arises from three types of cones, and how patterns of odors arise from the combinations of receptors being activated. The brain uses this same mixing-and-matching trick for taste. The tastes of all foods are made up of combinations of four tastes: sweet, sour, salty, and bitter (Bartoshuk & Beauchamp, 1994; Scott & Plata-Salaman, 1991). In addition, however, free nerve endings in the mouth appear to be irritated by spicy foods (Lawless, 1984). These provide another source of information about taste, one that is not directly related to the taste buds. Different parts of the mouth and tongue are more or less sensitive to different tastes; you can detect bitter flavors best in the back of your mouth (Shallenberger, 1993). However, these different sensitivities are a matter of degree: All kinds of taste buds are found in most locations on the tongue. Curiously, there is a "taste hole" in the middle of the tongue, an area where there are no taste buds at all.

For the most part, you cannot taste something unless it can be at least partially dissolved by your saliva (Seuling, 1986); that is why you can't taste a marble. However, an exception to this principle can occur if the stimulus changes the temperature of your tongue. For example, warming the front edge of your tongue can lead you to taste sweetness, but cooling this region can lead you to taste saltiness or sweetness. Moreover, changing temperature produces different tastes on different parts of the tongue (Cruz & Green, 2000). Finally, the tongue is sensitive to texture, which influences the way we experience different foods. In fact, the tongue is so sensitive that it is now being used to help blind people see! Researchers have devised machines that translate visual forms into patterns of stimulation on the tongue, and blind people can interpret these patterns to "see" rough outlines of objects (Sampaio et al., 2001).

Taste and Smell

Most people think that the flavor of food arises from its taste (Rozin, 1982), but in fact much of what we think of as taste is actually smell, or a combination of smell and taste. For example, aspartame (NutraSweet) tastes sweeter if you are simultaneously smelling vanilla (Sakai et al., 2001). In rats the two types of information converge on a region of the frontal lobes that is critical for the perception of flavor (Schul et al., 1996). Next time you have a stuffy nose, notice the flavor of your food, or lack thereof—particularly when you close your eyes and eliminate top-down processing to fill in your perception of the flavor. Researchers have found that people have a much harder time detecting most flavors when smell is blocked (Hyman et al., 1979). Kahlo might like the idea of not being able to smell her husband's body odor, but not smelling at all would ruin the taste of everything from chocolate to chili peppers.

Somasthetic Senses: Not Just Skin Deep

The traditional five senses—sight, hearing, smell, taste, and touch—were listed and described by Aristotle more than 2,000 years ago. It would be a sad commentary on the value of science if we couldn't do better after all this time. Today, we are able to argue that there are nine senses, perhaps ten: sight, hearing, smell, taste, and then a collection of five senses that together are called **somasthetic senses.** These senses all have to do with perceiving the body and its position in space: kinesthetic (sense of where the limbs are and how they move), vestibular (sense of balance), touch, temperature sensitivity, and pain. There may be a sixth somasthetic sense, magnetic sense. And, finally, there is possibly one more sense: extrasensory perception, or ESP (also sometimes called psi).

Kinesthetic Sense: A Moving Sense

Read this, and then close your eyes and hold out your left arm in an odd position. Now, keeping your left arm in place, touch your left hand with your right hand. You shouldn't have any trouble doing this because you know where your hands are without having to see them. You know because of your **kinesthetic sense,** which registers the movement and position of the limbs. Two types of specialized cells sense this information: One type is in the tendons (the material that connects muscles to bones) and is triggered by tension; the other is in the muscles themselves and is triggered by the length of the muscle (Pinel, 1993).

Vestibular Sense: Being Oriented

The inner ear is used not only for hearing, but also for balance. The **vestibular sense,** which provides information about how you are oriented relative to gravity, relies on an organ in the inner ear that contains three *semicircular canals* (illustrated in Figure 4.20). If these structures are disrupted, say by infection or injury (or by spending too much time in weightlessness in outer space, as happens to astronauts), people have a difficult time keeping their balance.

The vestibular and kinesthetic senses often work together. These people would be out of a job (or worse) if either sense failed. The vestibular sense lets them know where their bodies are relative to gravity, and the kinesthetic sense lets them know where their limbs are relative to their bodies.

Touch: Feeling Well

Here's another trick question: What's your body's largest organ? The lungs? The intestines? The answer is the skin. As well as protecting our bodies from the environment (such as dirt, germs, flying objects, changes in temperature), making crucial vitamins, and triggering the release of various hormones, the skin is also a massive sensory organ. Millions of receptors in the skin produce impulses when stimulated in specific ways. Moreover, using the same mechanism as other senses, it is the particular combination of receptors being stimulated that produces a specific sensation. The mix-and-match principle is at work here, too: We can feel many more types of sensations than we have types of receptors. Receptors in the skin in different parts of the body send impulses to different parts of the somatosensory cortex (see Chapter 3); in general, the more cortex devoted to a particular area of the skin, the more sensitive we are there (Weinstein, 1968).

Women tend to be more sensitive to touch than are men (Weinstein, 1968). Moreover, women are especially sensitive (relative to men) on some parts of their bodies, such as their backs and stomachs.

Temperature

The skin has separate systems for registering hot and cold; indeed, there are distinct spots on your skin that register *only* hot or *only* cold. These spots are

● **Somasthetic senses:** Senses that have to do with perceiving the body and its position in space—specifically, kinesthetic sense, vestibular sense, touch, temperature sensitivity, pain sense, and possibly magnetic sense.

● **Kinesthetic sense:** The sense that registers the movement and position of the limbs.

● **Vestibular sense:** The sense that provides information about the body's orientation relative to gravity.

about 1 mm across (Hensel, 1982). If a cold spot is stimulated, you will feel a sensation of cold even if the stimulus is something hot. This phenomenon is called **paradoxical cold.** People are not very good at telling exactly where a hot or cold stimulus is located, particularly if it is near the skin but not touching it (Cain, 1973).

Pain

Despite the discomfort, even the agony, pain brings, the inability to feel pain is even worse in the long run than the inability to smell odors. Sternbach (1978) described children who could not feel pain normally and who picked off the skin around their nostrils and bit off their fingers because they didn't notice what they were doing. Pain serves to warn us of impending danger, and it is crucial to survival.

The sensation of pain arises when three different kinds of nerves are stimulated. These nerves differ in size and in the speed with which they transmit impulses. Thus, we can feel **double pain:** the first phase, of sharp pain, occurs at the time of the injury; it is followed by a dull pain. The two kinds of pain arise from different fibers sending their messages at different speeds (Rollman, 1991).

One of the ways we deal with pain is by producing substances in our brains, called **endorphins,** that have painkilling effects. Some drugs, such as morphine, bind to the same receptors that accept endorphins, which explains how those drugs can act as painkillers (Cailliet, 1993). However, pain involves more than simple bottom-up processing. In fact, a placebo—which relies on your belief that a medically inert substance in fact has medicinal value—activates some of the same brain structures as do drugs such as morphine (Petrovic et al., 2002). In addition, although the parts of the brain that are activated when we feel pain are distinct from the parts that are activated when we *anticipate* feeling pain, the two sets of areas are very nearby (Ploghaus et al., 1999), which suggests that anticipating pain could interact with the real thing. And in fact, top-down processing can directly inhibit the interneurons that regulate the input of pain signals to the brain (Gagliese & Katz, 2000; Melzack & Wall, 1982; Wall, 2000). This **gate control** mechanism (as it is known) may explain how hypnosis can control pain (Kihlstrom, 1985); indeed, hypnosis can selectively alter our experience of the unpleasantness of pain without affecting how intense it feels. Hypnosis thus may alter processing in only some of the brain areas that register pain (Rainville et al., 1997). Inhibitory impulses from the brain to neurons that send signals from the body may also occur when pain is reduced by a *counter-irritant*—a painful stimulus elsewhere in the body (Willer et al., 1990). Such effects may explain how acupuncture, the placing of small needles to treat pain, works (Carlsson & Sjoelund, 2001; Chapman & Nakamura, 1999).

People differ widely in the amount of pain they can withstand; Rollman and Harris (1987) found that some people could put up with as much as 8 times as much pain as others. However, women at certain phases of the menstrual cycle have a lower threshold for pain (Hapidou & De Catanzaro, 1988). MacGregor and colleagues (1997) found that the threshold for pressure-based pain was highly correlated among twins, but this correlation was equally high for both identical and fraternal twins. Because identical twins share all their genes, but fraternal twins share only half their genes, the finding of the same correlation suggests that there is no substantial genetic component to pain thresholds. Instead, this common correlation is more likely a result of common family environment.

● **Paradoxical cold:** Occurs when stimulation of nerves by something hot produces the sensation of cold.

● **Double pain:** The sensation that occurs when an injury first causes a sharp pain, and later a dull pain; the two kinds of pain arise from different fibers sending their messages at different speeds.

● **Endorphins:** Painkilling chemicals produced naturally in the brain.

● **Gate control** of pain: The top-down inhibition of interneurons that regulate the input of pain signals to the brain.

Other Senses

Two additional senses are more controversial. One of these—magnetic sense—may not exist in humans, and one—extrasensory perception—may not exist at all.

Magnetic Sense: Only for the Birds?

Many birds migrate long distances each year, guided in part by the magnetic field of the earth. Tiny bits of iron found in crucial neurons of these birds apparently play a role in this sense (Gould, 1998; Kirschvink et al., 2001). Researchers have not only documented that at least some mammals also have this ability, but they have zeroed in on the crucial part of the brain that underlies it (a subcortical structure called the superior colliculus, at least for mole rats; Nemec et al., 2001). There is evidence that humans have a weak form of this sense (Baker, 1980), but the phenomenon has not yet been studied in enough detail to conclude with certainty that we all possess it. Magnetic fields have been shown to disrupt spatial learning in mice, at least for brief periods of time (Levine & Bluni, 1994). This is a sobering finding because the magnetic fields used in these studies were weaker than those commonly used in magnetic resonance imaging (MRI) machines.

Extrasensory Perception (ESP)

The ability to perceive and know things without using the ordinary senses is described as **extrasensory perception** (**ESP**, also sometimes called *anomalous cognition* or *psi*). Many forms of ESP have been asserted, including *telepathy*, the ability to send and transmit thoughts directly, mind to mind; *clairvoyance*, the ability to know about events directly, without using the ordinary senses or reading someone else's mind; and *precognition*, the ability to foretell future events. In addition, *psychokinesis* (PK), the ability to move objects directly, not by manipulating them physically, has also been reported (this ability does not derive from ESP proper, since it does not involve perception or knowing). Louisa and Joseph Rhine are often credited with beginning the scientific study of ESP and PK (J. B. Rhine, 1934; L. E. Rhine, 1967), and many experiments have been conducted in an effort to demonstrate the existence of the different forms of ESP (for example, Bem & Honorton, 1994; Haraldsson & Houtkooper, 1992). Many ESP experiments use the Ganzfeld procedure: Participants wear either half-pingpong balls over each eye or tight-fitting translucent glasses that allow only a blur to be seen; at the same time, they hear a dull hiss through headphones (Bem & Honorton, 1994; Haraldsson & Gissurarson, 1987). This procedure shuts off competing stimuli and thus, supposedly, increases the participant's sensitivity to ESP signals. Another person, sealed in a different room, tries to project an image of a particular card or scene to the participant, who later is asked to pick out the image from a set of alternatives.

Some researchers have argued that the results from some of these experiments suggest that the "recipient" can pick out the image "transmitted by the sender" more accurately than expected by chance (Bem & Honorton, 1994; Rosenthal, 1986). Nevertheless, most psychologists are skeptical about ESP and PK, for at least the three following reasons (Alcock, 1987, provides additional ones): First, the effects are difficult to repeat. For example, it wasn't long after Bem and Honorton (1994) claimed finally to have discovered how to produce

● **Extrasensory perception (ESP):** The ability to perceive and know things without using the ordinary senses.

reliable telepathy before Milton and Wiseman (1999a, 1999b) reported failures to replicate. To be fair, some ESP researchers have argued that such failures to replicate occur because the phenomena depend on personality, details of the setting, and other variables (Brugger et al., 1990; Honorton, 1997; Watt & Morris, 1995). But as more such qualifications are added, the harder it becomes to disprove the claims, and the field is thus nudged further away from science. Second, it is not known how the brain could possibly produce or pick up ESP signals or produce PK signals. Third, it is not known what form these signals might take. For example, physical energy (such as magnetic or electrical waves) typically declines in strength with increasing distance from the source, but there is no hint that the same is true for ESP or PK signals.

In spite of many years of hard work by many dedicated scientists, this field remains highly controversial (Bem & Honorton, 1994; Child, 1985; Thalbourne, 1989).

Looking *at* Levels

Is Body Odor a Problem?

Can culture affect senses as basic as smell? It can, and it does. Norwegians are less compulsive about eliminating all trace of natural human odors than are Americans (who, according to the *Los Angeles Times*, spent about $6 billion in 1997 on products to eliminate or mask body odor). Hence, the garments of Norwegians often retain more body odor than ours typically do. A young child, when his or her mother is gone, is sometimes given one of the mother's blouses to smell and is said to be comforted by this smell. To our knowledge, no rigorous studies of this phenomenon have been done, but observation alone is sufficient to make our point—that the interpretation of smell is in large part determined by cultural norms. In a pinch, one could probably hand the child a blouse from the mother's sister; Porter (1991) showed that people who share more genes also have more similar body odors. Body odor arises mostly from chemicals (specifically, steroids) produced by the sweat glands, and the genes determine the composition of these chemicals. Bacteria, which digest the chemicals, then produce the odor. Bartoshuk and Beauchamp (1994) have identified the genes that produce the distinguishing characteristics of body odor. Perhaps fortunately, simply living with someone will not make your body odor similar to his or hers, or vice versa (Porter et al., 1985).

So, consider the problem of body odor: It is only a problem if the culture defines it as such. If a person believes it is a problem, he or she will act accordingly—by buying deodorants (or feeling embarrassed). Consider the interactions among events at the different levels: If you feel threatened, the sympathetic branch of your autonomic nervous system is activated, producing sweat. The sweat contains chemicals that feed the ever-present bacteria, which produce more odor. The smell, in turn, at least in the United States, may make others turn away from you.

TEST YOURSELF!

1. How does the sense of smell work?
2. How does the sense of taste work?
3. How do we sense our bodies?
4. Do a magnetic sense and extrasensory perception (ESP) exist?

CONSOLIDATE!

Vision

- Vision begins with light, which consists of physical energy of certain wavelengths.

- The retina, a thin sheet of tissue at the back of the eye, contains types of cells that convert light to nerve impulses.

- Rods are sensitive to light but do not register color, whereas cones register color but are not as sensitive to light. Ganglion cells also transduce physical energy into neural signals, but these signals do not produce an image of the stimulus.

- The operation of the three types of cones (each tuned to be most sensitive to a different wavelength of light), in combination with the opponent cells, underlies our ability to see color. These neural signals are sent into the brain and initiate the processes of visual sensation and perception.

- Sensation is the immediate registration of basic properties of an object or event, such as its color, whereas perception is the organization and interpretation of the sensory input as signaling a particular object or event.

- You detect signals when they cross a threshold, but the level of that threshold depends in part on how hard you try to detect the signals. In addition, you can adjust your criteria so that you are more or less willing to guess.

- Visual perception can be divided into two main phases. The first takes the outputs from sensory processing and organizes them into sets of perceptual units that correspond to objects and surfaces.

- The Gestalt laws of organization (such as similarity, proximity, good continuation, good form, and closure) describe how the visual system organizes lines, dots, and other elements into perceptual units.

- The distance, size, and shape of figures are also specified in ways that do not vary when the object is seen from different viewpoints.

- The final phase of visual processing involves making the input meaningful.

- "What" and "where" are processed by separate neural pathways during the final phases of visual perception. In the "what" pathway, the input is matched to information already stored in memory, which allows you to know more about the stimulus than you can see at the time. In the "where" pathway, locations are coded, using either spatial categories or spatial coordinates.

- Perception relies on a combination of bottom-up processes, which are initiated by stimulus properties striking receptors, and top-down processes, which are guided by knowledge, expectation, or belief.

- Attention can be guided both by stimulus properties (bottom-up) and by personal knowledge, expectation, and belief (top-down). Shifting the focus of our attention usually allows you to detect signals more easily.

- When simple features are embedded in other simple features (like a red light in a sea of green lights), the stimulus "pops out" and attention is not necessary for easy detection.

- Finally, some information can be identified outside visual awareness.

THINK IT THROUGH Do you think "boosted" or enhanced sensory sensitivities would be an advantage or a disadvantage? (What if you could hear a pin drop 50 feet away, or you could see the dirt in the pores on a friend's face across the room?) In what ways would such superabilities be a benefit? a drawback? What if you were able to adjust your sensory sensitivity and bias at will? Would such abilities help an artist such as Frida Kahlo? In what kinds of situations would this power be desirable?

What do you think would happen if you had been born blind and suddenly had vision at age 50? Such cases have been studied in depth (Gregory, 1974; Sacks, 1995), and even though light was being properly transduced in the eyes, these people failed to realize they were viewing a human face (that of the person who took off their bandages) until the person spoke. Why? If you had to help such a person adjust after the sight-giving operation, what would you do? Why might part of your training involve attention?

Hearing

- Auditory sensation arises when you register sound waves—pressure waves that move molecules (usually in air, but also in liquids and solids).

- Sounds differ in pitch (which reflects variations in frequency) and loudness (which reflects variations in amplitude).

- For most frequencies, the ear uses the position of maximal activity on the basilar membrane to specify the frequency, but for low frequencies the rate of vibration of the basilar membrane may also indicate frequency.

- Hair cells along the basilar membrane, when stimulated, produce nerve impulses, which are sent to the brain. Hair cells that respond to specific frequencies can be impaired by exposure to loud sounds.

- The primary auditory area (the first cortical area to receive auditory input) is laid out as a strip, and the location of activation in this area depends on the frequency of the sound.

- Auditory perception begins with processes that organize sound into units and specify the locations of those units in space. Sounds are organized using Gestalt principles (such as similarity in pitch) and are localized using a combination of cues that rely on the two ears (differences in the phase, loudness, and arrival times) and cues that rely only on a single ear (loudness, distortions resulting from the shape of the outer ear, and changes in loudness resulting from movement).

- Auditory perception occurs when input matches information stored in memory. Top-down processing can actually fill in missing sounds, as occurs in the phonemic restoration effect.

- Not only can you understand speech sounds by accessing the appropriate stored memories, you can also understand environmental sounds (such as the meaning of a siren) and music.

- Some people can identify specific pitches, but most people identify only relative differences among pitches.

THINK IT THROUGH Will wearing a motorcycle helmet affect your ability to recognize sounds and localize them to the same extent? Why or why not? If one side of the helmet were made of thicker plastic than the other, which cues would be most affected?

Do you think that the way a musician looks or behaves when he or she is performing could influence the way the music sounds? How could this occur?

Sensing and Perceiving in Other Ways

- The senses of smell and taste are considered to be the "chemical senses" because they detect the presence of particular chemicals.

- Both smell and taste involve a lock-and-key arrangement in which the right molecule triggers a specific receptor, which in turn sends neural signals to the brain. Both smell and taste rely on combinations of receptors being activated.

- Instead of the traditional five senses, you have at least nine, and possibly up to eleven: In addition to sight, hearing, smell, taste, and touch, you have a kinesthetic sense, vestibular sense, temperature sensitivity, pain sense, and possibly a magnetic sense.

- These additional senses all inform you about the state of your bodies (where limbs are located, how we are positioned or located, what is touching us or otherwise affecting our skin).

- Each part of the skin is mapped out on the somatosensory cortex, with the amount of brain surface reflecting the relative sensitivity in that region.

- Pain is registered by two different systems, which can produce the feeling of double pain. Top-down processing can affect interneurons involved in pain, allowing your beliefs and desires to affect the degree to which you feel pain.

- Finally, some researchers have argued that extrasensory perception (ESP) exists. However, the evidence for ESP is shaky, and there has yet to be a reliable demonstration that any form of ESP actually exists.

THINK IT THROUGH Say your uncle is a food fanatic, loving every morsel and seeking out only the best. Should you recommend that he blow his nose before each meal and not waste his money going to fancy restaurants when he has a bad cold? Why or why not?

Should researchers spend time studying ESP instead of studying the nature of learning, reasoning, or the ordinary senses? What are the potential pros and cons of studying ESP rather than abilities that clearly are used by everyone every day?

Key Terms

absolute pitch, p. 158
absolute threshold, p. 124
accommodation, p. 126
afterimage, p. 131
amplitude, p. 126
attention, p. 145
attentional blink, p. 150
bias, p. 125
binocular cues, p. 137
bottom up processing, p. 142
categorical perception, p. 155
chemical senses, p. 159
cocktail party phenomenon, p. 157
color blindness, p. 132
color constancy, p. 137
conduction deafness, p. 154
cones, p. 128
cornea, p. 127
dark adaptation, p. 129
dichotic listening, p. 157

divided attention, p. 147
double pain, p. 164
endorphins, p. 164
extrasensory perception (ESP), p. 165
figure, p. 134
fovea, p. 127
frequency, p. 126
frequency theory, p. 153
gate control, p. 164
Gestalt laws of organization, p. 134
ground, p. 134
hair cells, p. 153
iris, p. 126
just-noticeable difference (JND), p. 125
kinesthetic sense, p. 163
loudness, p. 152
monocular (static) cues, p. 138

motion cues, p. 139
nerve deafness, p. 154
opponent cells, p. 131
opponent process theory of color vision, p. 131
optic nerve, p. 128
paradoxical cold, p. 164
perception, p. 123
perceptual constancy, p. 136
perceptual set, p. 143
pheromones, p. 160
pitch, p. 152
place theory, p. 153
pop-out, p. 145
psychophysics, p. 124
pupil, p. 127
repetition blindness, p. 150
retina, p. 127
retinal disparity, p. 137
rods, p. 128
selective attention, p. 145
sensation, p. 123

sensitivity, p. 125
shape constancy, p. 137
signal detection theory, p. 125
size constancy, p. 137
somasthetic senses, p. 163
speech segmentation problem, p. 155
stereopsis, p. 137
taste buds, p. 161
texture gradients, p. 138
threshold, p. 124
tinnitus, p. 154
tonotopic organization, p. 154
top-down processing, p. 142
transduction, p. 127
trichromatic theory of color vision, p. 130
vestibular sense, p. 163
wavelength, p. 126
Weber's law, p. 125

chapter 5

Tate Gallery, London/Art Resource, NY

Consciousness

Consider Lewis Carroll's classic tale *Alice's Adventures in Wonderland* through a psychologist's looking glass, and you may see it in a new light—not as a charming children's story but as a reflection on different levels and states of consciousness. Let's take a look at the story. A young girl, Alice, tumbles down a rabbit's burrow and finds herself in a fantastic, topsy-turvy world. There, animals speak English, regularly become invisible (and reappear), and wear waistcoats with pocket watches. Alice finds things to eat and drink, but they make her grow and shrink. Although she understands the *words* that the strange inhabitants say to her, rarely do their *statements* make sense. And, beyond all this, at times she feels not quite herself:

"Dear, dear! How queer everything is to-day! And yesterday things went on just as usual. I wonder if I've been changed in the night? Let me think: was I the same when I got up this morning? I almost think I can remember feeling a little different. But if I'm not the same, the next question is, Who in the world am I? Ah, THAT'S the great puzzle!" (Carroll, 1992, p. 15)

> "I wonder if I've been changed in the night? Let me think: was I the same when I got up this morning?"

Alice's situation immediately reveals one aspect of the nature of consciousness: It is a private, subjective experience, and one that can change so dramatically—from one moment to the next—that you may sometimes wonder, as Alice did, whether you are still the same person. Suppose you work intently for 10 solid hours in a windowless room, reading by the yellowish artificial light of a desk lamp. Finally finished with your research, you stumble out into the bright sunlight, dazed and disoriented. You feel distinctly different from the way you felt just hours before, when you were rested and full of vigor. This difference in feeling, like Alice's, is a difference in consciousness.

Why should psychologists care about consciousness? For one thing, our sense of the world and ourselves emerges from consciousness. **Consciousness** refers to our ongoing awareness of our own thoughts, sensations, feelings—our very existence. So a full understanding of what it is to be a person requires that we understand consciousness. William James (1890) argued that a "stream of consciousness" fills each moment of our waking lives (and even some of our non-waking lives); this stream of consciousness is "a teaming multiplicity of objects and relations," where individual sensations are crammed together and are often difficult to distinguish. Francis Crick, codiscoverer of DNA and subsequently a major theorist and researcher on the nature of consciousness, was asked by one of us what he meant by the term *consciousness*. He suggested the following exercise: "Hold both hands in front of you, but with one closer to you. Now look at the front one; now look at the back one. See how the front one seems different when you are focusing on the back one? That's what consciousness is all about." "Oh," his questioner remarked, "so consciousness is just attention!" "No," Crick replied with a tinge of amused annoyance, having no doubt heard similar responses before. "Consciousness is enriched by attention, but attention is not necessary for it." Crick and Koch (1998) develop this idea in detail and suggest that particular portions of the frontal lobes are crucial for consciousness.

Many researchers and thinkers have grappled with the very concept of consciousness. Consciousness isn't just about neurons; it necessarily involves subjective experience (Searle, 2000). The problem of consciousness breaks down into two parts—the "easy problem" and the "hard problem" (Chalmers, 1996). The easy problem is figuring out what consciousness is for ("easy" is a relative term!); the hard problem is figuring out the nature of consciousness itself, the nature of subjective experience. The easy problem is (relatively) easy because scientists already have tools for addressing it; the hard problem is hard not only because it is difficult to devise rigorous ways to study the raw stuff of experience, but also because it isn't clear how to conceptualize a theory of experience. Nevertheless, some researchers have begun to make progress even on this problem, using sophisticated types of introspection to study the nature of experience itself (Natsoulas, 2001; Varela & Shear, 1999).

Theories of the functions of consciousness abound. One influential theory suggests that consciousness plays a key role in allowing us to bring information together in novel ways (Baars, 2002). For example, the first time you drive a new route, you are likely to be aware of every turn, every stoplight, every landmark. But after a dozen trips, chances are you no longer notice them. (It can be surprisingly difficult to describe a familiar route to someone who's never taken it before.) What has changed? On your initial journey, new experiences required you to coordinate input and output in novel ways. But, as the experiences became habitual, the new connections you established between input and output allowed you to drive without the need to respond to stimuli that were no longer novel. Even after a hundred trips, however, if you unexpectedly found a tree lying in the road, your sudden consciousness of it would direct you to make the necessary response—and step on the brakes!

Other researchers argue that consciousness serves to bind our enormously complex perceptual and mental processes into a single coherent whole (Crick, 1994; Llinas et al., 1994; Singer, 1998; von der Malsburg, 2002). Still others focus on the idea that consciousness lets us know whether perceptual and mental processes are fitting together correctly (Kosslyn, 1992; Mangan, 2001). Yet other

● **Consciousness:** A person's awareness of his or her own existence, sensations, and cognitions.

researchers emphasize that consciousness plays a key role in self-awareness (Keenan et al., 2001), which in turn can help you control your emotions (Silvia, 2002).

One way to regard consciousness, in some ways an intuitive view, is as a single, central, internal lightbulb illuminating the mind. Philosopher Daniel Dennett (1991), however, argues against such a single "consciousness center." His view is supported by recent studies indicating that different parts of the brain appear to be involved in the experience of consciousness. Depending on exactly what a person is aware of at a given time, different parts of the brain "light up" as they are activated (Alkire et al., 1998; Barbur et al.,

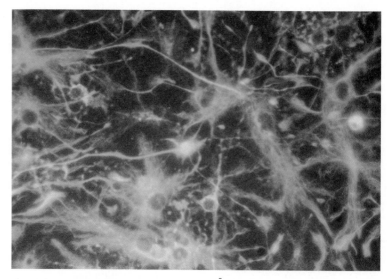

Edelman and Tononi (2000) argue that only complex, highly integrated patterns of neural activity give rise to consciousness.

1993; Bottini et al., 1995; Kosslyn, 1994b; Leopold & Logothetis, 1996; Vanni et al., 1996). But not all brain areas that are active when a person performs a task contribute directly to the experience of consciousness. In particular, consciousness apparently does not arise from activity in those parts of the brain that first register perceptual information, such as the primary visual cortex or primary auditory cortex (Crick & Koch, 1995, 1998). Instead, consciousness appears to rely on a number of areas in the brain (such as the right parietal lobe and frontal lobes) involved in the interpretation and integration of information (Bisiach & Luzzatti, 1978; Gazzaniga, 1995; Keenan et al., 2001).

The fact that many different brain areas contribute to consciousness helps to explain why consciousness is multifaceted and fluid, and why, at times, you experience yourself or the world very differently from the way you do ordinarily, in **normal consciousness** (also called *waking consciousness*). These **altered states of consciousness (ASC)** may be natural states, such as sleeping, dreaming, hypnosis, and meditation, or may be induced by substances such as drugs and alcohol.

In many cultures, inducing an altered state of consciousness is a socially acceptable, and sometimes even mandated, ritual. The members of some cultures, for example, enter into altered states through apparent communication with spirits or souls of deceased people. Others, such as certain Native American tribes, use hallucinogenic mushrooms and other drugs as the route to altered consciousness. Such practices are often considered sacred (Bourguignon, 1973). In Bourguignon's study of 488 societies, 90% had at least one "institutionalized," or culturally approved, altered state. One such case is that of a group of religious women in Trinidad. For one week, the women enter a period of "mourning," spending much of the time lying down, often in darkness and isolation. They also engage in praying, chanting, and singing. During the week, the women experience lifelike hallucinations (mental images so vivid that they seem real) and revelations into their spiritual lives (Ward, 1994). These same practices (periods of isolation accompanied by praying and chanting) are used by members of many cultures seeking to attain such altered states.

Although consciousness is a state we all experience, its definition can be tricky to pin down. The story of Alice and her experiences provides a springboard for an exploration of the nature of consciousness and its various facets. For example: Alice's adventures, we learn at the end of Carroll's book, have been only a dream.

- **Normal consciousness:** State of awareness that occurs during the usual waking state; also called *waking consciousness*.

- **Altered state of consciousness (ASC):** State of awareness that is other than the normal waking state.

One of Alice's disconcerting experiences in Wonderland is the often-changing size of her body—an experience that can be obtained through hypnosis. Might odd experiences like Alice's be the result of a meditative state? Do our heroine's adventures parallel the experience of a drug- or alcohol-induced state? Following Alice's adventures may help describe this shifting awareness of ourselves and the world around us that are part of what makes us uniquely human.

To Sleep, Perchance to Dream

Alice's story begins with an apparent change of consciousness on a hot afternoon:

> Alice was beginning to get very tired of sitting by her sister on the bank, and of having nothing to do, so she was considering in her own mind (as well as she could, for the hot day made her feel very sleepy and stupid), whether the pleasure of making a daisy-chain would be worth the trouble of getting up and picking the daisies, when suddenly a White Rabbit with pink eyes ran close by her. (p. 7)

It certainly appears that Alice is about to fall asleep, and perhaps by the end of the paragraph she has. As Alice's story closes, a crowd of the odd characters she met in Wonderland

> . . . rose up into the air, and came flying down upon her: she gave a little scream, half of fright and half of anger, and tried to beat them off, and found herself lying on the bank, with her head in the lap of her sister, who was gently brushing away some dead leaves that had fluttered down from the trees upon her face. . . .
>
> "Oh, I've had such a curious dream!" said Alice, and she told her sister, as well as she could remember them, all these strange Adventures of hers that you have just been reading about; and when she had finished, her sister kissed her, and said, "It WAS a curious dream, dear, certainly: but now run in to your tea; it's getting late." So Alice got up and ran off, thinking while she ran, as well she might, what a wonderful dream it had been. (pp. 97–98)

Stages of Sleep: Working Through the Night

Sleep is perhaps the most obvious example of an altered state of consciousness. Some people think that sleep is a single state, and you are either asleep or awake. Until the invention of the electroencephalograph (EEG; see Chapter 3) in 1928, that is what scientists used to think as well (Hobson, 1995). With the use of this new technology, they learned that **sleep,** a naturally recurrent experience during which normal consciousness is suspended, is not a single state. By using EEGs to record brain activity during sleep, researchers discovered several different types of sleep, which occur in five stages during the night. Everyone proceeds through these stages, but people differ in how much time they spend in each stage (Anch et al., 1988).

Stage 1

This initial sleep stage, lasting approximately 5 minutes and sometimes described as **hypnogogic sleep,** marks the transition from relaxed wakefulness to sleep. In Stage 1 sleep, your breathing becomes deeper and more regular, and the EEG registers brain waves that are less regular and of lower amplitude than those that mark the waking state (see Figure 5.1). You can be awakened relatively easily

● **Sleep:** The naturally recurrent experience during which normal consciousness is suspended.

● **Hypnogogic sleep:** Occurs in the first minutes of sleep and can include the experience of gentle falling or floating, or "seeing" flashing lights and geometric patterns.

FIGURE 5.1 Brain Waves During the Stages of Sleep

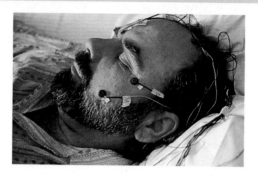

Awake

Stage 1

Stage 2

Stage 3

Stage 4

REM Sleep

Recordings show that brain waves differ by both amplitude (the height of the wave) and frequency (how often they occur). By examining individuals' EEG patterns when asleep, which differ from their EEG patterns when awake, researchers have identified five phases of sleep, each with its own unique EEG pattern.

from Stage 1 sleep and, if you are, you do not feel as if you have been asleep at all. In this stage you may "see" flashing lights and geometric patterns, experience a gentle falling or floating sensation, or feel your body jerk suddenly and rather violently in a movement called a hypnic jerk.

Stage 2

Once you are clearly asleep, your EEG pattern begins to record *sleep spindles*, brief bursts of brain activity measuring 12 to 14 Hz (a Hz is a cycle per second), and single high-amplitude waves (this pattern, known as the *K-complex*, is shown in Figure 5.1). You are now more relaxed and less responsive to your environment, although still relatively easy to awaken. But if you are awakened now, you will most likely report that you have been asleep. This phase lasts for approximately 20 minutes.

Stages 3 and 4

In Stages 3 and 4, your brain produces *delta waves*—slow, high-amplitude waves of 1 to 2 Hz on your EEG (see Figure 5.1). In Stage 3, 20 to 50% of EEG-recorded brain activity is in the form of delta waves; in Stage 4, the proportion is greater than 50%. In Stage 3, your heart rate and body temperature decrease, and you are no longer easily awakened. By the time you reach Stage 4, you are in a very deep sleep indeed, so deep that attempts by a friend (or an alarm clock) to wake you won't readily succeed. If you do wake up directly from this stage, you are likely to be briefly disoriented. During Stage 4 sleep, your heart rate, blood pressure, breathing, and body temperature slow down; all are now at their lowest ebb.

REM Sleep

About an hour after going to sleep, you begin to reverse the sleep cycle, coming back from Stage 4 through Stages 3 and 2. Instead of going all the way back to Stage 1, though, you now enter a state of *rapid eye movement (REM)* under the lids and, as shown in Figure 5.1, your EEG registers marked brain activity—even more activity than when you are awake. It is in this stage of sleep that you are likely to have dreams vivid enough to remember. During **REM sleep,** your breathing and heart rate are fast and irregular, and your genitals may show signs of arousal (men may have an erection; women may have increased genital blood flow and vaginal lubrication). These events occur in REM sleep regardless of the content of your dreams, unless a dream is particularly anxiety-provoking, in which case genitals may not be aroused (Karacan et al., 1966). During REM sleep, your muscles are relaxed and unresponsive; in fact, except for the muscles needed for the respiratory and vascular systems, your muscles are so paralyzed that you could not physically enact the behaviors in your dreams.

Sleep Cycles

After REM sleep, you descend again through at least some of the earlier stages, and then return, as shown in Figure 5.2. Each cycle takes about 90 minutes and occurs four or five times each night. However, the time you spend in each stage varies over the course of the night, and the course of a lifetime.

FIGURE 5.2 The March of Sleep Cycles

During the earlier part of the night, more time is spent in Stages 3 and 4, but later in the night, REM periods lengthen and Stages 3 and 4 shorten, eventually disappearing.

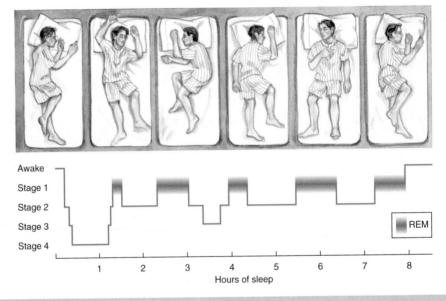

The phrase "I slept like a baby" turns out to have more truth to it than most of us realize. Infants sleep longer than adults (13 to 16 hours per night in the first year; see Figure 5.3) and have a higher percentage of REM sleep. They often enter REM immediately after falling asleep and change stages often. With age, this percentage changes so that when you enter your 40s, the amount of time spent in deep, slow-wave sleep begins to decrease. With less slow-wave activity, your sleep is shallower and more fragmented, you wake more easily, and the sleep you do get is less satisfying (Hobson, 1995). Stage 4 sleep is even less frequent as you move from middle age to older adulthood. With increasing age, the decreased slow-wave

● **REM sleep:** Stage of sleep characterized by rapid eye movements and marked brain activity.

FIGURE 5.3 Proportion of REM Sleep Over a Lifetime

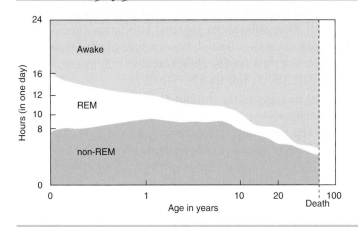

As we get older, we spend less time sleeping overall and less time in REM sleep.

Reprinted with permission from H. P. Roffwarg, J. N. Muzio, and W. C. Dement, "Ontogenic development of human sleep–dream cycle," *Science, 152,* 604–619. Copyright 1966 American Association for the Advancement of Science.

sleep and production of hormones involved in the sleep process make restful sleep difficult (Center for the Advancement of Health, 1998; Klinkenborg, 1997). As the quality of your sleep declines, so does its restorative effect on the cardiovascular and endocrine systems.

Suppose you share a bed with someone. Do you affect each other's sleep cycles? Yes. Because most people who share a bed go to sleep at around the same time, they are likely to enter REM sleep at about the same time during the night. And if one partner is tossing and turning, the other is less likely to fall asleep until the first one does (Hobson, 1995). Thus, bed partners tend to dream together—although not necessarily about each other.

The Function of Sleep

Why do we sleep? What purpose does it serve? Moreover, does not getting enough sleep merely leave you tired, or are there other negative effects? Research on sleep is beginning to piece together answers to these questions.

Sleep Deprivation: Is Less Just as Good?

In today's world of overscheduled lives and 10-hour workdays, can anyone claim to be getting a natural amount of sleep? A 2002 survey by the National Sleep Foundation found that two out of three people are not getting enough sleep (defined as approximately 8 hours), and one of those three gets less than 6 hours each night. Falling asleep in a dull class *may* signal sleep deprivation: "boredom doesn't cause sleepiness, it merely unmasks it" (Dement, as cited in Brody, 1998). What else happens when you don't get enough sleep, or miss a night's sleep entirely?

When you don't get enough REM sleep on a given night, a higher percentage of the next night's sleep will be REM sleep (Brunner et al., 1990); this phenomenon is called **REM rebound.** You can become REM deprived by not getting enough sleep at either end (going to bed late or waking up early) or by using

"WHEN I GROW UP I'D LIKE TO BE LIKE YOU, EXCEPT I DON'T KNOW IF I COULD SLEEP THAT MUCH."

Is this cartoon based on fact? How can we understand Dennis's comment if we know that children sleep more than adults, and *much* more than older adults?

● **REM rebound:** The higher percentage of REM sleep following a night's sleep deprived of REM.

depressants of the central nervous system such as alcohol or sleep medications, which suppress REM sleep. If these substances are used habitually and then discontinued, REM rebound dreams can be so vivid, bizarre, and generally unpleasant that people resume their use to fall asleep, and to suppress dreaming as well. Some people with posttraumatic stress disorder (victims of rape or assault, for example) cite disturbing dreams or nightmares (Inman et al., 1990) as a reason for using alcohol or drugs before sleep.

If you have ever stayed up late, say, studying or partying, and then awakened early the next morning, you have probably experienced sleep deprivation. In fact, you may be sleep deprived right now. If so, you have company: 40% of adults claim to be so sleepy during the day that daily activities are affected (National Sleep Foundation, 2002). In trying to determine the function of sleep, a common research method is to interfere with participants' sleep in some way, and see what the effects might be. What happens as a result of sleep deprivation? Young adults who volunteered for a sleep deprivation study were allowed to sleep for only 5 hours each night, for a total of 7 nights. After 3 nights of restricted sleep, volunteers complained of cognitive, emotional, and physical difficulties. Moreover, their performance on a visual motor task declined after only 2 nights of restricted sleep. Visual motor tasks usually require participants to concentrate on detecting a change in a particular stimulus, and then to respond as quickly as they can after they perceive the change by pressing a button (Dinges et al., 1997). Although you may be able to perform short mental tasks normally when sleep deprived, if a task requires sustained attention and a motor response, your performance will suffer. Driving a car is an example of such a task. In fact, in a survey by the National Sleep Foundation (1998), 25% of the respondents reported that they had at some time fallen asleep at the wheel; sleepy drivers account for at least 100,000 car crashes each year.

Moods are also affected by sleep deprivation (Dinges et al., 1997; Monk et al., 1997). Those who sleep less than 6 hours each weekday night are more likely to report being impatient or aggravated when faced with common minor frustrations such as being stuck in traffic or having to wait in line, and they were more dissatisfied with life in general (National Sleep Foundation, 2002). The loss of even one night's sleep can lead to increases in the next day's level of cortisol (Leproult, Copinschi et al., 1997). As mentioned in Chapter 3 (and discussed in more detail in Chapter 13), cortisol helps the body meet the increased demands imposed by stress. However, sleep deprivation can lead to a change in cortisol level that, in turn, alters other biological functions, creating an increased risk for diabetes. Chronically increased cortisol levels can cause memory deficits (Sapolsky, 1996) and decreased immune system functioning (Kiecolt-Glaser et al., 1995).

And, what about a series of all-nighters, when you get no sleep at all, as might occur during finals period? Results from volunteers who have gone without sleep for long stretches (finally sleeping after staying awake anywhere from 4 to 11 days) show profound psychological changes, such as hallucinations, feelings of losing control or going crazy, anxiety, and paranoia (Coren, 1996). Moreover, going without sleep alters the normal circadian rhythms of changes in temperature, metabolism, and hormone secretions (Leproult, Van Reeth et al., 1997). These findings are also seen in adult rats that are forced to stay awake. Within two weeks, they show major negative bodily changes; despite eating two and a half

Some students may stay up all night before an exam or a paper is due, but not without a cost. Sleep deprivation alters circadian rhythms, decreases immune system functioning, and temporarily impairs some cognitive abilities, such as maintaining prolonged attention.

times their usual amount, they begin to lose weight. Moreover, their temperature does not stay in the normal range, and they die within 21 days (Rechtschaffen et al., 1983). Even rats deprived only of REM sleep (they are awakened each time they enter the REM stage) experience temperature regulation changes, but these changes are less extreme (Shaw et al., 1998). Results of a PET study on sleep-deprived humans found a different pattern of brain activation when learning verbal material, compared to the pattern of activation when not sleep deprived, suggesting an attempt to compensate for the brain changes induced by sleep deprivation (Drummond et al., 2000).

Thus, sleep deprivation affects us in at least three important psychological areas: attention, mood, and performance.

Restorative Theory

One theory about the function of sleep is that sleep is important in helping the body repair the wear and tear from the day's events (Hobson, 1989). Support for this view comes from research on sleep deprivation and the adverse effects of lack of sleep. Moreover, in studies where participants were asked to discriminate among different visual stimuli, both slow wave sleep in the first quarter of the night and REM sleep in the last quarter of the night were crucial for visual learning: Participants deprived of these phases of sleep did not remember what they had previously learned (Stickgold, 1998; Stickgold et al., 2000). Thus, sleep not only "repairs" the body from the efforts of the day, but it is critical in laying down memories associated with at least certain kinds of learning.

Evolutionary Theory

Another explanation for the function of sleep is that it provided an evolutionary advantage—it kept our ancestors metaphorically off the streets and out of trouble. That is, sleeping removes us from potential life-threatening conflicts with predatory animals at night when humans do not have the advantage of night vision. Also, sleep (and its associated biological changes) allows energy conservation as the body's temperature lowers and caloric demands decline. In this view, when humans were not actively involved in securing and producing food (during the day), sleep provided the advantages of conserving energy and minimizing the risk of injury or death. Although interesting, this theory at present must be regarded as speculation.

Dream On

In addition to the biological changes that occur in sleep, there is a distinct change in consciousness—that of dreaming. It is *not* true that dreams take place only during REM sleep, but it *is* true that the dreams that take place during REM sleep are more memorable than those occurring during non-REM, or NREM, stages (Dement, 1974). If awakened during REM sleep, people recall dreams 78% of the time, compared with 14% recall during NREM sleep; moreover, NREM dreams are less vivid, less storylike, and less emotional (Farthing, 1992).

What Triggers Particular Dreams?

Although dreams may seem bizarre, disjointed, and nonsensical, their content is not necessarily totally random. President Gerald Ford once spoke the lines, "Thank you. Thank you. Thank you," in his sleep. He later told his wife, Betty, that he had dreamed he was in a receiving line (Seuling, 1978). By awakening dreamers at different stages of sleep and asking them about their dreams, or asking people to keep "dream diaries" at their bedsides, researchers have learned that certain types of dreams appear to be related to events occurring during the day (Hauri, 1970). Often these reflect the short-term lack of particular stimuli: Water-deprived people dream of drinking (Bokert, 1968), for example, and people socially isolated for a day dream of being with other people (Wood, 1963). Long-term deprivation seems to have a different effect, however: For individuals chronically deprived of an experience, over time there is a decrease in dreams related to the missing element (Newton, 1970).

Why Do We Dream?

Dreams can offer us a pleasant respite from the daily grind, bring us terror in the form of a nightmare, or leave us puzzled about their confusing or curious content.

Researchers and nonresearchers alike have long sought to know why we dream. The first modern dream theory was proposed by Sigmund Freud. Freud (1900/1958), convinced that dream content originates in the unconscious—outside our conscious awareness—dubbed dreams the "royal road to the unconscious." Further, Freud believed that dreams allow us to fulfill unconscious desires. Such *wish fulfillment* may not always be apparent from the **manifest content** of a dream, that is, its obvious, memorable content. We have to dig to find the **latent content** of the dream, its symbolic content and meaning, which, according to Freud, might reflect sexual or aggressive themes associated with an inner conflict. In this view, the manifest content of Alice's dream includes her specific adventures in Wonderland; the latent content, according to Freud, might reflect her underlying anxiety about the integrity of her body in general, and her sexuality in particular (Schilder, 1938). Although Freud's theory of the unconscious origin of the content of dreams has yet to be supported by solid, objective evidence, the idea of dream interpretation has both ancient appeal and present fascination—witness the large number of dream interpretation books and Web sites on the Internet. Can someone interpret your dreams? Although dream interpretation can be interesting and fun, it is unclear that any meaning inferred from the content of dreams is accurate.

Freudians find dreams brimming over with meaningful, albeit disguised, content. The opposite view is at the heart of the **activation-synthesis hypothesis,** which contends that dreams arise from random bursts of nerve cell activity. These bursts may affect brain cells involved in hearing and seeing, as well as storing information, and the brain's response is to try to make sense of the hodgepodge of stimuli (Hobson & McCarley, 1977), but the dreams do not disguise meaning, as Freud suggested (Goode, 1999a). The brain synthesizes the sensory images and activates stored information to create the experience of a dream. This theory would explain why dreams sometimes seem so bizarre and unrelated: Stickgold and colleagues (1994) asked people to write down their dreams and then literally cut their reports in half. They asked other people to reassemble each dream, deciding which half came first. This proved a very difficult task, a result that is understandable if dreams are merely attempts to interpret random activity and have no cohesive story line.

As part of his effort to understand consciousness, Crick also investigated dreams, which he believes are used to edit out unnecessary or accidental brain

● **Manifest content:** The obvious, memorable content of a dream.

● **Latent content:** The symbolic content and meaning of a dream.

● **Activation-synthesis hypothesis:** The theory that dreams arise from random bursts of nerve cell activity, which may affect brain cells involved in hearing and seeing; the brain attempts to make sense of this hodgepodge of stimuli, resulting in the experience of dreams.

connections formed during the day (Crick & Mitchison, 1983, 1986). Other theories of dreaming focus on the reverse notion: that dreams are used to *strengthen* useful connections. This view is supported by a study by Karni and colleagues (1994). Participants learned to discriminate between two visual stimuli before falling asleep; those who slept normally improved their performance on the task when tested the following morning. But participants who were awakened when they entered REM sleep did not improve when tested in the morning. In contrast, participants who slept but were deprived of slow-wave, Stage 4 sleep showed normal learning—which suggests that REM sleep is crucial for cementing in memory information gleaned during the day. However, more

In some societies, such as the Maya, telling dreams to others can provide a way to communicate feelings or solve problems (Degarrod, 1990; Tedlock, 1992).

recent research suggests that such memories do not absolutely depend on REM; at least in some circumstances, slow-wave sleep may play a role (Stickgold, 1998; Stickgold et al., 2000).

The largest and most systematic study of the neurological bases of dreaming was reported by Solms (1997), of the London Hospital Medical College. Solms interviewed more than 350 stroke patients about the changed nature of their dreams after their strokes. Consistent with the idea that consciousness arises from many parts of the brain, Solms found that dreaming was affected by damage to any number of brain areas. Perhaps Solms's most intriguing discovery was that dreaming stopped completely if a patient had damage that disconnected parts of the frontal cortex from the brainstem and the limbic system. These connections coordinate brain areas involved in curiosity, interest, and alert involvement with goals in the world (Panskepp, 1985, cited in Solms, 1997). This finding suggests that dreaming is not simply the brain giving itself a neurological tune-up, but is connected with our needs, goals, and desires. Solms speculates that dreaming may occur in response to any type of arousal that activates brain structures involved in motivation (Goode, 1999a). However, the inhibiting mechanisms of sleep prevent us from acting on these thoughts or desires, thus converting them into symbolic hallucinations.

So, although we cannot yet definitively answer *why* we dream, we do know something about *how* we dream. We know that dreaming is a neurological process, involving brain activity. We don't know whether dreams represent deep desires and conflicts, random bursts of nerve cell activity, the editing of unneeded neural connections, or the strengthening of neural connections. But it is interesting that all of these theories, despite their differences, agree that in some way the day's events, or the neural connections they instigate, affect dreams.

The Brain Asleep

We spend about one third of our lives asleep. During that time our brains and bodies are working away, responding to outside stimuli such as light and dark, and sending out fluctuating levels of neurotransmitters and hormones. These chemical changes are crucial to our daily functioning.

● **Circadian rhythms:** The body's daily fluctuations in response to the dark and light cycle, which affects blood pressure, pulse rate, body temperature, blood sugar level, hormone levels, and metabolism.

● **Suprachiasmatic nucleus (SCN):** A small part of the hypothalamus just above the optic chiasm that registers changes in light, which lead to production of hormones that regulate various bodily functions.

The Chemistry of Sleep: Ups and Downs

When you are awake, the cells in the system that release the neurotransmitter acetylcholine are inhibited, but when you are in REM sleep, they are activated (Hobson et al., 2000; McCarley & Hobson, 1975). Your dreams of walking, flying, or falling may occur because of the increased acetylcholine during REM, which activates the motor and visual areas of your brain and may cause you to dream of a wild roller-coaster ride or other types of motion (Hobson, 1995). Moreover, the cells in parts of your brainstem that release other neurotransmitters, specifically serotonin and norepinephrine, are most active when you are awake. Sleeping pills work in part by blocking production of these two "wake-up" neurotransmitters (Garcia-Arraras & Pappenheimer, 1983).

The hormone melatonin, which is secreted by the pineal gland, plays a role in promoting sleep. The body normally begins secreting melatonin around dusk, tapering off production at dawn; this cycle appears to be regulated, at least in part, by a recently discovered type of light receptor in the eye (Brainard et al., 2001). A person who takes melatonin in pill form may soon feel drowsy and, if undisturbed, may fall asleep within half an hour. Unlike other sleep aids, melatonin appears to induce a natural sleep, with the appropriate amount and time of REM and NREM sleep (Zhdanova & Wurtman, 1996). Some have argued that taking melatonin at the right times can help a traveler overcome jet lag, but this effect has not yet been demonstrated scientifically.

Circadian Rhythms

Our brain activity and internal chemistry dance in time to the daily rhythm of light and dark in a pattern called **circadian rhythms** (*circadian* means "about a day"). Daily fluctuations governed by circadian rhythms include blood pressure, pulse rate, body temperature, blood sugar level, hormone levels, and metabolism. Every one of us has an internal clock that coordinates these fluctuations; this clock is regulated by a small part of the hypothalamus just above the optic chiasm, called the **suprachiasmatic nucleus (SCN),** which is illustrated in Figure 5.4. Through photoreceptors in the retina, the suprachiasmatic nucleus registers changes in light, which lead it to produce hormones that set the body's clock and regulate various bodily functions (Berson et al., 2002). Researchers have found a gene in mice that is responsible for the regulation of their daily clocks; tissues in the eyes and the SCN generate the signals that let the mice know, among other bodily functions, when to sleep and when to awaken (Antoch et al., 1997). The rudiments of circadian rhythms appear in human infants as early as 1 week after birth (McGraw et al., 1999).

What happens to the human sleep–wake cycle in the absence of external cues of dark and light (except for electric light, which can be turned on and off at will) and cultural cues such as clocks? Volunteers who have lived this way as part of a research project ended up living a 24.9-hour day. In a variant of this study, in which only

FIGURE 5.4 The Suprachiasmatic Nucleus and the Optic Chiasm

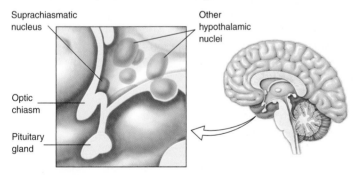

This illustration of a human brain shows the proximity of the SCN to the optic chiasm. Given the SCN's role in regulating circadian rhythms, it is not surprising that it is so close to the optic chiasm, which relays visual input about light and dark to the brain.

subdued lighting was provided, with no opportunity for stronger reading light, participants were more likely to have a 24.2-hour day (Czeisler et al., 1999).

But what about people who are completely blind and cannot detect light at all? They too show evidence of a 24.9-hour day, with 76% of the blind people studied reporting difficulty falling asleep at their usual bedtimes, based on a 24-hour day (Coren, 1996; Miles et al., 1977). Thus, the 24-hour schedule, so ingrained in us by the daily rotation of the earth, is not necessarily "natural" but instead is maintained by exposure to light–dark cycles, whether natural or artificial, and by cues from mechanical instruments such as clocks and radios.

Working Against Your Rhythms. Even within a 24-hour day, however, not everyone prefers to wake up or go to sleep at the same time. As you have no doubt noticed, some people are energetic and alert early in the morning, whereas others do not perk up until late morning or afternoon. People differ in the timing of their circadian rhythms: Morning people, or "larks," experience peak body temperature, alertness, and efficiency in the morning; evening people, or "owls," peak at night (Luce, 1971). Normally you are not aware of your circadian rhythms until you try to function well at your nonpeak time. If you're a night owl, for example, how do you feel when faced with a 9:00 A.M. class? Flying across time zones is bound to make you aware of your own circadian rhythms, especially if it's a long trip. Regardless of the time of day that finds you most alert, however, most people have a late-afternoon dip in energy level. More industrial and traffic accidents occur between 1:00 and 4:00 P.M. than at any other time of day (Klinkenborg, 1997).

Many cultures have a rest time in the afternoon, perhaps related to the circadian rhythm dip in energy during that part of the day.

Are you grouchy on a Monday morning? If so, it might be more than simply "waking up on the wrong side of the bed." Boivin and colleagues (1997), who studied mood and circadian rhythms, found that bad moods occurred during times of day when the participants' circadian clocks said they should be asleep. These results suggest that even minor alterations in a sleep schedule, relative to individual circadian rhythms, can have a noticeable effect on mood after awakening. Thus, if you go to bed later and sleep later on weekends, you may be adversely altering your circadian rhythms. You are, in a sense, putting yourself in another time zone for the weekend, so when Monday morning rolls around, you are hit with jet lag. Even fifth-grade children are affected by having to wake up earlier to go to school. Regardless of how much sleep they had, those children who had to be in school by 7:10 A.M. reported more daytime fatigue and poorer attention and concentration at school than those whose school day started at 8:00 A.M. (Epstein et al., 1998).

What can you do if your schedule conflicts with your natural circadian tendencies? One remedy is to sleep on a disciplined schedule 7 days a week. If, as in the case of jet lag, that isn't possible, try exposing yourself to plenty of light on Monday mornings; this may help reset your internal clock.

Shift Work: Work at Night, Sleep All Day. Can work schedules affect sleep? Just ask people who have worked the swing shift (4:00 P.M. to midnight) or

● **Night terrors:** Vivid and frightening experiences while sleeping; the sleeper may appear to be awake during the experience but has no memory of it the following day.

the graveyard shift (midnight to 8:00 A.M.)—a group that includes up to 20% of American workers (Klinkenborg, 1997). Some jobs even involve daily changes in the shift worked. Working during hours when you would normally be asleep can cause an increase in accidents, insomnia, and medical and psychological difficulties. The near-meltdown at the Three Mile Island nuclear power facility occurred after workers were placed on the night shift following six weeks of constant rotation; during their disastrous shift, they did not notice several warning indicators (Moore-Ede, 1982).

Researchers studying the effects of shift work have found that it is easier to switch to progressively later shifts (from the night to the day shift, and from the day to the evening shift) than to move in the opposite direction. In general, people differ in their ability to adjust to such schedule changes; those with a greater range of body temperatures in their circadian cycles have an easier time (Reinberg et al., 1983). If your work involves swing or graveyard shifts, one way to minimize the negative effects on your circadian rhythms (as well as on your social life) is to try not to stay on these shifts for more than 3 days (Knauth, 1997). This way, your sleep won't be disrupted by being on the night shift for extended periods of time, and you can still socialize with family and friends regularly. In addition, shift operators at an industrial plant who took planned naps of up to an hour while at work were more vigilant after the naps, and they viewed the naps as having improved their overall quality of life (Bonnefond et al., 2001).

Troubled Sleep

When a young girl like Alice falls asleep in the middle of the day, the reason is often simply drowsiness. In some instances, however, the cause may be a sleep disorder. Too much sleep, too little sleep, and odd variations in between can disturb our needed rest and, therefore, our bodily and psychological functioning (see Table 5.1). Sleep disorders stem from a number of causes, in particular, hereditary, environmental, and physical problems.

TABLE 5.1 Sleep Disorders

Disorder	Main Symptom(s)
Night terrors	Vivid, frightening experiences; the dreamer cannot be woken and does not remember the terrors.
Nightmares	Dreams with negative emotion; they may be remembered the next day.
Narcolepsy	Sudden attacks of extreme drowsiness and possibly sleep.
Insomnia	Difficulty getting to sleep, difficulty staying asleep, or awakening too early.
Sleep apnea	Brief, temporary cessation of breathing during sleep for up to 70 seconds, following a period of difficult breathing accompanied by snoring; the sleeper then startles into a lighter state of sleep and may have no memory of these events and may not feel rested after sleeping.

Night Terrors: Not Your Usual Nightmare

Most common among boys 3 to 7 years old, **night terrors** are vivid and frightening experiences. Night terrors occur in Stages 3 and 4, usually in the first third of a night's sleep. During a night terror, the child may sit bolt upright, screaming and sweating, and may be impossible to wake. In the morning, the child usually has no memory of the terrors, not even that they happened. For parents, however, the memory of their terrified child, eyes open and wild with fear, unresponsive to their attempts to comfort and help, is apt to linger.

Fortunately, night terrors usually subside as the child grows older. No one knows why they occur, although genetics plays a part: Night terrors can run in families. Night terrors are qualitatively different from **nightmares,** which are essentially dreams with strong negative emotion. Nightmares often take place during morning REM sleep; the dreamer can be roused during the nightmare and generally retains at least some memory of it.

Narcolepsy: Asleep at the Drop of a Hat

At the March Hare's tea party in Wonderland, Alice meets a Dormouse who is always falling asleep; occasionally he wakes, says something, then drifts off again.

> "Wake up, Dormouse!" And they pinched it on both sides at once.
> The Dormouse slowly opened his eyes. "I wasn't asleep," he said in a hoarse, feeble voice: "I heard every word you fellows were saying."
> "Tell us a story!" said the March Hare.
> "Yes, please do!" pleaded Alice.
> "And be quick about it," added the Hatter, "or you'll be asleep again before it's done." (p. 58)

The Dormouse could be suffering from **narcolepsy.** This sleep disorder causes sudden attacks of extreme drowsiness so powerful that the person with narcolepsy finds it almost impossible *not* to fall asleep, typically for 10–20 minute spells (American Psychiatric Association, 1994). Once asleep, people with narcolepsy often enter REM sleep almost immediately. The overwhelming drowsiness sufferers experience may be triggered by a large meal or intense emotions, but it can occur at any time—even during such inopportune moments such as while driving. A deficit in the neurotransmitter *orexin* (also referred to as *hypocretin*) appears to cause narcolepsy (Mignot, 2001). Behavioral treatment is often recommended, and stimulant medication may also be prescribed (Guilleminault et al., 1976); as orexin's role in narcolepsy is uncovered more fully, treatments involving orexin-based medication may be more effective than stimulants (Tuller, 2002). Like some other sleep disorders, narcolepsy tends to run in families, a sign that the disorder has a genetic component.

Insomnia

At the opposite end of the sleep spectrum from narcolepsy is a sleep disorder that may be more familiar to you, especially if you find it hard to get a good night's sleep. The symptoms of **insomnia** include repeated difficulty falling asleep or staying asleep, or waking too early. If you suffer from this disorder, you are certainly not alone. Half the adults in the United States experience occasional insomnia. Temporary insomnia may be related to environmental factors such as stress, which can cause increased sympathetic nervous system activity and can make sleep difficult. When sleep does not occur rapidly, the stressed person becomes frustrated. The frustration serves to increase arousal, compounding the problem.

For many Americans insomnia is a way of life. Chronic insomnia may stem from other disorders, such as anxiety and depression, as you will see in Chapter 14. Sleeping pills are the most common, but not necessarily the most effective, treatment for insomnia. They not only suppress needed REM sleep but also are addictive. Moreover, people develop tolerance to sleeping pills, requiring larger and larger dosages to get the same effect.

● **Nightmare:** A dream with strong negative emotion.

● **Narcolepsy:** Sudden attacks of extreme drowsiness.

● **Insomnia:** Repeated difficulty falling asleep, difficulty staying asleep, or waking up too early.

What can you do if you have trouble sleeping? The following nonmedicinal techniques may help (Hobson, 1995; Lacks & Morin, 1992; Maas, 1998):

Restrict your sleeping hours to the same nightly pattern. When living in the White House, both Martha and George Washington went to bed promptly at 9:00 P.M. each evening (Seuling, 1978). The Washingtons were on to something: Keep regular sleeping hours. Avoid sleeping late in the morning, napping longer than an hour, or going to bed earlier than usual, all of which will throw you off schedule, creating even more sleep difficulties later. And try to get up at the same time every day, even on weekends or days off.

If you have insomnia, lying in bed should only be associated with actually going to sleep, not with watching television or reading when you are unable to fall asleep. The person in the photograph should sit in a chair or sofa while watching television if he can't sleep.

Control bedtime stimuli so that things normally associated with sleep are associated only with sleep, not with the frustration of insomnia. Use your bed only for sleep or sex (don't read or watch TV in bed). If you can't fall asleep within 10 minutes, get out of bed and do something else.

Avoid ingesting substances with stimulant properties. Don't smoke cigarettes or drink beverages with alcohol or caffeine in the evening. Alcohol may cause initial drowsiness, but it has a "rebound effect" that leaves many people wide awake in the middle of the night. Don't drink water close to bedtime; getting up to use the bathroom can lead to poor sleep.

Consider meditation or progressive muscle relaxation. Either technique can be helpful (see Chapter 15). Regular aerobic exercise four times a week may be a long-term solution, but it can take up to 16 weeks for the effect on insomnia to kick in (King et al., 1997).

Sleep Apnea

Snoring can be a nuisance to those sharing a room with a snorer, but it can also be a sign of a more troublesome problem. As discussed in Chapter 2, **sleep apnea** is a disorder characterized by a temporary cessation of breathing during sleep, usually preceded by a period of difficult breathing accompanied by loud snoring. Breathing may stop for up to 70 seconds, startling the sleeper into a lighter state of sleep. This ailment, which affects 1 to 4% of American adults, can produce many such events each hour, preventing restful sleep (Klinkenborg, 1997). Perhaps this explains the results of a research study of medical students who snore versus those who do not: 13% of nonsnorers failed their exams, compared with 42% of frequent snorers (Ficker et al., 1999). If the snorers had sleep apnea, they would not function as well because of their troubled sleep.

Sleep apnea results when muscles at the base of the throat relax and consequently block the airway. In obese patients, weight loss can help reduce the obstruction, although normal-weight people also can have sleep apnea. Sleep apnea can be fatal, so treatment is imperative. A device called Continuous Positive Airway Pressure (CPAP) can assist a person's breathing while asleep; alternatively, surgery is sometimes recommended. In addition, recent research suggests that a complex interplay of heart rate, functioning of parts of the nervous system, and breathing may also influence sleep apnea: Men with heart problems and

● **Sleep apnea:** A disorder characterized by a temporary cessation of breathing during sleep, usually preceded by a period of difficult breathing accompanied by loud snoring.

implanted pacemakers who also had sleep apnea found that their apnea symptoms improved when their pacemakers increased the number of heartbeats by 15/minute (Garrigue et al., 2002). Finally, those with undiagnosed sleep apnea may take barbiturates to get a good night's sleep—this is unfortunate because barbiturates seriously compound the problem by depressing the central nervous system, interfering with the normal reflex to begin breathing again.

Looking *at* Levels

Recovery From Jet Lag

If you ever doubted that sleep, or its disruption, has an effect on consciousness, one good case of jet lag will convince you otherwise. *Jet lag* is that tired, grouchy, disoriented feeling you get after flying across different time zones. If you leave California on a 2:00 P.M. nonstop flight, after about 6 hours in the air (assuming the plane is on schedule) you will arrive in Boston, where it is about 11:00 P.M. local time—time for bed. But your body ignores the 3-hour difference between the Pacific and Eastern time zones and experiences the time as 8:00 P.M. You are nowhere near ready to go to sleep. And, come morning in Boston, your body will want to continue sleeping when the alarm says it is time to get up. The bodily changes, including altered hormonal and neurotransmitter activity, occur when your circadian rhythms are out of synch with the new time zone's physical and social cues. For example, your cortisol levels, which usually decrease before bedtime, are still high, and even if you do manage to get to sleep at what your body considers an early hour, the high level of cortisol is likely to lead to shallow and fragmented sleep (Center for the Advancement of Health, 1998).

How can you make a speedy recovery from jet lag? At the level of the brain, exposing yourself to light in the new time zone is thought to help reset the SCN in the hypothalamus, changing the levels of sleep- and wake-related hormones to suit the new time zone (Cassone et al., 1993). At the level of the person, motivation affects how easily you can adjust to jet lag (Bloom & Lazerson, 1988). Your willingness to get up in the morning when your alarm rings will help. In addition, exercise or activity can help shift circadian rhythms (Van Cauter & Turek, 2000). At the level of the group, adjusting to the new time zone's environmental and social cues for meal times and bedtimes, called *zeitgebers* (literally, "time givers" in German), facilitates the resetting of your biological clock (Van Cauter & Turek, 2000). Events at the different levels interact. Suppose you have flown east all night, leaving New York at 8:00 P.M. and arriving in London 6 hours later (7:00 A.M., U.K. time); further, you are meeting an old friend as soon as you arrive (which is the middle of the night to your body). You may be reasonably motivated to stay awake so you can enjoy your reunion over breakfast. But if no one is meeting you and you have no particular plans for the day, it may not seem worth the effort to ignore the activity of your neurotransmitters and hormones and try to stay awake.

TEST YOURSELF!

1. Brain and body function differently in sleeping and waking. What is the biology of sleep?
2. Why do we dream? Do dreams have meaning?
3. What happens when we don't sleep enough? What are sleep disorders?

Hypnosis and Meditation

When Alice fell down the rabbit hole, her descent seemed endless; she kept tumbling so long she thought she might be nearing the center of the earth. Although

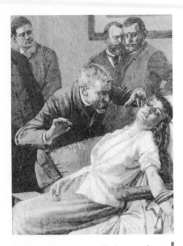

Franz Mesmer's technique of "manipulating bodily fluids" by repeatedly passing his hands near participants' skin successfully induced a hypnotic trance. Benjamin Franklin was part of a committee that used the scientific method to evaluate whether Mesmer's technique had the biological effect on patients that Mesmer claimed it did, namely that it unblocked electromagnetic forces in the body. The committee found Mesmer's theory to be unfounded.

- **Hypnosis:** A state of mind characterized by a focused awareness on vivid, imagined experiences and decreased awareness of the external environment.

- **Hypnotic induction:** The procedure used to attain a hypnotic trance state.

- **Trance state:** A hypnotically induced altered state of consciousness in which awareness of the external environment is diminished.

- **Generalized reality orientation fading:** A tuning out of external reality during hypnosis.

- **Trance logic:** An uncritical acceptance of incongruous, illogical events during a hypnotic trance.

- **Posthypnotic suggestion:** A suggestion regarding a change in perception, mood, or behavior that will occur *after* leaving the hypnotic state.

this feeling could have been a result of Stage 1 sleep at the beginning of Alice's nap, it's also somewhat similar to the sensations associated with one method of entering a hypnotic trance. In this technique, participants are asked to imagine gradually descending an elevator or staircase, becoming more deeply relaxed (and hypnotized) as they go lower and lower.

What Is Hypnosis?

When you think of hypnosis, you probably imagine a stage hypnotist speaking in a soft monotone, instructing a volunteer from the audience to look at a shiny pocket watch as it swings back and forth. The volunteer's eyelids grow heavier and heavier, he feels sleepier and sleepier. . . . Then, presto, he is hypnotized. At the hypnotist's suggestion, he will happily strut like a chicken, lie rigid between two chairs, or do the hula. Hypnosis as theatrical entertainment is rare. In fact, those whom the savvy hypnotist picks from the audience are highly hypnotizable, unlike some 90% of the U.S. population (Hilgard, 1965).

Scientific interest in hypnosis began in earnest in the 18th century when Franz Mesmer claimed to be able to heal people by unblocking their bodies' flow of electromagnetism. Although his healing technique seemed effective, his theories about how it worked did not stand up to scientific inquiry (Winter, 1998). Scientists are still trying to understand exactly how hypnosis confers its effects. **Hypnosis** is characterized by a focused awareness on vivid, imagined experiences and a decreased awareness of the external environment. The state is brought on by **hypnotic induction,** a process in which the participant is encouraged to relax and focus his or her awareness in a particular way, often with closed eyes.

Once you enter a **trance state,** an altered state of consciousness in which your awareness of the external environment is diminished, the hypnotist suggests that you focus your attention or alter your perception or behavior in some particular way, as illustrated in Figure 5.5.

There are at least two hallmarks of a trance state. One is called **generalized reality orientation fading,** a term used to describe a tuning out of external reality. As this occurs, you have a heightened awareness of "inner reality," your own imaginings and perceptions, and you experience this reality more vividly than in a daydream. Another hallmark of the trance state is the operation of **trance logic,** an uncritical acceptance of incongruous, illogical events, without being distracted by their impossibility. For instance, if you were instructed to imagine a place where you can feel safe and extremely relaxed, you might imagine a gazebo under a waterfall, or a beach colony on the moon. These images would come to you without your thinking twice about how such a place could exist or how safe it would really be.

Although these and other changes in awareness can occur because the hypnotist suggests them, they can also occur, with or without the hypnotist's suggestion, because of your expectations of the hypnotic situation (Kirsch & Lynn, 1999). People who expect their limbs to feel heavier during a trance have that experience, whereas people who don't expect their bodies to feel different do not, unless specifically directed to do so by the hypnotist. The hypnotist may also give you a **posthypnotic suggestion,** a suggestion for specific changes in perception, mood, or behavior that will occur *after* you leave the hypnotic state (see Figure 5.5, lower left).

People who are highly hypnotizable do not even have to be in the same room with the hypnotist to become hypnotized. A hypnotist on television once suggested

FIGURE 5.5 Examples of Hypnotic Alterations in Perception, Mood, Memory, and Behavior

Altered perception: The hypnotist says, "Imagine water splashing on your skin. Notice the sensation on your skin, the coolness of the water."

Altered mood: The hypnotist says, "While lying by the waterfall, you will feel very relaxed and peaceful."

Altered memory: The hypnotist says, "You will still remember the experience of the fire, but the fear and anxiety about it will become less and less over time."

Altered behavior: The hypnotist says, "Imagine magnets in the palms of your hands, pulling the hands toward each other."

to a volunteer in the studio that the volunteer's arm would become numb; a highly hypnotizable television viewer also became hypnotized. She lost feeling in her hand and did not come out of the trance state until she smelled the burning flesh of her own hand, which had been resting on the stove near an open flame (Kennedy, 1979).

Individual Differences: Who Is Hypnotizable?

Some people are more hypnotizable than others (see Figure 5.6, p. 190), and some people are more skilled at particular aspects of hypnosis than others. For example, some people can create extremely vivid visual images, whereas others are better at creating auditory, olfactory, or kinesthetic effects. Even those who are not very hypnotizable can go into a trance state if motivated strongly enough (Rossi & Cheek, 1988). In Western cultures, hypnotic ability appears to peak before adolescence and decline during the middle adulthood years. In contrast, in non-Western cultures, the ability to go into a trance state is often valued and encouraged throughout the lifespan, and thus does not diminish (Ward, 1994).

FIGURE 5.6 The Distribution of Hypnotizability

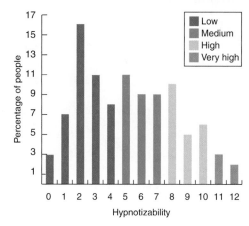

Not everyone is equally hypnotizable, and only a small percentage of people are *very* hypnotizable.

Hypnotizability is not highly correlated with biological indicators such as heart rate (Ray et al., 2000) nor with personality characteristics, such as shyness, emotionality, or thrill seeking. **Absorption,** or the capacity to concentrate totally on material outside oneself, is moderately correlated with hypnotizability (Council et al., 1996; Kirsch & Council, 1992; Tellegen & Atkinson, 1974). Some people seem better able to lose their awareness of themselves than others; these people become deeply engrossed when watching a movie or reading a book. In highly hypnotizable individuals, absorption may account for brief hypnotic experiences that can occur when driving on a highway for a long time or when watching a fire in a fireplace. Hypnosis also appears to be modestly related to "openness to experience," a willingness to experience new things. People with posttraumatic stress disorder also appear to be more hypnotizable. (Spiegel & Cardeña, 1991).

UNDERSTANDING RESEARCH

Hypnosis and Memory

The accuracy of information remembered while under hypnotic trance has been a controversial subject, in part because of its occasional role in eyewitness testimony and child sexual abuse cases. Psychologists are working to understand both the accuracy of people's memories when they are hypnotized and how confident they then become in those memories; the confidence with which they recount their memories can make a difference in jurors' perceptions of the testimony.

QUESTION: Joe Green and Steven Lynn (2001) asked two questions:

1. Does hypnosis enhance memory accuracy?
2. Does hypnosis enhance confidence in the accuracy of memories?

ALTERNATIVES:

1. Question 1 (*accuracy* of memories): (a) Hypnosis enhances the accuracy of memories or (b) hypnosis does not enhance the accuracy of memories.

● **Absorption:** The capacity to concentrate totally on external material.

2. Question 2 (*confidence* in the accuracy of memories): (a) Hypnosis increases the confidence in the accuracy of memories or (b) hypnosis does not increase the confidence in the accuracy of memories.

LOGIC:

1. Question 1: If participants who are hypnotized are able to recall events more accurately than those who are not hypnotized, then hypnosis should increase scores on a memory test.

2. Question 2: If participants who are hypnotized are more confident of their memories' accuracy, *even if the memories were not actually more accurate,* then the fact that they were hypnotized should increase their reported confidence in their memories.

METHOD: Ninety-six college students were asked questions about the exact date of 20 national and international news events from the prior 11 years, and they were asked to rate their confidence that their dates were correct, plus-or-minus 3 months of the event. Half of the participants were questioned after 20 minutes of hypnosis; the other half were questioned after performing a relaxation technique.

The participants in the hypnotic group were hypnotized using a standard procedure, and were then given the following instructions:

> "You are doing well. You are deeply hypnotized. Keep your eyes closed and listen carefully to what I say. In a moment, I am going to tell you to open your eyes and to complete the [test] booklet in front of you. You will remain deeply hypnotized as you complete the questions. When I tell you to, you will be able to open your eyes, think about each question, and write your answers while remaining hypnotized. It is very important that you do not talk or look at others' answers. When you are finished, close your booklet and then close your eyes and sit quietly."

After participants completed the test booklet, the hypnotic experience ended, and they opened their eyes.

The participants in the relaxation group were asked to close their eyes and alternatively tense and relax different muscle groups in their bodies in sequence (a procedure called *progressive muscle relaxation,* see pp. 625–626 in Chapter 15) and were then given the following instructions for visualization:

> "I want you to imagine a blue sphere and as you do you recognize that this sphere is very special because it can change its shape and turn into anything you want. It may turn into a beautiful landscape—perhaps of an ocean and a beach on a warm sunny day. Or perhaps, it turns into a beautiful meadow on a clear cloudless day. Take a moment and imagine this blue sphere gently changing into something pleasant and interesting."

After the questioning phase was complete (and hypnosis ended for those in that group) students watched an Introductory Psychology video while their test answers were checked for accuracy and, regardless of their actual accuracy, all students were told that they had gotten at least one answer wrong. They were then allowed to review and change their answers and asked to rank their degree of confidence in their revised answers.

RESULTS:

1. Question 1 (accuracy): The hypnotized and relaxed groups were equally accurate.

2. Question 2 (confidence): The groups expressed comparable levels of confidence in their answers both immediately after answering each question (before being told that there was at least one error) and after they revised their answers. However, those in the hypnotized group did not change as many answers when they were given the opportunity to do so.

INFERENCES: First and foremost, hypnosis did not enhance recall. But what about confidence in their answers? Green and Lynn suggest that hypnosis increased people's confidence in their memories (in that they changed fewer answers when given the opportunity to do so), although they did not *report* more confidence in their answers. The study's authors attribute this paradoxical result to prevailing beliefs that hypnosis can help people recover lost memories (and therefore they have more confidence in those memories); moreover, research suggests that people's behavior may be affected by the knowledge that they were hypnotized without their necessarily being conscious of this change in behavior (Green, 1999). If this interpretation is correct, then in this study, participants' assumption that hypnosis increases memory accuracy may have led them to have more faith in their memories than they themselves believed was appropriate—and hence the inconsistency between their reported belief and their behavior. These findings are consistent with those from previous research, which did find that hypnosis increased people's confidence in the accuracy of their memories, but not the accuracy itself (Steblay & Bothwell, 1994).

Hypnosis: Role Play or Brain State?

Do people really enter an altered state of consciousness during a trance? Or, are they behaving the way they think people behave when hypnotized? Psychologists have debated two major theories of how hypnosis works, and recent neuroimaging results help sort out these theories.

Trance Theory

One view, trance theory, focuses on the cognitive changes that occur during a trance (Conn & Conn, 1967; Hilgard, 1992). According to **trance theory,** someone in a state of trance in fact experiences an altered state of consciousness, one characterized by increased susceptibility and responsiveness to suggestions. As a result, the person is dissociated, or separated, from his or her normal level of awareness (that is, consciousness). When, for instance, people are successfully hypnotized for relief of pain, while in the trance they report that they feel no pain. If, however, they are asked to write about their experience while in the trance, some people *do* report experiencing pain. This "inner" experience has been attributed to the **hidden observer,** a part of the self that experiences (and can record) what the entranced part of the self does not consciously experience (Hilgard, 1992; Hilgard et al., 1978).

Sociocognitive Theory

Whereas trance theory suggests that hypnosis occurs because the trance state does in fact induce an altered state of consciousness, **sociocognitive theory** (Barber, 1969; Barber et al., 1974; Coe, 1978; Kirsch, 1999; Sarbin & Coe, 1972)

● **Trance theory:** The view that a person in a trance experiences an altered, dissociated state of consciousness characterized by increasing susceptibility and responsiveness to suggestions.

● **Hidden observer:** A part of the self that experiences (and can record) what the part of the self responding to hypnotic trance does not consciously experience.

● **Sociocognitive theory:** The view that a person in a trance voluntarily enacts the role of a hypnotized person as he or she understands it, which leads to behaviors and experiences believed to be produced by hypnosis.

focuses on the social context in which hypnosis takes place and the motivation to attend and respond to the suggestions of the hyponotist. In this view, the behavioral and experiential changes associated with a trance result from the hypnotized person's expectations of the hypnotized state rather than from a true trance. According to this view, the person in a trance enacts the role of a hypnotized person as he or she understands it, which leads to behaviors and experiences believed to be produced by hypnosis (Wagstaff, 1999). Thus, volunteers who are appropriately motivated can perform hypnotic feats even if they are not hypnotized.

Evidence From Neuroimaging

The sociocognitive theory stresses that hypnosis alters people's performance, not necessarily their consciousness, and does not presume a special cognitive state with distinctive changes in brain activity. Such a distinct internal state would be more in keeping with trance theory. Thus, important information about the nature of hypnosis can come from studies of the brain.

Studies done in the 1980s that recorded electrical current on the scalp found that hypnosis does alter brain events (Barabasz & Lonsdale, 1983; Spiegel et al., 1985, 1989), and more recent PET studies indicate that hypnosis changes specific brain states (Baer et al., 1990; Crawford et al., 1993; Sabourin et al., 1990–1991). However, most of the neurological changes observed during a hypnotic trance can be explained as arising from the *actions*, either actual or imagined, that people perform in hypnosis. To isolate the source of neurological changes more precisely, Kosslyn and colleagues (2000) showed that when highly hypnotizable people in a trance are told to view a pattern in color, a brain area that processes color is activated even if the pattern shown to them is actually in shades of gray. Similarly, if these people are told to see a pattern as shades of gray, a color area is deactivated, even if the pattern is brightly colored. Hypnosis could not only turn on or off this color area in accordance with what a person was experiencing (regardless of what was actually presented), but could also override the actual perceptual input. Clearly, hypnosis is not simply role playing or motivated behavior; people cannot intentionally alter brain processing in these particular ways.

Hypnosis as a Tool: Practical Applications

Hypnosis is much more than a stage trick; it has many therapeutic applications, including the treatment of anxiety, compulsive habit behaviors (such as smoking or hair pulling), certain medical conditions (such as asthma and warts), and stress-related problems (such as high blood pressure). Hypnosis has even been used to treat a particular complication during pregnancy. A study examined the use of hypnosis with 100 women pregnant with babies in the breech (feet first) position. One group was hypnotized and given the suggestion to relax bodily tensions and let nature take its course; another group did not receive hypnosis. The babies of 81% of the hypnotized women changed position to head first, compared with only 48% of the control group (Mehl, 1994).

Before the widespread availability of chemical anesthetics, hypnosis was used for the relief of pain (Winter, 1998). Pain can be controlled by top-down processing that directly inhibits the interneurons that regulate the input of pain signals to the brain (see Chapter 4); hypnosis is a particularly good way to affect this processing. Hypnosis is still used for pain control in many circumstances today—in the dentist's chair, the operating room, during childbirth, and at home and work

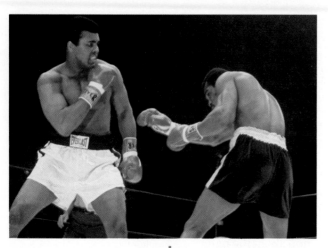

As part of his boxing training, Ken Norton used hypnosis before his match against Muhammed Ali (Spiegel, 1999). During that match, he broke Ali's jaw. Can hypnosis help athletes perform feats they would otherwise be unable to accomplish? No, but it can help them feel less anxious and free of distractions during competition, and it can help alleviate pain.

(Chaves, 1989; Hilgard & Hilgard, 1994). Hypnosis is used to induce relaxation before surgery, to lessen pain, and to speed healing (Forgione, 1988; Lang et al., 2000), as well as to alleviate tension and the fear of pain, both of which can worsen the *experience* of pain.

Hypnosis works to reduce pain by changing the way the sensation of pain is interpreted. Under hypnosis, a surgical patient might be led to experience an icy-cold numbness in the area where an incision will be made (Rossi & Cheek, 1988). Another use of hypnosis is to create imagined analgesia, or insensitivity to pain (Hilgard & Hilgard, 1994). For instance, one method used to treat headaches calls for the person in a trance first to create **glove anesthesia** (Barber & Adrian, 1982)—that is, to anesthetize the hand hypnotically. Once this is accomplished, the patient touches the painful part of the head with the anesthetized hand, transferring, by suggestion, the anesthetic effect to the head.

Hypnosis has also been used to enhance performance through hypnotic and posthypnotic suggestions; many athletes work with hypnosis consultants. Will a basketball player make more baskets or block more shots because of a hypnotic suggestion? Research findings reveal that hypnosis does not improve athletic performance per se but that it can help decrease anxiety, and thereby increase the athlete's focus; hypnosis also provides an opportunity for mental practice of athletic skills, a known benefit (Druckman & Bjork, 1994).

Meditation

In the last pages of *Alice's Adventures in Wonderland*, after Alice awakens from her dream and goes home for her tea, her sister remains behind under the tree. As she watches the setting sun and thinks about Alice's adventures, she too begins to dream, after a fashion, of the characters in Wonderland:

> So she sat on, with closed eyes, and half believed herself in Wonderland, though she knew she had but to open them again, and all would change to dull reality—the grass would be only rustling in the wind, and the pool rippling to the waving of the reeds—the rattling teacups would change to tinkling sheep-bells, and the Queen's shrill cries to the voice of the shepherd boy—and the sneeze of the baby, the shriek of the Gryphon, and all the other queer noises, would change (she knew) to the confused clamor of the busy farm-yard—while the lowing of the cattle in the distance would take the place of the Mock Turtle's heavy sobs. (pp. 98–99)

Might Alice's sister be in a meditative state? or simply a relaxed state of mind?

Types of Meditation

Meditation is an altered state of consciousness characterized by a sense of deep relaxation and *loss* of self-awareness, in contrast to hypnosis, which is characterized by ongoing self-awareness. Nevertheless, meditation and hypnosis do share similar elements. Both forms of altered consciousness involve increased, focused awareness of a particular signal. In hypnosis, this signal may be the hypnotist's voice. In meditation, the signal can be an object in the environment (such as a flower or a geometric pattern called a *mandala*), a rhythmic physical motion

● **Glove anesthesia:** Hypnotically induced anesthesia of the hand.

● **Meditation:** An altered state of consciousness characterized by a sense of deep relaxation and loss of self-awareness.

of the body (such as breathing), or a *mantra* (a chant or phrase that the meditator repeats). Whereas the person in a hypnotic trance often uses focused attention imaginatively and creatively, the meditator focuses attention on a single stimulus during the meditation period with the goal of clearing his or her awareness of other thoughts and sensations. Meditators experience a "relaxed, blissful, and wakeful state" (Jevning et al., 1992, p. 415).

A mandala is a complex circular geometric design used to facilitate meditation.

Prayer can be a form of meditation, as seen in the Buddhist and Hindu traditions. Other religions also incorporate meditative elements. For instance, Christians might focus attention on the cross, a verse of Scripture, or a mental image of Christ in a meditative manner. Rosary beads can be thought of as a meditative aid, helping to maintain the focus on prayer. In Judaism, the Torah may serve as the object of meditation, and many Orthodox Jews sway rhythmically while praying.

There are a number of other forms of meditation (Ornstein, 1986), all of which involve focused attention on an unchanging or repetitive stimulus. If you wanted to explore **concentrative meditation,** you would try to concentrate on one stimulus alone, disregarding everything else around you. Yoga and transcendental meditation (TM) are examples of this type of meditation. In **opening-up meditation,** a more advanced form of concentrative attention, you would focus narrowly on a stimulus and then try to broaden your focus to encompass your entire surroundings, almost as if you were merging with your environment. Both types of meditation bring about an altered sense of awareness or consciousness. **Mindfulness meditation** (also known as awareness meditation) is a combination of the two. Using this technique, you would try to maintain a "floating" state of consciousness, one that allows you to focus on whatever is most prominent at the moment. Whatever comes into your awareness—a physical sensation, sound, or thought—is what you focus on in a meditative way, fully aware of the stimulus but not judging it. In this way, everything around you can become part of your meditation.

For a sense of what a beginning meditator may experience, try the following exercise: Set a timer or alarm clock for 5 minutes and focus your attention on the word *one.* Close your eyes and try to clear your mind of distracting thoughts, sounds, smells, and sensations in your body; just focus on *one.* At the end of the 5 minutes, you may find that you have experienced a type of concentrative meditation. Another way to induce a meditative experience is to look at and focus on a crack in the ceiling or some other spot or object. As you do, try to maintain your focus on the object, letting distracting thoughts or sensations pass, and continually refocusing on your awareness of the crack. These suggested exercises may show you why meditation can be challenging for beginners; many people find themselves distracted by other thoughts or sensations and find it difficult to maintain their focus on the meditation. With practice, however, this type of focused attention becomes easier, and increasingly the meditator experiences the positive benefits of meditation.

HANDS ON

● **Concentrative meditation:** A form of meditation in which the meditator restricts attention and concentrates on one stimulus while disregarding everything else.

● **Opening-up meditation:** A form of meditation in which the meditator focuses on a stimulus but also broadens that focus to encompass the whole of his or her surroundings.

● **Mindfulness meditation:** A combination of concentrative and opening-up meditation in which the meditator focuses on whatever is most prominent at the moment; also known as *awareness meditation.*

- **Substance abuse:** Drug or alcohol use that leads to legal difficulties, causes distress or trouble functioning in major areas of life, or occurs in dangerous situations.

- **Substance dependence:** Chronic substance abuse that is characterized by seven symptoms, the two most important being tolerance and withdrawal.

- **Tolerance:** The condition of requiring more of a substance to achieve the same effect (or the usual amount providing a diminished response).

"Come, my head's free at last!" said Alice in a tone of delight, which changed into alarm in another moment, when she found that her shoulders were nowhere to be found: all she could see, when she looked down, was an immense length of neck, which seemed to rise like a stalk out of a sea of green leaves that lay far below her. (pp. 41–42)

Many of the odd things that happen to Alice on her travels in Wonderland occur after she has eaten or drunk something. She drank from a bottle labeled "DRINK ME" and shrank; she ate cakes labeled "EAT ME" and grew. And, of course, there's the famous mushroom. Could changes such as those experienced by Alice be produced by the use of stimulants, depressants, or other chemical substances?

Although neither drugs nor alcohol can actually cause our bodies to change shape the way Alice's did, they can alter our perceptions, mood, thoughts, and behavior. So far, we've discussed natural ways of altering consciousness such as hypnosis and meditation, methods that rely solely on the abilities and skills that reside within a person. But it's also possible to alter consciousness through external means, with the use of psychoactive substances. These substances, which can be ingested, injected, or inhaled, affect the user's thoughts, feelings, and behaviors. Some substances—marijuana, tobacco, cocaine, and alcohol, certain types of mushrooms, and caffeine—can be found in nature and have long been used to alter consciousness, often in the context of religious ceremonies (Bourguignon, 1973). More recently, synthetically produced substances such as amphetamines, LSD, PCP, and barbiturates have also been used as consciousness-altering agents.

Substance Use and Abuse

A woman drinks heavily, but only over the weekend, and she never misses work because of it. Is she an alcoholic? How about the man who smokes marijuana at the end of the day to feel relaxed, or the student who downs four cups of caffeinated coffee each evening while studying? Have these people crossed some biological or psychological line between use and abuse? The American Psychiatric Association (2000) has developed three main criteria for **substance abuse:** (1) A pattern of substance use that leads to significant distress or difficulty functioning in major areas of life (for instance, at home, work, or school, or in relationships); (2) Substance use that occurs in dangerous situations (for instance, while or before driving a car); and (3) Substance use that leads to legal difficulties.

Substance dependence results from chronic abuse. It is characterized by seven symptoms (see Table 5.2), the two most important of which are tolerance and withdrawal (American Psychiatric Association, 2000). **Tolerance** is the condition, resulting from repeated use, in which the same amount of a substance produces a diminished effect (thus, more of the substance is required to achieve the same ef-

TABLE 5.2 The Seven Symptoms of Substance Dependence

1. Tolerance.	6. Important work, social, or recreational activities given up as a result of the substance.
2. Withdrawal.	
3. Larger amounts of substance taken over a longer period of time than intended.	7. Despite knowledge of recurrent or ongoing physical or psychological problems caused or exacerbated by the substance, continued use of substance.
4. Unsuccessful efforts or a persistent desire to decrease or control the substance use.	
5. Much time spent in obtaining the substance, using it, or recovering from its effects.	

Source: American Psychiatric Association (2000). Reprinted with permission from the *Diagnostic and Statistical Manual of Mental Disorders,* Fourth Edition, Text Revision. Copyright © 2000 American Psychiatric Association.

fect). Tolerance typically occurs with the use of alcohol, barbiturates, amphetamines, and opiates such as morphine and heroin. Withdrawal is the cessation of the use of a substance; **withdrawal symptoms** are the uncomfortable or life-threatening effects that may be experienced during withdrawal. Substance abuse presents costs to society as a whole as well as to the individual: The costs related to crime, drug treatment, medical care, social welfare programs, and time lost from work total an estimated $67 billion per year (National Institute on Drug Abuse, 2003).

The various types of psychoactive drugs and their key properties are listed in Table 5.3.

TABLE 5.3 Psychoactive Substances: Their Biological Actions and Effects

Type of Drug	Example	Biological Action	Main Effects	Tolerance/ Withdrawal Symptoms
Depressants	Alcohol Barbiturates	Depresses the central nervous system.	Decreases behavioral activity, anxiety, and awareness; impairs cognition and judgment.	Yes / Yes
Stimulants	Amphetamines Cocaine	Stimulates the central nervous system.	Increases behavioral activity and arousal; creates a perception of heightened physical and mental abilities.	Yes / Yes
Narcotic- analgesics	Heroin	Depresses the central nervous system.	Dulls pain and creates an experience of euphoria and relaxation; with chronic use, the body stops producing endorphins.	Yes / Yes
Hallucinogens	LSD	Alters serotonergic functioning.	Hallucinations and perceptual alterations; the user's expectations shape the drug experience.	Yes / No
	Marijuana	Affects neurons in the hippocampus involved in learning, memory, and integrating sensory experiences.		For heavy users only: Yes / Yes

Depressants: Focus on Alcohol

The **depressants**, also called *sedative-hypnotic drugs*, include barbiturates, alcohol, and antianxiety drugs such as Valium. Drugs in this category tend to slow a person down, decreasing the user's behavioral activity and level of awareness. Because of its prevalence and the fact that so much is known about its effects, we focus at length on alcohol in the section.

Approximately 40% of adults in the United States report that they currently drink alcohol (National Institute on Alcohol Abuse and Alcoholism, 2001); 9% of adults in the United States (14 million people) are considered to have either alcohol abuse or dependence (Leary, 1997), and more than 5% are considered to be heavy drinkers. The younger people are when they start drinking, the more likely

● **Withdrawal symptoms:** The onset of uncomfortable or life-threatening effects when the use of a substance is stopped.

● **Depressant:** A class of substances, including barbiturates, alcohol, and antianxiety drugs, that depress the central nervous system, decreasing the user's behavioral activity and level of awareness; also called *sedative-hypnotic drugs*.

People's expectations of what will happen to them as a result of drinking alcohol can affect their behavior (Kirsch & Lynn, 1999).

they are to develop an alcohol disorder (Grant & Dawson, 1997). Binge drinking, defined as four or more drinks per episode, occurs on some college campuses, in some states more than others. College students in California are less likely to be binge drinkers than their counterparts across the nation, perhaps because California students are older on average and more likely to be married (Wechsler et al., 1997), and thus presumably more mature. Men are more likely than women to be binge drinkers (Schulenberg et al., 1996); women at women's colleges tend to binge drink less than do their female counterparts at coeducational colleges (Dowdall et al., 1998). Binge drinking is likely to occur in contexts in which the object is to get drunk (Schulenberg et al., 1996).

People who engage in binge drinking are also at risk for other alcohol-related behaviors, such as driving while their functioning is impaired (Wechsler et al., 1998), or having unprotected sexual intercourse or more sexual activity than planned (Center for Addiction and Substance Abuse, 2002).

Biological Effects of Alcohol

Alcohol is classified as a depressant because it depresses the nervous system through its inhibiting effect on excitatory neurotransmitters. Although the exact mechanisms are not yet known, alcohol changes the structure of the membrane of the neuron, altering neural transmission (Goldstein, 1994; Grilly, 1994). But depressants such as alcohol can also inhibit the action of inhibitory neurons, so some neurons fire that otherwise would be inhibited. Thus, in addition to depressing some neural activity, depressants also activate neurons that otherwise would not fire. This phenomenon is called **disinhibition.**

Although it takes about an hour for alcohol to be fully absorbed into the blood, drinkers can feel an effect within a few minutes. The effects of alcohol depend on the dosage. At low doses, alcohol can cause a sense of decreased awareness and increased relaxation, and the drinker may become talkative or outgoing. At moderate doses, the drinker experiences slowed reaction time and impaired judgment (which is why drinking and driving don't mix). At higher doses, cognition, self-control, and self-restraint are impaired, and the drinker may become emotionally unstable or overly aggressive. "Barroom brawls" often occur because a drunk patron misconstrues a casual remark that otherwise might have passed unnoticed. As the effects of the alcohol take hold, the drinker's responses are more likely to be out of proportion to the situation. At very high doses, the drinker can have a diminished sense of cold, pain, and discomfort (which is why some people drink when in pain). At these high doses, alcohol causes dilation of the peripheral blood vessels, which increases the amount of blood circulating through the skin and makes the drinker both feel

● **Disinhibition:** The inhibition of inhibitory neurons, which make other neurons (the ones that are usually inhibited) more likely to fire and usually occurs as a result of depressant use.

warmer and lose heat faster. Thus, heavy drinking in the cold increases the chance of hypothermia (that is, decreased body temperature) and frostbite. Such high doses can bring on respiratory arrest, coma, or death.

Psychological Effects of Alcohol

Steele and Southwick (1985) conducted a meta-analysis of the effects of alcohol on social behavior, specifically in "high-conflict" and "low-conflict" situations. The type of conflict considered here is within the person, between two opposing desires. Specifically, Steele and Southwick wanted to see whether the use of alcohol changes the way people behave when they experience such internal conflict. They found a pattern of what they called **inhibitory conflict:** If a person in a high-conflict situation was sober, his or her response was "both strongly instigated and inhibited"; that is, the person would both want to act and not want to. A person might very much want to engage in a particular behavior, but the consequences (moral, legal, social, personal) were great enough to inhibit it. After drinking, however, the same person would not restrain his or her behavior. And the more alcohol consumed, the greater the likelihood of engaging in the act despite societal or other sanctions. When the conflict level was low, it was still possible to inhibit the behavior; only in high-conflict situations was inhibition overcome by alcohol. This finding explains how date rape can happen: When sober, a man might want to have sexual relations but be inhibited from using force. But under the influence of alcohol, he might be more likely to act—in a high-conflict, sexually charged situation, he might have difficulty attending to the consequences that would otherwise cause him to inhibit such aggressive behavior.

Steele and his colleagues also looked at the effect of alcohol on conflict in helping situations (Steele et al., 1985). After doing tedious and boring paperwork for 30 minutes, participants in the study were asked whether they would agree to do more of the same, without additional pay, while waiting for the investigator to arrange for their payment. Some participants were given an alcoholic drink before the request for additional help, and some were given water. Some participants received more pressure to help (high-conflict), and some were asked simply if they would mind helping but were not pressured by personal appeal (low-conflict). In the low-conflict situation, alcohol had no effect, and participants were able to inhibit themselves from continuing the boring task. In the high-conflict situation, alcohol affected participants' ability to inhibit their response, and they were more likely to agree to help. This result is consistent with the earlier findings: Alcohol made it more difficult for participants to inhibit their responses in the high-conflict situation. This set of findings may explain why, after drinking some alcohol, people might have a harder time saying no to a sexual proposition in high-conflict circumstances, such as the conflict between the desire for sexual intimacy and the simultaneous wish (for either moral or personal reasons) to delay a sexual encounter. One solution is to abstain from alcohol if a high-conflict situation is likely to occur.

The results of many studies have shown that the use of alcohol facilitates aggressive behavior (Bushman & Cooper, 1990). You have already seen one path for increased aggression with alcohol use: Alcohol can make it difficult to inhibit behavior in a high-conflict situation. Aggression can also result from misreading a situation, as in the barroom brawl example. Alcohol impairs the ability to abstract and conceptualize information (Tarter et al., 1971) and to notice many situational cues (Washburne, 1956). This impairment results in **alcohol myopia,** "a state of shortsightedness in which superficially understood, immediate aspects of experience have a

● **Inhibitory conflict:** A response that is both strongly instigated and inhibited.

● **Alcohol myopia:** The disproportionate influence of immediate experience on behavior and emotion due to the effects of alcohol use.

disproportionate influence on behavior and emotion" (Steele & Josephs, 1990, p. 923). Thus, stimuli that elicit aggression (such as someone's clenched fists or a date's refusal to have sexual intercourse) loom larger than stimuli that must be abstracted or require more thought (such as considerations that the aggressive behavior may be immoral, illegal, or unnecessary). Drinking also makes it more difficult to process ambiguous social situations, such as occasions when someone's words and body language are contradictory. For example, suppose friends have gone out drinking and all are now quite drunk. One of them might announce he is sick, but laugh about it. The others might not understand that their friend really *is* sick and needs medical care.

Noting the fact that more than 50% of on-campus date rapes occur when men are under the influence of alcohol (Muehlenhard & Linton, 1987), researchers (Johnson et al., 2000) set out to determine exactly how drinking might be involved. They asked male volunteers to drink different levels of alcohol, then watch one of two videos of a woman on a blind date. In one video, she exhibited friendly, cordial behavior; in the other, she was unresponsive. The men were then asked how acceptable it would be for a man to be sexually aggressive toward his date (see Figure 5.7). Among the men who viewed the video with the unresponsive woman, alcohol intake made no difference in the men's answers. However, alcohol intake

FIGURE 5.7 Alcohol and Sexual Aggression

Male participants were assigned to one of four alcohol consumption groups: moderate alcohol intake, low alcohol intake, placebo alcohol intake (alcohol rubbed on the rim of glasses holding nonalcoholic drinks), and control group (drank ice water). The three alcohol groups did not know the strength of their drinks.

One group of men watched a video about a blind date in which the woman was very friendly; the other group watched a video about a blind date in which the woman was unresponsive and cold.

Regardless of alcohol intake, the participants who watched the unresponsive date were not very accepting of the idea of sexual aggression by the man, and attributed any responsibility for aggression to *him.* In contrast, there was clear alcohol myopia in those who watched the friendly date: The more alcohol they drank, the more the men accepted the idea of sexual aggression toward the woman, and the more they attributed any aggression by the man as being the *woman's* responsibility (Johnson et al., 2000).

did make a difference for the men who viewed the video of the friendly woman: Those men who had more to drink thought that sexual aggression toward a friendly date was acceptable. The alcohol impaired the men's ability to understand that the friendliness the woman showed did not mean that it was all right for a man to force her to have sex. This type of reasoning, which involves conceptualization and abstraction, was compromised.

Chronic Abuse: A Bad Habit

Alcoholics come from all socioeconomic classes. Historically, more males than females have become alcoholics, and this pattern continues today, although the gap is narrowing (G. B. Nelson et al., 1998). Almost all cultures recognize that drinking can create both tolerance and withdrawal symptoms, although problematic alcohol use is defined differently in different cultures (Gureje et al., 1997). Chronic alcohol abuse can cause severe memory deficits, even **blackouts,** periods of time for which the alcoholic has no memory of events that occurred while he or she was intoxicated. The chronic alcoholic often experiences difficulty with abstract reasoning, problem solving, and perceptual motor functions.

Different cultures have different social norms about what constitutes appropriate and inappropriate drinking. Moreover, in many cultures, people do not drink to "get drunk" but drink as part of sharing a meal and talking together.

It has been difficult for researchers to sort out to what degree these memory deficits are caused by the action of the alcohol itself or by the malnutrition that often accompanies alcoholism. Alcohol is highly caloric but contains very little in the way of nutrients; consequently, many heavy drinkers are inadequately nourished.

What does a hangover indicate? That the body is experiencing alcohol withdrawal (Cicero, 1978). This explains why drinking more alcohol will make hangover symptoms recede: After taking in large quantities of alcohol, your body needs more of it; otherwise, uncomfortable symptoms develop. Withdrawal symptoms for a heavy drinker include weakness, tremor, anxiety, and increased blood pressure, pulse rate, and respiration rate. Extremely heavy drinkers can experience convulsions and delirium tremens (the DTs), irritability, headaches, fever, agitation, confusion, and visual hallucinations; these typically begin within 4 days of stopping drinking (Romach & Sellers, 1991).

If you drink alcohol, answer these questions to see whether your drinking is problematic:

- Do you have a hangover the morning after drinking?
- Do you need to drink more now than you did 6 months ago to get the same feeling?
- Have you tried unsuccessfully to cut back on your alcohol intake?
- Have you ever had an accident during or after drinking?
- Do you spend a fair amount of money on alcohol?
- Have you missed work, class, or social obligations because of drinking or its after-effects?
- Do you find yourself thinking about drinking, or counting the time until it's a "decent hour" to have a drink?
- Have you had blackouts while drunk?

● **Blackout:** A period of time for which an alcoholic has no memory of events that transpired while intoxicated.

If you answered yes to any of these questions (particularly the first two, concerning tolerance and withdrawal), then you may have a problem with alcohol. You should seek more information from your doctor, counselor, or Alcoholics Anonymous.

Other Depressants

Barbiturates, including Amytal, Nembutal, and Seconal, mimic the effects of alcohol in that they depress the central nervous system. Barbiturates cause sedation and drowsiness and are therefore usually prescribed to aid sleep or to reduce anxiety, but they can be lethal when combined with alcohol. In higher doses, barbiturates cause slurred speech, dizziness, poor judgment, and irritability. Users will develop both tolerance and withdrawal symptoms: Withdrawal may be accompanied by agitation and restlessness, hallucinations, and delirium tremens. Sedation and drowsiness are also effects of benzodiazepines (such as Ativan, Xanax, and Valium, sometimes prescribed because they can reduce symptoms of anxiety). Because benzodiazepines are less habit-forming than barbiturates, the former are more frequently prescribed for sleep problems.

Stimulants: Focus on Cocaine

In contrast to depressants, **stimulants** excite the central nervous system, stimulating behavioral activity and heightened arousal. Low doses of amphetamines and cocaine can lead to a perception of increased physical and mental energy, diminished hunger, and a sense of invulnerability. Because "coming down" from this state is a disappointment, stimulant users often want to repeat the experience and so are at risk for continued drug use. Of all drugs, stimulants are the most likely to induce dependence.

Cocaine is commonly inhaled in its powdered form, and it has a local anesthetic effect. The user has an enhanced sense of physical and mental capacity and a simultaneous loss of appetite. Chronic users develop paranoia, teeth grinding, and repetitive behaviors and may also experience disturbances in the visual field, such as seeing snow, or feeling that insects ("cocaine bugs") are crawling on the skin. This latter sensation arises from the spontaneous firing of sensory neurons, caused by the cocaine.

Cocaine exerts its effects by inhibiting the reuptake of dopamine and norepinephrine (Figure 5.8). This increased presence of neurotransmitter in the synaptic cleft leads to a pleasurable, even euphoric, feeling. With continued use of cocaine, the drug becomes the main trigger for activation of the reward system, leading other sources of pleasure, such as food or sex, to have little or no effect (National Institute on Drug Abuse, 1998).

Crack

Cocaine in crystalline form, or **crack,** is usually smoked in a pipe ("freebasing") or rolled into a cigarette. Crack is faster acting and more intense in its effect than is cocaine powder inhaled through the nostrils; however, because its effects last for only a few minutes, the user tends to take greater amounts of crack than of powdered cocaine. Crack cocaine has more potential for abuse and dependence (Cone, 1995). The user experiences a feeling of euphoria, perceived clarity of thought, and increased energy. Crack increases heart rate and blood pressure and constricts blood vessels—a potentially lethal combination. After the drug wears off, the user experiences a massive "crash," with an intense depression and intense

● **Stimulant:** A class of substances that excite the central nervous system, leading to increases in behavioral activity and heightened arousal.

● **Crack:** Cocaine in crystalline form, usually smoked in a pipe (free-basing) or rolled into a cigarette.

FIGURE 5.8 Action of Stimulants on Neurotransmitters

Cocaine and other stimulants create their stimulant effects by blocking reuptake—preventing the normal reabsorption into the terminal button—of some norepinephrine and dopamine at the synaptic cleft. The net effect is more of these neurotransmitters in the synaptic cleft.

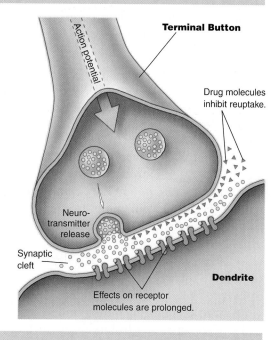

craving for more crack. Both cocaine and crack can create strong dependence, particularly if injected or smoked. The user can develop tolerance; with crack, the development of tolerance is particularly swift. Sudden death can occur even in healthy people who use the drug occasionally.

Other Stimulants

Amphetamines are synthetic stimulants such as Benzedrine and Dexedrine; they are usually taken in pill form or injected. With high doses, the user can suffer amphetamine psychosis, which is similar to paranoid schizophrenia (discussed in Chapter 14); symptoms include delusions, hallucinations, and paranoia. Chronic use of amphetamines stimulates violent behaviors (Leccese, 1991) and can cause long-term neural changes associated with impaired memory and motor coordination (Volkow et al., 2001). MDMA (also known as ecstasy, or "e") is a neurotoxic amphetamine—it destroys certain serotonin neurons. Research on animals indicates that MDMA, used even once, can permanently damage neurons that produce serotonin, affecting memory, learning, sleep, and appetite (Fischer et al., 1995). Many of the side effects that occur with other stimulants also occur with MDMA.

Caffeine is present in coffee, tea, chocolate, and colas, among other foods. It causes increased alertness, raises pulse and heart rate, and can produce insomnia, restlessness, and ringing in the ears. There is some degree of tolerance, and chronic users will experience withdrawal headaches if they miss their customary morning coffee. *Nicotine*, present in cigarettes and tobacco in any form, can cause increased alertness and relaxation, as well as irritability, increased blood pressure, stomach pains, dizziness, emphysema, and heart disease. Nicotine works by triggering the release of several neurotransmitters that lead to a pleasurable sensation. Nicotine is addictive, causing some level of tolerance and withdrawal symptoms when its use is stopped.

● **Amphetamines:** Synthetic stimulants.

● **Narcotic analgesic:** A class of strongly addictive drugs, such as heroin, that relieves pain.

● **Opiate:** A narcotic, such as morphine, derived from the opium poppy.

● **Hallucinogen:** A substance that induces hallucinations.

Alice wanted to be smaller and hoped to find a "book of rules for shutting people up like telescopes" (p. 31). Instead, she found a bottle (labeled DRINK ME) and, after drinking it, said, "What a curious feeling! . . . I must be shutting up like a telescope" (p. 31). This scene illustrates the effect of a user's *expectations* on his or her experience. Alice was hoping to find a way to shut herself up like a telescope, and that is just what she experienced after drinking the liquid. User expectations play a large role in the emotional tone of the LSD experience.

Narcotic Analgesics: Focus on Heroin

Certain drugs, including heroin, morphine, codeine, Percodan, and Demerol, are called **narcotic analgesics** because they are strongly addictive drugs that dull the senses and provide analgesia; that is, they relieve pain. These drugs affect certain endorphin receptors (see Chapter 4). Generally, drugs of this type are prescribed to relieve pain, severe diarrhea, protracted coughing, and troubled sleep. Heroin, an illegal drug, is one of the stronger narcotic analgesics. Like morphine, from which it is derived, heroin is an **opiate** (or *opioid*), produced from the opium poppy.

Heroin can bring about a feeling of relaxation and euphoria, but these effects are very short-term and are followed by negative changes in mood and behavior. Like other opiates, heroin is a central nervous system depressant, causing a slowing of neural activity in brainstem areas responsible for respiration and coughing, as well as in other areas of the brain. When heroin is in the body, the user may experience pupil constriction, slower breathing, and lethargy. Tolerance and withdrawal symptoms occur, usually with periods of yawning, chills, hot flashes, restlessness, diarrhea, and goose bumps on the skin, followed by up to 12 hours of sleep.

As well as activating the dopamine-based reward pathway in the brain, heroin and other opiates work by binding to the brain's opioid receptors, where the body's own opioids, such as endorphins, usually bind. This creates a negative feedback loop, leading the body to decrease its production of endorphins, and leaving the heroin user without natural means to relieve pain. Thus, more heroin is needed to achieve the analgesic effect. When the user tries to quit, endorphins do not kick in to alleviate the withdrawal symptoms, thus heightening the discomfort—and making it difficult to quit.

Hallucinogens: Focus on LSD

A **hallucinogen** is a substance that induces the perceptual experiences known as hallucinations. Although Alice's imaginings of Wonderland were a dream, other people, such as the 60s rock group Jefferson Airplane in their song "White Rabbit," inferred that Alice's experiences stemmed from a hallucinogenic drug. Hallucinogens include mescaline, peyote, psilocybin, lysergic acid diethylamide (LSD), phencyclidine (PCP), ketamine ("Special K"), and marijuana. In general, all but marijuana can cause visual hallucinations at moderate dosages; much higher dosages are needed before marijuana will do so.

LSD is a synthetic substance that produces perceptual alterations. Exactly how LSD works is not well understood, but it is known to alter the functioning of serotonin. Users commonly experience visual hallucinations, which often include geometric shapes, vivid colors, and violent movement. At higher doses, geometric shapes give way to quickly changing meaningful objects. Users may feel as if they are becoming part of whatever they observe. Auditory hallucinations include hearing invented foreign languages or symphonies. These symptoms may last several hours, and the user's expectations can shape the experience induced by LSD.

A Creativity Boost?

Although some people report that they feel more creative as a result of taking LSD, research does not support the subjective experience of increased creativity after use (Dusek & Girdano, 1980). On the contrary, LSD can produce frightening experiences ("bad trips"), which could be caused by a change in dose, mood, expectations, and environment. A user may panic during a bad trip and need to be "talked down," repeatedly reminded that the frightening experience is in fact a drug-induced state that will wear off. Occasionally, suicide or murder takes place in the course of a user's hallucination. Hallucinations can recur without use of the drug; these spontaneous, perhaps alarming, **flashbacks** can happen weeks, even years, afterward, and can be triggered by entering a dark environment (Abraham, 1983).

Other Hallucinogens

The most common hallucinogen in America is marijuana, whose active ingredient is tetrahydrocannabinol (THC), which is chemically similar to the naturally occurring neurotransmitters in the body called *cannabinoids* (such as anandamide). There are receptors for cannabinoid molecules throughout the body and brain, including in the hippocampus (see Chapter 3); cannabinoids can affect appetite, memory, and pain, and can modulate other neurotransmitters (Wilson & Nicoll, 2001). The effects of marijuana are dependent on the user's mood, expectations, and environment: If alone, the user may experience drowsiness and go to sleep; if with others, the user may feel euphoric. The effects of the drug can be subtle, including perceptual alterations in which sights and sounds seem more vivid. Distortions of space and time are also common, and perceptual motor skills may be impaired, making driving unsafe (Petersen, 1977, 1979; Sterling-Smith, 1976). Although marijuana is less powerful than most other hallucinogens, every year approximately 100,000 Americans attend treatment centers in an effort to stop using it (Blakeslee, 1997).

The substance ketamine, similar to PCP, is legally used as an anesthetic for animals. Use by humans can induce hallucinations, anesthesia, and stimulation of the cardiovascular and respiratory systems. Ketamine use is also associated with violence, a loss of contact with reality, and impaired thinking (White & Ryan, 1996). Users are likely to develop tolerance and dependence.

For people with glaucoma, nausea-inducing chemotherapy, or other medical problems, marijuana can ease some of the effects. Such medical uses of marijuana are convincing some people that marijuana should be legalized, at least for appropriate medical uses. Not everyone agrees with this position.

● **Flashback:** An hallucination that recurs without the use of a drug.

Looking *at* Levels

Princess Diana's Death

Whatever the full circumstances of the automobile accident that killed Lady Diana, former Princess of Wales, along with her boyfriend and the driver of the car, it is known that chemically altered states of consciousness played a role. The driver, Henri Paul, had a blood alcohol level of 1.75 grams per liter (more than 3 times the legal limit in France of 0.5 gram per liter); the antidepressant Prozac was detected in his blood, as well as tiapride, a medication commonly prescribed in France for alcoholics to ameliorate aggression and anxiety. Paul had been off duty for several hours but was called back to work at the last minute. With what you know about drugs and consciousness, you can see how events at the three levels of brain, person, and group might interact in this situation.

At the level of the brain, a high dosage of alcohol causes disinhibition, which creates slower reaction time and impaired cognition and judgment. At the level of the person, intoxicated people may have difficulty assessing their own abilities, feel euphoric and invulnerable, yet also be more aggressive or emotionally volatile. Paul would no doubt have been a poor judge of his driving ability. Thus impaired, chased by a horde of motorcycling *paparazzi* (level of the group), he would be more likely to fall prey to aggressive or impulsive behavior. Moreover, events at the level of the group led to his drinking: His social environment tolerated (or even approved of) alcohol use. These events would interact: For example, with inhibitory mechanisms impaired and in a tense social situation, the decision of how fast was safe to drive through a narrow, curving tunnel would not be grounded in a realistic assessment. And had Paul been part of a different social or cultural group, his alcohol intake might have been lower or nonexistent.

TEST YOURSELF!

1. What is substance abuse, as defined in our society?
2. What are depressants? How do they work?
3. What are stimulants? What are their effects?
4. What are the effects of narcotic analgesics?
5. What are hallucinogens? What do they do?

CONSOLIDATE!

To Sleep, Perchance to Dream

- There are five stages of sleep: Stages 1 through 4 (NREM sleep), and REM sleep, in which memorable, vivid dreams occur. REM rebound—a higher proportion of REM sleep—occurs on the night following deprivation of sufficient REM sleep.

- Although researchers do not yet know with certainty why we dream, various theorists have proposed that dreams represent unconscious desires (Freud), random bursts of nerve cell activity (Hobson & McCarley), the elimination of unneeded connections in the brain (Crick & Mitchison), the strengthening of needed brain connections (Karni), or an interplay of goals and desires, and arousal and inhibition (Solms).

- The content of dreams can be affected by certain types of events before sleep, such as thirst and the lack of social interaction.

- Lack of adequate sleep impairs performance on tasks that require vigilance and attention. Sleep deprivation also adversely affects mood and cortisol functioning (which, in turn, can affect learning and memory).

- Some sleep disorders, such as night terrors and narcolepsy, have a genetic basis; others, such as insomnia and sleep apnea, may have physical causes; still other types of insomnia are environmentally caused, such as those related to jet lag and shift work.

THINK IT THROUGH While trying to finish two papers, Antonio pulled two all-nighters in a row during finals week. It is the morning after the second sleepless night, and he has a final exam. What is his mental and physical state likely to be when he walks into the examination room? Which areas of functioning are likely to be impaired, and which are likely to remain undisturbed? What can you predict about the length and type of sleep Antonio will have when he finally sleeps?

Hypnosis and Meditation

- Hypnosis involves a tuning out of the external environment and increased attention and openness to suggestion. Aspects of consciousness that change with hypnosis are generalized reality orientation fading and trance logic. Hypnotizability varies from person to person.

- There are two theories that explain how people behave when hypnotized: trance theory and sociocognitive theory.

- Recent neuroimaging results indicate that hypnosis is not simply role playing, but in fact leads to a distinct brain state.

- Hypnosis has been used to treat a variety of psychological and medical disorders, including pain.

- Meditation, which focuses awareness on a single stimulus, generally brings a subjective sense of well-being and relaxation, along with such biological changes as decreased heart and respiratory rates and shifting EEG patterns of brain activity.
- There are three main types of meditation: concentrative, opening-up, and mindfulness.

THINK IT THROUGH Anna disliked her smoking habit and had been trying to quit for a year. Because her own efforts had failed, she decided to see a hypnotist. Can she be certain that the hypnotist will be able to hypnotize her successfully? How might the hypnotist use hypnosis to help her quit? If hypnosis helps her to quit smoking, how might the sociocognitive theory account for Anna's experience? If Anna smoked when she was stressed, might meditation help her stop smoking? Explain.

Drugs and Alcohol

- Depressants such as alcohol depress the central nervous system and can create an altered state of consciousness through disinhibition, decreased awareness, and an increased sense of relaxation. Disinhibition may make it difficult for the user to inhibit (or stop) behaviors in high-conflict situations that he or she would otherwise be able to prevent, and thus alcohol can promote aggressive behavior.
- Chronic alcohol abuse can lead to blackouts, as well as tolerance and withdrawal symptoms.
- Stimulants excite the central nervous system, leading to increases in behavioral activity, heightened arousal, and perceptions of increased physical and mental energy.
- The user of stimulants will "crash" after the drug wears off, become depressed and irritable, and crave more of the drug. Chronic use of some stimulants (such as amphetamines and cocaine) can cause paranoia and violence.
- Even moderate doses of hallucinogens (except marijuana) can cause visual hallucinations and perceptual alterations of other senses.
- The altered state of consciousness produced by a hallucinogen is influenced by the user's mood and expectations. Marijuana users may experience euphoria and relaxation. Flashbacks can occur after LSD use.
- Narcotics such as heroin act as an analgesic and also produce a sense of euphoria and relaxation; they are depressants of the central nervous system.
- Users of narcotics experience tolerance and extremely uncomfortable withdrawal symptoms; chronic use can suppress the body's production of endorphins.

THINK IT THROUGH A male, approximately 20 years old, was brought into the emergency room. He had been found in a local park, threatening passersby and muttering about bugs crawling on his skin. After waiting in the emergency room for an hour, he became extremely depressed and agitated. Assuming that he had no medical disorder other than drug use, what class of drug and what specific substance had he most likely taken? Suppose he hadn't complained of bugs but had trouble walking in a straight line and was slow to understand questions asked of him. What class of substance might be responsible for his actions? What specific substance?

In your opinion, did Alice exhibit symptoms only of dreaming? If not, what specific experiences lead you to suggest alternative hypotheses?

Key Terms

absorption, p. 190
activation-synthesis hypothesis, p. 180
alcohol myopia, p. 201
altered state of consciousness (ASC), p. 173
amphetamines, p. 205
blackout, p. 203
circadian rhythms, p. 182
concentrative meditation, p. 195
consciousness, p. 172
crack, p. 204
depressant, p. 199
disinhibition, p. 200
flashback, p. 207
generalized reality orientation fading, p. 188
glove anesthesia, p. 194
hallucinogen, p. 206
hidden observer, p. 192
hypnogogic sleep, p. 174
hypnosis, p. 188
hypnotic induction, p. 188
inhibitory conflict, p. 201
insomnia, p. 185
latent content, p. 180
manifest content, p. 180
meditation, p. 194

mindfulness meditation, p. 195
narcolepsy, p. 185
narcotic analgesic, p. 206
night terror, p. 184
nightmare, p. 185
normal consciousness, p. 173
opening-up meditation, p. 195
opiate, p. 206
posthypnotic suggestion, p. 188
REM rebound, p. 177
REM sleep, p. 176
sleep, p. 174
sleep apnea, p. 186
sociocognitive theory, p. 192
stimulant, p. 204
substance abuse, p. 198
substance dependence, p. 198
suprachiasmatic nucleus (SCN), p. 182
tolerance, p. 198
trance logic, p. 188
trance state, p. 188
trance theory, p. 192
withdrawal symptoms, p. 199

chapter 6

Réunion des Musées Nationaux/Art Resource, NY

Learning

Jackie Chan, actor, director, martial arts choreographer, and stuntman, begins his autobiography, *I Am Jackie Chan* (Chan & Yang, 1998) at the moment he is 45 years old and about to jump from the 21st floor of an office building in Rotterdam, the Netherlands, for his movie, *Who Am I?* The stuntmen on the film had only done the jump from the 16th floor, and Chan never asks his stuntmen to do stunts that he himself would not do. Jackie Chan did, in fact, jump from the 21st floor and land safely.

Chan had begun kung fu training in early childhood: his father woke him up each morning before sunrise and required him to work out for hours as the sun rose progressively higher into the sky. His father came from a long line of Chinese warriors, and had the view that "pain gives you discipline. Discipline is at the root of manhood. And so, to be a real man, one must suffer as much as possible" (p. 10).

Chan's early childhood years were spent living in the French embassy in Hong Kong, where his father was the cook and his mother the housekeeper and laundress; the Ambassador's youngest daughter was his friend, and he spent all day at home. When Chan was around 6 years old, he went to first grade, but had a hard time sitting still in the classroom. He was always making jokes and getting into trouble, often being forced to stand in the hallway, holding a desk over his head. Chan writes in his autobiography: "Sometimes I'd have to wear a sign around my neck, explaining the nature of my crime. Like, 'This is a noisy, ill-behaved boy.' Or, 'This boy lost all of his books.' Or, 'This boy has not done his homework.' Sometimes it would just say, in a couple of [Chinese] characters, 'Useless!' " Chan describes standing out in the hall as "peaceful." "And, if no one was looking," he says, "I'd gently put the desk down, lean against the wall, and catch a few winks. Learning how to sleep standing up was probably the most useful thing school ever taught me" (p. 16).

Jackie Chan found the process of learning to read and write tedious, boring, and difficult. He was not promoted to second grade, and did not return to school the following year, remaining at home all day with his parents. That year his father was offered, and accepted, a better paying job as the cook at the American

Embassy in Australia. Because of financial difficulties in relocating the whole family to Australia, his mother remained at her job as housekeeper at the French Embassy at Hong Kong, but Chan was getting too old to hang around with his mother all day.

"Learning how to sleep standing up was probably the most useful thing school ever taught me."

Before his father left for Australia, his parents brought him to visit Yu Jim-Yuen's Chinese Drama Academy, a residential school that trained students in the ancient art of Chinese Opera. However, this school was not like any acting or martial arts school with which you might be familiar. In fact, schools like this no longer exist in Hong Kong because the training methods are now considered abusive, with the children rising at 5 A.M., training in martial arts, singing, and drama, for more than 12 hours, then doing chores and perhaps receiving a couple of hours of traditional "school" a few evenings a week. The children went to sleep at midnight, on the hard wooden floor with only a blanket, in the same room in which they trained during the day. Their "day" was 19 hours long, 365 days each year. School discipline included being hit repeatedly with a cane, often past the point where blood was drawn.

Jackie Chan doing a stunt on his film *Tuxedo*.

Chan has undertaken many dangerous stunts in his career. Why does he put himself at such risk (so great, in fact, that no insurance company will provide insurance on his films!)? According to Chan, the answer is that he wants to please his fans; their approval is very important to him. Both Chan's ability to make the type of films he does, and the fact that the audience's approval is important to him reflect the capacity to learn—to learn skills and goals toward which to strive.

To learn is to discover, and the need to discover compels us from birth to the end of our days. Learning helps us both to survive and to realize our deepest dreams. It underlies virtually all of our behavior: what we eat and the way we eat it, how we dress, how we acquire the knowledge contained in books like this one, and how we live in a society with other people. And yet not all learning is positive in its results: Sometimes we "learn" to do things that either may not be good for us (such as when Chan does his own death-defying stunts?) or may not be what we wished to learn (as when Chan came to live out his father's view that manhood equals suffering). We can learn to do things that hurt as well as help.

Whereas many fields focus on the content of what people learn (historians add to their knowledge by finding out more facts about history), psychologists interested in the field of learning focus on the *process* of learning as well as the content. How does learning occur? To discover this, researchers have investigated both humans and animals and, in this chapter, we look at some of the principles their research has revealed.

What did Chan learn from Master Yu Jim-Yuen's beatings? How did he learn to do martial arts so successfully? How did the audience's response to his movies influence Chan's subsequent movies and his public behavior? Psychologists attempt to answer these questions, in part, through theories of learning.

Psychologists define **learning** as a relatively long-term change in behavior that results from experience. When, for example, you have mastered tying your shoelaces, you will likely be able to secure your shoes properly for the rest of your life. This durability is true of all learned behavior, in virtually every domain of life, from riding a bicycle to participating in a conversation.

But, what about the following case? Suppose you watch someone write your name in Chinese characters: Having seen it done, can you claim that you have learned how to do it? What if you are able to duplicate the characters successfully? Can you legitimately say that you have learned to write your name in Chinese?

In the first instance, unless you have a photographic memory and excellent drawing ability, the answer is probably no. Merely watching someone do something complex and unfamiliar on a single occasion is usually not enough to allow you to learn it. In the second instance, even if you copy the characters correctly, the answer is still likely to be no. Just performing an action once is not enough; unless you can do it repeatedly and without assistance, you cannot claim that you have really learned to do it. You may have learned some elements of the task, but not the entire pattern, and so you cannot claim to have mastered it.

Learning can take place in a variety of ways. The simplest form of learning is when repeated exposure to a stimulus decreases an organism's responsiveness; this is termed **habituation.** For instance, if you are walking in a city and hear a car horn honk nearby, you may well be startled; if other horns chime, you will not startle as much (if at all). Here's another example: When a wild animal, such as an elk, comes into contact with a human hiker (who does not scare the elk or try to harm it), that elk will habituate to humans; the next time a peaceful hiker comes by, the elk will likely allow the hiker to come even closer before it runs away.

Many other types of learning are by association—relating one object or event with another object or event. This general phenomenon is what psychologists call *associative learning*. This chapter will explore different types of learning. For all types, the criterion for learning is that we demonstrate a relatively long-term change brought about by experience.

Let's begin by exploring the model of associative learning investigated not quite a hundred years ago—classical conditioning.

Classical Conditioning

Unfortunately, Chan's early life was filled with adversity, often in the form of physical punishment. Within a few weeks of living at the Chinese Drama Academy, Chan received his first caning:

- **Learning:** A relatively permanent change in behavior that results from experience.

- **Habituation:** The learning that occurs when repeated exposure to a stimulus decreases an organism's responsiveness to the stimulus.

Master pushed me down to the ground and told me to lie flat on my belly. I closed my eyes and gritted my teeth. I felt my pants being roughly drawn down to my knees, as my belly and thigh collapsed on the polished wooden floor. Then a whistle and a crack, a sound that I registered in my brain just a flash before the pain raged from my buttock up my spine. (Chan & Yang, 1999, p. 38)

That whistling sound came to elicit fear in Chan; *elicit* means that the response (fear) is drawn out of the organism (in this case, Chan). When other students received a caning (in front of the rest of the students), the entire class would cringe on hearing the sound. This fear response (and cringe) is a complex example of classical conditioning.

In its simplest form, **classical conditioning** is a type of learning in which a neutral stimulus becomes associated, or paired, with a stimulus that causes a reflexive behavior and, in time, becomes sufficient to produce that behavior.

In Chan's case, the whistling sound of the fast-moving cane became paired with the extreme pain of the beating, thereby eliciting the fear and the cringe. The simplest example of the way classical conditioning works is found in the famous experiments that established the principle: the work of Pavlov and his dogs.

Pavlov's Experiments

Classical conditioning is also sometimes called *Pavlovian conditioning* because it was discovered, accidentally, by Ivan Pavlov (1849–1936), a Russian physiologist. As part of his work on the digestive processes, which won him a Nobel Prize, Pavlov studied salivation in dogs. To measure the amount of saliva that dogs produced when given meat powder (food for the dog), Pavlov collected the saliva in tubes attached to the dogs' salivary glands (see Figure 6.1). Pavlov and his colleagues noticed that even though salivation usually occurs during rather than

- **Classical conditioning:** A type of learning that occurs when a neutral stimulus becomes paired (associated) with a stimulus that causes a reflexive behavior and, in time, is sufficient to produce that behavior.

- **Unconditioned stimulus (US):** A stimulus that elicits an automatic response (UR), without requiring prior learning.

- **Unconditioned response (UR):** The reflexive response elicited by a particular stimulus.

- **Conditioned stimulus (CS):** An originally neutral stimulus that acquires significance through the "conditioning" of repeated pairings with an unconditioned stimulus (US).

- **Conditioned response (CR):** A response that depends, or is conditional, on pairings of the conditioned stimulus with an unconditioned stimulus; once learned, the conditioned response occurs when the CS is presented alone.

- **Acquisition:** The technical name given to the initial learning of the conditioned response (CR).

- **Trace conditioning:** A type of forward classical conditioning where the presentation of the conditioned stimulus (CS) ends before the presentation of the unconditioned stimulus (US) begins.

FIGURE 6.1 Pavlov's Apparatus for Measuring Salivation

Ivan Pavlov started out measuring saliva production in dogs as part of his research on the digestive system. He went on to use this same saliva collection technique with his investigations into classical conditioning.

before eating, his dogs were salivating before they were fed: They would salivate simply on seeing their food bowls or on hearing the feeder's footsteps.

Intrigued, Pavlov pursued the issue with more experiments. His basic method is still in use today (see Figure 6.2). Pavlov would sound a tone on a tuning fork just before the food was brought into the dogs' room. After hearing the pairing of the tone with the food several times, the dogs would salivate on hearing the tone alone. Because food by itself elicits salivation, Pavlov considered the food the **unconditioned stimulus (US)**—that is, a stimulus that elicits an automatic response and is not conditional on prior learning. The dogs' salivation is termed the **unconditioned response (UR)**, the reflexive or automatic response elicited by a US. The UR does not require learning, but it does depend on certain circumstances. For example, if an animal has just eaten and is full, it will not salivate when presented with food. In Pavlov's experiment, the tone is the **conditioned stimulus (CS)**—that is, an originally neutral stimulus that acquires significance through the "conditioning" of repeated pairings with a US. After hearing the tuning fork a number of times before they were fed, the dogs began to associate the tone with food. Thereafter, whenever the dogs heard the tone, even when presented by itself, they salivated. Salivation in response to the tone alone is thus a **conditioned response (CR)**, a response that depends (is conditional) on pairings of the CS with a US (Pavlov, 1927). Not surprisingly, psychologists call the initial learning of the conditioned response **acquisition.** In an attempt to see what factors might affect the process of conditioning, Pavlov and researchers after him altered the variables involved in creating a conditioned response. Initially, researchers thought that to create a conditioned response, the US (the food) must immediately follow the CS (the tone) in a procedure called *forward conditioning*, which occurs when the CS begins before the US begins. There are two types of forward conditioning. One is *delayed conditioning*, when the CS occurs both before and during the presentation of the US (see Figure 6.3, p. 216); an example with Pavlov's dogs would be when the tone sounds before and during the presentation of the food. The other type of forward conditioning is **trace conditioning,** when the presentation of the CS ends before the presentation of the US begins (Figure 6.3). A trace conditioning procedure used on Pavlov's dogs would occur if the food was not presented until the tone had already sounded and stopped. In general, trace conditioning is most effective if there is a very short interval of time between the CS and US (such as 0.5 second). If the food were presented 30 minutes after the tone, conditioning would be weak, if it occurred at all.

Pavlov tried the reverse order, called *backward pairing*, where the US comes first, followed quickly by the CS (Figure 6.3): He fed the dogs first and presented

FIGURE 6.2 The Three Phases of Classical Conditioning

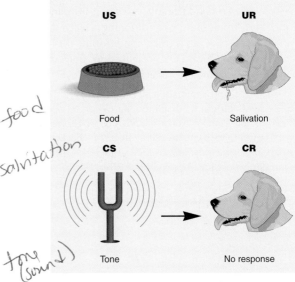
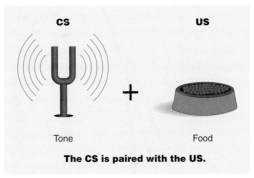
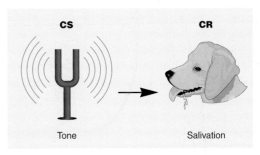

Before conditioning occurs, the CS does not lead to a conditioned response, but the US does. Then the CS is paired with the US—here, the tone is sounded and then the food is presented. Classical conditioning is complete when the CS elicits the conditioned response—here, the dog salivates after hearing the tone.

FIGURE 6.3 Variations of the Classical Conditioning Procedure

The sequence and timing of the presentation of the CS and US can vary: delayed conditioning, trace conditioning, backward pairing, and simultaneous conditioning. Delayed conditioning is generally effective, as is trace conditioning if there is a brief interval between CS and US presentation. Backward and simultaneous conditioning are generally not effective.

(Delayed, Trace, and Simultaneous) From *Psychology: Themes and Variations* (with Infotrac), 5th edition, by Weiten. © 2001. Reprinted with permission from Wadsworth, a division of Thomson Learning: www.thomsonrights.com. Fax: 800 730-2215. (Backward) From *Psychology,* 3e, by Kassin, Saul, © 2000. Adapted by permission of Pearson Education, Inc., Upper Saddle River, NJ.

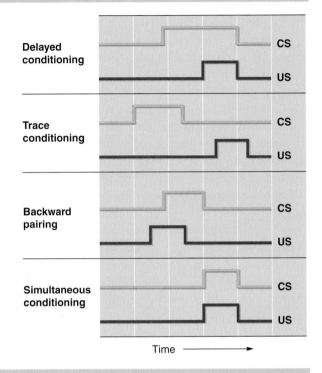

the tone 10, 5, or 1 second later. He found no conditioning; the dogs did not salivate when hearing the tone after eating the food. This is true of backward pairing in general. Even presenting the US and CS simultaneously, called *simultaneous conditioning* (Figure 6.3), does not lead to a conditioned response (Hall, 1984). Generally, in order for conditioning to occur, the US (food, in this example) should follow the CS (tone) immediately; however, there are exceptions, as is the case with certain food aversions, in which there may be a longer interval between the presentation of conditioned and unconditioned stimuli. As we will see, food aversion is one of the rare examples where strong conditioning can occur when there is a long interval between CS and US pairing.

Classical Conditioning: How It Works

Researchers studying classical conditioning have discovered a good deal about how organisms (human or otherwise) engage in this form of learning. Some conditioned responses remain with us all of our lives; others fade and even disappear altogether.

Another Russian researcher, Vladimir Bechterev (1857–1927), also conducted conditioning experiments. Here the US was a shock, and the UR was the dog's withdrawal of its foot. When a neutral stimulus such as a bell (CS) was paired with the shock, the dog learned to withdraw its foot (CR) after the bell but before the shock, thus successfully learning to avoid pain. Bechterev's findings were an important extension of Pavlov's work in that he extended the conditioned response to motor reflexes. Bechterev also established the basis for **avoidance learning** (Viney, 1993)—classical conditioning with a CS and an unpleasant US that leads the

• **Avoidance learning:** In classical conditioning, learning that occurs when a CS is paired with an unpleasant US that leads the organism to try to avoid the CS.

organism to try to avoid the CS. Does avoidance learning explain why some people put off going to the dentist for many years?

Conditioned Emotions: Getting a Gut Response

Seeing a cane in and of itself does not usually make people cringe or become afraid. If you saw such a cane leaning against a chair, chances are that it would not cause you fear. The cane is a *neutral* stimulus. However, for Jackie Chan and his schoolmates at the Chinese Drama Academy, the cane that director Master Yu held in his hand was no longer a neutral object or stimulus. Repeated beatings with it created a specific type of conditioned response called a **conditioned emotional response (CER)**—an emotionally charged conditioned response elicited by a previously neutral stimulus.

A landmark study by John B. Watson, the founder of behaviorism (see Chapter 1), and his assistant Rosalie Rayner (Watson & Rayner, 1920) illustrates how classical conditioning can produce a straightforward conditioned emotional response of fear, and how fear can lead to a **phobia,** an irrational fear of a specific object or situation. Watson and Rayner classically conditioned fear and then a phobia in an 11-month-old infant—Albert B.—whom they called "Little Albert" (see Figure 6.4). Through the use of classical conditioning, Watson and Rayner created in Albert a

- **Conditioned emotional response (CER):** An emotional response elicited by a previously neutral stimulus.

- **Phobia:** An irrational fear of a specific object or situation.

FIGURE 6.4 Classical Conditioning of a Phobia: Little Albert

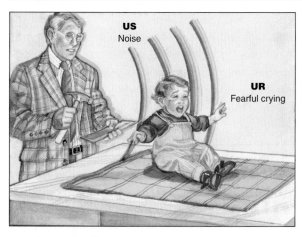

Initially, Little Albert did not show a fear of animals, but he did exhibit fear if a loud noise was made behind his back (a hammer striking a steel bar).

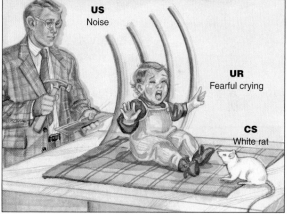

Then the researchers presented a white rat (CS) and made the loud noise (US).

After five presentations of the CS and US, Albert developed a phobia of rats—he began whimpering and withdrawing (the conditioned emotional response) and trying to avoid the rat. After two more presentations of CS and US, he immediately began crying on seeing the rat. "He . . . fell over on his left side, raised himself . . . and began to crawl away so rapidly that he was caught with difficulty before reaching the edge of the table" (Watson & Rayner, 1920, p. 5).

fear of rats; on seeing a white rat, Albert would cry and exhibit signs of fearfulness. This study could not be done today because of the rigorous ethical principles that govern psychological research (see Chapter 1), which did not exist at the time the study was undertaken. Neither Watson nor Rayner ever mentioned what became of Albert after the study, and they did nothing to help the child overcome the fear of white furry objects that they had induced (Benjafield, 1996).

Inadvertent classical conditioning can occur in people with certain kinds of heart problems who have a device, called a defibrillator, implanted under their skin. When their heartbeat gets too fast, the device emits an electric shock to the heart that causes the heart to resume beating normally. However, the shock can be quite an uncomfortable and alarming jolt for the device-wearer. The more frequent and intense the shocks are, the more likely the wearer is to develop severe anxiety—due to the conditioned fear in response to the shocks (Godemann et al., 2001).

Although it was initially thought that any response could be conditioned by any stimulus (Kimble, 1981), this supposition is not entirely true. Organisms seem to have a **biological preparedness,** a built-in readiness for certain conditioned stimuli to elicit particular conditioned responses, so that less learning is necessary to produce such conditioning. For instance, you may learn to avoid a certain kind of cheese if the first time you eat that variety you become nauseated. The fact that it takes only one pairing of the cheese and nausea for you to develop an aversion to that food is an example of preparedness. Similarly, research has shown that it is easier to condition a fear response to some objects than to others. Ohman and colleagues (1976) used pictures as the CS and shock as the US. They found that the fear-related response of sweaty hands is more easily conditioned, and less easily lost, if the CS is a picture of a snake or a spider than if it is a picture of flowers or mushrooms. Snakes, rats, and the dark are typical objects of a phobia. Some have argued that this makes sense from an evolutionary perspective—sensitivity to the presence of such possibly dangerous elements could help an organism survive (Seligman, 1971).

Contrapreparedness is a built-in disinclination (or even an inability) for certain conditioned stimuli to elicit particular conditioned responses. For example, Marks (1969) described a patient he was treating as an adult. When this woman was 10 years old, she was on a car trip and had to go to the bathroom. Her father pulled off the road so that she could relieve herself in a ditch. As she stepped out of the car, she saw a snake in the ditch—and at that moment her brother accidentally slammed the door on her hand. At 43, she was still deathly afraid of snakes, but she was not afraid of car doors, which had actually done the damage. Similarly, Bregman (1934) failed—with 15 different infants—to replicate Watson and Rayner's experiment when, instead of a rat as the CS, she used various inanimate objects, such as wooden blocks and pieces of cloth. There was no evidence of conditioning when the US was a loud noise and the CS was an inanimate object. These two examples highlight the point that certain stimuli, such as a car door and a wooden block, do not make successful conditioned stimuli.

Extinction and Spontaneous Recovery in Classical Conditioning: Gone Today, Here Tomorrow

It is indeed tragic that Watson never followed the history of Little Albert because even after a conditioned response (such as Albert's fear of white rats) is acquired, it is possible to diminish a conditioned response significantly in the presence of the

● **Biological preparedness:** A built-in readiness for certain conditioned stimuli to elicit certain conditioned responses so that less learning is necessary to produce conditioning.

● **Contrapreparedness:** A built-in disinclination (or even an inability) for certain conditioned stimuli to elicit particular conditioned responses.

CS. This process is called **extinction** because the CR is gradually eliminated, or "extinguished," by repeated presentations of the CS without the US. How would this work with Pavlov's dogs? If the tone continues to be presented, but is not followed by the presentation of food, after a while the dogs will no longer salivate at the tone: The CR will be extinguished. This process is graphed in Figure 6.5.

FIGURE 6.5 Acquisition, Extinction, and Spontaneous Recovery in Classical Conditioning

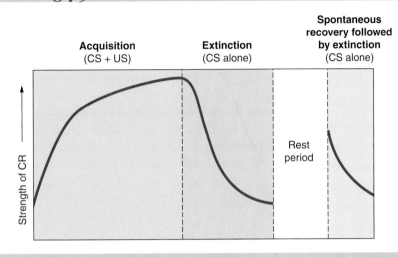

When the CS and US are paired, the organism quickly acquires the CR (left panel). However, when the CS occurs without the US, the CR quickly weakens (blue panel). After a rest period, the CR returns in response to the CS alone followed by extinction (right panel).

However, when a conditioned response has been extinguished and the CS presented again, the CS will again elicit the CR, although sometimes not as strongly as before extinction. This event is called **spontaneous recovery** (see Figure 6.5). Look again at the case of the dogs: As just noted, after the tone has been presented several times without any food forthcoming, the dogs' salivation response will extinguish, and they will stop salivating to the tone alone. However, if the tone is not presented for a period of time before it is presented again, the previously learned conditioned response of salivation on hearing the tone alone will return. The dogs have spontaneous recovery of the response, but they may not salivate as much as they did when they were first classically conditioned to the tone.

Once classical conditioning has occurred, the connection between the CS and US apparently never completely vanishes. After extinction occurs, the organism can then be retrained so that the CS again elicits the conditioned response; in this case, learning takes place more quickly than it did during the original training period. It is much easier to condition again, after extinction, than it is to condition in the first place.

In his work on extinction and spontaneous recovery, Bouton (1993, 1994) showed that what occurs during extinction is not the forgetting of old learning, but rather the overlayering of old learning by new learning. This new learning interferes with the previous classically conditioned response. Thus, according to Bouton's work, if Little Albert's fear of rats had been extinguished (that is, if the rat had been presented without the loud noise), it is not that Albert's association between the rat and the noise would have disappeared, but rather that new learning would have occurred "on top of" his previous learning. Thus, the CS (rat) no longer signals that the US (noise) will occur.

● **Extinction:** In classical conditioning, the process by which a CR comes to be eliminated through repeated presentations of the CS without the presence of the US.

● **Spontaneous recovery:** In classical conditioning, the process by which the CS will again elicit the CR after extinction has occurred.

- **Stimulus generalization:** A tendency for the CR to be elicited by neutral stimuli that are like, but not identical to, the CS; in other words, the response generalizes to similar stimuli.

- **Stimulus discrimination:** The ability to distinguish among similar conditioned stimuli and to respond only to actual conditioned stimuli.

Generalization and Discrimination in Classical Conditioning: Seen One, Seen 'em All?

Watson and Rayner wrote that, 5 days after the conditioning of Little Albert, a rabbit, a dog, a fur coat, cotton, and a Santa Claus mask all elicited the conditioned response of fear. This is an example of **stimulus generalization,** a tendency for the conditioned response to be elicited by neutral stimuli that are like, but not identical to, the conditioned stimulus; in other words, the response generalizes to similar stimuli. Moreover, because of a *generalization gradient*, the more closely the new stimulus resembles the original CS, the stronger the response. Stimulus generalization can be helpful for survival because often a dangerous stimulus may not occur in exactly the same form the next time. Without stimulus generalization, we might not know to be afraid of lions as well as tigers.

In addition to stimulus generalization, organisms are also able to distinguish, or discriminate, among stimuli similar to the CS and to respond only to actual conditioned stimuli; this ability is called **stimulus discrimination.** Stimulus discrimination can be extremely helpful for survival; consider that one type of mushroom may be poisonous, but another type is food. Should Albert have been shown a pile of cotton balls without a loud noise occurring (but continued to be presented with a rat paired with the loud noise), only the rat would elicit fear. Albert would have been able to discriminate between the two similar stimuli.

Classical conditioning can account for the learning of more complex behaviors through *higher order conditioning*: Once conditioning occurs, the CS (referred to as CS_1) serves as a US when paired with a new CS (referred to as CS_2). For Pavlov's dogs, once the original conditioning occurred, another stimulus, such as a black square, could be paired with the tone (see Figure 6.6). After a number of pairings, the presentation of the black square alone would lead to the salivation response, although the response would not be as strong as it was originally, to the tone. An example of higher order conditioning with Little Albert would be if a cane (CS_2) was presented immediately before the white rat (CS_1). With enough pairings, Albert would likely become afraid of the cane as well.

Cognition and the Conditioned Stimulus

Although strict behaviorists might not agree that thoughts play a role in classical conditioning, research suggests otherwise (see Chapter 1 for an explanation of behaviorism). The context in which classical conditioning occurs and the expectations that arise following classical conditioning influence the learning (Hollis, 1997). For example, Rescorla (1967) presented rats with a tone (CS) immediately before delivering a shock (US); these rats quickly learned a fear response to the

FIGURE 6.6 Higher Order Conditioning

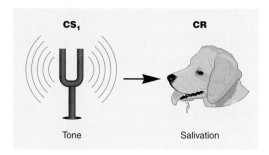

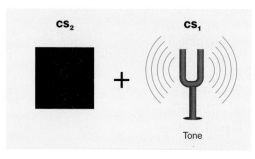

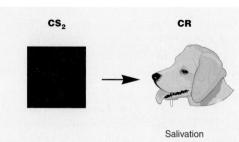

Once classical conditioning to the CS (now labeled CS_1) occurs, a new neutral stimulus is paired with the original CS_1. Here the new stimulus is a black square (CS_2). With repeated pairings, the new stimulus will elicit the conditioned response, although it will likely be weaker than the response to CS_1.

tone. However, another group of rats heard the tone and were shocked, but sometimes the tone was presented after the shock. As Pavlov had found years earlier, backward pairing does not produce conditioning (see Figure 6.3): This group did not come to fear the tone.

Apparently, the CS provides information by signaling the upcoming US (and therefore UR), and conditioning occurs because the animal is learning that relationship: The CS is a signal that the US will occur.

Kamin (1969) provided more evidence that mental processes lie between stimulus and response during conditioning. He conditioned rats by pairing a tone with a brief shock; the rats developed a conditioned fear response to the tone. But when he added a second CS by turning on a light with the tone, the rats did not develop a conditioned fear response to the light alone. Kamin hypothesized that the original pairing of tone and shock was blocking new learning. The light did not add new information and was therefore of no consequence and not worth their attention. The tone was enough of a signal, and the rats didn't seem to view the light as a signal. Thus, Kamin concluded that classical conditioning takes place only if the pairing of CS and US provides useful information about the likelihood of occurrence of the US.

In addition, a mental image of an object—what you see in your "mind's eye" when you visualize something—can play a role in classical conditioning, either as a CS or a US. For instance, imagining food can lead to salivation in humans (Dadds et al., 1997): Visualize the most scrumptious dessert you've ever eaten (was it a banana split? baked Alaska? ice cream drowning in chocolate sauce?). Imagine it in vivid detail. If the image is vivid enough, you may start salivating—the image is an unconditioned stimulus, the salivation is an unconditioned response.

Dissecting Conditioning: Brain Mechanisms

Classical conditioning has at least three distinct components; we know this because it has been shown that three different brain processes are involved. LeDoux (1995, 1996; also Beggs et al., 1999) and his colleagues have studied conditioned fear in detail and have established that registration of the stimulus, production of the response, and the connection between the two rely on distinct parts of the brain. Consider the case of a driver who has been honked at by a huge truck as it roars by and has barely missed being crushed; the driver has experienced fear. (1) When he later hears the sound of a horn and sees a truck drive by, the images and sounds are registered in the visual and the auditory cortex. (2) Following this, a specific part of the amygdala registers the sound and sight that triggers the conditioned fear. In experimental studies with animals, it has been shown that if this particular part of the amygdala is removed, animals cannot learn that a shock will soon follow a tone. (3) Finally, another part of the amygdala, the central nucleus, leads to the behaviors that express conditioned fear—for example, wincing when an 18-wheeler blasts its horn. When this part of the amygdala is removed, the movements, autonomic responses, and other signs of fear are not produced.

Why was conditioned fear triggered by this stimulus? Conditioning causes brain cells that register the stimulus (in the case of the honking truck, cells in the auditory cortex in the temporal lobe) to fire in tandem with cells in the amygdala that produce the fear response. Activity in the two sets of neurons becomes hooked together, so that whenever the stimulus occurs, the response is automatic. A crucial finding is that this linked activity never disappears entirely: Even after conditioning has been extinguished, linked activity remains, making it very easy for an animal to relearn a conditioned response. Indeed, extinction depends on the active suppression of the response, which is accomplished in part by the frontal lobe's inhibiting the amygdala (LeDoux, 1995, 1996).

Classical Conditioning Applied

If the investigation of classical conditioning had ended with the study of dogs' salivation, the great psychological importance of this kind of learning might not have been recognized. But classical conditioning showed that emotional responses, such as the fear response, can be conditioned, and emotional responses exert a powerful effect on people's lives. If a friend slaps you hard on the back every time you see him, you are likely to wince even as he lifts his arm to begin his greeting, and in time classical conditioning affects how you feel about him. Classical conditioning can play a role in the effectiveness of medicines, in the operation of our immune systems, and in other aspects of health and illness (as you will see in Chapter 13). Even without our awareness, it contributes to our feelings about events and objects (Bunce et al., 1999), even our sexual interests (Lalumiere & Quinsey, 1998).

Classical conditioning plays a role in deaths caused by drug overdoses. A user who generally takes a drug in a particular setting—the bathroom, for instance—develops a conditioned response to that place (Siegel, 1988; Siegel et al., 2000). Here's what happens. Because of classical conditioning, as soon as the user walks into the bathroom, his or her body begins to compensate for the influx of drug that is soon to come. This conditioned response is the body's attempt to counteract, or dampen, the effect of the drug. When the user takes the drug in a new setting, perhaps a friend's living room, this conditioned response does not occur. Because there is no conditioned response to the new setting, the user's body does not try to counteract the effect of the drug. The net result is a higher effective dose of the drug than the user can tolerate, leading to an overdose.

Similarly, classical conditioning also helps explain why people addicted to cocaine experience drug cravings merely from handling money (Hamilton et al., 1998). Part of the experience of using cocaine is buying it, often just before using it. Thus, handling money becomes a CS. In the same way, among cigarette smokers certain environmental stimuli can elicit a desire for a cigarette (Lazev et al., 1999), and virtual reality simulations of opioid-related cues can elicit a craving for the drug in opioid addicts (Kuntze et al., 2001). So, classical conditioning explains why some smokers automatically reach for a cigarette when they get a phone call or have a cup of coffee, often without realizing what is happening.

Classical conditioning also serves as the basis for a number of therapy techniques, including systematic desensitization, which has been used to treat phobias (this therapeutic technique and others are discussed in more detail in Chapter 15). Systematic desensitization is the structured and repeated presentation of a feared conditioned stimulus in circumstances designed to reduce anxiety. Systematic desensitization works to extinguish the phobia response by teaching people to be relaxed in the presence of the feared object or situation, such as an elevator for those with an elevator phobia. With systematic desensitization, the CS no longer elicits the CR of fear; extinction has occurred.

Watson formalized the use of behavioral principles when he took a job in advertising. The use of "sex appeal" to sell products stems from Watson's ideas. Sex isn't the only unconditioned stimulus that can work to produce a desired

Through the obvious sex appeal of this man and woman, Polo Sport® is trying to get you to buy its swimwear. If you find the ad to have sex appeal, then classical conditioning principles suggest that your mild arousal or pleasure on seeing the ad (and thereafter on seeing the product itself, following its pairing with the attractive couple) would lead you to buy the product.

response; Razran (1940) did a study showing that political slogans (CS) when paired with the eating of food (US) led people to view those slogans favorably. Classical conditioning continues to be used in advertising to promote consumers' positive attitudes about products (Grossman & Till, 1998; Kim et al., 1998; Till & Priluck, 2000). This is referred to as *evaluative conditioning*: The goal is to change your liking, or evaluation, of the conditioned stimulus—the product the advertisers want you to buy (De Houwer et al., 2001). Two special cases of the application of classical conditioning are taste aversion and the conditioning of the immune system.

Food and Taste Aversion

When animals or people have an unpleasant experience during or after eating a particular food or taste (and then try to avoid it), they may develop a **food** or **taste aversion.** This type of classical conditioning usually involves learning after only a single experience of the CS-US pairing. Generally, the US is a nausea- or vomiting-inducing agent, and the CS is a previously neutral stimulus that was paired with it, such as the sight or smell of food. The UR is nausea or vomiting, and so is the CR.

If you have ever had food poisoning, you may have developed a classically conditioned food aversion. A likely scenario is that the food that made you sick had some unhealthy and unwanted ingredient, such as salmonella bacteria. The bacteria are the US, and the ensuing nausea and vomiting are the UR. If the salmonella was in your dinner of broiled trout, trout might become a CS for you; whenever you eat it (or perhaps another fish similarly prepared), you become nauseated (the CR). Rather than put yourself through this experience, you are likely to avoid eating broiled trout, and a food aversion is born.

UNDERSTANDING RESEARCH

The Discovery of Taste Aversion

Garcia and Koelling (1966) accidentally discovered the existence of taste aversion when studying the effects of radiation on rats. The rats were exposed to high enough doses of radiation that they became sick. The researchers noticed that the rats drank less water from the plastic water bottle in the radiation chamber than from the glass water bottle in their "home" cage.

● **Food aversion (taste aversion):** A classically conditioned avoidance of a certain food or taste.

Although this preference could have been due to many factors, it turned out that the water in the plastic bottle had a slightly different taste, thanks to the plastic, than the water in the glass bottle. The researchers shifted their focus to discover why the rats drank less from the plastic than the glass bottle.

QUESTION: Was classical conditioning at work? Did the taste of the water, through its association with the radiation-induced nausea, become a conditioned stimulus, leading to a conditioned taste aversion?

FIGURE 6.7 Taste Aversion Conditioning

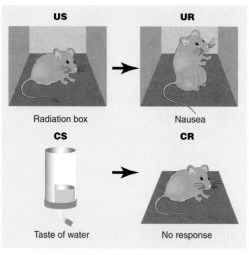

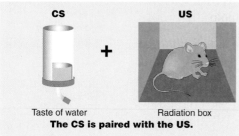

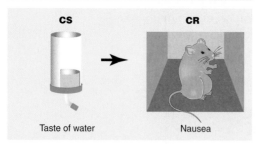

Had Garcia and Koelling (1966) inadvertently created a classically conditioned taste aversion where the US was the radiation, the CS was the taste of water in the plastic bottle in the radiation chamber, the UR was the rat getting nauseated, and the CR was the rat's taste aversion?

ALTERNATIVES: (1) Garcia and Koelling's preferred alternative (that is, their hypothesis) was that the radiation was the US, the taste of the water from the plastic bottle the CS, getting sick (nauseated) the UR, and the taste aversion was the CR (see Figure 6.7); (2) Their original finding was due to chance; if they had the rats go through the same setup a second time, the rats would drink equivalent amounts of water from the different types of water bottles; (3) Any type of negative stimulation (such as an electric shock), not just nausea, would lead the rats to avoid drinking water that had an unusual taste.

LOGIC: By repeating the original experiment (and adding other elements to rule out the last possibility), Garcia and Koelling would be able to determine whether the rats' response in the original study was due to chance, a response to an aversive stimulus, or a result of classical conditioning of a taste aversion.

METHOD: Rats were placed in cages with bottles of water. Drinking from one bottle caused flashes of light and a clicking noise. Drinking from the other bottle did not produce any of these effects. The cage was capable of giving shocks to the rodents' feet. During the first phase of this experiment, half of the rats drank water from the bottle that produced flashes of light and a clicking noise; the researchers thus referred to the water in this condition as bright-noisy water. Note that these are novel visual (flashing light) and auditory (clicking sound) stimuli. The other half of the rats drank water that was sweet (due to the addition of saccharin), but neither bright nor noisy; in this condition the rats were exposed to a novel gustatory stimulus (saccharine taste).

In the second phase of the experiment, half of each of these two groups had their feet shocked after drinking water. The other half of each group was exposed to radiation (as was originally done) or was given lithium chloride (a compound that causes nausea) after drinking water. In the final phase of the experiment, the rats were allowed to drink, and researchers noted which type of water each group would, and would *not,* drink; that is, did any of the groups of rats develop a conditioned taste aversion?

RESULTS: The results are summarized in Table 6.1.

TABLE 6.1   Results of Garcia and Koelling's Experiment

The rats that previously drank bright-noisy water and had been shocked would not drink this type of water again, although they would drink sweet water. And those who drank bright-noisy water but had nausea induced did not avoid any type of water. Those who drank sweet water followed by nausea would not drink sweet water again, although they would drink bright-noisy water. Those who drank sweet water followed by shock did not avoid either type of water.

	Type of Aversive Stimulus	
Type of Water	**Received shock**	**Received radiation/ lithium chloride**
Bright-noisy water	Avoided bright-noisy water, but not sweet water	No evidence of classical conditioning
Sweet water	No evidence of classical conditioning	Avoided sweet water, but not bright-noisy water

INFERENCES: Garcia and Koelling were able to classically condition a taste aversion in rats. Moreover, certain aversive, unconditioned stimuli were more likely to become associated with particular conditioned stimuli. A taste aversion could be conditioned to a gustatory stimulus (the sweet water), but not to visual and auditory stimuli (lights and noise). Similarly, visual and auditory stimuli could be conditioned to an aversive tactile stimulus (shock), but not to a gustatory stimulus. No matter how the researchers manipulated these visual and auditory stimuli, they could not elicit a conditioned response of nausea. Thus, taste aversion can only be conditioned to appropriate stimuli—tastes. More generally, not all stimuli can be conditioned to elicit a given response. This is additional evidence of both preparedness for some associations and contra-preparedness for others.

Garcia's research led to another important discovery. (As often occurs in science, following up on a curious result can lead to unexpected but interesting and important discoveries.) Continuing with experiments on conditioned taste aversion, Garcia, Ervin, and Koelling (1966) found that the rats avoided the novel-tasting water even if the nausea didn't occur until several hours after the novel-tasting water was presented. Garcia's research showed that, at least in this case, the US doesn't need to come immediately after the CS.

Garcia's findings stirred considerable controversy because they described exceptions to the "rules" of classical conditioning. Taste aversion can lead to a more generalized response; just the sight of the food can elicit a conditioned response. President Ulysses S. Grant, a soldier who had seen the carnage of the Civil War, became nauseated at just the sight of rare meat (Seuling, 1978). Classically conditioned taste aversion is the mechanism behind the use of Antabuse to treat alcoholism. Antabuse is a medicine that causes violent nausea and vomiting when mixed with alcohol. If an alcoholic took Antabuse and then drank, he or she would vomit. If the drug was successful in its larger purpose, an alcoholic would then develop a taste aversion to alcohol. Unfortunately, Antabuse has not been as successful as was originally hoped; those who were having difficulty refraining from drinking tended to stop taking their Antabuse so that they could drink without getting sick. If Antabuse is used consistently, it does decrease how often alcoholics drink, but it does not increase the likelihood of total abstinence (Fuller et al., 1986; Sereny et al., 1986). More recent findings suggest that if the person taking Antabuse is regularly supervised when taking it, thereby ensuring that the person actually takes it, then Antabuse is more effective at decreasing the amount of alcohol consumed (Brewer et al., 2000; Chick, Gough et al., 1992). This may explain why married alcoholics whose spouses help ensure that Antabuse is taken at regular intervals have the best success with it (Azrin et al., 1982).

Classical conditioning is adaptive, whether it involves an animal's (including a human's) ability to learn which foods are poisonous, or which animals or objects in the environment (such as predators or guns) to fear and avoid. The more readily an organism learns these associations, the more likely that organism is to survive. Learned food aversions based on one exposure can be particularly adaptive: Animals who readily learn what not to eat will probably live longer and have more offspring.

Conditioning the Immune System

Let's suppose you once worked day and night for a week, hardly taking the time to eat or sleep, and so severely weakened your immune system that you became very sick. During that exhausting work-filled week, you spent all of your waking hours with a laptop computer on your bed, which is covered by a bright red bedspread. Do you think that, after your recovery, simply sitting on that same bedspread could cause your immune system to weaken? Ader and his colleagues (Ader, 1976; Ader & Cohen, 1975) have shown that this kind of conditioning does in fact happen in rats. Ader and Cohen paired saccharin-flavored water with injections of cyclophosphamide, a drug given to organ transplant donors that suppresses the immune system and has a side effect of nausea. Ader had intended to use this drug not for its immune-suppressing qualities, but as a way to induce nausea in a study of taste aversion. He wanted to see how long the taste aversion would last once injections of cyclophosphamide stopped, but the rats continued to drink sweet water (the CS).

A few rats died on day 45 of the experiment, and more died over the next several days. Ader was confused; he had done similar experiments before with a different nausea-inducing drug and none of his animals had died. He eventually showed that the taste of the sweetened water was triggering not just the nausea, but a suppression of the immune system (as the actual drug would do), causing the eventual death of the rodents. Each time the rats drank the sweetened water, their immune systems were weakened—even without the immune-suppressing drug! The taste of the saccharine-sweetened water was acting as a CS and was in essence a placebo. The rats' bodies responded to the CS as if it were cyclophosphamide.

Ader's accidental discovery and his follow-up studies were noteworthy for two reasons: First, they showed that the placebo effect could be induced in animals, not just humans; second, they showed that the organism doesn't have to believe that the placebo has medicinal properties in order to produce a placebo response. Although Ader and Cohen could not ask the rats what they believed would happen when drinking sweet water, we have no reason to think that they "believed" it would impair their immune systems (Dienstfrey, 1991). Ader and Cohen have reported a number of follow-up studies, all trying to rule out other explanations of their results, and their hypothesis about the conditioning of the immune system has stood up well. Indeed, another study with rats showed that the immune response could actually be boosted by conditioning (Gorcynski, cited in Dienstfrey, 1991). There is evidence that the placebo response may be a conditioned immune response that occurs in humans (Voudouris et al., 1985).

Looking *at* Levels

Sick at the Thought of Chemotherapy

Like most psychological phenomena, classical conditioning provides an opportunity to understand how many events at the different levels of analysis affect one another in various organisms, including Pavlov's dogs and Ader's rats. The interplay of events at the levels of the brain, person, and group are easy to understand even in humans.

Cancer patients undergoing chemotherapy may experience intense nausea and vomiting as side effects of the treatment. But some patients develop anticipatory nausea, a classically conditioned response to chemotherapy triggered by a previously neutral CS (Burish & Carey, 1986; Carey & Burish, 1988; Davey, 1992). Such a stimulus might be as innocuous as a florist's shop seen en route to the hospital. For others undergoing chemotherapy, just thinking about the hospital where the treatment is received can produce nausea (Redd et al., 1993).

What is happening? At the level of the brain, the activity of neurons that feed into the patient's immune and autonomic nervous systems, stimulated by the US of the chemotherapeutic drugs that induce the UR and CR of nausea, becomes paired with the activity of neurons that register certain sights and sounds, for example the CS of the florist shop. After enough such pairings, the two groups of neurons become functionally connected, and activity in one group triggers activity in the other.

In addition, some patients are more likely than others to develop anticipatory nausea. Some people are generally more autonomically reactive than others; that is, they have a tendency toward a stronger autonomic response to given levels of stimulation. Such autonomically reactive people are more likely to develop anticipatory nausea (Kvale & Hugdahl, 1994). At the level of the person, such adverse effects can lead to a sense of helplessness and can cause some chemotherapy patients to stop the treatment altogether (Siegel & Longo, 1981). Fortunately, behavioral interventions such as relaxation training can be helpful in controlling anticipatory nausea, as can newer antinausea medications (Vasterling et al., 1993).

At the level of the group, chemotherapy involves a social component. It is administered by medical staff, in the social setting of a hospital or clinic, and the patient may be escorted to treatment by a friend or family member. Those involved in the chemotherapy treatment can become the CS, leading a patient to become nauseated at the sight of a particular nurse who always administers the treatment (Montgomery & Bovbjerg, 1997). Events at these levels interact. Autonomic reactivity influences the likelihood of developing anticipatory nausea, which can create yet another challenge for chemotherapy patients, affecting how they see the illness and their ability to fight it, and how they deal with medical staff, family, and friends. Moreover, the social interaction of being taught behavioral interventions for the anticipatory nausea (such as relaxation techniques) can influence events at the level of the brain and the person by giving the patient some sense of control over the nausea.

TEST YOURSELF!

1. What is classical conditioning? How was it discovered?
2. How are conditioned responses eliminated?
3. What are common examples of classical conditioning in daily life?

Operant Conditioning

Classical conditioning is not the only way that Jackie Chan learned. At times Master Yu would give some of the students special rewards—extra food or a meal in a restaurant—or special punishments. Chan's classmates were also sources of rewards and punishments: Younger classmate Yuen Baio (who later acted in several of Chan's films) was a friend, giving Chan support, camaraderie, and sometimes snacks from Yuen Baio's parents' weekly gift of food. Moreover, Chan was honored with the most powerful reward at the school—a much desired place in the Seven Little Fortunes, a troupe of seven schoolmates performing nightly in front of a paying audience (the income from the performances, however, went to Master Yu to pay for the running of the school).

How did the food treats come to be such a powerful force in Chan's life? And, how did the possibility of being picked to perform in the Seven Little Fortunes exert such a powerful influence on Chan and the other students, motivating them to practice even harder and more intensely than they otherwise would have?

The answer might lie with another kind of learning, **operant conditioning**, the process whereby a behavior becomes associated with its consequences.

The Roots of Operant Conditioning: Its Discovery and How It Works

If your behavior is followed by a positive consequence, you are more likely to repeat the act in the future; if it is followed by a negative consequence, you are less likely to repeat it. This observation underlies the mechanism of operant conditioning. Unlike classical conditioning, in which the organism is largely passive, operant conditioning requires the organism to "operate" in the world, to do something. Whereas classical conditioning usually involves involuntary reflexes, such as cringing in response to hearing the whistling of a cane whipping

- **Operant conditioning:** The process by which a behavior becomes associated with its consequences.

through the air, operant conditioning usually involves voluntary, nonreflexive behavior, such as singing a song, assuming a kung fu stance, or eating with chopsticks or a fork.

Thorndike's Puzzle Box

At about the same time that Pavlov was working with his dogs, American psychologist Edward L. Thorndike (1874–1949) was investigating a different kind of learning. Thorndike created a puzzle box, a cage with a latched door that a cat could open by pressing down on a pedal inside the cage (see Figure 6.8). Food was placed outside the cage door. Although the cat took a while to get around to pressing down the pedal, once it did (and the door opened), the cat was quicker to press the pedal in its subsequent sessions in the box: It had learned that pressing the pedal opened the door and enabled it to get the food (see Figure 6.9). Thorndike called this type of learning "trial-and-error learning." His finding led to his famous formulation of the **Law of Effect** (Thorndike, 1927), which lies at the heart of operant conditioning: Actions that subsequently lead to a "satisfying state of affairs" are more likely to be repeated (Thorndike, 1949, p. 14).

The Skinner Box

B. F. Skinner (1904–1990), the 20th century's foremost proponent of behaviorism, is important in the history of psychology not only because he most fully developed the concept of operant conditioning, but also because he showed how conditioning could explain much of our daily behavior. Working mostly with pigeons, he developed an apparatus to minimize his handling of the birds, which is now often referred to as a Skinner box. The box (see Figure 6.10, p. 230) could both feed the animals and record the frequency of their responses, making it easy to quantify the responses (this enormously helpful feature was, in fact, an unintended bonus of the box's design; Skinner, 1956). If a rat is put in a Skinner box, it learns to associate pressing the lever or bar with the likelihood of a food pellet's appearing. Here, the lever is the stimulus, pressing the lever is the response, or behavior, and receiving the food pellet is the consequence.

Principles of Operant Conditioning

Operant conditioning involves an association between a stimulus, the response to the stimulus (a behavior), and its consequence. (In classical conditioning, the association is between a neutral stimulus and an unconditioned stimulus.) Operant conditioning relies on **reinforcement,** the process by which consequences

FIGURE 6.8 Thorndike's Puzzle Box

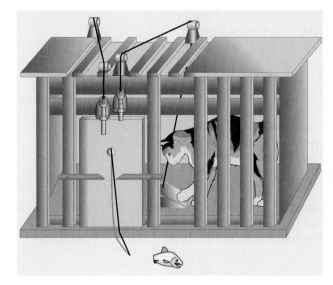

Thorndike placed a hungry cat inside the box and a piece of fish just outside the door, within the cat's sight. The cat tried to get out of the box to the fish by producing many behaviors, but only pressing the pedal would open the door. Eventually the cat pressed the pedal, and the door opened. When the cat was put back inside the box, it pressed the pedal more quickly, improving each time.

FIGURE 6.9 The Phases of Operant Conditioning

| **Stimulus** Pedal | **Response** Pushing pedal | **Consequence** Food |

Unlike classical conditioning, operant conditioning requires the organism to produce the desired behavior (the response). That behavior is then followed by positive or negative consequences.

● **Law of Effect:** Actions that subsequently lead to a "satisfying state of affairs" are more likely to be repeated.

● **Reinforcement:** The process by which consequences lead to an increase in the likelihood that the response will occur again.

FIGURE 6.10 Skinner Box and Cumulative Recorder

In a Skinner box, a hungry rat presses a lever (or pigeons peck a key). As with Thorndike's cat, the rat will emit random behaviors, eventually pressing the lever, causing a food pellet (reinforcement) to come down the chute into the food dish, increasing the likelihood of the response in the future. It presses the lever again, and another food pellet appears. It presses the lever (and eats) more frequently—it has learned that pressing the lever will be followed by the appearance of a food pellet. On the outside of the box is a device that records each lever press and the time interval between presses.

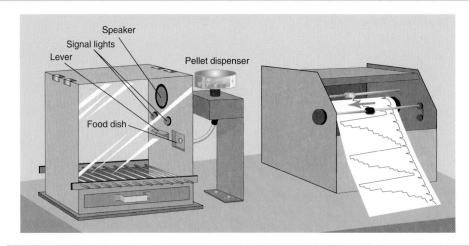

lead to an increase in the likelihood that the response will occur again. To be most effective, the reinforcement should be contingent on a desired response. Not surprisingly, this relationship between the response and the consequence is called **response contingency**; it occurs when a consequence is dependent on the organism's producing the desired behavior. In contrast to the responses that are elicited in classical conditioning, responses in operant conditioning are *emitted*; the responses are voluntarily produced.

An example of operant conditioning occurred in Chan's life when, as a young adult, he and many other martial arts experts were seeking work as stuntmen in the Hong Kong film industry. There were more junior (young, inexperienced) stuntmen than there were jobs, and Chan desperately needed the work in order to pay his bills. One day, a director wanted a stunt done; it was deemed so unsafe by the stunt coordinator that he refused to have any of his stuntmen do it. Chan volunteered to do it, figuring that this was the only way he'd be likely to get work. He did the dangerous stunt (twice), and *did* get more jobs after that—he shifted from being a junior stuntman to a full fledged stuntman with regular work. What Chan learned from this experience was that trying very dangerous stunts (behavior) would get him work (the desired response).

A **reinforcer** is an object or event that comes after a response that strengthens the likelihood of its recurrence. In Thorndike's puzzle box and in the Skinner box, the reinforcer, or consequence, is food. Which reinforcer works best? The answer to this question is tricky: What one person considers a "reward" might leave another person cold. Reinforcement, therefore, is in the eyes of the recipient. For instance, for one person, a night at the ballet might be a wonderful reinforcer for doing well on a test. To another, a night at the ballet might seem like punishment.

Chan recounts an example of this at the start of filming his first *Rush Hour* movie, when he was already considered a "star" in America:

The studio [spared] nothing to make me feel like I'm a star. I have a beautiful rented mansion, a luxurious trailer on the set, a personal trainer, and a car standing by at all times. Even my stuntmen have their own private rooms. In my Hong Kong movies, we squeeze together, share what we have to, and eat lunch together, all out of the same big pot. I do everything and anything I want to—I'm the director, the producer, the

● **Response contingency:** The relationship that occurs when a consequence is dependent on the organism's emitting the desired behavior.

● **Reinforcer:** An object or event that comes after a response that changes the likelihood of its recurrence.

cameraman, the prop guy, the janitor. Anything. Here, they won't let me do anything except act. They won't even let me stand around so they can check the lighting—they have a stand-in, my height, my color, wearing my clothes, come in, and they check the lighting off of him while I sit in my trailer. (Chan & Yang, 1999, p. 303)

The producers apparently thought that this "star treatment" would reinforce Chan for acting in American movies—but in fact he didn't like it and was itching to be more involved between scenes.

Parents who give stickers to their child for good behavior might conclude that behavioral programs don't work if that child makes no effort to win them. They'd be wrong: The problem is that their child doesn't view stickers as a reward. The parents simply need to find a reinforcer that will work, increasing the likelihood that their child will repeat a particular behavior. For instance, when we were toilet training our children, we used reinforcers whenever they tried to use the potty. We had asked each child to name a reinforcer, and one of our children requested black olives. This is a reminder that the proof is in the pudding—the degree to which an object or event is a reinforcer is determined by its effect on the individual organism. Just calling something a reinforcer doesn't make it so.

Reinforcement: Getting Your Just Desserts

There are two types of reinforcement, positive and negative. In **positive reinforcement,** a desired reinforcer is presented after a response, thereby increasing the likelihood of a recurrence of that response (see Figure 6.11, p. 232, first row). The food for Thorndike's cat and black olives for our toddler are examples of positive reinforcement. Food is the usual positive reinforcer for animals; for humans, toys, money, and intangibles such as praise and attention can also be positive reinforcers, as was Jackie Chan's acceptance into the Seven Little Fortunes. Chan also describes how, when he was about 6 years old, using kung fu against other kids could produce positive reinforcement: he would fight other kids who were "stupid enough to get in my way . . . I found out quickly that fighting was fun—when you won anyway—and it soon became one of my favorite hobbies, next to eating" (p. 12).

Sometimes even "bad attention," such as a scolding, can be a positive reinforcer if the only time a child receives any attention at all is when he or she misbehaves. Chan did not view having to stand outside his first-grade classroom with a sign around his neck as punishment for his classroom antics. Therefore, he did not learn what his teachers wanted him to learn. Again, reinforcement is particular to the individual.

In contrast, **negative reinforcement** is the removal of an unpleasant event or circumstance following a desired behavior, thereby increasing the probability of the behavior's occurring again (see Figure 6.11, second row). If a rat is being mildly shocked in its cage, and the shocks stop when it presses a bar, then bar pressing is negatively reinforced. A teacher who gives a "time out" to a continually disruptive child may inadvertently be negatively reinforcing the disruptive behavior if the child views the time out as relief from having to sit at a desk and do schoolwork (Piazza et al., 1998). Imagine this common scenario: A child whines to get his way; his father gives in to the whining; the child stops whining. What has happened? The aversive stimulus—the whining—has been removed, and so the father's behavior of giving in to the child has been negatively reinforced. Dad is then more likely to give in the next time his child whines. This principle is at work when people use substances, such as alcohol, to decrease their anxiety (Hohlstein et al., 1998; Samoluk & Stewart, 1998); by removing the aversive state, the alcohol is negatively reinforced.

● **Positive reinforcement:** Occurs when a desired reinforcer is presented after a behavior, thereby increasing the likelihood of a recurrence of that behavior.

● **Negative reinforcement:** Occurs when an unpleasant event or circumstance is removed following a desired behavior, thereby increasing the likelihood of a recurrence of the behavior.

FIGURE 6.11   Positive and Negative Reinforcement and Punishment

Chan's behavior (a correct landing of a flying side kick) is positively reinforced; after he does the behavior correctly, he receives a treat.

In contrast, the same behavior is negatively reinforced: the Master has a frown as Chan is going into the move (an aversive stimulus), but the aversive stimulus is removed when Chan lands from the flying sidekick correctly. The Master's goal is the same in both examples—to maximize the likelihood of the behavior (a perfect flying side kick landing) occurring again.

Chan's behavior (falling when landing from a flying side kick) is being positively punished: the Master gives an unpleasant consequence (a caning) so as to minimize the likelihood of the behavior (an incorrect flying side kick landing) occurring again.

Chan's behavior (falling when landing from a flying side kick) is being negatively punished: the Master removes a pleasant event (Master's smile at Jackie) so as to minimize the likelihood of the behavior (an incorrect flying side kick landing) occurring again.

Negative reinforcement is sometimes referred to as *escape conditioning*, because the organism has learned to perform a behavior that decreases or stops an aversive stimulus (thereby escaping from the aversive stimulus). Imagine that your bedroom window overlooks an area where trash barrels are placed for pickup by a garbage truck. You've just moved in and find that early one Saturday morning, as you are catching up on much needed sleep, you awaken to the sound of glass bottles and other trash being compacted in the rear of the truck. Several minutes go by, and still the noise continues. You stuff wads of tissue in your ears to muffle the sound, put a pillow over your head, and go back to sleep. Putting tissue in your ears (and the pillow over your head) is negatively reinforced because it stops an aversive stimulus (the noise of the garbage truck). You have performed a behavior that allows to you "escape" the aversive situation. After a few weeks of this, you are likely to experience *avoidance learning*: you avoid the unpleasant stimulus altogether by making sure to shut your windows and wear sound filtering ear plugs when you go to sleep Friday night.

Both positive and negative reinforcement are described as reinforcing because they increase the likelihood that a behavior will be repeated. Negative reinforcement is *not* the same thing as punishment. Let's see why.

Punishment

A punishment is an unpleasant event that occurs as a consequence of a behavior. Punishment *decreases* the probability of the recurrence of a behavior, in contrast to reinforcement (both positive and negative), which *increases* the likelihood of recurrence. Although punishment is commonly confused with negative reinforcement, they are not the same: punishment decreases the probability of a recurrence of a behavior; negative reinforcement increases the probability by removing an unpleasant consequence of the behavior.

Just as there is positive and negative reinforcement, so there is positive and negative punishment. **Positive punishment** occurs when a behavior leads to an undesired consequence, thereby decreasing the probability that the behavior will occur again (see Figure 6.11, third row). **Negative punishment** is the removal of a pleasant event or circumstance following a behavior, thereby decreasing the probability that the behavior will occur again (see Figure 6.11, fourth row).

Chan and his classmates were required to do handstands for at least half an hour at a time, despite distressing physical experiences as a result of remaining upside down for so long: "after fifteen minutes, our arms would grow limp, our blood would rush to our heads, and our stomachs would begin to turn flip-flops. But we couldn't show any weakness at all. A limb that moved would receive a whack from the master's rattan cane" (p. 43). This was an example of positive punishment: moving a limb led to a whack of the cane.

Punishment is most effective if it has three characteristics. First, punishment should be swift, occurring immediately after the undesired behavior. The old threat "Wait till you get home!" undermines the effectiveness of the punishment. Second, punishment must be consistent. The undesired behavior must be punished each and every time it occurs. If the behavior is punished only sporadically, the person or animal doesn't effectively learn that the behavior will be followed by punishment, and so doesn't decrease the frequency of the behavior as consistently. Finally, the punishment should be sufficiently aversive without being so aversive as to create problems such as high levels of fear or anxiety, injury, or new, undesired behaviors.

We must make several cautionary points about the use of punishment. First, although punishment may decrease the frequency of a behavior, it doesn't eliminate the capacity to engage in that behavior. Your little sister may learn not to push you because your mother will punish her, but she may continue to push her classmates at school because the behavior has not been punished in that context. She

● **Positive punishment:** Occurs when a behavior leads to an undesired consequence, thereby decreasing the likelihood of a recurrence of that behavior.

● **Negative punishment:** Occurs when a behavior leads to the removal of a pleasant event or circumstance, thereby decreasing the likelihood of a recurrence of the behavior.

Simply punishing someone does not provide that person with appropriate alternative behaviors. This mother clearly stated an appropriate alternative to biting someone when angry—using words to express feelings.

has learned not to push when she will be punished for it. Moreover, sometimes people are able to avoid punishment, but continue to exhibit the response, as when your little sister figured out that if she hit you, but then apologized, she would not get punished.

Second, physical punishment, such as a spanking, may actually increase aggressive behavior in the person on the receiving end (Haapasalo & Pokela, 1999; Straus, 2000; Straus et al., 1997). Although punishment provides an opportunity for operant learning, seeing others use physical violence also creates an opportunity for learning by watching the behavior of others. Such learning would account for the finding that abusive parents (and physically aggressive juvenile delinquents) tend to come from abusive families (Straus & Gelles, 1980; Straus & McCord, 1998).

A third problem created by punishment is that, through classical conditioning, the one being punished may come to fear the one doing the punishing. This may happen even if the punishment is infrequent. If the punishment is severe, a single instance may be enough for the person being punished to learn to live in fear of the punisher, as Chan and his classmates lived in fear of Master Yu. Constantly living in fear can make people and animals chronically stressed, and can lead to depression (Pine et al., 2001).

Punishment alone hasn't been found to be as effective as punishment used in combination with reinforcement. This is because punishment doesn't convey information about what behavior should be exhibited in place of the undesired, punished behavior. Consider a preschool-age boy who draws on the wall. You don't want him to ruin the wallpaper so you punish him, and he learns not to draw on the wall. But, at a later time, when he's feeling creative, he might draw on the floor or the door instead. However, if you punish him for wall- or floor-drawing and then provide him with paper and reinforce him for drawing on the paper, he can be artistically creative without inviting punishment. Because of the disadvantages of punishment, many training programs for parents emphasize positive reinforcement for good behavior; if children don't feel their parents are noticing and appreciating their efforts at good behavior, the incentive to keep it up may diminish.

Primary and Secondary Reinforcers

There are different levels of reinforcers: **Primary reinforcers** are events or objects that are inherently reinforcing (such as food, water, or relief from pain). At the Chinese Drama Academy, the children barely had enough to eat, and food became a much sought-out and fought-after item. Master Yu rewarded the Seven Little Fortunes with a trip to a restaurant after a particularly good performance. **Secondary reinforcers,** such as attention, praise, money, good grades, or a promotion, are learned reinforcers and do not inherently satisfy a physical need. The theme park Sea World uses food as a primary reinforcer for its dolphins. It also uses secondary reinforcers such as squirting the dolphins' faces with water. Secondary reinforcers are generally not instinctually satisfying.

● **Primary reinforcer:** An event or object that is inherently reinforcing, such as food, water, or relief from pain.

● **Secondary reinforcer:** An event or object that is reinforcing but that does not inherently satisfy a physical need, such as attention, praise, money, good grades, or a promotion.

When Chan was at the Academy, secondary reinforcers included being picked to be part of a troupe performing in public, and the kind words or deeds of a schoolmate. In his adult life, Chan received very powerful secondary reinforcement for making movies that were his own creation: 4.2 million Hong Kong dollars, and control over how the movies were made—the new studio would not require him to get their final approval over budgets or ideas.

Behavior modification is a technique that brings about therapeutic change in behavior through the use of secondary reinforcers. Programs involving mentally retarded children and adults, psychiatric patients, and prisoners have made use of secondary reinforcement. Participants in such programs earn "tokens" that can be traded for candy or for privileges such as going out for a walk or watching a particular television show. Behavior modification techniques using secondary reinforcement have also been used in the workplace; when employees received bonus vouchers for arriving at work on time, management found a significant reduction in tardiness (Hermann et al., 1973).

An unusual use of behavior modification with secondary reinforcers was undertaken by researchers in the rural Philippines who wanted to improve nutrition among poor children (Guthrie et al., 1982). The study was designed to discover whether reinforcement would be more beneficial than simply providing mothers with information about health and nutritional care for children. All of the mothers were given appropriate information. Then the health clinic provided reinforcement in various forms for increases in the children's heights and weights. Three different villages participated in the study. In one, the reinforcement was a ticket in a clinic lottery in which the prize was food; the reinforcer used in the second village was a photograph of the child. The third village was a control group, and these people received no reinforcement for height or weight gains. One year later, children in the two villages that received reinforcement grew more and had less malnutrition than did those in the third village; no differences were observed between the first and second village.

Immediate Versus Delayed Reinforcement

The interval of time between behavior and its consequence can affect operant conditioning. In the Skinner box, for instance, if the rat receives a food pellet immediately after pressing the bar, it is receiving **immediate reinforcement,** reinforcement given immediately after the desired behavior. If the food pellet doesn't appear immediately but comes, say, 30 seconds later, the rat is receiving **delayed reinforcement.** With delayed reinforcement, the rat has some difficulty learning that bar pressing is followed by food. After pressing the bar but before receiving reinforcement, the rat may have sniffed some other section of the cage, scratched its ear, or done any number of things. It would be hard for the rat to "figure out" which behavior had produced the pellet.

Humans often work hard for delayed reinforcement. We practice kicking the soccer ball into the goal so that we'll be able to score at the next game; we study hard in college to get into graduate school or to land a good job; we put in extra hours at work to get a promotion or a raise; we push our bodies to the limit of what's possible to please an audience. Walter Mischel and his colleagues (1989) found that among the 4-year-olds they studied, those who would forego a small reward now for a big one tomorrow became more socially competent and were more likely to be high achievers during adolescence.

● **Behavior modification:** A technique that brings about therapeutic change in behavior through the use of secondary reinforcers.

● **Immediate reinforcement:** Reinforcement given immediately after the desired behavior is exhibited.

● **Delayed reinforcement:** Reinforcement given some period of time after the desired behavior is exhibited.

Choosing a delayed reinforcement over an immediate one has its advantages, but the choice is not necessarily easy. A dieter trying to obtain the delayed reinforcement of looking and feeling better sacrifices immediate reinforcement (ice cream, now!) for future personal benefits. But immediate reinforcement can be very powerful, and often difficult to reject in favor of some future good. At some point, the dieter may yield to the satisfaction of eating the ice cream, or even just a normal-sized portion of dinner, instead of making yet another sacrifice for the sake of eventual slimness.

Chan experienced a long-delayed reinforcement: once his acting career began, he had two wishes. One was to be part of a Hollywood "opening night" ceremony, with plush ropes to keep fans back. The other wish was to put his handprints next to his "star" outside Grauman's Chinese Theatre in Los Angeles. He had been working and hoping for that reward for more than 10 years, with two previous Hollywood films, without success. After years of work, he achieved both goals.

Beyond Basic Reinforcement

Operant conditioning can play a powerful role in people's lives. To see how, let's look at ways in which conditioning can be more than simply learning to respond when reinforcement is likely to result.

Generalization and Discrimination in Operant Conditioning

Just as in classical conditioning, the abilities to generalize and discriminate occur during operant conditioning, but in relation to responses as well as stimuli. Thus, in operant conditioning, **generalization** is the ability to generalize from a learned response to a similar response. When a child has a runny nose, most parents teach her to wipe her nose on a tissue. She may then generalize the response of wiping her nose and begin to wipe it on any available soft surface—her sleeve, her parent's shirt, her pillow. On the other hand, in order to get into a house, Chan may climb up an outside wall and crawl in through a window when filming a stunt, but he undoubtedly doesn't enter his own home this way. **Discrimination** is the ability to distinguish between the desired response (wiping a runny nose on a tissue or handkerchief) and a similar but undesirable one (wiping a runny nose on a shirt sleeve). The child's parents could help her make this discrimination by reinforcing her every time she wipes her nose with tissues or handkerchiefs (making sure they are readily available), and by not reinforcing her when she wipes her nose on her sleeve or on theirs.

Discrimination depends on the ability to distinguish among the different situations in which a stimulus may occur. Animals can be trained to press a bar to get food only if a tone is sounding, or only if they hear a high tone (not a low or medium tone). A **discriminative stimulus** is the cue that tells the organism whether a specific response will lead to the expected reinforcement. Experienced drivers react to a red light without thinking, automatically putting a foot on the brake pedal. In this situation, the red light is the stimulus, stopping the car is the response, and the reinforcement (negative, in this case) is escaping a dangerous situation. But drivers don't stomp their right feet down if they encounter a red light while walking on the sidewalk. Driving a car is the discriminative stimulus that cues the response to stomp the right foot.

Extinction and Spontaneous Recovery in Operant Conditioning: Gone Today, Back Tomorrow

Have you ever lost money in a vending machine? If so, does this sequence of behaviors sound familiar? You deposit coins in the machine and press the button for your selection because you have learned that the reinforcement (the food) will come down the chute. When you press the button and no food appears, you press

Do you think that if a baseball player touches his elbow and drags his feet before going up to bat he will improve his hitting? It seems that Boston Red Sox player Nomar Garciaparra does. This behavior would seem to qualify as superstitious: good hitting is not a consequence of his touching his elbow and dragging his heel, but somewhere along the line Mr. Garciaparra associated the former as a consequence of the latter.

● **Generalization:** The ability to generalize both to similar stimuli and from a learned response to a similar response.

● **Discrimination:** The ability to distinguish between the desired response and a similar but undesirable one.

● **Discriminative stimulus:** The cue that tells the organism whether a specific response will lead to the expected reinforcement.

the button again. You then have a burst of pressing the button several times (and maybe a few other buttons for good measure) and, only after these responses fail to make the machine deliver the goods, do you give up. As this example shows, when someone has learned a behavior through operant conditioning (putting money in a vending machine), and the reinforcement stops (the food doesn't appear), initially there is an increase in responding. After this initial burst of behavior, the response fades. This is how **extinction** works in operant conditioning.

As with classical conditioning, the original response isn't lost through extinction; what happens is that new, opposing learning takes place. In the vending machine example, the opposing learning is that dropping coins in the slot does not lead to the appearance of food. As with classical conditioning, **spontaneous recovery** occurs: If a break follows extinction, the old behavior will reappear. So if you don't use that vending machine for a month, you might very well put money in it again, expecting it to dispense your bag of chips.

Building Complicated Behaviors: Shaping Up

Many complex behaviors are not learned all at one time, but rather are acquired gradually. Moreover, complex behaviors may often be built on previously learned behaviors. How do the animal trainers at Sea World train the dolphins to do a high jump? The dolphins don't naturally do it, so they can't be reinforced for that behavior.

Shaping is the gradual process of reinforcing an organism for behavior that gets closer and closer to the behavior you ultimately wish to produce. It is the method that helps train dolphins to do high jumps (see Figure 6.12), and it is also the method by which Jackie Chan learned kung fu: the complex behaviors were

- **Extinction:** In operant conditioning, the fading out of a response following an initial burst of a behavior after the withdrawal of reinforcement.

- **Spontaneous recovery:** In operant conditioning, the process by which an old response reappears if there is a break after extinction.

- **Shaping:** The gradual process of reinforcing an organism for behavior that gets closer to the desired behavior.

FIGURE 6.12 Shaping Dolphins at Sea World

At Sea World, training dolphins to jump requires a number of phases, each getting closer to the final goal.

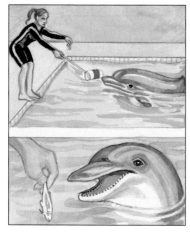 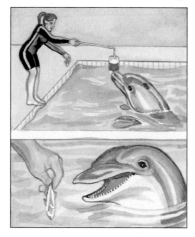 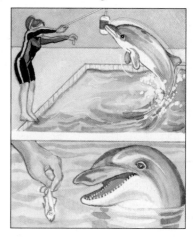

First the dolphin receives reinforcement (a food treat) after touching a target on the surface of the water.

The target is raised slightly out of the water. When the dolphin touches the target, it receives food.

The target continues to be raised until eventually the dolphin's body must come out of the water for it to touch the target. The dolphin receives a treat for doing so.

gradually shaped, first by his father when he was very young, and later by Master Yu. It is used when the desired response is not one that the organism would emit in the normal course of events. Shaping must be done in phases, nudging the organism closer and closer to the desired response. In shaping, the final behavior is considered as a series of smaller behaviors, which become increasingly similar to the desired behavior; these smaller behaviors are called **successive approximations.**

Reinforcement Schedules: An Hourly or a Piece-Rate Wage?

A critical element that can change the frequency of an organism's response is the schedule on which the reinforcement is delivered. Reinforcement can be given every time a desired response occurs, or it can be given less frequently. When an organism is reinforced for each desired response, it is receiving **continuous reinforcement.** When reinforcement does not occur after every response, but only intermittently, the organism is receiving **partial reinforcement.** Initial learning is slower with partial reinforcement than with continuous reinforcement. For this reason, when trying to shape a new behavior, continuous reinforcement is the best method until the desired behavior is stable. Thus, Sea World trainers reward a dolphin every time it touches the target on the surface of the water. An advantage of a partial reinforcement schedule, however, is that it is more resistant to extinction: The organism learns that it won't receive reinforcement after each response, so it doesn't stop doing the behavior right away when no reinforcement is forthcoming. Some partial reinforcement schedules, called **interval schedules,** are based on time; reinforcement is given for responses after a specified interval of time. Other schedules, called **ratio schedules,** are based on a specified number of the desired responses; reinforcement is given after that number of responses is emitted.

On a **fixed interval schedule,** the organism receives reinforcement for a response emitted after a fixed interval of time. In a Skinner box, a rat on a fixed interval schedule of 10 minutes would receive reinforcement for the first bar press that occurs 10 minutes after the previous reinforcement was given, but not during that 10 minutes, regardless of how many times it pressed the bar. The same applies for the next 10-minute interval: The rat would receive a food pellet only for the first bar press after 10 minutes since the last reinforcement. With animals on a fixed interval schedule, the frequency of desired behavior tends to slow down right after reinforcement and pick up again right before reinforcement. When working as a stuntman, if Chan received a bonus every week for performing highly dangerous stunts, regardless of whether he did one or five of that type of stunt, he would be on a fixed interval schedule of 1 week. A study break after every hour of studying is reinforcement on a fixed interval schedule. So is a weekly paycheck: No matter how hard you work, you will not get an additional paycheck that week. Companies recognize that the fixed interval schedule is not necessarily the best way to reward employees, and promotions are not always available nor desirable to award. To reward employees' performance, Discovery Communication (the company that owns the Discovery Channel, among other networks) instituted a new pay incentive structure in 2001: In addition to a significant pay raise for exceptional performance, employees are also eligible for bonuses that are largely determined by initiative, responsibility, and supervisors' evaluation. Mediocre employees earn only the minimum salary and do not get bonuses (Glater, 2001). As shown in Figure 6.13, responses to a fixed interval schedule produce a scallop shape on the graph of cumulative responses.

● **Successive approximations:** The series of smaller behaviors involved in shaping a complex behavior.

● **Continuous reinforcement:** Reinforcement given for each desired response.

● **Partial reinforcement:** Reinforcement given only intermittently.

● **Interval schedule:** Partial reinforcement schedule based on time.

● **Ratio schedule:** Partial reinforcement schedule based on a specified number of emitted responses.

● **Fixed interval schedule:** Reinforcement schedule in which reinforcement is given for a response emitted after a fixed interval of time.

In **variable interval schedules**, the interval is an average over time. If a rat were reinforced for its first response after 8 minutes, then 12 minutes later, then 13 minutes later, then 7 minutes later, it would be on a variable interval schedule of 10 minutes. If you took a study break after approximately an hour of studying, but sometimes after 45 minutes, sometimes after an hour and 15 minutes, sometimes after half an hour, sometimes after an hour and a half, the average would be every hour, and so you would be on a variable interval 60-minute schedule. If Chan received a bonus on average every week for daredevil stunts, but sometimes sooner, sometimes later, he would be on a variable interval schedule of reinforcement of 1 week. In animals, this schedule creates consistent although somewhat slow responding (see Figure 6.13).

Fixed ratio schedules provide reinforcement after a fixed number of responses. If a rat is on a "fixed ratio 10," it receives a food pellet after its tenth bar press, then again after another 10, and so on. Factory piecework is paid on a fixed ratio schedule; for example, in the garment industry, workers may be paid a certain amount for every 10 completed articles of clothing. When responses on this schedule are graphed, they assume a step-like pattern (see Figure 6.13): there is a high rate of response until reinforcement is delivered, then a lull, followed by a high rate of response until the next reinforcement, and so on. This schedule has

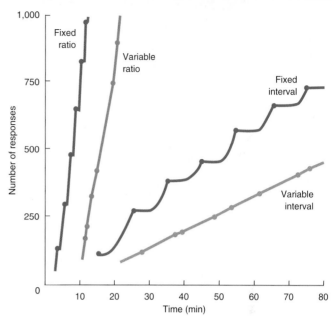

FIGURE 6.13 Schedules of Reinforcement

Research findings are mixed with regard to how well rodents' and humans' cumulative frequencies on four schedules of reinforcement correspond. Some studies with humans have found similar patterns of responding (Higgens and Morris, 1984); others have not (Lowe, 1979; Matthews et al., 1977). For both humans and rodents, however, variable reinforcement schedules induce a more consistent rate of responding than do their fixed reinforcement schedule counterparts.

a high rate of responding when compared with fixed interval responding. For this reason, piecework can be exhausting, whether the work is inputting data (being paid for every 100 lines of data entered), sewing garments, or assembling machinery. On this schedule, workers have a good reason not to take breaks (they will not be paid for that time), but as people work long hours without breaks, efficiency and accuracy decline (Proctor & Van Zandt, 1994). If Chan received a bonus for every fifth daredevil stunt, he would be receiving reinforcement on a fixed ratio schedule.

Variable ratio schedules present reinforcement at a variable rate. If reinforcement occurs on average after every tenth response, reinforcement could be presented after 5, 18, 4, and 13 responses, or it could presented after 24, 1, 10, and 5 responses. You never really know when the reinforcement will come. This is often called the "gambling reinforcement schedule" because most gambling relies on this type of unpredictable reinforcement. Slot machines hit the jackpot on a variable ratio reinforcement schedule. If you play long enough (and spend enough money), eventually you will win; unfortunately, you might spend years, and tens of thousands of dollars, trying to hit the jackpot. The variable ratio schedule is the most resistant to extinction (which is part of the reason some people get hooked on gambling). Because you don't know exactly when you will be reinforced (but expect that eventually reinforcement will come), you keep responding. Animals on

● **Variable interval schedule:** Reinforcement schedule in which reinforcement is given for a response emitted after a variable interval of time.

● **Fixed ratio schedule:** Reinforcement schedule in which reinforcement is given after a fixed ratio of responses.

● **Variable ratio schedule:** Reinforcement schedule in which reinforcement is given after a variable ratio of responses.

The variable ratio reinforcement schedule, often referred to as the gambling reinforcement schedule, is the most resistant to extinction. If you were playing a slot machine and didn't hit the jackpot, how long would you need to play before you might think there was a problem with the machine?

this schedule tend to respond frequently, consistently, and without long pauses, and this schedule tends to get the highest response rate; for example, Skinner (1953) found that when he shifted to reinforcing a pigeon on a variable, infrequent schedule, the pigeon continued to peck at a disk 150,000 times without reinforcement, as if still expecting reinforcement! Commission sales jobs are based on the same principle: The hope of an eventual sale (and therefore reinforcement in the form of an eventual commission) keeps salespeople pushing their wares.

After Chan moved out of the Academy and started making some money, he began to gamble. He described how powerful the gambling reinforcement schedule is. During the day, he would risk his life for money (get paid for doing dangerous stunts), and then after work would risk his pay on gambling—a game of chance, not skill. Some nights he had to be dragged from the gambling table; other times he woke up in the morning with no money, hungry, and hung over. But because Chan was reinforced for gambling on a variable ratio schedule, it was a behavior that was very hard to extinguish. Even when he tried to go straight home after work, he was often unable to resist the temptation of gambling: " . . . as soon as I stepped off of the Star Ferry and set foot in Kowloon, I felt the same old sizzle in the air: fast games. High risk. Big money. As hard as I tried to walk toward my apartment, I felt myself being drawn in the direction of an old familiar alley, where I knew I'd find the hottest action in town" (Chan & Yang, 1999, p. 155).

The Learning Brain

Until recently, learning theorists ignored the role of the brain in learning, focusing instead on overt behaviors. We now know, however, that an understanding of how the brain works can shed considerable light on this fundamental process (as shown by Beggs et al., 1999, among others). Recent research suggests, for example, that two neurotransmitters, acetylcholine and dopamine, play critical roles in several different aspects of learning.

Different Parts for Different Jobs

Learning isn't a single process. As discussed earlier, when you walk down a street you don't stomp your right foot every time you see a red light. From this we can infer that learning involves at least two major aspects. First, we learn to discriminate the proper situation in which to make a response. Here the hippocampus plays an important role. The neurotransmitter acetylcholine (ACh) is critical for this function of the hippocampus, and scopolamine is an antagonist for this chemical—in other words, it blocks it. Animals that are given scopolamine can't learn which stimuli should be grouped together as a signal for an appropriate response (Mishkin & Appenzeller, 1987).

Second, we learn the response-consequences association itself. The key to operant conditioning is that specific consequences follow a response. Various parts of the brain produce the neurotransmitter dopamine, but one part—the nucleus accumbens, located behind the amygdala—appears to be particularly important for reward to be effective. When researchers block dopamine receptors, animals fail to respond to reinforcement, either positive (Spyraki et al., 1982) or negative (Beninger et al., 1980). Moreover, studies show that animals trained to press a lever to get a squirt of a dopamine agonist (which causes the production of dopamine) into their veins will work hard to obtain such reinforcement (Koob &

Bloom, 1988). Similarly, amphetamines and cocaine, as well as nicotine and caffeine, are dopamine agonists; people with a dependence on stimulants (see Chapter 5) will work hard to acquire these substances.

Thus, at the level of the brain, the fact that different neurotransmitters are crucial for different aspects of learning again shows us that learning is not a single activity.

Classical Versus Operant Conditioning: Are They Really Different?

Table 6.2 presents a comparison of classical and operant conditioning. Both classical and operant conditioning involve extinction and spontaneous recovery, generalization, and discrimination. Both types of learning are subject to moderating factors that affect response acquisition, such as time (in classical conditioning, the length of time between CS and US; in operant conditioning, immediate versus delayed reinforcement), and for both types of learning, biological factors influence what can be learned easily.

Noting these similarities, some researchers have debated whether these two types of conditioning are really so distinct after all. Perhaps they are just different procedures toward a similar end. Indeed, the differences are not so clear cut. Some studies, for example, show that voluntary movements can be shaped via classical conditioning (Brown & Jenkins, 1968). Similarly, involuntary responses, such as learning to control tense jaw muscles to decrease facial pain, can be operantly conditioned (Dohrmann & Laskin, 1978). However, the fact that the same ends can be reached with either type of conditioning does not imply that the means to those ends are the same. After all, bats, birds, and helicopters fly, but they do so in different ways.

TABLE 6.2 **Classical and Operant Conditioning Compared**

	Classical Conditioning	Operant Conditioning
Similarities	• Learning is based on an association between the unconditioned stimulus and the conditioned stimulus.	• Learning is based on an association between response and reinforcement.
	• Avoidance learning.	• Avoidance learning.
	• Extinction.	• Extinction.
	• Spontaneous recovery.	• Spontaneous recovery.
	• Stimulus generalization.	• Generalization.
	• Stimulus discrimination.	• Discrimination.
	• Moderating factors can affect learning.	• Moderating factors can affect learning.
Differences	• The organism is passive.	• The organism is active, "operating" on the world.
	• Responses are reflexes (limited number of possible responses).	• Responses are voluntary behaviors (limitless possible responses).
	• Responses are elicited.	• Responses are emitted.
	• "Reinforcement" is unrelated to learning the association.	• Reinforcement is contingent on the desired response.

Perhaps the best evidence that the two kinds of conditioning are truly different is that different neural systems are used in each. Although the debate over making neat distinctions between classical and operant conditioning continues, recent research on the brain appears to discount the position that they are variations of the same process. Not only do classical and operant conditioning clearly draw on different mechanisms, but different forms of classical conditioning also rely on different brain structures, depending on the response to be conditioned. For example, whereas classical conditioning of fear draws on the amygdala (LeDoux, 1996), classical conditioning of eye blinks relies heavily on the cerebellum (Thompson & Krupa, 1994). In contrast, operant conditioning involves neither structure, using instead the dopamine-based "reward system" centered in the nucleus accumbens (Robbins & Everitt, 1998). By providing evidence that different neural systems are used in the different types of learning, studies of the brain establish that the two types of conditioning are essentially different.

Looking *at* Levels

Facial Expressions as Reinforcement and Punishment

Like most people, you've probably been out with a family member or friend, said or done something while with that person, and had that person respond with a smile or a frown. Do you think that person's smile or frown affected your behavior? Recent research suggests that other people's facial expressions can act as reinforcement or punishment (as it is in Figure 6.11, which shows the impact of the Master's expression as reinforcement or punishment). Edmund Rolls and colleagues (Kringelbach et al., 2001) found that when participants were asked to make a visual discrimination (that is, to discriminate one visual stimulus from another), different brain areas in the orbitofrontal cortex were active when their performance led to an angry face (positive punishment) rather than a happy face (positive reinforcement). Consider this finding from a levels of analysis approach: When we behave in a particular way, an observer's smile or frown (level of the group) creates motivation for us to repeat or stop the behavior (level of the person); the facial expression also changes our brain activation (level of the brain) that can lead to an experience of reward or punishment (level of the person). From an infant's earliest interactions with parents (in particular, their smiles and frowns) to our deepest friendships and romantic relationships, other people's facial expressions can change our behavior through operant conditioning.

TEST YOURSELF!

1. What is operant conditioning? How does it occur?
2. What is the difference between reinforcement and punishment?
3. How are complex behaviors learned? How are these new behaviors maintained?

Cognitive and Social Learning

Chan's first huge film success came with the film *Project A*, a pirate movie that deviated from the previously accepted formula for kung fu movies. It broke box office records in Asia. Prior to *Project* A, films starring martial arts expert and actor, Bruce Lee, were all the rage, and Lee's hero was always a "noble" man, avenging some injustice. Chan broke the mold by having the hero of *Project* A be just a regular guy. But to understand Chan's success, we need to look beyond classical and operant conditioning to how he figured out what kind of movies he should make, and how he learned to make them. When Chan was first given the opportunity to star in films and coordinate the stunts, he also began watching directors and film editors, observing what they did, how and why they included certain scenes and deleted others from the finished film. Chan's behavior was not being changed primarily through classical or operant conditioning, but through cognitive and social learning. Similarly, he learned how to do these dangerous stunts, in part, by watching others.

Cognitive Learning

The learning we have discussed so far focuses on behavior. In classical conditioning, the learned behavior is the conditioned response (CR); in operant conditioning, the learned behavior is the reinforced response. But even these types of learning involve the storing of new information, which guides the behavior. **Cognitive learning** is the acquisition of information that is often not immediately acted on but is stored for later use. Information acquired through cognitive learning may be used in planning, evaluating, and other forms of thinking, without producing any behavior—only, perhaps, more information to be stored. Learning how to add is an example of cognitive learning, as is learning the names of the 50 states or the meaning of a new word. You are engaged in cognitive learning right now.

Examples of Jackie Chan's cognitive learning include how he learned the lesson of what underlies a successful kung fu movie, and learned how to incorporate stunts into a successful film. "I think that a lot of the success of *Project* A was the result of the three of us [Chan, Samo Hung, and Yuen Baio—students with him at the Academy when they were younger] working as one. On the other hand, *Project* A was also the first film in which I did something that has since become my signature: The really, really, really dangerous stunt . . . the thrill of high risk. No blue screen and computer special effects. No stunt doubles. Real action. Real danger. And sometimes, real and terrible injury" (Chan & Yang, 1999, p. 283).

Illustrating the fact that cognitive learning is more than simple associations between stimuli and responses, Tolman and Honzik (1930b, 1930c) conducted a series of classic studies of learning with rats. One group of rats was put in a maze that led to a food box, thus receiving a food reward for completing the maze (Figure 6.14, p. 244, left panel). The other group was also put in the maze but received no reinforcement; the rats were simply removed from the maze after a certain amount of time. Sometimes routes were blocked, and the rats had to find a different way to the end. The first group of rats, those that were rewarded with food, quickly increased their speed in the maze and decreased the number of mistakes; the speed and accuracy of the unrewarded second group did not particularly improve. This finding was consistent with what behaviorists would predict. However, when rats in the second group received a food reward on the 11th day, their speed increased and their errors decreased, both dramatically (Figure 6.14, right panel). It appears that these rats had learned how to run the maze quickly and correctly before the 11th day, but had no reason to do so.

● **Cognitive learning:** The acquisition of information that often is not immediately acted on but is stored for later use.

FIGURE 6.14 Tolman and Honzik's Discovery of Latent Learning

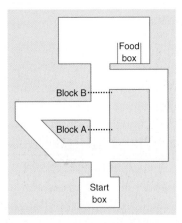

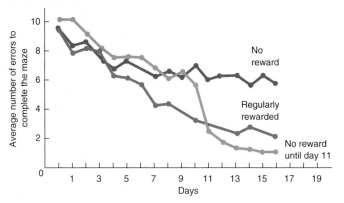

Three routes of differing lengths wind from start to finish. If two points along the most direct route are blocked, it is still possible to get to the end.

Rats that were rewarded for getting to the end of the maze made fewer "navigational" errors than rats that were not rewarded. Once rewarded (on day 11), the previously unrewarded rats made fewer mistakes than regularly reinforced rats, illustrating that the unrewarded rats had learned the spatial arrangement of the maze but did not apply that knowledge until reinforced.

Learning that occurs without behavioral signs is called **latent learning**. Tolman reasoned that the unreinforced rats, in their wanderings around the maze, had developed a *cognitive map* of the maze, storing information about its spatial layout. However, they did not use the map until they were motivated to do so by the reinforcement. This study, and the concept of latent learning, also reminds us of the important distinction between learning something and performing it. Researchers now know that latent learning depends on the hippocampus (Myers et al., 2000), which is generally used when new events are stored (Schacter, 1996). Note that although latent learning is a form of cognitive learning, not all cognitive learning is latent learning—you can rehearse to-be-memorized words aloud and otherwise produce observable behaviors when acquiring new information.

The study of learning focuses on the acquisition of information; in contrast, the study of memory focuses on the retention of information. By its very nature, cognitive learning relies crucially on how information is stored in memory, and most of the recent research on this topic (explored in the next chapter) focuses on the way information is stored in memory.

Insight Learning: Seeing the Connection

Insight learning consists of suddenly grasping what something means and incorporating that new knowledge into old knowledge. It is based on the phenomenon known as the "aha experience," the triumphal moment when an idea becomes crystal clear. By its very nature, insight learning, unlike other types of learning, is accompanied by a sudden flash of awareness that one has learned. Drawing on his experience with past films, Chan uses insight learning frequently on the set when choreographing martial arts sequences. He looks around at the items on the set right before filming a scene and gets insight into how those objects can be used in the scene:

● **Latent learning:** Learning that occurs without behavioral signs.

● **Insight learning:** Learning that occurs when a person or animal suddenly grasps what something means and incorporates that new knowledge into old knowledge.

A garden rake can be used to pull out someone's legs or to vault up to a ledge, can be spun like a staff or swung like a club. A rope becomes a whip, a restraining device, a tangling net. A barrel, a ladder, a chain-link fence—all can be thrown together in a dozen different ways, and until I'm actually there with my stunt team, weaving the scene together, I don't know which way will look best on screen. (p. 302)

The most famous psychological experiments regarding insight learning were done by Wolfgang Köhler (1887–1967), a German Gestalt psychologist. Köhler (1925–1956) put a chimpanzee named Sultan in a cage; outside the cage, and out of reach, Köhler put fruit. Also outside the cage and out of reach, but closer than the fruit, he placed a long stick. Inside the cage, Köhler placed a short stick. Initially, Sultan showed signs of frustration as he tried to reach the food. Then he stopped. He seemed suddenly to have an insight into how to snag the fruit: He used the short stick to get the long one, and then capture the fruit. In another study, Köhler put bananas in the cage but high, out of Sultan's reach. Also in the cage were stacks of boxes. At first, Sultan tried to jump up to grab the bananas. Eventually, he looked around at the objects in the cage and again appeared to have a flash of insight; he saw that stacking the boxes and climbing on them would enable him to reach the bananas.

In another instance of opportunity for insight learning, Sultan is faced with a variant of the two-stick solution to help him retrieve food that is out of reach. Here, there are four sticks of different lengths.

Observational Learning: To See Is to Know

Piaget (1962) described a situation in which one of his daughters watched another child have a dramatic temper tantrum, complete with writhing on the floor and howling. His daughter also saw the other child's parents react with concern. Days later, his daughter tried out this behavior, presumably to see whether she would be given the attention she thought a tantrum deserved. She did not have to engage in the behavior at the time in order to learn it. Everyone, like Piaget's daughter, has had the experience of watching someone else's behavior and then being able to reproduce it. The behavior is probably voluntary (and thus not the result of classical conditioning) and may not have been reinforced (and thus not the result of operant conditioning), but it was learned nonetheless. A group of

Observational learning explains why people may not make an effort to get to meetings on time: They see that latecomers do not suffer any negative consequences.

psychologists, led by Albert Bandura, developed *social learning theory*, which emphasizes the fact that much learning occurs in a social context. This kind of learning, which results simply from watching others and does not depend on reinforcement, is called **observational learning.** Observational learning helps people learn how to behave in their families (Thorn & Gilbert, 1998) and in their cultures: By watching others, we learn how to greet people, eat, laugh, tell jokes. Observational learning has helped you figure out how to behave in your class and on campus. Do you remember your first few days at college? By watching others, you learned how people talked to each other, what clothes were "fashionable," and how to interact with instructors.

Observational learning influenced Chan's behavior: at a basic level, he learned how to do kung fu and acrobatics largely by watching others, and then practiced. (Kung fu or acrobatics would be very difficult to learn from a book!) Later in his career, Chan learned to direct and edit through years of watching others direct and edit.

Bandura focused much of his work on *modeling,* a process in which someone learns new behaviors through observing other people. These other people function as models, presenting a behavior to be imitated. With modeling, you observe others' behaviors, and then none, some, or all of these behaviors may be learned and repeated, or modified. In one of Bandura's famous studies involving a Bobo doll, an inflated vinyl doll that pops back up when punched (Figure 6.15; Bandura et al., 1961), children were divided into three groups: One group watched an adult beating up a Bobo doll, one group watched an adult ignoring the Bobo doll, and the third didn't see an adult at all. After being mildly frustrated by being placed in a room with toys, but not being allowed to play with some of them, all of the children were then placed in another room with many toys, including a Bobo doll. Children who had observed the adult behaving aggressively with Bobo were themselves more aggressive. Similar studies have found similar results, including the observation that watching aggression by a live person has more of an impact than does watching a video of a person exhibiting the same behaviors. In turn, a realistic video has more of an impact than does a cartoon version of the same behaviors (Bandura et al., 1963).

Learning From Models

Learning from models has many advantages over other sorts of learning. By learning from models, you can avoid going through all the steps that learning usually requires and go directly to the end product.

"Do as I Do"

Observational learning can produce both desired and undesired learning. Models may say one thing and do another, and the observer learns both, saying what the model said and doing what the model did (Rice & Grusec, 1975; Rushton, 1975). If you are surrounded by positive models, you have the opportunity to learn a lot of positive behaviors; but if you don't have that opportunity, you may find it difficult to learn certain "skills." If adults in a family have trouble holding jobs, become explosively angry, exhibit little patience, and treat others rudely, it can be harder for the children to learn the skills involved in maintaining a job, effectively controlling anger, managing impatience and frustration, and treating others kindly. On a more positive note, Bandura and colleagues (1967) conducted a study in which preschool children who were afraid of dogs observed another

● **Observational learning:** Learning that occurs through watching others, not through reinforcement.

FIGURE 6.15 Bandura's Study on Observational Learning

Three groups of children were tested; the groups differed only in the first part of the study. Children in one group watched an adult abuse a Bobo doll, for example, by slamming it with a mallet, kicking it, and yelling at it.

Children in a second group watched adults play with Tinkertoys and ignore the Bobo doll.

Children in a third group never saw a model (an adult) in the playroom.

In the second part of the study, all of the children played in a room with a variety of toys, including Bobo. Children in the first group tended to imitate what they had seen, mistreating the doll (and inventing new ways to abuse it) and being more aggressive with the other toys in the room.

Children who observed the adult ignoring the Bobo doll were even less aggressive toward it than were children in the control group!

child who had no fear of dogs. During eight sessions, as prearranged, the model, on each successive occasion, played more closely with a dog and for a longer time. Fearful children who watched the model play with the dog had significantly more "approach" behaviors (those oriented toward a dog) than did a control group of fearful children who did not observe the model.

Both modeling and operant conditioning are involved in learning about culture and gender. You may learn how to behave by observing others, but whether you'll actually perform those behaviors depends, in part, on the consequences that occur when you try.

Chan recounts how he learned to minimize the number of beatings he received after arriving at the Academy: "I quickly learned to watch the other children carefully. Whenever they stood up, I stood up. If they sat down, I sat down. Whatever

Observational learning occurs frequently in everyday life: An apprentice spends large amounts of time observing a master before ever doing anything more than handing over a tool. How-to videos ranging from cooking to bike repair may be more effective than how-to books because they allow the viewer to see the desired behavior. Observational learning is the way we learn first languages, form standards of judgment, and even discover ways to solve many types of problems (Bandura, 1986).

they said, I said, and whatever they did, I did . . . it made it less likely that Master would single me out for punishment" (Chan & Yang, 1999, p. 40).

To further understand the way modeling and operant conditioning together help children learn about culture, imagine the following family interaction in a culture that has different expectations of what constitutes appropriate play for girls and boys. A boy observes his older sister asking her parents for a new doll and sees that they buy it for her. He then asks his parents for a doll for himself and is severely punished. His request was prompted by modeling, but because it resulted in punishment, he is unlikely to make that request again. Similarly, ninth and tenth graders were more likely to get involved in community activities if their parents were involved, or if parents reinforced them for minor involvement (Fletcher et al., 2000).

Researchers have discovered that several characteristics of models can make learning through observation more effective (Bandura, 1977a, 1986). Not surprisingly, the more you pay attention to the model, the more you learn. You are more likely to pay attention if the model is an expert, is good looking, has high status, or is socially powerful (Brewer & Wann, 1998). Perhaps intuitively realizing the importance of models for children's learning through observation, and recognizing the high-status position of his office, cigar enthusiast President William McKinley refused to be photographed with a cigar (Seuling, 1978). However, tobacco companies are using the same principles toward other ends, through product placement in films—showing actors smoking on screen. Unfortunately, research suggests that such use of observational learning has some success: 9- to 15-year-olds watching films with more incidents of smoking were more likely to try smoking themselves (Sargent et al., 2001). We know that children learn by observing others, and powerful, high-status models such as presidents, athletes, or celebrities are likely to be more influential.

"Television Made Me Do It"

We learn from models by seeing which of their responses are reinforced and which are punished. We are then able to make predictions about the reactions that our behaviors will provoke. This pattern of learning is one of the reasons parents and others have become increasingly concerned about the amount and type of violence, foul language, and sexuality portrayed on television. A large, year-long study of violence on television found not only that 57% of programs contained some violence, but also that in those programs the perpetrators of violence received no punishment 73% of the time. Moreover, in almost half of the violent interactions, no harm came to the victim, and 58% of the victims showed no pain. Only 4% of violent programs included any emphasis on alternative, nonviolent solutions to problems (Farhi, 1996). From an observational learning perspective, this is disconcerting because children watching TV learn from the bulk of shows portraying violence that there are no negative consequences for the violent person.

Further support for television's role in children's aggression comes from a study that randomly assigned third and fourth graders to either a classroom curriculum aimed at reducing television, videotape, and video game use, or to a control group. Children in the "reduction" group were reported by peers and parents to be less physically and verbally aggressive than were children in the control group (Robinson et al., 2001).

Since Bandura's work on modeling, his findings have been replicated many times over, with many variations, and the findings have largely been consistent (Clapp, 1988; Huesmann & Eron, 1986). The establishment of a rating system for television programs grew out of this body of psychological research. Many studies have been designed to identify which aspects of violence on television lead observers to behave violently later. Their results suggest that age, time spent watching television, identification with the television character, and the portrayal of violence all influence behavior (Clapp, 1988; Smith, 1993). At the same time, positive, nonviolent programs (such as *Sesame Street* or *Mr. Rogers' Neighborhood*) promote nonviolent observational learning: Preschool children who watched these programs were more likely to exhibit positive, helpful behaviors than were children who did not watch these shows (Forge & Phemister, 1987).

Many television shows geared toward children contain violence, which is frequently imitated by viewers. Moreover, television violence often shows no harm to the victim and no negative consequences for the perpetrator.

Smoking and aggression are not the only behaviors that may be modeled from television. On situation comedy shows, significantly more negative comments are made about and to overweight (as compared to underweight) women, and these comments are often followed by audience laughter (providing reinforcement for such comments; Fouts & Burggraf, 2000). Although it may not be sitcom writers' intention to "teach" such behavior, modeling and operant conditioning nonetheless lead at least some people to learn these behaviors.

Looking *at* Levels

Mom and Dad on Drugs

In the 1980s, a long-running TV public service advertisement showed a father confronting his son with what is obviously the boy's drug paraphernalia. The father asks his son incredulously, "Where did you learn to do this?" The son, half in tears, replies, "From you, okay? I learned it from watching you!" Observational learning clearly appears to be a factor in an adolescent's willingness to experiment with drugs and alcohol. Andrews and her colleagues (1997) found that adolescents' relationships with their parents influence whether they will model the substance use patterns of the parents. Specifically, they found that adolescents who had a positive relationship with their mothers modeled her use (or nonuse) of cigarettes, and those who had a close relationship with their fathers modeled the father's marijuana use (or nonuse). Similarly, those who had a negative relationship with their parents were less likely to model their parents' use of drugs or alcohol. Although some of the more complex results of this study depended on the age and sex of the adolescent, the general findings can be understood by thinking about them from the three levels of analysis and their interactions.

At the level of the brain, observing someone engage in a behavior causes you to store new memories, which involves the hippocampus and related brain systems. These memories later can guide behavior, as they do in all types of imitation. At the level of the person, if you are motivated to observe someone, you are likely to be paying more attention to them (and therefore increasing the likelihood of your learning from them and remembering what you learn). At the level of the group, you are more likely to be captivated by models who have certain attractive characteristics. In this case, adolescents who had a positive relationship with their parents were more likely to do what their parents did; if their parents didn't smoke, the adolescents were less likely to do so. The events at these levels interact: Children who enjoy a positive relationship with their parents may accord their parents higher status than do children who have a negative relationship with their parents. Thus, the former group of children probably increase the amount of attention they give to their parents' behavior. And, as you will see in the following chapter, paying attention engages the frontal lobes and other brain areas that are crucial for storing new information effectively.

TEST YOURSELF!

1. What is cognitive learning? How does it differ from classical and operant conditioning?
2. What is insight learning?
3. How can watching others help people learn?
4. What makes some models better than others?

CONSOLIDATE!

Classical Conditioning

- Classical conditioning, which was discovered by Ivan Pavlov, has four basic elements:

  1. The unconditioned stimulus (US), such as food, reflexively elicits an unconditioned response.
  2. The unconditioned response (UR), such as salivation, is automatically elicited by a US.
  3. The pairing of a conditioned stimulus (CS), such as a tone, with a US, such as food, elicits a conditioned response (CR), such as salivation. (Note that salivation can be either a conditioned or an unconditioned response, depending on the stimulus that elicits it.)
  4. The presentation of the CS alone then elicits the UR (the tone presented alone elicits the response of salivation now as a CR).

- A conditioned emotional response is involved in the development of fear and phobias, as shown by Watson and Rayner in the case of Little Albert.

- Extinction is the unpairing of the CS and US; spontaneous recovery is the return of a classically conditioned response after a rest period following extinction.

- In stimulus generalization, a similar, but not identical, stimulus elicits the CR.

- In stimulus discrimination, the organism learns to distinguish among similar stimuli so that only a particular stimulus elicits the CR.

THINK IT THROUGH Dog obedience classes suggest that the following procedure will train a dog to stop barking. When the dog starts to bark, squirt water (from a water bottle) in its face. Right before you squirt, say, "Don't bark!" The dog startles because of the water and stops barking. Is this classical conditioning? If so, identify the US, CS, UR, and CR. What would be happening if the dog stops barking as soon as you say, "Don't bark"? What learning process has occurred if the dog stops barking only when you give the command in a particular tone of voice?

Operant Conditioning

- Operant conditioning is the process whereby a behavior (usually a voluntary one) becomes associated with the consequences of performing that behavior. Operant conditioning has three basic elements:

  1. The stimulus, such as a pedal.
  2. The response, such as pressing the pedal.
  3. The consequence, such as a cage door opening.

- Shaping makes it possible to learn, by successive approximations, behaviors that would otherwise not be emitted.

- Both negative and positive reinforcement increase the behavior that precedes it.

- Both positive and negative punishment decrease the behavior that precedes it.

- Extinction, spontaneous recovery, generalization, and discrimination all occur in operant conditioning.

- Reinforcers can be primary or secondary; the latter can be tokens that are exchanged for a primary reinforcer.

- Reinforcement schedules can be continuous or partial; if partial, reinforcement may be given for responses after an interval of time (interval schedule), or after a set number of responses (ratio schedule). For both these types of schedules, reinforcement can be given on a fixed or variable basis.

THINK IT THROUGH You are babysitting, and the child's parents have explicitly instructed you not to give her any more food. She whines for dessert, you say no, and she has a temper tantrum. What can you conclude about how her parents have handled her requests for snacks in the past? If you want her to stop carrying on, what would be two different types of operant conditioning you could use to increase the likelihood of changing her behavior? (Physical or emotional violence, threats of cruelty, and yelling are not options.) Which technique do you think will be the most effective? Why? Which techniques were most effectively used by Master Yu?

Cognitive and Social Learning

- Cognitive learning involves the acquisition of information that may be used in planning, evaluating, and other forms of thinking, but is not necessarily acted on immediately.

- Latent learning, learning that occurs without behavioral signs, and insight learning, suddenly grasping what something means and incorporating that new knowledge into old knowledge, are examples of cognitive learning.

- Observational learning is learning by watching the behavior of others. The more you pay attention to the model, the more you are likely to learn.

- Children may learn to behave aggressively from watching violent television shows.

THINK IT THROUGH Curare is a drug that so totally paralyzes an animal, a heart-lung machine is necessary to keep it alive. Although the animal can't move, it can perceive and remember normally. Imagine showing a person in that situation how to open a simple combination lock on a box to obtain the $1,000 inside. When the effect of the curare has worn off and the person is able to move normally, will he know how to open the lock to get the reward? Why or why not?

Key Terms

acquisition, p. 215
avoidance learning, p. 216
behavior modification, p. 235
biological preparedness, p. 218
classical conditioning, p. 214
cognitive learning, p. 243
conditioned emotional response (CER), p. 217
conditioned response (CR), p. 215
conditioned stimulus (CS), p. 215
continuous reinforcement, p. 238
contrapreparedness, p. 218
delayed reinforcement, p. 235
discrimination, p. 236
discriminative stimulus, p. 236
extinction (in classical conditioning), p. 219
extinction (in operant condictioning), p. 237
fixed interval schedule, p. 238
fixed ratio schedule, p. 239
food aversion (taste aversion), p. 223
generalization, p. 236
habituation, p. 213
immediate reinforcement, p. 235
insight learning, p. 244
interval schedule, p. 238
latent learning, p. 244
Law of Effect, p. 229

learning, p. 213
negative punishment, p. 233
negative reinforcement, p. 231
observational learning, p. 246
operant conditioning, p. 228
partial reinforcement, p. 238
phobia, p. 217
positive punishment, p. 233
positive reinforcement, p. 231
primary reinforcer, p. 234
ratio schedule, p. 238
reinforcement, p. 229
reinforcer, p. 230
response contingency, p. 230
secondary reinforcer, p. 234
shaping, p. 237
spontaneous recovery (in classical conditioning), p. 219
spontaneous recovery (in operant conditioning), p. 237
stimulus discrimination, p. 220
stimulus generalization, p. 220
successive approximations, p. 238
trace conditioning, p. 215
unconditioned response (UR), p. 215
unconditioned stimulus (US), p. 215
variable interval schedule, p. 239
variable ratio schedule, p. 239

chapter 7

© 2003 Artists Rights Society (ARS), New York/ADAGP, Paris

Memory: *Living With Yesterday*

A Latvian newspaper reporter, known simply as "S." (short for S. V. Shereshevskii), had an almost superhuman memory. Each morning the editor of his newspaper would describe the day's stories and assignments, often providing addresses and details about the information the reporters needed to track down. The editor noticed that S. never took notes and initially thought that S. was simply not paying attention. When he called S. on the carpet for this apparent negligence, he was shocked to discover that S. could repeat back the entire briefing, word-perfect. When he quizzed S. about his memory, S. was surprised; he assumed that everyone could accurately remember what they had heard and seen. The editor suggested that S. visit the noted Russian psychologist Alexander Luria, who then studied him over the course of almost 30 years. Luria soon discovered that S.'s memory "for all practical purposes was inexhaustible" (Luria, 1968/1987, p. 3). S. could memorize a list of words or numbers of any length, and could recall it backward or forward equally easily! In fact, if given an item from the list, he could recall which items came immediately before it or after it. He generally made no errors. Moreover, he performed as well when he was tested years later, recalling perfectly not only the list itself but also when he learned it, where he and the examiner had been sitting, and even what the examiner had been wearing at the time.

Luria focused on unlocking the secrets behind S.'s formidable abilities. The results of this massive project are summarized in Luria's celebrated monograph, *The Mind of a Mnemonist: A Little Book about a Vast Memory.* Luria found that S. recalled objects, events, words, and numbers by using mental imagery. His mental imagery was rich and complex:

> "... I recognize a word not only by the images it evokes but by a whole complex of feelings that image arouses.... Usually I experience a word's taste and weight, and I don't have to make an effort to remember it—the word seems to recall itself" (p. 28).

Sounds were accompanied by images of colored lines, puffs, splotches and splashes, and these visual images could later remind him of

chapter outline

Storing Information: Time and Space Are of the Essence

Sensory Memory: Lingering Sensations

Short-Term Memory: The Contents of Consciousness

Long-Term Memory: Records of Experience

Working Memory: The Thinking Person's Memory

Genetic Foundations of Memory

Encoding and Retrieving Information From Memory

Making Memories

The Act of Remembering: Reconstructing Buried Cities

Fact, Fiction, and Forgetting: When Memory Goes Wrong

False Memories

Forgetting: Many Ways to Lose It

Amnesia: Not Just Forgetting to Remember

Repressed Memories: Real or Imagined?

Improving Memory: Tricks and Tools

Storing Information Effectively: A Bag of Mnemonic Tricks

Improving Memory Retrieval

> "Usually I experience a word's taste and weight, and I don't have to make an effort to remember it—the word seems to recall itself."

the sound. Moreover, S. used associations between images and concepts, which allowed the images to stand for other things. For example, "When I hear the word green, a green flowerpot appears. . . . Even numbers remind me of images. Take the number 1. This is a proud, well-built man; 2 is a high-spirited woman; 3 a gloomy person (why, I don't know) . . . 8 a very stout woman—a sack within a sack" (p. 31). S. could recall items in any order because he placed images along a scene, and could imagine "seeing" the imaged objects in any order. For example, "I put the image of the pencil near a fence . . . the one down the street, you know" (p. 36).

S.'s ability may sound like a dream come true, especially to a student slaving away to memorize the contents of several textbooks. As we shall see, S. was extraordinary but not supernatural. You, too, can learn many of the tricks he used. S.'s memory, like yours, relied on three fundamental types of processing: **Encoding** is the process of organizing and transforming incoming information so that it can be entered into memory, either to be stored or to be compared with previously stored information. S. was a master at this process. **Storage** is the process of retaining information in memory. As we shall see, the processes involved in storing information continue to operate for years after you've learned a fact. **Retrieval** is the process of digging information out of memory. For example, have you ever seen someone you know you've met before, but at first can't recall her name? In this situation, you get to watch the process of retrieval at work, as you struggle to bring her name to mind. S. never had such struggles, in part because his encoding and storage processing was so efficient that he could virtually always locate the information he sought in memory.

Storing Information: Time and Space Are of the Essence

S. relied heavily on mental images, but he also used language. S. eventually became a professional stage performer, and people paid to see him demonstrate his amazing memory. As part of his act, he asked audience members to produce any list or set of phrases, and he would memorize them. The audiences often tried to trip him up by giving him meaningless words or phrases. When given such verbal material to memorize, S. found it best to "break the words or meaningless phrases

- **Encoding:** The process of organizing and transforming incoming information so that it can be entered into memory, either to be stored or to be compared with previously stored information.

- **Storage:** The process of retaining information in memory.

- **Retrieval:** The process of accessing information stored in memory.

down into their component parts and try to attach meaning to an individual sylla-ble by linking it up with some association" (Luria, 1968/1987, p. 43). These asso-ciations often relied on verbal knowledge, both about the meaning of words and their sounds. S. clearly relied on many different sorts of memory—and so do the rest of us. In this section, we will consider these different types of memory.

Until someone asks for your address, chances are you aren't consciously aware of it—or even that you have one. But, once you are asked, the information is at your mental fingertips. This difference, between memories we are aware of holding and those we are not, is one sign that different types of "memory stores" are at work. A **memory store** is a set of neurons that serves to retain information over time.

Although we sometimes talk as if our "hands remember" how to shoot baskets and our "fingers remember" how to play the guitar, all memories are stored in the brain. We can distinguish among three types of memory stores, which differ in the time span over which they operate and in the amount of information they can hold (Shiffrin, 1999). These three types of structures are known as sensory, short-term, and long-term memory stores. The fundamental distinctions among these types of mem-ories were first characterized in detail by Atkinson and Shiffrin (1968, 1971) and Waugh and Norman (1965), as illustrated in Figure 7.1.

FIGURE 7.1   The Three-Stage Model of Memory

The three-stage model emerged from Atkinson and Shiffrin (1968, 1971) and Waugh and Norman (1965). This model not only identified distinct types of memory stores, but also specified how information flows among them. Later research showed that information can, in fact, flow to long-term memory without necessarily passing through short-term memory, and that rehearsal—repeating items over and over—only helps memorization if people think about the information (counter to what was initially claimed). Nevertheless, this model provided the framework for subsequent studies and theories of memory.

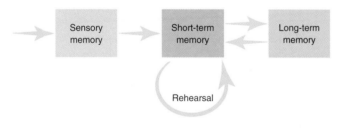

Sensory Memory: Lingering Sensations

Have you ever looked at scenery rushing past the window of a moving car and noticed that although you see literally miles and miles of landscape slipping by, you need to make an effort to remember more than fleeting images, which last about as long as the instant it takes for the image to flash by? **Sensory memory (SM)** holds a large amount of perceptual input for a very brief time, typically less than 1 second. Sensory memory happens automatically, without effort (via bottom-up processes; see Chapter 4); sensory memory arises because the activation of per-ceptual areas of your brain by the stimulus persists for a few brief moments.

● **Memory store:** A set of neurons that serves to retain information over time.

● **Sensory memory (SM):** The "lowest" level of memory, which holds a large amount of percep-tual input for a very brief time, typically less than 1 second.

George Sperling (1960) reported an experiment, presented in Figure 7.2 and now regarded as a classic, that demonstrated this lingering sensory memory in vision (the visual form of sensory memory is called *iconic memory*). When shown sets of many letters or digits very briefly, people can report only a handful afterward. However, they claim that they can remember all the items for an instant or two, but then the memory fades too quickly to "read off" all of them during recall. Sperling was able to demonstrate that this claim was, in fact, correct. He briefly showed participants displays of items, more than they could report, and then presented a tone that cued which row to report. The participants were able to report the cued row almost perfectly. Because the cue was presented *after* the display was removed, the participants had to have retained some memory of all of the rows in order to perform so well. This finding shows that iconic memory stores a large amount of information but that it fades very quickly. The sense of a fleeting memory after the stimulus has ceased holds true for hearing as well. For example, you can continue to hear the sound of a voice after it finishes speaking for the brief time it is still in auditory SM (Cherry, 1953; the auditory form of sensory memory is called *echoic memory*).

In iconic memory, sensory input lingers only briefly.

FIGURE 7.2 The Sperling Study

Participants saw sets of letters arranged in three rows. When the letters were flashed very quickly (for less than 0.25 second), people were able to report around 4 or 5 letters, even though they recalled seeing more.

In another part of the study, a high, medium, or low tone was presented immediately *after* the rows of letters were flashed. Participants reported the top row if the tone was high, the middle row if it was medium, and the bottom row if it was low. They could report the appropriate row almost perfectly, showing that they had briefly stored more than they could report aloud.

● **Short-term memory (STM):**
A memory store that holds relatively little information (typically 5 to 9 items) for a few seconds (but perhaps as long as 30 seconds); people are conscious only of the current contents of STM.

Short-Term Memory: The Contents of Consciousness

Whereas sensory memory retains information for the briefest of time, **short-term memory (STM)** holds information for several seconds; if people name the stimuli and say the names over and over, they can retain information in STM (typically for about 30 seconds). Also in contrast to SM, which can hold a large amount of information, STM holds only a handful of separate pieces of information. You are conscious only of the information you have currently stored in STM. The very fact that you are aware of information, such as a telephone number you've just looked up and are rushing to the telephone to dial, is a sure sign that the information is in STM.

How much remembered information can we be aware of at one time—in other words, how much information can STM hold? Miller (1956) argued that STM can hold only about 7 plus-or-minus 2 (that is, from 5 to 9) "chunks" at once, but more recent research suggests that the number is more like 4 (Cowan, 2001). A **chunk** is a unit of information, such as a digit, letter, or word. Generally speaking, STM can handle somewhere between 5 and 9 items (organized into about 4 chunks); this is why telephone and license plate numbers are fairly easy to remember. The definition of a chunk is not precise, however, and research has shown that the amount of information STM can hold depends on the type of materials and the individual's experience with them (Baddeley, 1994; Broadbent, 1971; Mandler, 1967). For instance, a word is usually treated as a chunk, but you can store more one-syllable words than five-syllable ones. Can you intentionally retain information such as telephone numbers in STM? Yes, indeed. When you see something you want to remember (such as the numbers on the license plate of a car involved in an accident), you can hold this information in STM by **rehearsal,** repeating the information over and over. When you dash from telephone book to telephone, repeating like a mantra the number you've just looked up, you are rehearsing. To get a sense of the importance of chunking, try the exercise in Figure 7.3.

- **Chunk:** A unit of information, such as a digit, letter, or word.
- **Rehearsal:** The process of repeating information over and over to retain it in STM.

FIGURE 7.3 "Chunking in Action"

A	E
7 9 1 2	5 1 8 6 1 9 2 4
8 9 8 9	7 7 7 5 5 5 8 8

B	F
1 4 2 5 9	9 6 5 2 4 6 3 7 9
2 2 4 4 1	2 2 2 2 7 7 7 7 1

C	G
9 1 3 9 2 6	1 3 8 5 2 6 2 1 7 4
4 2 4 2 4 2	3 3 5 5 9 9 4 4 2 2

D	H
6 4 1 7 6 2 8	7 2 5 8 3 1 8 4 3 2 1 6
3 3 3 8 8 5 5	2 2 5 5 8 8 1 1 6 6 3 3

HANDS ON

Read the first row in box A, left to right, and then look up from the book and say it aloud. Check to see whether you could recall all the digits. Then read the second row in box A, left to right, and do the same. Work your way down the table, and keep going until you can't recall either of the two equal-length rows in a pair perfectly. You should find that for the shorter rows, you can remember both rows with equal ease. But for the longer ones, the second row in each pair is easier to remember than the first one. Now that you know about chunking, you know why: It's not the number of digits, it's the number of chunks that's important—and the second member of each pair is easier to organize into fewer chunks.

Long-Term Memory: Records of Experience

Rehearsal is important in part because it provides us with an opportunity to move information into a third type of memory store, **long-term memory (LTM)**. LTM holds a huge amount of information for a long time, from hours to years. You are not directly aware of the information in LTM; it has to move into STM before you are conscious of it. As an analogy, think of the difference between storing a file on your hard drive versus having it only in RAM, or random-access memory, the active memory in a computer. Once information is saved on the hard drive, it can be stored indefinitely; it cannot be disrupted if the power fails. If information faded rapidly from RAM (instead of being lost instantly when you close without "saving"), the difference between storing words simply by typing them into RAM and saving them on the hard drive would be much like the difference between memories stored in STM versus LTM.

LTM stores the information that underlies the meanings of pictures, words, and objects, as well as your memories of everything you've ever done or learned. Unlike the single general-purpose hard drive on a computer, LTM is divided into specialized parts, as if (to continue the analogy) it had different drives for different sensory modalities (such as vision and audition), verbal information, and motor memories. The storage capability of LTM is so large that some researchers question whether it has a limit. Shepard (1967), for example, investigated the capacity of LTM by showing people more than 600 pictures (photographs, colored prints, illustrations), mostly from magazines, and then testing for recognition. Pairing pictures seen in the first round with new, previously unseen ones, Shepard asked his participants to pick out those they had been shown in the first part of the study. He found that the participants could recognize over 99% of the images correctly 2 hours after seeing them, and 87% a week later. This remarkable degree of retention was found even though the participants had spent an average of only 5.9 seconds looking at each picture.

STM and LTM in Action

The distinction between STM and LTM matters in everyday life, sometimes a great deal. If you see the license number of a car that has just hit a cyclist but lose that information from STM, it is gone forever unless it has moved into LTM. But, if the information has been stored in LTM, you should be able to retrieve it.

Evidence for distinct short-term and long-term memory stores has been shown in many studies. The earliest of these took place over 100 years ago, when German philosopher and pioneering memory researcher Hermann Ebbinghaus (1850–1909) undertook a series of experiments to discover the factors that affect memory. Although he didn't realize it at the time, Ebbinghaus's findings were the first solid evidence that STM and LTM are distinct, and that they operate differently. Here's what he did: To see how well he could memorize letters, digits, and *nonsense syllables* (such as *cac*, *rit*, and the like, which are not words but can be pronounced), Ebbinghaus (1885) wrote out a set of these stimuli, each on its own card. He then studied them, one at a time, seeing, later on, how many he could recall. Ebbinghaus found—as many researchers have since confirmed—that the first and last items studied were more easily remembered than those in the middle. The left panel of Figure 7.4 illustrates this *memory curve*. The increased memory for the first few stimuli is called the **primacy effect;** the increased memory for the last few stimuli is the **recency effect.**

● **Long-term memory (LTM):** A memory store that holds a huge amount of information for a long time (from hours to years).

● **Primacy effect:** Increased memory for the first few stimuli in a set.

● **Recency effect:** Increased memory for the last few stimuli in a set.

FIGURE 7.4 The Memory Curve

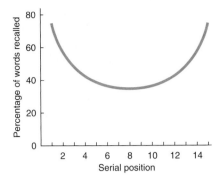
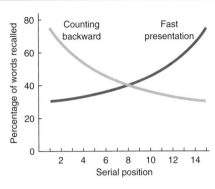

Memory is typically better for the first few and last few items in a set, producing the "memory curve" shown on the left. Less time between items reduces memory for the first few items, whereas counting backward impairs memory for the last few items. These different effects are evidence that different memory stores are involved in the two phases.

Primacy and recency effects are evidence that short-term and long-term memories rely on distinct stores. To see how, we need to look at additional studies. First, it has been found that presenting items to be learned in rapid succession reduces the primacy—but, crucially, not the recency—effect; as the right panel of Figure 7.4 shows, memory is still enhanced for the later items, but not for those learned early. The simple fact that the time between items affects only one part of the memory curve is evidence that both parts cannot arise from the same mental processes. Why does reducing the presentation time affect only the primacy effect? The primacy effect occurs because we have more time to think about the earlier items than the later ones, and thus the earlier ones are more likely to be stored in LTM. By rehearsing information in STM for those early items, we stretch out the time we have available for storing it in LTM and, in general, the more time we have to rehearse information, the more likely we are to store it effectively in LTM. If a list is presented quickly, the retention advantage of storing material in LTM is lost for the early items; but because STM is not affected, the items learned last are still available.

There is also a reverse effect. Counting backward out loud immediately after the last item of a list is presented disrupts the recency effect (see Figure 7.4) but not the primacy effect. Why? The recency effect occurs because the last few items are still in STM and thus can be recalled immediately (when told to recall a list, people typically start with the last few items, as if they are retrieving these items before the information stored temporarily in STM is lost). Counting backward disrupts information in STM, thus disrupting the recency effect. But counting backward does not affect the information in LTM any more than unplugging a computer affects what is stored on the hard drive. The different effects of presentation rate and the interference of backward counting indicate that different memory stores are used.

Modality-Specific Memories: The Multimedia Brain

The fact that memory is not a single capacity becomes especially clear when we look closely at how different kinds of information are stored in LTM. For example, note what seems to happen when you decide which is the darker green, a pine tree or a frozen pea? Or, as we asked in Chapter 4, do the first three notes of "Three Blind Mice" go up or down? When answering such questions, most people report recalling visual or auditory memories, "seeing" a tree and a pea,

HANDS ON

"hearing" the nursery song. S. was superb at these kinds of memories. In fact, virtually all of his memories were rooted in images of one sort or another; even when he used elaborate verbal associations or stories, they eventually led to specific mental images. As we saw in the discussion of perception in Chapter 4, our brains store visual memories so that we may recognize previously seen objects, auditory memories to recognize environmental sounds and melodies, olfactory memories to recognize previously encountered scents, and so on. These **modality-specific memory stores** retain input from a single sense or processing system (Fuster, 1997; Karni & Sagi, 1993; Squire, 1987; Squire & Kandel, 1999; Ungerleider, 1995). In addition to visual, auditory, and olfactory memory stores, we have separate memory stores for touch, movement, and language. Interestingly, nearly everyone finds visual memories easier to recall than verbal memories. If you have a vivid mental image of an event, your chances of accurately remembering the event increase (Brewer, 1988; Dewhurst & Conway, 1994). S.'s reliance on images may have been an accident of how his brain functioned, but it clearly helped his memory.

How do we know that memories for different modalities are stored separately? Damage to particular parts of the brain can disrupt each of these types of LTM (visual, auditory, and so forth) separately while leaving the others intact, which indicates that the information is stored separately (Gardner, 1975; Schacter, 1996; Squire, 1987; Squire & Kandel, 1999). Furthermore, neuroimaging studies have found that when people recall visual versus auditory information from LTM and store it temporarily in STM (as you did when you answered the questions about the tree and the pea and the tune), different perceptual areas of the brain are activated (Halpern & Zatorre, 1999; Mellet, Petit et al., 1998; Thompson & Kosslyn, 2000). The fact that different brain areas are used for the different memories is one form of evidence that distinct memory stores are at work.

Semantic Versus Episodic Memory

In each modality-specific LTM store, you can retain two types of information. **Semantic memories** are memories of the meanings of words (a pine is an evergreen tree with long needles), concepts (heat moves from a warmer object to a cooler one), and general facts about the world (the original 13 colonies were established by the British). For the most part, you don't remember when, where, or how you learned this kind of information. Information in semantic memory is organized into *semantic memory networks*, of the sort illustrated in Figure 7.5 (Collins & Loftus, 1975; Lindsay & Norman, 1977).

In contrast, **episodic memories** are memories of events that are associated with a particular time, place, and circumstance (when, where, and how); in other words, episodic memories provide a *context*. The meaning of the word "memory" is no doubt firmly implanted in your semantic memory, whereas the time and place you first began to read this book are probably in your episodic memory. At first, a new word may be entered in both ways, but after you use it for a while you probably don't remember when, where, or how you learned its meaning. However, even though the episodic memory may be gone, the word's meaning is retained in semantic memory. Episodic memory for events of your own life are called *autobiographical memories* (Conway & Rubin, 1993).

Neuroimaging studies have provided evidence that semantic and episodic memories are distinct. The frontal lobe, for instance, plays a key role in looking up stored information (Hasegawa et al., 1998). However, when we recall semantic memories, many researchers have found that the left frontal lobe tends to be acti-

● **Modality-specific memory stores:** Memory stores that retain input from a single sense, such as vision or audition, or from a specific processing system, such as language.

● **Semantic memories:** Memories of the meanings of words, concepts, and general facts about the world.

● **Episodic memories:** Memories of events that are associated with a particular context—a time, place, and circumstance.

FIGURE 7.5 Structure of Semantic Memory Networks

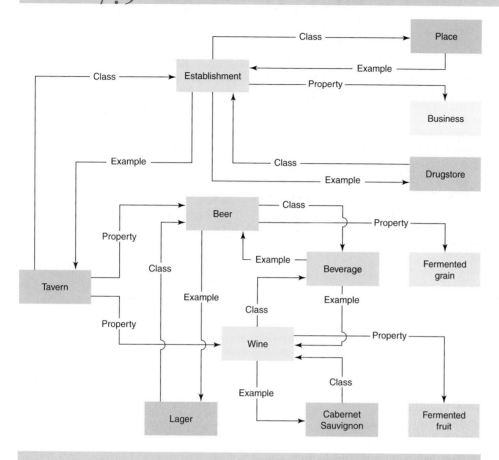

Semantic memory is organized so that activating a concept tends to activate other concepts that are associated with it. In this diagram, the boxed words stand for concepts and the lines stand for associative links between them. Semantic memory not only contains different sorts of concepts—such as objects, living things, and characteristics—but also different sorts of associations among them—such as whether one thing is an example of a category or has specific characteristics.

Adapted from Lindsay & Norman, 1977.

vated more than the right, but vice versa when we recall episodic memories. If the two types of memories were the same, generally the same parts of the brain should access both (Cabeza & Nyberg, 1997; Nyberg et al., 1996; Shallice et al., 1994).

Explicit Versus Implicit Memories: Not Just the Facts, Ma'am

When you consciously think about a previous experience, you are recalling an **explicit** (also called a **declarative**) **memory**. Explicit memories can be "looked up" at will and represented in STM; verbal and visual memories are explicit if you can call them to mind in words or images (as you did with the pine tree and the pea). Episodic and semantic memories are explicit memories. Explicit memories are what is stored after cognitive learning occurs (see Chapter 6). When explicit memories are activated, they can be operated on in STM: You can think about the recalled information in different ways and for different purposes, and build on them with new ideas.

But think of how exhausting it would be if every time you met a friend, you had to try consciously to recall everything you knew about how people interact socially before you could have a conversation. The reason you don't have to go through such a tedious process is that you are guided through the world by **implicit** (also called **nondeclarative**) **memories**, memories you are unaware of having that nonetheless predispose you to behave in certain ways in the presence of specific

● **Explicit (or declarative) memories:** Memories that can be retrieved at will and represented in STM; verbal and visual memories are explicit if the words or images can be called to mind.

● **Implicit (or nondeclarative) memories:** Memories that cannot be voluntarily called to mind, but nevertheless influence behavior or thinking.

You can voluntarily recall explicit memories, such as a particularly important birthday, but you cannot voluntarily recall implicit memories, such as how to ride a bike. Implicit memories guide much of our behavior, leaving the mental processes that underlie consciousness freed up to focus on novel or particularly important stimuli or events.

stimuli or that make it easier to repeat an action you performed previously (Roediger & McDermott, 1993; Schacter, 1987, 1996). Unlike explicit memories, implicit memories cannot be voluntarily called to mind—that is, brought into STM and thus into awareness.

The first hint that memory can be either explicit or implicit arose from the dreadful accidental consequences of a brain operation. H. M., whom you met in Chapter 3, suffered before his surgery from such a severe case of epilepsy that nothing could control his body-wracking convulsions. Finally, in 1953, at age 27, he underwent surgery to remove his hippocampus (and related parts of the brain in the front, inside part of the temporal lobe; Corkin, 2002). His doctors, whom H. M. had met many times, were pleased that the operation lessened his epileptic symptoms, but they were bewildered when he seemed not to recognize them. He could not remember ever having met them, and every time he saw them, he introduced himself and shook hands. To discover just how thorough this memory loss was, one of the doctors repeated an experiment first reported by Claparède in 1911: He concealed a pin in his hand and gave H. M. a jab at the handshake. The next day, H. M. again behaved as if he had never seen the doctor before but, as he reached out to shake hands, he hesitated and pulled his hand back. Even though he had no conscious memory of the doctor, his actions indicated that he had learned something about him. He had acquired a type of implicit memory (Hugdahl, 1995a).

Implicit memories are of three major types. The first type is classically conditioned responses of the sort H. M. developed after the pin prick (see Chapter 6; Hugdahl, 1995b). The second type of implicit memory is habits (which are sometimes called *procedural memories*). A **habit,** as the term is defined by memory researchers, is a well-learned response that is carried out automatically (without conscious thought) when the appropriate stimulus is present. Habits include the entire gamut of automatic behaviors we engage in every day. When you see a red light,

● **Habit:** A well-learned response that is carried out automatically (without conscious thought) when the appropriate stimulus is present.

you automatically lift your foot from the accelerator, shift it left, and press it on the brake (we hope!); if you think something is automatic, that's a give-away that the action is being guided by implicit memory. Even S., who relied so strongly on mental images (which are explicit memories), must have relied heavily on implicit memories. For example, S. could play the violin, and such knowledge is stored as implicit memories. Some of H. M.'s implicit memory was revealed by the working of habit. When one of us examined him some years ago, H. M. was using a walker because he had slipped on the ice and injured himself. The walker was made of aluminum tubes, and several operations were needed to fold it properly for storage. H. M. did not remember falling on the ice (which would have been an explicit memory), but he could fold and unfold the walker more quickly than the examiner could—thanks to the habit learned through using the device. He clearly had acquired a new implicit memory, even though he had no idea how he had come to need the walker in the first place. The intact ability to learn new habits, but not new episodic memories, is evidence that implicit and explicit memory are distinct.

We know that habits are actually stored differently from explicit memories because different brain systems underlie the two types of memory. First, consider the neural bases of explicit memories. Explicit memories cannot form unless the hippocampus and the nearby areas that feed into the hippocampus and receive information from it are functional (Sperling, 2001; Spiers et al., 2001). The removal of the hippocampus (in monkeys) disrupts memory for facts (Mishkin, 1982; Squire, 1987, 1992; Squire & Kandel, 1999; Zola et al., 2000), and brain-scanning studies have shown that the hippocampus and nearby parts of the cortex are activated when people learn and remember information (Dolan & Fletcher, 1997; Schacter, 1996; Schacter & Wagner, 1999; Squire et al., 1992). Differences in how effectively these brain areas operate could in part explain S.'s spectacularly good memory: Nyberg and colleagues (1996) found that people who had more active hippocampi when they studied words later recognized more of the words (Brewer et al., 1998 and Wagner et al., 1998, report similar findings). Second, in contrast to explicit memories, habits can be acquired by animals and humans (remember H. M.) even when the hippocampus and nearby cortex are not functional (Squire, 1987, 1992; Squire & Kandel, 1999). In fact, another circuit that bypasses the hippocampus allows us to learn habits (Mishkin & Appenzeller, 1987). Moreover, other brain structures, such as the cerebellum and basal ganglia, are crucial for habits but don't play a major role in memory for facts—which again is evidence that the two kinds of memory are different (Poldrack et al., 2001).

The third major type of implicit memory is **priming,** the result of having just performed a task (such as recognizing a particular object) that makes it easier to perform the same or an associated task more easily in the future (Schacter, 1987, 1996). If you just saw an ant on the floor, you would be primed to see other ants and, thus primed, you would now notice them in places where you might previously have missed them (such as on dark surfaces). Priming occurs when a preexisting memory or combination of memories is activated and the activation lingers. Priming that makes the same information more easily accessed in the future is called **repetition priming** (this is the kind of priming that enables you to see more ants). Many studies have shown that you can recognize a word or picture more quickly if you have seen it before than if it is novel. Such priming can be very long-lasting; for example, Cave (1997) found that people could name previously seen pictures faster when shown them again 48 weeks after the initial, single viewing. Your first exposure to the stimulus "greases the wheels" for your later reaction

● **Priming:** The result of having just performed a task that facilitates repeating the same or an associated task.

● **Repetition priming:** Priming that makes the same information more easily accessed in the future.

to it; in fact, after priming with a familiar object, the brain areas that perform the task work less hard when repeating it than they did initially (Gabrieli et al., 1995, 1996; Henson et al., 2000; Schacter & Badgaiyan, 2001; Squire et al., 1992).

Priming is clearly different from explicit memory. For one thing, priming occurs even in brain-damaged patients who cannot store new explicit memories (Cave & Squire, 1992; Guillery et al., 2001; Schacter, 1987; Squire & Kandel, 1999; Verfaellie et al., 2001). Priming is also different from habits. Some brain-damaged patients can learn motor tasks but don't show priming; other patients show the opposite pattern (Butters et al., 1990; Salmon & Butters, 1995). These results demonstrate that more than one type of implicit memory exists. S. apparently was easily primed by perceptual information (sights and sounds set up images that, later, were easily triggered), but this says nothing about how well he could acquire skills. The major different types of memory are summarized in Figure 7.6.

FIGURE 7.6 Types of Memories

Not only are there many types of memories, as shown here, but also each type can occur in multiple stimulus modalities (visual, auditory, and so on).

Reprinted with permission from L. R. Squire and S. Zola-Morgan, "The medial temporal lobe memory system," in *Science, 253,* 1380–1386. Copyright 1992 American Association for the Advancement of Science.

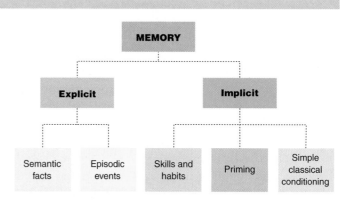

Working Memory: The Thinking Person's Memory

When S. was asked to memorize a set of meaningless sounds, he would think about each one of them and try to find an association to something familiar. What kind of memory was he using? He was doing more than retrieving items from STM or LTM; he was *using* that information to draw inferences. Whenever you reason something out, whether determining the best route to a destination, buying a com-

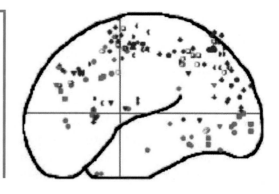

During working memory tasks, both the frontal lobes and perceptual areas of the brain are often activated. Different sets of areas are activated by different types of working memory tasks. The areas indicated by blue spots were activated when participants had to hold locations in mind, whereas the areas indicated by red spots were activated when participants had to hold shapes in mind (Smith, 2000).

forter that matches your sheets, or deciding which candidate to vote for, you remember relevant facts and use them to help you evaluate the options. In these kinds of situations, you have moved specific information into STM because you are using it or preparing to use it in some way (Zhang & Zhu, 2001).

Using information relies on yet another form of memory. **Working memory (WM)** comprises the components of the whole system that includes STM and the processes that interpret and transform information in STM (Baddeley, 1986; Cohen, Peristein, et al., 1997; D'Esposito et al., 1995; Smith, 2000; Smith & Jonides, 1999). As shown in Figure 7.7, we now know that there is more than one type of STM and that they differ in the kinds of information stored. In addition, there is a **central executive** function that operates on information in one or another of these STMs to plan, reason, or solve a problem. Baddeley (1986, 1992) distinguishes between an STM that holds verbally produced sounds, which he calls the *articulatory loop*, and another STM that holds visual and spatial information, which he calls the *visuospatial sketchpad*. The articulatory loop is like a continuous-play loop on a tape recorder, on which the sound impulses fade when the tape isn't being played; you need to rehearse repeatedly to continue to store sounds. In contrast, the visuospatial sketchpad is like a pad with patterns drawn in fading ink, which briefly retains mental images of the locations of objects (Logie, 1986; Logie & Baddeley, 1990; Logie & Marchetti, 1991; Quinn, 1991). Both STMs are temporary stores of the information you are working on; depending on what you are doing, you add and delete sounds from the taped loop or you sketch and revise diagrams on the pad. In this analogy, you are the central executive, using the two STMs, tape recorder, and pad to help you do different sorts of reasoning (Garden et al., 2002). The fact that these STMs are distinct is demonstrated not only by the different neural patterns of activation that occur when they are used (Raemae et al., 2001; Smith, 2000), but also by the fact that spatial working memory is more strongly influenced by genetics than is verbal working memory (Ando et al., 2001).

The central executive in your brain is at work when you plan what you will say on a first date or when you think about what you would like to do tomorrow. A crucial part of planning is the ability to use the fruits of past experiences, stored in LTM, to anticipate what would happen in a new situation. Thus, the contents of

FIGURE 7.7 Working Memory

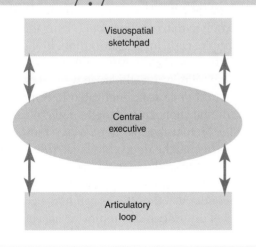

Working memory is a system that involves a central executive and different types of short-term memory stores (STM). The two forms of STM most often studied are one that holds pronounceable sounds (the articulatory loop) and one that holds visual-spatial patterns (visuospatial sketchpad).

Adapted from *Working Memory* by Alan Baddeley, Clarendon Press (1986). Reprinted by permission of Oxford University Press.

● **Working memory (WM):** The system that includes specialized STMs and the "central executive" processes that operate on them.

● **Central executive:** The set of processes that operates on information in one or another STM; part of working memory.

working memory are often retrieved from LTM. Working memory is used when you consider how to adapt previous experience to present or future circumstances. The importance of working memory is sobering when you consider that people who regularly used the club drug ecstasy (also known as "e"; see Chapter 5) have impaired working memory even 2 years after they've sworn off the drug (Morgan et al., 2002).

Genetic Foundations of Memory

The next time someone complains that they have a bad memory, you now know to wonder, What sort of memory? Short-term or long-term? Which modalities? Explicit or implicit? Surprisingly, in most cases, the different types of memory operate independently of one another. Evidence is emerging that different genes underlie different types of memory, serving to demonstrate further that the different types of memory are in fact distinct. To see how genes affect memory, we need to look more closely at the brain.

Linking Up New Connections

Many researchers believe that new information is stored in LTM when a sending neuron releases a particular neurotransmitter (glutamate) at the same time that the receiving neuron reaches a specific voltage level. When these two events occur at the same time, the neurotransmitter activates a special receptor, called the NMDA receptor (for N-methyl-D-aspartate). NMDA activation causes the receiving neuron to change so that the sending neuron needs to send less neurotransmitter to get the same effect in the future. This change, called **long-term potentiation (LTP),** essentially strengthens the connection between the sending and receiving neurons. According to this view, depending on which connections among neurons are altered, different types of memories are stored (Baudry & Lynch, 2001; Blair et al., 2001; Borroni et al., 2000; Geinisman, 2000; Villarreal et al., 2002).

Genes and Memory: Knockout Mice and Blinking Rabbits

How could we tell whether different genes affect different aspects of memory? One answer comes from the study of *knockout mice*, so named because a particular gene has been "knocked out". Genes are knocked out when a part of the genetic code has been snipped away, deleting all (or crucial parts) of the gene so that it is disabled. The basic idea is that if a gene is used in a particular function, then knocking out the gene should create a deficit in that function. But tracing that connection is easier said than done. For example, early investigators thought they had found that knocking out particular genes disrupted a mouse's ability to remember the location of a concealed platform in a pool of water (the mice wanted to swim to the platform so that they could rest, and hence were motivated to remember where it was; Morris, 1984). However, in one such study, Huerta and colleagues (1996) observed that the mice without the "remembering" gene weren't lost; they just wouldn't swim. When the researchers tickled the mice's hind feet, the animals swam and learned where the platform was located as quickly as normal mice. Their inability to find the platform wasn't caused by poor memory but by a lessened motivation to swim. (We have to wonder whether the researchers may have stumbled on a laziness gene!) One moral of this story is that removing a given gene can have multiple effects, which can cause the animal to do poorly on a test for any number of reasons (Gerlai, 1996).

● **Long-term potentiation (LTP):** A receiving neuron's increased sensitivity to input from a sending neuron, resulting from previous activation.

In spite of these confounded results in early experiments, subsequent research with knockout mice revealed that certain genes do influence memory, but their effects are limited to specific types of memory. In one set of studies (McHugh et al., 1996; Tsien et al., 1996) a *control sequence*, which turns specific genes on and off, was inserted into the DNA. This control sequence turned off the gene of interest only after the mouse had grown up, and thus the gene would stop working in an otherwise normal adult mouse. Researchers were able to eliminate the functioning of a gene that affects a single part of the hippocampus. Thereafter, these animals did not show general problems, such as a lack of enthusiasm for swimming, but they did exhibit difficulty remembering locations. Without the gene, the environmental event—trying to remember the location of a submerged platform—could not turn on the machinery that allows memories to be stored in the brain. However, the knockout mice were not totally clueless in memory tasks. They did retain some information, and hence this part of the hippocampus alone cannot be responsible for all memory. Consistent with this finding, Corkin (2002) reports that the patient H. M., who has no hippocampus, can learn some aspects of spatial layout. Again, we see evidence that memory is not a single ability.

Another way to study the effects of genes on memory is to observe which proteins are produced during a task. Specific genes produce specific proteins, and thus researchers can infer which genes were active by tracking their signature proteins. In one such study, Cavallaro and colleagues (2001) studied rabbits that were conditioned to blink their eyes when they heard a tone (see Chapter 6 for a discussion of classical conditioning). The most interesting result was that many genes decreased their production of proteins during conditioning; only a relatively few selected ones (which, for example, affected the cerebellum and hippocampus) were activated. Clearly, memory is a precise process, which involves intricate fine-tuning of that most marvelously complex of organs, the brain.

Genes and Memory Variation

Since the completion of the first phase of the human genome project, human genes have been identified that play a role in memory. For example, the apolipoprotein E (apo E) gene is present in many people who develop Alzheimer's disease, which devastates memory. But this gene does more than disrupt memory; versions (different alleles) of it also affect how well the normal brain can store information. For example, Hubacek et al. (2001) found that one allele of this gene tends to be present in people who have higher education than in people who dropped out of school by age 15, and vice versa for another version of this gene.

Looking *at* Levels

Stressed Memories

When you are stressed, your brain sends signals to your body to prepare it for a fight-or-flight response. One of these signals increases the production of the hormone cortisol (see Chapter 3), which converts protein and fat into sugar, readying the body for rapid action. However, cortisol is a two-edged sword. Sapolsky and his colleagues have shown that in rats and monkeys long-term exposure to cortisol actually kills neurons in the hippocampus

(McEwen, 1997; Sapolsky, 1992). And the loss of hippocampal neurons disrupts memory.

Sapolsky studied a troop of monkeys in Africa. The monkeys had a well-defined social order, with some members of the troop being "on top" (getting the first choice of food, mates, and shelter), and others "on the bottom." The monkeys on the bottom were found to have higher levels of cortisol in their blood; their social circumstances put them in a state of near-constant stress. When Sapolsky examined the brains of some of the monkeys who died, he found that those near the bottom of the social order had smaller hippocampi than those who were not continually stressed.

Think about this from the levels perspective: The social situation caused the monkeys to be stressed; the stress caused them to produce high levels of cortisol; the cortisol degraded their hippocampi; the impaired hippocampi caused them to have poorer memories. Now shift to the monkeys' evolutionary cousins—ourselves. MRI studies of the brains of people who have undergone prolonged stress during combat have shown that they have smaller hip-pocampi than people who were spared these experiences (Bremner et al., 1993). These and similar findings suggest that the results from monkeys may apply to humans. People may become irritated with someone who forgets tasks, putting stress on the forgetful person. The irritation and implied or stated criticism would probably affect the forgetter's view of him- or herself, and that lowered self-esteem would likely affect whether the forgetter could rise in the social order. So, social circumstances (the level of the group) cause stress, which triggers events in the brain that disrupt memory; bad memory can lead to more stress and lowered self-esteem and beliefs about abilities (the level of the person)—which in turn affect behavior in social settings (the level of the group). Fortunately, in humans the effects of stress on the hippocampus may be reversed if the environment changes (McEwen, 1997), a circumstance that introduces yet another set of possible interactions among events at the different levels of analysis.

TEST YOURSELF!

1. What is a memory store? How do memory stores differ?
2. How are different types of information stored over a long period of time?
3. What role do genes play in memory?

Encoding and Retrieving Information From Memory

As he learned to use his memory better and better, S. became a master at organizing information so that he could later remember it quickly. A key part of this activity was transforming what he was given to make it memorable. For example, when given a complex (and meaningless) mathematical formula to recall, he generated a story that described each term. The first term was N, which he recalled by thinking of a gentleman named Neiman; the next symbol was a dot (indicating multiplication), which he thought of as a small hole where Neiman had jabbed his cane in the ground; next came a square-root sign, which he converted to Neiman's looking up at a tree that had that shape; and so on (Luria, 1968/1987, p. 49). But S. was not simply adept at readying material to be memorized; he was also an expert at later digging out material from memory. In this section we will explore both types of processes—putting new information into memory and retrieving information.

HANDS ON

Making Memories

Look at Figure 7.8. Do you remember which way Abraham Lincoln faces on a penny? Most people don't. Unless you've had reason to pay attention to this fea-

FIGURE 7.8 Which Coin Is Correct?

Nickerson and Adams (1979) found that people perform poorly when asked to choose the correct coin from a set of choices. Because we need only to identify pennies versus other coins, not to notice which way Abe faces, we do not encode the profile information very well.

ture and encode it, you probably didn't store this information explicitly. In this section we will examine what it means to "store" information in memory and then look at several factors that determine whether this storage will occur.

Information not only can go from STM to LTM, but often moves in the other direction, from LTM to STM. Indeed, in order for a stimulus to be meaningful, information in LTM must have been activated because this is where meaning is stored. And most information in STM is *meaningful*: that is, you don't see the squiggle "6" as a curved line but as a recognizable number that conveys meaning; similarly, without conscious thought you see the letter pattern WORD as a recognizable word. (Remember the Stroop effect, described in Chapter 4: You can't ignore the meaning of color words when you try to report the color of the ink used to print them.) So, when you look up a telephone number, you must first access LTM in order to know how to pronounce the numbers and then keep them in STM as you prepare to make the call. Nevertheless, STM is important in storing information in LTM because working memory relies on STM, and working memory plays a crucial role in helping you organize information in a memorable way.

Coding: Packaged to Store

How convenient it would be if every time you scanned a picture into a computer, the computer automatically named it and stored a brief description. With such a feature, you could easily search for the picture (and its characteristics). As it happens, humans have this capacity and then some. In fact, we often register information using more than one memory system. Paivio and his collaborators (Paivio, 1971) not only showed that pictures are generally remembered better than words, but also made a convincing case that this difference is because pictures can be stored using *dual codes*. A **code** is a type of mental representation, an internal "re-presentation" of a stimulus or event. Just as you can print letters, draw pictures, or write the dots and dashes of Morse code on a blackboard (all of these forms are different representations), your brain can use many types of representations. Pictures can be stored with both a visual and a verbal code; that is, you can describe what you see in words as well as store it visually, so you can later recall it in your mind's eye. Research shows that illustrations improve memory for text (Levie & Lentz, 1982; Levin et al., 1987), particularly if the picture appears before the text.

As part of the encoding process, you can create new codes for storing material. For example, you can verbally describe visually perceived objects, creating a verbal code, or you can visualize verbally described information, creating a visual code. By creating and storing a verbal code when you perceive information, you

● **Code:** A type of mental representation, an internal "re-presentation" of a stimulus or event (such as words or images).

don't need to use visual parts of the brain when later recalling the information. Thus, when people were asked to name from memory the colors of objects shown to them in black and white drawings, such as fire trucks and tractors, the "color areas" of the brain were not activated (Chao & Martin, 1999). In this study, participants claimed not to use visual mental imagery; the associations apparently were stored verbally, and thus it was not necessary to access modality-specific memories themselves, which would be stored in the perceptual areas that originally registered the information.

Portions of the frontal lobes are often active when people encode new information, an indication that organizational processing is at work (Buckner et al., 1999; Kelley et al., 1998). Indeed, the degree of activation of the frontal lobes when information is studied predicts how well it will be remembered later (Brewer et al., 1998; Wagner et al., 1998).

Consolidation

If you were ever in a play, you probably found that although you knew your lines well for the performances, a week or two later you had almost forgotten them. What happened? Consider the following metaphor: Say you want to remember a path you are supposed to take in a few days. Someone shows it to you on a lawn and, to remember it, you walk the path over and over, repeatedly tracing its shape. This is a metaphor for *dynamic memory*; if it is not continually active, it is lost. But, if you stick with your chosen route long enough, the path you're tracing becomes worn, and grass no longer covers it; this kind of memory is called *structural memory* and, like the path, it no longer depends on continuing activity. When memories are stored in a dynamic form, they depend on continuing neural activity; when they are stored in a structural form, they no longer require ongoing activity to be maintained. The process of wearing a dirt path, of storing the memory as a new structure, is called **consolidation.** One goal of our *Consolidate!* sections is to help you accomplish just this process.

Many studies have shown that memories are initially stored in LTM in a dynamic form and are consolidated only after considerable amounts of time. For example, patients receiving electroconvulsive therapy for major depression—powerful jolts of electricity to the head (see Chapter 15)—experience disruption of memory for recent events, even those that are no longer in STM, but memory for older information is unaffected (McGaugh & Herz, 1972). In general, memories are well along the way to being consolidated after a couple of years (but this process may continue for much longer; Nadel & Moscovitch, 1997).

The plight of H. M. is another piece of evidence that very long-term explicit memories are stored in a structural form, but more recent memories are stored dynamically. After his operation, H. M. satisfactorily recalled events that occurred 11 years or more before the surgery, but he couldn't recall more recent information—and could not, of course, store new explicit memories. The hippocampus and related brain areas are crucial to the consolidation process, but afterward they are no longer necessary. Consolidation also occurs for implicit memories of sequences of movements, but in that process a different set of brain areas is involved (Brashers-Krug et al., 1996).

Depth and Breadth of Processing

If you want to remember the material in each of the sections of this book, we recommend you do the *Think It Through* exercises at the end of each chapter. We

● **Consolidation:** The process of converting information stored dynamically in long-term memory into a structural change in the brain.

have designed these exercises to take advantage of a fundamental fact about memory: The more you think through information, the better you will remember its meaning. Craik and Lockhart (1972) account for this effect in terms of **depth of processing,** the number and complexity of the operations used when you process information. They argue that the greater the depth of processing, the greater the likelihood of remembering what you have processed. Craik and Tulving (1975) reported a particularly effective demonstration of this effect. They asked participants to read a list of 60 words, telling them that the experiment was a study of perception and "speed of reaction." On seeing each word, the participants were asked a question about it. Three types of questions were posed (but only one for any particular word, randomly interspersed): One question required participants simply to look at the appearance of the word (to decide whether it was printed in capital letters), which did not require accessing detailed information stored in memory; the second led them to access stored information about the sound (for example, to decide whether it rhymes with train), requiring a bit more processing; and the third, to access complex semantic information (for example, to decide whether the word would fit into the sentence "The girl placed the _____ on the table"), requiring the most processing. Following this exercise, the participants were unexpectedly asked to recognize as many words from the list as they could in a new list of 180 words (containing the 60 original words and 120 new words). Craik and Tulving found that the greater the depth of processing required to answer the question, the more likely participants were to recognize the word.

What you pay attention to plays a key role in what is encoded into memory. However, the effect is not simply one of "depth," of a matter of degree: If you are shown words and asked which ones rhyme with train (which forces you to pay attention to the sounds of the words), you later will recall the *sounds* of the words better than if you were initially asked to decide which words name living versus nonliving objects. But the reverse effect occurs if you are shown words and asked later to recall their *meanings*; in this case, you will later recall better if you initially judge whether the words named living versus nonliving objects than if you initially evaluated their sounds. The most effective processing is tailored to the reasons the material is being learned (Fisher & Craik, 1977; Morris et al., 1977; Moscovitch & Craik, 1976). Practice on one task will help you perform another to the extent that the two tasks require similar processing. In particular, you will be able to remember information more easily if you use the same type of processing when you try to retrieve it as you did when you originally studied it; this is the principle of **transfer appropriate processing** (Morris et al., 1977; Rajaram et al., 1998).

If your goal is to understand the material presented in this book, you would do best to think of examples that demonstrate statements made in the text (or, conversely, to think of examples that seem to refute these statements). As to success on tests, you should try to find out what kind of test the instructor will give: If it is an essay test, you would be better off figuring out the connections between the various facts you have read and asking yourself "why" questions about them (Pressley et al., 1995); this sort of studying will be much more helpful than simple memorization, both for success on the test and for lasting understanding. For a multiple-choice or true-false test, however, simple memorization might do as well as more complicated strategies designed to integrate and organize the material, but even here you probably will retain more of the relevant information if you understand the material better.

● **Depth of processing:** The number and complexity of the operations involved in processing information, expressed in a continuum from shallow to deep.

● **Transfer appropriate processing:** Memory retrieval will be better if the same type of processing is used to retrieve material as was used when it was originally studied.

Information is encoded more effectively if it is *organized and integrated* into what you already know, thus engaging greater **breadth of processing.** Encoding that involves great breadth of processing is called **elaborative encoding** (Bradshaw & Anderson, 1982; Craik & Tulving, 1975). Perhaps the most dramatic demonstration of the benefits of elaborative encoding involved an undergraduate, S. F., who after a few month's practice could repeat lists of over 80 random digits (Chase & Ericsson, 1981). This is many, many more digits than can be held in STM, so how could he do it? S. F. was on the track team and was familiar with the times for various segments of races; thus, he was able to convert the numbers on the list into times, data with which he had associations. The digits 2145, for example, might be the times (with two digits each) needed to run two segments of a particular course. But in spite of his spectacular memory for numbers, S. F. was no better than average with letters. His memory, in general, had not improved over the months of practice with lists of numbers, only his tricks for organizing and integrating information about numbers.

The ability to organize and integrate explains why people in non-Western cultures recall stories better if the contents are familiar than if they are novel (Harris et al., 1992), and why Japanese abacus experts can remember 15 digits forward or backward, but have only average memory for letters or fruit names (Hatano & Osawa, 1983). The power of effective organization is illustrated in Figure 7.9. Indeed, people in Western cultures spontaneously organize words into categories, and later recall words in the same category before moving on to words from another category (Bousfield, 1953). However, in order to do this, the categories must be noticed; thus, it's a big help if the categories are presented explicitly.

FIGURE 7.9 Hierarchical Organization

Bower and colleagues (1969) asked participants to learn lists of words that named objects in different categories. For some of the people, the words were presented in random order; for others, they were arranged hierarchically, as shown here. The participants who had the diagram to help them organize the list remembered over three times as many words.

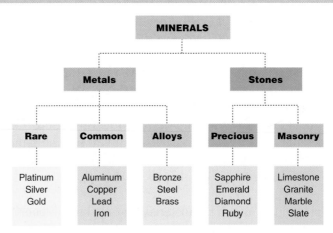

- **Breadth of processing:** Processing that organizes and integrates information into previously stored information, often by making associations.

- **Elaborative encoding:** Encoding that involves great breadth of processing.

One of the most remarkable discoveries in the study of memory is that it barely matters how much or how hard you *try* to learn something; what matters is how well you integrate and organize the material. Bower (1972) describes experiments in which participants were asked to form a mental image connecting each pair of words in a list (for example, pairing *car* and *desk*, perhaps by imagining a desk strapped to the roof of a car). In one part of the study, the participants were told to use the image to memorize the pairs of words; this kind of learning, in which you *try* to learn something, is called **intentional learning.** In another part, the participants were told simply to rate the vividness of the image, and they did not try to learn the pairs of words; learning that occurs without intention is called **incidental learning.** The interesting finding was that participants in the incidental learning part did as well as those who were told to memorize the words. But, this is not to say that motivation and effort aren't important. Instead, the effort that went into organizing the objects into an image appears to have helped the participants learn, even without a specific instruction. This effect has been found repeatedly, with different kinds of learning tasks (J. R. Anderson, 2000; Hyde & Jenkins, 1973).

Cramming is a good way to learn material for an exam, right? Wrong. Research has shown that people remember material much better if they rely on *distributed practice,* which takes place over a period of time, than if they rely on *massed practice,* which is crammed into one or two intense sessions.

Emotionally Charged Memories

S.'s memory was so good that the scientists who studied him could not perform ordinary memory experiments, which typically are aimed at discovering the factors that lead to better or worse memory. For most of us, the amount that we remember depends on specific aspects of the situation, and one important aspect is emotion: People store emotionally charged information in episodic memory better than they do neutral information. Bradley and colleagues (1992) showed people slides with positive, negative, and neutral images—for example, an attractive nude young man hugging an attractive nude young woman, a burned body, a table lamp. The participants later remembered the arousing stimuli, both positive and negative, better than the neutral ones.

Why does emotion boost memory? Cahill, McGaugh, and colleagues (Cahill et al., 1994) have begun to answer this question in detail. They showed people pictures that illustrated a story. For some participants, the pictures were all described

in a neutral way ("While walking along, the boy sees some wrecked cars in a junk yard, which he finds interesting."); for others, the pictures at the beginning and end were described in a neutral way, but those in the middle were described as depicting a bloody accident ("While crossing the road, the boy is caught in a terrible accident which critically injures him."). An hour before seeing the slides, half of each set of participants was given a medically inactive sugar pill; the other half was given a drug that interferes with noradrenaline, a neurotransmitter essential for the operation of the hippocampus (which, in turn, plays a crucial role in encoding new information into

Women remember emotional stimuli better than men, in part because emotion boosts the brain's memory circuits more effectively in women than in men (Canli et al., 2001). It is also possible, however, that socialization has led women to pay closer attention to emotion—and thus to encode it more effectively.

● **Intentional learning:** Learning that occurs as a result of trying to learn.

● **Incidental learning:** Learning that occurs without intention.

memory). A week later, all of the participants were given surprise memory tests. As expected, the group that received the sugar pill showed better memory for the pictures that had an emotional context, but the group that received the noradrenaline blocker failed to show this memory boost for emotional material.

Why does emotion cause more noradrenaline to be produced, which in turn causes enhanced memory encoding? Cahill and McGaugh thought that the boost in memory for emotional material reflects the activity of the amygdala, which is known to play a key role in emotion. To test this idea, Cahill and his colleagues (1996) used PET scanning to examine the relation between activity in the amygdala and the degree to which people could recall emotionally arousing or neutral film clips. The amount of activity in the right amygdala when the participants had seen the clips later predicted remarkably well how many clips they could recall. Thus, the enhanced memory for emotional material relies on the activation of the amygdala, which in turn influences the hippocampus.

A special case of emotionally charged memory is **flashbulb memory,** an unusually vivid and accurate memory of a dramatic event. It is as if a flashbulb in the mind goes off at key moments, creating instant records of the events. Perhaps you have such a memory for the moment you heard about the planes crashing into the World Trade Center towers on September 11, 2001. Brown and Kulik (1977) coined the term "flashbulb memory" and conducted the first studies of the phenomena. They polled people about a number of events, counting the recollections as flashbulb memories if respondents claimed to remember details about where they were when they learned of the event, from whom they heard about it, and how they or others felt at the time. Most of the people they polled at the time had flashbulb memories of President John F. Kennedy's assassination. In contrast, although three quarters of the African Americans interviewed had flashbulb memories for the assassination of Martin Luther King, Jr., fewer than one third of white interviewees had such memories. Brown and Kulik suggested that only events that have important consequences for a person are stored as flashbulb memories. Neisser and Harsch (1992) studied college students' memories of the crash of the space shuttle *Challenger,* interviewing them within a day of the accident and again two and a half years later. They found that although people may be very confident of their flashbulb memories, these memories often become distorted over time. Moreover, this distortion becomes progressively worse with the passage of time (Schmolck et al., 2000). In addition, as your current view of an emotional event changes, your memory of how you felt at the time also changes (Levine et al., 2001). Nevertheless, in general, flashbulb memories are more accurate than other types of memories (Schacter, 1996, pp. 197–201), perhaps because of their emotional content.

Would it have been a good idea if we had written a more emotionally charged opening story, perhaps discussing a horrible accident that S. had witnessed? By making the story more memorable in this way, we could have distracted you from remembering the other contents of the story—and perhaps even of the chapter itself! When people are shown a set of neutral stimuli and then a highly emotionally charged stimulus, not only do they recall the emotional one best, but they also tend to forget the stimuli that came immediately before and after this arousing one. This disruptive effect, called the *von Restorf effect,* occurs with any attention-

Many people remember where they were and what they were doing when they first heard about the events of September 11, 2001. Do you?

● **Flashbulb memory:** An unusually vivid and accurate memory of a dramatic event.

grabbing stimulus, not just those that are emotionally charged. Apparently, people are so busy thinking about the key stimulus that those occurring earlier and later are not encoded into LTM. Memory for items after the attention-grabbing stimulus is sometimes disrupted more severely than memory for items that came before it (Schmidt, 2002), especially when the materials are visual and not likely to be named and rehearsed.

The Act of Remembering: Reconstructing Buried Cities

It is tempting to think of memory as a collection of file drawers that contain assorted documents, books, tapes, and disks, and that to recall something we simply open a drawer and fetch the sought contents, all neat and complete in labeled folders. But memory doesn't work this way. When we open that file drawer, we don't find a book, but instead a bunch of partially torn pages that are not necessarily in order. Remembering is in many ways similar to the work archaeologists do when they find fragments of buildings, walls, furniture, and pottery, and reconstruct from them a long-buried city; they fit the pieces together in a way that makes sense, and they fill in the missing parts (Neisser, 1967). We store in episodic memory only bits and pieces of a given event, and we use information from episodic memories of similar situations and from semantic memories of general facts about the world to fit the pieces together and fill in the gaps.

The most famous demonstration that memory involves reconstruction was reported by British psychologist Frederic C. Bartlett in 1932. Bartlett had college students read a version of a Native American legend, previously unfamiliar to them, called *The War of the Ghosts* (these Cambridge University students knew little about Native American culture). According to the legend, a young Indian was hunting seals when he was recruited into a war party. He was wounded during a battle and thought he was being taken home by ghosts but, in fact, he was rescued by others in his war party. Although he did not feel himself to be injured, he soon died—then something black came out of his mouth.

At different intervals after their first readings, the students were asked to recall the story. Bartlett found that as time went on, the students' memories of the story changed. Sometimes they added new events; for example, one student misremembered hearing that someone cried out that the enemies were ghosts. Sometimes they reorganized the events in the story, scrambling the order. Bartlett concluded that we store key facts and later use them to reconstruct a memory by filling in the missing information. Although this conclusion has been borne out by many subsequent studies (Alba & Hasher, 1983), real-life events sometimes can be recalled repeatedly with very little distortion (Wynn & Logie, 1998).

The fragmentary nature of memory is also revealed in the *tip-of-the-tongue phenomenon*. Have you ever had the feeling that you know a word but just can't remember it? Brown and McNeill (1966) studied this phenomenon by reading definitions of relatively rare words and asking the participants to recall the words being defined. As expected, people often "knew they knew it" but couldn't quite summon up the entire word. Instead, they recalled only some of the aspects of a word, such as its relative length and perhaps even its first syllable. We don't store words as unitary wholes but as collections of different specifications—which we can sometimes recall individually.

Recognition Versus Recall

All remembering involves tapping into the right fragments of information stored in long-term memory. We remember information in two ways. **Recall** is the intentional bringing to mind of explicit information or, put more technically, the transfer of explicit information from LTM to STM. Once information is in STM, you are aware of it and can communicate it. **Recognition** is the matching of an encoded input to a stored representation, which allows you to know that it is familiar and that it occurred in a particular context, such as on a list (as used by memory researchers, the term recognition also implies identification; see Chapter 4). Essay tests demand recall; the essay writer must retrieve facts from memory. Multiple-choice tests call for recognition; the test-taker must recognize the correct answer among the options.

All else being equal, tests that require you to recognize information are easier than tests that demand recall. But recognition can become difficult if you must discriminate between similar choices. The more similar the choices, the harder it is to recognize the correct one. Similar objects or concepts have more characteristics in common than do dissimilar ones. If the choices are dissimilar, you can pick out the correct one on the basis of just a few stored features. But if the choices are similar, you must have encoded the object or concept in great detail in order to recognize the correct answer. Professors who want to make devilishly hard multiple-choice tests put this principle to work. If the alternative answers on the test have very similar meanings, the test-taker must know more details than if the choices are very different. In general, the more distinctive properties of a stimulus you have stored in memory, the better you can recognize it.

Of course, you do not always know in advance which details you will need to remember. Suppose S. witnessed a theft and later was asked to pick the thief from a police lineup. S., unlike the rest of us, typically remembered exactly what he saw. In the lineup both the thief and another man in the group of six are tall, a bit overweight, and have brown hair. The major difference between them is that the thief has a scar on his left cheek. S. would have probably noticed and remembered the thief's cheek and would be able to identify him. But, the rest of us may not have encoded this detail at the time, and thus would be hard pressed to identify the culprit. Both recognition and recall rely on activating collections of fragments stored in LTM. If the appropriate fragments are not present, you cannot distinguish among similar alternatives, and you will have difficulty recalling information.

UNDERSTANDING RESEARCH

A Better Police Lineup

You've probably seen police lineups on television shows or in movies, where a group of suspects is standing against a wall and a witness (usually behind a one-way mirror) picks out the culprit. If entertainment holds true to reality, you won't be seeing such scenes much longer. One of the great success stories of psychological research on memory resulted in a better way to have witnesses evaluate suspects (Steblay et al., 2001; Wells et al., 2000). The classic study was reported by Lindsay and Wells (1985).

QUESTION: After a witness has viewed a crime and is asked to identify the perpetrator, which is better: showing a set of suspects at the same time, or showing the suspects one at a time?

● **Recall:** The act of intentionally bringing explicit information to awareness, which requires transferring the information from LTM to STM.

● **Recognition:** The act of encoding an input and matching it to a stored representation.

ALTERNATIVES: (1) Simultaneous presentation could be better because it allows witnesses to notice and compare subtle characteristics; (2) Sequential presentation could be better because it doesn't encourage witnesses to pick out the choice that is most like the person's memory of the actual criminal (even if it isn't identical); (3) Both methods could be about the same, with the advantages of one being cancelled out by the advantages of the other.

LOGIC: If one method is better than the other, then participants should make fewer false identifications while not making fewer correct identifications when that method is used.

METHOD: In preparation for this study, the investigators assembled four sets of photographs. Two sets included the culprit and five other similar men; one set included each of the six men mounted on a separate card, and the other included all six photos mounted together on a single large card. The other two sets were the same as the initial two except that the photo of the culprit was removed (and replaced with a similar looking person).

    The 240 undergraduate participants did not know the purpose of the study in advance. Each participant was seated in a room (alone or in pairs), and the experimenter then left briefly "to get some forms." Thirty seconds later a confederate, acting as a criminal, came in, rifled several drawers and cupboards, and finally took a calculator and left the room. The experimenter then returned and told the participant that the thief was a confederate, and that the "crime" was staged. The witnesses were then told the purpose of the study (to study eyewitness accuracy), and signed an informed consent form. Approximately 5 minutes after the "crime," the participant was randomly assigned to receive one of the four sets of photographs. Two groups of participants received the photos mounted together and were asked to select the culprit. The other two groups received the individual photos, shown one at a time in sequence, and were asked to say "yes" or "no" to each one.

RESULTS: When the culprit's photo was not actually present, participants made many more errors (falsely selecting one of the alternatives) when all six photographs were presented at the same time than when they were presented sequentially. Thirty-five percent of the witnesses fingered an innocent person in a simultaneous lineup compared to only 18.3% who viewed a sequential lineup. When the culprit's photo was actually present, accuracy rates were comparable in the two presentation conditions.

INFERENCES: When the photos are presented together, the participants look for the one that is most similar to the person they saw commit the crime; when the photos are presented one at a time, they judge each on its own merits, not relative to the others. These findings, and those that followed this classic study, were so compelling that police departments are now changing their standard line-up procedures (Kolata & Peterson, 2001).

The Role of Cues: Hints on Where to Dig

How does an archaeologist know where to dig to find the right bits of pottery to reconstruct a water jug? A logical place to start might be in the ruins of a kitchen. The archaeologist digs, finds bits of a typical kitchen floor from the period, and then is encouraged to continue digging in the same area. Similarly, a good cue directs you to key stored fragments, which then allow you to remember. **Cues** are stimuli that help you remember; they are reminders of an event.

Imagine running into an acquaintance in a bookstore and trying to remember his name. You might recall that when you met him, he reminded you of someone else with the same name who had a similar hairline. Here the hairline is a cue, reminding you of your friend Sam and allowing you to greet this new Sam by name. S. at first memorized entire images but soon discovered that he was better off just remembering a specific "abbreviated or symbolic version" of the object. For example, when hearing the word "horseman" he would remember an image of a foot in a spur instead of a man on horseback. He tried "to single out one detail [he would] need in order to remember a word" (Luria, 1968/1987, p. 42). The fragments he recalled were good retrieval cues for the words. Whereas a man on horseback might bring to mind many associations (to statues, battles, historical figures, horse races, and so forth), a good retrieval cue narrows down the possibilities. Perhaps even more important, as illustrated in Figure 7.10 (Barclay et al., 1974), a helpful cue matches fragments of information stored in LTM.

FIGURE 7.10 What Makes Something a Good Cue?

Participants were asked to memorize two sets of sentences. What sort of mental images come to mind when you read these examples? Participants then received cues to help them recall the noun *piano* (in this example). The top cue would be more effective for the top sentence, and the bottom cue would be more effective for the bottom sentence.

Adapted from Barclay et al., 1974.

Godden and Baddeley (1975) dramatically illustrated the role of cues in an ingenious experiment. They asked scuba divers to learn a list of words either when they were underwater or when they were on land. They then tested half the divers in the same setting where they had learned the list, and the other half in the other setting. The results showed that the participants remembered more words if they were tested in the environment in which they had originally learned the words. The significance of this finding is that when we learn, we are learning not only the material, but also the general setting and other incidental events that occur at the same time. And these events can later help cue us to recall the information (Flexser & Tulving, 1978; Koutstaal & Schacter, 1997; Parker & Gellatly, 1997;

● **Cues:** Stimuli that trigger or enhance remembering; reminders.

Smith & Vela, 2001). The idea that memory is better when people are given cues that were present during learning is called the *encoding specificity principle* (Tulving, 1983; Tulving & Thomson, 1973). So, if at all possible, study as much as you can in circumstances similar to those of the testing room—if there won't be music playing during the test, don't study while listening to music.

Supplying Your Own Cues

Some cues are internally generated. We remember information better if we are in the same mood or psychological state (such as being hungry or sleepy) when we try to remember it as when we first learned it. If you were hungry when you studied material, you will remember it better if you are hungry at the time of recall than if you are stuffed. This can be a sobering thought if you are preparing for an exam: If you drink alcohol while studying, you will recall the information better if you are drinking later when you try to remember it. This effect is called **state-dependent retrieval** (Eich, 1989): Information is better remembered if recall is attempted in the same psychological state as when the information was first encoded. A closely related effect occurs with mood: If you are in a happy mood at the time you learn something, you may remember it better when you are feeling happy than when you are feeling sad (Bower, 1981, 1992). The effects of mood are not always very strong, however, and they can be overshadowed by other factors, such as how well the information is organized (Eich, 1995). Neither your psychological state nor your mood appears to be a very powerful retrieval cue.

When participants were cued verbally to recall an event while at the same time smelling a common odor, the memory was more emotional than when no odor was present (Herz & Schooler, 2002).

As shown in Godden and Baddeley's study of divers, the properties of the environment in which you learn something become associated with that information in memory and can also serve as retrieval cues. If you are not in the original environment when you want to remember particular information, try to "supply the environment yourself" by visualizing it; memory is improved when you can mentally supply cues from the original setting in which the material was learned (Smith, 1988). If you lose your keys or wallet, retrace your steps in your mind's eye, if not in reality. This retracing puts you in the same environment as when you last saw the missing item, so that you are more likely to remember where you left it.

Cues can also arise when you remember information associated with a sought memory. Psychologists were surprised to discover that if they showed people pictures and then asked them to recall the names of the pictures over and over, after a while recall improved, even though the participants were not given feedback or other additional cues. If at first you don't remember, try, try again. Improved memory over time, without feedback, is called **hypermnesia** (Erdelyi, 1984; Payne, 1987). Hypermnesia probably occurs because you remember different aspects of the information each time you try to recall it, and each bit that is remembered is then used as a retrieval cue. Some of these self-supplied cues will be effective, and thus you remember pictures better as you keep trying to remember them. So, if at first you cannot recall someone's name, don't give up. Eventually you may hit on the memory of a retrieval cue, such as the shape of a hairline, which in turn will allow you to remember the name. Unlike S.—who almost never had this problem—when the rest of us cannot recall at first, we are well advised to try and try again.

● **State-dependent retrieval:** Recall that is better if it occurs in the same psychological state that was present when the information was first encoded.

● **Hypermnesia:** Memory that improves over time without feedback, particularly with repeated attempts to recall.

People who feel better about themselves in general recall more positive memories, even when they are in a bad mood, than do people who do not have a high regard for themselves. Both groups, however, are in a better mood after they've recalled positive memories (Setliff & Marmurek, 2002).

Looking *at* Levels

Memory in Tribal Africa

Michael Cole and his colleagues (Cole et al., 1971, p. 120) tested members of the Kpelle tribe in rural western Africa by giving them names of objects in different categories and then asking them to recall these words. What would you do if you were asked to remember the words *shirt, apple, pear, sock, pants, banana, grapes,* and *hat?* We've seen that Westerners tend to organize the words into categories (in this case, clothing and fruit). But the tribal members did not. They could use this strategy when it was pointed out to them, but they did not do so on their own. Why not? Their culture stresses the importance of each object, animal, and person as an individual being. Organizing according to categories is not important in their society and, in fact, might impede them in going about their daily lives.

At the level of the group, learning the words was affected by the fact that categorization is not important to this culture. At the level of the person, the culture led tribe members to hold beliefs about the worth and uniqueness of each object and event in the world. At the level of the brain, it is known that parts of the frontal lobes are critically involved in categorization. Indeed, patients with brain damage to these regions often fail to group objects normally when recalling them (Gershberg & Shimamura, 1995; Stuss et al., 1994).

Think about how events at these levels interact: The training that the members of the tribe receive when growing up, during which time they absorb their culture's worldview, affects how their brains work. At the level of the person, according to their values, categorizing is not particularly useful and categorizing words is not useful at all. It was also clear that when asked by the investigators to categorize (which is a social interaction), the members of the tribe could perform the task—which is another example of the influence of events at the level of the group on the operation of the brain. All normal adults can categorize; whether they choose to do so is another question.

TEST YOURSELF!

1. What factors affect whether we retain information in memory?
2. How are memories reconstructed?

Fact, Fiction, and Forgetting: When Memory Goes Wrong

S. had a near-perfect memory. When he made an error, it almost always was a "defect of perception," a result of the specific images he formed. For instance, he once forgot the word "egg" in a long list. He reported "I had put it up against a white wall and it blended in with the background. How could I possibly spot a white egg up against a white wall?" (Luria, 1968/1987, p. 36). His memory was so good that he had a problem many of us might envy: He could not forget even when he wanted to. This became a problem when he performed on stage because material from a previous session could spring to mind unbidden, confusing him about the current list. He initially tried to imagine erasing the blackboard, or burning sheets of paper on which the information had been written, but he could just as easily imagine undoing these acts or seeing the writing on the charred embers—and thus the memories persisted. Finally, S. realized that the key to forgetting was simple: He just had to want the information not to appear, and if he did not think about it, it would not return. For S., this technique worked. Was S. like the rest of us in how his memories competed with each other? Could, for the rest of us, such interference cause losses and failures of memory? How accurate are our memories?

False Memories

Not everything we remember actually happened. **False memories** are memories of events or situations that did not, in fact, occur.

Implanting Memories

Deese (1959) and Roediger and McDermott (1995) showed that people regularly make errors of the sort illustrated by Figures 7.11 and 7.12. (If you weren't fooled, read the list of words to a friend and wait 5 minutes before testing; this will increase the likelihood of an error.) We associate the idea of "sweet" with all of the words listed, so its representation in LTM becomes activated and associated with the context of the list, and we misremember having seen it. Here is the critical point: In general, we do not necessarily remember what actually happened but rather what we *experience* as having happened.

Lest you think that misremembering only occurs when associated material is stored, consider this disturbing study reported by psychologist Elizabeth Loftus (1993). She asked one member of a pair of siblings to tell his younger, 14-year-old

HANDS ON

FIGURE 7.11 False Memory

Please read this list of words. Now go to Figure 7.12 on page 283.

candy	caramel
soda pop	chocolate
honey	cake
pie	icing
fudge	cookie
cotton candy	

● **False memories:** Memories of events or situations that did not, in fact, occur.

Twins sometimes have false memories of events that actually occurred to their sibling, such as being sent home from school for wearing a skirt that was too short. The same thing can happen (although less frequently) to non-twin siblings who are close in age, and even among same-sex friends (Sheen et al., 2001). Roediger and his colleagues (2001) describe a kind of "social contagion," where one person's recounting memories can lead another to adopt them.

brother about the time the younger brother had been lost in a shopping mall when he was 5 years old. This story was told as if it were fact, but it was entirely fiction. The youngster later gave every indication of having genuine memories of the event, adding rich detail to the story he had been told. For example, the boy claimed to remember the flannel shirt worn by the old man who found him, his feelings at the time, and the scolding he later received from his mother. When this study was repeated with many participants, about one quarter of them fell victim to the implanting of such false memories (Loftus & Pickrell, 1995). Moreover, these participants clung steadfastly to their false memories, refusing even on debriefing to believe that they had been artificially created. Similar results have been reported by Hyman and his colleagues (Hyman & Billings, 1998; Hyman & Pentland, 1996). Indeed, when participants were told to make up information about an event they viewed, they later falsely remembered some of those invented facts; these false memories were more likely to occur if the investigator had confirmed the invented fact at the time it was produced (even though the participant knew that he or she had invented it!). Some of these false memories persisted for at least 2 months (Zaragoza et al., 2001).

However, some false memories are easier to create than others. Pezdek and colleagues (1997) found that whereas some participants did acquire false memories of being lost in a shopping mall, none acquired false memories of having been given a rectal enema during childhood. People may have an intuitive grasp of the role of emotion in memory, which leads us to know that we would be sure to remember such an incident if it had actually happened. (The ethics of carrying out such studies might be an interesting topic for discussion.)

Distortions of memory can be implanted in very simple ways. In a now-classic experiment, Loftus and colleagues (1978) asked people to watch a series of slides that showed a red Datsun stopping at a stop sign and then proceeding into an accident. The participants were then asked either "Did another car pass the red Datsun while it was stopped at the stop sign?" or "Did another car pass the red Datsun while it was stopped at the yield sign?" The questions differed only by a single word, stop or yield. Loftus and her colleagues found that many more people who had been asked the yield-sign version of the question later mistakenly recalled that a yield sign had been present. In this case, the question itself interfered with memory. Loftus initially speculated that the misleading question erased the accurate memory; later evidence suggests that the original memory was still present but difficult to access after the misleading question was presented (McCloskey & Zaragoza, 1985). In addition, at least some false memories may reflect how willing people are to agree that they had encountered a previous stimulus (a difference in "criterion," using the language of signal detection theory; see Chapter 4; Hekkanen & McEvoy, 2002).

These kinds of memory errors have direct practical—and often quite serious—implications. After a crime is committed, for instance, witnesses are interviewed by the police, read newspaper stories about the crime, perhaps see television reports. This information can interfere with actual memories. Moreover, during a trial, the way a question is asked can influence a witness's faith in his or her recollection, or even change the testimony altogether.

Distinguishing Fact From Fiction

Does any aspect of false memories distinguish them from real memories? Daniel Schacter and his colleagues (1996) performed the "sweet" experiment, using similar key terms, while the participants' brains were being scanned. The participants were then asked which words were on the list and which words were merely implied by those listed. The hippocampus, which plays a key role in encoding new information into memory, was activated both when participants recognized actual words listed *and* when they identified associated words not on the original list. Crucially, when words actually on the list were correctly recognized, brain areas in the temporal and parietal lobes that register the sound and meaning of spoken words also were activated. In contrast, these areas were *not* active when people encountered words not on the list. Apparently, the construction of memory activates the representations of the perceptual qualities of stored words. Because the false words were not actually heard when the original list was read, this information was not activated. This cue of a "missing perception" may not be used all the time, but it clearly operates in many situations (Johnson et al., 1997).

The same principle applies to remembering a real versus an imagined event. Johnson and her colleagues (Johnson & Raye, 1981; Johnson et al., 1993) found that people often confuse actually having seen something with merely having imagined seeing it (which may be the basis of some false memories; Garry & Polaschek, 2000). Indeed, Dobson and Markham (1993) found that people who experience vivid mental images are more likely to confuse having read a description of an event with having seen it (similar findings have also been reported by Eberman & McKelvie, 2002). S., once again, is an extreme example; his "vivid images broke down the boundary between the real and the imaginary" (Luria, 1968/1987,

FIGURE 7.12 True or False?

candy	chocolate	Did all of these words, including *candy, chocolate,* or *sweet,* appear on the list you read on page 281? Are you sure? In fact, the word *sweet* does not appear. If you think it did, you are not alone; most people do. This exercise is an example of a false memory that was easily implanted in your head.
soda pop	cake	
honey	sweet	
pie	icing	
fudge	cookie	
cotton candy		

Remember when you shook Mickey's hand during a childhood trip to Disneyland? Even if this never happened, seeing an advertisement that leads you to imagine this happy event will later make you more confident that this event actually occurred. Researchers found the same thing even when an ad led participants to imagine that they had shaken hands with Bugs Bunny at Disneyland, which could never have happened (Bugs is not a Disney character)—and thus the ad could not have activated actual memories (Braun et al., 2002).

- **Reality monitoring:** An ongoing awareness of perceptual and other properties that distinguish real from imagined stimuli.

- **Source amnesia:** A failure to remember the source of information.

- **Forgetting curve:** A graphic representation of the rate at which information is forgotten over time: Recent events are recalled better than more distant ones, but most forgetting occurs soon after learning.

p. 144). He commented "To me there's no great difference between the things I imagine and what exists in reality" (p. 146).

Reality monitoring is the ongoing awareness of the perceptual and other properties that distinguish real from imagined stimuli. Reality monitoring can be improved greatly if people are led to pay attention to the context in which stimuli occur (Lindsay & Johnson, 1989). Mather and colleagues (1997) and Schacter and his colleagues (Norman & Schacter, 1997; Schacter et al., 2001) found that when people are asked to pay attention to the amount of perceptual detail in their memories (as would occur if they tried to notice the texture of objects, other nearby objects, and shadows), they are better able to distinguish actual memories from false memories. In fact, people generally experience fewer false memories for visual material than auditory material (Cleary & Greene, 2002; Kellogg, 2001). However, there is a limit to how well people can use such cues to distinguish real from false memories; false memories produced in the "sweet" task, for example, are remarkably persistent, even when people are warned in advance about the possibility of such memories (McDermott & Roediger, 1998).

When S. was a reporter, he often interviewed people—and never took notes. Let's say that S. remembered that Mrs. Borsht had mentioned that a burglar wore a checked shirt. But later it turned out that it wasn't Mrs. Borsht at all; another witness had provided that news. This would have been an example of **source amnesia**, a failure to remember the source of information. Patients who have suffered frontal lobe damage sometimes have an extreme version of this impairment; they generally cannot remember who said what, or when and where they heard it. But, even people without brain damage, like the authors or you, can experience source amnesia; all it requires is forgetting the source of information in episodic memory (Schacter, 1996). In spite of the fact that S. apparently never had this difficulty, such problems are surprisingly common; indeed, some cases of unintentional plagiarism may be a result of source amnesia (Marsh et al., 1997; Schacter, 1999). In general, false memories are not always easy to distinguish from actual ones.

Forgetting: Many Ways to Lose It

Once S. stored information in memory, it apparently was there for good; his recall was as accurate years later as it was immediately after learning. As first shown in 1885 by Hermann Ebbinghaus, the rest of us recall recent events better than more distant ones, and most forgetting occurs soon after learning. However, as time goes on, people lose less and less additional information from memory (Wixted & Ebbesen, 1991, 1997). Ebbinghaus discovered the **forgetting curve**, illustrated in Figure 7.13, which shows the rate at which information is forgotten over time.

Why do people lose information from memory? Sometimes the information was not well encoded in the first place. Remember the path traced over and over

FIGURE 7.13 Ebbinghaus's Forgetting Curve

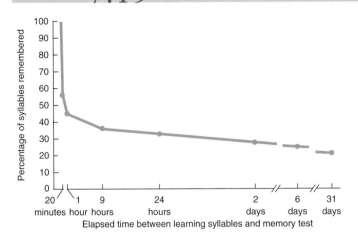

The forgetting curve shows that information becomes harder to recall over time, but that most forgetting occurs relatively soon after learning.

again into the grass? If the walker abandons the path before it is completely worn through to bare dirt, the pattern of the path is not stored structurally. Similarly, you must not "abandon" information—you must actively think about it if it is to be encoded effectively in LTM. An **encoding failure** results if you do not process information well enough to begin consolidation (Schacter, 1999).

An encoding failure produces huge losses of information shortly after learning, which may be one reason for the sharp drop at the beginning of the forgetting curve. But, even if information is properly encoded, it can be lost later. Why? For many years memory researchers hotly debated the fate of information that was once stored but then forgotten. One camp argued that once memories are gone, they are gone forever. The memory decays and disappears, just as invisible ink fades until nothing is left. The other camp claimed that the memories themselves are intact but cannot be "found." The ink hasn't faded, but the message has been misfiled. In fact, both camps had put their finger on important aspects of forgetting.

Decay: Fade Away

The invisible ink theory proposes that memories **decay;** that is, they degrade with time. The relevant connections between neurons are lost. What evidence supports this theory? In the sea slug, Aplysia, which has a relatively simple nervous system, it has been possible to document that the strength of the connections between neurons established by learning fades away over time (Baily & Chen, 1989). If human neurons are similar, as seems likely, memories may in fact decay over time. Indeed, researchers have produced evidence not only that certain genes promote stronger connections among neurons, but also that other genes prevent such connections and, hence, block memory (Abel et al., 1998). When these "memory suppressor genes" are turned on, they could cause the decay of connections that store memories.

Evidence refuting the decay theory seemed to come from dramatic findings described by Penfield (1955). Before performing brain surgery, neurosurgeons such as Penfield sometimes put small electrodes on the exposed cortex of awake patients and stimulated neurons electrically. A few patients reported vivid images and memories of long-forgotten events. For example, on having a particular area

● **Encoding failure:** A failure to process to-be-remembered information well enough to begin consolidation.

● **Decay:** The fading away of memories with time because the relevant connections between neurons are lost.

of the brain stimulated, one patient said, "Yes, sir, I think I heard a mother calling her little boy somewhere. It seemed something that happened years ago." However, at least some of these reports may not have been memories but images created on the spot (Squire, 1987; Squire & Kandel, 1999). There is no strong evidence that all memories stay stored forever. In fact, these oft-cited results occurred for only a minority of patients, and later work failed to reveal compelling evidence that memories are stored forever.

Interference: Tangled Up in Memory

The view that a mix-up in memory often explains forgetting has long been supported by strong direct evidence. If every summer you work with a group of kids as a camp counselor, you will find that learning the names of the current crop impairs your memory of the names of last year's campers. This is an example of interference. **Interference** is the disruption of the ability to remember one piece of information by the presence of other information. Two types of interference can plague your memories: retroactive and proactive.

Retroactive interference is interference that disrupts memory for something learned earlier. Learning the names of the new campers can interfere with your memory of the names of the previous group. **Proactive interference** is interference by something already learned that makes it difficult to learn something new. Your having learned the names of previous groups of kids may interfere with your learning the names on this summer's roster, particularly if some of the new names are similar to old ones.

Why does interference occur? The capacity of LTM is not the problem. You are not overloading a "memory-for-people" box in your brain; some politicians, after all, can remember the names of thousands of people with little or no difficulty. Interference probably occurs because the retrieval cues for various memories are similar, and thus a given cue may call up the wrong memory. The more similar the already-known and to-be-remembered information, the more interference you get (Adams, 1967).

The first president of Stanford University, David Starr Jordan, apparently worried that he might eventually fill up his memory if he learned too much. (But you shouldn't worry; we now know that the capacity of LTM is so vast that it hasn't yet even been measured.) President Jordan was an ichthyologist, an expert on fish who knew the names and habits of thousands of underwater species. At the beginning of each year he met the new students and politely smiled as they were introduced, but ignored their names. One bold student asked President Jordan if he had heard his name clearly, and repeated it. Jordan listened and realized he had now learned the student's name. He slapped himself on the forehead and exclaimed, "Drat, there goes another fish!"

Amnesia: Not Just Forgetting to Remember

Even S., if he received a strong blow to the head, might not recall anything that had happened to him after the incident. Why? Neither normal decay nor interference accounts for such unusual losses of memory. Instead, such memory failure is an example of **amnesia**, a loss of memory over an entire time span, typically resulting from brain damage caused by accident, infection, or stroke. Amnesia is not like normal forgetting, which affects only some of the material learned during a given period.

● **Interference:** The disruption of the ability to remember one piece of information by the presence of other information.

● **Retroactive interference:** Interference that occurs when new learning impairs memory for something learned earlier.

● **Proactive interference:** Interference that occurs when previous knowledge makes it difficult to learn something new.

● **Amnesia:** A loss of memory over an entire time span, resulting from brain damage caused by accident, infection, or stroke.

● **Retrograde amnesia:** Amnesia that disrupts previous memories.

● **Anterograde amnesia:** Amnesia that leaves consolidated memories intact but prevents new learning.

Amnesia produced by brain damage usually affects episodic memories while leaving semantic memories almost entirely intact (Warrington & McCarthy, 1988). Most people who have an accident that causes amnesia have no idea what they were doing immediately before the accident, but they can remember semantic information such as their names and birth dates. Sometimes, however, amnesia has the opposite effect, and mostly impairs semantic memory. For example, De Renzi and colleagues (1987) report a patient who forgot the meanings of words and most characteristics of common objects. Nevertheless, she remembered details about key events in her life, such as her wedding and her father's illness.

Amnesia may be retrograde or anterograde (Mayes & Downes, 1997; Parkin, 1987). **Retrograde amnesia** disrupts previous memories (Fast & Fujiwara, 2001). This is the sort of amnesia often popularized in soap operas and movies. Most of us suffer from a special form of retrograde amnesia called *infantile amnesia* or *childhood amnesia* (Newcombe et al., 2000): We don't remember much about our early childhood experiences, although some people apparently do remember very significant events (such as the birth of a sibling) that occurred when they were less than 2 years old (Eacott & Crawley, 1999). **Anterograde amnesia** leaves already consolidated memories intact but prevents the learning of new facts. It affects all explicit memories—that is, memories of facts that can be brought to consciousness voluntarily—and produces massive encoding failure. H. M. had a form of anterograde amnesia. Its manifestation is well presented in an old joke. A man runs into a doctor's office, screaming, "Doc! I've lost my memory!" The doctor asks him, "When did this happen?" The man looks at him, puzzled, and says, "When did what happen?" It is no joke for people with anterograde amnesia, who live as if frozen in the present moment of time.

What happens in the brain to produce amnesia? Often, as in the case of H. M., the cause involves damage to the hippocampus or its connections to or from other parts of the brain (Spiers et al., 2001). In addition, sometimes amnesia can result when areas of the cortex that serve as memory stores become degraded. As noted earlier, all memories are a result of changes in the interactions of individual neurons, and most neurons involved in memory are in the cortex. Alzheimer's disease, for example, typically begins with small memory deficits, which become progressively worse. In the later stages of the disease, people with Alzheimer's cannot remember who they are, where they are, or who their family and friends are. Alzheimer's disease not only affects the hippocampus but also degrades other parts of the brain that serve as memory stores.

Leonard Shelby, the lead character in the 2001 movie *Memento,* appears to suffer from anterograde amnesia as a result of brain damage from a brutal attack. Shelby remembers things he learned before the accident, but he apparently is unable to create new memories.

Approximately 4 million Americans are afflicted with Alzheimer's disease (Alzheimer's Association, 2003; St. George-Hyslop, 2000), and some estimate that this disease will affect as many as 14 million Americans by 2050. But not everybody is equally susceptible. In one study, nuns who had better linguistic ability, as judged from their autobiographies, developed this disease less often than nuns with poorer linguistic ability (Snowdon et al., 2000).

Depending on which other parts of the brain are affected, Alzheimer's patients can have greater amnesia for one form of information or another; for example, some patients have worse spatial memory than verbal memory, and vice versa for others (Albert et al., 1990).

Repressed Memories: Real or Imagined?

Recent years have witnessed many dramatic reports of suddenly recollected memories. Some people claim to have suddenly remembered that they were sexually molested by their parents decades before, when they were no more than 3 years old. One person claimed that as a child he had been strapped to the back of a dolphin as part of a bizarre devil worship ritual. Are these false memories, or are they **repressed memories,** real memories that have been pushed out of consciousness because they are emotionally threatening, as Freud believed? Whether or not repressed memories exist is perhaps the most heated issue in memory research today (Benedict & Donaldson, 1996; Golding et al., 1996; Knapp & VandeCreek, 1996; Melchert, 1996; Pope, 1996; Rubin, 1996).

Evidence for repressed memories comes from studies reported by Williams (1994). She interviewed 129 women 17 years after each had been admitted to a hospital emergency room for treatment of sexual abuse in childhood. Thirty-eight percent of the women had no memory of an event of sexual abuse; in fact, 12% claimed that they had never been abused. These results suggest that some people may forget traumatic memories. Could this finding simply reflect infantile amnesia, the forgetting of events that occurred in early childhood? Not likely, for two reasons: First, whereas 55% of the women who had been 3 years old or younger at the time of abuse had no recall, fully 62% of those who were between 4 and 6 years old at the time had no recall; if forgetting were simply a reflection of age, the women abused at a younger age should have had poorer memory. Second, more of the women who were abused by someone they knew, as was determined from independent evidence, claimed to have forgotten the incident than women who were abused by a stranger. Again, this difference should not have occurred if the forgetting simply reflected infantile amnesia. Indeed, a review of 28 studies of memory for childhood sexual abuse found robust evidence that such memories can be forgotten and later recalled (Scheflin & Brown, 1996). In some cases, people who suddenly remembered being abused as children then proceeded to track down the evidence for the event (Schacter, 1996).

There is a mystery here. As noted earlier, highly charged, emotional information is typically remembered *better* than neutral information. So, why should this particular kind of emotionally charged information be recalled poorly, or forgotten for decades? Schacter (1996) suggests that, in these cases of forgetting, the person has not really unconsciously pushed the memories out of awareness. Instead, it is as if the individual were "someone else" during the abuse and, thus has few retrieval cues later for accessing the memories. Nevertheless, the memories may be stored and may, under some circumstances and with appropriate cues, be retrieved. If so, it seems people sometimes forget emotionally charged events, but after long periods of time they could come to remember them. Clancy, Schacter, McNally, and Pitman (2000) have found that people who experience recovered memories of childhood abuse are more likely to mistakenly remember words such as "sweet" when asked to remember a previously presented list of sweet things in experiments that use the Deese-Roediger-McDermott technique discussed earlier.

● **Repressed memories:** Real memories that have been pushed out of consciousness because they are emotionally threatening.

This finding might suggest that these people are unusually sensitive to stored fragments of information. Leavitt (1997) has shown that people who recover memories are not especially prone to making up information when given suggestions, which indicates that they are not simply prone to forming false memories. That said, not all claims of recovered memories can be taken at face value; you've already seen how false memories (perhaps including being strapped to the back of a dolphin) can be implanted.

Looking *at* Levels

False Truths

Social psychologist Daniel Gilbert (1991) reports experiments in which people are given statements about nonsense objects, such as "A bilicar is a spear." For each statement, participants are told that it is true or false. Later, memory for the truth of the statements is tested. When people forget whether a statement was true or false, they are biased to say it was true. Thus, the participants end up with unwarranted beliefs about objects. The same principle probably operates regarding facts about people. For example, if you hear that a beloved high school teacher does not seduce students, you may later misremember that he does seduce them. It's fascinating, but disturbing, that a person's reputation could easily be ruined because of a simple psychological principle.

According to Gilbert, it requires extra effort to realize that a statement is false than to accept it as true; to determine that it is false, you must search for stored information that is inconsistent with the statement, which requires using working memory. Thus, because of properties of the brain, specifically the increased processing in the frontal lobes to look up and process stored information, events at the level of the person are affected: The person's beliefs are distorted. And the influences work the other way, too: Depending on your beliefs, you will be inclined to work more or less hard to search memory to verify a statement. If you are not strongly motivated to put in the extra work, you will be more inclined to fall prey to the bias to believe an assertion is true. This distortion in turn affects social interactions. And, of course, social interactions lead us to hear about characteristics of people, "So-and-so is this or that," statements that may lead to false beliefs.

TEST YOURSELF!

1. How can actual memories be distinguished from false ones?
2. Is a forgotten memory necessarily gone forever, or is it still stored but difficult to retrieve?
3. What is amnesia?
4. Are memories ever repressed?

Improving Memory: Tricks and Tools

No matter how hard you try, you probably will never develop a memory as good as S.'s. He apparently was born with something special, which he later learned to cultivate. However, you can use many of the same tricks he developed, and these tricks will improve your memory too—perhaps dramatically so. In many bookstores you can find at least a dozen books on how to improve your memory, all

● **Mnemonic devices:** Strategies that improve memory, typically by using effective organization and integration.

containing similar messages. Ways of improving your odds of retaining information in memory include linking visual images with text (dual coding); thinking through information (depth and breadth of processing); and studying in small chunks while trying to integrate and organize material (distributed practice). Let's now look at techniques that take advantage of such principles to improve memory.

You can improve the accuracy of your memory at both ends: when information goes in and when it is taken out. The fact that memory is so dependent on the strategies people use explains why it has among the lowest heritabilities (see Chapter 3) of all specific cognitive abilities. Even if a number of people in your family have fabulous memories, their gifts probably won't help you much, if at all (Nichols, 1978). For memory, the crucial differences between "good" and "bad" memories appear to be the strategies and tricks used when storing and retrieving information.

Storing Information Effectively: A Bag of Mnemonic Tricks

Tricks for improving memory typically require elaborative encoding and often involve either visualizing objects interacting with other objects or forming organized units where none previously existed. The essential element is that you *organize* the material so that you *integrate* it, making connections between what you want to remember and what you already know. Here are some **mnemonic devices,** or strategies that improve memory (mnemonic is derived from the Greek word for "memory"). Such memory tricks rely on organization and integration. Mnemonics can easily double your recall and are well worth the effort of learning and using. Using mnemonic devices not only helps you learn something in the first place but, should you forget it, you will be able to relearn it more effectively.

Interactive Images: Images That Play Together, Stay Together

Probably the single most effective mnemonic device is the use of *interactive images*. As discussed earlier, forming images of objects interacting will improve memory even without any effort to learn the material (Bower, 1972; Paivio, 1971). For example, if you want to learn someone's first name, visualize someone else you already know who has the same name, and imagine that person interacting with your new acquaintance in some way. You might envision them hugging, or fighting, or shaking hands. Later, when you see the new person, you can recall this image, and thus the name.

Method of Loci: Putting Objects in Their Place

A related method was discovered by the ancient Greek orator Simonides. He was attending a banquet one evening when he was called out of the room to receive a message. Shortly after he left, the ceiling collapsed, mangling the guests' bodies so badly that they were difficult to identify. When asked who had been at the feast, Simonides realized that he could remember easily if he visualized each person sitting at the table. This led him to develop a technique now called *the method of loci* (loci, the plural of locus, means "places" in Latin). To use this method, first memorize a set of locations. For example, you could walk through your house and memorize 12 distinct places, such as the front door, the computer desk, the potted plant, and so on. Later, when you want to memorize a list of objects, such as those on a shopping list, you can imagine walking along this path and placing an image of one object in each location. For instance, you might visualize a lightbulb leaning against the front door, a box of tissues on the computer desk, a can of coffee beside the plant, and so on. When you want to recall the list, all you need to do is visualize the scene and walk through it, "looking" to see what object is at each place.

However, not just any image will do. We can learn a lesson from S., who discovered some properties of effective images: "I know that I have to be on guard if I'm not to overlook something. What I do now is to make my images larger. Take the word egg I told you about before. It was so easy to lose sight of it; now I make it a larger image, and when I lean it up against the wall of a building, I see to it that the place is lit up by having a street lamp nearby . . . I don't put things in dark passageways any more . . . Much better if there's some light around, it's easier to spot then" (Luria, 1968/1987, p. 41).

To use the method of loci, pick out a set of locations in your house, and visualize each to-be-remembered object in a different location as you mentally walk through the house. To recall, later repeat this mental walk and "see" what's in each location.

Pegword System: Numbered Images

The pegword system is similar to the method of loci, except that instead of places, you first memorize a set of objects in order. For example, you might memorize a list of rhymes, such as "One is a bun, two is a shoe, three is a tree, four is a door," and so on. Then you can treat the memorized objects (bun, shoe, tree, door) in the same way as the locations in the method of loci. You could associate the first item on your grocery list, for example, with a bun, the second with a shoe, and so on. In this case, when you want to remember the list, you remember each of the *pegwords* (such as *bun* and *shoe*) in order and "see" what is associated with it.

When Henry Roediger (1980) asked people to use different mnemonic devices to remember sets of words, he found that these three methods—interactive imagery, the method of loci, and the pegword system—were the most effective. However, as you know, there are many types of memory, and people differ in how well they can use various techniques. You might find some other mnemonic devices more useful.

Other Mnemonic Devices

We can use many different sorts of tricks to improve our memories, not just the three discussed so far. For example, *rhyming words* provide a simple method for keeping concepts straight. For instance, learning the rhyme "rhyming priming rhyming" might help you remember that priming makes the same processing (like the same word repeated) easier to repeat in the future.

Hierarchical organization, as in the experiment by Bower and colleagues (1969; summarized on p. 241), can improve learning and memory. You might memorize the errands you need to do by organizing your tasks in the same way you organize your trip: Break the trip down into separate segments and organize the events in each segment separately. Think about which tasks need to be done at one end of town, or in one part of the store, which need to be done at another specific location, and so on. The key is to think of ways to organize the material hierarchically, so that the big task breaks down into smaller ones, which themselves may break down into yet smaller ones; the goal is to group together relatively small sets of material.

Acronyms are pronounceable words made from the first letters of the important words in a phrase, such as NOW for National Organization for Women; *initialisms* are simply the initial letters, pronounceable or not, such as DNA for deoxyribonucleic acid. Initialisms may be easier to make up for most situations; the idea in both cases is to create a single unit that can be unpacked as a set of cues for something more complicated.

In short, the key to mnemonics is figuring out a way to organize information so that you can link something new with something you already know. For example,

MNEMONIC. A memory aid. Think of trying to remember something by putting a name on it: putting a NEM-ON-IC.

You can use mnemonics throughout this book, setting up mental connections or associations from one thing to another, perhaps with the use of imagery. For example, to remember that the word *suppression* means "voluntarily forcing unwanted thoughts back into the unconscious," you might visualize SUPerman PRESSing down demons that are bursting out of someone's head, shoving them back inside. When you form the image, you need to remember that the first part of Superman's name and what he's doing (pressing) are critical, so make sure the S on his cape is very vivid and visible, and that he is clearly pressing with his hands. Showing you a drawing of the scene would work almost as well, but challenging you to make up your own image has the added advantage of forcing you to "process" the information more thoroughly, which in and of itself improves memory.

In addition, you can remember information by stringing it into a story. For example, if you wanted to remember that Freud came before the cognitivists, you can make up a story in which Freud wishes he had a computer to help him bill his patients but gets depressed when he realizes it hasn't been invented yet. Making the story a bit silly or whimsical may actually help memory (McDaniel & Einstein, 1986; McDaniel et al., 1995) and certainly makes it more fun to think about!

One of the fundamental facts about learning is that you will learn better if you are actively involved. Instead of just reading, try to find connections across areas, try to think of your own mnemonics. You won't go wrong if you simply form a visual image, make up an association, invent a rhyme or a joke. You will be better off if you try to be an active learner.

Improving Memory Retrieval

S.'s ability to remember what he saw and heard was so good that he didn't need to notice patterns in the stimuli. For example, memorizing a table of numbers that were arranged in order was no easier for him than memorizing a table of random numbers. For us, however, once we notice such a pattern, we can store the pattern in its own right—which will help us later to reconstruct the material. However, S.'s method does have one major advantage over the one we would use: Sometimes you need to remember things that you didn't expect to need or didn't have the opportunity to store effectively. Police officers are regularly faced with the effect of this unexpected demand on witnesses' memories. The need for accurate witness statements has been one impetus for developing methods to help people remember after the fact. Fisher and colleagues (Fisher & Geiselman, 1992; Fisher et al., 1989) used the results of laboratory studies to develop a method to help witnesses and victims of crimes recall what actually happened. Detectives trained with their methods were able to lead witnesses to recall 63% more information than was obtained with the standard police interview format. Their methods made use of the following memory principles and techniques:

HANDS ON

1. Recall is better when you mentally reinstate the environment in which information was learned. If you want to remember something, try to think of where you were when you learned it, what the weather was like, how you felt at the time, and so on.
2. Focus. Searching for information in LTM requires effort and is easily disrupted by other stimuli. To remember well, focus on the task, shutting out distractions.
3. Keep trying. The more times you try to remember something, the more likely you are eventually to retrieve it (Roediger & Thorpe, 1978).
4. If you cannot recall something immediately, try to think of characteristics of the information sought. Fisher and colleagues, in their 1989 study, advised detectives that if a witness could not remember a criminal's name, they should try to remember its length, first syllable, ethnic origin, and so on. This information can serve as retrieval cues.
5. For certain kinds of memory retrieval, you can arrange the world in such a way that you are reminded about what to remember. In other words, use *external cues* as mnemonic devices. If you are prone to forgetting your backpack, leave it by the door; if you forget to check the weather forecast before you leave home in the morning, put an umbrella on the door handle. A clever use of external cues was developed by historian Alistair Cooke, who hit on a novel way to remember where he shelved his books. He had a large

Arranging your world properly can aid memory. In this case, the pill holder makes it easy to recall whether or not you've taken your medication each day.

number of books on the United States and its regions, but he couldn't always recall the author of a particular book. Arranging the books alphabetically by state didn't work because he couldn't decide where to put books about regions, such as the Rocky Mountains. The system that finally worked was simple: He arranged the books about western regions on the left, eastern regions on the right, northern regions at the top, and southern regions at the bottom. The location in the bookcase mirrored the location in the country, and his problem was solved—all he had to do was look in the right place on his bookcase "map" (Morris, 1979).

If you can find a method that is fun and easy, and that works for you, you are more likely to use it, and benefit by it. As in the case of mnemonic devices, we advise you to try each of the methods we have noted and see which suits you.

Looking *at* Levels

Hypnosis and Memory

S. had very vivid mental images, which apparently allowed him to recall information with ease. If someone hypnotized you and told you that your images were especially vivid, would that boost your recall? Possibly. Hypnosis sometimes improves memory of prior events. In 1976 in Chowchilla, California, a school bus was hijacked, all of the children within kidnapped. The bus and all those inside were buried and held for ransom. When freed, the bus driver remembered the car driven by his assailants but no other details. In a hypnotic trance, he was able to recall the car's license plate, which ultimately led to the arrest of the kidnappers.

In many—if not most—cases, however, hypnosis increases people's confidence in their recollections but not their accuracy (Sheehan, 1988; Worthington, 1979) (see Chapter 5). Indeed, studies have found no overall differences in accuracy of memory between witnesses who were hypnotized and those who were interviewed using techniques based on cognitive strategies such as those summarized earlier (Geiselman et al., 1985). In

addition, hypnosis may actually lead people to believe that suggested events happened, rather than simply help them to recall actual events (e.g., Barber, 1997; Bryant & Barnier, 1999; Green et al., 1998). Thus, after hypnosis you might not, in fact, recall better than before, but you would probably be more confident that you did. Recognizing these problems, courts in many states will not consider testimony based on recall during hypnosis.

As discussed in Chapter 5, hypnosis affects the brain, in part by focusing attention. But attention can be focused on material suggested by an interviewer (a social interaction), and such suggestions can change the interviewee's beliefs. Thus, the social interaction between the hypnotist and the person hypnotized need not alter the ability to access memories, but instead can implant false memories. And false memories, if taken at face value, can have a devastating impact on how other people are treated.

TEST YOURSELF!

1. How should you try to organize and integrate new information in order to remember it?
2. What tricks will help you dig out information you want to retrieve?

CONSOLIDATE!

Storing Information: Time and Space Are of the Essence

- There are three types of memory stores: sensory memory (SM), short-term memory (STM), and long-term memory (LTM). The memory stores differ in the amount of information they can retain and how long they can retain it.

- Working memory (WM) is the use of STM to reason or to solve problems. Working memory involves specialized STMs (such as the articulatory loop and visuospatial sketchpad) and a central executive, which is a set of processes that manipulates information in these temporary storage structures.

- There are multiple types of LTMs, which store information in different sensory modalities, such as the visual and auditory. Some of the information stored in LTM is episodic, pertaining to events that occurred at a specific time, place, and circumstance.

- Some of the information in LTM is semantic, pertaining to meaning, concepts, and facts about the world. Some memories in LTM are explicit (stored so information can voluntarily be retrieved).

- Some memories in LTM are implicit (stored as tendencies to process information in specific ways). Implicit memories in LTM include classical conditioning, habits (automatic responses to appropriate stimuli), and priming (repetition priming makes it easier to repeat a process in the future).

- All memories arise when neurons change their patterns of interaction, so that new connections become strengthened. Long-term potentiation (LTP) is one mechanism whereby new memories are stored. The process of storing new memories depends on the actions of specific genes.

THINK IT THROUGH   S. was extraordinarily good at storing images. If he only relied on this sort of storage, what sorts of material might be difficult for him to understand? Can you think of reasons why it would make sense that someone would be extraordinary at only some types of memory, and not all? If a new drug were created that would improve one sort of memory, which sort of memory would you most prefer to improve?

Encoding and Retrieving Information From Memory

- Encoding is the act of organizing and transforming incoming information so that it can be entered into memory. Effective encoding depends in part on what is perceived to be important.

- Memory is improved as more time is spent thinking about the material to be stored and how it relates to your current knowledge. Memory is most effective if the learner focuses on the properties that will be relevant later. Depth of processing involves thinking about the more complex properties of objects.

- Elaborative encoding involves thinking of relations and associations of material to be stored. It takes time to consolidate information to be stored, converting it from a dynamic form to a structural form.

- Memory retrieval depends on a constructive process; you must retrieve the right pottery fragments to build the right jug. Recognition is often easier than recall, but the ease of recognition depends on the choices you must distinguish among; the more attributes the choices have in common, the harder it is to distinguish among them.

- Effective retrieval depends on having cues, or reminders, that match part of what is in memory, allowing you to reconstruct the rest.

THINK IT THROUGH   Can you think of any advantages to storing fragments and later reconstructing memories as opposed to storing mental photographs or other complete sets of information? At first glance, the fact that memory requires time to consolidate may appear a disadvantage. Can you think of any advantages to having to wait awhile before memories are consolidated? We generally find recognition easier than recall; can you think of any way to convert a recall task into a recognition task?

Fact, Fiction, and Forgetting: When Memory Goes Wrong

- False memories occur when a person stores information about an event that did not happen, or that did not happen in the way that is "remembered." False memories may not include information about the perceptual features of the stimuli, which may allow you to distinguish them from actual memories. Reality monitoring can be used to check for perceptual features in memory.

- Forgetting occurs in various ways: Decay results when neural connections are weakened to the point where they are no longer functional. Interference (either retroactive or proactive) prevents the digging out of stored information.

- In contrast to ordinary forgetting, amnesia wipes out explicit memory for a span of time, not just isolated aspects of memories.

- Strong emotion typically amplifies memory, not diminishes it.

- Memories may be difficult to recall because the stored information may not match later retrieval cues.

THINK IT THROUGH   Why does it make sense that we have better memory for emotional events? Would this help us make decisions or lead our lives in effective ways? Can you think of ways that this feature of memory is a drawback? If your mental images were as sharp and vivid as a picture, would this necessarily improve your memory? For all kinds of materials? Can you think of drawbacks to having such powerful memory images? Can you think of anything that would be easier or better for a person with amnesia?

If methods for implanting false memories effectively are demonstrated conclusively, should they be outlawed? In general, or only in certain circumstances (such as their being used by advertisers who want you to "remember" how much you like their products)? Can you think of any circumstances under which implanting a false memory might be a good idea? Explain.

Improving Memory: Tricks and Tools

- Some techniques help you store information effectively by organizing it and integrating it into other information in memory; these include interactive images, the method of loci, the pegword system, rhyming words, hierarchical organization, acronyms and initialisms. Mental imagery is generally the most effective of these techniques when it is used to organize information in a meaningful way.

- Other techniques have also been shown to help dig out information previously stored in long-term memory. One trick is to provide effective retrieval cues by thinking about where you were and how you felt at the time. Another major factor is effort: Focus and keep trying and, if you cannot recall the information, then try to recall its characteristics or associated information (which in turn can serve as retrieval cues). Finally, sometimes just arranging external cues to remind you can be enormously helpful.

THINK IT THROUGH   S. discovered new techniques as he became aware of his gift, and worked to hone it to a fine edge. Many of these techniques can be used by anyone. Should memory improvement techniques be taught in school? If so, in which courses? Can you think of any reason not to teach such techniques? Can you think of ways to use objects or events in your room to help remind you of tasks you need to do? Why do you think that many people don't use memory improvement techniques, even after they've discovered for themselves how powerful these techniques are?

Would you use the same memory aid to study for a multiple-choice test and an essay exam? What would be different about your methods?

If you were setting up a new business to teach executives how to improve their memories, what would you need to know about your clients' daily activities? What would you include in your curriculum?

If you were advising detectives, how could you help them determine which witness was remembering more accurately? What new retrieval cues could you produce that might be effective?

Key Terms

amnesia, p. 286
anterograde amnesia, p. 287
breadth of processing, p. 272
central executive, p. 265
chunk, p. 257
code, p. 269
consolidation, p. 270
cues, p. 278
decay, p. 285
depth of processing, p. 271
elaborative encoding, p. 272
encoding, p. 254
encoding failure, p. 285
episodic memories, p. 260
explicit (or declarative)
    memories, p. 261
false memories, p. 281
flashbulb memory, p. 274
forgetting curve, p. 284
habit, p. 262
hypermnesia, p. 279
implicit (or nondeclarative)
    memories, p. 261
incidental learning, p. 273
intentional learning, p. 273
interference, p. 286
long-term memory (LTM),
    p. 258
long-term potentiation
    (LTP), p. 266

memory store, p. 255
mnemonic devices, p. 290
modality-specific memory
    stores, p. 260
primacy effect, p. 258
priming, p. 263
proactive interference, p. 286
reality monitoring, p. 284
recall, p. 276
recency effect, p. 258
recognition, p. 276
rehearsal, p. 257
repetition priming, p. 263
repressed memories, p. 288
retrieval, p. 254
retroactive interference,
    p. 286
retrograde amnesia, p. 287
semantic memories, p. 260
sensory memory (SM), p. 255
short-term memory (STM),
    p. 256
source amnesia, p. 284
state-dependent retrieval,
    p. 279
storage, p. 254
transfer appropriate
    processing, p. 271
working memory (WM),
    p. 265

chapter 8

Digital Image © The Museum of Modern Art/Licensed by SCALA/Art Resource, NY

Language and Thinking

Albert Einstein had one of the most remarkable minds in history. He didn't simply revolutionize physics, he changed the way the human species looks at the world. Einstein is often thought of today as he was in his later years—a saintly figure, patient and benevolent, his head framed by a white halo of hair. However, as a young man he had a rebellious streak. He hated his experiences in the rigid and authoritarian German schools (experiences so alienating that he renounced his German citizenship when he was 17 years old, and was stateless until he was granted Swiss citizenship 5 years later). Einstein's father wanted him to have a practical career, and so insisted that young Albert apply to study electrical engineering. He failed the entrance exam, probably intentionally. He did attend university, but he regularly missed classes—either staying home to play his violin or to study physics on his own. When he did show up, he managed to annoy so many of his teachers that they shunned him after graduation, and he had great difficulty finding a job. Indeed, because of these personal characteristics, Einstein only held temporary teaching positions until he was 23 years old, when a friend's father helped him land an entry-level job at the Swiss patent office. He worked in the patent office for 7 years.

Even though he was cut off from universities and good libraries, Einstein later recounted that he was very lucky to be working in the patent office at that point in his life (Clark, 1971). In those days in Switzerland, hopeful inventors had to supply physical models along with their patent applications. Einstein became adept at studying such models and drawings, discerning the underlying principles; his job was to rewrite the often vague and muddled descriptions, cleaning them up so that they could be protected by law. Einstein learned to abstract clear-cut principles that explained how devices worked. He later noted that this was good training for discerning the Laws of Nature. In his spare time, he thought long and hard about the fundamental properties of the universe, and he published a series of papers that shook the world.

In general, Einstein's work was marked by "out of the box" thinking, by enormous intellectual flexibility. He did not accept the common wisdom of the day, but instead was comfortable breaking all the rules. He revealed not only that light can be viewed both as particles and as waves, but also that time isn't constant and light transfers mass. Moreover, he put together what had previously been viewed as distinctly different—for example, showing how mass and energy are in fact the same thing.

> "When I examine myself and my methods of thought, I come to the conclusion that the gift of fantasy has meant more to me than my talent for absorbing positive knowledge."

Einstein's insights often arose only after years of thought and intense work. For example, he labored for 10 years to produce his famous Special Theory of Relativity (which showed why the laws of physics apply only in the context of specific frames of reference, except that the speed of light is always constant). But don't think of Einstein as a kind of supercomputer, working through problems methodically and systematically, a step at a time. Einstein's methods of thinking often resembled that of an artist. He said, "When I examine myself and my methods of thought, I come to the conclusion that the gift of fantasy has meant more to me than my talent for absorbing positive knowledge" (Clark, 1971, p. 88).

What is thinking? How do people solve problems and reach decisions? Can you learn to think more effectively? In this chapter, we consider some of the most fundamental ways in which we humans tower over the other animals, namely in our thinking and language.

Einstein was an unconventional thinker, but he used the same tools of thought available to the rest of us.

Language: More Than Meets the Ear

Albert Einstein did not begin to talk until he was 3 years old, and he wasn't entirely fluent even by the time he was 9 (Clark, 1971, p. 10). His language skills were so poor that his parents seriously worried that he might be mentally retarded! Nevertheless, he eventually learned to speak not only his native German, but also French and English. However, he mixed German with his French, and he had a strong accent. His English, learned later in life, never became fluent—as countless satirists have noted, he made grammatical mistakes and had a heavy German accent. If we judged him by his language alone, we wouldn't be impressed. Clearly, language is something different from the abilities that allow us to reason and solve problems.

The Essentials: What Makes Language Language?

Language is a two-pronged process of sending and receiving. **Language production** is our ability to speak or otherwise use words, phrases, and sentences to convey information. Perhaps the most remarkable thing about language production is that it is *generative*. We create, or "generate," new sentences all the time; we don't simply retrieve and repeat stored sentences. The number of new sentences we can produce is astounding. Psychologist Steven Pinker (1994, p. 86) estimates that we would need at least 100 trillion years to memorize all the sentences any one of us can possibly produce. **Language comprehension** is the ability to understand the message conveyed by words, phrases, and sentences. We humans are endowed with the extraordinary ability to comprehend even fragments of speech, mispronounced words, and scrambled syntax. For example, you can probably extract the general meaning from the following: "Me speech badly with grammar, but words use appropriately." We can understand the speech of the very young, speech flavored with foreign or regional accents, and lisping speech, even though in each case the actual sounds made are very different. Even Albert Einstein, who spoke French and English with difficulty, could make himself understood in those languages. To put things in perspective, even today's most sophisticated speech recognition devices can decode only a fraction of what a competent 5-year-old can do effortlessly.

So, if language is a process of sending and receiving information, what about a dog that whines when it is hungry, barks to go for a walk, and sits when told to? In fact, the Takara Company of Japan has developed a device (smaller than a credit card) that "translates" your dog's barks, yelps, whines and growls into emotions, supposedly allowing you to know when she's lonely, hungry, and so on (Associated Press, 2001). Your pet can send and receive information, all right, but is it using language? The intuitive answer is no, and the intuitive answer is right—there's more to language than that. Language units are built from simple building blocks that can be combined in many ways, but only according to specific rules. Four types of units, and the rules for combining them, distinguish language from other communicative sounds such as whines. These units and rules are the key to both language production and language comprehension, and are described by the phonology, syntax, semantics, and pragmatics of a language. Let's look at each of these aspects of language in turn.

Phonology: Some Say "Tomato"

Phonology is the structure of the sounds of the words in a language. Linguists Roman Jakobson and Morris Halle (1956) provided evidence that the sounds of any language are built up from sets of **phonemes,** which are the basic building blocks of speech sounds (Halle, 1990). The difference between *boy* and *toy* is one phoneme.

Humans can produce about 100 phonemes, but no single language uses all 100; English, for instance, uses about 45. Back-of-the-throat, soft French *r*'s do not exist in the world of hard American *r*'s, and Japanese has no *r*'s at all. One of the reasons French is difficult to learn for people who learned English as their native tongue is that the two languages use some different phonemes (such as those for *r* and *u*).

In English, some sounds in each word are accented, given extra emphasis. Some say *toMAYto*, and some say *toMAHto*, but in both cases the second syllable

● **Language production:** The ability to speak or otherwise use words, phrases, and sentences to convey information.

● **Language comprehension:** The ability to understand the message conveyed by words, phrases, and sentences.

● **Phonology:** The structure of the sounds that can be used to produce words in a language.

● **Phoneme:** The basic building block of speech sounds.

Curiously, the left cerebral hemisphere is primarily activated when males process phonemes, but both hemispheres are strongly activated when females process phonemes (Shaywitz et al., 1995); perhaps this is one reason females tend to be better with language than males (Halpern, 1997).

is stressed. Some other languages do not usually stress only one of the syllables in a word. In French, for example, each sound typically is given equal emphasis. Linguist Lisa Selkirk (personal communication) suggests that this difference explains why French rock and roll often sounds bland: French rock artists can't synchronize the "beats" in the language with the rhythm of the music.

The ability to produce phonemes clearly depends on your having heard others say them. In fact, when deaf children are given cochlear implants—devices that directly stimulate the part of the inner ear that sends neural impulses to the brain—they not only can hear, but they also learn to speak more clearly. Four years after the operation, at least 90% of the syllables each participant spoke could be understood, whereas only one child could be understood at least 10% of the time prior to the operation (Blamey et al., 2001).

The process of organizing sounds into phonemes isn't just a matter of how good your hearing is; it also depends on your knowledge of language. You use knowledge about which words are likely to appear in a given context to narrow down the possible words you are hearing (e.g., Pecher, 2001; Farrar et al., 2001). For example, if you hear "Would you like to sit on the __air," you can fill in the missing part of the final word. Even though if you heard the sound by itself, it might equally well sound like part of "hair," "lair," or even "snare"—but you know that you wouldn't be invited to sit on one of these things! In addition, your experience with language shapes which parts of your brain respond to speech (Hsieh et al., 2001). When researchers sped up speech (but kept the pitch constant, so that it didn't sound like chipmunks chirping when the speed was increased), language parts of the brain in the left cerebral hemisphere had increasingly more activation as the speech grew faster, until the speech was so fast that it was incomprehensible, at which point the activation level in these language areas decreased (Poldrack et al., 2001). Clearly, our brains have learned to detect speech per se, and to treat speech sounds differently from other types of sounds (Phillips et al., 2000).

Syntax: The Rules of the Road

- **Syntax:** The internal grammatical structure of a sentence, determined by how words that belong to different parts of speech are organized into acceptable arrangements.

- **Aphasia:** A disruption of language caused by brain damage.

- **Broca's aphasia:** Problems with producing language following brain damage (typically to the left frontal lobe).

- **Wernicke's aphasia:** Problems with comprehending language following brain damage (typically to the left posterior temporal lobe).

Every language has building blocks of sound and rules for cementing them together into words. Similarly, all languages include rules for how words can be organized into sentences. Sentences in any language contain an internal structure, an acceptable arrangement of words called **syntax.** The syntax of a sentence is determined by a set of rules for combining different categories of words, such as nouns, verbs, and adjectives. For example, in English you cannot say, "Kicked girl ball the blue." The basic units of syntax are parts of speech, not the individual words that fall into each category. A sentence in English needs a noun phrase (which must at a minimum have a noun—a word that names a person, place, or thing) and a verb phrase (at a minimum a single verb—a word that describes an action or a state of being). Thus, the shortest possible sentence in English has only three letters: "I am." A typical analysis of the syntactic structure of a sentence is shown in Figure 8.1.

Ask a friend to help you perform the following experiment, which should help you understand the syntactic structures that underlie sentences: At night, turn on

FIGURE 8.1 Syntactic Analysis of a Sentence

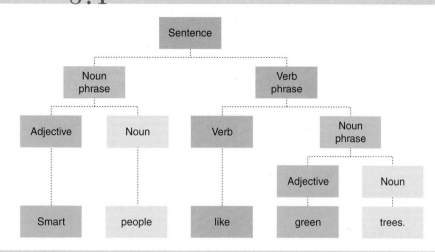

The syntactic structure of a sentence specifies the relations among words that belong to different syntactic categories such as nouns, verbs, and adjectives. All sentences have a noun phrase and a verb phrase.

the lights and shut all the blinds in the room. Read aloud from any book. Ask your friend to turn off the lights at some random point. You should find that you can keep saying the words leading up to the next major syntactic boundary (usually indicated by a verb, a conjunction, or a comma, period, or other punctuation mark). Fluent readers take in entire parts of the syntactic structure, one part at a time.

Moreover, we tend to interpret syntax in the simplest way. For example, read the following sentence and notice how you interpret each word when you first encounter it "The model embraced the designer and the photographer laughed." When you first read the noun phrase "the photographer," did you assume that it referred to one of the things that was embraced, or that it was the subject of a new clause? If you are like the participants in a study reported by Hoeks and colleagues (2002), you probably initially assumed that the model embraced the photographer, along with the designer. And then you were thrown off when you read "laughed." People automatically try to organize sentences so that there is only one topic—the model embracing, for instance—and prefer not to impose two topics, such as the model embracing and the photographer laughing.

The effects of brain damage on language reveal that it involves a system of mechanisms, not simply stored associations among words (Shelton & Caramazza, 1999). Patients with brain damage that disrupts language are said to have **aphasia.** In 1861 French anthropologist and neuroanatomist Paul Broca described how damage to the left frontal lobe—in an area later named *Broca's area*— disrupts speech much more than comprehension; this disorder is now called **Broca's aphasia.** These patients often produce long pauses between words and leave out function words, such as *and, if,* and *but.* For example, Goodglass (1976, p. 278) describes such a patient who said, "And, er Wednesday . . . nine o'clock. And er Thursday, ten o'clock . . . doctors. Two doctors . . . and ah . . . teeth. . . ." A little more than a decade after Broca's discovery, Carl Wernicke, a German neurologist, reported that damage to the back parts of the left temporal lobe has the reverse effect, disrupting comprehension more than production; this area was later named *Wernicke's area* (see Figure 8.2, p. 304), and this disorder is now called **Wernicke's aphasia.** These patients not only have difficulty

HANDS ON

At least some of the neural machinery of language is shared by other species. MRI scans were taken of the brains of 20 chimpanzees, 5 baboons, and 2 gorillas. Similar to humans, these great apes had more cortex in the region of the left hemisphere that corresponds to Broca's area in humans (Cantalupo & Hopkins, 2001).

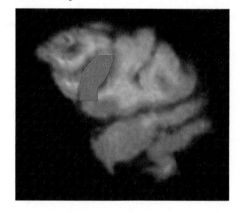

FIGURE 8.2   Major Language Areas of the Brain

Traditionally, Broca's area has been identified with speech production and Wernicke's area with speech comprehension, but we now know that Broca's area is involved in the use of syntax to understand sentences (Stromswold et al., 1996).

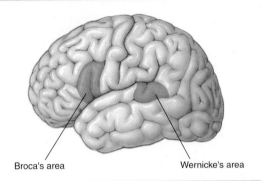

Broca's area   Wernicke's area

comprehending, but also produce "empty speech," which doesn't make sense. For example, when asked about the kind of work he did before being hospitalized, one such patient said, "Never, now mista oyge I wanna tell you this happened when happened when he rent" (Kertesz, 1981, p. 73, as cited in Carlson, 1994, p. 517). Part of the problem may have been that the patient didn't understand the request, but this man clearly had trouble producing coherent speech. When these patients are tested within 24 hours of having a stroke, researchers have found that the longer Wernicke's area requires to become activated (measured using fMRI) as the patients try to comprehend words, the more severe their language problems will be (Hillis et al., 2001).

However, even though production and comprehension rely on largely different mechanisms, the effects of brain damage demonstrate that both activities rely on at least some of the same processes. Damage to Broca's area and related brain areas can produce difficulties not only in forming sentences with correct syntax but also in understanding syntactic relations (Caramazza & Zurif, 1976; Grodzinsky, 1986; Zurif, 1995, 2000; Zurif et al., 1972). Moreover, PET studies have shown that Broca's area is activated when people must comprehend sentences with increasingly complex syntax (Stromswold et al., 1996). Thus, Broca's area is involved in the use of syntax in both production and comprehension. Comprehension, however, being tied to the meanings of words, may be less disrupted than production when syntax is impaired.

Semantics: The Meaning Is the Message

Language is, of course, more than sounds and sentence structures. To do its job, language must convey meaning. The **semantics** of a word or sentence is its meaning. Just as the sounds of words are represented by smaller elements (phonemes) and the syntactic aspects of a sentence are represented by its elements (parts of speech), semantics is represented by **morphemes,** the smallest units of *meaning* in a language. The word *wet* includes but a single morpheme, but the meanings of many words are determined by more than one morpheme. Prefixes and suffixes are obvious examples of such morphemes used in combination with other morphemes. For example, adding the morpheme *-ing* to a verb, as in *walking, talking, flirting,* creates a word expressing a continuing state, whereas adding the morpheme *-ed* indicates a completed state. Just as the other elements of language are combined according to rules, so, too, with morphemes. We cannot add *-ing* at the front of a word, or *mis-* (another morpheme) to the end. Different sets

● **Semantics:** The meaning of a word or sentence.

● **Morpheme:** The smallest unit of meaning in a language.

of morphemes underlie the different meanings of ambiguous words, words with more than one meaning; thus *park* as in "park the car" has different morphemes than does *park* as in "place with benches and pigeons." Many jokes rely on the fact that words can have more than one meaning. For example, "Energizer Bunny arrested—charged with battery."

Sometimes only context can indicate which morphemes should be assigned to words that have the same sounds. William Wang (cited in Komarova & Hauser, 2001, p. 413) tells of a speech given by Chairman Mao, when he was saying goodbye to visitors. The visitors heard him say, "I am a lone monk walking through the world with a leaky umbrella," but the exact same sounds in Chinese also translate as, "I am above the law, defying the powers of heaven." Apparently Chairman Mao was not in a poetic mood at the time, and he actually meant the latter.

Meanings are often assigned arbitrarily to different sounds or written words; the sound *dog* could easily have been assigned to refer to that feline we keep as a pet, and *cat* to the animal that likes to gnaw on bones and slippers. Specific events in the past have a lot to do with how particular words have come to have their meanings. For example, early medieval Scandinavian warriors wore bearskin shirts, for which the Old Norwegian word is *berserkr*; from the ferocity of the Vikings' frenzied attacks in battle we inherit the expression "going berserk." Of more recent vintage is the word *bedlam*, which since the 16th century has meant "chaos and confusion"; its origins are in the name of the Hospital of St. Mary of Bethlehem in London ("bedlam" is a shortened version of Bethlehem), where "lunatics" were confined. Sometimes the meanings of words seem to reveal deeper aspects of a culture: The Chinese character for *crisis* is composed of two other characters, one signifying "risk" and the other "opportunity."

The meaning of a sentence and its syntax are to a large extent distinct. For example, Chomsky (1957) pointed out that the sentence "Colorless green ideas sleep furiously" has an acceptable English syntax but is meaningless. On the other hand, "Fastly dinner eat, ballgame soon start" has the opposite properties: It is syntactically incorrect but understandable. The wise alien Yoda of the *Star Wars* movies often uttered such sentences, probably in part to remind the audience that he was not an ordinary person.

That semantics, understanding what words and sentences mean, is distinct from phonology, understanding sounds as signaling certain words, was demonstrated convincingly by Damasio and her collaborators (1996), who used PET scanning to show that different brain areas are involved in processing the sounds of words versus their meanings. (Devlin et al., 2003, also describe brain areas that respond differently during the two types of processing.) Damasio and colleagues also found that a third brain area literally bridged the meaning and sound regions; this third area may serve to cross-reference representations of sounds and meanings.

Just as morphemes are combined into representations of the meanings of words, the representations of words in turn are combined into *propositions*. **Propositional representations** are mental sentences that express the meaning of assertions. The same sets of words can express different propositions, depending on how they are organized. For example, consider this anecdote:

> An English professor wrote the words "Woman without her man is a savage" on the blackboard and directed his students to punctuate the sentence. The men wrote, "Woman, without her man, is a savage." The women wrote, "Woman: Without her, man is a savage."

● **Propositional representation:** A mental sentence that expresses the unambiguous meaning of an assertion.

As you see, the punctuation has organized the words in different ways to express different propositions. Propositional representations are not ambiguous; they specify the meanings that underlie the particular sense of a statement. Many studies have shown that people typically store not the literal words used in sentences, but rather the propositions that specify the meaning. For example, Sachs (1967) had participants in a study listen to paragraphs and then tested their memories for specific sentences. The participants had to indicate whether each test sentence had been presented in a paragraph or was changed from one that had been presented. The participants remembered the meanings well, but not the particular wordings (Bransford & Franks, 1971, report comparable results).

Pragmatics: Being Indirect

At least in German, Einstein was perfectly able to understand the semantics of words (he understood morphemes and how they are combined into words) and sentences (he understood how the meanings of words are combined into phrases and sentences and their underlying propositional representations); but he often failed at another aspect of meaning. Utterances have not only a literal meaning but also an *implied* meaning. For example, Einstein once sat through a series of vicious attacks on his theory of relativity by Nazis, who claimed the theory was part of a plot to disrupt the proper thought processes of the German people (Clark, 1971). Einstein laughed and apparently had a great time listening to the diatribes, oblivious to the barely concealed threats beneath them. The **pragmatics** of a language are concerned with the way language implies meaning. Have you ever asked a 13-year-old, "Do you know where the restroom is?" and got back the response "Yes"? This question can be interpreted literally as an inquiry, about your knowledge of, say, the layout of a large building or, indirectly, as a request for directions. In some contexts, such as children being addressed by a parent who is dropping them off at an auditorium by themselves, the question might really be meant literally. But in most instances you would understand that the questioner has a need for the facilities. This understanding depends on your grasp of pragmatics, which often involves knowledge of the world as well as of language and its specific conventions about how to communicate (Grice, 1975; Lindblom, 2001).

Although some aspects of pragmatics depend on being able to understand the meaning of rising or falling pitch in a sentence, as in spoken questions, pragmatics are pervasive in linguistic communication—even in reading (Kintsch, 1998). Pragmatics depend critically on our ability to draw correct inferences. The fact that we humans can draw the correct inferences quickly and seemingly without effort obscures how difficult these processes really are. Indeed, the use of pragmatics has stymied attempts to create computer programs that can truly understand language.

Pragmatics play a key role in understanding metaphor, a direct comparison of two things in which one is described as being the other (Gentner & Bowdle, 2001). To say that somebody's lawyer is a shark means that the attorney is vicious—but it doesn't mean that he or she can breathe under water or has pebbly skin. To understand metaphors we actively inhibit the irrelevant aspects of the meaning (Glucksberg et al., 2001). The fact that metaphor involves different mechanisms than the rest of language is attested to by the role of the right cerebral hemisphere. Other language abilities depend primarily (in right-handed people) on the left hemisphere, but metaphor, as well as the ability to understand humor, depends crucially on the brain's right hemisphere. Patients who have suffered damage to the right hemisphere might understand a metaphorical statement such as "Can you lend me a hand" as

● **Pragmatics:** The way that language conveys meaning indirectly, by implying rather than asserting.

asking literally for a hand on a platter. Indeed, in normal people, the right hemisphere is particularly active (as measured in PET) when they are interpreting metaphors (Bottini et al., 1994).

The role of the right hemisphere in the comprehension of humor was documented by Brownell and his colleagues (1990; Bihrle et al., 1986; Brownell et al., 1983, 1995), who told jokes to brain-damaged patients and asked them to select the appropriate punch line from a few choices. For example: "A woman is taking a shower. All of a sudden, her doorbell rings. She yells, 'Who's there?' and a man answers, 'Blind man.' Well, she's a charitable lady, so she runs out of the shower naked and opens the door." At this point, the patient is asked to select the appropriate punch line from five choices:

1. The man says, "Can you spare a little change for a blind man?"
2. The man says, "My seeing eye dog is 10 years old."
3. The man says, "I really enjoy going to the symphony."
4. The blind man throws a pie in the woman's face.
5. The man says, "Where should I put these blinds, lady?"

The patients with damage to the right hemisphere preferred the surprising but non sequitur endings, such as choice 4.

However, other studies have shown that patients with left-hemisphere damage have more difficulty than do patients with right-hemisphere damage in other aspects of pragmatics, such as producing the proper emphasis when they speak (for example, by raising pitch at the end of a question; Gandour & Baum, 2001). Pragmatics is not a single process, and different aspects of pragmatics rely on different parts of the brain.

It's worth underscoring a point that cuts across the four aspects of language. We've seen that although speech production and comprehension at first may seem entirely different, they actually draw on many of the same mechanisms. We learn phonological production through phonological perception, and the mechanisms that produce syntactically correct utterances also help us comprehend them. Moreover, the semantic representations that underlie our ability to speak coherently also allow us to comprehend; propositions express ideas, both our own (which we can

Patients with left-hemisphere damage that disrupted their ability to comprehend speech nevertheless could detect lies better than normal people (Etcoff et al., 2000). Apparently, the meanings of words can obscure other telltale features, such as changes in intonation or facial expression, that reveal deception.

express by speaking) and those of others (which we have decoded from their speech). Finally, we use the principles of pragmatics both when producing speech (guiding our patterns of intonation and use of metaphor and humor) and when comprehending speech.

However, there is one special problem posed in comprehension that is not present in production: How do we resolve ambiguity? When we speak, we know which meaning of an ambiguous word we intend, but it often isn't so clear when we comprehend. In the following section, we focus on a classic study that revealed how we sort out the proper meanings of ambiguous words during comprehension.

no such difficulty (Jusczyk, 1995). Infants 2 to 3 months old can register in less than half a second that a syllable has been changed ("ga" to "ba"; Dehaene-Lambertz & Dehaene, 1994). However, after about 6 months of age, they start to ignore distinctions among sounds that are not used in the language spoken around them (Kuhl et al., 1992). At around 8 months, infants can use patterns of sound regularity to identify individual words, even when the actual sounds run together into a single continuous stream (Saffran, 2001). More-over, by 14 months, infants pay attention to different sound distinctions in different tasks: When they are re-quired to distinguish between speech sounds, they are sensitive to differences in the sounds that they ignore when they are learning to pair words with particular objects (Stager & Werker, 1997).

Sign language resembles spoken language in crucial ways. For example, when communicating with infants, speakers slow down and exaggerate their vocalizations or hand and arm movements in order to communicate more clearly.

The ability of infants to discriminate and organize sounds outstrips their ability to produce them. All babies, even deaf ones, begin by babbling at around 6 months of age (Stoel-Gammon & Otomo, 1986). Initial babbling includes the sounds made in all human languages. However, as the child is exposed to speaking adults, the range of sounds narrows; at about 1 year, the child's babbling begins to have adultlike intonation patterns (Levitt & Wang, 1991). Deaf children do not develop the more advanced types of babbling but, if they are exposed to sign language, their hand and arm motions develop in corresponding ways—beginning with a wide range of motions and eventually narrowing down to those used in the sign language they see around them (Petitto & Marentette, 1991). The first words children in all languages say grow directly out of their babbles, such as "ma-ma" and "da-da."

Getting the Words

Most children begin to speak when they are about a year old. Two-year-olds can learn words even when the object or action being named is not present (Akhtar & Tomasello, 1996). By the time they are 6 years old, children know approximately 10,000 words (Anglin, 1993). The rate of learning differs for boys and girls, however, as shown in Figure 8.3. Children begin by understanding words far in advance of their ability to say them. Indeed, they can understand about 50 words at about 13 months but cannot say this many words until about 18 months (Menyuk et al., 1995). Studies of brain activity in children, as measured by electrical activity on the scalp, have shown that when they are just beginning to learn words (at about 13 to 17 months), brain activity is widely distributed over both cerebral hemispheres. In contrast, at 20 months, adultlike patterns of activation are found in the temporal and parietal areas of the left cerebral hemisphere (Mills et al., 1997). Such findings suggest that the brain is changing as language is learned or that maturational changes in the brain facilitate language learning, or—as seems most likely (Mills et al., 1997)—that both events occur.

Even 3-year-olds can often learn words, or facts about objects, after hearing them only a single time (Carey, 1978; Markson & Bloom, 1997). Which words children learn first depends partly on their cultures; in Vietnam, children learn the respectful pronouns used to refer to elders before learning the words for many objects (Nelson, 1981). However, rather than learning the entire meaning of words in one fell swoop, children sometimes make **overextensions**, using words over-

● **Overextension:** An overly broad use of a word to refer to a new object or situation.

FIGURE 8.3 The Number of New Words Understood During the First 2 Years of Life

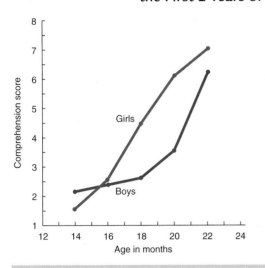

Notice the difference in comprehension rates for boys and girls.

broadly when referring to new objects or situations. They might call a dog a dog, and a cat a dog, and a horse a dog, and even a sawhorse a dog. This makes sense if their initial idea of "dog" is anything with four legs. With learning, they discover which features—in the case of a dog, more than just four-leggedness—restrict the appropriate use of the word (Clark, 1983, 1993). Overextensions may sometimes occur simply because the child has trouble recalling the appropriate word and uses the apparently next best one instead. Children sometimes also make **underextensions,** using words too narrowly. For example, a child may only refer to dogs with the word "animal." This may occur because an adult uses a superordinate term (such as "animal") when referring to a typical member of a category (such as a dog), and the child does not experience the term being used broadly for less typical members of the category (Kay & Anglin, 1982; White, 1982). However, as knowledge of distinctions within a domain (such as dinosaurs) increases, both children and adults tend to make more underextensions and fewer overextensions (Johnson & Eilers, 1998).

Grammar: Not From School

The heart of any language is its **grammar,** which is the rules that allow you to combine words into an infinite number of acceptable sentences in a language. Traditionally, the term "grammar" has referred to syntax and some aspects of semantics (including those aspects of word meaning that must be in agreement in a sentence, such as using a plural verb for a plural subject). However, some researchers argue that the concept of grammar should be extended to include features of all aspects of language except pragmatics (and even treating pragmatics as part of grammar is being discussed; Hu, 1990, 1995; Payne, 1992). By looking at the patterns of sounds to which babies became habituated, Marcus and colleagues (1999) showed that even 7-month-old babies have the capacity to abstract grammarlike rules. However, it is only around 2 years of age that children start putting words together into the simplest sentences, two-word utterances such as "Go dog." These utterances are often called **telegraphic speech** because, like the telegrams of days gone by and the text messages people send to cell phones today, they pack a lot of

- **Underextension:** An overly narrow use of a word to refer to an object or situation.

- **Grammar:** The rules that determine how words can be organized into acceptable sentences in a language.

- **Telegraphic speech:** Speech that packs much information into few words typically omitting words such as "the," "a," and "of."

People with dyslexia have difficulty both writing and reading. With extensive training in listening to speech and dividing the continuous stream into separate words, many reading-impaired children have dramatically improved their reading abilities, presumably because they have learned to store separate representations of words in memory (Merzenich et al., 1996; Tallal et al., 1996).

information into a few choice words. By about 3 years of age, children who speak English start to use sentences that follow the sequence subject–verb–object ("Dog chase cat"). Words such as *the*, *a*, and *of* are left out. The particular order of the words depends on the language being learned, but in all cases the child at this stage makes sentences with words in the appropriate order (de Villiers & de Villiers, 1992).

Adults do not teach grammatical rules to children, or even systematically correct grammatical errors (de Villiers & de Villiers, 1992; Pinker, 1994), but even 4-year-olds acquire such rules. Berko (1958) showed that most children this age generalize grammatical rules. This is true even when sentences contain nonsense words. For example, a child is given this problem:

This is a wug.
Now there is another one. Now there are two _____.

When asked to say the missing word, most 4-year-olds have no trouble saying "wugs."

Most verbs in a language are *regular*, following an easily derived rule for changes in tense—*play* becomes *played*, *work* becomes *worked*. But typically the most frequently used verbs in a language are *irregular*—for example, *eat* becomes *ate*. Children may start off using irregular verbs properly, but then begin to make mistakes such as *runned* instead of *ran*. These **overregularization errors,** mistakes caused by the misapplication of the rule for regular verb formation, occur because the child has now learned the rule and begins to apply it systematically, even when it is inappropriate (Pinker, 1999). The same thing happens with plurals; a child who could use *feet* correctly last week may suddenly start saying, "Mommy, my feets are tired."

The 5-year-old's language is in most ways like that of the adults in the community. Indeed, subtle testing is required to observe ways in which the language ability of 7-year-olds is less than complete. By such testing Carol Chomsky (1969) has shown that even 7-year-olds may confuse the meanings of statements such as "Please *tell* Sally" and "Please *ask* Sally"; but remarkably, even 3-year-olds understand that "I need a pencil" is a request, not a statement, and respond appropriately (Garvey, 1974). Subtle pragmatics and conversational skills emerge between the ages of 5 and 9—for example, learning to change topics by gradually, not suddenly, altering the direction of the conversation (Wanska & Bedrosian, 1985, 1986). The major milestones of language are listed in Table 8.1.

Is There a Critical Period for Learning Language?

Throughout history, there have been reports of children who grew up in the wild, never exposed to human language. Reports of such "feral," that is, wild, children include the story of Romulus and Remus, the legendary founders of Rome, who supposedly were abandoned as children and raised by a wolf; Edgar Rice Burroughs's novels about Tarzan of the Apes; and the true account of Victor, the Wild

● **Overregularization error:** A speaking error that occurs because the child applies a rule even to cases that are exceptions to the rule.

TABLE 8.1 Major Milestones in Language Acquisition

Approximate Age	Major Linguistic Development
2–3 months	Perceive all phonemes, notice changes in phonemes
6 months	Ignore distinctions among sounds that are not used in the languages spoken around them; begin babbling
8 months	Identify words in the continuous speech stream
1 year	Babbling has adultlike intonation patterns; speaking begins
13 months	Understand about 50 words
18 months	Speak about 50 words
2 years	Telegraphic speech
3 years	Simple pragmatics
4 years	Rules of grammar, such as plural
6 years	Know about 10,000 words
9 years	Subtle pragmatics

Boy of Aveyron. This boy was found naked and filthy in the woods near Paris, France, in 1799; he bit and scratched those who annoyed him and generally acted more like a wild animal than a human. He was incapable of speech, making only animal-like sounds (Ball, 1971; Lane, 1976; Pinker, 1994). When cases like these occur in real life, they provide a key test of the theory that language can only be learned during a narrow window of time called the **critical period.** This theory holds that the brain is "set" for the development of language (or other attributes) at a particular point, and trying to acquire it either earlier or later is fruitless. Critical periods are different from **sensitive periods,** which define time windows when learning is *easiest,* but are not the only times when such learning can occur. Lennenberg (1967) claimed that language had to be learned prior to puberty, during the period when the two halves of the brain were becoming fully specialized; if language was not learned before this, he believed, it would never be learned well (see also Grimshaw et al., 1998).

Although the Wild Boy of Aveyron and other such children did have language difficulties, it is impossible to know whether they were mentally deficient to begin with; that may even be why they were abandoned. However, more recently scientists have been able to study similar children in detail. Consider, for example, the dreadful case of a girl called Genie, whose deranged parents locked her up, nearly immobilized, in a back room from the age of 20 months until she was slightly over 13 years old (Curtiss, 1977, 1989; Rymer, 1993). Genie was not allowed any contact with other people, was not talked to, and was punished if she made any sounds. She was not intellectually slow, nor had she had difficulty beginning to speak as a toddler. After she was discovered, she received intensive training in language, with mixed success. Genie was able to learn many words and eventually had reasonably good language comprehension, so there doesn't seem to be a critical period for acquiring all aspects of language. But she was never able to grasp the rules of

● **Critical period:** A narrow window of time when certain types of learning are possible.

● **Sensitive period:** A window of time when a particular type of learning is *easiest,* but not the only time it can occur.

grammar fully, and thus there does seem to be a critical period for acquiring grammar (Grimshaw et al., 1998; Pinker, 1994).

The existence of a critical period for grammar explains why brain damage has much greater long-term effects on language in adults than in children. Bates and her colleagues (1997) studied language acquisition in 53 infants and preschoolers with brain damage and concluded that although there are in fact innate biases for certain parts of the brain to take on language functions, if those parts are damaged in children's brains, other parts can take over these functions. Indeed, if the entire left half of a young child's cortex, including the areas normally used in language, has to be removed because of disease or injury, the child will nevertheless learn language. In fact, such children can sometimes learn language so well that careful testing is necessary to detect deficits (for example, Aram et al., 1992; Bishop, 1983; Vargha-Khadem et al., 1991). In contrast, it is very difficult for an adult to recover language abilities following brain damage that produces aphasia.

Other Ways to Communicate: Are They Language?

True language must have phonology, syntax, semantics, and pragmatics. Think about that as you read the following sections. Which of these examples of communication do you think truly qualify as language?

Nonverbal Communication

In ancient Egypt, law courts met in the dark so that the judges could not see the accused, the accuser, or the witnesses (Seuling, 1988), so as not to be swayed by their demeanors. People are remarkably good at **nonverbal communication**, such as interpretation of facial expressions and body language (Ambady & Rosenthal, 1992, 1993). Indeed, we can detect whether someone is lying by registering *microexpressions*, flickers of expressions—such as frequent eyeblinks, sideways glances, or downcast eyes that last as little as a tenth of a second (DePaullo et al., 2003; Ekman, 1985; Ekman & Friesen, 1975). We recognize different types of nonverbal information and can detect lies when inconsistent information arises from different sources, such as a stiff body posture combined with trusting, direct eye contact. We are also sensitive to the fact that the pitch of the voice tends to go up when someone is lying (Zuckerman et al., 1981), as well as that liars often speak more slowly and less fluently, and may exaggerate their facial expressions.

Pretty impressive, we agree. But is such nonverbal communication language? Consider again the four criteria: phonology, syntax, semantics, and pragmatics. Nonverbal communication does not have a set of perceptual units like phonemes that are combined according to rules to form new units. Instead, it consists of a set of specific physical signs and gestures. In addition, these specific signs cannot be combined in novel ways to create brand new, meaningful expressions. For instance, if you arch your eyebrows, open your mouth, and scrunch up your nose, people may think you're weird, but they won't read a distinct message. Nonverbal communication lacks the generative power that comes from having a true grammar; whereas language can convey an infinite number of messages, nonverbal communication lends itself to a relatively small set of messages. Finally, no clear distinction separates the literal from the implied meaning of nonverbal cues. Although nonverbal communication *is* communication, it is not truly language. Still, we shouldn't underestimate its importance.

● **Nonverbal communication:** Facial expressions and body language that allow others to infer an individual's internal mental state.

Sign Language

One of the most remarkable things about language is that any normal person will develop it without being formally taught (Pinker, 1994). This is true for people in all cultures, including the culture of the deaf. Deaf children who are raised by speaking parents who do not sign will spontaneously invent sign languages (Goldin-Meadow & Mylander, 1998). Sign languages are not like the motions you might make when playing charades. Rather, the gestures specify the manual equivalent of phonemes, small units that are combined to make appropriate perceptual signals. Symbols for individual words are combined according to syntactic, semantic, and pragmatic rules (Emmorey, 1993; Klima & Bellugi, 1979). Just as there are different spoken languages, there are different sign languages: American Sign Language (ASL), for example, is not understandable to someone who uses British Sign Language (BSL), and vice versa.

One indication that sign language is a true language is that brain damage can disrupt it in ways that parallel the impairments of spoken language of hearing people (Bellugi et al., 1993; Poizner et al., 1987; Poizner & Kegl, 1992). Damage in the same brain areas results in corresponding effects in hearing speakers and deaf signers. For example, damage to Broca's area, in the left frontal lobe, can cause signers to have trouble using grammar when producing and comprehending sentences (Poizner et al., 1987), just as with people who use oral languages.

Even though a teacher's gestures might occasionally be distracting, they are actually helping that person explain material more clearly by freeing up cognitive capacity. Note that gesturing in this way isn't sign language: such gesturing supplements spoken language, but is not itself a language.

Gesture: Is It Just for Show?

The gestures hearing people make when they talk are not sign language. But they do enhance communication, partly because they lighten the cognitive load of the speaker. For example, in one study researchers asked participants to explain a math problem while they were also trying to remember a list of words or letters. Both children and adults later remembered more of the material if they had used gestures while explaining the math problem (Goldin-Meadow et al., 2001). Gestures apparently took some of the load off of processes used in verbal explanation, freeing up more cognitive resources for memorization. Such gesturing is not learned: Even people blind from birth gesture as they talk (and make similar gestures as those used by sighted people), and they even gesture when they know that they are talking to another blind person (Iverson & Goldin-Meadow, 1998, 2001). Gestures can supplement information conveyed in speech (Alibali et al., 1999), but are not themselves a distinct language.

Aping Language?

In evolutionary terms, chimpanzees are very close to humans: We have about 99% of our genes in common. Nevertheless, no one has succeeded in teaching a chimpanzee or other nonhuman primate to talk. Some heroic researchers have gone so far as to raise a chimp alongside their own child, but even then the animal did not learn to speak (Kellogg & Kellogg, 1933). More recent studies have told much the same story (Terrace et al., 1976; Terrace, 1979). Because part of the problem seems to be that the animal's throat cannot make the sounds of speech, some researchers have tried to teach chimps sign language (Gardner & Gardner, 1969; Terrace, 1979) or how to use arbitrary symbols such as cut-out plastic shapes or computer icons to communicate (Greenfield & Savage-Rumbaugh, 1990; Savage-Rumbaugh et al., 1986). With

Some nonhuman primates can be trained to understand the meaning of symbols, such as these pieces of plastic, and to arrange them to form simple sentences. But is this true language?

both sign language and arbitrary shapes, animals can in fact be taught to string symbols together to make "sentences." However, Terrace (1979) found that the chimps usually were simply imitating sequences they had previously seen and could not learn rules for reordering the signs to produce novel sentences. Nevertheless, members of one species of chimp, the pygmy chimpanzee, have spontaneously created new statements using the symbols (Greenfield & Savage-Rumbaugh, 1990), and at least some researchers believe that certain nonhuman primates are capable of using true language (Fouts & Mills, 1997). However, only humans spontaneously invent language (Pinker, 1994).

Bilingualism: A Window of Opportunity?

All normal people learn a language, and most of the people in the world learn a second language at some point in life (Fabbro, 2001). Is learning a second language the same as learning a first one? Using functional magnetic resonance imaging (fMRI), Kim and his colleagues (1997) scanned the brains of two groups of bilingual people while they thought about what they had done the previous day, using each of their two languages in turn. One group had learned their second languages as young children, the other as adults. Wernicke's area, involved in comprehension, was activated the same way in both languages and in both groups. But Broca's area told a different story: If the participants had learned the second language as young children, the same part of Broca's area displayed activity for both the first and the second languages. If they had learned the second language after childhood, however, activity for that language appeared in a different part of the left frontal lobe—in a part used in working memory. One theory is that if you learn grammar early enough, it becomes "procedural knowledge," which is mediated in part by subcortical structures; if you don't learn grammar early enough, it is stored as explicit memories—which you need to think about to recall (Ullman, 2001).

Different languages may rely to differing degrees on specific processes (such as working memory), and may incorporate more or less complex phonology, syntax, and semantics. Thus, brain damage can have different effects on different languages, even if the same underlying process is disrupted (Paradis, 2001). Indeed, Paradis and Goldblum (1989) describe a patient who had been fluent in French, Malagasy, and Gujariti prior to brain surgery; after the surgery, only Gujariti was impaired (in spite of the fact that the patient had learned both Gujariti and Malagasy as an infant). Curiously, 8 months after surgery he regained his ability to speak Gujariti, but no longer could speak Malagasy well! French, learned during school (and the only language in which he could read and write) remained intact. After 2 years, he regained complete control of all of his languages. In any case, second (and third) languages rely primarily on the left hemisphere, as do first languages (Paradis, 1990, 1992).

In spite of the fact that languages learned as an adult generally are not as well learned as those acquired during childhood, it is remarkably easy to learn some aspects of second languages. Dupuy and Krashen (1993) asked third-semester college students who were taking French to read five scenes from a script from a French movie, after having seen the first five scenes to get the story line. The scenes that were read contained many highly colloquial words that the students were unlikely to have seen or heard before. A surprise vocabulary test after reading showed that participants were learning almost five words per hour, without trying! This rate is remarkably close to the learning rates of children who are reading in their native languages.

Unfortunately, as you would expect from knowing that there is a critical period (or at least a sensitive period) in childhood for learning grammar, it is not so easy to learn the grammar of a second language as an adult. In addition, it is not easy to learn the sound pattern of a second language after childhood. Indeed, the vast majority of people who learn a second language after puberty will make grammatical errors and will speak with an accent. But even for these difficult tasks, some people can learn to pronounce words in another language almost flawlessly (Marinova-Todd et al., 2000; Snow, 2002). In general, the more formal education you have, and the younger you are when you start, the better you will learn a second language (Hakuta et al., 2003). People differ greatly (perhaps even genetically?) in their abilities to acquire second languages.

● **Specific language impairment:** A specific problem in understanding grammar and complex words that is not related to more general cognitive deficits.

Looking *at* Levels

Is There a Language Gene?

If you think about what makes people special, different from other animals, language probably comes to mind immediately. We are the talking animal. Some researchers have claimed that we humans have special genes for language. The best evidence for this claim involves two steps. First, researchers (Gopnik 1990, 1997, 1999; Gopnik & Crago, 1991) found families in which many members have a disorder called **specific language impairment.** These people have trouble understanding grammar and even complex words, those made up of many morphemes, such as *predisposing.* Basing their conclusions on results from many types of tests, Pinker (1994) and others have argued that this disorder is not caused by general cognitive difficulties or an overall lack of intelligence— hence the name *specific* language impairment. This disorder has been identified in speakers of English, Greek, French, and Japanese, even though these languages convey information very differently.

Second, having established a very specific disorder of language, the next step is to link it to the genes. There is evidence for a genetic contribution to specific language impairment. In particular, the disorder is more likely to occur in both identical twins (who

have the same genes) than in both fraternal twins (who share only half their genes). Moreover, language difficulties in general often run in families (Plomin, 2001). Both siblings and parents of children with reading problems also display difficulties in reading (DeFries et al., 1986, 1987). In fact, a gene has been identified that is associated with specific language impairment (Lai et al., 2001), but it remains to be seen whether this gene also affects other aspects of cognition. Communication disorders in general—that is, impairments in the ability to express ideas in words and understand others when they do—are about 80% heritable (that is, about 80% of the variability in these disorders can be explained by variation in the genes; Bishop et al., 1995; Lewis & Thompson, 1992); stuttering, for example, is in part genetic (Ambrose et al., 1993; Kidd, 1993).

Does all of this mean that there is a single gene for language? Probably not (Gilger, 1995). As you are discovering, language is a complex phenomenon, and it is as unlikely that it is controlled by one gene as it is that a bakery would rely on a single ingredient for a cake. To bake a cake, you need not only the multiple ingredients, but also the oven and the means to make it hot and to time the baking process. An intricate system of events is involved in baking cakes and in using language. In either case, knocking out a link in the process disrupts the end result: No flour or liquid, no source of heat, no timing—any one of these failures means no cake. Similarly, language involves many key factors, any one of which may be affected by a different gene or genes. Indeed, many cases of language disorder involve many facets of language (Ahme et al., 2001a, 2001b; Botting & Conti-Ramsden, 2001; Vargha-Khadem et al., 1995).

At the level of the group, language is clearly a social phenomenon. In fact, it is doubtful that language would have developed if not for the group. Being exposed to a community of speakers appears to turn on certain genes (see Chapter 3) that allow language learning to operate. If those genes don't work quite right, not only are our abilities to interact with other people affected but also the way we feel about ourselves is changed. Pinker (1994) describes in vivid detail the anxiety that people with specific language impairment experi-

ence, even in common social interactions, because they worry about their difficulties using language. Again, we see events at all three levels interacting: To understand the effects of this disorder, we need to consider events in the brain, the person, and the group.

TEST YOURSELF!

1. What are the essential characteristics of all languages?
2. How do we acquire language?
3. Which sorts of nonspeech communication are language, and which are not? Can animals be taught to use language?
4. Are first and second languages used in different ways?

Means of Thought: Words, Images, Concepts

Einstein was a theoretical physicist. He didn't perform experiments; he didn't collect new data. Instead, he tried to put together known facts and to synthesize specialized principles into larger and simpler overarching theories. At first glance, these abilities and skills might suggest that Einstein reasoned at a very abstract level, using complex mathematical symbols to manipulate arcane ideas. But Einstein denied thinking in that way. Instead, he said that he relied on mental imagery, playing with images of objects and events, "seeing" what would happen in certain circumstances. In fact, the initial insight that led to his Special Theory of Relativity came when he imagined himself chasing a beam of light, matching its speed, and "seeing" what it would look like. He reported that, "Conventional words or other signs have to be sought for laboriously only in a secondary stage, when the mentioned associative play is sufficiently established and can be reproduced at will" (Einstein, 1945, pp. 142–143).

Thinking involves manipulating information in your head. Sometimes it involves solving problems; sometimes it involves simply determining what is implied by or associated with information at hand. We do think partly by using language, but this isn't always the case. In fact, as Einstein noted, language may come into play rather late in the thinking game. As you will see, language is a tool that may be used in thinking, but it is not the sole basis of thought.

We are usually aware of what we are thinking about, but our awareness appears to be limited to language and mental images. Inner speech—talking to ourselves—and images are manipulated in working memory, and thus they play a key role in thinking; as discussed in Chapter 7, working memory operates on stored information to allow us to perform a task. Language and images help us to think but cannot themselves be the only means by which we think. To see why, let's consider each in turn, and then look at another way in which information is specified in the mind.

Words: Inner Speech and Spoken Thoughts

Many people, if asked, would say that they think with words. And, at first glance, that seems plausible: After all, to communicate with someone, we usually have to express ourselves in words, so why not use words when thinking?

Putting Thoughts Into Words

There are at least three problems with the idea that thinking is just talking to yourself, as was claimed by the founder of behaviorism, John B. Watson (1913). First, if this were true, why would you ever have trouble "putting a thought into words"? If thoughts were already formed in language, expressing them in language should be child's play. Second, words are often ambiguous, but thoughts are not. If you are thinking about "the port," you don't wonder whether you are thinking about a wine or a harbor. Third, anyone who has owned a dog or cat probably has sensed that at least some animals can think, and yet they don't use language. In fact, there is ample evidence that many animals can not only think but can also solve problems—remember Köhler's work with the chimpanzee Sultan, discussed in Chapter 6.

Does Language Shape Thought?

Even if thought is not the silent equivalent of talking to yourself, many people have been fascinated by the possibility that our perceptions and thoughts are shaped by the particular language we speak. This idea, known as the **linguistic relativity hypothesis,** was championed by Benjamin Lee Whorf (1956). For example, some have suggested that because the Inuit of northern Canada have many words for the different types of snow they recognize, they can see and think about subtle differences in snow better than speakers of English can with their paltry single word for the white stuff. If this idea is correct, then people who speak languages with lots of color words should be able to perceive more distinctions among colors than people who speak languages with few such words. Rosch (1973, 1975) tested this idea by studying the Dani, a remote tribe living in Papua New Guinea. The Dani use only two words for color, corresponding to *light* and *dark.* However, they perceive variations in color and are able to learn shades of color as readily as people who speak languages with words that label many colors.

● **Linguistic relativity hypothesis:** The idea that perceptions and thoughts are shaped by language, and thus people who speak different languages think differently.

Even though the Dani have only two words for color, *light* and *dark,* they can perceive and learn shades of color as easily as people who speak languages with many terms for color.

● **Mental images:** Internal representations like those that arise during perception, but based on stored information rather than on immediate sensory input.

Nevertheless, even if language does not entirely determine how we can think, it does influence some aspects of thought and memory. In some cases, we do appear to use words as a crutch to help us think, particularly when working memory is involved. In such circumstances, we often perform relatively slow, step-by-step reasoning—for example, memorizing a series of directions and recalling them one at a time, holding them in working memory long enough to turn the right way and continue to the next landmark. In addition, language can enhance memory. For example, if you look at clouds, you can remember their shapes better if you come up with a distinctive characterization for each (such as "a rabbit sticking out of a tube" or "a face without a chin") than if you use a single label for them all (Ellis, 1973). In addition, the written version of a language may affect thought. For example, speakers of English tend to think of time as if it is horizontal, but speakers of Mandarin Chinese think of time as if it were vertical ("Wednesday is lower than Tuesday"; Boroditsky, 2001). However, the relationship among language, memory, and perception is not the same thing as language's actually shaping the nature of our thoughts.

Mental Imagery: Perception Without Sensation

If language is not the basis of thinking, what might be? Virtually all the great thinkers who applied themselves to this question in the past, including Plato and Aristotle, and later John Locke and other British philosophers, identified thought with a stream of mental images (Kosslyn, 1980). **Mental images** are representations like those that arise during perception, but they arise from stored information rather than from immediate sensory input. Visual mental images give rise to the experience of "seeing with the mind's eye," an experience you probably will have if someone asks you, for example, whether the Statue of Liberty holds the torch in her left or right hand. To "get" some jokes you need to form an image, for example: "Corduroy pillows are making headlines" (hint: think about what your cheek would look like if you slept on a corduroy pillow all night). Auditory mental images give rise to the experience of "hearing with the mind's ear," as likely happened when you were deciding whether the first three notes of "Row, Row, Row Your Boat" change in pitch. Because visual imagery is the most common form of imagery (Kosslyn et al., 1990; McKellar, 1965), we will focus on it here.

Mental Space

There are many types of mental images (Kosslyn, 1994b); the most common seems to occur in a kind of "mental space." This space has three properties: spatial extent, limited size, and grain (grain is the equivalent of resolution on a television screen or computer monitor). Let's investigate these properties in turn.

First, visualize your living room, and count the number of windows. Does it feel as if you are scanning the walls? As illustrated in Figure 8.4, the greater the extent of your scan, the longer it takes to do the job; these results show that when you visualize something, its mental representation has a definite *spatial extent* (Denis & Kosslyn, 1999).

Second, how large can an object in a mental image be? When you mentally counted the windows in your living room, you scanned across each wall one by one because you couldn't "see" the whole extent at once; you have only a limited field of view in a mental image. Now imagine you are walking toward an elephant, mentally staring at the center of its body. Imagine walking closer and closer to it, keeping your mental gaze fixed on its center. Most people doing this exercise

FIGURE 8.4   Scanning Visual Mental Images

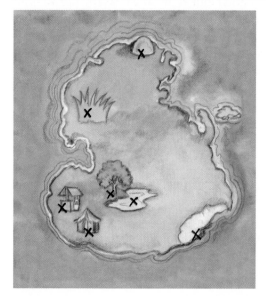

Participants memorized a map like this one, paying special attention to the locations of the seven objects.

Later, the participants were asked to close their eyes and focus on one location (such as the hut) and then to scan to another named location if it was on the map; they were to press one button if they found the second object and another if they could not (and the time was recorded). Participants scanned between every possible pair of objects.

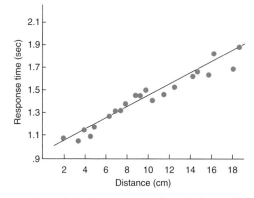

Even though their eyes were closed, the farther the participants had to scan from the first object to the second, the longer it took.

report that when they are at a certain distance from the elephant, its edges seem to blur, to "overflow" their field of vision—that is, their mental space. Note the distance at which the edges of the elephant seem to blur. Now try the same exercise with a rabbit. Fixate on its center, and imagine seeing it loom up as you get closer and closer to it. When you imagine walking toward the rabbit, can you get closer to it than you could to the elephant before the edges seem to blur? When this study was done carefully, the larger the object, the farther away it seemed to be in the mental image when it began to overflow (Kosslyn, 1978). This result is as expected if mental space has a *limited size*: Bigger objects must be "seen" from farther away to fit within it.

HANDS ON

Third, try this: Imagine stretching out your arm and looking at a butterfly perched on your fingertip. Can you see the color of its head? Many people find that they have to "zoom in" mentally to answer that question. Now move the butterfly to your palm and gently bring it to within 10 inches from your eyes; this time, zooming probably isn't necessary to "see" its head. Studies have shown that people require more time to "see" properties of objects that are visualized at small sizes than those visualized at larger sizes (Kosslyn, 1975, 1976). It is as if the imagery space has a *grain*. If you look at a television screen close up, you will see that the picture is made up of many small dots. The dots are the grain of the screen; if an object is too small, there will not be enough dots to define the details, and thus the details will be blurred.

In short, objects in images have many of the properties of actual objects, and thus images can "stand in" for objects. You can think about an object in its absence by visualizing it. Moreover, as shown in Figure 8.5, you can manipulate objects in images much like you manipulate actual objects.

FIGURE 8.5 Manipulating Objects in Images

Are the figures in the pairs of figures the same or mirror-images of each other? Notice that the pair at the far left must be rotated like a clock, not in depth (they are said to be rotated in the "picture plane"), whereas the other 2 pairs must be rotated in depth.

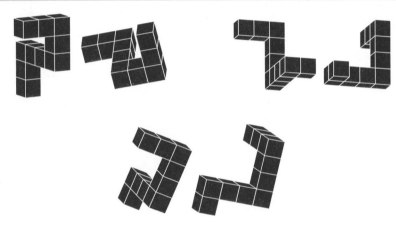

The time to make the decision increases the farther you must rotate a figure. To answer this question, people mentally rotate one figure until it lines up with the other member of the pair. It is as if the mental images were objects and required more time the farther you have to twist them.

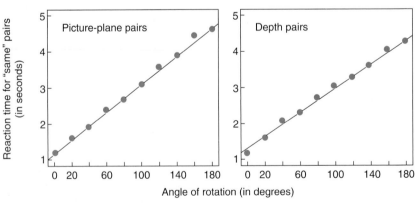

Reprinted with permission from R. N. Shephard and J. Metzler, "Mental rotation of three dimensional objects," *Science, 171,* 701–703. Copyright 1971 American Association for the Advancement of Science.

The Visualizing Brain

Visual images rely on many—about two-thirds—of the same parts of the brain that are used in visual perception (Kosslyn et al., 1997). This overlap may explain some of the key facts about imagery. First, how can we explain the fact that objects in images have *spatial extent*? Many of the areas of the brain that process visual input are organized so that images on the retina are laid out on the cortex in what are called "topographically organized areas" (from the Greek *topos*, "place"). As shown in Chapter 4 (see p. 135), there are literally "pictures in the brain" in these areas. Many researchers have found that when people visualize with their eyes closed, these areas are active (Kosslyn, Alpert et al., 1993; Kosslyn et al., 1995, 1999, 2001; LeBihan et al., 1993). Moreover, if these areas are temporarily impaired by the effect of strong magnetic pulses, visual mental imagery is disrupted (Kosslyn et al., 1999).

Second, let's consider why there are *limits* on the spatial extent of objects in images, why they seem to overflow if they loom too large. The brain needed to evolve only to process input from the eyes, and we don't see behind our heads. Objects in images overflow at about the same size that actual objects seem to become blurred in perception (Kosslyn, 1978). Like screens, topographically organized areas have definite boundaries, and images cannot extend beyond them. Of course, these areas are not literally screens, functioning like movie or television screens: No hidden observer in the brain looks at them—rather, the areas organize and process signals, which are sent to other areas in the brain.

Third, characteristics of these brain areas also can explain why images have *grain*. Topographically organized visual areas of the brain have a property called *spatial summation*: If a neuron is excited by a point of light in a particular place in space, another point of light close to it typically will add to the effects of the first. In contrast, if the spots are far enough apart, they are registered by different neurons. Spatial summation produces a kind of grain: If objects are small enough, points on their surfaces are too close together to be discriminated, and hence details are lost.

In short, we can understand the properties of this sort of mental imagery, which clearly depicts the surfaces of objects, because images arise in brain areas used in vision. Other types of images, such as the sense you have of where things are around you at any given moment, do not depict surfaces but rather specify locations; such spatial images, which even blind people can have, do not activate topographically organized areas (Mellet, Petit, et al., 1998). In addition, in at least some tasks for some people, it is possible that images arise on the basis of memories originally formed by topographically organized areas, but may no longer rely on such areas (Behrmann, 2000). Finally, we can manipulate objects in images by imagining that we physically manipulate them, which actually engages parts of the brain involved in physical movement (Grèzes & Decety, 2001; Jeannerod & Frak, 1999; Kosslyn, 1998; Lamm et al., 2001).

But images take us only so far. Their limitations prevent them from being the only tools of the mind, even in combination with words. For one thing, images cannot represent abstract concepts. Take justice, for example. How would you represent "justice" with an image? You might choose a blindfolded woman holding a pair of scales. But how would you know if that image represented the familiar statue or was supposed to stand for the abstract concept of justice? Another problem is that images are often ambiguous. An image of a box seen from the side could just as easily be an image of that side alone, detached from the box. Furthermore, not everybody can produce good images; perhaps 2% of the population have poor visual imagery (McKellar, 1965). Yet another problem is, how do you "decide" which images to form? Some other process must pick out which images will be useful. Like language, imagery can contribute to our thought processes, and like language, it cannot be the only means by which we think.

- **Concept:** An unambiguous, sometimes abstract, internal representation that defines a grouping of a set of objects (including living things) or events (including relationships).

- **Category:** A grouping in which the members are specific cases of a more general type.

- **Typicality:** The degree to which an entity is representative of its category.

Concepts: Neither Images nor Words

A **concept** is a grouping of a set of objects (which may include living things) or events (which can specify relations between things, such as "falling" or "on"). A concept is an unambiguous internal representation that may be abstract (such as the concept of truth or justice). Concepts may be *expressed* by images and words, but they are not the same as either (Kosslyn, 1980; Pinker, 1994). Thought arises from the manipulation of concepts, but words and images are used to express thoughts and further expand on them in working memory. Words and images play much the same role that a notepad does when you are planning a shopping trip; they not only help you work through and organize your thoughts, but also provide a way to store them.

The oldest idea of the nature of concepts was proposed by Aristotle in the 4th century B.C. According to this view, a concept corresponds to a set of features. For example, for the concept "bird" the features might be "wings, feathers, a beak, and the ability to fly." The features not only describe perceivable characteristics (such as wings and beak), but also specify appropriate activities (such as flight). The morphemes that underlie the meaning of the word *bird* would capture each of these properties. Some concepts are captured by the meanings of words, but others require a phrase or two to be fully expressed. Like the meanings of words, concepts are unambiguous.

Prototypes: An Ostrich Is a Bad Bird

According to Aristotle, the features of a concept must be both necessary and sufficient. A *necessary* feature is one that all members of the group must have; a *sufficient* condition is one that is enough—that "suffices"—to put an entity into a given category (so feathers would be a sufficient condition for "birdness"; if it has feathers, it's a bird). A **category** is a grouping in which the members are specific cases of a more general type. But Aristotle's formula doesn't always work: Although "the ability to fly" is a feature of birds, it is also a feature of insects and bats, but they're not birds; so flying is not a sufficient condition for birds. And an ostrich is a bird, but it can't fly, so flying is not a necessary condition for birds.

In addition, Aristotle's notion leads us to make wrong predictions. For example, according to his theory of how concepts are specified, if an object has the required properties, it is a member of the concept, period; all members of concepts have equally good standing. But Rosch (1978) showed that some objects are actually "better" members of their concept category than others. How good an example of its category an object is depends on its **typicality**—that is, how representative it is of that type of thing. As illustrated in Figure 8.6, people name objects that are typical members of a concept category faster than objects that are not typical members. Typi-

FIGURE 8.6 Name These Animals

Research has shown that you will name the center animal most readily and, in fact, the mutt is most typical for the category "dog."

cality affects not only the time it takes you to identify an object, but also your confidence in naming the object as an example of a specific concept (Garrard et al., 2001; Smith & Medin, 1981).

Most such effects can be explained if a concept corresponds to a set of features that describe the **prototype** of the category—that is, its most typical member—but only a *percentage* of those features need to be present in any particular member. In this case, the more features that apply above the bare minimum, the faster you can name the object—and more prototypical members of a concept have more such distinguishing features (Rips et al., 1973). Thus, people take longer to name ostriches as birds because fewer bird features apply to them (they cannot fly; they are not the size of the standard bird); on the other hand, robins are named faster because more of the features of birds, in general, apply to them.

If you want to impress your friends, ask them to participate in a "mind reading" exercise. Pick a category that has a well-defined prototype, for example "vegetables." And then say, "Quick, think of a vegetable!" Predict that they have selected "carrot"—because in most cases, "carrot" (the prototype) is the vegetable they will have chosen.

However, some researchers have argued that at least some concepts may be stored as prototypes that are not collections of features, such as the prototype of an odd number between 1 and 10 (Armstrong et al., 1983). Quick, think of an odd number between 1 and 10. Most people select 3, and on that basis 3 can be considered as the most typical member of this category. But such concepts are unusual in that, by definition, they require selecting a single example, so these special cases may be represented by a single example stored individually. Other researchers have made the case that not all concepts are stored as prototypes, but rather some concepts rely on storing sets of examples of the category (Medin & Schaffer, 1978; Smith & Medin, 1981). For example, your concept of a chair might correspond to representations of a collection of chairs (rocking, desk, easy chair, and so on), not a single prototype. In addition, concepts of movement or action, such as those labeled by verbs, may largely rely on "functional" features (for instance, whether an object can be lifted; Bird et al., 2000). At least some concepts may be stored in multiple ways or using combinations of methods, and different representations may be used in different situations (Anderson & Betz, 2001; Medin et al., 2000; Rips, 2001; Smith et al., 1998).

How Are Concepts Organized?

Many concepts can be applied to any given object. We can name an object with words that correspond to concepts at different levels of specificity: "Granny Smith apple" is very specific, "apple" is more general, and "fruit" more general still. How are different concepts organized?

Look at the objects in Figure 8.7 (p. 326) and name them as fast as you can. We bet that you named them "apple," "tree," and "dog." We strongly suspect that you didn't name the apple a "fruit" or a "Granny Smith," or call the tree an "oak" or the dog a "mammal" or an "animal." People consistently name objects at what Rosch and her colleagues (1976) have called the **basic level.** The basic level is like the middle rung of a ladder, with more general concepts above it and more specific concepts below it. So "apple" is the basic level; "fruit" is on a rung above it, and "Granny Smith" on a rung below. Each more general concept includes a number of more specific concepts; for example, "apple" includes "Granny Smith," "Delicious," "McIntosh," and many more.

● **Prototype:** A representation of the most typical example of a category.

● **Basic level:** A level of specificity, which is usually the most likely to be applied to an object.

FIGURE 8.7 Basic-Level Names

Name these objects as fast as you can. It is remarkable that most people choose the same three names, a feat no computer vision system can match.

At each level there are prototypes for the concept. For example, apple might be the prototypical fruit, and McIntosh might be the prototypical apple. The basic level indicates the level of specificity with which we are likely to apply a concept to an object. Rosch offered several ways to identify the basic level. For example, one way is based on shape: At the most specific level, if we compare individual Delicious apples with other Delicious apples, their shapes are very similar. Moving up a rung of generality, if we compare Delicious apples with McIntosh apples, Cortland apples, and so on, their shapes are pretty similar. But, moving up another rung, if we compare apples with other fruits, such as bananas, watermelons, or grapes, their shapes are not similar at all. The basic-level category is the one that is as general as possible while still limited to objects having similar shapes.

Some researchers theorize that sets of concepts are organized not only according to levels that vary in specificity, but also into schemas (Rumelhart, 1975; Schank & Abelson, 1977). If the basic level is like a rung on a ladder that organizes concepts in terms of specificity, a schema is like a basket that contains things that usually go together. A **schema** is a collection of concepts that specify necessary and "optional" aspects of a particular situation. For example, the schema for "room" indicates that it must have walls, a floor, a ceiling, and at least one door. In addition, this schema indicates that a room can also have windows, carpeting, and various types of furniture. If you know that something is a room, the "room" schema is activated, the necessary concepts apply to this case, and the schema guides you to look to see which other, optional features also apply. Such schemas can also organize objects into concepts based on "thematic relations," such as candles and cake (Lin & Murphy, 2001).

Concepts in the Brain

Studies of how concepts are stored in the brain have shown that they are organized not only in terms of specificity and their interrelations in schemas, but also according to how they are used. For example, brain damage can impair the ability to name living things but not manufactured objects (Warrington & Shallice, 1984), or vice versa (Warrington & McCarthy, 1987). This finding suggests that the brain organizes concepts according to these two general classes. In addition, Martin and colleagues (1996) found that when the participants in their study named tools, one of the areas of the brain that was activated (as measured by PET) is used to direct movements. In contrast, this area was not activated when the participants named animals, although in this case visual areas were activated. Characteristic actions are important for specifying the concept "tool," whereas visual properties are particularly important for specifying the concept "animal."

● **Schema:** A collection of concepts that specify necessary and optional aspects of a particular situation.

Looking *at* Levels

Prototypes and Heavy Drinking

Prototypes not only play a key role in thinking, they also affect how we behave. Gibbons and Gerrard (1995) theorized that whether someone will engage in a health-risk behavior, such as excessive drinking of alcohol, depends on how similar they think they are to a prototype of the typical person who engages in that behavior. Blanton and colleagues (1997) tested this theory by studying 463 adolescents (roughly half male, half female) who lived in rural Iowa. To assess prototypes for drinking, the participants were told, "We would like you to think for a minute about the *type of person your age who drinks (alcohol)* frequently." They stressed that they were not interested in anyone in particular, just "the typical teenage drinker." Following this introduction, the participants were given a set of adjectives and rated the degree to which those adjectives described their prototype. On the basis of these ratings, Blanton and colleagues inferred the degree to which the typical teenage drinker was generally viewed by the participant as "self-assured–together (such as self-confident and independent), unattractive (unattractive and dull), or immature (immature and careless)." To the extent that an individual participant rated people who drink high on the first factor and low on the other two, he or she was said to have a "positive prototype" of drinkers.

Three results are of particular interest. First, participants who had more positive prototypes of drinkers reported drinking more. Second, the more their peers tended to drink, the more the participants tended to drink. Third, adolescents who had poor relationships with their parents were more likely to associate with a drinking peer group.

These results are correlational, and you already know that correlation does not imply causation—and thus the prototype could be the cause, the effect, or both the prototype and the behavior could arise for other reasons. According to one interpretation, feeling that you are similar to the prototype shapes your behavior, a positive prototype of drinking develops from interactions with the drinking peer group, and poor relationships with your parents lead you to associate with a drinking peer group. But, according to another interpretation, people who drink more tend to develop positive prototypes of drinkers (not the other way around); heavy drinkers may select peers who are also heavy drinkers, and drinking and hanging out with others who do sours relationships between parents and their children.

Say you were in charge of a program to reduce teen drinking. Your program needs to affect events at the different levels of analysis, but precisely what you would do depends on which interpretation of the findings you believe. If you think that poor parenting (level of the group) leads kids to be disgruntled (level of the person), which then leads them to hang out with drinkers (level of the group) and eventually to glorify drinking and form a positive prototype of drinkers (level of the brain), you might concentrate on helping the parents develop better ways to interact with their children. In contrast, suppose you think some teens are inclined to drink, which is represented in part by their prototypes, and these inclinations lead them to pick unsavory peers, which in turn upsets the parents. If so, then you might focus less on the parents and more on the teens themselves. In either case, you will be mindful of how the prototype affects events at the other levels of analysis, and vice versa. Before you set out to develop such a program, however, it would be helpful to sort out how events at the different levels do, in fact, interact in these circumstances.

TEST YOURSELF!

1. Does language mold our thoughts?
2. Can we think with mental images? How might the brain give rise to these images?
3. What is a concept?

Problem Solving

Einstein never shied away from proposing radically new concepts, such as the idea that light consists of both particles and waves. But formulating concepts is only a small part of what we do while thinking. Once we form concepts, we use them in various ways, such as in solving problems. For example, Einstein used mental imagery to think about the nature of gravity. He reasoned that if you stood with some objects (such as keys and some coins) in an elevator that was falling down a long shaft, you and the objects would float within the elevator. But if the elevator started accelerating upwards, you and the objects would fall to the floor—exactly like what would happen if you were in a gravity field. In fact, you couldn't tell whether you were in a gravity field or were simply accelerating. So, gravity and acceleration seemed to have something in common.

Einstein continued to use his imagery to perform a "thought experiment": Say you shined a beam of light through the left side of a glass-walled elevator. If the elevator were moving upwards, the light would exit the right side a little closer to the floor than the height at which it entered on the left side, because the elevator had moved upwards a bit during the interval while the light was crossing through it. From the point of view of someone in the elevator, light would seem to bend as it moved across it. Einstein realized that if acceleration and gravity are comparable, then light should also bend in gravity. And this highly counterintuitive idea turned out to be correct!

Many different skills feed into your ability to solve problems—but your ability to solve problems is not simply the sum of those abilities. Solving a problem depends crucially on how you set it up. You can use language, images, or word–image combinations to specify the problem, but first you must conceptualize it—otherwise you won't know which words and images to use. Once you set up a problem in a particular way, you can manipulate your mental images and verbal descriptions to try to solve it. In this section we explore the differences among various kinds of problem solving.

How to Solve Problems: More Than Inspiration

A **problem** is an obstacle that must be overcome to reach a goal. Problems come in many types and can often be solved in many ways. In this section, we consider the tools at your disposal for solving a diverse range of puzzles and predicaments.

Solving the Representation Problem: It's All in How You Look at It

The first step to solving any problem is figuring out how to look at it. This fundamental challenge is called the **representation problem.** If you hit on the right way to represent a specific problem, the solution can be amazingly simple. Consider the example of the hiking monk in Figure 8.8 (based on Duncker, 1945). You have to decide whether, *at any one time of day,* the monk would be at precisely the same spot on the path going up and coming down. At first glance, this problem may seem difficult. If the precise specifications of departure times, speed, and so on lure you into trying to use algebra, you may work on it for hours. But if you hit on the right representation, it's easy: Imagine a mountain with a monk leaving from the top at the same time that another monk leaves from the bottom. It is clear that the two monks must pass each other at a particular point on the path—and the same will be true if instead of two monks leaving at the same time on the same day, a single monk goes up on one day and goes down on another day (provided that he departs at the same time in the morning for both treks). And so the answer is simply yes.

HANDS ON

● **Problem:** An obstacle that must be overcome to reach a goal.

● **Representation problem:** The challenge of how best to formulate the nature of a problem.

FIGURE 8.8 The Hiking Monk Problem

A monk leaves the bottom of a mountain every Monday at 5:00 A.M. and walks up a twisty path, climbing at a rate of 1.5 miles an hour, until he reaches the top at 4:00 P.M., having taken off a half-hour for lunch. He meditates on the mountain until sundown. At 5:00 the next morning he departs and walks down the path, going 3.5 miles an hour, until he reaches the bottom. Is there *any* point in the two journeys when he is at precisely the same location on the path at precisely the same time of day? You don't need to say what that time is, just whether there would be such a time.

● **Functional fixedness:** When solving a problem, getting stuck on one interpretation of an object or one part of the situation.

Finding the right representation for a problem can be tricky because once you think of a problem in a certain way, you may find it difficult to drop this view and try out others (Smith & Blankenship, 1989, 1991). For example, consider the problem in Figure 8.9; after you think about it, look at its solution in Figure 8.10 on page 330 (adapted from Duncker, 1945). At first, you probably thought of the box simply as a container, and not as a potential part of the solution. Becoming stuck on one interpretation of an object or aspect of the situation is called **functional fixedness.** Neuroimaging studies have shown that extra brain activity is required

FIGURE 8.9 The Candle Problem

Participants are asked to use the materials provided to mount the candle on the wall so that it can be lit. Some participants are given the materials as shown in the left panel; others, as shown in the right panel. Participants given the materials as shown in the right panel are more likely to solve the problem.

FIGURE 8.10 Solution to the Candle Problem

When the box is presented as a container, functional fixedness prevents people from imagining the box as a shelf.

when you need to inhibit one kind of performance and switch to another (Konishi et al., 1999).

Algorithms and Heuristics: Getting From Here to There

To solve a problem, you need a **strategy,** an approach to solving a problem determined by the type of representation used and the processing steps to be tried. There are two types of strategies: algorithms and heuristics. Let's say you hear about a fantastic price being offered on a hit alternative music CD by an independent record store, but you don't know the name of the store. You could try to find it by calling every relevant listing in the yellow pages. This process involves using an **algorithm,** a set of steps that, if followed methodically, will guarantee the right answer. But you may not have time to call every store. Instead, you might guess that the record store is in a part of town where many students live. In this case, having reduced the list of candidates to those located near the campus, you might find the store after calling only a few. This process reflects use of a **heuristic,** a rule of thumb that does not guarantee the correct answer but offers a likely shortcut to it. One common heuristic is to divide a big problem into parts and solve them one at a time.

Another heuristic is to guess at a solution and then work backwards, looking for evidence that supports that conclusion (Norman et al., 1999). And yet another heuristic is simply to see whether you recognize one alternative solution, and assume that if you do, then it's likely to be the best (Goldstein & Gigerenzer, 2002). Heuristics don't guarantee that you'll find the correct answer, but as Einstein put it, "Anyone who has never made a mistake has never tried anything new." As shown in Figure 8.11, different algorithms or heuristics may be used for the same problem, depending on the type of answer you seek.

Heuristics are particularly useful for ill-defined problems, in which the goal, what you have to work with (such as the amount of money available), or the method of reaching it are not clearly specified. For instance, the problem of "finding some entertainment" is ill-defined. In contrast, both heuristics and algorithms are useful for well-defined problems, where the goal, what you have to work with, and the method of reaching it are clearly specified. "Finding a cheap CD in New York" is a well-defined problem.

● **Strategy:** An approach to solving a problem, determined by the type of representation used and the processing steps to be tried.

● **Algorithm:** A set of steps that, if followed methodically, will guarantee the solution to a problem.

● **Heuristic:** A rule of thumb that does not guarantee the correct answer to a problem but offers a likely shortcut to it.

FIGURE 8.11 Different Heuristics for the Same Problem

Depending on the precise solution that is required, problems may be solved in different ways—even when you reason purely in your head. For example, when people compute exact arithmetic they use language, and brain areas involved in word-association are activated. In contrast, when people compute only approximate values, they don't use language but instead rely on a mental "number line"; in such processing, parts of the parietal lobes used in visuospatial processing are activated (Dehaene et al., 1999).

Solving Problems by Analogy: Comparing Features

Another way to solve problems requires you to compare the features of two situations, noticing what they have in common and what's different (Gentner & Gunn, 2001; Hummel & Holyoak, 1997). Let's begin with the following problem (based on Duncker, 1945): A surgeon has to remove a cancerous tumor from deep within a patient's brain. The use of a scalpel would cause permanent brain damage. An alternative is to use a beam of X rays to demolish the cancerous cells. However, the beam will also kill healthy cells in its path. Is there a way to reach only the cancerous cells and spare the healthy ones?

HANDS ON

The solution is to split the beam into several minibeams, each aimed from a different angle but crossing at the location of the tumor. Each minibeam is so weak that it will not hurt the healthy tissue, but their combined impact will destroy the tumor. Gick and Holyoak (1980, 1983) found that most people do not realize this solution. However, if they are first presented with an analogous problem and are told to think about how it relates to the second problem, success rates skyrocket. In this case, they first read about a problem faced by a general who wants to attack a fortress. If he advances all of his troops along a single road, mines will blow them to pieces. But smaller groups could travel on various approach roads without exploding the mines. The solution is to divide the army into smaller parties and have each take a separate road to the fortress. Once people see this solution and know it is relevant, the solution to the tumor problem becomes much easier (in fact, close to 80% get the problem right). If the participants are not told that the army problem is relevant to the tumor one, however, thinking about it does not help them much. At first glance, the two problems are unrelated. One involves soldiers and a fortress; the other, beams of radiation and a tumor. But beneath these surface differences, the problems have the same structure: Something too big is broken into parts, the parts are delivered separately, and then they are recombined. To see how a previous experience can be applied to a present case, you must recognize the similarities in the structure of the problems.

Analogical thinking relies on having solutions to previous problems stored in memory, spotting similarities between a new and a previous problem, and seeing how the structure of the previous problem allows its solution to be applied to the new problem. This process is guided by your goals, which lead you to seek a particular kind of solution to the present problem (Holyoak & Thagard, 1997; Hummel & Holyoak, 1997).

Sudden Solutions

People do not always have to work consciously through a problem, step by step. In some cases, they can "see" the solution right away; in others, the solution dawns on them after they have set the problem aside for a while.

Many researchers have suggested that people sometimes can see a solution to a problem in a flash, full-blown and complete (Guilford, 1979; Olton, 1979; Torrance, 1980). This phenomenon results from an **insight,** a new way to look at a problem that implies the solution. Insights can arise following a trial-and-error exploration in which the problem is represented in different ways. Once the problem is represented in the right way, the answer is obvious. A good example of insight is the *Wheel of Fortune* experience; once you solve the word puzzle yourself, the solution becomes so obvious that you can't imagine how the stumped television contestants can be so dense. *Insight learning,* discussed in Chapter 6, can follow such problem solving—making it easier to cope with similar problems in the future.

Insights may occur after a period of **incubation.** Olton (1979, p. 10) defines incubation as "a facilitation of thinking that is evident after a period during which no conscious work was done on the task (assuming an earlier period of substantial conscious work)." To study incubation, Goldman and colleagues (1992) asked participants to solve difficult anagrams—words or phrases created by rearranging the letters of other words or phrases ("dormitory" is an anagram of "dirty room"). Those who did not solve the anagrams within the allotted time were given the same problems again, either immediately, 20 minutes later, or 24 hours later. New anagrams were presented along with those previously seen but not solved. However, Goldman and colleagues found that the participants solved more old anagrams than new ones if they had a break, and performed even better after a longer break. They point out that this finding need not indicate that the unconscious works on problems even when you aren't thinking about them. For example, participants could have forgotten strategies that were not useful but that had kept them fixated during the initial session (Smith & Blankenship, 1989, 1991, have shown such effects) or could simply have been better rested after the break.

Metcalfe (1986) tested the idea that insight involves unconscious restructuring by asking people to predict in advance whether they could solve specific problems. If people solve all problems by remembering relevant information, then they should be good at predicting their performance. In contrast, if problems can be solved by insight, a sudden shift in the way you look at a problem, success

● **Insight:** A new way to look at a problem that implies the solution.

● **Incubation:** Improved thinking following a period of not consciously working on solving a problem or performing a task.

should be difficult to predict. Metcalfe found that although people could accurately predict their ability to answer questions about real-world trivia, they could not predict their performance on insight problems.

The mechanisms underlying insight and incubation are not well understood, but it would be surprising if they turned out to be much different from the mechanisms used in problem solving discussed earlier in this chapter. Many insights may emerge after we try out a new way to represent a problem, or after we spot an analogy. The fact that processes may occur unconsciously does not make them any more mysterious than the implicit memory mechanisms discussed in Chapter 7 (Kihlstrom, 1987).

Expertise: Why Hard Work Pays Off

Einstein had his priorities clear: Nothing, not friends, family, fame, or fortune could stand in the way of work. On visiting him in his study, a friend asked about a large meat hook that was hanging from the ceiling, ". . . bearing a thick sheaf of letters. These, Einstein explained, he had no time to answer." The friend, ". . . asking what he did when the hook was filled up, was answered by two words: 'Burn them.'" (Clark, 1971, p. 199). Einstein spent his years in the patent office thinking, studying, and working—and later credited that time as allowing him to develop expertise in his chosen field.

Expertise in any given field typically takes about 10 years to achieve, in part because it comes from encountering many examples of the types of problems in a particular area (Ericsson et al., 1993; Simon & Chase, 1973). For example, researchers have studied why you have to play chess for years to become a master. Chase and Simon (1973) tried to find out what made chess masters different from novices and very good chess players. Basing their study on the pioneering work of DeGroot (1965, 1966), Chase and Simon asked their participants to study chessboards with pieces on them for 5 seconds, and then to place the pieces properly on another board. The masters proved far superior to the novices and very good players, but only when the positions to be remembered were ones that could occur in an actual game. When the pieces were placed randomly on the board, the masters performed no better than the novices and very good players.

Chase and Simon inferred that the experts had seen so many games that they could recognize familiar positions in new games and so were able to group the pieces into single units (chunks); the novices and the very good players did not possess this information from experience. Chase and Ericsson (1981) subsequently showed that a key to enhancing problem-solving abilities is not storing larger chunks in short-term memory, but rather learning strategies (including organizing the board into chunks) for storing relevant information quickly and effectively in long-term memory, thus making an end run around the limitations of short-term memory (Ericsson & Charness, 1994, elaborate on this idea). Note that becoming an expert at chess is not merely a matter of developing a better memory for actual chess positions: Charness (1981) tested players who ranged in age from 16 to 64 and found that even the older players who had relatively poor memories could still make good decisions about which pieces to move.

Many researchers have shown that expertise involves numerous attributes (Chi et al., 1982; Chi & Glaser, 1985). Mayer (1997) reviews four types of knowledge that distinguish experts from nonexperts: (1) Experts organize their knowledge around fundamental principles, whereas nonexperts have more fragmented organizations;

(2) Experts use specific concepts, such as "momentum" in physics, whereas novices rely on vaguer ideas; (3) Experts categorize problems based on the relevant underlying principles, whereas novices categorize them on the basis of the literal objects or other directly observable features; and (4) Experts develop strategies more carefully in advance, whereas novices try to solve parts of the problem without an overall scheme in mind. Some aspects of these strategies involve knowing what to pay attention to, and how to use attention effectively (Posner et al., 1997). In addition, experts are more flexible when solving problems and, if necessary, can reorganize their strategies.

An interesting aspect of expertise is that it is limited to a specific field. Being an expert in one area does not generalize to another: Chess masters are no better than anyone else at solving different sorts of problems. The skills that are acquired by experience apply only to the specific area in which they were originally developed.

Ericsson and Charness (1994) and Ericsson and colleagues (1993) review much literature on expertise and reach a surprising conclusion: Talent plays little, if any, role in determining who becomes an expert. Rather, the crucial variable is simply how much deliberate practice is invested in performing a task. **Deliberate practice** is practice motivated by the goal of improving performance. When you engage in deliberate practice, you aren't necessarily having fun, and you aren't necessarily getting any kind of immediate reward (Ericsson & Charness, 1993). Deliberate practice involves spotting a weakness in a given domain (such as having a poor backhand in tennis, weak breath control in singing, or difficulty integrating functions in math), and specifically targeting that weakness for practice. Einstein constantly engaged in such practice. In fact, he was an avid sailor, but always took a notebook with him when he sailed. When the wind died down, he immediately brought out his notebook and started working (Clark, 1971, p. 31). Ericsson and colleagues (1993) found that the sheer amount of time spent in deliberate practice is the primary mechanism for achieving expert levels of performance (Bloom, 1985).

Artificial Intelligence

In 1997, our species seemed to suffer a minor setback: A computer (with special hardware and custom software) called Deep Blue beat the world's best human chess player, Garry Kasparov. Does this mean that computers will soon be able to solve all sorts of problems better than we can? Not to worry. Deep Blue relied, basically, on a boring program. Because Deep Blue was so fast, it could work out and evaluate an enormous number of possible moves, one at a time. Deep Blue, unlike its human challengers, used a "brute force" algorithm, similar to calling every music store in the phone book alphabetically to find a particular CD. Deep Blue was an advance over earlier computer programs partly because it could "anticipate" more possible consequences of any given move, and partly because it was better at noting which moves eventually led to disaster and which put the opponent in a bad position. Moreover, it had access to information on hundreds of thousands of important previous games (including every one of its opponent's games), and thus could detect whether Kasparov was doing anything that ever had been done before.

Another program, called Deep Fritz, has beaten every human player it has been pitted against. Unlike Deep Blue, which ran on a super computer and required 20 people to keep it going, Deep Fritz can run on a laptop. However, whereas Deep

● **Deliberate practice:** Practice that is motivated by the goal of improving performance, usually by targeting specific areas of weakness and working to improve them.

Blue could search about 200 million possible moves per second, Deep Fritz "only" evaluates about 2 million moves per second—but people are lucky to consider even one move a second!

Computers can now play a mean game of chess, to be sure, but the fact is that they couldn't figure out how to open a tin can or buy a bottle of milk. In contrast, chess-playing humans use analogical thinking, knowledge of principles, and various heuristic strategies in pursuing a checkmate. A surprisingly complex network of brain areas is involved in playing chess, tapping areas used in recognizing objects, registering spatial relations, and formulating plans (Nichelli et al., 1994).

Artificial intelligence (AI) is the name of the field devoted to building smart machines, machines that can "think." The existence of the human brain is the only proof that a mechanism can embody intelligence, and thus many AI researchers believe that the best way to make computers truly intelligent is to make them in our image. AI research has led to the creation of *expert systems*, computer programs that can solve problems in ways that human experts would pursue. Although these programs sometimes are impressive, so far they have lacked the flexibility and creative flair of human thought.

An innovation in AI has been the programming of **neural networks** to imitate (roughly) the way the brain works. These computer programs have many small units that interact via connections, akin to the networks of neurons in the brain. Unlike most computer programs, these programs depend on having many processes operating at the same time (McClelland & Rumelhart, 1986; Rumelhart & McClelland, 1986). Neural networks can recognize objects remarkably well and can generalize to novel examples of a familiar category. Furthermore, when parts are disrupted, the networks often mimic the effects of human brain damage (Kosslyn & Koenig, 1995).

Computers—specialized hardware plus customized software—can now beat the human world chess champion. What's next?

Overcoming Obstacles to Problem Solving

You can improve your ability to overcome obstacles to solving problems if you keep the following points in mind (Ellis & Hunt, 1993; Newsome, 2000):

1. A major challenge is to represent the problem effectively. One way to meet this challenge is to make sure you really understand the problem. Explain the problem to somebody else; sometimes, the simple act of explaining leads to a representation that immediately implies a solution.

2. Keep your eye on the ball: Don't lose sight of what actually constitutes the problem. People sometimes tend to transform the problem—resist this. If the problem is "how to get to Hawaii for Spring break," don't redefine the problem as "how to talk your parents into subsidizing the trip." This advice also applies to debates and arguments; you'd be surprised at how much more effective you'll be if you keep the issue in mind and don't allow yourself to be drawn off on tangents.

3. Don't get locked into viewing your resources in only one way, which is a form of functional fixedness. See whether you can come up with more than one strategy for approaching the problem. Einstein noted, "I am enough of an artist

● **Artificial intelligence (AI):** The field devoted to building smart machines.

● **Neural network:** A computer program whose units interact via connections that imitate (roughly) the way the brain works.

● **Mental set:** A fixed way of viewing the kind of solution you seek.

● **Cognitive engineering:** The field devoted to using facts and theories about human information processing to guide the design of products and devices.

to draw freely upon my imagination. Imagination is more important than knowledge. Knowledge is limited. Imagination encircles the world" (as cited in Viereck, 1929).

4. Don't get stuck with a certain **mental set,** a fixed way of viewing the kind of solution you seek. It's okay to begin by focusing on one possible solution, but recognize that there may be more than one happy outcome. Be willing to consider alternatives. (Southern California is a great Spring break destination, too.)

5. If you do get stuck, walk away from the problem for a while. A fresh look can lead to new ways of representing it or devising new strategies for solving it.

Looking *at* Levels

Cognitive Engineering at Home and at the Nuclear Power Plant

Researchers in the field of **cognitive engineering** design products and devices on the basis of theories and facts about how humans process information (Norman, 1988). This field rests on the premise that we humans have specific strengths and weaknesses, and good products should play to our strengths and avoid our weaknesses (which include our being startled by sudden loud noises, distracted by flashing lights, and overwhelmed by too much information being presented at the same time). For an everyday example, look at car stereos. Are the more important controls, those for power, volume, and tuning, more easily spotted than the less important ones, such as those for tone or balance? Do you move logically from left to right to adjust the controls, in the same order used when reading, or do you have to search? Are the controls labeled with terms you can easily read and understand, or are there cryptic symbols (which may even be too small to see clearly)? Cognitive engineers would build a stereo with those questions in mind, and would build the control room of a nuclear power plant so that technicians could understand the readouts at a glance, and not be overwhelmed by too much information.

Cognitive engineering must be understood from all three levels of analysis. First, it is grounded in basic facts about how our brains process information. For example, we can only hold so much infor-

mation in mind at once, and so it makes no sense to have a hundred lights flashing simultaneously. Second, cognitive engineering relies on prior knowledge and beliefs. For example, if customers are used to finding the "on" switch at the lower left on the front panel of a DVD player, that's where it should be. Third, the culture defines certain conventions, such as red means "stop" and green means "go," which must be respected in product design (lights signaling danger should not be green). Clearly, events at the different levels interact: Information processing is shaped by learning (such as learning to read left-to-right), which is a result of the culture. Beliefs, similarly, are shaped by the culture, and in turn affect information processing. Finally, if information processing cannot proceed properly, this can have adverse effects on the group—ranging from drivers not being able to operate a stereo easily to someone's not monitoring a nuclear power plant effectively and thereby endangering the surrounding community—as actually happened during the near meltdown of the Three Mile Island nuclear reactor in 1979.

TEST YOURSELF!

1. What methods can we use to solve problems?
2. Do experts solve problems differently from the rest of us? How so?
3. What is artificial intelligence?
4. How can you improve your problem-solving abilities?

Logic, Reasoning, and Decision Making

Einstein did not always make good decisions. For example, when offered a job at Princeton, he was asked to tell the new Institute for Advanced Study what he would need to live and work there. His request for salary and support was so unrealistically low that it was turned down, and the administrators turned to his wife to arrive at a more reasonable arrangement. Nevertheless, this same man derived equations that explained a previously inexplicable slippage in the orbit of Mercury. When his theory produced the correct result, he was satisfied but not exuberant, noting that "I did not for one second doubt that [my calculations] would agree with observation. There was no sense in getting excited about what was self-evident" (Clark, 1971, p. 206). Self-evident? It is logic that leads someone to think that something is self-evident. How do we humans—Einstein included—reason logically? And why do we sometimes make bad decisions?

Are People Logical?

Not all thinking consists of figuring out how to overcome obstacles; sometimes thinking is considering what follows from what, evaluating alternatives, and deciding what to do next. Decision making requires us to evaluate possible outcomes and choose one alternative or course of action over the others. **Logic** is the process of applying the principles of correct reasoning to reach a decision or to evaluate the truth of a claim. "Hector is a man; all men are human; therefore Hector is a human" is correct logic. But note that "Hector is a man; all men are Martians; therefore Hector is a Martian" is *also* correct logic. The first two statements in each case are the *premises*, and the only question in logic is whether the final statement, the *conclusion*, follows from the premises. The *content*—the actual meaning of the premises—is irrelevant to logic; only the *form*, the sequence of what-implies-what, counts in logic. If you accept the premises, logic dictates the conclusions you must also accept. In this process of **deductive reasoning**—that is, reasoning from the general to the particular—the rules of logic are applied to a set of assumptions stated as premises to discover what conclusions inevitably follow from those assumptions.

Logical Errors

Much research has shown that humans—even extraordinary ones such as Albert Einstein—are not entirely logical. For example, people often make the error of **affirming the consequent**; that is, we assume that a specific cause is present because a particular result has occurred. Here is a cause–effect relation: "If it is sunny out, Hector wears a hat." Does it follow that this statement is true: "Hector is wearing a hat; therefore, it is sunny out"? Not necessarily. Maybe Hector's on his way to a ballgame and has put on a hat with his team's logo. Maybe after checking The Weather Channel, he has put on a rain hat. Maybe he simply thinks a particular hat looks good with his outfit. Maybe—well, there might be any number of reasons, including that it is in fact sunny out. Affirming the consequent occurs because we incorrectly work backward, from result to cause. Armed with this knowledge, you now can tell what's wrong with the following reasoning:

1. Japanese do not eat much fat and have fewer heart attacks than the Americans and British.
2. The French eat a lot of fat and have fewer heart attacks than the Americans and British.

- **Logic:** The process of applying the principles of correct reasoning to reach a decision or evaluate the truth of a claim.

- **Deductive reasoning:** Reasoning that applies the rules of logic to a set of assumptions (stated as premises) to discover whether certain conclusions follow from those assumptions; deduction goes from the general to the particular.

- **Affirming the consequent:** A reasoning error that occurs because of the assumption that if a result is present, a specific cause must also be present.

3. Japanese do not drink much red wine and have fewer heart attacks than the Americans and British.

4. Italians drink large amounts of red wine and have fewer heart attacks than the Americans and British.

5. Conclusion: Eat and drink what you like. It's speaking English that causes heart attacks.

HANDS ON

Wason and Johnson-Laird (1972) devised a task that laid bare more of our reasoning frailties. Look at Figure 8.12: What would you do? The answer is that both A and 7 must be flipped. People tend to flip A, to see whether an even number is on the other side; if not, the rule would be wrong. If there is an even number on the reverse of A, most people assume the rule is confirmed. Very few think to turn over the 7: If there is a vowel on the other side, then the rule is wrong no matter what's on the reverse of A. Most people do not think about what it would take to *disconfirm* the rule. A **confirmation bias** occurs when people seek information that will confirm a rule but do not seek information that might refute it.

FIGURE 8.12 Wason and Johnson-Laird's Card Task

Here is a rule: If a card has a vowel on one side, then it will have an even number on the other side. How many and which of these cards must be flipped over to decide whether this rule is true?

Now consider a variation of this task. Instead of A, D, 4, and 7, the cards say *beer, coke, 22,* and *16,* and the rule relates to drinking age: If a person is drinking beer, then he or she must be over 21 years old. Griggs and Cox (1982) found that participants in this version of the task had little problem realizing that they had to turn over both the *beer* and the *16* cards. Instead of using the rules of logic, they used their knowledge of state drinking laws.

Much deductive reasoning appears to rely on setting up **mental models** (Johnson-Laird, 1995, 2001), images or descriptions of a specific situation used as an aid in reasoning about abstract entities. Try this: Sam is hungrier than Susan, but Susan is less hungry than George; is Susan the least hungry? Problems like this are very easy to solve if you imagine a line with a dot for each entity and place the dots standing for entities with more of the value (here, hunger) farther to the right (Huttenlocher, 1968; Huttenlocher et al., 1970). If you do this, when asked about the relative positions of the entities, you can simply "look" at your image and "read" the position of the dot of interest (Demarais & Cohen, 1998). Neuroimaging of people performing such reasoning shows activity in the spatial processing structures in the parietal lobes (Baker et al., 1996; Osherson et al., 1998), as expected if people are mentally manipulating spatial relations. Mental models can help us overcome some reasoning errors (Figure 8.13).

HANDS ON

FIGURE 8.13 Mental Model and Reasoning

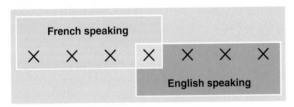

A crucial part of reasoning is to look for counterexamples. For instance, if told, "More than half of the people at a meeting speak French, and more than half of the people at the meeting speak English; does it follow that more than half of the people at the meeting speak both French and English?" The mental model shown here allows you to see the answer: No. (Adapted from Johnson-Laird, 2001, p. 441).

Reasoning can be inductive as well as deductive. The opposite of deductive reasoning, **inductive reasoning** works toward a conclusion by moving from the particular case to a generalization. Induction uses individual examples to figure out a rule that governs them. If you ate two green apples and each was sour, you might induce that green apples in general are sour. However, your conclusion would be faulty: You ignored the evidence of Granny Smiths (which are sweet).

Here's another example. What number comes next: 2, 4, 6, _? You probably said 8, but what if the underlying rule were simply "larger numbers"? Then 21, or 101, would also work. Or the rule might be "even numbers," and 2 would satisfy the condition, or "one-digit numbers," in which case 7 would work, and so on. The point is that every one of these additional generalizations is just as consistent with the set 2, 4, 6 as is the number 8 (Goodman, 1983). That inductive reasoning works at all is something of a miracle—nevertheless, it often does (Prasada, 2000), and much of scientific discovery relies on just this kind of reasoning. To remember the difference between deductive and inductive reasoning, try these mnemonics: To DEduce is to move DOWN FROM something larger; to INduce is to move INTO something larger.

Much reasoning involves a combination of deductive and inductive processes. Although evolutionary theories have been used to explain why our reasoning abilities work as well as they do and have the quirks they have (Cosmides, 1989; Gigerenzer & Hug, 1992; Oaksford & Chater, 1994), other, more general explanations also apply (Almor & Sloman, 1996; Fodor, 2000). Sperber and colleagues (1995) provide evidence that people try to minimize cognitive effort when reasoning, and Kirby (1994) showed that people assess the relative cost and benefit of each decision. It has proven very difficult to provide evidence for evolutionary theories of reasoning that cannot be explained just as easily and satisfactorily by other types of theories.

Framing Decisions

A key factor that determines how well we reason is how we *frame* a decision. A decision frame defines not only the decision to be made, but also the alternative possible outcomes and the criteria for a good decision (Bazerman, 1997; Russo & Schoemaker, 1989, 2002). Depending on how a decision is framed, the exact same outcome will seem more or less appealing to us. For example, people commonly tend to frame losses as more important than gains. Say you are a doctor faced with a new epidemic. The drug company gives you a choice between two new experimental drugs. WonderDrug-A will save 1,000 lives whereas WonderDrug-B has a 33% chance of saving 3,000 lives but a 67% chance of saving no lives. Which would you choose?

Most people go for the first alternative, even though statistically the two outcomes are the same. But now think about a decision framed this way: WonderDrug-X will lead to the loss of 2,000 lives whereas WonderDrug-Y has a 67% chance of losing no lives but a 33% chance of losing 6,000 lives. Again, the outcomes are the same statistically, but now the second choice is more palatable for most people. People avoid risk when it comes to thinking about possible gains, but actually prefer risk when it comes to avoiding losses (Druckman, 2001; Kahneman & Tversky, 1979, 1984; Tversky & Kahneman, 1992).

Heuristics and Biases: Cognitive Illusions?

If the laws of logic lead to inescapable conclusions, why do people make errors in reasoning? The answer is implied in the question: because people do not always use the laws of logic, but rely instead on sets of heuristics. While often useful, these

HANDS ON

Many supermarkets provide free food samples. Researchers gave shoppers a selection of either 6 or 24 different jams. In which case do you think the shoppers would then go on to buy jam? If you guessed 24, you were probably thinking that the larger selection would be more likely to have a flavor that pleased the customer. But the results turned out exactly the opposite (Iyengar & Lepper, 2000). After a point, the more choices consumers have, the more frustrated and less satisfied they are. Too many choices result in too much cognitive effort, which people find aversive.

- **Confirmation bias:** A tendency to seek information that will confirm a rule, and not to seek information that is inconsistent with the rule.

- **Mental model:** An image or description of a specific situation used to reason about abstract entities.

- **Inductive reasoning:** Reasoning that uses examples to figure out a rule; induction goes from the particular (examples) to the general (a rule).

- Young children learn language without explicit instruction. Language is acquired gradually over time. There is a critical (or sensitive) period for learning phonology and grammar.
- Gestures can help you communicate, largely by freeing up processing, but gestures themselves are not language.
- Animals that are taught to use sign language (which is a true language) may not grasp key aspects of grammar—but some animals have exhibited remarkable abilities to form novel utterances, which reveal the use of simple grammar.
- Adults can learn semantics and pragmatics of new languages as well as children can, but unless they learn a second language early in life they probably will never use it as well or "automatically" as they do their first language.
- Although it is unlikely that a single gene is involved in the uniquely human ability to use language, it seems probable that our genes do, directly or indirectly, bless us with this capacity.

THINK IT THROUGH Would it be technically correct to say that Einstein could speak French and English? In these languages, his phonology and grammar were faulty, and he never mastered pragmatics in any language. Is there a difference between speaking a language imperfectly versus not speaking it at all? At which point would you decide that his command of one or more of the aspects of language was so poor that you would no longer say he could use language? Can you think of a way to decide when a student studying a new language has reached the point of "speaking the language"?

Some forms of representation play critical roles in pragmatics. Consider this joke: A man showed up for work one day with huge bandages over each ear. A coworker asked him what happened. He replied, "I was ironing and was lost in thought. The phone rang, and without thinking I lifted my hand to answer it." The coworker was aghast, but then asked, "But what about the other ear?" "Oh," he replied, "then I had to call the doctor." This is a visual joke, and people who do not form images well don't seem to get it. Can you think of other such jokes?

Means of Thought: Words, Images, Concepts

- We use words and images in thinking as a way of keeping track of thoughts and storing them effectively, akin to making notations on a pad of paper while devising a plan. Language does not determine thought, but may influence it in subtle ways.

- Objects in visual mental images preserve many of the properties of actual objects, such as their spatial extent and relative size; at least some of these properties may arise from characteristics of the brain areas that give rise to imagery.
- Thought cannot rely solely on words or images: Both types of representations are ambiguous, and thoughts are not; if thoughts were based only on words, we would never have difficulty figuring out how to put our thoughts into words; if thought were based only on images, we would have trouble thinking about abstractions (such as truth and justice).
- Thoughts arise from manipulations of concepts, which specify groupings of objects or events.
- Representations of concepts are unambiguous and can be concrete (such as the concept of a bird) or abstract (such as the concept of justice). Concepts have an internal structure, with some examples being "better" (more typical) than others. Concepts are organized according to how specific or general they are and according to how they are grouped to apply to a particular situation (via a schema).

THINK IT THROUGH Einstein claimed that imagination was more important than knowledge. Do you think this is true? Think of the extreme case, where you had only one or the other—which situation (having only knowledge or only imagination) would be more limiting for getting by in daily life? Could you use imagination to solve problems if you had no knowledge?

Einstein claimed to think largely in images. Why might this make sense for a physicist? Would you expect the advantages of thinking in images to apply to psychologists? Would it depend on the type of psychology?

Problem Solving

- If the problem is not specified appropriately from the outset, it will be difficult to solve.
- People can solve problems by using heuristics (rules of thumb) and algorithms (sets of steps that are guaranteed to produce the answer). People can use both algorithms and heuristics with mental simulations and analogies.
- Both images and words can play important roles in helping you keep track of where you are in a problem and in providing insights into how to proceed.
- Sometimes it pays to put a problem aside and let it incubate, but the emergence of insight depends on first having thought hard about the problem.

- Experts develop skills in a particular area, which do not generalize beyond that area. Deliberate practice is essential as the would-be expert learns the relevant information and strategies.

- Artificial intelligence (AI) is based on the idea that human abilities can be duplicated in a machine. Present-day efforts are impressive, but still a far cry from human abilities.

- Knowing about the pitfalls of problem solving can help you to overcome them.

THINK IT THROUGH   Can someone be a creative scientist if they always use algorithms? What is the most important unsolved problem you can think of (for example, poverty, crime, AIDS, the greenhouse effect)? Which approach to problem solving is most likely to be useful? In what ways might different methods of problem solving be combined to approach such a megaproblem?

Is it better to use words or images when thinking? in general, or for certain purposes? If only for certain purposes, which kinds of thinking would best be accomplished with words? with images?

Logic, Reasoning, and Decision Making

- Reasoning involves seeing what follows from a given set of circumstances and making decisions at pivotal points. Decisions require you to evaluate possible outcomes and choose one alternative or course of action over the others.

- People are not, strictly speaking, logical; for example, we fall prey to biases, such as the confirmation bias.

- The same decision is made in different ways when it is framed differently.

- We often rely on heuristics, such as availability, when reaching decisions.

- Heuristics often lead us to draw the correct conclusion faster than we could with a step-by-step algorithm; however, they also sometimes lead to errors.

- Although many people may consider emotion a weakness when reasoning, in fact emotion often helps us to develop hunches and good intuitions.

THINK IT THROUGH   In what ways are the human weaknesses in logic and decision making the flip-side of processes that actually help us? Can you think of how to use any of the material you just learned to be a better debater? What is the most important aspect of the findings on "decision framing"?

Do you think our universal human weakness in using logic adversely affects world politics? Why or why not?

Key Terms

affirming the consequent, p. 337
algorithm, p. 330
aphasia, p. 303
artificial intelligence (AI), p. 335
availability heuristic, p. 341
base-rate rule, p. 340
basic level, p. 325
Broca's aphasia, p. 303
category, p. 324
child-directed speech (CDS), p. 309
cognitive engineering, p. 336
concept, p. 324
confirmation bias, p. 338
critical period, p. 313
deductive reasoning, p. 337
deliberate practice, p. 334
empiricism (approach to language), p. 309
functional fixedness, p. 329
grammar, p. 311
heuristic, p. 330
incubation, p. 332
inductive reasoning, p. 338
insight, p. 332
language acquisition device (LAD), p. 309
language comprehension, p. 301
language production, p. 301
linguistic relativity hypothesis, p. 319
logic, p. 337

mental images, p. 320
mental model, p. 338
mental set, p. 336
morpheme, p. 304
nativism (approach to language), p. 309
neural network, p. 335
nonverbal communication, p. 314
overextension, p. 310
overregularization error, p. 312
phoneme, p. 301
phonology, p. 301
pragmatics, p. 306
problem, p. 328
propositional representation, p. 305
prototype, p. 325
representation problem, p. 328
representativeness heuristic, p. 340
schema, p. 326
semantics, p. 304
sensitive period, p. 313
specific language impairment, p. 317
strategy, p. 330
syntax, p. 302
telegraphic speech, p. 311
typicality, p. 324
underextension, p. 311
Wernicke's aphasia, p. 303

chapter 9

Réunion des Musées Nationaux/Art Resource, NY

Types of Intelligence
What Does It Mean to Be Smart?

J anet never seemed able to do anything right. When she was little, her mother constantly yelled at her and called her "stupid" whenever she made a mistake. In time Janet realized that her mother was unreasonable, but Janet still couldn't shake the idea that she was dumb. It didn't help that she did poorly in school, that she dressed more shabbily and talked more slowly than her classmates. In fourth grade, a classmate had called her "Retard"; now, 4 years later, she still feared that someone might resurrect that dreaded label. Janet sometimes wondered whether something had gone wrong when she was born. She knew her mother wasn't stupid. Janet had seen her bargain at the flea market and had heard her analyze political speeches they had watched on television. And although she didn't remember her father, she knew he hadn't been stupid either. Although her mother resented his leaving their family a few days after Janet was born, she still paid grudging respect to his business skill.

One of her teachers had called her gifted and creative, and even said that her poems were good enough to be published.

Janet tried to talk to her mother about her feelings, but her mother just brushed her aside every time, sending her to do her chores or homework. Fortunately, Janet had a hobby: She kept a diary and wrote poetry—good poetry. One of her teachers had called her gifted and creative, and even said that her poems were good enough to be published.

In this chapter we discuss the nature of intelligence, intelligence testing, kinds of intelligence, how nature and nurture affect intelligence, mental retardation, giftedness, and, lastly, creativity—which may be the highest form of intelligence.

Is There More Than One Way to Be Smart?

Despite all of her problems in school, Janet was interested in most of her classes. One day she mustered up enough courage to stay after class and talk with her English teacher about a book they were reading. How, she asked, could the author have written such a lighthearted story when he was so poor? The teacher stared at her. Thinking she had said something stupid again, Janet turned to leave. The teacher leapt up and insisted that she stay. The two ended up talking for over an hour. Janet couldn't help noticing the dawning respect on her teacher's face and left feeling elated. Janet wondered whether she might not be so stupid after all; perhaps she should ask to have an IQ test to find out once and for all if she was smart.

What does it mean to say that someone is or is not intelligent? Intelligence is certainly not a concrete entity that can be quantified, like the amount of water in a jug; rather, it is a concept. Psychologists have offered many definitions of intelligence, and there is considerable disagreement about what intelligence is and whether it can be accurately measured (Gardner, 2002; Gardner et al., 1996; Sternberg, 1986b, 1990; Sternberg & Detterman, 1986). What most researchers mean by intelligence is pretty close to the standard dictionary definition: **Intelligence** is the ability to solve problems well and to understand and learn complex material. Researchers also typically stress that a key aspect of intelligence is the ability to adapt to the environment (Sternberg, 2000). Intelligence is often associated with mental quickness, but this need not be so; sometimes still waters really do run deep. However, researchers typically assume that "solving problems well" implies "in a reasonable amount of time." There is a limit to how much time you could take when solving a problem or learning complex material and still be considered "intelligent"; if it took Janet 3 days to solve a problem that most people could solve in 10 minutes, we would be reluctant to congratulate her on her intellectual accomplishment. Virtually all tests of intelligence rely on the assumption that intelligent people can solve problems and understand and learn complex material relatively easily, and hence do not require a lot of time to do so.

Measuring Intelligence: What Is IQ?

If Janet finds out that she has a "low IQ," should she decide not to apply to college? We think this would be a bad idea. To see why, let's look at exactly what "IQ" is.

A Brief History of Intelligence Testing

IQ is short for **intelligence quotient,** a test score used in Western countries as a general measure of intelligence. To understand the IQ test, and the meaning of IQ scores, it will be helpful to see how this test has evolved over time.

Binet and Simon: Testing to Help. The original test from which modern IQ tests derive had a more specific and different purpose than the modern tests. Responding to a call from the French government, which had recently enacted universal elementary education, a French physician named Alfred Binet (1857–1911) and his collaborator, Theodore Simon (1873–1961), devised the first intelligence test between 1904 and 1911 (Matarazzo, 1972). Their aim was to

● **Intelligence:** The ability to solve problems well and to understand and learn complex material.

● **Intelligence quotient (IQ):** A score on an intelligence test, originally based on comparing mental age to chronological age but later based on norms.

develop an objective way to identify children in the public schools who needed extra classroom help. They started with the idea that intelligence shows itself in a wide variety of things people do, a perspective that led them to construct a test consisting of many sorts of tasks. Among other things, children were asked to copy a drawing, repeat a string of digits, recognize coins and make change, and explain why a particular statement did not make sense. Binet and Simon assumed that the children's performance on the tests reflected educational experience, and thus that special classes could help those who did poorly.

To assess performance, Binet and Simon first gave the test to a group of normal children of various ages. They noted which problems were solved by most of the 6-year-olds, most of the 10-year-olds, and so forth; then they compared the performance of other children of the same age with those "normal" scores. So if a child could solve all of the problems solved by most 9-year-olds, but failed those passed by most 10-year-olds, the child's *mental age (MA)* was said to be 9. Children with a mental age lower than their *chronological age (CA)* were considered relatively slow.

Terman and Wechsler: Tests for Everyone. Binet and Simon's test was quickly adopted and adapted to suit new purposes. In 1916 Lewis Terman and his colleagues at Stanford University developed the Stanford-Binet Revision of the Binet-Simon test, which is still used to test people ages 2 to adult. To refine the testing further (especially for adults, by expanding the range at the "top"), to test a wider range of abilities, and to improve the method of scoring and interpreting results, David Wechsler (1958) developed another set of intelligence tests, the **Wechsler Adult Intelligence Scale (WAIS)** and the *Wechsler Intelligence Scale for Children (WISC)*. Today, the WAIS-III and the WISC-III ("III" denoting the third major version) are the most widely used IQ tests in the United States.

Believing that Binet's test relied too much on verbal skills, Wechsler divided his test into two major parts, summarized in Table 9.1 (p. 350). The *verbal subtests* assess the test-taker's ability to understand and use language by assessing vocabulary, comprehension, and other aspects of verbal ability. The *performance subtests* consist of nonverbal tasks such as arranging pictures in an order that tells a story and spotting the missing element in a picture. Because the performance subtests do not focus on the ability to use and manipulate words, they probably rely less heavily than do the verbal subtests on the test-taker's education or cultural experiences.

The WISC-III is administered to children individually by a trained examiner.

Scoring IQ Tests: Measuring the Mind

Modern IQ tests have been modified from earlier versions both in the nature of the tasks and in the way they are scored. Binet and Simon were satisfied with simply knowing whether a child was below or at par for his or her age, but later researchers wanted a more precise measure of the degree of intelligence. Early in the 20th century, William Stern, a German psychologist, developed the idea of an *intelligence quotient,* computed by dividing mental age (MA) by chronological age (CA) and multiplying by 100 to avoid fractional scores. Thus, a score of 100 meant that a child's mental age exactly matched the child's actual age. Computing IQ scores using the MA/CA ratio presents a major disadvantage, however: Because mental age does not keep developing forever, whereas chronological age marches on, older test-takers

● **Wechsler Adult Intelligence Scale (WAIS):** The most widely used intelligence test; consists of both verbal and performance subtests.

TABLE 9.1   WAIS-III Subtests with Simulated Examples of Questions

I. Verbal Subtests	II. Performance Subtests
• *Vocabulary:* Written and spoken words, which must be defined; the words are ordered in terms of increasing difficulty. *Example:* "What does 'trek' mean?" • *Similarities:* Questions that require explaining how the concepts named by two words are similar. *Example:* "How are an airplane and a car alike?" • *Arithmetic:* Problems, all but one presented orally (one involves using blocks); the test is timed. *Example:* "If 2 men need 4 days to paint a house, how long would 4 men need?" • *Digit Span:* Lists of digits, 2–9 numbers long, are presented. The test-taker repeats the digits, either in the same or reverse order. *Example:* "6, 1, 7, 5, 3." • *Information:* Questions that draw on literature, history, general science, and common knowledge. *Example:* "Who was Martin Luther King, Jr.?" • *Comprehension:* Questions that require understanding of social mores and conventions. *Example:* "Why are there taxes?"	• *Picture Completion:* Drawings of common objects or scenes, each of which is missing a feature. The test-taker must point out what's missing. What is missing?:  • *Digit Symbol-Coding:* The test-taker learns a symbol for each of the numbers 1–9 and then sees numbers and must write their appropriate symbols; the test is timed. Shown: Fill in: 1 2 3 4 4 1 3 2 + − × ÷ __ __ __ __ • *Block Design:* Problems that require the test-taker to arrange blocks colored on each side—white, red, or half white and half red—to reproduce a white-and-red pattern in a fixed amount of time. Assemble blocks to match this design: • *Matrix Reasoning:* Items that require the test-taker to study a progression of stimuli in a sequence from which a section is missing. The test-taker must choose which of 5 given possibilities completes the sequence (for an example of a similar task, see page 360). • *Picture Arrangement:* Sets of cards that must be arranged to tell a story. Put the pictures in the right order: 

Actual test items cannot be published; part of this table was adapted from Gardner et al., 1996, pp. 80–81.
This version is intended for people aged 16 to 89. Three additional tests are included as "spares," to be used
if there are problems in administering the basic set summarized here.

cannot help but appear to become less intelligent with age. For example, if your mental age is 25 and you are 25 years old, you would be average; but if your mental age is the same in 5 years, your IQ would drop from 100 to 83, even though you are just as smart at 30 as you were at 25. And at 40, your IQ would be about 62. But people do not automatically become stupider with age. Therefore, today's IQ tests are scored not by the MA/CA ratio but by specifying how a test-taker stands relative to the performance of other people of the same age. A score of 100 is set as the average score.

Although the average IQ score is set at 100, most people do not achieve this precise score. How can we interpret the meaning of scores above or below this benchmark? IQ test scores are based on a large **standardized sample,** a random selection of people from the appropriate population. In this sense, a *population* is defined as a group of people who share certain characteristics such as age, sex, or any other relevant variables. Almost always, scores are spread along a normal distribution, illustrated in Figure 9.1. When the distribution of scores follows a normal distribution, most scores fall near the middle, with gradually fewer scores toward either extreme (see Chapter 2).

After the test has been given to a standardized sample, the developers "norm" the test to make it easy to interpret the meaning of any one test-taker's score relative to the others in the standardized sample. **Norming** a test involves setting two measures: The first is the mean, or average; the mean of an IQ test is set at 100. The second is the standard deviation, which indicates the degree to which the individual scores deviate from the mean. The greater the number of standard deviations from the mean, the farther above or below the score is from the mean (see Chapter 2 for details). If the scores fall into a normal distribution, a certain percentage of them occur at each standard deviation from the mean, as shown in Figure 9.1 (each marked unit on the bottom corresponds to one standard deviation).

For the WAIS-III IQ test, scores are adjusted so that a standard deviation is 15 points. As shown in Figure 9.1, about two thirds of all people have IQs from 85 to 115 points (that is, within one standard deviation above or below the mean), but only a bit more than a quarter have IQs between 70 and 85 or between 115 and 130 (within the second standard deviation above or below the mean). Only 4.54% are above or below those scores.

- **Standardized sample:** A random selection of people, drawn from a carefully defined population.

- **Norming:** The process of setting the mean score and standard deviation of a test, based on results from a standardized sample.

FIGURE 9.1 The Normal Curve and WAIS-III IQ Scores

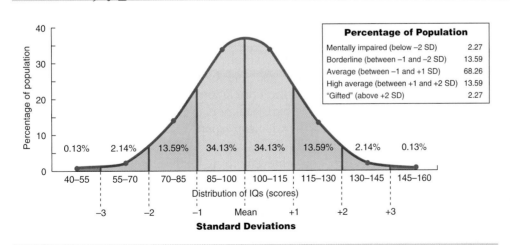

Percentage of Population	
Mentally impaired (below –2 SD)	2.27
Borderline (between –1 and –2 SD)	13.59
Average (between –1 and +1 SD)	68.26
High average (between +1 and +2 SD)	13.59
"Gifted" (above +2 SD)	2.27

Because of its shape, the normal curve is also known as the bell curve. In nature, most characteristics clump around the midpoint, and progressively fewer have very high or very low measures. This diagram indicates the percentage of people who have scores on the WAIS-III IQ test that fall within different regions of the distribution. An *SD* is a standard deviation.

For IQ scores to be meaningful or useful, the test must be *reliable*. A reliable test produces consistent results; that is, if you test the same group of people on two occasions, the two scores will be highly positively correlated. The WAIS-III has been shown to be highly reliable. In addition, a useful test must be *valid*. A valid test measures what it is supposed to measure. Do IQ tests really measure intelligence; do they measure the ability to solve problems well and to understand and learn complex material? One way to find out whether IQ tests in fact measure intelligence is to see whether scores on these tests are related to measures of performance in other tasks that seem to require intelligence, an investigation we will pursue in the next section.

The issue of validity has become more complex recently with the realization that more than one type of intelligence may exist. Many of today's tests, such as the WAIS-III, provide both an overall score and scores for various subtests, such as those that measure arithmetic and vocabulary. Thus "intelligence" is broken down into abilities of different types, and we can ask whether each measure is valid for a particular type of intelligence. This is a crucial idea, to which we will return repeatedly: The single-number "IQ score" can signify very different things depending on the relative scores on the subtests that contribute to it.

IQ and Achievement: IQ in the Real World

More than likely, IQ scores would have ceased to interest us long ago if they did not somehow relate to performance in the real world. In the United States, people with higher IQ scores, particularly in the verbal component, overall earn higher grade point averages in high school and college (Cronbach, 1990; Jensen, 1980; Snow & Yalow, 1982). IQ also predicts job success to some extent (Cronbach, 1990; Wagner, 1997). People with higher IQs tend to land higher-prestige jobs and make more money; they are also more likely to enjoy stable marriages and to stay out of jail (Herrnstein & Murray, 1994).

The IQ scores of college students typically fall between 112 and 120, considerably above the population average of 100 (Gottfredson, 1997). But before you get too giddy over this news, note that not everybody who is successful has a high IQ, nor are all people with high IQs necessarily successful. Correlations between IQ and job performance show that, at most, only about a quarter of the variation in levels of job success can be predicted by IQ (Hunter, 1983; Jensen, 1980; Streufert & Swezey, 1986; Wagner & Sternberg, 1986). This means that the lion's share of the variation reflects motivation, education, and other factors (Lubinski, 2000). Culture clearly plays a role. For example, Asian cultures, with their strong family bonds and emphasis on hard work, foster achievement (Stevenson et al., 1986), and IQ actually underpredicts job success among Japanese and Chinese Americans (Flynn, 1991, 1999a,b). Furthermore, the correlations between IQ and achievement decrease for people who have had more experience on the job. As workers become experienced, they develop expertise, which has little to do with IQ (Hunt, 1995).

Even when IQ and achievement are highly correlated, the relationship may be difficult to interpret: The positive correlation between IQ and success may occur because another variable is separately affecting them both, not because IQ itself leads to success. For example, healthy people, or people who had healthy parents, would be expected both to score higher on IQ tests and to be more successful than people who are not healthy or who

Achievement is only partly determined by intelligence; motivation counts for at least as much. Subcultures differ in the degree to which they value education, and thus the degree to which their members are strongly motivated to obtain education.

had chronically sick parents. Similarly, people who were raised to have high self-esteem might not be flustered in test-taking circumstances or in real-world job situations, and thus would tend to do well in both (indeed, this idea is consistent with findings reported by Steele, 1997). Janet did not score well on her IQ test, which may reflect the high level of anxiety she experienced while taking the test.

IQ tests do produce useful information. Janet's teachers could use the results of her IQ test to identify some of her cognitive strengths and weaknesses. They might use her scores to try to predict how well she could do in college or in certain types of jobs. But like other standardized tests, such as those that assess academic achievement, they are in part measures of how well a person performs in a test-taking situation. Performance under test conditions is influenced by many factors: anxiety, skills (or lack of them) in the mechanics of taking a test, and earlier experiences with tests. IQ is a test score that reflects many variables.

Intelligence: One Ability or Many?

As noted earlier, in the United States a high IQ score predicts, to some degree, success in school and in life. To interpret these findings, we need to know more about what, precisely, IQ tests measure. Is there some general ability, some basic intelligence, that determines IQ score? And do IQ tests tap everything meant by "intelligence"? There are different ways to solve problems, and so it seems reasonable that there should be different forms of intelligence. There is ample evidence that this is true.

Psychometric Approaches: IQ, *g*, and Specialized Abilities

How do researchers determine whether IQ scores reflect some basic, overall type of intelligence or a collection of various cognitive abilities such as the ability to solve puzzles or identify patterns? Psychologists who have investigated this question have used a *psychometric approach*; they have designed tests to measure psychological characteristics and have devised ways to use correlations and other statistical techniques to analyze the results from such tests.

Spearman's *g* Factor. As discussed, IQ tests include a variety of subtests, such as the picture completion, vocabulary, block design, and arithmetic subtests included in the WAIS-III. It turns out that people who do well on one subtest tend to do well on others; that is, scores on different types of tests are positively correlated. This finding has led researchers to infer that there is a single form of intelligence that cuts across the different subtests. Early in the last century, British psychologist Charles Spearman (1927) argued that the positive correlations among scores on different types of mental tests indicate the existence of a single underlying intellectual capacity, which he labeled *g*, for "general factor."

But if intelligence is simply *g*, then all of the scores from the different subtests should be correlated to the same degree. This is not the case: Spearman also noted a wide variation in the sizes of the correlations, which he took to reflect the influence of "specific factors," or *s*. When you perform a task, according to Spearman, you are drawing on *g* as well as on a particular type of ability, *s*, specific to that task. For example, spelling draws on a specialized ability, which is largely independent of other abilities. Some tasks, such as being able to analyze Shakespeare, rely more on *g* than on *s*; yet others, such as discriminating musical tones, rely more on a particular *s* than on *g*. Nevertheless, in Spearman's view, IQ scores depend mostly on

● **g:** "General factor," a single intelligence that underlies the positive correlations among different tests of intelligence.

● **s:** "Specific factors," or aspects of performance that are particular to a given kind of processing—and distinct from *g*.

● **Factor analysis:** A statistical method that uncovers the particular attributes (factors) that make scores more or less similar; the more similar the scores, the more strongly implicated are shared underlying factors.

● **Primary mental abilities:** According to Thurstone, seven fundamental abilities that are not outgrowths of other abilities.

● **Crystallized intelligence:** According to Cattell and Horn, the kind of intelligence that relies on knowing facts and having the ability to use and combine them.

● **Fluid intelligence:** According to Cattell and Horn, the kind of intelligence that underlies the creation of novel solutions to problems.

For the veteran angler, fishing relies on well-worn routines (such as putting the bait on the hook, casting the line in the water, knowing when to yank and when to wait, reeling in the fish, and so on), and thus it relies on crystallized intelligence. But what would happen if you didn't have bait, a hook, line, and sinker? Now you would need fluid intelligence to figure out how to catch fish.

g; how smart you are overall depends on how much of this general intellectual capacity you have.

A second perspective on what IQ scores reflect comes from Louis L. Thurstone (1938). Thurstone devised a battery of 56 tests and then analyzed the correlations of scores on these tests using a method, worked out by Spearman, called factor analysis. **Factor analysis** is a statistical method that uncovers the particular attributes ("factors") that make scores more or less similar. A factor analysis of the correlations among different measures of performance would show, for example, that speed of processing is one important factor in many tasks, and the amount of information that can be held in short-term memory is another.

When Thurstone analyzed his test results, he found that how well you can do arithmetic has little if anything to do with how well you can notice whether a scene has changed or how well you can figure out the best way to get home when traffic is heavy (Thurstone & Thurstone, 1941). Instead of believing in a single general capacity, such as *g,* Thurstone found evidence that intelligence consists of seven separate **primary mental abilities,** fundamental abilities that are the components of intelligence and that are not outgrowths of other abilities. Verbal comprehension and spatial visualization are two of Thurstone's primary mental abilities. According to this view, Janet's low IQ score might reflect deficiencies in one or two abilities, dragging down her overall score.

In the decades since Thurstone proposed his list of primary abilities, other researchers seeking to discover the facets of intelligence have analyzed and reanalyzed similar data with varying results. Carroll (1993) infers over 70 separate abilities, and some (such as J. P. Guilford, 1967) have reported finding more than a hundred distinct factors that underlie intelligence.

Cattell's Fluid Versus Crystallized Intelligence. One especially influential alternative to Thurstone's approach, however, was proposed by Raymond B. Cattell (1971), and then developed further by his student and collaborator John Horn (1985, 1986, 1989, 1994; Horn & Cattell, 1966). These researchers suggested that instead of possessing one general capacity, *g,* people possess two types of intelligence: crystallized and fluid. **Crystallized intelligence** relies on knowing facts and having the ability to use and combine them. This is the sort of intelligence that develops as you become an expert in an area. If you make good use of your college experience, you should boost your crystallized intelligence. In contrast, **fluid intelligence** is the more free-form ability to figure out novel solutions, such as how to write when a pen or pencil isn't available (one creative rock song-smith scribbled the lyrics to a new song using the heads of burnt matches). Fluid intelligence can be measured with tests that do not rely on language, and thus some researchers have argued it may reflect a fairer, less culturally bound measure of intelligence (Athanasiou, 2000; Braden, 2000). As we grow older, crystallized intelligence does not suffer much, if at all; we are still able to maintain our expertise in areas of strength. But the ability to shift gears quickly to solve new problems tends to decrease (Horn, 1985, 1986, 1994; Horn & Noll, 1994; Salthouse, 1996). That age affects the two types of intelligence differently is evidence that they are in fact different; if there were only a single form of intelligence, aging should have one effect on it. After the discovery of crystallized and fluid intelligence, Cattell and Horn provided evidence for a number of other "broad" factors (to use Jensen's term [Jensen, 1998]).

Today, psychologists generally agree with Spearman's theory that people have a collection of special mental abilities (s), and most agree that something like g exists. However, there is considerable disagreement over exactly what g is. Researchers have found that the higher people score on IQ tests overall, the more often there are sharp disparities in the scores on different subtests: In other words, the relative strengths and weaknesses of people with high IQs are likely to differ greatly from individual to individual (Deary & Pagliari, 1991; Detterman & Daniel, 1989; Hunt, 1995; Spearman, 1927). For example, some high scorers may be particularly good at vocabulary and digit span; others at digit span, matrix reasoning, and block design; and still others at yet additional combinations of abilities. In contrast, people who score low on IQ tests tend to perform consistently and generally poorly on all of the tasks. As Hunt (1995) observed, "It appears that general intelligence may not be an accurate statement, but general lack of intelligence is!" (p. 362).

Multiple Intelligences: More Than One Way to Shine

Howard Gardner (1983/1993b, 1995, 1999) developed a very influential view of intelligence, the **theory of multiple intelligences,** which holds that there are eight basic forms of intelligence:

1. *Linguistic intelligence.* The ability to use language well, as relied on by journalists and lawyers.
2. *Spatial intelligence.* The ability to reason well about spatial relations, as relied on by architects and surgeons.
3. *Musical intelligence.* The ability to compose and understand music, as relied on by audio engineers and musicians.

● **Theory of multiple intelligences:** Gardner's theory of eight distinct types of intelligence, which can vary separately for a given individual.

Linguistic intelligence is the ability to use language well, as relied on by journalists and lawyers.

Spatial intelligence is the ability to reason well about spatial relations, as relied on by architects and surgeons.

4. *Logical-mathematical intelligence.* The ability to manipulate abstract symbols, as used by scientists and computer programmers.
5. *Bodily-kinesthetic intelligence.* The ability to plan and understand sequences of movements, as drawn on by dancers and athletes.
6. *Intrapersonal intelligence.* The ability to understand oneself, as used by clergy.
7. *Interpersonal intelligence.* The ability to understand other people and social interactions, as used by politicians and teachers.
8. *Naturalist intelligence.* The ability to observe carefully, as used by forest rangers. (Gardner, 1995)

Finally, in more recent formulations of the theory, Gardner (1999) has tentatively suggested a ninth form of intelligence: *existential intelligence*, which is the ability to address "the big questions" about existence. Gardner's classifications are not isolated "special abilities" that allow a person to become skilled at a narrow range of particular tasks. Rather, these are separate *types* of intelligence, which involve a collection of abilities working together. Each type of intelligence allows you to solve a range of problems well and to understand and learn complex material of the appropriate type (Fasko, 2001).

We have shown repeatedly that different parts of the brain perform different functions; the brain is like an orchestra with separate sections playing different parts of the improvisational symphony of thinking, feeling, and behaving. Gardner's theory is unique in that it grew not out of correlations among test scores, but rather from a variety of distinct types of neurological and behavioral observations. Gardner worked for many years at the Boston Veterans Administration Medical Center, where he studied people who had suffered brain damage. He noticed that

Musical intelligence is the ability to compose and understand music, relied on by audio engineers and musicians.

brain damage often resulted in the loss of a certain ability while leaving others relatively intact. For example, language would be disrupted but patients could still sing, and vice versa; mathematical ability would be disrupted but patients could still speak, and vice versa; social skills would be disrupted while ordinary reasoning was unimpaired, and vice versa. In developing his theory, Gardner also considered other kinds of data. He noted, for example, that although everybody learns their first language in a few years, very few people master complex mathematics so easily. If two abilities develop at different rates during childhood, he reasoned, they must rely on different underlying processes. In addition, he observed that some abilities, such as music and mathematics, can be extraordinarily well developed in child prodigies, whereas these same children perform at average levels in other areas. This coexistence of the extraordinary and the ordinary, Gardner believes, suggests that some capacities, such as those related to music and mathematics, may be psychologically distinct from other capacities.

According to Gardner, most professions require combinations of different types of intelligence; to be a good novelist, for example, you need linguistic, intrapersonal, and interpersonal intelligence. Each person can be characterized by a *profile of intelligences*, with some types of intelligence being relatively strong and others relatively weak (Connell et al., in press; Walters & Gardner, 1985). Part of being successful in life is matching your particular profile to your career goals.

As appealing as Gardner's theory of multiple intelligences is to many, it has not been embraced by all researchers. One problem is that the theory is difficult to test rigorously because some of the types of intelligence (such as bodily-kinesthetic, intrapersonal, and interpersonal) are difficult to measure reliably (although people can rate themselves and others according to each type of intelligence; Furnham et al., 2002). Another problem is more fundamental: Some question whether the word *intelligence* should be applied so liberally; many of the abilities Gardner identifies, they say, have more to do with talents and skills than with intelligence per se.

Robert Sternberg (1985, 1988b) has also developed a theory of multiple intelligences, but he proposes only three types: analytic, practical, and creative. *Analytic intelligence*, the ability to learn to write clearly, do math, and understand literature, is critical for academic performance. *Practical intelligence* involves knowing how to do such things as fix a car or sew on a button, and sometimes relies on implicit memories, the unconscious biases and tendencies that guide our actions (see Chapter 7); "street smarts" are a form of practical intelligence. *Creative intelligence*, which seems closely related to Cattell and Horn's fluid intelligence, is the ability to formulate novel solutions to problems.

How do these three types of intelligence relate to IQ? Analytic intelligence is what IQ tests measure. According to Sternberg and his colleagues (Sternberg & Wagner, 1993; Sternberg et al., 1993, 2001), however, measures of practical intelligence are better predictors of how well someone will do on the job than are standard measures of IQ, and practical intelligence is largely distinct from analytic intelligence. One study found that some Brazilians who as children failed math in school nevertheless could do the math required in their business lives (Carraher et al., 1985). However, the level of a person's practical intelligence does not predict his or her academic achievement (Heng, 2000). Creative intelligence is also distinct from IQ, but people do need a certain level of IQ to be able to find creative solutions to problems or to create novel products that have specific uses (Guilford, 1967; Runco & Albert, 1986; Sternberg, 1985).

People unquestionably differ in their relative strengths and weaknesses in various aspects of intelligence. Sternberg and his colleagues (summarized in Sternberg, 1997) found that if you are taught in a way that is compatible with your strongest type of intelligence, you will learn better. Thus, if you tend toward the practical, you would more easily learn how to construct something by observing a hands-on demonstration than by reading a set of directions. This is exciting research, which may eventually allow the detailed characterization of learning styles, permitting the development of teaching methods that play to the strengths of different students. Table 9.2 (p. 358) summarizes five prominent views about the nature of intelligence.

Children learn more easily if the teaching technique is compatible with their particular cognitive strengths.

TABLE 9.2 The Nature of Intelligence: Five Views

Theorist	Key Ideas
Spearman (1927)	• *g* (generalized ability, contributes to all intellectual activities). • *s* (specialized abilities, such as spelling or distinguishing among tones). • IQ mostly reflects *g*.
Thurstone and Thurstone (1941)	• 7 primary mental abilities, such as verbal comprehension and spatial visualization. • No *g*.
Cattell (1971) and Horn (1985, 1986, 1989)	• Crystallized intelligence (using previously acquired knowledge appropriately, such as when doing arithmetic). • Fluid intelligence (producing novel solutions to problems, such as by using burnt match heads to write).
Gardner (1983/1993, 1999)	• At least 8 types of multiple intelligences (including such non-traditional ideas as bodily-kinesthetic and interpersonal intelligence). • Based on a wide variety of types of data (such as effects of brain damage, or areas in which child prodigies excel).
Sternberg (1985, 1988b)	• Analytic intelligence (the kind of reasoning relied upon in academic studies). • Practical intelligence (the kind of reasoning used to solve everyday, real-world problems). • Creative intelligence (the kind of reasoning needed to invent new things or to solve problems in new ways).

Emotional Intelligence: Knowing Feelings

In everyday life, whether you act intelligently or not often depends in large part on how well you understand both your own emotions and how your actions will affect others. Have you ever seen someone you *know* is smart do something incredibly dumb—for instance, unintentionally or uncontrollably make a remark that infuriates a spouse or boss? Salovey and Mayer (1990) refer to the ability to understand and regulate emotions effectively as **emotional intelligence (EI)**.

Emotional intelligence comprises five key abilities (Goleman, 1995; Salovey & Mayer, 1990, p. 5):

1. *Knowing your emotions*, which involves the ability to recognize emotions as they occur. For example, if you have high EI, you notice when you are becoming angry or depressed; by recognizing emotions as they arise, you are in a position to manage them rather than be managed by them.
2. *Managing your feelings*, which is essential for controlling impulses and bouncing back from failures. For example, when you feel yourself getting angry, you know that you should take a deep breath, count to 10, and bite back the reflexive nasty response on the tip of your tongue. Similarly, if you have high EI, you can put your disappointment at not reaching a goal in perspective and not let that emotion cloud your judgment.
3. *Self-motivation*, which is essential for persistence and self-control. For example, if you have high EI, you are able to decide that you want a good grade in a particular course (perhaps this one?) and are disciplined enough to study hard in spite of the tempting social distractions of college life.

● **Emotional intelligence (EI):** The ability to understand and regulate emotions effectively.

4. *Recognizing others' emotions*, which is crucial for empathy. If you have high EI, you are able to infer how someone else feels, and to respond to them accordingly. People with high EI can easily learn to become good negotiators.
5. *Handling relationships*, which involves knowing how others will react emotionally to you. If you have high EI, you not only can recognize and understand your own emotions and those of others, but you also can anticipate what emotions your actions will trigger in others.

Women tend to score higher than men on some aspects of emotional intelligence (Carrothers et al., 2000), particularly those aspects that relate to "social skills" (Petrides & Furnham, 2000). Nevertheless, men may believe that they have higher emotional intelligence than do women (Petrides & Furnham, 2000).

Emotional intelligence would seem to underlie at least part of what Sternberg means by practical intelligence, but it extends beyond that (Fox & Spector, 2000). Emotional intelligence can help you reason analytically by not allowing emotion to distract you or cloud your judgment; it can also inspire creative acts. Emotional intelligence can play a role in each of Gardner's multiple intelligences. Clearly, there is more than one type of intelligence, and IQ tests assess only some of them.

Boosting IQ: Pumping Up the Mind's Muscle

Can experience change IQ? As you have seen in Chapter 3, even if a characteristic is heavily influenced by genetics, the environment can make a difference. So it is not surprising that varying the environment can boost general intelligence as measured by IQ—but how, and by how much?

The Flynn Effect: Another Reason to Live Long and Prosper

Apparently, one of the most potent ways to improve your IQ is simply to keep on living! Many researchers had informally noted a trend that was documented by Flynn (1984, 1999a; Dickens & Flynn, 2001) and is now called the **Flynn effect**: In the Western world, IQ scores have generally risen about 3 points every 10 years. This means that the average IQ today would be 115 if the tests were scored the same way they were 50 years ago. (The way tests are scored is periodically adjusted, to keep the mean at 100.) Flynn (1999a) reports that the largest gains are on tests that are probably the most free of cultural influence, such as the Raven's Progressive Matrices (Figure 9.2, p. 360). This test requires you to discover how a series of patterns is progressively changing, and then to select from a set of possible choices the one that comes next in the sequence (Raven, 1965, 1976). The rule governing the change in the patterns can be very subtle and difficult to discern. Scores on the **Raven's Progressive Matrices** assess fluid intelligence and *g*.

There is even evidence that the Flynn effect is accelerating: Between 1972 and 1982, IQ increased by an average of 8 points. The Flynn effect has even boosted IQ scores of people who have learning difficulties, and has done so to the same degree for people of different races and genders (Truscott & Frank, 2001). In addition, as IQs have risen over time, *g* ("general intelligence") has accounted for progressively less of the variability in intelligence scores (Kane & Oakland, 2000). That is, not only has IQ in general risen, but some specific abilities have gained more than others—and the particular abilities that have gained vary for different people.

Neisser and colleagues (1996) offer three possible explanations for the Flynn effect. First, daily life today is more challenging than life in previous years, and the very

● **Flynn effect:** Increases in IQ in the population with the passage of time.

● **Raven's Progressive Matrices:** A nonverbal test that assesses fluid intelligence and *g*.

FIGURE 9.2 Raven's Progressive Matrices

Two problems similar to those in the Raven's Progressive Matrices test, which is often taken to measure fluid intelligence and *g*. Which of the numbered selections fits in the empty shape in each rectangle? The top example relies on visual-spatial ability, the bottom on analytic ability.

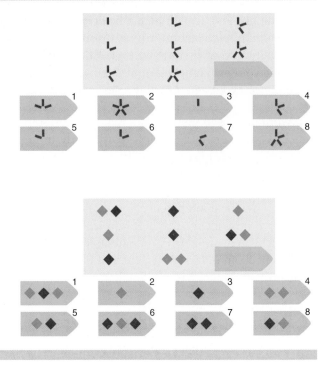

act of coping with life's complexities may have increased IQ (Kohn & Schooler, 1973). Second, nutrition is better. Lynn (1990) noted that height has increased along with IQ, and characteristics that improve brain functioning might also have increased along with height. Third, perhaps intelligence itself has not risen, but only the kind of reasoning ability that is useful in taking tests (Flynn, 1999a); technology may have led people to become more comfortable with abstract thinking. Indeed, television shows such as *Sesame Street* and interactive computers help children and adults alike learn to pay attention and to think more quickly, and also expose them to tasks similar to those on IQ tests. However, this account fails to explain why real-world indicators of "intelligent" behavior, such as how many people play intellectual games and the level of scientific productivity, have risen along with IQ scores (Howard, 2001). Flynn (1999a) and Williams (1998) offer other possible accounts, but at present the definitive explanation for this rising curve is not known.

Intelligence Enhancement Programs: Mental Workouts

Many educational and social programs have been developed with the aim of raising intelligence. Probably the most famous is Project Head Start, which was a grand initiative of the 1960s designed to provide additional intellectual stimulation for disadvantaged children and to prepare them to succeed in school. Unfortunately, most such programs show only short-term gains in IQ, and the gains evaporate with time (Baumeister & Bacharach, 2000; Consortium for Longitudinal Studies, 1983; Neisser et al., 1996). However, a few studies have shown that IQs can be raised if children are given hours of daily supplemental schooling, beginning at a young age and continuing for years (Brody, 1997). Perhaps the best known is the Abecedarian Project (Campbell & Ramey, 1994), which was started at the University of North Carolina in 1972. It provided intensive intellectual enrichment (as well as pediatric care, nutritional supplements, and help from social workers) for children at risk of failing in school. Entering the program as young as 6 weeks of age, children were placed in a specially designed daycare setting between 6 and 8 hours a day, 5 days a week. After 5 years, they entered a public kindergarten. By age 15, children who had been in the program still had higher IQ scores (by about 5 points) than those in a control group. Although a 5-point boost is not very large (a third of a standard deviation), the enhanced intellectual skills and abilities that underlie it may help participants succeed at school and at work.

What determines whether enrichment programs succeed in raising intelligence? The key may be whether they help the participants reorganize how they think (Perkins & Grotzer, 1997). In particular, successful programs teach people new strategies for making decisions, organizing problems, and remembering information. People are also taught how to plan and monitor progress as they try to solve problems, and how to know when to stop and change strategies. They are also taught to learn to detect situations that require particular patterns of thinking. (For example, remember problems that began like this: "A box of candy has twice as many chocolates as . . ."? The trick is often being able to figure out how to translate the situation into a specific kind of problem that you already know how to solve.) Wagner (1997) reviews ways in which people develop cognitively, many of which rely on "cognitive apprenticeship." Cognitive apprenticeship involves, among other things, intellectual coaching—having a mentor who can show you how to think.

Rauscher and colleagues (1993) reported that listening to Mozart could briefly improve spatial reasoning. However, before changing your musical tastes or investing in a new set of CDs, note that efforts to repeat this effect have produced spotty results (Carstens et al., 1995; Chabris, 1999; Newman et al., 1995; Steele et al., 1997, 1999; Wilson & Brown, 1997), and researchers disagree about when the effect is likely to occur (for example, Chabris, 1999, versus Rauscher, 1999). In any event, at best the effect is short-lived.

Looking *at* Levels

A Threat in the Air

Taking IQ tests isn't simply a matter of flexing your intellectual muscles. As you no doubt know from experience, test-taking of any kind, whether an achievement test such as the SAT, or an IQ test, can be anxiety provoking. Test stress may manifest itself in distinct physical symptoms, such as a speeded-up heart rate and sweaty palms. And as you feel literally "put to the test," your thinking may become clouded by a variety of distracting thoughts. Thus, factors unrelated to intelligence may affect IQ scores and other test scores.

Researchers Steele and Aronson (1995) conducted a study to investigate the possible effects of negative racial stereotypes on the test-taking performance of African Americans. They asked African American and white college students to take a test that included the most difficult items from the verbal portion of the Graduate Record Examination (GRE), a SAT-like test for graduate school. Some students, both African Americans and whites, were told that the test assessed intellectual ability; another mixed group was told that it was a study conducted by the laboratory. African Americans and whites did equally well when they were told that the test was simply a laboratory experiment, but African American students did much worse than whites when they thought the test measured intelligence. In another study, Steele and Aronson (1995) asked half the participants of each race to list their race immediately before taking the test. The test was always described as a laboratory study, not a test of intelligence. African Americans and whites performed the same when they did not list their races, but the simple act of being asked to list race drastically reduced the African American students' scores (such effects have since been reported by others, such as Croizet & Claire, 1998).

These studies dramatically illustrate the interactions of events at the levels of the brain, the person, and the group. According to Steele (1997), asking African Americans about race activates information in long-term memory about negative stereotypes, such as that African Americans are not smart. If you believe that a negative stereotype addresses issues that are important to you, then the mere possibility that others will see you as conforming to that view is threatening, even if you do not believe that you have the properties of the stereotype. Steele terms this phenomenon *stereotype threat*. When you are threatened, the autonomic nervous system is aroused (see Chapter 3) and leads you to become highly focused. In this case, the African American students may

have focused on the threat presented by the stereotype. If so, then they would not focus as well on the task at hand.

Thus, a social invention—stereotypes about groups—can become part of an individual's knowledge (level of the person). And that knowledge in turn can be activated by social situations. When activated, the knowledge produces events in the brain (as well as in the body—pounding heart, sweaty palms, and so on; see Chapter 13 for a discussion of the stress response), which in turn disrupt performance. And the disrupted performance can then reinforce the stereotypes. However, the precise instructions and context may be crucial; not all such tasks result in equally large effects of "stereotype threat" (McKay et al., 2002)—thus, it's your perception of the social situation that's crucial, which rests on yet another set of interactions among events at the different levels of analysis.

TEST YOURSELF!

1. What is IQ?
2. Is intelligence a single characteristic, or a complex set of characteristics?
3. Can "exercising the mind" raise IQ?

What Makes Us Smart?
Nature and Nurture

Janet was brought up by her mother alone in a home with few financial resources. Janet's mother was harsh and sometimes even abusive toward her, and the girl had few companions her own age. Her schoolbooks were the only books in her house, and, in any event, Janet rarely bothered to read because it took her so long to finish anything. She often wondered whether this slowness was caused by something wrong with her brain. Janet spent a great deal of time watching television, but she was not a passive viewer. Often she tried to guess what would come next in the story, and sometimes she thought about other ways the plots could have unfolded.

How might the circumstances of Janet's life have molded her intellectual strengths and weaknesses? It's difficult to know, in part because the vast bulk of research on intellectual development has focused on IQ alone. However, psychologists have learned a great deal about the forces that underlie those aspects of intelligence that are indexed by IQ scores.

The Machinery of Intelligence

Intelligence is the ability to solve problems well and to understand and learn complex material. Thus, it seems reasonable to expect that smart people would be good at the information processing required to solve problems, such as retrieving information from long-term memory or using information in working memory. Many researchers have examined the information processing that underlies intelligence (Anderson, 1992; Ceci, 1990; Sternberg, 1985, 1988b). But pinpointing just how the intellectual "machinery" of smart people differs from that of others has not been easy. Are some people smarter than others because they have bigger, faster, or more efficient brains?

Brain Size and Intelligence: Is Bigger Always Better?

Many studies have shown that the larger a person's brain, the greater his or her intelligence as measured by IQ tests (Neisser et al., 1996; Rushton & Ankney, 1996). Larger brains do tend to contain more neurons (Haug, 1987, as cited in Rushton & Ankney, 1996). But it isn't clear whether larger brain size causes greater intelligence or whether acting intelligently causes larger brain size. As discussed earlier, interacting with the environment can change your brain, even causing it to grow. For example, as discussed in Chapter 3, rats raised in stimulating environments developed larger brains.

In addition, the key variable may not be overall brain size, but the size of crucial areas. For instance, the part of the brain that controls the left hand is larger in professional musicians who play stringed instruments than in other musicians, or in other people in general (Elber et al., 1995). Consider also the brain of Albert Einstein, whose name has become nearly synonymous with genius. Shortly after Einstein died, his brain was removed and preserved. When it was initially examined, researchers found that his brain had an unusually large number of glial cells (which help to support neurons; Chapter 3), particularly in the bottom portions of the left parietal lobe (Gardner et al., 1996). This part of the brain is involved in mathematical thinking (Dehaene, 1997) and spatial visualization (Kosslyn, 1994b); as discussed in Chapter 8, Einstein made extraordinarily good use of these abilities. These cells may have helped that part of his brain function more efficiently than normal. A more recent analysis of Einstein's brain showed that he actually had more neurons in this key area in both hemispheres (Witelson et al., 1999). Indeed, Einstein's parietal lobes were about 15% wider than normal. In addition, the Sylvian fissure, the major horizontal crease in the brain (above the temporal lobe) was largely missing, perhaps because extra neurons were squeezed in. However, other areas of Einstein's brain were relatively small, making the overall size of his brain only average.

From such research findings, can we conclude that the larger your brain, or the larger certain key parts, the smarter you are? No, the relation between brain size and intelligence is not so simple. First, females have about the same average intelligence as males, but generally have smaller brains (Ankney, 1992; Rushton & Ankney, 1996). Second, the Neanderthals had larger brains than we do, but there is no evidence that they were smarter. Third, the correlation between brain size and IQ is typically small and does not apply to particular individuals. Fourth, correlation does not imply causation—as usual, some third variable (perhaps related to maternal nutrition or stress) might separately affect brain size and intelligence. At present, the meaning of correlations between brain size and intelligence is not clear. Moreover, skull size and brain size are weakly correlated, so resist the temptation to measure your friends' heads before forming a study group!

Speed: Of the Essence?

Janet is generally slow; is she therefore stupid? President John F. Kennedy could read 2,000 words per minute, understanding almost all of it (Seuling, 1978); does this mean he was smart? The answers depend in part on what you mean by "stupid" and "smart." Intelligence is a complicated beast, and most research on it has focused only on what is measured by IQ. IQ does correlate with the time taken to respond to a stimulus such as a light in a laboratory experiment—the higher the IQ, the faster the response (Jensen, 1980, 1987, 1991; Neubauer et al., 2000). At first glance, this correlation does not seem surprising: Many of the subtests in the WAIS-III are timed, and thus faster test-takers will tend to complete more of the questions and therefore have a chance at higher scores. However, people with higher IQs also require less exposure time to a stimulus in order to judge accurately which of two lines is longer (Anderson, 1992; Bates & Eysenck, 1993; Kranzler & Jensen, 1989; Nettelbeck, 1987). From such evidence, many researchers conclude that IQ reflects, at least in part, the speed of mental processes (Anderson, 1992; Ceci, 1990; Deary, 1995). Indeed, there may be a relation between the size of the brain areas used in a task and how quickly it can be performed: If more neurons are working on a task, the task may be processed more quickly than if fewer neurons are available.

Close examination, however, shows that just as the relationship between brain size and intelligence is complicated, so is the relation between speed and intelligence. Much of the underlying basis of IQ has nothing to do with how quickly you can make choices (Luciano et al., 2001). Moreover, measures of brain function have not shown that the brain itself "runs faster" in people who have high IQs (Posthuma et al., 2001). How do we reconcile such findings with the fact that IQ is often related to speed? Sternberg has devised ingenious ways to measure the speed of specific aspects of information processing. He finds that people who score high on IQ tests are faster only at certain steps in processing information. For example, people with higher IQs tend to spend *more* time digesting a problem and figuring out what kind of reasoning will be needed; as a result, they can then produce responses more quickly. So it's not that people with high IQs are necessarily faster; rather, they process information more effectively. In some cultures the importance of deliberation is recognized and considered to be a sign of intelligence (Gardner et al., 1996). Speed alone cannot determine intelligence.

Working Memory: Juggling More Balls

Some researchers have reported that the correlation between IQ and speed is best for tasks that are neither too easy nor too difficult (Jensen, 1993; Lindley et al., 1995). The highest correlation between IQ and speed is found when the task exercises working memory as much as possible without exceeding its capacity. This correlation reflects, in part, how efficiently working memory operates (for a further discussion, see Chapter 7). If Janet's mother quickly read her a list of 5 things to buy at the market, Janet could use working memory to organize the list so that she could remember it. But if her mother quickly read a list of 20 unrelated items, the task would tax working memory beyond the capacity of most people. IQ may index, at least in part, how well the central executive of working memory can manage information when the going gets tough, but not so tough as to be impossible (Carpenter et al., 1990; Lehrl & Fischer, 1990).

Studies of the brain have also supported the relationship between working memory and intelligence. On the one hand, some studies have shown that parts of the frontal lobes used in working memory are recruited in tasks that require high *g* (Duncan et al., 2000). On the other hand, neuroimaging studies have also revealed the neural bases of different forms of intelligence. For example, Prabhakaran and colleagues (1997) used functional magnetic resonance imaging (fMRI) to study which brain areas are activated while participants perform Raven's Progressive Matrices (see Figure 9.2). This test includes two sorts of items, which either require visual-spatial reasoning or simply finding an abstract rule. Prabhakaran and colleagues found that items on this test that require visual-spatial reasoning activated parts of the frontal lobes used in holding information about objects and spatial relations in working memory (see Chapter 7), and items requiring analytical reasoning (that is, items that require finding an abstract rule) activated these brain areas as well as parts of the frontal lobes used in verbal working memory. The frontal lobes are also important in directing the course of reasoning, and thus frontal lobe damage can disrupt fluid intelligence (Duncan, 1995; Duncan et al., 1995, 1996).

In response to research on the nature of intelligence, the WAIS-III, which was released in 1997, can be scored to assess four general aspects of intellectual ability: verbal comprehension, perceptual organization, working memory, and processing speed.

Smart Genes, Smart Environment: A Single System

Intelligence is related to the way the brain functions; to what extent are differences in such functioning linked to genes? Could Janet be bright in some ways and less bright in others, because of the genetic deck of cards she was dealt by her parents?

How Important Are Genes for Intelligence?

Because there is more than one kind of intelligence, we would not expect intelligence to be determined by a single gene, or even a small number of genes. And, in fact, researchers have had trouble identifying individual genes that are related to general intelligence as measured by IQ (Ball et al., 1998; Hill et al., 1999, 2002; Petrill, Ball, et al., 1997; Skuder et al., 1995). Studies have shown that multiple genes contribute to intelligence (for instance, Fisher et al., 1999), and it is now possible to use genetic data to help identify the different types of intelligence. For example, a portion of DNA has been found to be associated with one type of spatial ability (Berman & Noble, 1995) but not with general cognitive ability (Petrill, Plomin, et al., 1997), and a specific gene has been shown to predict performance IQ per se (Tsai et al., 2002).

How can we begin to sort out the relative contributions to intelligence of the genetic component and of other factors? How strong is the genetic influence? The most common method of assessing the contribution of genes to a characteristic is to observe correlations among relatives who share different proportions of their genes versus unrelated people (see Chapter 3). Virtually all research on the genetics of intelligence has focused on IQ scores, and this research is worth considering; however, we must always keep in mind the limited implications of such scores.

One way that researchers have tried to sort out the effects of genes versus environment is through *adoption studies*. In these studies the scores of adopted children are compared to those of their adoptive versus biological relatives. In some of these studies, tests are given to twins who were separated soon after birth and adopted into different families (for example, Bouchard et al., 1990). Because these twins were reared in different homes, any similarities between them are thought to reflect their common genetics. What do adoption studies find? The correlation of IQs of adult identical twins who were raised apart is higher than that both for fraternal twins and for nontwin siblings raised together (Bouchard & McGue, 1981; Bouchard et al., 1990; Plomin, 1990). In addition, an adopted child's IQ correlates higher with the biological mother's IQ than with the adoptive mother's IQ. Moreover, although the IQs of an adopted child and the biological children in a family are positively correlated, by the time the children grow up, virtually no correlation remains (Plomin, 1990; Scarr & Weinberg, 1983). These findings provide clear evidence that genes affect IQ.

Other studies have tried to find out exactly how large a role genes play in determining IQ by comparing IQs of people with different numbers of genes in common. The results clearly show that the more genes in common, the higher the correlations (Figure 9.3). The usual estimate is that the heritability of IQ is around .50, which means that about half the variation in IQ can be attributed to inherited characteristics (Chipuer et al., 1990; Loehlin, 1989). (Heritability scores indicate what proportion of observed variability in a characteristic is caused by inherited factors [Bell, 1977; Lush, 1937]; see Chapter 3 for a further discussion of heritability.) Keep in mind that heritability estimates have no bearing on how much of *your* personal intelligence is the result of your genes versus environmental factors. The number that denotes heritability refers to the proportion of causes of variation within a population, not to the proportion of the characteristic that is inherited; and because it is an average, it does not apply to individuals.

FIGURE 9.3 Genetic Relatedness and Similarities in IQ

The correlations between people who are unrelated, cousins, siblings (nontwin brothers and sisters), and twins are graphed, along with their shared amounts of genes (in parentheses).

Adapted from *Behavioral Genetics* by R. Plomin, J. C. DeFries, G. E. McClearn, and M. Rutter. © 1980, 1990, 1997, 2001 by Worth Publishers. Used with permission.

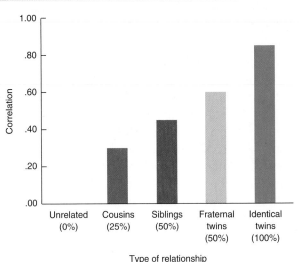

Finally, researchers have begun combining twin studies with neuroimaging studies to discover whether the sizes of specific brain areas are under particularly tight genetic control. Thompson and colleagues (2001) found that the amount of gray matter (cell bodies) in various portions of the frontal lobes and in Wernicke's area (which is crucial for language; Chapter 8) is substantially more similar in identical twins than in fraternal twins—the hallmark of high heritability. In addition, the IQ scores of these twins were highly correlated with the amount of gray matter in the frontal lobes. Note, however, that the amount of gray matter need not be the *cause* of intelligence: both the amount of gray matter and the IQ scores could *result* from other factors. For example, perhaps some twins tend to be peppy and others lethargic, which leads them to engage in more or less stimulating activities—and these activities cause neural growth in key brain areas (Chapter 3) and increase IQ. (In fact, 3-year-olds who tend to seek out stimulation actually score higher on IQ tests at age 11 [Raine et al., 2002].) These differences in temperament could themselves be genetically determined or could depend on the environment. The environment and genes engage in an intimate and intricate dance, as we consider in more detail in the following section.

Effects of the Environment: More Real Than Apparent?

Take another look at Figure 9.3, and compare the correlations between fraternal twins and those between other siblings. These pairs have the identical amount of common genes, 50%, and thus their IQ scores should be the same if intelligence is wholly determined by genes (Lyons & Bar, 2001). But, as you can see in the figure, the IQs of nontwin siblings are less correlated than those of fraternal twins (.45 versus .60), even though they have the same percentage of genes in common. What can account for this difference? Researchers assume that if scores are not related to genes, they must reflect effects of the environment.

It is clear that the environment affects intelligence as assessed by IQ. The observed relationship between IQ and achievement, noted earlier, can also run in the opposite direction: People who achieve more can develop higher scores (for example, see Kohn & Schooler, 1973; Neisser et al., 1996). Perhaps the best evidence for this comes from studies of the effects of formal schooling. For example, when poor black children moved from the rural South to Philadelphia in the 1940s, their IQs increased by a bit more than half a point for each year they spent in their new schools (Cahan & Cohen, 1989; Ceci, 1991; Ceci & Williams, 1997; Lee, 1951).

The correlations on which heritability scores are based may overestimate the role of genes and underestimate the role of the environment, even when the correlations are drawn from adoption studies. Consider some factors that make it difficult to interpret heritability scores based on studies of twins and relatives.

First, twins share much the same environment in the womb before birth and are subject to most of the same pluses and minuses of that residence. The fetus suffers when the mother has a bad diet, takes drugs or alcohol, smokes, or experiences a great deal of stress; the fetus profits when the mother eats well, takes vitamins, and doesn't drink, smoke, or take drugs. In addition, about two thirds of identical twins even share the same placenta and amniotic sac in the uterus (see Figure 9.4, p. 368), which increases the similarity of the prenatal environment compared with that of fraternal twins, who are almost always in separate sacs (Phelps et al., 1997). Twins in the same sac share blood, which contains chemicals that affect brain development. Aspects of this common environment affect later IQ (Devlin et al., 1997; Jacobs et al., 2001) and are shared even by twins separated at birth and raised apart (Phelps et al., 1997). Thus, the high correlations between identical twins separated at birth may reflect their early shared environment as well as their shared genes.

FIGURE 9.4   Fraternal and Identical Twins

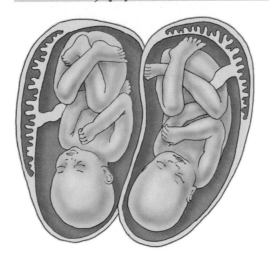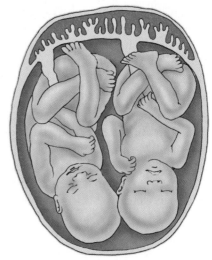

Twins can have separate placentas and separate amniotic sacs or can share a single placenta and sac; sharing results in greater similarity prior to birth. Virtually all fraternal twins are in separate sacs (left), whereas about two thirds of identical twins are in the same sac (right).

Second, after birth, it is not clear just how different the environmental influences on twins raised in different homes really are. Families that seek to adopt a child share many characteristics, and these similarities are further enhanced by the fact that adoption agencies frown on placing children in deprived conditions. The households in which twins are placed often are more similar than not. When Stoolmiller (1999) mathematically corrected for the small variations among adopting families, he estimated the effects of environment on IQ to be 57%. It is not clear, however, whether this estimate applies only to this special situation of twins raised apart or can be taken as a general estimate.

Third, aspects of the genes can help shape the environment itself. The **microenvironment** is the environment you create by your very presence. For one thing, identical twins may have more aspects of their environments in common than fraternal twins because much of our environment is social, and people respond to us in part because of the way we look and behave. So if both twins are physically appealing, they will be treated very differently than if both are homely; ditto for twins who are sluggish and overweight or are athletic and trim. Also, to the extent that children have similar inborn tendencies, their behavior may shape their environments in similar ways. For example, children who enjoy being read to will reinforce adults for this activity, leading the adults to buy or borrow more books and thus providing more opportunity for stimulating interactions. In addition, depending on their personalities, people select aspects of the environment that appeal to them (perhaps, initially, for genetic reasons), and thus what appear to be different environments may in fact function as very much the same environment for two people with similar inclinations. For example, two homes may differ in the number of books they contain, but a child who likes to read may seize on whatever is available and end up reading as much in a home with few books as a child

● **Microenvironment:** The environment created by a person's own presence, which depends partly on appearance and behavior.

We create part of our environments simply by the way we look and act, which influences how others treat us. This *microenvironment* is similar for twins, and their common characteristics may in part reflect common aspects of their microenvironment, not the direct effects of the genes.

who lives in a home with many books. In short, identical twins share many characteristics that define the microenvironment, and so they live in more similar microenvironments than do other siblings. Even twins separated at birth may create similar microenvironments, and so it is not clear exactly how different the environmental influences on the twins are in the different homes.

Finally, researchers have typically observed that only about a quarter or a third of the variability in g can be explained by shared environment, aspects of the family setting that are present for all siblings in a household, such as the number of books in the house (Plomin et al., 1997, p. 142). If genes account for about half the variability, and shared environment for less than half of what remains, what accounts for the rest? Some aspects of the environment don't have the same effect on all children growing up in the household; the same event can be a very different experience for different people. Watching television can be the mindless pastime of a couch potato, but Janet made watching TV into a stimulating experience. Even when the environment of two siblings appears to be identical, its influence depends in part on each child's predispositions and inclinations, which may be partly innate (Kagan, 1989; Turkheimer & Waldron, 2000). A shy child, for example, will be pleased to be left alone to find solitary amusements; but the same treatment would be a punishment for an outgoing, gregarious child. The *perceived* environment, not the objective environment, is the important one.

In general, any effects of a shared family environment on children's IQs, which produce positive correlations among the scores of all children who grow up in the same house, wear off by adulthood, and genetic influences become increasingly evident with age (McCartney et al., 1990; McGue et al., 1993; Plomin, 1990). Why? One theory is that, as people age, they are increasingly able to select their environments, and genetically determined properties, such as temperament, lead people to select some environments over others. For example, if you are temperamentally shy, you will not take a job in sales; if you are outgoing, you might enjoy managing a hotel. Thus, as you grow older and have more choices about how to live, the effects of your environment are increasingly related to the effects of genes

Our genes determine the range within which the environment can mold us. For example, Japanese youth are commonly much taller than their parents. Why? Same genes, but different environment (especially nutrition)—which led the genes to operate differently. Similarly, genes for intelligence define a range of possible intelligences, and the person you meet embodies just one instance of what was possible given the reaction range of the genes.

(Neisser et al., 1996). This does not mean, however, that the environment is not playing a crucial role in helping you function well (Cleveland et al., 2000).

Within this context, the concept of a "reaction range" (Scarr, 1976; Scarr & McCartney, 1983) offers a framework for understanding the significance of heritability. The **reaction range** (also sometimes called the *range of reaction*) is the range of possible reactions to environmental events that is established by the genes; the environment sets your position within that range (Weinberg, 1989). In general, the greater the reaction range, the more evident the effects of the environment. Conversely, the narrower the reaction range, the more deterministic the effects of the genes. For some genes, notably those associated with certain diseases (such as Huntington's disease; De Marchi & Mennella, 2000; Gontkovsky, 1998), simply having the gene is enough to produce an effect—these genes have very narrow reaction ranges. But most genes that affect our psychologies do not seem to be like these; rather, the operation of these genes is regulated by our interactions with the environment.

Group Differences in Intelligence

How would you feel if you were told that you are a member of a group that is genetically stupid? Many groups have faced such charges, often with far-reaching consequences. The Immigration Act of 1924 aimed to minimize immigration to the United States of "biologically weak stocks," a term that was defined to include Italians and Jews of southern and eastern Europe. During congressional testimony, supporters of the bill pointed to the results of intelligence tests, on which recent immigrants scored less well than established Americans with northern European roots. There is debate about the extent to which this testimony mattered (Snyderman & Herrnstein, 1983), but no debate over the catastrophic effects of this bill less than 20 years later, during World War II, when Jews attempting to escape Nazi Germany were severely restricted from immigrating to the United States.

Contemporary studies comparing IQ scores find that some groups score lower than others on IQ tests; for example, Jews of European descent in Israel score about 15 points higher than Jews of North African descent. What do such findings mean?

Within-Group Versus Between-Group Differences

If, as most experts have concluded, about 50% of the differences in IQ can be accounted for by differences in genes, is it reasonable to say that differences in IQs between groups are largely genetic? Absolutely not. The genetic contribution to intelligence *within* a given group cannot say anything about possible genetic differences *between* groups (Block, 1995; Lewontin, 1976a, 1976b; Plomin, 1988). To see why not, imagine that you have two orchards with the same kind of apple trees. You make sure that each orchard receives exactly the same amounts of sunlight, fertilizer, water, and so on. If you succeed in making the environments identical,

● **Reaction range:** The range of possible reactions to environmental events that is set by the genes.

FIGURE 9.5 Within-Group Differences Do Not Explain
Between-Group Differences

The state of an organism is a result of interactions between the genes and environ-ment. The two groups of trees could have the same genes, but differences in the environment cause the genes to produce different characteristics. Differences among trees in the *same* environment may reflect differences in genes, but this says nothing about differences among trees in different environments.

then any differences in the sizes of apples from the two orchards should reflect genetic differences among the trees. However, say the two orchards have overall different conditions, that one gets more sunshine and water than the other (see Figure 9.5). *Within* each orchard, differences in the sizes of the apples would reflect genetic differences. But those differences say nothing about the differences *between* the orchards. The disadvantaged environment puts the trees in one or-chard in a generally lower part of the reaction range than those benefiting from the advantaged environment. It is even possible that the differences within the "ad-vantaged" orchard reflect the operation of one set of genes, whereas the differences within the "disadvantaged" orchard reflect the operation of another set that allows the trees to make the most of skimpy amounts of sunshine or water. No question about it: Differences within one group cannot be used to explain differences between groups or within another group.

When you see an apple, all you have to go on is its present size; you have no way of knowing the range of possible sizes. Similarly, when you meet Janet, you have no way of knowing the range of her possible intelligence. Further, heritabil-ity only tells you about the effects of a *certain environment* on the genes; it says nothing about the possible effects of *other environments* (Hirsch, 1971, 1997). There is no way to know how tall, or smart, Janet would have been if she (or her mother, while pregnant) had had a different diet, experienced less stress at certain periods of her life, and so on.

Race Differences: Bias in Testing?

Asian Americans tend to score higher on IQ tests than do White Americans, who in turn tend to score higher than African Americans (Neisser et al., 1996; Rushton, 1995; Suzuki & Valencia, 1997); Hispanics tend to score between Whites

Participating in spatial activities means that the neural systems that underlie those activities are exercised. Subrahmanyam and Greenfield (1994) showed that spatial abilities could be improved by having children play certain video games, and that boys and girls in their studies improved the same amount. However, sex differences in spatial abilities can be measured even in early childhood, and so are unlikely to be totally the result of learning (Reinisch & Sanders, 1992; Robinson et al., 1996).

Researchers have even found that a woman's spatial abilities shift during the course of her monthly cycle, as the balance of hormones changes (Hampson, 1990; Hampson & Kimura, 1988; Hausmann et al., 2000). By the same token, the level of male hormones shifts during the course of the day and over the seasons, and researchers have found that American males are worse at spatial abilities in the fall, when their levels of male hormones are highest, than in the spring. The effects of these hormones are not more-is-better, but apparently are like an upside-down U: Too little or too much is worse than intermediate amounts (Kimura, 1994). Elderly men have low levels of male hormones, and thus it is interesting that testosterone supplements can boost their scores on spatial tests (Janowsky et al., 1994). However, these relationships between hormone levels and behavior are not always found (Liben et al., 2002; Wolf et al., 2000), and the effects of these hormones probably depend on a variety of other currently unknown factors.

Researchers are also now discovering differences in the structure and function of the brains of men and women. For example, it has long been known that the cerebral hemispheres are not as sharply specialized in women as in men (Jancke & Steinmetz, 1994; Springer & Deutsch, 1998), and such anatomical differences may underlie some functional differences (Gur et al., 1999; Mansour et al., 1996; Shaywitz et al., 1995).

In addition, at least part of the sex differences may arise from how boys and girls are treated in our society. Boys and girls are encouraged to take part in "sex appropriate" activities (Lytton & Romney, 1991). This is important in part because if you do not perform spatial activities, spatial abilities do not develop (Baenninger & Newcombe, 1989). And traditionally, girls have not been encouraged to participate in as many spatial activities, such as climbing trees and playing ball, as boys.

Finally, keep in mind that many females are better at spatial reasoning than many males, and many males are better at verbal abilities than many females. Here, too, differences in the means of groups say nothing about differences among particular individuals.

Looking *at* Levels

Accidentally Making Kids Smarter

For Janet, and for the rest of us, genes and the environment have interacted to create a complex mix of strengths and weaknesses. Neither theories about information processing in the brain nor data about group differences in IQ can predict what

Janet will be able to accomplish. The right conditions might help her perform better, but their effects would depend on the interaction of events at three levels of analysis: the brain, the person, and the group.

The importance of these interactions is highlighted in a study by Rosenthal and Jacobson (1968; Rosenthal, 1993, 1994). They showed that if teachers thought the children in their classes were going to become smarter, those expectations led the teachers to behave in such a way that those children actually *did* become smarter. Rosenthal and Jacobson performed a large-scale study in a public elementary school in the San Francisco area (in grades 1–6). The students first were given a nonverbal intelligence test, which was disguised as a "test of intellectual potential" (and called, nonsensically, the "Harvard Test of Inflected Acquisition"). Rosenthal and Jacobson chose at random about 20% of the children in each of three classrooms at each of six grade levels; they then told the teachers that these children had scored exceptionally well on the test and that they should expect to see these children bloom intellectually over the next 8 months. The teachers did not know that the children had been assigned randomly to this group, and there was no difference in intelligence between them and the remaining students. At the end of the year, the children were tested again, and lo and behold, those whom the teachers thought were going to develop intellectually actually showed larger gains in intelligence scores than did their classmates, especially in grades 1 and 2.

How could this have happened? Rosenthal and his colleagues observed the teachers interacting with the kids and found that the teachers treated the students they thought had greater "intellectual potential" differently. Most important, the teachers not only behaved more warmly to these students, but also put more effort into teaching them more information and more difficult material. In addition, the teachers called on these children more often and gave them more time to answer questions; they also gave them more informative feedback about their performance, providing correct answers after wrong ones were offered. These findings have since been repeated (Babad, 1993; Eden, 1990; Raudenbush, 1984; Rosenthal, 1993), and the effects are especially pronounced if the teachers don't know the children very well (Raudenbush, 1984).

Think about this effect: At the level of the group, the teachers were given information about students, information that changed their beliefs. These beliefs, in turn, led them to treat the children differently, which, in turn, required some of the children's brains to process more information—and, as we saw in Chapter 3, having to solve challenging tasks causes neurons to become more intricately connected, and the brain actually becomes heavier. The teacher's performance could have affected how well the children's brains worked! This is a *self-fulfilling prophecy*. The favored children may also have developed different views about themselves (at the level of the person), which affected how they treated other people (at the level of the group), and so on. Similar effects—positive and negative—may occur if expectations are invoked because the students have personal characteristics, such as skin color, way of talking, gender, and other characteristics that define a microenvironment; teachers make inferences, and the self-fulfilling prophecy rolls on.

TEST YOURSELF!

1. What aspects of brain function underlie intelligence?
2. How do environment and genetics contribute to intelligence?
3. How can we interpret group differences in IQ?

Diversity in Intelligence

By the time Janet became a teenager, she was showing a talent for writing in general and for writing poetry in particular. But she was no better than average at other things, and in some school subjects she did poorly. Her writing gave her a sense of confidence in her intellectual abilities, but this confidence could be quickly offset by failures or disappointments in other areas. As a result, her fears of being intellectually deficient, or even mentally retarded, persisted. The fourth grade label "Retard" stayed in her mind, sowing doubts. But rather than being mentally impaired, in some ways Janet was gifted. In this section we consider the extreme forms of intelligence, high and low. Moreover, we consider the bases of perhaps the highest form of intelligence, creativity.

Mental Retardation:
People With Special Needs

How could Janet, seriously worried about her mental abilities, settle her concerns once and for all? For want of a better definition, people with an IQ score of 70 or lower (that is, who fall more than two standard deviations below the mean) are traditionally considered to be **mentally retarded.** The American Association for Mental Retardation (1992) specifies two additional criteria: "significant limitations" in two or more everyday abilities, such as communication, self-care, and self-direction; and the presence of the condition since childhood.

Although estimates vary widely, at least 4 million Americans are mentally retarded (Larson, et al., 2001), and possibly as many as 7 million (Fryers, 1993). Mental retardation (also called *intellectual disability*) affects about 100 times more people than does total blindness (Batshaw & Perret, 1992). One out of every 10 families in the United States is directly affected by mental retardation (American Association for Mental Retardation, 1992). The good news is that just as IQ is on the rise, mild mental retardation appears to be on the decline (Howard, 2001).

Retardation does not imply an inability to learn. Mildly retarded people can learn to function well as adults, and behavioral techniques that involve explicit shaping and reinforcement (see Chapter 6) can allow even severely retarded people to master many tasks.

Furthermore, many otherwise retarded children display **islands of excellence,** areas in which they perform remarkably well. *Savants* (previously called *idiot savants*), such as the main character, Raymond, in the movie *Rain Man*, have dramatic disparities in their abilities (Hermelin, 2001; Miller, 1999). For example, a savant may be able to determine the day of the week for any calendar date, including dates centuries from now or in the past (Horwitz et al., 1965), or to draw outstandingly vivid, detailed pictures (Hou et al., 2000). But these same people may be incapable of doing simple addition.

The medical disorder, *Williams syndrome*, includes both retardation and islands of excellence (Bellugi et al., 1993, 1999a, 1999b; Kaplan et al., 2001; Udwin & Yule, 1990, 1991). Although people with Williams syndrome are in general retarded, they have large vocabularies and often detailed knowledge of facts. Frequently, however, they fail to understand the facts they apparently have at their command. For example, consider this interview of S.K., a 21-year-old woman with Williams syndrome, who liked novels about vampires:

> When asked what a vampire is, she replied, "Oooh, a vampire is a man who climbs into ladies' bedrooms in the middle of the night and sinks his teeth into their necks." When asked why vampires do this, she was visibly taken aback—she hesitated and said, "I've never thought about that." She then thought for a long time before finally answering, "Vampires must have an inordinate fondness for necks." (Johnson & Carey, 1998)

S.K. apparently had absorbed facts about vampires from the books she had read, but had never put them together. She did not understand that vampires sucked blood, that they were dead and killed people to create new vampires, and so on. But note her use of the word *inordinate*—she had an impressive vocabulary and could use it appropriately. Again, we see that intelligence is not a single capacity and that various aspects of intelligence can be affected separately from the rest.

● **Mentally retarded:** People who have an IQ of 70 or less and significant limitations in at least two aspects of everyday life since childhood.

● **Islands of excellence:** Areas in which retarded people perform remarkably well.

Mental retardation results when the brain fails to develop properly, which can happen in the womb or during childhood. Although hundreds of causes have now been identified, the causes of about one third of all cases are still mysteries. However, it is clear that both genetic and environmental factors can lead to retardation.

Genetic Influences: When Good Genes Go Bad

The most common type of mental retardation (occurring in about 1 in 1,000 births) is known as **Down syndrome,** first described by British physician J. Langdon Down in 1866. Down children have an average IQ of 55, but the degree of retardation varies widely—and may disrupt everyday activities less severely than other forms of mental retardation (Chapman & Hesketh, 2000). The most common form of Down syndrome is not inherited, but it is caused by a genetic problem—the creation of an extra chromosome (number 21) during conception. This genetic abnormality apparently prevents neurons from developing properly, so that action potentials (neural "firings") do not operate normally (Galdzicki et al., 2001). Down syndrome is more likely to occur in older mothers, whose eggs have been dormant for many years.

The second most common cause of mental retardation is also genetic, but in this case the child inherits a genetic quirk: a small bit of DNA on the X chromosome repeats itself many times (Eliez & Reiss, 2000). Because this defect makes the chromosome prone to breaking up when observed in the laboratory, the disorder is called **fragile X syndrome** (Madison et al., 1986; Murray et al., 1996; Sudhalter & Belser, 2001). About twice as many males as females suffer from this disorder because males have only one X chromosome, and females have two. It is rare that both of a female's X chromosomes carry the disorder; only one of her two X chromosomes is actually functional, and about half the time the functioning one does not have the disorder. The repetition of the bit of DNA is compounded over generations, and the more repeats, the more severe the symptoms (Levitas, 2000; Siomi et al., 1996). Thus, with each succeeding generation, the syndrome becomes worse.

Mental retardation also typically accompanies **autism,** a condition of intense self-involvement to the exclusion of external reality (Tager-Flusberg et al., 2001). Only about 25% of autistic people have IQs higher than 70, and thus most people with this disorder are also mentally retarded (Fombonne, 1999; Volkmar et al., 1994). Depending on the severity of the disease, people with autism are socially bizarre, disoriented, may sometimes engage in repetitive body movements such as rocking or hand flapping, and have severe attentional difficulties; they may also be self-destructive. Although the disorder is rare (estimates range from as low as 3 out of 10,000 live births to as high as 1 out of 500), it is highly heritable: If one identical twin has it, the chances are around 60% that the other does, too. In contrast, if one fraternal twin is autistic, the chances are only 10% that the other is. Four times as many boys as girls are afflicted with autism.

Environmental Influences: Bad Luck, Bad Behavior

Drinking and driving don't mix; neither do drinking and pregnancy. If the mother drinks heavily during pregnancy, her child can be born with **fetal alcohol syndrome.** Part of this syndrome is mental retardation (Streissguth et al., 1989, 1999). Indeed, many environmental factors can lead to mental retardation. If the pregnant mother experiences malnutrition, rubella, diabetes, HIV infection, high doses of X rays, or any of a number of infections, her child may be born with

- **Down syndrome:** A type of retardation that results from the creation of an extra chromosome during conception; it is genetic but not inherited.

- **Fragile X syndrome:** A type of retardation that affects the X chromosome; it is both genetic and inherited.

- **Autism:** A condition of intense self-involvement to the exclusion of external reality; about three quarters of autistic people are mentally retarded.

- **Fetal alcohol syndrome:** A type of retardation caused by excessive drinking of alcohol by the mother during pregnancy.

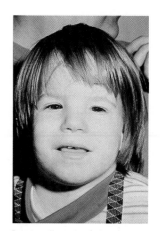

If a mother drinks alcohol heavily during pregnancy, her child can be born with fetal alcohol syndrome—one aspect of which is mental retardation.

mental retardation. Streissguth and colleagues (1989) found that taking antibiotics and even aspirin during pregnancy also can adversely affect the developing baby's brain. Because in these cases the condition is environmentally induced, people whose retardation is due to such circumstances tend not to have retarded children themselves.

Mental retardation can also arise if the birth is unusually difficult and the infant's brain is injured. Premature birth and low birth weight put the child at risk for retardation. In addition, some childhood diseases, such as chicken pox and measles, can sometimes cause brain damage, as can ingesting lead, mercury, or poisons. Vaccines and other treatments have greatly reduced the incidence of mental retardation over the past several decades (Alexander, 1991; Croen et al., 2002). Both genetic and environmental factors are summarized in Table 9.3.

TABLE 9.3 Causes of Retardation: Common Examples

Genetic conditions	Problems after birth
• Down syndrome • Fragile X syndrome **Problems during pregnancy** • Use of alcohol or drugs • Malnutrition • Rubella • Glandular disorders and diabetes • Illnesses of the mother during pregnancy • Physical malformations of the brain • HIV infection in the fetus **Problems at birth** • Prematurity • Low birth weight	• Childhood diseases such as whooping cough, chicken pox, and measles, which may lead to meningitis and encephalitis, which can in turn damage the brain • Accidents such as a blow to the head or near drowning • Lead and mercury poisoning **Poverty and cultural deprivation** • Malnutrition • Disease-producing conditions • Inadequate medical care • Environmental health hazards

Source: From http://thearc.org/faqs/mrqa.html

The Gifted

There is no hard and fast way to determine whether a person is *gifted* (Robinson et al., 2000); the term is sometimes used to refer to people who have IQs of at least 135, but more commonly **gifted** denotes the 150–180 range (Winner, 1997). Much of the research on the gifted has focused on people with very high IQs, greater than 150, and that is the criterion we will adopt here. It is not known how genes and the environment, including the environment in the womb, contribute to the condition. However, gifted boys tend to have lower testosterone levels than nongifted boys, whereas gifted girls may actually have higher amounts of testosterone than nongifted girls (Dohnanyiova et al., 2001; Ostatnikova et al., 2000, 2002); these findings hint at biological factors that could predispose some people to become gifted.

● **Gifted:** People who have IQs of at least 135, but more commonly between 150 and 180.

As expected from the idea of multiple intelligences, children can be gifted in some domains while not being gifted in others (Winner, 2000a, 2000b). **Prodigies**, children with immense talent in a particular area, may be perfectly normal in other domains; for example, mathematically gifted children often are not gifted in other domains (Benbow & Minor, 1990). Achter and colleagues (1996) found that over 95% of the gifted children they tested had sharply differing mathematical and verbal abilities.

According to some researchers (such as Jackson & Butterfield, 1986) gifted children do the same kinds of processing as average children but simply do it more effectively. As Winner (1997) notes, however, some children "as young as three or four years of age have induced rules of algebra on their own (Winner, 1996), have memorized almost instantly entire musical scores (Feldman & Goldsmith, 1991), and have figured out on their own how to identify all prime numbers (Winner, 1996)" (p. 1071). Such intellectual feats suggest that the cognition of gifted children may be qualitatively different from that of the rest of us. Specifically, Winner suggests that gifted children may be exceptionally able to intuit solutions to problems and may be driven by an extraordinary passion to master tasks.

The gifts are sometimes bestowed with a price. Gifted children are at times socially awkward and may be treated as "geeks" and "nerds" (Silverman, 1993a, 1993b; Winner, 1996). In addition, they may tend to be solitary and introverted (Silverman, 1993b). They have twice the rate of emotional and social problems as nongifted children (Winner, 1997).

If you aren't gifted as a child, does this mean you have no hope of becoming a gifted adult? Not at all. Many distinguished adults—Charles Darwin, for example—showed no signs of being gifted as children (Simonton, 1994); and, vice versa, most gifted children grow up to be rather ordinary adults (Richert, 1997; Winner, 2000a, 2000b).

Many eminent adults had the help of able mentors at critical phases of their lives (Bloom, 1985; Gardner, 1993a). Having an apprentice relationship with an appropriate role model can make a huge difference. That is one reason why graduate education in the sciences in the United States is based on apprenticeship: Students in Ph.D. programs in the sciences learn at the elbows of their supervisors, not simply from reading books or listening to lectures.

Creative Smarts

Creativity lies at the heart of many forms of intelligence. **Creativity** is the ability to produce something original of high quality or to devise effective new ways of solving a problem. Creativity necessarily involves the ability to recognize and develop a novel approach; the ability to consider a problem from multiple angles and to change points of view repeatedly; and the ability to develop a simple idea in different ways. Creative thought can be applied to practical problems (such as raising money), intellectual tasks (making new connections in a term paper), or artistic work (writing a poem).

Creative Thinking: Not Just Inspiration
Many theorists have suggested that creativity relies on a two-stage process. In the first stage, you generate a variety of possible solutions to a problem; in the second stage, you interpret and select among them (Campbell, 1960; Martindale, 1990; Simonton, 1995, 1997).

- **Prodigies:** People who early in life demonstrate immense talent in a particular domain, such as music or mathematics, but who are normal in other domains.

- **Creativity:** The ability to produce something original of high quality or to devise effective new ways of solving a problem.

FIGURE 9.6 Creative Cognition

Shapes used in the Finke and Slayton (1988) experiments on visual synthesis. On a given trial, three of the shapes were selected.

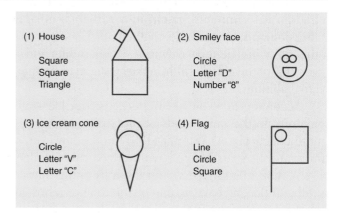

The participants mentally arranged the shapes and, after 2 minutes, named and drew a picture of what they had created. Judges decided that the patterns were recognizable in 40.5% of the trials, and that 15% of those patterns were creative.

The two-stage technique is a key aspect of an approach called *creative cognition*, in which the processes of normal cognition, such as memory and imagery, function to produce novel solutions to problems (Finke, 1996; Finke et al., 1992; Ward, 2001). Much research on creative cognition has grown out of the task illustrated in Figure 9.6. Finke and Slayton (1988) gave participants a set of simple shapes and asked them to combine the shapes mentally to create a recognizable form or object. In these studies, the first stage involves "mental play" with images of the forms, by rotation, size adjustment, and repositioning. To be effective in this first phase, the participants should produce many candidate creations. The right cerebral hemisphere appears to be involved in reaching for remote associations among concepts, and thus may play a special role in this phase (Seger et al., 2000). Finke and colleagues (1992) found that participants were more creative if they combined shapes without a particular goal in mind at the outset (such as creating a device that removes peach pits), and instead attempted an interpretation only after producing novel combinations.

In Finke and colleagues' mental combination task, the second stage involved recognizing what a combination of the forms could represent. Finke et al. (1992) found that participants were more creative if they were asked to produce objects in a certain category, such as toys or furniture (which are not specific goals), than if they were allowed to produce objects in any category. In this task, asking for objects in particular categories prevented the participants from thinking about the forms in conventional ways, and forced them to consider novel interpretations.

It is possible that either stage of creativity can occur consciously or unconsciously (as can aspects of problem solving; see Chapter 8). Consciously, each stage can be approached with different forms of thinking, and optimal creativity probably involves a mixture of them. Creativity often involves an interplay between two types of thinking, *convergent* and *divergent* (Guilford, 1967; Mumford, 2001). With convergent thinking, you stay focused on one particular approach to a problem and work through a series of steps to arrive at a solution. With divergent thinking, you come at a problem from a number of different angles, exploring a variety of approaches to a solution before settling on one (Mednick, 1962; Reese et al., 2001).

What Makes a Person Creative?

Some people are undoubtedly more creative than others. Why? Eysenck (1995) claims that very creative people tend to make loose associations and engage in divergent thinking. However, studies of creative people suggest that they have special abilities that affect both stages of the creative process: Not only can they generate more possible solutions, but they are also able to select among them more effectively. Amabile (1983, 1998) found that creative people keep options open, do not make snap decisions about the likely outcome of an effort, and are good at seeing a problem from a new vantage point. Similarly, when Guilford used factor analysis to discover which underlying abilities are tapped by various tests of creativity, he found that flexibility and the ability to reorganize information were key (similar conclusions were drawn by Aguilar-Alonso [1996] and Eysenck [1995]). Martindale (1989, 2001) stresses that creative people tend to think in terms of analogies, tend to have high intelligence, have wide interests, don't like traditional dogmas, have high self-esteem, and like to work hard. In addition, creative people are often highly motivated and persistent, driven to create (Sulloway, 1996). Amabile (2001) underscores the role of hard work and strong motivation in creativity.

Moreover, in keeping with the importance of events at the different levels of analysis, creativity flourishes only when the social circumstances are right; Nakamura and Csikszentmihalyi (2001) conceive of creativity by analogy to natural selection during evolution: the individual provides the variation, but the social world selects, preserves, and propagates only some of those innovations.

Are creative people born that way? Unlike IQ, differences in creativity are not strongly related to genetic differences, if at all. Moreover, and also in contrast to IQ, shared aspects of the home (such as exposure to cultural resources, home libraries, or parents' mechanical or artistic hobbies) strongly affect creativity (Canter, 1973; Nichols, 1978; Simonton, 1988).

Other researchers have looked for the roots of creativity by examining the lives of creative people. Simonton (1984, 1988, 1990) found that in spite of romantic images of the moody Russian composer, the drunken Irish poet, and the poor Southerner beaten as a child, the amount of stress people experience is not related to how creative they are, and social recognition of a person's accomplishments neither increases nor decreases creativity. In addition, the most creative people had intermediate amounts of formal education; either too much or too little formal education apparently stifles creativity (Simonton, 1988).

Are highly creative people mentally unstable? It has long been believed that certain mental disorders promote creativity (Kraepelin, 1921). Manic-depressive (bipolar) mental illness can result in shifts between very "high" energetic moods and very "low" depressed ones. Kay Redfield Jamison and her colleagues (Goodwin & Jamison, 1990; Jamison, 1989; Jamison et al., 1980; see also Hershman & Lieb, 1988, 1998) have argued that a "loosening" of thought that occurs during the manic phase enhances creativity. If so, the manic phase may spur creativity by increasing the number of possible solutions a person can formulate during the first phase of the creative process. Isaac Newton, Charles Dickens, and Kurt Cobain apparently suffered from this disorder, and Andreasen (1987) found that almost half

How many uses can you think of for a brick? Divergent thinking might lead you to consider bricks as doorstops, supports for bookshelves, or as bookends. Plucker (1999) reports that the ability to engage in divergent thinking is at least three times more important than intelligence in predicting creativity. Convergent thinking also has an important role in creativity—in setting up a problem in the first place, or in cutting back the lush jungle of ideas created by divergent thinking.

In some ways creativity is like pitching in baseball. Cy Young was the pitcher with the greatest number of wins in baseball history. The pitcher with the most losses? Cy Young. People who produce increased numbers of creative works are also likely to produce increased numbers of mundane works.

HANDS ON

the visiting faculty in the University of Iowa Writers' Workshop, an intensive course for creative writers, had experienced it. Jamison (1989) reports similar findings, particularly for poets.

Others have claimed, however, that mental illness is independent of creativity; these claims are consistent with analyses of Dennis (1966) and Simonton (1984, 1997), who showed that the quality of a creative person's work tends to be constant over their productive years; in years when a large number of particularly good works are produced, a correspondingly large number of inferior works are also produced.

In short, many different factors underlie creativity.

Enhancing Creativity

Many techniques, focusing on ways to find novel effective solutions to problems, have been developed in an effort to enhance creativity. When designing an object, for example, Crawford (1954) suggests listing its attributes, and then considering how to modify each attribute to improve the object. Say you are developing a beach chair; you would first list the essential attributes—it must support weight, recline at different angles, and so on. Then you would think about how to design different systems for supporting weight (webbing fabric, air cushions) and for adjusting the angle (ropes, gears, air pressure), and so forth. Another useful technique is to consider how to combine attributes in new ways (Davis, 1973). For example, consider how the properties of knives, spoons, and forks could be combined to create new multipurpose eating tools.

Sternberg (2001) claims that everyone can make decisions that will lead them to become creative. He proposes ten such decisions: (1) *Redefine problems.* Don't accept the way a problem is characterized; think about different ways to pose it; (2) *Analyze your own ideas.* Be your own harshest critic, and change your ideas when they aren't working; (3) *Sell your ideas.* In the process of trying to persuade others, your ideas will sharpen; (4) *Knowledge is a double-edged sword.* Don't trust experts; knowing too much can be as much of a hindrance as knowing too little; (5) *Surmount obstacles.* Any truly original idea won't be embraced by everyone immediately; expect to struggle; (6) *Take sensible risks.* If an idea means a lot to you, be willing to press forward even if others resist (but take *sensible* risks—consider carefully the reasons why others are resisting); (7) *Be willing to grow.* Keep open eyes and an open mind, and be willing to change course when necessary; (8) *Believe in yourself.* If you don't, others won't either; (9) *Tolerate ambiguity.* Even very good ideas take time to work out in detail; (10) *Find what you love to do and do it.* Do your own thing—you'll be more creative if you do (Amabile, 1996).

Some techniques for enhancing creativity rely on interactions among people (Garfield et al., 2001; Taggar, 2001). Probably the most well known of these is *brainstorming* (Osborn, 1953), in which members of a group say the first thing that comes to mind, volunteering ideas almost at random, thus triggering new ideas from one another. For this technique to be productive, the members of the group must suspend judgment and agree not to criticize one another's ideas at this stage. However, research findings suggest that relying on a group discussion to find creative solutions may be a bad idea. People may actually produce fewer ideas in groups than when they work alone, perhaps because they are more inhibited with others than they are in the private recesses of their own minds (Dennehy et al., 1991, as cited in Finke et al., 1992; Diehl & Stroebe, 1987). However, how

Destination Imagination (DI) is an international organization that encourages team brainstorming and creativity in the context of preparing the most creative possible "solution" to the team's choice of a challenging problem. This group performed a commercial for a nutritional product that they created.

effective a group will be depends on whether it has highly creative members and how the group is managed; groups can help or hinder creativity (Taggar, 2001).

UNDERSTANDING RESEARCH

Constrained Creativity

QUESTION: Many people believe that true creative thought requires freedom, but others have argued that creativity thrives when there is a great deal of structure. When a problem is specified precisely and the approach is made very clear, is it easier to be creative?

ALTERNATIVES: (1) Structure can facilitate creativity, (2) structure can inhibit creativity, or (3) structure can make no difference.

LOGIC: Goldenberg and colleagues (1999) programmed a computer to engage in the most extreme form of structured thinking: following an algorithm, a step-by-step set of rules. If such structure facilitates creativity, then the computer should be able to produce creative solutions—perhaps more of them than humans who are not working within such a strict structure.

METHOD: The researchers first studied effective advertisements and noticed that they seemed to rely on a few simple ideas (which are involved in creativity in general; Boden, 2000). For instance, many involved replacing properties of one thing with those of another: An ad for Bally shoes, for example, suggested that their shoes gave wearers a sense of freedom by showing clouds or an inviting island in the shape of a shoe; the sense of freedom conveyed by clouds and the island were intended to transfer to the shoes. After being armed with such rules, the computer was asked to describe ads for specific products in order to convey certain messages; its suggestions were then compared to those from humans (who were not in the ad business).

RESULTS: Table 9.4 (p. 384) presents some examples of what the computer and humans produced (as reported by Angier, 1999). Which ideas do you think are more creative? When the ads were judged by both advertising professionals and others, the computer's ideas came out on top: The judges rated its suggestions as more creative and original than those of the humans. In fact, the computer's suggestions were often judged virtually as good as actual award-winning ads.

TABLE 9.4 Problems and Solutions: Humans Versus Computer

Problem	Human Idea	Computer Idea
Convey that Apple computers are user-friendly.	An Apple computer next to a PC, with the claim: "This is the friendliest computer."	An Apple computer offers flowers.
Convey that Jeeps have very quiet engines.	A car alone in the country.	Two Jeeps communicating in sign language.
Convey that an airline has on-time performance.	A family running to an airplane, with one of the parents screaming, "Let's run, I know this airline's planes are always right on time."	A cuckoo in the shape of a jumbo jet popping out of a cuckoo clock.

Computer programmed by Goldenberg and colleagues (1999; examples from Angier, 1999).

INFERENCES: At least in some situations, structure helps creativity rather than hindering it (Perez Y Perez & Sharples, 2001). In fact, when humans were taught the rules programmed into the computer, they did as well as, and sometimes better than, the computer. However, such training is highly limited to a particular type of problem, such as writing advertisements.

Looking *at* Levels

Which Termites Were Successful?

The quality of being gifted in adulthood depends on a complex interplay between genes and various life experiences, as was well illustrated by the work of Lewis Terman and his colleagues at Stanford University (Terman & Oden, 1959). They selected 1,470 children who had IQs between 135 and 196 (and hence scored in the top 1% of the population) from over a quarter million students in the California public schools. These children (along with 58 of their siblings who were added to the study later) were tested and interviewed every 7 years or so as they grew up; they came to be known as "Termites." Many of them did remarkably well in life (Ceci, 1996; Minton, 1988).

Oden (1968) found that by about age 50, the 759 men she studied had published over 200 books, 2,500 papers, 400 short stories, poems, and musical compositions, as well as television and movie scripts. They had also filed more than 350 patents.

However, Ceci (1990, 1996) observed that success could not be predicted from IQ scores alone. Motivation apparently played a big role. Termites from modest backgrounds did much worse than those from more upper-income families, and people raised during the Great Depression did less well than those raised later. Researchers have suggested that for groups who performed less well, economic circumstances affected the Termites' perceptions of what was possible, and thus what was worth striving to achieve. Some Termites were notorious underachievers who never did very well. Few of these underachievers came from families that were as successful as those of the high-achieving Termites. The underachievers apparently were not highly motivated to succeed, in large part because their families did not instill in them the value of success.

Thus, events at all three levels of analysis must be considered to understand why one high-IQ child becomes a successful adult and another does not. The ability to score well on an IQ test is not enough; as you've seen, there are multiple types of intelligence, many of which are not tapped by an IQ score. At the level of the brain, you must have the ability to solve problems and to understand and learn complex material in the context in which you work, and different abilities are relevant for different jobs. At the level of the person, you must also be motivated to succeed. And the origins of such values and beliefs depend partly on factors at the level of the group: Motivation comes in part from the way you are raised and in part from your perceptions of what is possible. If you grow up during a time when there are few opportunities, you may not see the point in straining to succeed. As usual, events at the different levels interact: If you don't have the mental machinery, the opportunity to succeed may not be enough; if you don't have the motivation, the mental machinery is not enough.

TEST YOURSELF!

1. What is mental retardation? What causes it?
2. What does it mean to be "gifted"?
3. What is creativity? What makes some people more creative than others? Is there any way to enhance creativity?

CONSOLIDATE!

Is There More Than One Way to Be Smart?

- The most common measure of intelligence is the score on an intelligence test, IQ. IQ scores are a composite of many different underlying abilities, and the same IQ score can arise from different mixtures of relative strengths and weaknesses.

- The most common IQ tests, the Wechsler Adult Intelligence Scale (WAIS) and the Wechsler Intelligence Scale for Children (WISC), consist of two main parts, one that assesses verbal performance and one that assesses nonverbal performance.

- When first devised, IQ was a measure of mental age compared to chronological age. Today, IQ scores are based on norms, which are updated periodically so that the mean score on the WAIS and WISC is always 100 and a standard deviation is 15.

- There are many theories of intelligence, some of which posit a single overarching "general intelligence" (g), and most of which posit a set of specific or special abilities. According to one theory, g may be broken down into crystallized and fluid intelligence.

- Most researchers believe that there are many forms of intelligence; you can be smart in some ways, not so smart in others. The theory of multiple intelligences posits a wide range of types of intelligence, defined by the types of problems that are solved and material that is learned and understood.

- Scores on IQ tests are positively correlated with achievement in school and on the job, at least during the initial phases of performance; they are also correlated with many aspects of success in life, such as staying out of prison or having an enduring marriage.

- IQ scores in general have been rising with the passage of time, perhaps because the environment has become more complex and our brains have risen to the challenge.

- Intensive early training can raise IQ, but not by very much. Successful programs for boosting IQ generally teach people new strategies for making decisions, organizing problems, and remembering information, as well as strategies for noting when it is appropriate to use a particular kind of thinking in a given situation.

THINK IT THROUGH
For what purposes does it make sense to have only a single overall IQ score? For what purposes might it be better to have separate scores for the subtests? Can you think of ways in which making all high school students take an IQ test would be potentially harmful? helpful?

If you were designing the ideal school, how would you organize it so that different types of intelligence were properly nurtured? Can you think of ways of disguising tests to minimize test-taker anxiety and to eliminate stereotype threat?

Given what you've read, answer the question, "Is Janet smart?". Can you do this easily? Does it make sense to classify Janet as either "smart" or "stupid"? What is an "intelligence profile," and how is that concept relevant to these questions?

What Makes Us Smart? Nature and Nurture

- Differences in intelligence among individuals may arise because key parts of people's brains vary in size or efficiency. People with larger brains tend to have higher IQ scores, but size per se cannot be all that is important. Although additional neurons in a larger brain area could allow it to process more complex information, and to do so faster, simple speed is not crucial. Instead, the speed of the "central executive" aspect of working memory may be key.

- Crucially for some forms of intelligence, parts of the frontal lobes involved in working memory may allow a person to hold more information "on-line" simultaneously.

- Variations in intelligence probably reflect an intimate dance between genes and the environment. Genes set the reaction range, the extreme upper and lower limits, of different aspects of an individual's intelligence; the environment positions an individual within this range.

- Although about 50% of the variability in scores on IQ tests can be explained in terms of inheritance, this number is an average and does not apply to individuals.

- Group differences in IQ have been well documented; it is impossible to sort out the relative contributions of genes and the environment to such differences. Some group differences in some abilities, such as sex differences in spatial abilities, may reflect biological differences, for example, in hormone levels. However, other group differences—in IQ scores, for example—may arise in part from the ways in which environments affect individuals. Group differences may also reflect the way in which individuals' characteristics create their microenvironments and influence the reactions of others to them.

- Environmental effects can also occur at the time an IQ test is administered; when this happens, test scores are not valid indicators of ability.

- All distributions of abilities within any group overlap those of other groups, and hence group differences cannot be applied to particular individuals.

THINK IT THROUGH
Say that you could measure someone's reaction ranges for particular types of intelligence (some abilities for a given person could have larger reaction ranges than others). What could you do with this information?

Do you think tests should be designed so that there are no differences between men and women or between other groups? What are the pros and cons of such an approach? If someone came to you feeling intellectually doomed because he thought his parents were stupid, what would you say? What concrete advice could you offer for raising intelligence?

What implications, if any, would group differences in IQ scores have for the way schools should be organized? How would you explain the fact that group differences in IQ scores are actually shrinking with time?

Diversity in Intelligence

- Today's definitions of both mental retardation and genius are based in large part on IQ scores. Mental retardation is traditionally defined on the basis of overall IQ score *plus* significant difficulty with 2 or more everyday tasks, both conditions existing since childhood. By this definition, someone who is retarded cannot be gifted; giftedness is defined by a very high IQ score (typically well over 2 standard deviations above the mean, often 3 or more).

- Nevertheless, even people who perform much worse than the average in many tasks can have "islands of excellence" and perform superbly in one or two areas.

- Mental retardation can arise for many reasons, some genetic and some environmental. Not all of the genetic reasons reflect inherited defects, but rather some reflect accidents during conception or environmental damage to genes.

- Creativity leads to the production of original works or to innovative effective solutions to problems. Various tests of aspects of creative thinking (such as divergent thought) have been devised, and creativity can be assessed in the laboratory by observing whether people generate novel products or solutions. At least some forms of creativity depend on specific knowledge and skills, but there may also be a general creative ability.

- Creative people tend to make loose associations, engage in divergent thinking, keep options open, avoid snap decisions, be flexible, organize information well, and see problems from many points of view. Creativity has a very low heritability and is strongly influenced by shared environment. Although creative people are typically highly motivated, their creativity is not a gift of mental instability.

- Many techniques have been developed to enhance creativity, such as thinking of ways to vary attributes of an object or to combine them in new ways. Sometimes brainstorming is used but, in general, individuals are more creative than groups. At least sometimes, making sure that the problem is clearly specified and working within a well-structured framework can enhance creativity.

THINK IT THROUGH If you knew Janet, and she confided in you that she thought she might be retarded, how would you respond?

The eugenics movement seeks to improve the human species by encouraging those with extremely low IQ scores not to have children. What do you think of this idea? What counts as "smart" depends on the problems that need to be solved. Can you think of ways in which the problems of everyday life have changed since prehistoric times, since the Middle Ages, since the 19th century, or even since the 1920s? How has this affected what counts as "being smart"? What kinds of abilities do you think "being smart" will require in the future? Do you think it is useful to define people as mentally retarded or gifted? Why or why not?

Is creativity always desirable? What would the world be like if everyone were supercreative, always trying to change things? In what circumstances might creativity be more of a drawback than a benefit?

Key Terms

autism, p. 377
creativity, p. 379
crystallized intelligence, p. 354
Down syndrome, p. 377
emotional intelligence (EI), p. 358
factor analysis, p. 354
fetal alcohol syndrome, p. 377
fluid intelligence, p. 354
Flynn effect, p. 359
fragile X syndrome, p. 377
g, p. 353
gifted, p. 378
intelligence, p. 348
intelligence quotient (IQ), p. 348

islands of excellence, p. 376
mentally retarded, p. 376
microenvironment, p. 368
norming, p. 351
primary mental abilities, p. 354
prodigies, p. 379
Raven's Progressive Matrices, p. 359
reaction range, p. 370
s, p. 353
standardized sample, p. 351
test bias, p. 372
theory of multiple intelligences, p. 355
Wechsler Adult Intelligence Scale (WAIS), p. 349

chapter 10

© 2003 Artists Rights Society (ARS) New York/ProLitteris, Zürich

Emotion and Motivation
Feeling and Striving

John had been looking forward all day to his evening's date. Dinner with his girlfriend, Barbara, would mark the first anniversary of their meeting. But he had become absorbed working on his computer. With a start he noticed the time and realized that he might be late. Agitated at the thought of beginning a romantic evening on the wrong foot, he dashed out of the building and rushed down the street. He decided to take a shortcut down an alley. In the last of the daylight, the narrow alley was in deep shadow, but he could see the other end and felt sure he could get through quickly. But there was so little light between the old warehouses that he had to look carefully to avoid bumping into trash cans and dumpsters. As he hurried along, he thought he heard a noise behind him, and he became edgy. He walked faster. The noise seemed to be coming closer. He walked even faster. He tried to convince himself that what he heard was only a cat, but in his heart he knew better.

Suddenly he felt a strong hand grab his shoulder and then an arm snake around his neck, while something sharp dug into his ribs. His entire body froze; he felt literally paralyzed by fear. He handed over his wallet as he was told, although his heart was pounding so hard that he could barely hear the mugger's demand. Without another word, the mugger ran away, leaving John shaken but not really hurt. John ran ahead and gasped with relief when he emerged into the main street.

John hurried on to the restaurant, now far more interested in the comfort of talking to Barbara than in his romantic fantasies. Although he had been hungry when he left work, he was no longer thinking about food. He just wanted to be away from that alley, safe in his girlfriend's company.

In that harrowing experience, John was driven by emotion and motivation. What these two forces have in common is their power to "move" us. (The root of both of these English words comes from the Latin *movere*, "to move.") Our motivations and emotions are intimately interwoven: We are often motivated to do something because we are feeling an emotion, as happens when love leads us to hug someone; or we

> Our emotions and motivations are not always obvious; they may confuse us, or compel us to do things that surprise us.

are motivated because we look forward to changing our emotions, as happens when we work on a project in the expectation of replacing guilt with pride. Our emotions and motivations are not always obvious; they may confuse us, or compel us to do things that surprise us. In this chapter we consider first the nature of emotion and how it affects our behavior. This leads us to consider motivation—what makes us act. Finally, we focus on two of the most important motivations: hunger and sex.

Emotion: I Feel, Therefore I Am

John felt an odd mixture of emotions as he continued to the restaurant after his encounter with the mugger. He had no thought of what might happen later in the evening; his romantic after-dinner plans were no longer on his mind. Instead, he was trembling with fear. Now he felt nervous when he passed an alley, even though the mugger who had assaulted him was surely far away. Also, he was surprised at the strength of his feelings both when he was grabbed by the mugger and after the terrifying episode was over. When he saw Barbara, he was overwhelmed with intense feelings of warmth and relief.

An **emotion** is a positive or negative reaction to a perceived or remembered object, event, or circumstance; emotions are accompanied by subjective feelings (Damasio, 1999). Emotions not only help guide us to approach some things and withdraw from others, but they also provide visible cues that help other people know key aspects of our thoughts and desires.

Types of Emotion: What Can You Feel?

Think of the emotions you have experienced in your life. Fear? Guilt? Guilt tinged with fear? Love? Love tinged with joy? The range of human emotions is huge. In the realm of emotion the brain apparently uses the trick of producing many gradations and types of experienced reactions by combining sets of simple signals (Plutchik & Kellerman, 1980). Just as all colors can be produced by mixtures of three primary colors, researchers have argued that all emotions, even the most complex, arise from combinations of a simple set we all possess, which, like primary colors on an artist's palette, lie ready for us to blend, experience, and present to the world.

● **Emotion:** A positive or negative reaction to a perceived or remembered object, event, or circumstance, accompanied by a subjective feeling.

Basic Emotions

Charles Darwin (1872/1965), for one, believed that many emotional behaviors—the outward acts that arise from our emotions—are inborn. He noticed that people of many races and cultures appear to have very similar facial expressions to signal similar emotional states. Moreover, blind people show those same expressions, even if they have never had the chance to observe the way others look when they have particular emotional reactions. Are we all born with a built-in set of emotions? If so, these emotions would be an essential part of what we call "human nature," constituting a defining characteristic of what it means to be human in every time and culture.

Ekman and Friesen (1971) described the results of experiments that were designed to investigate this possibility (see Figure 10.1, p. 392). They wanted to know whether people who had never seen Caucasian faces could nevertheless identify the emotions underlying their facial expressions. They visited a New Guinea tribe, the Fore, who had rarely if ever seen White people in person, in movies, or on television. Nonetheless, the Fore were able to identify expressions of happiness, anger, sadness, disgust, fear, and surprise. The one difficulty they had was in distinguishing the expression of fear from that of surprise, probably because the two are very similar emotions. Also, it is possible that in Fore culture the two often go together: Most surprises in the jungle, such as the unexpected wild boar, are life-threatening, fear-inducing ones.

Ekman (1984) concludes that surprise, happiness, anger, fear, disgust, and sadness are **basic emotions,** emotions that are innate and shared by all humans. Other theorists have proposed slightly different lists of basic emotions. For example, Tomkins (1962) proposes surprise, interest, joy, rage, fear, disgust, shame, and anguish. Some of the apparent disagreements may be simply a matter of word choice; *joy* and *happiness*, for example, probably label the same emotion (LeDoux, 1996). Although the precise number of basic emotions is debated (LeDoux, 1996), there is widespread agreement that humans do have a set of built-in emotions that express the most basic types of reactions. Evidence about the way the brain gives rise to emotion also supports the existence of distinct basic emotions; for example, damage to the brain can selectively disrupt the ability to detect another person's fear and sadness without disrupting the ability to discern other emotions (Adolphs et al., 1996).

But even when there is agreement that a particular emotion is "basic," that does not mean it is "simple." Basic emotions may be complex. For example, Rozin and colleagues (1994) distinguish among three types of disgust, each of which is signaled by a different facial expression. A nose-wrinkling expression of disgust is associated with bad smells (and, sometimes, bad tastes); an open mouth with the tongue hanging down is associated with foods perceived as disgusting (the "yech" reaction); and a raised upper lip accompanies feelings of disgust such as those associated with death and filth.

Finally, although the perception of basic emotions is partly innate, learning also plays a role. Hillary Anger Elfenbein and Nalini Ambady (2002) carried out a meta-analysis of studies of the perception of emotion, looking carefully at the effects of many variables. For one, they found that although participants could recognize basic emotions of members of other racial groups better than you would expect by chance alone, they generally recognize emotions from their own group better than from other groups. However, Elfenbein and Ambady found that in some cases members of a minority group may actually recognize emotions on

● **Basic emotion:** An innate emotion that is shared by all humans, such as surprise, happiness, anger, fear, disgust, and sadness.

FIGURE 10.1   Recognition of Basic Emotions

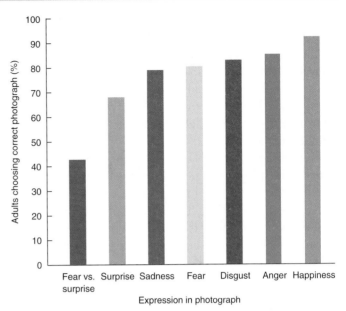

Note: Chance performance would be 33.3%.

Ekman and Friesen told the participants a story, and then presented three pictures of faces displaying different emotions. The participants chose the face that showed the appropriate emotion for the story.

Participants could distinguish all of the emotions except they tended to confuse fear and surprise.

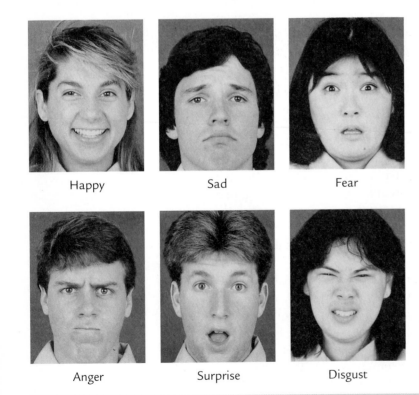

| Happy | Sad | Fear |
| Anger | Surprise | Disgust |

The six basic emotions that Ekman and others identified and studied. In the Ekman and Friesen study (1971), all the faces were Caucasian, however.

faces of members of the majority group better than they recognize emotions on faces of their own group. This finding is a clear testament to the role of learning.

Thus, even with "basic" emotions, the contribution of the genes (which produce inborn tendencies) cannot be considered in isolation from events at the levels of the person (such as learning) and group (such as whether one is a member of a specific race and culture).

Separate But Equal Emotions

Have you ever watched a movie that was a four-star tear-jerker and found yourself racked with sobs *and* rolling with laughter? There is good evidence that positive and negative emotions are not really opposite sides of the same coin. Rather, positive and negative emotions can occur at the same time, in any combination (Bradburn, 1969; Cacioppo et al., 1997; Diener & Emmons, 1984; Goldstein & Strube, 1994). For example, have you ever found yourself both enjoying a dessert and simultaneously feeling disgusted because you are such a glutton? Cacioppo and his colleagues (1997) asked students to rate how positively they felt about their roommates on one scale, and how negatively they felt about their roommates on another scale. The researchers found that the degree of negative feelings students had toward their roommates was not related to the degree of positive feelings they had toward them. The students typically felt both positively and negatively toward their roommates, at the same time.

The notion that positive and negative emotions are independent is also supported by what happens in the brain when people experience emotions. Davidson and his colleagues have provided several types of evidence that there are separate systems in the brain for two general types of human emotions: *approach* emotions (such as love and happiness) and *withdrawal* emotions (such as fear and disgust; Davidson, 1992a, 1992b, 1993, 1998, 2002; Davidson et al., 2000a; Lang, 1995; Solomon & Corbit, 1974a). In general, approach emotions are positive, and withdrawal emotions are negative. EEG recordings show that the left frontal lobe tends to be more active than the right when people have approach emotions, whereas the right frontal lobe tends to be more active when people have withdrawal emotions. Moreover, people who normally have more activation in the left frontal lobe tend to have a rosier outlook on life than do people who have more activation in the right frontal lobe. And brain scanning has shown that clinically depressed patients have relatively diminished activity in the left frontal lobe (Davidson, 1993, 1994a, 1998; Davidson et al., 1999).

What Causes Emotions?

Distinguishing among and characterizing different emotions is interesting, but it doesn't tell us what emotion is for, or why particular emotions arise as they do, any more than a theory of how color arises can explain how Leonardo painted the *Mona Lisa*. Why did John feel fear *after* the mugger had left? What possible good would that do him? The major theories of emotion, and the ideas arising from them, provide the impetus for much of the research into these questions.

Theories of Emotion: Brain, Body, and World

It seems both obvious and logical that emotion would work like this: You are in a particular situation; that situation induces a specific emotion; that emotion leads you to behave in a certain way. John is mugged, becomes afraid, and runs. This may seem obvious, but research has shown it's not quite right. Each of the following theories has succeeded in capturing at least a grain of truth about how emotions actually operate.

James–Lange Theory. More than 100 years ago, William James (1884) argued that this intuitively plausible relation between emotion and behavior is exactly backward. James believed that you feel emotions after your body reacts (see Figure 10.2). For example, if you come across someone who begins acting like a mugger, James would say that you would first run and then feel afraid, not the other way around. The emotion of fear, according to James, arises because you sense your bodily state as you are fleeing. You are aroused, and you sense your heart speeding up, your breathing increasing, and the other signs of your sympathetic nervous system's becoming active (see Chapter 3). According to his theory, different emotions arise from different sets of bodily reactions, and that's why emotions feel different. Carl Lange (1887), a Danish physiologist, independently developed a similar theory, and thus the theory has come to be called the *James–Lange theory* (Lange, 1994).

FIGURE 10.2 Four Theories of Emotion

Theories of emotion differ in the relationship they assume between bodily events, interpretations of events, and distinct brain systems.

From Lester A. Lefton, *Psychology,* 7/e. Published by Allyn and Bacon, Boston, MA. © 2000 by Pearson Education. Reprinted by permission of the publisher.

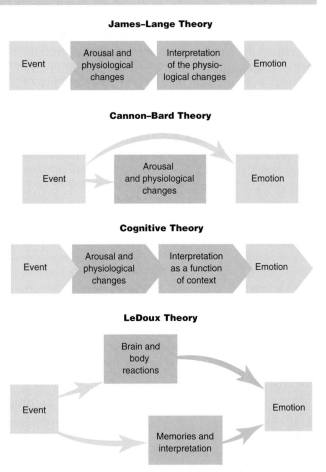

Cannon–Bard Theory. Walter Cannon (1927) claimed that the James–Lange theory focused too much on noticing bodily signals, such as heart and breathing rates. He raised a telling criticism of the James–Lange theory—that it takes many seconds for the body to become aroused and yet emotions are usually present well before this happens. Instead, he claimed, the brain itself is all that matters. You perceive the potential mugger, and the results of that perception marshal the body's resources for fleeing or fighting *at the same time* that they generate an emotion. According to the *Cannon–Bard theory* (see Figure 10.2), formulated by Cannon and another physiologist, Philip Bard, bodily arousal and the experience of emotion arise in tandem.

Cognitive Theory. *Cognitive theory* holds that an emotion arises when you interpret the situation as a whole—your bodily state in the context of everything that surrounds it. According to this theory, unlike James–Lange, you don't react to a stimulus and then feel an emotion after the reaction; and unlike Cannon–Bard, you don't have separate bodily and emotional reactions. Rather, your reactions and the general situation together form the basis of emotions. For example, the act of running and the accompanying arousal have equal chances of accompanying the emotions of joy (as you rush to embrace someone you love), fear (as you flee a pursuing mugger), or excitement (as you join the crowd on the field to celebrate a football victory). The difference is not in the bodily state, but in how you interpret it at the time it occurs. Richard Lazarus, Stanley Schachter, and Magda Arnold were pioneers in developing this view. In general, cognitive theories of emotion rest on the idea that, as Lazarus puts it, emotion "cannot be understood solely in terms of what happens in the person or in the brain, but grows out of ongoing transactions with the environment that are evaluated" (Lazarus, 1984, p. 124). This statement of course embodies our by-now familiar approach of looking at events at the levels of brain, person, and group.

LeDoux's Theory. Joseph LeDoux (1996) modified the cognitive theory in an important way. He claims that there are different brain systems for different emotions. Some of these systems operate as reflex systems do, *independent* of thought or interpretation, whereas others *depend* on thought and interpretation. Fear, for example, relies on activation of the amygdala, a small brain structure located at the front inside part of the temporal lobes (see Chapter 3), without need for cognitive interpretation. But other emotions, such as guilt, rely on cognitive interpretation and memories of previous similar situations. Thus, the emotions we feel at any moment arise from (1) a mixture of brain and body reactions and (2) interpretations and memories pertaining to the situation.

Which theory comes closest to the mark? To find out, let's take a closer look at the nature of emotion.

Physiological Profiles: Are Emotions Just Bodily Responses?

Suppose John had been so anxious about his anniversary date that he had taken a powerful tranquilizer beforehand. If this drug kept his heart from pounding and otherwise prevented his sympathetic nervous system from becoming fully activated, would he still have felt fear after the mugging? Yes, he probably would have. Let's see why.

Perhaps the strongest evidence against James's idea that emotions arise when people interpret their own bodily states is the finding that even people with spinal cord injuries so severe that they receive no sensations from their bodies still report having emotions (Bermond et al., 1991). However, it is possible that these patients experience emotions differently than do people with intact spinal cords. For example, one such patient described in this way what it felt like when a lit cigarette fell onto his bed: "I could have burned up right there, but the funny thing is, I didn't get all shook up about it. I just didn't feel afraid at all, like you would suppose." Speaking about another common emotion, he said, "Sometimes I act angry when I see some injustice. I yell and cuss and raise hell, because if you don't do it sometimes, I've learned people will take advantage of you, but it doesn't have the heat to it that it used to. It's a mental kind of anger" (Hohman, 1966, pp. 150–151). These quotations suggest that this man's emotions were largely rational evaluations, not reactions to events that were accompanied by feelings.

The James–Lange theory implies that we feel different emotions because each emotion corresponds to a different bodily state. John's heart was pounding and his palms began to sweat when he felt a sharp object jabbing into his ribs, and these events may have played a key role in the emotions he felt. The lag in time for these bodily events to arise after the mugging could explain why John continued to feel fear after he had fled the alley. In contrast, the Cannon–Bard theory implies that our bodies are aroused similarly in different arousing situations. According to this view, arousal is arousal; it occurs not only if you are mugged but also if you win the lottery. But physiological evidence leads us to question the Cannon–Bard theory. Many emotions are accompanied by *distinct patterns* of heart rate, temperature, sweat, and other reactions. For example, when you feel anger, your heart rate increases and so does the temperature of your skin; and when you feel fear, your heart rate increases but your skin temperature actually decreases (Levenson et al., 1990). Even if some of these distinct bodily responses arise because of the different levels of effort required to respond to various emotion-causing situations (Boiten, 1998), distinguishing bodily events do accompany at least some different emotions.

It is possible that emotion also corresponds to another bodily state, one that is not defined in terms of autonomic reactions. At least 20 muscles in your face do nothing but vary your facial expressions (Fridlund, 1994). When you move these muscles, your brain receives feedback from them. According to the **facial feedback hypothesis,** you feel emotions in part because of the way your muscles are positioned in your face (Izard, 1971; Tomkins, 1962).

There is evidence that "putting on a happy face" is not just a good lyric; it can actually make you feel happier. Following up on other studies (Duclos et al., 1989; Laird, 1974, 1984), Ekman and colleagues (Ekman, 1992; Ekman et al., 1990) tested this idea by leading participants to shift parts of their faces until they held specific expressions—for example, lifting the corners of the mouth until a smile and other signs of happiness were formed. The participants maintained these configurations while they rated their mood. If their faces

HANDS ON

Stick a pencil sideways (not point first) in your mouth, so that as you bite down on it, the corners of your lips turn up. Simply making this motion will actually make you feel happier (Strack et al., 1988). For more dramatic results, try to make a big smile, raising your cheeks.

● **Facial feedback hypothesis:** The idea that emotions arise partly as a result of the position of facial muscles.

were posed in a positive expression, they tended to rate their mood more positively than if their faces were posed in a negative expression.

However, putting on a happy face does not lead our brains to be in exactly the same state as when we are genuinely happy (Ekman & Davidson, 1993). Thus, although facial feedback may affect emotions, smiles, frowns, and glowers are not the only causes of our emotional experiences.

Cognitive Interpretation

Bodily factors are not enough to explain the range of feelings we have. What's missing? Our own interpretation of objects and events, and the context in which they occur, both of which affect our feelings.

The classic experiment in this area was reported by Stanley Schachter and Jerome Singer in 1962; it is illustrated in Figure 10.3. The participants, who believed that they would be taking part in a test of vision, received an injection of what they were told was a vitamin supplement. The injection was really a shot of epinephrine, which causes general arousal. Each participant then waited in a room before beginning the "vision test." Also waiting in the room was a "confederate"— that is, someone posing as a participant who in fact cooperates with the investigators in establishing the conditions of the experiment. The experiment consisted of having the confederate act in different ways during the "waiting period" and recording the effects of his behavior on the participant. In one condition, the confederate was manic, playing with a hula hoop, tossing paper airplanes, and generally acting silly. In another condition, the confederate was sullen and irritable; he tried to make the participant angry, and eventually stormed out of the room. The participants who had waited with the manic confederate reported that they felt happy, whereas the participants who had waited with the angry confederate reported that they felt angry.

Although the participants had the same bodily arousal induced by the drug, they experienced this arousal very differently, depending on the context in which it occurred; and this difference apparently led them to attribute different causes to the arousal. In contrast, when participants were told in advance about the drug and its effects, they did *not* feel differently in the different contexts; it was only when they interpreted the arousal as arising from the context that their feelings differed. In addition, participants in a control group, who did not receive an injection, experienced no effects of context. It is worth noting that this study took place more than 40 years ago; today, giving participants drugs without their knowledge is considered unethical and would not be done.

FIGURE **10.3** The Schachter–Singer Experiment

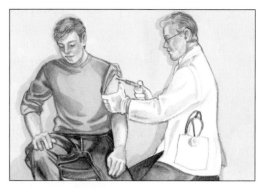

Participants received an epinephrine injection.

Confederates acted very differently while the participants waited.

The participants reacted very differently to the drug, depending on what the confederate was doing.

If you interpret signs of bodily arousal incorrectly, making a cognitive error called the **misattribution of arousal,** you may experience emotions that ordinarily would not arise in that situation. For example, in one study male participants were given false feedback about their own internal responses (Valins, 1966). They had been asked, while looking at slides of partially nude women, to listen to what they were told was their own heartbeat. The heartbeats they heard were in fact not their own; they were sometimes faster and sometimes slower than their actual heart rates. When the participants later were asked to rate the attractiveness of each woman, their ratings were based not just on what they saw but also on what they had heard: If they had associated a rapid heartbeat with a picture, they rated the woman as more attractive. It is clear that our interpretation of bodily feedback depends on the situation—and how we interpret the situation depends at least in part on bodily feedback (Palace, 1999). Emotion is a complex mixture that arises from the "whispers and shouts" of the body as filtered through the expectations and interpretations of the mind.

The fact that cognitive interpretations affect how we feel does not imply that the interpretations must be conscious. You have seen that unconscious associations between stimuli and their value can lead to hunches, which can in turn guide reasoning (Chapter 8).

Fear: The Amygdala and You

Because it is one of the emotions scientists understand best, fear has become a testing ground for theories of emotion. Fear causes changes in the brain, in the autonomic nervous system, in hormones, and in behavior. When people are afraid, they tend to freeze (to be "paralyzed by fear"), and they have an increased tendency to be startled, a tendency called *fear-potentiated startle* (Davis, 1992; Lang, 1995; Vrana et al., 1988). As John walked down the alley, the noises he heard made him afraid, which made him even more susceptible to being startled, so that he was particularly thrown off balance when the mugger grabbed him.

Researchers have discovered four important facts about fear from studying the brain systems that produce it. First, after you have learned to fear an object, fear can well up later as a kind of "emotional reflex," with no thought or interpretation at all (LeDoux, 1996). The amygdala plays a crucial role in producing the reactions you have when you are afraid. It sends signals to other brain areas, such as the hypothalamus, that cause your heart to speed up, your muscles to freeze (as John's did when he was grabbed), and all the other autonomic reactions associated with fear. In fact, conscious awareness is not needed for a stimulus to trigger the amygdala into producing a fear response (Öhman, 2002). For example, in an fMRI neuroimaging study, the amygdala responded when participants were briefly shown faces with fearful expressions—so briefly that they were not even aware of having seen the expressions (Whalen et al., 1998).

Second, there is evidence that once you learn to associate fear with an object or situation, you will always do so. To this day, whenever John sees that alley, his palms sweat and his heart beats a little faster. Even after he thought he was finally over the experience, he found himself avoiding that block. Fear is a classically conditioned response, and even after extinction, the sets of neurons that were created by an association still fire together (see Chapter 6). This is one reason why it is so easy to reinstate conditioned fear. Even though you are not aware of the association, it is never fully lost (LeDoux, 1996).

● **Misattribution of arousal:** The failure to interpret signs of bodily arousal correctly, which leads to the experience of emotions that ordinarily would not arise in that particular situation.

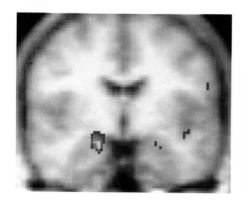

Even though participants were not aware of seeing pictures of angry faces, their amygdalae responded (Whalen et al., 1998). In addition, people who have a gene (SLC6A4, the human serotonin transporter gene) that affects serotonin levels have increased activation of the amygdala when they see emotional stimuli (Hariri et al., 2002).

Third, in spite of its reflexive nature, fear interacts with mental processes. For example, if you merely visualize yourself in a scary situation, you become susceptible to being startled (Cook et al., 1991; Lang et al., 1990; Vrana & Lang, 1990). The parts of the brain involved in cognition play a key role in "setting you up" to be easily startled.

Finally, in spite of its role in regulating fearful behaviors, the amygdala does not play a direct role in producing the emotional "feel" of fear; patients with damaged amygdalae report experiencing positive and negative emotions (such as fear) as often and as strongly as those reported by normal people (Anderson & Phelps, 2002). In contrast, the amygdala does play a role in perceiving that *other* people feel fear. People with damage to the amygdala (but with little other brain impairment) cannot recognize fear or anger in the tone of other people's voices (Adolphs et al., 1996; Calder et al., 1996; Hamann et al., 1996; Scott et al., 1997; Young et al., 1996).

What does all this tell us about emotion in general? First, there are distinct events that underlie fear, a finding that is consistent with the James–Lange theory. However, these states are not just bodily reactions; they also involve specific brain systems. Second, the events underlying fear appear to produce both the experience and the bodily reaction at the same time, which fits the Cannon–Bard theory. However, the experience and reaction are not entirely separate; rather, your interpretation of the event can affect both. Third, although interpretation is not always necessary, it is clear that mental events do interact with emotion. Thus, aspects of cognitive theory are supported. And, fourth, emotions cannot be identified with the operation of a single brain area. For example, fear is typically the strongest emotion, and some researchers have suggested that the amygdala may be responding when we perceive or feel strong emotions—not fear per se (Davis & Whalen, 2001). In fact, researchers have found that the amygdala responds when people experience both positive and negative emotions (Aalto et al., 2002), when they read words that name positive and negative emotions (Hamann & Mao, 2002), and even when they think they've won or lost a simple game (Zalla et al., 2000). Thus, the study of fear is revealing the inner workings of emotion more generally.

In short, the three oldest theories all contain a grain of truth. However, the sum total of the findings is most consistent with LeDoux's revision of cognitive theory, which includes roles for both brain-based, reflexive reactions and for the interpretation of bodily states in particular contexts. As illustrated in Figure 10.4 (p. 400), a host of brain systems has been identified that play roles in particular aspects of emotion. One specific brain area, the ventral medial frontal cortex (which is located in the center, lower, rear portions of the frontal lobes), is particularly interesting because it seems to play a role in emotional memory (Damasio, 1994).

FIGURE 10.4   Key Brain Areas Involved in Emotion

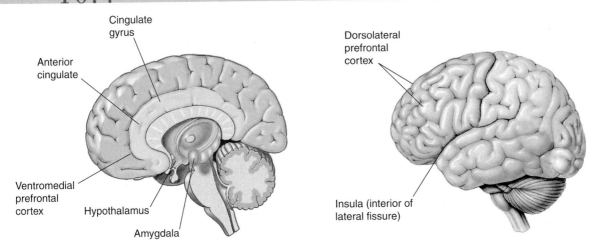

Many areas of the brain are involved in emotion, which may explain why we have such complex and rich emotional lives.

Happiness: More Than a Feeling

Lest you think that psychologists have a morbid fascination with the dark side, we must note that much has also been learned about happiness (Diener, 2000; Fredrickson, 2001; Lyubomirsky, 2001; Myers, 2000; Peterson, 2000; Ryan & Deci, 2000). What kinds of events make us happy? Self-reported measures of happiness depend on many variables, which affect events at the different levels of analysis. Many of these factors reflect events at the level of the group. Not surprisingly, a survey of happiness in 40 countries found that money *can* buy happiness, at least to some extent: People tend to be happier when they are living in better economic conditions (Schyns, 1998). In addition, happiness was correlated with the number of opportunities for cultural enrichment only in rich countries, which may suggest that basic needs (such as adequate shelter and nutrition) take precedence and, until they are satisfied, other events or opportunities cannot substitute for them in producing happiness. This notion might explain the results of surveys, taken over the period 1972–1993, showing that in the United States Whites tended to be happier than African Americans (Aldous & Ganey, 1999). However, other factors must be at work; although White women generally make less money than White men, they were generally happier than White men. One possible additional contributor is social support, the degree to which you feel that other people are willing and able to listen and help (Myers, 2000). In China, the strongest predictor of happiness was a measure of social support (Lu, 1999; Lu et al., 1997).

But we must be cautious about generalizing from one culture to another. When asked about the sources of happiness, Chinese people focused on interpersonal interactions and external evaluation, whereas Westerners focused on the achievement of personal goals and internal evaluation (Lu & Shih, 1997a). Culture also mitigates the effects of other variables. For example, many overweight people are troubled by their weight, but this concern is particularly acute for those who live in a culture in which thinness is the norm. In addition, ethnic group plays a role; Pinhey and colleagues (1997) found that Asians and Filipinos in Guam who were overweight reported being less happy than did Chamorros and Micronesians, who generally have larger average body mass. These results suggest that people gauge themselves relative to a reference group, and the same personal characteristics can be viewed as acceptable or unacceptable, depending on the results of comparison with that group. However, the effects of such social comparisons seem to depend on how happy you are to begin with: Researchers have found that happy people tend to pay less attention than do unhappy people to what they have or have not achieved relative to other people (Lyubomirsky, 2001; Lyubomirsky et al., 2001).

It is also clear that events at the level of the person affect happiness. For example, at least in Western countries, assertive people tend to be happier than nonassertive people (Argyle & Lu, 1990). But more than that, happy people tend to perceive the world through rose-colored glasses; they construe situations to "maintain and even promote their happiness and positive self views" (Lyubomirsky, 2001, p. 241).

At the level of the brain, at least some of the factors that affect whether or not you are happy are biological. We have already noted that people with more activation in the left frontal lobe (not only during a particular task, but in general) tend to be happier than people with more activation in the right frontal lobe (Davidson, 1992a, 1992b, 1993, 1994a, 1998, 2002). But why do people differ in these ways? One possibility lies in their genetic make-up. At least 50% of the variability in happiness may arise from genetics (Lykken & Tellegen, 1996). Does this mean that if you are unhappy, you should just adjust because you can't change? Not at all! As we discussed in Chapter 3, genes are not destiny.

Researchers have found that in 16 of 17 countries they examined (the exception was Northern Ireland), marriage is linked to greater happiness than is either being single or living with someone to whom you aren't married. This increase in happiness was comparable for both men and women (Ross, 1995; Stack & Eshleman, 1998; Weerasinghe & Tepperman, 1994). Apparently, most of the effects of marriage on happiness are indirect: increasing satisfaction with household finances and improving perceived health. However, this is not all there is to it; the simple fact of being married, all by itself, contributes to happiness.

Expressing Emotions: Letting It All Hang Out?

Emotions occur in the social context of family, friends, and culture. As in John's story, many of our emotions arise from social interactions, both positive (the comforting dinner with Barbara) and negative (his fear during and in the wake of the mugging). Not only do social stimuli trigger emotions, but emotions in turn serve social roles; these roles range from communicating to providing connections among people.

Culture and Emotional Expression: Rules of the Mode

In many ways emotional experience is a private affair, inaccessible to others. But emotional expression is crucial for our daily interactions with other people.

According to Ekman (1980), each of us learns a set of **display rules** for our culture that indicate when, to whom, and how strongly certain emotions can be shown. For example, he notes that in North America people will find it suspicious if at a man's funeral his secretary seems more upset than his wife. In the display rules of North American culture, the closer the relation to the deceased, the more emotion may be displayed. Display rules are partly a function of habit (individuals do differ in their styles), but they largely reflect "the way things are done" in a particular region, class, or ethnic culture.

UNDERSTANDING RESEARCH

Culture and Emoting

Ekman (1984) describes a fascinating test of his theory that all people share the same basic emotions but that emotional expression may be different because of different display rules.

QUESTION: How is the experience or expression of emotion different between Westerners and Japanese?

ALTERNATIVES: (1) The stereotype that Japanese are less emotional than Westerners may be correct, and they display what they feel; (2) Japanese may experience emotions the same way as Westerners, but display them differently; (3) Japanese may both experience and display emotions differently from Westerners; (4) Japanese and Westerners may experience and display emotions in the same ways.

LOGIC: If the two groups are equally emotional but respect different displays rules that regulate how they show their emotions in public (Alternative 2), then they both should show emotions when in private but behave differently when in public.

METHOD: Americans in Berkeley and Japanese in Tokyo were shown the same films, one positive (scenery) and one negative (a surgical procedure). Participants viewed the films either alone or in the company of a white-coated scientist. Unbeknownst to the participants, a hidden camera monitored their facial expressions as they watched the films, both when alone and with company.

RESULTS: Both national groups showed the same range of emotional expression when they viewed the films in individual screenings, one person at a time, but the Japanese participants were notably more restrained when they were in company. Ekman analyzed slow-motion videotapes of the participants as they watched, which revealed that a Japanese participant watching alone reacted in the same way as an American. But a Japanese watching in the presence of company would begin showing an emotional reaction, then quickly squelch it.

INFERENCES: According to Ekman, the initial Japanese reaction reflected the basic, innate emotions; then—when company was present—display rules came to the fore, and the participants regulated their show of emotions accordingly. Thus, Japanese experience emotions as do Westerners, but display them differently.

Culture affects not only how willing you are to express emotion in specific situations, but also how sensitive you are to the emotional expressions of others (Stephan et al., 1996). It is almost as if when a culture makes emotions harder to detect, its members develop better abilities to detect them. For example, although China has

● **Display rule:** A culture-specific rule that indicates when, to whom, and how strongly certain emotions can be shown.

more restrained display rules than Australia, Chinese children can detect basic emotions more accurately than Australian children (Markham & Wang, 1996).

Body Language: Broadcasting Feelings

Nonverbal communication isn't really language (see Chapter 8), but it is a form of communication that is particularly effective at conveying emotion. We are remarkably good at reading cues about emotion, acquiring information from even minimal cues. Dittrich and colleagues (1996) attached 13 small lights to the bodies of each of two professional dancers and had them perform dances that conveyed fear, anger, grief, joy, surprise, and disgust. Undergraduate students who later watched videotapes of the dances were able to recognize the intended emotions, even in the dark when only the lights were visible. Similarly, Bassili (1978) showed that people can recognize facial expressions of emotion in the dark from only the movement of lights attached to faces; the specific locations of the lights did not seem to matter.

Men and women differ in their characteristic nonverbal behavior. Hall (1978) performed a meta-analysis of studies of nonverbal behavior and found that men tend to be more restless (for instance, they had more frequent leg movements) and expansive (such as by leaving their legs open) than women, but women tend to be more expressive, as evidenced by their gestures (Gallaher, 1992). These conclusions are consistent with the finding that women are more expressive than men when watching emotional films (Kring & Gordon, 1998). There are also gender differences in the ability to decode nonverbal cues. Apparently women can register nonverbal signs of happiness better than men, but men can register unspoken signs of anger better than women (Coats & Feldman, 1996).

Emotion is conveyed not only by facial expression, but also by tone of voice and "body language" movements. People can sense happiness more accurately than other emotions from facial expressions—but sense happiness least accurately from tone of voice. In contrast, of all the emotions, anger is most easily sensed from the tone of voice, and it is less well sensed from the face (Elfenbein & Ambady, 2002). Nonverbal information is not entirely conveyed by facial expression, so it's wise to pay attention to all sources of information.

As these differences may suggest, at least some of our nonverbal behaviors may result from innate factors. Although there has yet to be a good rigorous study of this, one anecdote is highly suggestive. In reviewing 30 studies of identical twins who were separated and raised apart, Faber (1981) wrote: "As with voice, the way the twins held themselves, walked, turned their heads, or flicked their wrists was more alike than any quantifiable trait the observers were able to measure. . . . If one twin had a limp, moist handshake, so did the other. If one had a spirited prance, so did the partner" (pp. 86–87). However, the ability to *read* nonverbal communications is at least partly determined by experience. For example, children who watch more television tend to be better at judging emotional expressions (Feldman et al., 1996).

"Body language" plays an important role in conveying sexual interest. For example, studies have shown that men and women hold their bodies differently with someone of the opposite sex if they are interested in that person than if they are not interested. However, interest is not conveyed in exactly the same way by men and women. Grammer (1990) found that interested men had "open postures" (with the legs relaxed and open) and watched the women, whereas interested women avoided eye contact, presented their body rotated slightly to the side (so that their breasts were seen in profile), and uncrossed their arms and legs. For both males and females, a closed posture conveyed lack of interest.

Body language also plays a role in unwanted sexual encounters. This is important for students to recognize because college women experience sexual victimization three to four times more frequently than women in general (Cummings, 1992; Hanson & Gidycz, 1993). Researchers asked observers to view videotapes of ordinary people walking down the street and to rate how vulnerable they were to physical assault (Grayson & Stein, 1981). Those viewed as victims tended to move awkwardly and disjointedly, whereas "nonvictims" moved smoothly, in a coordinated, confident way. Murzynski and Degelman (1996) conducted an experiment to discover exactly which aspects of body language lead women to be perceived as vulnerable to sexual assault. They defined two victim profiles. In one, potential victims tend to walk with a long, exaggerated stride and lift their feet up rather than smoothly swinging them; in the other, they may walk with short, mincing steps. Both police officers and college students rated the women who walked in the manner of the victim profiles as more likely to be sexually assaulted than the women who walked in the style of the nonvictim profile.

Controlling Emotions

The very fact that display rules exist implies that we have at least some voluntary control over our emotional expression. Researchers have shown that we also have at least some control over how our brains respond emotionally. For example, in one study participants saw neutral or negative pictures while their brains were being scanned using fMRI. The participants were told either simply to view the pictures or to maintain their emotional responses. In fact, when they maintained the negative emotion, their amygdalae continued to be activated over a longer period of time. Moreover, the more strongly the participants rated their negative reaction to the picture, the more strongly their amygdalae were activated (Schaefer et al., 2002).

Can people also voluntarily dampen down the mechanisms that underlie emotion? The answer seems to be yes. In one neuroimaging study, researchers showed male participants erotic videos and asked them to respond normally or to try to inhibit sexual arousal (Beauregard et al., 2001). When reacting normally, various brain areas involved in emotion were activated, such as the amygdala and hypothalamus. When inhibiting their reactions, parts of the frontal lobe became activated—and the areas normally activated were no longer activated. Such processing apparently is not restricted to erotic stimuli. In another study, researchers showed participants neutral and negative pictures, and then measured their reactions to loud noise (by measuring eye blink and other facial reactions; Jackson et al., 2000). The trick was that the participants were asked to maintain, suppress, or enhance their emotional reaction to the picture. In fact, the participants were more strongly startled by the noise when they were asked to enhance their emotional reaction to a picture, and were less strongly startled when asked to suppress this reaction. One interesting twist in the results was that people who could effectively suppress negative emotion couldn't enhance it very well, and vice versa. Such individual differences may have important real-world consequences; in fact, difficulty controlling negative emotions could be a source of violent aggression (Davidson et al., 2000b).

Being able to control emotion is also important because emotion affects cognition (especially working memory; Gray, 2001). Positive emotions actually facilitate verbal tasks but interfere with spatial tasks (such as remembering an object's location or recognizing faces); negative emotions have the opposite effects. (Could these findings say something about how you might prepare to study for an English versus a geometry test?) The different effects of positive and negative emotions on cognition may arise from the fact that positive emotion activates the left frontal lobe during a verbal task whereas negative emotion activates the right frontal lobe during a spatial task (J. R. Gray et al., 2002).

● **Polygraph:** A machine that monitors the activity of the sympathetic and parasympathetic nervous systems, particularly changes in skin conductance, breathing, and heart rate. These machines are used in attempts to detect lying.

Looking *at* Levels

Lie Detection

John reported the mugging to the police but was frustrated when they failed to identify a suspect. And even if they did make an arrest, would they be able to prove anything? Lie detector tests may not be admissible evidence in court, but they are used in various investigations nonetheless. What do they really "detect"?

If different brain states and bodily states accompany different emotions, researchers have reasoned, then there might be distinct biological "footprints" of the feelings of guilt or fear of being caught. This idea underlies a long history of attempts to detect deception objectively. One result has been machines called **polygraphs,** known misleadingly as lie detectors. These machines don't "detect lies" directly; they monitor the activity of the sympathetic and parasympathetic nervous systems—in particular, changes in skin conductance, breathing, and heart rate.

The most basic technique used with a polygraph is the *relevant/irrelevant technique* (RIT; Larson, 1932). Suppose you are trying to determine whether the suspect in a crime is telling the truth. When the RIT technique is used, the suspect is asked crime-related questions ("Did you break into Mr. Johnson's house last night?") and neutral questions ("Do you live at 43 Pleasant Street?"). The responses to the two types of questions are then compared. However, there is clearly a large difference in the emotional weight of the two types of questions. Thus, a greater physiological response to a crime-related question may reflect not guilt but simply the fact that the idea posed by the question is more arousing. To avoid this possibility, the *control question technique* (CQT; Reid, 1947) includes comparison questions that should have an emotional weight roughly equivalent to that of the crime-related questions. For example, in addition to the two questions above, the suspect might be asked, "Did you ever do anything you were ashamed of?"

A more recent technique is the *guilty knowledge test* (GKT; sometimes called the "concealed information test"), developed by Lykken (1959, 1960). In contrast to the RIT and CQT, the GKT does not rely on asking direct questions about the crime. Instead, this test uses indirect questions that presumably only the guilty person would be in a position to answer correctly. In addition, the GKT relies on multiple-choice questions. So the suspect might be asked, "Was the color of the walls in Mr. Johnson's bedroom white? yellow? blue?" Someone who has never been in the room should have comparable responses to each of the choices, whereas someone who has guilty knowledge should respond selectively to the actual color. A modification of this approach is the *guilty actions test* (Bradley & Warfield, 1984; Bradley et al., 1996), which observes responses when people are given statements about actions they may have committed.

Do these techniques work? Ben-Shakhar and Furedy (1990) report that in the laboratory the CQT on average correctly classifies 80% of the guilty and 63% of the innocent. Thus, this technique unfortunately leads too often to the classification of honest responses as lies. The GKT has a better track record; the guilty were detected 84% of the time, and the innocent 94%. However, the range of accuracy in the reviewed studies was from 64% to 100% for detecting the guilty, and 81% to 100% for detecting the innocent. More recent techniques that measure electrical activity in the brain can sometimes be as high as 95% accurate, but there is still enough variability to cast doubt on the test's ability to classify individual answers

Polygraphs are used to detect changes in autonomic nervous system activity, which may signal that the person being interviewed is lying.

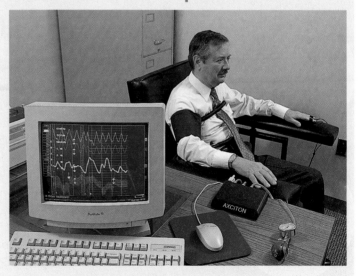

or reports from individual people as untruthful (Allen & Iacono, 1997).

Are these tests any better than simply asking observers to detect lies and taking seriously only those cases in which they are very confident? DePaulo and her collaborators (1997) reported a meta-analysis of research on the relation between an individual's confidence that he or she has spotted a lie and the level of accuracy, and found essentially no relation between the two (a correlation of essentially zero). Similarly, in another study, police officers viewed videotapes of an interview with a man who was lying about a murder (which he later confessed to committing); these officers correctly classified 70% of the true statements but only 57% of the lies (Vrij & Mann, 2001). However, other evidence suggests that *some* people can distinguish truth from lies extraordinarily accurately, particularly some (but not all) of those who have been trained in law enforcement or clinical psychology with an interest in deception (Ekman et al., 1999). Rarely, some people are intuitively able to pick up tell-tale cues of deception, but scientists have yet to isolate those cues. How can we best understand lie detection? The goal of lie detection is to assess a particular social interaction in which one person is misleading another person. However, the technique depends on interactions among events at the three levels of analysis. Perhaps the greatest problem with all the traditional techniques is that they are methods of detecting guilt or fear (the level of the person). If the person being tested lies but does not *feel* guilty or afraid, the palms won't become sweaty, heart rate won't increase, and so forth; the brain will not produce the autonomic responses associated with the feeling. And the interviewer will not have any basis for detecting the lie, which in turn may alter how the person is being treated during the interview (a social interaction), and that treatment in turn affects the person's reactions to the questions. Thus, in order to understand lie detection, we need to consider all three levels of analysis: The activity in the brain that produces the autonomic results; the personality differences that could lead a person to feel guilty or afraid; and the rules of the society, together with the person's understanding of them, which would lead the person to feel guilty under certain circumstances.

TEST YOURSELF!

1. What are the different emotions?
2. What causes emotion?
3. How does culture affect our emotional lives?

Motivation and Reward: Feeling Good

John enjoyed his work so much that on the afternoon of his first anniversary celebration he completely forgot his plans for dinner and thereafter—until he looked at the clock. When he saw the time, all thoughts of work flew from his head and he focused entirely on getting to the restaurant. Because of the pleasures that he believed lay in store for him—and because he didn't want to risk spoiling the evening by being late—John was highly *motivated* to get to the restaurant from the moment he left work, and even more so after the mugging. We often take a particular action because we expect to feel good afterward; in this sense, emotions motivate us. To motivate is to set in motion, and in psychology the term **motivation** is used to refer to the requirements and desires that lead animals (including humans) to behave in a particular way at a particular time and place.

● **Motivation:** The requirements and desires that lead animals (including humans) to behave in a particular way at a particular time and place.

Many different goals motivate us, ranging from the promise that good grades will lead to a bright future, to needing to keep warm, to being the object of others' attention. What goals motivate you most strongly?

Getting Motivated: Sources and Theories of Motivation

There is no single, widely accepted, grand theory that can explain all of human motivation. There are motives based on biological needs (such as the need to keep warm) and motives based on learning (such as the desire for money); motives rooted in the internal state of a person (such as hunger) and motives sparked by the external world (such as exploration); motives based on a current situation and motives based on an expected future situation. Psychologists have analyzed, classified, and identified human motives in numerous ways, developing a variety of theories of motivation. Let's look at the key concepts in these theories and find out what each has to offer as an explanation of human behavior.

Instincts: My Genes Made Me Do It

Why do birds fly south for the winter and spiders make certain kinds of webs? Instinct. For many animals, instincts provide the main motivation for behaviors. An **instinct** is an inherited tendency to produce organized and unalterable responses to particular stimuli. For several decades at the beginning of the 20th century, some psychologists tried to explain human motivation in terms of instincts (for example, McDougall, 1908/1960); their approach is termed *instinct theory*. Much of Freud's theory, for example, hinges on ideas about how we grapple with our sexual urges, which he considered to be instinctive (these ideas are discussed in Chapter 11). But unlike many other animals, we humans are remarkably flexible in the way we can respond to any stimulus, so it is difficult to assign an important role to instincts in human motivation.

Evolutionary psychology has offered an alternative to instinct theory. Instead of proposing that a behavior itself is "hard-wired," these theorists believe that goals that motivate us (such as finding attractive mates) and general cognitive strategies for achieving goals (such as deception) are inborn (Barkow et al., 1992; Buss, 1998; Cosmides & Tooby, 1996; Pinker, 1997, 2002; Plotkin, 1997). However, evolutionary theories of motivation are notoriously difficult to test because we can never know for sure what our ancestors were like and how they evolved.

● **Instinct:** An inherited tendency to produce organized and unalterable responses to particular stimuli.

Nevertheless, evolutionary thinking can be a source of inspiration and can lead to novel hypotheses that can be tested in their own right (Pinker, 1997).

Drives and Homeostasis: Staying in Balance

Instinct theory and evolutionary theory focus on specifying particular innate behaviors or goals and strategies. In contrast, *drive theory* focuses on the mechanisms that underlie such tendencies, whether or not they are innate. A **drive** is an internal imbalance that pushes you to reach a particular goal, which in turn will reduce that imbalance. Drives differ in terms of the goals to which they direct you, but all are aimed at satisfying a requirement (decreasing an imbalance). For example, hunger is a drive that orients you toward food; thirst is a drive that impels you toward drink; being cold is a drive that nudges you toward a source of warmth. Some drive theories link drives and reinforcement: Something is reinforcing if it reduces an imbalance. According to this theory, if you are hungry, food is reinforcing because it reduces the imbalance experienced when you have the hunger drive; if you are not hungry, food is not reinforcing.

What is the nature of the imbalance that is quelled by reinforcement? In 1932 Walter B. Cannon published a groundbreaking book titled *The Wisdom of the Body*, in which he pointed out that for life to be sustained, certain characteristics and substances of the body must be kept within a certain range, neither rising too high nor falling too low. These characteristics and substances include body temperature and the amounts of oxygen, minerals, water, and food taken in. Bodily processes such as digestion and respiration work toward keeping the levels steady. The process of maintaining a steady state is called **homeostasis.** Homeostasis works not simply to keep the system in balance, but to keep it in balance in the range in which the body functions best. The usual analogy to homeostasis is a thermostat and furnace: the thermostat turns the furnace on when the temperature drops too low and turns it off when the temperature reaches the desired level. But Cannon pointed out that in living creatures, homeostasis often involves active behavior, not simply the passive registering of the state of the environment. To stay alive, you must nourish yourself by obtaining and taking in food and water, and you must maintain body temperature by finding shelter and wearing clothing. If the homeostatic balance goes awry, an imbalance results—and you are motivated to correct the imbalance.

The power of homeostasis in motivation was dramatically illustrated by the classic case of a boy, referred to as D.W., who developed a craving for salt when he was a year old (Wilkins & Richter, 1940). He loved potato chips, salted crackers, pretzels, olives, and pickles. He would also eat salt directly, upending salt shakers and pouring their contents directly into his mouth. When his parents took away his salt, he would cry and carry on until they relented. When he began to talk, one of his first words was "salt." At 3½ years of age, he was hospitalized and forced to eat standard hospital fare. Deprived of his usual salt intake, D.W. died within a few days. An autopsy revealed that he died because his adrenal glands were deficient and could not produce a hormone that is essential for the body to retain salt, which is crucial to the maintenance of homeostasis. Because D.W. needed an abnormal supply, his strong drive for salt led to behavior that caused his parents to give it to him.

Arousal Theory: Avoiding Boredom, Avoiding Overload

People are also motivated to maintain another kind of balance, one that has nothing to do with physiological homeostasis: Simply put, we don't like stimuli that are either too boring or too arousing, and instead seek to maintain an inter-

● **Drive:** An internal imbalance that motivates animals (including humans) to reach a particular goal that will reduce the imbalance.

● **Homeostasis:** The process of maintaining a steady state, a constant level of a bodily substance or condition.

mediate level of stimulation. Berlyne (1960, 1974) showed that people like random patterns, paintings, or music best when they are neither too simple nor too complex, but rather somewhere in the middle. What counts as "simple" or "complex" depends partly on the person as well as the nature of the stimulus. For example, children find patterns complex that adults find less so.

These findings conform to what is now known as the *Yerkes–Dodson law* (Figure 10.5), named after the researchers who first described a similar principle. This law states that we perform best when we are at an intermediate level of arousal. If we are underaroused, we are sluggish; if we are overaroused, we can't focus and sustain attention. Intermediate levels of arousal may occur when we are challenged not too much and not too little. For example, if you have to speak before a large group, you may become tongue-tied because of overarousal; if you are rehearsing the speech alone in your room, you may be understimulated and give a lackluster presentation. Indeed, people adapt to a constant set of stimuli, become bored, and then seek additional stimulation (Helson, 1964). We are apparently drawn to moderate stimulation. As intuitive as this idea may seem, not all studies have supported it (for example, Messinger, 1998), perhaps because it is difficult to define precisely levels of stimulation and how they vary.

FIGURE 10.5 The Yerkes–Dodson Law

People perform best at intermediate levels of arousal.

Incentives and Reward: Happy Expectations

Homeostasis is a useful concept for understanding thirst, hunger, and certain other drives (such as those for salt, oxygen, and temperature control), and arousal theory helps explain why people select certain activities and situations and reject others. However, neither principle helps to explain other motivations, such as for sex (Beach, 1956). Your body doesn't actually need sex in the way you need food and oxygen; you can't die from celibacy. Moreover, sex is an example of seeking high arousal, not the intermediate levels we apparently prefer in other areas of stimulation. Like sex, much of what motivates us is best understood in terms of **incentives,** which are stimuli or events that draw us to achieve a particular goal in anticipation of a reward. Sex is a good example of incentive-related motivation; so, too, is any money-making activity. To see the difference between a drive and an incentive, consider the fact that hunger is a drive, which is often long gone before dessert—but dessert can nevertheless still be an incentive to keep eating (as exploited by countless generations of parents, who use dessert as an incentive to get their kids to eat their spinach).

The notion that much of motivation can best be understood in terms of incentives has led theorists to think about some aspects of motivation in terms of *expectations* of reinforcement. We tend to behave in ways that experience has shown us produce a desirable outcome (see Chapter 6), either a positive consequence of the behavior (positive reinforcement) or the removal of a negative condition (negative reinforcement). If working 20 hours a week in a store has led to a regular paycheck, you will likely want to keep working (assuming that the check is large enough!).

Imagine you are standing in line for a roller coaster or sitting in the audience waiting for the newest *Star Wars* movie to screen. If you are eagerly anticipating

● **Incentive:** A stimulus that draws animals (including humans) toward a particular goal, in anticipation of a reward.

Rewarding a child merely for performing an activity can undermine *intrinsic motivation*—it can make children less likely to engage in that activity for its own sake (Deci et al., 1999b; Lepper et al., 1973). But this need not occur. For example, praise can increase intrinsic motivation, provided it has a number of characteristics, including being perceived as sincere, focusing on personal competence and positive traits (but not by relying on social comparisons), and helping the recipient feel autonomous (Cialdini et al., 1998; Eisenberger & Cameron, 1996; Henderlong & Lepper, 2002).

the upcoming event, a host of brain areas has become active. For one, your amygdala is probably triggering your autonomic nervous system—a tingling excitement is part and parcel of the anticipation of having a particularly good time. The amygdala—which we've just seen is a key player in emotion—is connected to the hypothalamus, and thereby can trigger activation of the sympathetic nervous system; it also has connections to brain areas that produce the neurotransmitters dopamine and adrenaline (Cardinal et al., 2002). In addition, researchers have discovered a "cheerleader" signal in the brain, which increases as an animal nears its goal and stops right before the goal is actually reached. This signal arises in the anterior cingulate cortex, a brain area that is also involved in detecting errors and monitoring conflict between what you expect and what you get (Shidara & Richmond, 2002). Moreover, your feeling of happy anticipation also arises from neurons in other parts of the brain that are involved in emotion, notably areas of your frontal lobes and basal ganglia (O'Doherty et al., 2001; Schultz et al., 2000). In particular, areas that rely on dopamine—such as the nucleus accumbens (which is often considered part of the basal ganglia)—are activated when humans expect reward, even with rewards as varied as money (Breiter et al., 2001) and looking at attractive faces (Aharon et al., 2001). Indeed, such brain areas are activated more strongly by an attractive face in which the eyes look right at you than by the same face when the eyes are averted (Kampe et al., 2001, 2002).

Classical conditioning may play a role in determining what is an incentive by making a previously neutral stimulus desirable (Bindra, 1968; see Chapter 6). Patients with damage to the ventral medial frontal lobe seem unable either to draw on the results of such learning or to set up new emotional associations that can guide them to make good decisions in the future (Bechara et al., 2000).

Needs and Wants: The Stick and the Carrot

Different things motivate different people: A monk is not motivated to make money; an entrepreneur is not motivated to give away all earthly possessions and seek enlightenment on a mountaintop. Moreover, you are not motivated by the same forces day in and day out; rather, motivations may shift over the course of the day (or year, or life span). A particular motivation comes to the fore when you have a *need* or *want*. A **need** is a condition that arises from the lack of a requirement. Needs give rise to drives, which push you to reach a particular goal that will reduce the need. Lacking nutrients creates a need; hunger is a drive that will lead you to fill that need. In contrast, a **want** is a condition that arises when you have an unmet goal that will not fill a requirement. A want causes the goal to act as an incentive. You might *need* to eat, but you don't *need* a fancier car, although you might desperately *want* one—and the promise of a new car for working hard over the summer would be an incentive for you to put in long hours on the job. You are not necessarily aware of your needs or wants; **implicit motives** are needs and wants that direct your behavior unconsciously. After the mugging John wasn't aware of his need to eat, but he was only too well aware of his wanting to be with Barbara.

● **Need:** A condition that arises from the lack of a requirement; needs give rise to drives.

● **Want:** A condition that arises when you have an unmet goal that will not fill a requirement; wants turn goals into incentives.

● **Implicit motive:** A need or want that unconsciously directs behavior.

Is There More Than One Type of Reward?

For all needs and wants, we think of the goal as reinforcing the behaviors that lead to it. But what makes the goal rewarding? What is "reward"? Even the strongest regulatory needs, creating drives such as hunger and thirst, arise from the brain—and those needs are satisfied not by what we do directly, but rather by the effects of our actions on the brain. To understand why something is rewarding, we must look more closely at the brain's response to events in the world. By looking at the brain mechanisms underlying reward, we find support for the distinction between needs and wants.

In Chapter 3 we discussed the idea of a "pleasure center." Olds and Milner (1954) found that rats who received electrical stimulation in certain brain areas acted as if they desired more of it. Later research showed that Olds and Milner had stumbled on a brain system that underlies reward when an animal has been deprived of the reinforcer. **Deprived reward** is reward that occurs when you have filled a biological need. Such reward arises from the brain pathway that runs from certain parts of the brain stem, through the (lateral) hypothalamus, on up to specific parts of the limbic system and the frontal lobes (Baxter et al., 2000; Kalivas & Nakamura, 1999; Rolls & Cooper, 1974; Wise, 1996). Many of the neurons in this circuit use, or are affected by, dopamine. Drugs that block the action of dopamine also block the rewarding effect of brain stimulation (Nader et al., 1997) and of normal reinforcers such as food or water. When given these dopamine-blockers, experimental animals (usually rats) begin to respond normally to obtain reinforcement, but then lose interest. Because the drugs are blocking the rewarding effect of the reinforcer, the animals' response undergoes extinction (Geary & Smith, 1985; Schneider et al., 1990). Blocking dopamine can disrupt both unconditioned and conditioned positive reinforcement (Beninger, 1983, 1989; Wise, 1982). At least in some situations, the dopamine may actually signal that a reward is expected, not simply that a reward has been obtained (Cardinal et al., 2002; Garris et al., 1999; Hollerman & Schultz, 1998; Hollerman et al., 1998; Schultz, 1997; Schultz et al., 1997).

There is good evidence that the brain has a second system, which operates for **nondeprived reward,** reward that occurs when you haven't actually required the rewarding stimulus or activity—in other words, when you had a want but not a need. For example, John hadn't eaten since noon on the day of the mugging. After the fear and excitement of that experience, and the calming effect of Barbara's company, he realized how hungry he was. The pleasure he then found in eating was mediated by brain circuits used in deprived reward, which rely on dopamine. In contrast, at the end of the meal, even though he was no longer hungry, he ordered a sinful ice-cream-drenched-in-hot-chocolate-sauce dessert simply because he wanted it. In this case, he was nondeprived. Although dopamine plays a crucial role in producing the rewarding effects of a stimulus or activity that fills a deprivation, it does not play a role when you are not deprived. A key part of the brain involved in nondeprived reward is in the brain stem. Lesions in this area knock out the system that registers reward when an animal is not deprived, but leave intact the system for deprived reward (Bechara & Van der Kooy, 1992; Berridge, 1996; Nader et al., 1997).

Did John want dessert simply because he *liked* the taste? Possibly, but *wanting* something is not the same thing as *liking* it. For example, you can like a particular tree, bridge, or sunset very much without wanting it—and most of us can even like chocolate very much but not always want it. In fact, distinct neural circuits underlie

● **Deprived reward:** Reward that occurs when a biological need is filled.

● **Nondeprived reward:** Reward that occurs even when a requirement is not being met.

● **Need for achievement (nAch):** The need to reach goals that require skilled performance or competence to be accomplished.

liking something (receiving pleasure from perceiving it or thinking about it) and wanting it (Cardinal et al., 2002; Robinson & Berridge, 2001; Wyvell & Berridge, 2000). Nevertheless, liking the taste of something can motivate you to eat it, and the nondeprived reward system will make the experience gratifying even if you aren't hungry.

The existence of different brain systems for deprived and nondeprived reward is grounds for drawing a psychological distinction between needs and wants, between motivation that arises when a requirement must be filled and motivation that arises when a goal that is not a requirement is desired. Figure 10.6 summarizes the relation between these different facets of motivation.

FIGURE 10.6 Needs and Wants

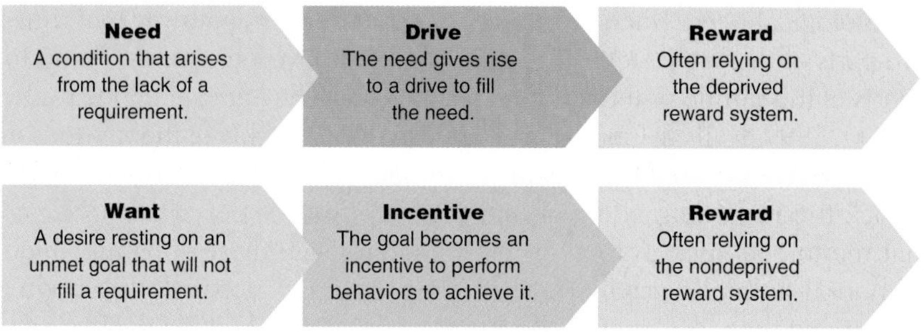

| **Need** A condition that arises from the lack of a requirement. | **Drive** The need gives rise to a drive to fill the need. | **Reward** Often relying on the deprived reward system. |

| **Want** A desire resting on an unmet goal that will not fill a requirement. | **Incentive** The goal becomes an incentive to perform behaviors to achieve it. | **Reward** Often relying on the nondeprived reward system. |

Needs and wants typically trigger different sorts of events.

Types of Needs: No Shortage of Shortages

There are psychological as well as bodily needs. Researchers have proposed that these include a need to be competent, to be autonomous (Sheldon et al., 1996), to have social approval, to be dominant or in control (Kim & Kim, 1997), to be affiliated with others, to be powerful (McClelland et al., 1989), to reach closure (Kruglanski & Webster, 1996; Taris, 2000), to understand, to maintain self-esteem, and even to find the world benevolent (Stevens & Fiske, 1995). Most of the pertinent studies examine individual differences in various needs. These individual differences probably arise from differences in personal inherited temperament (Kagan, 1994a) and differences in personal experiences, such as interactions with peers (Harris, 1998) and family (Sulloway, 1996).

A classic example of a psychological need is the **need for achievement** (nAch; McClelland & Atkinson, 1953), which is the need to reach goals that require skilled

What sorts of needs do you suppose motivated President Franklin Delano Roosevelt? During all the days of FDR's presidency (1933–1945), he could not walk without the use of metal braces or crutches (he contracted polio in 1921 and was paralyzed thereafter). However, this did not stop him from getting around the White House on his own by using his hands to crawl from one room to another.

performance or competence to be accomplished. There is a large body of research assessing the consequences of differences in this need (for example, Neel et al., 1986; Spangler, 1992). People who have a high need for achievement tend to assume that their successes are due to their personal characteristics, whereas their failures are due to environmental circumstances (Nathawat et al., 1997; Weiner & Kukla, 1970). In a meta-analysis, Spangler (1992) found that measures of "implicit" (that is, not conscious) need for achievement predict actual success better than "explicit" (or conscious) need, as measured by questionnaires filled in by participants.

Another need that has attracted considerable research is the *need for cognition* (NC), which is the need to engage in and enjoy thinking (Cacciopo & Petty, 1982; Cacciopo et al., 1996). To assess whether an individual is motivated by the need for cognition, John Cacciopo and his colleagues developed a test that includes true–false items such as "I really enjoy a task that involves coming up with new solutions to problems." People whose test scores indicate that they have high NC share key characteristics. They tend to draw more inferences when they evaluate an advertisement (Stayman & Kardes, 1992), think more about a persuasive communication and subsequently remember more of it (Cacciopo, et al., 1986), think more about attitudes they have just expressed (Lassiter et al., 1996; Leone & Ensley, 1986), are less affected by the way a problem is stated when they reason (Chatterjee et al., 2000; Smith & Levin, 1996), and tend to get better grades (Sadowski & Guelgoez, 1996).

Abraham Maslow (1970) created a hierarchy of physical and emotional needs, illustrated in Figure 10.7. Lower-level needs are considered more essential to life,

FIGURE 10.7 Maslow's Hierarchy of Needs

According to Maslow's theory, needs lower in the pyramid must be met before needs higher in the pyramid become the focus of concerns.

Self-Actualization Needs
Be all that you are capable of becoming

Aesthetic Needs
Harmony and order

Cognitive Needs
Understand the world, creating curiosity

Esteem Needs
Mastery and feeling appreciated by others

Belongingness Needs
Sense of belonging and love

Safety Needs
Shelter, protection

Physiological Needs
Water, food, air

and must be met before needs further up the hierarchy can be addressed and satisfied. Ascending the hierarchy, the needs are considered less basic because they arise less frequently and, if not met, do not seriously impair the quality of life. You can live without understanding the world, but not without air or food. According to Maslow's theory, once a need is met, it becomes less important, and unmet, higher-level needs become more important. During crises (such as loss of a home by fire), needs regress to a lower level and higher-level needs are put on hold.

Maslow's hierarchy of needs has had an enormous impact on how people think about motivation, particularly in the business world (Soper et al., 1995). But is it right? There are three major difficulties with Maslow's theory. First, research has produced mixed evidence, at best, for the idea that needs are organized into a hierarchy. Results of questionnaire studies generally show that the levels are not clearly distinct from one another, as revealed by factor analysis (Wahba & Bridwell, 1976). In addition, there is no clear-cut ordering of needs (Soper et al., 1995; Wahba & Bridwell, 1976). Beer (1966), for example, found that female clerks reported strong social needs and a strong need for self-actualization but not a strong need for self-esteem. Moreover, the importance of different needs appears to vary in different cultures (Diaz-Guerrero & Diaz-Loving, 2000). Second, there is no good evidence that unmet needs become more important and that met needs become less important. In fact, Hall and Nougaim (1968) found that the longer a need was satisfied, the more important it became. Third, this theory fails to explain various phenomena—for example, why people voluntarily go to war and put themselves in the line of fire (Fox, 1982).

Achievement in Individualist Versus Collectivist Cultures

Many of the goals that motivate us are provided by groups, and the structure of the society determines what sorts of activities will be reinforced. Cultures can be divided into two general types that affect achievement motivation differently (although these differences may often be matters of degree and may vary for subgroups within a culture; Oyserman et al., 2002). **Individualist cultures,** such as that of the United States, emphasize the rights and responsibilities of the individual over those of the group. **Collectivist cultures,** such as that of China, emphasize the rights and responsibilities of the group over those of the individual. Such cultural differences have been shown to affect achievement goals. For example, Anglo-Australians (from an individualist culture) have been found to be focused more on personal success than on family or groups, whereas Sri Lankans (from a collectivist culture) are oriented more toward their families and groups (Niles, 1998). Similarly, Sagie, Elizur, and Hirotsugu (1996) found that Americans had higher achievement motivation (as measured by scales that emphasize individual achievement) than did Japanese or Hungarians, members of collectivist cultures.

Thus, growing up in one or the other type of culture influences a person's needs and wants. The effects of growing up in an individualist culture are not without a cost: Tafarodi and Swann (1996) found that Americans like themselves less than do Chinese. Why? Tafarodi and Swann believe that members of collectivist cultures are raised in a way that leads others to like them, in part by de-emphasizing competition among individuals. This may lead to greater self-liking if we assume that our self-liking is increased if other people like us. In individualist cultures, on the other hand, members are raised to strive for freedom and independence, which tends to produce competition and conflict. In such cultures, there are more feelings of self-competence, but fewer of self-liking.

● **Individualist culture:** A culture that emphasizes the rights and responsibilities of the individual over those of the group.

● **Collectivist culture:** A culture that emphasizes the rights and responsibilities of the group over those of the individual.

● **Learned helplessness:** The condition that occurs after an animal has an aversive experience in which nothing it does can affect what happens to it, and so it simply gives up and stops trying to change the situation or to escape.

Looking *at* Levels

Learned Helplessness

People not only can learn new strategies for coping with problems, but they also can learn to give up trying. Martin Seligman and his colleagues first described **learned helplessness,** which occurs when an animal has an aversive experience in which nothing it does can affect what happens to it, and so it simply gives up and stops trying to change the situation or to escape (Mikulincer, 1994). As shown in Figure 10.8 (Overmeier & Seligman, 1967), when dogs were put in a cage in which they could not escape shocks, they eventually gave up responding and just huddled on the floor and endured—and they continued to do so even when they were moved to a new cage in which it was easy to escape the shocks. This condition can also afflict humans who experience a lack of control over negative events: If nothing you do seems to make an abusive spouse stop tormenting you, you may eventually just give up and stop trying. Learned helplessness can lead to depression and a range of stress-related problems.

It is clear that learned helplessness depends on events at the different levels of analysis. At the level of the group, others may create the situation from which you cannot escape. For example, a child trapped in an abusive family, who has no control over the situation, may eventually exhibit learned helplessness. Events at the level of the group can directly interact with an individual's experience, which then affects the tendency toward learned helplessness. This connection has been clearly demonstrated with rats, which were given inescapable shock either alone or in pairs. When in pairs, the rats fought with each other when they were being shocked. When tested individually 2 days later, the rats that were stressed in pairs displayed less learned helplessness than those stressed alone (Zhukov & Vinogradova, 1998). The fighting may simply have distracted them from the shock, or this effect may reflect neural events that occurred when the rats fought, which in turn protected them against learned helplessness.

In addition, many studies have examined what happens in the brain when an animal has received uncontrollable shock and descends into learned helplessness. The findings indicate that learned helplessness has a wide range of complex effects throughout the brain. For

FIGURE 10.8 The Classic "Learned Helplessness" Experiment

An animal is placed in a cage and shocked. Initially, the animal tries to escape, but it can do nothing to avoid or prevent the shocks.

The animal eventually gives up.

When the animal is moved into a new cage in which only a small barrier separates the side where shocks are delivered from the side where no shocks occur, it does not try to escape the shock, even when the shock is signaled by a tone.

example, there is evidence that learned help-lessness can lower the levels of the neuro-transmitter serotonin, or decrease the num-bers of receptors that are affected by it, in various parts of the brain (Amat et al., 1998; Papolos et al., 1996). Although some of these effects may be caused by stress per se (Wu et al., 1999), at least some are caused by the effects of the impossi-bility of escaping shock, not solely the shock itself (Edwards et al., 1992; Petty et al., 1994). It is possible to breed rats that are particularly sus-ceptible to this syndrome (Lachman et al.,

1993), which suggests that some people could conceiv-ably be genetically prone to this problem. Clearly, events at the different levels interact, and all must be taken into account if we are to understand when and why animals and humans come to behave as if they were helpless—even when they're not.

TEST YOURSELF!

1. What are the sources of motivation?
2. What is the difference between "needs" and "wants," and how does culture affect them?

Hunger and Eating: Not Just About Fueling the Body

When he sat down to dinner the evening of the mugging, John ate mechanically, paying little attention to what was in front of him. Food was now the last thing on John's mind, and he didn't have much of an appetite, even after joining Barbara in the safety and warmth of the restaurant. But after the first few bites, he realized that he was terrifically hungry and had no trouble polishing off a large dinner. He particularly liked Italian food, partly because it was one of his mother's specialties. Now, just smelling the richness and flavor of the homemade ravioli and fresh tomato sauce relaxed him and made his mouth water.

One of the drives that is best understood—and that motivates us each and every day—is hunger. Hunger is the classic drive that relies on the deprived reward system; by definition, to be hungry is to be deprived of food. However, not all eat-ing occurs because we are hungry (Wilson, 2002). Sometimes we eat simply be-cause it's fun, in which case the pleasure ultimately relies on the operation of the nondeprived reward system. Hunger, and its satisfaction, affects many aspects of our lives, social and experiential as well as biological.

Eating Behavior: The Hungry Mind in the Hungry Body

Your life is sustained by your body's **metabolism,** the sum of the chemical events in each of your cells, events that convert food molecules to the energy needed for the cells to function. Eating is necessary to maintain your metabolism. What factors determine what and when we eat?

Is Being Hungry the Opposite of Being Full?

Although you might think of hunger as a continuum from starvation to satiety, hunger in fact arises from the action of two distinct brain systems. One system leads you to feel a need to eat; another leads you to feel satiated (Davis & Levine, 1977; Yeomans & Gray, 1997).

● **Metabolism:** The sum of the chemical events in each of the body's cells, events that convert food molecules to the energy needed for the cells to function.

The feeling of a need to eat arises when your brain senses that the level of food molecules in your blood is too low. The brain registers the quantities of two major types of food molecules: *glucose* (a type of sugar) and *fatty acids* (Friedman, 1991; Friedman et al., 1986b). In contrast, "feeling full" does not depend on the level of food molecules in the blood: You feel full well before food is digested and food molecules enter the bloodstream. If you suspect that feeling full has something to do with the state of your stomach, you're on the right track. If food is removed with a flexible tube from the stomach of a rat that has just eaten to satisfaction, the rat will eat just enough to replace the loss (Davis & Campbell, 1973). But a full stomach is not enough to tell an animal to stop eating. Filling an animal's stomach with saltwater does not diminish appetite as much as filling it with milk, even if the fluids are placed directly into the stomach so that the animals cannot taste them (Deutsch et al., 1978). The stomach contains detectors that register the food value of its contents, and this information is transmitted to the brain. People know when to stop eating largely because of signals sent by sensory neurons in the stomach to the brain. Similar signals are also sent by other organs, including the upper part of the small intestine and the liver.

The brain system that regulates eating is surprisingly complex, as is revealed when it is disrupted by a stroke. For example, a person can develop what is known as *gourmand syndrome,* a neurological disorder in which people become obsessed with fine food. Such people do not report being hungry all of the time, and may not overeat—but their entire lives become centered on food.

What part of the brain detects these signals? Some 50 years ago researchers thought they had found "start" and "stop" eating centers in the brain. They had discovered that even small lesions (holes) in the lateral (side) part of the hypothalamus caused an animal to lose interest in food, even to the point of death by starvation. When this structure was electrically stimulated, the animal ate more and worked harder for food (Anand & Brobeck, 1952; Teitelbaum & Stellar, 1954). In contrast, the ventromedial (bottom, central) part of the hypothalamus was thought to be the center in the brain that told an animal it was full and should stop eating.

Other research, however, soon highlighted the difficulties in interpreting these findings. Lesions to the lateral hypothalamus suppressed the animals' interest not only in eating but also in drinking, sex, and even caring for their young; the result was often a general sluggishness. Researchers found that the lesions were disrupting not only the neurons in the lateral hypothalamus, but also connections between other areas. Similarly, when the ventromedial hypothalamus is damaged, animals don't just fail to stop eating, they become picky eaters (Ferguson & Keesey, 1975); indeed, they initially overeat carbohydrates (Sclafani & Aravich, 1983; Sclafani et al., 1983).

Improved methods allowed researchers to clear these muddy waters. When chemicals are used to destroy only neurons in the lateral hypothalamus and none of the connections that pass through it, hunger *is* reduced more than most other drives (Dunnett et al., 1985; Stricker et al., 1978). The ventromedial hypothalamus appears to affect other brain regions that allow stored food molecules to be released; thus, when it is damaged, the animal has no choice but to keep eating (Weingarten et al., 1985). Rather than having centers in the hypothalamus that say "eat" or "don't eat," we, and other animals, have some neurons that signal when nutrient levels are low, and others that signal when stored food molecules should be released (Shiraishi et al., 2000). These neurons act not so much like buttons or switches as like sensors that provide information that guides attention and behavior. In fact, learning plays a role in how an animal interprets such signals; only after prior experience that eating reduces hunger signals and drinking reduces thirst signals do young rats intentionally seek out food or drink (as appropriate) when they are food deprived or dehydrated (Changizi et al, 2002).

Appetite: A Moving Target

The early phases of eating depend on the taste of food. When you take the first bites of a meal or snack, you probably experience the *appetizer effect*; if those first bites taste good, your appetite is stimulated. This effect is driven in part by *opioids* in the brain; as you might suspect from their name, opioids are chemicals that behave like opium-derived drugs and cause you to experience pleasure. The opioids are released when you first eat food that tastes good (Yeomans & Gray, 1997).

As you continue to eat, your responses to food-related stimuli change. After eating some fresh-baked cookies, the smell of them doesn't seem quite as heavenly as it did before you ate them. If people have had their fill of a certain food, they rate its odor as less pleasant than they did before eating it (Duclaux et al., 1973). However, when the flavor, texture, color, or shape of a food is changed, people will eat more of the same food (Rolls et al., 1981b). After you've eaten a few chocolate chip cookies, you might find yourself not interested in more cookies, but happy to have some fresh-baked bread.

Not surprisingly, these changes in your appetite are linked to events in the hypothalamus. Neurons in the lateral hypothalamus initially fire to the sight or taste of a food, and then reduce their firing after an animal has eaten its fill of that food (Burton et al., 1976). These neurons are selective: After they stop responding to one food, they can still be stimulated by another (Rolls et al., 1981b; Critchley & Rolls, 1996, report similar findings in regions of the frontal lobe that are involved in emotional responses). But appetite, like most psychological phenomena, is governed by a complex set of brain areas. In one study, participants' brains were scanned as they ate their fill of chocolate, and then kept on eating and eating (Small et al., 2001). As they ate beyond the point when the candy was appetizing, activity changed in parts of the frontal lobes and the insula (which registers bodily sensations).

And appetite isn't just about the brain. To understand why you eat the amount you do, you need to consider events at the different levels of analysis. When alone, you vary the size of a meal depending on the size and length of time since your last meal—for example, by eating less for dinner if you had a late lunch (Woods et al., 2000). But this biological process doesn't work so well when you eat with others (De Castro, 1990). When people eat in groups, they do not vary the size of their meals to reflect their degree of hunger. Moreover, people report eating a greater amount when more people are present for a meal. Part of this effect may simply reflect the fact that when more people are present, the meal takes longer to complete. At the level of the person, men want chocolate (and report that they enjoy it more) when they are in a good mood, for example after they've watched films that make them happy (such as *When Harry Met Sally*; Macht et al., 2002). Moreover, anything that reminds you of good food you've eaten on a previous occasion—an event at the level of the person—can increase hunger. As usual, events at the different levels interact. For example, you get hungry when reminded of good food in part because your body responds both to perceptions of food and to thoughts of food by secreting insulin. **Insulin** is a hormone that stimulates the storage of food molecules in the form of fat. Thus, insulin reduces the level of food in the blood, which may increase hunger.

● **Insulin:** A hormone that stimulates the storage of food molecules in the form of fat.

Why Does It Taste Good?

What about preferences for specific foods? Some of our tastes clearly are a consequence of beliefs that develop with experience. Some people develop disgust reactions to certain foods (Rozin & Fallon, 1986), and the very idea of that food then keeps them away from it. Such *cognitive taste aversion* is apparently long-lasting and can be formed without classical conditioning (for instance, without being nauseated after eating the food; see Batsell & Brown, 1998). Rozin and his colleagues have shown that people apparently believe that "once in contact, always in contact." If a neutral food was in contact with an aversive food, the aversive properties seem to transfer. Suppose someone dunked a sterilized, dead cockroach briefly in your glass of water. Would you want to take a sip? The answer is probably a resounding no. Similarly, if a morsel of premium chocolate fudge were molded into the shape of feces, the shape alone would make it unappealing. Rozin and his colleagues have also shown that Americans harbor exaggerated beliefs about the harmful effects of some foods; in fact, many incorrectly believe that salt and fat are harmful even at trace levels (Rozin et al., 1996).

Beliefs also play another role in determining what we want to eat: Perhaps unconsciously, people believe that "you are what you eat." Nemeroff and Rozin (1989) asked people to rate qualities of people who "ate boar" and those who "ate turtle." The boar eaters were believed to be more likely to have boarlike qualities, such as being bearded and heavy-set.

Culture plays a key role in shaping our tastes in food: the French would never give up their beloved snails or frogs; Koreans find pickled snakes delicious; Filipinos enjoy unhatched chicks in the shell; the Germans savor stuffed pig intestines; and Chileans eat a kind of sea anemone whose looks would qualify it to star in a science-fiction movie.

Overeating: When Enough Is Not Enough

We humans like the taste of fatty foods, which is bad news because eating too much fat can lead to a variety of diseases, such as diabetes, cardiovascular disease, cancer, high blood pressure, and gallbladder disease (Schiffman et al., 1999). Diet books and cookbooks are best-sellers. Does this seem ironic to you? Do we want to lose weight so that we can eat more? Or does our love of eating make us need to diet? Our culture places a premium on being thin. Nonetheless, some of us overeat, and some of us are obese—why?

Set Point: Your Normal Weight

If you lose weight, fat cells become less likely to give up their stored energy. In addition, receptors in your brain that are sensitive to low levels of fat then become active and make you hungry, you eat more, and thus you end up gaining weight. This mechanism reminded researchers of the way a thermostat turns on the heater when the room is too cold, bringing it back to a constant temperature. This analogy led to the notion that animals, including humans, settle at a particular body weight that is easiest to maintain; this weight is called the **set point**. For many years, researchers thought of the set point as relatively constant, and homeostatic mechanisms kept it that way (Nisbett, 1972; Stunkard, 1982). However, more recently some researchers have argued that your set point doesn't maintain weight the way a thermostat maintains room temperature (Berthoud, 2002; Levine & Billington, 1997). Rather, although this process usually keeps your weight relatively stable, your weight can change if your environment changes (for example, so that you are tempted by more and fattier foods), your activities change (for example, you walk to work and thus exercise more often), or your emotional state changes (for example, you become depressed and listless).

● **Set point:** The particular body weight that is easiest for an animal (including a human) to maintain.

Why would you ever eat more than your body needs? Cognitive systems in the brain are connected to the hypothalamic systems that underlie hunger, and apparently can "overpower" these hypothalamic mechanisms (Berthoud, 2002). Thus, we sometimes eat not because we're hungry, but because we're bored, lonely, or simply because we think we ought to eat (perhaps because the clock says it's lunchtime). If you eat when your body doesn't need the energy, you are "overeating"; if you overeat for a prolonged time, the number of fat cells in your body increases to store the additional energy. Thus, you gain weight. In contrast, when you lose weight, each fat cell becomes thinner, but you don't lose fat cells. This may explain why it's generally easier to gain weight than to lose it. Regular, moderately vigorous exercise can speed up your metabolism, leading your cells to need more energy even when you are not exercising. This is the best method of changing your balance of energy input and output, and thereby of losing weight.

Obesity

An obese person is defined as one who is more than 20% heavier than the medically ideal weight for that person's sex, height, and bone structure. By this standard, almost one third of Americans are obese. But why? Consider three theories.

Obese people have the same "will power" to resist eating junk food as nonobese people.

Fat Personalities? Do these people have weak characters that make them slaves to food? No. The personality characteristics of obese and nonobese people are similar (Nilsson et al., 1998; Poston et al., 1999). Indeed, President William Howard Taft (president from 1909–1913) was a grossly obese man, weighing over 300 pounds. He was so overweight that, after getting stuck in a White House bathtub, he had a new tub constructed that would hold four average-sized men. However, his size did not deter him from achieving the highest office in the land.

So, why are some people obese? Some explanations have grown out of psychodynamic theory. According to one such theory, obese people eat when they feel stress, as a kind of defense. The evidence for this theory is mixed: Obese people do not always overeat when they feel stress and may instead tend to overeat when aroused, positively or negatively (Andrews & Jones, 1990; McKenna, 1972). Overeating is not the same thing as an eating disorder (see Chapter 14); people don't necessarily overeat because they have a psychological problem.

Fat Genes? There is good reason to believe that at least some forms of obesity have a genetic basis—which may not even be connected to how much a person actually eats. If one identical twin is obese, the other probably is too; variations in weight may be as much as 70% heritable (Berthoud, 2002; Ravussin & Bouchard, 2000). In fact, 58 distinct genes and portions of all chromosomes but chromosome Y (the male sex chromosome) have been related to obesity (Rankinen, et al., 2002). Bouchard, a researcher in this area, notes that genes may affect weight in numerous ways: "Some affect appetite, some affect satiety. Some affect metabolic rate" (quoted in Gladwell, 1998, p. 53). Thus, the genetics of obesity will not be a simple story, but the story is beginning to be told. First, the neurons involved in brain regions that register satiety appear to rely in part on the neurotransmitter serotonin (Blundell, 1977, 1984, 1986; Blundell & Halford, 1998), and mutant mice that lack specific receptors for this neurotransmitter will keep eating until they become obese (Tecott et al., 1995). The notion that humans may act the same way is supported by the finding that people gain weight if they take medication that happens to block these receptors (Fitton & Heel, 1990); moreover, people who take drugs that activate these receptors report being less hungry, and actually lose weight while on the medication (Sargent et al., 1997).

In addition, a gene known as *ob* (short for *obese*) has been shown to play a role in governing eating and weight. This gene governs the release of a hormone called *leptin* (*leptos* is Greek for "thin"), which is released by fat cells. The more fat, the more leptin is in the blood. Leptin decreases food intake and increases energy expenditure (in part by increasing heat production; Wang et al., 1999). Leptin affects eating in part by interfering with a neurotransmitter called Neuropeptide Y (NPY), which induces eating (Inui, 1999). This interference occurs in the hypothalamus, by activating or inhibiting specific neurons (Yokosuka et al., 1998); indeed, hungry rats will work hard to receive electrical stimulation of key parts of the hypothalamus, but giving them leptin decreases the rate of such responding (Fulton et al., 2000). Rosenbaum and Leibel (1999) suggest that leptin may serve to maintain a constant level of body fat by acting as a signal to the brain that the amounts of stored fat and food intake are adequate.

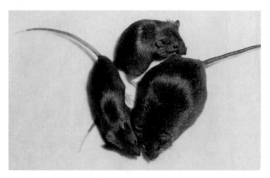

Genes can make a big difference. Researchers found that by altering a single gene, they could increase the production of substances that make a rat obese.

Given its role in regulating eating, some researchers hypothesized that obese people might have a defective ob gene—which, unlike the normal gene, fails to decrease eating after more fat is stored. However, studies have shown that only extremely obese people have a deficit in the ob gene, and this problem is unlikely to underlie most obesity (Berthoud, 2002; Mantzoros, 1999). Another candidate gene is involved in the regulation of the stress hormone cortisol. Scientists altered the genes of mice so that this particular gene was turned on only in fat cells (Masuzaki et al., 2001). These mice became obese, developing a "spare tire" around their middles—much like those of tubby humans who have an "apple shape." However, some obese humans have a "pear shape," gaining weight mostly in their thighs; these mice clearly didn't have that problem, so this one gene cannot explain all forms of obesity. Yet another gene has been discovered that determines whether the excess fat in food is converted to body fat or is turned into surplus body heat (Fleury et al., 1977). Animals that do not have this gene become fat when they eat amounts that normally do not increase weight. How does such a gene work? One mechanism could be the "fidget factor"; that is, the gene could affect the overall level of physical activity (Bouchard, as quoted in Gladwell, 1998, p. 53). Consider the findings reported by Levine, Eberhardt, and Jensen (1999), who asked a group of normal people to overeat a large amount each day for 8 weeks. At the end of this period there were large differences in how much fat the volunteers gained—some people gained literally 10 times as much as others. Levine and his colleagues found that the single biggest factor that determined whether people gained fat was the number of physical movements unrelated to sports or fitness regimens—"activities of daily living, fidgeting, spontaneous muscle contraction" and the effort of maintaining posture when not reclining. Each movement burned up extra energy in the extra food so that it was not stored as fat. We know that temperament is partly innate (Kagan et al., 1994), and it is possible that differences in temperament lead to differences in such activity levels, which in turn affect whether extra calories are burned or stored.

Fat Environment. As we have seen, genes determine a reaction range, and the environment sets individuals within that range (Chapter 9). Some people have a propensity to become fat, but do so only in certain environments (Ravussin & Bouchard, 2000). Overeating is encouraged by many aspects of our environment: Food is relatively cheap, fast foods are high in fat, and portions have grown larger in the United States (but not in many parts of Europe). At the same time, people exercise less not only because most of us drive or ride to work, but also because our amusements, such as watching television and surfing the Web, are sedentary. Hill and Peters (1998) suggest approaches to "curing the environment," which is supporting a virtual epidemic in obesity: (1) Educating people to eat smaller portions; (2) Making foods that are low in fat and calories more available; and (3) Encouraging more physical activity.

Some obese people are capable of losing large amounts of weight, and keeping the weight off (Tinker & Tucker, 1997). These people are able to adopt healthier eating and exercise habits. Note, however, that changes in the environment will be effective only if the reaction range for weight is relatively large (that is, if the genes define a wide range of possibilities). If the reaction range of certain genes that result in obesity is small, then people who have those genes may not have much choice in determining how heavy they are.

Looking *at* Levels

The Starvation Diet

In American culture, many of us are at some point concerned about our weight and thus may go on a diet. The most commonly recommended diet for obese people requires them to cut their normal food intake in half (Stallone & Stunkard, 1994). Keys and his colleagues (1950) studied the effects of such a diet on a group of 36 healthy young men. After 6 months, these men weighed on average 25% less than they had at the outset. In addition, they experienced many dramatic psychological changes, resulting from events at all three levels of analysis. At the level of the brain, their perceptual processes and sleep patterns changed. They slept less, became more sensitive to light and noise, had less tolerance for cold, and showed various other physical symptoms (and later studies have shown that dieting disrupts your ability to focus attention; Williams et al., 2002).

At the level of the person, the content of their thoughts changed. They became obsessed with food. Many began to hoard not only food, but also random junk. (This also happens with rats who are put on such diets [Fantino & Cabanac, 1980] and with people who have eating disorders and put themselves on similar diets [Crisp et al., 1980].) At the level of the group, they lost interest in sex and in interacting with other people. They also became irritable, anxious, depressed, and argumentative. Many of these symptoms persisted for months after the men began to eat normally again.

Of course, the effects at the three levels also interacted. Because the men were more irritable, others were less likely to seek their company and thus provide distraction from thoughts of food. Because their senses had become more acute, they were likely to avoid social situations. The most sobering point about this study is the realization that many people today voluntarily put themselves on stringent diets, without realizing the consequences.

TEST YOURSELF!

1. What makes us hungry and leads us to eat particular foods at particular times?
2. How is your weight kept relatively constant, and what factors will cause your weight to change?
3. Why do some people become obese?

Sex: Not Just About Having Babies

John had planned his anniversary dinner with Barbara carefully. He picked a restaurant that was a sentimental favorite of theirs, with fabulous food, soft lighting, and relaxing music. He suggested that they eat early so that there would be time for a romantic evening at his apartment. Unfortunately, after the mugging, he wasn't in the mood. But when they arrived at his apartment, he found that romantic thoughts returned and he enjoyed Barbara's company more than ever.

Sexual Behavior: A Many-Splendored Thing

People engage in sexual relations for two general reasons: to have babies (*reproductive sex*) and for pleasure (*recreational sex*). The vast majority of sexual acts, on the order of 98% (Linner, 1972), are for pleasure, as opposed to procreation. Sex leads to some of the most intense of all positive emotions, and hence it is valued highly by members of our species. The earliest known attempts at contraception were developed 4,000 years ago by the Egyptians; they thought dried crocodile dung would do the job.

Alfred Kinsey began the first systematic surveys about human sexual behavior in the late 1940s. He and his colleagues interviewed thousands of Americans about their sex lives. Kinsey found that people frequently reported sexual practices then considered rare or even abnormal. However, attempts to study sexual behavior ran into some unique problems. As Freud wrote (1910, p. 41), "People in general are not candid over sexual matters, they do not show their sexuality freely, but to conceal it wear a heavy overcoat of a tissue of lies, as though the weather were bad in the world of sexuality." Psychologists have had difficulty getting beyond this "tissue of lies," and even today there is debate about whether we have reliable information about many facets of human sexuality.

Most studies of sexual behavior rely on surveys. But would you volunteer to be in a study of sexual behavior? How about filling in a questionnaire about your most intimate moments? Researchers have found that not everybody is equally willing to participate in studies of sexual behavior, and thus the data are likely to come from a biased sample. Bogaert (1996), for example, found that the undergraduate males who volunteered for a study on human sexuality differed in many ways from males who volunteered for a study on personality: The former group had more sexual experience, were more interested in sexual variety, were more inclined to seek out sensation and excitement, and were less socially conforming and less likely to follow rules (Trivedi & Sabini [1998] report similar findings). In addition, people from different cultures may respond differently when asked about their sexual and reproductive behavior: Researchers found that Hispanic women reported less sexual activity when their interviewers were older, but African American women did not display this bias as strongly (Ford & Norris, 1997). The researchers suspected that this bias arose because the Hispanic culture has traditionally frowned on premarital sex for women, leading Hispanic women to underreport their sexual activity to older women who might disapprove.

In short, interview data about sex are suspect. Sampling bias as well as response bias can distort the results.

Sexual Responses: Step by Step

William Masters and Virginia Johnson (1966) were the first researchers to study systematically actual sexual behavior, not just reports of descriptions of it, with a large sample of participants. Their effort was the first that provided a look behind the "tissue of lies" about sex. Over the course of many years, Masters and Johnson brought thousands of men and women into their laboratory and devised ways to measure what the body does during sex. The outcome was a description of the stages the body passes through during sexual activity. They discovered that both men and women pass through four such stages: (1) *Excitement* (during the initial phases, when the person becomes aroused); (2) *Plateau* (a full level of arousal); (3) *Orgasm* (accompanied by muscle contractions, and in men ejaculation); and (4) *Resolution* (the release of sexual tension). These stages meld into one another, with no sharp divisions separating them (Levin, 1980, 1994).

The mountain of research they conducted led Masters and Johnson to reach four general conclusions: (1) Men and women are similar in their bodily reactions to sex; (2) Women tend to respond more slowly than men, but stay aroused longer; (3) Many women can have multiple orgasms, whereas men typically have a *refractory period*, a period of time following orgasm when they cannot become aroused again; and (4) Women reported that penis size is not related to sexual performance, unless the man is worried about it.

Others have built on Masters and Johnson's research and have developed a comprehensive description of the **sexual response cycle.** Our current understanding is that *sexual attraction* leads to *sexual desire, sexual excitement* (arousal), and possibly *sexual performance* (which involves becoming fully aroused, reaching orgasm, and then experiencing resolution followed by—for men—a refractory period).

Why do we have sexual responses at the times, and with the partners, we do? Not unexpectedly, events at all three levels of analysis play crucial roles in our sexual behavior.

The Role of Hormones: Do Chemicals Dictate Behavior?

In 1849, German scientist Arnold Berthold wondered why castrated roosters acted like hens. They stopped crowing, mating with hens, fighting, and engaging in other typical rooster behaviors. So he castrated roosters and then put the testes into their abdominal cavities. Shortly thereafter, the roosters started behaving like roosters again. Berthold reasoned that the testes produced their effects not because of nerves or other physical connections, but because they released something into the bloodstream. We now know that what the testes release is the male hormone *testosterone.*

Hormones are chemicals that are secreted into the bloodstream primarily by endocrine glands and that trigger receptors on neurons and other types of cells (see Chapter 3). Hormones are controlled in large part by the pituitary gland, the brain's "master gland." The pituitary gland in turn is controlled by the hypothalamus, which plays a major role in emotion and motivation and is affected by hormones produced in the body. When you are sexually aroused, hormones from the gonads (the testes and ovaries) act on the brain and genital tissue. **Androgens** are male hormones (such as testosterone), which cause many male characteristics such as beard growth and a low voice. **Estrogens,** female hormones, cause many female characteristics such as breast development and the bone structure of the female pelvis. The presence of the different hormones is not all-or-none between the sexes. Both types of hormones are present in both males and females, but to different degrees. Unlike their direct effects on physical characteristics, hormones don't directly dictate behavior. Rather, they lead to a tendency to *want* to behave

● Sexual response cycle (SRC): The stages the body passes through during sexual activity, now characterized as including sexual attraction, desire, excitement, and performance (which includes full arousal, orgasm, and resolution).

● Androgens: Male hormones, which cause many male characteristics such as beard growth and a low voice.

● Estrogens: Female hormones, which cause many female characteristics such as breast development and the bone structure of the female pelvis.

in certain ways in the presence of particular stimuli. That is, they modify motivation. For example, giving young women a dose of testosterone later caused their heart rates to speed up when they saw angry faces. This response could indicate that the women were more ready to "fight or defend status in face-to-face challenges" (van Honk et al., 2001; p. 241). Testosterone does more than influence sexual behavior.

In addition, changes in the level of sex hormones over the course of a woman's menstrual cycle affect the degree to which she is inclined to become sexually aroused. Slob and colleagues (1996) found that erotic videos increased the temperature of the female genital area more during the days just before ovulation than during the days following ovulation, and the women who were about to ovulate generally had increased sexual desire and sexual fantasies for the next 24 hours. In fact, researchers have found that women who were about to ovulate tended to classify very briefly presented pictures as sexual stimuli, both when the stimuli were in fact in this category (pictures of nude men) and when they were not (pictures of babies or objects related to body care; Krug et al., 1994). And when women are ovulating, they prefer "ruggedly handsome" male faces more than when they are not ovulating (Penton-Voak & Perrett, 2000). Moreover, women are more likely to be interested in men who are not their partners while they are ovulating (Gangestad et al., 2002). However, the effects of shifting hormone levels are only tendencies, affecting different people to different degrees (Regan, 1996). For example, Van Goozen and colleagues (1997) found that only those women who had premenstrual complaints had peak sexual interest during the ovulatory phase.

The relationship between hormones and motivation runs in both directions. In a famous study, a researcher who signed his paper only as "Anonymous" (1970) reported the effects of his building anticipation of female companionship after sustained periods of enforced celibacy. This man was a scientist who worked on a small island and only occasionally visited the mainland, where he would have brief periods of contact with the opposite sex. He apparently had time on his hands when he was alone, and decided to measure his beard growth every day by weighing his beard clippings after shaving. He found that his beard grew thicker as his visits to the mainland approached. Just thinking about the visit apparently caused increases in male hormones, which in turn caused increased beard growth. Researchers have also documented the reverse effect: Although single and married men have the same levels of testosterone in the morning, by the end of the day married men have less than unmarried men (testosterone normally decreases over the course of the day, but does so more sharply for married men; P. B. Gray et al., 2002). This was true for men who did or did not have children. Moreover, for those who did not have children, the more hours a man spent with his wife on his last day off work, the lower his testosterone levels.

But we are not simply creatures of our hormones. To study the role of testosterone on sexual behavior and mood, Schiavi and colleagues (1997) injected men who had difficulty having erections with the hormone twice a week for 6 weeks; this course was followed by injections of a placebo for 4 weeks (the change was not known to the participants). Although the participants did ejaculate more often when they were receiving the testosterone than when they were receiving the placebo, little else changed. Testosterone did not affect the amount of sexual satisfaction, the rigidity of the penis during sex, or mood.

The so-called sex hormones aren't the only ones that affect our sex lives (Meston & Frohlich, 2000). *Oxytocin* is a hormone (produced by the pituitary gland) that increases dramatically in women immediately after they give birth, and probably helps to forge the mother–infant emotional bond (Insel, 2000). Oxytocin is also released after orgasm, and may bond sex partners—perhaps even if they consciously don't like each other. Could oxytocin explain why "love is blind"? Future research will tell us.

Sexual Stimuli

We humans are visual creatures—probably about half the cerebral cortex is concerned with vision. Visual stimuli play a major role in sexual attraction, particularly for men (Przybyla & Byrne, 1984). How do visual sexual stimuli affect us? Karama and colleagues (2002) scanned the brains of men and women as they watched either erotic or neutral videos. Many of the brain areas involved in reward and the anticipation of reward were activated in both sexes when watching the erotic stimuli. Critically, the hypothalamus was only activated in the males—and the more strongly it was activated, the more strongly the male (but not the female) participants reported being aroused. This activation suggests that the erotic material not only stimulated the men but also motivated them to want to respond accordingly. In general, men reported being more strongly aroused than did women, which could either be the cause or the effect of the differences in how their brains were activated.

However, the tendency for visual stimuli to be less important for women is modified by culture. Effa-Heap (1996) reports that Nigerian 15- to 20-year-olds of both sexes preferred adult videos over other formats of pornography. In addition, the precise nature of the video material matters. Pearson and Pollack (1997) assessed women's level of sexual arousal when they watched sexually explicit films. The researchers compared two types of films, those designed for men and those designed specifically for women or male–female couples. The women who viewed the latter films reported greater arousal. Moreover, there are clear sex differences in the importance of other types of stimuli. Notably, women reported that body odor was the most important sensory quality that could turn them off sexually, whereas men were neutral regarding body odor (Herz & Cahill, 1997).

People use sex to satisfy different psychological needs. Cooper and colleagues (1998) showed that motivations for having sex can be thought of in terms of the two dimensions illustrated in Figure 10.9, which range from avoidance to approach (the horizontal dimension) and from social connection to independence (the vertical di-

FIGURE 10.9 Motives for Having Sex

People engage in sex for many reasons, which Cooper and colleagues (1998) characterize as falling along two dimensions.

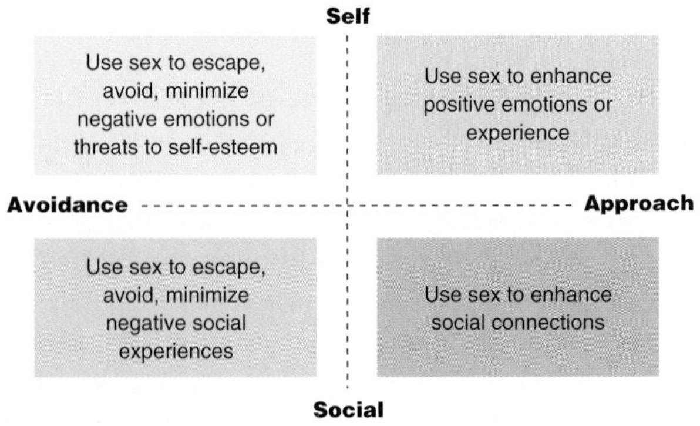

Self

Use sex to escape, avoid, minimize negative emotions or threats to self-esteem

Use sex to enhance positive emotions or experience

Avoidance — — — — — — — — — — — — — — — — — Approach

Use sex to escape, avoid, minimize negative social experiences

Use sex to enhance social connections

Social

mension). The importance of these dimensions is different for different people and in different contexts—for instance, for people in stable relationships, exclusive relationships, or relationships that are both stable and exclusive.

Finally, sexual responses can be triggered in many ways, affecting events at the different levels of analysis. For example, adolescents apparently model their behavior after that of their friends, and hence are more likely to have sexual relations early if their friends are having sexual relations early (DiBlasio & Benda, 1990). However, such social interactions can be mediated by biological events—including whether the adolescent has certain genes (Miller et al., 1999).

Mating Preferences

Think about it: What sort of person would be your ideal mate? Or just a good date for tomorrow night? Evolutionary psychology has offered theories of what makes someone seem desirable as a potential mate. Some of these theories derive from Trivers's (1972) influential theory of "parental investment." He argued that males, who typically invest less than do females in the nurturing and raising of children, should be more interested in short-term sex and less particular about mates; females, who typically are very invested in nurturing and raising children, should have opposite preferences. How-

Certain genes that affect the brain receptors for the neuro-transmitter dopamine influence the age at which people first have sexual intercourse (Miller et al., 1999).

ever, when Pedersen and colleagues (2002) tested this idea, they found that 98.9% of men and 99.2% of women hoped to have a long-term stable relationship. Very few of either gender were motivated by continued short-term sex. In addition, the two genders spend comparable amounts of time and money in "short-term mating," such as trying to meet someone at a party (Miller et al. 2002).

Another evolutionary theory relies on the observation that because fertilization occurs in the privacy of a woman's fallopian tubes, a man can never be absolutely certain that a baby carries his genes; thus, according to this theory, men should be particularly alert to their mates' possible sexual infidelity. In contrast, because women value a man who will devote time, energy, and resources to her children, women should be particularly alert to their mates' becoming emotionally involved with someone else. When asked which would be more upsetting, their mates' falling in love with someone else or having sex with someone else, most men chose the latter and most women chose the former (Buss et al., 1992; Cramer et al., 2001–2002). However, these results may not be found when participants use a continuous scale to specify their reaction to each event (DeSteno & Salovey, 1996) or when they are asked to reflect about actual experiences (Harris, 2002). Moreover, other researchers have found that men and women value remarkably similar characteristics in a potential mate (Miller et al., 2002). To avoid methodological problems (such as demand effects; see Chapter 2) that arise when participants are asked to make these kinds of judgments, some researchers have recorded bodily reactions to such questions (Buss et al., 1992; Grice & Seely, 2000). One particularly careful study of such reactions was reported by Harris (2000). She asked participants to imagine different scenarios while she recorded their blood pressure, heart rate, and skin conductivity. Men did show greater reactions to imagining their mate having sex versus being emotionally involved with someone else. But they showed the same reactions when they imagined *themselves* having sex versus being emotionally involved with their mate. Moreover, women who had been in a committed sexual relationship produced results very much like those of the men— clearly counter to the predictions of evolutionary theory.

Does all of this mean that evolution had no role in shaping mate preferences? Not necessarily. However, these findings do show that mate selection, like all other human behavior, does not arise solely from events at a single level of analysis.

Sexual Orientation: More Than a Choice

People who are sexually attracted to the opposite sex are termed **heterosexual**; people attracted to the same sex are termed **homosexual**; people attracted to both sexes are termed **bisexual.** Sexuality might best be regarded as a continuum, with most people being primarily heterosexual, and somewhere between 4% and 10% of the U.S. population being primarily homosexual in their behavior (Fay et al., 1989). Studies of bisexual men have shown that many of them tend to become more homosexually oriented over time (Stokes et al., 1997). For many years, homosexuality was considered either a personal choice or the result of being raised a certain way (for instance, with a weak father and an overly strict mother). However, programs to train homosexuals to prefer the opposite sex have failed, even those that relied on extreme techniques such as electric shock to punish homosexual thoughts or behavior (Brown [1989] offers a personal account).

There is now evidence that people do not simply choose to be homosexual or heterosexual, nor are homosexuals or heterosexuals created by the ways their parents treat them as young children. Rather, biological events appear to play a major role in determining sexual orientation. LeVay (1991) studied the brains of homosexual men and found that a small part of the hypothalamus, about as large as an average-sized grain of sand, was about twice as small in them as in the brains of heterosexual men (Allen & Gorski, 1992, report related evidence). This is interesting in part because others had previously found that this same structure typically is smaller in women than in men. However, all of the brains LeVay studied came from men who had died of AIDS, and it is possible that the disease had something to do with the structural abnormality. But this possibility seems unlikely because when this same structure was surgically disrupted in monkeys, they displayed atypical sexual behavior (Slimp et al., 1978). These and similar data suggest that there is a biological predisposition for some people to become homosexual (LeVay & Hamer, 1994).

Other differences between heterosexual and homosexual people point toward biological differences. Consider, for example, the sound that is emitted from the ears of some people in some circumstances (see the discussion in Chapter 4). In some cases the sound is a response to a heard click, and the ears of some people actually emit sound even without such a trigger event. It turns out that this response to a click is less frequent and weaker for homosexual and bisexual women than for heterosexual women—in fact, men in general have less frequent and weaker ear responses than do heterosexual women (McFadden & Pasanen, 1999). Apparently, parts of the ear are different in these women. However, no such difference appears among heterosexual, bisexual, and homosexual men. Thus, these results not only show a biological difference for homosexual and

● **Heterosexual:** A person who is sexually attracted to members of the opposite sex.

● **Homosexual:** A person who is sexually attracted to members of the same sex.

● **Bisexual:** A person who is sexually attracted to members of both sexes.

bisexual women, but may also hint at different biological bases for male and female homosexuality.

The findings of biological differences between homosexual and heterosexual people do not indicate whether the causes are hereditary (that is, genetic), the result of experiences in the womb, or the result of experiences during early childhood. Hamer and his colleagues (1993) studied 114 families that included a homosexual man and found that inheritance of homosexuality seemed to be passed from the mother. This result led them to examine the X chromosome, which is the sex chromosome from the mother (females have two X chromosomes, one from the mother and one from the father; males have only one X chromosome, from the mother, and a Y chromosome from the father). These researchers concluded that a small portion of the X chromosome is related to homosexual preference and behavior. However, not all studies have supported this view (McKnight & Malcolm, 2000). Moreover, although Bailey and Pillard (1991) conducted a study with twins that supported the idea that homosexuality is at least partly inherited, a later study failed to find this effect (Rice et al., 1999).

The mixed findings from genetic studies may mean that there is more than one way homosexuality can arise. One intriguing possibility is suggested by the finding that more gay men have older brothers than do heterosexual men (Blanchard, 2001; Ellis & Blanchard, 2001). In fact, the sexual orientation of about 15% of gay men appears to arise from the fact that they had older brothers (Cantor et al., 2002). Why? It appears that the mother's body somehow "remembers" the number of boys she bore (possibly by building up specific antibodies; Ellis & Blanchard, 2001), and alters the level of testosterone accordingly. Boys with older brothers receive proportionally more testosterone during gestation, which appears to increase the likelihood that they will be homosexual. One intriguing— if preliminary—bit of evidence for this theory relies on the fact that prenatal levels of testosterone regulate genes (the so-called Homeobox or *Hox* genes, Kondo et al., 1997) that not only determine how the genitals develop, but also regulate testosterone levels in the fetus and dictate the relative lengths of the ring and index fingers. Some researchers have in fact found that the relative lengths of the ring and index fingers differ for homosexual and heterosexual men (Robinson & Manning, 2000). Additional research with a large number of participants suggests that this relation only occurs for gay men who have older brothers (T. J. Williams et al., 2000b).

To say that homosexuality has biological roots is not to rule out a role for the environment. Bem (1996, 1998) has argued that young boys who are not typical of their sex, in that they are not physically strong and have gentle temperaments, prefer to play with girls—and it is this socialization experience that later leads them to become homosexual. In Bem's view, "exotic becomes erotic": If young boys identify with girls and engage in girl-like behavior, it is boys who become "dissimilar, unfamiliar and exotic" and thus "erotic." For girls, the reverse would hold true, with "tomboy" girls choosing to associate with boys and engage in boy-like activities, and thus later finding girls exotic and hence erotic. According to this theory, biology would affect the body and temperament, and only indirectly affect sexual orientation. However, in order to explain why it has proved so difficult to alter sexual orientation in adulthood, we would need to assume that at a certain age sexual orientation is set and thereafter difficult to modify.

What's Normal?

For many years the manual of the American Psychiatric Association classified homosexuality as a psychological disorder, but (after conducting a poll of its members) in 1973 this classification was deleted. What is normal sexual behavior?

FIGURE 10.10 Major Factors That Affect Human Sexual Activity

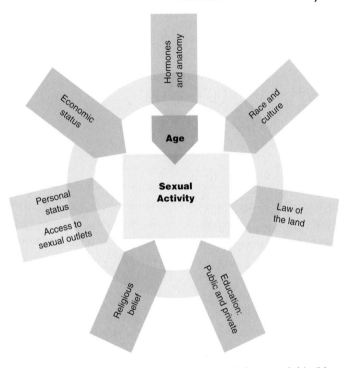

From "Human male sexuality: Appetite, arousal, desire and drive" by R. J. Levin, in *Appetite, Neural and Behavioral Bases* edited by Charles R. Legg and David Booth (1994). Reprinted by permission of Oxford University Press.

Cultural Variations: Experience Counts

Sexual behavior is partly instinctive but, like eating, it is also molded by personal tastes and by culture (see Figure 10.10). For example, among the people of the Grand Valley Dani in Indonesia the men apparently have extraordinarily little interest in sex (Heider, 1976). They reportedly do not have intercourse with their wives for 5 years after a child is born; nor do they seem to have other sexual outlets. Nonetheless, these people do not seem unhappy. At the opposite extreme, the Mangaians, who live on an island in the South Pacific, may have sex up to the time when a woman goes into labor and may resume sex within a few days after the birth of a child, although they typically wait a few months (Marshall, 1971).

Cultural variations occur over time, even within a single group. In the 20 years that followed the decade of the 1950s, attitudes about sex changed dramatically in the United States, in large part because of the development of effective birth control. "Free sex," a motto of the '60s generation, encouraged sexual liberation; people should be free, proponents said, to have sex when and where they choose (in those days, young women sometimes brought a condom and toothbrush with them on the first date). Today, with the spread of AIDS and the resurgence of fundamentalist and evangelical religions, sexual behavior is changing again, becoming less casual. Culture clearly affects how, when, and where sexual behavior occurs.

Sexual Dysfunction: When Good Things Go Wrong

Despite the many variations in human sexual behavior in different times and places, psychologists do consider some sexual behaviors to be dysfunctional. Categorizing a behavior as "dysfunctional" depends in part on the individual, in part on the relationship, and in part on the standards of the surrounding culture. *Sexual dysfunctions*, according to the fourth edition of the *Diagnostic and Statistical Manual of Mental Disorders* (American Psychiatric Association, 2000), "are characterized by a disturbance in the processes that characterize the sexual response cycle or by pain associated with sexual intercourse" (p. 535). Included in this description are disorders of sexual desire, arousal, orgasmic disorders, and sexual pain. Many, if not most, problems in the sexual response cycle have psychological causes; they are not caused by physical problems with the sex organs. An example is the inability to reach orgasm. In men, the disorder is called *male erectile dys-*

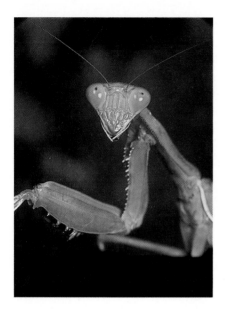

The male praying mantis can copulate only after its head has been ripped off, a service readily provided by the receptive female. Some lions copulate over 50 times a day. Human sexual behavior is also shaped by our biologies, but it is much more variable than that of other animals.

function (or *impotence*); in women, it is known as *female arousal dysfunction* (previously called *frigidity*). Masters and Johnson found that such sexual disorders often arise because of a preoccupation with personal problems, fears about the possible consequences of sexual activity, or anxiety about sexual performance.

However, at least some sexual dysfunction may have a biological cause. The drug Viagra caused quite a stir when it was first released in the late 1990s because it provided a safe and effective medical treatment for impotence. Viagra doesn't cause an erection. Rather, the drug operates only when a man is sexually excited, by increasing the flow of blood to the penis. Thus, Viagra is not a cure but a treatment for impotence, and it is effective only if it continues to be taken. The user of this drug who would derive the most benefit would be a middle-aged man who has difficulty keeping an erection and wants to be sexually active. Some women also use this drug now that it has proved to have a similar effect on the clitoris. However, Viagra commonly has side effects, which range from headache and stomachache to changes in color vision (such as difficulty discriminating between green and blue). Furthermore, in some cases impotence is an early warning sign of something more serious: the veins carrying blood to the penis can become narrowed by buildup of plaque in the blood vessels, which can also lead to heart attacks and stroke. Thus, purchasing Viagra over the Web without seeing a physician is not medically sound.

Atypical Sexual Behavior

Some forms of sexual behavior are atypical but not considered "sexual dysfunction." For example, objects can sometimes become conditioned stimuli for sexual arousal; a common example is a shoe, or even a picture of a shoe. When an object that has no inherent sexual meaning comes to be sexually arousing, it is called a *fetish*. Mental health professionals consider fetishes a problem only if they are necessary for arousal or if they are objectionable to the partner.

Sexual dysfunction is not the same thing as sexual abnormality, which may or may not be dysfunctional. For example, people with *androgen insensitivity syndrome* have XY chromosomes and a genetic mutation that does not allow androgen receptors to develop. Thus, the lock is missing for the hormonal key, and the hormone has no effects either during development or afterward. These people, who should have been boys, grow into girls, but with testes tucked up in the belly and no uterus or ovaries. In some cases, the vagina is too shallow and must be surgically altered later in life. In spite of their genetic identities as males, the failure of male hormones to have an effect does not allow the genes to influence their sexuality. In fact, although they sometimes require appropriate female hormone supplements, these people look like women, often marry, and have normal female sex lives (which include normal orgasms during intercourse).

Such people must be distinguished from *transvestites*, men who dress as women. Docter and Prince (1997) asked more than 1,000 men who sometimes dressed as women to complete a survey about their lives, sexual identities, and behavior. One finding of interest is that the vast majority (87%) claimed to be heterosexual, not homosexual. Eighty-three percent had been married at one time, and 60% were married when they filled in the survey. These men apparently enjoyed their male and female modes of behavior equally.

Looking *at* Levels

Homophobia

To study one possible basis of strong negative views of homosexuals, Adams and colleagues (1996) asked two groups of male heterosexuals to watch videotapes that showed heterosexuals, lesbians, or gay men engaging in explicit sex acts. One group of men had scored high on a test of *homophobia*, which is a strong aversion to homosexuality; the other group scored low. While both groups watched the tapes, the researchers recorded changes in penile circumference as an indication of sexual arousal. All the participants became aroused when they saw the heterosexual and lesbian videos, but only the homophobic males were aroused by the homosexual male videos. The investigators note that psychodynamic theory might explain these results by claiming that the homophobic men had repressed homosexual impulses. Alternatively, they note that another theory would explain the results in terms of anxiety (Barlow, 1986). In this view, the homosexual stimuli produce negative emotions, which in turn lead to anxiety, which in turn enhances arousal, which leads to erection.

Consider this result from the levels perspective. First, it is clear that visual stimuli can trigger the brain

mechanisms that lead to arousal. Second, which stimuli are arousing depends on personal characteristics: Men who disliked homosexuals had stronger penile responses to the homosexual videos than did men who were not homophobic. Third, we are led to ask the question, Why did the men who were most aroused by the homosexual video express the greatest dislike of homosexuals? It is easy to speculate that they would not have felt this way in a different culture, such as that of ancient Greece, in which homosexuality was accepted. If the arousal was in fact sexual, these men may actually have been denying their own homosexual tendencies because cultural norms stigmatized such behavior. On the other hand, if the arousal was a consequence of a negative reaction to the films, this response too may have been mitigated had they grown up in a different culture. Moreover, such a reaction affects how these people behave and think. For example, they may avoid certain bars or have negative reactions to gays or embrace socially restrictive policies regarding homosexuals.

TEST YOURSELF!

1. What is the nature of sexual response? What factors lead to it?
2. What determines whether we are attracted to the same or to the opposite sex?
3. What is "normal sexual behavior"? How does culture affect our standards of normality?

CONSOLIDATE!

Emotion: I Feel, Therefore I Am

- Ekman and his collaborators have identified six basic emotions: happiness, anger, sadness, disgust, surprise, and fear. Research results have shown that surprise and fear are more easily confused with each other than they are with any of the others.

- Culture and experience influence how easily emotions can be read; although humans can read emotions from any other human better than chance, they do better with members of familiar cultures.

- Although theories of emotion are often considered alternative views, each in fact has captured a grain of the truth. The James–Lange theory holds that you feel emotion after your body reacts to a situation. The Cannon–Bard theory holds that emotions and bodily reactions occur at the same time. Cognitive theory claims that emotions arise when you interpret your bodily reactions in the context of the specific situation. LeDoux's revision of cognitive theory rests on the idea that some emotions arise from brain responses that do not involve interpretation, whereas others arise from cognitive interpretation.

- As James–Lange predicts, emotions may be caused in part by differences in bodily reactions, such as heart rate, breathing rate, and facial expression. As Cannon–Bard predicts, some emotions, such as fear, are reflexes that produce the experience and the bodily reaction simultaneously. As cognitive theory predicts, how you interpret the causes of your bodily reactions does in fact influence which emotion you feel. As claimed by LeDoux, some emotions, such as fear, arise via brain mechanisms (particularly those involving the amygdala) that do not rely on interpretation, whereas others do rely on interpretation.

- Fear is the most salient of our emotions, and the amygdala may play a role in salient emotions more generally. Environmental events influence emotion; our happiness, for example, depends in part on our economic and cultural context. Emotions also arise in response to other people's emotional signals, which vary depending on their cultures. In addition, the emotions we feel depend on how we construe a situation; happy people tend to remain happy, in part because of how they view the world.

- Culture shapes the emotional reaction we will have to moral violations. Culture also affects how effectively we can read body language to determine another person's emotion.

- We can control our emotions, both by prolonging them over time and by suppressing them; this control is directly reflected in the activation of brain mechanisms. Culture affects the display rules we use, the rules that determine when and how we express emotion.

- Lies cannot be reliably detected by current methods, although some individuals are particularly adept at spotting deception.

THINK IT THROUGH Which theory of emotion best explains all of John's reactions during and after the mugging?

Would the world necessarily be a better place if people could control their emotions perfectly? Do you think children have the same emotions as adults? If interpretation plays a key role, in what ways would this limit the emotions very young children feel? How might this change with increasing development?

What would be the advantages and disadvantages of a machine that always detected lies and never mistook the truth for lies? If your school offered a course in reading "body language," would you take it? Why or why not?

Motivation and Reward: Feeling Good

- Some of our motivations arise from evolutionarily shaped instincts, sex being an obvious example. Other motivations are drives, such as thirst; some drives are designed to maintain homeostasis, such as occurs when we are cold and seek warmth. Other motivations center on a preference for an intermediate level of arousal.

- We are often motivated by incentives, such as the potential rewards (including money) for engaging in a behavior.

- Brain systems that rely on the neurotransmitter dopamine goad us on in the anticipation of a reward.

- A need is a condition that arises when you lack a requirement, which in turn gives rise to a drive to acquire specific rewards to fulfill the requirement. A want is a condition that arises when you have an unmet goal that will not fulfill a requirement, which in turn causes the goal to act as an incentive.

- Needs may be related to a brain system that provides an internal reward when a deprivation is satisfied, such as by eating when you are hungry. In contrast, many wants may be related to a system that provides a reward when you are not deprived but you achieve a desired goal.

- There are many types of needs; the importance of a given need depends partly on your culture, particularly on whether the culture is individualist or collectivist.

- Animals can learn to be helpless if their behavior fails to reduce punishment.

THINK IT THROUGH　If you could design a school for young children, how would you organize it so that the children were motivated as strongly as possible? How can you find out what motivates a particular person?

You could argue that wants are never satisfied for very long. If this is correct, does it make sense to try to fulfill them at all? How could you tell if a motivation is a need or a want?

Do you think it might be useful to develop a drug that blocks the deprived reward system? the nondeprived system? Why might such a drug be dangerous? beneficial?

Hunger and Eating: Not Just About Fueling the Body

- We eat for many reasons: pleasure, nutrition, as a social activity. The brain senses when the quantity of nutrients in the blood is too low and causes us to feel hungry. We often eat until signals from the stomach (and other digestive organs) indicate that we've consumed enough food.

- The hypothalamus plays a particularly important role in hunger and thirst. At the beginning of a meal, taste plays an especially important role in determining whether you want to eat. As a meal progresses, changes in the type of food will keep your appetite up, and tastes (as well as thoughts) that cause insulin to be released will increase hunger.

- Beliefs about the history of a food item (for example, whether it was ever in contact with something repulsive), and even associations with the shape of the food affect how appealing it is.

- Overeating can cause your body weight to increase, and once increased it is often difficult to move down again. However, weight is determined by many factors that affect metabolism and behavior, including your en-

vironment, types of activities, and emotional state. Cognitive mechanisms in the brain can over-ride the hypothalamus, allowing us to eat when we aren't actually hungry.

- Obese people do not have "weak characters" but rather may be genetically predisposed to becoming obese. Many genes play a role in obesity, and affect body weight in different ways. Being underweight or dieting alters cognition, emotion, and personality.

THINK IT THROUGH　In the 1930s, Coke bottles held 6.5 ounces; today, they hold a liter—more than 5 times the original amount. We tend to think of a bottle as a single serving or perhaps two servings.

What effects do you think this sort of change has on consumption? Does it make a difference that a lot of Coke is consumed on social occasions with a lot of people? If so, how could such a difference be minimized?

Sex: Not Just About Having Babies

- Sexual attraction leads to sexual desire, sexual excitement (arousal), and possibly sexual performance (which involves becoming fully aroused, reaching orgasm, and then experiencing resolution followed, for men, by a refractory period).

- Hormones play a key role in sexual development and modify motivation toward sexual behavior. Fluctuations in sex hormones affect cognition and emotion.

- Sexual desire and arousal can be triggered by various cues, with visual stimuli often playing a critical role (and odor playing a particularly important role for women). The hypothalamus is affected by visual sexual stimuli in men, but not in women.

- Mating preferences may be influenced by evolutionary characteristics, but they are not determined by them.

- There is evidence that male homosexuals have differences in certain brain structures, and that female homosexuals have differences in the operation of certain neural systems (involved in hearing), from heterosexuals. Such biological differences, and homosexuality itself, are probably caused either by genes or by events in the womb or during childhood.

- Sexual behaviors differ in different cultures, and what constitutes normal sexual behaviors varies widely. Sexual variations are considered disorders only if they cause "marked distress and interpersonal difficulty."

THINK IT THROUGH Could John have been sexually aroused because of his traumatic experience? In what circumstances is misattribution of arousal likely to occur?

Could someone feel sexual desire for a partner but have a difficult time becoming sexually aroused? Why or why not? Imagine that researchers figured out in detail the factors that lead to sexual arousal. Would it be ethical to use your knowledge of such factors to make yourself sexually attractive when you were going out on a date?

Do you think researchers should be trying to find a gene (or genes) for homosexuality? What positive uses could such knowledge have? what negative uses? Would it be ethical to try to alter such genes either before conception or in the womb?

Key Terms

androgens, p. 424
basic emotion, p. 391
bisexual, p. 428
collectivist culture, p. 414
deprived reward, p. 411
display rule, p. 402
drive, p. 408
emotion, p. 390
estrogens, p. 424
facial feedback hypothesis, p. 396
heterosexual, p. 428
homeostasis, p. 408
homosexual, p. 428
implicit motive, p. 410
incentive, p. 409
individualist culture, p. 414

instinct, p. 407
insulin, p. 418
learned helplessness, p. 415
metabolism, p. 416
misattribution of arousal, p. 398
motivation, p. 406
need, p. 410
need for achievement (nAch), p. 412
nondeprived reward, p. 411
polygraph, p. 405
set point, p. 419
sexual response cycle (SRC), p. 424
want, p. 410

chapter **11**

Victoria & Albert Museum, London/Art Resource, NY

Personality
Vive la Différence!

Tina and Gabe met in their introductory psychology class. They were immediately attracted to each other and started studying together. After a few conversations, they were pleased to discover they had similar values and political views. Predictably, they began going out together. On their fourth date, though, Tina began to realize that she and Gabe weren't as much alike as she had thought; she was surprised by this because their views on so many issues were so similar. Tina sometimes had trouble "reading" Gabe because he was shy and emotionally steady, without many highs or lows; his manner was "mellow." She wondered why he wasn't more enthusiastic when she proposed activities she thought would be fun to do together, such as in-line skating, bungee-jumping, or biking. "Well, opposites attract, I guess," she thought. And although Gabe enjoyed Tina's spirit, her outgoingness and emotional vibrancy, her interest in trying new things, now and then he asked her why she was so emotional and always in such a hurry. Tina began to worry that, even though they were strongly attracted to each other, a long-term relationship might reveal persistent problems between them that would be difficult to overcome.

Do these differences reveal something fundamental about Tina and Gabe as people?

Do these differences reveal something fundamental about Tina and Gabe as people? Do they reflect their personalities? And if so, are personalities set in stone? This chapter explores the idea of personality, how psychologists measure it, and the perspectives of a number of different theorists who have sought to describe and explain it. We'll consider issues such as the genetic influence on personality development; the relation of inner motives, thoughts, and feelings to personality; and the effects of the social environment on personality.

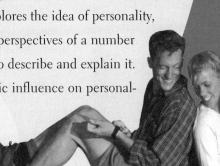

● **Personality:** A consistent set of behavioral characteristics that people display over time and across situations, and that distinguish individuals from each other.

● **Personality trait:** A relatively consistent characteristic exhibited in different situations.

What Is Personality?

As Tina got to know Gabe, she began to make certain assumptions about him, about who he was as a person. He studied hard and did well on psychology exams and quizzes, so Tina figured he was smart, hard-working, and conscientious. (Tina did well on her psychology exams and quizzes, too, but she didn't study much. She considered herself smart, but not particularly hard-working.) So she was surprised to discover that Gabe's apartment was a disaster area—she had assumed he would be as orderly and neat in his personal space as he was in his approach to schoolwork, and so she wondered whether his "personality," as she thought of it, was altogether consistent. Tina also noticed that, on dates, Gabe preferred to get together for dinner and a movie, not for lunch or an afternoon break ("Too much studying," he said). If she suggested going to a party together, Gabe invariably declined; he didn't like parties. Tina attributed this reluctance to his shyness.

The concept of personality infuses daily life. When you describe an acquaintance as "intense," wonder how a friend will handle a piece of bad news, or think about the type of partner you would like to have in life, personality is exerting its influence. What exactly is this quality, which is part and parcel of each of us? **Personality** has been described as a consistent set of behavioral characteristics that people display over time and across situations, and that distinguish individuals from each other. Thus the very concept of personality implies that people have enduring, stable qualities such as, say, talkativeness or curiosity. These qualities are called **personality traits,** relatively consistent characteristics exhibited across a range of situations. But notice the "relatively" in the preceding sentence. Let's see just what that means.

Personality: Traits or Situations?

Traits exist on a continuum (for example, from extremely quiet to extremely talkative). Gabe's shyness and Tina's adventurousness can be considered traits. Many trait theorists—personality psychologists who study traits and believe that personality is built on traits—assume that everyone has the same set of traits, but that for each person each trait falls at a different point on its continuum. Some trait theorists propose that our traits lead us to behave in certain ways; this view would suggest that Gabe avoided parties because of his trait of shyness. Not all trait theorists share the belief in this cause-and-effect relationship, however; some trait theorists regard traits simply as labels for collections of behaviors rather than as causes of them (Buss & Craik, 1984).

Traits by definition imply consistency. But are our personality traits always consistent? Bem and Allen (1974) found that people are not equally consistent on *all* traits. When they asked participants to rate how *consistently* friendly and conscientious they were, they found large variability in consistency; not all participants felt that they were consistent on each of these traits. People who rated themselves as consistent on the trait of friendliness

The names of Snow White's seven dwarves fit their personalities. Imagine the personalities of dwarves named Dirty, Hungry, Shifty, Flabby, Puffy, Crabby, Awful, Doleful, all of which were on Disney Studios' list of possible names (Seuling, 1976). The final choices work so well because we view their personalities as consistent with their names; but what if Grumpy were, in fact, upbeat and easy-going!

were more likely to have their behaviors reflect that trait than people who viewed themselves as inconsistent on the trait of friendliness. For instance, those consistent on the trait of friendliness were more likely to strike up a conversation with a sales clerk. Similar results were found for the trait of conscientiousness: People who rated themselves as consistent on this trait were more likely to exhibit relevant behaviors, such as carefully double-checking term papers for typing and spelling errors. Kenrick and Stringfield (1980) further refined Bem and Allen's research by showing that everyone is consistent on some traits, but that the particular traits on which people differ vary across individuals. Thus, some traits are just irrelevant for some of us—they aren't important in our lives (Britt & Shepperd, 1999). For example, Gabe may be inconsistent on the general dimension of conscientiousness, which would explain the coexistence of his conscientious attention to schoolwork and his careless housekeeping at home. This explanation for people's inconsistency on some traits dovetails with early trait theorist Gordon Allport's (1897–1967) idea that some personality traits can be grouped as *central traits*, those traits that affect a wide range of behavior; the particular traits that are central will vary from individual to individual (Allport, 1937). Whether or not traits are viewed as causing behavior, they certainly aren't always accurate in *predicting* behavior (witness Gabe's domestic messiness). The situations in which we find ourselves can exert powerful influences on behavior, thoughts, and feelings.

Situationism: Different Traits for Different Contexts

Does the following paragraph represent an accurate description of your personality?

HANDS ON

> You have a strong need for other people to like you and for them to admire you. You have a tendency to be critical of yourself. You have a great deal of unused capacity which you have not turned to your advantage. While you have some personality weaknesses, you are generally able to compensate for them. Your sexual adjustment has presented some problems for you. Disciplined and controlled on the outside, you tend to be worrisome and insecure inside. At times you have serious doubts as to whether you have made the right decision or done the right thing. You prefer a certain amount of change and variety and become dissatisfied when hemmed in by restrictions and limitations. You pride yourself as being an independent thinker and do not accept others' opinions without satisfactory proof. You have found it unwise to be too frank in revealing yourself to others. At times you are extroverted, affable, sociable, while at other times you are introverted, wary, and reserved. Some of your aspirations tend to be pretty unrealistic. (Ulrich et al., 1963, p. 832)

Does this sound like you? If you had taken a personality test and this paragraph was given to you as a summary of your test results, you probably would have agreed with it. That is exactly what happened in a study in which undergraduate participants were asked to take a personality test and then *all of the participants* were given this same paragraph as a summary of their results, *regardless of their responses on the test.* The students rated the summary interpretation as good or excellent (Snyder & Larson, 1972; Ulrich et al., 1963). But how could "one size fit all"—how can we make sense of these results? Because most people experience some of the traits described in the summary *in some situations* and at *some points in their lives.* Hence, the statements were true—some of the time. Reread the paragraph, and note how many of the statements present descriptions of two opposing characteristics, such as being extroverted at times, introverted at other

● **Situationism:** A view of personality that regards behavior as mostly a function of the situation, not of internal traits.

Situationism would hold that people have a certain view of an individual's personality because we usually only see that person in a particular type of situation (perhaps work related, as in the photo on the left), but not in other types of situations (as in the photo on the right). If we did, the individual's personality would not appear to be so consistent.

times. This kind of dual presentation is what makes horoscopes so often seem to be on the mark.

A larger question arises, then, about the consistency of personality traits (known as the *person-situation controversy*): If much of our behavior depends on the situation in which we find ourselves, then perhaps there aren't consistent personality traits at all. To examine children's behavioral consistency across different types of situations, Hartshorne and May (1928) gave grade-school children the opportunity for undetected deceit: to lie about how many push-ups they were able to do, to lie to their parents about how much work they did at home, to cheat on a school test, and to keep money they were given for other purposes. The researchers found that children who were dishonest in one situation were not necessarily dishonest in another; a child who cheated on a test would not necessarily lie to his or her parents. Although the children showed some consistency across situations, less than 10% of the variation of behaviors across situations could be explained by a single, common, underlying trait of honesty. Not surprisingly, though, the less similar the situations, the lower were the correlations of honesty between situations; lying and stealing were not highly correlated. Remember that a correlation (see Chapter 2) is an index of how closely related two sets of measured variables are, in this case lying and stealing.

Similarly, Mischel and Peake (1982) observed college students and recorded 19 different behaviors reflecting conscientiousness, as defined by how regularly they attended class, how promptly they completed assignments, how neatly they made their beds, and how neatly they recorded class notes. They found that the students were likely to be consistent in similar situations, but not across different types of situations.

In later research, Mischel (1984) found that inconsistency across situations is pervasive; he found this not only with the traits of honesty and conscientiousness, but also with other traits, such as aggression and dependency. Furthermore, different measures of what should be the same trait often were only weakly correlated, or not related at all. Such findings led to the theory of **situationism,** which holds that a person's behavior is mostly a function of a given situation, not of internal traits. Situationism recognizes that, in part, we create our own situations, not necessarily by our actions but simply by who we are. In other words, characteristics such as age, sex, race, religion, ethnicity, and socioeconomic status can influence other people's behavior toward us, often in culturally determined ways, creating a different "situation," which can in turn lead to differences in people's behavior (see the discussion of microenvironments in Chapter 9). Nineteen-year-old Tina behaves very differently with Gabe—drinking from his cup, calling him after midnight—than she does with her 52-year-old female economics professor. In each case, Tina's age, sex, and status relative to the other person might be said to change her be-

havior. If you knew Tina only from economics lectures, you might be surprised by how different her "personality" seemed when she was with Gabe.

Taken to its extreme, situationism views traits as mere illusions. People we know seem to have stable personalities because we tend to see them in the same kinds of situations. Thus, when we label someone's behavior as part of a personality trait, we are imposing order on his or her behavior, much as the Gestalt laws of organization (see Chapter 4) impose an order on what is before our eyes. It makes us more comfortable to think that we can "peg" someone, that we can predict how he or she will behave.

Interactionism: Who, Where, and When

Not surprisingly, situationism has had strong critics who point out that, over long periods of time and over many situations, people are fairly consistent, and personality traits become reliably evident (Funder, 2001; Funder & Colvin, 1991; Kenrick & Funder, 1988; Roberts et al., 2001). Moreover, the more precisely a trait is defined, the more accurate it is in predicting behavior (Wiggins, 1992). Thus, saying that someone is sociable will not predict his or her behavior at a party nearly as well as saying the person appears at ease in interactions with new people. This is the tradeoff: The more narrowly a trait is defined, the better it predicts behavior, but the fewer circumstances there are to which it can be applied. However, even

when a trait is narrowly defined, there is not necessarily a one-to-one correspondence between the point at which someone falls on a trait continuum and that person's behavior. Rather, several traits may interact, along with situational factors, to influence behavior (Ahadi & Diener, 1989).

Nevertheless, the power of the situation cannot be denied: People do behave differently in different contexts. Thus, a synthesis of the traditional trait view and situationism evolved, called **interactionism,** which suggests that traits, situations, and their interactions affect thoughts, feelings, and behavior. For instance, Tina is generally outgoing and enjoys parties (trait); she has also noticed that the more crowded the party

As predicted by interactionism, whether or not an individual enjoys a job as a park ranger (or librarian, or actor, or chemist, with the job requirements constituting some aspects of the situation) will depend in part on his or her constellation of personality traits.

and the louder everyone has to speak to be heard (all part of the situation), the more she enjoys herself. Had Tina disliked parties, the situation would not have exerted itself in this way. It is the interaction of her traits, along with qualities about her (such as her appearance), that affect how people behave toward her. And the situation, in turn, affects her thoughts (such as planning to arrive at a party when she thinks it will be in full swing and sufficiently crowded), feelings (being excited about the party), and behavior (making an effort to attend parties, even if it means leaving her work undone).

As another example, Asian Americans tend to show lower levels of assertiveness than do Whites on personality tests. However, Zane and colleagues (1991) found that this is true only when the people involved are strangers. Thus, the interactionists say, it isn't really accurate to describe Asian Americans as "low on the assertiveness trait" in general; a better characterization would be the more specific "unassertive when among strangers."

● **Interactionism:** A view of personality in which both traits and situations are believed to affect thoughts, feelings, and behavior.

Thus, people's personalities can affect their situations in two major ways. First, people often can choose their situations—their jobs, their friends, their leisure activities. And, insofar as they are able, people tend to choose environments that fit their personalities. It's up to you, for instance, to decide whether to go bungee-jumping or sunbathing at the beach for the day. Second, people also find opportunities to create their environments. An aggressive person, for instance, will create a tense situation by words or deeds (A. H. Buss, 1995), and others will react accordingly.

Factors of Personality: The Big Five? Three? More?

How many personality traits are there? The answer depends on how specific you want to be about a given trait. You could be very specific, narrowing down behavior all the way to a "shy-so-only-goes-on-dates-to-dinner-and-a-movie-but-not-to-parties" trait. Narrowing traits to this level of precision, however, poses certain problems. Each trait explains only particular patterns of thoughts and behaviors in very specific instances. For example, you could consider sociability (which personality psychologists call "extraversion") a trait. Or you could say that extraversion is really a combination of the more specific traits of warmth, gregariousness, and assertiveness. In this case, you could say that extraversion is a *personality dimension*, a set of related personality traits. Using the statistical technique of factor analysis (see Chapter 9), some researchers have sought to discover whether specific traits are in fact associated and, together, constitute a more general trait; such a personality dimension is sometimes called a *superfactor*. An early proponent of factor analysis to determine personality factors was Raymond Cattell (1905–1998); he proposed 16 personality factors (listed in Figure 11.1 on page 445) (Cattell, 1943), although further factor analyses lead to fewer factors (which are in turn less predictive of specific behaviors).

Many factor analytic studies have revealed that traits can be reduced to five superfactors, which are listed along with their included traits in Table 11.1 (Digman, 1990; McCrae & Costa, 1987); each superfactor and trait are on a continuum,

TABLE 11.1 The Big Five Superfactors and Their Traits

Superfactor	Traits
Extraversion (also called *Sociability*)	Warmth, gregariousness, assertiveness, activity, excitement seeking, positive emotions.
Neuroticism (also called *Emotionality*)	Anxiety, hostility, depression, self-consciousness, impulsiveness, vulnerability.
Agreeableness	Trust, straightforwardness, altruism, compliance, modesty, tender-mindedness.
Conscientiousness (also called *Dependability*)	Competence, order, dutifulness, achievement striving, deliberation, self-discipline.
Openness	Fantasy, aesthetics, feelings, actions, ideas, values.

Source: Adapted from Costa, McCrae, & Dye (1991).

with the name of the superfactor or trait identifying only one end of that continuum. Thus, the other end of the neuroticism superfactor is called *emotional stability*. These superfactors are sometimes referred to as the Five Factor Model, or the **Big Five** (Goldberg, 1981): extraversion, neuroticism (also called *emotionality*), agreeableness, conscientiousness (also called *dependability*), and openness to experience (Costa et al., 1991). To remember these factors, which are supposed to "plumb the depths" of personality, use the mnemonic OCEAN (Openness, Conscientiousness, Extraversion, Agreeableness, and Neuroticism). Depending on the personality inventory used, different individual traits may make up each of the five superfactors, and hence some of the superfactors are given different names by different researchers. Some versions of extraversion and neuroticism, however, are found in almost all lists, perhaps reflecting how fundamental these two dimensions are to personality.

Psychologist Hans Eysenck identified not five but three superfactors or, as he labeled them, *personality dimensions:* extraversion, neuroticism, and psychoticism. While Eysenck's first two dimensions resemble the Big Five's superfactors of the same names, the third—psychoticism—was originally thought to measure a propensity toward becoming psychotic, that is, toward loss of touch with reality, as occurs in schizophrenia (Eysenck, 1992). It is true that people with schizophrenia score high on this dimension; however, psychoticism as defined by Eysenck also contains traits related to social deviance, such as criminality and substance addiction, and to a lack of conventional socialization, such as respect for rules and the feelings of others (Costa & McCrae, 1995). For this reason, Eysenck's psychoticism includes some of the traits listed under the Big Five's superfactors of agreeableness and conscientiousness (or lack thereof) (Draycott & Kline, 1995; Saggino, 2000).

Instead of using the term *psychoticism*, others have suggested using a broader term such as *nonconformity* or *social deviance* in order to highlight the traits of creativity and nonconformity that are also a part of this dimension. Artists, for example, tend to score higher on this personality dimension than people who are truly psychotic (Zuckerman et al., 1988). The Big Five's openness superfactor has no direct counterpart in Eysenck's model.

Although personality dimensions may be a useful way of conceptualizing personality, they are less predictive of behavior than the traits on which they are built (Paunonen, 1998). And although the identification and description of traits and personality dimensions were and continue to be important contributions to the process of understanding personality, this sort of cataloging work doesn't take the crucial next step—attempting to explain and thereby predict human behavior. For this exploration we must turn to theories of personality that focus on explaining and predicting behavior. An essential tool in all such theories is reliable measurement.

Measuring Personality: Is Grumpy Really Grumpy?

Let's assume for the moment, despite the view taken by situationism, that personality does exist. If so, psychologists, employers, teachers, and parents—indeed, all of us—might be able to understand and predict the behavior of others by discovering as much as possible about their personalities. Various instruments for assessing personality attempt to do just that. Most personality assessments focus on measuring overt behaviors that psychologists believe to be manifestations of a given

● **Big Five:** The five superfactors of personality—extraversion, neuroticism, agreeableness, conscientiousness, and openness— determined by factor analysis.

trait, inferring the strength of a trait from an individual's behavior. The use of behavior to infer personality traits is at the heart of all methods of personality assessment discussed here.

Interviews

Interviews to assess personality are usually *structured*; that is, the interviewer asks all interviewees questions from predetermined sets, adding or omitting specific questions spontaneously based on the interviewees' responses. The questions often focus on specific behaviors or beliefs and do not require the person being interviewed to reflect on his or her personality. An advantage of the structured interview is that the interviewer comes away with a sense of knowing the interviewee and is able to infer different aspects of his or her personality.

The interview also has disadvantages: Unless the interviewee answers the questions honestly and accurately, the personality assessment is not valid. In addition, from a research perspective, it is difficult to generalize about personality characteristics beyond one interviewee. An interviewer might discover that Gabe has many conscientious behaviors, yet he confesses to keeping a messy apartment. It does not follow that all people who have those same conscientious behaviors are terrible housekeepers.

Observation

Whether we are aware of it or not, we all use observation to learn about other people's personalities; that's what Tina did to get a sense of Gabe's personality. When psychologists use observation to assess personality, they assign observers, known as "judges," to rate participants' behaviors. Each participant's personality is then inferred from the ratings.

How accurate are observations? The better the judge knows the person about whom ratings are being made, the more accurate the ratings (Paulhus & Bruce, 1992; Wiggins & Pincus, 1992). But strangers can also provide accurate ratings as long as their judgments are based on observations of the appropriate behaviors related to the personality trait being assessed (Ozer & Reise, 1994). For example, if you attempt to assess assertiveness by counting how often someone raises a hand in class, your conclusion may not be very accurate: Reluctance to volunteer may reflect reading assignments that were never read!

Inventories: Check This

Perhaps the most common method of personality assessment is a **personality inventory**, a paper-and-pencil test that requires those being assessed to read statements and indicate whether each is true or false about themselves (only two choices) or how much they agree or disagree with each statement along a multi-point rating scale (three or more choices). Personality inventories usually assess many different traits and contain a great number of statements, often more than 300. This comprehensiveness, including statements on different aspects of each trait, ensures the validity of the inventory.

Rather than producing a single indicator of personality (such as "friendly" or "seeks excitement"), the results of a personality inventory provide information about a number of traits in the form of a *personality profile*, a summary of the different traits that constitute someone's personality (see Figure 11.1). Personality inventories are used in a variety of settings and for a variety of purposes: by mental health professionals to assess mental illness; by research psychologists to assess how

● **Personality inventory:** A pencil-and-paper method for assessing personality that requires the test-taker to read statements and indicate whether each is true or false about themselves.

FIGURE 11.1 Personality Profiles and Employment

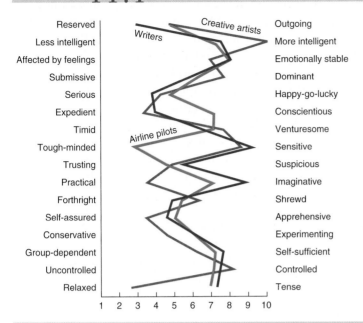

Reserved										Outgoing
Less intelligent										More intelligent
Affected by feelings										Emotionally stable
Submissive										Dominant
Serious										Happy-go-lucky
Expedient										Conscientious
Timid										Venturesome
Tough-minded										Sensitive
Trusting										Suspicious
Practical										Imaginative
Forthright										Shrewd
Self-assured										Apprehensive
Conservative										Experimenting
Group-dependent										Self-sufficient
Uncontrolled										Controlled
Relaxed										Tense

1 2 3 4 5 6 7 8 9 10

Completed personality inventories provide personality profiles of different traits. According to Cattell's personality inventory (the 16PF for 16 personality factors), writers, creative artists, and airline pilots show different profiles.

personality traits are related to other variables; by employers to assess how personality characteristics are related to aspects of the job (Borman et al., 1997). For example, many employers use scores on the trait of conscientiousness to predict employee theft, absenteeism, termination, and "good citizenship" at work (Organ & Ryan, 1995; Sackett, 1994). But not all jobs are well served by very conscientious people; work that requires artistic ability appears to fare better in the hands of those low on conscientiousness (Hogan & Hogan, 1993).

One of the key advantages of personality inventories is that they are easy to administer; a major drawback is that responses can be biased in several ways. Some people are more likely to check off "agree" than "disagree," regardless of the content of the statement. This response style, called *acquiescence*, can be reduced by wording half the items negatively. Thus an item such as "I often feel shy when meeting new people" would be reworded as "I don't usually feel shy when meeting new people." Another bias is **social desirability**: answering questions in a way that you think makes you "look good," even if the answer is not true. For instance, some people might not agree with the statement, "It is better to be honest, even if others don't like you for it" but think that they should agree, and respond accordingly. To compensate for this bias, many personality inventories have a scale that assesses the respondent's propensity to answer in a socially desirable manner. This scale is then used to adjust or, in the language of testing, to "correct" the scores on the part of the inventory that measures traits. Some researchers have found relatively high correlations between personality assessment by inventory and judges' ratings of personality (J. A. Johnson, 2000; McCrae & Costa, 1989b), lending support for the idea that the easier-to-administer personality inventories yield information similar to personality assessment by judges. However, self-reports of personality traits do not predict all types of personality-related behaviors equally well: in one study, extraversion-related behaviors were better predicted by self-report than were neuroticism-related behaviors (Spain et al., 2000).

● **Social desirability:** A bias in responding to questions such that people try to make themselves "look good" even if it means giving untrue answers.

● **Minnesota Multiphasic Personality Inventory-2 (MMPI-2):** A personality inventory primarily used to assess psychopathology.

● **Projective test:** A method used to assess personality and psychopathology that involves asking the test-taker to make sense of an ambiguous stimulus.

● **Rorschach test:** A projective test consisting of a set of inkblots that people are asked to "interpret."

One personality inventory is Raymond Cattell's 16PF (Cattell et al., 1970; see Figure 11.1). People's responses on this inventory are categorized into Cattell's 16 personality factors. Another, the **Minnesota Multiphasic Personality Inventory-2 (MMPI-2),** is commonly used to assess psychopathology (Butcher & Rouse, 1996). It has 567 questions that the test-taker checks off as either true or false; it usually takes 60–90 minutes to complete. (There is a short form consisting of 370 questions.) In contrast to the MMPI-2, which primarily assesses psychopathology or maladaptive extremes of personality, the NEO Personality Inventory (NEO-PI-R) is designed to assess 30 personality traits along the Five-Factor Model (*N* for Neuroticism, *E* for Extraversion, *O* for Openness—three of the Big Five factors—and *R* for Revised). There are both self-report and other-report (such as spouses or roommates) versions of the inventory. As with the MMPI-2, the NEO-PI-R has been extensively used, and is considered to be both a valid and reliable assessment tool.

Projective Tests: Faces in the Clouds

A **projective test** presents the respondent with an ambiguous stimulus, such as a shapeless blot of ink or a drawing of people, and asks the respondent to make sense of the stimulus. The respondent is then asked to provide the story behind the stimulus: What does the inkblot look like? What are the people in the drawing doing? The theory behind projective tests is that people's personalities can be revealed by what they project onto an ambiguous stimulus as their minds impose structure on it. This is the reasoning behind the **Rorschach test** (see Figure 11.2). Developed by Herman Rorschach (1884–1922), this commonly used projective technique has 10 cards, each with a different inkblot. The ambiguous shapes of the inkblots allow people to use their imaginations as they decide what the shapes might represent or resemble (for example, a bat or a butterfly) and what features of the inkblot made them think so.

A common complaint about the use of projective tests (and the Rorschach in particular) is that their validity and reliability are questionable. For instance, an individual taking the test on different days may answer differently, leading to different assessments of the person's personality (Anastasi, 1988; Entwisle, 1972). To increase the Rorschach's reliability and validity, a comprehensive and systemic

FIGURE 11.2 The Rorschach Test

This inkblot is similar to those used in the Rorschach test, which asks the viewers to decide what the inkblot resembles or represents and to tell why they think so.

scoring method was developed (Exner, 1974), which has been extensively tested and normed on different populations and judged to have reasonable reliability and validity by some (Meyer & Archer, 2001), but not by others (Lilienfeld et al., 2000; Wood, Lilienfeld et al., 2001). Also controversial is how truly representative those norms are, and whether someone free of psychological disorders would appear to have psychopathology in comparison to those norms (Wood, Nezworski et al., 2001).

The *Thematic Apperception Test (TAT)*, developed in the 1930s by Henry Murray, relies on the same concept as the Rorschach but uses detailed black-and-white drawings, often with people in them. Several criticisms are leveled at the TAT: (1) Although systematic scoring systems exist, only 3% of clinicians actually use a scoring system to interpret the TAT, preferring to rely on intuitive interpretations of participants' responses (Pinkerman et al., 1993); (2) From a person's response to the cards, the test administrator cannot distinguish between how the person actually thinks, feels, and would behave versus how the person *wishes* to think, feel, and behave (Lilienfeld et al., 2000).

Defenders of the TAT and Rorschach point out that the tests' abilities to predict future behavior depend not only on the test administrator's experience, but on the specific behavior(s) that the tests are being used to predict (Karon, 2000).

People are shown a drawing like this one from the Thematic Apperception Test (TAT) and asked to explain what is happening in the picture, what led up to it, what will happen later, and what the characters are thinking and feeling.

Looking *at* Levels

Genes and Personality Dimensions

As you have seen, psychologists have categorized personality traits by clustering them into personality dimensions, or superfactors. Is this the best way to categorize traits, or is there perhaps a better way? Cloninger and his colleagues (1993) suggest organizing personality traits so that they correspond to distinct biological systems. These researchers believe that people differ on four basic personality dimensions: novelty seeking (an "exhilaration or excitement in response to novel stimuli"); harm avoidance; dependence on rewards; and persistence. Cloninger further proposes that there are distinct biological systems that correspond to these four traits, each of which cuts across the Big Five.

For example, novelty seeking corresponds to a combination of a high score on extraversion and a low score on conscientiousness in the Big Five (as cited in Benjamin et al., 1996). Cloninger and his colleagues hypothesized that the novelty-seeking dimension arises directly from the functioning brain systems that use dopamine. Earlier studies with animals had shown that dopamine is involved in exploratory behavior, and a lack of dopamine in people with Parkinson's disease leads to low novelty seeking (Cloninger et al., 1993). In normal people, according to Cloninger, differences in novelty seeking are caused by genetically determined differences in the regulation of dopamine.

To test this hypothesis, Ebstein and colleagues (1996) examined people who have a particular gene that produces a type of dopamine receptor. They found that people who have this gene score higher on novelty seeking than do people without it. This result held true for men and women, for different age groups, and for different ethnic backgrounds. Although the effects of this gene were evident (in opposite ways) on extraversion and conscientiousness when the Big Five scales were used, these effects were captured more simply by the single trait of novelty seeking.

Consider in more detail what this novelty-seeking scale measures, and the implications of genetic influence. Ebstein and colleagues note that people who score higher than average on this measure are "impulsive, exploratory, fickle, excitable, quick-tempered and extravagant, whereas those who score lower than average tend to be reflective, rigid, loyal, stoic, slow-tempered, and frugal" (p. 78). Take loyalty, for example. This is a key aspect of most intimate human relationships. Is it possible that genes affect whether a person is likely to be loyal? If so, we would then have startling interactions among events at the different levels of analysis, with genes affecting events in the brain, which affect personality, which in turn affects relationships and the social activities to which people are drawn. According to this theory, genes can produce consistent impulsive, extravagant behavior; what sort of person would be attracted to someone with that personality? If in this instance "opposites attract" and

someone at the other end of the range becomes the partner, how are things likely to go for this couple in which one member is not particularly loyal and loves novelty and excitement?

It is important to emphasize, however, that although genes do bias people in certain ways, these influences are biases only and do not inevitably and unvaryingly lead to those behaviors (see Chapters 3 and 9). The average difference in novelty-seeking scores between people who did and did not have the dopamine receptor gene were about half a standard deviation (this is a difference similar to that between an IQ of 110 and an IQ of 118, which is not a huge difference). Nevertheless, it is clear that, to understand personality, we need to look at all three levels of analysis: events at the level of the brain (in this case dopamine), the person, and the group (including the situation and physical environment), as well as the interactions among those events.

TEST YOURSELF!

1. Does such a thing as a consistent personality really exist, or do our behaviors, thoughts, and feelings depend primarily on the situation?
2. How do psychologists group personality traits into sets of personality types?
3. What methods do psychologists use to measure personality?

The Brain: The Personality Organ

As their relationship progressed, Tina began to notice a host of ways in which she and Gabe were different: She loved in-line skating, biking, dancing, and skiing; he liked to read outdoors (weather permitting), go on long walks, and watch movies. She liked to meet new people or hang out with her friends and generally didn't enjoy being alone; Gabe had a few close friends but was happy spending time by himself. Tina was fairly straightforward and, up to a point, flexible; Gabe seemed less direct and more rigid. Tina was spontaneous and a bit anxious; Gabe was not spontaneous and never seemed anxious, depressed, or worried. Tina could be impatient, sometimes even snappish; Gabe was always kind and gentle. When Tina was finally able to drag Gabe to a party (he kept forgetting he had agreed to go), she was surprised by his reaction: He stayed in a corner talking to one person for half an hour, then announced that he'd had enough and was ready to leave. Tina, on the other hand, felt like the party was just beginning. Taken together, the differences between them left Tina increasingly puzzled and wondering why they were attracted to each other.

As described in Cloninger's classification of personality, some aspects of personality are biologically based, so personalities are partly born, not made. Is Gabe shy and mellow because of his biology? Is Tina outgoing and a bit anxious because of her genes or hormones? Let's explore how biology contributes to personality.

Eysenck's Theory

Eysenck used factor analysis to derive his three superfactors: extraversion, neuroticism, and psychoticism. However, Eysenck went beyond simply describing personality dimensions: He also attempted to discover the origins of their variations. For each superfactor, Eysenck conceived of a hierarchy. At the base of the hierarchy are sets of stimulus–response associations (in the Specific Response level; see Figure 11.3) derived from learning principles and an individual's biological responses to stimuli, which might make you have a good (or bad) time at a party. Further up the hierarchy is the Habit Response level, which consists of automatic responses that are in turn based on the specific responses in the lowest level; for example, Tina automatically gets excited when hearing about a party; Gabe does the opposite. These habit responses build toward the next level in the hierarchy—personality traits. The highest level of the hierarchy is the superfactor. Eysenck viewed the three dimensions and their associated traits as hereditary and universal among humans, and even among some other animals, such as rhesus monkeys. From his own research and that of other investigators, he came to view personality differences as arising in large part from biological differences, not differences in environment or social surroundings. Eysenck argued that these biological differences affect everyday behaviors and thus personality (Eysenck, 1967). As you will see, there is support for Eysenck's idea of a biological basis of personality (Matthews & Gilliland, 1999). Let's consider Eysenck's three dimensions in more detail.

FIGURE 11.3 Eysenck's Pyramid

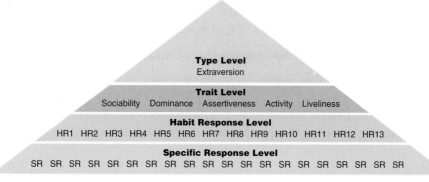

From Eysenck, *The Biological Basis of Personality,* 1967. Courtesy of Charles C. Thomas, Publisher, Ltd., Springfield, Illinois.

Eysenck proposed a hierarchy of personality in which the base of the pyramid consists of single stimulus-response associations. At the next level are habit responses such as shyness when meeting new people. Higher up are traits (which are composed of correlated habit responses), and at the top is one of the superfactors—extraversion, neuroticism, or psychoticism. A separate pyramid exists for each superfactor; this figure illustrates only extraversion.

Extraversion

Think about someone (a real or fictitious person) whom you'd describe as subdued, quiet, perhaps shy and solitary; now think of someone who enjoys people and social stimulation. The first person would probably score low on Eysenck's extraversion dimension and would be termed an *introvert*; the second, scoring high, would be an *extravert*. Researchers have identified differences at the level of the brain between introverts and extraverts. The nature of these differences seems at first surprising, but less so after a little thought.

In contrast to introverts, extraverts are less "arousable" (Haier et al., 1984); it takes more stimulation to arouse or overstimulate them (Eysenck & Eysenck, 1967). This at first seems an unlikely finding, but consider what it means: Because of this greater need, extraverts seek out activities that are more stimulating and arousing

Research suggests that extroverts are more easily conditioned by reward (such as winning money), whereas introverts are more easily conditioned by punishment (such as losing money). These differences may be related to differences in brain structure or function (Gray, 1987).

(recreational activities such as hang gliding, or occupations such as espionage). Introverts and extraverts also have different biological responses to caffeine, nicotine, and sedatives (Corr & Kumari, 1997; Corr et al., 1995; Stelmack, 1990). Differences are also found in skin conductance and EEG recordings (Eysenck, 1990a; Matthews & Amelang, 1993). The biological influence of this dimension has been further refined by Gray (1987), who suggests a mechanism based on activation or "reward," and a mechanism based on inhibition or "punishment." Extraverts are more sensitive to, and more easily conditioned by, reward, whereas introverts are more sensitive to, and more easily conditioned by, punishment. Gray views these differences as attributable to specific brain structures, neurotransmitters, and neuromodulators, and research has shown differences in EEG activation in introverts and extraverts during a card game in which money is lost (punishment) or won (reward; Bartussek et al., 1993). However, more recent research has shown that it may be the trait of anxiety, not introversion per se, that moderates the effect of punishment (Corr et al., 1997).

Neuroticism

Those who score high on the dimension of neuroticism are easily and intensely emotionally aroused and so are more likely to experience conditioned emotional responses—that is, emotional responses elicited by previously neutral stimuli (see Chapter 6; Eysenck, 1979). Thus, someone high on this dimension who is stuck in an elevator is more likely to develop a fear of elevators than someone low on this dimension. Zuckerman (1991) hypothesizes that an increased sensitivity of the amygdala is responsible for this ease of emotional arousal (see Chapter 10).

Neuroimaging data confirm that extraversion and neuroticism measure different types of processing. Canli and colleagues (2001) used fMRI to monitor brain activity while women looked at positive pictures (such as puppies playing, a happy couple) and negative pictures (such as people crying, a cemetery). The investigators then looked at the relation between the women's extraversion and neuroticism scores and their brain activity in several regions. Extraversion scores were correlated with activation in one set of brain areas when the women looked at the positive pictures (compared with negative ones); in contrast, neuroticism scores were correlated with activation in another set of brain areas when the women looked at negative pictures (compared with positive ones).

Psychoticism

Eysenck views those high on psychoticism as having less control over their emotions and therefore as more likely to be aggressive or impulsive. In the same vein, Zuckerman (1989, 1991) suggests that those high on psychoticism have difficulty learning not to engage in particular behaviors. Both tendencies could lead to criminal behavior. In fact, Eysenck (1990b) claimed that 50–60% of the variability in such tendencies is inherited. This does not mean that some people are born crooks, but rather that some are born with autonomic and central nervous system underarousal that indirectly leads them to seek risks—and some of these risks, given exposure to certain environmental influences, may be associated with criminal behavior (Eysenck, 1977). Low arousal may occur in part because of low levels of activity of the neurotransmitter serotonin in the central nervous system, a condition that has been associated with impulsive behavior (Klinteberg et al., 1993; Linnoila et al., 1983). Indeed, Raine and colleagues (1990) showed that underarousal at age 15 (as assessed by three different measures of autonomic and central nervous system activity) predicted criminality at age 24 in 75% of cases.

Although showing an impressive link between biology and criminality, these findings do not prove that biology is destiny, in this or most other areas. By analogy, our biology leads us all to need to eat, but how, what, and when we eat are determined in large part by the way we are raised. Environmental factors play a strong role in the development of criminality (Eysenck & Gudjonsson, 1989; Henry et al., 1996). Indeed, twin studies document the influence of environmental factors in criminality (McGuffin & Gottesman, 1985; Plomin et al., 1997).

Temperament: Waxing Hot or Cold

Psychologists use the term **temperament** to refer to innate inclinations to engage in a certain style of behavior. Arnold Buss (1995) views temperament as having more influence on behavior than personality traits or factors, affecting not just *what* people do, think, and feel, but *how* they act, think, and feel. Such inborn tendencies can appear at an early age and persist through adulthood. Longitudinal studies have found that children's temperaments at age 3 are correlated with their personalities, as assessed by a personality inventory, at age 18 (Caspi, 2000; Chess & Thomas, 1996). A study of 21-year-olds also linked temperament with health-risk behaviors such as unsafe sex, alcohol dependence, violent crime, and dangerous driving (Caspi et al., 1997). One aspect of temperament is *sensation seeking*: the pursuit of novelty, often in high-stimulation situations, such as sky diving, fast driving, or drug and alcohol use, or occupations, such as working in a hospital emergency room (Zuckerman, 1979). A study of personality predictors of driving accidents found that those drivers who had car accidents or traffic violations were more likely to be thrill seekers and risk takers compared with drivers who had neither (Trimpop & Kirkcaldy, 1997). Tina appears to have a sensation-seeking temperament, and Gabe, who actively shies away from adventurous activities, doesn't. Sensation seeking is associated with lower levels of the chemical monoamine oxidase (MAO) in the blood, at least in males (Shekim et al., 1989).

● **Temperament:** Innate inclinations to engage in a certain style of behavior.

People who engage in highly stimulating hobbies such as race car driving, downhill skiing, or snowboarding are more likely to be *sensation seekers*.

● **Activity:** A temperament dimension characterized by the general expenditure of energy; activity has two components—vigor (intensity of the activities) and tempo (speed of the activities).

● **Sociability:** A temperament dimension characterized by a preference to be in other people's company rather than alone.

● **Emotionality:** A temperament dimension characterized by an inclination to become aroused in situations in which the predominant emotions are distress, fear, and anger.

● **Impulsivity:** A temperament dimension characterized by the propensity to respond to stimuli immediately, without reflection or concern for consequences.

Buss and Plomin (1984; A. H. Buss, 1995) propose four dimensions of temperament: activity, sociability, emotionality, and impulsivity. **Activity** is the general expenditure of energy; it has two components: *vigor* (intensity of activity) and *tempo* (speed of activity). People can differ in the intensity of vigorous activity they prefer (for example, preferring skiing to bowling), and the pace of the activities (for instance, preferring fast-paced activities and performing activities more quickly). Tina seems to have a temperament that is vigorous *and* has a fast tempo, as evidenced by her enjoyment of in-line skating, biking, and skiing, and by the impression she gives of perpetually being in a hurry.

Other dimensions of temperament are **sociability**, the preference to be in the company of other people rather than alone, and **emotionality**, the inclination to become aroused in emotional situations, but only when the emotions of distress, fear, and anger are involved. Emotionality is similar to the Big Five superfactor of neuroticism, also known as "emotional instability." Studies of identical versus fraternal twins have shown that a person's degree of emotionality is partly inherited. In these studies, twins answered questionnaires about their own temperaments (Eaves et al., 1989; Saudino et al., 1999) and about their cotwins' temperaments (Heath, Neale, et al., 1992); parents were asked about the temperaments of their twin children (these questionnaires also included ratings of activity and sociability, with results that also indicated genetic influence) (Buss & Plomin, 1975; Plomin & Foch, 1980). Research on twins who are raised apart has also produced evidence that activity level and sociability are partly inherited (Loehlin et al., 1985; emotionality was not assessed).

The fourth dimension of temperament, **impulsivity,** is the propensity to respond to stimuli immediately, without reflection or concern for consequences. Impulsivity refers to the time lag from stimulus to response, as opposed to tempo, which refers to the rate of a response once it is initiated.

Genes and Personality

We pointed out earlier that the personality dimension of novelty seeking can be influenced by a single gene, which in turn influences your biology. Since biology can influence personality, the question arises, are all personality differ-

These identical twins were separated in infancy and adopted by different working-class families. In school, neither liked spelling, but both liked math; as adults, both worked as part-time deputy sheriffs, vacationed in Florida, had first wives named Linda, second wives named Betty, and gave their sons the same names (although with different spellings: James Alan and James Allan). They both drove Chevys, had dogs named Toy, liked carpentry (Holden, 1980), and built nearly identical benches around trees in their backyards (Rosen, 1987). Moreover, their medical histories were remarkably similar, including the onset of migraine headaches at age 18. However, they wore their hair differently and preferred different ways of expressing themselves: one preferred writing, the other talking (Holden, 1980). Are these similarities a result of coincidence, or of their shared genetics? How many similarities would any two random people have if they compared such detailed information?

ences genetically determined? Behavioral geneticists seek to ascertain the influence of heredity on behavior, and in so doing investigate a wide range of psychological phenomena, including personality. One way these researchers try to tease apart the effects of heredity from those of the environment is to compare twins separated at birth and raised apart with twins raised together (see Chapter 9). Also compared are identical and fraternal twins who share an environment but have exactly the same genes (identical twins) or on average only half their genes in common (fraternal twins). If the identical twins are more similar than the fraternal twins, that difference is usually attributed to effects of the genes.

UNDERSTANDING RESEARCH

The Minnesota Study of Twins Reared Apart

QUESTION: The question had two parts: First, how much of personality is genetically determined? Second, how much of personality is environmentally determined? Personality psychologists generally consider two aspects of the environment: One of these is the shared family environment; the other is the individual's unique experiences (such as winning a spelling bee or single-handedly causing the team to lose the soccer finals). Which type, if either, contributes to personality?

ALTERNATIVES: (1) Heritability is relatively high, and effects of shared environment low; (2) heritability is relatively low, and effects of shared environment high; (3) heritability and effects of shared environment both are relatively low, which would imply large effects of nonshared environment.

LOGIC: To the extent that personality traits have a genetic component, identical twins should be more similar than fraternal twins on personality measures. Similarly, to the extent that personality traits have a component due to the shared family environment, twins reared together should be more similar in their personality profiles than twins reared apart.

METHOD: A group of psychologists at the University of Minnesota undertook the largest study of twins reared apart (identical and fraternal) to shed light on this issue. Called the Minnesota Study of Twins Reared Apart (MISTRA), the researchers located 59 pairs of identical twins, 47 pairs of fraternal twins, and four sets of triplets adopted into different families at some point after birth (Bouchard, 1994). Once enrolled in the program, adult twins spent 6 days taking personality (including the MMPI), intelligence (including the WAIS), biological, medical, and dental tests, and answering a total of 15,000 written questions (Rosen, 1987; Segal, 1999). The researchers correlated the results within each pair in order to assess similarity.

RESULTS: In addition, about 24,000 pairs of twins raised together were studied to produce the correlations in Table 11.2 (p. 454; Loehlin, 1992). As the results indicate, both extraversion and neuroticism have substantial heritability—the fraction of observed variability of a characteristic that arises from inherited factors (see Chapter 9). In addition, both dimensions are influenced to some degree by shared environment, but this effect is more pronounced for extraversion.

INFERENCES: The results of the MISTRA and other studies provide evidence indicating that at least part of the variation in personality traits is caused by genetics (Bouchard & Loehlin, 2001). Other twin studies have shown high heritabilities for temperament (accounting for up to two thirds of the total variance), and have

TABLE 11.2 Correlations of Twin, Family, and Adoption Studies for Extraversion and Neuroticism

Note that low numbers indicate little if any correlation, and higher numbers indicate a stronger correlation. Notice that identical twins' levels of extraversion and neuroticism are more similar to each other than those of fraternal twins, and that twins reared together are generally more similar than twins reared apart.

Type of Relative	Correlation	
	Extraversion	Neuroticism
Identical twins reared together	.51	.46
Fraternal twins reared together	.18	.20
Identical twins reared apart	.38	.38
Fraternal twins reared apart	.05	.23
Nonadoptive parents and offspring	.16	.13
Adoptive parents and offspring	.01	.05
Nonadoptive siblings	.20	.09
Adoptive siblings	−.07	.11

Source: Adapted from Loehlin (1992).

found comparable results for German and Polish samples. These findings suggest that shared environmental differences have much less impact than genes on temperament (Zawadzki et al., 2001). Similarly, researchers report that Russians have very much the same levels of heritability for personality dimensions as those found in the West (Saudino et al., 1999). This makes sense given the additional finding that shared environment has only a small effect on twins' personalities. However, the combined effects of heritability and shared environment do not explain all the results—which suggests that the nonshared environment plays a role.

It is worth stressing that, although personality traits may be partly caused by your genes, even in research on twins not all traits are equally heritable, as shown in Figure 11.4 (Heath & Martin, 1990; Loehlin, 1992; Pederson et al., 1988). Even within a superfactor, heritability of traits is variable. For instance, the heritability of traits within the superfactor Extraversion vary from .23 (Warmth) to .36 (Excitement Seeking; Jang et al., 1998). Similar results have been found when twins rate themselves and when others rate them (Angleitner et al., 1995).

The method of using twins to obtain heritability has been criticized on both statistical and methodological grounds (Joseph, 2001; Stoolmiller, 1999), and studies of adoptive families have not found such high correlations (Loehlin et al., 1981). Criticisms include the idea that the adoptive homes for the twins reared

FIGURE 11.4 Heritability of Personality

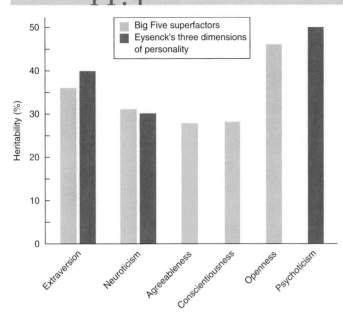

Heritability of the Big Five superfactors and Eysenck's three dimensions of personality based on research with twins.

Data for Big Five superfactors from Loehlin 1992. Data for Eysenck's three dimensions of personality—extraversion and neuroticism from Pederson et al., 1988; psychoticism from Heath & Martin, 1990.

apart were more similar to each other than a random selection of homes would be, and that some of the twin pairs reared apart lived together through infancy or saw each other sporadically throughout childhood. Both of these events would thereby increase the correlations among the twin pairs, but not because of genetics.

Despite such criticisms, some researchers propose a genetic origin for very specific behaviors (Bergeman et al., 1990; Kendler et al., 1992; Lyons et al., 1993), from the amount of time spent watching television (Prescott et al., 1991) and childhood accidents (Phillips & Matheny, 1995) to divorce (McGue & Lykken, 1992) and religious attitudes (Waller et al., 1990). Genes apparently influence the way people with these traits respond to specific situations (Lensvelt-Mulders & Hettema, 2001a). Similarly, Lykken and colleagues (1993) found a heritability of 50% in work and leisure interests in a twin study and estimate that a subjective sense of well-being (what some might call happiness) has a heritability of between 44% and 80% (Lykken & Tellegen, 1996)! Other researchers have found that the "subjective sense of well-being" has a higher heritability in women (.54) than in men (.46) (Roysamb et al., 2002); a particularly interesting result of this study was a suggestion that different genes may underlie variations in happiness for men and women.

Of course, nobody claims that the amount of time you spend watching television is explicitly coded in your genes. What some researchers do claim, however, is that the genes may influence characteristics such as how easily your autonomic nervous system is triggered (Lensvelt-Mulders & Hettema, 2001b; Tesser et al., 1998)—and such factors, in turn, influence personality traits. Indeed, even physical traits—such as how attractive and athletic you are—may indirectly allow the genes to influence personality (Olson et al., 2001). If, for instance, your activity level is both "low vigor" and "low tempo" and you tend to be shy, you are more likely to spend time alone in sedentary pursuits (such as watching television) than

Your temperament (such as your preferred level of *vigor*) and personality traits will likely determine whether your idea of a good time at the beach will lead you to be physically active or inactive (assuming you like beaches).

if you are a gregarious person who likes vigorous, fast-paced activities. It is also important to note that simply because some aspects of personality have a genetic component, this does not mean that personality is fixed from birth to death. All researchers agree that other factors, such as personal experience, also shape personality. Even Eysenck (1993), who argued that much of behavior is biologically determined, conceded that the environment makes a difference in whether someone high in psychoticism will become a creative, productive researcher or artist, or be disabled by schizophrenia. As we have tried to show through this textbook, the environment can affect the body (and the brain), which in turn leads to other psychological changes (Davidson, 2001).

As noted earlier, the MISTRA group has generally not found the family environment to be a large contributor to personality traits. The exceptions are "social closeness," that is, the desire for intimacy with others (Tellegen et al., 1988), and "positive emotionality," a trait "characterized by an active engagement in one's environment" (p. 1037). The relatively small contribution of a common family environment to other personality traits may simply reflect the fact that adoptive families are more similar to each other than are families in general, thereby diminishing the correlation for shared family environment (Stoolmiller, 1999). Moreover, many important aspects of the family environment are not in fact shared. The same family event, such as a divorce, will be experienced differently by children of different ages and cognitive abilities (Hoffman, 1991). In addition, parents do not treat each of their children exactly the same. Children create their own microenvironments based on their own temperaments and personalities at birth, leading parents to develop different patterns of interaction with each of their children and different expectations of each child (Graziano et al., 1998; Plomin & Bergeman, 1991; Scarr & McCartney, 1983; see Chapter 9). It is also possible that there are individual differences in their susceptibility to environmental forces in personality development (Holden, 1980). Genes not only have direct effects, but indirect ones as well—which may in turn alter the environment, which in turn can alter the operation of the genes. As we discussed earlier (Chapters 3 and 9), genes and environment are best regarded as a single system.

Looking *at* Levels

The Wallflower Personality

Are you shy, or do you know someone who is? Have you ever wondered what causes one person to be shy and another outgoing? Is shyness innate? To understand the origins of shyness, it is necessary to look at shy people from the vantage points of events at all three levels—the brain, the person, and the group.

At the level of the brain, Kagan and his colleagues (1988) have found that some babies are more reactive, or sensitive, to environmental stimuli and thus are more fussy than other babies. These "high-reactive" infants are more likely than "low-reactive" babies to respond to a recording of a woman's voice or to a colored toy with crying, general distress, and increased motor activity. Such infants tend to have a reactive nervous system, as indicated by faster heart rates and higher levels of the stress hormone cortisol. Kagan and his colleagues have shown that babies with a fast heart rate in the womb are more likely later to become inhibited, fearful children who startle more easily; in fact, the heart activity of even 2-week-old infants can predict later inhibition (Snidman et al., 1995). These children's sympathetic nervous systems are more easily aroused, leading to a preference for situations less likely to create high arousal. As these inhibited children get older, they are usually the ones who hide behind their parents in a room full of adults.

At the level of the person, shy people are extremely self-conscious, so much so that they may painfully and ruthlessly analyze their behavior after a social interaction, an unhappy process that leads them to avoid interaction with others in the future. They become preoccupied with their shyness and its effects ("I can't stop imagining what they're thinking about me"). These preoccupying thoughts can occur in response to autonomic nervous system reactions (a pounding heart), to behavior (what to do with the hands), and to thoughts ("No one wants to talk to me"). Fear and distress in social situations are common feelings for inhibited people.

But not all inhibited toddlers are still inhibited at age 7, and not all inhibited children become shy adults (Kagan, 1989a). Events at the level of the group can play a role either in diminishing the effects of shyness or in maintaining shyness into adulthood. Fox (cited in Azar [1995]) found that the home environment, specifically parents, can help inhibited children by recognizing and supporting the children's temperaments. As one previously inhibited 7-year-old explained, "My parents introduced me to new things slowly" (Azar, 1995).

Events at the three levels all interact: Having a reactive autonomic nervous system may produce a bias toward shyness, but the view taken by the environment of family and culture toward such behavior will determine how a person thinks and feels about him- or herself. American culture tends to favor outgoing people, a social bias that puts shy people at a disadvantage. Their self-image as social beings is more likely to be negative, and this negative self-concept increases the likelihood of an autonomic reaction in social situations, thereby perpetuating the cycle. Moreover, Kagan (1989a) has found that a larger proportion of inhibited children are later-borns, whereas a larger proportion of uninhibited children are firstborns. He hypothesizes that those with an inhibited temperament who have older siblings live in a more stressful environment, which exaggerates their autonomic responses. Those who are firstborn or only children grow up in a less stressful environment and are less likely to become shy children or adults.

TEST YOURSELF!

1. What are "introverts" and "extraverts"? How does Eysenck's theory explain the origin of personality?
2. What, exactly, is temperament?
3. What does the field of behavioral genetics say about the genes' effects on personality?

The Person: Beliefs and Behaviors

Tina wanted to understand why Gabe was the way he was—or, put another way, why he had the personality he did. Lately when they studied together, he'd have a big bag of pistachio nuts and sit there cracking and eating nuts while they read. It

● **Psychological determinism:**
The view that all behavior, no matter how mundane or insignificant, has a psychological cause.

was driving Tina, well, nuts. She couldn't understand how he could just sit there hour after hour, cracking and crunching nuts. She wanted to ask him about it—why didn't he just buy shelled nuts—but she didn't feel comfortable asking him. Why were they so different? How do our personalities develop, and why do they develop differently? Does experience build on the genetic and biological framework of our personalities, affecting our beliefs, motivations, and views of ourselves? Among the notable theories that attempt to answer these questions are the psychodynamic theory of Sigmund Freud, humanistic theory, and the cognitive view of personality.

Freud's Theory: The Dynamic Personality

Sigmund Freud viewed personality as a bubbling cauldron, rocked by unconscious, irrational forces at war with one another, competing for expression and preventing the individual's exercise of free will. He believed in **psychological determinism,** the view that all behavior, even something as mundane as forgetting someone's name or being late for an appointment, has an underlying psychological cause. Freud proposed that two major drives, sex and aggression, are the primary motivating forces of human behavior. Tension occurs when these drives are not given opportunity for expression.

The Structure of Personality

In order to understand Freud's view of the structure of personality, it is necessary first to understand his view of consciousness. Freud proposed that consciousness is not one thing, but rather can be thought of as divided into three layers (see Figure 11.5). The topmost layer is normal awareness, or the *conscious*, which includes thoughts, feelings, and motivations of which you are aware. The second layer, the *preconscious*, holds subjective material that can easily be brought into conscious awareness but of which you are not aware most of the time. For example, your telephone number is in your preconscious until someone asks you what it is, at which point it moves into your conscious awareness. The final layer is the *unconscious*, which houses the thoughts, feelings, and motivations that you cannot bring into consciousness but which nevertheless influence you. A much greater

FIGURE 11.5 Freud's View of Personality Structure

In Freud's view, only part of the mind is available for inspection and provides normal awareness (conscious); some of it is occasionally conscious (preconscious), and some is hidden, not available for observation (unconscious). Repressed thoughts, feelings, and wishes are hidden from awareness.

Adapted from Lester A. Lefton, *Psychology*, eighth edition. Published by Allyn and Bacon, Boston, MA. © 2003 by Pearson Education. Reprinted by permission of the publisher.

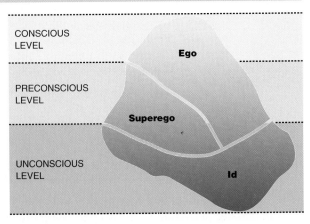

CONSCIOUS LEVEL

Ego

PRECONSCIOUS LEVEL

Superego

UNCONSCIOUS LEVEL

Id

proportion of your thoughts, feelings, and motivations are in the unconscious than are in the conscious.

As part of the dynamic nature of personality, Freud proposed three personality structures—the id, superego, and ego (see Figure 11.5). These are not physical structures, but abstract mental entities. The **id,** which exists from birth, houses the sexual and aggressive drives, physical needs such as the need to sleep or eat, and simple psychological needs such as the need for comfort; these needs and drives constantly vie for expression. The id lives by the *pleasure principle,* wanting immediate gratification of its needs by a reduction in pain, discomfort, or tension, regardless of the consequences. Because of this insistent urge for immediate gratification, the id is sometimes compared with a demanding infant. Freud proposed that when the id's instincts threaten to erupt, anxiety can develop. When that anxiety reaches a sufficiently high level, abnormal behavior and mental illness can result.

A second structure, the **superego,** forms during early childhood; this entity houses the child's (and later the adult's) sense of right and wrong. The child learns morality by internalizing—that is, taking in—the values of the parents and of the immediate culture. The superego tries to prevent the expression of the id's sexual and aggressive impulses. The superego thus isn't a Jiminy Cricket whispering in your ear, but the internalized voice of society. However, the superego's morality, because it was internalized during early childhood, remains childlike in nature.

The superego is the home of the conscience, and depending on the parents' way of teaching right and wrong, it can be more or less punishing. If your superego is very harsh, you experience much anxiety and strive for perfection. The superego can cause feelings of *guilt,* an uncomfortable sensation of having done something wrong, which results in feelings of inadequacy. The superego's morality is responsible for the *ego ideal,* which provides the ultimate standard of what a person should be (Nye, 1992).

A third structure, the **ego,** also develops in childhood, before the superego, and works very hard to balance the demands of the id and superego. The ego tries to give the id enough gratification to prevent it from making too much trouble, while at the same time making sure that no major moral lapses lead the superego to become too punishing. The ego must also make sure that the actions of the id and superego, as well as its own actions, don't create problems in the real world. The ego is guided by the *reality principle,* which leads it to assess what is realistically possible in the world. Although he believed that the ego develops out of the id, in his later life Freud (1937/1964) wrote that the ego's characteristics may be determined by heredity (Nye, 1992). According to Freud's theory, the ego is also responsible for cognitive functions such as problem solving and reasoning.

Personality Development: Avoiding Arrest

Freud viewed childhood as central in determining the formation of personality. He proposed five distinct phases, or stages, of development, each having an important task requiring successful resolution for healthy personality development. Four of Freud's five stages involve specific erogenous zones, areas of the body (mouth, anus, and genitals) that can provide satisfaction of instinctual drives. Freud believed that each zone demanded some form of sexual gratification, with a different zone prominent during each stage. For this reason, Freud's stages are called **psychosexual stages.**

If a child does not satisfy the needs of a given stage, he or she will develop a *fixation,* a state in which energy is still focused on an earlier stage of development

● **Id:** A psychic structure, proposed by Freud, that exists at birth and houses sexual and aggressive drives and physical needs.

● **Superego:** A psychic structure, proposed by Freud, that is formed during early childhood and houses the sense of right and wrong, based on the internalization of parental and cultural morality.

● **Ego:** A psychic structure, proposed by Freud, developed in childhood, that tries to balance the competing demands of the id, superego, and reality.

● **Psychosexual stages:** Freud's developmental stages based on erogenous zones; the specific needs of each stage must be met for its successful resolution.

even as the child moves on to the next stage. A fixation results from incomplete resolution of an earlier stage. In times of stress, Freud argued, the person will regress to the thoughts, feelings, and behaviors of the fixated stage. Such arrested development could create a **neurosis**: an abnormal behavior pattern relating to a conflict between the ego and either the id or the superego. According to Freud (1938), conflict between the ego and reality results in *psychosis*, a break from reality.

Oral Stage. The *oral stage* extends from birth until approximately the age of 1½. In this stage, the child's pleasures come from the mouth, primarily via sucking and biting; the developmental task in the oral stage is successful weaning from mother's breast or the bottle. If oral needs are frustrated at this stage, the child will develop a fixation, resulting in one of two kinds of personality. One is the *oral–receptive*, which is characterized by oral pleasure seeking, such as putting food or cigarettes into the mouth. According to Freud, people with oral–receptive personalities tend to become dependent on others and expect others to take care of them. The other personality style, the *oral–aggressive*, is characterized by a predilection for oral pleasures that emphasize biting, such as chewing ice or smoking pipes. Freudian theory proposes that oral–aggressive people are often verbally hostile in relationships. Would Freud have interpreted Gabe's preference for pistachio nuts as a sign of an oral–aggressive personality? Possibly, although Gabe doesn't exhibit other signs of the oral–aggressive personality; maybe he just likes pistachios.

According to Freud, children whose oral needs were frustrated in the oral stage will remain fixated on pleasure from that erogenous zone.

Anal Stage. The developing child leaves the oral stage for the *anal stage*, which lasts from about age 1½ to age 3. The primary zone of pleasure shifts from the mouth to the anus. Retaining and expelling feces are the primary pleasures in this stage, and the developmental task is successful toilet training. Freud believed that parents who are rigid about toilet training, requiring their children to "go" on demand, can create a battle of wills, resulting in a fixation in adulthood. One type of fixation, the *anal–retentive*, can be thought of as producing a constipated personality that waits until the last moment to "go." Such people are more likely to delay gratification and, according to Freudian theory, are neat, methodical, miserly, and stubborn. In contrast, the *anal–expulsive* personality is characterized by cruelty, destructive acts, emotional outbursts, and a disregard for conventional rules. Although a Freudian might see in Gabe's personality some traits akin to the anal–retentive type (his methodical manner, his organized schoolwork, his fairly inflexible nature), he does not entirely fit the bill because he isn't neat in other aspects of his life and is not miserly, but in fact quite generous.

Phallic Stage. The third stage, the *phallic stage*, occurs from around 3 to 6 years old. The locus of pleasure is now the clitoris or penis, gratification occurring primarily through masturbation. The developmental task is successful identification with the same-sex parent. Freud proposed that children of this age are preoccupied with the discovery that girls don't have penises, a discovery that in girls creates jealousy of the male's penis, and in boys fear of castration. Freud took inspiration from the ancient Greek story of Oedipus, who unknowingly killed his father and married his mother. Freud believed that boys in this stage jealously love their mothers and view their fathers as competitors for their mothers' love, so they

● **Neurosis:** An abnormal behavior pattern relating to a conflict between the ego and either the id or the superego.

both fear and hate their fathers. Freud called this dynamic the *Oedipus complex*. A boy fears that, as punishment for loving his mother and hating his father, his father will cut off his penis, the primary zone of pleasure; this concern leads to the boy's **castration anxiety.** For successful resolution, a boy must renounce his passionate love for his mother and make peace with his father, choosing to identify with him and accept his position instead of viewing him as a competitor. In doing so, the boy "introjects," or internalizes, his father's morality as part of his superego. According to Freud, fixations at this stage can create either a Don Juan personality, obsessed with attaining sexual gratification, or, following poor identification with the father, a less masculine, more feminine personality, possibly although not necessarily homosexual.

Girls' personality development at this stage, according to Freud, is different from that of boys; girls' version of the Oedipal complex has been labeled the *Electra complex*, after a Greek myth about a girl who avenges her father's murder, committed by her mother and her mother's lover, by persuading her brother to kill their mother. Girls at this stage experience *penis envy*, a sense of being ineffectual owing to the lack of a penis and the ensuing desire to have a penis. Girls also struggle with feelings of anger and jealousy toward the mother: anger for neither providing a penis for her daughter nor having one herself, and jealousy because of the mother's relationship with the father. Girls ambivalently identify with their mothers. As a product of the Victorian era, Freud justified women's inferiority to men by explaining that they only partially resolved this stage. Because they do not experience castration anxiety, they are not motivated to resolve fully this ambivalent identification with their mothers. They remain fixated at this stage, and as a result have a less-well-developed superego, less ego strength, and less ability to negotiate reality and the id.

Latency Period. After the phallic stage the sexual impulses in both boys and girls become subdued for a time during the *latency period*, which lasts from approximately age 6 until puberty. In this stage sexual urges are repressed, and the developmental task is transforming these repressed urges into socially acceptable activities. Stimulation of an erogenous zone is not the focus of this stage; rather, sexual urges are transformed into more culturally acceptable, nonsexual behaviors.

Genital Stage. Freud's final psychosexual stage is the *genital stage*, which begins at puberty; the erogenous zones now are the vagina for girls and the penis for boys. Gratification occurs in sexual intimacy, and one of the two developmental tasks of this stage, the ability to form a sexual love relationship, marks the beginning of mature sexual relationships. The other task of this stage is to develop interests and talents related to productive work. Freud believed that individuals with fixations at earlier developmental stages would have problems in the genital stage. According to Freud, girls' erogenous zones now shift from the "immature" clitoris to the "mature" vagina, and the "vaginal orgasm" is evidence of successful resolution of this stage. There is no evidence, however, that women experience two different kinds of orgasm; rather, the female orgasm involves both clitoris and vagina, not "either/or" (Harris, 1976; Kaplan, 1981; Masters & Johnson, 1966).

Defense Mechanisms: Protecting the Self

The ego's job of handling threatening material is made easier by its use of **defense mechanisms,** unconscious psychological means by which we try to

● **Castration anxiety:** A boy's anxiety-laden fear that, as punishment for loving mother and hating father, his father will cut off his penis (the primary zone of pleasure).

● **Defense mechanism:** An unconscious psychological means by which a person tries to prevent unacceptable thoughts or urges from reaching conscious awareness.

TABLE 11.3 Common Defense Mechanisms

Note: Defense mechanisms are used by the ego to prevent threatening thoughts from entering awareness.

Denial
Threatening thoughts are denied outright. *Example:* You have a drinking problem but deny that it is a problem (and truly believe this).

Intellectualization
Threatening thoughts or emotions are kept at arm's length by thinking about them rationally and logically. *Example:* While watching a frightening part of a horror movie, you focus on the special effects, make-up, camera angles, and other emotionally nonthreatening details.

Projection
Threatening thoughts are projected onto (attributed to) others. *Example:* You accuse your partner of wanting to have an affair rather than recognizing your own conscious or unconscious wish to have one yourself.

Rationalization
Creating explanations to justify threatening thoughts or actions. *Example:* In response to watching a football game instead of studying, and subsequently doing poorly on an exam, you say, "Oh, I can make up for it on the final exam."

Reaction Formation
Unconsciously changing an unacceptable feeling into its opposite. *Example:* You harbor aggressive impulses toward your boss, but instead you experience warm, positive feelings toward him, transforming your anger about his obnoxious behavior into an appreciation of "his fairness as a manager."

Repression
Anxiety-provoking thoughts, impulses, and memories are prevented from entering consciousness. *Example:* After failing an exam, you keep forgetting to tell your parents about it.

Sublimation
Threatening impulses are directed into more socially acceptable activities. *Example:* You sublimate your unacceptable aggressive urges to engage in physical fights by playing ice hockey.

Undoing
Your actions try to "undo" a threatening wish or thought. *Example:* After having the thought of eating several slices of chocolate cake, you go to the gym and work out for an hour.

Source: From Freud (1933/1965), p. 70.

prevent unacceptable thoughts or urges from reaching conscious awareness, thereby decreasing anxiety (see Table 11.3). Freud proposed a number of defense mechanisms; these were further developed by his daughter, Anna Freud (1895–1982), herself a noted psychoanalyst. The most important defense mechanism is **repression,** a process that occurs when the unconscious prevents threatening thoughts, impulses, and memories from entering consciousness. An example of repression might be "forgetting" to go to a dreaded dentist appointment. According to Freud, overreliance on particular defense mechanisms may lead to the development of neuroses.

Freud's Followers

Freud attracted many followers, a number of whom modified his theory of personality or added ideas of their own. Among those who expanded on Freud's work, termed *neo-Freudians*, were Carl Jung, Alfred Adler, and Karen Horney.

Carl Jung. Carl Jung (1875–1961) was a Swiss psychiatrist whom Freud befriended but with whom he later severed communication over disagreements about theory. Jung agreed with Freud's concepts of the unconscious, ego, and id but

● **Repression:** A defense mechanism that occurs when the unconscious prevents threatening thoughts, impulses, and memories from entering consciousness.

diverged from Freud over his emphasis on the centrality of sexuality in personality development. Jung developed his own theory of personality that added to Freud's concepts of the unconscious, the ego, and the id, an entity Jung termed the *collective unconscious*. According to Jung, the collective unconscious contains a rich storehouse of ideas and memories common to all humankind, which we all share on an unconscious level. The common themes in myths and stories around the world and throughout the ages, Jung claimed, spring forth from the collective unconscious in each generation. Stored in the collective unconscious are many **archetypes,** symbols that represent "aspects of the world that people have an inherited tendency to notice" (Carver & Scheier, 1996, p. 268). Among these archetypes are God, the shadow (that is, the dark side of personality), and Mother Earth.

Alfred Adler. Whereas Freud viewed sexual and aggressive impulses as integral to personality development, Alfred Adler (1870–1937) viewed feelings of inferiority and helplessness as important in forming personality (1956). Feelings of inferiority fuel a *striving for superiority*, which Adler viewed as the source of all motivation. When severe, such inferiority feelings can hamper strivings for superiority and lead to strong feelings of inferiority—an **inferiority complex.** This can arise from parents' neglect or hatred. Adler viewed the Oedipus complex not as universal, but as experienced only by children who are overindulged by the opposite-sex parent (Adler, 1964).

Karen Horney. Karen Horney (1885–1952) agreed with Freud that anxiety-inducing childhood experiences are central to later psychological problems. She disagreed, however, about the role and primacy of sexual and aggressive drives. Horney emphasized the importance of parent–child interactions in early childhood. If parents do not provide their children with consistent and real interest, warmth, and respect, Horney claimed, the children are likely to grow up with *basic anxiety*, an "all-pervading feeling of being lonely and helpless in a hostile world" (Horney, 1937, p. 89). Horney offered an alternate explanation for penis envy, which she called *privilege envy*. Rather than wanting a penis per se, Horney theorized, girls desire the privileges that go along with having a penis. Even privilege envy, however, is not a cultural universal; in some cultures, Horney noted, men are envious of women's reproductive ability. Horney felt that Freud had disregarded the cultural and social factors that influence personality development.

Critiquing Freudian Theory: Is It Science?

Psychoanalytic theory remains fascinating a century after Freud first conceived it, and legions of people worldwide—psychologists, writers, filmmakers, and others—have seen truth in its observations about personality. But as fascinating as Freud's theory may be, is it grounded in good science? First, as you saw in Chapter 2, a scientific theory must be testable, but many aspects of Freud's theory are difficult to test. Some key concepts were not concretely defined, some changed over time, and often the interpretation of these concepts was left open. Freud believed that many actions and objects have symbolic meanings. For example, long thin objects are *phallic symbols*—they stand for a penis. However, when Freud was asked about the meaning of his sucking on a cigar, he replied, "Sometimes a cigar is only a cigar." Maybe so, but a good theory would tell us when it is and when it isn't "only a cigar."

A second criticism of Freud's theory is that it is so complicated that it can explain, or explain away, almost anything. When there is an apparent contradiction

● **Archetype:** A Jungian concept of symbols that represent basic aspects of the world.

● **Inferiority complex:** The experience that occurs when inferiority feelings are so strong that they hamper striving for superiority.

within someone's personality, it is almost always possible to appeal to a defense mechanism to explain that contradiction. If Gabe had had a difficult time with toilet training, resulting in frequent constipation, we could predict that he would have an anal–retentive personality. But how do we then explain that he is often generous and, at home, downright sloppy? Psychodynamic theory could say that his generosity and sloppiness are an undoing of his desire to be selfish and orderly.

Third, Freud developed his theory by analyzing patients, mostly women, and by analyzing himself. And Freud's views of women, of proper parenting, and of appropriate development were all biased by his sensibilities and surroundings, as we are biased by ours. He and his patients were upper-middle-class or upper-class products of late 19th-century Vienna; their sensibility was not necessarily representative of other classes, times, or cultures. Applying a theory based on a particular group of people at a particular time to other people at another time raises issues of validity.

However, some aspects of Freud's theory have received support from contemporary research (see Westen, 1998, 1999). For example, the type of attachment we have to our parents predicts the type of attachment we will have to a partner and to our own children (Shaver & Hazan, 1994). Although not supporting Freud's specific psychosexual stages, such findings support the general idea that relationships with parents can affect aspects of later development. Moreover, research on defensive styles has supported some aspects of Sigmund and Anna Freud's views on defense mechanisms (Bond et al., 1983; Mikulincer & Horesh, 1999; Newman, Duff et al., 1997; Silverman, 1976). More generally, research on conditioned emotional responses (see Chapter 6), implicit memory (see Chapter 7), and aspects of thinking (see Chapter 8) support the broad idea that some mental processes can be unconscious—that is, without awareness. Despite the difficulty in evaluating most of Freud's theory, many aspects of it remain with us because it offers a truly comprehensive, and sometimes insightful, view of people and of personality.

Humanistic Psychology

Partly as a reaction to Freud's theory, which in many ways draws a pessimistic picture of human nature and personality formation, the humanist psychologists focused on the positive aspects of the individual—on people's innate goodness, creativity, and free will. Rather than being driven by forces outside of their control, as the Freudians claimed, the humanists believe that people can create solutions to their problems. A cornerstone of their theories is that we all have a drive toward **self-actualization,** an innate motivation to attain our highest emotional and intellectual potential. The work of two psychologists, Abraham Maslow and Carl Rogers, represents the humanistic perspective on personality.

Maslow

The personality theory developed by Abraham Maslow (1908–1970) is really a theory of motivation based on a hierarchy of physical and emotional needs (see Chapter 10). Lower-level needs, said Maslow, must be met before needs further up the hierarchy can be satisfied; the highest level need is that for self-actualization. During crises, needs regress to a lower level, and higher-level needs are put on hold.

Maslow studied the lives and characteristics of historical figures he considered to be at the self-actualizing level, including Albert Einstein, Mahatma Gandhi, Abraham Lincoln, and Eleanor Roosevelt. His investigation led him to propose

● **Self-actualization:** An innate motivation to attain the highest possible emotional and intellectual potential.

TABLE 11.4 Characteristics of Self-Actualizing People

- Perceive reality accurately and efficiently
- Accept themselves, others, and nature
- Appreciate ordinary events
- Try to solve cultural rather than personal problems
- Form deep relationships, but only with a few people
- Often experience "oceanic feelings" (a sense of oneness with nature that transcends time and space)

Source: Maslow (1968).

● **Flow:** The experience of complete absorption in and merging smoothly into an activity and losing track of time.

● **Unconditional positive regard:** Acceptance without any conditions.

that people who are self-actualizing have these qualities: a true perception of reality, an acceptance of themselves and their environments, an appreciation of the ordinary, a focus on cultural rather than personal problems, few but deep personal relationships, and what Maslow called "oceanic feelings" (see Table 11.4). Maslow regarded oceanic feelings as *peak experiences*, moments of intense clarity of perception (Privette & Landsman, 1983), a suspended sense of time, and wonderment at the experience. Oceanic feelings are similar to the idea of **flow**, the feeling of complete absorption with and merging smoothly into an activity and losing track of time (Csikszentmihalyi & Csikszentmihalyi, 1988); you may have had such an experience, becoming totally engrossed in, say, sketching, listening to music, or playing a musical instrument. Various researchers have studied Maslow's theory, particularly as it relates to motivation on the job. In the end, many of Maslow's concepts are difficult to test, and the validity of his theory remains questionable (Fox, 1982; Soper et al., 1995; Wahba & Bridwell, 1976).

Rogers

Carl Rogers (1902–1987) is noted for his formulation of client-centered therapy (see Chapter 1) and his notions of personality and its development. Like Maslow, Rogers viewed humans as possessing a need for self-actualization. But rather than viewing the satisfaction of lower- to higher-order needs as the driving force behind personality, he believed that the *self-concept*—our sense of ourselves and of how others see us—is central to personality development. Rogers proposed that our feelings about ourselves are in part a function of how others see us. Thus we have a basic need for **unconditional positive regard**, acceptance without any conditions. Receiving unconditional positive regard, according to Rogers, is crucial for the development of a healthy self-concept. Of course, it is impossible to receive or provide unconditional positive regard all the time, and the socialization process praises children for behaving in accordance with societal rules. This praise for specific behaviors leads us to learn *conditions of worth*, or "what it takes" to be treated as worthwhile. According to Rogers, people whose lives revolve around meeting such conditions of worth will not achieve their full

Good or bad child? Rogers argues that a child may at times behave unsuitably, but that does not mean he or she is a bad child. Labeling children as "bad" may affect their developing self-concepts or self-worth (Kamins & Dweck, 1999).

- **Expectancies:** Expectations that have a powerful influence on thoughts, feelings, and behavior, and in turn on personality.

- **Locus of control:** The source perceived to be the center of control over life's events.

human potentials. In order to prevent such obstruction of potential, yet meet society's need for children to learn what it considers appropriate behavior, Rogers advised parents to make the distinction between a child's inappropriate *behavior* and his or her *worth* as a human being.

Humanistic theories appeal to many because of their emphasis on the uniqueness of each person and on free will. According to this view, how you live your life is determined not by unconscious forces but through the use of your conscious awareness and the freedom to choose your experiences. Critics of humanistic theory point out that, as with psychodynamic theory, many of its concepts are difficult to test and have received little research support. Moreover, the uplifting, positive view of human nature has struck a discordant note for many in light of the amount of violence and evil in the world.

The Cognitive View of Personality: You Are What You Expect

The cognitive approach to personality emphasizes that the development of personality is affected by people's thoughts: Thoughts influence feelings and behavior, and consistent thoughts (consistent at least in a given situation) create personality.

Expectancies

One aspect of the cognitive view of personality development is the idea of **expectancies:** What you *expect* to happen has a powerful influence on your thoughts, feelings, and behavior, and in turn on your personality. Expectancies about the outcomes of behavior, often based on past experiences, can explain why operant conditioning works. You learn that a certain stimulus signals a likely outcome if you behave in a certain way, so you come to expect certain outcomes from particular behaviors in certain situations. Perhaps Gabe doesn't like parties because, from his previous experience of them, he expects that he will have a miserable time and feel socially isolated (in the language of conditioning, this would be "punishment" for attending the party; see Chapter 6). Such expectancies have a powerful influence on behavior even without our awareness. Killen and his colleagues (1996) found that among ninth-grade nondrinkers, both male and female, those who had the expectancy that drinking would enhance social behavior (that is, the outcome of drinking would be more or better social behavior) were more likely to begin drinking within a year.

One type of personality difference related to expectancy focuses on **locus of control,** the source we perceive as exerting control over our life events—that is, determining the outcome (Rotter, 1966). People who have an internal locus of control, called *internals*, are more likely to see control over events as coming from within themselves when the situation is ambiguous; that is, they feel personally responsible for what happens to them. Gabe's responsible approach to studying would indicate that he has an internal locus of control. In contrast, *externals* are people with an external locus of control; these people are more likely to see control as coming from outside forces, and they feel less personal responsibility. Because Tina does well in her classes without studying much, she chalks up her good grades to easy tests. She feels less personally responsible for her success than does Gabe. In this way, she seems to have more of an external locus of control.

Although we don't know what Hillary Clinton believed about herself when she graduated from high school, it is likely that she had a high level of self-efficacy.

Internals and externals have different responses to success and failure. Internals are more likely to increase their expectancies in response to success and to lower their expectancies in response to failure. Externals are likely to do the opposite, lowering their expectancies after success and raising them after failure; externals apparently reason that the present situation may change in the future—for better or worse. Thus, what you believe about a situation depends on whether you attribute the consequences to your own behavior or to outside forces. As an internal, Gabe has lowered expectations about future parties because of what he sees as his failures at past ones. Tina, as an external, doesn't fully expect to maintain her high grades because she doesn't feel completely responsible for them in the first place.

Self-Efficacy

People also differ with respect to **self-efficacy,** the sense that we have the ability to follow through and produce the specific behaviors we would like to perform (Bandura, 1977b). Thus, those who are high on self-efficacy believe they will be able to perform a specific behavior if they want to do so (Ajzen, 2002). Self-efficacy is distinct from locus of control, which focuses on internal or external causes. (Note, however, that the two types of expectancies appear to have an underlying concept in common; Judge et al., 2002.) Albert Bandura hypothesized that self-efficacy helps people believe in themselves and in their ability to change or perform behaviors previously viewed as difficult or impossible. Those with high self-efficacy persist more than others when working on difficult problems (Brown & Inouye, 1978). Both Gabe and Tina have high self-efficacy, a correspondence that partly accounts for the initial sense they had of being a lot alike. Bandura (2001) also proposed another important cognitive element of personality: *self-reflectiveness*, reflecting on yourself and determining whether your behaviors and thoughts (such as predictions and expectations) are accurate.

Another aspect of the cognitive view of personality stems from the idea of self-regulation (Bandura, 1976, 1977a)—that is, the reinforcement we give ourselves for our behavior. Tina might reward herself for studying all day by going skating the next day. Self-regulation can occur by just thinking about your actions. When you like the way you behaved in a given situation, you praise yourself (providing reinforcement), and when you disapprove of your behavior, you blame yourself (providing punishment). Self-regulation is a powerful tool in determining behavior and feelings, which in turn contribute to personality.

Reciprocal Determinism

Bandura (1978, 2001) regarded human behavior as part of an interactive process involving psychological and social forces: Thoughts, expectancies, feelings, and other personal factors influence both the environment (including the social world) and behavior; in turn, the environment and personal factors influence, and are influenced by, behavior (see Figure 11.6). Bandura called this interactive relationship **reciprocal determinism.** In essence, Bandura was calling attention to the interaction among events at different levels of analysis, as we do in our Looking at Levels sections, except that he did not include biologically based factors. Reciprocal

- **Self-efficacy:** The sense of being able to follow through and produce the specific behaviors one would like to perform.

- **Reciprocal determinism:** The interactive relationship between the environment, cognitive/personal factors, and behavior.

FIGURE 11.6 Reciprocal Determinism

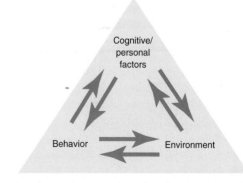

Behavior, the environment, and cognitive/personal factors all influence one another.

determinism might explain Tina's desire for highly stimulating activities (such as bungee-jumping) by pointing out that because of certain aspects of her environment, such as moving a lot as a child, Tina came to *expect* a certain level of newness, excitement, even danger, from her experiences (cognitive/personal). These expectations influence her thrill-seeking behavior (bungee-jumping), but all of the factors influence one another. Because Tina has a great time bungee-jumping, she expects to enjoy doing something similarly thrilling, and she seeks out such stimuli in her environment.

Looking *at* Levels

The Cyberstudent Personality

Have you ever taken a course via the Web instead of going to lectures? If so, how well did you do? If not, how well do you think you would do? Wang and Newlin (2000) studied the personality characteristics of students who chose to take a conventional course in statistical methods for psychology versus those who chose to take a Web-based version of the same course ("cyberstudents"). The students in the two versions of the course generally were very similar, the same material was covered in both versions of the course, and the teaching methods were the same. Moreover, the same instructor, text, syllabus, assignments, and tests were used in both versions of the course. The only difference in content was that cyberstudents were asked to participate in chatroom discussions both to prepare for quizzes and to do homework.

Three findings are of interest: First, most of the cyberstudents had higher scores on a measure of external locus of control than did the students in the conventional version of the course. In fact, this was the only personality difference between the two groups. Second, the students in the conventional version of the course got higher grades than did the cyberstudents. Third, not all the cyberstudents did poorly. Among the cyberstudents themselves, several characteristics predicted the final grade, namely whether they "maintained a high level of on-line course activity, displayed a high degree of inquisitiveness, and had an internal locus of control. . . ." (p. 140). Wang and Newlin point out that an earlier study had already reported that cyberstudents with an internal locus of control fared better than those with an external locus of control (Dille & Mezack, 1991).

Why did students who were inclined to view the world in terms of an external locus of control choose the Web-based course? Such "externals" feel that events are driven by forces outside their control and thus might be attracted to the idea that a machine will deliver material to them predictably and reliably. Apparently, a characteristic at the level of the person affected their social interactions; cyberstudents had much less "face time" with other people than did the students in the conventional course. But why did the cyberstudents do relatively poorly? Externals tend to take less personal responsibility; they assume that events are not under their control. Such people might not take the initiative in learning. They would be especially likely to benefit from a professor who notices nonverbal cues, such as their looking bored or puzzled, asks how they are doing, and helps out if there is a problem. And in fact, among the cyberstudents, those who scored more toward the "internal" end of the scale—and hence took more personal responsibility—did better in the course. A characteristic at the level of the person affected not only social interactions but also the brain: how well the students learned. Events at the three levels interacted: Their personality characteristics affected the sorts of social interactions they had, which in turn affected how well the students learned. And depending on how well they did, they may decide that in the future that they do or do not need the added interactions afforded in conventional classrooms.

TEST YOURSELF!

1. What is the Freudian view of personality?
2. What is the main emphasis of humanistic theories?
3. What is the cognitive approach to personality?

The World: Social Influences on Personality

Tina wondered whether some of the differences between Gabe and herself might reflect the different environments in which they had grown up. Gabe was an only child; Tina was the youngest of three, with two older brothers. Gabe grew up in a rural part of the United States and, before college, had lived in the same town his whole life. Tina, an Air Force "brat," had lived in half a dozen countries before she was 12.

Although some percentage of personality has genetic or biological components, the environment also plays a role. Our family environments and the ways in which we are raised contribute substantially toward personality traits of social closeness and positive emotionality. Other environmental influences on personality that psychologists have investigated include birth order, peer relationships, gender differences, and culture.

Birth Order: Are You Number One?

Have you ever noticed that people who are firstborns seem more responsible and better organized, and that last-borns seem more agreeable and accommodating? If you have, you're not the first person to make a connection between personality and birth order. Alfred Adler (1964), himself a younger sibling raised in the shadow of a high-achieving brother, was one of the early personality theorists who proposed that birth order affects personality. In the past, research has not shown clear-cut evidence for the impact of birth order on personality development (Ernst & Angst, 1983), but more recent reviews of birth order research, using meta-analytic procedures, have found consistent and interesting results.

Science historian Frank Sulloway (1996) used meta-analyses to support his proposal that at least one aspect of personality, openness to experience (one of the Big Five superfactors), is shaped by birth order. But Sulloway was careful to point out that birth order acts along with other factors, such as the number of children in a family and the level of conflict between each child and his or her parents. Moreover, a person's sex (and that of his or her siblings), the number of years between siblings, temperament, social class, and loss of a parent can also affect this aspect of personality.

Sulloway developed his theory in an attempt to understand why, throughout history, some people have supported scientific and political revolutions whereas others have insisted on maintaining the status quo, and especially why such opposite views occur within the same family. From available information about the lives of historical figures, Sulloway proposed that, in general, firstborns, because of their place in the birth order, are more likely to support parental authority, see things as their parents do, and be less open to new ideas and experiences. Younger siblings, because they must find a different niche in the family and in the world around them, are more likely to be open to new ideas. In their personalities, "only" children are similar to firstborn children.

Although not all psychologists agree with his meta-analytic conclusions about birth order and personality development (Modell, 1996), and not all subsequent research has supported his theory (Freese et al., 1999), Sulloway (1999) has

TABLE 11.5 The Effects of Birth Order on Personality

Firstborns and Only Children	Middle-borns	Later-borns
• More responsible, ambitious, organized, academically successful, energetic, self-disciplined • More temperamental, more anxious about their status • More assertive, dominant (Sulloway, 1996)	• Less closely identified with family • Less likely to ask for parental help in an emergency • Less likely to report having been loved as a child • Compared with siblings, more likely to live farther from parents and less likely to visit parents (Salmon, 1999; Salmon & Daly, 1998)	• More tender-minded, easy-going, trusting, accommodating, altruistic • More adventurous, prone to fantasy, attracted by novelty, untraditional • More sociable, affectionate, excitement-seeking, fun-loving • More self-conscious (Sulloway, 1996)

extended and replicated his results with over 5,000 adults; the results are summarized in Table 11.5. And other researchers have also contributed to this research. For example, Salmon's work (1998, 1999; Salmon & Daly, 1998) has focused on middle-born children. She found that middle-borns were less close to their families than were their elder or younger siblings. For instance, when hearing political speeches, middle-borns responded most positively to the speeches when the speaker used the term *friend* than when the terms *brothers* and *sisters* were used. In contrast, first- and last-borns responded most positively to speeches in which family terms were used (Salmon, 1998). Further, when asked to define themselves, middle-borns were least likely to define themselves by their last names, that is, their family names (Salmon & Daly, 1998).

Findings about the importance of birth order come from more than self-report measures. When spouses were asked to complete a personality inventory about their partners, firstborn partners were described as having different personality characteristics than later-born partners (Sulloway, 1999). As rated by their partners, later-born spouses were less conscientious and more extraverted, agreeable, and open to experience than the firstborn spouses. A similar correlation between personality and birth order was found among college roommates: Firstborn roommates were perceived differently than later-born roommates. However, a study of birth order effects among families with both biological and adoptive children (so that the first biological child may not have the "firstborn" position), found that conscientiousness was the only trait common among those in the firstborn position (Beer & Horn, 2000).

Peer Relationships: Personality Development by Peer Pressure

In 1995, Judith Harris wrote an article (and later a book, *The Nurture Assumption*) proposing that, beyond the genes they give their children, parents do not really affect their children's personalities and social behavior. She claimed that it is children's peers, not their families, who shape how they behave and determine the nongenetic elements of their personalities. For example, she proposed that both contact with their peers and the desire to fit in lead children quickly to learn how to speak the new language without an accent—even if their parents spoke with a thick accent.

According to Harris (1998), there are only two main ways that parents' behaviors can have enduring effects on their children's personalities and social behavior. These are severe abuse and choice of where to live and where to send their children to school (and the latter is significant only because it gives parents some small control over their children's peer group). Beyond this, she theorizes, parents have little lasting influence on their children's personalities and social behavior.

Harris's view of minimal parental influence on childhood development rests on the assumption that all children in the same family experience the same environment, but there are several flaws with this assumption. First, as we have noted, people create their own microenvironments based on their temperaments, past experiences, and appearances, and different temperaments among siblings may elicit different types of parenting style from the same parent (Jenkins et al., 2003). Thus, there is no single "family environment" that is the same for each child, and any measure of an aspect of family environment, such as the number of books in the house, does not necessarily reflect the actual environment for a particular child. To say that families affect each child differently is a far cry from saying that families do not affect the child at all (Rutter, 2002). Second, if families had no effect on children's personalities, then birth order effects would not exist (Sulloway, 1998). The fact that firstborns have been shown to have consistently different personalities than their younger brothers and sisters speaks to the fact that interactions within the family—including the manner in which parents treat their children—*does* affect personality.

Third, the same event in a family has different meaning for each of its members, based on age and cognitive ability (Hoffman, 1991). This can be clearly seen in studies of the effects of parents' divorce on their children. Children who are 5 years old when parents divorce respond in predictable ways that are *different* from the predictable ways that 11-year-olds respond. Five-year-olds assume the divorce is a result of something they did, whereas 11-year-olds can reason and understand that the divorce may be caused by other factors. Thus, siblings of different ages may

Parents can influence how each of their children feels about him- or herself, which in turn affects the child's thoughts, feelings, and behaviors (in essence, personality). Parents can also affect their children's values, which ultimately affect their personalities.

have the same stimulus, in this case the divorce, but the effects on their personalities are very different (Hoffman, 1991).

Another flaw in Harris's general theory is that she ignores the role that parents, and the family in general, can play in the way people feel about themselves, and how these feelings, in turn, lead to the particular thoughts, feelings, and behaviors that constitute personality. For example, if the youngest child in a family is always belittled, that consistent experience, in tandem with his or her temperament, can create a child who longs to grow up and prove his or her worth (Dunn & Plomin, 1990). Harris's

critique of parental influence is based on research conducted more than two decades ago; more recent research takes into account parent and child temperaments (genetic influence) and still finds that parenting style can affect children's consistent behavior. Moreover, peers generally affect day-to-day behavior (such as what to wear) more than they influence enduring personality traits (Collins et al., 2000).

Finally, Harris does not address the literature showing that parents influence their children's values, which in turn influence how they think, feel, and behave. Although peer relationships can affect personality development, these relationships are not the only environmental factor to affect personality. Research designed to test elements of Harris's hypothesis directly has thus far provided mixed results (Iervolino et al., 2002; Loehlin, 1997; Vernon et al., 1997).

Gender Differences in Personality: Nature and Nurture

In general, personality differences between females and males are not very great, especially when compared with the large differences among people within each sex (Costa et al., 2001). In fact, some have proposed that it is counterproductive to look for sex differences in personality, arguing that the context in which behavior takes place has a larger role in personality development (Lott, 1996). For example, there are no notable sex differences in social anxiety, locus of control, impulsiveness, or reflectiveness (Feingold, 1994).

Nonetheless, some consistent differences have been found (Feingold, 1994). Women tend to score higher on traits reflecting *social connectedness*, which is a focus on the importance of relationships (Gilligan, 1982). In contrast, men tend to score higher on traits reflecting *individuality* and *autonomy*, with a focus on separateness from others, achievement, and self-sufficiency. Women tend to be more empathic than men (Lennon & Eisenberg, 1987) and report more nurturing tendencies (Feingold, 1994). In addition, as noted in Chapter 10, women do better on tasks assessing emotion in other people (Hall, 1978, 1987; McClure, 2000). For example, women are better than men at spotting when their partners are deceiving them (McCornack & Parks, 1990).

The observed sex differences in individuality and social connectedness show themselves in part in the way males and females try to resolve moral dilemmas. Gilligan (1982) and others have argued that females think through moral dilemmas differently from, not less well than, males. Females are more likely to pay attention to the interpersonal context of a moral decision, to whether and how others will be hurt by the decision; males are more likely to make a moral decision based on laws or abstract principles. We will discuss this in more detail in Chapter 12. Note, however, that not all studies find this sex difference (Archer & Waterman, 1988).

Males and females also differ in their degree of neuroticism, with men scoring lower (Costa et al., 2001; Lynn & Martin, 1997; Zuckerman et al., 1988). However, women generally score lower on anger and aggression (Shields, 1987) and on assertiveness (Costa et al., 2001; Feingold, 1994).

These findings are consistent with stereotypes about men and women, but the fact that a difference exists doesn't tell us *why* it exists—what might be the role of biological or cultural factors (sex differences caused by cultural factors are sometimes referred to as *gender differences*)? Several cultural and social theories attempt to explain personality differences between men and women. Social role theory proposes that boys and girls learn different skills and beliefs. For example, some computer games pitched to girls emphasize social interactions and a concern for others, and portray getting along as more important than winning. This emphasis is in contrast to the more typical genre, which involves killing the enemy, capturing others' territory, and defending against capture or death. These two types of computer games let the user cultivate different skills and lead to different moral lessons. Expectancy effects can also play a role in gender differences in personality; through direct interaction with their environments, boys and girls come to have different expectancies about likely responses when gender-role appropriate or inappropriate behavior is exhibited (Henley, 1977).

Another cultural explanation for personality differences between men and women rests on the fact that women are most often the primary caretakers of children. Choderow (1978) proposes that between the ages of 3 and 5, boys realize they are a different sex from their mothers, a realization that leads them to feel a loss of identification and connection with their mothers and to experience themselves as autonomous individuals. In contrast, girls do not experience this loss because they and their mothers are the same sex, and girls maintain a sense of connection to others. An additional cultural explanation for gender differences in assessing others' emotions is the difference in power between men and women. Traditionally, women have been less likely to hold positions of power. In such circumstances, being able to read the emotions of others provides some degree of safety by being able to make rapid assessments of a situation (Snodgrass, 1985; Tavris, 1991).

One cultural explanation for gender differences in personality is that as boys between the ages of 3 and 5 realize they are a different sex than their mothers, they lose their identification and connection with her, and come to experience themselves as more autonomous than do girls (Choderow, 1978).

The importance of context, or situation, has raised the question of whether examining sex differences in personality is valid; after all, different situations can yield contradictory findings (Eagly, 1987, 1995; Lott, 1996). For example, Moskowitz (1993) found differences between men and women when participants interacted with same-sex friends (males were more dominant, females were more friendly), but those differences disappeared when the interactions were between opposite-sex strangers. Thus, although differences between men's and women's personalities have been observed, they do not necessarily hold in all situations. Moreover, a large, 26-country meta-analysis using the NEO-PI-R found that, in general, differences between men and women are not as large as differences within each sex. If sex (or gender) exerts a large role on personality, then there should have been differences between men and women in addition to the usual ones in individuality and social connectedness. However, this was not the case (Costa et al., 2001).

In spite of the evidence that culture and context shape gender differences, we must also note that there are biological explanations for these differences. Biological explanations for sex differences include the effects of testosterone (see Chapters 3 and 10) (Berenbaum, 1999; Dabbs et al., 1997, 2001), as well as the premise that men and women have evolved differently because of differences in mate selection and parenting strategies (D. Buss, 1995). According to this view, women have a greater investment in their offspring because they cannot have as many children as can men. This greater investment, and their caretaker role, supposedly causes women to become more strongly attached to their children, which has an evolutionary advantage: These women are more likely to have children who survive into adulthood and have children themselves.

From what we know of Tina and Gabe, we cannot say with certainty that the personality differences between them are explained by sex or gender differences. Although he prefers to be alone more than she, he does have friends, and we can't say if their contrasting preferences reflect a gender difference, a difference in social connectedness and individuality, temperament, or their learning histories.

Culture and Personality

It is more difficult to compare personalities across cultures than you might think. Although it is possible to translate personality assessment measures into other languages, some concepts don't translate very well, even if the words themselves can be rendered in different languages. For example, it is possible to translate the phrase *self-esteem* into French, but the concept of self-esteem as we understand it has not been generally familiar in France, and so a simple translation of words from English to French doesn't convey the meaning of the idea.

Nevertheless personality measures that have been carefully translated to compensate for such problems reveal the same Big Five personality factors in many, although not all, cultures (Katigbak et al., 1996, 2002; McCrae & Costa, 1997; McCrae, Costa, et al., 1998; Paunonen & Ashton, 1998; Paunonen et al., 2000). Personality measures developed in the native language of a culture, rather than translated into it, may be more accurate for that culture, depending on the behaviors of interest (Katigbak et al., 2002). For example, Chinese college students were asked to rate other people on qualities described by Chinese adjectives (not English adjectives translated into Chinese); five factors were identified, but they were not the same as the Big Five found in English-language tests (Yang & Bond, 1990).

In general, personality differences have been found between collectivist and individualist cultures (see Chapter 10). Collectivist cultures often find the needs of the group more important than those of the individual: Asian, African, Latin American, and Arab cultures tend to have this orientation (Buda & Elsayed-Elkhouly, 1998). In contrast, individualist countries such as the United States, Great Britain, Canada, and Australia emphasize the individual, even at the expense of others. Collectivist countries tend to value humility, honoring the family, and efforts to maintain the social order (Triandis et al., 1990), and are more likely to have a populace that cares about others, even strangers (Hui & Triandis, 1986). Individualist countries value personal freedom, equality, and enjoyment. This distinction between cultures has been used to explain differences in crime rates, which are higher in individualist cultures: Collectivist cultures exert more social control over the individual, and criminals' actions

People in collectivist cultures tend to define themselves as part of a group, are very attached to the group, and see their personal goals as secondary to the group's goals. People from individualist cultures define themselves as individuals, are less attached to the group, and see their personal goals as more important than the group's goals (Triandis et al., 1988).

reflect not only on themselves but also on their families. In fact, as the global economy leads collectivist cultures to shift their work habits and values to those of individualist countries, crime rates and other social ills increase (Strom, 2000).

Not surprisingly, individualist countries also differ from collectivist countries in their citizens' self-concepts: People from individualist countries report "self" as a composite of traits, independent from the group; people from collectivist countries see "self" in relation to specific situations and contexts (Markus & Kitayama, 1991). That is, other people are incorporated into the definition of self in the latter type of culture. Perhaps for this reason, traits may be less predictive of behavior in collectivist cultures such as the Philippines (Church & Katigbak, 2000). These cultural differences also affect individuals' behaviors and views of themselves: Americans are more likely to behave in ways to enhance their view of themselves through individualist-oriented behaviors, whereas Japanese are more likely to enhance their view of themselves through collectivist-oriented behaviors (Kitayama et al., 1997; Sedikides et al., 2003).

Are these cultural differences associated with differences in personality profiles? Using the five-factor approach, bilingual Hong Kong university students were given a personality inventory. Results showed that, compared with North American university students, Hong Kong students were low in extraversion in general, and low in the particular traits of excitement seeking, competence, and altruism. Moreover, they were high in vulnerability, straightforwardness, and compliance (McCrae et al., 1998). As proof of the impact of culture on personality, after Chinese immigrants move to North America, their personality profiles begin to resemble those of native-born North Americans; the longer they have lived in North America, the more similar the profiles (McCrae, Costa, et al., 1998).

Although the United States is an individualist country, individualism varies by region (Vandello & Cohen, 1999) (see Figure 11.7, p. 476). The Deep South (perhaps because of its strong self-identification as a cultural region, its history of collective farming, and the prominence of religion) is the most collectivist. The states

FIGURE 11.7 Individualism Versus Collectivism, by State

Even regions within a country differ on the individualism–collectivism dimension. Utah, with its strong collectivist orientation, ranks as one of the top 10 states in collectivism, along with some states in the Deep South and the Southeast. Some of the Great Plains and western mountain states are the most individualist, perhaps because of the individualist "frontier" mentality and rugged geographic features.

Data from Vandello & Cohen, 1999.

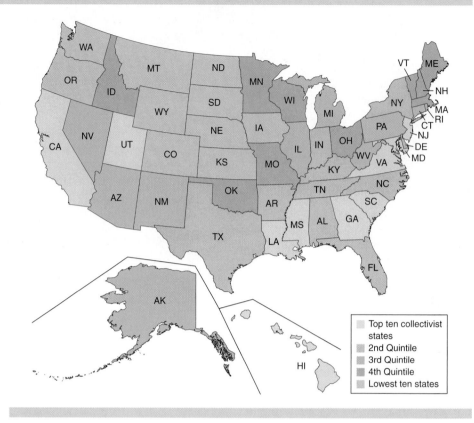

Top ten collectivist states

2nd Quintile

3rd Quintile

4th Quintile

Lowest ten states

of the Southwest are also relatively collectivist; these states have a distinct history and an influx of immigrants from Mexico, a collectivist country. In contrast, the Great Plains and western mountain states are particularly individualistic, perhaps because of the "vast distances, sparse population, and harsh, unpredictable weather" in this part of the country (Shortridge, 1993, p. 1011), as well as the frontier values of individuality. Thus, although people may live in a country that falls on a particular point on a collectivist–individualist continuum, there are regional, as well as individual, differences. So, to the extent that experience shapes personality, Tina's and Gabe's different experiences during their childhood years may well have contributed to their different approaches to life.

Looking *at* Levels

Two's Company

How can we explain cultural differences in personality? Could it be that people from different cultures have different genes, or the environment leads different genes to be expressed in certain cultures and not others? Let's look again at a study by Ekman (1980) described in Chapter 10. Japanese and Americans watched emotional films, either alone or with a white-coated investigator in the room. When alone, the Japanese and the Americans reacted to various events in the films in very similar ways. But in company, the Japanese tended to respond more politely and with a narrower range of emotions, whereas the Americans responded much as they did when alone. Thus, it isn't the case that the Japanese actually had different emotional responses than the Americans, that they had lower levels of emotionality. Rather, their learned behaviors (politeness and less expression of emotion) masked their true emotional responsiveness.

When in the company of authoritative strangers (such as the white-coated investigator), the Japanese do not display the same range of emotions that is permissible when alone. The collectivist Japanese culture leads to a change in behavior (changing facial expressions), and the Japanese have learned to make this change very well, extremely quickly, and apparently automatically. Both their initial responses to the films and their subsequent learned responses can be considered elements of personality, although they are influenced by different factors. The initial responses may be influenced more by temperament (emotionality, at the level of the brain), whereas the subsequent responses are influenced more by the social environment (in this case, culture). The cultural differences in personality between the Americans and the Japanese trace back to learning during childhood (level of the person), learning that not only shapes the individual's personality, but also regulates the expression of biological responses.

TEST YOURSELF!

1. To what extent does birth order shape personality?
2. Can friends affect the way personality develops?
3. Do social factors produce gender differences in personality?
4. Do different cultures produce different types of personalities?

CONSOLIDATE!

What Is Personality?

- Personality is a consistent set of behavioral characteristics that people display over time and across situations, and that distinguish individuals from each other.
- People do not behave in the same manner in all situations: The context, or situation, influences the way people behave, and people can influence the situation.
- Some researchers have found that personality traits can be statistically grouped into five superfactors (extraversion, neuroticism, agreeableness, conscientiousness, and openness) or, according to Eysenck, three personality dimensions (extraversion, neuroticism, and psychoticism).
- Personality can be measured by interviews, observation, inventories (such as Cattell's 16PF), and projective tests (such as the Rorschach test and the Thematic Apperception Test, or TAT), with inventories being the most common method.
- Cloninger proposes four personality dimensions, based on distinct biological systems: novelty seeking, harm avoidance, dependence on rewards, and persistence.

THINK IT THROUGH Suppose you are interested in dating someone and wanted to assess his or her personality before getting too involved. Why would you choose a particular type of assessment method? If you could assess a prospective employer's personality, why might you use the same method or a different one? Would you be able to predict your future employer's behavior if you knew his or her Big Five characteristics? Why or why not? Why might it change the accuracy of your predictions if you knew more about the scores on the specific traits that make up the five superfactors?

The Brain: The Personality Organ

- Eysenck proposed that each of his three personality dimensions (extraversion, neuroticism, and psychoticism) has a corresponding biologically distinct system. Aspects of this theory have been supported by neuroimaging and other biological research.

- Some psychologists and behavioral geneticists estimate that approximately 50% of the variations in personality are inherited, although some traits appear to be more heritable than others.

- Innate inclinations, often referred to as temperament, include activity, sociability, emotionality, and impulsivity.

- Differences in biology, such as emotional arousability, can affect thoughts, feelings, motivation, and behavior, and can make people more or less prone to conditioned emotional responses and shyness.

THINK IT THROUGH Imagine that you know a family in which both parents are highly extraverted, emotionally stable, not particularly creative, and very conscientious. Would you predict that their child would have the same personality features? Why or why not? If their child was very shy (one of Kagan's "inhibited" children), would that mean that the child will always be shy, or might he or she become like the parents? (Hint: Think about what you have learned about temperament.) Might Gabe have been one of Kagan's "inhibited" children? Explain your answer.

The Person: Beliefs and Behaviors

- Questions of motives, thoughts, and feelings are at the heart of Freud's psychodynamic theory, which focuses on the three structures of personality (id, ego, and superego, and their dynamic relationships), three levels of awareness (unconscious, preconscious, and conscious), as well as sexual and aggressive drives, defense mechanisms, and psychosexual stages (oral, anal, phallic, latency, and genital).

- According to Freud, when resolution of a psychosexual stage is incomplete, development is arrested, creating a neurosis. Moreover, sexual and aggressive impulses can create anxiety, causing the use of defense mechanisms.

- Neo-Freudians (such as Jung, Adler, and Horney) have added to or altered aspects of Freud's theory, generally rejecting his emphasis on sexual drives.

- Maslow's and Rogers's humanistic theories also address motives, feelings, and the self, but celebrate each person's uniqueness, stress positive qualities of human nature and free will, and emphasize self-actualization.

- The cognitive view of personality focuses on the roles of expectancies on people's thoughts, feelings, and behav-

iors: What we expect to happen will influence our personality development.

- Personality differences in expectancies include locus of control, the source we perceive as exerting control over life events, and self-efficacy, the sense that we have the ability to follow through and produce the behaviors we would like to perform.

THINK IT THROUGH If you used Freudian theory to understand a historical figure's personality and motivations, do you think you could be sure of your analysis? Why or why not? Could you use a humanist theory to understand this person? What would you need to know about him or her? Which aspects of this person's life would you need to know about in order to apply a cognitive theory of personality?

The World: Social Influences on Personality

- Birth order, along with other moderating factors, such as the number of children in a family and the level of conflict between parents and children, can influence openness to experience and other aspects of personality.

- Although there are a few broad personality differences between women and men (social connectedness versus individuality, and high versus low emotionality), in general differences between the sexes tend to be small, and it is not clear whether they are due to biological or social factors. Social explanations for these differences range from social role theory, to identification with the primary caretaker and differences in power. Context may predict personality better than does sex.

- Personality differences have also been found between citizens of cultures that are collectivist as opposed to individualist, with people in each culture tending to have personality traits that are more valued in their cultures.

THINK IT THROUGH What are two possible explanations for regional personality differences between "mellow" Californians and "fast-paced" northeasterners? (Hint: Genetic? environmental?) How might you go about trying to determine whether your explanation is supported by research data? What type of study could you design, and what kinds of participants would you need? What is your hypothesis—that is, what kind of results would you expect to find?

Key Terms

chapter 12

Smithsonian American Art Museum, Washington, DC/Art Resource, NY

Psychology Over the Life Span

Growing Up, Growing Older, Growing Wiser

"Spielbug," some of his classmates called him. Girls thought he was nerdy and unattractive. His father, Arnold, a pioneer in the use of computers in engineering, was hardly ever around and, to make matters worse, frequently uprooted his family, moving from Ohio to New Jersey, to Arizona, and finally to Northern California. Steven Spielberg was a perpetual new kid on the block. He was also, by all accounts, an unusual child, both in his appearance (he had a large head and protruding ears) and in his fearful and awkward behavior (McBride, 1999). Spielberg himself has said that he "felt like an alien" throughout his childhood. He desperately wanted to be accepted, but didn't fit in. So, at age 12 he began making films, "little 8mm things. I did it to find something that, for me, could be permanent" (quoted in R. Sullivan, 1999, p. 66). Spielberg continued to make movies as a teenager, often casting his three sisters in roles. He discovered that making movies was one way to win his peers' acceptance, as well as some small measure of power—for he sometimes induced his worst enemies to appear in his films.

When he was 16, Spielberg's parents divorced, and Spielberg blamed his father's constant traveling for the breakup. His unhappiness only deepened when his father remarried, taking for his second wife a woman Spielberg couldn't stand. At the same time that he withdrew from his father, Spielberg continued to have a close relationship with his mother, Leah, a concert pianist and artist. The split with his father lasted some 15 years.

In many ways, Spielberg's films, like the rest of his life, are shaped by his childhood. Spielberg himself has said about E.T., The Extra-Terrestrial, "The whole movie is really about divorce. . . . Henry's [the main character's] ambition to find a father by bringing E.T. into his life to fill some black hole—that was my struggle to find somebody to replace the dad who I felt had abandoned me" (R. Sullivan, 1999, p. 68). Many of Spielberg's other films include children who are separated from their parents (such as the girl in *Poltergeist* and the boy in *Close Encounters of the Third Kind*). And *Back to the Future* might represent his longings to change the past, if only he could. Only when he turned 40 did he turn to adult contexts. As he matured, Spielberg's identification with oppressed people in general (not just oppressed children) led him to make movies such as *The Color Purple*, *Schindler's List*, and *Amistad*.

Steven Spielberg married and had a child, but eventually divorced his first wife, actress Amy Irving. His own experiences made him extremely sensitive to the effect of the divorce on his son, Max, and he made every attempt to ensure that Max did not feel abandoned. When he married again, he became deeply involved with his family (which includes seven children, some of them adopted). There was a happy development in the previous generation's father–son relationship as well: Arnold became a well-loved grandfather who is now a regular presence in the Spielberg household.

> Spielberg himself has said that he "felt like an alien" throughout his childhood.

Spielberg's journey is one version of the universal story of human development: A skinny kid beset by fears and with few friends becomes one of the most powerful figures in the global entertainment industry; from a family with a fragmented family life develops a man's resolve to make the best possible life for his own family; across generations, a father and a son come to like each other, now as father and grandfather, after 15 years of estrangement. *Developmental psychologists* study exactly these sorts of events in our lives—the fascinating and varied process of human development over the life span. In this chapter, we begin by considering prenatal development and the newborn, and we see that even here genes and environment are intimately intertwined. We next turn to infancy and childhood and observe the interplay between maturation and experience in the shaping of the child's physical, mental, emotional, and social development. Then we consider adolescence, a crucial time in development. And finally, we discuss adulthood and aging, and gain insights that help us understand how Arnold could develop from a less-than-optimal father into a terrific grandfather.

In the Beginning: From Conception to Birth

Steven Spielberg has been celebrated as one of the most successful moviemakers of all time. He just seemed to have a natural bent for making movies (he never attended film school). Where did his talent come from? In this section we begin at the beginning and think about the foundations of our skills and abilities.

Prenatal Development: Nature and Nurture From the Start

For each of us, life began with the meeting of two cells, a sperm and an egg (or *ovum*, which in Latin means "egg"). These specialized cells are sex cells, or *gametes.* The sperm penetrated the egg, and the genetic material of the sperm melded with that of the ovum. The ovum is not a passive partner in this dance of life; the sperm is drawn to the egg by chemical reactions on the surface of the egg. And when a sperm has been accepted within the egg, other reactions prevent additional sperm from penetrating. The ovum is a supercell, the largest in the human body. Even so, it is barely the size of a pinprick, and sperm are much smaller (about 1/500 of an inch). But despite their small sizes, within the ovum and sperm reside all the machinery necessary to create a new life. And, even at this earliest stage of development, *genes* (*nature*) and the *environment* (*nurture*) are intimately intertwined.

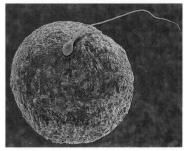

At the moment of conception, a sperm penetrates an ovum. The egg, however, is not a passive recipient; by changing its surface properties, it actively regulates the behavior of the sperm.

Getting a Start in Life

The genetic heritage of every normal human being is 23 pairs of chromosomes, one member of each pair coming from an egg and the other from a sperm. A *chromosome* is a strand of DNA (*deoxyribonucleic acid*) in the nucleus of the cell. A molecule of DNA is shaped like a twisted ladder—the famous "double helix"—in which the rungs are formed by the bonds between pairs of chemicals. Each *gene* on the chromosome is a series of particular "rungs" (see Chapter 3). All cells in the body except the gametes (eggs and sperm) contain all 23 pairs of chromosomes; each gamete contains only a single member of each chromosome pair. In an egg, one of these 23 is a chromosome known as X; in a sperm, the corresponding chromosome is either an X chromosome or a shorter version called a Y chromosome.

The fertilization of the egg by the sperm creates a cell called a **zygote,** in which the chromosomes from the egg and from the sperm pair up so that the zygote contains the full complement of 23 pairs. If the sperm contributes an X chromosome, the offspring will be female (XX); if Y, male (XY). The Y chromosome contains a gene (the SRY gene, for "sex-determining region of the Y chromosome") that produces a chemical substance that ultimately causes the zygote to develop into a male; if this substance is not present, genes on the X chromosome will produce other substances that cause the baby to be female (Goodfellow & Lovell-Badge, 1993; Hawkins, 1994).

Much of early development is determined by **maturation,** the process that produces genetically programmed changes with age. But from the very start, genes and the environment interact. Although the genes of the sperm that fertilizes the egg (along with the genes of the egg) will have a major impact on what kind of person develops, the environment plays a crucial role in whether the sperm ever reaches the egg. Sperm actually "surf" on subtle muscle contractions in the uterus; these waves usually move in the correct direction in fertile women, but they either move in the wrong direction or are weak in infertile women (Kunz et al., 1997; Lyons & Levi, 1994). In addition, the fluid in the uterus must be the right consistency and have the right chemical composition for the sperm to complete their journey (Mori et al., 1998; Shibahara et al., 1995; Singh, 1995).

The members of each pair of chromosomes (other than XY for males) are similar—but they are not identical. For example, the gene for the shape of your earlobes is on the same spot on both chromosomes, but because of its particular chemical composition, the gene on one chromosome may code for an attached earlobe and the gene on the other for an unattached earlobe. The gametes are formed from specialized cells that, while themselves containing the full 23 pairs, in the course of division produce cells with half that number, with only one member of each pair. So, because the members of each pair are not identical, the genetic contents of the resulting gametes are not all the same. And there's another

● **Zygote:** A fertilized ovum (egg).

● **Maturation:** The developmental process that produces genetically programmed changes with increased age.

FIGURE 12.1   The Long Road to a Zygote

The chromosomes in eggs and sperm are not simply copies of those of the parent, but rather unique combinations of the material in the two chromosomes in each pair of the parent's chromosomes. The sperm and egg combine to form the basis of a unique individual (or individuals, in the case of identical twins).

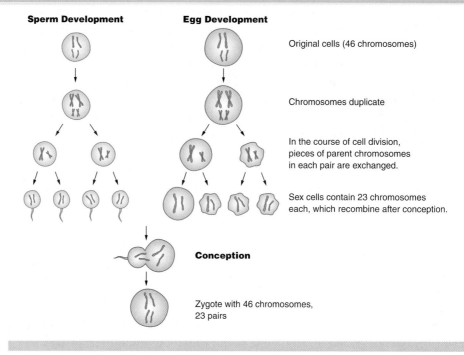

Sperm Development   **Egg Development**

Original cells (46 chromosomes)

Chromosomes duplicate

In the course of cell division, pieces of parent chromosomes in each pair are exchanged.

Sex cells contain 23 chromosomes each, which recombine after conception.

Conception

Zygote with 46 chromosomes, 23 pairs

● **Embryo:** A developing baby from the point where the major axis of the body is present until all major structures are present, spanning from about 2 weeks to 8 weeks after conception.

● **Fetus:** A developing baby during the final phase of development in the womb, from about age 8 weeks until birth.

wrinkle, which further contributes to our wonderful human variety: In the course of cell division, the chromosomal decks of cards are shuffled so that pieces of the parent chromosomes in each pair are exchanged, as shown in Figure 12.1, to form new combinations of genes.

Each zygote thus consists of a unique combination of genes. In fact, in theory, each human couple can produce some 70 trillion genetically different children! Moreover, the same genetic material can produce different results, depending on whether it is inherited from the mother or the father. This effect is called *genomic imprinting* (or *gametic imprinting*; Keverne, 1997; Kirkness & Durcan, 1992). For example, a deletion of part of chromosome 15 leads to Angelman's syndrome if it is inherited from the mother; this syndrome includes an awkward way of walking, inappropriate laughter, and severe mental retardation. When the same deletion comes by way of the father, it leads to Prader-Willi syndrome, which involves depression, overeating, and "having a temper" (Barlow, 1995; Clarke et al., 1995; Dykens & Cassidy, 1999). Researchers have yet to discover how such genomic imprinting works.

Once formed, the zygote begins to divide. The production of certain hormones causes genes to turn on and off in a specific sequence, guiding the zygote's development (Brown, 1999; as discussed in Chapter 3, genes produce specific proteins only when they are "turned on"). Soon a cluster of cells has developed. After 3 days, about 60 to 70 cells have formed and organized themselves into a sphere called a *blastocyst*. This cluster proceeds through an orderly progression, first rolling up into a tube, then developing features that in early stages look much like those of relatively primitive animals, then more complex ones.

Human development in the womb is divided into *trimesters*, three equal periods of 3 months each. The first trimester is divided into three stages: the developing baby starts off as a zygote, becomes an **embryo** when the major axis of the body is present (about 2 weeks of age), and then becomes a **fetus** when all major body structures are present (about 8 weeks of age, and the developing baby is called a fetus thereafter, until he or she is born). At the end of the second trimester, the great bulk of the neurons each individual possesses are in place (Nowakowski, 1987; Rakic, 1975; Rodier, 1980), but they are not completely fixed; researchers have recently found that new neurons can be produced in adult brains (Gould et al., 1999).

The path from zygote to birth is not always smooth. Perhaps surprisingly, about half of all fertilized eggs contain some kind of abnormality in their chromosomes. Most of these eggs are spontaneously aborted (in fact, about 30% of zygotes don't even make it to the embryo phase), but even so, about 1 in 250 babies is born with an abnormality that is obvious (for example, he or she may not respond appropriately to light or loud noises), and probably more have abnormalities that are not obvious (such as subtle defects in particular brain areas, which will become evident only later in life; Plomin et al., 1997; Sadler, 1995).

In the Womb

A popular—and misleading—image shows the fetus floating peacefully asleep in the womb. But in truth, the fetus is active nearly from the start, at first with automatic movements, such as the heart beating, and then with large-scale coordinated behaviors. As the fetus develops, the heart rate slows down (but becomes more variable), the fetus moves less often but more vigorously when it does stir, and the heart rate and movement patterns become coordinated. Some researchers have even reported sex differences in behavior in the womb, with male fetuses more active than females (DiPietro et al., 1996). After 20 to 25 weeks of gestation, the fetus is sensitive to both sound and light (Nilsson & Hamberger, 1990; Pujol et al., 1990). How do we know this? Because if a fetus is examined, as is sometimes medically necessary, by a special light-emitting instrument called a *fetoscope*, it will actually move its hands to shield its eyes. As the fetus develops, its movements become increasingly coordinated, and by 28 weeks, it responds to external stimulation. A bit later its heart rate can change if the mother is startled (DiPietro et al., 1996; Kisilevsky & Low, 1998), and between 25 and 34 weeks, a fetus can detect human speech (Cheour-Luhtanen et al., 1996; Zimmer et al., 1993).

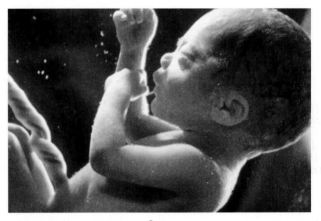

This fetus may look primitive and passive, but looks can be deceiving; the fetus in fact is capable of a rich range of behaviors well before birth.

In addition, there is evidence that fetuses can learn. In a classic study (DeCasper & Fifer, 1980), pregnant women read the story *The Cat in the Hat* aloud twice each day during the 6 weeks before their babies were born. A few hours after birth, the babies were tested. The researchers put earphones on the babies' little heads, and put a special pacifier-like device in their mouths. By sucking faster or slower, the device allowed the infants either to hear their mother's voice or another woman's voice reading the story. The infants sucked at the speed that produced their own mother's voice. Perhaps even more impressive, the researchers also gave the infants the opportunity to choose between hearing their mother read *The Cat in the Hat* or another story—and the infants preferred the story their mother had read aloud before they were born!

Teratogens: When the Environment Hurts

A **teratogen** is a chemical, virus, or type of radiation that can cause damage to the zygote, embryo, or fetus. Because of events at different stages in the course of development, different organs are vulnerable to teratogens at different times.

● **Teratogen:** Any chemical, virus, or type of radiation that can cause damage to the zygote, embryo, or fetus.

Unfortunately, the central nervous system is vulnerable at virtually every phase. For example, the development of the brain can be disrupted if the mother catches a virus, such as chicken pox or rubella (3-day German measles); more than half the babies born to mothers who contract rubella will be mentally retarded if the developing child is in the embryonic period at the onset of the disease. In addition, a mother who is HIV-positive can pass the virus on to the baby during gestation or birth (but only about one third of these babies contract the virus). The HIV virus causes brain damage, leading to problems in concentration, attention, memory, movement control, and the ability to reason (Clifford, 2000; Grant et al., 1999).

Another potential teratogen is alcohol, which can damage the eggs before fertilization (Kaufman, 1997) as well as affect the developing baby throughout pregnancy, starting with the embryo phase. If the mother drinks enough alcohol during pregnancy, the baby may be born with *fetal alcohol syndrome*; part of this syndrome is mental retardation (Streissguth et al., 1989, 1999; see Chapter 9). Using heroin or cocaine during pregnancy can cause a host of problems: physical defects (Singer et al., 2002a), irritability, and sleep and attentional problems in the newborn (Fox, 1994; J. M. Miller et al., 1995; Vogel, 1997). Although prenatal exposure to cocaine may have only subtle effects in infancy (such as slowed language development, Lester et al., 1998), such exposure may have long-lasting consequences—some of which may become more marked in subsequent years (Chapman, 2000; Lester, 2000; Singer et al., 2002b). Moreover, various environmental pollutants and ionizing radiation can have effects ranging from birth defects and cancer to behavioral difficulties, such as in paying attention. It is known that, in other animals at least, these effects can be passed on to the third generation, to the offspring of the offspring (Friedler, 1996). Certain drugs (both prescription and illegal, such as cocaine) can affect the sperm and thereby affect the growing fetus and child (Yazigi et al., 1991).

Major diseases and strong drugs are not the only threats to healthy prenatal development. Excessive amounts of caffeine (three cups of coffee a day, according to one study) can lead to miscarriage or low birth weight, irritability, and other symptoms (Eskenazi, 1993; Eskenazi et al., 1999). Smoking during pregnancy affects both mother and fetus; it is correlated with higher rates of miscarriage, lower birth weights, smaller head size, stillbirth, and infant mortality, and can cause attentional difficulties in the infant (Cornelius & Day, 2000; Floyd et al., 1993; Fried & Makin, 1987; Fried & Watkinson, 2000). A mother's smoking also significantly increases the chance that her baby will die from *sudden infant death syndrome* (SIDS; Pollack, 2001). Smoking during pregnancy alters the way the infant's autonomic nervous system operates, which may contribute to SIDS (Browne et al., 2000). In addition, a mother's poor diet can lead her infant to have fewer brain cells than normal (Morgane et al., 1993), and the lack of even a single important vitamin or mineral can have significant effects. For example, insufficient folic acid (vitamin B) can disrupt the early development of the nervous system (Nevid et al., 1998).

Stressors in the mother's life can also endanger the developing fetus, and when the stress is severe enough, infants may subsequently experience attentional difficulties, be unusually anxious, and exhibit unusual social behavior (Weinstock, 1997). In fact, fetuses of mothers of lower socioeconomic status, who are often more stressed than those of higher socioeconomic status, move less often and less vigorously, and show other differences from fetuses of better-off mothers (Pressman et al., 1998). There are several biological reasons for these effects. When the mother is stressed, more of her blood flows to parts of the body affected by the fight-or-flight response (such as the limbs and heart), and less to the uterus. She produces hormones such as cortisol, which slows down the operation of genes that guide prenatal development of the brain, suppressing brain growth (Brown, 1999). There is evidence that the babies of stressed mothers are born with smaller heads than those of unstressed mothers, which may be related to the poorer behavioral functioning scores seen for such babies (Lou et al., 1994).

Positive Environmental Events: The Earliest Head Start

The previous paragraphs might seem to suggest that our species would be better off if maturation alone controlled development. But environmental effects are not all bad, and some prenatal experiences help the fetus, as shown in the following study by Lafuente and colleagues (1997).

UNDERSTANDING RESEARCH
Stimulating the Unborn

QUESTION: Can playing music to an unborn child enhance development during infancy?

ALTERNATIVES: (1) Playing music to a fetus enhances development during infancy; (2) playing music to a fetus impairs development during infancy; (3) playing music to a fetus does not affect development during infancy.

LOGIC: If playing music to a fetus enhances subsequent development, then as infants they should be advanced on standard measures of cognitive and motor function.

METHOD: Each of 172 pregnant women was randomly assigned to an experimental or a control group. The participants in the experimental group were given a waistband with a tape recorder and small speakers, on which they played tapes of violin music for an average of 70 hours, starting at about 28 weeks after conception and continuing until the birth of the baby. The researchers then tracked the development of the babies during their first 6 months of life. The pregnant women in the control group did not play music to their fetuses.

RESULTS: The children of mothers in the experimental group were more advanced than those in the control group; for example, they had better motor control and better vocal abilities of the sort that precede language.

INFERENCES: Playing music to a fetus (and perhaps other forms of stimulation) can in fact enhance subsequent development. Steven Spielberg's mother played piano frequently while she was pregnant; could these prenatal concerts have had long-term positive effects on him? (Note that this study in its design and conclusions is very different from the "Mozart effect" discussed in Chapter 9, in which music is played for very brief periods to adults who are then tested on aspects of IQ.)

A particularly powerful example of interactions among events at different levels of analysis is the fact that social interactions with friends and family can lead to healthier babies being born to stressed mothers (McLean et al., 1993). Social support presumably helps to reduce the mother's stress, which in turn keeps her from the fight-or-flight state and its accompanying unfortunate consequences for the developing baby.

The Newborn: A Work in Progress

In many ways, the human infant compares unfavorably with the infants of some other species. A baby kitten is much more competent, able to walk on its own and explore its environment at only 6 weeks, an age when the human infant has no hope of even crawling. The human brain is not fully developed at birth, perhaps because if it were, the baby's head would not fit through the birth canal. Much human brain development continues after birth (Johnson, 2001), which affects the newborn's abilities to think, feel, and behave. For example, newborns cannot be classically conditioned to associate a tone with an air puff that causes them to blink (Naito & Lipsitt, 1969; Sommer & Ling, 1970); in the rat, researchers have shown that this ability emerges only after key parts of the cerebellum have matured during infancy (Freeman & Nicholson, 2001; Rush et al., 2001).

Nevertheless, although the typical infant may seem thoroughly incompetent, capable of eating, sleeping, cooing, crying, drooling, and not much else, such an assessment would be off the mark. The baby is not a blank slate, waiting for learning or maturity to descend. On the contrary, babies come equipped with a surprising range of abilities and capacities.

Sensory Capacities

Even at the earliest phases of development, babies have the beginnings of sophisticated sensory capabilities. They are born sensitive to the range of frequencies of women's voices (Hauser, 1996) and have a relatively sensitive sense of smell. Even babies who are fed by bottle prefer the odor of a woman who is breast-feeding another infant to that of a woman who is not breast-feeding (Porter et al., 1992).

Two-day-old infants can learn to pair information coming from senses, such as vision and hearing. For example, Slater and colleagues (1997) showed infants two visual stimuli, which differed in both color and orientation; at the same time that they presented one of the stimuli, they also presented a distinctive sound. They then switched the pairings and found that the infants paid more attention to the new combinations. These results showed that even 2-day-old infants can put visual and auditory stimuli together; if they couldn't, they wouldn't have noticed the changed pairings.

Reflexes

Infants also come equipped with a wide range of reflexes, the most important of which are summarized in Table 12.1. A *reflex* is an automatic response to an event, an action that does not require thought. Some of these reflexes have obvious survival value, such as sucking, and some may have had survival value for our ancestors, such as the Moro reflex, in which the startled baby throws its arms wide, as if to grab hold of someone. Other reflexes, such as the Babinski reflex, in which the baby's big toe flexes while the other toes fan out when the sole of his or her foot is stroked, are less obviously useful.

Curiously, many of the reflexes that babies have at birth disappear after a while. Some of the reflexes appear to be simpler versions of later behaviors, such as walking or swimming. Should we try to preserve these reflexes? It has been shown, for example, that the stepping reflex can be retained longer if the baby's leg muscles are exercised and become stronger (the reflex appears to disappear in part because the baby gains weight and the legs can no longer support the body;

TABLE 12.1 Major Reflexes Present at Birth

	Reflex	Stimulus	Response	Duration (approx.)
Stepping	**Withdrawal**	Sharp stimulus to sole of foot	Leg flexes	Weakens after 10 days of age
	Stepping	Held upright over flat surface	Stepping movements	Until about 2 months of age
	Sucking	Finger in mouth	Sucking	Until about 3 months of age
	Rooting	Stroking cheek lightly	Turns head toward stimulus, starts trying to suck	Until about 3 or 4 months of age
Rooting	**Palmar grasp**	Pressing the palm	Grasps object pressing the palm	Until about 4 months of age
	Moro (startle)	Sudden loud sound	Throws apart arms and extends legs, then brings arms together, cries	Until 5 months of age
	Swimming	Face-down in water	Kicks and paddles in water	Until about 6 months of age
	Tonic neck	Head turned to one side	One arm straightens while other bends, and one knee bends (resembling a "fencing" position)	Until 7 months of age
Moro (startle)	**Plantar**	Pressing the ball of the foot	All toes curl under	Until about 1 year of age
	Babinski	Stroking sole of the foot	Big toe flexes, other toes fan out	Until about 1 year of age
	Eye blink	Bright light in eyes	Eyes close	Life

Thelen, 1983, 1995). However, infants who walk earlier do not walk *better* than infants who walk later.

Temperament: Instant Personality

A friend describing the birth of his second son expressed amazement as he realized, when handed the child immediately after birth, that the infant was *already different* from his first son, calmer and steadier. Our friend should not have been surprised. From their earliest hours, babies show the makings of individual personalities. They demonstrate differences in *temperament*, in their innate inclinations to engage in a certain style of behavior (see Chapter 11). Some babies may be inclined toward "approach," others toward "withdrawal" (Thomas & Chess, 1996). Infants characterized by an approach response generally react positively to

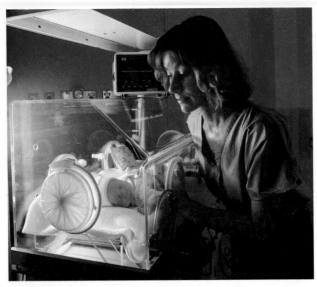

Social support can help babies who are born prematurely. Field and her colleagues (1986) found that such infants who were touched three times a day, in 15-minute sessions (moving the babies' limbs, stroking their bodies), grew 50% faster, developed more quickly behaviorally, were more alert and active, and were discharged from the hospital sooner than those premature infants who were not touched three times a day.

new situations or stimuli, such as a new food, toy, person, or place. Infants characterized by a withdrawal response typically react negatively to new situations or stimuli, either by crying, fussing, or otherwise indicating their discomfort (Chess & Thomas, 1987). Some babies are considered "easy" in that they do not cry often and are not demanding, whereas others are "difficult" in that they are fussy and demanding.

That such differences are present virtually from birth suggests, at least in part, biological factors. As we saw in Chapter 11, babies who had a fast heart rate in the womb are more likely to become inhibited, fearful children (Kagan, 1994b). Indeed, heart rate differences between inhibited, fearful babies and uninhibited, relaxed babies have been found at 2 weeks of age (Snidman et al., 1995). Further, at 14 and 21 months of age, inhibited babies often have narrow facial structures, whereas uninhibited babies often have broader faces. These differences may reflect the fact that facial growth at these ages can be affected by high amounts of cortisol (Kagan, 1994a). Babies who had greater EEG activation in the right frontal lobe at 9 months of age tend to be inhibited at 14 months (Calkins et al., 1996); this is interesting because greater EEG activation over the right frontal lobe in adults has been identified with a relatively depressed mood (see Chapter 10). The importance of biological variables in temperament is also evident in the fact that 24-month-old identical twins have more similar temperaments than do fraternal twins (DiLalla et al., 1994). Indeed, this study of twins showed that the tendency to be inhibited has a high heritability (that is, the variability in this tendency among people is largely accounted for by genetic differences).

For temperament, like other characteristics, the story of development over the life span reveals themes of both stability and change. As you saw in Chapter 11, not all inhibited infants became shy children and adults. In fact, only children who are extremely inhibited or uninhibited are likely to stay that way; the majority of children, who fall in the middle ranges, can change dramatically (Kerr et al., 1994; Robinson et al., 1992; also Kagan et al., 1998; Schwartz et al., 1996). Nevertheless, for those infants who exhibit marked inhibited or uninhibited behavior, these early temperaments are likely to be enduring core characteristics of later personality.

Some of the stability of temperament may arise not from inherited predispositions, but from early nurturing experiences. Probably the most compelling evidence of this comes from research with nonhuman animals. Meaney and his colleagues (Anisman et al., 1998; Liu et al., 1997; Meaney et al., 1991; Zaharia et al., 1996) have shown that simply handling rat pups during the first 10 days after birth has enormous effects on the way the animals later respond to stressful events. As adults, these animals don't become as nervous as other rats when put in a large open field (as reflected by fewer feces, less "freezing" responses, and more exploration), and have lower cortisol responses (and thus are less vulnerable to the negative effects of prolonged exposure to cortisol, as discussed in Chapter 7). They are also less prone to learned helplessness (discussed in Chapter 10; Costela et al., 1995). The effects of handling occur naturally when the mother rat licks her pups and engages in nursing with an arched back (so the pups are directly under her); offspring of mothers that behaved this way later had lower amounts of the type of

RNA that produces cortisol (Liu et al., 1997). We have good reason to believe that similar effects extend to humans: Touching infants not only can enhance growth and development, but also can reduce the right frontal lobe EEG activation that is associated with depression (even in 1-month-old infants!) and can boost immune function (Field, 1998; Field et al., 1986; Jones et al., 1998).

Looking *at* Levels

Cued Emotions

Babies spend much of their waking hours in the arms of a caregiver. At first glance, you might think the baby is a mere passenger, being carted from one place to another. In fact, the baby is learning a lot through interactions with the caregiver—including emotional reactions. Matthew Hertenstein and Joseph Campos (2001) neatly demonstrated one way in which nonverbal interactions between mother and child could shape the child's emotional responses. They asked mothers to hold their 12-month-old infants while viewing various objects. When an object was presented, the mother was asked to do one of three things: she tensed her fingers around the baby's belly and suddenly drew in her breath, she loosed her fingers around the baby's belly, or she did not change her grip or breath. When the mother tightened her grip and drew a sharp breath, the infant waited longer before touching the stimulus object, touched it less, and also showed more negative emotion than when the mother either relaxed her grip or had no reaction. In short, the social interaction between mother and infant affected the brain events that produced the infant's response to the stimulus. Moreover, the infant probably was learning and developed new expectations and beliefs (level of the person) via this interaction. And, of course, events at the three levels were interacting: Mothers respond differently when their babies have a negative reaction (for example, by removing the offending object, level of the group), which in turn would affect what the baby learns to expect (level of the person) and how his or her brain responds. Clearly, from an early age, events at the three levels of analysis shape emotional responses.

TEST YOURSELF!

1. How does development progress in the womb?
2. What are the capabilities of newborns?

Infancy and Childhood: Taking Off

Spielberg has repeatedly noted that his ability to make movies that appeal to children and to "the child inside adults" stems from the fact that he's never grown up himself. But although he may retain many childlike characteristics, the filmmaker has indeed matured. That is, his motor, perceptual, cognitive, and even social abilities have long outstripped those of even a preadolescent child. In this section we will see how this development occurs.

Physical and Motor Development: Getting Control

If we continued to grow throughout childhood at the same rate as during infancy, we would all be giants. A newborn can look forward to being 50% longer on his or her first birthday and 75% longer on his or her second. But growth does not continue at this rate; rather, it usually occurs in a series of small spurts. Similarly, control over various parts of the body does not occur simultaneously and smoothly, but in phases. Good motor control (that is, control of the muscles) is a necessary first step for normal interaction with the world.

Developmental psychologists have spent many years studying the precise ways in which babies' movements change as they grow. Two of the early pioneers, Arnold Gesell (Gesell & Thompson, 1938) and Myrtle McGraw (1943), described a series of milestones that all babies, from all races and cultures, pass in an orderly progression. In general, control progresses from the head down the trunk to the arms, and finally to the legs; at the same time, control extends out from the center of the body to the periphery (hands, fingers, toes). By the age of 2, the child has good control over all the limbs. However, fine motor control—of the sort needed to play piano or type on a keyboard—develops more slowly. And some of us do this better than others; Steven Spielberg, for example, was notoriously clumsy and un-coordinated throughout his childhood.

The early theorists believed that the consistent and universal order of motor development implies that it is entirely maturational. However, later studies of motor control showed that this view cannot be correct (Thelen & Ulrich, 1991). For example, consider the unanticipated consequences of having infants sleep on their backs, in an effort to reduce the chances of SIDS (this is the so-called "Back to Sleep" movement, and SIDS in the U.S. has been reduced by about 30% since this program began in 1994; Association of SIDS and Infant Mortality Programs, 2002). Ratliff-Schaub and colleagues (2001) found that premature infants who slept on their backs had more difficulty holding their heads up and lowering them with control than did infants who slept on their bellies. Moreover, back-sleeping babies were slow to roll from their backs to bellies, to sit up, to creep, crawl, and to pull themselves to a standing position (Davis et al., 1998). However, the children walked at the same age, regardless of how they slept. In fact, since babies have begun sleeping on their backs, some never actually learn to crawl. "It was an occasional phenomenon before, and now about a third of babies skip the step of crawling and go right to walking," says Dr. Karen Dewling (quoted by Seith, 2000). Thus, developing some aspects of motor control involves more than maturation; it also involves learning about the body and the world (Adolph, 2000; Thelen, 1995).

Developing motor control is important not simply because it allows the child to get around, but also because it helps the child develop capacities as varied as distance perception, visual search, and even using gestures to communicate. As Campos and colleagues (2000) put it, "travel broadens the mind." Table 12.2 presents average age ranges for major motor developments (but keep in mind that various factors, such as the opportunities to use specific muscles, affect these ages).

Perceptual and Cognitive Development: Extended Horizons

A parent probably would not tell as elaborate a story to a 3-year-old as to a 10-year-old. The reason is obvious: The younger child not only has a shorter attention span and understands fewer concepts about objects and events, but also can grasp only concepts of simple relations (such as that one object can physically cause another to move). Where do these concepts come from? In part from perception, the

TABLE 12.2 Typical Ages for Developmental Motor Milestones

Approximate Age	Milestones
2–5 Mo.	Follow movements with eyes; lift head and chest while on stomach; hold head steady; hold an object placed in hand.
6–9 Mo.	Roll over; sit upright; pick up small objects with thumb and fingers; shift objects between hands; crawl.
10–12 Mo.	Pull to upright standing, and "cruise" (walk by supporting body against objects); turn pages of book.
13–18 Mo.	Scribble; walk unaided; feed self; point to pictures when asked; throw a ball.

Source: Adapted from LaRossa, 2000.

organization and identification of information received through our senses; in part from cognition, our mental processes; and in part from our social environment.

Perceptual Development: Opening Windows on the World

Along with the rest of the body, the sensory organs develop with age. For example, young infants view the world blurrily, as if through thick gauze; with age, their visual acuity increases, in part because of developments in the eye, particularly in the lens and the retina (Banks & Bennett, 1988).

How do we know that infants can't see well? You obviously can't ask them, so how might you determine what babies are capable of seeing? Psychologists working in this area have developed a number of clever techniques. For example, to determine depth perception, infants are placed on a level sheet of glass that at first lies directly on the floor, but then extends over a part of the floor that has been stepped down. In this *visual cliff* experiment, researchers have found that even 6-month-old infants don't want to crawl over the "deep end"—even when coaxed by their mothers—thus demonstrating that they can perceive depth before they can talk (Gibson & Walk, 1960).

But the visual cliff task is of no use with babies who are not yet able to crawl, so it is possible that even younger babies can see depth. How can we tell? In one study, researchers measured infants' heart rates when they were placed on the shallow or deep end of the visual cliff, and found that 2-month-old babies had slower heart rates on the deep side (Campos et al., 1970); slower heart rates indicate that someone is paying closer attention, which suggests that the infants could in fact tell the difference between the two depths. Other techniques for examining infants' visual perception measure the amount of time they look at stimuli. For example, the *habituation technique* (also sometimes called the *looking time technique*), illustrated in Figure 12.2 (p. 494), is based on the fact that all animals—including humans of all ages—*habituate* to a stimulus: if a baby looks at a particular shape long enough, he or she will no longer find it interesting—and thus will prefer to look at

Babies are placed on the sheet of glass over a floor that appears to be directly under the glass. A short distance ahead, the floor drops down (although the glass remains level). If the baby can perceive depth, he or she will be reluctant to crawl on the glass that is over the "deep end." This is the famous "visual cliff" invented by Gibson and Walk (1960).

FIGURE 12.2   The Habituation Technique

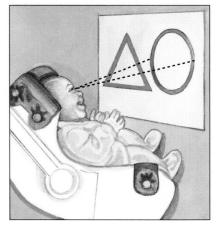

In the habituation task, the baby is first shown one stimulus and allowed to look at it until he or she is bored with it (has habituated to it).

After habituation, the baby is shown the original stimulus along with another stimulus. The baby prefers to look at something new. This technique can be used to determine what shape differences babies see and whether they see depth or other physical properties.

something new. This technique can be used to discover what babies can see, hear, or feel as "different." If you simply added a copy of the habituated stimulus, it would be no more interesting than the original—the infant has to perceive it as different to find it interesting. By varying how two stimuli differ (in shape, distance, color, pattern of movement, and so on), and seeing in what circumstances babies will prefer a new stimulus after habituating to a previous one, it is possible to discover what differences they can detect. Habituation techniques have shown that babies can detect depth between 2 and 3 months of age. In fact, 8-week-old babies can see depth as represented by sets of points flowing on a screen, the way we do when we see a spaceship whizzing through a cloud of meteors in a movie—and these infants can even see shapes that are depicted three dimensionally by sets of flowing points (Arterberry & Yonas, 2000). As noted earlier, researchers have also relied on the opposite idea to study what infants can see. Instead of observing what bores infants, investigators note what interests them. If an infant pays more attention to one stimulus than another, he or she must notice the difference. For example, even 8-month-olds look longer at a display when different depth cues are inconsistent than when they are consistent. This technique has shown that by 8 months of age, infants can not only see visual illusions of depth, but also understand how an illusory square (created by presenting only brackets at the corners) should look if it partially covered another picture (Csibra, 2001).

Newborns aren't very attentive companions, but they will notice if you make direct eye contact with them; in fact, even infants 2–5 days old prefer to look at faces that look directly at them than faces in which the eyes are averted (Farroni et al., 2002). However, at first infants only notice isolated portions of objects; within

2 or 3 months, they can perceive overall shapes (Spelke et al., 1993). By about 6 months of age they can even organize sets of isolated squares into horizontal or vertical stripes (Quinn et al., 2002). And infants organize forms better when three-dimensional objects are depicted—even 3-month-olds apparently see 3–D shapes instead of isolated line fragments (Bhatt & Bertin, 2001). As they grow older, babies need less stimulus information to recognize patterns. It is tempting to speculate that their enjoyment of playing "peek-a-boo" may reflect this developing ability, in which they can use top-down processing (see Chapter 4), using their knowledge about objects to infer a whole from a part.

Steven Spielberg is counting on the fact that you will relate emotionally to his images on film in the same way you would relate to the events and characters if you met them in reality. Nonetheless, you are in no doubt that you are seeing an image, not the thing itself. Apparently, however, 9-month-old infants aren't quite sure about which properties of objects are captured by pictures. DeLoache and her colleagues (1998) showed infants high-quality color photographs and observed the babies' reactions. The babies reached for and touched the pictures as if they were seeing the actual objects, and sometimes actually tried to pick them off the page! It wasn't as if the babies thought that the pictures *were* objects; they weren't surprised or upset when they couldn't pluck them off the page. Rather, they apparently *did not know* what pictures were and so were exploring their properties in the way that seemed most sensible. But 10 months later, at 19 months of age, the babies pointed toward the objects in the pictures and no longer tried to manipulate them. Babies apparently have to learn what pictures are, and this learning takes time. This learning transcends culture: Babies from the Ivory Coast of Africa and babies from the United States acted the same way in this experimental situation.

Compared with visual perception, auditory perception appears to be more fully developed at an earlier age. Even 6-month-old infants seem to hear well enough to detect different musical intervals. Schellenberg and Trehub (1996) showed that when infants hear pairs of tones, one after the other, they notice a change (as is evidenced by their turning their heads toward the appropriate audio speaker) from the first to the second only when the second is different according to a simple frequency ratio, such as a perfect fifth. In another study, researchers played to 4-month-old infants consonant or dissonant versions of two sequences of tones. When the sequence was consonant, the infants looked longer at the speakers than when it was dissonant. Not only did they look away when the stimulus was dissonant, but they were more physically active. The authors suggest that infants are innately tuned to find consonance more pleasing than dissonance (Zentner & Kagan, 1998). Apparently, to appreciate dissonant music, you must learn to overcome preferences that may be innate. But infant audition is unlike that of adults in a crucial way: When listening to sequences of tones that "do not conform to the rules of musical composition" (Saffran & Griepentrog, 2001, p. 74), even 8-month-old infants initially focus on absolute pitches, not relations among pitches. Adults, in contrast, focus on relations among pitches. Thus, part of auditory development is a shift away from attending to absolute pitch to attending to relative pitch, which is more useful for music and for speech (because individual voices differ in absolute pitch).

Perceptual development continues beyond the first year of life. When, for instance, toddlers (2- and 3-year-olds) are shown an array of objects and asked whether it includes a specific object, they look haphazardly from place to place (Vurpillot, 1968). But 6- to 9-year-olds will search the array systematically, left to right, then top to bottom, as if they were reading a page. In general, by about age 11, children have perceptual abilities that are similar to (although often slower than) those of adults (Lobaugh et al., 1998; Piaget, 1969; Semenov et al., 2000), but some aspects of perceptual processing (used in organizing complex patterns) probably continue to develop until late adolescence (Sireteanu, 2000).

Memory Development: Living Beyond the Here and Now

As discussed in Chapter 7, we adults have both implicit and explicit memories. Is the same true of infants? Many studies have documented that even 3-month-old infants can store information both implicitly and explicitly (Rovee-Collier, 1997). How could researchers find this out? The key idea is that recognition taps explicit memory, whereas priming taps implicit memory (priming occurs when performing a task "greases the wheels," making the same or a related task easier to perform in the future). To assess recognition, in one study researchers attached one end of a ribbon to an infant's foot and the other to a mobile that hung over the crib. The mobile was decorated with plus marks of a particular size. The infants soon learned that kicking would move the mobile, which they found reinforcing—and hence kicked at a higher rate. The researchers waited a day and then showed the infants either the identical mobile, or one with plus marks that were either larger or smaller than the original. The infants remembered the original mobile, and kicked at a high rate only when the plus marks were the initial size. This is evidence that they recalled the stimulus explicitly (Gerhardstein et al., 2000).

What about implicit memory? To test whether even 3-month-old infants have such memory, these researchers used the kicking test but now waited 2 weeks before testing memory, which is well after the time infants can recall that kicking would move the mobile (typically only up to 6–8 days after learning). They had each infant watch while the investigator held the ribbon attached to the mobile and moved it at about the same rate that the infant had moved it before. This prime was sufficient to reactivate the memory, leading the infant to recall the relationship between kicking and moving the mobile. However, the explicit memory was not activated: Now infants increased their kicking when they saw mobiles that had all sizes of plus marks, not just when the plus marks were the original size (Gerhardstein et al., 2000). Additional studies have shown that only 7.5 seconds of priming are necessary to reactivate the memory (Sweeny & Rovee-Collier, 2001). Moreover, the prime doesn't have to be part of the to-be-remembered event; even at 6 months of age a "forgotten" memory can be reactivated by showing the infant another event that was associated with a to-be-remembered event (Barr et al., 2001, 2002). In fact, other researchers have shown that at 6 months of age the brain responds differently when infants see a novel face than when they see one that's been primed (by having been shown previously; Webb & Nelson, 2001).

You might be tempted to think that memory is like height and weight: You get more of it as you age. Not exactly. For example, in one study researchers found that although adults recognize location better than do children, older children actually recognize color better than do adults (Gulya et al., 2002). Such findings are additional evidence that "memory" is not a single entity, but instead is comprised of multiple systems—and these systems develop at different rates.

Language-based types of memory take on increased importance as a child gets older. For example, in one study Simcock and Hayne (2002) asked young children to learn to operate a machine that apparently shrank the sizes of toys. Six months or a year later the researchers tested the children's memory for this event. They found that the children never used words to recall an aspect of the event that they could not have used at the time when they initially experienced it. This finding suggested to the researchers that "children's verbal reports of the event were frozen in time, reflecting their verbal skill at the time of encoding, rather than at the time of test" (p. 229). We noted in Chapter 7 that adults have remarkably poor memory for events that occurred during early childhood—perhaps this is one explanation.

For the most part, memory does improve from early childhood to adulthood. Why? Some improvement is probably due to the development of the brain (Bauer, 2002). For example, the brains of both 4-year-olds and adults are activated when they see a previously studied item, but more of the adult brain is activated—and is activated more quickly after the item is seen (Marshall et al., 2002). In fact, even 14-year-olds differ from adults in how their brains are activated during memory tasks (Hepworth et al., 2001). But not all improvement in memory with age is due to brain development—events at other levels of analysis are also important. For example, adults, in particular mothers, systematically help young children learn to label and organize to-be-remembered material (Labrell et al., 2002; Low & Durkin, 2001).

Piaget was an extraordinarily sensitive observer of children's behavior.

Stages of Cognitive Development: Piaget's Theory

Thinking is more than perceiving and remembering; it also involves reasoning. It's obvious that babies don't have the mental capacity of adults; they can't even understand most problems, let alone solve them. The gradual transition from baby to adult cognitive capacity is known as *cognitive development*. The great Swiss psychologist Jean Piaget (1896–1980) developed a far-reaching and comprehensive theory of cognitive development. Interest in Piaget's theory helped generate other lines of research that have focused on how changes in information processing, the maturation of the brain, and the social environment contribute to cognitive development.

Piaget was originally trained in biology, but early in his career, he worked in Paris with Alfred Binet's collaborator, Theodore Simon, helping to standardize Binet's newly developed intelligence tests for children (see Chapter 9). Piaget was curious about the types of reasoning mistakes children were likely to make. This new interest connected with his long-term fascination with biology and the nature of the mind, and led him to a general investigation of the reasoning processes of children at various ages. Piaget believed that babies begin with very simple, innate **schemas,** mental structures that organize perceptual input and connect it to the appropriate responses. For the youngest infant, such schemas trigger grasping and sucking at the nipple when the infant is hungry and in the presence of a bottle or breast. According to Piaget, the process of **assimilation** allows the infant to use existing schemas to take in new stimuli and respond accordingly. For example, the schema for sucking a breast can also be used for sucking a bottle or thumb. In contrast, the process of **accommodation** results in schemas' changing as necessary to cope with a broader range of situations. As the child develops, the schemas develop in two ways. First, they become more fully *articulated*; for example, more precise motions are used to locate the nipple and suck.

● **Schema:** In Piaget's theory, a mental structure that organizes perceptual input and connects it with the appropriate responses.

● **Assimilation:** In Piaget's theory, the process that allows use of existing schemas to take in new sets of stimuli and respond accordingly.

● **Accommodation:** In Piaget's theory, the process that results in schemas' changing as necessary to cope with a broader range of situations.

TABLE 12.3 Piaget's Periods of Cognitive Development

Period	Age	Essential Characteristics
Sensorimotor	0–2 years	The child acts on the world as perceived and is not capable of thinking about objects in their absence.
Preoperational	2–7 years	Words, images, and actions are used to represent information mentally. Language and symbolic play develop, but thought is still tied to perceived events.
Concrete operations	7–11 years	Reasoning is based on a logic that is tied to what can be perceived. The child is capable of organizing information systematically into categories, and can reverse mental manipulations.
Formal operations	11 years (at the earliest)	Reasoning is based on a logic that includes abstractions, which leads to systematic thinking about hypothetical events.

Second, they become *differentiated*; an original schema may give rise to two separate schemas, one for bottles and one for thumbs, which in turn may give rise to schemas for drinking with a straw, drinking from a cup, and eating solid food.

These two processes—assimilation and accommodation—together are the engine that powers cognitive development. Piaget's theory of development hinges on the results of assimilation and accommodation working in tandem, which he claimed produce a system of rules—in Piaget's terms, a "logic"—that guides the child's thought. Depending on the available schemas, different kinds of logical operations are possible. Thus, according to Piaget, the child's thinking changes systematically over time as new schemas develop.

Piaget described four major stages, or *periods*, of cognitive development, as shown in Table 12.3; each period is governed by a different type of logic and includes many substages, with key characteristics. The periods overlap slightly, and they may occur at different ages for different children; thus, the ages given in the table are only approximate.

Sensorimotor Period. The infant's experience begins in the *sensorimotor period*, which extends from birth to approximately 2 years of age. According to Piaget's theory, infants initially conceive of the world solely in terms of their perceptions and actions. In this period infants lack the ability to form mental representations that can be used to think about an object in its absence (see Chapter 8). In the early stages of the sensorimotor period, the infant does not yet have the concept of **object permanence**, the understanding that objects (including people) continue to exist even when they cannot be immediately perceived. For example, a rattle dropped by an infant over the side of the high chair is quickly forgotten—and more than forgotten: Out of sight means not just out of mind but out of existence! Piaget claimed that by the end of the sensorimotor period, by about age 2,

● **Object permanence:** The understanding that objects (including people) continue to exist even when they cannot be immediately perceived.

the toddler understands that objects exist even when they are no longer perceived. In addition, Piaget claimed that a second major achievement of the sensorimotor period—at around 9 months of age—is the ability to imitate.

Preoperational Period. Once out of the sensorimotor period, the toddler enters the *preoperational period*, from roughly age 2 until age 7. Armed with the ability to form mental representations, children in the preoperational period are able to think about objects and events that are not immediately present. As a result, they can imitate actions that occurred in the past. This newfound capacity for mental representation allows the child to engage in fantasy play. Whereas the infant might play with a bar of soap in the bath by squeezing it and watching it pop out, the preoperational child, performing the same actions, might think of the soap as a submerged submarine that is breaking the surface.

A cook asks two boys who have just ordered a large pizza, "How many slices do you want me to cut your pizza into, 8 or 12?" One boy immediately answers, "Please cut it into 12 pieces, because I'm very hungry!" This is a joke for older children and grown-ups, but not for preoperational children, whose thoughts are limited in part because they do not yet have a "logic" for manipulating, or *operating* on, mental representations. Therefore, they often reason on the basis of appearances. One important result is that they do not understand **conservation**, the principle that properties of an object, such as its amount or mass, remain the same even when the appearance changes, provided that nothing is added or removed. Many studies have documented that preoperational children do not conserve, and so they would not realize that cutting a pizza into 12 pieces instead of 8 does not increase the total amount of pizza. A classic example, illustrated in Figure 12.3, is that preoperational children do not understand that pouring liquid from a short wide glass into a tall thin glass does not alter the amount of liquid.

Only after a baby has object permanence does he or she understand that objects continue to exist even after they are no longer being perceived.

● **Conservation:** The Piagetian principle that certain properties of objects remain the same even when their appearance changes, provided that nothing is added or removed.

FIGURE 12.3 Conservation of Liquids

In the classic conservation of liquids test, the child is first shown two identical glasses with water at the same level.

The water is poured from one of the short, wide glasses into the tall, thin one.

When asked whether the two glasses have the same amount, or if one has more, the preoperational child replies that the tall, thin glass has more. This is a failure to conserve liquids.

Similarly, they typically think that flattening a ball of clay decreases the amount of clay and that spreading the objects in a row farther apart changes the number of objects in the row.

Both sensorimotor and preoperational children show **egocentrism,** which does not mean "selfishness" in the ordinary sense of the word, but instead the inability to take another's point of view. For example, children in this period will hold a picture they've drawn up to the telephone, to "show" it to Grandma. They mistakenly assume that others see the same things they do.

Concrete Operations Period. By the end of the preoperational period, at about age 7, children develop the ability to take another person's perspective. This ability is linked to the fact that they can now perform **concrete operations,** manipulating mental representations in much the same way they could manipulate the corresponding objects. So the child is now able to begin to classify objects and their properties, to grasp concepts such as length, width, volume, and time, and to understand various mental operations such as those involved in simple arithmetic. This *period of concrete operations* is Piaget's third period of cognitive development, which takes place roughly between the ages of 7 and 11. Concrete operations allow the child to reason logically, partly because this mode of conceptualizing is *reversible*; that is, it can be used to make or undo a transformation. For example, having seen the liquid being poured into a tall thin glass, the child can mentally reverse the process and imagine the liquid being poured back into the original container. Seeing that no liquid has been added or subtracted in the process, the child realizes that the amount in both glasses must be the same.

Formal Operations Period. By definition, concrete operations cannot be used for reasoning about abstract concepts; children in the period of concrete operations cannot figure out, for example, that whenever 1 is added to an even number, the result will always be an odd number. To be able to reason abstractly, Piaget said, requires that the child be capable of **formal operations,** reversible mental acts that can be performed even with abstract concepts. This ability emerges roughly during the ages of 11 or 12, at the onset of what Piaget termed the *period of formal operations*. Rather than simply understanding the logic of "what is," as occurs with concrete operations, the emerging adolescent is now able to imagine the possibilities of "what could be." Formal operations allow children to engage in abstract thinking, to think about "what-would-happen-if" situations, to formulate and test theories, and to think systematically about the possible outcomes of an act by being able to list alternatives in advance and consider each in turn. For example, formal operations would permit a child to think about how best to spend his or her money and to weigh the benefits and drawbacks of each possible budget decision.

The Child's Concepts: Beyond Piaget

Do children follow the stages Piaget described? When researchers use techniques different from Piaget's in order to see what children do or do not understand, they often come up with results that differ from his. Although Piaget conducted very clever tasks (such as those used to assess conservation), they typically assessed only easily observable aspects of behavior. When more subtle measurements are taken, evidence sometimes emerges that children can show competence well before they have reached the appropriate Piagetian stage.

● **Egocentrism:** In Piaget's theory, the inability to take another person's point of view.

● **Concrete operation:** In Piaget's theory, a (reversible) manipulation of the mental representation of perceived events and actions that corresponds to the actual physical manipulation.

● **Formal operation:** In Piaget's theory, a mental act that can be performed (and reversed) even with abstract concepts.

For example, Andrew Meltzoff and his colleagues (notably, Meltzoff & Moore, 1977) have found that 2- to 3-week-old infants can show true imitation, and others have found that even 2-day-old infants can imitate happy and sad facial expressions (Field et al., 1982). Given what's been learned about infant memory, you won't be surprised that other researchers have shown that babies as young as 3 months old can have object permanence—they know that previously seen objects continue to exist after they are removed from sight. This refutes the idea that object permanence does not establish itself until the child is a toddler (Baillargeon, 1993; Spelke et al., 1992). Moreover, when appropriately tested, children as young as 3 years show that they understand the conservation of amount or mass (Gelman, 1972).

Piaget's theory seems to underestimate the sophistication of young children's conceptions of the world. Infants demonstrate an understanding of some physical laws even before they have developed the kinds of perceptual–motor schemas that Piaget claimed are the foundations of such knowledge. For example, even 4-month-old infants are aware of temporal intervals, showing surprise when a predictable sequence of flashing lights is interrupted (Colombo & Richman, 2002). Moreover, by using looking-time methods, researchers have concluded that even young infants realize that objects need to be physically supported to remain stable (Figure 12.4), that objects can't move *through* other objects, and that objects don't flit from place to place but shift along connected paths (Spelke, 1991; Spelke et al., 1992).

In contrast to Piaget's idea that formal operations are necessary to formulate and test theories, other research suggests that in many ways the young child relates to the world as a young scientist. Faced with a bewildering set of phenomena, children try to organize stimuli and events into categories and develop theories of how those categories interact (Carey, 1985, 1988, 1995b; Keil & Silberstein, 1996; Spelke et al., 1992; Wellman, 1990). Even 1-year-old babies begin to organize categories (Waxman, 1992), and preschoolers develop sophisticated ways to determine whether an object belongs in a particular category. For example, they begin to understand that animals beget animals of the same type and that the internal biology—not the external appearance—defines the type (Keil, 1989a, 1989b).

In addition, current thinking suggests that children develop a **theory of mind,** a theory of other people's mental states—their beliefs, desires, and feelings. This theory allows them to predict what other people can understand and how they will react in a given situation (Flavell, 1999; Frye et al., 1998; S. Johnson, 2000; Lillard, 1999; Wellman, 1990). One way to assess children's theory of mind is to tell a story and see whether the children draw the proper inferences about the protagonist's mental state. In one story used for this purpose, a boy hides his candy in a drawer, but after he leaves the room, his mother moves the candy to a cupboard. Children are then told that the boy returns and is asked where he thinks his candy is hidden. By age 4 (which is before the age at which Piaget believed that children rise above their egocentric outlook), chil-

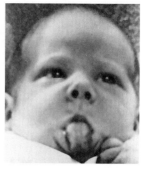

Very young infants can imitate some facial expressions, as shown in these photos from Meltzoff and Moore's study.

● **Theory of mind:** A theory of other people's mental states (their beliefs, desires, and feelings) that allows prediction of what other people can understand and how they will react in a given situation.

FIGURE 12.4 Early Perception of Possible Events

Possible Event

This panel shows a possible event: A box on top of another box is slid over to the edge, but it is still fully supported.

Impossible Event

This panel shows an impossible event: The top box is slid so far over that only 15% of it is supported, and yet it does not fall. Between 3 and 6½ months, babies realize that one box must rest on top of the other to be supported.

Infancy and Childhood: Taking Off **501**

dren believe that the boy thinks the candy is still where he put it originally, but children under 4 do not—they often think that the boy believes the candy is in the cupboard. In order to get this right, the child must understand that belief does not necessarily reflect reality.

How does a theory of mind develop? It is possible that children learn to "put themselves in another person's place," seeing things through another's eyes (J. R. Harris, 1995). It is also possible that children build a theory of the situations that give rise to other people's feelings (for example, seeing a child scream after being stung by a bee leads to the theory that bee stings hurt; Wellman, 1990); this approach has been called the *theory theory* (see Gopnik, 1996).

The particular theory of mind a child develops depends in part on the surrounding culture. Among many African tribes, calamities such as AIDS or fires are believed to have supernatural causes (Lillard, 1999). Even within a culture, different subgroups can develop different types of theories. Lillard and colleagues (1998, as cited in Lillard, 1999) asked children to explain the behavior of a character in a story and found that children growing up in cities tended to use psychological explanations—for example, referring to the character's likes and dislikes—even at 7 years of age. In contrast, children growing up in the country rarely used such explanations (20% of the time, compared with 60% for children growing up in the city). Instead, rural children usually relied on aspects of the situation to explain behavior. It is not clear why this difference exists.

Although researchers agree that culture plays a role in the development of a theory of mind, how do we explain the evidence that children as young as 6 months begin to develop a theory of mind? For example, after being habituated by watching someone reach for the same toy repeatedly, these infants looked longer when a person reached for a new toy than when the person used a new movement to reach for a familiar toy (Woodward, 1998). Apparently the infant inferred that the person had the goal of reaching for the first toy and was surprised when the goal changed—but not when the motion changed. Such effects were not found when inanimate objects were used to do the reaching (Baldwin, 2000, and S. Johnson, 2000, report similar findings).

In short, the finding that many abilities are evident much earlier than Piaget expected challenges his idea that all of a given child's thought reflects a single underlying logic, a logic that changes with increasing age and development. Moreover, later research showed that many children do not enter the period of formal operations until high school, and some never enter it at all (Hooper et al., 1984; Lunzer, 1978). Nevertheless, Piaget has been proven correct in his observation that there are qualitative shifts in children's performance as they age. He must also be credited with discovering many counterintuitive phenomena, such as a failure to conserve and egocentrism, that all theories of cognitive development must now be able to explain.

Information Processing and Neural Development

Efforts to explain the findings sparked by Piaget's theory have looked at specific changes in the way children process information and how their brains mature. The *information processing approach* is based on the idea that perception and cognition rely on a host of distinct processes, and not all necessarily develop at the same rate. Researchers have thus studied very specific aspects of development and have found that some mental processes do indeed develop more quickly than others. For example, even very young children are adept at using *sensory memory* (the very brief memory of perceptual stimulation) and at accessing *long-term memory* (the relatively permanent store of information). However, anyone who has spent time with children knows that young children often perform more poorly than older children in many tasks. There are many reasons for this: Young children are not able to focus attention effectively; they are not able to formulate and follow plans effectively (Scholnick, 1995); and they do not have stored information that can be used in organizing and remembering input (Chi, 1978). Moreover, young children are simply slower than older children and adults (Kail, 1988, 1991).

One common reason young children may perform more poorly than older children is that their *working memory*—their ability to use information held in an active state—does not stack up well against that of older children or adults. Working memory capacity increases with age throughout childhood (Case, 1977, 1978). When the child has enough working memory capacity, he or she can perform tasks that were previously beyond reach.

The finding that working memory increases with age allows us to explain many of the phenomena documented by Piaget, such as the out-of-sight/out-of-mind behavior that he took to show a lack of object permanence (Baird et al., 2002). In this case, a *quantitative* change (simple increase in size) in capacity can lead to *qualitative* changes in performance (the transition to new stages; Case, 1992b; Pascual-Leone, 1970). By analogy, if you have a relatively small amount of RAM memory in your computer, then only relatively simple programs will run (such as basic word processing or e-mail), but not more complicated ones (such as a large slide-show presentation). If you increase the amount of memory, you not only can run more complex programs, but also multiple programs at the same time. A quantitative change in the amount of memory underlies qualitative changes in performance.

Increases in working memory can also affect other factors that change with age—such as the number and types of strategies a child can use. Robert Siegler's (1996) *wave model* rests on the idea that cognitive development is like a series of waves, where the waves are sets of strategies. Each wave crests at a different age, and more sophisticated strategies become possible with age—but older strategies are not abandoned altogether, they just come to be used less often. For example, when shown a square grid that contains blocks in some of its cells, and asked to report the number of blocks, children use three strategies: they count clusters of blocks and add them up, they count the number of empty cells and subtract them from the total possible, or they guess based on an overall impression. Younger children have difficulty using the subtraction strategy, in part because they don't accurately calculate the total number of cells (Luwel et al., 2001). As children become older, they have more strategies to select among (Chen & Seigler, 2000; Jansen & van der Maas, 2002; Lautrey & Caroff, 1996; Siegler, 1989, 1996; Siegler & Svetina, 2002). Some strategies are automatic, and once learned will continue to be used in familiar settings; other strategies require conscious thought, and it is these that are most affected by the growth of working memory (Crowley et al., 1997, 1999).

What accounts for the child's improvements in working memory with age? The initial immaturity of the brain may be key. The brain undergoes rapid growth spurts (Epstein, 1980) around the times of transitions to new periods in Piaget's scheme. Some of the increase in brain weight with age may be due to myelinization (the laying down of myelin, a fatty substance that serves as an insulator, on the axons), which increases the speed and efficiency of neural transmission, and some to larger numbers of synapses and long-distance connections (Case, 1992c;

Thatcher, 1994; Thompson et al., 2000). These changes would not only increase the speed of information processing (Demetriou, et al., 2002), but also would allow more information to be activated at the same time—which in turn would increase working memory capacity.

Vygotsky's Sociocultural Theory: Outside/Inside

Appreciating the importance of events at different levels of analysis leads us to look beyond any single source to explain psychological events. Thus, it isn't surprising that at least some aspects of cognitive development reflect social interactions. Russian psychologist Lev S. Vygotsky (1896–1934) emphasized the role of social interaction during development (Vygotsky, 1978, 1934/1986). Whereas Piaget believed that the child constructs representations of the world in the course of experiencing it firsthand, Vygotsky believed that the child constructs representations of the world by absorbing his or her culture, and the culture, as represented in the child's mind, then serves to guide behavior (Beilin, 1996; Kitchener, 1996). According to Vygotsky, adults promote cognitive development by guiding and explicitly instructing the child, and cultural creations, particularly language, play a crucial role in development (Cole & Wertsch, 1996; Karpov & Haywood, 1998).

One of Vygotsky's key ideas is that once children learn language, they begin to use "private speech" to direct themselves (Berk, 1994a; Smolucha, 1992; Vygotsky, 1962, 1988). **Private speech** (also sometimes called *inner speech*) is language used by the child in planning or prompting him- or herself to behave in specific ways. Children initially begin to use language in this way by actually speaking aloud to themselves, but then language becomes internalized and silent. As Vygotsky predicted, researchers have found that young children use private speech more when trying to solve a difficult task (such as folding paper in a particular way or arranging events into a story) (Berk, 1992a, 1994b; Duncan & Pratt, 1997) than when working on an easy task. They also use private speech more after they have made an error (Berk, 1992a, 1994b). Preschoolers (ages 3 to 5) also use private speech more frequently when they have to decide what to do in a free play situation than when they are put in a highly structured play situation (Krafft & Berk, 1998).

It might be tempting to think that culture is one influence on cognitive development, the brain another. But this would be an error. The two factors interact: Culture affects the brain, and vice versa. For example, culture determines which languages you learn, which in turn affects how the brain processes sounds. By the same token, aspects of the brain affect culture; for example, we don't have customs that require more working memory capacity than the brain provides.

Children in different cultures master different skills; for example, middle-class North Americans often master the visual-motor skills needed to play computer games, whereas street children in Brazil may master the kinds of arithmetic needed to bargain with tourists over the prices of goods (Saxe, 1988).

● **Private speech:** The use of language in planning or in prompting oneself to behave in specific ways.

Social and Emotional Development: The Child in the World

The psychological development of a child includes more than improvements in mental processing and the acquisition of knowledge and beliefs. Equally impressive development occurs in the child's social interactions, such as the ability to form relationships.

Attachment: More Than Dependency

In our closest relationships we develop deep attachments to other people. **Attachment** is an emotional bond that leads us to want to be with someone and to miss him or her when we are separated. The tendency to form such an emotional bond begins during infancy, when normal infants become attached to their primary caregivers.

What is the origin of the infant's attachment? Decades ago, a prominent theory—sometimes called the "cupboard theory" because it centered on food—held that infants become attached because their caregivers feed them and thus become associated with positive feelings (Sears et al., 1957). However, classic experiments by Harry Harlow and his collaborators disproved this and similar theories (for example, Harlow, 1958). These researchers found that baby monkeys became much more attached to a model "mother" that had a pleasing texture and more realistic face than to one without these characteristics, even though it was the only one that fed them. The impulse to seek comfort from something soft is an innate rather than a learned characteristic of mammals.

British psychoanalyst John Bowlby (1969) developed a theory of attachment that has become widely accepted among developmental psychologists. According to Bowlby, children go through phases during the development of attachment. Just as in Piaget's stages, the order of the phases is thought to be determined biologically, but the precise ages depend on experience. A major shift, usually occurring between 6 months and 2 years, is characterized by **separation anxiety,** which is fear of being away from the primary caregiver. This shift may arise on the heels of cognitive development, specifically because infants can now think about and remember objects for relatively long periods (including the primary caregiver) when they are no longer present.

Not all babies become attached to their caregivers in the same way. Ainsworth and her colleagues (1978) developed a way to assess attachment using a scenario they called the *Strange Situation*. The setup involves a staged sequence of events designed to discover how a child reacts when left with a stranger or alone in an unfamiliar situation. If the child has developed secure attachment, he or she should show separation anxiety, becoming upset when the mother leaves, and should not be soothed equally well by a stranger as by the mother. Studies using the Strange Situation revealed four types of attachment:

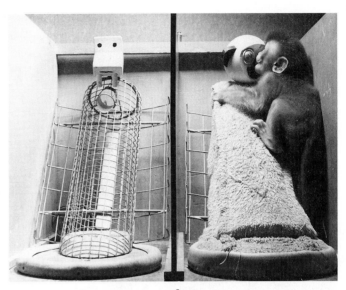

Baby monkeys were separated from their mothers shortly after birth and were raised with two substitute "moms." One was wire and held the baby bottle, and each young monkey needed to climb on this one to be fed. The other was covered with terry cloth and did not provide food. Baby monkeys preferred to cling to the fuzzy model, even though it never provided food.

Secure attachment (about 60–70% of American babies) is evident if babies venture away from the mother, are upset when she leaves and not well comforted by a stranger, but calm down quickly when the mother returns.

Avoidant attachment (about 15–20% of American babies) is evident if babies don't seem to care very much whether the mother is present or absent, and are equally comfortable with her and a stranger; when she returns, they do not immediately gravitate to her.

Resistant attachment (about 10–15% of American babies) is evident if babies do not use the mother as a base of operations but rather stay close to her and

● **Attachment:** An emotional bond that leads us to want to be with someone and to miss him or her when we are separated.

● **Separation anxiety:** Fear of being away from the primary caregiver.

We know that at least some aspects of attachment are learned because infants in different cultures become attached differently. For example, American infants show less resistant attachment than do Japanese infants. In Japan, many more women are full-time mothers than in the United States, and their children are not used to being left with other adults (Takahashi, 1990).

become angry when she leaves; some of these babies may go so far as to hit the mother when she returns and do not calm down easily thereafter.

Disorganized/disoriented attachment (5–10% of American babies) is evident if the babies become depressed and have periods of unresponsiveness along with spurts of sudden emotion at the end of the procedure.

Various factors influence how an infant will become attached. For example, if the mother takes drugs while pregnant, her infant is more likely at age 18 months to have disorganized/disoriented attachment (Swanson et al., 2000). The type of early attachment can have long-lasting effects. Infants with secure attachment who were later studied at age 11 were found to have closer friendships and better social skills than children who had not been securely attached as infants (Shulman et al., 1994). Moreover, secure attachment can lead the child to be more comfortable exploring, which leads to better learning and can lead to more intimate love relationships later in life (Sroufe & Fleeson, 1986; Weiss, 1986).

Is Daycare Bad for Children?

Obviously, a child will not have an opportunity to become attached to a parent who is never around. This was a major concern of Steven Spielberg's, whose own father was often absent. However, according to Scarr (1998), "Exclusive maternal care of infants and young children is a cultural myth of an idealized 1950's, not a reality anywhere in the world, either now or in earlier times" (p. 95). Since 1940 less than half of all persons in the United States have lived in a "traditional" family with a full-time working father and a mother who works only in the home, and the percentage has been declining since 1950. In the United States today, over half of the mothers of babies younger than 1 year old work outside the home (Behrman, 1996). Most of these children are in some form of daycare.

Is daycare bad for children? This question has been the subject of a long and sometimes intense debate; parents have felt trapped between guilt about leaving their children and the necessity to support their families. Research examining the strength of attachment of children raised at home versus those raised partly in daycare centers has found that children who entered daycare relatively early in life were as strongly attached to their mothers as those who entered relatively late (Scarr, 1998; see also NICHD Early Child Care Research Network, 1997; Roggman et al., 1994). However, other research has shown that slightly more of the home-raised children are securely attached in the Strange Situation (Scarr, 1998). Moreover, there is evidence that children who spend more time in "nonmaternal care" during their first 4½ years behave more aggressively and defiantly than children who spend more time with their mothers (Belsky, 2001, 2002). But, these behaviors are fluid, and change as children grow older (Barry, 2002).

Self-Concept and Identity: The Growing Self

A critical aspect of social development is the emerging sense of who you are and how you stand relative to other people. Psychologists use the term **self-concept** to refer to the beliefs, desires, values, and attributes that define a person to him- or

● **Self-concept:** The beliefs, desires, values, and attributes that define a person to himself or herself.

herself. A key aspect of Steven Spielberg's self-concept as a child was his many fears, both large and small (McBride, 1999).

For young children, the self-concept is necessarily grounded in their level of cognitive development. Thus, preschoolers think of themselves in very concrete terms, in terms of behaviors and physical appearance (Keller et al., 1978). At what age do children begin to conceive of themselves as having specific characteristics? To find out, a dab of red paint was placed on babies' noses without their knowledge, and the babies then looked in a mirror. Some babies of about 15 months of age will notice the smudge and rub it off. By age 2, virtually all children have this response (Amsterdam, 1972; Lewis & Brooks-Gunn, 1979). However, this test may in fact assess understanding of temporary changes in appearance, not self-concept (Asendorpf et al., 1996). Other researchers have argued that the roots of the self-concept are present much earlier than toddler age. Bahrick and her collaborators (1996) found that even 3-month-olds prefer to look at the face of another child of the same age rather than at their own faces, which suggests that they are already familiar with the appearance of their own faces. Even newborns distinguish between touching themselves and being touched by someone else, a distinction that may mark the beginning of a self-concept (Rochat & Hespos, 1997).

Knowledge of your appearance is part of your self-concept.

By 3 years of age, children begin to appreciate that they have distinct psychological characteristics, such as being happy in certain situations and not in others (Eder, 1989). Children of about 8 to 11 begin to describe themselves in terms of personality traits, perhaps as "energetic" or "musical." The oldest children also describe themselves in terms of social relations (Rosenberg, 1979), such as the relationships they have with their siblings and friends. This ability to self-label depends on reasoning abilities that develop during the period of formal operations.

Culture clearly affects a person's self-concept. In the collectivist cultures of Japan, China, and other Asian countries, children's self-concepts typically revolve around their relations to the group (Markus & Kitayama, 1991). In contrast, in the individualist cultures of most Western countries, children's self-concepts typically revolve around defining themselves as distinct entities that must negotiate with, and navigate through, the group.

Gender Identity: Not Just Being Raised With Pink or Blue

A crucial aspect of the self-concept is **gender identity,** which is the belief that you are male or female. Part of your gender identity arises from how you are raised (Tenenbaum & Leaper, 2002), and part of it comes from the social context in which you grow up (Horowitz & Newcomb, 2001). Given the pervasive influence of events at all three levels of analysis, you might expect biological factors also to play a role—and they do. The role of such factors is vividly illustrated in the following case history (Colapinto, 2000): At 8 months of age, a boy's penis was accidentally sliced off as a split foreskin was being surgically repaired. The family and surgeons decided that it would be best to raise the boy as a girl, and so his testicles were removed and a vagina was surgically formed. The boy, previously known as "John," was now called "Joan," and her past as a boy was never discussed. Joan was treated in every way like a girl, and her friends and classmates had no reason to suspect that she was in any way extraordinary. When Joan was 9 years old, psychologist John Money (1975) wrote a famous paper in which he reported that Joan had a female gender identity, in sharp contrast to her identical twin brother, who had a strong male gender identity. This report, and others like it, led researchers to

● **Gender identity:** A person's belief that he or she is male or is female.

believe that gender identity was essentially neutral at birth and was formed by culture and upbringing.

However, Diamond and Sigmundson (1997) revisited John/Joan some 20 years later and recounted a very different story. They found that as a young child she sometimes ripped off her dresses and tried to urinate standing up. At 14, she refused to have any more vaginal surgery or to live as a girl. She was not attracted to boys and considered suicide. Even though she had been treated as a girl and even received female hormones that caused breasts to develop, she was deeply unhappy and confused. Her father finally broke down and told her about the accident. Instead of being upset on learning that she had been born a boy, she was greatly relieved. She renounced her female identity, underwent surgery to remove her breasts and reconstruct a penis, and was determined to establish a relationship with a woman. Joan became John once again. He eventually married and adopted his wife's children from a previous marriage.

What was going on here? John's brain had been exposed to high levels of male sex hormones in the womb, which led his brain to develop in male-typical ways. These male predispositions were not something that could be arbitrarily changed simply by treating him as a female. Indeed, certain disorders result in a fetus's being exposed to high levels of male hormones in the womb, even if the fetus is genetically female. Studies of such children have shown that the hormones can affect gender identity. These girls later preferred to play with boys' toys and to participate in boys' games (Berenbaum, 1999; Berenbaum & Hines, 1992). Boys can also be affected by the hormonal environment; boys who receive relatively little male sex hormone in the womb engage in less rough-and-tumble play than do boys who are exposed to the usual amount (Hines & Kaufman, 1994).

Moral Development: The Right Stuff

A key aspect of social development is the emergence of more complex ideas of morality, which center on the ability to tell right from wrong. As children grow older, their developing cognitive abilities allow them to draw more subtle inferences. The young child may feel that a girl who knocks over a lamp and breaks it is equally to blame if she smashed it intentionally, bumped it by accident while horsing around, or fell against it accidentally when the dog jumped on her. The older child would make clear distinctions among the three cases, seeing decreasing blame for each in turn. Piaget was a pioneer in the study of moral as well as cognitive development. His studies often involved telling children stories in which he varied the intentions of the characters and the results of their actions, then asking the children to evaluate the characters' morality. Lawrence Kohlberg extended Piaget's approach and developed an influential theory of moral development. He presented boys with **moral dilemmas**, situations in which there are moral pros and cons for each of a set of possible actions. Kohlberg asked participants to decide what the character should do, and why. This is the famous dilemma that confronted Heinz (Puka, 1994):

> In Europe, a woman was near death from a special kind of cancer. There was one drug that the doctors thought might save her. It was a form of radium that a druggist in the same town had recently discovered. The drug was expensive to make, but the druggist was charging 5 times what it cost him to make the drug. He paid $400 for the radium, and charged $2,000 for a small dose of the drug. The sick woman's husband, Heinz, went to everyone he knew to borrow the money, but he could only get together about $1,000, half of what it cost. He told the druggist that his wife was dying, and asked him

● **Moral dilemmas:** Situations in which there are moral pros and cons for each of a set of possible actions.

to sell it cheaper or let him pay later. But the druggist said, "No, I discovered the drug and I'm going to make money from it, so I won't let you have it unless you give me $2,000 now." So Heinz got desperate and broke into the man's store to steal the drug for his wife.

Should Heinz have done that? Why?

Kohlberg was not so much interested in what the children decided as in the way that they reached their decisions. What kinds of factors did they consider? Which conflicts did they identify (such as the conflict between the value of human life and the value of private property), and how did they try to resolve these conflicts? Kohlberg interviewed boys and men at length, and from their responses he identified three general levels of moral development (Kohlberg, 1969; Rest, 1979). The *preconventional level* rests on the idea that good behaviors are rewarded and bad ones are punished. Correct action is what an authority figure says it is. A preconventional response to the Heinz dilemma might be, "If you let your wife die, you will get in trouble" (this and the following examples are adapted from Kohlberg, 1969, and Rest, 1979). The *conventional level* rests on the role of rules that maintain social order and allow people to get along. For example, the child wants to be viewed as a "good person" by friends and family and tries to follow the Golden Rule ("Do unto others as you would have them do unto you"). Morality is still closely tied to individual relationships ("If he lets his wife die, people would think he was some kind of heartless lizard"). The *postconventional level* (also called the *principled level*) rests on the development of abstract principles that govern the decision to accept or reject specific rules. In the most advanced stage at this level, principles are adopted that are believed to apply to everyone. ("Human life is the highest principle, and everything else must be secondary. People have a duty to help one another to live").

Some researchers have questioned the generality of Kohlberg's stages. For example, some have found that the stages don't apply well to people in non-Western cultures. Okonkwo (1997) studied Igbo students in Africa with Kohlberg's methods, and found that in some cases the responses did not fit into any stage. Although the responses clearly relied on moral reasoning, the reasoning sometimes involved factors such as family interdependence and the supreme authority of a divine being. Perhaps the strongest objection to Kohlberg's theory came from Carol Gilligan (1982), who argued that because it was based on studies of boys and men, it applies only to males. She believed that females tend to focus on an *ethic of care*, a concern and responsibility for the well-being of others. In contrast, Kohlberg's higher stages of moral development focus on abstract rights and justice, which Gilligan saw as a male-oriented perspective.

However, later studies have shown that the differences between the moral reasoning of males and females do not reflect fundamental differences in the way their minds work. Although there is evidence that males and females do emphasize different principles in their moral reasoning (Wark & Krebs, 1996), this seems more a reflection of their daily activities (and the assumptions and general orientations that result from such activities) than an enduring gender difference. For example, if people are presented with dilemmas that feature concerns about raising children, men and women reason in the same ways (Clopton & Sorell, 1993). In addition, males and females score comparably on Kohlberg's tests, and both sexes reveal concerns with both caring and justice (Jadack et al., 1995; Walker, 1995). Furthermore, it is not clear that the stages are like traits, which characterize a person in all situations. Rather, people may use different types of moral reasoning, depending on the details of the dilemma (Trevethan & Walker, 1989).

● **Gender roles:** The culturally determined appropriate behaviors of males versus females.

In addition, we must distinguish between *moral reasoning* and *moral behavior*: The fact that someone reasons in a particular way doesn't guarantee that he or she will act on this reasoning. Moral behavior may be governed not simply by reasoning, but also by various aspects of your character, such as your *conscience*—which leads you to appreciate what is morally correct and feel obligated to follow this path. A conscience may develop far earlier than sophisticated moral reasoning. For example, Grazyna Kochanska and her colleagues (1994) have found that conscience typically develops at about age 3. However, having a conscience at an early age has a lot to do with temperament and how a child interacts with his or her mother (Kochanska, 1997). Fearful children, who are shy and anxious, learn moral standards best if their mothers gently discipline them and encourage them to do right instead of threatening them about the consequences of doing wrong. Fearless children, who are outgoing and who actively explore their surroundings, learn moral standards best when their mothers provide direct feedback, such as taking a toy away or making angry comments. But such direction has the greatest impact if these fearless children have a close, emotionally secure relationship with their mothers (Fowles & Kochanska, 2000). Fearful children may actually develop a conscience earlier than fearless children, in part because the fearful children may become anxious and guilty at the mere thought of doing something wrong (Kochanska et al., 2002).

And conscience is not the only aspect of character that can direct moral behavior. Another is the capacity to feel *empathy*, the ability to put yourself in another person's situation and feel what they feel. Indeed, Martin Hoffman (2000) shows that by early adolescence most children have sophisticated abilities to feel and act on empathy in a wide range of moral situations. For example, children appreciate the unfairness of another person's not receiving a just reward for his or her efforts.

In short, many factors affect how people behave in moral situations, and many of the key factors develop much earlier than does the ability to reason logically about morality. Our behavior is not just a result of how we reason, but also of who we are.

Looking *at* Levels

Gender Role Development

Gender roles are the culturally determined appropriate behaviors of males versus females. It is one thing to identify yourself as male or female, but something else again to understand what behaviors are appropriate for your gender. Gender roles vary in different cultures, social classes, and time periods; for example, a proper woman in Victorian England (or, perhaps, 19th-century America) would probably be very surprised to learn that a woman can be a senator or the president of a major corporation today. Conceptions about gender roles develop early. Indeed, by age 2 children have apparently learned about gender role differences (Caldera & Sciaraffa, 1998; Witt, 1997). Even preschool boys apparently believe that if they played with cross-gender toys (say, dishes instead of tools), their fathers would think that was "bad" (Raag & Rackliff, 1998).

Freud argued that children identify with the same-sex parent, and that this is the main way in which gender roles develop (see Chapter 11). But Eleanor Maccoby believes that identification with the same-sex parent may be the *result* of sex-role development, not the cause. Her account rests on events at all three levels. At the level of the group, in Maccoby's view, peer-group interactions are key to learning gender roles. It is in the peer group, she argues, that boys first learn about how to gain and maintain status in the hierarchy, and that girls develop their styles of interaction (Maccoby, 1990, 1991). Maccoby and Jacklin (1987) found that by age 4 children spent about 3 times as much time playing with same-sex peers as with opposite-sex peers, and this ratio shot up to 11 times more when the children were 6 years old. According to Maccoby (1990, p. 514), "Gender segregation . . . is found in all the cultural settings in which children are in social groups large enough to permit choice."

Why does gender segregation occur? Maccoby (1988) suggests that part of the answer may rest on biological, particularly hormonal, differences. Boys play more aggressively than do girls, and their orientation toward competition and dominance may be aversive to many girls. However, shifting to the level of the person, Maccoby (1990) also notes that girls may not like playing with boys because they believe that boys are too difficult to influence; the polite manner in which girls tend to make suggestions apparently doesn't carry much weight with boys. Girls find this response (or lack of response) frustrating and retreat to the company of other girls.

In short, even for something as clearly influenced by culture as gender role development, we must consider events at all three levels of

Boys and girls play in characteristic ways, partly because of biological differences.

analysis. As usual, these events interact: If not for hormonal differences between the sexes, girls probably would not come to believe that boys are difficult to influence, and if not for that belief, they would have different interactions with boys.

TEST YOURSELF!

1. How does the ability to control the body develop with age?
2. What perceptual and cognitive abilities emerge during the course of development?
3. How do social and emotional development occur?

Adolescence: Between Two Worlds

Steven Spielberg's adolescence was different from that of many of his peers in many ways; nonetheless, the challenges he faced in those years—forming friendships, testing limits, coming to terms with a new and unfamiliar body—are essentially universal. Because his family had moved so often, in high school none of his friends from early childhood were still with him; most of his classmates, on the other hand, were firmly established in cliques. Spielberg craved their acceptance and used his new-found love of moviemaking and storytelling as a way of gaining it. Nevertheless, his obsession with movies and his lack of interest in most of the usual teenage pursuits of dating, sports, and schoolwork continued to set him apart.

Not surprisingly, Spielberg's adolescence was not an easy time for him or, sometimes, for those around him. On one occasion he and some friends spent 3 hours throwing rocks through plateglass windows at a shopping mall, causing about $30,000 worth of damage (McBride, 1999, p. 88). He later said that *Poltergeist* was "all about the terrible things I did to my younger sisters" (McBride, 1999, p. 89). He fought his father's wishes for him to study math and science, declaring that someday he was going to be a famous movie director and didn't need to know those kinds of things (McBride, 1999). Extreme behavior, yes. Adolescent behavior, yes.

Physical Development: In Puberty's Wake

Adolescence begins with **puberty,** the time when hormones cause the sex organs to mature and secondary sexual characteristics to appear, such as breasts for women and a beard for men. These changes typically begin between ages 8–14 for girls and between ages 9–15 for boys. **Adolescence** is the period between the appearance of these sexual characteristics and, roughly, the end of the teenage years. Although girls usually experience their first period (*menarche*) about 2 years after the onset of puberty, typically between 12 and 13 years of age today, various factors influence when this occurs. In fact, in the mid-19th century girls had their first period at about 17 years of age. In recent years, the age of puberty has declined—both for girls and boys—throughout the developed and developing world, including the United States (Finlay et al., 2002; Herman-Giddens et al., 2001), Europe (de Muinck Keizer-Schrama & Mul, 2001), China (Huen et al., 1997), and Brazil (Kac et al., 2000). This may reflect a *secular trend* in society: As children receive better health care and consistently better nutrition, and lead less physically strenuous lives, puberty occurs earlier. For example, in rural Brazil, girls whose fathers were unemployed and those from low-income families had their first periods later than girls from more prosperous backgrounds (Tavares et al., 2000). Another study documented that African American, Mexican American and Caucasian American boys are taller and heavier today than in previous generations, and these boys also develop pubic hair and mature genitalia at a younger age than was previously considered the norm (Herman-Giddens et al., 2001). Could better nutrition explain this trend? Studies have shown that overweight girls tend to experience their first periods before those who are not overweight (Kaplowitz et al., 2001), which suggests a link between diet and the age of onset of puberty. However, African American girls tend to be overweight less often than Caucasian American girls, but are younger when they have their first periods (Herman-Giddens et al., 1997). Thus, diet alone cannot explain the secular trend. Many theories have been proposed to explain the trend, ranging from the effects of additives in food (such as hormones added to animal feed and then passed on to human consumers; Teilmann et al., 2002) to various chemical pollutants in the environment (such as polybrominated biphenyls, or PBBs) (Blanck et al., 2000)—but the reason or reasons for this trend are still not understood.

Physical development during adolescence also, of course, includes growth. During infancy and childhood, the body grows from the trunk outward; the upper arms grow before the lower arms, which in turn grow before the hands. At puberty, the trend is reversed: Rapid growth of the hands, feet, and legs is followed by growth of the torso (Wheeler, 1991). Do you remember when you stopped needing larger shoes but still needed larger coats? That's why. The uneven growth during adolescence can lead to an awkward, gawky look, which doesn't do wonders for a teen's sense of self-confidence.

Once the sex hormones start operating in earnest, the shoulders of young boys grow large relative to their hips, and vice versa for girls. At age 11, girls typically are taller and heavier than boys because their major growth spurt starts about 2 years before that of boys. By age 14, however, boys' heights and weights have taken off,

- **Puberty:** The time when hormones cause the sex organs to mature and secondary sexual characteristics appear, such as breasts for women and a beard for men.

- **Adolescence:** The period between the onset of puberty and, roughly, the end of the teenage years.

Girls tend to mature faster than boys.

whereas girls have stopped growing or have begun to grow more slowly. American girls typically stop growing at around age 13 (some may continue to grow until about age 16), but American boys usually continue to grow until about their 16th birthdays (and some may continue growing until they are almost 18 years old; Malina & Bouchard, 1991; Tanner, 1990).

Cognitive Development: Getting It All Together

The adolescent's ability to reason can become dramatically more powerful, but nevertheless can be plagued with biases and distortions.

More Reasoned Reasoning?

The major cognitive development of adolescence, achieved by some but not all adolescents, is the ability to reason abstractly. Piaget's period of formal operations describes the adolescent's cognitive achievements. According to Piaget, formal operational thinking allows a person not only to think abstractly, but also to think systematically about abstract concepts and possible scenarios. In one of his experiments, now regarded as a classic, Piaget gave a child a set of weights, string that could be attached to the weights, and a bar to which the string could be attached, allowing the weight to swing like a pendulum. The child was asked to vary both the weight and the length of the string in order to discover what factors would make the weight swing most quickly. Adolescents in the formal operational period are not only able to figure out the possibly relevant factors (size of weight, length of string, how high the weight is raised before being dropped, force with which it is pushed), but also to understand that to discover the role of each variable, they must alter only one thing at a time. These adolescents have grasped the very essence of scientific experimentation: holding everything else constant while systematically varying one factor at a time. In short, all the cognitive machinery necessary to think scientifically can be present by about 11 or 12 years of age. But not all adolescents develop these abilities this early, and some never do.

Most adolescents in Western societies are able to grasp the rules that underlie algebra and geometry. The ability to think systematically about abstractions also allows them to think about concepts such as justice and politics, as well as relationships and the causes of human behavior.

How does the ability to think abstractly and logically emerge? It might be tempting to conclude that it is a result of the final stages of brain maturation (and the brain does in fact continue to develop well into adolescence—Sowell et al., 1999), but the assumption that events at any one level alone could account for such a sweeping change would be rash indeed. Cole (1990) has found that, in many traditional African societies, even the adults cannot use the kinds of abilities described by "formal operations," but there is no indication that their brains have failed to develop fully. Culture must play a role, perhaps shaping the developing child's thought, as Vygotsky theorized.

Adolescents have sometimes been portrayed as prone to distortions in their thinking. For example, at least some adolescents may use self-serving distortions, such as deciding that there's no need to ask because their parents really wouldn't mind if they borrow the family car late at night (Barriga et al., 2000; Gerrard et al., 2000). In particular, they have been seen as unable to make well-reasoned judgments about themselves. This assumption contains a grain of truth, but bear in mind that adults aren't so good at making judgments about themselves either. The authors of one study asked adults and adolescents to assess the probability of various misfortunes happening either to them or to someone else. Adolescents and adults made remarkably similar estimates (Quadrel et al., 1993). It is sobering to note that both age groups tended to *underestimate* the amount of risk they would face in various circumstances (such as having a car accident or being mugged). Both groups exhibited signs that they thought they were, to some extent, invulnerable. Both adults and children sometimes use heuristics and shortcuts that can produce faulty reasoning (Jacobs & Klaczynski, 2002; see Chapter 8).

Adolescent Egocentrism: It's All in Your Point of View

The enhanced cognitive abilities of adolescents allow them to take other points of view easily—in particular, to see themselves as they imagine others see them. Theorists have claimed that these new abilities can lead to two kinds of distortions in adolescents' conceptions of how others view them.

First, the *imaginary audience* is a belief sometimes held by adolescents, in which they view themselves as actors and everyone else as an audience (Elkind, 1967; Elkind & Bowen, 1979). This view would lead teenagers to be extremely self-conscious and easily embarrassed; a pimple feels like a beacon, not unlike Rudolph's nose. Although many adolescents do not succumb to such cognitive distortions (Vartanian, 2001), those who do—perhaps because they believe others may be watching them—are less likely to engage in risky behaviors (Galanaki, 2001).

Second, some teenagers have a *personal fable*, which is a story in which they are the star, and as the star they have extraordinary abilities and privileges. Teenagers may have unprotected sex and drive recklessly because they believe that they are immune to the possible consequences (Lapsley, 1990; Lapsley et al., 1988). These tendencies, and

Who is the "imaginary audience"?

other social behaviors, are clearly influenced by peers. However, in spite of these tendencies, adolescents remain influenced primarily by their families with regard to basic values and goals (Brown et al., 1986a, b).

Social and Emotional Development: New Rules, New Roles

A bridge between childhood and adulthood, adolescence is a time of transition. The adolescent must forge a new identity, which emerges as he or she negotiates a new place in the world (Marcia, 1993). This negotiation involves not only coming to grips with changing roles in the larger society, which requires obeying new sets of rules, but also learning to live with cognitive and biological changes that affect interactions with others in many ways.

"Storm and Stress": Raging Hormones?

The picture of adolescents as moody and troubled is nothing new. In the 18th century, German authors developed an entire genre of stories (the best known is Johann Wolfgang von Goethe's *The Sorrows of Young Werther*) about passionate, troubled young people so immersed in anguish and heartache that they committed impetuous acts of self-destruction. This body of literature came to be called *Sturm und Drang*, which translates roughly as "storm and stress." G. Stanley Hall (1904) popularized this term among psychologists when he wrote his now-classic two-volume work on adolescence.

The notion that adolescents experience a period of "storm and stress" has waxed and waned in popularity (Arnett, 1999). Anna Freud (1958) not only believed that adolescent "angst" was inevitable but also that "normal" behavior during adolescence was in itself evidence of deep *abnormalities* in the individual. A strong reaction to this view soon followed, and only a few years ago, many psychologists were dismissing the idea as another popular misconception. However, additional studies have shown that there is in fact a normal tendency for adolescents to have three sorts of problems (Arnett, 1999).

First, adolescents tend to have conflicts with their parents (Laursen et al., 1998). The *frequency* of the conflicts is greatest in early adolescence, whereas the *intensity* of the conflicts is greatest in midadolescence (Laursen et al., 1998). Adolescent–parent conflicts occur most often between mothers and daughters on the brink of adolescence (Collins, 1990). These conflicts can be even worse if the parents are not getting along or become divorced. Steven Spielberg claims that *E.T.* is really about the trauma he suffered during the divorce of his parents (McBride, 1999, p. 72); he broke down sobbing at the end of its first screening (p. 333).

Second, adolescents experience extreme mood swings (Buchanan et al., 1992; Larson & Richards, 1994; Petersen et al., 1993), and by the middle of the teen years about one third of adolescents are seriously depressed (Petersen et al., 1993). Adolescents also often report feeling lonely and nervous.

Third, adolescents may be prone to taking risks. Anticipating Anna Freud's view, Hall (1904) went so far as to say that "a period of semicriminality is normal for all healthy boys" (Vol. 1, p. 404, referring to adolescent boys). Steven Spielberg's rock-throwing episode at the shopping mall is a perfect example of what Hall had in mind. Adolescents are relatively likely to commit crimes, drive recklessly, and have high-risk sex (Arnett, 1992; Gottfredson & Hirschi, 1990; Johnston et al., 1994). Such behaviors tend to peak in late adolescence.

Many adolescents don't have these problems; rather, as Arnett (1999) documents, these problems are simply "more likely to occur during adolescence than at other ages." (p. 317). But, why do they occur at all? Many people assume that they are an unavoidable result of the hormonal changes that follow puberty. The notion that the emotional turmoil of adolescence is rooted in biology was neatly captured by Greek philosopher Aristotle's remark that adolescents "are heated by Nature as drunken men by wine."

In fact, the hormonal changes that follow puberty do make the adolescent prone to emotional swings (Brooks-Gunn et al., 1994; Buchanan et al., 1992). But hormones only predispose, they do not cause; environmental events trigger these emotional reactions. Moreover, the biological effects can be indirect. For example, such changes can lead adolescents to want to stay up late at night and sleep late in the morning (Carskadon et al., 1993). If they are forced to wake up early to go to school, their mood and general emotional tenor will no doubt be affected.

In sum, adolescents are more likely than others to experience "storm and stress," which arises in part from the workings of hormones. However, this is only a tendency, and the degree to which an adolescent will experience such turmoil depends on personal and cultural circumstances.

Evolving Peer Relationships

The adolescent's relationship with his or her parents casts a long shadow. Both young men and women who have a more positive relationship with their mothers later have more positive intimate relationships with others (Robinson, 2000). But many kinds of life experiences affect whether a young man or woman will develop intimate relationships. For example, perhaps counterintuitively, military service can actually enhance the ability to form intimate relationships (for example, by helping someone learn to trust and rely on others; Dar & Kimhi, 2001).

Most adolescents develop predominantly same-gender networks of friends, and women's friendships tend to be stronger than men's (Roy et al., 2000). The one exception to this generalization is gay young men—who tend to have more female than male friends; moreover, young gay men tend to be less emotionally attached to their love interests than are heterosexual young men (Diamond & Dube, 2002). In addition, as portrayed in countless Hollywood "nerd films," some adolescents can be rejected by their peers. For example, girls can effectively use indirect aggression (such as by spreading false rumors) to exclude other girls from their circle (Owens et al., 2000). Hurt pride or lowered self-esteem are not always the only results of such rejection. Many gay or bisexual students report being victimized at school, which apparently contributes to their being at risk for suicide and substance abuse and for their engaging in high-risk behaviors (Bontempo & D'Augelli, 2002).

Looking *at* Levels

Teenage Pregnancy

In general, U.S. teenage girls engage in amounts of sexual activity comparable to those of girls in other industrialized societies, but U.S. teens do not use contraception as effectively. In 2001, 33.4% of births in the U.S. were to unmarried mothers. However, teens are having fewer children; in 2001, teens had 25.3 births per 10,000, compared to 27.4 in 2000—an 8% decline (Wetzstein, 2002).

Which teenagers are likely to become pregnant? Those at greatest risk are poor students who do not have clear career plans. Maynard (1996) reports that a third of the teenagers who become pregnant drop out of school even before they become pregnant. Further, over half of teenage mothers were living in poverty when they had their children. For many of these young women, particularly African Americans, having a baby is part of "coming of age," and is in many ways equivalent to a career choice (Burton, 1990; Merrick, 1995). Unfortunately, the adult children of teen mothers are likely to leave school early, be unemployed, and be in trouble with the law for violent offences—and they themselves tend to become parents at an early age (Jaffee et al., 2001).

Consider these events from the different levels of analysis. First, sex is a biological drive, but your brain is constructed so that you can regulate your urges. The frontal lobes allow us to inhibit impulses, if we so choose. Second, why would someone choose to forgo immediate pleasure? They would do so only if there were a good reason—so good that it overshadowed the passions of the moment. If you don't believe that staying in school will give you a future, and if you believe that having a child is the easiest way to create meaning in your life, why worry about becoming pregnant? Third, cultures create norms about when and in what circumstances—married, not married, financially secure, financially insecure—people should have babies. Once again, events at the different levels interact. Your belief structure leads you to either heed societal norms or ignore them in favor of your own goals. Moreover, the specific consequences of having a child depend on your behavior and social group: If teenage mothers do not drop out of school, they are about as likely to graduate as girls who did not give birth, and African Americans appear to suffer the fewest economic consequences of having given birth as a teenager. Apparently, African American girls tend to live at home, continue school, and benefit from the assistance of other members of their families (Burton, 1990, 1996; Rosenheim & Testa, 1992). Thus, the consequences of having a baby for changing the mother's brain via education are very different for members of different social groups. Events at the different levels of analysis clearly interact, even when we consider a decision as personal as whether to have a baby.

TEST YOURSELF!

1. How does puberty affect the body?
2. How do thought processes change in adolescence?
3. Does adolescence always lead to emotional upheaval?

Adulthood and Aging: The Continuously Changing Self

Steven Spielberg was an unhappy teenager and—in some aspects of life—a spectacularly successful young adult. But being successful in his chosen career did not mean that he was successful in all aspects of life. His first marriage ended; his relationship with his father was strained; and he was concerned that he himself would not measure up as a father (several of his movies deal with difficult relationships between fathers and sons). When he had children of his own, he realized that he needed to be an adult for them; he, and his relationships, had to change, and they did.

Famous moviemaker or not, the grown-up Steven Spielberg is in a very different phase of life than his children; he is also in a very different phase of life than his father. This is the human condition, and we now turn to an exploration of the stages of adult development.

The Changing Body: What's Inevitable, What's Not

By your early 20s, it is unlikely that you will grow taller, and your weight has typically stabilized for many years to come. For the next several decades, changes in your body should be relatively minor. True, you may come to need bifocals, and your hair may begin to gray or to thin. But the basic systems continue to function well. However, after age 50 or so, noticeable changes in the body begin to occur (Lemme, 1995).

Aging has two aspects: changes that are programmed into the genes and changes that arise from environmental events (Busse, 1969; Rowe & Kahn, 1998). Many aspects of aging may in fact arise not from inevitable processes, but rather from lack of adequate nutrition (such as fragile bones that result from osteoporosis-related calcium deficiency), or lack of exercise (resulting in obesity in some elderly people and frailty in others), or lack of meaningful activities (which can lead to feelings of helplessness or apathy; Avorn & Langer, 1982; Langer & Rodin, 1976; Rodin & Langer, 1977; Rowe & Kahn, 1998). By the same token, environmental events—such as taking calcium supplements or lifting weights—can help to counter or diminish such problems.

A major challenge of aging is to accommodate to those changes that are inevitable and to forestall undesirable changes when you can. Many older people develop diseases or conditions that are uncomfortable or even painful, such as arthritis or collapsed vertebrae. However, in most cases, older people can cope with pain effectively, particularly if they adopt a "can-do" attitude (Melding, 1995; Rowe & Kahn, 1998). One of the inevitable age-related changes in women is *menopause*, the gradual ending of menstruation that typically occurs between the ages of 45 and 55; following menopause, eggs are no longer released and pregnancy is not possible (Wise et al., 1996). Hormone changes that accompany menopause can lead to various bodily sensations (such as "hot flashes"); the knowledge that childbearing is no longer possible, along with the decline in youthful appearance, can adversely affect a woman's self-concept and self-esteem. On the other hand, for many women the physical discomforts are slight, if present at all, and the idea of sexual intercourse without the threat of an unwanted pregnancy provides new pleasure. Some women discover "post-menopausal zest" and are reinvigorated by this change and the freedom it represents. For men, after about age 40, sperm production begins to fall off—

It's not just diet that can help prevent osteoporosis; behavior can also play a role. Lifting weights helps the bones retain calcium.

but, unlike the cessation of egg production after menopause, men never fully lose the ability to produce sperm. Men do experience declining vigor (strength and energy) with age, which can affect sexual performance.

Why do all of us inevitably become less vigorous as we age? The combined effects of changes in the body have been likened to the effect of hitting a table with a hammer over and over (Birren, 1988). Eventually, the table will break, not because of the final blow, but because of the cumulative effects of all the blows. Some researchers believe that aging and death are programmed into the genes. An oft-cited piece of evidence for this idea was reported by Hayflick (1965), who found that human cells grown in the lab will divide on average only about 50 times, and then simply stop. However, all the findings that suggest programmed death can also be interpreted in other ways. Instead of accepting that the genes have been programmed for death, we might assume that over time errors accumulate, and finally there are so many errors that the genes no longer function properly. If you photocopy a drawing or page of text, and then copy the copy, and so on, you'll see how errors in reproduction multiply over repeated copying. In the case of the body, the damage may not be caused by the copying process itself, but rather by the repeated effects of bodily chemicals on each copy (Arking, 1991; Harman, 1956; Levine & Stadtman, 1992).

Perception and Cognition in Adulthood: Taking the Good With the Bad

Cognitive abilities remain relatively stable through most of adulthood, but by age 50 signs of decline begin to appear in some abilities. The good news is that aging per se probably doesn't cause neurons to die (Long et al., 1999; Stern & Carstensen, 2000), but the bad news is that aging does impair communication among neurons, possibly by disrupting neurotransmitter function (S-C. Li et al., 2001) or by degrading the white matter of the brain—the connections among neurons (Guttmann et al., 1998). These changes in the brain will eventually catch up with you and lead you to perform more slowly and be more prone to making errors. Indeed, by age 60 people perform most cognitive tasks more slowly than do younger people (Birren et al., 1962; Cerella, 1990; Salthouse, 1991b). The harder the task, the larger the difference in time taken by young adults and the elderly.

But how large is a "large" difference in time? Although even healthy elderly people require more time to carry out most tasks, the elderly are usually only a second or so slower than young people (Cerella et al., 1980), a difference that is often barely noticeable in daily life.

Shortly before death, however, many people exhibit *terminal decline* (Kleemeier, 1962). Their performance on a wide range of cognitive tasks takes a dramatic turn for the worse (Berg, 1996). This decline appears most dramatically in those who will die from cerebrovascular diseases, such as strokes and heart attacks, and may be related to such disease states (Small & Bäckman, 2000). Thus, terminal decline is probably not an inevitable final chapter of the book of life (Bosworth & Siegler, 2002).

Perception: Through a Glass Darkly?

During early and middle adulthood, worsening vision can usually be corrected with eyeglasses. Later in life, however, more severe visual difficulties emerge. More than half the population 65 and up has *cataracts*, a clouding of the lens of the eye, and in older people, the pupil, the opening of the eye through which light enters, becomes smaller. Surgery can remove cataracts and result in greatly improved vision. Until that point, even moderate optical difficulties cause older people to need greater contrast to see differences in light (Fozard, 1990). Contrasts between lit and unlit surfaces, such as shadows caused by steps, can define differences in depth, and if older people cannot perceive such definition, they are more likely to stumble over a step. Simply providing more light will not necessarily help older people to see well; because of the clouding of the lens, more light causes more glare. Thus, the best level of illumination is a compromise between what produces the best contrast and the least glare.

Hearing is also affected by age. After age 50 or so, people have increased difficulty hearing high-frequency sounds (Botwinick, 1984; Lemme, 1995). Because consonants (such as *k*, *c*, *p*, and *t*) are produced with higher frequency sounds than are vowels, older people will have trouble distinguishing between words that differ by a single consonant, such as *kill* and *pill*. Older people also have more difficulty shutting out background noise, a problem that may actually be worsened by hearing aids, which boost the loudness of irrelevant background sounds as well as of relevant sounds.

A flood of herbs, vitamins, and other medicinal remedies promise to reverse the negative cognitive effects of aging. For example, the herb Ginkgo biloba and the drug acetyl-L-carnitine have been reported to improve blood flow to the brain (Dean et al., 1993). However, much more research is necessary before we will know for sure whether such treatments work as advertised for everyone.

Unlike vision and hearing, taste per se does not decline with age (Bartoshuk et al., 1986; Ivy et al., 1992). Even in 80-year-olds, the taste buds are replaced frequently. But much of what we think of as the sensation of taste actually comes in part from smell, and the sense of smell does decline after the middle 50s (Doty et al., 1984; Ivy et al., 1992; Schiffman, 1992). As a result, as people move beyond middle age, they may prefer spicier foods; they may also have difficulty noticing if food has gone bad (Lemme, 1995).

Memory: Difficulties in Digging It Out

Parts of the brain that produce the neurotransmitter acetylcholine become impaired with age (Albert & Moss, 1996; D. E. Smith et al., 1999); this neurotransmitter is crucial for the proper functioning of the hippocampus, which plays a key role in memory. The loss of efficient processing in this part of the brain is probably one reason why older people often have trouble with some kinds of memory (Schacter, 1996).

Even so, aging affects some aspects of memory more than others. *Semantic memory* (memory for facts, words, meanings, and other information that is not associated with a particular time and place) remains relatively intact into very old age (Light, 1991), and the storing of new *episodic memories* (memory for specific events) is often relatively intact. People in their 70s and 80s do relatively well if they are given a list of words and then asked to pick out these words from a longer list that also contains other words (Craik & McDowd, 1987). Moreover, they can recall the gist of a description and its implications at least as well as younger people (Radvansky, 1999).

However, the elderly have difficulty when they must actively recall specific episodic memories: For example, they do poorly if they are given a list of common words to remember and later asked to recall them (Craik & McDowd, 1987). Tasks that require the *recall* of specific information appear to rely on the frontal lobes to dig the information out of memory, and processes accomplished there are not as efficient in the elderly as they are in younger people. Indeed, the frontal lobes become proportionally smaller in old age than other brain areas (Ivy et al., 1992). In fact, even healthy people over age 67 or so have trouble with the same tasks that are difficult for patients with frontal lobe damage (such as sorting cards first by one rule, then switching to another rule; Schacter, 1996). Moreover, just as patients with frontal lobe damage sometimes show "source amnesia," forgetting the source of a learned fact, so do elderly people (Craik et al., 1990; Glisky et al., 1995; Schacter et al., 1991, 1997; Spencer & Raz, 1995). For example, Schacter and colleagues (1991) asked people to listen to novel facts (such as "Bob Hope's father was a fireman"), which were read aloud by either a man or a woman. When later asked to recall which voice read the facts, 70-year-olds were much less accurate than young people, even when they could recall the facts themselves (Schacter et al., 1994, describe similar findings).

Frontal lobe impairment probably also is responsible for difficulties the elderly have with tasks involving working memory. Such deficits are particularly evident when the elderly must hold information in mind while doing something else at the same time (Craik et al., 1995). If strategies are needed to perform a task (such as figuring out the most efficient way to move through a store to collect different items), the frontal lobe impairments of the elderly can affect their performance (Gabrieli, 1996; S-C. Li et al., 2001). As Salthouse (1985) suggests, slowed cognitive processes may also lead the elderly to use inefficient strategies, strategies composed of many steps, each relatively simple.

Intelligence and Specific Abilities: Different Strokes for Different Folks

It might seem likely that as you age, your accumulated life experience adds up to an increasingly important determinant of your intelligence. But this is not so. Researchers were surprised to discover that genetic influences on general intelligence actually *increase* with age (Finkel et al., 1995; Plomin et al., 1994). Investigators have asked whether aging affects all types of intelligence in the same way. In particular, they have examined the effects of age on *fluid intelligence*, which involves flexibility in reasoning and the ability to figure out novel solutions, and *crystallized intelligence*, which involves using knowledge as a basis of reasoning (see Chapter 9). It might seem that crystallized intelligence, which by definition relies on effects of experience, would be less influenced by age than would fluid intelligence. How could we tell? These two types of intelligence have been assessed in **longitudinal studies**, which test the same group repeatedly, at different ages. These findings suggest that *both* types of intelligence are stable until somewhere between the mid-50s and early 70s, at which point both decline (Hertzog & Schaie, 1988). However, the very strength of longitudinal studies, the continuing use of the same group, also leads to a weakness: The participants become familiar with the type of testing, and this familiarity can influence their performance on later assessments. **Cross-sectional studies** involve testing different groups of people, with each group at a different age. The key here is to ensure that the groups are equated on all possible measures other than age (such as sex, educational level, and health status). Such studies have led most researchers to believe that fluid intelligence begins to decline as early as the late 20s (Salthouse, 1991a), whereas crystallized intelligence may actually grow with age and decline only late in life (Baltes, 1987; McArdle et al., 2002).

Crystallized intelligence, rooted in experience, may be thought of as underlying much of what we mean by "wisdom." The ability to draw on such intelligence may explain why researchers found that older adults were rated as telling more interesting, higher quality, and more informative stories than younger adults (James et al., 1998). This should be cheering news for Steven Spielberg, who plans to keep telling stories as long as he can.

Moreover, in some respects old people actually reason better than young people. For example, in one study researchers asked young and old participants to indicate their preferences when given two or three alternatives—for example, chocolate or vanilla ice cream versus chocolate, vanilla, or strawberry ice cream. Young people were inconsistent, perhaps choosing vanilla when only two choices were offered, but chocolate when strawberry was included. Old people were much more consistent and "logical" in their choices (Tentori et al., 2001).

General intelligence is distinct from special abilities, such as the ability to do arithmetic or to imagine objects rotating. Not all the special abilities of a given person are affected by aging to the same degree. For example, a longitudinal study by Schaie (1983, 1989, 1990b) examined the effects of aging on five measures of special abilities, including the ability to recognize and understand words and the ability to rotate shapes mentally. He found that by age 60 about three fourths of the participants maintained their level of performance from the previous 7 years on at least four of the five abilities tested, and by age 81 more than half the participants maintained this level of performance. For any given person, some aspects of intelligence were affected by aging more than others (Schaie & Willis, 1993). The same is true for many types of skills, which age affects in different ways for different people (Stern & Carstensen, 2000).

● **Longitudinal study:** A study in which the same people are tested repeatedly, at different ages.

● **Cross-sectional study:** A study in which different groups of people are tested, with each group at a different age.

The Flynn effect (see Chapter 9) is the finding that average IQ has risen steadily through the years throughout the industrialized world. Additional research has shown that during the 20th century, one of the best ways to preserve cognitive ability into old age was simply to have been born later. Although nobody knows for sure why this is true, obvious possibilities are improved nutrition and more enriching intellectual experiences (for example, as provided by experience operating technology). People who were born at about the same time form a **cohort,** which means that they move through life at the same time and go through many of the same experiences.

People can often compensate for declining abilities by using abilities that are still intact (Baltes, 1987; Baltes et al., 1984). Some typists can retain their speed as they age by looking farther ahead on the page, thus taking in more as they go (Salthouse, 1984). Similarly, tennis players may compensate for reduced speed and vigor by developing better strategies (Lemme, 1995; Perlmutter, 1988). In fact, people with more education tend to function better than those with less education when their brains have been impaired by diseases, such as Alzheimer's disease (AD). The *cerebral reserve hypothesis* states that education either strengthens the brain itself (for example, by building in backup circuits) or helps people develop multiple strategies; thus, when part of the brain is damaged, they can draw on these reserves and continue to function reasonably well (Cohen et al., 1996; Stern, 2002). In fact, simply having more leisure activities in old age may help build such reserves (Scarmeas et al., 2001).

Social and Emotional Development During Adulthood

The term "grow up" might seem to imply that psychological development is like height: After a certain age, you reach a plateau, and that's where you stay. Not so. At least in mentally healthy people, psychological development continues through the life span. In discussing Steven Spielberg's 15-year split with his father, an expert on father–son relationships, James Levine, commented: "In such a split, you don't recognize that under the anger is sadness. There's denial: pretending it's not important to heal the rift. But a split in the father–child relationship always has an effect" (quoted in Sullivan, 1999, p. 67). Still, as in Spielberg's case, relationships change and evolve over time.

Theories of Psychosocial Stages in Adulthood

Some theorists, Freud included, believed that personality stops developing in childhood. But Erik Erikson (1921–1994) believed there are three stages of adult **psychosocial development,** or *effects of maturation and learning on personality and relationships,* in addition to five stages of psychosocial development through childhood and adolescence (see Table 12.4). The adult stages were defined by issues that adults are most likely to confront and need to resolve. The first, *intimacy versus isolation,* occurs in young adulthood. To navigate this phase successfully, the young adult must develop deep and intimate relations with others and avoid becoming socially isolated. Steven Spielberg had serious difficulty being intimate with people, which may be one reason why his first marriage dissolved (McBride, 1999). The second adult stage, characterized by *generativity versus self-absorption,* occurs during the middle adult years. The challenge now is for men and women to think about the future and decide what their contributions will be for their children or

● **Cohort:** A group of people who were born at about the same time and thus move through life together and share many experiences.

● **Psychosocial development:** The effects of maturation and learning on personality and relationships.

for society at large. People who are highly generative agree with the African proverb, "The world was not left to us by our parents. It was lent to us by our children" (which is inscribed on a wall in the UNICEF office in New York). People in this stage who fail to accomplish these goals will be faced with a sense of meaninglessness in life. Steven Spielberg not only cares for his own children but also makes it a point to help young directors who are just starting out; such altruism is another type of generativity. The third adult stage, characterized by *integrity versus despair*, occurs during old age. The task here is to be able to reflect back on life and feel that it was worthwhile, thereby avoiding feelings of despair and fear of death.

Many theorists have picked up where Erikson left off (Gould, 1978; Havinghurst, 1953; Vaillant, 1977). Some have focused on one aspect of Erikson's theory. For example, McAdams and his colleagues developed ways to assess generativity (McAdams & de St. Aubin, 1992), and have found that adults who are concerned about providing for future generations tend to be more satisfied with their lives (McAdams et al., 1993) and to view life optimistically—believing that even bad events will eventually have a happy outcome (McAdams et al., 2001).

After a 15-year split, Steven Spielberg developed a new relationship with his dad.

TABLE 12.4 Erikson's (1950) Psychosocial Stages

Issue to Be Resolved	Average Age	Summary
Basic trust vs. mistrust	0–1 year	Depending on how well they are treated by caregivers, infants either develop a basic trust that the world is good or fail to develop such a basic trust.
Autonomy vs. doubt	1–3 years	The child either is allowed to choose and make independent decisions or is made to feel ashamed and full of self-doubt for wanting to do so.
Initiative vs. guilt	3–6 years	The child either develops a sense of purpose and direction or is overly controlled by the parents and made to feel constrained or guilty.
Industry vs. inferiority	6–11 years	The child either develops a sense of competence and ability to work with others or becomes beset with feelings of incompetence and inferiority.
Identity vs. role confusion	Adolescence	The adolescent either successfully grapples with questions of identity and future roles as an adult or becomes confused about possible adult roles.
Intimacy vs. isolation	Young adulthood	The young adult either develops deep and intimate relations with others or is socially isolated.
Generativity vs. self-absorption	Middle adulthood	The adult in the "prime of life" must look to the future and determine what to leave behind for future generations; failing this task leads to a sense of meaninglessness in life.
Integrity vs. despair	Old age	In reflecting back on life, a person either feels that life was worthwhile as it was lived or feels despair and fears death.

Many roles are open to us as we age, despite stereotypes to the contrary!

Other theorists have extended Erikson's approach by proposing additional stages. For example, Levinson (Levinson, 1977, 1978, 1986, 1990; Levinson et al., 1978), basing his work on interviews with 40 men, developed an influential theory of developmental transitions in men's lives. Perhaps the most important and interesting aspect of Levinson's theory is the *midlife transition*, which occurs when a man begins to shift from thinking of his life as marked by the time that's passed since birth to thinking of his life as marked by the time left until death. This transition typically occurs somewhere between the ages of 40 and 45. This change in perspective can have profound consequences, often leading a man to question the path he has chosen. According to Levinson, many men have *midlife crises*, which can lead them to end marriages and begin others, change jobs, or make other major life changes. In Steven Spielberg's case, this crisis seems to have caused him to deal with conflicting emotions about being Jewish; one result was his movie *Schindler's List*, in which he confronted his fears and ambivalence about his Jewish identity (which were particularly severe because of his strong need for acceptance; McBride, 1999).

We must distinguish between such changes in perspective and changes in personality; evidence indicates that personality does not change substantially during adulthood (Costa et al., 2000). In fact, Costa and McCrae (1988) tested more than a thousand adults, both men and women, using standardized measures (not interviews) of the Big Five personality dimensions: openness to experience, conscientiousness, extroversion, agreeableness, and neuroticism (see Chapter 11). The participants ranged in age from 21 to 96 years. In addition to asking the participants to complete the measures, they also asked 167 spouses to fill in the measures about the participants. Eighty-nine men and 78 women were tested twice, 6 years apart; thus, both cross-sectional and longitudinal data were collected. The results were clear: There were very few differences in any of the dimensions of personality over the years, and when such differences were found, they were very small. Moreover, Costa and McCrae found that personality was equally stable over time for men and women. They concluded that "aging itself has little effect on personality. This is true despite the fact that the normal course of aging includes disease, bereavement, divorce, unemployment, and many other significant events for substantial portions of the population" (p. 862). As a matter of fact, objective tests have shown that even when people feel that their personality has changed (over the course of 6–9 years) during middle age, it really hasn't (Herbst et al., 2000).

Apparent changes in personality over time probably reflect not so much changes in the person as changes in the life challenges he or she is confronting at the time: For many people, aging is accompanied by changes in marital status, parenting, and positions at work. Such major life changes often become less frequent or severe as a person grows older, which could explain the finding that until around age 50, people become increasingly consistent in the degree to which they can be described by particular traits, and thereafter are stable (Roberts & DelVecchio, 2000). Consistency, in this sense, refers to the relative ordering of people according to a trait—with increasing age, your ranking relative to other people will become more stable. This stability could reflect, in part, your settling into a niche in life, and thus restricting the range and variety of situations you encounter.

Mature Emotions

The poet Robert Browning wrote, "Grow old along with me!/ The best is yet to be/The last of life, for which the first is made./" He may have been more right than he realized. In one study, people of different ages were prompted to report their emotions at various times over the course of a week (Carstensen et al., 2000). The researchers found that as people enter old age, they tend to experience extended periods of highly positive emotions and less enduring spells of negative emotions than do younger people. Moreover, positive emotions were evoked as regularly for the elderly as for the young. Negative emotions, on the other hand, arose increasingly less often until about age 60 (when they leveled off).

But the news is even better than this. Older people are, well, more "mature" in their emotional responses. With age, people become better able to regulate emotions (Gross et al., 1997). In fact, elderly European and Chinese Americans had smaller changes in heart rate when watching emotional films than did younger people (Tsai et al., 2000). But this doesn't mean that their emotions are blunted or diminished; even when heart rate changes were smaller, older participants had subjective responses comparable to those of younger participants.

Adult Relationships: Stable Changes

Perhaps as a result of their increased ability to grapple with emotions, older people tend to change their outlook on life. Laura Carstensen and her collaborators have developed *socioemotional selectivity theory*, which rests on the idea that older people come to focus on the limited time they have left, which in turn changes their motivations (Carstensen & Charles, 1998; Lang & Carstensen, 2002). Consistent with this theory, these researchers find that as people age they come increasingly to value emotionally fulfilling relationships. This leads older people to prefer the company of only those who are emotionally close. The same findings hold true both for European and African Americans (Fung et al., 2001).

In general, as people age they interact with fewer people, but these interactions tend to be more intimate (Carstensen, 1991, 1992)—older people don't miss the broader social networks that they had when they were young (Lansford et al., 1998). Relationships earlier in life tend to include more friends than relatives, but with age the mix reverses, with more time spent with relatives than with friends. This pattern is even more pronounced among Latinos than European Americans (Levitt et al., 1993). In later life, a relationship long dormant can be picked up and reestablished with minimal effort (Carstensen,1992); after young adulthood, temperament and personality variables are relatively stable, which makes it easy to "know" someone again even after a long lapse.

During young adulthood, people are concerned that their relationships with friends and relatives are equitable—that neither

At one point, approximately 2,500 people well over 100 years old were reported to be living in countries comprising the former Soviet Union. One purportedly 168-year-old gentleman, who was still walking half a mile daily and gardening, attributed his longevity to the fact that he didn't marry until he was 65 (Seuling, 1986). Many elderly people, such as this Belgian couple—he's 98 and she's 74!—enter second marriages.

party gives more than he or she receives (Lemme, 1995; Walster et al., 1978). As people age, such concerns recede into the background. In successful marriages, the members of the couple think of themselves as a team, not separate people who are in constant negotiations (Keith & Schafer, 1991). Because they are in it for the long haul, people trust that the balance of favors and repayment will even out over time. Thus, older couples resolve their differences with less negative emotion than found with younger couples (Carstensen et al., 1995).

Death and Dying

We began this chapter with the very earliest phase of development, and we close it with the last of life's experiences. The psychology of death has two faces: The effects on the person who is dying and the effects on friends and family.

Grief is the emotion of distress that follows the loss of a loved one, and **bereavement** is the experience of missing a loved one and longing for his or her company. People in the United States tend to go through the grieving process in three phases (Lemme, 1995; Lindemann, 1991). First, until about 3 weeks after the death, the bereaved person is in a state of shock. He or she feels empty, disoriented, and, sometimes, in a state of denial and disbelief; these feelings eventually settle into a state of deep sorrow. (This shock may be buffered by having to make funeral arrangements, deal with lawyers, and so on, but nevertheless apparently develops during this period.) Second, from 3 weeks to about a year following the death, the bereaved person experiences emotional upheavals, from anger to loneliness and guilt. During this time, people often review their relations with the deceased, wondering whether they should have done things differently, whether the death was inevitable. During this phase, people may think that they catch glimpses of the deceased in crowds or hear the person talk to them. Third, by the beginning of the second year, grief lessens. The bereaved person may largely stop thinking of the deceased and, in the case of a spouse's death, be ready to become committed to a new intimate relationship. However, bereavement may continue indefinitely, particularly when a person is reminded of the deceased by special places or events, such as anniversaries or birthdays. Indeed, even years after an adult child has died, parents tend to be more depressed and their health declines more rapidly than in a control group. But such a tragedy may also bring the parents closer together, leading them to become more satisfied in their marriages (de Vries et al., 1997).

Wortman and Silver (1989) shook up this field of research by challenging key assumptions about the response to the death of a loved one. In particular, they challenged the idea that we must "work through" our loss, and that eventually we should expect to recover from the loss. That is, for many years, mental health clinicians urged the bereaved to "work through" their grief, which involves talking to others about their feelings and striving to finish the relationship with the dead (Lindstrom, 2002). But there is little evidence that such practices help (Davis et al., 2000). In fact, many clinicians now recommend suppressing or avoiding negative thoughts and emotions (not discussing them freely), focusing on positive emotions, and actually maintaining an internal relationship with the deceased.

The effects of the death of a friend or loved one depend on many factors. You might think that the death of a mate would be more severe if the marriage was conflicted, given the "unfinished business" at the end. But this has not turned out to be true (Carr et al., 2000). You also might think that the situation would be easier if you had a lot of forewarning. Again, this is not necessarily so (Carr et al., 2001).

● **Grief:** The emotion of distress that follows the loss of a loved one.

● **Bereavement:** The experience of missing a loved one and longing for his or her company.

When forewarned, some people begin grieving before the death, and the accompanying depression doesn't necessarily let up afterwards; however, if women don't become depressed when forewarned that their husbands will die, this leaves them particularly vulnerable to becoming depressed after his death (Carnelley et al., 1999). In addition, a woman's reaction to her husband's death will be different if she was dependent on him (more anxiety after his death) than if she was not (less anxiety; Carr et al., 2000). And a person's reaction depends in part on the age of the deceased. Most deaths in the United States and Canada tend to occur at a relatively old age; the average age of death in some Latin American countries is much younger. The grief for someone who has had a full life is different from the grief for someone who has been cut down in his or her prime.

Concern about our own deaths apparently does not increase with age: Death anxiety either stays the same over the course of life, or may actually decrease near the end (Lemme, 1995). Women report fearing death more than do men (Lonetto & Templer, 1986). However, this finding could simply mean that women are more honest or self-aware, or that men—consciously or unconsciously—avoid confronting the topic. In addition, because women tend to live longer than men, they may have had more opportunity to witness and to become concerned about death.

Cultural differences clearly influence the ways in which people view and react to death (Kalish & Reynolds, 1977; Platt & Persico, 1992). Researchers who studied the Mayan people of South America found that they did not try to fight death. Elderly people announce that their time has come and then retire to a mat or hammock and wait to die. They refuse food or water, ignore attempts by others to talk to them, and soon die. Their attitude toward death is fostered by their strong belief in an afterlife in paradise (Steele, 1992). In contrast, the Kaliai, a tribe in Papua New Guinea, almost never die of old age, instead meeting death in battle or as a result of an accident. Thus, they do not view death as a natural occurrence; they look for someone to blame for such deaths, usually a sorcerer (Counts & Counts, 1992).

Looking *at* Levels

Keeping the Aging Brain Sharp

In old age, particularly the years just before death, many people do not function as well mentally as they did earlier in life, even if they are physically healthy (Small & Bäckman, 2000). Is this deterioration inevitable? As people age, the brain receives less blood, which means that it is sustained by fewer nutrients and oxygen (Ivy et al., 1992). The blood supply to the brain decreases with age because the vessels themselves become smaller. Why does this happen? One reason may be that the brain cells are not working as hard, so they need less blood—which in turn leads the vessels to adjust (Ivy et al., 1992). This is a catch-22: The neurons don't work as effectively because they receive fewer blood-borne nutrients and less oxygen, but the reason they don't receive as much is that they haven't been functioning as effectively as they did before. Thus, if your otherwise healthy parents or grandparents are understimulated by their surroundings (as occurs in some nursing homes as well as in many home environments), this could affect their brains. The lack of mental challenge and engagement can lead to a change in their self-concepts and levels of self-esteem. These changes then may lead them to become lethargic and not to try to challenge themselves (including with other people), which could lead to even less effective neural functioning, and so on. Events at all three levels clearly interact.

Although the appropriate research has yet to be conducted, it is tempting to hypothesize that if you managed to engage your elderly parents, grandparents, or other family members in more challenging tasks, you could literally increase the blood supply to their brains and improve their thinking abilities. This result is plausible because "mental workouts" appear to enhance cognitive function in the elderly (Rowe & Kahn, 1998). Moreover, dendrites continue to grow normally even into old age (Coleman & Flood, 1986), and as neurons die, new connections may be formed to compensate for losses (Cotman, 1990). In one study, when elderly rats were moved from their standard cages into a rat playpen full of toys and other rats, they developed heavier brains with more extensive connections among neurons. Moreover, other researchers have found that mice who live in an enriched environment (complete with lots of attractive toys, other rats to play with, and opportunities to explore and exercise) actually retain more neurons (Kempermann et al., 1998). Indeed, simply giving animals the chance to exercise enhances neural growth and survival (Cotman & Berchtold, 2002; van Praag et al., 1999). Very likely the same would be true for humans who were moved to more stimulating environments (Avorn & Langer, 1982; Langer & Rodin, 1976; Rodin & Langer, 1977; Rowe & Kahn, 1998). In fact, researchers have found that the brain generally becomes smaller with aging, but that people with more education have less severe reductions (Coffey et al., 1999).

But focusing on the brain alone is not enough. At least in the U.S., the elderly have absorbed societally transmitted negative conceptions about aging—and these stereotypes apparently can undermine the will to live. In one study, young and elderly people were shown positive or negative words concerning old age; the words were presented too briefly to be seen consciously. But after being primed with negative words, the elderly were more likely to say they would reject treatment for serious illness than they were after being primed with positive words; the negative words appar-

Research with mice suggests that it's not the pure amount of stimulation that boosts brain function, but rather the amount of novelty that's encountered (Kempermann & Gage, 1999). If this result generalizes to humans, travel may truly broaden the mind even for the elderly!

ently activated stored negative concepts about aging. For the young, the type of prime made no difference (Levy et al., 1999–2000).

However, it is unlikely that all of the functions that are impaired with age can be helped simply by getting your grandparents to use their brains more, or even by changing their conceptions of what it means to be elderly. MRI scans of more than 3,600 apparently normal elderly people (aged

65 to 97) revealed that slightly over one third had brain lesions. These were often small and usually affected subcortical structures, but some of the lesions may have been large enough to affect a specific cognitive function (Bryan et al., 1997). Damage to the white matter can also disrupt cognition in the elderly (Koga et al., 2002). Thus, possible effects of changing beliefs and social interactions must be considered within the context of the state of the brain. As always, events at the three levels interact.

TEST YOURSELF!

1. How do changes in bodily organs affect us as we age?
2. How does aging affect perception, memory, and intelligence?
3. What is the course of social and emotional development during adulthood?
4. How do people cope with the knowledge of their own impending deaths, and with the deaths of friends and family members?

CONSOLIDATE!

In the Beginning: From Conception to Birth

- Your mother's and father's genes recombined when their gametes (eggs and sperm) were formed, leading you to have a unique combination of alleles. The development of both the brain and the body relies on the activation of specific genes, which are regulated in part by environmental events.

- Development progresses in an orderly process through a series of stages, or trimesters; during the first, the zygote becomes an embryo, then a fetus.

- The developing fetus is active, and becomes increasingly coordinated over time. The fetus can detect human speech, and prefers the mother's voice.

- Maturational processes can be disrupted by teratogens or enhanced by certain environmental events, such as those that reduce the level of stress experienced by the mother.

- Newborns have a good sense of smell, and can learn that different stimuli tend to occur together. Newborns are equipped with a host of inborn reflexes, such as sucking and Moro reflexes. These reflexes often disappear during the course of development.

- However, aspects of temperament that are present at birth may persist for many years to come.

- In addition, a newborn has sophisticated sensory capacities, including those necessary to begin organizing sounds into words and recognizing objects.

THINK IT THROUGH Do you think that Steven Spielberg was born with his abilities to make movies? In what ways might his abilities have been affected by a combination of innate factors, effects of teratogens, nutrition, and appropriate stimulation (perhaps even the sounds of his mother's piano playing) during his prenatal development? If you were going to design a program to teach newly pregnant women how best to care for their unborn children, what would you emphasize?

Infancy and Childhood: Taking Off

- In general, motor control progresses from the head, down the trunk to the arms, and finally to the legs; at the same time, control extends out from the center of the body to the periphery (hands, fingers, toes).

- Perception develops so that the child can make finer discriminations, needs less stimulus information to recognize objects, can focus attention more deliberately, and can search more systematically.

- Even 3-month-old infants have both implicit and explicit memory. Not all aspects of memory develop at the same rate. Although perceptual memory is present before verbal memory, not all aspects of perceptual memory change with age in the same way.

- Piaget posited that during cognitive development the child moves through a series of major periods. However, these stages may not be fixed, and many abilities are evident at earlier ages than originally believed. Researchers have since found that children have at least the rudiments of many abilities far earlier than Piaget's theory would predict.

- Children develop a theory of mind at a very early age, which becomes increasingly sophisticated with development.

- Cognitive development arises in part from improved information processing, particularly more efficient working memory, which probably in part reflects increased neural development. However, as Vygotsky stressed, culture and instruction also play a role in cognitive development.

- Children become attached to their caregivers, going through a series of stages, but may end up being attached in different ways.

- Attending day care as an infant does not necessarily lead to poorer attachment to the mother or father.

- The self-concept begins to develop during very early infancy, which in turn probably affects many social interactions, including gender roles. Gender identity is part of the self-concept, which is determined in part by biological factors present since conception.

- People may move through a series of stages in the way they tend to reason about moral issues, and males and females may tend to reason slightly differently at the later stages—but this is mostly a function of their different concerns in daily life, not something intrinsic to their genders.

- A conscience may develop early in life (around 3 years old), but its development depends on a combination of temperament and the child's interactions with his or her mother.

THINK IT THROUGH Why would you expect variations in the age at which stages of cognitive development are reached? Do you think schools should focus on speeding up cognitive development, so that children pass through the stages more quickly? Why or why not? If you had a child who was born with sexual organs that were partly male and partly female, as sometimes happens, on what basis would you decide whether the child should be raised as a boy or a girl?

Can a child experience normal emotional development if he or she spends much of the day watching television? Which aspects of emotional development do you think would be affected by watching television?

Adolescence: Between Two Worlds

- The extremities (arms and legs) grow rapidly during adolescence, with the trunk lagging behind, a pattern that can produce a gawky appearance. During this period the body acquires pubic hair and other sex characteristics. Puberty occurs earlier today than previously.

- If the adolescent reaches the period of formal operations, he or she can reason about abstract concepts systematically—and thus becomes capable of true scientific thought. This enhanced reasoning ability affects all aspects of thinking, including one's conceptions of oneself and society.

- Although hormones do prime the adolescent to experience more conflicts with parents as well as to have large mood swings and be prone to taking risks, these tendencies are neither inevitable nor necessarily severe.

- Enhanced cognitive capacities during adolescence allow the child to think about relationships in more sophisticated ways, and can lead to the formulation of an imaginary audience and personal fable.

- Most adolescents develop strong same-gender friendships, but these bonds tend to be stronger among young women than young men.

THINK IT THROUGH If you were going to design a school program that takes into account the biological changes that occur during adolescence, how would it differ from your own middle school or high school experience? What kinds of classes, activities, or schedule might make the transition to adulthood easier?

Why was adolescence a particularly important period for Steven Spielberg? Do you think it played such a large role in your own life? Why or why not?

Adulthood and Aging: The Continuously Changing Self

- The body remains relatively stable until around age 50. At about this point, women experience menopause, and both men and women may begin to become less vigorous. Many of the changes in the body can be treated, either by dietary supplements (such as calcium for bone weakness) or with changes in activities (which can reduce obesity and strengthen bones).

- With age the lens of the eye clouds and the pupil doesn't expand as much as it did before, leading to difficulty in seeing contrast. The elderly also have difficulty hearing high-frequency sounds such as consonants, and their sense of smell declines.

- With advancing old age, working memory operates less effectively, memory retrieval becomes more difficult, and people sometimes experience source amnesia.

- Although intelligence declines with advanced age, fluid intelligence may be more affected than crystallized intelligence, and the special abilities need not be affected much, if at all (but in different people, different abilities tend to be affected). In some respects, the elderly can reason more logically than younger people.

- Many theorists, including Erik Erikson and Daniel Levinson, have proposed that people pass through psychosocial stages as they age. These stages may be a result of challenges posed by a particular culture; there is little evidence that personality changes substantially during adulthood.

- Adult relationships focus on fewer people (often relatives) and tend to be stable over long periods of time. The elderly tend to have greater emotional control than younger people.

- Grief for another's death may pass through stages, which may extend over 2 years following the death. The sense of bereavement may never entirely disappear. Concern about one's own death does not increase with age, and for some people may actually decrease with age.

- In old age, the brain may stop functioning as well as it did before, in part because the person is no longer being intellectually challenged; at least in rats, such challenge can in part reverse this state of affairs.

- Although many people experience terminal decline, this does not appear to be an inevitable final phase of life.

THINK IT THROUGH If you could choose several of your own abilities to protect from decaying with age, which would they be? Why? If you could choose between becoming wise or having a perfect memory, which would you choose? Why? As you age, what factors do you think will influence whether you stay close to friends you made earlier in life?

Key Terms

accommodation, p. 497
adolescence, p. 512
assimilation, p. 497
attachment, p. 505
bereavement, p. 526
cohort, p. 522
concrete operation, p. 500
conservation, p. 499
cross-sectional study, p. 521
egocentrism, p. 500
embryo, p. 484
fetus, p. 484
formal operation, p. 500
gender identity, p. 507
gender roles, p. 510

grief, p. 526
longitudinal study, p. 521
maturation, p. 483
moral dilemmas, p. 508
object permanence, p. 498
private speech, p. 504
psychosocial development, p. 522
puberty, p. 512
self-concept, p. 506
separation anxiety, p. 505
schema, p. 497
teratogen, p. 485
theory of mind, p. 501
zygote, p. 483

chapter 13

Copyright Scala/Art Resource, NY

Stress, Health, and Coping

Lisa, a college sophomore, was becoming worried about her father, Al. Only 54 years old, he always seemed exhausted, regardless of the time of day or the amount of work he'd been doing. Whenever Lisa asked him why he was so tired, he answered in generalities: "Oh, work's crazy. That's all, honey." He'd also been coughing a lot, and when Lisa asked about this, he'd reply, "I've been sick more than usual—it's just been a bad winter."

Lisa used to look forward to her visits home and her telephone conversations with her father, but now she dreaded talking to him because he always sounded so tired and dejected. Lisa suggested that he see his doctor, exercise, maybe learn some type of relaxation technique. Al finally told her the real reason he was so tense and tired: His company had laid off several of his colleagues, and he was afraid he'd be next. It also meant that now Al's department was responsible for more work with less staff. In addition, as part of the downsizing, the company had moved to smaller premises. His new office was cramped, noisy, and generally unpleasant. He had trouble concentrating, and he knew his work was suffering, which made him even more concerned that he'd be fired. There was a possibility of a job offer from another company, but at a substantially lower salary. Lisa, listening to his story, understood that he had tried to protect her by not telling her. If he was fired, or took the other job, he wouldn't be able to help with her college expenses, and she was already working 25 hours a week. If Al's fears materialized, she would probably have to leave school, at least for a while, or take out very large loans. He was worried about his own situation, and worried about his daughter;

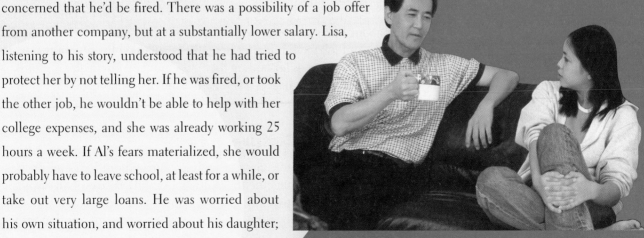

Lisa used to look forward to her . . . conversations with her father, but now she dreaded talking to him because he always sounded so tired and dejected.

Lisa understood the burden of those worries, which she now shared. She worried, too, about his persistent cough—was it just from lots of winter colds, or was it something more?

This situation produced stress in both father and daughter. Just what is "stress"? Can it affect our health? How can we deal with it? Such questions, and the search for answers, are in the domain of **health psychology:** the area of psychology concerned with the promotion of health and the prevention and treatment of illness as it relates to psychological factors.

What Is Stress?

Al began to hate going to work. Often as he worked at his desk, he felt as if he'd just finished a race—heart beating, palms sweating, breath coming hard—but without any accompanying sense of relief or accomplishment. He was simply exhausted all of the time and felt as if his heart wasn't pumping his blood fast enough for his body's needs. He began to be seriously worried about his health, as well as his job.

But Maya, a colleague who so far had survived at the company, didn't seem disturbed by the changes happening around them. Maya had two children and, like Al, needed her job, but she seemed to be taking this difficult situation in stride. Al didn't understand how Maya was able to stay so calm—didn't she understand what was going on?

And what about Lisa's response to pressures? She had been managing the demands of college and job well; but after her father explained his situation at work and the possible repercussions for both of them, she noticed physical symptoms in herself—sweaty palms, racing heart—even while studying or taking class notes. Al and Lisa are responding to stress.

Stress: The Big Picture

Today even third graders complain of feeling "stressed out," and adults take evening courses in "stress management." But what exactly *is* stress? **Stress** is the general term describing the psychological and bodily response to a stimulus that alters your equilibrium (Lazarus & Folkman, 1984). The stimulus that throws

● **Health psychology:** The area of psychology concerned with the promotion of health and prevention and treatment of illness as it relates to psychological factors.

● **Stress:** The general term describing the psychological and bodily response to a stimulus that alters a person's state of equilibrium.

the body's equilibrium out of balance is called a **stressor;** for instance, stepping on a piece of glass while walking barefoot and getting a puncture wound is a stressor. The body's response to a stressor is the **stress response,** also called the *fight-or-flight* response; this is the bodily changes that occur to help you cope with the stressor. If you get a puncture wound, your body may produce chemicals called endorphins and enkephalins, its own version of painkillers, and cause white blood cells to congregate at the site of the injury to fight off any infectious agents. These responses work to bring the body back to normal, to restore homeostasis.

The list of potential stressors is long, and categorized according to a number of criteria (Table 13.1). Stressors can be short-term (**acute stressor**) or long-term (**chronic stressor**); they can be physical, "psychological" (which affect events at the level of the person), or social (or, of course, some combination). Physical stressors, such as not eating for 2 days, generally apply to most people; psychological and social stressors, on the other hand, can be much more subjective. Going to a dance club for hours can be a party animal's idea of a great time or a shy person's nightmare. In general, it is our *perception* of a stimulus that determines whether it will elicit the stress response, not necessarily the objective nature of the stimulus itself.

TABLE 13.1 Examples of Types of Stressors

Type of Stressor	Duration of Stressor	
	Acute	**Chronic**
Physical	Being injured in a car crash	Being underfed; having cancer
Psychological (level of the person)	Working against a deadline	Chronically feeling pressured by work
Social	Being humiliated	Chronic isolation; overcrowding

The Biology of Stress

Austrian-born researcher Hans Selye (1907–1982), who pioneered the study of stress, established that the body responds to stressors in generally predictable ways (Selye, 1976). He called the overall stress response the **general adaptation syndrome (GAS)** and suggested that it has three distinct phases: alarm, resistance, and exhaustion (Figure 13.1, p. 536).

The Alarm Phase: Fight or Flight

Perception of a stressor triggers the **alarm phase,** which is characterized by the fight-or-flight response. In this response, the body mobilizes itself to fight or to flee from a threatening stimulus, which can be a physical threat, such as a knife at the throat, or a psychological one, such as working against a deadline.

When you perceive a threat, your brain responds to it by activating the sympathetic nervous system and inhibiting the parasympathetic nervous system (see Chapter 3 and Figure 3.9). Neurotransmitters and hormonal secretions such as epinephrine and norepinephrine (also referred to as adrenaline and noradrenaline, respectively) cause breathing, heart rate, and blood pressure to increase. (Norepinephrine is considered a neurotransmitter when it is found in the brain, but a

● **Stressor:** A stimulus that throws the body's equilibrium out of balance.

● **Stress response:** The bodily changes that occur to help people cope with a stressor; also called the *fight-or-flight response.*

● **Acute stressor:** A stressor of short-term duration.

● **Chronic stressor:** A stressor of long-term duration.

● **General adaptation syndrome (GAS):** The technical name for the three phases of the body's response to stress.

● **Alarm phase:** The first phase of the GAS, in which a stressor is perceived and a fight-or-flight response is activated.

LOOKING *at* LEVELS *(continued)*

surgery, whereas most of those who were unusually apprehensive about the surgery, but not convinced of death, did not die. Moreover, research with people with asthma has found a powerful nocebo effect: One group of sufferers was asked to inhale what they were told was an irritant or allergen, but that was in fact a harmless saline solution. Almost half of this group experienced an asthmatic reaction. Another group of people with asthma received the same saline solution but without any such information and had no reaction (Luparello et al., 1968).

How can we understand the nocebo response? At the level of the brain, classical conditioning appears to trigger a response consistent with the expected outcome (Barsky et al., 2002). At the level of the person, the *expectation* of a negative outcome leads the person to be hypervigilant for any bodily changes and to attribute any changes to the nocebo in-

stead of to some other stimulus (Barsky et al., 2002). At the level of the group, the culture promotes certain ideas and expectations about sickness and health. Events at these levels interact: For the people with asthma who were told they were inhaling a noxious stimulus, their culture provided the context (level of the group), which led them to be hypervigilant (level of the person) to their physical response (level of the brain), which in turn led them to interpret the bodily changes in a particular way (level of the person).

TEST YOURSELF!

1. What are the different types of coping strategies?
2. Are some people better equipped than others to handle stress?
3. How do relationships affect stress and health?
4. What are mind–body interventions?
5. Do gender and culture play a role in coping?

CONSOLIDATE!

What Is Stress?

- Stress is the general term describing the psychological and bodily response to a stimulus that alters your equilibrium. The stress response of the autonomic nervous system increases heart rate and blood pressure and suppresses the immune system.

- Continued stressors can lead the body's response to stress to become harmful.

- The perception of stress helps determine what constitutes a stressor. Common sources of stress include a sense of a lack of control and predictability, internal conflict, and daily hassles.

- The workplace can cause stress through environmental factors such as noise or work-related conflict. Work can also be a stressor because of a perceived lack of control over how the job is done, or because the job entails responsibility for other people's lives or welfare. Low socioeconomic status can also cause stress.

- The personality trait *hostility* is associated with increased stress, heart rate, blood pressure, and cortisol production. Men are generally more hostile than women.

THINK IT THROUGH Suppose you wanted a job that wasn't very stressful. What job-related factors would you look for as being least stressful— the nature of the job itself, deadlines, the physical work environment, or other factors? What stressful employment-related factors would you want to avoid? Once you start work, what bodily indicators might suggest that your new job was, in fact, fairly stressful? Why do those bodily changes occur?

Stress, Disease, and Health

- Frequent activation of the stress response can lead to changes in the immune system, which can make you vulnerable to contracting a cold or can promote the growth of existing tumors. However, stress does not cause tumors to develop.

- Stress can create cardiovascular changes and can contribute to the development of heart disease through increased blood pressure.

- Stress can increase the likelihood of engaging in unhealthy behaviors such as smoking, substance abuse, or poor eating habits.

- Whether an individual adopts an unhealthy behavior is related to his or her perceived risk of developing a health problem by engaging in an unhealthy behavior and the perceived severity of the problem.

- People often go through stages of change, and relapse, when trying to alter a health-impairing behavior.

THINK IT THROUGH Suppose you were caught in a thunderstorm and were soaking wet by the time you got home. Would you now be more likely to catch a cold? Why or why not? What factors might make you more or less likely to catch a cold? What if you had been out very late, or if you had had a lot of sleep? Why might these factors matter, or would they not matter? Why might Al become sicker as time goes on?

Strategies for Coping

- A realistic appraisal of whether your actions can affect a stressor will help you to determine what coping strategies will be effective.

- Emotion-focused coping strategies are best when the situation can't be changed, and problem-focused strategies work best when it can.

- Mind–body techniques, such as relaxation training, meditation, and hypnosis, can decrease the physical effects of stress.

- Some people are more stress-resistant, or hardy, than others; such people tend to have a sense of commitment and control, view stressors as challenges, and tend to be optimists.

- Social support (particularly perceived social support) can help decrease the experience of stress.

- Culture can affect both the appraisal of a stimulus as a stressor and the choice of coping strategies for managing the stressor.

THINK IT THROUGH If your next-door neighbor plays music very loudly every night when you are trying to go to sleep, and you find this to be a stressor, what could you do to lower your stress response? What type of coping strategies would work best in this situation? What personality characteristics would make you less likely to feel stressed by a noisy neighbor? If you were in a non-Western culture, could the nightly serenade be less stressful? Why or why not?

Key Terms

acute stressor, p. 535
aggression, p. 557
alarm phase, p. 535
approach–approach conflict, p. 539
approach–avoidance conflict, p. 540
atherosclerosis, p. 547
avoidance–avoidance conflict, p. 539
B cell, p. 545
burnout, p. 542
chronic stressor, p. 535
coping, p. 538
emotion-focused coping, p. 553
enacted social support, p. 564
exhaustion phase, p. 536
general adaptation syndrome (GAS), p. 535
glucocorticoids, p. 536

hardy personality, p. 561
health psychology, p. 534
hostile attribution bias, p. 558
hostility, p. 543
internal conflict, p. 539
natural killer (NK) cell, p. 545
nocebo effect, p. 567
perceived social support, p. 564
problem-focused coping, p. 553
resistance phase, p. 536
social support, p. 563
stress, p. 534
stressor, p. 535
stress response, p. 535
T cell, p. 545
thought suppression, p. 556

Copyright Scala/Art Resource, NY

chapter 14

Psychological Disorders

Museum-goers worldwide throng to see exhibits of the works of Vincent van Gogh. Born in Holland in 1853, van Gogh created extraordinary art and took much joy in painting, but his life is a tale of misery. The son and grandson of Protestant ministers, van Gogh was the second of six children. A memoir by his sister-in-law records, "As a child he was of difficult temper, often troublesome and self-willed" (Roskill, 1963, p. 37). According to his parents, when punished, Vincent became more "difficult." As a child he showed no particular awareness of his great gifts; however, on two occasions, once when he modeled a clay elephant and again when he drew a cat, he destroyed his creations when he felt a "fuss" was being made about them (Roskill, 1963).

When van Gogh was 16, he worked as a clerk in an art gallery, but his long, moody silences and irritability isolated him from his coworkers. After 4 years, he was transferred to the gallery's London office, where he fell in love with his landlady's daughter, Ursula. They spent many months together until she revealed her engagement to a previous tenant and rejected van Gogh. Feeling utterly defeated, he found it difficult to concentrate at work. He frequently argued with his coworkers and was soon fired.

Van Gogh next decided on a career in the ministry but could not master the Greek and Latin necessary for the entrance exams. Instead, he became a lay pastor, preaching to miners in the Borinage, a coal-mining area in Belgium. He went without bathing and slept in a hut on bare planks as the miners did. But the miners feared this unkempt, wild-looking man, and the church elders dismissed him. Increasingly, van Gogh found comfort in painting and drawing.

His life continued to be marked by instability. After he left the Borinage, he lived in and out of his parents' home and wandered around the country. Whereas once his interest in religion had been intense, if not obsessional, he now turned his back on religion. He developed a relationship with a pregnant prostitute, Sien, but their liaison ended after about a year and a half. Van Gogh reported that he had "attacks" during which he would hear voices; at times he believed he was being poisoned.

When he was 35, van Gogh convinced fellow painter Paul Gauguin to share a house with him in Arles, France. As was true for all of van Gogh's relationships, he and Gauguin frequently quarreled. According to Gauguin, after one particularly violent argument, van Gogh approached him threateningly with an open razor, but Gauguin stared him down. Van Gogh then ran to their house, where he cut off his earlobe, which he then sent to a local prostitute (not Sien). The next day he was found at home, bleeding and unconscious, and was taken to a hospital, where he remained for 2 weeks. His brother Theo spent time with him in the hospital and found Vincent in great spiritual anguish.

After his release from the hospital in January 1889, van Gogh's behavior became increasingly bizarre, so much so that within 2 months the residents of Arles petitioned that he be confined, and he again stayed for a time in the hospital. In May, van Gogh moved to the asylum at Saint-Remy, not far from Arles, where he lived on and off for the next year and a half, and where he produced many paintings. Shortly after his last release, less than 2 years after the incident with Gauguin, he purposefully ended his anguish and his life by going out into a field with a gun and shooting himself in the stomach. Yet, a few weeks before his death, he could say, "I still love art and life very much indeed" (Roskill, 1963).

Questions of art aside, van Gogh's experiences focus our attention on psychological disorders: What defines a psychological disorder? Who establishes criteria for determining what is abnormal behavior? What are the symptoms and origins of some specific disorders?

> "As a child he was of difficult temper, often troublesome and self-willed"

Identifying Psychological Disorders: What's Abnormal?

What distinguishes unusual behaviors from behaviors that are symptoms of a psychological disorder? Before he rejected religion, van Gogh was tormented by religious ideas and believed in ghosts. Are these signs of psychological disturbance? What about his self-mutilation? What would you want to know about him before drawing any conclusions?

Mental health professionals face questions such as these every day. In this section you will see how formulations of and findings about psychological disorders suggest answers to those questions.

Defining Abnormality

It is difficult to give an exact definition of psychological disorders—also referred to as psychiatric disorders, mental disorders or, less systematically, mental illnesses—because they can encompass many aspects of behavioral, experiential, and bodily functioning. However, a good working definition is that a **psychological disorder** is signaled by a constellation of cognitive, emotional, and behavioral symptoms that create significant distress; impair work, school, family, relationships, or daily living; or lead to significant risk of harm. This definition takes into account three factors: distress, disability, and danger.

Distress

People with psychological disorders may display or experience *distress*. An example of distress that is obvious to others is repeatedly bursting into tears and expressing hopelessness about the future, for no apparent reason. However, a person's distress is not always observable to others, as when people chronically worry, feel profoundly sad for long periods of time, or hear voices that only they can hear.

Disability

People with psychological disorders may experience a *disability* or dysfunction in some aspect of life. Examples include a police officer who becomes so anxious that while on duty he cannot perform his job, or an individual (such as van Gogh) whose emotional outbursts drive others away. An individual's dysfunction may not necessarily cause him or her distress.

Psychological disorders can be very debilitating, and worldwide they rank second among diseases that lead to death and disability, a higher ranking than cancer (Murray & Lopez, 1996). According to some estimates, up to 48% of Americans have experienced 1 of 30 common psychological disorders at some point in their lives (Kessler et al., 1994), and 20% of Americans have a diagnosable mental disorder in any given year (Regier et al., 1993; Satcher, 1999). Psychological disorders can affect people's relationships, their ability to care for themselves, and their functioning on the job. For every 100 workers, an average of 37 work days per month are lost either because of reduced workloads or absences stemming from psychological disorders (Kessler & Frank, 1997).

Danger

Danger can occur when symptoms of a psychological disorder cause an individual to put life (his or her own, or another's) at risk, either purposefully or accidentally. For instance, depression may lead someone to attempt suicide, extreme paranoia may provoke someone to attack other

● **Psychological disorder:** The presence of a constellation of cognitive, emotional, and behavioral symptoms that create significant distress or impair work, school, family, relationships, or daily living.

Van Gogh's painting of the church at Auvers is unusual because of its unconventional perspective, use of color, and brushstrokes. Do these differences reflect a psychological disorder, or just a different way of seeing or conveying the structure and its surroundings?

people, or a parent's disorder may be sufficiently severe that the children's safety is put at risk (as when Andrea Yates, who suffered so severely from depression that she lost touch with reality, drowned her five young children in 2001, thinking that she was rescuing them from Satan's grasp).

Are Deviant Behaviors Necessarily Abnormal?

Mathematician John Nash (left), whose life was the basis for the movie *A Beautiful Mind*, starring Oscar-winning actor Russell Crowe (right), had delusions that aliens were communicating with him. Although the movie portrayed Nash as having both hallucinations and delusions, in real life he did not have hallucinations.

Picture someone hopping on one leg, thumb in mouth, trying to sing the French national anthem during a hockey game. You would probably think this was abnormal; but what if the behavior was part of a fraternity initiation ritual, or a new kind of performance art? A behavior that is bizarre or inappropriate in one context may be entirely appropriate in another. To be considered "disordered," it is not enough for a behavior or a set of behaviors to be deviant from the mainstream culture. Being unconventional or different in religious, political, or sexual arenas does not qualify as abnormal. What is considered deviant changes from generation to generation, and can differ across cultures.

Consider that, in 1851, Dr. Samuel Cartwright of Louisiana wrote an essay in which he declared that slaves' running away was evidence of a serious mental disorder, which he called "drapetomania" (Eakin, 2000). Until 1973, homosexuality was officially considered a psychological disorder in the United States, and then it was removed from the *Diagnostic and Statistical Manual of Mental Disorders* (this manual is used by mental health clinicians to classify psychological disorders). And in the last decade, the determination of abnormality has taken a new turn in the United States; as health maintenance organizations (HMOs) and other types of managed care organizations try to keep costs down, they have developed their own criteria for the symptoms and disorders they will pay to have treated—and have also regulated the frequency and duration of the treatment.

The line between normal and abnormal behavior is perhaps easiest to draw in the case of **psychosis,** which is an obvious impairment in the ability to perceive and comprehend events accurately, combined with a gross disorganization of behavior. People with psychoses may have **hallucinations,** mental images so vivid that they seem real, or **delusions,** which are entrenched false beliefs that are often bizarre (such as that their thoughts are being controlled by aliens). However, such beliefs, even if false (or at least not susceptible to rational proof), should not be considered abnormal if they are an accepted part of the culture. For instance, in some religious groups, such as Pentecostals, it is not considered abnormal to hear voices, especially the voice of God (Cox, personal communication, 2000). Another example is *zar*, or spirit possession, experienced in some North African and Middle Eastern cultures. Those affected may shout, laugh, hit their heads against a wall, or exhibit other behavior that otherwise would be considered inappropriate; an experience of zar is not considered abnormal in the cultures in which it occurs (American Psychiatric Association, 2000).

Explaining Abnormality

Explanations for abnormal behavior have changed with the times and reflect the thinking of the culture. In ancient Greece, abnormal behaviors, as well as med-

- **Psychosis:** An obvious impairment in the ability to perceive and comprehend events accurately, and a gross disorganization of behavior.

- **Hallucinations:** Mental images so vivid that they seem real.

- **Delusions:** Entrenched false beliefs that are often bizarre.

ical problems, were thought to arise from imbalances of the body's four fluids, or "humors": yellow bile, phlegm, blood, and black bile. Too much phlegm, for instance, made you sluggish and "phlegmatic"; too much black bile made you melancholic. In 17th-century New England, abnormality was thought to be the work of the devil. In the middle of the 20th century, Sigmund Freud's work was influential, and psychodynamic theory was the instrument used to understand abnormality. Currently, in order to understand psychological disorders, many psychologists and others in the field have used the *biopsychosocial model*. This model focuses on factors at the levels of the brain, the person, and the group. In this discussion, we go one step further and show how events at those three levels are not discrete but affect one another in various interactions.

The Brain

Van Gogh's family history points to a possible cause of his psychological problems. Van Gogh's brother Theo was often depressed and anxious, and he committed suicide within a year after Vincent's suicide; his sister Wilhelmina exhibited a long-standing psychosis; his youngest brother Cor is thought to have committed suicide. Does this history indicate that van Gogh inherited some vulnerability to a psychological disorder? Not necessarily, but researchers are finding increasing evidence that genetic factors frequently contribute to the development of some disorders.

Biological factors, including, for example, neurotransmitters (such as serotonin), hormones (such as adrenaline, which functions as a hormone in the body), and abnormalities in the structure of the brain, appear to play a role in the development of some psychological disorders. From this point of view, depression can be seen as a manifestation of an abnormal serotonin level. Similarly, the cause of an irrational fear of spiders could be the outcome of an overreactive amygdala. Although these explanations may be valid, they are only a part of the picture. *Why* are someone's serotonin levels abnormal? *Why* is someone else's amygdala overreactive to the sight of a spider? As previously noted in many contexts, our own thoughts, feelings, and behaviors, as well as our interactions with others and our environment, can affect the workings of our brains.

Thus, abnormality cannot be considered solely as a function of brain chemistry or structure. Many researchers and clinicians today believe that psychological disorders can best be explained by a **diathesis–stress model** (*diathesis* means a predisposition to a state or condition). This conceptualization, illustrated in Figure 14.1, states that "for a given disorder, there is both a predisposition to the disorder (a *diathesis*) and specific factors (*stress*) that combine with the diathesis to trigger the onset of the disorder" (Rende & Plomin, 1992, p. 177). According to the diathesis–stress model, because of certain biological factors (such as their genes, abnormality of brain structures, or neurotransmitters), some people may be more vulnerable to developing a particular disorder, but without certain

● **Diathesis–stress model:** A way of understanding the development of a psychological disorder, in which a predisposition to a given disorder (diathesis) and specific factors (stress) combine to trigger the onset of the disorder.

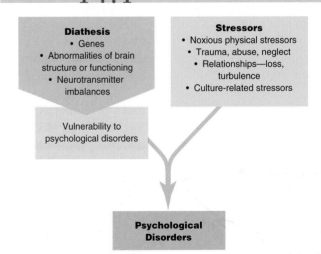

FIGURE 14.1 The Diathesis–Stress Model

Most mental health researchers and professionals believe that both biological factors (diathesis) and environmental stressors (stress) together cause psychological disorders.

environmental stressors, the disorder is not triggered. By the same token, when experiencing a stressor, people without a biological vulnerability for a disorder may not develop that disorder. From this perspective, neither factor alone can cause illness, and as noted in Chapter 13, not everyone perceives a particular event or stimulus to be a stressor. Whether because of learning or biology, or an interaction of the two, some people are more likely to perceive more stressors (and therefore to experience more stress) than others. For instance, although schizophrenia appears to have a genetic component, even if an identical twin has schizophrenia, the co-twin will not necessarily develop the disorder. The diathesis–stress model proposes that it is the *combination* of biological vulnerability and specific other factors, such as a trauma or the death of a loved one, that elicits the disorder.

The Person

Several factors at the level of the person also play a role in psychological disorders. One factor is the results of classical conditioning, as in the case of Little Albert (Chapter 6), who developed a fear of white furry things based on his classical conditioning experiences with a white rat and a loud noise. Operant conditioning and observational learning can also help explain some psychological disorders, as can the pattern of a person's thoughts. For instance, chronic negative thought patterns ("I'm incompetent; I can't do anything right") can lead to depressing feelings and can contribute to the development or maintenance of depression. Learning, thoughts, and feelings may help explain why certain psychological disorders develop in some people.

The Group

Factors at the level of the group play a role in triggering psychological disorders, as well as in increasing the risk of a disorder's recurrence. For example, the "stress" part of posttraumatic stress disorder is usually caused by other people (such as a terrorist or a rapist) or the physical environment (natural disasters such as floods and earthquakes).

Culture can also influence the conception of psychological disorders. For a period during the 1960s, a number of mental health professionals proposed the idea that mental illness is a myth, merely a label applied to culturally undesirable behavior (Szasz, 1961). In this view, the label determines how people are treated and, in a self-fulfilling prophecy, may even play a role in how the "mentally ill" person behaves, once labeled.

David Rosenhan (1973) tested an aspect of this idea. In his study, people without a psychological disorder gained admittance to psychiatric hospitals by claiming that they heard voices. Once in the hospital they behaved normally. But because they were given a psychiatric diagnosis, their normal behavior was interpreted as pathological, and they were treated accordingly. For example, when these "pseudopatients" asked about eligibility for grounds privileges, the psychiatrists responded to such questions only 6% of the time; in 71% of the encounters, the doctors just moved on.

Rosenhan claimed that his study illustrated the power of labels and contexts. But does it tell us anything about the reality of mental disorders? The pseudopatients originally reported auditory hallucinations that were troubling enough to drive them to request admission to a mental hospital; people do not normally have such symptoms. How was the staff to know that the pseudopatients were lying when they described their "symptoms"? Similarly, the fact that the staff in Rosenhan's study labeled and treated the pseudopatients as if their symptoms were genuine does not indicate that psychological disorders with these symptoms do not exist, only that doctors did not recognize that the pseudopatients were "faking it" (Spitzer, 1975). In fact, the doctors *did* notice that something was amiss because, when the "patients" were discharged from the hospital, the diagnosis they were given was "schizophrenia, in remission," a rarely given diagnosis. Moreover, the generalizability of Rosenhan's findings are limited because he did not use any type of control or comparison group (Millon, 1975).

Diagnosing individuals involves making judgments that, like all judgments, are subject to error, and this is part of what Rosenhan felt his study illustrated. A systematic type of error in diagnosis is called a *diagnostic bias* (Meehl, 1960), often with the result that some people receive certain diagnoses based on nonmedical factors, such as race. For instance, studies of racial bias show that African American patients in the United States are more likely to be evaluated negatively than are white patients (Garb, 1997; Jenkins-Hall & Sacco, 1991; Strakowski et al., 1995) and are prescribed higher doses of medication (Strakowski et al., 1993).

However, the reality of certain disorders—schizophrenia being one—is attested to by the fact that these disorders are recognized worldwide. Nevertheless, cultures differ in which behaviors they consider abnormal, and the symptoms, course, and prognosis of disorders may vary from culture to culture (Basic Behavioral Science Task Force, 1996).

Events at all three levels and the interactions among them must be examined to understand the various psychological disorders discussed in this chapter. Biological factors; learning and thought patterns; familial, cultural, and environmental factors; and the relationships among them all play a role in explaining psychological disorders.

Categorizing Disorders: Is a Rose Still a Rose by Any Other Name?

Suppose a man comes to a clinical psychologist's office complaining that he feels he is going crazy and that he has a strong sense of impending doom. How would the clinical psychologist determine the nature of this man's difficulties and figure out how best to help him? What questions should the psychologist ask? One guide to help the psychologist and other mental health clinicians is the *Diagnostic and Statistical Manual of Mental Disorders*, known to its users simply as the *DSM*.

In 1952 the American Psychiatric Association published the inaugural edition of the *DSM*, the first manual of mental disorders designed primarily to help clinicians diagnose and treat patients. This edition was based on psychodynamic theory. In later editions of the manual, its developers tried to avoid relying on any one theory of the causes of disorders and to base the identification of disorders on a growing body of empirical research. The fourth edition, the *DSM-IV*, published in 1994, was an attempt to refine the diagnostic criteria and make the diagnostic categories more useful to mental health researchers and practitioners.

Since the third edition, the *DSM* has described five *axes*, or types of information, that should be considered in the assessment of a patient. Clinical disorders are noted on Axis I, and personality disorders and mental retardation on Axis II. Axis III notes any general medical conditions that might be relevant to a diagnosis on Axis I or II. Psychosocial and environmental problems are identified on Axis IV,

TABLE 14.1 *DSM-IV-TR*'s 17 Major Categories of Disorders

Major Category of Disorders	Explanation
Disorders usually first diagnosed in infancy, childhood, or adolescence	Although describing disorders usually first evident early in life, some adults are newly diagnosed with disorders in this category, such as attention-deficit/hyperactivity disorder.
Delirium, dementia, and amnestic and other cognitive disorders	Disorders of consciousness and cognition.
Mental disorders due to a general medical condition not elsewhere classified	Disorders in which mental and psychological symptoms are judged to be due to a medical condition (coded on Axis III).
Substance-related disorders	Disorders of substance dependence and abuse, as well as disorders induced by a substance, such as a substance-induced psychotic disorder.
Schizophrenia and other psychotic disorders	Disorders related to psychoses.
Mood disorders	Disorders of mood/feelings.
Anxiety disorders	Disorders of anxiety.
Somatoform disorders	Disorders in which physical/medical complaints have no known medical origin (or the symptoms are not proportional to a medical condition) and so are thought to be psychological in nature.
Factitious disorders	Disorders in which the person intentionally fabricates symptoms of a medical or psychological disorder, but not for external gain (such as disability claims).
Dissociative disorders	Disorders in which there is a disruption in the usually integrated functions of consciousness, memory, or identity.
Sexual and gender identity disorders	Disorders of sexual function, the object of sexual desire, and/or of gender identity.
Eating disorders	Disorders related to eating.
Sleep disorders	Disorders related to sleep.
Impulse-control disorders not elsewhere classified	Disorders related to the ability to contain impulses (such as kleptomania).
Adjustment disorders	Disorders related to the development of distressing emotional or behavioral symptoms in response to an identifiable stressor.
Personality disorders	Disorders related to personality traits that are inflexible and maladaptive, and that cause distress or difficulty with daily functioning.
Other conditions that may be a focus of clinical attention	A problem receiving treatment for which there is no psychological disorder, or the symptoms do not meet criteria for a disorder.

Source: Adapted from American Psychiatric Association (2000). Reprinted with permission from the *Diagnostic and Statistical Manual of Mental Disorders,* Fourth Edition, Text Revision. Copyright 2000 American Psychiatric Association.

and Axis V records the patient's highest level of functioning in major areas of life within the past year. An appendix to the manual outlines aspects of the patient's cultural context that clinicians should take into account when making a diagnosis. Most of the manual, however, is devoted to describing disorders. It defines 17 major categories of psychological problems. All told, almost 300 mental disorders are specified. A revision called *DSM-IV-TR* (TR stands for *Text Revision*) in 2000 included more up-to-date information on incidence rates and cultural factors, but did not change the diagnostic categories nor the criteria.

The sheer number of disorders included in the *DSM-IV* has provoked criticism of the manual; the breadth of the major diagnostic categories is shown in Table 14.1. As the *DSM* has evolved, it has introduced categories that define medical problems as psychological disorders, leading to a pathologizing of people's mental health. For example, a new diagnosis in the *DSM-IV* is "Breathing-Related Sleep Disorder" (one cause of which is sleep apnea; see Chapter 5). Thus, the *DSM-IV* created a *psychological* or *psychiatric* disorder for a medical problem. Moreover, the *DSM-IV* does not provide a discrete boundary separating abnormality from normality (Double, 2002; Frances, 1998); a clinician's judgment determines whether an impairment is "clinically significant." Another criticism leveled at the *DSM-IV* is that some of the disorders are not clearly distinct from one another (Blais et al., 1997), although they are often presented as if they were (Tucker, 1998).

Despite these criticisms, the *DSM-IV* is the predominant means of categorizing psychological disorders in the United States. The discussion of disorders in this chapter uses the *DSM-IV* system of categorization.

Looking *at* Levels

Did Charles Whitman Have a Psychological Disorder?

If a person is violent, does this automatically mean that he or she has a psychological disorder? No; there is no simple, single criterion. Psychological disorders can most clearly be identified by looking at events at all three levels of analysis. Consider the case of Charles Whitman. On August 1, 1966, long before anyone imagined today's far more common occasions of violence in schools and workplaces, Whitman, a 25-year-old student at the University of Texas in Austin, climbed to the top of a tower on the campus and opened fire on students casually walking below. After an hour and a half, 16 were dead and another 30 wounded. As Gary Lavergne, author of *A Sniper in the Tower: The Charles Whitman Murders* (1997) wrote, Whitman "introduced America to public mass murder" (p. xi). At the time, a local reporter described Whitman as "a good son, top Boy Scout, an excellent Marine, an honor student, a hard worker, a loving husband, a fine scout master, a handsome man, a wonderful friend to all who knew him—and an expert sniper" (Lavergne, 1997, p. xi).

What drove Whitman to murder? Was he unhappy at school? Yes; he was extremely frustrated by his heavy course load (an explanation at the level of the person). What about his relationship with his family? His parents were about to divorce, a circumstance that upset him greatly. He also had a long history of bad blood with his abusive father. In fact, the night before his rampage, he killed his mother and his wife, and then wrote an angry letter about his father. In this same note, Whitman asked that his brain be examined after his death, to see whether "there is any mental disorder."

Charles Whitman's hunch was correct—something *was* wrong with his brain. An autopsy uncovered a pecan-sized tumor near his hypothalamus, a part of the brain involved in emotion. Whitman had complained of massive headaches for weeks before the shooting and was seen regularly gobbling huge doses of aspirin.

Can we conclude that with the discovery of the tumor the case is closed—that Whitman had a medical disorder, not a psychological one? Probably not. It's unlikely that the brain tumor was the sole cause of his behavior. After all, most people with similar brain tumors don't become mass murderers. Perhaps the tumor intensified Whitman's violent feelings, but this still doesn't tell us how and why those feelings led to violent acts. Whitman was clearly deeply unhappy (level of the person), but again, this by itself was probably not enough to trigger his violent rampage.

Whitman's killing spree can best be understood by looking for interactions among events at all three levels. He may have interpreted the discomfort and feelings produced by the tumor in terms of his frustration over his school work and his unhappiness (level of the person), and his rage toward his parents and others (level of the group). Such thoughts may have caused severe stress, which amplified the headaches caused by the tumor (level of the brain), thereby ratcheting up his misery and rage. This in turn may have led him to finally revert to his training as a Marine and lash out at a world of innocent people on the ground below.

TEST YOURSELF!

1. How is abnormality defined?
2. How are psychological disorders explained?
3. How are psychological disorders classified and diagnosed?

Mood Disorders

We cannot diagnose from a distance, but we know enough about van Gogh's life and behavior to make some educated guesses about the nature of his moods and turmoil. He frequently spoke of feeling sad; still, he clung to the commonality of human feeling, saying, "I prefer feeling my sorrow to forgetting it or becoming indifferent" (Lubin, 1972, p. 22). Painting was the one thing that drove away his sadness, and sometimes he painted in a frenzy. He would have bouts of irritability, had difficulty concentrating, was often miserable, and was frequently quarrelsome. People described him as odd, argumentative, very sensitive, and unpredictable. He described himself as an alcoholic. He had frequent thoughts of suicide, and in the end, at the age of 37, he died after he intentionally shot himself (Lubin, 1972).

Mood disorders are conditions marked by persistent or episodic disturbances in emotion that interfere with normal functioning in at least one realm of life. Among the most common mood disorders are *major depressive disorder, dysthymia* (a less intense but longer lasting form of depression), and *bipolar disorder* (formerly known as manic-depressive disorder).

Major Depressive Disorder: Not Just Feeling Blue

When people are feeling sad or blue, they may say they are "depressed," but generally they do not mean they are suffering from a psychological disorder. **Major depressive disorder (MDD)** is characterized by at least 2 weeks of depressed mood or loss of interest in nearly all activities, along with at least four of the other symptoms of depression listed in Table 14.2 (American Psychiatric Association, 2000).

● **Mood disorder:** A category of disorders marked by persistent or episodic disturbances in emotion that interfere with normal functioning in at least one realm of life.

● **Major depressive disorder (MDD):** A disorder characterized by at least 2 weeks of depressed mood or loss of interest in nearly all activities, along with sleep or eating disturbances, loss of energy, and feelings of hopelessness.

TABLE 14.2 Diagnostic Criteria for Major Depressive Disorder

During a period of at least 2 weeks, five or more of the following symptoms have occurred and represent a change in functioning.

- Depressed mood most of the day, almost daily (based on subjective report or observations of others).
- Markedly diminished interest or pleasure in nearly all daily activities (based on subjective or objective reports).
- Significant weight loss, not through dieting.
- Daily insomnia or hypersomnia (sleeping a lot).
- Daily psychomotor agitation (intense restlessness) or retardation (physical sluggishness).
- Daily fatigue, or loss of energy.
- Almost daily feelings of worthlessness, or inappropriate or excessive guilt.
- Almost daily diminished ability to think or concentrate, or indecisiveness (based on subjective or objective reports).
- Recurrent thoughts of death or suicide with or without a specific plan.

Source: American Psychiatric Association (2000). Reprinted with permission from the *Diagnostic and Statistical Manual of Mental Disorders*, Fourth Edition, Text Revision. Copyright 2000 American Psychiatric Association.

Thus, major depression affects a person's "ABC's": affect (mood), behavior (actions), and cognition (thoughts). It is estimated that up to one in five people in the United States will experience this disorder in their lifetimes (American Psychiatric Association, 1994; Ross, 1991), and in the workplace, it is the leading cause of both absenteeism and "presenteeism," which occurs when a depressed person is less effective at work (Druss et al., 2001). By the year 2020, depression will probably be the second most disabling disease in the nation, after heart disease (Schrof & Schultz, 1999). Some people with depression may experience only one episode; others experience recurrent episodes that may be frequent or separated by years; or the depression may become more chronic (Judd et al., 1998). A 10-year study of over 300 people diagnosed with major depressive disorder found that more than one third of the participants did not have a recurrence of depression (Solomon et al., 2000).

Artist Kate Monson, who experienced depression, describes her painting as a reflection of her depression.

Major Depressive Disorder From the Inside

The experience of depression is captured in words by Elizabeth Wurtzel, author of *Prozac Nation*:

> In my case, I was not frightened in the least bit at the thought that I might live because I was certain, quite certain, that I was already dead. The actual dying part, the withering away of my physical body, was a mere formality. My spirit, my emotional

being, whatever you want to call all that inner turmoil that has nothing to do with physical existence, were long gone, dead and gone, and only a mass of the most . . . god-awful excruciating pain . . . was left in its wake. (Wurtzel, 1995, p. 22)

Elizabeth Wurtzel's description of her depression captures the essence of the painful, extremely disturbing quality of many of the symptoms. In some cases, severely depressed people also have delusions or hallucinations. Often these psychotic symptoms feature themes of guilt, deserved punishment, and personal inadequacy, such as voices asserting the individual's worthlessness.

However, not all cultures share exactly the same symptom list. People from Zimbabwe who are depressed often complain of headache and fatigue (Patel et al., 2001), as do people in Latin and Mediterranean cultures. They do not necessarily report sadness and guilt. In Asian cultures, people with major depression are likely to report weakness, tiredness, a sense of "imbalance," or other bodily symptoms (Parker et al., 2001).

UNDERSTANDING RESEARCH

Symptoms of Depression in China and the United States

For several decades, mental health professionals have been told that Chinese people more frequently report bodily symptoms (compared to cognitive or emotional symptoms) of depression. Such symptoms include poor appetite, tiredness, and concentration problems. Psychologists Yen, Robins, and Lin (2000) set out to compare symptoms of depression among college students in China and American students of Chinese descent, as well as students of Caucasian descent.

QUESTION: These researchers asked: Do Chinese students report more bodily symptoms of depression than Chinese American students, who in turn report more bodily symptoms than Caucasian American students?

ALTERNATIVES: (1) Chinese students report more bodily symptoms of depression than the other two groups, and Chinese Americans, in turn, report more bodily symptoms of depression than Caucasian Americans; (2) Chinese students report more bodily symptoms than the two American groups, but the American groups report comparable numbers of such symptoms; (3) The three groups report equivalent levels of bodily symptoms of depression; (4) In some other way, the three groups differ from each other in the amount of bodily symptoms.

LOGIC: If their culture leads Chinese people to experience bodily symptoms when depressed (as opposed to cognitive or emotional symptoms), then the Chinese group should score highest on questions assessing bodily symptoms, followed by Chinese Americans (who are influenced by Chinese culture, but less so than Chinese in China), with Caucasian Americans scoring lowest.

MEASURES: Three groups of college students participated in the study, each including both males and females: (1) Chinese; (2) Chinese Americans; and (3) Caucasian Americans. All participants completed questionnaires assessing depressive symptoms; Chinese American participants also were asked about their level of immersion in American culture.

RESULTS: In contrast to the expected results, the Chinese group had the *lowest* scores on the questions pertaining to bodily symptoms of depression; that is, they reported experiencing fewer such symptoms of depression than did either American group. The Chinese American and Caucasian American groups were not significantly different from each other. Moreover, among the Chinese Americans, there was no relation between how "Americanized" they were and their amount of bodily symptoms.

INFERENCES: These results are inconsistent with previous studies on this topic. When a study's results differ substantially from related studies and from the study's hypotheses, researchers wonder whether methodological factors could have affected the results—that is, whether the unexpected results were obtained because different research methods were used. This study used a questionnaire that directly asked about different types of symptoms, whereas some previous studies assessed symptoms during visits to doctors or mental health professionals (where the participants were asked about their symptoms). Perhaps in these face-to-face encounters in China, participants only felt comfortable mentioning the more culturally sanctioned bodily symptoms (Nikelly, 1988) and not other symptoms, particularly in a medical setting. Moreover, in the current study, participants' answers were anonymous; perhaps this method of assessment led to differences in the reporting of symptoms. In any event, it's clear that the previous cultural stereotype is either inaccurate or applies only in restricted situations.

Major depressive disorder, the most common psychological disorder in the United States (Kessler et al., 1994), is found among all cultural and ethnic groups (Weissman et al., 1991), as well as across the economic spectrum. In developing countries, rates are estimated to be about the same for men and for women (Culbertson, 1997), but American women are diagnosed with depression two to three times more frequently than American men (APA, 1994; Culbertson, 1997; Gater et al., 1998). Further, the overall rate of depression is increasing in the United States (Lewinsohn et al., 1993).

Many, if not most, suicide attempts seem to be motivated by the sense of hopelessness that is often a part of depression. Approximately 30% of people with depression attempt suicide, and half of those succeed. One estimate is that 19,200 to 30,000 depressed people in the United States commit suicide every year (American Foundation for Suicide Prevention, 1996) making it the 8th leading cause of death in the U.S. (Monthly Vital Statistics Report, 2000). Suicide prevention programs try, in part, to treat depression and alcohol use, both of which are associated with suicide (Reifman & Windle, 1995). Several common misconceptions about suicide are listed in Table 14.3 (p. 584). Test yourself to see whether your views of suicide are accurate.

Some people—approximately 6% of the American population—experience a less intense but longer lasting type of depression called **dysthymia** (American Psychiatric Association, 1994). People who are given this diagnosis do not suffer an episode of extreme depression but do have a depressed mood for most of the day for at least 2 years and experience two other symptoms of depression (see Table 14.2; APA, 2000).

HANDS ON

● **Dysthymia:** A mood disorder similar to major depressive disorder, but less intense and longer lasting.

TABLE 14.3 Common Misconceptions of Suicide

- *If you talk about suicide, you won't really do it.* (False: Most people who commit suicide gave some clue or warning. Threats or statements about suicide should not be ignored.)

- *People who attempt suicide are "crazy."* (False: Suicidal people are not "crazy"; they *are* likely to be depressed, upset, or to feel hopeless.)

- *Someone determined to commit suicide can't be stopped.* (False: Almost all suicidal people have mixed feelings about living and dying up until the last moment. Moreover, most suicidal people don't want to die; they want their pain to stop. And the suicidal impulse often passes.)

- *People who commit suicide weren't willing to seek help.* (False: Studies have shown that more than half of suicide victims sought medical help within the 6 months before death.)

- *Talking about suicide could give someone the idea, so you shouldn't talk or ask about it.* (False. Discussing suicide openly can be helpful to someone who is suicidal.)

Source: Adapted from Suicide Awareness\Voices of Education (SA\VE), P.O. Box 24507, Minneapolis, MN 55424; Phone: (612) 946-7998; Internet: http://www.save.org; E-mail: save@winternet.com.

Bipolar Disorder: Going to Extremes

In contrast to depression, **bipolar disorder** is a mood disorder marked by one or more manic episodes or by the less intense hypomania; some people with this disorder also experience depression. Approximately 1% of Americans have this disorder (Regier & Kaelber, 1995). A **manic episode** is a period of at least a week during which an abnormally elevated, expansive, or irritable mood persists (see Table 14.4). Being manic is not just having an "up" day. During a manic episode, the sufferer may be euphoric and enthusiastic about everything, starting conversations with strangers and making grandiose plans.

Bipolar Disorder From the Inside

Psychologist Kay Redfield Jamison describes her personal experience with mania:

There is a particular kind of pain, elation, loneliness, and terror involved in this kind of madness. When you're high, it's tremendous. The ideas and feelings are fast and frequent like shooting stars, and you follow them until you find better and brighter ones. Shyness goes, the right words and gestures are suddenly there, the power to captivate others a felt certainty. There are interests found in uninteresting people. Sensuality is pervasive and the desire to seduce and be seduced irresistible. Feelings of ease, intensity, power, well-being, financial omnipotence, and euphoria pervade one's marrow. But, somewhere, this changes. The fast ideas are far too fast, and there are far too many; overwhelming confusion replaces clarity. Memory goes. Humor and absorption on friends' faces are replaced by fear and concerns. Everything previously moving with the grain is now against—you are irritable, angry, frightened, uncontrollable, and enmeshed totally in the blackest caves of the mind. You never knew those caves were there. It will never end, for madness carves its own reality. (Jamison, 1995, p. 67)

● **Bipolar disorder:** A mood disorder marked by one or more episodes of either mania or hypomania.

● **Manic episode:** A period of at least 1 week during which an abnormally elevated, expansive, or irritable mood persists.

TABLE 14.4 Diagnostic Criteria for a Manic Episode

- Grandiosity or elevated sense of self-esteem.

- Less need for sleep.

- More talkative than usual, or feels pressure to keep talking, and may be difficult to interrupt.

- Racing thoughts (sometimes described as watching three different television programs simultaneously).

- Distractibility and difficulty screening out useful from extraneous material.

- Increase in goal-directed activity (this could be socially, at work, at school, or sexually) or psychomotor agitation.

- Excessive involvement in pleasurable activities that have a high potential for painful consequences (for example, unrestrained shopping sprees, sexual infidelity, unwise business investments).

Source: American Psychiatric Association (2000). Reprinted with permission from the *Diagnostic and Statistical Manual of Mental Disorders,* Fifth Edition. Copyright 2000 American Psychiatric Association.

Psychologist Kay Redfield Jamison, like many people with bipolar disorder, had difficulty recognizing that she had a psychological disorder and resisted attempts at treatment for a number of years. People experiencing **hypomania** have less severe symptoms of mania, and their symptoms are less likely to interfere with social functioning. Manic or hypomanic episodes are often preceded or followed by episodes of depression, and the cycling of the mood usually takes place over a number of years, although some people may experience rapid cycling, with four or more mood shifts in a year. If left untreated, mood swings often become more frequent over time, leading to a poorer prognosis. The early phase of an episode, before the symptoms become acute, is termed the *prodromal phase* (a *prodrome* is a warning symptom). Some people with bipolar disorder report prodromal indicators of manic or depressive symptoms that signal that an episode will occur (Keitner et al., 1996).

Explaining Mood Disorders

Although bipolar and major depressive disorders are distinct disorders, research has characterized these disorders, as well as dysthymia, as lying along a spectrum of mood disorders (Akiskal, 1996; Angst, 1998) that are related by biological and psychological factors. Mood disorders can best be understood by considering events at three levels of analysis and their interactions: the brain, the person, and the group.

Level of the Brain

Twin studies show that if one identical twin has a major depression, the co-twin is four times more likely to experience a depression than the co-twin of an affected fraternal twin (Bowman & Nurnberger, 1993; Kendler et al., 1999). This appears to be good evidence for genetic influence. However, adoption studies have not shown the same clear-cut evidence for a genetic role (Eley et al., 1998; Wender et al., 1986). More definitive support for biological factors comes from research with depressed

● **Hypomania:** A mood state similar to mania, but less severe, with fewer and less intrusive symptoms.

people whose relatives also suffer from depression: The depressed people studied had unusually low activity in one area of the frontal lobe that has direct connections to many brain areas involved in emotion, such as the amygdala. This part of the frontal lobe also has connections to the systems that produce serotonin, norepinephrine, and dopamine (Kennedy et al., 1997). Parts of this area of the frontal lobe have frequently been found to have abnormal patterns of activation in people who are depressed (Davidson et al., 2002). People with depression have also been found to have smaller hippocampi, a key brain area involved in memory (Bremner et al., 2000). Additional studies suggest that people with depression have increased activity in the amygdala, which is involved in emotional memory; the amygdala's involvement may account for the rumination about emotional events (Cahill et al., 2001).

Among those with bipolar disorder, there is evidence that the amygdala is enlarged (Altshuler et al., 1998; Strakowski et al., 2002). These abnormalities in or affecting the amygdala in people with mood disorders are consistent with the role of the amygdala in regulating mood and accessing emotional memories (LeDoux, 1996) (see Chapters 9 and 10). Neuroimaging studies of people with bipolar disorder have found shifts in temporal lobe activity during manic episodes that are not present during other mood states (Gyulai et al., 1997), which may be related to activity in parts of the limbic system that are located in this structure.

There is clear evidence for an underlying genetic relationship between bipolar and depressive mood disorders. For example, if an identical twin has bipolar disorder, the co-twin has an 80% chance of developing some kind of mood disorder (such as depression), although not necessarily bipolar disorder (Karkowski & Kendler, 1997; Vehmanen et al., 1995).

Unfortunately, it is not yet clear which neurotransmitters are most involved in depression; it is not even clear whether the problem is having too much or too little of those substances (Duman et al., 1997). What *is* clear, however, is that some change occurs in the activity of serotonin, norepinephrine, and possibly a more recently discovered neurotransmitter, *substance P* (Kramer et al., 1998), among people with depression.

Neurotransmitters are also implicated in bipolar disorder, although the exact mechanism is unknown. There is some support for the theory that bipolar disorder involves disturbances in the functioning of serotonin (Goodwin & Jamison, 1990). Moreover, it is known that lithium, the medication usually prescribed for bipolar disorder, lowers the activity level of norepinephrine in the brain (Bunney & Garland, 1983), but just how this happens is not yet known.

Level of the Person

Events at the level of the person can be associated with a higher risk of depression. Compared with people who are not depressed, depressed people make more negative comments and less eye contact, are less responsive, and speak more softly and in shorter sentences (Gotlib & Robinson, 1982; Segrin & Abramson, 1994). Aaron Beck (1967) found evidence of a "negative triad of depression" in the thoughts of depressed people. This triad consists of: (1) A negative view of the world, (2) A negative view of the self, and (3) A negative view of the future (see Figure 14.2).

FIGURE 14.2 Beck's Negative Triad

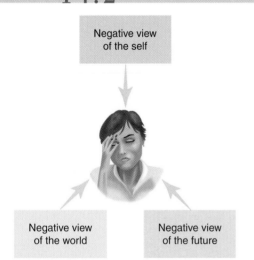

Negative view of the self

Negative view of the world

Negative view of the future

Among people who are depressed, Beck's triad of distorted, negative thinking about the world, the self, and the future add up to produce a negative view of life. However, these distortions can be corrected.

Beck proposes that people with depression commit errors in their thinking, or "cognitive distortions," based on these three sets of beliefs, and that these errors in logic maintain an outlook on life that perpetuates depressing feelings and behaviors. These cognitive distortions may be based on early learning.

The phenomenon of learned helplessness (see Chapter 10) also contributes to depression; when people feel they have no control over negative aspects of their environment, they are more likely to develop depression. Of particular interest is evidence that people's views of themselves and the world can influence their risk of developing depression. A person's characteristic way of explaining life events—his or her **attributional style**—affects the risk of depression. For people who attribute blame to themselves (versus external factors), the risk of depression rises, especially after a stressful event (Monroe & Depue, 1991). Research on attributional styles and depression find that those people who tend to attribute unfortunate events to internal causes (their own thoughts, abilities, behaviors, and the like), and who believe that these causes are stable, are more likely to become depressed. Thus, depressing thoughts (such as "I deserved to be fired . . . I wasn't as good at my job as some other people") are more likely to lead to depressing feelings. In contrast, patterns of attributing blame to external causes ("I was laid off because I didn't have enough seniority"), even if inaccurate, are less likely to lead to depression (Abramson et al., 1978).

Research has found that at the beginning of a semester, college students whose attributional style led them to blame internal causes are more likely to become depressed when receiving a bad grade than are those who blame external causes. These students are more likely to attribute a bad grade to their lack of ability rather than to the difficulty of the test, poor teaching, or other external factors (Peterson & Seligman, 1984).

Level of the Group

Occurrences at the level of the group have also been tied to depression. Life stresses that occur before depression develops can influence how severe it becomes. Moreover, as would be expected according to the principles of operant conditioning (see Chapter 6), the less opportunity there is for social reinforcement because of decreased activity and contact with other people, the more likely it is that depressive symptoms will occur (MacPhillamy & Lewinsohn, 1974). Similarly, environments that not only lack positive reinforcements but also provide many "punishing" experiences (such as being regularly criticized) put people at risk for depression. For example, although not necessarily associated with the *onset* of depression, the family environment can be influential in *recovery* from a depressive episode. Living with unsupportive and critical relatives can increase the risk of a relapse of depression (Hooley & Licht, 1997; Miller et al., 1992). Programs designed to help those with depression increase the frequency and quality of positive interactions with others (as well as help decrease the frequency and quality of punishing interactions) to minimize depressive symptoms (Teri & Lewinsohn, 1985).

Culture may also play a role in facilitating depression by influencing the type of events that are likely to lead to poor mood. For instance, among Malaysian students in a British university, depressed mood was more likely to follow negative social events, whereas, among British students, depressed mood was more likely to follow negative academic events (such as a poor grade; Tafarodi & Smith, 2001). These results are consistent with the different cultural values in collectivist versus individualist cultures (see Chapter 11).

In addition, at least some of the sex differences in the frequency of depression may be influenced by culture. For example, Nolen-Hoeksema (1987) offered a cultural explanation for the finding that women in developed countries experience depression more often than men. She and others (Nolen-Hoeksema & Morrow,

● **Attributional style:** A person's characteristic way of explaining life events.

1993; Vajk et al., 1997) have found that people in developed countries who ruminate about their depressed mood are more likely to have longer periods of depression. She proposes that as children, boys and girls are taught to respond differently to stressors, and they carry these response styles with them through adulthood. She contends that boys are encouraged to de-emphasize feelings and to use distraction and action-oriented coping strategies, whereas girls are encouraged to be introspective and not to take action. A ruminative response is known to promote depression; action and distraction can protect against depression. In fact, research has shown that depressed mood improves when college students learn to increase strategies of distraction and decrease their ruminations (Nolen-Hoeksema & Morrow, 1993). Other psychologists propose that the substantially higher rate of depression in women may also be due to biases in how the diagnosis is made and how depression is measured (Hartung & Widiger, 1998; Sprock & Yoder, 1997).

As with depression, there is evidence that more Americans are experiencing bipolar disorder than ever before, and at earlier ages (Goodwin & Jamison, 1990). One cause may be the unnaturally lengthened day in modern society brought about by electric lights. When a patient with rapid cycling bipolar disorder was put in an environment without electric lights (thereby experiencing 10–14 hours of darkness a night), the cycles lengthened, bringing more stability of mood (Wehr et al., 1998).

First episodes of bipolar disorder are invariably preceded by significant stressors (Goodwin & Ghaemi, 1998). And, as with depression, people with bipolar disorder are more likely to relapse if they live with critical families (Honig et al., 1997; Miklowitz et al., 1988). Life stressors can also impede recovery after a hospitalization for bipolar disorder (Johnson & Miller, 1997). On a positive note, programs designed to reduce the critical behavior of families appear to be effective in reducing relapses (Honig et al., 1997).

Events at the level of the group can affect the course of bipolar disorder. Social stressors that affect biological rhythms or schedules, such as frequent plane travel or repeated changes in work schedules, can adversely affect the course of the disease (Johnson & Roberts, 1995; Post, 1992), as can events that disrupt social rhythms, such as moving to a new residence (Malkoff-Schwartz et al., 1998).

Interacting Levels

Events at the three levels of analysis are not independent but interact in a number of ways. In particular, James Coyne (1976; Coyne & Downey, 1991) has proposed an interactional theory of depression. He theorized that the depressed person, who may be biologically vulnerable to depression, alienates others who might provide support through his or her verbal and nonverbal actions (Nolan & Mineka, 1997). Such actions include negative attitudes, dependent behavior, and an inclination to ignore or be unable to use help or advice from others. These actions eventually lead other people to reject or criticize the depressed person, confirming the depressed person's negative view of him- or herself, and increasing the likelihood of negative future events.

We know that van Gogh suffered from bouts of depression, at times had poor hygiene, narrowed his activities severely, and took pleasure only in painting. MDD seems like a possible diagnosis. Van Gogh's attempted assault on Gauguin, as well as the self-mutilation of his ear might be explained by MDD with psychotic features. Perhaps the auditory hallucination that told him to kill Gauguin was caused by his depression. Although MDD could explain the majority of these symptoms, it is not the only possibility. Bipolar disorder is another potential diagnosis. Perhaps van Gogh's episodes of frenzied painting were manic episodes, although they could also have been an intense restlessness that can occur with depression. His attacks, which became more frequent over time, might have been episodes of mania that became psychotic; untreated episodes of mania do become more frequent.

Looking *at* Levels

Depression Is as Depression Does

Have you ever noticed that it's no fun being with a depressed person? A depressed mood can be contagious, and family and friends of depressed people may find themselves being and acting somewhat depressed, further limiting their assistance to the depressed person (Coyne et al., 1987). Thomas Joiner (1994) found that college students who spent time with depressed roommates over a period of 3 weeks themselves became more depressed. Indeed, anger, anxiety, depression, and sadness have also been found to be contagious (Coyne, 1976; Hsee et al., 1990; Joiner, 1994; Katz et al., 1999; Segrin & Dillard, 1992; Sullins, 1991).

One possible way that you "catch" emotions from others is by acting like them, which leads you to feel similarly. At the level of the brain, just as putting on a happy face can make you feel better, putting on a frown can make you feel worse (Ekman et al., 1990; see Chapter 10). This response could be unconscious. In fact, just seeing a happy or an angry face causes muscles in your own face to respond, and to respond very quickly—in less than a half a second (Dimberg &

Thunberg, 1998). At the level of the person, when participants were asked to inhibit their facial movements when they watched happy films, they later reported enjoying the films less than when their facial muscles were allowed to move spontaneously as they watched; however, large differences were reported in the degree to which making an expression led to the experience of the corresponding emotion (Laird et al., 1994). Moreover, at the level of the group, someone's behavior may directly affect a close companion. For example, a depressed person is less responsive, which in and of itself may lead a companion to become depressed (Coyne, 1976). In addition, those who develop depression are more likely to behave in ways that create stress in their environments, which in turn can trigger the onset of depression in others (McGuffin et al., 1988; Rende & Plomin, 1992). Thus, your roomate's or family member's depression can lead you to feel depressed, perhaps changing your brain and bodily functioning (level of the brain).

TEST YOURSELF!

1. What are mood disorders?
2. What causes them?

Anxiety Disorders

We know that van Gogh had what he called "attacks." Were these anxiety attacks? He was also considered to be nervous and had concentration problems—signs of anxiety. Can we recognize a pattern in these symptoms? Could he have had an anxiety disorder? What is an anxiety disorder?

Many people are nervous when they have to speak in public. But suppose you become so nervous before an in-class presentation that your mouth is dry, you feel lightheaded, your heart begins to race, and you think you're having a heart attack and going crazy at the same time. These reactions are not normal "stage jitters." They are typical signs of an **anxiety disorder,** a state characterized by extreme fear (a response to an external stimulus, such as a snake) and extreme anxiety (a vague but persistent sense of foreboding or dread when not in the presence of the stimulus). Fear and anxiety are part of life, but people who have anxiety disorders experience *intense* or *pervasive* anxiety or fear, or *extreme* attempts to avoid these feelings. These experiences create exceptional distress that can interfere with the ability to function normally. Four major types of anxiety disorders are panic disorder, phobias, posttraumatic stress disorder, and obsessive-compulsive disorder.

Panic Disorder

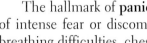

The hallmark of **panic disorder** is the experience of **panic attacks,** episodes of intense fear or discomfort accompanied by symptoms such as palpitations, breathing difficulties, chest pain, nausea, sweating, dizziness, fear of going crazy or doing something uncontrollable, fear of impending doom, and a sense of unreality. Symptoms reach their peak within a few minutes of the beginning of an attack, which can last from minutes to hours. Often these attacks are not associated with a specific situation or object and may even seem to occur randomly. One study of college students found that 12% of the participants experienced spontaneous panic attacks in college or in the years leading up to college (Telch et al., 1989). Internationally, approximately 3% of all people will experience panic disorder during their lifetimes (Rouillon, 1997). Some people may have episodic outbreaks of panic disorder, with years of remission; others may have more persistent symptoms.

Panic attacks can interfere with everyday functioning. Mob captain Tony Soprano seeks professional help to keep his panic attacks under control.

● **Anxiety disorder:** A category of disorders whose hallmark is intense and pervasive anxiety and fear, or extreme attempts to avoid these feelings.

● **Panic disorder:** A disorder whose hallmark is panic attacks.

● **Panic attack:** An episode of intense fear or discomfort accompanied by physical and psychological symptoms such as palpitations, breathing difficulties, chest pain, fear of impending doom or doing something uncontrollable, and a sense of unreality.

Panic Disorder From the Inside

Here is one person's description of a panic attack:

My breathing starts getting very shallow. I feel I'm going to stop breathing. The air feels like it gets thinner. I feel the air is not coming up through my nose. I take short rapid breaths. Then I see an image of myself gasping for air and remember what happened in the hospital. I think that I will start gasping. I get very dizzy and disoriented. I cannot sit or stand still. I start pacing. Then I start shaking and sweating. I feel I'm losing my mind and I will flip out and hurt myself or someone else. My heart starts beating fast and I start getting pains in my chest. My chest tightens up. I become very frightened. I get afraid that these feelings will not go away. Then I get really upset. I feel no one will be able to help me. I get very frightened I will die. I want to run to some place safe but I don't know where. (Beck et al., 1985, p. 107)

People with panic disorder worry constantly about having more attacks, and in their attempts to avoid or minimize panic attacks, they may change their behavior. People may go to great lengths to try to avoid panic attacks, quitting their jobs, avoiding places (such as hot, crowded rooms or events) or activities that increase their heart rate (such as exercise, sex, or watching suspenseful movies or sporting events). Some people fear or avoid places that might be difficult to leave should a panic attack occur—for example, a plane or car. They may avoid leaving home (Bouton et al., 2001), or do so only with a close friend or relative. Such fear and avoidance can lead to **agoraphobia** (literally, "fear of the marketplace"), a condition in which the avoidance of places or activities restricts daily life. In some cases, people have agoraphobia without panic attacks, avoiding many places because they fear either losing control of themselves in some way (such as losing bladder control) or they fear the occurrence of less severe but still distressing panic symptoms.

Level of the Brain

What causes panic attacks? A biological vulnerability for panic, an event at the level of the brain, is apparently inherited (Crowe et al., 1983; Torgersen, 1983; van den Heuvel et al., 2000). Evidence of one possible route to such a vulnerability comes from animal studies, which suggest that panic attacks may arise from a hypersensitivity involving the locus coeruleus, a small group of cells deep in the brainstem (Gorman et al., 1989). The locus coeruleus is the seat of an "alarm system" that triggers an increased heart rate, faster breathing, sweating, and other components of the fight-or-flight response (see Chapters 3, 10, and 13), and can lead to the experience of panic. EEG studies (Wiedemann et al., 1999) have also found unusually strong activation in the right frontal lobe relative to the left when people with panic attacks see potentially panic-inducing stimuli. This suggests that the "withdrawal" system (as characterized by Davidson, 1992b) (see Chapter 10) is relatively easily activated in people with panic attacks, further evidence of brain involvement in the development of panic symptoms. People with panic disorder may be more sensitive than others to changes in carbon dioxide inhalation (Beck et al., 1999; Papp et al., 1993, 1997), which can come about through hyperventilation. Changes in carbon dioxide levels can elicit panic, perhaps through a "suffocation alarm" in the brain that has an abnormally low threshold for firing (Coplan et al., 1998; Klein, 1993).

Level of the Person

How a person interprets and responds to these signals from the body—that is, events at the level of the person—may be critical to the development of panic disorder. For instance, people who have *anxiety sensitivity*, defined as the "belief that autonomic arousal can have harmful consequences" (Schmidt et al., 1997, p. 355), are at higher risk of experiencing spontaneous panic attacks (Plehn & Peterson, 2002; Schmidt et al., 1999). Those high in anxiety sensitivity believe that their experiences of shortness of breath necessarily indicate suffocation or that their heart palpitations must be signaling a heart attack. Studies have found that people with panic disorder are more accurate than other people at detecting changes in their heart rates when their breathing is restricted (Richards et al., 1996).

The misinterpretation of the cause of physiological events may itself increase sympathetic nervous system activity (Wilkinson et al., 1998) and lead to panic. Changes in the body can act like a *false alarm* (Beck, 1976), and after several false

● **Agoraphobia:** A condition in which people fear or avoid places that might be difficult to leave should panic symptoms occur.

alarms, the sensations associated with them become *learned alarms*, which themselves trigger panic (Barlow, 1988). People can also become hypervigilant for the signals that have led to panic in the past. Thus, in a vicious cycle, these people are more likely to experience anticipatory anxiety, which increases sympathetic nervous system activity (including increased heart rate and breathing changes), which in turn triggers panic.

Level of the Group

At the level of the group, although 80% of people with panic disorder reported a stressful life event before the panic disorder developed, the presence of such stress did not predict how severe the disorder would be, nor whether the symptoms would become chronic (Manfro et al., 1996; Rouillon, 1997). This is in contrast to other disorders, such as depression, in which the particular life stressor before an illness develops is associated with the severity or course of the disorder. However, other studies have found that people with panic disorder tend to have more stressful life events during childhood and adolescence, not the year before the disorder occurs, as compared to people without panic disorder. In addition, there is evidence that specific types of stressors, such as those occurring in love and family relationships in adulthood, are related to the onset of panic disorder (Horesh et al., 1997). Longitudinal studies of children who go on to develop, or not develop, panic disorder may help sort out the role of stressful events in the development of panic disorder.

For people with agoraphobia, group-level events can play an important role. When a person with agoraphobia feels anxious, the presence of a close relative or friend (referred to as a "safe person") can help decrease negative, panicky thinking. The presence of a safe person can also lower the amount of autonomic arousal experienced (Carter et al., 1995).

In addition, increasing dangers in the environment (increasing crime rate) and less social connections among people have increased the baseline level of anxiety. Today's "normal" children score higher on measures of trait anxiety than did children in the 1950s who had a psychiatric diagnosis (Twenge, 2000), suggesting that those born recently are more likely to develop anxiety disorders than those born earlier.

Culture can also influence the particular form of some panic-related symptoms. Among Khmer refugees, for example, panic attacks are associated with symptoms of *kyol goeu*, "wind overload"—a fainting syndrome that can occur when you stand up from a lying or sitting down position. Those who have experienced kyol goeu are more likely to be sensitive to signs of autonomic arousal in their bodies and to have negative beliefs about what the arousal means; this increased anxiety makes panic attacks more likely (Hinton et al., 2001).

Although van Gogh was anxious and irritable, we do not know enough about what happened during one of his so-called attacks to know whether these episodes were panic attacks or something else. In any event, panic disorder alone would not account for his symptoms of depressed mood, irritability, impulsiveness, and his bizarre behavior.

Phobias: Social and Specific

A **phobia** is an exaggerated fear of an object, class of objects, or particular situations, accompanied by avoidance that is extreme enough to interfere with everyday life. Phobias can be sorted into types, based on the object or situation that is

● **Phobia:** A fear and avoidance of an object or situation extreme enough to interfere with everyday life.

feared. **Social phobia** (social anxiety disorder), is the fear of public embarrassment or humiliation and the ensuing avoidance of social situations likely to arouse this fear (Kessler, Stein, et al., 1998). People with this disorder might try to avoid eating, speaking, or performing in public, or using public restrooms or dressing rooms. When unable to avoid these situations, they invariably experience anxiety or panic. This is one of the most common psychiatric diagnoses (major depression is *the* most common; American Psychiatric Association, 1994). Estimates are that approximately 13% of Americans currently experience social phobia (Fones et al., 1998).

A **specific phobia** is focused on a specific object or situation. Most people with phobias about blood, for example, faint if they see blood and may, because of their phobia, avoid getting appropriate treatment for medical problems (Kleinknecht & Lenz, 1989). People may have phobias about flying or of heights, spiders, or dental work (see Table 14.5). The fear may occur in the presence of the stimulus or in anticipation of it, despite an intellectual recognition that the fear is excessive or unreasonable. By avoiding the object or situation, the sufferer avoids the fear, anxiety, or panic that it might elicit. In contrast, **generalized anxiety disorder** involves excessive anxiety and worry that is not consistently related to a specific object or situation, and approximately 3% of people have this disorder at any given point in time (American Psychiatric Association, 2000).

TABLE 14.5 Five Subtypes of Specific Phobias

Phobia Subtype	Examples (Fear of . . .)
Animal fears	Snakes, rats, insects
Blood–injection–injury fears	Seeing blood or receiving an injection
Natural environment fears	Storms, heights, the ocean
Situation fears	Public transportation, tunnels, bridges, elevators, dental work, flying
Miscellaneous fears cued by stimuli not already mentioned	Choking, vomiting, contracting an illness, falling down

Source: American Psychiatric Association (2000). Reprinted with permission from the *Diagnostic and Statistical Manual of Mental Disorders,* Fourth Edition, Text Revision. Copyright 2000 American Psychiatric Association.

Level of the Brain

Studies with twins suggest that phobias have a genetic component that affects events at the level of the brain (Kendler et al., 1992, 2001, 2002; Li et al., 2001). The genetic vulnerability may rest on hyperreactivity of the amygdala and other fear-related brain structures (see Chapter 10) in certain situations (LeDoux, 1996). However, not all identical co-twins are phobic if their twins are phobic, so nongenetic factors must play a role. Humans seem biologically *prepared* to develop phobias about certain stimuli and not others (see Chapter 6).

Level of the Person

Some people who have social phobias may have been extremely shy as children (see Chapters 11 and 12; Biederman et al., 2001; Kagan, 1989b). Thus, they

- **Social phobia:** A type of phobia involving fear of public humiliation or embarrassment and the ensuing avoidance of situations likely to arouse this fear.

- **Specific phobia:** A type of phobia involving persistent and excessive or unreasonable fear triggered by a specific object or situation, along with attempts to avoid the feared stimulus.

- **Generalized anxiety disorder:** A disorder whose hallmark is excessive anxiety and worry that is not consistently related to a specific object or situation.

● **Obsessive-compulsive disorder (OCD):** A disorder marked by the presence of obsessions, and sometimes compulsions.

● **Obsession:** A recurrent and persistent thought, impulse, or image that feels intrusive and inappropriate, and is difficult to suppress or ignore.

● **Compulsion:** A repetitive behavior or mental act that an individual feels compelled to perform in response to an obsession.

do not *develop* a social phobia; rather, they never lost their discomfort in certain social situations (level of the group). The sufferer's thoughts about how other people might be evaluating him or her can become distorted and constant. This distorted thinking about social situations maintains the social phobia (Coupland, 2001; Rapee & Heimberg, 1997).

Learning may play a role in the development of a specific phobia. Classical and operant conditioning, in particular, could be involved in producing some phobias (Mowrer, 1939; see Chapter 6). If a stimulus such as a thunderstorm (the *conditioned stimulus*) is paired with a traumatic event (the *unconditioned stimulus*), anxiety and fear may become *conditioned responses* to thunderstorms. Furthermore, because fear and anxiety are reduced by avoiding the feared stimulus, the avoidant behavior is operantly reinforced.

Level of the Group

The phobic person need not experience classical conditioning directly: Observational learning from the behavior of other people who fear particular objects or situations can lead to the development of a phobia, by indicating what should be feared (Mineka et al., 1984). However, some research in this area questions the importance of classical conditioning because studies of people with phobias of spiders, heights, and water have not found evidence that such conditioning played the predicted role in the majority of cases (Jones & Menzies, 1995; Menzies & Clarke, 1993, 1995a, 1995b; Poulton et al., 1999). Some researchers propose that specific phobias may reflect a genetic predisposition to fear naturally occurring events or objects that were a danger to the human species (such as water or heights) and to which some people never habituate (Poulton & Menzies, 2002). Observational learning may also help explain why males and females tend to have different specific fears—boys are encouraged to interact more with potentially fearful objects (such as playing with spiders or climbing high places) and in the process may naturally be "exposed" to such stimuli (Antony & Barlow, 2002).

Obsessive-Compulsive Disorder (OCD)

Obsessive-compulsive disorder (OCD) is marked by the presence of obsessions, either alone or in combination with compulsions. **Obsessions** are recurrent and persistent thoughts, impulses, or images that feel intrusive and inappropriate, and that are difficult to suppress or ignore. These are more than excessive worries about real problems, and may cause significant anxiety and distress. Common obsessions involve thoughts of contamination ("Will I become contaminated by shaking her hand?"), repeated doubts ("Did I lock the door? Did I turn off the stove?"), the need to have things in a certain order (a perfect alignment of cans of food in a cupboard), or aggressive or horrific impulses (such as the urge to shout an obscenity in church).

Compulsions are repetitive behaviors or mental acts that some individuals feel driven to perform in response to an obsession. Examples of compulsive behaviors are *washing* in response to thoughts of contamination (washing the hands repeatedly until they are raw), *checking* (checking again and again that the stove is turned off or the windows closed so that it can take hours to leave the house), *ordering* (putting objects in a certain order or in precise symmetry, a task that may take hours until perfection is attained),

People with handwashing compulsion may spend hours washing their hands until they are raw.

and *counting* (counting to 100 after each obsessive thought, such as thinking about hitting one's child or shouting an obscenity). Some people with OCD believe that a dreaded event will occur if they do not perform their ritual of checking, ordering, and so on, but these compulsions are not realistically connected to what they are trying to ward off, at least not in the frequency and duration with which the compulsion occurs. Approximately 2 to 3% of Americans suffer from OCD at some point in their lives (Robins & Regier, 1991).

Obsessive-Compulsive Disorder From the Inside

One woman with OCD describes the ordeal of grocery shopping:

> Once I have attained control of the car, I have the burden of getting into it and getting it going. This can be a big project some days, locking and unlocking the doors, rolling up and down the power windows, putting on and off the seat belts, sometimes countlessly. . . . Sometimes while driving I must do overtly good deeds, like letting cars out of streets in front of me, or stopping to let people cross. These are things everyone probably should do, but things I *must* do. . . . My trip in the car may take us to the grocery store. Inside I have certain rituals I must perform. I am relatively subtle about how I do them to avoid drawing attention to myself. Certain foods must have their packages read several times before I am allowed to purchase them. Some things need to be touched repetitively, certain tiles on the floor must be stepped on by myself and my family. I'll find myself having to go from one end of an aisle to the other and back again, just to make everything all right. I fear being accused of shoplifting sometimes because of the way I behave and the way I am always looking around to see if people have noticed my actions. (Steketee & White, 1990, pp. 12–13)

OCD can be understood by looking at events at the three levels and their interactions.

Level of the Brain

At the level of the brain, studies of families have produced evidence for a genetic contribution, although not a straightforward link: If one member of a family has OCD, others are more likely to have an anxiety disorder, but not necessarily OCD itself (Black et al., 1992; Torgersen, 1983). Brain structures and neurotransmitters have been implicated: Obsessions and compulsions have been related to a loop of neural activity that occurs in the caudate nucleus of the basal ganglia (Breiter et al., 1996; Jenike, 1984; Rauch et al., 1994). Obsessions may occur when the caudate nucleus does not do its normal job of "turning off" recurrent thoughts before they become obsessions about an object or circumstance; carrying out a compulsion may temporarily end the obsessional thoughts (Insel, 1992; Jenike, 1984; Modell et al., 1989; Saxena & Rauch, 2000). The neurotransmitter serotonin appears to play a role in the presence of OCD symptomatology; serotonin-based medications such as Prozac reduce symptoms, although the exact mechanism is unknown (Greenberg et al., 1997; Micallef & Blin, 2001).

Level of the Person

As with other anxiety disorders, operant conditioning may be involved. Because compulsive behavior may momentarily relieve the anxiety created by obsessions, the compulsion is reinforced and thus more likely to recur. Research has found that

● **Posttraumatic stress disorder (PTSD):** A disorder experienced by some people after a traumatic event, whose symptoms include an unwanted re-experiencing of the trauma, avoidance of anything associated with the trauma, and heightened arousal.

obsessions themselves are not all that uncommon (Weissman et al., 1994)—many people experience obsessive thoughts during their lives, including thoughts about a partner during the early stages of a relationship, without developing a disorder. Salkovskis (1985) proposes that such obsessions develop into a disorder when someone with obsessive thoughts determines that those thoughts are about an unacceptable action (such as killing a newborn child). Obsessive thoughts of this nature may imply danger to the person with the obsession or to someone else. As a result, extremely uncomfortable feelings arise, and mental rituals are created and invoked in an effort to reduce these feelings. Paradoxically, these attempts to alleviate the uncomfortable feelings associated with the obsession perpetuate its ability to induce uncomfortable feelings, and, through negative reinforcement, strengthen the mental rituals. Similarly, Rachman and his colleagues (Rachman, 1997; Shafran et al., 1996) propose that people with OCD view a disturbing thought as the moral equivalent of carrying out the thought, leading to higher levels of distress in response to the initial obsessional thought.

Level of the Group

Although a similar percentage of people experience OCD in different countries (Horwath & Weissman, 2000), culture plays a role in the particular symptoms displayed (Weissman et al., 1994); for example, religious obsessions and praying compulsions are more common among Turkish men with OCD than among French men with OCD (Millet et al., 2000).

In addition, in research studies, people with more serious OCD tended to have families who were more rejecting of them and to have experienced more kinds of family stress (Calvocoressi et al., 1995). However, the direction of causation is unclear: Were families more rejecting because their OCD relatives were more symptomatic, and therefore more difficult to live with? Or did the strong rejection by the families produce stronger symptoms of OCD in the affected relatives? Perhaps future research will be able to say more about causation.

Posttraumatic Stress Disorder (PTSD)

Psychological symptoms can occur as a consequence of a traumatic event such as war, physical or sexual abuse, terrorism, or natural disasters. Victims of rape, for example, may be afraid to be alone, especially shortly after the attack. Women who have been raped may become afraid of and angry at all men, or they may experience more general feelings of anger, helplessness, guilt, pain, embarrassment, or anxiety. They may have sexual difficulties because the sexual act has been linked with such negative experiences and feelings. They may also develop physical symptoms of stress, such as stomachaches, headaches, back problems, inability to sleep, or diminished appetite. Depression may come and go over a long period. Long after the rape, they may remain afraid to trust anyone.

The diagnosis of **posttraumatic stress disorder (PTSD)** is made when three conditions are met. First, the person experiences or witnesses an event that in-

Some soldiers develop post-traumatic stress disorder.

volves actual or threatened serious injury or death. Second, the traumatized person responds to the situation with fear and helplessness. Third, the traumatized individual then experiences three sets of symptoms. One set is the persistent re-experiencing of the traumatic event, which may take the form of intrusive, unwanted, and distressing recollections, dreams, or nightmares of the event, or may involve flashbacks that can include illusions, hallucinations, and a sense of reliving the experience. The second set of PTSD symptoms is a persistent avoidance of anything associated with the trauma and a general emotional numbing. The third set of symptoms is heightened arousal, which can cause people with PTSD to startle easily (Shalev et al., 2000), have difficulty sleeping, or be in a constant state of hypervigilance. These symptoms do not always appear immediately after the traumatic event, and they can persist for months or even for years.

Posttraumatic Stress Disorder From the Inside

Mr. E, age 65, complained that ever since World War II he experienced extreme nervousness that was somewhat alleviated by chewing tobacco. . . . After this wartime nervousness—consisting of subjective feelings of anxiety, itching, and shaking—developed [it got to the point where he experienced] eight such episodes in the month before he came to the hospital.

During the war Mr. E manned a landing craft that transported soldiers to the beaches. He was particularly distraught about an experience in which he felt something underfoot on a sandy beach and discovered that he was stepping on the face of a dead GI. He also described an incident in which his ship had been torpedoed and several crewmen killed. He experienced intense survivor guilt about this incident. . . . (Hierholzer et al., 1992, p. 819)

The majority of people who experience trauma do not go on to experience PTSD (Breslau et al., 1998; Resnick et al., 1993; Shalev et al., 1998), and the type of trauma makes a difference in the outcome. For example, one study found that women were more likely to develop posttraumatic stress disorder when their traumas resulted from crimes rather than from natural disasters (Resnick et al., 1993), and other studies corroborate this finding (Breslau et al., 1998). Other factors that affect whether PTSD will occur can be found in the interactions of events at each level of analysis: the brain, the person, and the group.

Level of the Brain
Some people may be biologically at risk for developing symptoms of posttraumatic stress disorder, perhaps because of a genetic predisposition (Shalev et al., 1998; True et al., 1993) or trauma in childhood (Vermetten & Bremner, 2002). One possible way such a predisposition could manifest itself is in a hypersensitivity of the locus coeruleus, as occurs with panic disorder. In addition, the limbic system (including the amygdala) of people with this disorder appears to be more easily activated by mental imagery of traumatic events versus nontraumatic events (Rauch et al., 1996; Shin et al., 1997).

Level of the Person
Factors at the level of the person include the traumatized person's psychological characteristics before, during, and after a trauma (Ehlers et al., 1998; Ozer et al., 2003). A history of social withdrawal, depression, or a sense of not being able

to control stressors all increase the risk of developing PTSD after a trauma (Joseph et al., 1995). The perception that your life is at risk during the traumatic event or that you have no control over it can also facilitate development of PTSD, regardless of the actual threat (Foa et al., 1989). Risk of suffering the disorder rises, too, if you believe the world is a dangerous place (Keane et al., 1985; Kushner et al., 1992).

As in the case of phobias, classical and operant conditioning may help explain the avoidance symptoms of PTSD. In addition, operant conditioning also helps us understand why people with PTSD are at a higher risk of developing drug abuse or dependence than those who experienced trauma that did not lead to PTSD (Chilcoat & Breslau, 1998; Jacobsen et al., 2001): Substance use can lead to negative reinforcement because when the substances are taken, the symptoms of PTSD temporarily subside.

Level of the Group

Whether trauma will lead to PTSD also depends, in part, on events at the level of the group. Support from friends, family, or counselors immediately after a trauma may help decrease the likelihood that PTSD will develop (Kaniasty & Norris, 1992; Kaniasty et al., 1990). In the case of those exposed to trauma as part of military service, social support on arrival home can reduce the risk of PTSD (King, King, et al., 1998). Group factors play an integral role in creating the "trauma" part of the disorder, since these traumas almost always involve other people or environmental causes, and certain types of traumatic events (crimes versus natural disasters) are more likely to lead to PTSD.

Looking *at* Levels

Individual Differences in Responses to Trauma

Because of differences in physiological and psychological characteristics, different people are likely to experience and make sense of a traumatic event differently (Bowman, 1999) and to have different experiences with social support. Consider that among male Vietnam veterans who are identical or fraternal twins, a willingness to volunteer for combat, or to accept more risky assignments, is partly heritable (Lyons et al., 1993). This heritability (level of the brain) may be reflected in certain temperaments such as sensation seeking (see Chapter 11): High sensation seekers may be more likely to volunteer for combat and thus be more at risk for certain kinds of trauma. People's personality traits and ways of viewing the world

(level of the person) may also influence the level of available social support to them: Extraverts are likely to have more social support (level of the group) available to them than are introverts. Such traits and ways of thinking also influence how people use, or don't use, social support. In turn, the use of social support moderates the effects of the trauma. Moreover, the more severe the trauma, the less important are events at the levels of brain and the person in moderating the trauma's effects (Keane & Barlow, 2002).

TEST YOURSELF!

1. What are the main types of anxiety disorders?
2. What are their symptoms and causes?

Schizophrenia

In the last years of his life, van Gogh apparently had increasing difficulty distinguishing between his internal experiences and external reality. He would become disoriented and not know who he was. He had delusions of being poisoned and attacked. Gauguin claimed that van Gogh referred to himself as a ghost before cutting off part of his ear. During a period of mental clarity, when van Gogh was asked about the assault on Gauguin, he said that he was given to hearing voices, that he had heard voices telling him to kill Gauguin. Then he remembered the biblical injunction, "If thine own eye offend thee, pluck it out." His ear had offended him by "hearing" the voice that suggested he kill Gauguin, so he cut part of it off to do penance for his sin against Gauguin (Lubin, 1972).

These aspects of van Gogh's life and behavior suggest the possibility of schizophrenia. The word *schizophrenia* is derived from two Greek words, *schizo* meaning "to split" or "to cut," and *phren* meaning "mind" or "reason." Books or movies sometimes portray schizophrenia as if it meant having a split personality, but schizophrenia is characterized by a split from reality, not a split from different aspects of oneself. **Schizophrenia** is a psychotic disorder that profoundly alters affect, behavior, and cognition, particularly the pattern or form of thought.

Symptoms: What Schizophrenia Looks Like

The term *schizophrenia* actually embraces a number of subtypes of this disorder, each with distinct symptoms and prognoses (prospects of recovery). *DSM-IV* divides symptoms of schizophrenia into two groups (see Table 14.6). **Positive symptoms** involve an excess or distortion of normal functions, such as hallucinations.

TABLE 14.6 Positive and Negative Symptoms of Schizophrenia

Positive Symptoms	Negative Symptoms

• Delusions
 	
  of persecution (beliefs that others are out to "get" you)
 	
  of grandeur (beliefs that you are an important person)
 	
  of reference (beliefs that normal events have special meaning directed toward you)
 	
  of control (beliefs that your feelings, behaviors, or thoughts are controlled by others)
 	
• Hallucinations
 	
• Disordered behavior
 	
• Disorganized speech
	• Flat affect (appears to be without emotion)
	
	• Alogia (brief, slow, empty replies to questions)
	
	• Avolition (inability to initiate goal-directed behavior)

● **Schizophrenia:** A psychotic disorder in which the patient's affect, behavior, and thoughts are profoundly altered.

● **Positive symptom:** An excess or distortion of normal functions, such as a hallucination.

They are called positive not because they indicate something desirable, but because they mark the *presence* of certain unusual behaviors. **Negative symptoms,** on the other hand, involve a *diminution* or *loss* of normal functions, such as a restriction in speech or movement.

Positive symptoms include *delusions* (distortions of thought), and *hallucinations.* Positive symptoms are usually more responsive than negative symptoms to antipsychotic medication (discussed in the next chapter). Delusions can be complex, centering on a particular theme, such as the belief that someone, or some people, are out to "get" you. Hallucinations in schizophrenia are typically auditory; hearing voices is a common symptom. *Disorganized behavior* can include inappropriate, childlike silliness or unpredictable agitation. People with disorganized behavior may have difficulty with everyday tasks such as organizing meals, maintaining hygiene, and selecting their clothes (they might wear two overcoats in the summer). Another positive symptom is *disorganized speech,* as in the following example: "I may be a 'Blue Baby' but 'Social Baby' not, but yet a blue heart baby could be in the Blue Book published before the war" (Maher, 1966, p. 413).

Negative symptoms include flat affect, alogia, and avolition (see Table 14.6). *Flat affect* is a general failure to express or respond to emotion. There may be occasional smiles or warmth of manner, but usually the facial expression is constant; eye contact is rare and body language minimal. *Alogia,* or "poverty of speech," is characterized by brief, slow, empty replies to questions. Alogia is not an unwillingness to speak; rather, the thoughts behind the words seem slowed down. Someone with alogia speaks less than others and doesn't use words as freely. *Avolition* is an inability to initiate or persist in goal-directed activities. Someone exhibiting avolition may sit for long periods without engaging in any behavior or social interaction.

Not all of these symptoms are present in everyone affected with schizophrenia. According to the *DSM-IV,* a diagnosis of schizophrenia requires that two or more symptoms are displayed for at least a week and that other signs of socially inappropriate behavior are exhibited for at least 6 months. The average age of onset of schizophrenia is the 20s, although in some people (particularly women) onset does not come until later in life. Symptoms often occur gradually, with a prodromal phase characterized by slow deterioration in functioning, including withdrawal from other people, poor hygiene, and outbursts of anger (Heinssen et al., 2001). Eventually the symptoms reach an active phase, in which full-blown positive and negative symptoms arise.

Did van Gogh appear to exhibit symptoms of schizophrenia? We know that he had auditory hallucinations and that he exhibited inappropriate social behavior (including poor hygiene and outbursts of anger), but he does not appear to have had negative symptoms of schizophrenia (at least not between his attacks). Not enough is known about his behavior during his attacks to determine whether additional symptoms accompanied them.

Types of Schizophrenia

People with schizophrenia, as mentioned earlier, tend to suffer from only some of the full range of possible symptoms. The symptoms of schizophrenia tend to cluster into groupings, and from these groupings mental health professionals and researchers have identified subtypes of schizophrenia. The *DSM-IV* specifies four subtypes of schizophrenia (see Table 14.7): paranoid, disorganized, catatonic, and undifferentiated.

● **Negative symptom:** A diminution or loss of normal functions, such as a restriction in speech.

TABLE 14.7 Four Subtypes of Schizophrenia, According to *DSM-IV-TR*

Paranoid
Delusions of persecution are prominent; intellectual functioning and affect are relatively intact, but auditory hallucinations are common.

Disorganized
Disorganized speech and behavior and flat or inappropriate affect are prominent.

Catatonic
Catatonic (bizarre, immobile, or relentless) motor behaviors are prominent.

Undifferentiated
Symptoms do not clearly fall into any of the above three subtypes.

Source: American Psychiatric Association (2000). Reprinted with permission from the *Diagnostic and Statistical Manual of Mental Disorders,* Fourth Edition, Text Revision. Copyright 2000 American Psychiatric Association.

Paranoid Schizophrenia From the Inside

Jeffrey DeMann describes his first hospitalization for schizophrenia at the age of 27:

> I recall vividly the delusion of believing my mother was to take my place in the shock treatments. Then I was to be quietly murdered and placed in an acid bath grave, which would dissolve any physical evidence of my existence. At this time, auditory hallucinations also were present. I could actually hear the slamming of my mother's body on the table while being administered the deadly shock. I truly believed my mother was now dead in my place. I also recall curling up on an old wooden bench and repeatedly chanting the words "Die quickly now." (DeMann, 1994, p. 580)

If van Gogh did indeed suffer from schizophrenia, a diagnosis of the paranoid subtype would seem to fit him best because his intellectual functioning and affect remained relatively intact between attacks. But he apparently did not have extended periods of paranoid delusions, and schizophrenia would not account for his lengthy bouts of depression.

Why Does This Happen to Some People, But Not Others?

With few exceptions, schizophrenia occurs at about the same rate worldwide, about 1 in 100 (Gottesman, 1991). The reason some people and not others suffer from schizophrenia involves events at the three levels of analysis and the interactions among events at these levels.

The Brain
Twin, family, and adoption studies point to the influence of genetic factors in the development of schizophrenia (Gottesman, 1991; Kendler & Diehl, 1993; Tiernari, 1991). Having relatives with schizophrenia increases the risk of developing schizophrenia; the closer the relative, the greater the risk. However, it

Schizophrenia | **601**

is important to note that even for those who have a close relative with schizophrenia, the actual incidence is still quite low. More than 80% of people who have a parent or sibling diagnosed with schizophrenia do *not* have the disorder themselves (Gottesman & Moldin, 1998). Even in the case of the highest level of genetic resemblance, identical twins, the co-twin of a schizophrenic twin has only a 48% risk of developing schizophrenia. If the disease were entirely genetic, we would expect a 100% risk in this circumstance. And a fraternal co-twin has only a 17% likelihood of developing the disorder (Gottesman, 1991). Although genes do play a role in the etiology of schizophrenia, they are clearly not the only factor.

Evidence from autopsies and neuroimaging studies suggests that schizophrenia may involve abnormalities in brain structures. Someone with schizophrenia is more likely than others to have enlarged *ventricles*, cavities in the center of the brain filled with cerebrospinal fluid. Increased ventricle size means a reduction in the size of other brain areas, including the frontal cortex (Goldstein et al., 1999), which plays a central role in abstract thinking and planning. Impaired frontal lobe functioning has been the focus of a substantial amount of the research on schizophrenia. One explanation is that at least some deficits in functioning may occur because of excessive pruning of neural connections in the frontal lobe during adolescence (Keshavan et al., 1994). This explanation is supported by neuroimaging studies that have revealed abnormally low numbers of dopamine receptors in the frontal lobes of people with schizophrenia (Okubo et al., 1997); such studies also indicate brain abnormalities even before psychotic symptoms appear (Pantelis et al., 2002).

Researchers looking at different ways in which these brain abnormalities might arise have found several possible causes. One focus has been on the fetus's developing brain, and how normal brain development may go awry during gestation (the 9 months the fetus is developing in the mother's uterus). Possibilities include maternal malnourishment during pregnancy (Brown, van Os, et al., 1999; Wahlbeck et al., 2001), maternal illness (Buka et al., 1999; Gilmore et al., 1997; Mednick et al., 1998), and prenatal or birth-related medical complications that lead to oxygen deprivation (Cannon, 1997; Geddes & Lawrie, 1995; McNeil et al., 2000; Zornberg et al., 2000). Because research has found a higher incidence of prenatal and birth complications in babies born to mothers with schizophrenia, some have further argued that fetuses with a genetic predisposition to schizophrenia have an increased likelihood of abnormal development, which in turn leads to the higher rate of prenatal and birth complications (Goodman, 1988). However, other researchers suggest that complications in and of themselves do not create a risk for schizophrenia in the absence of genetic vulnerability (Buka et al., 1999). Rather, according to this view, it is the combination of the genetic vulnerability and the physical complications during gestation and birth that together heighten the risk for the alteration in brain development and later schizophrenia (Baaré et al., 2001).

In addition, children who are at risk for schizophrenia—those who show an extreme discomfort with close relationships and exhibit relatively high levels of quirky or odd behavior—are more reactive to stress and have higher baseline levels of the stress-related hormone cortisol (Walker et al., 1999; see Chapter 13). Some suggest that the increased biological changes and stressors of adolescence lead to higher levels of stress hormones (which in turn are thought to affect

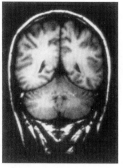 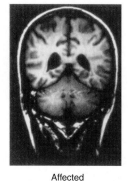

Well   Affected

28-year-old males

Those with schizophrenia have larger ventricles, smaller amounts of frontal and temporal lobe cortex, and a smaller thalamus. This decreased cortical volume probably accounts for some of the cognitive deficits found in people with schizophrenia (Andreasen et al., 1986, 1992).

dopamine activity). Prodromal symptoms of schizophrenia often begin to emerge during adolescence.

Similarly, using careful analyses of home movies taken during the childhoods of people who were later diagnosed with schizophrenia, Walker and colleagues (Grimes & Walker, 1994; Walker et al., 1993) found that those who went on to develop schizophrenia were different from their siblings. They found that from infancy through adolescence these people exhibited more involuntary movements, such as writhing or excessive movements of the tongue, lip, or arm (Walker et al., 1994). The more severe the involuntary movements, the more severe the schizophrenic symptoms in adulthood (Neumann & Walker, 1996). These results are consistent with other findings of a biological vulnerability to schizophrenia that exists prior to adulthood.

Neurotransmitters, particularly dopamine, have been implicated in schizophrenia (Walker & Diforio, 1997). It was once thought that an overproduction of dopamine, or an increased number or sensitivity of dopamine receptors, was responsible for schizophrenia. This *dopamine hypothesis* received support from research showing that medications that decrease the amount of dopamine reduce the positive symptoms of schizophrenia. Moreover, when people who do not have schizophrenia are given drugs that increase dopamine activity, they experience schizophrenia-like symptoms (Syvalathi, 1994). Perhaps, it was thought, excess dopamine triggers a flood of unrelated thoughts, feelings, and perceptions, and the delusions are attempts to organize these disconnected events into a coherent, understandable experience (Gottesman, 1991). However, research soon indicated that the dopamine hypothesis is too simple. Although dopamine clearly plays a role in schizophrenia, other neurotransmitters and neural processes are also involved (Laruelle et al., 1993; Nestler, 1997; Syvalathi, 1994; Walker & Diforio, 1997; Weinberger & Lipska, 1995).

In sum, researchers now agree that prenatal and birth complications may play a role in the development of schizophrenia, and some individuals are genetically vulnerable to the disorder. These factors may create abnormalities in brain structure, particularly in the frontal lobe, and in the structure and function of neurotransmitter systems.

The Person

The home movies study mentioned above also found that those children who went on to develop schizophrenia exhibited fewer expressions of joy than their unaffected siblings (Walker et al., 1993). (This emotional dampening may also cause other people to respond less positively because of emotional contagion, as described earlier.)

The Group

For someone who has had episodes of schizophrenia, a stressful life event may act as a trigger, leading to a recurrence of symptoms (Gottesman, 1991; Ventura et al., 1989). Events at the level of the group can produce such stress. For example, almost two thirds of people hospitalized with schizophrenia live with their families after leaving the hospital, and the way a family expresses emotion can affect the likelihood of a recurrence of acute schizophrenia symptoms, although it does not *cause* schizophrenia. Families that are critical, hostile, and overinvolved, termed **high expressed emotion** families, are more likely to include someone with schizophrenia who has had a recurrence; this higher rate is strongest for those with

● **High expressed emotion:** An emotional style in families that are critical, hostile, and overinvolved.

more chronic schizophrenia (Butzlaff & Hooley, 1998; Kavanagh, 1992; Vaughn & Leff, 1976). However, it is possible that the direction of causality runs the other way: Perhaps high expressed emotion families are responding to a relative with schizophrenia who is more bizarre or disruptive, and low expressed emotion families include someone whose schizophrenic symptoms are less extreme. Casting the social net wider, a longitudinal study of people with schizophrenia found that after their first psychotic episodes, those who had larger numbers of nonrelated people in their social support networks before their first episodes had the best recoveries 5 years later (Erikson et al., 1998).

A higher rate of schizophrenia is found in urban areas and in lower socioeconomic classes (Freeman, 1994; Mortensen et al., 1999). Why might this be? Two factors appear to play a role: *social selection* and *social causation* (Dauncey et al., 1993). **Social selection,** also called *social drift,* refers to the "drifting" to lower socioeconomic classes of those who have become mentally disabled (Mulvaney et al., 2001). This often happens to those who are no longer able to work and who lack family support or care (Dohrenwend et al., 1992). **Social causation** refers to the chronic psychological and social stresses of life in an urban environment, particularly for the poor. The stress of these living conditions may trigger the disorder in persons who are biologically vulnerable (Freeman, 1994).

Culture may influence the recovery rate of schizophrenia. Industrialized countries generally have lower recovery rates than do developing nations (American Psychiatric Association, 1994; Kulhara & Chakrabarti, 2001), although not all studies support this finding (Edgerton & Cohen, 1994; von Zerssen et al., 1990). If this finding is further substantiated, possible explanations include a more tolerant attitude and lower expressed emotion in extended families among people in developing countries (El-Islam, 1991). Moreover, developing countries also tend to have collectivist cultures, which place an emphasis on the community versus the individual (see Chapters 10 and 11). People in developing countries who have schizophrenia thus may have more support available to them.

Interacting Levels

Events at the three levels of analysis interact: As suggested by the finding that 48% of identical co-twins develop schizophrenia if the twin has schizophrenia, biological factors play a role in the development of the illness, leading to a vulnerability to the disorder. Such a biological vulnerability, in combination with environmental and social factors, and with the individual's learning history, help determine whether the disorder manifests itself. Walker and Diforio (1997) propose a specific diathesis–stress model to explain how stress can worsen schizophrenic symptoms. They note that although people who develop schizophrenia do not experience more life stressors than people who do not develop the disorder, individuals with schizophrenia who experience more stressful events are likely to have more severe schizophrenic symptoms and experience more relapses (Hultman et al., 1997). And, in fact, people with schizophrenia have higher baseline levels of cortisol, an indicator of the stress response. This relationship goes even further, since not only people with schizophrenia but also those at risk for the disorder (because of family history or evidence of some symptoms of schizophrenia) are more likely to have higher levels of cortisol. And antipsychotic medications decrease cortisol levels in people with schizophrenia.

Walker and Diforio further propose that this heightened susceptibility to stress comes about because of cortisol's effect on dopamine activity, namely an over-

● **Social selection:** The tendency of the mentally disabled to drift to the lower economic classes; also called *social drift.*

● **Social causation:** The chronic psychological and social stresses of living in an urban environment that may lead to an increase in the rate of schizophrenia (especially among the poor).

activation of dopamine pathways, which can worsen symptoms of schizophrenia. They propose that the negative symptoms of schizophrenia, such as social withdrawal, are attempts to reduce stress. Thus, genetic, prenatal, or birth factors increase a susceptibility to stress, and stress aggravates symptoms.

Van Gogh had a family history of schizophrenia, implicating a possible genetic factor, and some biographical material suggests that van Gogh's extremely strict father could be regarded as a high expressed emotion parent. And before becoming an artist, van Gogh repeatedly returned to live with his parents after leaving his various jobs. Moreover, after becoming an artist, he generally lived off monies sent by his brother Theo. He was so poor that he often experienced enormous stress; for example, he often had to choose between spending Theo's gift of money on painting supplies or on food, and frequently chose the former (Auden, 1989).

Looking *at* Levels

The Genain Quadruplets

Now that you know more about schizophrenia and its causes, you can see how the factors at the different levels are involved, and how they interact. We can apply this knowledge to the Genain quadruplets, four girls born in the early 1930s in the Midwest into a family of limited financial means with an abusive, violent, alcoholic father and a strict mother. All four girls developed schizophrenia, although each presented different symptoms. Myra attained a substantially higher level of functioning than her sisters before the onset of the disorder and had fewer and briefer relapses than they did. The youngest (by a few minutes) and most sickly, Hester, fared the worst (Rosenthal, 1963).

The sisters' paternal grandmother had symptoms of paranoid schizophrenia, so they probably had a genetic vulnerability for the disorder (level of the brain). Still, based on statistical probabilities, the odds of all four developing schizophrenia were one in a billion. However, the prenatal difficulties involved in carrying quadruplets, which may have led to impairment in brain development, would have increased the likelihood. CT scans of the quads when they were in their 50s showed similar brain abnormalities in

All four of these identical quadruplets—from oldest to youngest, Nora, Iris, Myra, and Hester—went on to develop schizophrenia. Their symptoms and the onset and course of their illness differed. Nora and Myra were paired off by the parents as the smartest. Hester and Iris were paired off as the least able, and their illness was more disabling.

all four sisters (Mirsky & Quinn, 1988). However, although they were genetically identical quadruplets, they varied biologically: Nora and Hester showed more evidence of neurological difficulties and fared much worse when off medication. Moreover, on tests of attention taken when the quads were 20 years old, Myra was the only one to perform well enough to predict a possibility of a normal life; Iris's and Hester's attentional abilities indicated that they would not be able to live independently for long periods of time. In fact, their performance on these attentional tests fairly accurately predicted the course of their lives.

At the level of the person, the quads, particularly Hester, exhibited odd behavior. Even as a child, Hester could not keep up mentally and physically with her sisters, and her bizarre behavior included putting on four new pairs of underwear over an old pair. In kindergarten, she appeared fearful and cried more than her sisters. In addition, Myra had the most social skills and social desire, even having a "boyfriend" at school, with whom she would exchange notes; she was not allowed to see him after school (Rosenthal, 1963). Nora and Myra made the most skilled pair, and Iris was often paired with Hester.

At the level of the group, the girls were forbidden to play with other children and had no outside social life; they didn't mix well with other children at school and were teased. The sisters were seldom separated from one another and appeared unhappy to neighbors.

The Genain family would be considered a high expressed emotion family (level of the group). Psychologist David Rosenthal (1963) reported that the quads' father was particularly critical, angry, and extremely controlling—he forbade his daughters to close any doors, even the one to the bathroom. Although Nora was less physically abused by him than were her sisters, her doctors and medical team thought that he may have sexually abused her. Nora was the closest to her father and was able to appease him. Myra was their mother's favorite. Hester, who was difficult to control, received the most physical punishment, including being whipped and having her head dunked in water. Other social stressors included a long history of financial problems.

Events at the different levels interact: A family history of schizophrenia as well as prenatal and birth complications made the quads more vulnerable to developing schizophrenia. Without this vulnerability, stressors—such as being socially isolated, teased by other children, and experiencing physical and emotional abuse—might not have led to schizophrenia. Myra, the most socially motivated and skilled sister, was the one whose schizophrenia was least severe, and she was able to remain off medication and out of the hospital for long periods of time; she eventually married and had two sons (Mirsky & Quinn, 1988). Hester, the sickliest sister, was the one most physically abused and the most bizarre as a child. Had the quads grown up in a different home environment, with parents who treated them differently, it is possible that not all four would have developed schizophrenia, or if they had, they might have suffered fewer relapses.

TEST YOURSELF!

1. What are the symptoms of schizophrenia?
2. What are the subtypes of schizophrenia?
3. Why do some people develop schizophrenia?

Other Axis I Disorders: Dissociative and Eating Disorders

Perhaps van Gogh, like many people, suffered from more than one psychological disorder. Consider that, at the age of 24, he spoke of an "evil self" that caused him to become a disgrace and bring misery to others. He sometimes had trouble with his memory. He wrote to Theo that his frail memory "also seems to me to prove that there is quite definitely something or other deranged in my brain, it is astounding to be afraid . . . , and to be unable to remember things" (Auden, 1989, p. 363).

At times van Gogh ate only breakfast and a dinner of coffee and bread. And while in the hospital during the last year of his life, he would eat only meager dinners of half-cooked chick-peas or alcohol or bread and a little soup (Auden, 1989). Were van Gogh to be seen by mental health professionals now, they would undoubtedly ask more about his restricted and bizarre eating habits. Particularly if van Gogh were female, mental health professionals might wonder whether his eating habits were symptoms of an eating disorder.

In addition to the disorders in the major diagnostic categories already discussed, there are several less common Axis I disorders; some of these unfortunately are becoming more common. In this section we consider the categories of dissociative and eating disorders.

Dissociative Disorders

The hallmark of **dissociative disorders** is a disruption in the usually integrated functions of consciousness, memory, or identity, often caused by a traumatic or very stressful event. The disruptions may be fleeting or chronic; they may come on suddenly or gradually. They can lead to several symptoms (Steinberg, 1994): *identity confusion*, a state of uncertainty about one's identity, or *identity alteration*, the adoption of a new identity; *derealization*, the sense that familiar objects have changed or seem "unreal"; *depersonalization*, the experience of observing oneself as if from the outside; and *amnesia*, the loss of memory. These symptoms are not necessarily signs of pathology; people often have dissociative experiences in the course of ordinary life. For example, it is common to experience derealization on returning home after a long absence: The ceiling may seem lower, the furniture smaller, and so on. Even identity alteration need not signify abnormality. Possession trance (discussed in Chapter 5), which is not uncommon in some cultures, can lead to dissociation of identity, but in those cultures the dissociation is not considered pathological. In dissociative disorders, as defined by the *DSM-IV*, the dissociative experiences are severe enough to cause distress or to impair functioning. It is unclear how many people suffer from these disorders, although they are more frequently diagnosed now than in the past. In fact, some researchers and clinicians believe that several of these disorders are now overdiagnosed: One estimate is that 10% of Americans have been diagnosed with a dissociative disorder (Loewenstein, 1994).

Renee Zellweger's character in the movie *Nurse Betty* has some symptoms of a dissociative fugue: after witnessing the brutal death of her husband, she abruptly leaves her job and has some difficulty remembering aspects of her past. She thinks she is the ex-fiancée of a character in a soap opera, but doesn't realize that he is from a television show.

Dissociative Amnesia and Dissociative Fugue

One type of dissociative disorder is **dissociative amnesia,** marked by an inability to remember important personal information, usually about a traumatic or extremely stressful event; this inability to remember is often experienced as "gaps" in memory. A soldier who has seen several days of intense and brutal combat but then cannot remember much about the battlefield experience might be suffering from dissociative amnesia. In time, some people are able to recall such terrible memories; others may never remember, developing instead a chronic form of amnesia.

Dissociative fugue is another dissociative disorder, marked by an inability to remember some or all of the past, combined with abrupt, unexpected disappearances from home or work. The disturbed state of consciousness may last hours, days, or months, and during it there are no obvious signs of a disorder, nor does the sufferer otherwise attract attention. People in a dissociative fugue may ultimately come to the attention of health care or law enforcement officials because of their loss of awareness of their identities. People suffering from this disorder do not usually create new identities for themselves. At any given point in time, only 0.2% of the American population experiences this disorder, but this rate may increase during times of war or large-scale natural disasters (American Psychiatric Association, 1994).

● **Dissociative disorder:** A category of disorders involving a disruption in the usually integrated functions of consciousness, memory, or identity.

● **Dissociative amnesia:** An inability to remember important personal information, often experienced as memory "gaps."

● **Dissociative fugue:** An abrupt, unexpected departure from home or work, combined with an inability to remember some or all of the past.

Dissociative Identity Disorder

The most controversial dissociative disorder, estimated to affect 1% of the American population (Loewenstein, 1994), is **dissociative identity disorder (DID)**, a condition in which two or more distinct personalities take control of the individual's behavior. This disorder was formerly known as *multiple personality disorder* and attracted immense interest after it was portrayed in the movies *The Three Faces of Eve* (1958) and *Sybil* (1976). Each personality, or *alter*, may be experienced as if it had a distinct personal history, self-image, and identity, including a separate name, mannerisms, and way of talking. Not all alters know of the existence of the other alters, a circumstance that can lead to amnesia. The gaps in memory are substantial enough that they cannot be considered ordinary forgetfulness. People with dissociative identity disorder have been reported to have from 2 to 100 alters, although 10 or fewer are more commonly reported. Stress can trigger a transition to a different alter; this switch often occurs within seconds, although it can be more gradual.

Wendy illustrates her experience with her trauma and dissociative identity disorder through her artwork. The drawing symbolizes a memory of being raped and severely beaten by her mother.

● **Dissociative identity disorder (DID):** A disorder in which a person has two or more distinct personalities that take control of the individual's behavior.

Dissociative Identity Disorder From the Inside

Wendy's story captures the essence of DID:

> As a child, Wendy . . . had been physically and sexually abused as far back as she could remember . . . and there were hospital records of severe physical abuse . . . that occurred before Wendy was 2 years old. Wendy's mother was extremely sadistic and had tortured her regularly with extreme and violent means. For example, without any provocation, Wendy's mother would burn and cut her on various parts of her body. . . . Wendy had learned to rely on her hypnotic abilities to psychologically distance herself from her distressing memories and emotions. . . . Since childhood, Wendy had developed more than 20 distinct personalities! . . . Each of Wendy's personalities had its own distinct pattern of behaviors (e.g., speech, posture, mannerisms), perceived ages, sex, and appearance . . . each of Wendy's personalities possessed different physical reactions or different physical abilities. . . . By dividing things up this way, Wendy was able to have parts of herself that could contain the feelings and knowledge about the tortures and abuse that were going on at home and thereby still be able to have other parts of herself that could handle going to . . . work. (Brown & Barlow, 1997, pp. 102–108)

What might cause dissociative identity disorder? According to some researchers, most people who suffer this disorder share two characteristics: They experienced severe and usually repeated physical abuse as young children (Ross et al., 1991), and they are very hypnotizable and can dissociate easily (Bliss, 1984; Frischholz, 1985). These two factors are related: Children who experience extreme abuse later recount a sense that their minds temporarily leave their bodies in order that they might endure the abuse. In other words, because of the severity of the situation, they dissociate. With continued abuse, and continued use of dissociation, the dissociated state develops its own memories, feelings, and thoughts, and becomes an alter (Putnam, 1989). This view is supported by work by Perry and his colleagues (1995), who found that young children who have been severely traumatized have a tendency to dissociate or become hyperaroused in response to an aversive stimulus.

There are reports that different alters have different EEG patterns, visual acuity, pain tolerance, symptoms of asthma, sensitivity to allergens, and response to insulin (American Psychiatric Association, 1994). Nevertheless, some researchers and clinicians question whether dissociative identity disorder is a verifiably distinct diagnosis, because similar physiological differences occur when researchers ask participants who do *not* have symptoms of the disorder to role-play the condition (Coons et al., 1982). Just as role play induces physiologically different states, some (Lilienfeld et al., 1999; Sarbin, 1995; Spanos, 1994) propose that DID is the product of the beliefs and expectations of the therapist, who, without realizing it, induces patients to behave in ways consistent with the condition known as dissociative identity disorder. Most people who are diagnosed with DID were not aware of their "alters" prior to being in therapy (Lilienfeld et al., 1999). However, researchers have found independent evidence of severe abuse histories in people diagnosed with DID (Lewis et al., 1997; Putnam, 1989; Swica et al., 1996). These same people had either amnesia or scant memories of the abuse (Lewis et al., 1997; Swica et al., 1996) and evidenced signs of dissociation in childhood (Lewis et al., 1997), as would be expected from the theory of how DID develops. However, there is some disagreement about how valid these studies are: The presence of abuse histories alone does not rule out the possibility that DID symptoms are shaped by cultural expectations and the therapist's behavior.

Another question about the diagnosis of DID is whether, because of an overlap in symptoms, it should be considered a subtype of PTSD (Dell, 1998). Furthermore, other researchers note that a substantial percentage of people who are diagnosed with DID have symptoms that also meet the criteria for a particular personality disorder (Lilienfeld et al., 1999). Despite the debate about the origins and causes of dissociative identity disorder, we do know that severe trauma can lead to disruptions in consciousness and to other dissociative disorders, and can have other adverse effects (Putnam, 1989; Putnam et al., 1995).

DID thus results from interacting events at the three levels: Severe trauma, cultural information about dissociative symptoms, and therapists' questions and responses (all events at the level of the group) lead to changes in bodily reactions such as hyperarousal (level of the brain) and psychological changes such as the increased use of dissociation (level of the person). These various types of changes are likely to become chronic responses to stressors. Repeated and lengthy dissociations can become the building blocks for DID.

Could van Gogh's "attacks" have been episodes of dissociation? He once referred to his "evil self," but there is no evidence that he had any alters; and although he may have suffered some memory loss during his attacks, he could very well have been psychotic, not dissociative, at those times. Amnesia alone is not an indication of a dissociative disorder.

Eating Disorders: You Are How You Eat?

Do you have a friend who's on a diet? If you do, the chances are that friend is a woman. Is her mood determined by the numbers on the scale? Does she want to lose more weight, even if she stops menstruating and others tell her she is too thin? If she eats more than she wants, does she feel that she must exercise, even if she's tired or sick? Is her view of herself dependent on whether she exercises today? Does she eat as little as possible during the day, and then find herself "losing control" with food in the afternoon or evening? A yes response, even to every question, does not necessarily indicate the presence of an eating disorder, but it does indicate a preoccupation with food, body image, and weight. These preoccupations are typical of people with **eating disorders,** disorders involving severe disturbances in

● **Eating disorder:** A category of disorders involving a severe disturbance in eating behavior.

- **Anorexia nervosa:** An eating disorder characterized by the refusal to maintain even a low normal weight, and an intense fear of gaining weight.

eating behavior. And although more than 90% of those diagnosed with eating disorders are females, males are increasingly suffering from these disorders too.

Anorexia Nervosa: You Can Be Too Thin

Anorexia nervosa is a potentially fatal disorder characterized by a refusal to maintain even a low normal weight. Someone with anorexia nervosa pursues thinness regardless of the physical consequences. Of those hospitalized with anorexia nervosa, 10% will eventually die of causes related to the disorder (American Psychiatric Association, 1994).

Anorexia Nervosa From the Inside

People with anorexia nervosa develop irrational and unhealthy beliefs about food, as recounted by one woman's experience:

> Yesterday . . . I had a grapefruit and black coffee for breakfast, and for dinner I had the . . . salad I eat every night. I always skip lunch. I had promised myself that I would only eat three-quarters of the salad since I've been feeling stuffed after it lately—but I think I ate more than the three-quarters. I know it was just lettuce and broccoli but I can't believe I did that. I was up all night worrying about getting fat. (Siegel et al., 1988, p. 17)

Included in the list of symptoms required for a diagnosis of anorexia nervosa are distortions of how they see their bodies ("body image"; see Figure 14.3), an intense fear of becoming fat, a refusal to maintain a healthy weight, and, among females, amenorrhea—the cessation of menstruation. It is common for extremely anorexic women to "know" that they are underweight, yet when they look in the mirror, they "see" fat that is not there, or generally overestimate their body size (Smeets et al., 1997). They are often obsessed by thoughts of food, and these thoughts are usually based on irrational or illogical thinking (such as what are "good" and "bad" foods). They often deny that their low weight is a problem, or even that they have a problem. Some symptoms of anorexia nervosa differ from

---

FIGURE 14.3 Body Image Distortion

Many women, not only those with anorexia nervosa, have distorted body images. *Ideal* is the average of women's ratings of the ideal figure; *Attractive to men* is the average rating of the figure women believe is most attractive to men; *Other* is the average actual selection of the female figure that men find most attractive; *Think* is the average figure women think best matches their figure; *Feel* is the average figure women feel best matches their figure.

Adapted from Thompson (1990, p. 11). From Thompson, J. K. (1990). *Body Image Disturbance: Assessment and Treatment.* Copyright 1990 by Pergamon Press. Reprinted by permission of The McGraw-Hill Companies.

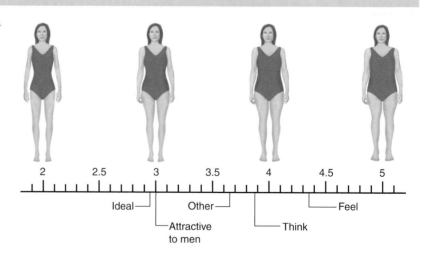

culture to culture. For example, half of young Chinese women with this disorder do not have the fear of being fat common among North Americans, but explain their restricted diet in terms of a distaste for food or bodily discomfort when eating (Lee, 1996).

Some, but not all, people with anorexia nervosa periodically engage in *binge eating* (eating substantially more food within a certain time period than most people would eat in similar circumstances) or *purging* (getting rid of unwanted calories through vomiting or the misuse of laxatives, diuretics, or enemas), or both. Thus, there are two types of anorexia nervosa: the *binge-eating/purging type* and the classic *restricting type*, in which weight loss is achieved primarily by undereating, without purging.

Bulimia Nervosa

People with bulimia nervosa, like those with anorexia nervosa, are usually women, but they may be of normal weight or even overweight, and thus continue to menstruate. **Bulimia nervosa** is marked by recurrent episodes of binge eating, followed by an attempt to prevent weight gain. When that attempt is made through purging (by vomiting or with the use of laxatives), the diagnosis of bulimia nervosa is further specified as *purging type*. Attempts to restrict weight gain may also occur through other methods such as fasting or excessive exercise, and in this case the disorder is the *nonpurging type*.

Some people with bulimia purge even when their eating does not constitute a binge: "If I had *one* bite of bread, just one, I felt as though I blew it! I'd stop listening to whomever was talking to me at the table. I'd start thinking, *How can I get rid of this?* I'd worry about how fat I'd look, how I couldn't fit into my clothes. My head would be flooded with thoughts of what to do now. . . . I had to undo what I'd done. The night was blown. I was a mess" (Siegel et al., 1988, p. 18). Although most people with bulimia do not realize it, in the long run, purging does not usually eliminate all the calories ingested and is, in fact, a poor method of weight loss (Garner, 1997).

Explaining Eating Disorders

Why do people, most often women, develop eating disorders?

Level of the Brain. There is evidence of a genetic predisposition for anorexia. In one study, 56% of identical co-twins were likely to have anorexia if their twins did, compared to 5% of co-twins of affected fraternal twins (Holland et al., 1988). Moreover, in a 1998 study, relatives of those with anorexia nervosa had a higher incidence of obsessive-compulsive symptoms than relatives of those with bulimia nervosa or control subjects. This finding suggests that obsessive personality traits in a family may increase the risk for anorexia nervosa (Lilenfeld et al., 1998). However, learning (resulting in changes at the level of the person) can also account for this finding: People with obsessional relatives may learn to be obsessional; those with eating disorders have focused the obsession on food and weight.

The data for bulimia nervosa in twins shows a sharply different pattern: Twenty-three percent of identical co-twins were likely to have bulimia if their twins did, compared with 9% of co-twins of affected fraternal twins (Kendler et al., 1991). In bulimia, the environment, not genes, clearly plays the larger role (Wade et al., 1998).

● **Bulimia nervosa:** An eating disorder characterized by recurrent episodes of binge eating, followed by some attempt to prevent weight gain.

As was shown by the University of Minnesota starvation study (see Chapter 10), decreased caloric intake leads to pathological eating behaviors and other symptoms of eating disorders. The malnutrition and weight loss that occur with anorexia nervosa lead to changes in neurotransmitters, particularly serotonin. This neurotransmitter is also involved in obsessive-compulsive disorder, and the obsessional thinking about food and pathological eating in anorexia is hypothesized to be related to alterations in serotonergic functioning (Barbarich, 2002; Kaye, 1995). Lower levels of serotonin have been implicated as a predisposing factor for bulimia nervosa (Pirke, 1995) since one effect of serotonin is to create a feeling of satiety (Halmi, 1996). The biological effects of dieting may also make women vulnerable to developing bulimia nervosa: Some, though not all, studies indicate that dieting sometimes precedes the onset of bulimia in some people (Garner, 1997). Although the research points to abnormalities or dysregulation of neurotransmitters, it is as yet unclear how the changes in different neurotransmitters are related; nor is it known whether these changes *precede* the development of an eating disorder and thus may create a susceptibility to it, or whether they are a *consequence* of an eating disorder (Halmi, 1995).

Level of the Person. Numerous personal characteristics have been linked with eating disorders. An increased risk of developing anorexia occurs among women who are perfectionists and have a negative evaluation of themselves (Fairburn et al., 1999; Tyrka et al., 2002). More generally, people with eating disorders often exhibit irrational beliefs and inappropriate expectations about their bodies, jobs, relationships, and themselves (Garfinkel et al., 1992; Striegel-Moore, 1993). They tend to engage in dichotomous, black-or-white thinking: Fruit is "good"; pizza is "bad."

Perhaps people with these characteristics are especially likely to find rewards in the behaviors associated with eating disorders. Preoccupations with food can provide distractions from work, family conflicts, or social problems. By restricting their eating, people may gain a sense of increased control—over food and over life

Cultural pressure on women to be thin and to attain an "ideal" body shape can contribute to eating disorders. Such pressure explains why there is a higher incidence of eating disorders now than 50 years ago, as the ideal figure has changed from the generous proportions of Marilyn Monroe to the rail-thin silhouette of today's runway models (Andersen & DiDomenico, 1992; Field et al., 1999; Nemeroff et al., 1994). Culture plays a role by promoting the idea that body shape can be changed and by determining the rationales people offer for their symptoms (Becker & Hamburg, 1996).

in general—although such feelings of mastery are often short-lived as the disease takes over (Garner, 1997). By purging, they may relieve the anxiety created by overeating.

Level of the Group. The family and the larger culture also play important roles in the development of eating disorders. They may contribute to these disorders by encouraging a preoccupation with weight and appearance. Children have an increased risk of developing eating disorders if their families are overly concerned about appearance and weight (Strober, 1995). Symptoms of eating disorders increase among immigrants from less weight-conscious cultures (such as the Chinese and the Egyptian) as they assimilate to American culture (Bilukha & Utermohlen, 2002; Dolan, 1991; Lee & Lee, 1996), although not all studies find this (Abdollahi & Mann, 2001). Eating disorders are increasing among men who regularly take part in appearance- or weight-conscious activities such as modeling and wrestling (Brownell & Rodin, 1992). Among U.S. women, the focus on appearance and weight may derive from their desire to meet the culture's ideal of femininity (Striegel-Moore, 1993). Westernization (or modernization) increases dieting (Gunewardene et al., 2001; Lee & Lee, 2000), a risk factor for developing eating disorders.

Van Gogh had abnormal eating habits; could he have had an eating disorder? It is unlikely; although van Gogh often purposefully ate sparingly and peculiarly, he did not appear to be preoccupied with weight gain or body image, and no information suggests that he purged in any way.

Looking *at* Levels

Binge Eating

You have learned what eating disorders are and explanations of why they might occur. Let's consider in detail a core aspect of bulimia nervosa—binge eating. Why do some people chronically binge eat? At the level of the brain, food restriction is a contributor to binge eating (Nakai et al., 2001; Polivy & Herman, 1993; Stice et al., 2002). In their efforts to be "in control" of food, people with bulimia generally consume fewer calories at nonbinge meals than do nonbulimics, thus setting the stage for later binge eating because they are hungry and have food cravings (Walsh, 1993), and the bingeing thereby is reinforced. A binge/purge episode may be followed by an endorphin rush (and the ensuing positive feelings that it creates), further reinforcing the binge/purge cycle. As one woman with bulimia reported, "I go to never-

never land. Once I start bingeing, it's like being in a stupor, like being drunk . . . I'm like a different person. It's very humiliating—but not then, not while I'm eating. While I'm eating, nothing else matters" (Siegel et al., 1988, p. 20).

The dichotomous thinking typical of people with eating disorders leads them to view themselves as either "good" (when dieting or restricting food intake), or "bad" (eating "forbidden foods" or feeling out of control while eating). This thinking (level of the person) sets the stage for bingeing if any small amount of forbidden food is eaten; a bite of a candy bar is followed by the thought, Well, I shouldn't have eaten *any* of the candy bar, but since I did, I might as well eat the whole thing, especially since I really shouldn't have a candy bar again. This line of reasoning is part of the *abstinence violation effect* (Polivy & Herman, 1993), the sense of letting go of self-restraint after transgressing a self-imposed rule about food: Once you violate the rule, why not go all the way? In addition, purging is negatively reinforcing (remember, negative reinforcement is reinforcement, not punishment; see Chapter 6): Eating too much, or eating forbidden foods, can cause anxiety, which is then relieved by purging. This reinforcement then increases the likelihood of purging in the future.

Bingeing and purging are usually done alone, increasing the affected person's sense of isolation and decreasing his or her social interactions; if social interactions are stressful, then bingeing and purging are reinforced by the isolation they provide (level of the group). Events at the different levels interact: Cultural pressures to be thin, or to eat small meals, lead vulnerable individuals to

try to curb their food intake. The hunger caused by this undereating may trigger a binge. The binge may also be triggered by stress, social interactions, negative affect, or viewing appearance as very important (Polivy & Herman, 1993; Stice et al., 2002; Vanderlinden et al., 2001); bingeing can create positive changes (such as decreased hunger, distraction from an uncomfortable feeling or thought, and removal from difficult social interactions). This immediate reinforcement often outweighs the negative consequences that are experienced later.

TEST YOURSELF!

1. What are dissociative disorders? What causes them?
2. What are the symptoms and causes of eating disorders?

Personality Disorders

By now, it should come as no surprise to know that van Gogh was more than just unconventional; his difficulties in life went beyond his attacks, his hallucinations, and his periods of depression. Van Gogh's relationships with other people were troubled, and they often followed a pattern: Initial positive feelings and excitement about someone new in his life (such as happened with Gauguin and Sien) were invariably followed by a turbulent phase and an eventual falling out. Throughout his life, he had emotional outbursts that sooner or later caused others to withdraw their friendship. His relationship with his brother Theo is the only one that endured. Does such a pattern suggest that he may have had a personality disorder?

Axis II Personality Disorders

Axis II of the *DSM-IV* allows the possibility of a **personality disorder** (see Table 14.8), which is a set of relatively stable personality traits that are inflexible and maladaptive, causing distress or difficulty with daily functioning. A personality disorder may occur alone, or it may be accompanied by an Axis I disorder.

Whereas Axis I symptoms feel as if they are inflicted from the outside, the maladaptive traits of Axis II are often experienced as parts of the person's personality. The maladaptive traits of personality disorders cause distress or difficulty with daily functioning in school, work, social life, or relationships. They can be so subtle as to be unnoticeable in a brief encounter. It is only after getting to know someone over time that a personality disorder may become evident.

Some researchers argue that the combinations of traits now defined as personality disorders should not be called "disorders" at all. Doing so, they contend,

● **Personality disorder:** A category of disorders where relatively stable personality traits are inflexible and maladaptive, causing distress or difficulty with daily functioning.

TABLE 14.8 Axis II Personality Disorders

Disorder	Description
Antisocial personality disorder	A pattern of disregard or violation of the rights of others.
Avoidant personality disorder	A pattern of social discomfort, feelings of inadequacy, and hypersensitivity to negative evaluation.
Borderline personality disorder	A pattern of instability in relationships, self-image, and feelings, and pronounced impulsivity (such as in spending, substance abuse, sex, reckless driving, or binge eating). Relationships are often characterized by rapid swings from idealizing another person to devaluing him or her. Recurrent suicidal gestures, threats, or self-mutilation, such as nonlethal cuts on the arm are common, as are chronic feelings of emptiness.
Dependent personality disorder	A pattern of clingy, submissive behavior due to an extreme need to be taken care of.
Histrionic personality disorder	A pattern of excessive attention seeking and expression of emotion.
Narcissistic personality disorder	A pattern of an exaggerated sense of self-importance, need for admiration, and lack of empathy.
Obsessive-compulsive personality disorder	A pattern of preoccupation with perfectionism, orderliness, and control (but no obsessions or compulsions, as occur with obsessive-compulsive disorder).
Paranoid personality disorder	A pattern of suspiciousness and distrust of others to the extent that other people's motives are interpreted as ill-intentioned. However, unlike the paranoid subtype of schizophrenia, there are no delusions or hallucinations.
Schizoid personality disorder	A pattern of detachment from social relationships and a narrow range of displayed emotion.
Schizotypal personality disorder	A pattern of extreme discomfort in close relationships, odd or quirky behavior, and cognitive or perceptual distortions (such as sensing the presence of another person or spirit).

Source: American Psychiatric Association (2000). Reprinted with permission from the *Diagnostic and Statistical Manual of Mental Disorders,* Fourth Edition, Text Revision. Copyright 2000 American Psychiatric Association.

either treats normal variations in personality as pathological or creates separate Axis II categories for conditions that could be part of an Axis I clinical disorder (Hyman, personal communication, 1998; Livesley, 1998). For example, the clinging, submissive behavior that *DSM-IV* categorizes as Axis II "dependent personality disorder" might also characterize a personality that is within the normal range. And the symptoms of avoidant personality disorder overlap those of Axis I social phobia—only the greater severity of anxiety and depressive symptoms distinguishes avoidant personality disorder from social phobia (Johnson & Lydiard, 1995); the two disorders are quantitatively, not qualitatively, different.

Other researchers argue that each personality disorder is not a research-validated disorder distinct from all others (Atre-Vaidya & Hussain, 1999; Horowitz, 1998). Furthermore, the criteria for the various personality disorders do not all require the same level of dysfunction. Thus, a lesser—and in some cases quite mild—degree of impairment is required for a diagnosis of obsessive-compulsive, antisocial, and paranoid personality disorders (Funtowicz & Widiger, 1999).

From what is known about his life, it is not impossible that van Gogh had a personality disorder; but we have no way of knowing if he in fact met all of the criteria.

Antisocial Personality Disorder

The most intensively studied personality disorder is **antisocial personality disorder (ASPD),** evidenced by a long-standing pattern of disregard for others to the point of violating their rights (American Psychiatric Association, 2000). Symptoms include a superficial charm; egocentrism; impulsive, reckless, and deceitful behavior without regard for others' safety; a tendency to blame others for any adversity that comes their way; and a lack of conscience, empathy, and remorse. People with this disorder talk a good line and know how to manipulate others, but they don't have the capacity to know or care how another person feels.

Antisocial Personality Disorder From the Inside

A common feature among people with ASPD is that they see *themselves* as the real victims. While discussing the murders he committed, John Wayne Gacy portrayed himself as the 34th victim:

> I was made an asshole and a scapegoat . . . when I look back, I see myself more as a victim than a perpetrator. . . . I was the victim; I was cheated out of my childhood. . . . [He wondered whether] there would be someone, somewhere who would understand how badly it had hurt to be John Wayne Gacy. (Hare, 1993, p. 43)

Antisocial personality disorder occurs three times more frequently in men than in women, and although only 1 to 2% of Americans are diagnosed with this disorder, 60% of male prisoners are estimated to have it (Moran, 1999). Cross-cultural studies have found a similar pattern of symptoms in both Western and non-Western cultures (Zoccolillo et al., 1999). Many people diagnosed with antisocial personality disorder also abuse alcohol and drugs (Nigg & Goldsmith, 1994).

● **Antisocial personality disorder (ASPD):** A long-standing pattern of disregard for others to the point of violating other people's rights.

Looking *at* Levels

Understanding Antisocial Personality Disorder

What causes antisocial personality disorder? Evidence for a biological basis (level of the brain) arises from a number of sources. Some of the data on antisocial personality disorder come from studies of certain types of criminality, which are related to some of the symptoms of antisocial personality disorder. These data show that the disorder runs in families (Nigg & Goldsmith, 1994). Moreover, adoption studies show that environment matters only if a child's biological parents were criminals; if they were, there was a slight increase in criminal behavior for boys adopted into a family of law-abiding people, but there was a whopping increase in criminal behavior if they were adopted into a family of criminals. If the biological parents were not criminals, the adopted child's later criminal behavior was the same when he or she grew up in law-abiding or criminal families (Mednick et al., 1984). Criminal behavior provides a clear example of how genes and environment can interact. The genes predispose; the environment triggers.

At the level of the person, research suggests that people with antisocial personality disorder have difficulty modulating their anger (Zlotnick, 1999). In addition, their difficulty in understanding how others feel and their lack of empathy may be related to a poor attachment to their primary caretaker (Gabbard, 1990; Pollock et al., 1990), perhaps because of emotional deprivation, abuse, and inconsistent or poor parenting (Patterson, 1986; Patterson et al., 1989).

As children, people with antisocial personality disorder often experienced or witnessed abuse, deviant behavior, or a lack of concern for the welfare of others by peers, parents, or others (level of the group). The behaviors of models who lack basic regard for others may later be imitated (Elliott et al., 1985).

How might events at these levels interact? To begin with, genes may lead to a relatively underresponsive central and autonomic nervous system (level of the brain). In turn, this might lead people with such genes to seek out highly arousing, thrilling activities (Quay, 1965). A depressed central and autonomic nervous system might also leave them relatively unaffected by social rejection or mild punishment. In other words, when people have an underresponsive nervous system, the normal social and legal consequences of inappropriate behavior might not make them feel anxious (level of the person). Conversely, a moderate level of arousal is optimal for performance (see Chapter 10). Together, these consequences of an underresponsive nervous system might produce another important result—difficulty in learning to control impulses. In fact, Schachter and Latané (1964) found that such people have difficulty learning to avoid shocks. But when they are injected with adrenaline so that their level of arousal is increased, they learn to avoid shocks at the same rate as other people.

This physiological underresponsiveness may also be related to poor parental bonding, in that the normal stimulation provided by parents may not be enough to engage these infants. Moreover, as they grow up, learning antisocial behavior from others in the immediate environment may be arousing enough to hold their interest and increase their learning, which creates a vicious cycle. Their underresponsiveness may have *caused* their caregivers to treat them differently. Poor attachment (a group-related factor) can then make it difficult for them to identify with others, which leads to a lack of empathy (Kagan & Reid, 1986), the inability to understand how others feel (level of the person). Thus, violating the rights of others does not lead people with antisocial personality disorder to feel for people they have hurt or wronged.

TEST YOURSELF!

1. What are personality disorders?
2. What is antisocial personality disorder?

A Cautionary Note About Diagnosis

The events of van Gogh's life present an opportunity to explore ways in which the human psyche can be troubled, and the ways in which the mental health field presently classifies disorders. But that is not the same as proposing a diagnosis of someone who, while in art is very close to us, is in his person very distant in time.

No mental health clinician can really know with certainty from what, if any, specific disorder van Gogh suffered. Major depressive disorder and schizophrenia are possibilities, as is bipolar disorder (Jamison, 1993). Alternatively, his attacks and hallucinations might have been due to *delirium tremens* (DTs), caused by withdrawal from alcohol (see Chapter 5); but such a diagnosis would not explain why van Gogh had attacks even during lengthy periods of sobriety (Lubin, 1972). Possibly he suffered from a form of epilepsy, and his "attacks" were seizures; before epileptic seizures, victims are sometimes overcome with religious feelings and delusions. The consideration of epilepsy, a neurological disorder not a psychological one, in our speculations points to the importance of ensuring that the patient does not have a medical disorder that can cause psychological symptoms. Only after ruling out medical illnesses can the mental health clinician or researcher have confidence in a diagnosis of a psychological disorder.

 **CONSOLIDATE!**

Identifying Psychological Disorders: What's Abnormal?

- A psychological disorder is signaled by a constellation of cognitive, emotional, and behavioral symptoms that create significant distress, disability, and danger.

- Behaviors that are merely deviant from the mainstream culture are not considered to be "disordered."

- Psychological disorders are best understood as events at the levels of brain, person, and group, and their interactions.

- The catalog of psychiatric disorders in the *DSM-IV* distinguishes among disorders by the symptoms exhibited or reported, and by the history of the symptoms. The *DSM-IV* includes both clinical and personality disorders.

> **THINK IT THROUGH** If a classmate tells you in all seriousness that someone you both know is "weird" and a "basket case," how would you respond? What would you want to know about the behavior that led your friend to this conclusion? What other questions should you ask? Why?

Mood Disorders

- Major depressive disorder is characterized by depressed mood, loss of pleasure, fatigue, weight loss, poor sleep, a sense of worthlessness or guilt, and poor attention and concentration.

- Dysthymia is a less intense, but longer lasting type of depression.

- Bipolar disorder involves episodes of mania or hypomania, which may or may not alternate with depression.

- Some people are biologically vulnerable to developing these disorders; further, neurotransmitters and neuromodulators are implicated in both major depressive disorder and bipolar disorder, although the exact mechanisms are not yet understood.

- People's worldviews and attributional styles, such as the negative triad of depression, also play a role in the development of major depressive disorder. Learned helplessness can also contribute to depression.

- Operant conditioning and the available rewards or punishments in the environment also may be related to the development of depression, as can life stresses.

- Women in developed countries experience depression more often than do men. This difference may occur because, as children, girls are taught to be introspective, and not to take action. As women, such ruminations may promote depression.

- Depressed people, through their actions, may inadvertently alienate others, who then reject those depressed people, who view the rejection as confirmation of their negative views.

- The rate of occurrence of bipolar disorder is increasing, and at earlier ages.

THINK IT THROUGH Suppose someone you know, someone whose sharp style of dress and confident manner you admire, starts looking unkempt and acting tired, nervous, and fidgety. Would this change suggest a psychological disorder? Why or why not? If so, what type of disorder do you have in mind and why? Would psychological impairment be the only explanation?

Anxiety Disorders

- Anxiety disorders include panic disorder, specific and social phobias, posttraumatic stress disorder, and obsessive-compulsive disorder.

- People with panic disorder may avoid places or activities in order to minimize the possibility of additional panic attacks; when such avoidance restricts daily life, it is referred to as agoraphobia.

- People can inherit a biological vulnerability for panic. Moreover, an anxiety sensitivity can increase the risk for panic disorder, as can a misinterpretation of certain bodily sensations.

- People can be biologically vulnerable to developing both social and specific phobias. Although learning can also contribute, it is unclear to what extent it does so.

- Not everyone who experiences a traumatic event goes on to develop PTSD. The type of trauma, the response to it, and other factors can increase or decease the risk of PTSD developing.

- Neutral activity in the caudate nucleus is related to OCD. Compulsions may momentarily relieve the anxiety that obsessions cause, operantly reinforcing the compulsions.

THINK IT THROUGH If your relative refuses to fly because of a fear of flying, do you think that he or she has an anxiety disorder (based on what you have read)? If no, why not; if yes, which disorder and why? Suppose that a classmate confided to you that he's been very anxious lately and that he has been going back to check that he's locked his door or his bike. What other questions might you want to ask if you think he might have symptoms of an anxiety disorder? What disorder and why (or why not)?

Schizophrenia

- Schizophrenia involves a markedly restricted range of affect, odd or disorganized thoughts, delusions or hallucinations, and behaviors; it is characterized by positive and negative symptoms.

- The *DSM-IV* specifies four subtypes of schizophrenia: paranoid, disorganized, catatonic, and undifferentiated.

- Research findings on schizophrenia point to genetic and biological abnormalities. These abnormalities include enlarged ventricles and a decrease in the frontal cortex. Such abnormalities may arise during fetal development, and may arise from maternal illness or malnutrition during pregnancy and prenatal or birth-related complications.

- Children at risk for schizophrenia show extreme discomfort with close relationships, exhibit high levels of odd or quirky behavior, are more reactive to stress, and have higher baseline levels of cortisol.

- Those with schizophrenia who have high expressed emotion families are more likely to suffer a recurrence. However, this finding is only a correlation.

- Social selection and social causation are factors that may account for the higher rates of schizophrenia in urban areas and in lower socioeconomic classes.

THINK IT THROUGH Would someone who has exhibited positive and negative symptoms of schizophrenia ever be able to function relatively normally again? Does having a parent with schizophrenia guarantee the development of the disorder? Can the environment of someone with schizophrenia affect the symptoms? If so, in what way? What is the best evidence that van Gogh did not have schizophrenia?

Other Axis I Disorders: Dissociative and Eating Disorders

- Dissociative disorders are characterized by identity confusion, derealization, depersonalization, and amnesia.
- Trauma or severe stress influences the development of these disorders.
- Types of dissociative disorders are dissociative amnesia, dissociative fugue, and dissociative identity disorder.
- People with DID experienced severe (and usually repeated) physical abuse as young children. They are also very hypnotizable and can dissociate easily.
- DID symptoms may be shaped by cultural expectations and therapists' behavior.
- Eating disorders (anorexia nervosa and bulimia nervosa) are characterized by preoccupations with weight and body image, as well as abnormal eating (restriction, binges, purges).
- Symptoms of anorexia nervosa include a refusal to maintain a healthy weight, a fear of becoming fat, a disturbed body image, and amenorrhea.
- Symptoms of bulimia include recurrent binge eating episodes, followed by an attempt to prevent weight gain.
- Genetic factors are more influential in the development of anorexia nervosa than bulimia nervosa, and environmental factors, specifically the cultural emphasis on thinness, affect the development of both eating disorders.
- Biological factors related to food restriction and binge eating can also lead to the development of an eating disorder.

THINK IT THROUGH If a friend began eating less and lost weight, what else would you want to know before concluding that she might have an eating disorder? If she confessed to you that she sometimes didn't "feel like herself" anymore, that she wasn't sure who she "really was," might you suspect she had a dissociative disorder? Why or why not?

Personality Disorders

- Personality disorders are sets of maladaptive and inflexible personality traits that can create difficulty in work, school, or in other social spheres.
- Such traits may be unnoticeable in a brief encounter, and only reveal themselves over time.
- In contrast to Axis I disorders, which seem to the sufferer to be inflicted from the outside, personality disorders, which are on Axis II, are experienced as part of the personality itself.
- Antisocial personality disorder is the most intensively studied personality disorder; the key symptom is a long-standing pattern of disregard for others to the point of violating their rights.
- Antisocial personality has a biological basis, perhaps an underresponsive central and autonomic nervous system.
- For those who are biologically vulnerable, the environment in which they are raised can influence whether they later develop criminal behavior.

THINK IT THROUGH At first, your new neighbor seemed like a really nice guy—then you got to know him better. Weeks ago he borrowed money because of an "emergency," but he never repaid you. When you ask for your money back, he always has an excuse. Whenever friends come by to see you, he seems to make a point of sticking his head out the door and charming your visitors. You become increasingly frustrated because your friends can't understand why you keep complaining about him. Would you suspect that antisocial personality disorder might be in the picture? Why? If you knew that a mental health clinician had diagnosed him as having antisocial personality disorder, what could you infer about his family history? What should you *not* infer?

Key Terms

Copyright Visual Arts Library/Art Resource, NY

Treatment

At 2 A.M., Beth sat hunched over her textbook and notes, studying for her midterm. Concentration was difficult; she had to struggle to make sense of the words before her eyes. She'd read the same page four times and still couldn't remember what it said. She tried to give herself a pep talk ("Okay, Beth, read it one more time, and then you'll understand it"), but her upbeat words would be drowned out by a different, negative internal monologue (*Well, Beth, you've really screwed yourself, and there's no way out of it now. You're going to fail, get kicked out of school, never be employed, end up destitute, homeless, hopeless, talking to yourself on the street*).

Beth was 21 years old, a junior in college. She'd already had to walk out of two exams because she couldn't answer most of the questions, although she had understood the material earlier. Her thoughts had been jumbled, and she'd had a hard time organizing her answers to the questions. She'd always been nervous before a test or class presentation, but this year her anxiety had spun out of control. Taking the first quiz of the semester, she simply drew a blank when she tried to answer the questions.

Since then, she'd become more anxious, and depressed as well. With each quiz she couldn't finish, with each paper that required more concentration than she could summon, she felt herself spiraling downward, helpless. She had no hope that the situation would change by itself, and no amount of good intentions or resolutions or even effort made a difference. She began cutting classes and spent much of her time in bed; she had no interest in doing anything with her friends because she felt she didn't deserve to have fun. She'd put off saying anything to her professors; at first she figured things would get better, and then she was too embarrassed to face them. But she knew that eventually she'd have to talk to them or else she'd definitely fail her courses.

She finally did talk to her professors. Several of them suggested that she seek treatment, or at least go to the campus counseling center, but she didn't want to do that. Taking that step, she felt, would be admitting to herself and to the world not only

that something was wrong with her, but also that she was too weak to deal with it herself.

Beth was reluctant to seek help partly because when she was growing up, her mother had experienced bouts of depression severe enough that she had been hospitalized several times. Beth recognized that she, too, was becoming depressed, and she was afraid that if she went to see a therapist, she'd end up in the hospital.

> Beth recognized that she, too, was becoming depressed, and she was afraid that if she went to see a therapist, she'd end up in the hospital.

Finally, Beth confided in a family friend, Nina, who had been the school nurse at Beth's elementary school. Nina told Beth that people with problems like hers often felt much better after psychotherapy and that her problems were not severe enough to warrant hospitalization. She also pointed out that there were many forms of therapy available to Beth that were not as readily available to her mother 20 years earlier. Modern treatments, Nina said, ranged from psychologically based therapies such as cognitive, behavioral, and insight-oriented therapies to biologically based treatments such as medication. Research has revealed that, for a given problem, some treatments may be more effective than others, and for Beth's problems there were a number of potentially helpful treatments. Beth agreed to see a therapist, but didn't know where to begin to find one. The campus counseling center could be useful, Nina said, but Beth might also explore other ways to find a therapist who would be right for her needs, such as the Internet and referral organizations.

Let's make a similar exploration in this chapter, examining the different schools of therapy, how they work, and what research has to say about the effectiveness of the therapies.

Behavior and Cognitive Therapy

Beth decided to see a therapist. A cognitive–behavior therapist would begin by asking Beth: What does she do before she sits down to study or take an exam? What does she think about when she starts to study or walks to a classroom to take an exam? What, in detail, does she do during the day? Has she ever tried any relaxation techniques? What does she believe about herself and her abilities? These are questions about thought patterns and behaviors.

Although therapists usually integrate cognitive and behavioral techniques, we first discuss them separately so that you can understand the unique focus of each approach.

Behavior Therapy

Behavior therapy focuses on changing observable, measurable behavior. Joseph Wolpe (1915–1997) profoundly altered the practice of psychotherapy in 1958 when he published *Psychotherapy by Reciprocal Inhibition*. He was a psychiatrist, but his focus on behavior created a new form of treatment that particularly appealed to psychologists because of its emphasis on quantifiable results. Moreover, behavior therapy rested on well-researched principles of learning (see Chapter 6; Wolpe, 1997).

Theory

In behavior therapy, distressing symptoms are seen as the result of learning. Through the use of social learning—that is, modeling—as well as through classical and operant conditioning, clients can change unwanted behaviors by learning new ones; it is easiest to change a problematic behavior by replacing it with a new, more adaptive one. The behavior therapist is interested in the ABCs of the behavior: its *antecedents* (what is the stimulus that triggers the problematic behavior?), the problematic *behavior* itself, and its *consequences* (what is reinforcing the behavior?). Behavior therapy's lack of interest or belief in an unconscious "root cause" was revolutionary. Behaviors and performance are emphasized, the therapist takes an active, directive role in treatment, and "homework"—between-session tasks on the part of the client—is an important component of the treatment. Therapists took a new look at treatment results: Did the client experience less frequent or less intense symptoms after therapy?

In Beth's case, a behavior therapist would be interested in the antecedent, or stimulus, of Beth's problematic behaviors. Consider her anxiety: The antecedent might be the act of sitting down to study for an exam, or waiting in class to receive her exam booklet. The behavior is the conditioned emotional response of fear and anxiety, evidenced by her sweating hands, racing heart rate, and other behaviors associated with anxiety (see Chapter 14). The consequences include negative reinforcement (the uncomfortable symptoms go away) when skipping an exam. Thus, related nonacademic avoidant behaviors such as sleeping through an exam are reinforced. In addition, her anxiety and subsequent social isolation lead to a loss of pleasant activities and opportunities for social reinforcement, which in turn leads to depression. Unlike cognitive therapy, which views depressive thoughts as producing depressive feelings and behaviors, behavior theory views depressive behaviors as leading to depressive thoughts (see Chapter 14; Emmelkamp, 1994).

Techniques

Behavioral techniques rest on classical conditioning, operant conditioning, and social learning principles.

Techniques Based on Classical Conditioning. One classical conditioning technique is **systematic desensitization,** a procedure that teaches people to be relaxed in the presence of a feared object or situation. This technique, developed by Wolpe for treating phobias, grew out of the idea that someone cannot be fearful (and hence anxious) and relaxed at the same time. Systematic desensitization uses **progressive muscle relaxation,** a relaxation technique whereby the muscles are sequentially relaxed from one end of the body to the other, often from feet to head. Although progressive muscle relaxation is used in systematic desensitization,

● **Behavior therapy:** A type of therapy, based on well-researched principles of that focuses on changing observable, measurable behaviors.

● **Systematic desensitization:** A behavior therapy technique that teaches people to be relaxed in the presence of a feared object or situation.

● **Progressive muscle relaxation:** A relaxation technique whereby the person relaxes muscles sequentially from one end of the body to the other.

HANDS ON

it can be used by itself to induce relaxation. You can try progressive muscle relaxation yourself by following the instructions below. Read them several times until you essentially know them and can say them to yourself with your eyes closed; or, have a friend read them to you; or tape record them for playback. The instructions should be recited slowly and clearly. If you're repeating the instructions to yourself from memory and you forget a group of muscles, the technique can still be effective. (If you have an injury in a particular part of your body, you may want to skip tensing the muscles in that area.) Like any new skill, relaxation induction becomes easier and more effective with practice.

> Sit in a comfortable position, take a deep breath, and close your eyes. Curl your toes, and hold that position for a few seconds . . . not so tightly that it hurts, just enough so that you can notice what the tension in your foot muscles feels like (5–10 seconds). . . . Relax. . . . Notice the difference between the tension and the relaxation, the pleasantness of the relaxation. . . . Now point your toes up toward the ceiling, keeping your heels on the floor. . . . Feel the tension, the pull . . . keep breathing. . . . Relax. . . . As before, notice the difference between the tension and the relaxation. . . . Press your knees toward each other . . . not so much that it hurts, just enough to notice the tension in those muscles. . . . Relax. . . . Tense your thighs and buttocks, and notice your body lift slightly. . . . Notice the tension in the muscles, remember to breathe. . . . Relax. . . . Notice how pleasant the relaxation feels. . . . Tense your abdominal muscles as if you were a prize fighter. . . . Feel the tension, keep breathing. . . . Relax. . . . Take a deep breath and hold it while counting to 5, then slowly exhale. . . . Notice the way the muscles in your chest feel as you hold the breath and then exhale, and how your sense of relaxation is enhanced. . . . Raise your shoulders up toward your ears and hold it. . . . Notice what the tension feels like in those muscles, breathe. . . . Relax. . . . Now push your shoulders down toward the floor, focusing your awareness on how this new tension feels. . . . Relax. . . . Notice a sense of relaxation spreading over your body. . . . Purse your lips together and notice the tension in the lower part of your face, your jaw, perhaps your neck. . . . Relax. . . . Notice the difference between the tension and the relaxation, and how much more pleasant relaxation is. . . . Close your eyes tightly, but not so tightly that it hurts. . . . Notice the tension. . . . Relax. . . . Notice the pleasantness of the relaxation. Take a moment and check your body for any residual tension; if you find any, tense and relax those muscles. . . . Enjoy the sensation of relaxation. In a few moments, open your eyes, and bring this sense of relaxation with you into the day. (Adapted from Jacobson, 1925)

When using systematic desensitization to overcome a phobia, the therapist and client begin by constructing a hierarchy of real or imagined activities related to the feared object or situation—such as a fear of elevators (see Figure 15.1). This hierarchy begins with the least fearful activity, such as pressing an elevator call button, progressing to the most fearful, being stuck in a stopped elevator. Over the course of a number of sessions, clients work on becoming relaxed when imagining increasingly anxiety-provoking activities. Once Beth successfully learned how to become relaxed, she and her therapist might begin systematic desensitization.

Another behavioral technique that relies on classical conditioning principles to treat anxiety disorders is **exposure.** It rests on the principle of habituation (see Chapter 6). Patients are asked to *expose* themselves to feared stimuli in a planned and usually gradual way. (Exposure and habituation do not generally occur naturally because people with fears that reach the level of an anxiety disorder often

● **Exposure:** A theraputic technique based on classical conditioning that rests on the principle of habituation.

FIGURE 15.1 Systematic Desensitization of an Elevator Phobia

With systematic desensitization, a man with an elevator phobia would list a hierarchy of activities related to using an elevator. Next, he would successfully learn to make himself relax, using techniques such as progressive muscle relaxation.

He then starts out imagining items at the low end of the hierarchy, such as pressing an elevator button. When he becomes anxious, he stops imagining that scene and uses relaxation techniques to become fully relaxed again.

When he can imagine the elevator-related situations on the lower end of the hierarchy without anxiety, he progresses to situations that make him more anxious, stopping to do the relaxation technique when he becomes anxious.

Systematic desensitization continues in this fashion until the man can imagine being fully immersed in the most feared situation (a stuck elevator) without anxiety. He would then follow the same procedure in a real elevator.

avoid the stimulus that instills fear.) People can be exposed to the feared stimulus in three ways:

- *Imaginal exposure*, where they imagine the feared stimulus;
- *In vivo exposure*, where they expose themselves to the actual stimulus; or,
- *Virtual reality exposure*, where they use virtual reality techniques to expose themselves to the stimulus.

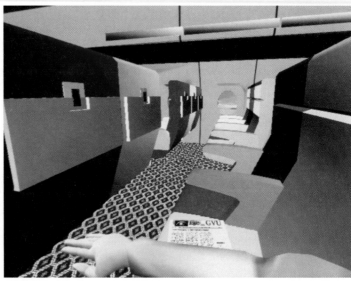

Virtual reality exposure appears to work as well as in vivo (actual) exposure for fears of flying and heights (Emmelkamp et al., 2001, 2002; Rothbaum et al., 2001, 2002).

● **Stimulus control:** A behavior therapy technique that involves controlling the exposure to a stimulus that elicits a conditioned response, so as to decrease or increase the frequency of the response.

● **Behavior modification:** A category of therapeutic techniques for changing behavior based on operant conditioning principles.

If an alcoholic drank to excess only in a bar, limiting or eliminating the occasions of going to a bar would be an example of stimulus control.

A related technique, *exposure with response prevention*, is a planned, programmatic procedure that exposes the client to the anxiety-provoking object but prevents the usual maladaptive response. For instance, clients with an obsessive-compulsive disorder that compels them to wash their hands repeatedly would purposefully get their hands dirty during a therapy session and then stop themselves from washing their hands immediately afterward. In this way, they would habituate to the anxiety. Exposure with response prevention has been found to be as effective as medication for OCD, and the behavioral treatment can have longer-lasting benefits (Marks, 1997). However, not all people who have OCD are willing to use this behavioral technique (Stanley & Turner, 1995). The technique is also used in treating bulimia nervosa: Clients would eat a food normally followed by forced vomiting, and then would not throw up (or would delay it as long as possible). Beforehand, client and therapist would develop strategies that the client could use while trying *not* to engage in the maladaptive behavior. The technique of **stimulus control** involves controlling the exposure to a stimulus that elicits a conditioned response, so as to decrease or increase the frequency of the response.

Techniques Based on Operant Conditioning. Techniques based on operant conditioning make use of the principles of reinforcement, punishment, and extinction, with the goal of **behavior modification**—that is, changing the *behavior*, not focusing on thoughts or feelings. Setting the appropriate *response contingencies*, or behaviors that will earn reinforcement, is crucial. If Beth used behavior modification techniques, she would establish response contingencies for behaving in desired new ways: She might reward herself with a movie or a dinner out after taking an exam, or allow herself an hour's conversation with a friend after studying for 2 hours. *Extinction*, eliminating a behavior by not reinforcing it, is another important tool of the behavioral therapist.

Self-monitoring techniques, such as keeping a daily log of a problematic behavior, can help identify its antecedents (see Figure 15.2). Daily logs are used for a variety of problems including poor mood, anxiety, overeating, smoking, sleep problems, and compulsive gambling.

FIGURE 15.2 Daily Self-Monitoring Log

| Name _____ Day _____ Date _____ |
Time of Day	Problematic Behavior	Where the Behavior Occurred	What happened before the behavior occurred (thoughts/feelings, interactions with others, etc.)?

This daily self-monitoring log helps clients become aware of the antecedents, or "triggers," to their problematic behaviors. The column for time of day helps determine whether there is a daily or weekly pattern. Noting where the behavior occurred helps establish whether certain environments play a role in the behavior, perhaps serving as conditioned stimuli. Writing down thoughts, feelings, interactions with others, or other factors (such as level of hunger) that preceded the problematic behavior helps identify irrational thought patterns, distressing feelings, states, or situations that lead to the behavior. With knowledge of the factors, the client and therapist can develop appropriate targets of change for the therapy.

Techniques Based on Observation Learning. Observational learning also plays a role in behavior therapy, particularly with children and in the treatment of some phobias, especially animal phobias (Goetestam & Berntzen, 1997). Patients observe other people interacting with the feared stimulus in a relaxed way and learn to do the same.

Cognitive Therapy: It's the Thought That Counts

The ripples of the cognitive revolution in psychology (see Chapter 1) were felt in therapy as well as in research. Therapists began to examine the mental processes that contribute to behavior, not simply physical stimuli. It became clear that people's thoughts ("cognitions"), not just their learning histories, influence their feelings and behavior, and do so in myriad ways. Just thinking about a past positive experience with love can put you in a good mood, and thinking about an unhappy love experience can have the opposite effect (Clark & Collins, 1993). A cognitive therapist would focus on Beth's thoughts and the way in which one thought leads to another, contributing to her emotional experience of anxiety and depression.

● **Self-monitoring techniques:** Behavioral techniques that help the client identify the antecedents, consequences, and patterns of a targeted behavior.

Behavior and Cognitive Therapy | 629

Theory

The way people perceive or interpret events can affect their well-being (Chapter 13). **Cognitive therapy** emphasizes the role of attempts to think rationally in the control of distressing feelings and behaviors. It is the perception of any experience that determines the response to that experience, and cognitive therapy highlights the importance of the way people perceive and think about events. Two particularly important contributors to cognitive therapy were Albert Ellis and Aaron Beck.

Albert Ellis (b. 1913) is a clinical psychologist who in the 1950s developed a treatment called *rational-emotive therapy (RET)*. RET emphasizes rational, logical thinking and assumes that distressing feelings or symptoms are caused by faulty or illogical thoughts. People may develop illogical or irrational thoughts as a result of their experiences and never assess whether these thoughts are valid. They elevate irrational thoughts to "godlike absolutist musts, shoulds, demands, and commands" (Ellis, 1994a, p. 103). According to RET, Beth's thought that she needs to do well in school is based on a dysfunctional, irrational belief that in order to be a lovable, deserving human being, she must earn good grades; if she does not, she believes she will be unlovable and worthless.

Ellis (1994a) proposed three processes that interfere with healthy functioning: (1) *Self-downing*—being critical of oneself for performing poorly or being rejected; (2) *Hostility and rage*—being unkind to or critical of others for performing poorly; and (3) *Low frustration tolerance*—blaming everyone and everything for "poor, dislikable conditions."

RET focuses on creating more rational thoughts. In Beth's case, they might be, *I might be disappointed or disappoint others if I don't do well this semester, but they will still love and care about me.* This more rational thought should then cause the problematic behavior to diminish, allowing her to choose more rational courses of action. Part of the goal of RET is educational, and clients should be able to use the techniques on their own once they have mastered them. Like behavior therapy, RET is oriented toward *solving* problems as opposed to exploring them psychologically. The RET therapist strives to have the client feel accepted and encourages self-acceptance and a new way of thinking; self-blame is viewed as counterproductive because it involves faulty beliefs. Shortcomings or failures are viewed as simply part of life, not as crimes or signs of moral weakness.

Psychiatrist Aaron Beck (b. 1921) developed a form of cognitive therapy that, like RET, rests on the premise that irrational thoughts are the root cause of psychological problems, and that recognition of irrationality and adoption of more realistic, rational thoughts cause psychological problems to improve. According to his theory, irrational thoughts that arise from a systematic bias, such as the belief that if you tell your friend you are mad at her she will reject you, are considered **cognitive distortions** of reality; several common distortions are presented in Table 15.1. However, unlike RET, which relies on the therapist's attempts to persuade the client that his or her beliefs are irrational, Beck's version of cognitive therapy encourages the client to view beliefs as hypotheses to be tested. Thus, interactions with the world provide opportunities to perform "experiments" to ascertain the accuracy of the client's beliefs (Hollon & Beck, 1994). Beck and his colleagues have approached treatment empirically, developing measures to assess depression, anxiety, and other problems, and to evaluate the effectiveness of treatment.

● **Cognitive therapy:** Therapy that focuses on the client's thoughts rather than his or her feelings or behaviors.

● **Cognitive distortion:** Irrational thoughts that arise from a systematic bias in the way a person thinks about reality.

TABLE 15.1 Five Common Cognitive Distortions

Distortion	Description	Example
Dichotomous thinking	Also known as black-and-white thinking, which allows for nothing in between the extremes; you are either perfect or a piece of garbage.	Beth thinks that if she doesn't get an A on a test, she has failed in life.
Mental filter	Magnifying the negative aspects of something while filtering out the positive.	Beth remembers only the things she did that were below her expectations but doesn't pay attention to (or remember) the things she did well.
Mind reading	Thinking you know exactly what other people are thinking, particularly as it relates to you.	Beth believes that she *knows* her professors think less of her because of what happened on the exams (when in fact they don't think less of her, but are concerned about her).
Catastrophic exaggeration	Thinking that your worst nightmare will come true and that it will be intolerable.	Beth's fear is that she'll be kicked out of school and end up homeless; a more likely reality is that she may have to take some courses over again.
Control beliefs	Believing either that you are helpless and totally subject to forces beyond your control, or that you must tightly control your life for fear that, if you don't, you will never be able to regain control.	Until talking to her family friend, Nina, Beth thought there was nothing she could do to change the downward spiral of events, and that she was either totally in control of her studying or else not in control at all.

Source: Adapted from Beck (1967).

Techniques

The RET therapist helps the client identify his or her irrational beliefs, relying on verbal persuasion (Hollon & Beck, 1994) and works through a sequence of techniques with the client, which can be remembered by the alphabetical sequence ABCDEF. Distressing feelings exist because an *activating event* (A) along with the person's *beliefs* (B) lead to a *highly charged emotional consequence* (C). It is not the event per se that created the problem, but rather the beliefs attached to the event that led to a problematic consequence. Thus, changing the beliefs will lead to a different consequence. This is done by helping the client *dispute* (D) the irrational beliefs and perceive their illogical and self-defeating nature. Such disputes lead to an *effect* (E; also called *effective new philosophies*), a new way of feeling and acting. Finally, clients may have to take *further action* (F) to solidify the change in beliefs. Each session is devoted to a specific aspect of the client's problem. Often at the outset of a session, client and therapist will determine what effect the client wants from the intervention.

Beth and a RET therapist might agree on what the effect should be when studying—namely, less anxiety—and would discuss the activating events (sitting down to study), beliefs (that if Beth does not do well on a test, she will be a failure as a person), and consequences (anxiety). The bulk of their work together would focus on disputing the beliefs: Beth is still a lovable person even if she doesn't do

Cognitive restructuring: The process of helping clients shift their thinking away from the focus on automatic, dysfunctional thoughts to more realistic ones.

well on a test, and even if she gets a B or C, her grade is not a failure, nor is she. The end result of this process is that Beth should feel less anxiety.

When working on a dispute, a RET therapist helps the client distinguish between a thought that is a "must" and one that is a "prefer." Beth's thought *I must get an A* is irrational and creates unpleasant feelings. Its more realistic counterpart is *I prefer to get an* A, which makes it clearer that she has some choice about the grade she sets as a goal. The therapist sometimes argues with the client to help him or her confront (and dispute) the faulty cognitions that contribute to the client's distress. The RET therapist may also use role playing to help the client practice new ways of thinking and behaving (Ellis, 1994b). RET can be helpful with anxiety, unassertiveness (Haaga & Davison, 1989), and unrealistic expectations. RET is generally not successful with psychotic disorders.

Beck's cognitive therapy often makes use of a daily record of dysfunctional thoughts (see Figure 15.3). Clients are asked to identify the situation in which their automatic negative thoughts (comparable to irrational beliefs) occurred, rate their emotional state (Emotions column), write down the automatic thought, their rational response to the automatic negative thoughts (comparable to the RET "dispute"), and then rerate their emotional state (Outcome column). Clients should rate their emotional state as lower after going through this process. Although this technique appears straightforward, it can be hard to use because the client has believed the "truth" of the automatic thought for so long that they don't seem to be distorted or irrational. The process of helping clients shift their thinking away from automatic, dysfunctional thoughts to more realistic ones is called **cognitive restructuring.** The therapist helps clients examine and assess the accuracy of the automatic thoughts, and search for alternative interpretations or solutions to their automatic thoughts and habitual ways of viewing themselves and the world.

FIGURE 15.3 Daily Record of Dysfunctional Beliefs

Situation	Emotion(s)	Automatic Thought(s)	Rational Response	Outcome
Actual event or stream of thoughts	Rate (1–100%)	ATs that preceded emotion Rate belief in ATs (1–100%)	Write rational response to ATs Rate belief in rational response (1–100%)	Rerate AT (1–100%)
1. Sit down to study	Anxious 70%	I won't be able to do as well on the test as I would like. —100% (Dichotomous thinking)	I might not be able to do as well as I want, but that doesn't mean that I will necessarily fail. —50%	Anxious 50%
2. In bed in the morning	Sad 80%	There's no point in getting out of bed—the day will be awful. I fail at everything I try. —90% (Mental filter)	Although I may not "succeed" in the goals I set for myself, it is possible that my expectations are too high, that I have too many expectations, or that I only notice the goals I don't attain, and don't notice the ones I do. —70%	Sad 6%

Keeping a written daily record like Beth's, shown here, can help identify triggers to dysfunctional, automatic thoughts and make them more rational.

Format adapted from Beck et al., 1979.

Cognitive therapy also makes use of **psychoeducation**—that is, educating clients about therapy and research findings pertaining to their disorders or problems. This knowledge is then used to help clients develop a more realistic, undistorted view of their problems. Beth was afraid to seek treatment because she was afraid she would be hospitalized; a cognitive therapist might explain to her the criteria for a hospital admission so this fear wouldn't become the basis for developing irrational automatic thoughts. Cognitive therapy has been found to be particularly helpful with panic and other anxiety disorders, depression, eating disorders, and anger management.

Cognitive–Behavior Therapy: An Assertiveness Training Example

In the last quarter of the 20th century, therapists began to use both cognitive and behavioral techniques within the same treatment. This merging of therapies grew out of the recognition that both cognitions and behaviors affect feelings and are a part of most psychological disorders. The two sets of techniques can work together to promote therapeutic change: Cognitive techniques change thoughts, which then affect feelings and behaviors; behavioral techniques change behaviors, which in turn lead to new experiences, feelings, ways of relating, and changes in how one thinks about oneself and the world. Assertiveness training is an example of cognitive–behavior therapy (CBT) that focuses on providing specific skills.

Assertiveness training is taught to people who have difficulty clearly communicating their preferences, feelings, thoughts, and ideas. They may be afraid of being ridiculed ("If I say what I think, they'll laugh at me") or of making others angry ("If I say what I think, he'll yell at me"); or they may never have really asked themselves their preferences because they were not taught to be assertive (historically, this has been more of an issue for women than for men). Or, they may become explosively angry when trying to express their desires. Assertiveness training involves helping people identify their irrational beliefs about being assertive ("If I tell them what's really on my mind, they might be upset" or "If I don't yell, they won't pay attention"). The cognitive component identifies irrational thoughts, and aims to change them. Moreover, although such thoughts may sometimes be irrational, at other times they may be appropriate. The therapy aims to help clients distinguish between the two types of situations. The behavioral component encourages people to try out assertive behaviors with the therapist (or other members of a therapy group) so that they can see how it feels to be assertive, discuss the reactions others might have, and learn how to respond to other people's reactions. If some of the people in the client's life really will be upset if some preferences or thoughts are articulated, part of the work in therapy will focus on how to handle that situation, identifying irrational thoughts about it, and developing appropriate ways to behave.

Despite differences between cognitive and behavioral therapies (see Table 15.2, p. 634), both approaches and the combined CBT are appropriate for a wide range of clients and disorders. Cognitive therapy, behavior therapy, and CBT provide the client with the opportunity to learn new coping strategies and to master new tasks.

● **Psychoeducation:** The process of educating clients about therapy and research findings pertaining to their disorders or problems.

TABLE 15.2 Differences Among Behavioral, Cognitive, and Cognitive–Behavior Therapies

Although behavioral, cognitive, and cognitive–behavior therapies all address a client's symptoms, focus on symptom relief as a goal in and of itself, and employ between-session homework, they also have differences.

Type of Therapy	Focus	Goal	Technique
Behavioral therapy	Maladaptive behaviors	Change the behavior, its antecedents, or its consequences	Relaxation techniques, systematic desensitization, exposure with response prevention, stimulus control, behavior modification, observational learning
Cognitive therapy	Automatic, irrational thoughts	Change dysfunctional, unrealistic thoughts to more realistic ones Recognize the relationships among thoughts, feelings, and behaviors	Cognitive restructuring (or Ellis's ABCDEF technique), psychoeducation, role playing
Cognitive–behavior therapy	Thoughts and behaviors	Goals of cognitive and behavioral therapies	Techniques of cognitive and behavioral therapies

Looking *at* Levels

Token Economies

As you have seen, behavioral techniques focus on changing maladaptive behaviors. They can also be used in inpatient psychiatric units. In these facilities, it is possible to change the response contingencies for an undesired behavior as well as for a desired behavior. Behavior modification can be used to change even severely maladaptive behaviors. Secondary reinforcers, those that are learned and don't inherently satisfy a biological need, are used in treatment programs not only with psychiatric patients but also with mentally retarded children and adults, and even in prisons. Patients and residents must earn "tokens" by behaving appropriately; these tokens then can be traded for small items such as cigarettes or candy at a "token store," or for privileges such as going out for a walk or watching a particular television show.

These **token economies**—treatment programs that use secondary reinforcers to change behavior—can be used to mold social behavior (level of the group) directly by modifying what patients say to one another and to nonpatients. For instance, using a token economy, hospitalized patients with schizophrenia can learn to talk to others, answer questions, or eat more normally. The token economy itself is a social creation, and it is only within the confines of the values of the culture that certain behaviors come to be reinforced and others extinguished. Choosing to reward patients for talking to each other (versus rewarding silence, for example) reflects the value placed on social interaction. Operant conditioning also modifies how patients perceive specific stimuli, such as when someone with schizophrenia begins to interpret a question as something that requires an answer (level of the person). At the level of the brain, operant conditioning can affect the dopamine-based reward system in the nucleus accumbens (see Chapter 6), increasing the likelihood that a reinforced behavior will occur again. Thus, behavior modification as a treatment for severely disturbed behavior can best be understood by regarding events at the three levels: how conditioning changes the brain and how it changes the meaning of stimuli, which in turn changes behavior. Moreover, such conditioning affects and is affected by social interactions. Although token economies can be effective, their use is declining because of ethical and moral questions about depriving patients and clients of secondary reinforcers (such as television, cigarettes, walks on the grounds) if they do not earn them through behavior change (Glynn, 1990).

TEST YOURSELF!

1. What is the focus of behavior therapy? What are some of its techniques?
2. What are the goals of cognitive therapy? What techniques are used?
3. How does cognitive–behavior therapy differ from cognitive or behavior therapy alone?

Insight-Oriented Therapies

If the therapist Beth contacted was an insight-oriented therapist, chances are that the therapist would begin by asking Beth about her past, how she felt about her family and her relationships with family members, and about her feelings in general. This therapist might ask surprisingly little about Beth's current anxiety or her depression.

Therapies that aim to remove distressing symptoms by leading someone to understand their causes through deeply felt personal insights are called **insight-oriented therapies.** The key idea underlying this approach is that once someone truly understands the causes of distressing symptoms (which often arise from past relationships), the symptoms themselves will diminish. Psychoanalysis is the original insight-oriented therapy; client-centered therapy is also considered an insight-oriented therapy because it rests on the belief that therapeutic change follows from the experience of insight.

Psychodynamic Therapy: Origins in Psychoanalysis

Developed by Sigmund Freud, **psychoanalysis** is a type of therapy directly connected to Freud's theory of personality, which holds that people's psychological difficulties are caused by conflicts among the three psychic structures of the mind: the id, ego, and superego. According to Freud, the id strives for immediate gratification of its needs, the superego tries to impose its version of morality, and the ego attempts to balance the demands of the id, superego, and external reality. These unconscious competing demands can create anxiety and other symptoms (see Chapter 11). The goal of psychoanalysis is to help patients understand the unconscious motivations that lead them to behave in specific ways; if the motivations and feelings remain unconscious, those forces are more likely to shape patients' behavior, without their awareness. According to this theory, only after true understanding—that is, insight—is attained can patients choose more adaptive, satisfying, and productive behaviors.

In psychoanalysis, patients talk about their problems, and the analyst tries to infer the root causes. Early on, this method was revolutionary because, before

● **Token economy:** A treatment program that uses secondary reinforcers (tokens) to bring about behavior modification.

● **Insight-oriented therapy:** Therapy that aims to remove distressing symptoms by leading people to understand their causes through deeply felt personal insights.

● **Psychoanalysis:** An intensive form of therapy, originally developed by Freud, based on the idea that people's psychological difficulties are caused by conflicts among the id, ego, and superego.

Psychoanalysis usually takes place 4 to 5 days a week for a number of years. Psychodynamic therapy can take place anywhere from several times a month to twice a week. The patient lies on a couch in psychoanalysis, and the analyst sits in a chair behind the couch, out of the patient's range of sight so that the patient can better free associate without seeing the analyst's reactions to his or her thoughts. In psychodynamic therapy, the client and therapist sit in chairs facing each other.

Freud, most European patients were treated medically for psychological problems. Freud started out using hypnosis but over time developed the method of **free association,** in which the patient says whatever comes into his or her mind. The resulting train of thought reveals the issues that concern the patient, as well as the way he or she is handling them. Because Freud (1900/1958) viewed dreams as the "royal road to the unconscious," another important feature of psychoanalysis is the use of **dream analysis,** the examination of the content of dreams to gain access to the unconscious. Freud did not believe that psychoanalysis was a cure, but rather that it could transform abject misery into ordinary unhappiness.

Psychoanalysis has declined in popularity over the last several decades for several reasons; one is the cost and time required for the four to five sessions per week. The average patient engages in 835 sessions before completing psychoanalysis (Voth & Orth, 1973), which usually lasts at least 4 years. Some patients who begin psychoanalysis never complete it. Psychoanalysis is rarely paid for by health insurance. A second reason for its decline is that studies have not generally found psychoanalytic treatment to be effective in treating various disorders, such as those discussed in Chapter 14.

A less intensive form of psychoanalytically oriented treatment, and one that is more common today, is **psychodynamic therapy.** Although based on psychoanalytic theory, its techniques differ in some important ways, including less frequent sessions and a decreased emphasis on sexual and aggressive drives. Recent trends in psychodynamic therapy include the development of short-term versions of psychotherapy (Bloom, 1997; Malan, 1976; Sifneos, 1992), which might involve therapy lasting 12 to 20 sessions and greater emphasis on current relationships (Greenberg & Mitchell, 1983; Kohut, 1977; Sullivan, 1953; Winnicot, 1958/1992). At

● **Free association:** A technique used in psychoanalysis and psychodynamic therapies in which the patient says whatever comes to mind and the train of thoughts reveals the patient's issues and ways of dealing with them.

● **Dream analysis:** A technique used in psychoanalysis and psychodynamic therapy in which the therapist examines the content of dreams to gain access to the unconscious.

● **Psychodynamic therapy:** A less intensive form of psychoanalysis.

least one study found that psychiatrists referring patients for psychological treatment do not refer all prospective patients to psychodynamic therapy, only those who are healthier and who do not have a personality disorder (Svanborg et al., 1999). Such patients seeking help for relationship difficulties may find insight attained through short-term therapy useful (Kivlighan et al., 2000).

Theory

The goal of psychodynamic therapy, like that of psychoanalysis, is to bring unconscious impulses and conflicts into awareness. Doing so leads to intellectual and emotional insights, which are supposed to give the patient more control over these impulses. With this control, the patient can actively and consciously *choose* behaviors instead of acting on unconscious impulses. Both psychoanalysis and psychodynamic therapy try to link the patient's current difficulties with past experiences, and both view the patient's relationship with the therapist as an integral part of treatment. Given the importance of relationships, the therapy relationship can provide a "corrective emotional experience"—that is, a new, positive experience of relationships, which can lead to changes in symptoms, behavior, and personality (Alexander & French, 1946).

From a psychodynamic perspective, Beth's anxiety and depression might reflect two competing desires. On the one hand, Beth wants to be different from her mother. Doing well in school and going on to graduate school represent a path different from that taken by her mother who, although she did well in college, elected not to pursue a graduate degree. Although her plan was not necessarily logically thought out, Beth hoped that by making different choices in her own life, she could avoid the intermittent depressions that had plagued her mother. On the other hand, Beth loves her mother, and the idea of academically passing a parent by, in essence, abandoning her, causes Beth to feel guilty about her accomplishments. Although Beth's anxiety and depression are upsetting and debilitating, part of her may feel relief that those symptoms prevent her from leaving her mother behind. Psychodynamic theory would say that, by gaining insight about these issues, Beth will not have to "act out" these ambivalent feelings (that is, impulsively or compulsively behave in a maladaptive way) and will have more control over her anxiety and depression.

Techniques

Along with dream analysis and free association, psychodynamic therapists rely on **interpretation,** deciphering the patient's words and behaviors and assigning unconscious motivations to them. Through the therapist's interpretations, the patient becomes aware of his or her motives and potential conflicts within the unconscious. The patient's own interpretations are not considered as accurate as those of the therapist because they are biased by the patient's own conflicts. Slips of the tongue—"Freudian slips"—are interpreted as having unconscious meanings. For example, should Beth tell her therapist that her mother recommended that she come to therapy (instead of her mother's friend, which was the case, and what she meant to say), her therapist might interpret this as Beth's wish that her mother would take care of her by suggesting that she seek therapy.

Through interpretation, patients also become aware of their defense mechanisms, unconscious mechanisms used to handle conflictual and distressing thoughts and feelings (see Chapter 11). At some point in the course of psychodynamic therapy, patients are likely to experience **resistance,** a reluctance or refusal

● **Interpretation:** A technique used in psychoanalysis and psychodynamic therapies in which the therapist deciphers the patient's words and behaviors, assigning unconscious motivations to them.

● **Resistance:** A reluctance or refusal to cooperate with the therapist, which can range from unconscious forgetting to outright refusal to comply with a therapist's request.

to cooperate with the therapist. Resistance can range from unconscious forgetting to outright refusal to comply with a therapist's request. Resistance can occur as the patient explores or remembers painful feelings or experiences in the past. Thus, if Beth comes late to a therapy session, a psychodynamic therapist might interpret this behavior as resistance: Perhaps Beth does not want to work on the issues currently being explored or is concerned about something that she doesn't want to share with her therapist.

Over the course of therapy, patients may come to relate to their therapist as they did to someone who was important in their lives, perhaps a parent. This phenomenon is called **transference.** If Beth began asking how the therapist is feeling, or if she began to talk less about her own distressing feelings because she worried that the therapist might become upset, Beth would be "transferring" onto her therapist her usual style of relating with her mother, in which she views her mother as fragile and needing protection. The therapeutic value of transference is that patients can talk about what they are experiencing (which they may very well have been unable to do with the parent) to heighten understanding. Moreover, the therapist's acceptance of uncomfortable or shameful feelings helps patients accept those feelings in order to *choose* whether to act on them. A psychodynamic therapist would likely interpret Beth's questions about the therapist's well-being as transference. Beth and her therapist would then talk about what it was like for Beth to feel so protective toward, and careful with, her mother.

Humanistic Therapy: Client-Centered Therapy

Like the humanistic approach to personality (see Chapter 11), humanistic therapy emphasizes free will, personal growth, self-esteem, and mastery. This approach is in contrast to psychodynamic therapy, which emphasizes the past, mental mechanisms, and the working through of conflictual impulses and feelings. One of the early proponents of humanistic psychology was Carl Rogers, who developed a therapeutic approach that came to be called **client-centered therapy,** which focuses on people's potential for growth and the importance of an empathic therapist.

Theory
Rogers viewed people's distressing symptoms as caused by a blocked potential for personal growth. The goal of client-centered therapy is to dismantle that block so that people can reach their full potential. Within the framework of Rogers, problems arise because of a lack of a coherent, unified sense of self. An example is a mismatch, or **incongruence,** between the *real self* (who you actually are) and the *ideal self* (who you would like to be). By helping people to become more like their ideal selves, client-centered therapy lessens the incongruence, and the client feels better. Within the framework of client-centered therapy, Beth's problems may stem from incongruence between her real self (a self that has to work hard for good grades and feels shame and guilt about the imperfections that remind her of her mother's depression) and her ideal self (a self that is without struggle—a good student who always does the "right thing" and who never experiences sadness, hopelessness, or anxiety). The tension between her real and ideal selves creates a fragmented sense of self, which drains Beth's time and energy; these different parts of herself are in conflict with each other and prevent her from reaching her full potential.

● **Transference:** The process by which patients may relate to their therapists as they did to some important person in their lives.

● **Client-centered therapy:** A type of insight-oriented therapy that focuses on people's potential for growth and the importance of an empathic therapist.

● **Incongruence:** According to client-centered therapy, a mismatch between a person's *real self* and his or her *ideal self.*

Techniques

The client-centered therapist should be warm, able to see the world as the client does, and able to empathize with the client. The therapist does not offer analyses to the client; instead the therapist reflects back the thrust of what the client has said. However, the therapist must not simply parrot the client's words or phrases but show *accurate* and *genuine* empathy. Such empathy lets the client know that he or she is really understood. If the therapist is inaccurate in reflecting what the client says, or if the empathy seems false, the intervention will fail. The therapist must also provide unconditional positive regard; that is, he or she must convey positive feelings for the client regardless of the client's thoughts, feelings, or actions. The therapist does this by continually showing the client that he or she is inherently worthy as a human being. According to the theory, genuine empathy and unconditional positive regard allow the client to decrease the incongruence between the real and ideal selves. Although Beth was unable to take some of her exams (real self), a client-centered therapist's empathy and unconditional positive regard would allow Beth to see that she is still smart (ideal self) and that everyone sometimes has negative, uncomfortable feelings. This therapeutic approach could help Beth see her real and ideal selves in a different light and allow her to think of herself more positively.

The client-centered therapist provides both genuine empathy and unconditional positive regard by making a distinction between the client as a person and the client's behaviors. The therapist could dislike a client's *behavior* but still view the client as a good person. If Beth were seeing a client-centered therapist, the topic of a therapy session might be what it was like for Beth during her mother's bouts of depression. A session might include this exchange:

BETH: I was so disappointed and ashamed when I'd come home from school and she'd still be in bed, wearing her bathrobe.

THERAPIST: Yes, it must have caused you to feel ashamed, anxious, and worried when you came home and found your mother still in bed.

BETH: And I felt that it was *my* fault, that I wasn't doing enough to make her feel better.

THERAPIST: Although you felt that it was your fault, you did all that you possibly could. You were concerned about her. You were, and still are, a good, worthwhile person.

BETH: And now I spend most of the day in bed and don't bother to get dressed . . . am I becoming like my mother?

THERAPIST: You and your mother are two separate individuals. Although you may have some things in common, and right now that may include depression, that doesn't mean that your path in life is identical to hers.

The therapist repeatedly emphasizes the worthiness of the client until the client comes to accept this valuation and is able to reach his or her potential, and make

Being rejected by a partner can leave a person feeling bad about him- or herself. Client-centered therapy would make a distinction between the person's *actions* in the relationship and the fact he or she is still a worthwhile, good person.

different, healthier choices and decisions. When successful, client-centered therapy can achieve its objective in a few months rather than years.

In sum, although there are differences between the insight-oriented therapies (Table 15.3), the clients most likely to benefit from these treatments are similar in that they are relatively healthy, articulate individuals who are interested in knowing more about their own motivations.

TABLE 15.3 Differences Between Psychodynamic and Client-Centered Therapies

Although psychodynamic and client-centered therapies have in common their use of insight, the treatments differ in some important ways, including the focus of treatment, its goals, and techniques.

Type of Therapy	Focus	Goal	Techniques
Psychodynamic therapy	Unconscious conflict and sexual/aggressive drives	To make unconscious conflict conscious	Free association, dream analysis, use of transference, interpretation
Client-centered therapy	Each person's unique experiences and potential for growth	To unblock the person's potential for growth by decreasing incongruence	Empathy, unconditional positive regard, genuineness toward the client

Looking *at* Levels

The Importance of Expressing Emotions

In both types of insight-oriented therapy, clients spend time focusing on and talking about their feelings. Does the expression of emotion have a therapeutic effect?

The answer appears to be yes. In studies where participants were asked to write about their feelings concerning a stressful event, participants had fewer doctor visits, improved immune functioning, and had a greater sense of well-being than those in the control group (these studies are discussed in greater detail in Chapter 13; see Esterling et al., 1999; Pennebaker et al., 1990). When participants were asked about their writing experiences, 76% described the benefits of writing as helping them attain insight: One said, "It made me think things out and really realize what my problem is" (Pennebaker et al., 1990). In fact, studies comparing the benefits of this particular form of expressive writing with the benefits of a few sessions of

psychotherapy have found both interventions to have similarly positive effects in the long run (Murray et al., 1989), although those participants seeing a psychotherapist had more positive moods immediately after therapy sessions compared with those using expressive writing, who had more negative moods immediately after writing. It is as if the act of deliberately processing the emotional experience, whether in writing or with a therapist, transforms the experience into a less upsetting event.

The psychotherapy sessions and writing exercises focused on feelings surrounding a traumatic event that occurred in the past, often an event about which the participants had not told anyone. Thus, the therapy and the writing provided opportunities for participants to think about issues that they had not previously explored. It should be noted, however, that most studies on emotional expression through writing have used relatively healthy college undergraduates as participants. It remains to be seen whether the therapeutic results would be the same with participants who are diagnosed with psychological disorders.

Nonetheless, these results about the positive effects of expressing emotions and gaining insight support some of the basic tenets of psychodynamic therapy specifically and of insight-oriented therapy more generally. Moreover, the outcome can be understood as emerging from events at different levels of analysis. Expressing feelings by making what is unconscious conscious and deriving insight (level of the person), may reduce stress, which in turn has an effect on the immune system (level of the brain; see Chapter 13). Further, participants in studies on emotional expressiveness report feeling better in the long run and attribute this positive emotional state to the insights gained (level of the person). At the level of the group, those gaining insight through therapy had less negative moods immediately after sessions in which they expressed emotions than did those writing about their feelings, illustrating the importance of expressing the feelings *with another person*. In addition, cultural factors led the participants to have certain beliefs about what would occur in the therapy sessions and how they might feel about the sessions.

TEST YOURSELF!

1. What is the focus of treatment in psychodynamic therapy? What are its main techniques?
2. How would client-centered therapists approach treatment? What techniques would they use?

Biomedical Therapies

Thinking about her mother's depression led Beth to wonder whether medication might help her own anxiety and depression. After her mother's last hospitalization 5 years earlier, Beth's mother had participated in a research study in the hospital, where she was treated successfully with antidepressant medication and cognitive–behavior therapy. Although her mother had tried medication many years before, it hadn't helped. Yet this new medication seemed to help a great deal. Might there be medications or other biomedical treatments that would help Beth feel better? With recent advances in knowledge about the brain have come advances in biomedical treatments of many disorders.

Psychopharmacology

The use of medication to treat psychological disorders and problems is known as **psychopharmacology.** In the last two decades, the number and types of medications for the treatment of psychological disorders have multiplied. As scientists learn more about the brain and neurotransmitter systems, researchers are able to develop new medications to target symptoms more effectively and with fewer side effects. Thus, for any given disorder, there are more medication options.

Schizophrenia and Other Psychotic Disorders

The most common type of medication for the treatment of schizophrenia and other psychotic disorders is **antipsychotic medication** (also called *neuroleptic medication*), which generally reduces psychotic symptoms but does not cure the disorder. Antipsychotic drugs have long been known to have an effect on the positive symptoms of schizophrenia (see Chapter 14), such as hallucinations. Traditional antipsychotic medications include Thorazine and Haldol. However, long-term use of these medications can cause **tardive dyskinesia,** an irreversible movement disorder in which the affected person involuntarily smacks his or her lips, displays

- **Psychopharmacology:** The use of medication to treat psychological disorders and problems.

- **Antipsychotic medication:** Medication that reduces psychotic symptoms.

- **Tardive dyskinesia:** An irreversible movement disorder in which the person involuntarily smacks his or her lips, displays facial grimaces, and exhibits other symptoms; caused by traditional antipsychotic medication.

facial grimaces, and exhibits other symptoms. *Atypical antipsychotics* are a new group of antipsychotic drugs that affect the neurotransmitter dopamine (as does traditional antipsychotic medication), as well as other neurotransmitters. For instance, the atypical antipsychotic medication Risperdal cuts down on the amount of free serotonin and dopamine available in the brain, which affects the ease with which signals cross synapses. In addition to decreasing positive symptoms, such as hallucinations, these newer drugs also counteract negative symptoms such as apathy, lack of interest, and withdrawal, and are effective in improving cognitive functioning (Keefe et al., 1999); all of which allow psychological therapies to be more effective (Ballus, 1997). These drugs also appear to have fewer side effects than traditional antipsychotic medication. There are increasing amounts of data suggesting that pharmacological treatment administered soon after the first psychotic episode is associated with a better long-term prognosis, compared to treatment begun later (see Chapter 14; Wyatt et al., 1997).

Mood Disorders

Effective pharmacological treatment for depression began in earnest in the 1950s with the discovery of **tricyclic antidepressants (TCAs),** named for the three rings in their chemical structure. Elavil is an example of this class of drug. For decades, TCAs were the only effective antidepressant medication readily available, although common side effects include constipation, dry mouth, blurred vision, and low blood pressure. These medications affect serotonin levels, and they can take weeks to work. Although another type of medication, **monoamine oxidase inhibitors (MAOIs),** was the first antidepressant medication discovered, MAOIs have never been as widely prescribed as TCAs, for two major reasons. First, MAOIs require users not to eat foods with tyramine (such as cheese and wine) because of potentially fatal changes in blood pressure. Second, they are particularly effective with atypical depression involving increased appetite and hypersomnia (increased need for sleep; Prien & Kocsis, 1995), and less effective with typical symptoms of depression.

Then **selective serotonin reuptake inhibitors (SSRIs),** such as Prozac, Zoloft, and Paxil, were developed in the 1980s. They have fewer side effects (they only work on *selective* serotonin receptors), and thus, people are less likely to stop taking them (Anderson, 2000); however, a common side effect is decreased sexual interest. In addition, many people experience a "Prozac poop-out" after a while, no longer attaining the same benefit from what had previously been an effective dosage. A meta-analysis of the use of Prozac in treating depression found an effectiveness rate comparable to that of TCAs, but not greater (Agency for Health Care Policy and Research, 1999).

Researchers continue to discover ways to alleviate symptoms of depression without as many side effects and to discover additional biological mechanisms so that those who do not respond to existing antidepressants can obtain relief from medication. Some newer antidepressants (such as Serzone, Effexor, and Remeron) don't fall into the existing categories; these drugs, which affect both the serotonin and norepinephrine systems, are sometimes referred to as **serotonin/norepinephrine reuptake inhibitors (SNRIs).** Antidepressant medications are also given to people experiencing dysthymia.

Studies of an extract from the flowering plant **St. John's wort,** *Hypericum perforatum,* suggest that it may be effective as a short-term treatment of mild to moderately severe depression (Agency for Health Care Policy and Research, 1999;

● **Tricyclic antidepressant (TCA):** A class of antidepressant medications named for the three rings in their chemical structure.

● **Monoamine oxidase inhibitor (MAOI):** A type of antidepressant medication that requires strict adherence to a diet free of tyramine-based foods.

● **Selective serotonin reuptake inhibitor (SSRI):** A type of antidepressant medication that affects only *selective* serotonin receptors, with relatively few side effects.

● **Serotonin/norepinephrine reuptake inhibitor (SNRI):** A newer type of antidepressant that affects both serotonin and norepinephrine neurotransmitter systems.

● **St. John's wort:** An herbal remedy for mild to moderate depression.

Gaster & Holroyd, 2000), although not without minor side effects. Further investigations about the exact dosages and long-term effects are under way. In addition, medications that block *substance P*, a neurotransmitter, show success in treating depression (Kramer et al., 1998; Rupniak, 2002), although further study will ultimately determine their effectiveness. Substance P–related medications do not operate by altering norepinephrine or serotonin, as do other antidepressants, but rather work by some other, as yet undetermined mechanism (Bender, 1998).

For bipolar disorder, mood stabilizers such as *lithium* can prevent a recurrence of both manic and depressive phases, although up to half of those with this disorder either will show no significant improvement or will be unable to tolerate the side effects. When this happens, a mood stabilizer such as Depakote or Tegretol is given to minimize the recurrence of manic episodes. During a manic episode, antipsychotic drugs or antianxiety drugs are often used. The usual medication regimen for schizophrenia and bipolar disorder may involve lifelong use of medication.

Anxiety Disorders

For most anxiety disorders (including panic disorder, the panic symptoms of phobias, and PTSD), **benzodiazepines** are often the medication prescribed. Xanax and Valium are types of benzodiazepines, which affect the target symptoms within 36 hours and do not need to be taken for 10 days or more to build up to an effective level, as is the case with antidepressants. However, they can cause drowsiness and are potentially lethal when taken with alcohol. In addition, a person using benzodiazepines can develop tolerance and dependence (see Chapter 5) and can experience withdrawal reactions. For these reasons, drugs of this class are often prescribed only for short periods of time, such as during a particularly stressful period. Antidepressants (TCAs, SSRIs, or SNRIs) may be prescribed for long-term treatment of anxiety disorders, although the dosage may be lower or higher than that used in the treatment of depression, depending on the anxiety disorder (Gorman & Kent, 1999; Kasper & Resinger, 2001; Rivas-Vazques, 2001). Obsessive-compulsive disorder can be treated effectively with SSRI antidepressants such as clomiprimine, although at a higher dose than that prescribed for depression or other anxiety disorders. Table 15.4 (p. 644) provides a summary of medications and their effects.

Electroconvulsive Therapy

Essentially a controlled brain seizure, **electroconvulsive therapy (ECT)** was developed in the 1930s as a treatment for schizophrenia. It was based on the idea that schizophrenia and epilepsy are incompatible, and thus that ECT-induced epilepsy would relieve the symptoms of schizophrenia. Although it did not cure schizophrenia, it is still a recommended treatment when medication does not work (Lehman & Steinwachs, 1998). ECT has been particularly helpful in treating certain mood disorders, specifically psychotic depression and manic episodes of bipolar disorder. In fact, 80% of those receiving ECT suffer from depression (Sackeim et al., 1995). Specifically, people most likely to receive ECT are those with severe depression who have not received much benefit from psychotherapy

Studies so far show that the herbal remedy St. John's wort can be effective in treating mild to moderately severe depression.

- **Benzodiazepine:** A type of antianxiety medication that affects the target symptoms within 36 hours and does not need to be taken for more than a week to be effective.

- **Electroconvulsive therapy (ECT):** A controlled brain seizure, used to treat people with certain psychological disorders such as psychotic depression or those for whom medication has not been effective or recommended.

TABLE 15.4 Summary of Medications and Their Effects

Type of Disorder	Type of Medication	Desired Effects	Side Effects
Schizophrenia and other psychotic disorders	Traditional antipsychotics	Decreases positive symptoms	Long-term use can cause tardive dyskinesia.
	Atypical antipsychotics	Decreases positive and negative symptoms	
Depression	Tricyclics SSRIs/SNRIs St. John's wort	More effective with typical depressive symptoms	Tricyclics: Constipation, dry mouth, blurred vision, low blood pressure. SSRIs: Decreased sex drive.
	MAOIs	More effective with atypical depressive symptoms	MAOIs: Potentially lethal in combination with tyramine-related foods.
Bipolar disorder	Lithium	Decreases mood swings	Kidney or gastrointestinal problems; dry mouth.
Anxiety disorders	Tricyclics, SSRIs/SNRIs	Decreases panic symptoms with regular use	See "Depression" side-effects above.
	Benzodiazepines	Short term use: Decreases panic symptoms	Drowsiness; tolerance and withdrawal with continued use; potentially lethal if combined with alcohol.

or medication (Lam et al., 1999), or those for whom drugs are inadvisable for medical reasons. Although the treatment can be effective, the reasons are not well understood. The patient is given a muscle relaxant before each ECT treatment and is under anesthesia during the procedure; because of the anesthesia, ECT is administered in a hospital and generally requires a hospital stay. Patients may experience temporary memory loss for events right before, during, or after each treatment. After a course of 6 to 12 sessions over several weeks, usually twice a week (Shapira et al., 1998; Vieweg & Shawcross, 1998), depression often lifts; relief may come sooner for the depressed elderly (Tew et al., 1999).

ECT was considered a major biomedical treatment in the 1940s and 1950s, but the ready availability of medications in subsequent decades led to a decline in its use. Another reason for its decreased use was that some patients seemed to experience significant cognitive impairment, including memory loss. And, as it became known that it was sometimes used in understaffed institutions to produce a docile patient population, ECT became politically unpopular. However, improvements in the way ECT is administered have significantly reduced the cognitive deficits and undesirable side effects, and since the 1980s, the use of ECT has increased (Glass, 2001). However, severely depressed patients helped by ECT are at risk to relapse, particularly if they do not take medication after ECT treatments end (Sackeim et al., 2001). The increase in ECT's use reflects a new appreciation of its effectiveness, and a recognition that not all people with depression, mania, or schizophrenia can either take medication or find it helpful. In recent years,

ECT is more frequently administered to affluent patients than to those in publicly funded hospitals (Sackeim et al., 1995).

Transcranial Magnetic Stimulation

A new treatment currently being researched is transcranial magnetic stimulation (TMS) (see Chapter 2), a procedure in which an electromagnetic coil on the scalp transmits pulses of high-intensity magnetism to the brain in short bursts lasting 100 to 200 microseconds. Although it is not yet known exactly how this magnetic field changes brain neurophysiology and neurochemistry, TMS has varying effects, depending on the exact location of the coil on the head. Placebo studies of TMS (in which the procedure of TMS is administered, but at an angle that does not affect the brain) have found actual TMS to be more effective than the placebo (George et al., 1999; Klein et al., 1999). Studies of people with depression who have not responded to medication have yielded positive results, with depressive symptoms decreasing after TMS (Epstein et al., 1998; Figiel et al., 1998; Klein et al., 1999). Some studies have found that severely depressed people receiving TMS respond as well as those receiving ECT (Dannon et al., 2002; Janicak et al., 2002). Should additional studies confirm these early positive results, TMS offers a number of advantages over ECT, including easier administration (it requires neither anesthesia nor hospitalization) and minimal side effects. The most common short-term side effect, experienced by 5 to 20% of patients, is a slight headache.

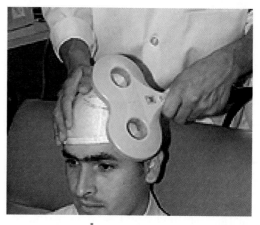

Unlike with ECT, the person receiving transcranial magnetic stimulation is awake and does not need anesthesia.

TMS has been administered to people with depression, bipolar disorder (Grisaru, Chudakov et al., 1998), schizophrenia (George et al., 1999; Hoffman et al., 2003), OCD (Alonso et al., 2001), and PTSD (Grisaru, Amir et al., 1998). But more research is necessary before TMS can definitively be declared a treatment of choice rather than an experimental one. Information about the precise optimum location of the coil and the frequency and intensity of the stimulation is needed.

Looking *at* Levels

Less Depression Through the Placebo Effect

The goal of any treatment for depression is to lessen the symptoms at the level of the person (such as distress, depressed mood, negative or unrealistic thoughts of the self) and group (such as social withdrawal), as well as to right imbalances in the brain (such as by normalizing neurotransmitter function) and decrease biological symptoms of depression (such as appetite and sleep changes). Treatments that target events at primarily one level will in turn affect events at other levels. For instance, successful cognitive therapy also causes changes in the biological symptoms of depression (appetite and sleep) as well as changes in neurotransmitters that are not yet well understood. Social relations are also improved.

Successful treatment with medication (level of the brain) also affects symptoms at the levels of the person and group. But the interaction among events at different levels doesn't stop there. Even when taking medication, the person's beliefs and expectations about the medication (level of the person) can affect the individual's symptoms through the *placebo effect*, the healing effect that occurs after taking a medically inactive substance that nevertheless seems to have medicinal effects. Consider that a meta-analysis of the effectiveness of antidepressants found that about 75–80% of the effect of antidepressants can be achieved with a placebo. Only about 25% of the response to an antidepressant arises from the active ingredients in the medication. Thus, among those helped by an antidepressant, much—if not most—of the positive response arises from expectations that symptoms will get better (Kirsch & Lynn, 1999; Kirsch et al., 2002a; Kirsch & Sapirstein, 1998; Walach & Maidhof, 1999). In addition, more than half of the antidepressant studies funded by drug companies found that medication and placebo were equally effective (Kirsch et al., 2002a; Kirsch et al., 2002b).

When the placebo has ingredients that mimic the side effects of antidepressants (so that the patients think they are taking the med-

ication and not a placebo), the difference in effectiveness between the true antidepressant and the placebo is even smaller (Greenberg & Fisher, 1989). Moreover, depressed people taking either an SSRI or a placebo medication had similar changes in brain functioning (Leuchter et al., 2002). Thus, someone's *beliefs* about what will happen after taking antidepressant medication (level of the person) affect what happens (level of the brain), which in turn affects their interactions with others (level of the group).

Note that this does *not* mean that people taking antidepressants should necessarily go off their medication. Taking a placebo is *not* the same as not taking a medication. Rather, it appears that the act of taking a placebo promotes biological changes that would not otherwise occur.

TEST YOURSELF!

1. What are different types of medications that can be used to treat psychological disorders?
2. What is ECT, and what disorders does it help alleviate?
3. Why might TMS be a better treatment for some than ECT?

Other Forms of Treatment

During the course of her therapy, Beth talked about her vivid memories of her mother's episodes of depression, about the times when she would lie in bed most of the day. However, her mother had not had an episode of severe depression in the last 5 years. Beth was surprised when her therapist raised the possibility of having her mother come in for a few sessions; the idea had not occurred to her.

Beth's questions about treatment continued. Cost-related forces were changing the way health care was delivered. How might these changes affect her mother and the course of her own therapy? As health insurance companies and health care professionals seek ways to provide effective treatment in a time- and cost-efficient manner, some psychological therapies have changed; today, there is more of an emphasis on considering a wider array of treatments that might be helpful and on intervening early.

Modalities: When Two or More Isn't a Crowd

● **Modality:** A form of therapy.

● **Individual therapy:** A therapy modality in which an individual client is treated by a single therapist.

Each therapy approach mentioned thus far can be implemented in a variety of **modalities,** or forms. **Individual therapy**—therapy in which one client is treated by one therapist—is a modality. Other modalities have one or more therapists working with a family, or with a group of people who share some commonality, such as a diagnosis of agoraphobia. Each theoretical orientation discussed earlier can be used in these various modalities: individual, group, or family.

Group Therapy

Clients with compatible needs who meet together with one or two therapists are engaging in **group therapy.** This modality became more frequently offered after World War II, when there were many more veterans seeking treatment than therapists available to treat them individually. The course of treatment can range from a single occasion (usually an educational session) to ongoing treatment lasting for years. Some groups are for members who have a particular problem or disorder, focusing on, for instance, recent divorce

Group therapy can help reduce shame and isolation and can provide support and an opportunity to interact differently with other people.

or posttraumatic stress disorder. These groups may offer emotional support, psychoeducation, concrete strategies for managing the problem or disorder. Other groups have members who may not share such a specific problem or disorder, but rather who want to learn more about maladaptive or inappropriate ways in which they are interacting with people; the therapy group provides an opportunity to change their patterns of behavior. Therapy groups can have theoretical orientations ranging from psychodynamic to client-centered, to CBT, or other orientations.

In addition to offering information, support, and (if the group has a cognitive–behavioral orientation) between-session homework assignments, group therapy provides something that individual therapy cannot: interaction with other people who are experiencing similar difficulties. The group experience can decrease the sense of isolation and shame that clients sometimes feel. In revealing their own experiences and being moved by others', clients often come to see their own lives and difficulties in a new light. Also, because some clients' problems involve interpersonal interactions, the group provides a safe opportunity for clients to try out new behaviors.

Family Therapy

In **family therapy,** a family as a whole, or a subset of some of its members, such as a couple, is treated. "Family" is often defined as those who think of themselves or function as a family; thus, blended families created by marriage are seen in family therapy, as are other nontraditional families. The most common theoretical orientation among those providing family therapy is **systems therapy,** which starts from the premise that no client is an island: A client's symptoms occur in a larger context, or system (the family and subculture), and any change in one part of the system will affect the rest of the system. Thus, the client is referred to as the "identified patient," although the system (the couple, the family) is considered the "patient" that is to be treated. Systems therapy was originally used exclusively with families; in fact, some of the pioneers in systems therapy would refuse to see individuals without their families. For this reason, systems therapy is sometimes referred to as "family therapy," although this is a misnomer. Some therapists treat entire families, but not necessarily from a systems approach. They may use a psychodynamic or behavioral approach. Similarly, some systems therapists see individuals without their families, but the therapy makes use of systems theory. Systems therapy can also be the theoretical framework used to treat couples in therapy.

● **Group therapy:** A therapy modality in which a number of clients with compatible needs meet together with one or two therapists.

● **Family therapy:** A therapy modality in which a family (or certain members of a family) is treated.

● **Systems therapy:** A type of therapy that views a client's symptoms as occurring in a larger context, or system (the family and subculture), in which a change in one part of the system affects the rest of the system.

FIGURE 15.4 Systems Therapy: Family Interaction

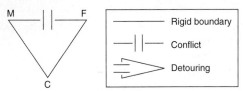

This triangle graphically represents the following type of family interaction: The mother and father criticize each other and then reroute their conflict by both attacking their child. Systems therapy would focus on decreasing the conflict between the parents and strengthening their relationship.

From Minuchin, 1974, pp. 53, 61. Adapted and reprinted by permission of the publisher from *Families and Family Therapy* by Salvador Minuchin. Cambridge, Mass.: Harvard University Press, Copyright © 1974 by the President and Fellows of Harvard College.

● **Paradoxical intention:** A systems therapy technique that encourages a behavior that seems contradictory to the desired goal.

● **Reframing:** A therapy technique in which the therapist offers a new way of conceptualizing, or "framing," the problem.

● **Validation:** A therapy technique in which the therapist conveys his or her understanding of the client's feelings and wishes.

● **Self-help group:** A group whose members focus on a specific disorder or event and do not usually have a clinically trained leader; also called a *support group*.

Systems therapy focuses on family communication, structure, and power relationships. The theory views the identified patient's symptoms as attempts to convey a message. Initially, a systems therapist takes a family history to discover which members of the family are close to one another or angry with one another, and to ascertain more generally how anger, sadness, and other feelings or issues are handled within the family. Systems therapists often illustrate these relationships graphically (see Figure 15.4). In some cases, one parent may be underinvolved and the other overinvolved; treatment would be directed to encourage the underinvolved parent to be more involved, and the overinvolved parent to be less involved. Or, the parents' relationship with each other may need strengthening, with consequences for other family members, because conflict between parents affects their children's behavior (Kitzmann, 2000). For instance, in a family in which the parents fight a lot, an adolescent boy's rebelliousness may serve to unite his parents in their anger and frustration at him. The systems therapist might explain to the family that their son was purposefully being rebellious to keep his parents united, for fear of what would happen to the parents' relationship if he weren't causing them problems. The family therapist might praise the son for his efforts at keeping his parents together, and even urge him not to stop rebelling yet, because his parents hadn't yet practiced how to relate to each other without fighting. This type of intervention is sometimes referred to as **paradoxical intention,** which encourages a behavior that seems contradictory to the desired goal (Stanton, 1981). This technique has also been called "prescribing the symptom" and is useful in treating families who appear resistant or unable to change, or who aren't able to implement suggestions from the therapist. Other techniques include **reframing,** in which the therapist offers a new way of conceptualizing, or "framing," the problem, and **validation,** in which the therapist conveys his or her understanding of clients' feelings and wishes (Minuchin, 1974; Minuchin & Fishman, 1981).

A therapist with a systems orientation treating Beth might, after taking a family history, reframe the problem. The therapist might propose that Beth is sacrificing herself: Beth's difficulties allow her mother to be a "good mother" to Beth in ways she had not been when Beth was younger, such as frequently checking how Beth is doing. Thus, Beth's illness serves the function of allowing her mother to feel good about herself as a mother. The therapist might also validate Beth's offering of herself in this way—suggesting that her concern for her mother is so great that she would allow herself to sacrifice her own current opportunities in order to provide this opportunity for her mother. The therapist might even give Beth a paradoxical intention: Beth should not get better until her mother becomes a "nervous wreck" worrying about Beth. This paradoxical intention serves the purpose of indirectly pointing out how Beth's behavior may in fact have the opposite effect of the one she desires.

Self-Help Therapies

Self-help groups (sometimes referred to as *support groups*) can be used on their own or as a supplement to psychotherapy, and are focused on a specific disorder or event. They do not usually have a clinically trained leader, although a mental health professional may be involved in some capacity (Shepherd et al.,

1999). Alcoholics Anonymous (AA), the first self-help program, is based on 12 steps of recovery. Most 12-step programs view a belief in a Higher Power (for most people, God) as crucial to recovery, and meta-analytic results show that weekly attendance in group meetings is associated with drug or alcohol abstinence, whereas less than weekly attendance is not (Fiorentine, 1999). People who are not religious can also benefit from attending AA meetings (Winzelberg & Humphreys, 1999), or meetings of Smart Recovery, an organization that is based on cognitive behavioral principles. Another self-help group that does not use the 12-step approach is the National Depressive and Manic Depressive Association, which helps those suffering from bipolar disorder or depression, and their families and friends. Self-help groups are not only valuable sources of information and support, they can also make referrals to therapists who are knowledgeable about the particular disorder or problem. Relatives of those with a psychological disorder report that such groups are helpful in providing support and self-understanding (Citron et al., 1999). As is true in group therapy, self-help groups can be invaluable in decreasing feelings of isolation and shame.

The last two decades have witnessed a proliferation of self-help books and tapes dealing with a wide range of problems; the use of such materials is sometimes referred to as **bibliotherapy.** Many of these materials incorporate philosophies and techniques of the therapies discussed in this chapter, and therapists often suggest that clients read particular books (Starker, 1988). Although such material can help with depression and anxiety, people trying to eliminate habits such as smoking, drinking, and overeating were not helped as much. Not surprisingly, those who complied with the materials' recommendations fared better than those who did not (Gould & Clum, 1993).

Another vehicle for self-help is the Internet, where there are "support groups" in chat rooms, self-help treatments, and psychoeducation. However, buyer beware: information on a Web site may not be accurate, and people in an online support group may not be who they claim to be (Finn & Banach, 2000; Waldron et al., 2000). Some of the Web-based self-help cognitive–behavioral programs are better than no treatment (Carlbring et al., 2001), but whether they are as effective as the treatment provided by a mental health clinician awaits further research.

Meta-analyses revealed that self-help materials help primarily people with depression (Cuijpers, 1997), headache, sleep disturbances, and fears (Gould & Clum, 1993), and these material can also reduce anxiety (Finch et al., 2000; Scogin et al., 1990). At least for many people, self-administered treatment programs available through books and audiotapes appear to be more effective than no treatment at all (Scogin et al., 1990).

Innovations in Psychotherapy

As psychologists learn more about effective treatments, treatment changes. Changes also occur as a result of technological and economic realities.

Psychotherapy Integration: Mixing and Matching

In the last quarter century, many therapists have moved away from identifying their work as exclusively from one theoretical orientation, such as psychodynamic or behavioral. Surveys found that between 68% (Jensen et al., 1990) and 98% (Smith, 1982) of mental health professionals identify themselves as eclectic in orientation. A therapist using **psychotherapy integration** uses techniques from different theoretical orientations, with an overarching theory of how the integrated techniques will achieve the goals of treatment. A therapist's integrating of specific techniques *without* regard for an overarching theory is referred to as **technical eclecticism** (Beutler & Hodgson, 1993). This integrative approach includes incorporating new techniques based on research findings and the clinical needs of a particular client at a specific point in the treatment (Stricker, 1993). Such an approach

● **Bibliotherapy:** The use of self-help books and tapes for therapeutic purposes.

● **Psychotherapy integration:** The use of techniques from different theoretical orientations with an overarching theory of how the integrated techniques will be used to achieve the goals of treatment.

● **Technical eclecticism:** The use of specific techniques that may benefit a particular client, without regard for an overarching theory.

provides the aspects of therapy that are common to all theoretical orientations (such as offering hope, a caring listener, and a new way of thinking about problems) and employs specific techniques for a given disorder (Weinberger et al., 1995), such as exposure with response prevention for people with OCD. Two clients with the same diagnosis may receive different integrative treatments from the same therapist, based on factors other than diagnosis—perhaps family issues, client preference for directive versus nondirective treatment, and other concerns.

Managed Care and Psychotherapy

The cost of health care in general became extremely expensive in the last two decades of the 20th century, and the system of health care administration known as *managed care* was developed as a way to contain costs. Managed care seeks to limit the expense of health care while providing services deemed medically necessary by health care administrators. In mental health, one way to reduce costs has been to limit the amount of inpatient and outpatient services. Thus, psychological therapies, regardless of theoretical orientation or modality, have tried to meet the challenge of attaining the same level of effectiveness in a reduced number of sessions. There is in fact some support for the idea that a time limit on psychotherapy can accelerate the rate of therapeutic change (Reynolds et al., 1996).

Although therapists have become adept at helping clients get better in fewer sessions, it is unclear whether brief therapy provides long-term positive change or protection against relapse. There is a dose–effect relationship between therapy and outcome: the more therapy, the greater its positive effect. The standard of what constitutes good care is being driven not by clinicians, but by the financial bottom line. Many of the studies examining the effectiveness of time-limited psychotherapy were based on treatments of approximately 20 sessions, more than is currently allowed by some insurance companies, except in the case of chronic mental illness such as schizophrenia. Note, however, that for many specific phobias, brief—even one session—treatments can be very effective (Hellström & Öst, 1995; Öst et al., 1997; Öst et al., 2001).

Strupp (1997; Strupp & Hadley, 1977) suggests that three groups should determine how mental health is defined: society (of which managed care is a part), which determines the use of funds and defines mental health via stability, conformity, and predictability; the individual client, who often defines mental health subjectively; and the mental health professional, who may define mental health according to a theoretical approach.

Time and Therapy: Therapy Protocols and Brief Therapy

The last 25 years has seen a rise in the use of *therapy protocols*, detailed session-by-session manuals of how therapy should proceed for a specific disorder from a certain theoretical orientation (such as behavioral treatment for panic disorder or cognitive therapy for depression). These manual-based treatments were created, in part, to ensure that when a research study was testing a given therapy's effectiveness (for example, CBT), all CBT therapists were actually using the same techniques in the same way. This meant, of course, that the results of the study were in fact relevant to the treatment's effectiveness because all therapies of the same orientation were comparable. Some clinicians advocate the use of therapy performed without deviation from treatment manuals (Addis, 1997). However, a large manual-based treatment study of panic disorder found that, even when therapists adhere to the manual, the therapist, as an individual, makes his or her own unique contribution to the treatment (Huppert et al., 2001; Malik et al., 2003).

A drawback of research studies using manual-based treatment is that they often exclude people whose symptoms do not meet the exact criteria for a disorder, or who may simultaneously have more than one diagnosis (such as depression *and* panic disorder). Even if a treatment is found to be helpful for people who have only one diagnosis, the same treatment may not be helpful for those with that diagnosis plus another disorder (Seligman, 1995).

Many of the protocols were developed for treatment lasting 15 to 20 sessions. Today, many managed care programs in different parts of the United States will approve 3 to 10 sessions, and the therapist must request additional sessions. Thus, although the course of treatment is becoming briefer, the total number of sessions cannot be used in a systematic way and may not fit into many of the existing protocols. Research indicates that those with focused problems in one sphere of life (such as work) receive more benefit from brief psychotherapy than those who have difficulties in multiple spheres (Barkham & Shapiro, 1990; Klosko et al., 1990; Strupp & Binder, 1984).

In the future, computer technology will be commonly used to facilitate brief treatment. Research on the use of palmtop computers preprogrammed with cognitive–behavioral tasks found that 4 weeks of computer-assisted treatment (plus 8 weeks of practice with the palmtop) was, as determined at follow-up, as effective as 12 weeks of regular cognitive–behavior therapy (Newman, Kenardy et al., 1997).

High-tech gadgets such as this palmtop computer are at the cutting edge of brief cognitive-behavior treatments, preprogrammed with cognitive–behavioral tasks to help participants self-monitor their thoughts.

Cybertherapy: Doctor Online

A new form of treatment is **cybertherapy,** or therapy over the Internet. This sort of therapy may be helpful for those who have no ready access to mental health services: rural residents, the severely medically ill, or people with agoraphobia. Several types of cybertherapeutic interactions are possible. One involves an Internet version of individual therapy, such as a "pay-for-each-response" e-mail exchange with a therapist. However, most therapists consider this type of cybertherapy to be less than an optimally desirable form of treatment. First, the anonymity offered via the Internet cuts two ways, and the "therapist" offering this service may not be professionally trained or licensed. Second, confidentiality and privacy cannot be guaranteed on the Internet. Third, the multitude of nonverbal cues (facial expressions, tone of voice) that pass between client and therapist are absent during cybertherapy (Bloom, 1998); although some people are using webcams to provide nonverbal cues, the video quality still leaves something to be desired. On the plus side, it has been argued that simply having to put thoughts and feelings on paper (or rather, on screen) can be therapeutic, as can the ability to have a complete transcript of the treatment for later reading and reflection (Murphy & Mitchell, 1998). Other types of cybertherapy include "live" two-person chat rooms or therapist-led on-line support groups. Although some studies show that cybertherapy is more effective than no treatment (Lange et al., 2001), there is little research on whether cybertherapy is as effective as face-to-face therapy. E-mail has also been used in family therapy in cases when members of the family lived too far away to attend sessions (King et al., 1998). The effectiveness of this tool in the realm of family therapy has yet to be rigorously tested.

● **Cybertherapy:** Therapy over the Internet.

Prevention: Sometimes Worth More Than a Pound of Cure

Programs intended to prevent mental illness aim to halt the development or progression of psychological disorders by using social or cultural interventions. *Universal preventive interventions* target all members of a general group, some of whom may be at higher risk to develop a given disorder (Mrazek & Haggerty, 1994). Examples of universal prevention programs might include school programs on suicide or drug abuse prevention.

Selective preventive interventions target subgroups of the population who have a higher risk to develop a given disorder than the general population (Mrazek & Haggerty, 1994). For instance, research suggests that children with a depressed parent are at higher risk than those without a depressed parent to develop psychological disorders such as depression, anxiety disorders, and alcohol dependence (Weissman et al., 1997). People at risk might receive cognitive therapy to help modify any irrational automatic thoughts that could lead to depression; a study that provided CBT to such at-risk adolescents helped minimize the later development of depression (Clarke et al., 2001). Programs in selective prevention may be administered by a community mental health center, hospital, or other facility providing mental health services.

Indicated preventive interventions target those at higher risk who have some symptoms of a disorder, but not a full disorder (Mrazek & Haggerty, 1994). An example involves an experimental treatment for adolescents at extremely high risk to develop schizophrenia: Some of these young people are given a low dose of an antipsychotic medication at the first signs of symptoms (but before psychosis develops) and others are given a placebo. The hope is that such an early intervention will minimize the frequency and duration of episodes of schizophrenia, and early results indicate that such intervention efforts can be effective (Cannon et al., 2002; McGorry & Edwards, 1998). Community mental health centers and hospitals, which came into existence to treat those with psychological disorders who could not otherwise afford help, offer selective interventions.

Some prevention programs are available through publicly funded services such as community rape crisis centers or Head Start preschool programs. Others may be offered through private sources, such as health insurance companies or employers. For example, these organizations may offer stress management programs or support groups for relatives of those diagnosed with Alzheimer's disease (who experience significant amounts of stress and are at risk for developing disorders such as anxiety and depression).

Employee stress management programs are an example of universal prevention.

Looking *at* Levels

Treating Obsessive-Compulsive Disorder

We know that some treatments are more effective than others for a given disorder. What about for OCD? Does effective behavior therapy exert its beneficial effect and work in a similar way as effective medication? Until recently this question could not have been answered. But neuroimaging has made it possible to begin to understand the positive effects of both medication and psychotherapy. We can understand their effects by looking at events at the three levels and their interactions.

Obsessive-compulsive disorder (OCD) is marked by intrusive, illogical thoughts and overpowering compulsions to repeat certain acts, such as hand washing to get rid of germs (see Chapter 14). In some cases, OCD can be disabling. The brain activity of nine people with OCD was examined by PET scanning before and after behavior therapy (which included exposure with response prevention) (Baxter et al., 1992), as were the brains of nine people with OCD before and after they received fluoxetine (Prozac), a serotonergic medication that suppresses some of the symptoms of OCD. The scans revealed that behavior therapy and Prozac both change the way a certain part of the brain works. In both cases, the activity in the right caudate (part of the basal ganglia involved in automatic behaviors) decreased following the intervention. The drug also affected the anterior cingulate and thalamus, both of which are involved in attention. The effects of behavior therapy on the brain were replicated by Schwartz, Stoessel and colleagues (1996).

At the level of the person, trying new behaviors (such as not washing dirty hands or not rechecking a locked door) and experiencing the success of not *having* to perform the compulsions gives the patient a sense of mastery and hope, which leads him or her to keep engaging in the new behavior. At the level of the brain, the therapy actually changed the way specific neural structures function. At the level of the group, it was interactions with another person—the therapist—that changed the brain. In addition, personal relationships changed. For example, some of the time and energy that was devoted to OCD rituals could now be spent on relationships. Thus, events at the three levels of analysis and their interactions inform us about different aspects of the disorder.

TEST YOURSELF!

1. What are other forms, or modalities, of therapy besides individual therapy?
2. Name and explain innovations in psychotherapy.
3. What are some types of prevention programs for psychological disorders?

Which Therapy Works Best?

After a number of sessions, Beth began to feel better. She was going to class more often, and felt better able to handle studying and preparing for tests. She wanted to know what it was about the therapy that was helping her, and why her therapist used specific techniques at certain times. Her treatment had not included medication, and she still wondered whether she would be feeling even better—or worse—if she had taken medication. She also wondered whether her therapy would be as effective for other people in her situation. If her best friend went to see Beth's therapist for anxiety and depression, would her friend fare as well as Beth?

Issues in Psychotherapy Research

More than 400 types of psychotherapy are currently available (Garfield & Bergin, 1994), but many of them do not rest on well-constructed and replicated research. Research on psychotherapy is crucial for determining how well a new or old therapy treats a particular problem. It is easy to claim that a new therapy is a wonder cure, but harder to back up that claim with solid data. There are many issues to consider when evaluating findings about psychotherapy.

Researching Psychotherapy

Research that asks whether the client is feeling better, functioning better, living more independently, or has fewer symptoms after treatment is called **outcome research.** These questions are trickier to answer than it would seem because they depend on how you define "outcome"; in research lingo, the answers to the questions depend on what you designate as the therapy's dependent variable. For example, you could have clients rate their thoughts, feelings, or behaviors, which are not necessarily highly correlated and might yield different outcomes (Kazdin, 1994). You must also decide how long after the end of treatment to assess outcome: immediately afterward? a month later? a year later? Moreover, in their review of studies, Luborsky and colleagues (1999) noticed an "allegiance effect": Researchers of a particular orientation tend to find evidence supporting that orientation.

Initially, much outcome research focused on assessing the superiority of one treatment over another, not taking into account clients' diagnoses. Results revealed that therapy was more effective than no therapy. Most often, the no-therapy group was a wait-list control, people who were on a waiting list for therapy but had not yet received treatment (Lambert & Bergin, 1994). The findings also seemed to suggest that therapies included in those research studies were equally effective, a position later described as the *dodo bird verdict* of psychotherapy (Luborsky et al., 1975), named for the Dodo bird in *Alice's Adventures in Wonderland*, who declared, "Everyone has won, and all must have prizes." (Note that this does *not* mean that all therapies are equally effective, only those that were studied; Beutler, 2000.)

But is the dodo bird verdict all there is to it? Several questions, listed in Table 15.5, should be addressed when designing or evaluating studies of psychotherapy,

TABLE 15.5 Questions About Psychotherapy Research

1. Are the participants randomly assigned?
2. Is a specific disorder being treated?
3. Are there exclusion criteria (must participants have only one diagnosis)?
4. Are the therapists' treatments representative of their stated approaches?
5. What types of outcome measures are selected, who is the evaluator, and how is success defined?
6. Are clients more likely to drop out of some types of therapy than others?
7. Is a follow-up assessment planned, and if so, at what interval of time after the end of treatment?

Source: Kazdin (1994).

● **Outcome research:** Research that asks whether, after psychotherapy, the client is feeling better, functioning better, living more independently, has fewer symptoms.

and the answers to these questions determine what conclusions can be reached and how far those conclusions can generalize. Let's look at one well-known investigation in detail.

Initiated in 1977, the National Institute of Mental Health sponsored a study called the Treatment of Depression Collaborative Research Program, or TDCRP, to assess the effectiveness of four different treatments for depression: cognitive–behavior therapy (CBT); interpersonal therapy (IPT); antidepressant medication (the TCA imipramine; the study predates SSRIs) with supportive visits with a psychiatrist (ICI-CM, "CM" for "clinical management"); and a placebo medication with supportive visits with a psychiatrist (PLA-CM). These groups are shown in Figure 15.5.

FIGURE 15.5 The Four Groups in the Treatment of Depression Collaborative Research Program

| Cognitive–behavior therapy **CBT** | Interpersonal therapy **IPT** | Imipramine and clinical management (an antidepressant and supportive medical visits) **ICI-CM** | Placebo medication and clinical management **PLA-CM** |

Interpersonal therapy (IPT) can be considered an insight-oriented therapy; it focuses on issues that arise in the client's current relationships, and attempts to link what happens in those relationships to mood. The goal of IPT is to help the client's relationships work better and become more satisfying. IPT rests on the assumption that if the relationships are functioning better, the depression will lessen. Therapeutic techniques include helping clients explore the consequences of their actions in their relationships and facilitating better personal communication, perhaps by encouraging clients to tell others how they feel. This type of therapy was developed in the late 1970s; most IPT treatments are based on IPT therapy protocol manuals. All treatments in all four TDCRP groups were brief, lasting 16 weeks.

Question 1: Are the Participants Randomly Assigned? Participants in the TDCRP were randomly assigned to one of the four treatment groups; the design of the study addressed Question 1 in Table 15.5. What would it mean if the assignments weren't random? Suppose those who were more depressed were put in the medication group, but the therapy groups turned out to be more effective; we couldn't then conclude that therapy was more effective than medication because the participants in the medication group were in worse shape to begin with. Random assignment is crucial if we want to be able to infer anything about the effectiveness of one treatment over another.

Questions 2 and 3: Specific Disorders and Exclusion Criteria. In trying to determine whether certain types of treatment are more effective for certain disorders (Question 2), many studies exclude participants with more than one diagnosis (Question 3). Although this exclusion makes research findings more clear-cut, it limits their generalizability, because many clients going to a therapist's office have more than one type of diagnosis. For example, more than half of those diagnosed with an anxiety disorder have at least one additional disorder, and 30 to 40% of those with a diagnosis of depression also have a diagnosis of a personality disorder (Sleek, 1997). The TDCRP study restricted inclusion to those who met the exact criteria for major depressive disorder, without any other disorder.

Question 4: Do Treatments Correspond to Their Stated Approach? One difficulty in assessing research on a particular therapeutic orientation is that therapists who by their own statements would seem to have different orientations may in fact be remarkably similar in the way they actually provide therapy (Lambert & Bergin, 1994). This makes comparisons among therapies difficult (Question 4). Suppose that in the TDCRP study, a self-defined CBT therapist focused on relationship issues, and a self-defined IPT therapist gave concrete suggestions, such as those given in assertiveness training, for improving relationships. If there were no differences in outcome between the two therapy groups, it could be because therapists in the two groups were doing much the same thing! In an effort to address this problem, the TDCRP developed therapist manuals for each of the four treatments, providing in each case a detailed guide and techniques to be used with clients for each session. These standardized forms of treatment ensured that all therapists categorized as using one approach (for example, CBT) were actually providing similar therapy.

Question 5: Outcome Measures. Question 5 addresses the difficult issue of how to measure outcome. Measures can focus on behaviors, thoughts, or feelings in relation to specific symptoms, or on more general patterns of functioning. Different types of therapy might be differentially effective with each of these possible outcome measures. In the TDCRP, medication might be more effective with some symptoms of depression (tiredness, poor appetite), but not help with relationships or negative thinking as much as psychological treatment (Segal et al., 1999). The type of outcome measures used can bias the results in favor of one form of therapy over another. In order to avoid this pitfall, the TDCRP study looked at multiple types of outcome measures, but surprisingly, it found comparable results for these different measures (Imber et al., 1991), except that patients in IPT and CBT reported that their relationships benefited from treatment, whereas this was not true of those in the other groups (Blatt et al., 2000).

Question 6: Drop Outs. In addition, there is the problem that 50% or more of those who begin treatment in a research study may drop out (Kazdin, 1994). And if more participants drop out of one group than another, the conclusions you can draw about the treatment are limited (Question 6). The TDCRP results showed that *of those completing the study*, all four groups improved, but CBT and IPT treatment were about as effective as antidepressant medication in decreasing depressive symptoms (Antonuccio et al., 1995; Elkin et al., 1995). However, more participants dropped out of the medication group before the completion of the program because of unpleasant side effects. So, if you consider all of those *starting* the TDCRP study rather than only those *completing* it, both CBT and IPT were *more* effective than medication-and-support or placebo-and-support groups (Elkin, 1994). Knowing the attrition rates can make a difference in understanding the results.

Question 7: Follow Up. Finally, it is important to determine what happens after treatment ends, and if the outcome results change with the passage of time (Question 7). In the TDCRP study, CBT had a more sustained effect at an 18-month follow-up, with fewer relapses, particularly when compared with the group given imipramine (Elkin, 1994; Shea et al., 1992). This result is consistent with other findings (Antonuccio et al., 1995). However, further analyses showed that, across all four treatment groups, both medication and IPT were slightly more effective than CBT for severely depressed clients (Elkin et al., 1995). Moreover, the quality of the collaborative bond between client and therapist (as measured by independent raters who watched videotapes of the sessions) affected outcome; this influence was stronger than that of the type of treatment (Krupnick et al., 1996). In both CBT and IPT, clients reported feeling supported and reassured and indicated that the therapy had given them new ways of relating to others and had encouraged their independent opinions (Ablon & Jones, 1999).

UNDERSTANDING RESEARCH

For OCD: CBT Plus Medication, Without Exclusion

Using a similar research design as the TDCRP, researchers have found that exposure with response prevention is helpful for OCD. However, such studies exclude people with an additional diagnosis. Franklin and colleagues (2002) set out to investigate whether similar results would occur when patients with both OCD and another disorder are not excluded.

QUESTION: When people who have OCD *and* another psychological disorder are not excluded from participating in research on treatment, is an exposure and response prevention-based CBT *plus* medication more effective for OCD than CBT alone?

ALTERNATIVES: For this broader sample, (1) combined treatment is as effective as CBT alone; (2) combined treatment is *more* effective than CBT alone; and (3) combined treatment is *less* effective than CBT alone.

LOGIC: If CBT *plus* medication increases the overall benefits of treatment, such combined treatment should lead to fewer OCD symptoms than CBT alone.

METHOD: Fifty-six people with OCD participated in this study; approximately half of the participants were taking medication at the time the study began (referred to as the CBT + medication group), and half were not (referred to as the CBT-alone group). Participants were not randomly assigned to these treatment groups; their membership in one or the other group was based on whether they happened to be taking medication at the time the study began. The members of the groups had comparable symptoms before CBT began. CBT was based on a manual intended as a flexible guide rather than an exact blueprint. Treatment lasted 18 sessions, typically 2 hours each.

RESULTS: CBT substantially reduced symptoms in both groups, and to the same extent.

INFERENCES: Medication neither interfered with nor enhanced the benefits of CBT. One drawback of the study, however, is that those who were taking medication prior to CBT could have had more symptoms before taking medication than they had at the time the study began. If they had had more symptoms before taking medication, the two treatment groups (CBT + medication and CBT alone) cannot be considered to have been equivalent before CBT began. An advantage of this study's design, however, is that it more closely resembles treatment that isn't part of a research project—where some people who seek CBT may have other disorders and may already be taking medication.

Psychotherapy Versus Medication

Is the TDCRP the only study to have found that psychotherapy can work as well to alleviate depression as medication? And are depression and OCD the only disorders that can claim this general result? The answer to these questions is no (Gloaguen et al., 1998; Reynolds et al., 1999; Thase et al., 1997).

Depression. Medication does alleviate depression for many people; why, therefore, might someone choose psychotherapy over medication? According to research, the main drawback of medication becomes apparent when you look at how people fare over the long haul. When medication is discontinued, the relapse rate is high, a fact that has led some doctors to recommend continued use of medication for those at risk for additional depressive episodes (Hirschfeld, 1997). Cognitive–behavioral treatment appears to provide an equivalent benefit without the side effects of drugs (Antonuccio et al., 1995). CBT may also be helpful in treating residual symptoms of depression following treatment with antidepressant medication. This supplemental use of CBT lowers the relapse rate when medication is discontinued (Fava et al., 1998a). At 6-year follow-up, those who had supplemental CBT were less likely to have had another episode of depression than those without CBT (Fava et al., 1998b). Similarly, a number of studies have found that medication and cognitive therapy combined may be more helpful than medication alone, even with severely depressed people (Macaskill & Macaskill, 1996; Thase et al., 1997), although not all studies have found an added benefit of combined treatment (Oei & Yeoh, 1999).

Anxiety Disorders. For anxiety disorders, research on the question of medication versus psychotherapy yields results similar to those of the research on depression: That is, particular types of psychotherapy (CBT, IPT) provide as much, if not more, long-term relief of symptoms as does medication (Gould et al., 1995). In the treatment of panic disorder, for instance, although medication and CBT may work about equally well, CBT does a better job of preventing symptom relapse (Chambless & Gillis, 1993; Otto et al., 1994). And as with OCD, behavior therapy is as helpful as medication. Early results of a large-scale study of OCD, similar in design to the TDCRP study, confirm that behavior therapy (in this case, exposure with response prevention) is as helpful as medication, and possibly more so over the long term. Moreover, combining the exposure treatment with medication wasn't more beneficial. However, as with other manual-based treatments that exclude participants with more than one diagnosis, there are questions as to whether these findings generalize to behavior therapy with clients diagnosed with more than one disorder (Kozak et al., 2000).

In the treatment of social phobias, research shows that MAOIs and group CBT are equally helpful (Heimberg et al., 1998). However, when medication is discontinued symptoms usually return, in contrast to CBT, whose effects continue after treatment ends.

Other Disorders. Meta-analytic studies of medication versus CBT with participants with bulimia nervosa have found CBT to be more effective (Whittal et al., 1999). However, for other disorders, such as schizophrenia and bipolar disorder, medication is clearly superior to psychotherapy, although CBT can help decrease psychotic symptoms (Gould et al., 2001; Rector & Beck, 2001). For people with these disorders, psychotherapy can play a role in helping them accept the need to take medication on a lifelong or long-term basis (Colom et al., 1998; Tohen & Grundy, 1999) and can provide an opportunity to learn new relationship skills after the medication has helped them to be more stable. Moreover, psychological treatment in conjunction with medication can be helpful in identifying triggers of psychotic, manic, or depressive episodes, and can help prevent relapses (Buchkremer et al., 1997; Goldstein, 1992). Recent guidelines for the treatment of schizophrenia advocate behavioral and cognitive skills training to encourage compliance with the medication regimen and to help improve functioning by social skills training (Lehman & Steinwachs, 1998). CBT can also be effective in helping reduce positive symptoms in schizophrenic patients who are not helped by medication (Kuipers et al., 1997, 1998; Sensky et al., 2000; Tarrier et al., 1998). A meta-analysis of nonmedication treatments for schizophrenia found that people with more chronic schizophrenia were more responsive to psychotherapy than those whose symptoms were less chronic (Mojtabai et al., 1998).

Although medication can work in treating social phobia, such as a fear of public speaking, it is not necessarily superior to cognitive–behavior therapy because symptoms often return after medication is stopped. Cognitive–behavior therapy's benefits usually last after treatment ends.

Caveat. However, like all research that has examined groups of people, the results do not necessarily apply to a particular individual. Thus, for any particular person, psychotherapy may be more effective than medication, and the opposite may be true for someone else with apparently identical symptoms.

The *Consumer Reports* Study

In 1994 *Consumer Reports* magazine asked its readers to evaluate not just their cars, dishwashers, and toasters, but their mental health treatments as well. Approximately 180,000 subscribers received a detailed questionnaire about cars, appliances, and mental health. Those who had experienced stress or other emotional problems over the preceding 3 years and had sought help from friends, relatives, members of the clergy, mental health professionals (such as psychologists), family doctors, or support groups were asked to complete the mental health section. Seven thousand subscribers responded to the mental health questions, with 3,000 reporting that they talked only to friends, relatives, or clergy, and 4,100 reporting that they went to some combination of mental health professionals, family doctors, and support groups. Of these 4,100, 2,900 saw mental health professionals. In addition, 1,300 joined self-help groups, and about 1,000 saw family doctors. The respondents had a median age of 46, were highly educated, and mostly middle class; men and women were almost equally represented.

TABLE 15.6 Findings From the *Consumer Reports* Survey

- Of those who reported doing very poorly before treatment, 54% said that treatment made things much better, and 33% said it made things somewhat better.

- Treatment by a mental health professional was superior to treatment by a family doctor; this result has also been found in subsequent studies (Meredith et al., 1996; Schulberg et al., 1996).

- Those respondents who went to Alcoholics Anonymous (AA) reported themselves as doing well.

- Those who actively sought out a therapist and, at the outset, discussed such matters as the therapists' qualifications and the frequency and duration of treatment were more likely to fare better than those who were more passive in their treatment.

- Those whose choice of therapist and duration of treatment were limited by their health insurance plan did worst overall.

- Generally, the dodo bird verdict seemed to hold true: No specific form of therapy generally had better results than any other.

Some of the survey's findings are summarized in Table 15.6. They found that treatment by a mental health professional is effective: Most of those who responded said they felt much better after treatment (Seligman, 1995). These findings are consistent with meta-analyses of research studies on the efficacy of therapy (Lipsey & Wilson, 1993; Shapiro & Shapiro, 1982; Smith & Glass, 1977). Moreover, long-term therapy provided more improvement than short-term therapy, a result that is consistent with other findings about the length of treatment (the dose–effect relationship). A meta-analysis of 2,431 patients over a 30-year period showed that 50% improved measurably by the eighth session, and 75% improved after 26 sessions of weekly therapy (Howard et al., 1986).

Several caveats are in order when interpreting the results of the *Consumer Reports* survey. First, very few respondents had schizophrenia or bipolar disorder, so no specific conclusions could be made about treatment of those disorders. Second, the results were not based on controlled, methodologically rigorous studies (as was the TDCRP), and generalization is therefore difficult. Many other criticisms have been leveled against the *Consumer Reports* study on methodological grounds (Jacobson & Christensen, 1996, provide a detailed criticism), limiting confidence in the results.

In its favor, the *Consumer Reports* study addressed the question of therapy as it is actually delivered for most people: not as part of a research study, without the use of therapy manuals, not in a prescribed number of sessions, nor restricted to those with a single diagnosis. Although controlled psychotherapy research studies can attempt to answer specific questions about outcome, or which treatment works best for which disorder, the *Consumer Reports* study chiefly addressed the question, "Do people have fewer symptoms and a better life after therapy than they did before?" The respondents generally answered yes. The survey also stimulated research about the generalizability of controlled psychotherapy studies ("research therapy") to therapy as it is actually done by most practitioners ("clinic therapy").

Another indication of the effectiveness of clinic therapy is found in a community study examining long-term mental health outcomes for some residents of Baltimore, Maryland. The study found that participants who had received individual or group therapy were less distressed at a 15-year follow-up than those who either received medication or did not seek out mental health treatment (Bovasso et al., 1999).

Curative Factors: The Healing Powers

Although therapy does not always reduce the frequency or intensity of the troublesome symptoms that bring people to treatment, it often works (Garfield & Bergin, 1994; Matt & Navarro, 1997). Despite the fact that people aren't necessarily "cured," as they might be cured of a bacterial sinus infection, psychologists refer to the therapy-related factors that help make clients better as **curative factors.** As psychologists have attempted to understand why psychotherapy works, they have isolated two types of factors—*common factors* and *specific factors.* **Common factors** are curative factors of therapy common to all types of treatment. For instance, just going to and being in therapy provides hope, a chance of emotional expression, support and advice, an explanation and understanding of one's difficulties, and an opportunity to experiment with new behaviors and thoughts (Garfield & Bergin, 1994). Carl Rogers appears to have been at least partly correct: A supportive and warm therapy relationship facilitates the success of the therapy (Beutler et al., 1994). In contrast, **specific factors** are those that relate to the particular type of therapy employed. For people with OCD, exposure with response prevention is a specific factor, and the most important factor in improvement (Abramowitz, 1997). Another example would be specific techniques of CBT that can be particularly helpful in treating panic disorder, leading to better outcomes than other types of therapy or medications (Gould et al., 1995).

Research on therapy also looks at broader outcome measures, such as quality of life—the client's psychological, social, and material well-being (Gladis et al., 1999). This new focus addresses complaints that looking at symptoms alone is too narrow a scope and takes the position that health is not simply the absence of disease (World Health Organization, 1948).

Which Therapy Works Best for Which Disorder?

For some disorders, the dodo bird verdict appears to be correct, possibly because of common curative factors among all therapies; for other disorders, particular types of therapy are preferred.

General Trends. The results of thousands of research studies and meta-analyses show that some treatments are better than others for certain disorders: Cognitive therapy and interpersonal therapy provide relief from depression (Blatt et al., 2000); exposure and response prevention provides long-term symptom relief for those with OCD (Jenike, 2000); cognitive therapy is helpful for people with panic disorder (Clark et al., 1999; Wolfe & Maser, 1994) and agoraphobia (Hoffart, 1998); exposure works well for those with specific phobias (Barlow, 2002).

Insight-Oriented Therapies. Psychodynamic therapy appears to work best with patients who are able to articulate their feelings and want to understand

- **Curative factor:** A therapy-related factor that helps make clients better.

- **Common factor:** In psychotherapy, a curative factor of therapy common to all types of treatment.

- **Specific factor:** In psychotherapy, a curative factor related to the specific type of therapy being employed.

their unconscious (and who have the time and money for lengthy treatment). Some meta-analyses find short-term psychodynamic therapy to be as effective as other short-term treatments (Crits-Christoph, 1992), but other studies contradict this result (Svartberg & Stiles, 1991), particularly studies with a 1-year follow-up (Barkham et al., 1999).

There are several difficulties in evaluating the effectiveness of psychodynamic therapies. One is that there isn't much actual research to evaluate. Consider that for every research article on transference, there are 500 on theory. Moreover, although psychodynamic therapists may believe in the accuracy of their interpretations, they may not be correct. For instance, research shows that interpretations of the transference relationship do not appear to be particularly helpful in psychodynamic treatment (Henry et al., 1994). Psychodynamic therapists have tended to view treatment failures as the patient's responsibility rather than the therapist's. It is possible that this view is correct—lack of behavioral change may result from insufficient insight—but insight is not objectively measurable, at least not yet.

Although Rogers did much to bring about the first real insight-oriented alternative to psychodynamic therapy and made the treatment amenable to research by tape recording therapy sessions, research has not been as supportive as he might have wished. Almost all forms of therapy incorporate Rogers's view that the therapist's warmth, empathy, and positive regard for the client are fundamental for a working relationship between client and therapist (Lambert, 1983). However, most therapies do not rest on the idea that these factors are *enough* to bring about change. Moreover, although client-centered therapy was the first major school of therapy to focus on assessing the effectiveness of the treatment, it can be difficult to measure which clients have achieved their potentials.

Behavioral and Cognitive Therapies. Although cognitive, behavioral, and CBT treatments have been found to be helpful for specific disorders, these classifications may be too broad, and it seems that specific techniques from each approach are the appropriate units of comparison. For example, in the treatment of OCD, although exposure with response prevention (a behavioral technique) has been the most well-documented technique to produce long-term symptom relief, there is evidence that cognitive therapy may be as effective. In contrast, progressive muscle relaxation, another behavioral technique, is not as beneficial (Abramowitz, 1997).

In addition, two distinct types of treatment, CBT without exposure and exposure therapy only, *both* worked well for social phobia (Feske & Chambless, 1995), although later research has found that the combination can be effective (Gould et al., 1997; S. Taylor, 1996). In the treatment of PTSD, both exposure with response prevention and cognitive restructuring worked equally well, and those two treatments combined were no more effective than each treatment by itself. However, all were superior to relaxation training (Marks et al., 1998). Similar results were found in a meta-analysis of various therapies for PTSD (Sherman, 1998).

And for depression, although cognitive therapy in general has been found to be as helpful as medication or IPT, recent research has looked at whether just a subset of CBT techniques is equally helpful. Jacobson and his colleagues (1996) found that techniques that increase a depressed person's activity level are as effective as CBT treatment, which changes dysfunctional attitudes or attributional styles. These results were consistent at follow-up 2 years later (Gortner et al., 1998).

For chronic PTSD, imaginal exposure (a behavioral technique that uses mental images of the distressing event or object) and cognitive therapy were equally helpful (Tarrier et al., 1999). Thus, asking about the effectiveness of behavioral, cognitive, or cognitive–behavior therapies appears to be too broad a question; further research will clarify which components of therapy are most helpful for particular disorders.

Matching Client to Therapeutic Approach. As well as attempting to match disorders and therapy, research has also attempted to match clients and therapy, asking "Which type of therapy works best with what type of client?" This question has been addressed by the National Institute on Alcohol Abuse and Alcoholism (NIAAA). This organization sought to discover whether certain types of treatment for alcohol abuse are more effective with certain types of clients. Some client characteristics thought to be potentially relevant were severity of the alcoholism, sex of the client, and presence of other psychiatric disorders. The study examined three treatments: CBT, a 12-step treatment program to prepare clients to join AA, and motivational enhancement therapy (which was directed toward increasing readiness to change drinking habits). Results found that all three treatments had good overall results, increasing the percentage of abstinent days from 20% before treatment to 80% after treatment, with only a slight dip after 1 year. However, none of the planned "matches" between client and assignment to a particular type of treatment enhanced treatment effectiveness (Project MATCH Research Group, 1997).

Research on matching a treatment to a given client has also looked at the possible effect of a client's personality style. For instance, among depressed clients in the TDCRP, those who also had an avoidant personality disorder (and thus didn't like to dwell on their experiences) were more likely to fare better with cognitive therapy, a result that was consistent with their externally oriented coping style. In contrast, depressed people who had an obsessive-compulsive personality style did better in interpersonal therapy, consistent with their internally oriented coping style (Barber & Muenz, 1996). Similar results have been found for the superiority of CBT in helping depressed people who are externalizers versus internalizers (Beutler et al., 1991, 1993b).

Treatment for an Ethnically Diverse Population

According to the 2000 census, 25% of the population of the United States are members of an ethnic minority, and this number continues to grow. As the composition of America changes, so too does the composition of those seeking mental health services. At least until the early 1990s, most psychotherapy research did not include information about race, education, or economic status. However, it has been shown that these factors may influence the effectiveness of a given treatment for a particular client (Francis & Aronson, 1990). Psychotherapists are now more aware of the need to consider a client's background, cultural values, and attitudes about psychotherapy (McGoldrick et al., 1996; Ramirez, 1999). For instance, a client's immigrant or refugee experience

Therapists try to be aware of unique ethnic and cultural factors that can play a role in treatment, such as immigrant, cultural, or racial stressors.

creates a stressor that can affect mental health. And members of minority groups who are born and raised in the United States may experience prejudice and other hardships that can affect mental health.

An example of the importance of understanding a symptom's cultural context can be found in *ataques de nervios* (Spanish for "attack of nerves"), which some Puerto Rican women experience. This condition is a physical expression of strong emotions and includes trembling, heart palpitations, numbness, difficulty breathing, loss of consciousness, and a hyperkinetic (overactive) state (Rivera-Arzola & Ramos-Grenier, 1997). The context for this illness is a culture in which women are likely to endure great hardships, have little real power, and are actively discouraged from expressing anger. *Ataque de nervios* provides a culturally sanctioned way for them to express an inability to cope with a current situation, and the community responds (Rivera-Arzola & Ramos-Grenier, 1997). It is clear that the most effective therapist is one who is aware of both the cultural and familial contexts of a disorder.

It is part of a therapist's responsibility to be aware of cultural or racial issues that can affect all aspects of treatment—diagnosis, the process of the therapy, and its goals (Helms & Cook, 1999; Ramirez, 1999). The therapist should inquire about the client's understanding of the meaning of the problem, so that therapist and client can discuss and come to agreement on the nature of the problem, interventions to be used, and expected goals (Higgenbotham et al., 1988; Kleinman, 1978).

Although age, sex, and ethnicity do not appear to play a systematic role in therapy outcomes generally (Beutler et al., 1994; Lam & Sue, 2001), research suggests that some people (such as some Asian Americans) prefer a therapist from their own ethnic group, and such matching leads to better outcomes for them (Sue et al., 1994). In general, however, there is no clear-cut evidence to date that matching by ethnicity for most ethnic groups results in better outcomes (Garfield, 1994). Some attempts have been made to develop particular therapies for different ethnic groups, with varying success; for example, *cuento therapy* (from the Spanish word for "fable"), which uses folktales or stories, has proved helpful with Latino American children (Sue et al., 1994).

How to Pick a Psychotherapist

Suppose you, like Beth, decide to seek psychotherapy. How do you pick a therapist? Keep several factors in mind when trying to find someone who could most effectively help you. If your problem is identifiable (such as depression or anxiety), it can be helpful to see someone who has experience in treating people with that problem. Many state and national referral agencies or professional associations are available, such as the American Psychological Association, the National Association of Social Workers, and the American Psychiatric Association. Regional organizations can also provide referrals for specific problems, such as the Massachusetts Eating Disorders Association or the Manic-Depressive and Depressive Association of Boston (MDDA-Boston). These organizations all have national associations that can also supply the names of therapists with expertise in treating specific problems.

It may be helpful to get the names of more than one therapist because any one therapist may not have compatible office hours, location, or available times. You can also ask friends, family, teachers, and religious leaders for recommendations, as well as the counseling center at your college or university (Practice Directorate, 1998). Many insurance companies will reimburse or authorize psychotherapy only if the provider is on their list. If this is true for you, tell the therapists you are considering what insurance coverage you have and ask whether their services are reimbursed by that company; if they don't know, call the company and check. Alternatively, call your insurance company and ask for referrals.

It is important that you feel comfortable with your therapist. If you don't, you may be less likely to talk about what's on your mind or share how you are really doing. And if you aren't able to talk about these things, the therapy can't be as helpful. It's also important to feel that the therapist is trustworthy—if the therapist doesn't have your trust, you will find it easy to discount what he or she says if it is something that you don't want to hear. If after one or two sessions, you realize you just don't feel comfortable, make an appointment with someone else and see whether the situation feels different. Therapists are used to this initial "try out" period, and you shouldn't worry about possibly hurting their feelings by switching to someone else.

Looking *at* Levels

How Do You Know Whether Psychotherapy Worked?

How could you determine whether a particular therapy had been successful? The answer depends on what you measure, and the measures can be defined at each of the three levels of analysis. At the level of the group, you could ask members of the clients' families to report their impressions about their interactions with the client, or you could measure the frequency of certain social behaviors, such as the amount of time the client spends talking to other people. At the level of the person, you could have clients rate their thoughts, feelings, or behaviors, or fill in questionnaires about their psychological states. And at the level of the brain, you could take PET scans or other measures of brain activity, or you could obtain biochemical measures and examine the levels of key neuromodulators and neurotransmitters (although not all new learning that occurs at the level of the brain can be assessed in this way). What would

you think if some measures showed changes, but not others? Would you be willing to say that someone had improved if only the brain-based measures showed a change after therapy? What if only other people's reports of clients' social interactions, or only the clients' own subjective reports, showed a change? Sure, if he or she feels better, that may be good enough for the client—but unless changes actually occur in the brain and in behavior, what grounds are there for thinking of the improvement as enduring? Any new learning, whether it is having insight into problems, changing maladaptive behavior patterns, or replacing irrational thoughts with rational ones, creates changes in the brain. Lasting changes following psychotherapy are reflected at all three levels of analysis.

TEST YOURSELF!

1. What key issues should be kept in mind when reading research studies of psychotherapy?
2. What are good ways to find a therapist?

CONSOLIDATE!

Behavior and Cognitive Therapy

- Behavior therapy is grounded in the idea that psychological problems are a product of a client's learning history. Treatment seeks to help the client develop more adaptive behaviors.

- Behavioral techniques based on classical conditioning include systematic desensitization, progressive muscle relaxation, exposure, and stimulus control.

- Behavioral techniques based on operant conditioning include behavior modification and self-monitoring.

- Cognitive therapy is grounded in the idea that psychological problems are caused by faulty perceptions or interpretations. Treatments seek to help the client develop more realistic thoughts.

- The RET sequence of techniques (ABCDEF) may involve the therapist's trying to persuade the client to give up his or her irrational beliefs.

- Beck's cognitive therapy involves the identification of dysfuntional automatic thoughts, cognitive distortions, and rational responses.

- Both types of cognitive therapy are generally active, focus on current problems, and often assign between-session homework.

THINK IT THROUGH   If you read about a study that claimed CBT treatment effectively reduces kleptomania (compulsive stealing done for pleasure, not for material need), what questions would you ask about how the study was done? Suppose each therapist in the study treated some clients with CBT and some with client-centered therapy. What would you need to know before agreeing with their conclusions about the superiority of CBT? Why? Would CBT be effective if the client was not motivated or had a poor memory? From what you know about her, would you recommend CBT to Beth? Explain your answers.

Insight-Oriented Therapies

- Insight-oriented therapies rest on the belief that psychological problems are caused by emotional forces.

- Such treatments focus on helping people gain insight into their problems and propose that such insight will lead to changes in thoughts, feelings, and behavior.

- Examples of insight-oriented therapies include psychodynamic and client-centered therapies.

- Psychodynamic therapy focuses on unconscious conflict and sexual and aggressive drives. The goal of the therapy is to make unconscious conflict conscious.

- Psychodynamic techniques include free association, dream analysis, interpretation, and the use of transference.

- Client-centered therapy focuses on each client's unique experiences and potential for growth. The goal of the therapy is to unblock each client's potential for growth by decreasing incongruence.

- Client-centered techniques include empathy, unconditional positive regard, and genuineness toward the client.

THINK IT THROUGH   Imagine two people, one of whom is the ideal candidate for insight-oriented therapy and one of whom is the worst possible candidate. How would you describe these two people? If a friend tells you that he is in insight-oriented therapy, what can you assume about his therapy? What can't you assume? From what you've read here, would you recommend insight-oriented therapy for Beth?

Biomedical Therapies

- Medication is one type of biomedical therapy. Medications are used to treat schizophrenia, mood and anxiety disorders, as well as other disorders.

- For schizophrenia and other psychotic disorders, traditional antipsychotic medication reduces positive symptoms but can cause serious side effects. Atypical antipsychotic medication can also reduce negative symptoms and have less serious side effects.

- TCAs, MAOIs, SSRIs, SNRIs, and, for moderate depression, St. John's wort, can be used to treat depression. Mood stabilizers such as lithium can help symptoms of bipolar disorder.

- Benzodiazepines may be used as a short-term treatment for anxiety disorders. For longer-term treatment, antidepressants can be helpful.

- Electroconvulsive therapy is used with severely depressed people when other treatments have failed.

- Treatment by transcranial magnetic stimulation is still considered experimental.

THINK IT THROUGH Suppose your best friend's mother had bipolar disorder. What might be her likely treatment? Why? Suppose instead that your friend's father had schizophrenia; what treatment might he receive? Under what circumstance might you consider ECT to be a reasonable treatment?

Other Forms of Treatment

- Psychological treatment exists in a variety of forms, including individual, family, and group therapy; self-help resources including books and tapes; and prevention programs.

- Systems therapy views a client's symptoms in a family context; it seeks to reduce the symptoms by changing the family system. Techniques include reframing, validation, and possibly paradoxical intention.

- Psychotherapy protocols and integrative psychotherapy have been more widely used in recent years, partly because of the demands of managed care.

- Cybertherapy refers to therapy over the Internet, through email, chat rooms, or therapist-led online support groups. Such treatment is considered less than optimal.

- Prevention programs include universal, selective, and indicated interventions.

THINK IT THROUGH Suppose a friend decides to seek help for a problem. He tells you his therapist is "eclectic"—what does that mean? He also tells you that he's agreed to participate in a study of manualized treatment. What can you infer about his treatment, and what should you *not* infer? Suppose a different friend showed no sign of any disorder, but was involved in a prevention program: What type of preventative intervention would that be?

Which Therapy Works Best?

- The answers to various questions about psychotherapy research will determine what conclusions can be drawn from the results of a given study, and how far the results generalize to other circumstances.

- Research on psychotherapy shows that, overall, those who receive psychotherapy fare better than those who don't receive treatment. This is generally true, regardless of the therapeutic approach.

- An effective therapy has both common and specific factors that contribute toward its success.

- For some disorders, symptoms can worsen when clients stop medication that had been helpful. Beneficial psychotherapies can continue to exert their positive influence after treatment ends.

- Research shows that certain types of psychotherapy are more effective with certain disorders than with others; for example, exposure with response prevention is a particularly effective treatment for OCD.

- It is also important to understand the ethnic and cultural factors related to a client's problems and goals.

THINK IT THROUGH Suppose you were designing a treatment program for depression for an ethnically diverse set of clients. What would you want to know about these clients? How would you use that information? How would you design a study to test the effectiveness of your new program? Why would you do it that way?

Key Terms

antipsychotic medication, p. 641
behavior modification, p. 628
behavior therapy, p. 625
benzodiazepine, p. 643
bibliotherapy, p. 649
client-centered therapy, p. 638
cognitive distortion, p. 630
cognitive restructuring, p. 632
cognitive therapy, p. 630
common factor, p. 661
curative factor, p. 661
cybertherapy, p. 651
dream analysis, p. 636
electroconvulsive therapy (ECT), p. 643
exposure, p. 626
family therapy, p. 647
free association, p. 636
group therapy, p. 647
incongruence, p. 638
individual therapy, p. 646
insight-oriented therapy, p. 635
interpretation, p. 637
modality, p. 646
monoamine oxidase inhibitor (MAOI), p. 642
outcome research, p. 654
paradoxical intention, p. 648
progressive muscle relaxation, p. 625

psychoanalysis, p. 635
psychodynamic therapy, p. 636
psychoeducation, p. 633
psychopharmacology, p. 641
psychotherapy integration, p. 649
reframing, p. 648
resistance, p. 637
selective serotonin reuptake inhibitor (SSRI), p. 642
self-help group, p. 648
self-monitoring techniques, p. 629
serotonin/norepinephrine reuptake inhibitor (SNRI), p. 642
specific factor, p. 661
stimulus control, p. 628
St. John's wort, p. 642
systematic desensitization, p. 625
systems therapy, p. 647
tardive dyskinesia, p. 641
technical eclecticism, p. 649
token economy, p. 634
transference, p. 638
tricyclic antidepressant (TCA), p. 642
validation, p. 648

chapter 16

Faith Ringgold © 1986

Social Psychology
Meeting of the Minds

In 1993 Sarah Delany, known as Sadie, and her younger sister Elizabeth, called Bessie, published their first book, *Having Our Say* (Delany, Delany, & Hearth, 1993). What's remarkable about these authors is that they were 104 and 102 at the time of publication. Their book recounts the story of their lives, their experiences as Black children and then as Black women during a century of American history. It was during their childhood that the South's Jim Crow laws came into effect, legalizing separate facilities—separate schools, separate water fountains, separate seats on the bus, separate toilets—for Blacks and Whites; it was during their adulthood that these laws were struck down.

Sadie and Bessie had 8 brothers and sisters. Their father, Henry, had been born a slave but was freed by emancipation. He became vice principal of St. Augustine's School (now St. Augustine's College), a Black college in Raleigh, North Carolina. Their mother, Nanny James, who had both Black and White grandparents, was light-skinned. In addition to managing her 10 children, she was the matron of the college, overseeing many of its daily functions. The Delany children were educated at "St. Aug's," where their father taught. All 10 children became college-educated professional men and women—a remarkable feat for anyone of that era, regardless of race or sex. Sadie earned both a bachelor's and a master's degree from Columbia University and became a teacher. In 1926 she became the first Black woman appointed to teach home economics at the high school level in New York City. Bessie went to dental school at Columbia in 1923, where she was the only Black woman, and she was the second Black woman licensed to practice dentistry in New York City.

The Delany family, well known in Black society in North Carolina and in New York City's Harlem neighborhood, was considered to be part of an elite group of educated Blacks. But the road was not easy for the sisters. People, Black and White, developed attitudes toward and stereotypes about the sisters, and some discriminated against them—because they were Black, because they were women, or simply because they were Delanys.

Like the Delanys, we are all targets of other people's attitudes and stereotypes,

and we have attitudes and stereotypes of our own about other people. And like the Delanys, we all feel pressure from others to behave in certain ways, and we exert pressure on others to behave in certain ways. How we think about other people and interact in relationships and groups makes up the subfield of psychology called **social psychology.**

Many of the phenomena psychology seeks to understand—sensation, learning, and memory, to name just a few—take place primarily at the levels of the brain and the person, but are influenced, as shown in the Looking at Levels features of this book, by the environment and the social world. In this chapter, the central emphasis is the level of the group. By definition, social psychology is about our relationships with other people. It focuses on two general topics: the way we think about others (*social cognition*) and the way we act toward them, individually and in groups (*social behavior*). And these interactions affect our thoughts, feelings, behavior, even our brains. Are there psychological principles that underlie the ways we think about and behave toward other people? If so, what are they?

> Like the Delanys, we are all targets of other people's attitudes and stereotypes, and we have attitudes and stereotypes of our own about other people.

Social Cognition: Thinking About People

The Delany sisters' parents worked hard to protect their children as much as possible from prejudice, discrimination, and intimidation. They also tried to instill in their children a sense of dignity, self-respect, and respect for and support of others. They encouraged their children to think about the world and their places in it, in specific ways. For example, their parents called each other Mr. and Mrs. Delany in front of others, including their children. This was a conscious decision. It was common for whites to call blacks by their first names in instances in which they would use surnames for whites; therefore, Mr. and Mrs. Delany deliberately chose to use formal titles to convey respect for each other and the expectation of respect from others.

In this chapter we focus largely on the ways people think about other people, in other words, on social cognition—*cognition* because it is about how we think, and *social* because the thoughts involve other people and the social world in general. **Social cognition** does not focus on the "objective" social world, but instead on how individuals perceive their social worlds, and how they attend to, store, remember, and use information about other people and the social world.

● **Social psychology:** The subfield of psychology that focuses on how people think about other people and interact in relationships and groups.

● **Social cognition:** The area of social psychology that focuses on how people perceive their social worlds, and how they attend to, store, remember, and use information about other people and the social world.

Making an Impression

The Delany children, like many other children, were always told to "make a good impression." Have you ever been told, even long after childhood, essentially the same thing—to comb your hair or dress up a bit before meeting someone for the first time? You may have wondered, "I know what kind of person I am. Why do I need to appear a particular way for other people?" An obvious answer is, of course, that other people *don't* know what kind of person you are, and they make inferences about you from things they notice at that initial meeting. Social psychologists have found that first impressions can make a difference (Schlenker, 1980); we tend to give earlier information more weight than later information. Even the position you assume when sitting shapes other people's impression of you: When females sit with their legs open and their arms held away from their upper bodies (more common among males), they are seen as less feminine; when males sit with their thighs against each other and their arms touching their upper bodies (more common among females), they are seen as less masculine (Vrugt & Luyerink, 2000).

The name psychologists use for the process by which we develop such impressions of others is **impression formation.** The creating and receiving of impressions is a two-way street, and the term **impression management** refers to our efforts to control the type of impression we try to create.

Thin Slices

In the process of forming impressions of others we take in large amounts of information (verbal and nonverbal) and, sometimes without conscious awareness, mold them into judgments. If you were observing a job applicant who was interviewing for a job, how much time do you think it would take you to form your impression of the candidate? Suppose you observed a video clip of the interview and the sound was off—how long should the clip be for you to

People use two common strategies to make a good impression. *Self-enhancement strategies* involve making yourself look good, perhaps by appearing particularly well groomed or knowledgeable about particular topics. *Other-enhancement strategies* involve eliciting a positive mood or reaction from the other person by asking for advice (Morrison & Bies, 1991), or being particularly attentive in an effort to convey the impression that you like him or her (Wayne & Ferris, 1990).

After watching a 15-second video clip of a man and woman interacting, observers were able to identify accurately the type of relationship between the two—whether they were strangers, platonic friends, or lovers (Ambady, Conroy et al., 2000).

● **Impression formation:** The process of developing impressions of others.

● **Impression management:** A person's efforts to control the type of impression he or she creates.

assess the candidate? Most of the time, our observations of "thin slices" of less than 5 minutes of behavior are remarkably accurate (Ambady, Bernieri, & Richeson, 2000). In fact, often just 10 seconds is enough. Consider that during mock "initial screening" job interviews, observers' ratings of 10-second video clips of interviewees walking in the door, greeting the interviewer, and sitting down predicted the interviewers' evaluations of the candidates (Prickett et al., in preparation). Similarly, after listening to 20 seconds of the tone of voice used by physicians during routine office visits, listener ratings predicted which physicians were most likely to have been sued in the past for malpractice (Ambady et al., under revision). Another study found that participants who observed 10-second video clips of teachers both interacting with students and talking about them could accurately gauge the teachers' expectations of their students (Babad et al., 1989).

From such nonverbal and verbal communications, we make meaning and infer other people's personality traits (see Chapter 11), particularly traits that we view as important. If you are at a party with many strangers and are interested in finding someone with whom you later can go bungee jumping, you probably will focus on verbal and nonverbal behavior that you think represents the personality trait of sensation seeking or adventurousness. In contrast, if you were looking for a good study partner among new classmates (or party guests), you would focus on other traits—and might even have a negative view of those same sensation-seeking behaviors, and form a negative impression of the person. Clearly, the context affects the impression you form of other people.

Primacy Effect

When forming impressions, you are also likely to respond to a *halo effect:* if you think someone has a positive and important trait (at least in one context), you are likely to infer that he or she has other positive and important traits. In North America, for instance, if you think someone is physically attractive, you will probably think he or she has other attributes that you consider to be positive (Feingold, 1992). However, not all positive traits contribute equally to your impression of another person. Information you notice early on is more likely to bias your impression, a tendency that is referred to as the *primacy effect* (Anderson & Barrios, 1961).

Self-Fulfilling Prophecy

The process of impression formation involves *perceiving* another person. This process requires you to direct your attention to particular behaviors and to interpret them. As we saw in Chapter 4, one process that guides our perceptions is top-down processing. Similarly, impression formation also can involve top-down processing: We often "see" what we expect to see and, in doing so, create a *self-fulfilling prophecy* (Darley & Gross, 1983). In a classic study, psychologists went into an elementary school classroom and administered a test to students. Teachers were then told which particular students would have extremely positive performance over the year, supposedly based on their test results. In fact, these particular students were chosen at random. At the end of the school year, those who had been noted as destined for great performance did in fact show this pattern relative to their classmates who were not so marked. Thus, the teachers' impressions and expectations of the students shaped the way they treated the students, which in turn shaped the students' performance (Rosenthal & Jacobson, 1968; see Chapter 9). Even when we are motivated to accurately perceive the other person's behavior and not use top-down processing, we are only accurate when we pay careful attention; when distracted, we fall victim to the self-fulfilling prophecy (Biesanz et al., 2001).

Another classic example of the self-fulfilling prophesy is the study by Snyder, Tanke, and Berscheid (1977; see Figure 16.1). They created 51 pairs of men and women, each member of the pair unknown to and unseen by the other. Each member was placed in a separate room. Before they began speaking on the phone, the men received photographs of a woman they were told was their partner. Half of the men received a photo of an attractive woman, the other half received a photo of an unattractive woman.

Each pair then spoke on the phone, and the woman's side of the conversation was taped. Independent judges (who did not know the women, nor did they know about the photographs) listened to the tapes. The judges rated as warm and friendly the women whose partners had been given "attractive" photos, whereas women who were rated less warm and friendly had partners who had received the "unattractive" photo. Thus, it appears that the men who thought they were speaking to an attractive woman asked questions of her, and responded to what she said, in ways that led her to be friendlier than the women in the

FIGURE 16.1 Self-Fulfilling Prophecy

Male and female participants who have never met are placed in separate rooms. Before they speak to each other on the phone, the men are shown a photograph of either an attractive or an unattractive woman. They are told the woman in the photo is their "partner," with whom they will speak on the phone.

The partners speak to each other. The woman's side of the conversation is taped separately.

Judges later listened to the woman's side of each conversation, and rated the women whose partners were given an attractive photo as more warm, likeable, and flirtatious than those whose partners had been given an unattractive photo. Men's beliefs about their partners became a self-fulfilling prophecy; they asked questions and responded to the "attractive" women in ways that elicited more attractive responses.

"unattractive" group. The men's expectations led to a self-fulfilling prophecy that shaped the women's behavior: The "attractive" women behaved in a friendlier way—more attractively—toward their partners.

Attitudes and Behavior: Feeling and Doing

When you read or hear the news, your attitudes affect your interpretation of the events being reported. In a smaller arena, your attitudes about people from a particular ethnic group will determine how you feel about them. For instance, your attitude about African Americans will determine how you *feel* about African Americans, which will in turn affect how you feel when you read about the Delanys. And in your own circle, if your friend tells you she's had an abortion, your attitude toward abortion will help determine how you feel about your friend. An **attitude** is an overall evaluation about some aspect of the world—people, issues, or objects (Petty & Wegener, 1998). This evaluation has three components: affective, behavioral, and cognitive, summarized by the acronym ABC (Breckler, 1984). *Affective* refers to your feelings about the object or issue. *Behavioral* refers to your predisposition to act in a particular way toward the object or issue (note that this component does not refer to an actual behavior, but an inclination to behave in a certain way). *Cognitive* refers to what you believe or know about the object or issue. Your attitudes can affect your behavior. The opportunity for the interplay of attitude and behavior can be seen in Sadie's father's comment to her: "Daughter, you are college material. You owe it to your nation, your race, and yourself to go. And if you don't go, then shame on you" (Delany et al., 1993, p. 91). His remarks reflected his attitude toward higher education for Blacks: He was passionately positive about it (affective); his inclination to promote higher education was reflected in his comment to Sadie (behavioral); he had no doubt about the power of education to elevate the position of Blacks in American society (cognitive).

Attitudes can be positive, such as being in favor of energy conservation; negative, such as disliking speed limits on highways; or neutral, such as not being moved one way or the other by a political candidate. The same issue—for instance, whether American troops should intervene in a foreign war—can evoke strong negative (NO!) or positive (YES!) attitudes. These different evaluations are accompanied by different changes in facial muscles (Cacioppo, Petty, Losch et al., 1986) and brain activation (Davidson, 1992a). We can also have ambivalent attitudes, with simultaneous negative and positive attitudes being equally strong.

Attitudes and Cognitions

Just as attention can play an important role in how we process and remember perceptual information in the physical world (see Chapters 4 and 7), attitudes play an important role in how we process information and remember events in our social world (Eagly & Chaiken, 1998). Particularly in ambiguous social situations, our attitudes help organize events and thus determine what information is attended to, processed, encoded, and remembered. This is one reason why people in the same social situation can come away with different versions of what occurred. In one study, Princeton and Dartmouth students watched a motion picture of a controversial Princeton–Dartmouth football game. Although all students saw the same motion picture of the game, students from the different schools described different events (Hastorf & Cantril, 1954), such as which team started rough play).

● **Attitude:** An overall evaluation about some aspect of the world.

Our attitudes also affect the way we shape our goals and expectations, and how we interpret obstacles we encounter in trying to achieve our goals, perhaps inducing stress. (As a general rule, it is not an event itself, but how it is perceived that determines whether it induces stress; see Chapter 13.) Our attitudes guide us as we selectively evaluate information; generally, we find information that is contrary to our attitudes to be unconvincing, and we may even try to disprove it (Eagly & Chaiken, 1998). As an example, consider the effect of socioeconomic class in the workplace (Gerteis & Savage, 1998). If you think that someone from a lower socioeconomic class will make a bad colleague, you will look for any evidence of shoddy work. You may not notice your colleague's well-performed tasks, and if you do notice them, you make up reasons that discount or discredit your colleague's abilities—perhaps, you say, those are easy tasks.

Attitudes are shaped by individual experiences as well as personality and temperment. If you are a sensation seeker, you will be more likely to have a positive attitude toward risky professions, such as being a war correspondent. However, learning (see Chapter 6) can also affect your attitudes. Suppose a friend's relative was a war correspondent who was murdered while on assignment. Observing how this death affected your friend (observational learning) will influence your attitudes. Similarly, operant conditioning can shape your attitudes: For example, imagine that you attended a local rally that became violent, and you were almost arrested (a consequence of your attending this event). This learning experience could affect your attitude toward high-risk journalism. Moreover, even classical conditioning can affect your attitudes: Did you acquire conditioned fear while attending the violent rally? If so, this fear might generalize to similar events in the future—which would impede your being an effective war correspondent.

Predicting Behavior

Suppose, after all of your experiences, you still have a positive attitude toward high-risk journalism. Does that mean that you'll actually become a war correspondent? More generally, if you know someone's attitudes, can you predict his or her behavior? Consider the experience of psychologist Richard La Piere (1934), who traveled the country in the 1930s with a young Chinese couple. They stayed in 67 paid lodgings and ate in 184 restaurants and cafés. Six months after each visit, La Piere sent a questionnaire to those establishments inquiring whether they would accept Chinese people as customers. More than 90% of the lodgings and restaurants said no. Yet on their trip, La Piere and his colleagues were refused only once. Attitudes influence behavior, but do not always lead to behavior consistent with attitudes.

Several factors determine how likely it is that an attitude toward a behavior will lead to the behavior's occurrence. An attitude is more likely to affect behavior when it is (1) strong, (2) relatively stable, (3) directly relevant to the behavior, (4) important, or (5) easily accessed from memory (Eagly & Chaiken, 1998). For instance, suppose you strongly dislike eating Moroccan food—an attitude. Against your better judgment, you went to a Moroccan restaurant recently and only picked at the food. If a friend invites you today to a meal at a Moroccan restaurant, you are likely to suggest another place to go: Your attitude about Moroccan food is strong, stable, directly relevant to your behavior, and easily accessed from memory. But if you haven't eaten this type of food in years, don't feel that strongly about it now, and have almost forgotten why you ever disliked it, you would be less likely to object to your friend's choice of a Moroccan restaurant (Sanbonmatsu & Fazio,

1990). Attitudes based on indirect experience, such as hearsay, have less influence on behavior than those based on direct experience (Regan & Fazio, 1977).

Behavior Affects Attitudes

If a professor assigned an essay on a topic about which you didn't have very strong feelings (say, supporting curbside recycling versus recycling at a local center), do you think writing the essay would influence your subsequent views? Research has shown that it can: When people are asked repeatedly to assert an attitude on a given topic, thus priming that attitude and making it easier to access, they are more likely to behave in ways consistent with that attitude, compared with those who did not repeatedly express the attitude (Fazio et al., 1982; Powell & Fazio, 1984). In fact, repeatedly asserting an attitude can make the attitude more extreme (Downing et al., 1992). Many self-help or self-improvement programs capitalize on this finding, encouraging participants to express frequent "affirmations," positive statements about themselves, their intentions, and their abilities. Such repeated affirmations can strengthen people's positive attitudes about themselves.

Implicit Attitudes

Did you prefer George Bush or Al Gore in the presidential election of 2000? Do you think women should pursue occupations in the sciences? Do you have a positive or negative attitude toward Whites? African Americans? As you answer these questions to yourself, you will undoubtedly answer based on your *explicit* attitude. Just as you have both explicit and implicit memories (see Chapter 7), you have explicit and implicit attitudes. Before you read on, if you have access to the Internet, please go to *www.yale.edu/implicit* and read about the Implicit Association Test (IAT; Greenwald et al., 1998); if you are interested, take one or more of the online attitude surveys and then come back to this page.

The IAT is often thought to measure implicit attitudes—those not available for conscious reflection. The IAT measures the strength of association between a concept, category, or person (such as George W. Bush) and an evaluation (bad or good), using response times as the dependent measure. In a typical version of the IAT, the task is to classify words as good or bad *and*, when appropriate, to indicate when a target stimulus is in one of two categories. These categories can, for example, pertain to two specific people (such as Bush versus Gore). It is crucial that the key on the keyboard you use to respond to a "good" target word (such as "marvelous") is *also* the key you use to respond to one of the categories (such as Bush), and the keyboard key you use to respond to a "bad" target word (such as "awful") is also the key you use to respond to the other category (Gore). The trick is in which category is paired with *good* and which is paired with *bad*. For example, Bush-related stimuli (such as his name or photograph) might be paired with *good* or Gore-related stumuli might be paired with *good*, and vice versa for *bad*. If you have a strong association between Al Gore and your evaluation of him (let's say *good*), then you are likely to classify a good-related target word, such as *marvelous*, faster if the concept *good* is paired with *Gore* than if *good* is paired with *Bush* (see Figure 16.2 for an example of this).

One study exposed participants to photos of admired African Americans and photos of disliked Whites. Subsequent IAT responses indicated that the typical "implicit" White response (White + Good) was weakened 24 hours later by exposure to the photos of disliked Whites (Dasgupta & Greenwald, 2001). Given that im-

FIGURE 16.2 The Implicit Association Test

In the version of the Implicit Association Test on the 2000 presidential election, respondents are asked to press the *e* key (on the left of the keyboard) when target words related to Gore or Good appear, and to press the *i* key (on the right of the keyboard) when target words related to Bush or Bad appear. Here the target word is *marvelous,* and respondents should press the *e* key because *marvelous* is related to *Good.* Response times are a measure of respondents' implicit attitudes; response times should be faster when the target word (such as *marvelous*) is consistent with both category words (such as *Gore* or *Good* if you were a Gore fan) rather than consistent with one but not the other (such as *Bush* or *Good*).

plicit associations were so readily shifted, this study and others raise doubt as to whether the IAT necessarily assesses deep, unconscious attitudes or simple associations based on context and recent experiences (Brendl et al., 2001; Fazio & Olson, 2003; Karpinski & Hilton, 2001). Moreover, when people are motivated to reduce a negative attitude, they can compensate—or even overcompensate—for their biases when taking the IAT (Banse et al., 2001; Devine et al., 2002; Payne, 2001). And although some studies have found IAT scores to predict relevant behaviors (McConell & Liebold, 2001), others do not (Karpinski & Hilton, 2001). Thus, whether the IAT measures implicit *attitudes* (versus associations) is an open question (Fazio & Olson, 2003).

Cognitive Dissonance

Attitudes and behavior don't always go hand in hand, as dramatically demonstrated by La Piere's study. But most people prefer that their attitudes and behavior are consistent (Snyder & Ickes, 1985). When an attitude and behavior—or two attitudes—are inconsistent, an uncomfortable state that psychologists refer to as **cognitive dissonance** arises. Cognitive dissonance is accompanied by heightened arousal (Losch & Cacioppo, 1990).

Festinger and Carlsmith's (1959) classic study on cognitive dissonance found that, counterintuitively, participants who were paid less to tell someone that a boring task was really enjoyable reported afterward that they enjoyed the task more than those who were paid a greater amount (Figure 16.3, p. 678). How can we understand this? By the effects of cognitive dissonance reduction. The participants who were paid less, only $1, could not have justified reporting that they enjoyed the task for that amount. To reduce dissonance, they appear to have convinced

● **Cognitive dissonance:** The uncomfortable state that arises because of a discrepancy between an attitude and behavior or between two attitudes.

FIGURE 16.3 Cognitive Dissonance

In Festinger and Carlsmith's classic 1959 study, participants were asked to perform a very boring, repetitive task: putting spools on a tray, then dumping them out, and starting all over again.

Participants were given either $1 or $20 (a lot of money in those days). They were then asked to tell another person that the task was in fact quite interesting.

After telling the other person about the task, the participants were asked to rate how much they liked the task. Those who were paid $1 to tell the other person they liked the task reported actually liking the task more than those paid $20 to do so!

Source: Festinger & Carlsmith, 1959.

themselves, unconsciously, that they really *did* enjoy the task, so much that they were willing to say they enjoyed it for little reimbursement. The participants who were paid more felt no such compulsion; the money they received, they apparently felt, adequately compensated for telling someone they liked the task, so there was no dissonance to be resolved. In general, research has shown that the less reason there is to engage in a behavior that is counter to our attitudes, the stronger the dissonance. Cognitive dissonance does not occur with every inconsistency; it is experienced only by people who believe that they have a choice and that they are responsible for their course of action, and thus for any negative consequences (Cooper, 1998; Goethals et al., 1979).

Ask yourself these questions: Do you think that giving to charity (either money or time) is a good thing? Do you think that homeless people should be helped? If you answered "yes" to these questions, when was the last time you donated time or money to a charity? The last time you helped a homeless person? Do you ignore homeless people on the street? You may feel uncomfortable after answering these questions. These feelings arise from the contradiction—the dissonance—between your attitudes about charity and homelessness and your behavior related to those issues.

Another explanation for cognitive dissonance findings comes from **self-perception theory,** which states that people understand themselves by making inferences from their behavior and the events surrounding their behavior—much as they would draw inferences from observing another person's behavior (Bem, 1972). The influence of such self-perception is especially clear when we do not have strong feelings or motivations that help us understand our behavior. This

HANDS ON

● **Self-perception theory:** The theory that people come to understand themselves by making inferences from their behavior and the events surrounding their behavior, much like those they would make about another person's behavior.

Cognitive dissonance can occur when our attitudes and behavior are inconsistent, even though we have a choice about how to behave.

theory would say that participants in Festinger and Carlsmith's study tried to understand why they would tell someone they liked a boring task when they were paid only $1. They explained it to themselves the same way they would explain the behavior in someone else: They must have actually liked the task. However, this explanation doesn't rule out cognitive dissonance.

Because cognitive dissonance creates an uncomfortable state, we try to decrease it. How do we minimize cognitive dissonance once it has occurred? We can use indirect strategies, such as trying to feel good about ourselves in other areas of life, or direct strategies, which involve actually changing our attitudes or behavior. Direct strategies also include attempts to obtain additional information supporting our attitude or behavior. Or, we can trivialize an inconsistency between two conflicting attitudes (or between an attitude and a behavior) as being unimportant, and therefore less likely to cause cognitive dissonance (Simon et al., 1995). For example, suppose you really believe in, and talk about, a desire to help feed starving people. Then a friend points out that you talk about this desire repeatedly but don't do anything about it. This observation would probably induce cognitive dissonance in you. To lessen it, you could use an indirect strategy by telling yourself what a good person you are, or by finding information about how hard it is for one individual to do anything about world hunger, or simply by saying, "Well, my heart's in the right place." Or, you could implement a direct strategy that has an impact on world hunger, such as then volunteering to work in a food bank.

Attempts to reduce dissonance can also explain why people who are not generally immoral may act immorally (Tsang, 2002). They can (1) change how they understand their immoral act in order to see it as having a higher moral purpose, or as being less immoral than what some other people do; (2) minimize their responsibility for it; (3) disregard the negative consequences (by avoiding knowledge of the results or minimizing the harm); and (4) blame and dehumanize the victims (Bandura, 1999; Tsang, 2002). For instance, those otherwise upstanding citizens who cheat on their taxes may tell themselves that it's not really cheating because they (1) view their lesser tax payment as a protest against a government policy; (2) argue that it's not really their fault, they need the money because the cost of living is so high; (3) claim that the government collects so much money that the small amount they don't pay is totally inconsequential; and (4) blame the President or Congress for having "such a high income tax" while giving themselves high salaries, lots of perks, and even tax breaks.

Cognitive dissonance has been used to increase behaviors that promote health. Stone and his colleagues (1997) set up a situation in which participants were induced to feel that they were being hypocritical. Sexually active college students were asked to write and videotape a talk on AIDS prevention for high school students. Participants who were asked to write speeches based on reasons they *personally* had not always used condoms were then more likely to purchase offered condoms than those who were asked to include in their speech reasons why *other* people might not use condoms.

Attitude Change: Persuasion

Walking to class, have you ever been approached by someone offering you a leaflet about an upcoming event, a political candidate, a new product? If so, someone (or some company) was trying to encourage you to do something: go to the event, vote for the candidate, buy the product. We are bombarded by attempts to change our attitudes about things, through advertisements, editorials, and conversations with friends. These efforts to change your attitudes are called **persuasion.**

Petty and Cacioppo (1986), in their *elaboration likelihood model* of attitude change, propose two routes to persuasion: central and peripheral. You are being affected by the *central* route when you pay close attention to the content of the argument—when you carefully read the leaflet to decide whether to attend the event, vote for the candidate, or buy the product. If you already hold the opposite view from that expressed in the leaflet, you will likely only be persuaded by strong arguments. But people who try to persuade us know that we don't always have the time, energy, or expertise to use central processing fully. When this occurs, they may rely instead on the *peripheral* route to persuade us. This route consists of attempts to sway us based not on the content of an argument, but rather on the attractiveness and expertise of the source (as in celebrity endorsements; Hovland & Weiss, 1951; Kiesler & Kiesler, 1969), the number of arguments (although not necessarily how "strong" we think they are), or how other people respond to the message. Furthermore, the **mere exposure effect** can change attitudes through the peripheral route: Simply becoming familiar with something (being exposed to it) can change your attitude toward it—generally, in a favorable way. And this attitude can generalize to similar objects or people (Zajonc, 2001).

Various characteristics of the person who tries to persuade us affect the peripheral route. Fast speakers are generally more persuasive than slow speakers (Miller et al., 1976). And if the attempt at persuasion arouses strong emotions in you, particularly fear, it is more likely to work, especially if it includes specific advice about what you can do to bring about a more positive outcome (Leventhal et al., 1965). This technique is used in public service messages that try to scare people into behaving differently, such as ads that graphically describe how someone contracted AIDS by not using a condom and then strongly recommend condom use. Not surprisingly, people who are perceived as honest are more persuasive (Priester & Petty, 1995).

After Katie Couric's colonoscopy was televised live into millions of homes, there was a 20% increase in the number of colonoscopy screenings performed (Dobson, 2002). This televised event undoubtedly persuaded more people to have the same procedure, using both central and peripheral routes. Can you describe how?

● **Persuasion:** Attempts to change people's attitudes.

● **Mere exposure effect:** Simply becoming familiar with something can change your attitude toward it—generally, in a favorable way.

If you are not paying full attention to an attempt at persuasion, you are less likely to be persuaded by a rational argument that requires you to think deeply about it, but more likely to be persuaded by a simplistic argument, at least in part because you have less ability to develop a counterargument (Allyn & Festinger, 1961; Romero et al., 1996). So, if you are watching a television commercial while sorting the laundry, you are more likely to be persuaded by it than if you're focused on it. If you've ever heard a Republican speaking to a group of Democrats (or vice versa), you may have noticed a persuasion technique used to convince people who hold the opposite view, whatever that view is: The would-be persuader uses a two-sided approach. The speaker presents both sides of an argument rather than only one side (as is common if the audience already agrees with the speaker). And when a message does not appear to be *trying* to persuade you to change your attitude, it is often more effective than one that is obviously trying to move you.

In an effort to persuade smokers to quit, this ad uses persuasion techniques. Which techniques are at work here?

Attempts at persuasion are often foiled by four common obstacles:

1. *Strong attitude.* If we, as listeners, already have a strong attitude about an issue, as opposed to a weak one, we are less likely to be persuaded to change our current attitude (Petty & Krosnick, 1996). Indeed, among identical twins reared apart (see Chapter 11), certain attitudes appear to be heritable, strong, and resistant to change. For instance, the attitude toward the death penalty has a high heritability; whatever is responsible for this attitude is, at least in part, affected by the genes (Tesser, 1993).

2. *Reactance.* Reactance is the development of a negative reaction to someone who is seen as trying too hard or too often to change our opinion. In this case, we may very well change our minds in the *opposite* direction from that intended by the persuader, even if we would not otherwise take that position; this response is called *negative attitude change* (Brehm, 1966).

3. *Forewarning.* If we know in advance that someone is going to try to persuade us of something, we are less likely to be persuaded (Cialdini & Petty, 1979; Petty & Cacioppo, 1981), although this is not always the case (Romero et al., 1996).

4. *Selective avoidance.* We may simply bypass someone's attempt to persuade us by deliberate selective avoidance, such as changing the channel during television commercials.

Social Cognitive Neuroscience

Attitudes are often unconscious, and therefore can be difficult to measure. As we've seen, one way to approach this thorny problem is to tap into unconscious processes by observing telltale behavioral signs (such as those measured by the IAT). Another way to tap into such unconscious processes is to query the brain itself. **Social cognitive neuroscience** attempts to understand social cognition not only by specifying the cognitive mechanisms (such as those involved in memory, attention, and perception) that underlie it, but also by discovering how those mechanisms are rooted in the brain (D. T. Gilbert, 2002; Ochsner & Lieberman, 2001). Social cognitive neuroscience bridges cognitive neuroscience and social cognition. On the one hand, as we saw in Chapter 1, cognitive neuroscience rests on the idea that "the mind is what the brain does"—and thus focuses on how mental processes can be

● **Social cognitive neuroscience:** The field that attempts to understand social cognition not only by specifying the cognitive mechanisms that underlie it, but also by discovering how those mechanisms are rooted in the brain.

related to brain structure and function. On the other hand, the field of social cognition addresses how social events are related to cognitive function. Social cognitive neuroscience ties together the two fields, attempting to fathom how social cognition arises from cognitive processes that in turn arise from the brain. This approach allows researchers to use the methods of neuroscience to grapple with questions that cannot easily be answered in other ways.

Here's an example: Do you think cognitive dissonance reduction depends on your consciously noticing the dissonance? The traditional view implies that you reason about the causes of cognitive dissonance in order to reduce this uncomfortable feeling. Lieberman and colleagues (2001) set out to test this idea. They studied patients with brain damage that produced amnesia; these patients could not consciously recall anything they had recently experienced. If you met the most severely affected of these patients and talked to him for 3 hours, and then left the room for 10 minutes, he would have no idea who you were when you returned (Schacter, 1996). Lieberman and colleagues realized that if cognitive dissonance reduction depends on recalling the events that led to the dissonance, then these patients should not experience this phenomenon. These researchers used a classic way to induce cognitive dissonance: If a researcher gives you two sets of stimuli that you like almost to the same degree, and requires you to decide which one you like better, you later will end up liking the one you chose even more than you did at the outset (and disliking the rejected set even more; Brehm, 1956). Because the two sets were in fact so similar, you could find reasons for liking either one — but when forced to choose, you need to reduce the dissonance that arises when you reject one that you do in fact like (but a hair less than the other) by exaggerating the differences between them. The question was, would amnesic patients behave the same way? The answer was "yes." Even amnesic patients become more positive about the chosen set and more negative about the rejected one. Their attitudes toward the sets shifted even though these patients had no conscious memory of ever having chosen between the two almost-equivalent sets! Thus, the traditional view is wrong: You don't need to be conscious of the causes of dissonance in order to try to reduce it.

The social cognitive neuroscience approach has illuminated many other aspects of social cognition (Ochsner & Lieberman, 2001). For example, in one study researchers used fMRI to monitor how strongly the amygdala was activated while White participants viewed unfamiliar African American and White faces (Phelps et al., 2000). The amygdala is a part of the brain that is activated when people encode aversive stimuli (see Chapter 10). The amygdala was more strongly activated by African American faces, compared to White faces, for people who had IAT scores that indicated negative attitudes about African Americans (consistent findings were also reported by Hart and colleagues, 2000). But the researchers did not find this relation between amygdala activation and IAT scores for the faces of *familiar* African American celebrities, such as Michael Jordan. Clearly, it was not just the race of individual faces that triggered the amygdala, but the participants' feelings about race more generally. To see why this effect occurs, we need to find out about stereotypes.

Stereotypes: Seen One, Seen 'Em All

In the social world around us, we could easily be overwhelmed by the torrent of information conveyed by other people — their words, postures, gestures, facial expressions—to say nothing of what we can infer about their attitudes and goals, and even further, what other people have said about them. The world is full of information and stimuli, and if we had no way of organizing this input flying at us from all directions, assaulting our senses, we would live in chaos. In the physical realm, we organize all of this information by principles such as Gestalt groupings of visual stimuli (see Chapter 4). To avoid drowning in this sea of social information, we create *stereotypes*, a type of schema (see Chapter 8) that helps provide a cognitive shortcut for processing all of this information about the social world (Allport, 1954; Gilbert & Hixon, 1991; Macrae et al., 1994). A **stereotype** is a belief (or set of beliefs) about people in a particular social category; the category can be defined by race, sex, social class, religion, hair color, sport, hobby, and myriad other characteristics. A stereotype may be positive, such as "women are nurturing"; neutral, such as "Mexicans eat spicy food"; or negative, such as "Australians drink too much."

When lawyers select a jury, they try to have certain potential jurors excluded because of stereotypes about how people of a certain race, sex, age, or profession are likely to view the case. But one study found that lawyers' stereotype-based expectations of whether jurors would be likely to convict were often incorrect (Olczak et al., 1991).

Not only can stereotypes affect how we feel about other people, but our expectations of others based on our stereotypes can lead *them* to behave in certain ways. (See Chapter 11 for an example of how expectations of others can change their behavior.) As with other types of classification, stereotypes can be useful shortcuts. But stereotypes are caricatures, not reasoned formulations, and are often incorrect. The effect of errors we make when using stereotypes is anything but trivial. Perhaps because we often strive for cognitive efficiency, we prefer to read information consistent with our stereotypes, and we process such information more quickly (Smith, 1998). As with attitudes, we are less likely to attend to, and therefore encode or remember, information inconsistent with our stereotypes (Johnston & Macrae, 1994), and in fact we may deny the truth of such information (O'Sullivan & Durso, 1984). Such stereotype-preserving actions are particularly likely if we believe that people's behavior is best explained by their traits (rather than the situation, see Chapter 11; Plaks et al., 2001).

Once a stereotype is activated, we respond to a person's membership in a social category, not to the characteristics of the individual person. Here's how this works. Suppose that you have a positive stereotype of New Englanders, believing them to be punctual and hard-working. When you meet someone from Maine, your "New Englander" stereotype is activated. You will then be more likely to notice aspects of her behavior that are consistent with your stereotype, and in thinking about her, you will be more likely to remember those aspects. You may not notice when she comes in late, or you will come up with plausible excuses for her tardiness. The stereotype thus lives on and may shape the rest of your thinking. One way this occurs is that information relevant to the stereotype is recalled faster than unrelated information (Dovidio et al., 1986). However, if you are motivated to be accurate, and do *not* assume that a stereotype applies to a particular individual, you can minimize the impact of stereotypes (Wyer et al., 2000).

Sometimes the conflict between a stereotype and actual behavior of someone from the stereotyped group is too great to be ignored—but rather than change a stereotype, we are more likely to create a new subtype within the stereotype

● **Stereotype:** A belief (or set of beliefs) about people in a particular social category.

(Anderson, 1983; Anderson et al., 1980). So in this case, when your New England acquaintance's chronic lateness and laziness are too great to ignore, you might create a subtype—"female New Englander having a hard time." This allows you to preserve your stereotype of New Englanders as punctual and hard-working. Because of this psychological phenomenon—creating subtypes in order to preserve a stereotype—stereotypes can be extremely difficult to change or eliminate. However, under certain circumstances, stereotypes *can* change, when the exception is made to appear typical of its group and when we are encouraged to think that the person's behavior results from his or her characteristics, *not* the situation (Wilder et al., 1996).

Cognition and Prejudice

Stereotyping can lead to **prejudice,** which is an attitude, generally negative, toward members of a group. Prejudice includes not only beliefs and expectations about the group but also an emotional component: Simply thinking about members of a disliked group can produce strong feelings about them (Bodenhausen et al., 1994). As is the case with attitudes and stereotypes, information inconsistent with a prejudice is less likely to be attended to and remembered accurately than is information consistent with a prejudice, making prejudice self-perpetuating.

Prejudice may be conscious and intentional; it may also be conscious and unintentional, or even unconscious and unintentional (Carter & Rice, 1997; Fazio et al., 1995; Greenwald & Banaji, 1995). And emotions can influence prejudice in two ways. The *presence of negative feelings* may account for conscious prejudice, whether intentional or unintentional. But even if someone does not have negative feelings toward a group, prejudice can also arise from the *absence of positive feelings* (Pettigrew & Meertens, 1995), leading to unconscious prejudice. Thus, someone can be prejudiced against a group with whom he or she has no experience; for instance, someone from an Asian country might have a prejudice against people with red hair that is engendered by the absence of any positive feelings or experiences.

UNDERSTANDING RESEARCH

How Stereotypes Can Prime Behavior

The case of Amadou Diallo may illustrate unconscious prejudice. In February, 1999, four New York City undercover police officers were driving down a Bronx street in an unmarked car. At 12:40 in the morning they noticed a man acting suspiciously in the stoop of a building, peering out, then "slinking" back. A serial rapist was still at large, and from what the police could see, the man on the stoop resembled the general description of the rapist. The plainclothes officers approached the man, Amidou Diallo, identified themselves as police, showed their badges, and ordered him to put his hands up. It is not known why Mr. Diallo pulled out his wallet in response, but the police officers reported that they thought it was a gun, and shot him 41 times. Mr. Diallo died.

Psychologist Keith Payne (2001) wanted to understand more about the psychological processes that would lead officers to see a wallet as a gun, and so he conducted the following study.

QUESTION: Can group stereotypes affect behavior without conscious awareness?

ALTERNATIVES: (1) Yes, group stereotypes can affect behavior without conscious awareness; (2) No, group stereotypes do not affect behavior outside of conscious awareness.

● **Prejudice:** An attitude (generally negative) toward members of a group.

LOGIC: If group stereotypes affect behavior outside of conscious awareness, then photos that prime racial stereotypes should automatically facilitate associations between the stereotype and objects consistent with it (see Chapter 7 for a discussion of priming).

METHOD: Thirty-one participants who were not African American saw the face of a White or African American man (as shown in the photos), which then disappeared. The face was followed by a picture of either a gun or a tool (see photo), and the participants were to press one key if they saw a gun, and another key if they saw a tool. They could take their time, and were asked to be as accurate as possible.

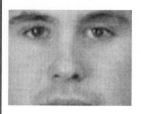 

RESULTS: The participants made very few errors (such as pressing a key for a gun when a tool was shown). When they saw the African American face followed by the gun, they pressed the appropriate key more quickly than they did when they saw the White face followed by the gun. In addition, when they saw the White face followed by the tool, they pressed the appropriate key more quickly than they did when they saw the African American face followed by the tool.

INFERENCES: The photos served to prime racial stereotypes, facilitating associations between the stereotype and objects consistent with it. Common stereotypes about African Americans are traits of hostility, aggression, and criminality (Devine & Elliot, 1995; Dovidio et al., 1986). Thus, guns are consistent with this stereotype. Similar results have been found with stereotype-consistent and inconsistent words primed by gender (Banaji & Hardin, 1996).

A follow-up study (Experiment 2, Payne, 2001) gave participants who were not African American only half a second to respond to each face–object pair, which pushed the participants to make more errors; thus, rather than focusing on response times, this study focused on the number of errors participants made after the different primes. White participants were more likely to identify a tool incorrectly as a gun when primed by an African American face than by a White one. Applying these results to the Diallo murder, we can understand how the police officers were primed to see an ambiguous shape (Mr. Diallo's wallet in the dim light) as a gun. Such stereotype-consistent prejudice is often unconscious and depends on the context; had these police officers been off duty and attending a movie when an African American took his wallet out of his pocket, they would not have reached for their guns.

According to social identity theory, members from both of these high school groups view their own group as superior to the other, and these views (conscious or not) may lead to prejudicial behavior against those in the other group.

Some cognitive operations perpetuate unconscious prejudice. *Social categorization* leads people to divide the world automatically into categories of "us" and "them," both consciously and unconsciously. According to social identity theory (Tajfal, 1982), in an effort to enhance self-esteem, people usually think of their own group—the **ingroup**—favorably. The other group, the **outgroup,** is usually disliked and assumed to possess more undesirable traits (Brewer & Brown, 1998; Fiske, 1998; Judd et al., 1991; Lambert, 1995; Linville & Fischer, 1993; Rustemli et al., 2000; Vonk & van Knippenberg, 1995). When we identify with an ingroup, we are more inclined to like, trust, help, and cooperate with other ingroup members than we are to like, trust, help, and cooperate with outgroup members (Brewer & Brown, 1998). Our views of the ingroup and outgroup can lead to unconscious prejudice (Fiske, 2002).

Another cognitive operation that can lead to unconscious prejudice is the *illusory correlation*, which is a tendency to overestimate the strength of a relationship between two things (Mullen & Johnson, 1990). This cognitive operation may explain why White people overestimate the number of crimes committed by African American men, and hence maintain their prejudice (Hamilton & Sherman, 1989). The *illusion of outgroup homogeneity* is an inclination to view an outgroup as more homogeneous (that is, it has members who are more similar to one another) than the ingroup. The corollary, *ingroup differentiation*, is the inclination to view members of an ingroup (that is, your own group) as more heterogeneous—members are more diverse than those of another group.

For example, a research study found that non-Hispanic Americans were less likely to distinguish among different types of Latinos (a perceived outgroup from the point of view of the non-Hispanics) than were Latinos themselves. However, Latinos only differentiated their own subgroup from all other Latino groups; thus, Mexican Americans were more likely to categorize themselves as a particular group—the ingroup—and to lump Cuban Americans and Puerto Ricans together as Latinos—the outgroup (Huddy & Virtanen, 1995).

● **Ingroup:** An individual's own group.

● **Outgroup:** A group different than an individual's own.

Discrimination

When Bessie Delany was in dental school, a White professor failed her on some work that she knew was good. A White girlfriend, also a dental student, offered to hand in Bessie's work as her own to see what grade the work would be given this time. Bessie's friend passed with the same work that had earned Bessie a failing grade.

Bessie's experience was one of discrimination; specifically, she suffered the effect of prejudiced behavior. Her professor's behavior was influenced by his prejudice against Bessie because of her race, her membership in a particular social category. As with stereotypes, people discriminate on the basis of just about anything that distinguishes groups: gender, race, social class, hair color, religion, college attended, height, and on and on. As with prejudice, discrimination may be subtle, and sometimes even unconscious.

Most Americans believe discrimination is wrong; when their own discriminatory behavior is pointed out to them, they are uncomfortable (Devine & Monteith, 1993), and they may subsequently reduce their discriminatory behaviors (Monteith, 1996). This phenomenon provides another example of the way we act to reduce cognitive dissonance: Becoming aware of the discrepancy between attitudes and behavior leads to the discomfort of cognitive dissonance, which can be reduced through changing future behaviors.

Why Does Prejudice Exist?

The effects of prejudice are limiting, damaging, and painful. Why then does prejudice exist? The *realistic conflict theory* (Bobo, 1983) suggests a reason—competition for scarce resources such as good housing, jobs, and schools. As groups compete for these resources, increasingly negative views of the other groups take form, eventually becoming prejudice.

A classic experiment, the Robber's Cave study, showed how easily prejudice can be created from competition (see Figure 16.4, p. 688; Sherif et al., 1961). A set of 11-year-old boys was divided into two groups, Eagles and Rattlers, at a special overnight camp called the Robber's Cave. The two groups competed for valued prizes. Conflict between the two groups quickly escalated into prejudice and discrimination, with the groups sometimes calling each other names and even destroying each other's property. However, such attitudes and behavior stopped when the two groups no longer competed for resources but cooperated for larger, mutually beneficial goals such as restoring the camp's water supply. Although the study has several limitations (it is unclear if the findings generalize to girls, non-White boys, or adults), it does illustrate how prejudice can both develop and dissipate (Sherif et al., 1961).

The Robber's Cave study supports the view of realistic conflict theory that competition between groups for scarce resources can produce prejudice. But are scarcity and competition necessary to produce prejudice? Apparently not. Social categorization theory provides one explanation for prejudice in the absence of scarcity or competition: In this view, the psychological forces leading to ingroup favoritism are so powerful that creating even an *arbitrary* "us" and "them" can lead to unconscious favoritism and discriminatory behavior (Feather, 1996; Perdue et al., 1990). This social categorization can lead to discrimination in two distinct ways: (1) The ingroup is actively favored; and (2) the outgroup is actively disfavored.

Eleven-year-old boys at a special overnight summer camp (called the Robber's Cave) were the participants in this study. In the initial phase of the study, the boys were randomly divided into two groups and separated from each other for a week. During this time, activities fostered a sense of cohesion in each group.

During the 2-week-long second phase, the two groups competed for highly desired prizes such as pocket knives and medals. Conflict between the two groups quickly escalated from name calling to direct acts (destroying the other group's personal property). Negative attitudes as well as negative behavior developed, with each group labeling the other with pejorative terms such as "coward."

In the third phase, the two groups were brought together to work on a number of superordinate goals such as restoring the camp's water supply. Tensions between the groups dissolved by the 6th day of this phase.

Although social categorization can perpetuate a skewed picture of other people, it is efficient because once we've made an "us" versus "them" distinction, we can then use our stereotypes about "us" and "them" to understand behavior, saving us the effort of paying close attention to other people and actively processing our observations of their behavior. Because we expect certain behaviors from outgroup members, just being in their presence can activate our stereotypes about them (Bargh et al., 1996). We may then behave in ways that elicit behavior from an outgroup member that is consistent with that stereotype, even if he or she wouldn't otherwise behave that way (Snyder, 1984, 1992). This process thus becomes a self-fulfilling prophecy: The elicited behavior confirms our stereotype, and we regard the outgroup member's behavior as "proof" of the validity of our prejudices (Fiske, 1998). However, our goals in a given situation or interaction can lessen the use of these cognitive shortcuts: If it is important to be accurate in our view of an outgroup member, we are more motivated to think actively, and perhaps accurately, about that person (Fiske, 1998).

Once a prejudicial attitude is in place, *social learning theory* (see Chapter 6) explains how it can be spread and passed through generations as a learned stereotype. Parents, peers, television, movies, and other aspects of the culture provide models of prejudice (Pettigrew, 1969). When prejudice is translated into words and actions, it may be reinforced. Scarce resources, competition, natural cognitive mechanisms, and learning may all contribute to the development and maintenance of prejudice.

Changing Prejudice: Easier Said Than Done

Psychology has shown us how prejudice develops and deepens; equally important, can psychology show us how to arrest the development of prejudice? The answer is yes, but the task is not easily accomplished.

One method of decreasing prejudice is described by the *contact hypothesis*, which holds that increased contact between different groups will decrease prejudice between them (Pettigrew, 1981). Increased contact serves several purposes: (1) Both groups are more likely to become aware of similarities between the groups, which can enhance mutual attraction; (2) Even though stereotypes resist change, when stereotypic views are met with enough inconsistent information or exceptions, those views *can* change (Kunda & Oleson, 1995); and (3) Increased contact can shatter the illusion that the outgroup is homogeneous (Baron & Byrne, 1997).

What are children in Bosnia being taught about Gavrilo Princip, the man who started World War I by assassinating Archduke Franz Ferdinand D'Este of Austria-Hungary in 1914? Textbooks in the Serb-controlled part of Bosnia call the act heroic; a Croatian textbook refers to Princip as an "assassin trained and instructed by the Serbs to commit this act of terrorism"; and a Muslim textbook refers to him as a nationalist and says the resulting anti-Serbian rioting "was only stopped by police from all three ethnic groups" (Hedges, 1997). Social learning theory explains how these different perspectives can lead to prejudice toward other ethnic groups.

Increased contact does reduce prejudice (Emerson et al., 2002), particularly under certain conditions, such as when working toward a shared goal and when all participants are deemed to be equal. For example, politically influential members of Israeli and Palestinian groups met informally and unofficially for sessions of intensive interactive problem solving. The increased contact that occurred while working on the larger goal of resolving obstacles to peace talks was partly successful in lowering the barriers between the two sides. After the Oslo Peace Accord in 1993, many of those involved viewed these informal group meetings as directly and indirectly laying the foundation for the beginning steps toward peace (Kelman, 1997). The meetings, although not designed to reduce prejudice, nonetheless fulfilled one of the steps in that direction: coming together to work toward a shared goal. Other conditions, however, were not met: The participants from the two sides were *not* equal (Brewer & Brown, 1998), nor did they view each other as typical of their respective populations. Although they were able to work together for this one overarching goal of beginning peace discussions, the larger task of hammering out an agreement and sticking to it did not progress smoothly.

Another way to decrease prejudice is through **recategorization**—that is, shifting the categories of "us" and "them" so that the two groups are no longer distinct entities. Examples of recategorization are familiar in everyday life. An assembly-line worker who is promoted to management experiences recategorization: The identity of "us" and "them" changes. When distinctions between groups are minimized so that different groups can be thought of as a single entity, recategorization can decrease prejudice. Working together toward a common goal facilitates recategorization, such as occurred in the Robber's Cave study

● **Recategorization:** A means of reducing prejudice by shifting the categories of "us" and "them" so that the two groups are no longer distinct entities.

when, instead of being Eagles or Rattlers, all boys became simply campers who had no running water.

Social psychologist Eliot Aronson and colleagues devised another way to decrease prejudice, which has been used in many American classrooms. This technique is called the "jigsaw classroom," and is a cooperative learning technique (Aronson & Osherow, 1980; Aronson & Platnoe, 1997). Integrated groups of five or six students from different backgrounds are formed and given an assignment, such as learning about the American War of Independence (see Figure 16.5). Each member of a jigsaw group researches a different aspect of the project (such as military strategy, George Washington's actions, women's roles); after doing their separate research, the members of each jigsaw group researching the same topic form a new group—an expert group—comprised of one member from each jigsaw

FIGURE 16.5 The Jigsaw Classroom

The classroom is divided into groups of 5 or 6 children from different backgrounds (jigsaw groups), and each group studies the same general subject. Each member of the group has a specific topic he or she must research.

After each student does his or her research, they reconfigure into expert groups, where one member from each jigsaw group meets with his or her counterparts from the other groups. Expert groups discuss the results of their research and practice their presentations. This is the "George Washington" expert group.

Each member of the jigsaw group presents his or her research to the rest of the group. Every student is tested on all of the information, so students must listen closely to every presentation. This method fosters interdependence and mutual respect and reduces prejudice.

group. For instance, all students researching George Washington will meet together after doing their research; this is the Washington expert group. These expert groups meet to share information and rehearse presentations. The expert groups then disband; each member writes a report and reads that report to his or her original jigsaw group. The only way jigsaw group members can learn about all of the topics is to pay close attention to everyone's reports; as with a jigsaw puzzle, each member's contribution is a piece of the whole, and each person depends on the others. The jigsaw method decreases prejudice (Aronson & Osherow, 1980; Walker & Crogan, 1998) in ways similar to other techniques: by increasing contact between individuals from different "groups" and creating new, integrated groups that require mutual interdependence in order to achieve a superordinate goal.

Attributions: Making Sense of Events

When you read about the Delany sisters' successes, how did you explain them? Did you say to yourself, *The sisters worked hard and persevered*? Or, *They were lucky*? Whatever your reaction, it reflects not only your attitudes, stereotypes, and prejudices, but the attributions you make. **Attributions** are our explanations for the causes of events or behaviors.

What Is the Cause?

Usually, events and actions have many possible causes. An unreturned telephone call to a friend might be an indication that your friend is very busy, is annoyed at you, or simply had problems with voicemail. If a politician you admire changes position on an issue, do you explain the behavior as a sincere change of heart, a cave-in to heavy campaign contributors, or a calculated attempt to appeal to new supporters?

The particular attributions people make are of two broad types: internal and external. **Internal attributions** (also called *dispositional attributions*) explain a person's behavior in terms of that person's preferences, beliefs, goals, or other characteristics. For instance, if a friend leaves a math lecture very confused, you could attribute his confusion to internal factors: "I guess he's not very good at math." **External attributions** (also called *situational attributions*) explain a person's behavior in terms of the situation (Kelley, 1972; Kelley & Michela, 1980). If you make an external attribution for your friend's confusion, you might say, "The professor gave a really bad lecture today."

The attributions you make about events affect both you and other people (see Table 16.1, p. 692): Blaming yourself for negative events (internal attribution) can suppress your immune system (Segerstrom et al., 1996; see Chapter 13). Blaming yourself or others affects behavior: Mothers who view their children's misbehavior as the children's fault are likely to discipline their children more harshly than mothers who attribute such misbehavior to other causes, such as their mothering (Slep & O'Leary, 1998).

How do you decide whether to attribute someone's behavior to internal or external causes? Take the following situation: When Sadie wanted a job teaching at a high school, there were no Black high school teachers in New York. At Bessie's urging, Sadie applied for the job. After her application was received, school administrators asked Sadie to come in for a meeting; she simply didn't go. (She later apologized, explaining she had "forgotten.") She subsequently received a letter that offered her the job. When she appeared on the first day of school, the school

● **Attribution:** An explanation for the cause of an event or behavior.

● **Internal attribution:** An explanation of someone's behavior that focuses on the person's beliefs, goals, or other dispositions; also called *dispositional attribution*.

● **External attribution:** An explanation of behavior that focuses on the situation; also called *situational attribution*.

TABLE 16.1 Examples of Types of Attributions

	Internal Attributions	External Attributions
Attributions about oneself	*Positive:* I did a good job because I'm smart.	*Positive:* I did a good job because the task was easy.
	Negative: I did a bad job because I'm inept.	*Negative:* I did a bad job because the time allotted for the task was too short.
Attributions about others	*Positive:* She did a good job because she's smart.	*Postive:* She did a good job because the task was easy.
	Negative: She did a bad job because she's inept.	*Negative:* She did a bad job because the time allotted for the task was too short.

administrators were very surprised to find out she was Black but did not deny her the job. Did Sadie's decision to miss the face-to-face interview reflect an enduring "doesn't play by the rules" trait, or was it based on the realities of that particular situation? How do we decide? Harold Kelley's **theory of causal attribution** identifies rules for deciding whether to attribute a behavior to a person's enduring traits or to the situation. In this view, when people try to understand the behavior of others, they automatically, without conscious awareness, take into account three dimensions: consensus, consistency, and distinctiveness.

Consensus. Would other people react similarly in the situation? If so, greater weight should be given to the situation than to personal traits. For example, would other Black women applying for the high school teaching job that Sadie eventually obtained not show up for the face-to-face interview? If so, the behavior has high consensus.

Consistency. Has the person responded in the same way in similar situations? If so, the cause of the behavior is likely to be stable (either internal or external). For example, if Sadie avoided personal interviews when applying for similar jobs, her behavior would have high consistency.

Distinctiveness. Has the person responded differently in situations that are not similar? If so, the cause may be situational. For example, if Sadie didn't usually miss meetings or appointments on purpose, her behavior in this case had high distinctiveness.

According to Kelley's theory, you attribute someone's behavior to internal causes if consensus and distinctiveness are low and consistency is high. In contrast, if consensus, consistency, and distinctiveness are all high, you attribute the behavior to external causes. You attribute behavior to both internal and external causes if consensus is low and consistency and distinctiveness are high. If we knew that Sadie's behavior during the application process had high consensus, consistency, and distinctiveness, we would be able to attribute her behavior to external causes.

Do people really think this way? If you follow Kelley's rules, making causal attributions involves a lot of cognitive work. Nonetheless, people apparently do use all of the factors proposed by Kelley if an event or behavior is either unexpected or

● **Theory of causal attribution:** Rules for deciding whether to attribute a given behavior to a person's enduring traits or to the situation.

has a negative outcome. In other cases, however, people usually take shortcuts, letting their general beliefs and biases guide their judgments.

Taking Shortcuts: Attributional Biases

Like stereotypes, **attributional biases** are cognitive shortcuts for determining attributions that generally occur outside our awareness. They help lessen the cognitive load required to make sense of the world, but they can lead to errors. These errors have implications for social relationships, the legal system, and social policy. Suppose, for example, you are a member of a jury and hear that the defendant confessed to the crime. It turns out that the confession was extracted after many hours of tough, coercive questioning by police. The judge then throws out the confession, striking it from the record, and tells you, the jury, to ignore it. Would you? Could you? Researchers using mock juries found that jurors in this situation assume that the confession was heartfelt and vote guilty more often than jurors who do not hear about a confession (Kassin & Wrightsman, 1981). The "jurors" are demonstrating the **fundamental attribution error** (Ross et al., 1977), the strong tendency to interpret other people's behavior as caused by internal causes rather than external ones. In the courtroom example, jurors would thus be more likely to view the confession as evidence of guilt (an internal attribute) than coercion (an external attribute).

As its name suggests, the fundamental attribution error is one of the most common attributional biases and a frequent source of error. The fundamental attribution error is at work, for example, when the sight of a homeless man on a bench leads us to assume his plight is due to an internal trait such as laziness rather than external factors such as a run of bad luck, a high unemployment rate, and a lack of affordable housing, or when a driver cuts in front of you on the road, and you attribute his lack of road etiquette to his despicable personality traits rather than situational factors (J. S. Baxter et al., 1990). The fundamental attribution error helps perpetuate discrimination because fault is attributed to the person, not to the circumstances. Once you make the fundamental attribution error, you are likely to ignore the context of future behavior (that is, the surrounding situation), and thus the effect of the initial error is multiplied.

Related to the fundamental attribution error is the **self-serving bias** (Brown & Rogers, 1991; Miller & Ross, 1975), the inclination to attribute your failures to external causes and your successes to internal ones, but to attribute other people's failures to internal causes and their successes to external causes. As a result, you consider the negative actions of others as arbitrary and unjustified, but perceive your own negative acts as understandable and justifiable (Baumeister et al., 1990). You are angry and slam things around because you've had a terrible day; your roommate throws tantrums because he or she has an awful temper. A society as a whole may engage in this type of bias, leading one culture, ethnic group, or nation to attribute positive values and traits to its own group, and negative values and traits to other cultures and ethnic groups, sustaining ethnic conflict (Rouhana & Bar-Tal, 1998).

Not all cultures exhibit these various biases to the same degree. Just as different cultures promote different personality traits (see Chapter 11), they also lead

When you see a homeless person, to what do you attribute his or her homelessness? Chances are that the fundamental attribution error is at work if you assume that his or her plight is due to an internal trait such as laziness rather than to external factors such as a run of bad luck, a high unemployment rate, and a lack of affordable housing.

● **Attributional bias:** A cognitive shortcut for determining attribution that generally occurs outside our awareness.

● **Fundamental attribution error:** The strong tendency to interpret other people's behavior as due to internal (dispositional) causes rather than external (situational) ones.

● **Self-serving bias:** A person's inclination to attribute his or her own failures to external causes and successes to internal causes, but to attribute other people's failures to internal causes and their successes to external causes.

● **Belief in a just world:** An attributional bias that assumes people get what they deserve.

people to use attributional biases somewhat differently. For example, accounts of crimes in Chinese-language newspapers are more likely to give external explanations, whereas for the same offense, English-language newspapers are more likely to emphasize internal factors (Morris & Peng, 1994).

Attributions can also be distorted by a **belief in a just world** (Lerner, 1980), the assumption that people get what they deserve. Because most Americans are richer than most Egyptians, Colombians, or Bulgarians, they must, according to this bias, also be smarter or work harder. According to the belief in a just world, if you get what you deserve, you must have done something to deserve what you get—notice the circular reasoning here! The belief in a just world can shape reactions to violent crime (particularly rape; Karuza & Carey, 1984) and contributes to the practice of *blaming the victim.* For example, those who strongly believe in a just world are more likely than others to view AIDS as a deserved punishment for homosexual behavior (Glennon & Joseph, 1993) and to view the plight of a disadvantaged group, such as immigrants, as deserved (Dalbert & Yamauchi, 1994). This belief maintains discriminatory behaviors (Lipkus & Siegler, 1993).

Looking *at* Levels

Punishing Rapists

Events at the levels of brain, person, and group interact to form our attitudes. Think about how we can understand a particular attitude. What's your attitude about rapists? More specifically, what's your attitude about how severely rapists should be punished? Should they get the death penalty? At the level of the brain, we have seen that among identical twins reared apart, certain attitudes, such as the attitude toward the death penalty, are in part heritable; genetic factors indirectly affect this attitude, which can range from very much in favor to very much opposed. These attitudes will affect how we evaluate information about whether the death penalty is a successful deterrent in reducing crime. However, your attitudes about the death penalty may not predict how you would vote on it unless your attitudes are strong, or based on direct experience with a capital crime.

At the level of the person, you have developed stereotypes about the kinds of people who are rapists or who are raped. Because of the nature of stereotypes, should you meet a convicted rapist who doesn't fit your stereotype, you are not likely to change your stereotype, but rather will create a separate subtype of rapist,

leaving the larger category unchanged. If you like this person, you might attribute blame for the rape to the victim, not the rapist.

This analysis at the level of the person may conflict with analysis at the level of the group. If a member of your group, perhaps defined by class, race, or family, has been raped by someone not in your group, you may vilify all members of outgroups, particularly those to which the rapist belongs. Thus, events at the three levels need not be entirely consistent and will interact in complex ways. Depending on the precise situation, events at one level or another may win out; if so, the result may be cognitive dissonance, perhaps leading you to modify your behavior or attitudes.

TEST YOURSELF!

1. Do first impressions really make a difference?
2. What is the relationship between people's attitudes and their behaviors?
3. What are stereotypes? Why do people have them? What are the differences between stereotypes and prejudice?
4. How do we determine responsibility for positive and negative events, and what difference does it make?

Social Behavior: Interacting With People

The Delanys had very definite ideas about how they were supposed to behave with people. Based on their ideas about marriage, both Sadie and Bessie decided early on not to marry. They both definitely wanted careers, and women of that era often had to choose between a career and marriage. Moreover, their father instilled in them a sense of self-reliance, as evidenced in his advice to Sadie about going to Columbia University: He advised her not to take a scholarship because she might then feel indebted to the people who offered it. He encouraged her to pay for her own education.

The Delanys also had definite ideas about how other people should be treated. They were taught to help others, regardless of skin color; the family motto was "Your job is to help someone." The Delanys stuck by their beliefs, even when others did not agree. Bessie recounts a time she vacationed in Jamaica with a darker-skinned Jamaican-born friend. There, Bessie learned that there were two official classes of Jamaican Negroes: "White Negroes," who had more privileges in society, and "Black Negroes," who were considered to be in a lower social class. The young women stayed with the family of Bessie's friend, who was a "Black Negro." "White Negroes" extended invitations to Bessie (a lighter-skinned African American) and ignored her friend. Bessie refused all invitations until her friend was invited as well.

Whereas social cognition focuses on individuals' perceptions of the social world, social behavior focuses on aspects of social situations that affect diverse types of behavior—from intimate relationships to obedience.

Relationships: Having a Date, Having a Partner

Sadie and Bessie's White maternal great-great-grandmother had a liaison with a slave while her husband was away fighting in the War of 1812. This relationship produced two daughters, half-sisters to the seven children she had already had with her husband. When her husband returned home, he adopted the two girls as his own. No one knew exactly what happened to her lover, although it was rumored that he ran away on the husband's return. The relationship between the Delanys' great-great-grandmother and biological great-great-grandfather would appear to have been based on more than a passing interest, given that the relationship spanned a number of years. Why were they attracted to each other? Why are we attracted to certain people? Why do we like particular people, and love others?

As the Delany children's ancestors undoubtedly experienced almost 2 centuries ago, and you may be experiencing now, relationships are strong stuff. They can lead to our most positive emotions and, as you saw in Chapter 13, can help us regulate our emotions in response to events outside the relationship (Berscheid & Reis, 1998). They can also be the source of negative emotions: When asked about the "last bad thing that happened to you," almost half the respondents reported conflict in a significant relationship (Cupach & Spitzberg, 1994).

Liking: To Like or Not to Like

Even though Sadie and Bessie decided not to marry, they still had boyfriends. Why were they attracted to certain men—why are you attracted to some people and

Recent research recognizes that physical distance itself may no longer be as important as it once was in defining "repeated contact": Internet chat rooms and interest groups make it possible for a couple to "meet" and have a relationship without any physical contact (Parks & Roberts, 1998).

not others? First impressions play an initial role, as does *repeated contact*, which usually leads to a more positive evaluation of someone (Moreland & Zajonc, 1982; Zajonc, 1968). The Delany sisters recount that a lot of "racial mixing, especially after slavery days, was just attraction between people, plain and simple, just like happened in our family, on Mama's side. You know, when people live in close proximity, they can't help but get attracted to each other" (p. 76).

Similarity is a second factor in the development of liking; the more similar a stranger's attitudes are to your own, the more likely you are to be attracted (Tesser, 1993). In this case, the adage "Opposites attract" has *not* been borne out by research. Similarity of preferred activities (Lydon, Jamieson et al., 1988), even similar ways of communicating, can lead to increased attraction and liking. For instance, we are more likely to be attracted to someone whose nonverbal cues are the same as those used in our own culture (Dew & Ward, 1993). In general, the greater the similarity, the more probable it is that our liking for another person will endure (Byrne, 1971).

A third, and major, factor is *physical attraction* (Collins & Zebrowitz, 1995; Hatfield & Sprecher, 1986). In part, the role of physical attraction in liking may be influenced by our stereotypes about attractive people—such as that they are smarter and happier. Although the stereotype that people who are physically more attractive possess more desirable attributes is found in different cultures, what constitutes "more desirable" differs across cultures. For instance, in Korea (a collectivist country; see Chapters 10 and 11), attractive people are thought to have greater integrity and concern for others—qualities more valued in that collectivist culture than in individualist Western ones (Wheeler & Kim, 1997).

Can all human beings agree on what makes someone attractive? Research that seeks to answer this question has generally focused on facial features. What makes a man attractive to women are large eyes, a large chin, prominent cheekbones, and a big smile (Cunningham et al., 1990); men prefer women with a small nose, prominent cheekbones, and a big smile (Cunningham, 1986). Findings of what constitutes attractiveness are consistent across cultures. For example, when shown photographs of faces of Hispanic, Asian, White, and African American women, ratings of attractiveness by recent Asian and Hispanic male immigrants were similar to those of White and African American men (Cunningham et al., 1995). There is some evidence that cultures rate as attractive faces that are "average" looking—that is, their proportions approximate the population average (Jones & Hill, 1993). One theory that explains this preference is that "average" faces are more likely to look familiar because they are more similar to the faces of the rest of the population, and familiarity, via the mere exposure effect, can lead to liking (Rhodes et al., 2001). We also prefer faces that are symmetrical (Grammer & Thornhill, 1994). Thus, one proposal is that people's preference for symmetry reflects a desire to choose a mate who "looks healthy" because facial asymmetries may reflect the presence of disease (Grammer & Thornhill, 1994; Thornhill & Gangestad, 1993). There is also evidence that people prefer men's and women's faces that are "feminized"—that is, faces that reflect higher levels of female hormones (Perrett et al., 1998; see Chapter 4). In addition, one study found that women were attracted or turned off not just by appearance, but also by a man's body odor (Herz & Inzlicht, 2002).

Loving: How Do I Love Thee?
Despite all the poems and plays, novels and movies, that chronicle, celebrate, and analyze love, its mystery endures. Its variations, components, styles, and fate

over time have all been examined by psychologists. Loving appears to be a qualitatively different feeling from liking, not simply very strong liking (Rubin, 1970). Moreover, attitudes about and experiences with love appear to be similar across cultures as diverse as those of Russia, Japan, and the United States (Sprecher, Aron, et al., 1994).

People talk about "loving" all sorts of things in all sorts of ways. You might say you love a pet, a friend, a parent, a mate, and pizza with anchovies; obviously you don't mean quite the same thing in each case. Love is usually studied in the context of relationships. Sexual or **passionate love**—the intense, often sudden feeling of being "in love"—involves sexual attraction, a desire for mutual love and physical closeness, arousal, and a fear that the relationship will end. **Compassionate love** is marked by very close friendship, mutual caring, liking, respect, and attraction (Caspi & Herbener, 1990).

What do the various sorts of love have in common, and how can we understand their differences? Robert Sternberg has proposed a **triangular model of love** (1986a, 1988a). Love, he says, has three dimensions: (1) passion (including sexual desire); (2) intimacy (emotional closeness and sharing); and (3) commitment (the conscious decision to be in the relationship). Particular relationships reflect different proportions of each dimension, in amounts that are likely to vary over time (see Figure 16.6). According to Sternberg's theory, most types of love relationships involve two of the three components; only "consummate love" has passion, intimacy, *and* commitment.

Attachment style is another way of thinking about different kinds of love relationships. The attachment style with a partner stems from the interaction pattern developed between parent and child (Waller & Shaver, 1994). For instance, adults who seek closeness and interdependence in relationships and are not worried about the possibility of the loss of the relationship, about 59% of an American sample, are said to have a *secure* style of attachment (Mickelson et al., 1997). Those who are uncomfortable with intimacy and closeness, about 25% of an American sample, have an *avoidant* style and structure their daily lives so as to avoid closeness (Tidwell et al., 1996). Those who want but simultaneously fear a relationship have an *anxious–ambivalent* style (Hazan & Shaver, 1990); about 11% of Americans have this style. Although by extrapolation from these studies, a majority of Americans have a secure style (Hazan & Shaver, 1987), an anxious–ambivalent style is more common in Japan and Israel, and an avoidant style more common in Germany (Shaver & Hazan, 1994).

Are our love relationships in part genetically determined? Apparently not. When twins were tested on six scales that measured different aspects of romantic relationships, little evidence of heritability was found (Waller & Shaver, 1994). As Plomin and his colleagues (1997, p. 205) put it, "Perhaps love *is* blind, at least from the DNA point of view." If our relationship style isn't genetically influenced, are we doomed to repeat the style of our childhood interactions with our parents?

FIGURE 16.6 Sternberg's Triangular Model of Love

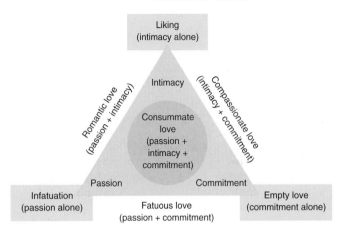

According to Sternberg's triangular theory of love, passion, intimacy, and commitment form three points of a triangle. Any given relationship may have only one component (at a point), two components (one of the sides of the triangle), or all three components (the center of the triangle).

- **Passionate love:** An intense feeling that involves sexual attraction, a desire for mutual love and physical closeness, arousal, and a fear that the relationship will end.

- **Compassionate love:** A type of love marked by very close friendship, mutual caring, liking, respect, and attraction.

- **Triangular model of love:** A theory of love marked by the dimensions of (1) passion (including sexual desire), (2) intimacy (closeness), and (3) commitment.

Although these early interactions affect attachment style, the outcome is not set in stone at childhood's end. The relationships we have as adults can change our attachment style (Shaver & Hazan, 1994).

As you may have experienced in your relationships, a sense of intimacy usually progresses in stages (Honeycutt et al., 1998), and how we feel in the relationship influences the relationship itself. A growing feeling of intimacy comes from three factors: (1) Feeling understood by your partner; (2) Feeling "validated," that is, feeling that your emotions and point of view are respected; and (3) Feeling that the other person cares for you (Reis & Shaver, 1988). As a relationship progresses, love seems to deepen over time (Sprecher, 1999). And just as mood can influence other aspects of our lives, such as memory, it influences us in this area as well: We are more likely to think our relationships are good when we're in a positive mood. Moreover, our attributions for serious conflicts in our relationships shift in response to our moods: In a bad mood, we are more likely to attribute relationship problems to vague, stable, internal factors; in a good mood, we are more likely to attribute the causes of conflict to specific, unstable, external factors (Forgas et al., 1994).

Making Love Last

As noted, the way we think about people, things, and events can have a powerful effect on our feelings, behavior, and subsequent thoughts. This is also true of relationships. If you are asked to think about the external reasons and pressures to stay in a relationship (having something to do on Saturday nights, your parents' approval), you will view commitment to the relationship as less likely, and report less love for your partner, than if you think about the enjoyment you experience in the relationship and other intrinsic motivational factors (Seligman et al., 1980).

Research results indicate that sex is only one facet of lasting love. Myers (1993) summarizes four factors that determine whether love will be sustained. First, "similarity breeds content" (p. 170): You are more likely to stay involved with someone who is similar to you. (Byrne, 1971). Second, successful couples have sex more often than they argue, and people in successful marriages have sex more often than those in less successful marriages. Third, successful couples are intimate: They share their innermost thoughts and feelings. Fourth, people in successful marriages share in decision making and in the daily burdens of maintaining a house and home.

Reciprocity also has a part in close relationships: If you want to sustain close relationships, you should help people who help you, and not hurt them (Gouldner, 1960). If someone does you a favor, you have an obligation to return the favor in the future, although this debt will not necessarily concern you indefinitely (Burger et al., 1997). However, in successful long-term relationships members do not keep track of debts, assuming that they will average out over time.

Mating Preferences: Your Cave or Mine?

Is love the reason people settle down and have children? According to evolutionary theory, among our ancestors those couples more closely bonded to each other and to their children were more likely to have offspring who survived. Thus, evolutionary theorists propose, humans today are genetically predisposed not only to search for sex but also to fall in love and to tend to their children (Trivers, 1972).

Finding someone attractive and liking, or even loving, that person is different from choosing him or her as a mate; we may date people we wouldn't necessarily want to marry. Why do we view certain people as potential mates, and not others?

Evolutionary theorists propose that a reason why men are attracted by a well-proportioned body and symmetrical features is that these characteristics, along with other features, signal fertility and health, (Thornhill & Gangestad, 1993). This view is supported by research with identical female twins; the twin whose face was more symmetrical was rated as more attractive (Mealey et al., 1999). In contrast, women find men attractive who appear to be able to protect and nourish them and their children; in modern society, researchers translate this as having good earning potential (D. M. Buss, 1989, 1999; Sprecher, Sullivan, et al., 1994).

Evolutionary psychologists have argued that characteristics associated with reproduction are particularly likely to have been shaped by natural selection. David Buss, (1989) asked people in 37 countries to rank order how important they believed 18 different characteristics are in ideal mates. In most respects, men and women valued the characteristics similarly; everybody agreed, for example, that kindness and intelligence are of paramount importance, and that emotional stability, dependability, and a good disposition are important (similar findings are reported by Li et al., 2002; Cramer et al., 1996). Respondents also valued mutual attraction and love. However, men and women did not have identical desires: Men tended to focus on physical attractiveness, whereas women tended to focus on wealth and power. Basing his view on evolutionary theory (Trivers, 1972, 1985), Buss (1994) has argued that women seek characteristics in men that would direct resources to their children, whereas men seek characteristics in women that indicate high fertility.

However, Speed and Gangestad (1997) found slightly different results when they collected less subjective ratings. In their study, they asked members of a sorority and a fraternity house to nominate other members whom they felt scored high on specific qualities such as physical attractiveness and likelihood of financial success. The investigators then examined which of these characteristics predicted the frequency with which those nominated were asked out on dates. Perhaps the most interesting results concerned the men. As expected, romantically popular men were seen by their peers as confident, outgoing, and "trend-setting." However, they were not seen as likely to succeed financially or as the best leaders, both characteristics that would seem to reflect the qualities that evolution is supposed to favor in males.

Other studies have shown that as women come to have more economic power, their preference in mates becomes more similar to men's—that is, physical attractiveness becomes more important (Eagly & Wood, 1999; Gangestad, 1993). Women's preference for men who make good providers may reflect women's historic economic dependence on men rather than a true biological preference. In general, then, the sex differences are more pronounced in studies that use self-reports versus actual behavior (Feingold, 1990) and in situations in which women have less economic power.

However, evolution is more than natural selection (see Chapters 1 and 3); we have inherited some characteristics

Evolutionary theorists propose that women are attracted to men who will be good providers, and men are attracted to women who have physical attributes associated with fertility. However, not all research supports this view: As women gain more economic power, they become more interested in a man's attractiveness.

What constitutes an "attractive" body type differs over time and across cultures. Women who today in America would be considered overweight or even obese have a body type that has been and continues to be attractive in some cultures.

- **Social exchange theory:** A theory that proposes that individuals act to maximize the gains and minimize the losses in their relationships.

- **Group:** A social entity characterized by regular interaction among members, emotional connection, a common frame of reference, and interdependence.

- **Deindividuation:** The loss of sense of self that occurs when people are in a group but are anonymous.

not because they are adaptive in themselves but rather because they are associated with other characteristics that are adaptive. Nor are the brain's circuits all dictated from birth: Learning rewires the brain, and development itself allows the environment to shape the way the brain works. Culture obviously plays an important role in shaping mate preferences: What is deemed an attractive body type changes with time (Wolf, 1991). Also, the characteristics that make a man a good provider depend in part on the culture; the properties that make a man a good rancher are not necessarily those of a good stockbroker. In short, it would be a serious error to assume that what people find attractive or unattractive can be entirely explained by analyses of what might have been useful for mating among our distant ancestors.

How else, then, do psychologists explain why we get into and stay in relationships? Another approach looks for explanations in the immediate situation. **Social exchange theory** offers a rather dry-eyed view, holding that individuals are like accountants, trying to maximize the gains and minimize the losses in their relationships. If the losses outweigh the gains, the relationship is likely to end. In order for a relationship to continue, it must be profitable enough for both parties (Kelley, 1979; Sprecher, 1998; Thibaut & Kelley, 1959). But what is "enough"? The profits and losses in a relationship are compared with expectations based on past relationships, or the *comparison level*. Thus, if you have just left an abusive relationship, your comparison level is likely to be low, and a relationship without abuse might be seen as one providing a big profit.

In short, we enter, maintain, and leave relationships for a multitude of reasons. Unless a relationship is arranged for us by others, as it is in some cultures, attractiveness and similarity are two key factors that influence whom we like and whom we love.

Social Organization: Group Rules, Group Roles

If you live with other people, in the same apartment or on the same dorm floor, you might agree that the people in your living unit constitute a group, even if you don't get along. But if you live in a building with a number of apartments, or a residence hall with many floors, would everyone living there be considered part of a group, even if they don't all know one another? What, exactly, constitutes a group? Social psychologists have long wrestled with such questions and have come up with a number of definitions. There are some commonalities, though, in the use of the term **group**: regular interaction among members, some type of emotional connection with one another, a common frame of reference, and some type of interdependence (Levine & Moreland, 1998). In a group, each of us may feel, think, and act less from the point of view of an individual and more from the point of view of a group member. Military training, such as boot camp, is a dramatic example of the shift from feeling like an individual to feeling like a group member: Loyalties and actions are no longer driven by individual goals but by group goals.

At the other extreme of group experience is **deindividuation**, traditionally defined as the loss of sense of self that occurs when people in a group are literally *anonymous*—their identities are un-

The military tries to instill a sense of "groupness" in new recruits: The group's goal, such as a successful military action, is supposed to become more important than an individual's goal, such as staying alive.

known to others in the group. This is often the situation in crowds. With deindividuation, attention is focused on external events, and a high level of arousal is experienced (Diener, 1977). When this occurs, people respond to external cues and immediate feelings and act on them without monitoring the appropriateness of their behaviors. Violence by fans at European soccer matches has usually been explained by deindividuation. However, a meta-analytic study on deindividuation suggests that loss of self is not the precipitating cause of the behaviors attributed to deindividuation, as has traditionally been thought. Rather, the behaviors result from the sense, shared by members of the crowd, that in this limited circumstance certain behaviors are permissible that would not be acceptable otherwise (Postmes & Spears, 1998).

Disappointed fans riot at a European soccer game. Are they violent because they've become deindividuated? Probably not. In this case they engage in situation-specific behaviors that are inconsistent with general expectations of appropriate behavior.

Norms

The Delany sisters recount that in their hometown of Raleigh, North Carolina, even strangers passing on the street would nod and say good morning or good evening. But when Sadie and Bessie moved to New York City, they discovered that courteous behavior toward strangers did not always end in a pleasant exchange, and they had to learn a new way of behaving in their new social context. Perhaps you, like them on their arrival in New York, have at one time or another been the "new kid on the block"—in school or college, in a new neighborhood, in an already established group of people. Chances are you didn't know the "rules"—how people were supposed to behave toward one another, and especially how you, a new member, were supposed to behave. Once you figured things out by watching other people (Gilbert, 1995)—an obvious case of observational learning—you probably felt more comfortable in the group. And, in fact, groups create such rules and structures to help the group function.

The rules that implicitly or explicitly govern members of a group are called **norms.** They are, in essence, shared belief systems that are enforced through the group's use of sanctions, or penalties (Cialdini & Trost, 1998). Just as individuals have attitudes, groups have norms (Wellen et al., 1998).

Norms pervade our everyday experience, defining the behaviors that make us good members of a family, friends, neighbors, partners, employees, employers, students, teachers, and so on. Norms may vary from group to group, or by age, sex, race, social class, or geographic region. For example, in the culture of the American South, honor is very important. Southern men are more likely than northern men to think their reputation is threatened when others swear at them in public, and thus they respond with more aggressive behavior (Cohen et al., 1996). Moreover, Cohen and his colleagues found that southerners in general were more likely than northerners to view such aggressive responses as appropriate. Southern norms of appropriate reactions to an insult are reflected in the more lenient judicial sentences given to certain types of violent offenders (Nisbett & Cohen, 1996).

Although norms can endure over time, even if the members of the group change (Jacobs & Campbell, 1961), norms too can change. This is the case with

● **Norm:** A shared belief that is enforced through a group's use of penalties.

the use of the title "Ms." When this form of address was introduced, it was seen as a title that would be used only by radical feminists. Now, however, Ms. is much more widely used and positively viewed (Crawford et al., 1998). Another example of changing norms is found among adolescents in India who watch Western television shows (and derive what they perceive of as Western norms). Their attitudes about drugs, alcohol, and sex change, and they reject the social norms of Indian society and become more Western (Varma, 2000).

How we *perceive* norms is important. Even if those perceptions are not necessarily accurate, we still behave in accordance with them. For instance, some antidrug programs emphasize both *why* you should say no to drugs and *how* to say no. But it appears that training students *how* to say no leads them to think that offers of drugs, and drug use in general, are more common than they really are, thereby creating the impression of a pro–drug-use social norm and leading to an increase in drug use. This is particularly true for alcohol use among college students (see Table 16.2; Berkowitz, 1997). Programs that focus only on *why* you should say no appear to be more successful (Botvin, 1995; Cialdini & Trost; 1998; Donaldson, 1995; Hansen et al., 1988). Programs aimed at emphasizing a drug-abstinent norm or a moderate-drinking norm also appear to be effective (Barnett et al., 1996; Berkowitz, 1997). Perceived norms can also affect how willing you are to become involved in social causes: If you perceive that becoming involved would violate an implicit group norm and make you "deviant" from others, you are less likely to work for social action (Ratner & Miller, 2001).

This problem of falsely perceived norms may explain why eating disorder prevention programs that feature speakers who have recovered from an eating disorder

TABLE 16.2 Personal Attitudes and Perceived Norms

What college students *think* are the norms for alcohol use are not necessarily accurate. Most students in a 1986 study had a more conservative view of alcohol use than they thought their peers did, but their peers were similarly conservative. This table shows the percentage of students personally agreeing with each item, and the percentage of students who thought that an item was the "norm" on campus. As you can see, the only time students' personal attitudes were near the perceived norm was in the lack of enthusiasm for total abstinence.

Item	Personal Attitudes (% of students agreeing)	Perceived Norm
Drinking is never a good thing to do.	1.4	0.1
Drinking is all right, but a student should never get "smashed."	12.7	0.8
An occasional "drunk" is okay as long as it doesn't interfere with grades or responsibilities.	66.0	35.4
An occasional "drunk" is okay even if it does occasionally interfere with grades or responsibilities.	9.3	33.2
A frequent "drunk" is okay if that's what the individual wants to do.	9.5	29.5

Source: Adapted from Perkins & Berkowitz (1986). Reprinted from Perkins and Berkowitz, "Perceiving the community norms of alcohol use among students," *International Journal of the Addictions, 21,* Sept/Oct 1986, pp. 961–974, by courtesy of Marcel Dekker, Inc.

may inadvertently lead students to develop eating disorder symptoms (Carter et al., 1997; Mann et al., 1997): Students inflate the perceived norm of eating disorders on campus after hearing and seeing the speaker and are thus led to change their behavior in the direction of the perceived norm.

Roles and Status

In contrast to norms, **roles** are the behaviors that members in different positions in a group are expected to perform. Groups often create different roles to fulfill different group functions. Sometimes roles are assigned officially, as when a group votes for a leader; sometimes roles are filled informally, without a specific election or appointment. Roles help a group delineate both responsibility *within* the group and responsibility *to* the group.

In a **status hierarchy,** different roles reflect the distribution of power in a group. The Delany sisters describe the status hierarchy of the South during and after Jim Crow laws: "White men were the most powerful, followed by White women. Colored people were absolutely below them and if you think it was hard for colored men, honey, colored women were on the bottom" (pp. 75–76). You can often tell who has a high-status position in a group from nonverbal cues: High-status members are more likely to maintain eye contact, be physically intrusive (somewhat "in your face"), and stand up straight (Leffler et al., 1982). You can also identify high-status members from what they say and how they say it: They are usually the ones who criticize or interrupt others or tell them what to do. In addition, other members direct their comments to the high-status member (Skvoretz, 1988). Perhaps because of the absence of nonverbal cues, social status differences have been found to be less prominent in groups communicating by e-mail as opposed to face to face (Dubrovsky et al., 1991).

Norms can affect all kinds of behavior, including a cold sufferer's willingness to wear a surgical mask when out in public. This Japanese woman is behaving according to one of her culture's norms: It is frowned on for a cold sufferer to go outside without a mask and spread cold germs to others.

Yielding to Others: Going Along With the Group

In Raleigh when the Jim Crow laws were in effect, Black customers in a White-owned shoe store were supposed to sit in the back of the store to try on shoes. On one occasion when Sadie shopped for shoes, she was asked by the White owner, Mr. Heller, to sit in the back. She asked, "Where, Mr. Heller?" And he gestured to the back saying, " 'Back there.' And I would say, 'Back *where?*' . . . Finally, he'd say, 'Just sit anywhere, Miss Delany.' And so I would sit myself down in the White section, and smile" (p. 84). What made Sadie able to resist Mr. Heller's request—or his order, backed by law? What made Mr. Heller give up his attempt to have Sadie comply with the law and social convention? What made him call her "Miss Delany" and not "Sadie"? What would you have done? In what circumstances do we go along with the group, do what someone asks of us, obey orders? When do we resist?

Conformity and Independence: Doing What's Expected

Social norms tell us how we ought to behave, and sometimes we change our beliefs or behavior in order to follow these norms. This change in beliefs or behavior because of pressure from others is known as **conformity.** For example, immigrants must decide how much to conform to the norms of their new country and how much to retain the ways of their homeland (Lorenzo-Hernandez, 1998).

● **Role:** The behaviors that a member in a given position in a group is expected to perform.

● **Status hierarchy:** The positioning of roles that reflect who has power over whom.

● **Conformity:** A change of beliefs or actions in order to follow a group's norms.

Two types of social influence can lead to conformity. One type is *informational social influence*, which occurs when we conform to others' views or behavior because we want to be right, and we believe they are correct. This type of conformity is most likely to occur when the situation is ambiguous, when there is a crisis, or when other people are the experts. Suppose you are working in a study group that is trying to solve a complex engineering problem, or that you are part of a medical team trying to agree on a diagnosis of a particularly perplexing case. The majority agree on an answer that doesn't seem right to you. What would make you more likely to go along with the majority view? Research indicates that *task difficulty* increases conformity: The harder the task, the more you are likely to conform—at least in part because you are less sure of yourself. *Social comparison theory* (Festinger, 1950) is consistent with this explanation: All people are driven to evaluate their abilities and opinions. When their abilities or views cannot be measured objectively, they seek out others, particularly people similar to themselves, to serve as a basis of comparison (Morris et al., 1976). Thus, even when we are initially certain, the disagreement of other members of our group can make us doubt (Orive, 1988).

Informational social influence, however, cannot be the only explanation for conformity. The second type of conformity arises from *normative social influence*, which occurs when we conform because we want to be liked or thought of positively, as demonstrated in pioneering research by Solomon Asch (1951, 1955). If you had been a participant in Asch's original study, you would have found yourself in a group with five to seven others asked to perform a task of visual perception. You are all shown a target line and asked to say which of three other lines matches the length of the target line. Each person gives an answer aloud; you are next to last. This sounds like an easy task, as you can see in Figure 16.7, but it soon becomes perplexing. For 12 of the 18 times you are shown the lines, everyone else gives the wrong answer! Will you agree with the answer everyone else is giving?

In fact, in Asch's experiment only one person in the group was the true participant; the others were confederates playing a role. Seventy-six percent of participants went along with the confederates at least once, and overall approximately one third of participants' responses conformed with the obviously wrong majority.

Why would these people conform with the norm established by the group? Variations on Asch's original experiment showed that characteristics of the situation are part of the answer. When participants *wrote* their answers instead of announcing them to the group, they gave the correct response 98% of the time, reflecting the fact that participants accurately perceived the lines. *Social support* also influences conformity. If another group member openly disagrees with the group consensus, conformity is less likely (Morris & Miller, 1975). When Asch had one confederate disagree—that is, give the correct answer—91% of actual participants did not conform with the group answer. Furthermore, the more *cohesive* a group—the more attraction and commitment members have toward it—the more likely members are to conform, as are members who identify more strongly with its norms (Prapavessis & Carron, 1997; Schofield et al., 2001; Terry & Hogg, 1996). And when a member of a less powerful group, such as a social or political minority, is in a group with more powerful members, the minority member may be more likely to conform (Roll et al., 1996). In general, despite the pressure to conform to group norms, not everyone is equally affected (Trafimow & Finlay, 1996).

One person not given to conformity for its own sake was Sadie and Bessie Delany's maternal grandfather, James Millam. A White man, he fell in love with a free woman, Martha Logan, who was one quarter Black; marriage between them

FIGURE 16.7 Asch's Conformity Study

Participants in Asch's classic study on conformity were shown lines similar to these and asked the following type of question: Here are three lines of different lengths and a fourth target line. Which of the three lines matches the target line?

Only two people have yet to give their opinions, but everyone else appears to have given the same incorrect answer. Which would you say was the correct line if you were next in line? Asch (1951, 1955) created this situation with the use of confederates, and the true participant was the next-to-last person. Although 76% of participants conformed to the incorrect group response at least once, over the entire experiment, approximately two thirds of responses were independent of the majority.

was, at the time, illegal. In such situations, it was usual for the man to marry a White woman and establish the Black woman as his mistress. Millam refused to conform to this convention; he lived openly with Martha Logan without benefit of marriage. Why would he not conform? Because to go along with the group, to conform, against one's beliefs or better judgment, leads to a loss of choice, of independence. The desire to retain a sense of individuality (Maslach et al., 1987) or control (Burger, 1992; Burger & Cooper, 1979) also provides reasons for not conforming. Thus, to understand someone's choice to conform, you need to look not only at the situation and the group but also at that person's characteristics—such as his or her commitment to the group or desire for individuality.

Were the people in Asch's study typical? All were men, but the results of later studies with women were similar (Eagly & Carli, 1981). However, Asch's original participants may have been influenced by their culture. His experiment has been repeated by many researchers in many countries, and studies in countries with a more collectivist orientation, such as China, found higher levels of conformity than did those in individualistic countries (R. Bond & Smith, 1996). Furthermore, the findings of conformity studies over the years suggest that conformity has decreased since Asch's original work (R. Bond & Smith, 1996). Thus, characteristics of the individual, his or her relationship to the group, characteristics of the group, and the larger culture can all affect conformity and independence.

Compliance: Doing What You're Asked

Even if you don't want to go along with a group's norms, you may be willing to comply with a direct request, as occurs when someone asks, "Could you please tell me how to get to the library?" **Compliance** is a change in behavior brought about through a direct request rather than by social norms. When the driver of the car in the next lane gestures to you, asking to be let into your lane in front of you, you will either comply or not.

Without realizing it, you are a target of multiple requests for compliance each day, from television commercials, in conversations with friends, or through questions on a survey form. Skill at getting people to comply is key to success in many occupations, from sales and advertising to lobbying, politics, and health prevention programs. Psychologist Robert Cialdini decided to find out from "compliance professionals"—people in jobs such as advertising, fundraising, and door-to-door sales—exactly what they know about the subject. He inferred that the essence of effective compliance technique lies in six principles (Cialdini, 1994):

1. *Friendship/liking.* People are more likely to comply with a request from a friend than from a stranger.
2. *Commitment/consistency.* People tend to comply more when the request is consistent with a previous commitment.
3. *Scarcity.* People are more likely to comply with requests related to limited, short-term, rather than open-ended, opportunities.
4. *Reciprocity.* People tend to comply more when the request comes from someone who has provided a favor.
5. *Social validation.* People are more likely to comply if they think that others similar to themselves would comply.
6. *Authority.* People tend to comply with a request if it comes from someone who appears to be in authority.

To see these principles at work, let's examine a few of the techniques most often used to win compliance. The commitment/consistency principle explains why a classic compliance technique, the **foot-in-the-door technique,** works so often. In this method, first you make an insignificant request; if you meet with compliance, you follow up with a larger request. Consider the study by Freedman and Fraser (1966), who had a male experimenter phone housewives, asking what brand of soap they used. Three days later, the same man telephoned and asked if five or six people could perform a 2-hour inventory of everything in the housewife's cupboards, drawers, and closets. Fifty-three percent of the housewives who had agreed to the simple first request agreed to this much larger second request. In contrast, when housewives did not receive the first request but were asked to allow the inventory, only 22% complied.

The foot-in-the-door technique appears to work, at least in part, because people want to seem consistent (Guadagno et al., 2001). If you agree to the first request, you are being a nice person; declining the second request would call this self-perception into question. The consistency principle also explains the success of an unethical sales technique, the **lowball technique,** which consists of first get-

● **Compliance:** A change in behavior prompted by a direct request rather than social norms.

● **Foot-in-the-door technique:** A technique that achieves compliance by beginning with an insignificant request, which is then followed by a larger request.

● **Lowball technique:** A compliance technique that consists of getting someone to make an agreement and then increasing the cost of that agreement.

ting someone to make an agreement, and then increasing the cost of that agreement. Suppose you see an advertisement for some shoes you've been eyeing—for a very low price. You go the store and are told that the shoes are no longer available at that price, but you can get them for a somewhat higher (although still discounted) price. What do you do? Many people would comply with the request to buy the shoes at the higher price.

Turning the foot-in-the-door procedure backward also works; this is the **door-in-the-face technique.** You begin by making a very large request; when it is denied, as expected, you make a smaller request, for what you actually wanted in the first place. For instance, in one study (Cialdini et al., 1975), college students were stopped on campus and asked to serve as unpaid counselors to a group of juvenile delinquents for 2 hours a week for 2 years. Not surprisingly, no one agreed. Then the same students were asked to take the group on a 2-hour field trip. Fifty percent agreed. In contrast, when students were asked only to make the field trip without the larger, first request, only 17% agreed.

The door-in-the-face technique is a staple of diplomacy and labor–management negotiations. Why does it work? The reciprocity principle may hold the answer. If your first request is denied and you then make a smaller one, you appear to be making concessions, and the other party tries to reciprocate.

People sometimes go to surprising lengths to comply with a request. Kassin and Kiechel (1996) provided one example in a study that involved the *appearance* that participants had destroyed some data after being explicitly warned not to touch the ALT key on a keyboard. Sixty-nine percent of the participants agreed with a request to sign a confession that they had destroyed data—even though they had done no such thing. Nine percent made up details to support their (false) admission of guilt. You might suspect that something about the laboratory situation created an unnatural, unrealistic result. But Kassin and Kiechel were reproducing a result found in life: Innocent suspects sometimes comply with requests for a (false) confession to having committed a crime, even one as serious as murder (Kassin, 1997). Even more surprising, some of those who falsely confessed to a crime came to believe they actually committed it (see Chapter 7 for a discussion of how this can occur).

Obedience: Doing as You're Told

If people can be so obliging in response to a polite request, what happens when they receive an order? Compliance with an order is called **obedience.** The nature of obedience attracted intense study in the United States after World War II, when the world heard about atrocities apparently committed in the name of obedience.

The most famous study of obedience was carried out by Stanley Milgram (1963). Milgram expected that Americans would not follow orders to inflict pain on innocent people. In testing this hypothesis, his challenge was to design a study that gave the appearance of inflicting pain without actually doing so. He hit on the following procedure: Suppose you volunteered to participate in a study of memory. You are asked to act the part of "teacher" (see Figure 16.8, p. 708). You are paired with a "learner" (a confederate), who, you are told, was asked to memorize a list of pairs of common words. You, the teacher, are to present one word from each pair

Car salespeople are notorious for using the lowball technique; however, some car makers have changed to a nonnegotiable pricing policy so that there is less opportunity for the lowball technique.

● **Door-in-the-face technique:** A compliance technique in which someone makes a very large request; when it is denied, as expected, a second, smaller request (the desired one) is made.

● **Obedience:** Compliance with an order.

FIGURE 16.8   The Milgram Obedience Study

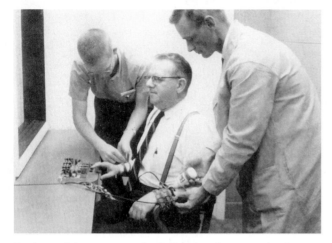

Each participant was paired with another man, having drawn lots to decide who would be the "teacher" and the "learner." In fact, the participant was always the teacher. The learner was always the same 47-year-old accountant who was a confederate in the study. The man who introduced himself as the experimenter was an actor. The learner was asked to memorize a list of pairs of common words; the teacher was to present the words, keep track of how well the learner did, and punish the learner for incorrect responses. The teacher watched as the learner was brought to a cubicle where the experimenter asked him to sit down and strapped him in a chair to "prevent excess movement" (above). The experimenter attached shock electrodes to his wrist. Throughout the remainder of the study, the teacher could not see the learner, and all communication was via an intercom.

The teacher was seated in front of the shock generator. The generator had 30 switches labeled in 15-volt increments from 15 to 450 volts. A description below each switch ranged from "Slight Shock" to "Danger: Severe Shock." The labels under the last two switches were ominous: "XXX." At the outset the teacher was given a sample shock of 45 volts so that he could know what it felt like.

and keep track of how well the learner does in correctly remembering the other word. If the learner makes a mistake, you are to administer a shock, increasing the voltage with each successive mistake. Although the shock generator is a phony and no shock at all is administered, you do not know this.

This is precisely what Milgram did; by prearrangement, at "120 volts" the learner shouted that the shocks were becoming too painful. At "150 volts" the learner asked to stop. At 180 he screamed that he couldn't stand the pain. At 300 volts he pounded on the wall and demanded to be set free. At 330 volts there was only silence—an "incorrect response" according to the directions of the experimenter, who stood beside the teacher.

How far would you go in obeying the experimenter's instructions? If you were like the participants in Milgram's study, when the learner cried out in pain or refused to go on, you would turn to the experimenter for instructions, who would reply that the experiment had to proceed and that he would take full responsibility. Would you obey? When Milgram described the experiment to a group of psychiatrists, they predicted that only a "pathological fringe" of at most 2% of the population would go to the maximum shock level. In fact, much to Milgram's surprise, 65% of the participants went to the highest level. Some of the participants, but apparently not all, felt terrible about what they were doing. But they still continued to administer the shocks.

The willingness of so many of Milgram's participants to obey orders to hurt others disturbed many people. Was there something distinctive about Milgram's participants that could explain the results? In the original studies, the participants were men. Later studies, however, found similar results with women (Milgram, 1965, 1974), as well as with people in Jordan, Germany, and Australia, and with children (Kilham & Mann, 1974; Shanab & Yahya, 1977).

Why did so many participants obey orders to hurt someone else? Were there particular characteristics of the situation that fostered obedience? Compliance research suggests two ways in which the study's design increased the likelihood of obedience. First, Milgram's experiment applied something like the foot-in-the-door-technique: Participants were first ordered to give a trivial amount of shock before going on to give apparently harmful ones. When the participants were allowed to set the punishment voltage themselves, none ever went past 45 volts. Second, additional research indicated that people become more likely to comply with a request if it comes from someone in authority; the same holds true for obedience (Bushman, 1984, 1988). In a variant of the study (Milgram, 1974), when a college student was the one who gave a fellow student the order to shock instead of an older, white-coated experimenter, obedience fell to only 20%. When the experimenters were two authority figures who disagreed with each other, no participants administered further shocks. It appears that the more authoritative the person who gives the order, the more likely it is to be obeyed; when someone in authority gives an order, the person obeying can deny responsibility for his or her actions.

Later variations of Milgram's original study point to other characteristics of the situation that have an important influence on obedience. *Proximity* to the learner is one. When teachers saw the learners while they were being shocked, and even held an electrode directly on the accomplice's skin (with a "special insulating glove"), 30% progressed to the maximum voltage, compared with 65% in the original design. Proximity to the experimenter also matters: When the experimenter telephoned his commands to the teacher instead of giving face-to-face instructions, obedience dropped to 21%.

Disturbing as Milgram's results were, it is important to remember that not all participants obeyed the experimenter, and in some conditions the great majority did not obey; it is the specifics of the situation (such as proximity to the learner) that influences an individual's willingness to obey an order to hurt someone else (Blass, 1999; Gibson, 1991; A. G. Miller et al., 1995).

Performance in Groups: Working Together

When Sadie and Bessie went to New York City, they moved into their brother Hubert's apartment, along with another brother and sister. Now there were five Delanys living in a three-room apartment. In such tight quarters, it helped to be very organized and to have clear rules and clear roles. Even though the apartment was Hubert's, and they all participated in making decisions, Sadie would have the final say because she was the oldest. How do groups make decisions? What are the advantages and disadvantages of working as a group?

Decision Making in Groups: Paths to a Decision

After living in Hubert's apartment for a while, Sadie and Bessie got a place of their own in New York, and their mother came to live with them. However, at some point, their mother's health began to fade, and it was no longer safe for her to be home alone all day while her daughters were at work. The situation required that one of them leave her job to stay home with Mrs. Delany (it never occurred to them to hire someone to stay at home with their mother while they were out at work). How did they decide who would stay home? This question faces many families today, and the path to a solution often involves group decision making. Such decision making also occurs in other contexts: Political parties, military planners, and athletic teams must decide on strategies; clinical groups must decide who receives what medical treatment and for how long; college admissions officers decide who is accepted and who is not. How are decisions made in groups?

In general, if a group is not initially unanimous in favor of a particular decision, it is likely that the view favored by the majority will prevail (Levine & Moreland, 1998). The larger the majority, the more likely it is that their choice will "win." This path is known as the *majority-win rule*, and it works well when the decision involves judgments or opinions. But there are times—you may have been present at some—when what began as the minority position eventually "wins." When there is an objectively correct answer, the *truth-win rule* works well because its inherent worthiness is recognized by the group (Kirchler & Davis, 1986). In general, groups reach a better decision when one solution can be shown to be correct (Hastie, 1986; Laughlin & Ellis, 1986).

Group decision making does not always lead to the best decision. The opinion of a powerful member can shift others' opinions by might rather than right. Group decisions can be marred by **group polarization,** the tendency of members of the group to take more extreme positions (in the same direction as their initial opinions) after discussion (Isenberg, 1986; Levine & Moreland, 1998). This polarization of attitude can last well beyond the initial discussion (Liu & Latané, 1998).

One reason group polarization develops is that some members of the group may give very compelling reasons for their initial views, and more of them. In listening to these reasons, members who are in general agreement may become more convinced of the correctness of that initial assessment and more extreme in their views (Burnstein, 1982). This route to group polarization is more likely to be a factor when an intellectual issue is at stake, or when the group's goal is to make a "correct" or task-oriented decision (Kaplan, 1987). Another reason behind group polarization is that, through discussion, members can figure out the group's consensus on the issue and may be tempted to increase their standing in the group (and improve their view of themselves) by taking a more extreme position in accordance with the group norm (Goethals & Zanna, 1979). This route to group polarization is likely when the issue requires judgments, and when the group is more focused on group harmony than on correctness (Kaplan, 1987).

Groupthink is another means by which decision making can go awry. **Groupthink** refers to the tendency of people who try to solve problems together to accept one another's information and ideas without subjecting them to critical analysis. According to Janis (1982), people are most likely to fall into groupthink when the group members are especially close. In such instances, rather than realistically thinking through a problem, members are more concerned with agreeing with one another. This concept has been used to explain many real-life disasters, such as why NASA launched the space shuttle *Challenger* despite widespread concerns about its booster rockets. (The failure of the booster rockets ended up causing the shuttle to crash.) Although the evidence that groupthink leads to bad decisions is mixed (Aldag & Fuller, 1993), a meta-analysis revealed that cohesive groups tend to make poorer decisions if the cohesiveness grew out of "interpersonal attraction"—the members' feelings about one another (Mullen et al., 1994). In such groups, the members want to seem cooperative, and so refrain from asking questions or making comments that they otherwise would, potentially leading to a different outcome from the group. Groups that have a norm of coming to consensus are more vulnerable to groupthink than those that have a norm of minority dissent (Postmes et al., 2001).

The variety of people in a group may also affect its decision-making process and performance. In general, as a group becomes more heterogeneous, it com-

● **Group polarization:** The tendency of group members' opinions to become more extreme (in the same direction as their initial opinions) after group discussion.

● **Groupthink:** The tendency of people who try to solve problems together to accept one another's information and ideas without subjecting them to critical analysis.

municates less effectively (Maznevski, 1994; Zenger & Lawrence, 1989), and subgroups of similar members may form, causing nonsimilar members to feel alienated (Jackson et al., 1991). Some of the negative effects of heterogeneous groups can be minimized in the following ways: education about similarities and differences; recategorization by increasing a sense of the group as a team (creating an "us"); increasing social skills among members; and learning conflict resolution skills (Caudron, 1994). Paradoxically, although heterogeneity can create some group conflict, it can also have a positive effect on the group's performance (McLeod & Lobel, 1992) because of the increased innovation and flexibility that diversity brings to a group (Levine & Moreland, 1998).

Social Loafing

When responsibility for an outcome is spread among the members of the group, some members may be likely to let other members work harder (Latané et al., 1979), a phenomenon that has been called **social loafing.** One way to prevent social loafing is to instill a sense of importance and responsibility in each person, even if the work is boring or if the member's contribution is anonymous (Harkins & Petty, 1982). Making the task attractive also reduces social loafing, as does knowing that individual as well as group performance will be evaluated (Harkins & Szymanski, 1989; Hoeksema-van Orden et al., 1998; Karau & Williams, 1993). If you have lived with other people, you may have experienced the effects of social loafing: When dishes pile up in the sink or the bathroom goes uncleaned for weeks, each member of the household is doing some social loafing, waiting for somebody else to do the cleaning.

> When a group as a whole is responsible for a task, some members may work less hard than they would if they were individually responsible for a task. This tendency toward social loafing can be countered by evaluating everyone's performance separately or by making the task attractive.

Although working in groups may lead some people to indulge in social loafing, it may lead others to engage in *social compensation,* working harder in a group than they do when alone. Social compensation usually occurs when some members of the group see the task to be done as important but don't expect that other members will pull their weight (Williams & Karau, 1991). Social compensation occurs when someone finally washes the dishes or cleans the bathroom: The mess bothers someone enough that he or she cleans it all up. But the person cleaning is doing more than his or her share.

Social Facilitation: Everybody Loves an Audience

Sometimes being part of a group, or just being in the presence of other people, can increase performance; this effect is called **social facilitation.** However, usually the presence of others enhances performance only on well-learned simple tasks; on complicated, less well-learned tasks, the presence of others can hinder performance (Guerin, 1993). The presence of others appears to increase arousal, which then facilitates the *dominant* response in that situation (Schmitt et al., 1986; Seta & Seta, 1992). Thus, well-learned responses are likely to come to the fore when you are aroused, and you will be less likely to execute complicated or recently learned behaviors. Hence, at a concert a musician may perform an old song better than a new one, whereas when practicing at home that same day, she probably could play them both equally well.

● **Social loafing:** The tendency to work less hard when responsibility for an outcome is spread over the group's members.

● **Social facilitation:** The increase in performance that can occur simply by being part of a group or in the presence of other people.

Helping Behavior: Helping Others

When Bessie Delany began her dentistry practice in 1923, both cleanings and extractions were $2 each, and a silver filling cost $5. When she retired in 1950, she charged the same rates and was proud of it. In fact, she treated people regardless of their ability to pay. The Delany family ethic was to help others. This quality is called **altruism,** which has been defined as "the motivation to increase another person's welfare" (Batson, 1998, p. 282). What made Bessie so willing to help others? Why do we help other people? What circumstances encourage altruism?

New York City's firefighters displayed their altruism both when they went into the burning World Trade Center towers in 2001 to rescue people inside, and when they searched through the burning rubble for survivors.

Prosocial Behavior

Acting to benefit others, called **prosocial behavior,** includes sharing, cooperating, comforting, and helping (Batson, 1998). Whether or not we help someone depends on factors about us and the person we could help. We are more likely to help others if we have certain personality traits, such as a high need for approval, or a predisposition to feeling personal and social responsibility, or an empathic concern for others (Batson et al., 1986; Eisenberg et al., 1989). People who tend to be helpers also have a sense of empathy, a belief in a just world, an internal locus of control, and less concern for their own welfare (Bierhoff et al., 1991). Bessie Delany seemed to feel a sense of personal and social responsibility toward others and could empathize with their plights. She also appeared to have less concern for her own welfare; when she was in dental school, a White girl born with syphilis came to the dental clinic—only Bessie volunteered to help her.

Group identity also plays a role in prosocial behavior. We are more likely to help and cooperate with other members of our group. Principles of learning (see Chapter 6) are also influential. Through our learning history, we may have been reinforced for helping, or punished for not helping. Parents, teachers, and others were models for observational learning. Thus, in time, we come to reward ourselves for helping, feel good after helping, and punish ourselves or feel guilty when we don't (Batson, 1998).

Prosocial behavior also appears to have a neurological correlate: Choosing to act for mutual benefit, rather than individual benefit, increases activation in the "reward" areas of the brain (Rilling et al., 2002). When we choose not to act for mutual benefit but for our own, our distressing feelings—often resulting from cognitive dissonance—may be assuaged in a number of ways. Some people perform a prosocial act other than the one facing them (McMillen & Austin, 1971); others minimize the impact they would have made had they chosen to cooperate—"I probably couldn't have made a difference anyway" (Kerr & Kaufman-Gilliland, 1997).

● **Altruism:** The motivation to increase another person's welfare.

● **Prosocial behavior:** Acting to benefit others.

Some people in need of assistance are more likely to be helped than others. Who are they? First, we are more likely to help people we view as similar to ourselves. Consider an experiment in which Americans in three foreign cities asked for directions: Residents of those cities who were similar in age to the Americans requesting help were more likely to give directions (Rabinowitz et al., 1997). Second, we are more likely to help friends or people we like (remember, similarity facilitates liking). Third, we are more likely to help people we believe are not responsible for their predicaments, or people who give a socially acceptable justification for their plight (Weiner, 1980). In fact, the more justification the requester gives, the more likely he or she is to receive help (Bohm & Hendricks, 1997).

Bystander Intervention

A great deal has been learned about a specific type of prosocial behavior—bystander intervention—as a result of research inspired by one dreadful incident. At about 3 A.M. on March 13, 1964, a 28-year-old woman named Catherine Genovese—known to her neighbors as Kitty—was brutally murdered in Queens, a borough of New York City, only minutes from her own apartment building. She was coming home from work as a manager of a bar. When her attacker first caught and stabbed her, she screamed for help. The lights came on in several apartments overlooking the scene of the crime, and a man yelled down to her attacker to leave her alone. Her attacker briefly stopped and walked away. The apartment lights went out. The attacker returned and stabbed her again; she screamed again, to no avail, although lights again came on in the surrounding apartments. The attacker left in a car, and Kitty Genovese dragged herself to the lobby of an apartment building near her own. The attacker returned again, and this time he kept stabbing her until she died. The gruesome ordeal took some 35 minutes and was viewed by at least 38 witnesses. Only one person called the police (Rosenthal, 1964).

Darley and Latané (1968) hypothesized that if only a few bystanders had witnessed the crime, those few would have been more likely to help Kitty Genovese. This relationship is known as the **bystander effect:** As the number of bystanders increases, offers of assistance decrease. To test this relationship, Darley and Latané, with the aid of confederates, created the following situation. Imagine yourself as a participant in a study, taking part in a telephone conference about campus life with a number of others. Each participant speaks without interruption, and when everyone has spoken, the first person gets to speak again, and so on. Suppose another participant mentions that when stressed he gets seizures; then you hear that person stutter, start to choke, and ask for help. Would you get help? If you were like most participants in Darley and Latané's study (1968) (see Figure 16.9, p. 714), and you believed there were only two people in the telephone conference—you and the person with seizures—you would very likely seek help. But if you had been told there were three participants, you would be less likely to seek help, and even less likely with a total of six participants. In short, attempts to help rose as the number of apparent bystanders dropped: When participants thought that they were the only one aware of the "emergency," 85% of them left the cubicle and got the experimenter within the first minute. When they thought there was one other bystander, 65% helped within the first minute. When participants thought there were four other bystanders, only 25% helped within the first minute. At the end of 4 minutes, all in the smallest group helped, as did 85% of those in the mid-sized group, but only 60% in the largest group.

● **Bystander effect:** The decrease in offers of assistance that occurs as the number of bystanders increases.

FIGURE 16.9 Bystander Intervention

Participants thought they were involved in a study of campus life but instead were exposed to an "emergency" with a varying number of bystanders. Participants went into a private cubicle and were told that they could all hear one another, but only one student would be able to speak during any 2-minute period; when all had spoken, the cycle would start again. They were also told that the experimenter would not be listening. Participants were led to believe that either four, one, or no other students ("bystanders") were listening. In fact, there was only one true participant at a time; the rest of the voices on the intercom were prerecorded tapes.

The crisis came after one (prerecorded) voice confessed to having seizures in stressful situations. This person subsequently seemed to be having a seizure, and asked for help.

Would participants leave their cubicles to get help? Their responses depended greatly on the perceived number of bystanders. The great majority of participants went to get help when they thought they were the only ones aware of the problem, but they helped less often the more bystanders they thought were aware of the problem.

From this and other studies, Darley and Latané (1970) described five steps, or "choice points," in bystander intervention (see Figure 16.10).

At each step, various factors, such as the number of bystanders and characteristics of the bystanders, shape the likelihood that someone will help. For example, consider Step 2, perceiving the event. If a situation is ambiguous, leaving you uncertain about whether the emergency is real, you may hesitate to offer help. If other bystanders are present, your hesitancy may be increased by *evaluation*

FIGURE 16.10   The Five Choice Points of Bystander Intervention

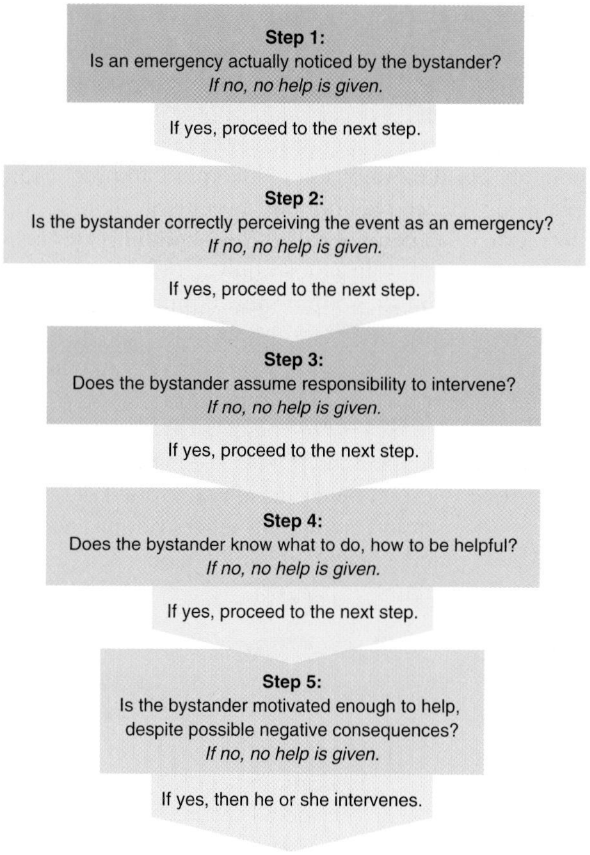

- **Diffusion of responsibility:** The diminished sense of responsibility to help that each person feels as the number of bystanders grows.

Step 1:
Is an emergency actually noticed by the bystander?
If no, no help is given.

If yes, proceed to the next step.

Step 2:
Is the bystander correctly perceiving the event as an emergency?
If no, no help is given.

If yes, proceed to the next step.

Step 3:
Does the bystander assume responsibility to intervene?
If no, no help is given.

If yes, proceed to the next step.

Step 4:
Does the bystander know what to do, how to be helpful?
If no, no help is given.

If yes, proceed to the next step.

Step 5:
Is the bystander motivated enough to help, despite possible negative consequences?
If no, no help is given.

If yes, then he or she intervenes.

Source: Darley and Latané (1970).

apprehension—a fear that you might be embarrassed or ridiculed if you try to intervene because there may be no emergency after all. The number of bystanders also influences Step 3, assuming responsibility. The more bystanders there are, the less each one feels responsible to help, creating a **diffusion of responsibility.** Fortunately, once people have learned about the bystander effect, they are subsequently more likely to intervene (Beaman et al., 1978).

Looking *at* Levels

Cults

In 1997 members of the Heaven's Gate cult killed themselves in order to ascend to join an alien spaceship that they believed was hidden behind the Hale–Bopp Comet; they believed that the spaceship would take them to the next level of existence. How is it that cults exert such a powerful influence on their members? We can best understand how

LOOKING *at* LEVELS *(continued)*

cults function by looking at the phenomenon from the three levels of analysis and their interactions. At the level of the brain, the bodily functions of cult members, such as eating, sleeping, and sexual relations (in those cults that permit them), are carefully monitored. New recruits in many cults are often physically and mentally exhausted after listening to music, chanting, or engaging in similar activities for hours on end (Streiker, 1984), which can induce a meditative or hypnotic-like state that alters brain function as well as the sense of reality.

At the level of the person, many cults try to eliminate members' experience of themselves as individuals. In the Heaven's Gate group, each day was structured down to the minute in order to minimize the sense of self and individual choice. Moreover, members were forbidden to trust their own judgments or to have "inappropriate" curiosity (Bearak, 1997). Members, particularly new ones, were not allowed to be alone, even in the bathroom. These measures, as well as the altered state of consciousness and the exhaustion, can induce a sense of depersonalization (the experience of observing oneself as if from the outside) and derealization (the sense that familiar objects have changed or seem unreal).

At the level of the group, the arousal and unpleasant effects of the derealization are calmed by listening to the group and by being cared for by others. This resulting dependency increases the desire to stay within the group. Performing actions at the behest of the group that would otherwise be refused, such as begging for money or having sexual relations, can induce cognitive dissonance; only a change in attitude can then resolve the discomfort aroused. Moreover, members receive enormous amounts of attention and reinforcement, sometimes called "love-bombing," for behaving in desired ways—in other words, conforming to their expected role and to group norms. Group polarization and groupthink may affect the group's decision making. Perhaps these group processes led to the decision that group suicide was an effective way to join the alien spaceship.

Events at these levels of analysis interact: The unpleasant bodily and psychological states are relieved when desired behaviors are performed, in a process of negative reinforcement; this relief leads to a change in self-concept and a heightened importance of, and dependence on, the group.

TEST YOURSELF!

1. What psychological principles explain why we like certain people and not others?
2. Why do all groups have rules for social behavior and organization?
3. Why do we sometimes "go along" with others even when we don't want to? What makes us able to refuse?
4. Does being part of a group change our behavior? How do groups make decisions?
5. Are some people more helpful than others? Why would we not help other people?

A Final Word: Ethics and Social Psychology

The researchers involved in many of the studies described in this chapter did not tell participants about the true nature of the experiments at the outset, and several used confederates. Many of the classic social psychology studies were carried out before the discipline established rigorous ethical guidelines (see Chapter 1). In fact, some of the guidelines were formulated *because* these studies raised serious ethical concerns. Keep in mind, however, several issues related to the use of deception in psychology. First, many of the pioneering researchers did not expect to cause psychological distress. For example, Milgram initially did not expect participants to be willing to shock learners at higher "voltage" levels, although he did continue to perform variants of his study after he knew the results of his first study. Second, some psychological phenomena are extremely difficult, if not impossible, to study if the participant knows the true nature of the experiment. For example, could you think of a way to design a study on conformity *without* using deception? Third, at present, in order to receive approval for a study that uses deception, researchers must show that the deception is absolutely necessary (that the information could not be ascertained without deception); that the information is valuable and the deception minimal; and that at the conclusion of the study, the investigators will fully explain to the participants the nature of the study and the reasons for deception. In short, today deception is permitted in research only if it is crystal clear that the participants will not be harmed and important knowledge will be gained.

CONSOLIDATE!

Social Cognition: Thinking About People

- We can form impressions of others quickly, in as little as 10 seconds. The primacy and halo effects can influence the impressions we form, and these impressions can become self-fulfilling prophecies.

- Attitudes and stereotypes help reduce the cognitive effort required to understand the social world. Our impressions, attitudes, stereotypes, and attributions affect how we encode, store, and retrieve information.

- Our attitudes can affect our behavior and are especially likely to do so when they are strong, stable, relevant, and salient.

- Conflict between attitudes and behavior (or between two attitudes) can lead to cognitive dissonance, which we are then driven to reduce.

- Efforts to change attitudes are attempts at persuasion. Central routes to persuasion require more time, energy, or expertise than peripheral routes.

- Persuasion attempts can be foiled by strong attitudes, reactance, forewarning, and selective avoidance.

- Social cognitive neuroscience has helped reveal that cognitive dissonance and other social cognitive phenomena can occur outside conscious awareness.

- The human process of categorizing objects (including people) leads to stereotypes, and our stereotypes of others affect our behavior, can affect the way others behave toward us, and can lead to prejudice and discrimination.

- Because stereotypes create biases in the way we process information, our stereotypes often seem more accurate than they really are and thus are difficult to change.

- Although we are driven to make attributions to understand events, our reasoning about the causes of these events may rely on attributional biases, such as the fundamental attribution error, the self-serving bias, and the belief in a just world. Such biases can lead us to understand people's behavior inaccurately.

THINK IT THROUGH If you were to design an antismoking campaign based on your knowledge of persuasion and stereotypes, what strategies might you include? What psychological factors might explain how people attribute their success in quitting or failure to quit smoking? If you wanted to help people resist the pull of advertisements or political campaigns, what information would be particularly important to convey? Explain.

Social Behavior: Interacting With People

- In our intimate relationships, we are more likely to be attracted to, and to like, people we view as similar to ourselves.

- Love can be understood using Sternberg's triangular model, or by looking at different styles of attachment.

- All groups have norms and roles and assign status to members; these factors guide members' behaviors in a group.

- Conformity is affected by informational and normative social influence, depending upon the situation. Asch's conformity experiment is an example of normative social influence.

- The foot-in-the-door, lowball, and door-in-the-face techniques are used to increase compliance.
- Obedience to an order can be affected by various factors, including the status and proximity of the person giving the order.
- The style of a group's decision making depends on the group's goals and on the ways in which group members articulate their views on an issue before the group.
- Being in a group can help or harm a given individual's performance.
- Psychological principles, such as the bystander effect and diffusion of responsibility, determine when and whom we help.

THINK IT THROUGH When Sadie Delany began her job as a New York high school teacher, how might she have learned the school's norms and members' roles? Imagine that you have started a new job working in a large corporation. Based on what you have learned, what colleagues are you likely to be attracted to and why? If your boss wants employees to do something "slightly illegal," what factors may make employees less likely to go along with this request (or order)? Will working as a group change the way the work is performed? Why or why not? If an employee is injured at work, what factors may make the employees who witness the incident more likely to help?

Key Terms

References

Aalto, S., Naeaetaenen, P., Wallius, E., Metsahonkala, L., Stenman, H., Niemi, P. M., & Karlsson, H. (2002). Neuroanatomical substrata of amusement and sadness: A PET activation study using film stimuli. *Neuroreport: For Rapid Communication of Neuroscience Research, 13*, 67–73.

Aarons, L. (1976). Sleep-assisted instruction. *Psychological Bulletin, 83*, 1–40.

Abdollahi, P., & Mann, T. (2001). Eating disorder symptoms and body image concerns in Iran: Comparisons between Iranian women in Iran and in America. *International Journal of Eating Disorders, 30*, 259–268.

Abel, T., Martin, K. C., Bartsch, D., & Kandel, E. R. (1998). Memory suppressor genes: Inhibitory constraints on the storage of long-term memory. *Science, 279*, 338–341.

Ablon, J. S., & Jones, E. E. (1999). Psychotherapy process in the National Institute of Mental Health Treatment of Depression Collaborative Research Program. *Journal of Consulting and Clinical Psychology, 67*, 64–75.

Abraham, H. D. (1983). Visual phenomenology of the LSD flashback. *Archives of General Psychiatry, 40*, 884–889.

Abramowitz, J. S. (1997). Effectiveness of psychological and pharmacological treatments for obsessive-compulsive disorder: A quantitative review. *Journal of Consulting and Clinical Psychology, 65*, 44–52.

Abrams, L. R., & Jones, R. W. (1994, August). *The contribution of social roles to psychological distress in businesswomen.* Paper presented at the 102nd annual convention of the American Psychological Association, Los Angeles, CA.

Abramson, L. Y., Seligman, M. E., & Teasedale, J. D. (1978). Learned helplessness in humans: Critique and reformulation. *Journal of Abnormal Psychology, 87*, 49–74.

Achter, J., Lubinski, D., & Benbow, C. P. (1996). Multipotentiality among the intellectually gifted: "It was never there and already it's vanishing." *Journal of Counseling Psychology, 43*, 65–76.

Adams, H. E., Wright, W. L., & Lohr, B. A. (1996). Is homophobia associated with homosexual arousal? *Journal of Abnormal Psychology, 105*, 440–445.

Adams, J. (1967). *Human memory.* New York: McGraw-Hill.

Adams, S. H., Cartwright, L. K., Ostrove, J. M., Stewart, A. J., & Wink, P. (1998). Psychological predictors of good health in three longitudinal samples of educated midlife women. *Health Psychology, 17*, 412–420.

Addis, M. E. (1997). Evaluating the treatment manual as a means of disseminating empirically validated psychotherapies. *Clinical Psychology: Science & Practice, 4*, 1–11.

Ader, R. (1976). Conditioned adrenocortical steroid elevations in the rat. *Journal of Comparative and Physiological Psychology, 90*, 1156–1163.

Ader, R., & Cohen, N. (1975). Behaviorally conditioned immunosuppression. *Psychosomatic Medicine, 37*, 333–340.

Ader, R., & Cohen, N. (1985), CNS-immune system interactions: Conditioning phenomena. *Behavioral and Brain Sciences, 8*, 379–394.

Ader, R., & Cohen, N. (1993). Psychoneuroimmunology: Conditioning and stress. *Annual Review of Psychology, 40*, 53–85.

Adler, A. (1956). *The individual psychology of Alfred Adler: A systematic presentation of selections from his writings.* (H. L. Ansbacher & R. R. Ansbacher, Eds.). New York: Basic Books.

Adler, A. (1964). *Social interest: A challenge to mankind.* New York: Capricorn Books. (Original work published 1933).

Adler, N. E., Epel, E. S., Castellazzo, G., & Ickovics, J. R. (2000). Relationship of subjective and objective social status with psychological and physiological functioning: Preliminary data in healthy white women. *Health Psychology, 19*, 586–592.

Adolph, K. E. (2000). Specificity of learning: Why infants fall over a veritable cliff. *Psychological Science, 11*, 290–295.

Adolphs, R., Damasio, H., Tranel, D., & Damasio, A. R. (1996). Cortical systems for the recognition of emotion in facial expressions. *Journal of Neuroscience, 16*, 7678–7687.

af Klinteberg, B., Andersson, T., Magnusson, D., & Stattin, H. (1993). Hyperactive behavior in childhood as related to subsequent alcohol problems and violent offending: A longitudinal study of male subjects. *Personality of Individual Differences, 15*, 381–388.

Agency for Health Care Policy and Research. (1999). Newer antidepressant drugs are equally as effective as older-generation drug treatments, research shows. AHCPR Pub. No. 99-E013. Rockville, MD.

Aglioti, S., Smania, N., Manfred, M., & Berlucchi, G. (1996). Disownership of left hand and objects related to it in a patient with right brain damage. *Neuroreport, 8*, 293–296.

Aguilar-Alonso, A. (1996). Personality and creativity. *Personality and Individual Differences, 21*, 959–969.

Ahadi, S., & Diener, E. (1989). Multiple determinants and effect size. *Journal of Personality and Social Psychology, 56*, 398–406.

Aharon, I., Etcoff, N., Ariely, D., Chabris, C. F., O'Connor, E., & Brieter, H. C. (2001). Beautiful faces have variable reward value: fMRI and behavioral evidence. *Neuron, 32*, 537–551.

Ahmed, S. T., Lombardino, L. J., & Leonard, C. M. (2001a) Specific language impairment: Definitions, causal mechanisms and neurobiological factors. *Journal of Medical Speech-Language Pathology, 9*, 1–15.

Ahmed, S. T., Lombardino, L. J., & Leonard, C. M. (2001b). "Specific language impairment: Definitions, causal mechanisms, and neurobiological factors": Erratum. *Journal of Medical Speech-Language Pathology, 9*, 211.

Ainsworth, M. D. S., Blehar, M. C., Waters, E., & Wahl, S. (1978). *Patterns of attachment: A psychological study of the Strange Situation.* Hillsdale, NJ: Erlbaum.

Ajzen, I. (2002). Perceived behavioral control, self-efficacy, locus of control, and the theory of planned behavior. *Journal of Applied Social Psychology, 32*, 665–683.

Akhtar, N., & Tomasello, M. (1996). Two-year-olds learn words for absent objects and actions. *British Journal of Developmental Psychology, 14*, 79–93.

Akiskal, H. S. (1996). The prevalent clinical spectrum of bipolar disorders: Beyond DSM–IV. *Journal of Clinical Psychopharmacology, 16* (Suppl. 1), 4S–14S.

Alan Guttmacher Institute. (1994). *Sex and America's teenagers.* New York.

Alba, J. W., & Hasher, L. (1983). Is memory schematic? *Psychological Bulletin, 93*, 203–231.

Albert, M. S., Duffy, F. H., & McAnulty, G. B. (1990). Electrophysiologic comparisons between two groups of patients with Alzheimer's disease. *Archives of Neurology, 47*, 857–863.

Albert, M. S., & Moss, M. B. (1996). Neuropsychology of aging: Findings in humans and monkeys. In E. L. Schneider, J. W. Rowe, T. E. Johnson, N. J. Holbrook, & J. H. Morrison (Eds.), *Handbook of the biology of aging (4th ed.).* San Diego, CA: Academic Press.

Alcock, J. E. (1987). Parapsychology: Science of the anomalous of search for the soul? *Behavioral and Brain Sciences, 10*, 553–565.

Alcoholics Anonymous. (1999). *12 Steps of Alcoholics Anonymous.* URL http://www.addictions.org/aa/steps.htm.

Aldag, R. J., & Fuller, S. R. (1993). Beyond fiasco: A reappraisal of the groupthink phenomenon and a new model of group decision processes. *Psychological Bulletin, 113*, 533–552.

Aldous, J., & Ganey, R. F. (1999). Family life and the pursuit of happiness: The influence of gender and race. *Journal of Family Issues, 20*, 155–180.

Alexander, C. N., Robinson, P., Orme-Johnson, D. W., Schneider, R. H., & Walton, K. G. (1994a). The effects of transcendental meditation compared to other methods of relaxation and meditation in reducing risk factors, morbidity, and mortality. *Homeostasis, 35*, 243–264.

Alexander, C. N., Robinson, P., & Rainforth, M. (1994b). Treating and preventing alcohol, nicotine, and drug abuse through transcendental meditation: A review and statistical meta-analysis of 19 studies. *Alcoholism Treatment Quarterly, Vol. II*, 13–87.

Alexander, D. (1991). Keynote Address. In *President's Committee on Mental Retardation, Summit on the National Effort to Prevent Mental Retardation and Related Disabilities.*

Alexander, F., & French, T. (1946). *Psychoanalytic theory.* New York: Ronald.

Alexander, M. G., Brewer, M. B., & Hermann, R. K. (1999). Images and affect: A functional analysis of out-group stereotypes. *Journal of Personality and Social Psychology, 77*, 78–93.

Alibali, M. W., Bassok, M., Solomon, K. O., Syc, S. E., & Goldin-Meadow, S. (1999). Illuminating mental representations through speech and gesture. *Psychological Science, 10*, 327–333.

Alkire, M. T., Haier, R. J., & James, H. F. (1998). Toward the neurobiology of consciousness: Using brain imaging and anesthesia to investigate the anatomy of consciousness. In S. Hameroff, A. Kaszniak, & A. Scott (Eds.), *Toward a science of consciousness II*. Cambridge, MA: MIT Press.

Allen, B. (1997). *Personality theories: Development, growth, and diversity*. (2nd ed.). Needham Heights, MA: Allyn & Bacon.

Allen, J. J. B., & Iacono, W. G. (1997). A comparison of methods for the analysis of event-related potentials in deception detection. *Psychophysiology, 34*, 234–240.

Allen, L. S., & Gorski, R. A. (1992). Sexual orientation and the size of the anterior commissure in the human brain. *Proceedings of the National Academy of Sciences of the United States of America, 89*, 7199–7202.

Allison, J. (1970). Respiratory changes during transcendental meditation. *Lancet, 1*(7651), 833–834.

Alloy, L. B., Abramson, L. Y., Hogan, M. E., Whitehouse, W. G., Rose, D. T., Robinson, M. S., Kim, R. S., & Lapkin, J. B. (2000). The Temple-Wisconsin Cognitive Vulnerability to Depression Project: Lifetime history of axis I psychopathology in individuals at high and low cognitive risk for depression. *Journal of Abnormal Psychology, 109*, 403–418.

Allport, G. W. (1937). *Personality: A psychological interpretation*. New York: Holt.

Allyn, J., & Festinger, L. (1961). The effectiveness of unanticipated persuasive communications. *Journal of Abnormal and Social Psychology, 62*, 35–40.

Almor, A., & Sloman, S. A. (1996). Is deontic reasoning special? *Psychological Review, 103*, 374–380.

Alonso, P., Pujol, J., Cardoner, N., Benlloch, L., Deus, J., Menchon, J. M., Capdevila, A., & Vallejo, J. (2001). Right prefrontal repetitive transcranial magnetic stimulation in obsessive-compulsive disorder: A double-blind, placebo-controlled study. *American Journal of Psychiatry, 158*, 1143–1145.

Alper, C. M., Doyle, W. J., Skoner, D. P., Buchman, C. A., Seroky, J. T., Gwaltney, J. M., & Cohen, S. (1996). Pre-challenge antibodies moderate infection rate, and signs and symptoms in adults experimentally challenged with rhinovirus 39. *Laryngoscope, 106*, 1298–1305.

Altshuler, L. L., Bartzokis, G., Grieder, T., Curran, J., & Mintz, J. (1998). Amygdala enlargement in bipolar disorder and hippocampal reduction in schizophrenia: An MRI study demonstrating neuroanatomic specificity. *Archives of General Psychiatry, 55*, 663–664.

Aluja-Fabregat, A., Colom, R., Abad, F., & Juan-Espinosa, M. (2000). Sex differences in general intelligence defined as g among young adolescents. *Personality & Individual Differences, 28*, 813–820.

Amabile, T. M. (1983). *The social psychology of creativity*. New York: Springer-Verlag.

Amabile, T. M. (1996). *Creativity in context*. Boulder, CO: Westview.

Amabile, T. M. (1998, September–October). How to kill creativity. *Harvard Business Review*, pp. 76–87.

Amabile, T. M. (2001). Beyond talent: John Irving and the passionate craft of creativity. *American Psychologist, 56*, 333–336.

Amat, J., Matus-Amat, P., Watkins, L. R., & Maier, S. F. (1998). Escapable and inescapable stress differentially alter extracellular levels of 5-HT in the basolateral amygdala of the rat. *Brain Research, 812*, 113–120.

Ambady, M., Bernieri, F. J., & Richeson, J. A. (2000). Toward a histology of social behavior: Judgmental accuracy from thin slices of the behavioral stream. In M. P. Zanna (Ed.), *Advances in experimental social psychology*, (Vol. 32, pp. 201–271). New York: Academic Press.

Ambady, N., & Rosenthal, R. (1992). Thin slices of expressive behavior as predictors of interpersonal consequences: A meta analysis. *Psychological Bulletin, 111*, 256–274.

Ambady, N., & Rosenthal, R. (1993). Half a minute: Predicting teacher evaluations from thin slices of behavior and physical attractiveness. *Journal of Personality and Social Psychology, 64*, 431–441.

Ambady, N., Conroy, M., Tobia, A., & Mullins, J. (in preparation). Friends, lovers, and strangers: Judging dyadic relationships from thin slices.

Ambady, N., LaPlante, D., Nguyen, T., Chaumeton, N., Rosenthal, R., & Levinson, W. (under revision). Physician affect and malpractice claims in primary care and surgery.

Ambrose, N. G., Yairi, E., & Cox, N. (1993). Genetic aspects of early childhood stuttering. *Journal of Speech & Hearing Research, 36*, 521–528.

Ambuel, B. (1995). Adolescents, unintended pregnancy, and abortion: The struggle for a compassionate social policy. *Current Directions in Psychological Science, 4*, 1–5.

American Association for Mental Retardation (1992). *Mental retardation: Definition, classification, and systems of supports* (9th ed.).

American Foundation for Suicide Prevention. (1996). http://www.afsp.org/suicide/facts.html.

American Psychiatric Association (1987). *Diagnostic and statistical manual of mental disorders* (3rd ed., rev.). Washington, DC: American Psychiatric Association.

American Psychiatric Association. (1994). *Diagnostic and statistical manual of mental disorder* (4th edition). Washington, DC: American Psychiatric Association.

American Psychiatric Association. (2000). *Diagnostic and statistical manual of mental disorders* (5th edition). Washington, DC: American Psychiatric Association.

Ames, A. (1952). *The Ames demonstration in perception*. New York: Hafner.

Amsterdam, B. (1972). Mirror self-image reactions before age two. *Developmental Psychology, 5*, 297–305.

Anand, B. K., & Brobeck, J. R. (1952). Food intake and spontaneous activity of rats with lesions in the amygdaloid nuclei. *Journal of Neurophysiology, 15*, 421–430.

Anastasi, A. (1988). *Psychological testing* (6th ed.). New York: Macmillan.

Anch, A. M., Bowman, C. P., Mitler, M. M., & Walsh, J. K. (1988). *Sleep: A scientific perspective*. Englewood Cliffs, NJ: Prentice-Hall.

Andersen, A. E., & DiDomenico, L. (1992). Diet vs. shape content of popular male and female magazines: A dose response relationship to the incidence of eating disorders? *International Journal of Eating Disorders, 11*, 283–287.

Andersen, B. (1997, July). Psychological interventions for individuals with cancer. *Clinician's Research Digest* (Suppl. bulletin) *16*, 1–2.

Andersen, B. L., Kiecolt-Glaser, K. K., & Glaser, R. (1994). A biobehavioral model of cancer stress and disease course. *American Psychologist, 49*, 389–404.

Anderson, A. K., & Phelps, E. A. (2002). Is the human amygdala critical for the subjective experience of emotion?: Evidence of intact dispositional affect in patients with amygdala lesions. *Journal of Cognitive Neuroscience, 14*, 709–720.

Anderson, B. L., & Nakayama, K. (1994). Toward a general theory of stereopsis: Binocular matching, occluding contours, and fusion. *Psychological Review, 101*, 414–445.

Anderson, C. A. (1983). Abstract and concrete data in the perseverance of social theories: When weak data lead to unshakable beliefs. *Journal of Experimental Social Psychology, 19*, 930–1108.

Anderson, C. A., & Bushman, B. J. (1997). External validity of "trivial" experiments: The case of laboratory aggression. *Review of General Psychology, 1*, 19–41.

Anderson, C. A., Lepper, M. R., & Ross, L. (1980). Perseverance of social theories: This role of explanation in the persistence of discredited information. *Journal of Personality and Social Psychology, 39*, 1037–1049.

Anderson, I. M. (2000). Selective serotonin reuptake inhibitors versus tricyclic antidepressants: A meta-analysis of efficacy and tolerability. *Journal of Affective Disorders, 58*, 19–36.

Anderson, J. R. (2000). *Cognitive psychology and its implications* (5th ed.). New York: Worth.

Anderson, J. R., & Betz, J. (2001). A hybrid model of categorization. *Psychonomic Bulletin & Review, 8*, 629–647.

Anderson, M. (1992). *Intelligence and development: A cognitive theory*. Oxford, England: Blackwell.

Anderson, M. C., Bjork, R. A., & Bjork, E. L. (1994). Remembering can cause forgetting: Retrieval dynamics in long-term memory. *Journal of Experimental Psychology: Learning, Memory and Cognition, 20*, 1063–1087.

Anderson, N. A. (1981). *Foundations of information integration theory*. New York: Academic Press.

Anderson, N. B. (1998). Levels of analysis in health science: A framework for integrating sociobehavioral and biomedical research. In S. M. McCann, J. M. Lipton, et al. (Eds.), *Annals of the New York Academy of Sciences: Vol. 840, Neuroimmunomodulation: Molecular aspects, integrative systems, and clinical advances* (pp. 563–576). New York: New York Academy of Sciences.

Anderson, N. H., & Barrios, A. A. (1961). Primacy effects in personality impression formation. *Journal of Abnormal and Social Psychology, 63*, 346–350.

Anderson, V. L., Levinson, E. M., Barker, W., & Kiewra, K. R. (1999). The effects of meditation on teacher perceived occupational stress, state and trait anxiety, and burnout. *School Psychology Quarterly, 14*, 3–25.

Ando, J., Ono, Y., & Wright, M. J. (2001). Genetic structure of spatial and verbal working memory. *Behavior Genetics, 31*, 615–624.

Andreasen, N. C. (1987). Creativity and mental illness: Prevalence rates in writers and their first-degree relatives. *American Journal of Psychiatry, 144*, 1288–1292.

Andreasen, N. C., Flashman, L., Flaum, M., Arndt, S., Swayze, V., O'Leary, D. S., Ehrhardt, J. C., & Yuh, W. T. (1994). Regional brain abnormalities in schizophrenia measured with magnetic resonance imaging. *Journal of the American Medical Association, 272*, 1763–1769.

Andreasen, N. C., Nasrullah, H., Dunn, V., Olson, S., Grove, W., Erhardt, J., Coffman, J., & Crosett, J. (1986). Structural abnormalities in the fronal system in schizophrenia. *Archives of General Psychiatry, 43*, 136–144.

Andreasen, N. C., Rezai, K., Alliger, R., Swayze, V., Flaum, M., Kirchner, P., Cohen, G., & O'Leary, D. (1992). Hypofrontality in neuroleptic-naïve patients and in patients with chronic schizophrenia: Assessment with xenon-133 single proton emission computed tomography and the Tower of London. *Archives of General Psychiatry, 49*, 943–958.

Andrews, H. B., & Jones, S. (1990). Eating behaviour in obese women: A test of two hypotheses. *Australian Psychologist, 25*, 351–357.

Andrews, J. A., Hops, H., Duncan, S. C. (1997). Adolescent modeling of parent substance use: The moderating effect of the relationship with the parent. *Journal of Family Psychology, 11*, 259–270.

Angier, N. (1999, September 7). Route to creativity: Following bliss or dots? *New York Times*, F3 (col. 1).

Angleitner, A., Riemann, R., & Strelau, J. (1995). A study of twins using the self-report and peer-report NEO-FFI sclaes. Paper presented at the seventh meeting of the International Society for the Study of Individual Differences, July 15–19, Warsaw, Poland.

Anglin, J. M. (1993). Vocabulary development: A morphological analysis. *Monographs of the Society for Research in Child Development, 58*(10, Serial No. 238).

Angst, J. (1998). The emerging epidemiology of hypomania and bipolar II disorder. *Journal of Affective Disorders, 50*, 143–151.

Anisman, H., Zaharia, M. D., Meaney, M. J., & Merali, Z. (1998). Do early-life events permanently alter behavioral and hormonal responses to stressors? *International Journal of Developmental Neuroscience, 16*, 149–164.

Ankney, C. D. (1992). Sex differences in relative brain size: The mismeasure of women, too? *Intelligence, 16,* 329–336.

Anonymous. (1970). Effects of sexual activity on beard growth in man. *Nature, 226,* 867–870.

Antoch, M. P., Song, E. J., Chang, A. M., Vitaterna, M. H., Zhao, Y., Wilsbacher, L. D., Sangoram, A. M., King, D. P., Pinto, L. H., Takahashi, J. S. (1997, May 16). Functional identification of the mouse circadian Clock gene by transgenic BAC rescue. *Cell, 89*(4), 655–667.

Antonuccio, D. O., Danton, W. G., & DeNelsky, G. Y. (1995). Psychotherapy versus medication for depression: Challenging the conventional wisdom with data. *Professional Psychology: Research & Practice, 26,* 574–585.

Antony, M. M., & Barlow, D. H. (2002). Specific phobias. In D. H. Barlow (Ed.), *Anxiety and its disorders* (2nd ed., pp. 380–417). NY: Guilford.

Aram, D. M., Morris, R., & Hall, N. E. (1992). The validity of discrepancy criteria for identifying children with developmental language disorders. *Journal of Learning Disabilities, 25,* 549–554.

Aranda, M. P., & Knight, B. G. (1997). The influence of ethnicity and culture on the caregiver stress and coping process: A socio-cultural review and analysis. *Gerontologist, 37,* 342–354.

Archer, S. L., & Waterman, A. S. (1988). Psychological indvidualism: Gender differences or gender neutrality? *Human Development, 31,* 65–81.

Arend, L. (1994). Surface colors, illumination and surface geometry: Intrinsic-image models of human color perception. In A. Gilchrist (Ed.), *Lightness, brightness, and transparency* (pp. 159–213). Hillsdale, NJ: Erlbaum.

Arguin, M., Cavanagh, P., & Joanette, Y. (1994). Visual feature integration with an attention deficit. *Brain and Cognition, 24,* 44–56.

Argyle, M. L., & Lu, L. (1990). Happiness and social skills. *Personality & Individual Differences, 11,* 1255–1261.

Arking, R. (1991). *Biology of aging: Observations and principles.* Englewood Cliffs, NJ: Prentice Hall.

Armstrong, S. L., Gleitman, L. R., & Gleitman, H. (1983). What some concepts might not be. *Cognition, 13,* 263–308.

Arnell, K. M., & Jolicoeur, P. (1999). The attentional blink across stimulus modalities: Evidence for central processing limitations. *Journal of Experimental Psychology: Human Perception and Performance, 25,* 630–648.

Arnett, J. (1992). Reckless behavior in adolescence: A developmental perspective. *Developmental Review, 12,* 339–373.

Arnett, J. J. (1999). Adolescent storm and stress, reconsidered. *American Psychologist, 54,* 317–326.

Arnold, M. B. (1960a). *Emotion and personality: Vol. I, Psychological aspects.* New York: Columbia University Press.

Arnold, M. B. (1960b). *Emotion and personality: Vol. II, Neurological and physiological aspects.* New York: Columbia University Press.

Aron, E. N., & Aron, A. (1997). Sensory-processing sensitivity and its relation to introversion and emotionality. *Journal of Personality and Social Psychology, 73,* 345–368.

Aronson, E., & Osherow, N. (1980). Cooperation, prosocial behavior, and academic performance: Experiments in the desegregated classroom. *Applied Social Psychology Annual, 1,* 163–196.

Aronson, E., & Patnoe, S. (1997). *The jigsaw classroom: Building cooperation in the classroom* (2nd ed.). New York: Addison Wesley Longman.

Aronson, J., Blanton, H., & Cooper, J. (1995). From dissonance to disidentification: Selectivity in the self-affirmation process. *Journal of Personality and Social Psychology, 68,* 986–996.

Arterberry, M. E., & Yonas, A. (2000). Perception of three-dimensional shape specified by optic flow by 8-week-old infants. *Perception & Psychophysics, 62,* 550–556.

Asch, S. E. (1951). Effects of group pressure upon the modification and distortion of judgment. In H. Guetzkow (Ed.), *Groups, leadership, and men* (pp. 177–190). Pittsburgh: Carnegie.

Asch, S. E. (1955). Opinions and social pressure. *Scientific American, 193,* 31–35.

Asendorpf, J. B., Warkentin, V., & Baudonniere, P-M. (1996). Self-awareness and other-awareness: II. Mirror self-recognition, social contingency awareness, and synchronic imitation. *Developmental Psychology, 32,* 313–321.

Ashbridge, E., Walsh, V., & Cowley, A. (1997). Temporal aspects of visual search studied by transcranial magnetic stimulation. *Neuropsychologia, 35,* 1121–1131.

Ashton, C. H. (2001). Pharmacology and effects of cannabis: A brief review. *British Journal of Psychiatry, 178,* 101–106.

Aslin, R. N., Saffran, J. R., & Newport, E. L. (1998). Computation of conditional probability statistics by 8-month-old infants. *Psychological Science, 9,* 321–324.

Associated Press. (2001, 9 August). Man's best friend finally understood: A bark deciphered. *Wall Street Journal Europe,* p. 18.

Association of SIDS and Infant Mortality Programs (2002). http://www.asip1.org/isp.html

Athanasiou, M. S. (2000). Current nonverbal assessment instruments: A comparison of psychometric integrity and test fairness. *Journal of Psychoeducational Assessment, 18,* 211–229.

Atkinson, R. C., & Shiffrin, R. M. (1968). Human memory: A proposed system and its control processes. In K. W. Spence & J. T. Spence (Eds.), *The psychology of learning and motivation: Advances in research and theory* (Vol. 2, pp. 89–195). New York: Academic Press.

Atkinson, R. C., & Shiffrin, R. M. (1971). The control of short-term memory. *Scientific American, 225,* 82–90.

Atre-Vaidya, N., & Hussain, S. M. (1999). Borderline personality disorder and bipolar mood disorder: Two distinct disorders or a continuum? *Journal of Mental and Nervous Disorders, 187,* 313–315.

Auden, W. H. (1989). *Van Gogh: A self-portrait.* New York: Marlowe.

Avorn, J., & Langer, E. (1982). Induced disability in nursing home patients: A controlled trial. *Journal of the American Geriatrics Society, 30,* 397–400.

Awh, E., Jonides, J., Smith, E. E., Schumacher, E. H., Koeppe, R. A., & Katz, S. (1996). Dissociation of storage and rehearsal in verbal working memory: Evidence from positron emission tomography. *Psychological Science, 7,* 25–31.

Ayton, P., & Wright, G. (1994). Subjective probability: What should we believe? In G. Wright, & P. Ayton (Eds.), *Subjective probability* (pp. 163–183). New York: Wiley.

Azar, B. (1995). Timidity can develop in the first days of life. *APA Monitor, 26* (11), 23

Azari, N. P. (1991). Effects of glucose on memory processed in young adults. *Psychopharmacology, 105,* 521–524.

Azrin, N. H., Sisson, R. W., Meyers, R., & Godley, M. (1982). Alcoholism treatment by disulfiram and community reinforcement therapy. *Journal of Behavior Therapy and Experimental Psychiatry, 13,* 105–112.

Baaré, W. F. C., van Oel, C. J., Pol, H. E. H., Schnack, H. G., Durston, S., Sitskoorn, M. M., & Kahn, R. S. (2001). Volumes of brain structures in twins discordant for schizophrenia. *Archives of General Psychiatry, 58,* 33–40.

Baars, B. J. (2002). The conscious access hypothesis: Origins and recent evidence. *Trends in Cognitive Sciences, 6,* 47–52.

Babad, E. (1993). Pygmalion—25 years after interpersonal expectations in classroom. In P. D. Blanck (Ed.), *Interpersonal expectations: Theory, research, and applications* (pp. 125–153). Cambridge: Cambridge University Press.

Babad, E., Bernieri, F., & Rosenthal, R. (1989). Nonverbal communication and leakage in the behavior of biased and unbiased teachers. *Journal of Personality & Social Psychology, 56,* 89–94.

Bachen, E. A., Manuck, S. B., Cohen, S., Muldoon, M. F., Raible, R., Herbert, T. B., & Rabin, B. S. (1995). Adrengergic blockage ameliorates cellular immune responses to mental stress in humans. *Psychosomatic Medicine, 57,* 366–372.

Baddeley, A. (1986). *Working memory.* Oxford, England: Clarendon.

Baddeley, A. (1994). The magical number seven: Still magic after all these years? *Psychological Review, 101,* 353–356.

Baenninger, M., & Newcombe, N. (1989). The role of experience in spatial test performance: A meta-analysis. *Sex Roles, 20,* 327–344.

Baer, J. (1998). The case for domain specificity of creativity. *Creativity Research Journal, 11,* 173–177.

Baer, L., Ackerman, R., Surman, O., Correia, J., Griffith, J., Alpert, N., & Hackett, T. (1990). PET studies during hypnosis and hypnotic suggestion. In P. Berner (Ed.), *Psychiatry: The state of the art, biological psychiatry, higher nervous activity* (pp. 293–298). New York: Plenum Press.

Bagwell, C. L., Newcomb, A. F., & Bukowski, W. M. (1998). Preadolescent friendship and peer rejection as predictors of adult adjustment. *Child Development, 69,* 140–153.

Bahrick, H. P. (1974). Semantic memory content in permastore: Fifty years of memory for Spanish learned in school. *Journal of Experimental Psychology: General, 120,* 1–31.

Bahrick, H. P., & Phelps, E. (1987). Retention of Spanish vocabulary over eight years. *Journal of Experimental Psychology: Learning, Memory and Cognition, 13,* 344–349.

Bahrick, L. E., Moss, L., & Fadil, C. (1996). Development of visual self-recognition in infancy. *Ecological Psychology, 8,* 189–208.

Bailey, J. M., & Pillard, R. C. (1991). A genetic study of male sexual orientation. *Archives of General Psychiatry, 48,* 1089–1096.

Baillargeon, R. (1993). The object concept revisited: New directions in the investigation of infants' physical knowledge. In C. E. Granrud (Ed.), *Visual perception and cognition in infancy* (pp. 265–315). Hillsdale, NJ: Erlbaum.

Baillargeon, R. (1994). How do infants learn about the physical world? *Current Directions in Psychological Science, 3*(5), 133–140.

Baillargeon, R. (1995). A model of physical reasoning in infancy. In C. K. Rovee-Collier & L. P. Lipsitt (Eds.), *Advances in infancy research* (Vol. 9, pp. 305–371). Norwood, NJ: Ablex.

Baillargeon, R., Graber, M., Devos, J., & Black, J. (1990). Why do young infants fail to search for hidden objects? *Cognition, 36,* 255–284.

Baillargeon, R., Kotovsky, L., & Needham, A. (1995). The acquisition of physical knowledge in infancy. In D. Sperber, D. Premack, & A. J. Premack (Eds.), *Causal understandings in cognition and culture* (pp. 79–116). New York: Oxford University Press.

Baily, C. H., & Chen, M. (1989). Time course of structural changes at identified sensory neuron synapses during long-term sensitization in Aplysia. *Journal of Neuroscience, 9,* 1774–1781.

Baird, A., Kagan, J., Gaudette, T., Walz, K., Hershlag, N., & Boas, D. (2002). Frontal lobe activation during object permanence: Data from near-infrared spectroscopy. *NeuroImage, 16,* 1120–1126.

Baird, J. C. (1982). The moon illusion: II. A reference theory. *Journal of Experimental Psychology, 111,* 304–315.

Baird, J. C., & Wagner, M. (1982). The moon illusion: I. How high is the sky? *Journal of Experimental Psychology, 111,* 296–303.

Baker, R. R. (1980). Goal orientation by blindfolded humans after long-distance displacement: Possible involvement of a magnetic sense. *Science, 210,* 555–557.

Baker, S. C., Dolan, R. J., & Frith, C. D. (1996). The functional anatomy of logic: A PET study of inferential reasoning. *NeuroImage, 3,* S218.

Baldwin, D. A. (2000). Interpersonal understanding fuels knowledge acquisition. *Current Directions in Psychological Science, 9,* 40–45.

Baldwin, J. D., & Baldwin, J. I. (1989). The socialization of homosexuality and heterosexuality in a non-Western society. *Archives of Sexual Behavior, 18,* 13–29.

Ball, D., Hill, L., Eley, T. C., Chorney, M. J., Chorney, K., Thompson, L. A., Detterman, D. K., Benbow, C., Lubinski, D., Owen, M., McGuffin, P., & Plomin, R. (1998). Dopamine markers and general cognitive ability. *NeuroReport, 9,* 347–349.

Ball, T. S. (1971). *Itard, Seguin, and Kephart: Sensory education—A learning interpretation.* Columbus, OH: Merrill.

Ballus, C. (1997). Effects of antipsychotics on the clinical and psychosocial behavior of patients with schizophrenia. *Schizophrenia Research, 28,* 247–255.

Baltes, P. B. (1987). Theoretical propositions of life-span developmental psychology: On the dynamics between growth and decline. *Developmental Psychology, 23,* 611–626.

Baltes, P. B., Cornelius, S. W., & Nesselroade, J. R. (1979). Cohort effects in developmental psychology. In J. R. Nesselroade & P. B. Baltes (Eds.), *Longitudinal reserach in the study of behavior and development* (pp. 61–87). New York: Academic Press.

Baltes, P. B., Dittmann-Kohli, F., & Dixon, R. A. (1984). New perspectives on the development of intelligence in adulthood: Toward a dual-process conception and a model of selective optimization with compensation. In P. B. Baltes & O. G. Brim, Jr. (Eds.), *Life-span development and behavior* (Vol. 6, pp. 33–76). San Diego, CA: Academic Press.

Banaji, M. R., & Hardin, C. D. (1996). Automatic stereotyping. *Psychological Science, 7,* 136–141.

Bandura, A. (1976). Self-reinforcement: Theoretical and methodological considerations. *Behaviorism, 4,* 135–155.

Bandura, A. (1977a). *Social learning theory.* Englewood Cliffs, NJ: Prentice-Hall.

Bandura, A. (1977b). Self-efficacy: Toward a unifying theory of behavior change. *Psychological Review, 84,* 191–215.

Bandura, A. (1978). The self-system in reciprocal determinism. *American Psychologist, 33,* 344–358.

Bandura, A. (1986). *Social foundations of thought and action: A social-cognitive theory.* Englewood Cliffs, NJ: Prentice-Hall.

Bandura, A. (1999). Moral disengagement in the perpetration of inhumanities. *Personality & Social Psychology Review, 3,* 193–209.

Bandura, A. (2001). Social cognitive theory: An agentic perspective. *Annual Review of Psychology, 52,* 1–26.

Bandura, A., & Rosenthal, T. L. (1966). Vicarious classical conditioning as a function of arousal level. *Journal of Personality and Social Psychology, 3,* 54–62.

Bandura, A., Grusec, J. E., & Menlove, F. L. (1967). Vicarious extinction of avoidance behavior. *Journal of Personality & Social Psychology, 5,* 16–23.

Bandura, A., Ross, D., & Ross, S. A. (1961). Transmission of aggression through imitation of aggressive models. *Journal of Abnomal and Social Psychology, 63,* 575–582.

Bandura, A., Ross, D., & Ross, S. A. (1963). Imitation of film-mediated aggressive models. *Journal of Abnormal & Social Psychology, 66,* 3–11.

Banich, M. T., & Federmeier, K. D. (1999). Categorical and metric spatial processing distinguished by task demands and practice. *Journal of Cognitive Neuroscience, 11,* 153–166.

Banks, M. S., & Bennett, P. J. (1988). Optical and photoreceptor immaturities limit the spatial and chromatic vision of human neonates. *Journal of the Optical Society of America, 5,* 2059–2079.

Banse, R., Seise, J., & Zerbes, N. (2001). Implicit attitudes towards homosexuality: Reliability, validity, and controllability of the IAT. *Zeitschrift fuer Experimentelle Psychologie, 48,* 145–160.

Bar, M., & Biederman, I. (1998). Subliminal visual priming. *Psychological Science, 9,* 464–469.

Bar, M., Tootell, R. B., Schacter, D. L., Greve, D. N., Fischl, B., Mendola, J. D., Rosen, B. R., & Dale, A. M. (2001). Cortical mechanisms specific to explicit visual object recognition. *Neuron, 29,* 529–535.

Barabasz, A., & Barabasz, M. (1989) Effects of restricted environmental stimulation: Enhancement of hypnotizability for experimental and chronic pain control. *International Journal of Clinical and Experimental Hypnosis, 37,* 217–231.

Barabasz, A. F., & Lonsdale, C. (1983). Effects of hypnosis on P300 olfactory-evoked potential amplitudes. *Journal of Abnormal Psychology, 92,* 520–523.

Barañano, D. E., Ferris, C. D., & Snyder, S. H. (2001). Atypical neural messengers. *Trends in Neurosciences, 24,* 99–106.

Barbarich, N. (2002). Is there a common mechanism of serotonin dysregulation in anorexia nervosa and obsessive compulsive disorder? *Eating & Weight Disorders, 7,* 221–231.

Barber, J. (1997). Hypnosis and memory: A cautionary chapter. In G. A. Fraser (Ed.), *The dilemma of ritual abuse: Cautions and guides for therapists.* (pp. 17–29). Washington, DC: American Psychiatric Press.

Barber, J., & Adrian, C. (1982). *Psychological approaches to the management of pain.* New York: Brunner/Mazel Publishers.

Barber, J. P., & Muenz, L. R. (1996). The role of avoidance and obsessiveness in matching patients to cognitive and interpersonal psychotherapy: Empirical findings from the Treatment for Depression Collaborative Research Program. *Journal of Consulting and Clinical Psychology, 64,* 951–958.

Barber, T. X. (1969). An empirically based formulation of hypnotism. *American Journal of Clinical Hypnosis, 12,* 100–130.

Barber, T. X., Spanos, N. P., & Chaves, J. F. (1974) *Hypnosis, imagination, and human potentialities.* New York: Pergamon.

Barbur, J. L., Watson, J. D. G., Frackowiak, R. D. G., & Zeki, S. (1993). Conscious visual perception without V1. *Brain, 116,* 1293–1302.

Barclay, J. R., Bransford, J. D., Franks, J. J., McCarrell, N. S., & Nitsch, K. (1974), Comprehension and semantic flexibility. *Journal of Verbal Learning and Verbal Behavior, 13,* 471–481.

Barefoot, J. C., Dahlstrom, W. G., & Williams, R. B. (1983). Hostility, CHD incidence, and total mortality: A 25-year follow-up study of 255 physicians. *Psychosomatic Medicine, 45,* 59–63.

Barefoot, J., Dodge, K., Peterson, B., Dahlstrom, W., & Williams, R. (1989). The Cook-Medley Hostility Scale: Item content and ability to predict survival. *Psychosomatic Medicine, 51,* 46–57.

Bargh, J. A. (1997). The automaticity of everyday life. In R. S. Eyer, Jr. (Ed.), *Advances in social cognition* (Vol. 10, pp. 1–61). Mahwah, NJ: Erlbaum.

Bargh, J. A., Chen, M., & Burrows, L. (1996). Automaticity of social behavior: Direct effects of trait construct and stereotype activation on action. *Journal of Personality and Social Psychology, 71,* 230–244.

Barinaga, M. (1995). Remapping the motor cortex. *Science, 268,* 1696–1698.

Barinaga, M. (2001). How cannabinoids work in the brain. *Science, 291,* 2530–2531.

Barkham, M., & Shapiro, D. A. (1990). Brief psychotherapeutic interventions for job-related distress: A pilot study of prescriptive and exploratory therapy. *Counseling Psychology Quarterly, 3,* 133–147.

Barkham, M., Shapiro, D. A., Hardy, G. E., & Rees, A. (1999). Psychotherapy in two-plus-one sessions: Outcomes of a randomized controlled trial of cognitive-behavioral and psychodynamic-interpersonal therapy for subsyndromal depression. *Journal of Consulting and Clinical Psychology, 67,* 201–211.

Barkow, J. H., Cosmides, L., & Tooby, J. (Eds.) (1992). *The adapted mind: Evolutionary psychology and the generation of culture.* New York: Oxford University Press.

Barlow, D. H. (1986). Causes of sexual dysfunction: The role of anxiety and cognitive interference. *Journal of Consulting and Clinical Psychology, 54,* 140–148.

Barlow, D. H. (1988). *Anxiety and its disorders.* New York: Guilford Press.

Barlow, D. H. (2002). *Anxiety and its disorders: The nature and treatment of anxiety and panic.* New York: Guilford Press.

Barlow, D. P. (1995). Gametic imprinting in mammals. *Science, 270,* 1610–1613.

Barnes, V. A., Treiber, F., & Davis, H. (2001). Impact of transcendental meditation on cardiovascular function at rest and during acute stress in adolescents with high normal blood pressure. *Journal of Psychosomatic Research, 51,* 597–605.

Barnett, L. A., Far, J. M., Mauss, A. L., & Miller, J. A. (1996). Changing perceptions of peer norms as a drinking reduction program for college students. *Journal of Alcohol & Drug Education, 41,* 39–62.

Barnett, M. A., Howard, J. A., King, L. M., & Dino, G. A. (1980). Antecedents of empathy: Retrospective accounts of early socialization. *Personality and Social Psychology Bulletin, 6,* 361–365.

Baron, R., & Byrne, D. (1997). *Social psychology* (8th ed.). Needham Heights, MA: Allyn & Bacon.

Baron, R. A. (1977). *Human aggression.* New York: Plenum.

Baron, R. A. (1988). Negative effects of destructive criticism: Impact on conflict, self-efficacy, and task performance. *Journal of Applied Psychology, 73,* 199–207.

Baron, R. B., & Richardson, D. (1994). *Human aggression.* New York: Plenum.

Baron, R. S., Vandello, J. A., & Brunsman, B. (1996). The forgotten variable in conformity research: Impact of task importance on social influence. *Journal of Personality and Social Psychology, 71,* 915–927.

Barr, R., Vieira, A., & Rovee-Collier, C. (2001). Mediated imitation in 6-month-olds: Remembering by association. *Journal of Experimental Child Psychology, 79,* 229–252.

Barr, R., Vieira, A., & Rovee-Collier, C. (2002). Bidirectional priming in infants. *Memory & Cognition, 30,* 246–255.

Barriga, A. Q., Landau, J. R., Stinson, B. L., Liau, A. K., & Gibbs, J. C. (2000). Cognitive distortion and problem behaviors in adolescents. *Criminal Justice & Behavior, 27,* 36–56.

Barry, E. (2002, 3 September). After day care controversy, psychologists play nice. *Boston Globe,* E1–E3.

Barsky, A. J., Saintfort, R., Rogers, M. P., Borus, J. F. (2002). Nonspecific medication side effects and the nocebo phenomenon. *Journal of the American Medical Association, 287,* 622–627.

Bartlett, F. C. (1932). *Remembering.* Cambridge, England: Cambridge University Press.

Bartoshuk, L. M., & Beauchamp, G. K. (1994). Chemical senses. *Annual Review of Psychology, 45,* 419–449.

Bartoshuk, L. M., Rifkin, B., Marks, L. E., & Bars, P. (1986). Taste and aging. *Journal of Gerontology, 41,* 51–57.

Bartussek, D., Diedrich, O., Naumann, E., & Collet, W. (1993). Introversion-extraversion and event-related potential (ERP): A test of J. A. Gray's theory. *Personality and Individual Differences, 14,* 565–574.

Basic Behavioral Science Task Force of the National Advisory Mental Health Council (1996). Basic behavioral science research for mental health, *American Psychologist, 51,* 722–731.

Bass, B. M. (1990). *Bass and Stogdill's handbook of leadership: Theory, research, and managerial applications* (3rd ed.). New York: Free Press.

Bass, M. B., & Avolio, B. J. (1993). Transformational leadership: A response to critiques. In M. M. Chemers & R. Ayman (Eds.), *Leadership theory and research: Perspectives and directions* (pp. 49–80). San Diego, CA: Academic Press.

Bassili, J. N. (1978). Facial motion in the perception of faces and of emotional expression. *Journal of Experimental Psychology: Human Perception & Performance, 4,* 373–379.

Bates, E., & MacWhinney, B. (1987). Competition, variation, and language learning. In B. MacWhinney (Ed.), *Mechanisms of language acquisition* (pp. 157–193). Hillsdale, NJ: Erlbaum.

Bates, E., Thal, D., Trauner, D., Fenson, J., Aram, D., Eisele, J., & Nass, R. (1997). From first words to grammar in children with focal brain injury. *Developmental Neuropsychology, 13,* 275–343.

Bates, T. C., & Eysenck, H. J. (1993). Intelligence, inspection time, and decision time. *Intelligence, 17,* 523–531.

Batsell, W. R., Jr., & Brown, A. S. (1998). Human flavor-aversion learning: A comparison of traditional aversions and cognitive aversions. *Learning & Motivation, 29,* 383–396.

Batshaw, M., & Perret, Y. (1992). *Children with disabilities: A medical primer.* Baltimore: Brookes.

Batson, C. D. (1998). Altruism and prosocial behavior. In D. T. Gilbert, S. T. Fiske, & G. Lindzey (Eds.), *The handbook of social psychology* (4th ed., pp. 282–316). New York: McGraw Hill.

Batson, C. D., Bolen, M. H., Cross, J. A., & Neuringer-Benefiel, H. E. (1986). Where is the altruism in the altruistic personality? *Journal of Personality & Social Psychology, 50,* 212–220.

Baudry, M., & Lynch, G. (2001). Remembrance of arguments past: How well is the glutamate receptor hypothesis of LTP holding up after 20 years? *Neurobiology of Learning & Memory, 76,* 284–297.

Baumeister, A. A., & Bacharach, V. R. (2000). Early generic educational intervention has no enduring effect on intelligence and does not prevent mental retardation: The Infant Health and Development Program. *Intelligence, 28,* 161–192.

Baumeister, R. F., & Boden, J. M. (1998). Aggression and the self: High self-esteem, low self-control, and ego threat. In R. G. Geen and E. Donnerstein (Eds.), *Human aggression: Theories, research, and implications for social policy* (pp. 111–137). San Diego, CA: Academic Press.

Baumeister, R. F., Catanese, K. R., & Wallace, H. M. (2002). Conquest by force: A narcissistic reactance theory of rape and sexual coercion. *Review of General Psychology, 6,* 92–135.

Baumeister, R. F., Smart, L., & Boden, J. M. (1996). Relation of threatened egotism to violence and aggression: The dark side of high self-esteem. *Psychological Review, 103,* 5–33.

Baumeister, R. F., Stillwell, A., & Wotman, S. R. (1990). Victim and perpetrator accounts of interpersonal conflict: Autobiographical narratives about anger. *Journal of Personality and Social Psychology, 59,* 994–1003.

Bauserman, R. (1996). Sexual aggression and pornography: A review of correlational research. *Basic & Applied Social Psychology, 18,* 405–427.

Bavelier, D., & Neville, H. J. (2002). Cross-modal plasticity: Where and how? *Nature Reviews Neuroscience, 3,* 443–452.

Baxter, J. S., Macrae, C. N., Manstead, A. S. R., Stradling, S. G., & Parker, D. (1990). Attributional biases and driver behavior. *Social Behaviour, 5,* 185–192.

Baxter, L. R., Schwartz, J. M., Bergman, K. S., Szuba, M. P., Guze, B. H., Mazziota, J. C., Alazraki, A., Selin, C. E., Ferng, H. K., Munford, P., & Phelps, M. E. (1992). Caudate glucose metabolic rate changes with both drug and behavior therapy for obsessive-compulsive disorder. *Archives of General Psychiatry, 49,* 681–689.

Baxter, L. R., Schwartz, J. M., Guze, B. H., Begman, K., & Szuba, M. P. (1990). Neuroimaging in obsessive-compulsive disorder: Seeking the mediating neuroanatomy. In M. A. Jenike, L. Baer, W. E. Minichiello (Eds.), *Obsessive compulsive disorder: Theory and management* (2nd ed., pp. 167–188). Chicago: Year Book Medical Publishers.

Baxter, M. G., Parker, A., Lindner, C. C. C., Izquierdo, A. D., & Murray, E. A. (2000). Control of response selection by reinforcer value requires interaction of amygdala and orbital prefrontal cortex. *Journal of Neuroscience, 20,* 4311–4319.

Bayley, N. (1969). *Bayley Scales of Infant Development.* New York: The Psychological Corporation.

Bazerman, M. (1997). *Judgment in managerial decision making* (4th ed.). New York: Wiley.

Beach, F. A. (1956). Characteristics of masculine "sex drive." In M. Jones (Ed.), *Nebraska Symposium on Motivation* (pp. 1–32). Lincoln, NE: University of Nebraska Press.

Beagley, G. H., & Beagley, W. K. (1978). Alleviation of learned helplessness following septal lesions in rats. *Physiological Psychology, 6,* 241–244.

Beaman, A., Barnes, P. Kletz, B., & McQuirk, B. (1978). Increasing helping rates through information dissemination: Teaching pays. *Personality and Social Psychology Bulletin, 4,* 406–411.

Beaman, A. L., Cole, C. M., Preston, M., Klentz, B., & Steblay, N. M. (1983). Fifteen years of foot-in-the-door research: A meta-analysis. *Personality and Social Psychology Bulletin, 9,* 181–196.

Bearak, B. (1997, March 29). Time of puzzles heartbreak binds relatives left behind. *New York Times,* 1.

Beatty, J. (1995). *Principles of behavioral neuroscience.* Dubuque, IA: Brown & Benchmark.

Beauregard, M., Levesque, J., & Bourgouin, P. (2001). Neural correlates of conscious self-regulation of emotion. *Journal of Neuroscience, 21,* 6993–7000.

Bebbington, P. E., Brugha, T., MacCarthy, B., Potter, J., Sturt, E., et al. (1988). The Camberwell Collaborative Depression Study: I. Depressed probands: Adversity and the form of depression. *British Journal of Psychiatry, 152,* 754–765.

Bechara, A. & Van der Kooy, D. (1992). A single brain stem substrate mediates the motivational effects of both opiates and food in nondeprived rats but not in deprived rats. *Behavioral Neuroscience, 106,* 351–363.

Bechara, A., Damasio, H., Tranel, D., Anderson, S. W. (1998). Dissociation of working memory from decision making within the human prefrontal cortex. *Journal of Neuroscience, 18,* 428–437.

Bechara, A., Damasio, H., Tranel, D., & Damasio, A. R. (1997). Deciding advantageously before knowing the advantageous strategy. *Science, 275,* 1293–1294.

Bechara, A., Tranel, D., & Damasio, H. (2000). Characterization of the decision-making deficit of patients with ventromedial prefrontal cortex lesions. *Brain, 123,* 2189–2202.

Beck, A. T. (1967). *Depression: Causes and treatment.* Philadelphia: University of Pennsylvania Press.

Beck, A. T., Emery, G., & Greenberg, R. L. (1985). *Anxiety disorders and phobias: A cognitive perspective.* New York: Basic Books.

Beck, A. T., Rush, A. J., Shaw, B. F., & Emery, G. (1979). *Cognitive therapy of depression: A treatment manual.* New York: Guilford Press.

Beck, A. T., Ward, C. H., Mendelson, M., Mock, J. E., & Erbaugh, J. K. (1961). An inventory for measuring depression. *Archives of General Psychiatry, 4,* 561–571.

Beck, H. (1976). Neuropsychological servosystems, consciousness, and the problem of embodiment. *Behavioral Sciences, 21,* 139–160.

Beck, J. G., Ohtake, P. J., & Shipherd, J. C. (1999). Exaggerated anxiety is not unique to CO2 in panic disorder: A comparison of hypercapnic and hypoxic challenges. *Journal of Abnormal Psychology, 108,* 473–482.

Beck, R., & Fernandez, E. (1998). Cognitive-behavioral therapy in the treatment of anger: A meta-analysis. *Cognitive Therapy & Research, 22,* 63–74.

Becker, A., & Hamburg, P. (1996). Culture, the media, and eating disorders. *Cross-Cultural Psychiatry, 4,* 163–167.

Bedford, F. L. (1999). Keeping perception accurate. *Trends in Cognitive Sciences, 3,* 4–10.

Beer, J. M., & Horn, J. M. (2000). The influence of rearing order on personality development within two adoption cohorts. *Journal of Personality, 68,* 789–819.

Beer, M. (1966). *Leadership, employee needs, and motivation* (Monograph No. 129). Columbus, OH: Ohio State University, Bureau of Business Research, College of Commerce.

Beggs, J. M., Brown, T. H., Byrne, J. H., Crow, T., LeDoux, J. E., LeBar, K., & Thompson, R. F (1999). Learning and memory: Basic mechanisms. In M. J. Zigmond, F. E. Bloom, S. G. Landis, J. L. Roberts, & L. R. Squire (Eds.), *Fundamental neuroscience* (pp. 1411–1454). New York: Academic Press.

Behrman, R. E. (Ed.). (1996). *The future of children: Financing child care* (Vol. 6, No.2). Los Altos, CA: Center for the Future of Children, The David and Lucile Packard Foundation.

Behrmann, M. (2000). The mind's eye mapped onto the brain's matter. *Current Directions in Psychological Science, 9,* 50–54.

Beilin, H. (1996). Mind and meaning: Piaget and Vygotsky on causal explanation. *Human Development, 39,* 277–286.

Beilock, S. L., Carr, T. H., MacMahon, C., & Starkes, J. L. (2002). When paying attention becomes counterproductive: Impact of divided versus skill-focused attention on novice and experienced performance of sensorimotor skills. *Journal of Experimental Psychology: Applied, 8,* 6–16.

Belcher, G., & Costello, C. G. (1991). Do confidants of depressed women provide less social support than confidants of nondepressed women? *Journal of Abnormal Psychology, 100,* 516–525.

Belkin, M. & Rosner, M. (1987). Intelligence, education, and myopia in males, *Archives of Opthamology, 105,* 1508–1511.

Bell, A. E. (1977). Heritability in retrospect. *Journal of Heredity, 68,* 297–300.

Beller, M., & Gafni, N. (1996). The 1991 international assessment of educational progress in mathematics and sciences: The gender differences perspective. *Journal of Educational Psychology, 88,* 365–377.

Bellugi, U., Adolphs, R., Cassady, C., & Chiles, M. (1999a). Towards the neural basis for hypersociability in a genetic syndrome. *NeuroReport, 10,* 1653–1657.

Bellugi, U., Birhle, A., Neville, H., Jernigan, T., & Doherty, S. (1992). Language, cognition, and brain organization in a neurodevelopmental disorder. In M. R. Gunnar and A. C. Nelson (Eds.), *Developmental behavioral neuroscience* (pp. 201–232). Hillsdale, NJ: Erlbaum.

Bellugi, U., Lichtenberger, L., Mills, D., Galaburda, A., & Korenberg, J. R. (1999b). Bridging cognition, the brain and molecular genetics: Evidence from Williams syndrome. *Trends in Neurosciences, 22,* 197–207.

Bellugi, U., Poizner, H., & Klima, E. S. (1993). Language, modality, and the brain. In M. Johnson (Ed.), *Brain development and cognition* (pp. 380–388). Cambridge, MA: Blackwell.

Belsky, J. (2001). Emanuel Miller Lecture: Developmental risks (still) associated with early child care. *Journal of Child Psychology & Psychiatry & Allied Disciplines, 42,* 845–859.

Belsky, J. (2002). Quantity counts: Amount of child care and children's socioemotional development. *Journal of Developmental & Behavioral Pediatrics, 23,* 167–170.

Bem, D. J. (1972). Self-perception theory. In L. Berkowitz (Ed.), *Advances in experimental social psychology* (Vol. 6, pp. 1–62). San Diego: Academic Press.

Bem, D. J. (1996). Exotic becomes erotic: A developmental theory of sexual orientation. *Psychological Review, 103,* 320–335.

Bem, D. J. (1998). Is EBE theory supported by the evidence? Is it androcentric? A reply to Peplau et al. *Psychological Review, 108,* 395–398.

Bem, D. J., & Allen, A. (1974). On predicting some of the people some of the time: The search for cross-situational consistencies in behavior. *Psychological Review, 81*, 506–520.

Bem, D. J., & Honorton, C. (1994). Does psi exist? Replicable evidence for an anomalous process of information transfer. *Psychological Bulletin, 115*, 4–18.

Ben-Shakhar, G., & Furedy, J. J. (1990). *Theories and applications in the detection of deception: A psychophysiological and international perspective.* New York: Springer-Verlag.

Benbow, C. P., & Minor, L. L. (1990). Cognitive profiles of verbally and mathematically precocious students: Implications for identification of the gifted. *Gifted Child Quarterly, 34*, 21–26.

Bender, K. J. (1998). "Substance P" antagonist relieves depression. *Psychiatric Times, 15*(11).

Benedict, J. G., & Donaldson, D. W. (1996). Recovered memories threaten all. *Professional Psychology: Research & Practice, 27*, 427–428.

Benes, F. M. (1996, November). Schizophrenia: Altered neural circuits in schizophrenia. *The Harvard Mental Health Letter, 13*(5).

Beninger, R. J. (1983). The role of dopamine in locomotor activity and learning. *Brain Research Reviews, 6*, 173–196.

Beninger, R. J. (1989). Dissociating the effects of altered dopaminergic function on performance and learning. *Brain Research Bulletin, 23*, 365–371.

Beninger, R. J., Mason, S. T., Phillips, A. G., & Fibiger, H. C. (1980). The use of extinction to investigate the nature of neuroleptic-induced avoidance deficits. *Psychopharmacology, 69*, 11–18.

Benjafield, J. G. (1996). *The history of psychology.* Needham, MA: Allyn & Bacon.

Benjamin, J., Li, L., Patterson, C., Greenberg, B. D., Murphy, D. L., & Hamer, D. H. (1996). Population and familial association between the D4 dopamine receptor gene and measure of novelty seeking. *Nature Genetics, 12*, 81–84.

Benson, D. F., & Greenberg, J. P. (1969). Visual form agnosia: A specific deficit in visual recognition. *Archives of Neurology, 20*, 82–89.

Berenbaum, S. A. (1999). Effects of early androgens on sex-typed activities and interests in adolescents with congenital adrenal hyperplasia. *Hormones & Behavior, 35*, 102–110.

Berenbaum, S. A., & Hines, M. (1992). Early androgens are related to childhood sex-typed toy preferences. *Psychological Science, 3*, 203–206.

Berg, S. (1996). Aging, behavior, and terminal decline. In J. E. Birren & K. W. Schaie (Eds.), *Handbook of the psychology of aging* (4th ed., pp. 323–337). New York: Academic Press.

Bergeman, C. S., Plomin, R., Pederson, N. L., McClearn, G. E., & Nesselroad, J. R. (1990). Genetic and environmental influences on social support: The Swedish Adoption/Twin Study of Aging (SATSA). *Journal of Gerontology: Psychological Sciences, 45*, P101–P106.

Berk, L. (1989). Eustress of mirthful laughter modifies natural killer cell activity. *Clinical Research, 37*, 115.

Berk, L. E. (1992a). Children's private speech: An overview of theory and the status of research. In R. M. Diaz & L. E. Berk (Eds.), *Private speech: From social interaction to self-regulation* (pp. 17–53). Hillsdale, NJ: Erlbaum.

Berk, L. E. (1992b). The extracurriculum. In P. W. Jackson (Ed.), *Handbook of research on curriculum* (pp. 1002–1043). New York: Macmillan.

Berk, L. E. (1994a). Vygotsky's theory: The importance of make-believe play. *Young Children, 50*, 30–39.

Berk, L. E. (1994b). Why children talk to themselves. *Scientific American, 271*(5), 78–83.

Berk, L. E. (1997). *Child development* (4th ed.). Boston: Allyn & Bacon.

Berkman, L. F., & Syme, S. L. (1979). Social networks, host resistance, and mortality: A nine year follow-up study of Alameda Country residents. *American Journal of Epidemiology, 109*, 186–204.

Berko, J. (1958). The child's learning of English morphology. *Word, 14*, 150–177.

Berkowitz, A. D. (1997). From reactive to proactive prevention: Promoting an ecology of health on campus. In P. C. Rivers & E. R. Shore (Eds.), *Substance abuse on campus: A handbook for college and university personnel.* Westport, CT: Greenwood Press.

Berkowitz, L. (1983). Aversively stimulated aggression: Some parallels and differences in research with animals and humans. *American Psychologist, 38*, 1135–1144.

Berkowitz, L. (1997). Some thoughts extending Bargh's argument. In R. S. Wyer, Jr. (Ed), *The automaticity of everyday life* (pp. 83–94). Mahwah, NJ: Lawrence Erlbaum.

Berkowitz, L. (1998). Affective aggression: The role of stress, pain, and negative affect. In R. G. Geen and E. Donnerstein (Eds.), *Human aggression: Theories, research, and implications for social policy* (pp. 49–72). San Diego, CA: Academic Press.

Berlyne, D. E. (1960). *Conflict, arousal, and curiosity.* New York: Mcgraw-Hill.

Berlyne, D. E. (Ed.). (1974). *Studies in the new experimental aesthetics: Steps toward an objective psychology of aesthetic appreciation.* Washington, DC: Hemisphere.

Berman, S. M., & Noble, E. P. (1995). Reduced visuospatial performance in children with the D2 dopamine receptor Al allele. *Behavior Genetics, 25*, 45–58.

Bermond, B. N., Fasotti, L., & Schuerman, J. (1991). Spinal cord lesions, peripheral feedback, and intensities of emotional feelings. *Cognition & Emotion, 5*, 201–220.

Bernier, D. (1998). A study of coping: Successful recovery from severe burnout and other reactions to severe work-related stress. *Work & Stress, 12*, 50–65.

Bernstein, I. L., Zimmerman, J. C., Czeisler, C. A., & Weitzman, E. D. (1981). Meal patterns in "free-running" humans. *Physiology & Behavior, 27*, 621–623.

Berridge, K. C. (1996). Food reward: Brain substrates of wanting and liking. *Neuroscience and Biobehavioral Reviews, 20*, 1–20.

Berscheid, E., & Reis, H. T. (1998). Attraction and close relationships. In D. T. Gilbert, S. T. Fiske, & G. Lindzey (Eds.), *The handbook of social psychology* (4th ed., pp. 193–281). New York: McGraw Hill.

Berson, D. M., Dunn, F. A., & Takao, M. (2002). Phototransduction by retinal ganglion cells that set the circadian clock. *Science, 295*, 1070–1073.

Berthoud, H-R. (2002). Multiple neural systems controlling food intake and body weight. *Neuroscience and Biobehavioral Reviews, 26*, 393–428.

Bess, B. E. (1997). Human sexuality and obesity. *International Journal of Mental Health, 26*, 61–67.

Best, J. (2001). *Damned lies and statistics: Untangling the numbers from the media, politicians, and activists.* Berkeley, CA: University of California Press.

Bettencourt, B. A., & Miller, N. (1996). Sex differences in aggression as a function of provocation: A meta-analysis. *Psychololgical Bulletin, 119*, 422–447.

Beutler, L. E. (2000). David and Goliath: When psychotherapy research meets health care delivery systems. *American Psychologist, 55*, 997–1007.

Beutler, L. E., & Hodgson, A. B. (1993). Prescriptive psychotherapy. In G. Stricker & J. R. Gold (Eds.), *Comprehensive Handbook of Psychotherapy Integration* (pp. 151–164). New York: Plenum Press.

Beutler, L. E., Engle, D., Mohr, D., Daldrup, R. J., Bergan, J., Meredity, K., & Merry, W. (1991). Predictors of differential response to cognitive, experiential, and self-directed psychotherapeutic procedures. *Journal of Consulting & Clinical Psychology, 59*, 333–340.

Beutler, L. E., Machado, P. P., Engle, D., & Mohr, D. (1993). Differential patient X treatment maintenance among cognitive, experiential, and self-directed psychotherapies. *Journal of Psychotherapy Integration, 3*, 15–31.

Beutler, L. E., Machado, P. P., & Neufeldt, S. A. (1994). Therapist variables. In A. E. Bergin & S. L. Garfield (Eds.), *Handbook of psychotherapy and behavior change,* (4th ed., pp. 229–269). New York: Wiley.

Bhatt, R. S., & Bertin, E. (2001). Pictorial cues and three-dimensional information processing in early infancy. *Journal of Experimental Child Psychology, 80*, 315–332.

Biederman, I. (1987). Recognition-by-components: A theory of human image understanding. *Psychological Review, 94*, 115–147.

Biederman, I., & Shiffrar, M. M. (1987). Sexing day-old chicks: A case study and expert systems analysis of a difficult perceptual-learning task. *Journal of Experimental Psychology: Learning, Memory, and Cognition, 13*, 640–645.

Biederman, J., Hirshfeld-Becker, D. R., Rosenbaum, J. F., Hérot, C., Friedman, D., Snidman, N., Kagan, J., & Faraone, S. V. (2001). Further evidence of association between behavioral inhibition and social anxiety in children. *American Journal of Psychiatry, 158*, 1673–1679.

Bierhoff, H. W., Klein, R., & Kramp, P. (1991). Evidence for the altruistic personality from data on accident research. *Journal of Personality, 59*, 263–280.

Biesanz, J. C., Neuberg, S. L., Smith, D. M., Asher, T., & Judice, T. N. (2001). When accuracy-motivated perceivers fail: Limited attentional resources and the reemerging self-fulfilling prophecy. *Personality & Social Psychology Bulletin, 27*, 621–629.

Bihrle, A. M., Brownell, H. H., Powelson, J. A., & Gardner, H. (1986). Comprehension of humorous and non-humorous materials by left and right brain-damaged patients. *Brain and Cognition, 5*, 399–411.

Bijeljac-Babic, R., Bertoncini, J., & Mehler, J. (1993). How do 4-day-old infants categorize multisyllable utterances? *Developmental Psychology, 29*, 711–721.

Bilukha, O. O., & Utermohlen, V. (2002). Internalization of Western standards of appearance, body dissatisfaction and dieting in urban educated Ukrainian females. *European Eating Disorders Review, 10*, 120–137.

Bindra, D. (1968). Neuropsychological interpretation of the effects of drive and incentive motivation on general activity and instrumental behavior. *Psychological Review, 75*, 1–22.

Bird, H., Howard, D., & Franklin, S. (2000). Why is a verb like an inanimate object? Grammatical category and semantic category deficits. *Brain & Language, 72*, 246–309.

Birenbaum, L. K., Stewart, B. J., & Phillips, D. S. (1996). Health status of bereaved patients. *Nursing Research, 45*, 105–109.

Birren, J. E. (1988). Behavior as a cause and a consequence of health and aging. In J. J. F. Schroots, J. E. Birren, & A. Svanborg (Eds.), *Health and aging* (pp. 25–41). New York: Springer.

Birren, J. E., Riegel, K. F., & Morrison, D. F. (1962). Age differences in response speed as a function of controlled variations of stimulus conditions: Evidence of a general speed factor. *Gerontologia, 6*, 1–18.

Bishop, D. V. M. (1983). Linguistic impairment after left hemidecortication for infantile hemiplegia? A reappraisal. *Quarterly Journal of Experimental Psychology, 35A*, 199–207.

Bishop, D. V. M., North, T., & Donlan, C. (1995). Genetic basis of specific language impairment: Evidence from a twin study. *Developmental Medicine and Child Neurology, 37*, 56–71.

Bishop, G. D. (1994). *Health psychology: Integrating mind and body.* Boston, MA: Allyn & Bacon.

Bisiach, E. (1981). Brain and conscious representation of outside reality. *Neuropsychologia, 19*, Pergamon Journals, Ltd.

Bisiach, E., & Luzzatti, C. (1978). Unilateral neglect of representational space. *Cortex, 14*, 129–133.

Bisiach, E., Capitani, E., Luzzatti, C., & Perani, D. (1981). Brain and conscious representation of outside reality. *Neuropsychologia, 19*, 543–551.

Bjork, R. A. (1989). Retrieval inhibition as an adaptive mechanism in human memory. In H. L. Roediger, III, & F. I. M. Craik (Eds.), *Varieties of memory and consciousness: Essays in honour of Endel Tulving* (pp. 309–330). Hillsdale, NJ: Erlbaum.

Black, D. W., Noyes, R., Goldstein, R. B., & Blum, N. (1992). A family study of obsessive-compulsive disorder. *Archives of General Psychiatry, 49,* 362–368.

Black, J. E., Jones, T. A., Nelson, C. A., & Greenough, W. T. (1998). Neuronal plasticity and the developing brain. In N. E. Alessi, J. T. Coyle, S. I. Harrison, & S. Eth (Eds.), *Handbook of child and adolescent psychiatry: Vol 6. Basic psychiatric science and treatment* (pp. 31–53). New York: Wiley.

Blair, H. T., Schafe, G. E., Bauer, E. P., Rodrigues, S. M., & LeDoux, J. E. (2001). Synaptic plasticity in the lateral amygdala: A cellular hypothesis of fear conditioning. *Learning & Memory, 8,* 229–242.

Blais, M. A., Hilsenroth, M. J., & Castlebury, F. D. (1997). Psychometric characteristics of the Cluster B personality disorders under DSM–III–R and DSM–IV. *Journal of Personality Disorders, 11,* 270–278.

Blakeslee, S. (1997). Brain studies tie marijuana to other drugs. *New York Times.* June 27:A16 (col. 4).

Blamey, P., Barry, J., Bow, C., Sarant, J., Paatsch, L., & Wales, R. (2001). The development of speech production following cochlear implantation. *Clinical Linguistics & Phonetics, 15,* 363–382.

Blanchard, R. (1997). Birth order and sibling sex ratio in homosexual versus heterosexual males and females. *Annual Review of Sex Research, 8,* 27–67.

Blanchard, R. (2001). Fraternal birth order and the maternal immune hypothesis of male homosexuality. *Hormones & Behavior, 40,* 105–114.

Blanck, H. M.,Marcus, M., Tolbert, P. E., Rubin, C., Henderson, A. K., Hertzberg, V. S., Zhang, R. H., & Cameron, L. (2000). Age at menarche and Tanner stage in girls exposed *in utero* and postnatally to polybrominated biphenyl. *Epidemiology, 11,* 641–647.

Blanton, H., Gibbons, F. X., Gerrard, M., Conger, K. J., & Smith, G. E. (1997). Role of family and peers in the development of prototypes associated with substance abuse. *Journal of Family Psychology, 11,* 271–288.

Blass, T. (1999). The Milgram Paradigm after 35 years: Some things we now know about obedience to authority. *Journal of Applied Social Psychology, 29,* 955–978.

Blatt, S. J., Zuroff, D. C., Bondi, C. M., & Sanislow, C. A., III. (2000). Short- and long-term effects of medication and psychotherapy in the brief treatment of depression: Further analyses of data from the NIMH TDCRP. *Psychotherapy Research, 10,* 215–234.

Bleibtreu-Ehrenberg, G. (1990). Pederasty among primitives: Institutionalized initiation and cultic prostitution. *Journal of Homosexuality, 20,* 13–30.

Bliss, E. L. (1984). Spontaneous self-hypnosis in multiples personality disorder. *Psychiatric Clinics of North America, 7,* 135–148.

Block, J. (1995). A contrarian view of the five-factor approach to personality description. *Psychological Bulletin, 117,* 187–215.

Block, N. (1995). How heritability misleads about race. *Cognition, 56,* 99–128.

Bloom, B. L. (1997). *Planned short-term psychotherapy: A clinical handbook* (2nd ed.). Boston, MA: Allyn & Bacon.

Bloom, B. S. (1985). Generalizations about talent development. In B. S. Bloom (Ed.), *Developing talent in young people* (pp. 507–549). New York: Ballantine Books.

Bloom, F. E., & Lazerson, A. (1988). *Brain, mind, behavior* (2nd ed.). New York: Freeman.

Bloom, J. W. (1998). The ethical practice of WebCounseling. *British Journal of Guidance & Counselling, 26,* 53–59.

Blumenthal, J. A., Babyak, M., Wei, J., O'Connor, C., Waugh, R., Eisenstein, E., Mark, D., Sherwood, A., Woodley, P. S., Irwin, R. J., & Reed, G. (2002). Usefulness of psychosocial treatment of mental stress-induced myocardial ischemia in men. *American Journal of Cardiology, 89,* 164–168.

Blundell, J. E. (1977). Is there a role for 5-hydroxytryptamine in feeding? *International Journal of Obesity, 1,* 15–42.

Blundell, J. E. (1984). Serotonin and appetite. *Neuropharmacology, 23,* 1537–1551.

Blundell, J. E. (1986). Serotonin manipulations and the structure of feeding behaviour. *Appetite, 7,* 39–56.

Blundell, J. E., & Halford, J. C. G. (1998). Serotonin and appetite regulation: Implications for the pharmacological treatment of obesity. *CNS Drugs, 9,* 473–495.

Bly, B. M., & Kosslyn, S. M. (1997). Functional anatomy of object recognition in humans: Evidence from PET and fMRI. *Current Opinion in Neurology, 10,* 5–9.

Bobo, L. (1983). Whites' opposition to busing: Symbolic racism or realistic group conflict? *Journal of Personality and Social Psychology, 45,* 1196–1210.

Boddy, J. (1992). Comment on the proposed DSM–IV criteria for trance and possession disorder. *Transcultural Psychiatric Research Review, 29,* 323–330.

Boden, M. A. (2000). State of the art: Computer models of creativity. *Psychologist, 13,* 72–76.

Bodenhausen, G. V., Kramer, G. P., & Susser, K. (1994). Happiness and stereotypic thinking in social judgment. *Journal of Personality and Social Psychology, 66,* 621–632.

Boeringer, S. B. (1994). Pornography and sexual aggression: Associations of violent and nonviolent depictions with rape and rape proclivity. *Deviant Behavior, 15,* 289–304.

Bogaert, A. F. (1996). Volunteer bias in human sexuality research: Evidence for both sexuality and personality differences in males. *Archives of Sexual Behavior, 25,* 125–140.

Bohm, J. K., & Hendricks, B. (1997). Effects of interpersonal touch, degree of justification, and sex of participant on compliance with a request. *Journal of Social Psychology, 137,* 460–469.

Boiten, F. (1996). Autonomic response patterns during voluntary facial action. *Psychophysiology, 33,* 123–131.

Boiten, F. A. (1998). The effects of emotional behavior on components of the respiratory cycle. *Biological Psychiatry, 49,* 29–51.

Boivin, D. B., Czeisler, C. A., Dijk, D., Duffy, J. F., Folkard, S., Minors, D. S., Totterdell, P., & Waterhouse, J. M. (1997). Complex interaction of the sleep-wake cycle and circadian phase modulates mood in healthy subjects. *Archives of General Psychiatry, 54,* 145–152.

Bokert, E. (1968). The effects of thirst and a related verbal stimulus on dream reports. *Dissertation Abstracts, Vol. 28(11-B),* 4753. (18192)

Bolger, F., & Harvey, N. (1993). Context-sensitive heuristics in statistical reasoning. *Quarterly Journal of Experimental Psychology, 46A,* 779–811.

Bond, M., & Gardiner, S. T., Christian, H., & Sigel, J. J. (1983). Empirical study of self-rated defense styles. *Archives of General Psychiatry, 40,* 333–338.

Bond, M. H., & Smith, P. B. (1996). Cross-cultural social and organizational psychology. *Annual Review of Psychology, 47,* 205–235.

Bond, R., & Smith, P. B. (1996). Culture and conformity: A meta-analysis of studies using Asch's (1952b, 1956) line judgment task. *Psychological Bulletin, 119,* 111–137.

Bonnefond, A., Muzet, A., Winter-Dill, A, Bailloeuil, C., Bitouze, F., & Bonneau, A. (2001). Innovative working schedule: Introducing one short nap during the night shift. *Ergonomics, 44,* 937–945.

Bonnel, A.-M., Faita, F., Peretz, I., & Besson, M. (2001). Divided attention between lyrics and tunes of operatic songs: Evidence for independent processing. *Perception & Psychphysics, 63,* 1201–1213.

Bontempo, D. E., & D'Augelli, A. R. (2002). Effects of at-school victimization and sexual orientation on lesbian, gay, or bisexual youths' health risk behavior. *Journal of Adolescent Health, 30,* 364–374.

Booth, R. J., Petrie, K. J., & Pennebaker, J. W. (1997). Changes in circulating lymphocyte numbers following emotional disclosure: Evidence of buffering? *Stress Medicine, 13,* 23–29.

Borg, E., & Counter, S. A. (1989). The middle ear muscles. *Scientific American, 261,* 74–80.

Boring, E. G. (1950). *A history of experimental psychology* (2nd ed.). New York: Appleton-Century-Crofts.

Borman, W. C., Hanson, M. A., & Hedge, J. W. (1997). Personnel selection. *Annual Review of Psychology, 48,* 299–337.

Bornstein, M. H. (1992). Perception across the life span. In M. H. Bornstein & M. E. Lamb (Eds.), *Developmental psychology: An advanced textbook* (pp. 155–209). Hillsdale, NJ: Erlbaum.

Bornstein, M. H., Tal, J., Rahn, C., Galperin, C. Z., et al. (1992). Functional analysis of the contents of maternal speech to infants of 5 and 13 months in four cultures: Argentina, France, Japan, and the United States. *Developmental Psychology, 28,* 593–603.

Bornstein, R. F. (1989). Exposure and affect: Overview and meta-analysis of research, 1968–1987. *Psychological Bulletin, 106,* 265–289.

Bornstein, R. F., & D'Agostino, P. R. (1992). Stimulus recognition and the mere exposure effect. *Journal of Personality and Social Psychology, 63,* 545–552.

Bornstein, R. F., & D'Agostino, P. R. (1994). The attribution and discounting of perceptual fluency: Preliminary tests of a perceptual fluency/attributional model of the mere exposure effect. *Social Cognition, 12,* 103–128.

Bornstein, R. F., Leone, D. R., & Galley, D. (1987). The generalizability of subliminal mere exposure effect: Influence on stimuli perceived without awareness on social behavior. *Journal of Personality and Social Psychology, 53,* 1070–1079.

Boroditsky, L. (2001). Does language shape thought? Mandarin and English speakers' conceptions of time. *Cognitive Psychology, 43,* 1–22.

Borroni, A. M., Fichtenholtz, H., Woodside, B. L., & Teyler, T. J. (2000). Role of voltage-dependent calcium channel long-term potentiation (LTP) and NMDA LTP in spatial memory. *Journal of Neuroscience, 20,* 9272–9276.

Bosch, J. A., Brand, H. S., Ligtenberg, A. J. M., Bermond, B., Hoogstraten, J., & Nieuw Amgerongen, A. V. (1998). The response of salivary protein levels and S-IgA to an academic examination are associated with daily stress. *Journal of Psychophysiology, 12,* 384–391.

Bosma, H., Stansfelt, S. A., & Marmot, M. G. (1998). Job control, personal characteristics, and heart disease. *Journal of Occupational Health Psychology, 3,* 402–409.

Bosworth, H. B., & Siegler, I. C. (2002). Terminal change in cognitive function: An updated review of longitudinal studies. *Experimental Aging Research, 28,* 299–315.

Bothwell, R. K., & Brigham, J. C. (1983). Selective evaluation and recall during the 1980 Reagan-Carter debate. *Journal of Applied Social Psychology, 13,* 427–442.

Botting, N., & Conti-Ramsden, G. (2001). Non-word repetition and language development in children with specific language impairment (SLI). *International Journal of Language & Communication Disorders, 36,* 421–432.

Bottini, G., Corcoran, R., Sterzi, R., Paulesu, E., Schenone, P., Scarpa, P., Frackowiak, R. S. J., & Frith, C. D. (1994). The role of the right hemisphere in the interpretation of figurative aspects of language: A positron emission tomography activation study. *Brain, 117,* 1241–1253.

Bottini, G., Paulesu, E., Sterzl, R., Warburton, E., Wise, R. J. S., Vallar, G., Frackowiak, R. S. J., & Frith, C. D. (1995). Modulation of conscious experience by peripheral sensory stimuli. *Nature, 376,* 778–781.

Botvin, G. J. (1995). Drug abuse prevention in school settings. In G. J. Botvin, S. Schinke, & M. A. Orlandi (Eds.), *Drug abuse prevention with multiethnic youth* (pp. 169–192). Newbury Park, CA: Sage.

Botwinick, J. (1984). *Aging and behavior: A comprehensive integration of research findings.* New York: Springer.

Bouchard, T. J. (1983). Do environmental similarities explain the similarity in intelligence of identical twins reared apart? *Intelligence, 7,* 175–184.

Bouchard, T. J. (1991). Identical twins reared apart: What they reveal about human intelligence. Paper presented at the American Association for the Advancement of Science, Washington, DC.

Bouchard, T. J., & McGue, M. (1981). Familial studies of intelligence: A review. *Science, 212*, 1055–1059.

Bouchard, T. J., Jr. (1994). Genes, environment, and personality. *Science, 264*, 1700–1701.

Bouchard, T. J., Jr., & Loehlin, J. C. (2001). Genes, evolution, and personality. *Behavior Genetics, 31*, 243–273.

Bouchard, T. J., Jr., Lykken, D. T., McGue, M., Segal, N. L., & Tellegen, A. (1990). Sources of human psychological differences: The Minnesota study of twins reared apart. *Science, 250*, 223–228.

Bourguignon, E. (1973). *Altered States of Consciousness and Social Change.* Columbus: Ohio State University Press.

Bousfield, W. A. (1953). The occurrence of clustering in the recall of randomly arranged associates. *Journal of General Psychology, 49*, 229–240.

Bouton, M. (1993). Context, time and memory retrieval in the interference paradigms of Pavlovian conditioning. *Psychological Bulletin, 114*, 80–99.

Bouton, M. (1994). Context, ambiguity and classical conditioning. *Current Directions in Psychological Science, 3*, 49–52.

Bouton, M. E., Mineka, S., & Barlow, D. H. (2001). A modern learning theory perspective on the etiology of panic disorder. *Psychological Review, 108*, 4–32.

Bovasso, G. B., Eaton, W. W., & Armenian, H. K. (1999). The long-term outcomes of mental health treatment in a population-based study. *Journal of Consulting and Clinical Psychology, 67*, 529–538.

Bower, B. (1996, May 18). Trauma syndrome traverses generations. *Science News, 149*, 315.

Bower, G. H. (1972). Mental imagery and associative learning. In L. Gregg (Ed.), *Cognition and learning and memory* (pp. 51–88). New York: Wiley.

Bower, G. H. (1981). Mood and memory. *American Psychologist, 36*, 129–148.

Bower, G. H. (1992). How might emotions effect learning? In S.-Å. Christianson (Ed.), *The handbook of emotion and memory: Research and theory* (pp. 3–31). Hillsdale, NJ: Erlbaum.

Bower, G. H., Clark, M. C., Lesgold, A. M., & Winzenz, D. (1969). Hierarchical retrieval schemes in recall of categorized word lists. *Journal of Verbal Learning and Verbal Behavior, 8*, 323–343.

Bowlby, J. (1969). *Attachment and loss: Vol. 1, Attachment.* New York: Basic Books.

Bowlby, J. (1980). *Attachment and loss: Vol. 3, Loss.* New York: Basic Books.

Bowman, E. S., & Nurnberger, J. I. (1993). Genetics of psychiatry diagnosis and treatment. In D. L. Dunner (Ed.), *Current psychiatric therapy* (pp. 46–56). Philadelphia: Saunders.

Bowman, M. L. (1999). Individual differences in posttraumatic distress: Problems with the DSM–IV model. *Canadian Journal of Psychiatry, 44*, 21–33.

Boyle, C. A., Decoufle, P., & Yeargin-Allsopp, M. (1994). Prevalence and health impact of developmental disabilities in US children. *Pediatrics, 93*, 399–403.

Bradburn, N. M. (1969). *The structure of psychological well-being.* Chicago: Aldine.

Braden, J. P. (2000). Editor's introduction: Perspectives on nonverbal assessment of intelligence. *Journal of Psychoeducational Assessment, 18*, 204–220.

Bradley, M. M., Greenwald, M. K., Petry, M. C., & Lang, P. J. (1992). Remembering pictures: Pleasure and arousal in memory. *Journal of Experimental Psychology: Learning, Memory, and Cognition, 18*, 379–390.

Bradley, M. T., & Warfield, J. F. (1984). Innocence, information, and the Guilty Knowledge Test in the detection of deception. *Psychophysiology, 21*, 683–689.

Bradley, M. T., MacLaren, V. V., & Carle, S. B. (1996). Deception and nondeception in Guilty Knowledge and Guilty Actions Polygraph Tests. *Journal of Applied Psychology, 81*, 153–160.

Bradshaw, G. L., & Anderson, J. R. (1982). Elaborative encoding as an explanation of levels of processing. *Journal of Verbal Learning & Verbal Behavior, 21*, 165–174.

Brainard, G. C., Hanifin, J. P., Greeson, J. M., Byrne, B., Glickman, G., Gerner, E., & Rollag, M. D. (2001). Action spectrum for melatonin regulation in humans: Evidence for a novel circadian photoreceptor. *Journal of Neuroscience, 21*, 6405–6412.

Braksiek, R. J., & Roberts, D. J. (2002). Amusement park injuries and deaths. *Annals of Emergency Medicine, 39*, 65–72.

Brannon, L. (1996). *Gender: Psychological perspectives.* Needham Heights, MA: Simon & Schuster.

Bransford, J. D., & Franks, J. J. (1971). The abstraction of linguistic ideas. *Cognitive Psychology, 2*, 331–350.

Brashers-Krug, T., Shadmehr, R., & Bizzi, E. (1996) Consolidation in human motor memory. *Nature, 382*, 252–254.

Braun, K. A., Ellis, R., & Loftus, E. F. (2002). Make my memory: How advertising can change our memories of the past. *Psychology & Marketing, 19*, 1–23.

Braverman, P. K., & Strasburger, V. C. (1993). Adolescent sexual activity. *Clinical Pediatrics, 32*, 658–668.

Brebner, J. (1998). Happiness and personality. *Personality & Individual Differences, 25*, 279–296.

Breckler, S. J. (1984). Empirical validation of affect, behavior, and cognition as distinct components of attitude. *Journal of Personality and Social Psychology, 47*, 1191–1205.

Bregman, A. S. (1990). *Auditory scene analysis: The perceptual organization of sound.* Cambridge, MA: MIT Press.

Bregman, A. S. (1993). Auditory scene analysis: Hearing in complex environments. In S. McAdams & E. Bigand (Eds.), *Thinking in sound: The cognitive psychology of human audition* (pp. 10–36). New York: Oxford University Press.

Bregman, E. O. (1934). An attempt to modify the emotional attitudes of infants by the conditioned response technique. *Journal of Genetic Psychology, 45*, 169.

Brehm, J. W. (1956). Post-decision changes in the desirability of alternatives. *Journal of Abnormal and Social Psychology, 52*, 384–389.

Brehm, J. W. (1966). *A theory of psychological reactance.* New York: Academic Press.

Breiter, H. C., Aharon, I., Kahneman, D., Dale, A., & Shizgal, P. (2001). Functional imaging of neural responses to expectancy and experience of monetary gains and losses. *Neuron, 30*, 619–639.

Breiter, H. C., Rauch, S. L., Kwong, K. K., Baker, J. R., Weisskoff, R. M., Kennedy, D. N., Kendrick, A. D., Davis, T. L., Jiang, A., Cohen, M. S., Stern, C. E., Belliveau, J. W., Baer, L., O'Sullivan, R. L., Savage, C. R., Jenike, M. A., & Rosen, B. R. (1996). Functional magnetic resonance imaging of symptom provocation in obsessive-compulsive disorder. *Archives of General Psychiatry, 53*, 595–606.

Breland, K., & Breland, M. (1961). The misbehavior of organisms. *American Psychologist, 16*, 661–664.

Bremner, J. D., Narayan, M., Anderson, E. R., Staib, L. H., Miller, H. L., & Charney, D. S. (2000). Hippocampal volume reduction in major depression. *American Journal of Psychiatry, 157*, 115–117.

Bremner, J. D., Stienberg, M., Southwick, S. M., Johnson, D. R., & Charney, D. S. (1993). Use of the structured clinical interview for DSM-IV dissociative disorders for systemic assessment of dissociative symptoms in posttraumatic stress disorder. *American Journal of Psychiatry, 150*, 1011–1014.

Brendl, C. M., Markman, A. B., & Messner, C. (2001). How do indirect measures of evaluation work? Evaluating the inference of prejudice in the Implicit Association Test. *Journal of Personality & Social Psychology, 81*, 760–773.

Brennan, A., Chugh, J. S., & Kline, T. (2002). Traditional versus open office design: A longitudinal study. *Environment & Behavior, 34*, 279–299.

Breslau, N., Kessler, R. C., Chilcoat, H. D. Schultz, L. R., Davis, G. C., & Andreski, P. (1998). Trauma and posttraumatic stress disorder in the community: The 1996 Detroit Area Survey of Trauma. *Archives of General Psychiatry, 55*, 626–632.

Brewer, C., Meyers, R. J., & Johnsen, J. (2000). Does disulfiram help to prevent relapse in alcohol abuse? *CNS Drugs, 14*, 329–341.

Brewer, J. B., Zhao, Z., Desmod, J. E., Glover, G. H., & Gabrielli, J. D. E. (1998). Making memories: Brain activity that predicts how well visual experience will be remembered. *Science, 281*, 1185–1187.

Brewer, K. R., & Wann, D. L. (1998). Observational learning effectiveness as a function of model characteristics: Investigating the importance of social power. *Social Behavior & Personality, 26*, 1–10.

Brewer, M. B., & Brown, R. (1998). Intergroup relations. In D. T. Gilbert, S. T. Fiske, & G. Lindzey (Eds.), The handbook of social psychology (4th ed., pp. 554–594). New York: McGraw Hill.

Brewer, M. B., & Kramer, R. M. (1986). Choice behavior in social dilemmas: Effects of social identity, group size, and decision framing. *Journal of Personality and Social Psychology, 50*, 543–549.

Brewer, W. F. (1988). Qualitative analysis of the recalls of randomly sampled autobiographical events. In M. M. Gruneberg & P. E. Morris (Eds.), *Practical aspects of memory: Current research and issues, Vol. 1: Memory in everyday life.* (pp. 263–268). New York: John Wiley & Sons.

Briggs, S. R., & Cheek, J. M. (1988). On the nature of self-monitoring: Problems with assessment, problems with validity. *Journal of Personality and Social Psychology, 54*, 663–678.

Britt, T. A., & Shepperd, J. A. (1999). Trait relevance and trait assessment. *Personality and Social Psychology Review, 3*, 108–122.

Broadbent, D. E. (1971). The magic number seven after fifteen years. In A. Kennedy & A. Wilkes (Eds.), *Studies in long-term memory* (pp. 2–18). New York: Wiley.

Brody, J. (1998, April 6). Dealing with sleep deprivation. *International Herald Tribune*, 9.

Brody, N. (1997). Intelligence, schooling, and society. *American Psychologist, 52*, 1046–1050.

Brooks, D. C., & Bouton, M. E. (1993). A retrieval cue for extinction attentuates spontaneous recovery. *Journal of Experimental Psychology: Animal Behavior Processes, 19*, 77–89.

Brooks-Gunn, J., Graber, J. A., & Paikoff, R. L. (1994). Studying links between hormones and negative affect: Models and measures. *Journal of Research on Adolescence, 4*, 469–486.

Brosschot, J. F., Benschop, R. J., Godaert, G. L. R., Olff, M., de Smet., M., Heijnen, C. J., & Ballieux, R. E. (1994). Influence of life stress on immunological reactivity to mild psychological stress. *Psychosomatic Medicine, 56*, 216–224.

Brown, A. L., & Campione, J. C. (1972). Recognition memory for perceptually similar pictures in preschool children. *Journal of Experimental Psychology, 95*, 55–62.

Brown, A. S., van Os, J., Driessens, C., Hoek, S. W., & Susser, E. S. (1999). Prenatal famine and the spectrum of psychosis. *Psychiatric Annals, 29*, 145–150.

Brown, B. (1999). Optimizing expression of the common human genome for child development. *Current Directions in Psychological Science, 8*, 37–41.

Brown, B. B., Clasen, D., & Eicher, S. (1986a). Perceptions of peer pressure, peer conformity dispositions, and self-reported behavior among adolescents. *Developmental Psychology, 22*, 521–530.

Brown, B. B., Lohr, M. J., & McClenahan, E. L. (1986b). Early adolescents' perceptions of peer pressure. *Journal of Early Adolescence, 6*, 139–154.

Brown, D. E. (1991). *Human universals.* Philadelphia: Temple University Press.

Brown, I., Jr., & Inouye, D. K. (1978). Learned helplessness through modeling: The role of perceived similarity in competence. *Journal of Personality and Social Psychology, 36*, 900–908.

Brown, J. D. (1991). Staying fit and staying well: Physical fitness as a moderator of stress. *Journal of Personality and Social Psychology, 60*, 555–561.

Brown, J. D., & Rogers, R. J. (1991). Self-serving attributions: The role of physiological arousal. *Personality and Social Psychology Bulletin, 17*, 501–506.

Brown, P. L., & Jenkins, H. M. (1968). Auto-shaping of the pigeon's key peck. *Journal of the Experimental Analysis of Behavior, 68*, 503–507.

Brown, R. (1989). Roger Brown. In G. Lindzey (Ed.), *A history of psychology in autobiography*, Vol. 8 (pp. 37–60). Stanford, CA: Stanford University Press.

Brown, R., & Kulik, J. (1977). Flashbulb memories. *Cognition, 5*, 73–99.

Brown, R., & McNeill, D. (1966). The "tip of the tongue" phenomenon. *Journal of Verbal Learning and Verbal Behavior, 5*, 325–337.

Brown, T. A., & Barlow, D. H. (1997). *Casebook in abnormal psychology.* Pacific Grove, CA: Brooks/Cole.

Browne, C. A., Colditz, P. B., & Dunster, K. R. (2000). Infant autonomic function is altered by maternal smoking during pregnancy. *Early Human Development, 59*, 209–218.

Brownell, H., Gardner, H., Prather, P., & Martino, G. (1995). Language, communication, and the right hemisphere. In H. S. Kirshner (Ed.), *Handbook of neurological speech and language disorders* (pp. 325–349). New York: Dekker.

Brownell, H. H., Michelow, D., Powelson, J., & Gardner, H. (1983). Surprise but not coherence: Sensitivity to verbal humor in right hemisphere patients. *Brain and Language, 18*, 20–27.

Brownell, H. H., Potter, H. H., Michelow, D., & Gardner, H. (1984). Sensitivity to lexical denotation and connotation in brain-damaged patients: A double dissociation. *Brain and Language, 22*, 253–265.

Brownell, H. H., Simpson, T. L., Bihrle, A. M., Potter, H. H., & Gardner, H. (1990). Appreciation of metaphoric alternative word meanings by left and right brain-damaged patients. *Neuropsychologia, 28*, 375–383.

Brownell, K. D., & Rodin, J. (1992). *Medical, metabolic, and psychological effects of weight cycling.* Unpublished manuscript, Yale University.

Brubaker, R. G., Prue, D. M., & Rycharik, R. G. (1987). Determinants of disulfiram acceptance among alcohol patients: A test of the theory of reasoned action. *Addictive Behaviors, 12*, 43–51.

Brugger, P., Landis, T., & Regard, M. (1990). A "sheep-goat effect" in repetition avoidance: Extrasensory perception as an effect of subjective probability? *British Journal of Psychology, 81*, 455–468.

Brugioni, D. A. (1996). The art and science of photoreconnaissance. *Scientific American*, 78–85.

Brunner, D. P., Dijk, D. J., Tobler, I., & Borbely, A. A. (1990). Effect of partial sleep deprivation on sleep stages and EEG power spectra: Evidence for non-REM and REM sleep homeostasis. *Electroencephalogr. Clin. Neurophysiol., 75*, 492–499.

Brussoni, M. J., Jang, K. L., Livesley, W. J., & MacBeth, T. M. (2000). Genetic and environmental influences on adult attachment styles. *Personal Relationships, 7*, 283–289.

Bryan, R. N., Wells, S. W., Miller, T. J., Elster, A. D., Jungreis, C. A., Poirier, V. C., Lind, B. K., & Manolio, T. A. (1997). Infarctlike lesions in the brain: Prevalence and anatomic characteristics at MR imaging of the elderly—data from the Cardiovascular Health Study. *Radiology, 202*, 47–54.

Bryant, R. A., & Barnier, A. J. (1999). Eliciting autobiographical pseudomemories: The relevance of hypnosis, hypnotizability, and attributions. *International Journal of Clinical & Experimental Hypnosis, 47*, 267–283.

Buchanan, C. M., Eccles, J., & Becker, J. (1992). Are adolescents the victims of raging hormones? Evidence for activational effects of hormones on moods and behavior at adolescence. *Psychological Bulletin, 111*, 62–107.

Buchkremer, G., Klingberg, S., Holle, R., Schulze-Moenking, H., & Hornung, W. P. (1997). Psychoeducational psychotherapy for schizophrenic patients and their key relatives or care-givers: Results of a 2-year follow-up. *Acta Psychiatrica Scandinavica, 96*, 483–491.

Buckalew, L. W., & Ross, S. (1981). Relationship of perceptual characteristics to efficacy of placebos. *Psychological Reports, 49*, 955–961.

Buckley, K. W. (1982). The selling of a psychologist: John Broadus Watson and the application of behavioral techniques to advertising. *Journal of the History of the Behavioral Sciences, 18*, 207–221.

Buckner, R. L., Kelley, W. M., & Petersen, S. E. (1999). Frontal cortex contributes to human memory formation. *Nature Neuroscience, 2*, 311–314.

Buda, R., & Elsayed-Elkhouly, S. M. (1998). Cultural differences between Arabs and Americans: Individualism-collectivism revisited. *Journal of Cross-Cultural Psychology, 29*, 487–492.

Buehler, R., Griffin, D., & Ross, M. (1994). Exploring the "planning fallacy": Why people underestimate their task completion times. *Journal of Personality & Social Psychology, 67*, 366–381.

Buka, S. L., Goldstein, J. M., Seidman, L. J., Zornberg, G. L., Donatelli, J. A., Denny, L. R., & Tsuang, M. T. (1999). Prenatal complications, genetic vulnerability, and schizophrenia: The New England Longitudinal Studies of Schizophrenia. *Psychiatric Annals, 29*, 151–156.

Bunce, S. C., Bernat, E., Wong, P. S., & Shevrin, H. (1999). Further evidence for unconscious learning: Preliminary support for the conditioning of facial EMG to subliminal stimuli. *Journal of Psychiatric Research, 33*, 341–347.

Bunney, W. E., & Garland, B. L. (1983). Possible receptor effects of chronic lithium administration. *Neuropharmacology, 22*, 367–372.

Burger, J. M. (1992). *Desire for control: Personality, social, and clinical perspectives.* New York: Plenum.

Burger, J. M., & Cooper, H. M. (1979). The desirability of control. *Motivation and Emotion, 3*, 381–393.

Burger, J. M., Horita, M., Kinoshita, L., Roberts, K., & Vera, C. (1997). Effects of time on the norm of reciprocity. *Basic & Applied Social Psychology, 19*, 91–100.

Burgoon, J. K., Buller, D. B., Hale, J. L., & DeTurck, M. A. (1984). Relational messages associated with nonverbal behaviors. *Human Communication Research, 10*, 351–378.

Burish, T. G., & Carey, M. P. (1986). Conditioned aversive responses in cancer chemotherapy patients: Theoretical and developmental analysis. *Journal of Counseling and Clinical Psychology, 54*, 593–600.

Burnstein, E. (1982). Persuasion as argument processing. In H. Brandstatter, J. H. Davis, & G. Stocker-Krechgauer (Eds.), *Group decision making* (pp. 103–124). London: Academic Press.

Burton, L. M. (1990). Teenage childbearing as an alternative life-course strategy in multigeneration Black families. *Human Nature, 1*, 123–143.

Burton, L. M. (1996). Age norms, the timing of family role transitions, and intergerational caregiving among aging African American women. *Gerontologist, 36*, 199–208.

Burton, M. J., Rolls, E. T., & Mora, F. (1976). Effects of hunger on the responses of neurons in the lateral hypothalamus to the sight and taste of food. *Experimental Neurology, 51*, 668–677.

Bushman, B. J. (1984). Perceived symbols of authority and their influence on compliance. *Journal of Applied Social Psychology, 14*, 501–508.

Bushman, B. J. (1988). The effects of apparel on compliance: A field experiment with a female authority figure. *Personality and Social Psychology Bulletin, 14*, 459–467.

Bushman, B. J. (1998). Threatened egotism, narcissism, self-esteem, and direct and displaced aggression: Does self-love or self-hate lead to violence? *Journal of Personality and Social Psychology, 75*, 219–229.

Bushman, B. J., & Cooper, H. M. (1990). Effects of alcohol on human aggression: An integrative research review. *Psychological Bulletin, 107*, 1–14.

Bushman, B. J., & Wells, G. L. (1998). Trait aggressiveness and hockey penalties: Predicting hot tempers on the ice. *Journal of Applied Psychology, 83*, 969–974.

Bushman, B. J., Baumeister, R. F., & Phillips, C. M. (2001). Do people aggress to improve their mood? Catharsis beliefs, affect regulation opportunity, and aggressive responding. *Journal of Personality and Social Psychology, 81*, 17–32.

Busjahn, A., Faulhaber, H. D., Freier, K., & Luft, F. C. (1999). Genetic and environmental influences on coping styles: A twin study. *Psychosomatic Medicine, 61*, 469–475.

Buss, A. H. (1989). Personality as traits. *American Psychologist, 44*, 1378–1388.

Buss, A. H. (1995). *Personality: Temperament, social behavior, and the self.* Needham Heights, MA: Allyn & Bacon.

Buss, A. H., & Plomin, R. (1975). *A temperament theory of personality development.* New York: Wiley Interscience.

Buss, A. H., & Plomin, R. (1984). *Temperament: Early developing personality traits.* Hillsdale, NJ: Erlbaum.

Buss, D. M. (1989). Sex differences in human mate preferences: Evolutionary hypotheses tested in 37 cultures. *Behavioral and Brain Sciences, 12*, 1–49.

Buss, D. M. (1994). *The evolution of desire: Strategies of human mating.* New York: Basic Books.

Buss, D. M. (1995). Psychological sex differences: Origins through sexual selection. *American Psychologist, 50*, 164–168.

Buss, D. M. (1998). The psychology of human mate selection: Exploring the complexity of the strategic repetoire. In C. B. Crawford & D. L. Krebs (Eds.), *Handbook of evolutionary psychology: Ideas, issues, and applications* (pp. 405–429). Mahwah, NJ: Erlbaum.

Buss, D. M. (1999). *Evolutionary psychology: The new science of the mind.* Boston: Allyn & Bacon.

Buss, D. M., & Craik, K. H. (1984). Acts, dispositions, and personality. In B. A. Maher & W. A. Maher (Eds.), *Progress in experimental personaity research* (Vol. 13). New York: Academic Press.

Buss, D. M., Larsen, R. J., Western, D., & Semmelroth, J. (1992). Sex differences in jealousy: Evolution, physiology, and psychology. *Psychological Science, 3*, 251–255.

Busse, E. W. (1969). Theories of aging. In E. W. Busse & E. Pfeiffer (Eds.), *Behavior and adaptation in later life* (pp. 11–32). Boston: Little, Brown.

Butcher, J. N., & Rouse, S. V. (1996). Personality: Individual difference and clinical assessment. *Annual Review of Psychology, 47*, 87–111.

Butters, N., Heindel, W. C., & Salmon, D. P. (1990). Dissociation of implicit memory in dementia: Neurological implications. *Bulletin of the Psychonomic Society, 28*, 359–366.

Butzlaff, R. L., & Hooley, J. M. (1998). Expressed emotion and psychiatric relapse: A meta-analysis. *Archives of General Psychiatry, 55*, 547–552.

Buunk, B. P., Angleitner, A., Oubaid, V., & Buss, D. M. (1996). Sex differences in jealousy in evolutionary and cultural perspective: Tests from the Netherlands, Germany, and the United States. *Psychological Science, 7*, 359–363

Byrne, D. (1971). *The attraction paradigm.* New York: Academic Press.

Byrne, D. (1982). Predicting human sexual behavior. In A. G. Kraut (Ed.), *The G. Stanley Hall Lecture Series* (Vol.2). Washingotn, DC: American Psychological Association.

Cabeza, R., & Nyberg, L. (1997). Imaging cognition: An empirical review of PET studies with normal subjects. *Journal of Cognitive Neuroscience, 9*, 1–26.

Cabeza, R., & Nyberg, L. (2000). Imaging cognition II: An empirical review of 275 PET and fMRI studies. *Journal of Cognitive Neuroscience, 12*, 1–47.

Cacioppo, J. T., & Petty, R. E. (1982). The need for cognition. *Journal of Personality & Social Psychology, 42*, 116–131.

Cacioppo, J. T., Gardner, J. T., & Berntson, W. L. (1997). Beyond bipolar conceptualizations and measures: The case of attitudes and evaluative space. *Personality & Social Psychology Review, 1,* 3–25.

Cacioppo, J. T., Petty, R. E., Feinstein, J. A., & Jarvis, W. B. G. (1996). Disposition differences in cognition motivation: The life and times of individuals varying in need for cognition. *Psychological Bulletin, 119,* 197-253.

Cacioppo, J. T., Petty, R. E., & Kao, C. F. (1984). The efficient assessment of need for cognition. *Journal of Personality Assessment, 48,* 306–307.

Cacioppo, J. T., Petty, R. E., Kao, C. F., & Rodriguez, R. (1986). Central and peripheral routes to persuasion: An individual difference perspective. *Journal of Personality & Social Psychology, 51,* 1032–1043.

Cacioppo, J. T., Petty, R. E., Losch, M. E., & Kim, H. S. (1986). Electromyographic activity over facial muscle regions can differentiate the valence and intensity of affective reactions. *Journal of Personality and Social Psychology, 50,* 260–268.

Cadoret, R. J., O'Gorman, T. W., Heywood, E., & Troughton, E. (1995). Genetic and environmental factors in major depression. *Journal of Affective Disorders, 9,* 155–164.

Cahan, S., & Cohen, N. (1989). Age versus schooling effects on intelligence development. *Child Development, 60,* 1239–1249.

Cahill, L., Haier, R. J., Fallon, J., Alkire, M. T., Tang, C., Keator, D., Wu, J., & McGaugh, J. L. (1996). Amygdala activity at encoding correlated with long-term free recall of emotional information. *Proceedings of the National Academy of Sciences, USA, 93,* 8016–8021.

Cahill, L., Haier, R. J., White, N. S., Fallon, J., Kilpatrick, L., Lawrence, C., Potkin, S. G., & Alkire, M. T. (2001). Sex-related differences in amygdala activity during emotionally influenced memory storage. *Neurobiology of Learning & Memory, 75,* 1–9.

Cahill, L., Prins, B., Weber, M., & McGaugh, J. L. (1994). Adrenergic activation and memory for emotional events. *Nature, 371,* 702–704.

Cailliet, R. (1993). *Pain: Mechanisms and management.* Philadelphia: Davis.

Cain, W. S. (1973). Spatial discrimination of cutaneous warmth. *American Journal of Psychology, 86,* 169–181.

Cain, W. S. (1979). To know with the nose: Keys to odor identification. *Science, 203,* 467–470.

Cain, W. S. (1982). Odor identification by males and females: Predictions and performance. *Chemical Senses, 7,* 129–141.

Cain, W. S., & Gent, J. F. (1991). Olfactory sensitivity: Reliability, generality, and association with aging. *Journal of Experimental Psychology: Human Perception and Performance, 17,* 382–391.

Calder, A. J., Young, A. W., Rowland, D., Perrett, D. I., Hodges, J. R. & Etcoff, N. L. (1996). Face perception after bilateral amygdala damage: Differentially severe impairment of fear. *Cognitive Neuropsychology, 13,* 699–745.

Caldera, Y. M., & Sciaraffa, M. A. (1998). Parent-toddler play with feminine toys: Are all dolls the same? *Sex Roles, 39,* 657–668

Calkins, S. D., Fox, N. A., & Marshall, T. R. (1996). Behavioral and physiological antecedents of inhibited and uninhibited behavior. *Child Development, 67,* 523–540.

Calvert, G. A., Bullmore, E. T., Brammer, M. J., Campbell, R., Williams, S. C. R., McGuire, P. K., Woodruff, P. W. R., Iverson, S. D., & David, A. S. (1997). Activation of auditory cortex during silent lipreading. *Science, 276,* 593–596.

Calvocoressi, L., Lewis, B., Harris, M., Trufan, S. J., et al. (1995). Family accommodation in obsessive-compulsive disorder. *American Journal of Psychiatry, 152,* 441–443.

Campbell, D. T. (1960). Blind variation and selective retention in creative thought as in other knowledge processes. *Psychological Review, 67,* 380–400.

Campbell, F. A., & Ramey, C. T. (1994). Effects of early intervention on intellectual and academic achievement: A follow-up study of children from low-income families. *Child Development, 65,* 684–698.

Campbell, J. I. D., & Charness, N. (1990). Age-related declines in working-memory skills: Evidence from a complex calculation task. *Developmental Psychology, 26*(6), 879–888.

Campos, J. J., Anderson, D. I., Barbu-Roth, M. A., Hubbard, E. M., Hertenstein, M. J., & Witherington, D. (2000). Travel broadens the mind. *Infancy, 1,* 149–219.

Campos, J. J., Langer, A., & Krowitz, A. (1970). Cardiac responses on the visual cliff in prelocomotor human infants. *Science, 170,* 196–197.

Canli, T., Zhao, Z., Desmond, J. E., Kang, E., Gross, J., & Gabrieli, J. D. E. (2001). An fMRI study of personality influences on brain reactivity to emotional stimuli. *Behavioral Neuroscience.*

Cannon, M., Jones, P., Huttunen, M. O., Tanskanen, A., Huttunen, T., Rabe-Hesketh, S., & Murray, R. M. (1999). School performance in Finnish children and later development of schizophrenia: A population-based longitudinal study. *Archives of General Psychiatry, 56,* 457–463.

Cannon, T. D., Kaprio, J., Lönnqvist, J., Huttunen, M., & Koskenvuo, M. (1998). The genetic epidemiology of schizophrenia in a Finnish twin cohort: a population-based modeling study. *Archives of General Psychiatry, 55,* 67–74.

Cannon, T. D., Huttunen, M. O., Dahlstroem, M., Larmo, I., Raesaenen, P., & Juriloo, A. (2002). Antipsychotic drug treatment in the prodromal phase of schizophrenia. *American Journal of Psychiatry, 159,* 1230–1232.

Cannon, W. B. (1927). The James-Lange theory of emotions: A critical examination and an alternative theory. *American Journal of Psychology, 39,* 106–124.

Cannon, W. B. (1932). *The wisdom of the body.* New York: Norton.

Cannon, W. B. (1942). Voodoo death. *American Anthropologist, 44,* 169–181.

Cantalupo, C., & Hopkins, W. D. (2001). Asymmetric Broca's area in great apes: A region of the ape brain is uncannily similar to one linked with speech in humans. *Nature, 414,* 505.

Canter, S. (1973). Personality traits in twins. In G. Claridge, S. Canter, & W. I. Hume (Eds.). *Personality differences and biological variations* (pp. 21–51). New York: Pergamon.

Cantor, J. M., Blanchard, R., Paterson, A. D., & Bogaert, A. F. (2002). How many gay men owe their sexual orientation to fraternal birth order? *Archives of Sexual Behavior, 31,* 63–71.

Cantor, N., & Norem, J. K. (1989). Defensive pessimism and stress and coping. *Social Cognition, 7,* 92–112.

Caramazza, A. (1984). The logic of neuropsychological research and the problem of patient classification in aphasia. *Brain and Language, 21,* 9–20.

Caramazza, A. (1986). On drawing inferences about the structure of normal cognitive systems from the analysis of patterns of impaired performance: The case for single-patient studies. *Brain and Cognition, 5,* 41–66.

Caramazza, A. (1992). Is cognitive neuropsychology plausible? *Journal of Cognitive Psychology, 4*(1), 80–95.

Caramazza, A., & Zurif, E. B. (1976). Dissociation of algorithmic and heuristic processes in language comprehension: Evidence from aphasia. *Brain & Language, 3,* 572–582.

Caramazza, A., McCloskey, M., & Green, B. (1981). Naive beliefs in "sophisticated" subjects: Misconceptions about trajectories of objects. *Cognition, 9,* 117–123.

Cardinal, R. N., Parkinson, J. A., Hall, J., & Everitt, B. (2002). Emotion and motivation: The role of the amygdala, ventral striatum, and prefrontal cortex. *Neuroscience and Biobehavioral Reviews, 26,* 321–352.

Carey, M. P., & Burish, T. G. (1988). Etiology and treatment of the psychological side effects associated with cancer chemotherapy: A critical review and discussion. *Psychological Bulletin, 104,* 307–325.

Carey, S. (1978). The child as word learner. In J. Bresnan, G. Miller, & M. Halle (Eds.), *Linguistic theory and psychological reality* (pp. 264–293). Cambridge, MA: MIT Press.

Carey, S. (1985). *Conceptual change in childhood.* Cambridge, MA: Bradford/MIT Press.

Carey, S. (1988). Conceptual differences between children and adults. *Mind and Language 3,* 67–82.

Carey, S. (1995a). Continuity and discontinuity in cognitive development. In E. E. Smith, & D. N. Osherson (Eds.), *Thinking: An invitation to cognitive science* (2nd ed.). Cambridge, MA: MIT Press.

Carey, S. (1995b). On the origin of causal understanding. In D. Sperber, D. Premack, & A. J. Premack (Eds.), *Causal cognition: A multidisciplinary debate* (pp. 268–302). Oxford: Clarendon Press.

Carlbring, P., Westling, B. E., Ljungstrand, P., Ekselius, L., & Andersson, G. (2001). Treatment of panic disorder via the Internet: A randomized trial of a self-help program. *Behavior Therapy, 32,* 751–764.

Carlson, N. R. (1992). *Foundations of physiological psychology* (2nd ed.). Boston: Allyn & Bacon.

Carlson, N. R. (1994). *Physiology of behavior.* Needham Heights, MA: Allyn & Bacon.

Carlson, R., & Levy, N. (1973). Studies of Jungian typology: I. Memory, social perception, and social action. *Journal of Personality, 48,* 87–94.

Carlsson, C. P. O., & Sjoelund, B. H. (2001). Acupuncture for chronic low back pain: A randomized placebo-controlled study with long-term follow-up. *Clinical Journal of Pain, 17,* 296–305.

Carmines, E. G., & Zeller, R. A. (1979). *Relability and validity assessment.* Beverly Hills, CA: Sage.

Carnelley, K. B., Wortman, C. B., Kessler, R. C. (1999). The impact of widowhood on depression: Findings from a prospective survey. *Psychological Medicine, 29,* 1111–1123.

Carney, R. M., Freeland, K. E., Veith, R. C., Cryer, P. E., Skala, J. A., Lynch, T., & Jaffe, A. S. (1999). Major depression, heart rate, and plasma norepinephrine in patients with coronary heart disease. *Biological Psychiatry, 45,* 458–463.

Carpenter, P. A., Just, M. A., & Shell, P. (1990). What one intelligence test measures: A theoretical account of the processing in the Raven Progressive Matrices test. *Psychological Review, 97,* 404–431.

Carr, D., House, J. S., Kessler, R. C., Nesse, R. M., Sonnega, J., & Wortman, C. (2000). Marital quality and psychological adjustment to widowhood among older adults: A longitudinal analysis. *Journals of Gerontology: Series B: Psychological Sciences & Social Sciences, 55B,* S197–S207.

Carr, D., House, J. S., Wortman, C., Neese, R., & Kessler, R. C. (2001). Psychological adjustment to sudden and anticipated spousal loss among older widowed persons. *Journals of Gerontology: Series B: Psychological Sciences & Social Sciences, 56B,* S237-S248.

Carraher, T. N., Carraher, D. W., & Schliemann, A. D. (1985). Mathematics in the streets and in schools. *British Journal of Developmental Psychology, 3,* 21–29.

Carrington, P. (1977). *Freedom in meditation.* Garden City, NY: Anchor Press/Doubleday.

Carroll, J. (1993). *Human cognitive abilities: A survey of factor-analytic studies.* New York: Cambridge University Press.

Carroll, L. (1992). Alice in wonderland. Authoritative texts of Alice's adventures in wonderland, Through the looking-glass, The hunting of the snark. Backgrounds. In D. J. Gray (Ed.), *Essays in criticism* (2nd ed.). New York: Norton.

Carrothers, R. M., Gregory, S. W., Jr., & Gallagher, T. J. (2000). Measuring emotional intelligence of medical school applicants. *Academic medicine, 75,* 456–463.

Carskadon, M., Vieria, C., & Acebo, C. (1993). Association between puberty and delayed phase preference. *Sleep, 16,* 258–262.

Carskadon, T. G. (1978). Use of the Myers-Briggs Type Indicator in psychology courses and discussion groups. *Teaching of Psychology, 5,* 140–142.

Carstens, C. B., Huskins, E., & Hounshell, G. W. (1995). Listening to Mozart may not enhance performance on the revised Minnesota Paper Form Board Test. *Psychological Reports, 77*, 111–114.

Carstensen, L. L. (1991). Socioemotional selectivity theory: Social activity in life-span context. In K. W. Schaie & M. P. Lawton (Eds.), *Annual review of gerontology and geriatrics* (Vol. 11, pp. 195–217). New York: Springer.

Carstensen, L. L. (1992). Social and emotion patterns in adulthood: Support for socioemotional selectivity theory. *Psychology and Aging, 7*, 331–338.

Carstensen, L. L., & Charles, S. T. (1998). Emotion in the second half of life. *Current Directions in Psychological Science, 7*, 144–149.

Carstensen, L. L., Gottman, J. M., & Levenson, R. W. (1995). Emotional behavior in long-term marriage. *Psychology & Aging, 10*, 140–149.

Carstensen, L. L., Pasupathi, M., Mayr, U., & Nesselroade, J. R. (2000). Emotional experience in everyday life across the adult life span. *Journal of Personality & Social Psychology, 79*, 644–655.

Carter, C., & Rice, C. L. (1997). Acquisition and manifestation of prejudice in children. *Journal of Multicultural Counseling and Development, 25*, 185–194.

Carter, C., Robertson, L., Nordahl, T., Chaderjian, M., Kraft, L., & O'Shora-Celaya, L. (1996). Spatial working memory deficits and their relationship to negative symptoms in unmedicated schizophrenia patients. *Biological Psychiatry, 40*, 930–932.

Carter, J. C., Stewart, D. A., Dunn, V. J., and Fairburn, C. G. (1997). Primary prevention of eating disorders: Might it do more harm than good? *International Journal of Eating Disorders, 22*, 167–172.

Carter, M. M., Hollon, S. D., Carson, R., & Shelton, R. C. (1995). Effects of a safe person on induced distress following a biological challenge in panic disorder with agoraphobia. *Journal of Abnormal Psychology, 104*, 156–163.

Cartwright-Hatton, S., & Wells, A. (1997). Beliefs about worry and intrusions: The Meta-Cognitions Questionnaire and its correlates. *Journal of Anxiety Disorders, 11*, 279–296.

Caruso, S., Grillo, C., Agnello, C., Maiolino, L., Intelisano, G., & Serra, A. (2001). A prospective study evidencing rhinomanometric and olfactometric outcomes in women taking oral contraceptives. *Human Reproduction, 16*, 2288–2294.

Carver, C. S., & Scheier, M. F. (1996). *Perspectives on personality.* Boston: Allyn & Bacon.

Carver, C. S., Scheier, M. F., & Weintraub, J. K. (1989). Assessing coping strategies: A theoretically based approach. *Journal of Personality and Social Psychology, 56*, 267–83.

Casada, J. H., Amdur, R., Larsen, R., & Liberzon, I. (1998). Psychophysiologic responsivity in posttraumatic stress disorder: Generalized hyperresponsiveness versus trauma specificity. *Biological Psychiatry, 44*, 1037–1044.

Case, R. (1977). Responsiveness to conservation training as a function of induced subjective uncertainty, M-space, and cognitive style. *Canadian Journal of Behavioral Sciences, 9*, 12–25.

Case, R. (1978). Intellectual development from birth to adulthood: A neo-Piagetian approach. In R. S. Siegler (Ed.), *Children's thinking: What develops?* (pp. 37–71). Hillsdale, NJ: Erlbaum.

Case, R. (1985). *Intellectual development: A systematic reinterpretation.* New York: Academic Press.

Case, R. (1992a). The role of the frontal lobes in the regulation of cognitive development. *Brain & Cognition, 20*, 51–73.

Case, R. (1992b). *The mind's staircase.* Hillsdale, NJ: Erlbaum.

Case, R. (1992c). The role of the frontal lobes in the regulation of cognitive development. *Brain and Cognition, 20*, 51–73.

Caspi, A. (1998). Personality development across the life course. In W. Damon (Series Ed.) & N. Eisenberg (Vol. Ed.), *Handbook of child psychology: Vol. 3. Social, emotional, and personality development.* (5th ed., pp. 311–388). New York: Wiley.

Caspi, A. (2000). The child is father of the man: Personality continuities from childhood to adulthood. *Journal of Personality and Social Psychology, 78*, 158–172.

Caspi, A., & Herbener, E. S. (1990). Continuity and change: Assortative marriage and the consistency of personality in adulthood. *Journal of Personality and Social Psychology, 58*, 250–258.

Caspi, A., Begg, D., Dickson, N., Harrington, H., Langley, J., Moffitt, T. E., & Silva, P. A. (1997). Personality differences predict health-risk behaviors in young adulthood: Evidence from a longitudinal study. *Journal of Personality and Social Psychology, 73*, 1052–1063.

Cassone, V. M., Warren, W. S., Brooks, D. S., & Lu, J. (1993). Melatonin, the pineal gland and circadian rhythms. *J. Biol. Rhythms, 8* (Suppl.), S73–S81.

Castillo, R. J. (1994). Spirit possession in South Asia, dissociation or hysteria? II. Case histories. *Culture, Medicine & Psychiatry, 18*, 141–162.

Catalan-Ahumeda, M., Degwgouj, N., De Volder, A., Melin, J., Michel, C., & Veraart, C. (1993). High metabolic activity demonstrated by positron emission tomography in human auditory cortex in case of deafness of early onset. *Brain Research, 623*, 287–292.

Cattell, R. B. (1943). The description of personality: Basic traits resolved into clusters. *Journal of Abnormal and Social Psychology, 38*, 476–506.

Cattell, R. B. (1971). *Abilities: Their structure, growth, and action.* Boston: Houghton Mifflin.

Cattell, R. B., Eber, H. W., & Tatsuoka, M. M. (1970). *Handbook for the Sixteen Personality Factor Questionnaire (16PF).* Champaign, IL: Institute for Personality and Ability Testing.

Caudron, S. (1994). Diversity ignites effective work teams. *Personnel Journal, 73*, 54–63.

Cavallaro, S., Schreurs, B. G., Zhao, W., D'Agata, V., & Alkon, D. L. (2001). Gene expression profiles during long-term memory consolidation. *European Journal of Neuroscience, 13*, 1809–1815.

Cavanagh, P. (1992). Attention-based motion perception. *Science, 257*, 1563–1565.

Cave, C. B. (1997). Very long-lasting priming in picture naming. *American Psychological Society, 8*, 322–325.

Cave, C. B., & Kosslyn, S. M. (1993). The role of parts and spatial relations in object identification. *Perception, 22*, 229–248.

Cave, C. B., & Squire, L. R. (1992). Intact and long-lasting repetition priming in amnesia. *Journal of Experimental Psychology: Learning, Memory, and Cognition, 18*, 509–520.

Cechetto, D. F., & Saper, C. B. (1990). Role of the cerebral cortex in autonomic function. In A. D. Loewy & K. M. Speyer (Eds.), *Central regulation of autonomic function* (pp. 208–223). New York: Oxford University Press.

Ceci, S. J. (1990). *On intelligence . . . more or less: A bio-ecological treatise on intellectual development.* Englewood Cliffs, NJ: Prentice-Hall.

Ceci, S. J. (1991). How much does schooling influence general intelligence and its cognitive components? A reassessment of the evidence. *Developmental Psychology, 27*, 703–722.

Ceci, S. J. (1996). *A bioecological treatise on intellectual development.* Cambridge, MA: Harvard University Press.

Ceci, S. J., & Williams, W. M. (1997). Schooling, intelligence, and income. *American Psychologist, 52*, 1051–1058.

Center for Addiction and Substance Abuse at Columbia University (2002). *Substance use and risky sexual activity.* http://www.casacolumbia.org/newsletter1457/newsletter_show.htm?doc_id=95635.

Center for the Advancement of Health (1998). Facts of life: An issue briefing for health reporters. 3(3), 2.

Centers for Disease Control. (1999, May 5). http://www.cdc.gov/nchswww/fastats/alcohol.htm.

Cerella, J. (1990). Aging and information-processing rate. In J. E. Birren & K. W. Schaie (Eds.), *Handbook of the psychology of aging* (3rd ed., pp. 201–221). San Diego, CA: Academic Press.

Cerella, J., Poon, L., & Williams, D. (1980). Age and the complexity hypothesis. In L. W. Poon (Ed.), *Aging in the 1980's* (pp. 332–340). Washington, DC: American Psychological Association.

Cernoch, J. M., & Porter, R. H. (1985). Recognition of maternal axillary odors by infants. *Child Development, 56*, 1593–1598.

Chabris, C. F. (1998). IQ since "The Bell Curve." *Commentary, 106*, 33–40.

Chabris, C. F. (1999). Prelude or requiem for the "Mozart effect"? *Nature, 400*, 826–827.

Chabris, C. F., & Kosslyn, S. M. (1998). How do the cerebral hemispheres contribute to encoding spatial relations? *Current Directions in Psychological Science, 7*, 8–14.

Chalmers, D. J. (1996). *The conscious mind.* New York: Oxford University Press.

Chamberlain, K., & Zika, S. (1990). The minor events approach to stress: Support for the use of daily hassles. *British Journal of Psychology, 81*, 469–481.

Chamberlain, M. C., Nichols, S. L., & Chase, C. H. (1991). Pediatric AIDS: Comparative cranial MRI and CT scans. *Pediatric Neurology, 7*, 357–362.

Chambers, J. M., Cleveland, W. S., Kleiner, B., & Turkey, P. A. (1983). *Graphical methods for data analysis.* Belmont, CA: Wadsworth.

Chambless, D. L., & Gillis, M. M. (1993). Cognitive therapy of anxiety disorders. *Journal of Consulting and Clinical Psychology, 61*, 248–260.

Chan, J., & Yang, J. (1999). *I am Jackie Chan.* New York: Ballantine Books.

Chan, R. W., Raboy, B., & Patterson, C. J. (1998). Psychosocial adjustment among children conceived via donor insemination by lesbian and heterosexual mothers. *Child Development, 69*, 443–457.

Changizi, M. A., McGehee, R. M. F., & Hall, W. G. (2002). Evidence that appetitive responses for dehydration and food-deprivation are learned. *Physiology & Behavior, 75*, 295–304.

Channouf, A., & Roubah, A. (1995). The effect of non-conscious perception of frequent stimuli on credibility judgement. *International Journal of Psychology, 30(2)*, 213–235.

Chao, L. L., & Martin, A. (1999). Cortical regions associated with perceiving, naming, and knowing about colors. *Journal of Cognitive Neuroscience, 11*, 25–35.

Chapman, C. (1989). Giving the patient control of opioid analgesic administration. In C. Hill & W. Fields (Eds.). *Advances in pain research and therapy* (Vol. 11). New York: Raven Press.

Chapman, C. R., & Nakamura, Y. (1999). A passion of the soul: An introduction to pain for consciousness researchers. *Consciousness and Cognition, 8*, 391–422.

Chapman, J. K. (2000). Developmental outcomes in two groups of young children: Prenatally cocaine exposed and noncocaine exposed: Part 2. *Infant-Toddler Intervention, 10*, 81–96.

Chapman, R. S., & Hesketh, L. J. (2000). Behavioral phenotype of individuals with Down syndrome. *Mental Retardation & Developmental Disabilities Research Reviews, 6*, 84–95.

Charness, N. (1981). Aging and skilled problem solving. *Journal of Experimental Psychology: General, 110*, 21–38.

Chase, W. G., & Ericsson, K. A. (1981). Skilled memory. In J. R. Anderson (Ed.), *Cognitive skills and their acquisition.* Hillsdale, NJ: Erlbaum.

Chase, W. G., & Simon, H. A. (1973). The mind's eye in chess. In W. G. Chase (Ed.), *Visual information processing* (pp. 215–281). New York: Academic Press.

Chassin, L., Curran, P. J., Hussong, A. M., & Colder, C. R. (1996). The relation of parent alcoholism to adolescent substance use: A longitudinal follow-up study. *Journal of Abnormal Psychology, 105*, 70–80.

Chatterjee, S., Heath, T. B., Milberg, S. J., & France, K. R. (2000). The differential processing of price in gains and losses: The effects of frame and need for cognition. *Journal of Behavioral Decision Making, 13,* 61–75.

Chaves, J. F. (1989). Hypnotic control of clinical pain. In N. P. Spanos & J. F. Chaves (Eds.), *Hypnosis: The cognitive-behavioral perspective,* pp. 242–272. Buffalo, NY: Prometheus Books.

Chee, M. W., Caplan, D., Soon, C. S., Sriram, N., Tan, E. W., Thiel, T., & Weekes, B. (1999). Processing of visually presented sentences in Mandarin and English studied with fMRI. *Neuron, 23,* 127–137.

Chen, Y., Levy, D. L., Nakayama, K., Matthysee, S., Palafox, G., & Holzman, P. S. (1998). Dependence of impaired eye tracking on deficient velocity discrimination in schizophrenia. *Archives of General Psychiatry, 56,*155–161.

Chen, Z., & Siegler, R. S. (2000). Across the great divide: Bridging the gap between understanding of toddlers' and older children's thinking. *Monographs of the Society for Research in Child Development, 65,* v-96.

Cheour-Luhtanen, M., Alho, K., Sainio, K., Rinne, T., & Reinikainen, K. (1996). The ontogenetically earliest discriminative response of the human brain. *Psychophysiology, 33,* 478–481.

Cherry, E. C. (1953). Some experiments on the recognition of speech with one and two ears. *Journal of the Acoustical Society of America, 25,* 975–979.

Chess, S., & Thomas, A. (1987). *Know your child.* New York: Basic Books.

Chess, S., & Thomas, A. (1996). *Temperament: Theory and practice.* New York: Brunner/Mazel.

Chi, M. T. H. (1978). Knowledge structures and memory development. In R. S. Siegler (Ed.), *Children's thinking: What develops?* (pp. 73–96). Hillsdale, NJ: Erlbaum.

Chi, M. T. H., & Glaser, R. (1985). Problem solving ability. In R. J. Sternberg (Ed.), *Human abilities: An information processing approach* (pp. 227–250). New York: Freeman.

Chi, M. T. H., Glaser, R., & Rees, E. (1982). Expertise in problem solving. In R. J. Sternberg (Ed.), *Advances in the psychology of human intelligence* (Vol. 1, pp. 7–75). Hillsdale, NJ: Erlbaum.

Chick, J., Gough, K., Falkowski, W., Kershaw, P., Hore, B., Mehta, B., Ritson, B., Ropner, R., & Torley, D. (1992). Disulfiram treatment of alcoholism. *British Journal of Psychiatry, 161,* 84–89.

Chilcoat, H. D., & Breslau, N. (1998). Posttraumatic stress disorder and drug disorders testing causal pathways. *Arch Gen Psychiatry, 55,* 913–917.

Child, I. L. (1985). Psychology and anomalous observations: The question of ESP in dreams. *American Psychologist, 40,* 1219–1230.

Chipuer, H. M., Rovine, M. J., & Plomin, R. (1990). LISREL modeling: Genetic and environmental influences on IQ revisited. *Intelligence, 14,* 11–29.

Choderow, N. (1978). *The reproduction of mothering.* Berkeley: University of California Press.

Chomsky, C. (1969). *The acquisition of syntax in children from 5 to 10.* Cambridge, MA: MIT Press.

Chomsky, N. (1957). *Syntactic structures.* Mouton: The Hague.

Chomsky, N. (1965). *Aspects of a theory of syntax.* Cambridge, MA: MIT Press.

Chomsky, N. (1972). *Language and mind.* New York: Harcourt Brace.

Chomsky, N. (1975). *Reflections on language.* New York: Pantheon.

Chomsky, N. (1976). *Reflections on language.* London: Temple Smith.

Christensen, K. A., Stephens, M. A. P., & Townsend, A. L. (1998). Mastery in women's multiple roles and well-being: Adult daughters providing care to impaired parents. *Health Psychology, 17,* 163–171.

Christman, S. D. (2002). Hemispheric asymmetries in categorical judgments of directions versus coordinate judgments of velocity of motion. *Psychonomic Bulletin and Review, 9,* 298–305.

Christopher J., Murray, L., & Lopez, A. D., Eds. (1998). The global burden of disease: Volume 2. Global Health Statistics. Cambridge, MA: Harvard University Press.

Chun, M. M. (1997). Types and tokens in visual processing: A double dissociation between the attentional blink and repetition blindness. *Journal of Experimental Psychology: Human Perception and Performance, 23,* 738–755.

Chun, M. M. (2000). Contextual cueing of visual attention. *Trends in Cognitive Sciences, 4,* 170–177.

Church, T. A., & Katigbak, M. S. (2000). Trait psychology in the Philippines. *American Behavioral Scientist, 44,* 73–94.

Cialdini, R. B. (1979). Interpersonal influence. In S. Shavitt & T. C. Brock (Eds.), *Persuasion* (pp. 195–218). Boston: Allyn & Bacon.

Cialdini, R. B. (1994). Interpersonal influence. In N. S. Shavitt & T. C. Brock (Eds.), *Persuasion: Psychological insights and perspectives* (pp. 195–218). Boston: Allyn & Bacon.

Cialdini, R. B., & Petty, R. (1979). Anticipatory opinion effects. In B. Petty, T. Ostrom, & T. Brock (Eds.), *Cognitive responses in persuasion.* Hillsdale, NJ: Erlbaum.

Cialdini, R. B., & Trost, M. R. (1998). Social influence: Social norms, conformity, and compliance. In D. T. Gilbert, S. T. Fiske, & G. Lindzey (Eds.), *The handbook of social psychology* (4th ed.). New York: McGraw Hill. 151–192.

Cialdini, R. B., Eisenberg, N., Green, B. L., Rhoads, K., & Bator, R. (1998). Undermining the undermining effect of reward on sustained interest. *Journal of Applied Social Psychology, 28,* 249–263.

Cialdini, R. B., Reno, R. R., & Kallgren, C. A. (1990). A focus theory of normative conduct: Recycling the concept of norms to reduce littering in public places. *Journal of Personality and Social Psychology, 58,* 1015–1026.

Cialdini, R. B., Trost, M. R., Newsom, J. T. (1995). Preference for consistency: the development of a valid measure and the discovery of surprising behavioral implications. *Journal of Personality and Social Psychology, 69,* 318–328.

Cialdini, R. B., Vincent, J. A., Lewis, S. K., Catalan, J., Wheeler, D., & Darby, B. L. (1975). Reciprocal concessions procedure for inducing compliance: The door-in-the-face technique. *Journal of Personality and Social Psychology, 31,* 206–215.

Cicero, T. J. (1978). Tolerance to and physiological dependence on alcohol: Behavioral and neurobiological mechanisms. In M. A. Lipton, A. DiMascio, & K. F. Killman (Eds.), *Psychopharmacology.* New York: Raven.

Citron, M., Solomon, P., & Draine, J. (1999). Self-help groups for families of persons with mental illness: Perceived benefits of helpfulness. *Community Mental Health Journal, 35,* 15–30.

Clancy, S. A., McNally, R. J., & Schacter, D. L. (2000). Effects of guided imagery on memory distortion in women reporting recovered memories of childhood sexual abuse. *Journal of Traumatic Stress, 12,* 559–569.

Clancy, S. A., Schacter, D. L., McNally, R. J., & Pitman, R. K. (2000). False recognition in women reporting recovered memories of sexual abuse. *Psychological Science, 11,* 26–31.

Claparède, E. (1911/1951). Recognition and "me-ness." Originally published in *Archives de Psychologie, 11,* 79–90. Reprinted in D. Rappaport (Ed.), (1951). *Organization and pathology of thought* (pp. 58–75). New York: Columbia University Press.

Clapp, G. (1988). *Child study research: Current perspectives and applications.* Lexington, MA: Lexington Books/D. C. Heath and Company.

Clarey, J. C., Barone, P., & Imig, T. J. (1992). Physiology of thalmus and cortex. In A. N. Popper & R. R. Fay (Eds.), *The mammalian auditory pathway: Neurophysiology* (pp. 232–334). New York: Springer-Verlag.

Clark, D. M., Ball, S., & Pape, D. (1991). An experimental investigation of thought suppression. *Behaviour Research and Therapy, 29,* 253–257.

Clark, D. M., Salkovskis, P. M., Hackmann, A., Middleton, H., Anastasiades, P., & Gelder, M. (1994). A comparison of cognitive therapy, applied relaxation and imipramine in the treatment of panic disorder. *British Journal of Psychiatry, 164,* 759–769.

Clark, D. M., Salkovskis, P. M., Hackmann, A., Wells, A., Ludgate, J., & Gelder, M. (1999). Brief cognitive therapy for panic disorder: A randomized controlled trial. *Journal of Consulting and Clinical Psychology, 67,* 583–589.

Clark, E. V. (1983). Meanings and concepts. In P. H. Mussen (Ed.), *Handbook of child psychology: Vol. 3, Cognitive development* (pp. 787–840). New York: Wiley.

Clark, E. V. (1993). *The lexicon in acquisition.* Cambridge: Cambridge University Press.

Clark, L. F., & Collins, J. E. (1993). Remembering old flames: How the past affects assessments of the present. *Personality & Social Psychology Bulletin, 19,* 399–408.

Clark, R. W. (1971). *Einstein: The life and times.* New York: The World Publishing Co.

Clark, S. A., Allard, T., Jenkins, W. M., & Merzenich, M. M. (1988). Receptive fields in the body-surface map in adult cortex defined by temporally correlated inputs. *Nature, 332,* 444–445.

Clarke, D. J., Boer, H., & Webb, T. (1995). Genetic and behavioural aspects of Prader-Willi syndrome: A review with a translation of the original paper. *Mental Handicap Research, 8,* 38–53.

Clarke, G. N., Hornbrook, M., Lynch, F., Polen, M., Gale, J., Beardslee, W., O'Connor, E., & Seeley, J. (2001). A randomized trial of a group cognitive intervention for preventing depression in adolescent offspring of depressed parents. *Archives of General Psychiatry, 58,* 1127–1134.

Clay, R. (1995). Working mothers: happy or haggard? *The APA Monitor, 26 (11),* 1, 37.

Cleary, A. M., & Greene, R. L. (2002). Paradoxical effects of presentation modality on false memory. *Memory, 10,* 55–61.

Clifford, D. B. (2000). Human immunodeficiency virus-associated dementia. *Archives of Neurology, 57,* 321–324.

Collins, A. M., & Loftus, E. F. (1975). A spreading activation theory of semantic memory. *Psychological Review, 82,* 407–428.

Clementz, B. A., & Sweeney, J. A. (1990). Is eye movement dysfunction a biological marker for schizophrenia? A methodological review. *Psychological Bulletin, 108,* 77–92.

Cleveland, H. H., Jacobson, K. C., Lipinski, J. J., & Rowe, D. C. (2000). Genetic and shared environmental contributions to the relationship between the HOME environment and child and adolescent achievement. *Intelligence, 28,* 69–86.

Cloninger, R., & Svarkic, D. M. (1997). Integrative psychobiological approach to psychiatric assessment and treatment. *Psychiatry, 60,* 120–141.

Cloninger, R., Svarkic, D. M., & Prysbeck, T. R. (1993). Psychobiological model of temperament and character. *Archives of General Psychiatry, 50,* 975–990.

Cloninger, S. C. (1996). *Personality: Description, Dynamics, and Development.* New York: Freeman.

Clopton, N. A., & Sorell, G. T. (1993). Gender differences in moral reasoning: Stable or situational? *Psychology of Women Quarterly, 17,* 85–101.

Clum, G. A., Clum, G. A., & Surls, R. (1993). A meta-analysis of treatments for panic disorder. *Journal of Consulting & Clinical Psychology, 61,* 317–326.

Coats, E. J., & Feldman, R. S. (1996). Gender differences in nonverbal correlates of social status. *Personality & Social Psychology Bulletin, 22,* 1014–1022.

Coe, W. C. (1978). The credibility of posthypnotic amnesia: A contextualists' view. *International Journal of Clinical & Experimental Hypnosis, 26,* 218–245.

Coffey, C. E., Saxton, J. A., Ratcliff, G., Bryan, R. N., & Lucke, J. F. (1999). Relation of education to brain size in normal aging: Implications for the reserve hypothesis. *Neurology, 53,* 189–196.

Cohen, C. I., Strashun, A., Ortega, C., & Horn, L. (1996). The effects of poverty and education on temporoparietal perfusion in Alzheimer's disease: A reconsideration of the cerebral reserve hypothesis. *International Journal of Geriatric Psychiatry, 11,* 1105–1110.

Cohen, D., Nisbett, R. E., Bowdle, B. F., & Schwarz, N. (1996). Insult, aggression, and the southern culture of honor: An "experimental ethnography." *Journal of Personality and Social Psychology, 70,* 945–960.

Cohen, H., Kotler, M., Matar, M. A., Kaplan, Z., Loewenthal, U., Miodownik, J., & Cassuto, Y. (1998). Analysis of heart rate variability in posttraumatic stress disorder patients in response to a trauma-related reminder. *Biological Psychiatry, 44,* 1054–1059.

Cohen, J. D., Peristein, W. M., Braver, T. S., Nystrom, L. E., Noll, D. C., Jonides, J., & Smith, E. E. (1997). Temporal dynamics of brain activation during a working memory task. *Nature, 386,* 604–608.

Cohen, N. J., & Squire, L. R. (1980). Preserved learning and retention of pattern analyzing skill in amnesia: Dissociation of knowing how and knowing that. *Science, 210,* 207–209.

Cohen, S., & Herbert, T. B. (1996). Health Psychology: psychological factors and physical disease from the perspective of human psychoneuroimmunology. *Annual Review of Psychology, 47,* 113–142.

Cohen, S., & Wills, T. (1985). Stress, social support and the buffering hypothesis. *Psychological Bulletin, 98,* 310–357.

Cohen, S., Doyle, W. J., Skoner, D. P., Fireman, P., Gwaltney, J., & Newsom, J. (1995). State and trait negative affect as predictors of objective and subjective symptoms of respiratory viral infections. *Journal of Personality and Social Psychology, 68,* 159–169.

Cohen, S., Doyle, W. J., Skoner, D. P., Rabin, B. S., & Gwaltney, J. M., Jr. (1997). Social ties and susceptibility to the common cold. *Journal of the American Medical Association, 277,* 1940–1944.

Cohen, S., Evans, F. W., Krantz, D. S., & Stokols, D. S. (1986). *Behavior, health, and environmental stress.* New York: Plenum Press.

Cohen, S., Frank, E., Doyle, W. J., Skoner, D. P., Rabin, B. S., & Gwaltney, J. M., Jr. (1998). Types of stressors that increase susceptibility to the common cold in adults. *Health Psychology, 17,* 214–223.

Cohen, S., Tyrrell, D. A. J., & Smith, A. P. (1991). Psychological stress and susceptibility to the common cold. *New England Journal of Medicine, 325,* 606–612.

Cohen, S., Tyrrell, D. A. J., & Smith, A. P. (1993). Negative life events, perceived stress, negative affect, and susceptibility to the common cold. *Journal of Personality and Social Psychology, 64,* 131–140.

Cohen, S., Tyrrell, D. A. J., & Smith, A. P. (1997). Psychological stress in humans and susceptibility to the common cold. In T. W. Miller (Ed.), *Clinical disorders and stressful life events.* (pp. 217–235). Madison, CT: International Universities Press.

Colapinto, J. (2000). *As nature made him: The boy who was raised as a girl.* New York: HarperCollins.

Colby, A., Kohlberg, L., Gibbs, J. C., & Lieberman, M. (1983). A longitudinal study of moral judgment. *Monographs of the Society for Research in Child Development, 48* (1–2, Serial No. 200).

Cole, M. (1990). Cognitive development and formal schooling: The evidence from cross-cultural research. In L. C. Moll (Ed.), *Vygotsky and education* (pp. 89–110). New York: Cambridge University Press.

Cole, M. (1996). *Cultural psychology: A once and future discipline.* Cambridge, MA: Harvard University Press.

Cole, M., & Bruner, J. S. (1971). Cultural differences and inferences about psychological processes. *American Psychologist, 26,* 867–876.

Cole, M., & Wertsch, J. V. (1996). Beyond the individual-social antinomy in discussions of Piaget and Vygotsky. *Human Development, 39,* 250–256.

Cole, M., Engestroem, Y., & Vasquez, O. A. (Eds.), (1997). *Mind, culture, and activity: Seminal papers from the Laboratory of Comparative Human Cognition.* New York: Cambridge University Press.

Cole, M., Gay, J., Glick, J. A., & Sharp, D. W. (1971). *The cultural context of learning and thinking.* New York: Basic Books.

Cole, P. M. (1998). Nepali children's ideas about emotional displays in hypothetical challenges. *Developmental Psychology, 34,* 640–646.

Coleman, P., & Flood, D. (1986). Dendritic proliferation in the aging brain as a compensatory repair mechanism. *Progress in Brain Research, 70,* 227–236.

Collings, V. B. (1974). Human taste response as a function of locus of stimulation on the tongue and soft palate. *Perception & Psychophysics, 16,* 169–174.

Collins, A. M., & Loftus, E. F. (1975). A spreading activation theory of semantic memory. *Psychological Review, 82,* 407–428.

Collins, M. A., & Zebrowitz, L. A. (1995). The contributions of appearance to occupational outcomes in civilian and military settings. *Journal of Applied Social Psychology, 25,* 129–163.

Collins, W. A. (1990). Parent-child relationships in the transition to adolescence: Continuity and change in interaction, affect, and cognition. In R. Montemayor, G. R. Adams, & T. P. Gullota (Eds.), *From childhood to adolescence: A transitional period?* (pp. 85–106). Newbury Park, CA: Sage.

Collins, W. A., Maccoby, E. E., Steinberg, L., Hetherington, E. M., & Bornstein, M. H. (2000). Contemporary research on parenting: The case for nature and nurture. *American Psychologist, 55,* 218–232.

Colom, F., Vieta, E., Martinez, A., Jorquera, A., & Gasto, C. (1998). What is the role of psychotherapy in the treatment of bipolar disorder? *Psychotherapy & Psychosomatics, 67,* 3–9.

Colombo, J., & Richman, W. A. (2002). Infant timekeeping: Attention and temporal estimating in 4-month-olds. *Psychological Science, 13,* 475–479.

Colome, A. (2001). Lexical activation in bilinguals' speech production: Language-specific or language-independent? *Journal of Memory & Language, 45,* 721–736.

Comery, T. A., Shah, R., & Greenough, W. T. (1995). Differential rearing alters spine density on medium-sized spiny neurons in the rat corpus striatum: Evidence for association of morphological plasticity with early response gene expression. *Neurobiology of Learning & Memory, 63,* 217–219.

Compas, B. E., Haaga, D. A. F., Keefe, F. J., Leitenberg, H., & Williams, D. A. (1998). Sampling of Empirically Supported Psychological Treatments From Health Psychology, *Journal of Consulting and Clinical Psychology, 66,* 89–112.

Comstock, G., & Paik, H. (1991). *Television and the American child.* San Diego, CA: Academic Press.

Cone, E. J. (1995). Pharmacokinetics and pharmacodynamics of cocaine. *Journal of Analytical Toxicology, 19,* 459–477.

Conn, J. H., & Conn, R. N. (1967). Discussion of T. X. Barber's "Hypnosis as a causal variable in present day psychology: A critical analysis." *International Journal of Clinical & Experimental Hypnosis, 15,* 106–110.

Connell, M. W., Sheridan, K., & Gardner, H. (in press). On abilities and domains. In R. Sternberg and E. Grigorenko (Eds.), *Perspectives on the psychology of abilities, competencies, and expertise.* New York: Cambridge University Press.

Connolly, J. B., Roberts, I. J. H., Armstrong, J. D., Kaiser, K., Forte, M., Tully, T., & O'Kane, C. J. (1996). Associative learning disrupted by impaired Gs signaling in Drosophila mushroom bodies. *Science, 274,* 2104–2107.

Connor, E. M., Sperling, R. S., Gelber, R., Kiselev, P., Scott, G., & Sullivan, M. J. (1995). Reduction of maternal-infant transmission of human immunodeficient virus 1 with zidovudine treatment. *Obstetrical and Gynecological Survey, 50,* 253–255.

Consortium for Longitudinal Studies (Ed.). (1983). *As the twig is bent . . . Lasting effects of preschool programs.* Hillsdale, NJ: Erlbaum.

Conti, R., Coon, H., & Amabile, T. M. (1996). Evidence to support the componential model of creativity: Secondary analyses of three studies. *Creativity Research Journal, 9,* 385–389.

Conway, A. R. A., Cowan, N., & Bunting, M. F. (2001). The cocktail party phenomenon revisited: The importance of working memory capacity. *Psychonomic Bulletin & Review, 8,* 331–335.

Conway, M. A., & Rubin, D. C. (1993). The structure of autobiographical memory. In A. F. Collins, S. E. Gathercole, M. A. Conway, & P. E. Morris (Eds.), *Theories of memory* (pp. 103–137). Hillsdale, NJ: Erlbaum.

Cook, E. W., III, Hawk, L. W., Davis, T. L., Stevenson, V. E. (1991). Affective individual differences and startle reflex modulation. *Journal of Abnormal Psychology, 100,* 5–13.

Cook, M., & Mineka, S. (1991). Selective associations in the origins of phobic fears and their implications for behaviour therapy. In P. Martin (Ed.), *Handbook of behavior therapy and psychological science :An integrative approach.* New York: Pergamon Press.

Coons, P. M., Milstein, V., & Marley, C. (1982). EEG studies of two multiple personalities and a control. *Archives of General Psychiatry, 39,* 823–825.

Cooper, J. (1998). Unlearning cognitive dissonance: Toward an understanding of the development of dissonance. *Journal of Experimental Social Psychology, 34,* 562–575.

Cooper, M. L., Shapiro, C. M., & Powers, A. M. (1998). Motivations for sex and risky sexual behavior among adolescents and young adults: A functional perspective. *Journal of Personality and Social Psychology, 75,* 1528–1558.

Cooper, R. P., Abraham, J., Berman, S., & Staska, M. (1997). The development of infants' preference for motherese. *Infant Behavior & Development, 20,* 477–488.

Coplan, J. D., Goetz, R., Klein, D. F., Papp, L. A., Fyer, A. J., Liebowitz, M. R., Davies, S. O., & Gorman, J. M. (1998). Plasma cortisol concentrations preceding lactate-induced panic: Psychological, biochemical, and physiological correlates. *Archives of General Psychiatry, 55,* 130–136.

Corbetta, M., & Shulman, G. L. (2002). Control of goal-directed and stimulus-driven attention in the brain. *Nature Reviews Neuroscience, 3,* 201–215.

Corbetta, M., Miezin, F. M., Dobmeyer, S., Shulman, G. L., & Petersen, S. E. (1990). Attentional modulation of neural processing of shape, color, and velocity in humans. *Science, 248,* 1556–1559.

Corbetta, M., Miezin, F. M., Dobmeyer, S., Shulman, G. L., & Petersen, S. E. (1991). Selective and divided attention during visual discriminations of shape, color, and speed: Functional anatomy by positron emission tomography. *Journal of Neuroscience, 11,* 2383–2402.

Corbetta, M., Miezen, F. M., Schulman, G. L., & Petersen, S. E. (1993). A PET study of visuospatial attention. *Journal of Neuroscience, 13,* 1202–1226.

Coren, S. (1996). *Sleep thieves: An eye-opening exporation into the science and mysteries of sleep,* New York: Free Press.

Corkin, S. (2002). What's new with the amnestic patient H. M.? *Nature Reviews Neuroscience, 3,* 153–160.

Cornelius, M. D., & Day, N. L. (2000). The effects of tobacco use during and after pregnancy on exposed children. *Alcohol Research & Health, 24,* 242–249.

Corr, P. J., & Kumari, V. (1997). Sociability/impulsivity and attenuated-dopaminergic arousal: Critical flicker/fusion frequency and procedural learning. *Personality and Individual Differences, 22,* 805–815.

Corr, P. J., Pickering, A. D., & Gray, J. A. (1995). Sociability/impulsivity and caffeine-induced arousal: Critical flicker/fusion frequency and procedural learning. *Personality and Individual Differences, 18,* 713–730.

Corr, P. J., Pickering, A. D., & Gray, J. A. (1997). Personality, Punishment, and Procedural Learning: A Test of J. A. Gray's Anxiety Theory. *Journal of Personality and Social Psychology, 73,* 337–344.

Cosmides, L. (1989). The logic of social exchange: Has natural selection shaped how humans reason? Studies with the Wason selection task. *Cognition, 31,* 187–276.

Cosmides, L., & Tooby, J. (1996). Are humans good intuitive statisticians after all? Rethinking some conclusions from the literature on judgment under uncertainty. *Cognition, 58*, 1–73.

Costa, P. T., & McCrae, R. R. (1988). Personality in adulthood: A six-year longitudinal study of self-reports and spouse ratings on the NEO personality inventory. *Journal of Personality and Social Psychology, 54*, 853–863.

Costa, P. T., & McCrae, R. R. (1995). Primary traits of Eysenck's P-E-N System: Three- and five-factor solutions. *Journal of Personality and Social Psychology, 69*, 308–317.

Costa, P. T., McCrae, R. R., & Dye, D. A. (1991). Facet scales for agreeableness and conscientiousness: A revision of the NEO Personality Inventory. *Personality and Individual Differences, 12*, 887–898.

Costa, P. T., Terracciano, A., & McCrae, R. R. (2001). Gender differences in personality traits across cultures: Robust and surprising findings. *Journal of Personality and Social Psychology, 81*, 322–331.

Costa, P. T., Jr., Herbst, J. H., McCrae, R. R., & Siegler, I. C. (2000). Personality at midlife: Stability, intrinsic maturation, and response to life events. *Assessment, 7*, 365–378.

Costela, C., Tejedor-Real, P., Mico, J. A., & Gilbert-Rahola, J. (1995). Effect of neonatal handling on learned helplessness model of depression. *Physiology and Behavior, 57*, 407–410.

Cotman, C. (1990). The brain: New plasticity/new possibility. In R. N. Butler, M. R. Oberlink, & M. Schechter (Eds.), *The promise of productive aging: From biology to social policy* (pp. 70–84). New York: Springer.

Cotman, C. W., & Berchtold, N. C. (2002). Exercise: A behavioral intervention to enhance brain health and plasticity. *Trends in Neurosciences, 25*, 295–301.

Council, J. R. (1993). Contextual effects in personality research. *Current Directions in Psychological Science, 2*, 31–34.

Council, J. R., Kirsch, I., & Grant, D. L. (1996). Imagination, expectancy and hypnotic responding. In R. G. Kunzendorf, N. P. Spanos, & B. J. Wallace (Eds.), *Hypnosis and imagination* (pp. 41–65). Amityville, NY: Baywood.

Counts, D. A., & Counts, D. R. (1992). "I'm not dead yet!" Aging and death: Process and experience in Kaliai. In L. A. Platt & V. R. Persico, Jr. (Eds.), *Grief in cross-cultural perspective: A casebook* (pp. 307–343). New York: Garland.

Coupland, N. J. (2001). Social phobia: Etiology, neurobiology, and treatment. *Journal of Clinical Psychiatry, 62*, 25–35.

Courtney, S. M., Ungerleider, L. G., Keil, K., & Haxby, J. V. (1997). Transient and sustained activity in a distributed neural system for human working memory. *Nature 386*, 608–611.

Cover, H., & Irwin, M. (1994). Immunity and depression: Insomnia, retardation, and reduction of natural killer cell activity. *Journal of Behavioral Medicine, 17*, 217–223.

Cowan, N. (2001). The magical number 4 in short-term memory: A reconsideration of mental storage capacity. *Behavioral and Brain Sciences, 24*, 87–114.

Cowan, W. M., Fawcett, J. W., O'Leary, D. D. M., & Stanfield, B. B. (1984). Regressive events in neurogenesis. *Science, 225*, 1258–1265.

Cowey, A., & Stoerig, P. (1995). Blindsight in monkeys. *Nature, 373*, 247–249.

Cox, H. (2000). Personal communication.

Coyne, J. C. (1976). Toward an interactional description of depression. *Psychiatry, 39*, 28–40.

Coyne, J. C., & Downey, G. (1991). Social factors in psychopathology: Stress, social support, and coping processes. *Annual Review of Psychology, 42*, 401–425.

Coyne, J. C., Kessler, R. C., Tal, M., Turnbull, J., Wortman, C., & Greden, J. (1987). Living with a depressed person: Burden and psychological distress. *Journal of Clinical and Consulting Psychology, 55*, 347–352.

Crago, M., & Crago, H. (1983). *Prelude to literacy.* Carbondale, IL: Southern Illinois University Press.

Craig, R. L., & Siegel, P. S. (1978). Does negative affect beget positive affect? A test of the opponent-process theory. *Bulletin of the Psychonomic Society, 14*, 404–406.

Craik, F. I., & McDowd, J. M. (1987). Age differences in recall and recognition. *Journal of Experimental Psychology: Learning, Memory, & Cognition, 13*, 474–479.

Craik, F. I., Morris, L. W., Morris, R. G., & Loewen, E. R. (1990). Relations between source amnesia and frontal lobe functioning in older adults. *Psychology and Aging, 5*, 148–151.

Craik, F. I. M., & Lockhart, R. S. (1972). Levels of processing: A framework for memory research. *Journal of Verbal Learning and Verbal Behavior, 11*, 671–684.

Craik, F. I. M., & Tulving, E. (1975). Depth of processing and the retention of words in episodic memory. *Journal of Experimental Psychology: General, 104*, 268–294.

Craik, F. I. M., & Watkins, M. J. (1973). The role of rehearsal in short-term memory. *Journal of Learning and Verbal Behavior, 12*, 599–607.

Craik, F. I. M., Anderson, N. D., Kerr, S. A., & Li, K. Z. H. (1995). Memory changes in normal aging. In A. D. Baddeley, B. A. Wilson, & F. N. Watts (Eds.), *Handbook of memory disorders* (pp. 211–241). New York: Wiley.

Cramer, R. E., Abraham, W. T., Johnson, L. M., & Manning-Ryan, B. (2001–2002). Gender differences in subjective distress to emotional and sexual infidelity: Evolutionary or logical inference explanation? *Current Psychology: Developmental, Learning, Personality, Social, 20*, 327–336.

Cramer, R. E., Schaefer, J. T., & Reid, S. (1996). Identifying the ideal mate: More evidence for male–female convergence. *Current Psychology: Developmental, Learning, Personality, Social, 16*, 157–166.

Crawford, H. J., Gur, R. C., Skolnick, B., Gur, R. E., & Benson, D. (1993). Effects of hypnosis on regional cerebral blood flow during ischemic pain with and without suggested hypnotic analgesia. *International Journal of Psychophysiology, 15*, 181–195.

Crawford, M., Stark, A. C., & Renner, C. H. (1998). The meaning of Ms.: Social assimilation of a gender concept. *Psychology of Women Quarterly, 22*, 197–208.

Crawford, R. P. (1954). *The technique of creative thinking: How to use your ideas to achieve success.* New York: Hawthorn Books.

Crick, F. (1994). *The astonishing hypothesis: The scientific search for the soul.* New York: Scribners.

Crick, F., & Koch, C. (1995). Are we aware of neural activity in primary visual cortex? *Nature, 375*, 121–123.

Crick, F., & Koch, C. (1998). Consciousness and neuroscience. *Cerebral Cortex, 8*, 97–107.

Crick, F., & Mitchison, F. (1983). The function of dream sleep. *Nature, 304*, 111–114.

Crick, F., & Mitchison, G. (1986). REM sleep and neural nets. *Journal of Mind and Behavior, 7*, 229–250.

Crick, N. R., & Grotpeter, J. K. (1995). Relational aggression, gender, and social-psychological adjustment. *Child Development, 66*, 710–722.

Crisp, A. H., Hsu, L. K., & Harding, B. (1980). The starving hoarder and voracious spender: Stealing in anorexia nervosa. *Journal of Psychosomatic Research, 24*, 225–231.

Crist, R. E., Li, Wu, & Gilbert, C. D. (2001). Learning to see: Experience and attention in primary visual cortex. *Nature Neuroscience, 4*, 519–525.

Critchley, H. D., & Rolls, E. T. (1996). Hunger and satiety modify the responses of olfactory and visual neurons in the primate orbitofrontal cortex. *Journal of Neurophysiology, 75*, 1673–1686.

Crits-Christoph, P. (1992). The efficacy of brief dynamic psychotherapy: A meta-analysis. *American Journal of Psychiatry, 149*, 151–158.

Croft, R. J., Klugman, A., Baldeweg, T., & Gruzelier, J. H. (2001). Electrophysiological evidence of serotonergic impairment in long-term MDMA ("ecstasy") users. *American Journal of Psychiatry, 158*, 1687–1692.

Croizet, J.-C., & Claire, T. (1998) Extending the concept of stereotype and threat to social class: The intellectual underperformance of students from low socioeconimic backgrounds. *Personality & Social Psychology Bulletin, 24*, 588–594.

Cronbach, L. J. (1990). *Essentials of psychological testing.* New York: Harper & Row.

Crowe, R., Noyes, R., Pauls, D., & Slyman, D. (1983). A family study of panic disorder. *Archives of General Psychiatry, 40*, 1065–1069.

Crowley, K., & Siegler, R. S. (1999). Explanation and generalization in young children's strategy learning. *Child Development, 70*(2), 304–316.

Crowley, K., Shrager, J., & Siegler, R. S. (1997). Strategy discovery as a competitive negotiation between metacognitive and associative mechanisms. *Developmental Review, 17*, 462–489.

Crozier, J. B. (1997). Absolute pitch: Practice makes perfect, the earlier the better. *Psychology of Music, 25*, 110–119.

Cruz, A., & Green, B. G. (2000). Thermal stimulation of taste. *Nature, 403*, 889–892.

Csibra, G. (2001). Illusory contour figures are perceived as occluding surfaces by 8-month-old infants. *Developmental Science, 4*, F7–F11.

Csikszentmihalyi, M., & Csikszentmihalyi, I. S. (Eds.). (1988). *Optimal Experience: Psychological studies of flow in consciousness.* New York: Cambridge University Press.

Cuijpers, P. (1997). Bibliotherapy in unipolar depression: A meta-analysis. *Journal of Behavior Therapy & Experimental Psychiatry, 28*, 139–147.

Culbertson, F. M. (1997). Depression and gender: An international review. *American Psychologist, 52*, 25–31.

Cummings, N. (1992). Self-defense training for college women. *Journal of American College Health, 40*, 183–188.

Cunningham, M. R. (1986). Measuring the physical in physical attractiveness: Quasi-experiments on the sociobiology of female facial beauty. *Journal of Personality and Social Psychology, 50*, 925–935.

Cunningham, M. R., Barbee, A. P., & Pike, C. L. (1990). What do women want? Facialmetric assessment of multiple motives in the perception of male facial physical attractiveness. *Journal of Personality and Social Psychology, 59*, 61–72.

Cunningham, M. R., Roberts, A. R., Barbee, A. P., Druen, P. B., & Wu, C. H. (1995). "Their ideas of beauty are, on the whole, the same as ours": Consistency and variability in the cross-cultural perception of female physical attractiveness. *Journal of Personality and Social Psychology, 68*, 261–279.

Cupach, W. P., & Spitzberg, B. H. (1994). *The dark side of interpersonal communication.* Hillsdale, NJ: Erlbaum.

Curtiss, S. (1977). *Genie: A psycholinguistic study of a modern-day "wild child."* New York: Academic Press.

Curtiss, S. (1989). The independence and task-specificity of language. In M. H. Bornstein & J. S. Bruner (Eds.), *Interaction in human development* (pp. 105–137). Hillsdale, NJ: Erlbaum.

Czeisler, C. A., Duffy, J. F., Shanahan, T. L., Brown, E. N., Mitchell, J. F., Rimmer, D. W., Ronda, J. M., Silva, E. J., Allan, J. S., Emens, J. S., Dijk, D. J., & Kronauer, R. E. (1999). Stability, precision, and near-24-hour period of the human circadian pacemaker. *Science, 284*, 2101–2103.

Dabbs, J. M., Jr., Strong, R., & Milun, R. (1997). Exploring the mind of testosterone: A beeper study. *Journal of Research in Personality, 31*, 577–587.

Dabbs, J. M., Jr., Riad, J. K., & Chance, S. E. (2001). Testosterone and ruthless homicide. *Personality & Individual Differences, 31*, 599–603.

Dackis, C. A., and O'Brien, C. P. (2001). Cocaine dependence: A disease of the brain's reward centers. *Journal of Substance Abuse Treatment, 21*, 111–117.

Dadds, M. R., Bovberg, D. H., Redd, W. H., & Cutmore, T. R. H. (1997). Imagery in human classical conditioning. *Psychological Bulletin, 122*, 89–103.

Dahloef, P., Norlin-Bagge, E., Hedner, J., Ejnell, H., Hetta, J., & Haellstroem, T. (2002). Improvement in neuropsychological performance following surgical treatment for obstructive sleep apnea syndrome. *Acta Oto-Laryngologica, 122,* 86–91.

Dai, X. Y., & Lynn, R. (1994). Gender differences in intelligence among Chinese children. *The Journal of Social Psychology, 134,* 123–125.

Dalbert, C., & Yamauchi, L. (1994). Belief in a just world and attitudes toward immigrants and foreign workers: A cultural comparison between Hawaii and Germany. *Journal of Applied Social Psychology, 24,* 1612–1626.

Dalderup, L. M., and Fredericks, M. L. C. (1969). Colour sensitivity in old age. *Journal of the American Geriatric Society, 17,* 388–390.

Dale, R. (1997, November 25). A psychoanalyst's view of Japan's ills. *International Herald Tribune,* 13.

Damasio, A. R. (1985). Disorders of complex visual processing: Agnosias, achromatopsia, Balint's syndrome, and related difficulties of orientation and construction. In M.-M. Mesulam (Ed.), *Principles of behavioral neurology* (pp. 259–288). Philadelphia: Davis.

Damasio, A. R. (1994). *Descartes' error: Emotion, reason, and the human brain.* New York: Grosset/Putnam.

Damasio, A. R. (1996). The somatic marker hypothesis and the possible functions of the prefrontal cortex. *Philosophical Transactions of the Royal Society London Series B, 351,* 1413–1420.

Damasio, A. R. (1999). *The feeling of what happens: Body and emotion in the making of consciousness.* New York: Harcourt Brace.

Damasio, H., Grabowski, T. J., Tranel, D., Hichwa, R. D., & Damasio, A. R. (1996). A neural basis for lexical retrieval. *Nature, 380,* 499–505.

Dannon, P. N., Dolberg, O. T., Schreiber, S., & Grunhaus, L. (2002). Three and six-month outcome following courses of either ECT or rTMS in a population of severely depressed individuals—Preliminary report. *Biological Psychiatry, 51,* 687–690.

Dar, Y., & Kimhi, S. (2001). Military service and self-perceived maturation among Israeli youth. *Journal of Youth & Adolescence, 30,* 427–448.

Darley, J. M., & Gross, P. H. (1983). A hypothesis-confirming bias in labeling effects. *Journal of Personality & Social Psychology, 44,* 20–33.

Darley, J. M., & Latané, B. (1968). Bystander intervention in emergencies: Diffusion of responsibility. *Journal of Personality and Social Psychology, 10,* 202–214.

Darley, J. M., & Latané, B. (1970). Norms and normative behavior: Field studies of social interdependence. In J. Macauley and L. Berkowitz (Eds.), *Altruism and helping behavior.* (pp. 83–101). New York: Academic Press.

Darwin, C. (1872). *The expression of the emotions in man and animals.* Chicago: University of Chicago Press, 1965.

Das, A., & Gilbert, C. D. (1995). Long-range horizontal connections and their role in cortical reorganization revealed by optical recording of cat primary visual cortex. *Nature, 375,* 780–784.

Dasgupta, N., & Greenwald, A., (2001) On the malleability of automatic attitudes: Combating automatic prejudice with images of admired and disliked individuals. *Journal of Personality & Social Psychology, 81,* 800–814.

Dauncey, K., Giggs, J., Baker, K., & Harrison, K. (1993). Schizophrenia in Nottingham: Lifelong residential mobility of a cohort. *British Journal of Psychiatry, 163,* 613–619.

Davey, G. C. L. (1992). Classical conditoiting and the acquisition of human fears and phobias: A review of synthesis of the literature. *Advances in Behavior Research and Therapy, 14,* 29–66.

David, J. P., & Suls, J. (1999). Coping efforts in daily life: Role of Big Five traits and problem appraisals. *Journal of Personality, 67,* 265–294.

Davidson, R. J. (1992a). Emotion and affective style: Hemispheric substrates. *Psychological Science, 3,* 39–43.

Davidson, R. J. (1992b). A prolegomenon to the structure of emotion: Gleanings from neuropsychology. *Cognition and Emotion, 6,* 245–268.

Davidson, R. J. (1993). Parsing affective space: Perspectives from neuropsychology and psychophysiology. *Neuropsychology, 7,* 464–475.

Davidson, R. J. (1994a). Honoring biology in the study of affective style. In P. Ekman & R. J. Davidson (Eds.), *The nature of emotion: Fundamental questions* (pp. 321–328). New York: Oxford University Press.

Davidson, R. J. (1994b). The role of prefrontal activation in the inhibition of negative affect. *Psychophysiology, 31,* S7.

Davidson, R. J. (1998). Affective style and affective disorders: Perspectives from affective neuroscience. *Cognition and Emotion, 12,* 307–330.

Davidson, R. J. (2001). Toward a biology of personality and emotion. *Annals of the New York Academy of Sciences, 935,* 191–207.

Davidson, R. J. (2002). Anxiety and affective style: Role of prefrontal cortex and amygdala. *Biological Psychiatry, 51,* 68–80.

Davidson, R. J., Abercrombie, H., Nitschke, J. B., & Putnam, K. (1999). Regional brain function, emotion and disorders of emotion. *Current Opinion in Neurobiology, 9,* 228–234.

Davidson, R. J., Jackson, D. C., & Kalin, N. H. (2000a). Emotion, plasticity, context, and regulation: Perspectives from affective neuroscience. *Psychological Bulletin, 126,* 890–909.

Davidson, R. J., Pizzagalli, D., Nitschke, J. B., & Putnam, K. M. (2002). Depression: Perspectives from affective neuroscience. *Annual Review of Psychology, 53,* 545–574.

Davidson, R. J., Putnam, K. M., & Larson, C. L. (2000b). Dysfunction in the neural circuitry of emotion regulation—A possible prelude to violence. *Science, 289,* 591–594.

Davies, K. A. (1997). Voluntary exposure to pornography and men's attitudes toward feminism and rape. *Journal of Sex Research, 34,* 131–137.

Davis, B. E., Moon, R. Y., Sachs, H. C., & Ottolini, M. C. (1998). Effects of sleep position on infant motor development. *Pediatrics, 102,* 1135–1140.

Davis, C. G., Wortman, C. B., Lehman, D. R., & Silver, R. C. (2000). Searching for meaning in loss: Are clinical assumptions correct? *Death Studies, 24,* 497–540.

Davis, G. A. (1973). *Psychology of problem solving. Theory and practice.* New York: Basic Books.

Davis, J. D., & Campbell, C. S. (1973). Peripheral control of meal size in the rat: Effects of sham feeding on meal size and drinking rate. *Journal of Comparative & Physiological Psychology, 83,* 379–387.

Davis, J. D., & Levine, M. W. (1977). A model for the control of ingestion. *Psychological Review, 84,* 379–412.

Davis, J. O., Phelps, J. A., & Bracha, H. S. (1995). Prenatal development of monozygotic twins and concordance for schizophrenia. *Schizophrenia Bulletin, 21,* 357–366.

Davis, K. D., Kiss, Z. H., Luo, L., Tasker, R. R., Lozano, A. M., & Dostrovsky, J. O. (1998). Phantom sensations generated by thalamic microstimulation. *Nature, 391,* 385–387.

Davis, M. (1992). The role of the amygdala in conditioned fear. In J. P. Aggleton (Ed.), *The amygdala: Neurobiological aspects of emotion, memory, and mental dysfunction* (pp. 255– 306). New York: Wiley-Liss.

Davis, M., & Whalen, P. J. (2001). The amygdala: Vigilance and emotion. *Molecular Psychiatry, 6,* 13–34.

Davis, M. C., Matthews, K. A., McGrath, C. E. (2000). Hostile attitudes predict elevated vascular resistance during interpersonal stress in men and women. *Psychosomatic Medicine, 62,* 17–25.

Davis, M. S. (1973). *Intimate relations.* New York: Free Press.

Dean, H. J., McTaggart, T. L., Fish, D. G., & Friesen, H. G. (1986). Long-term social follow-up of growth hormone deficient adults treated with growth hormone during childhood. In B. Stabler & L. E. Underwood (Eds.), *Slow grows the child: Psychosocial aspects of growth delay.* (pp. 73–82). Hillsdale, NJ: Erlbaum.

Dean, W., Morgenthaler, J., & Fowkes, S. W. (1993). *Smart drugs: II. The next generation: New drugs and nutrients to improve your memory and increase your intelligence (Smart Drug Series, Vol. 2).* Petaluma, CA: Smart Publications.

Deary, I. J. (1995). Auditory inspection time and intelligence: What is the direction of causation? *Developmental Psychology, 31,* 237–250.

Deary, I. J., & Pagliari, C. (1991). The strength of g at different levels of ability: Have Detterman & Daniel rediscovered Spearman's "law of diminishing returns"? *Intelligence 15,* 247–250.

DeCasper, A. J., & Fifer, W. P., (1980) On human bonding: Newborns prefer their mothers' voices. *Science, 208,* 1174–1176.

DeCasper, A. J., & Spence, M. J. (1986). Prenatal maternal speech influences newborns' perception of speech sounds. *Infant Behavior and Development, 9,* 133–150.

De Castro, J. M. (1990). Social facilitation of duration and size but not rate of the spontaneous meal intake of humans. *Physiology & Behavior, 47,* 1129–1135.

Decety, J. (2001). Is there such a thing as functional equivalence between imagined, observed, and executed actions? In A. N. Meltzoff and W. Prinz (Eds.), *The imitative mind: Development, evolution, and brain bases.* Cambridge, UK: Cambridge University Press.

Decety, J., Chaminade, T., Grèzes, J., & Meltzoff, A. N. (2002). A PET exploration of the neural mechanisms involved in reciprocal imitation. *NeuroImage, 15,* 265–272.

Deci, E. L., Koestner, R., & Ryan, R. M. (1999). The undermining effect is a reality after all—Extrinsic rewards, task interest, and self-determination: Reply to Eisenberger, Pierce, and Cameron (1999) and Lepper, Henderlong, and Gingras (1999). *Psychological Bulletin, 125,* 692–700.

Deese, J. (1959). On the prediction of occurrence of particular verbal intrusions in immediate recall. *Journal of Experimental Psychology, 58,* 17–22.

Deffenbacher, J. L., Oetting, E. R., Huff, M. E., Cornell, G. R., & Dalleger, C. J. (1996). Evaluation of two cognitive-behavioral approaches to general anger reduction. *Cognitive Therapy & Research, 20,* 551–573.

DeFries, J. C., Fulker, D. W., & LaBuda, M. C. (1987). Evidence for a genetic aetiology in reading disability of twins. *Nature, 329,* 537–539.

DeFries, J. C., Vogler, G. P., & LaBuda, M. C. (1986). Colorado Family Reading Study: An overview. In J. L. Fuller & E. C. Simmel (Eds.), *Perspectives in behavior genetics* (pp. 29–56). Hillsdale, NJ: Erlbaum.

Degarrod, L. N. (1990). Coping with stress: Dream interpretation in the Mapuche family. *Psychiatric Journal of the University of Ottawa, 15,* 111–116.

DeGroot, A. D. (1965). *Thought and choice in chess.* The Hague: Mouton.

DeGroot, A. D. (1966). Perception and memory versus thought. In B. Kleinmuntz (Ed.), *Problem solving* (pp. 19–50). New York: Wiley.

Dehaene, S. (1997). *The number sense: How the mind creates mathematics.* New York: Oxford.

Dehaene, S., Spelke, E., Pinel, P., Stanescu, R., & Tsivkin, S. (1999). Sources of mathematical thinking: Behavioral and brain-imaging evidence. *Science, 284,* 970–974.

Dehaene-Lambertz, G., & Dehaene, S. (1994). Speed and cerebral correlates of syllable discrimination in infants. *Nature, 370,* 292–295.

Dehaene-Lambertz, G., & Pena, M. (2001). Electrophysiological evidence for automatic phonetic processing in neonates. *Neuroreport, 12,* 3155–3158.

De Houwer, J., Thomas, S., & Baeyens, F. (2001). Associative learning of likes and dislikes: A review of 25 years of research on human evaluative conditioning. *Psychological Bulletin, 127,* 853–869.

Deiber, M. P., Passingham, R. E., Colebatch, J. G., Friston, K. J., Nixon, P. D., & Frackowiak, R. S. J. (1991). Cortical areas and the selection of movement: A study with positron emission tomography. *Experimental Brain Research, 84,* 393–402.

Delany, S. L., Delany, A. E., & Hearth, A. H. (1993). *Having Our Say: The Delany Sisters' First 100 Years.* New York: Delta.

Delbridge, M. L., & Graves, J. A. M. (1999). Mammalian Y chromosome evolution and the male-specific functions of Y chromosome-borne genes *Reviews of Reproduction, 4,* 101–109.

Delis, D. C., Robertson, L. C., & Efron, R. (1986). Hemispheric specialization of memory for visual hierarchical stimuli. *Neuropsychologia, 24,* 205–214.

DeLisi, L. E. (1999). Structural brain changes in schizophrenia. *Archives of General Psychiatry, 56,* 195.

Delk, J. L., & Fillenbaum, S., (1965). Difference in perceived color as a function of characteristic color. *American Journal of Psychology, 78,* 290–293.

Dell, G. S. (1990). Effects of frequency and vocabulary type on phonological speech errors. *Language & Cognitive Processes, 3,* 17–22.

Dell, G. S., Burger, L. K., & Svec, W. R. (1997). Language production and serial order: A functional analysis and a model. *Psychological Review, 104,* 123–147.

Dell, P. F. (1998). Axis II pathology in outpatients with dissociative identity disorder. *Journal of Nervous & Mental Disease, 186,* 352–356.

DeLoache, J. S., Pierroutsakos, S. L., Uttal, D. H., Rosengren, K. S., & Gottlieb, A. (1998). Grasping the nature of pictures. *Psychological Science, 9,* 205–210.

DeLongis, A., Coyne, J. C., Dakof, G., Folkman, S., & Lazrus, R. S. (1982). Relationship of daily hassles, uplifts, and major life events to health status. *Health Psychology, 1,* 119–136.

DeMann, Jeffrey A. (1994). First person account: The evolution of a person with schizophrenia. *Schizophrenia Bulletin, 20,* 579–582.

Demarais, A. M., & Cohen, B. H. (1998). Evidence for image–scanning eye movement during transitive inference. *Biological Psychology, 49,* 229–247.

De Marchi, N., & Mennella, A. (2000). Huntington's disease and its association with psychopathology. *Harvard Review of Psychiatry, 7,* 278–89.

Demare, D., Briere, J., & Lips, H. M. (1988). Violent pornography and self-reported likelihood of sexual aggression. *Journal of Research in Personality, 22,* 140–153.

Demare, D., Lips, H. M., & Briere, J. (1993). Sexually violent pornography, anti-women attitudes, and sexual aggression: A structural equation model. *Journal of Research in Personality, 27,* 285–300.

Dement, W. C. (1974). *Some must watch while some must sleep.* San Francisco, CA: W. H. Freeman.

Demetriou, A., Christou, C., Spanoudis, G., & Platsidou, M. (2002). The development of mental processing: Efficiency, working memory, and thinking. *Monographs of the Society for Research in Child Development, 67,* vii-154.

de Muinck Keizer-Schrama, S. M. P. F., & Mul, D. (2001) Trends in pubertal development in Europe. *Human Reproduction Update, 7,* 287–291.

DeNeve, K. M., & Cooper, H. (1998). The happy personality: A meta-analysis of 137 personality traits and subjective well-being. *Psychological Bulletin, 124,* 197–229.

Denis, M., & Kosslyn, S. M. (1999). Scanning visual images: A window on the mind. *Current Psychology of Cognition, 18,* 409–465.

Dennehy, E. B., Bulow, P., Wong, F. Y., Smith, S. M., & Aronoff, J. B. (1991). *A test of cognitive fixation in brainstorming groups.* Unpublished manuscript. Department of Psychology, Texas A&M University, College Station, TX.

Dennett, D. C. (1991). *Consciousness explained.* Boston: Little, Brown & Co.

Dennis, W. (1966). Goodenough scores, art experience, and modernization. *Journal of Social Psychology, 68,* 211–228.

Dennis, W. (1973). *Children of the creche.* New York: Appleton-Century-Crofts.

Department of Health and Human Services: Substance Abuse and Mental Health Services Administration. Preliminary Results from the 1997 National Household Survey on Drug Abuse. Rockville: SAHMSA, 1998.

DePaulo, B. M., Charlton, K., Cooper, H., Lindsay, J. J., & Muhlenbruck, L. (1997). The accuracy-confidence correlation in the detection of deception. *Personality & Social Psychology Review, 1,* 346–357.

DePaulo, B. M., Lindsay, J. J., Malone, B. E., Muhlenbruck, L., Charlton, K., and Cooper, H. (2003). Cues ot deception. *Psychological Bulletin, 129,* 74–118.

DeQuardo, R. (1998). Pharmacologic treatment of first-episode schizophrenia: Early intervention is key to outcome. *Journal of Clinical Psychiatry, 59,* 9–17.

De Renzi, E. (1982). *Disorders of space exploration and cognition.* New York: Wiley.

De Renzi, E., Liotti, M., & Nichelli, P. (1987). Semantic amnesia with preservation of autobiographic memory. A case report. *Cortex, 23,* 575–597.

Derogatis, L. R., Lipman, R. S., Rickels, K., Uhlenhuth, E. H., & Covi, L. (1974). The Hopkins Symptom Checklist (HSCL): A self-report symptom inventory. *Behavioral Science, 19,* 1–15.

Desimone, R., Albright, T. D., Gross, C. G., & Bruce, C. (1984). Stimulus-selective properties of inferior temporal neurons in the macaque. *Journal of Neuroscience, 8,* 2051–2062.

D'Esposito, M., Detre, J. A., Alsop, D. C., Shin, R. K., Atlas, S., & Grossman, M. (1995). The neural basis of the central executive system of working memory. *Nature, 378,* 279–281.

DeSteno, D. A., & Salovey, P. (1996). Evolutionary origins of sex differences in jealousy? Questioning the "fitness" of the model. *Psychological Science, 7,* 367–372.

Detterman, D. K., & Daniel, M. H. (1989). Correlates of mental tests with each other and with cognitive variables are highest for low IQ groups. *Intelligence, 13,* 349–359.

Deutsch, J. A., Young, W. G., & Kalogeris, T. J. (1978). The stomach signals satiety. *Science, 201,* 165–167.

De Valois, R. L., & De Valois, K. K. (1975). Neural coding of color. In E. C. Carterette & M. P. Friedman (Eds.), *Handbook of perception* (pp. 117–166). New York: Academic Press.

De Valois, R. L., & De Valois, K. K. (1988). *Spatial vision.* New York: Oxford University Press.

De Valois, R. L., & De Valois, K. K. (1993). A multi-stage color model. *Vision Research, 33,* 1053–1065.

DeVane, C. L. (2001). Substance P: A new era, a new role. *Pharmacotherapy, 21,* 1061–1069.

de Villiers, P. A., & de Villiers, J. G. (1992). Language development. In M. H. Bornstein & M. E. Lamb (Eds.), *Developmental psychology: An advanced textbook* (3rd ed., pp. 337–418). Hillsdale, NJ: Erlbaum.

Devine, P. G., & Elliot, A. J. (1995). Are racial stereotypes really fading? The Princeton trilogy revisited. *Personality & Social Psychology Bulletin, 21,* 1139–1150.

Devine, P. G., & Monteith, M. J. (1993). The role of discrepancy-associated affect in prejudice reduction. In D. M. Mackie & D. L. Hamilton (Eds.), et al. *Affect, cognition, and stereotyping: Interactive processes in group perception* (pp. 317–344). San Diego, CA: Academic Press.

Devine, P. G., Plant, E. A., Amodio, D. M., Harmon-Jones, E., & Vance, S. L. (2002). The regulation of explicit and implicit race bias: The role of motivations to respond without prejudice. *Journal of Personality & Social Psychology, 82,* 835–848.

Devlin, B., Daniels, M., & Roeder, K. (1997). The heritability of IQ. *Nature, 388,* 468–471.

Devlin, J. T., Matthews, P. M., & Rushworth, M. F. S. (2003). Semantic processing in the left inferior prefrontal cortex: A combined functional magnetic resonance imaging and transcranial magnetic stimulation study. *Journal of Cognitive Neuroscience, 15,* 71–84.

de Vries, B., Davis, C. G., Wortman, C. B., & Lehman, D. R. (1997). Long-term psychological and somatic consequences of later life parental bereavement. *Omega: Journal of Death & Dying, 35,* 97–117.

deVries, M. W. (1984). Temperament and infant mortality among the Masai of East Africa. *American Journal of Psychiatry, 141,* 1189–1194.

De Wijk, R. A., & Cain, W. S. (1994). Odor identification by name and by edibility: Life-span development and safety. *Human Factors, 36,* 182–187.

De Wijk, R. A., Schab, F. R., & Cain, W. S. (1995). Odor identification. In F. R. Schab & R. G. Crowder (Eds.), *Memory for odors* (pp. 21–37). Mahwah, NJ: Erlbaum.

Dew, A. M., & Ward, C. (1993). The effects of ethnicity and culturally congruent and incongruent nonverbal behaviors on interpersonal attraction. *Journal of Applied Social Psychology, 23,* 1376–1389.

Dewhurst, S. A., & Conway, M. A. (1994). Pictures, images, and recollective experience. *Journal of Experimental Psychology: Learning, Memory, and Cognition, 20,* 1088–1098.

DeZazzo, J., & Tully, T. (1995). Dissection of memory formation: From behavioral pharmacology to molecular genetics. *Trends in Neuroscience, 18,* 212–218.

Diamond, L. M., & Dube, E. M. (2002). Friendship and attachment among heterosexual and sexual-minority youths: Does the gender of your friend matter? *Journal of Youth & Adolescence, 31,* 155–166.

Diamond, M. (1997). Sexual identity and sexual orientation in children with traumatized or ambiguous genetalia. *Journal of Sex Research, 34,* 199–211.

Diamond, M., & Sigmundson H. K. (1997). Sex reassignment at birth. Long-term review and clinical implications. *Archives of Pediatrics & Adolescent Medicine, 151,* 298–304.

Diamond, M. C., Rosenzweig, M. R., Bennett, E. L., Lindner, B., & Lyon, L. (1972). Effects of environmental enrichment and impoverishment on rat cerebral cortex. *Journal of Neural Biology, 3,* 47–64.

Diaz-Guerrero, R., & Diaz-Loving, R. (2000). Needs and values in three cultures: Controversy and a dilemma. *Interdisciplinaria, 17,* 137–151.

DiBlasio, F. A., & Benda, B. B. (1990). Adolescent sexual behavior: Multivariate analysis of a social learning model. *Journal of Adolescent Research, 5,* 449–466.

Dick, F., Bates, E., Wulfeck, B., Utman, J. A., Dronkers, N., and Gernsbacher, M. A. (2001). Language deficits, localization, and grammar: Evidence for a distributive model of language breakdown in aphasic patients and neurologically intact individuals. *Psychological Review, 108,* 759–788.

Dickens, W. T., & Flynn, J. R. (2001). Heritability estimates versus large environmental effects: The IQ paradox resolved. *Psychological Review, 108,* 346–369.

Dickinson, A., & Dawson, G. R. (1987). Pavlovian processes in the motivational control of instrumental performance. *Quarterly Journal of Experimental Psychology: Comparative & Physiological Psychology, 39(3, Section B),* 201–213.

Diehl, M., & Stroebe, W. (1987). Productivity loss in brainstorming groups: Toward the solution of a riddle. *Journal of Personality & Social Psychology, 53,* 497–509.

Diener, E. (1977).Deindividualtion: Causes and consequences. *Social Behavior and Personality, 5,* 143–155.

Diener, E. (2000). Subjective well-being: The science of happiness and a proposal for a national index. *American Psychologist, 55,* 34–43.

Diener, E., and Emmons, R. A. (1984). The independence of positive and negative affect. *Journal of Personality and Social Psychology, 47,* 1105–1117.

Dienstfrey, H. (1991). *Where the mind meets the body.* New York: HarperCollins.

DiGiuseppe, R., & Tafrate, R. C. (2003). Anger treatment for adults: A meta-analytic review. *Clinical Psychology: Science and Practice, 10,* 70–84.

Digman, J. M. (1990). Personality structure: Emergence of the five-factor model. *Annual Review of Psychology, 41,* 417–440.

DiLalla, L. F., Kagan, J., Reznick, J. S. (1994). Genetic etiology of behavioral inhibition among 2-year-old children. *Infant Behavior & Development, 17,* 405–412.

Dill, P. L., & Henley, T. B. (1998). Stressors of college: A comparison of traditional and nontraditional students. *Journal of Psychology, 132,* 25–32.

Dillbeck, M. C., & Orme-Johnson, D. W. (1987). Physiological differences between transcendental meditation and rest. *American Psychologist,* 879–881.

Dille, B., & Mezack, M. (1991). Identifying predictors of high risk among community college telecourse students. *The American Journal of Distance Education, 5,* 24–35.

Dimberg, U., & Thunberg, M. (1998). Rapid facial reactions to emotion facial expressions. *Scandinavian Journal of Psychology, 39,* 39–46.

Dinges, D., Pack, F., Williams, K., Gillen, K., Powell, J., Ott, G., Aptowicz, C., & Pack, A. (1997). Cumulative sleepiness, mood disturbance, and psychomotor vigilance performance decrements during a week of sleep restricted to 4–5 hours per night. *Sleep, 20,* 267–277.

Dion, K., Berscheid, E., & Walster, E. (1972). What is beautiful is good. *Journal of Personality & Social Psychology, 24,* 285–290.

DiPietro, J. A., Hodgson, D. M., Costigan, K. A., Hilton, S. C., & Johnson, T. R. B. (1996). Fetal neurobehavioral development. *Child Development, 67,* 2553–2567.

Ditto, P. H., & Lopez, D. A. (1993). Motivated skepticism: use of differential decision criteria for preferred and nonpreferred conclusions. *Journal Personality and Social Psychology, 63,* 568–584.

Dittrich, W. H., Troscianko, T., Lea, S., & Morgan, D. (1996). Perception of emotion from dynamic point-light displays represented in dance. *Perception, 25,* 727–738.

Dobbins, A. C., Joe, R. M., Fiser, J., & Allman, J. M. (1998). Distance modulation of neural activity in the visual cortex. *Science, 281,* 552–555.

Dobkin, P. L., Tremblay, R. E., Másse, L. C., & Vitaro, F. (1995). Individual and peer characteristics in predicting boys' early onset of substance abuse: A seven-year longitudinal study. *Child Development, 66,* 1198–1214.

Dobson, M., & Markham, R. (1993). Imagery ability and source monitoring: Implications for eyewitness memory. *British Journal of Psychology, 32,* 111–118.

Dobson, R. (2002, 11 May). Broadcast of star's colonoscopy puts up screening by 20%. *British Medical Journal, 324,* 1118.

Docter, R. F., & Prince, V. (1997). Transvestism: A survey of 1032 cross-dressers. *Archives of Sexual Behavior, 26,* 589–605.

Dodge, K. A., & Newman, J. P. (1981). Biased decision-making processes in aggressive boys. *Journal of Abnormal Psychology, 90.*

Doheny, M. (1993). Effects of mental practice on performance of a psychomotor skill. *Journal of Mental Imagery, 17*(3–4), 111–118.

Dohnanyiova, M., Ostatnikova, D., & Laznibatova, J. (2000). Physical development of intellectually gifted children. *Homeostasis in Health & Disease, 40,* 123–125.

Dohnanyiova, M., Ostatnikova, D., & Laznibatova, J. (2001). Spatial imagery, testosterone and anthropometric characteristics in intellectually gifted and control children. *Homeostasis in Health & Disease, 41,* 53–55.

Dohrenwend, B. P., Levav, I., Shrout, P. E., Schwartz, S., Naveh, G., Link. B. G., Skodol, A. E., & Stueve, A. (1992). Socioeconomic status and psychiatric disorders: The causation-selection issue. *Science, 255,* 946–952.

Dohrmann, R. J., & Laskin, D. M. (1978). An evaluation of electromyographic biofeedback in the treatment of myofascial pain-dysfunction syndrome. *J Am Dent Assoc, 96,* 656–62.

Dolan, B. (1991). Cross-cultural aspects of anorexia nervosa and bulimia: A review. *International Journal of Eating Disorders, 10,* 67–79.

Dolan, R. J., & Fletcher, P. C. (1997). Dissociating prefrontal and hippocampal function in episodic memory encoding. *Nature, 388,* 582–585.

Dolinski, D., & Nawrat, R. (1998). "Fear-then-relief" procedure for producing compliance: Beware when the danger is over. *Journal of Experimental Social Psychology, 34,* 27–50.

Domar, A. D., Noe, J. M., & Benson, H. (1987). The preoperative use of the relaxation response with ambulatory surgery patients. *Journal of Human Stress, 13,* 101–107.

Domjan, M. (1992). Adult learning and mate choice: Possibilities and experimental evidence. *American Zoologist, 32,* 48–61.

Donaldson, S. O. (1995). Peer influence on adolescent drug use: A persepctive rom the trench of experimental evaualtion research. *American Psychologist, 50,* 801–802.

Doty, R. L., Bartoshuk, L. M., & Snow, J. B., Jr. (1991). Causes of olfactory and gustatory disorders. In T. V. Getchell, R. L. Doty, L. M. Bartoshuk, & J. B. Snow, Jr. (Eds.), *Smell and taste in health and disease* (pp. 449–462). New York: Raven.

Doty, R. L., Shaman, P., Applebaum, M. S. L., Gilberson, R., Siksorski, L., & Rosenberg, L. (1984). Smell identification ability: Changes with age. *Science, 226,* 1441–1443.

Double, D. (2002). The limits of psychiatry. *British Medical Journal, 324,* 900–904.

Dovidio, J. F., Brigham, J. C., Johnson, B. T., & Gaertner, S. L. (1996). Sterepyting, prejudice, and discrimination: Another look. In N. Macrae, C. Stangor, & M. Hewston (Eds.), *Stereotypes and stereotyping* (pp. 276–319). New York: Guilford.

Dovidio, J. F., Evans, N., & Tyler, R. B. (1986). Racial stereotypes: The contents of their cognitive representations. *Journal of Experimental Social Psychology, 22,* 22–37.

Dowdall, G. W., Crawford, M., & Wechsler, H. (1998). Binge drinking among American college women: A comparison of single-sex and coeducational institutions. *Psychology of Women Quarterly, 22,* 705–715.

Dowling, J. E. (1992). *Neurons and networks: An introduction to neuroscience.* Cambridge, MA: Harvard University Press.

Downing, J. W., Judd, C. M., & Brauer, M. (1992). Effects of repeated expressions on attitude extremity. *Journal of Personality and Social Psychology, 63,* 17–29.

Draycott, S. G., & Kline, P. (1995). The Big Three or the Big Five—the EPQ—R vs the NEO-PI: A research note, replication and elaboration. *Personality & Individual Differences, 18,* 801–804.

Drayna, D., Manichaikul, A., de Lange, M., Snieder, H., & Spector, T. (2001). Genetic correlates of musical pitch recognition in humans. *Science, 291,* 1969–1972.

Dreary, I. J. (1995). Auditory inspection time and intelligence: What is the direction of causation? *Developmental Psychology, 31,* 237–250.

Drevets, W. C., Price, J. L., Simpson, J. R., Jr., Todd, R. D., Reich, T., Vannier, M., & Raichle, M. E. (1997). Subgenual prefrontal cortex abnormalities in mood disorders. *Nature 386,* 824–827.

Driskell, J., Copper, C., & Moran, A. (1994). Does mental practice enhance performance? *Journal of Applied Psychology, 79*(4), 481–492.

Druckman, D. & Bjork, R. A. (1994). *Learning, remembering, believing: Enhancing human performance;* Washington, D.C.: National Academy Press.

Druckman, D., & Swets, J. A. (Eds.). (1988). *Enhancing human performance: Issues, theories, and techniques.* Washington, D.C.: National Academy Press.

Druckman, J. N. (2001). Evaluating framing effects. *Journal of Economic Psychology, 22,* 91–101.

Drummond, S. P. A., Brown, G. G., Gillin, J. C., Stricker, J. L., Wong, E. C., & Buxton, R. B. (2000). *Nature, 403,* 655–657.

Druss, B. G., Schlesinger, M., & Allen, H. M. Jr. (2001). Depressive symptoms, satisfaction with health care, and 2-year work outcomes in an employed population. *American Journal of Psychiatry, 158,* 731–734.

Dubrovsky, V. J., Kiesler, S., & Sethna, B. N. (1991). The equalization phenomenon: stauts effoects in computer-mediated and face-to-face decision-making groups. *Hum.-Comput. Interact., 6,* 119–146.

Duclaux, R., Feisthauer, J., & Cabanac, M. (1973). The effects of eating on the pleasantness of food and nonfood odors in man. *Physiology & Behavior, 10,* 1029–1033.

Duclos, S. E., Laird, J. D., Schneider, E., Sexter, M., Stern, L., & Van Lighten, O. (1989). Emotion-specific effects of facial expressions and postures on emotional experience. *Journal of Personality and Social Psychology, 57,* 100–108.

Dudai, Y. (1996). Consolidation: Fragility on the road to the engram. *Neuron, 17,* 367–370.

Duman, R. S., Heninger, G. R., & Nestler, E. J. (1997). A molecular and cellular theory of depression. *Archives of General Psychiatry, 54,* 597–606.

Duncan, H. F., Gourlay, N., & Hudson, W. (1973). *A study of pictorial perception among Bantu and White primary school children in South Africa.* Johannesburg, South Africa: Witwatersrand University Press.

Duncan, J. (1995). Attention, intelligence, and the frontal lobes. In M. S. Gazzaniga (Ed.), *The cognitive neurosciences.* (pp. 721–733). Cambridge, MA: MIT Press.

Duncan, J., Burgess, P., & Emslie, H. (1995). Fluid intelligence after frontal lobe lesions. *Neuropsychologia, 33,* 261–268.

Duncan, J., Emslie, H., Williams, P., Johnson, R., & Freer, C. (1996). Intelligence and the frontal lobe: The organization of goal-directed behavior. *Cognitive Psychology, 30,* 257–303.

Duncan, J., Seitz, R. J., Kolodny, J., Bor, D., Herzog, H., Ahmed, A., Newell, F. N., & Emslie, H. (2000). A neural basis for general intelligence. *Science, 289,* 457–460.

Duncan, R. M., & Pratt, M. W. (1997). Microgenetic change in the quantity and quality of preschoolers' private speech. *International Journal of Behavioral Development, 20,* 367–383.

Duncker, K. (1945). On problem solving. *Psychological monographs, 58* (No. 270).

Dunn, J., & Plomin, R. (1990). *Separate lives: Why siblings are so different* (pp. 63, 74–75). New York: Basic Books.

Dunnett, S. B., Lane, D. M., & Winn, P. (1985). Ibotenic acid lesions of the lateral hypothalamus: comparison with 6-hydroxydopamine-induced sensorimotor deficits. *Neuroscience, 14,* 509–518.

Dupuy, B., & Krashen, S. D. (1993). Incidental vocabulary acquisition in French as a foreign language. *Applied Language Learning, 4,* 55–63.

Dusek, D., & Girdano, D. A. (1980). *Drugs: A factual account.* Reading, MA: Addison Wesley.

Dykens, E. M., & Cassidy, S. B.(1999). Prader-Willi syndrome. In S. Goldstein & C. R. Reynolds (Ed.) *Handbook of neurodevelopmental and genetic disorders in children* (pp. 525–554). New York: Guilford.

Eacott, M. J., & Crawley, R. A. (1999). Childhood amnesia: On answering questions about very early life events. *Memory, 7,* 279–292.

Eagly, A. (1987). *Sex differences in social behavior: A social-role interpretation.* Hillsdale, NJ: Erlbaum.

Eagly, A. H. (1995). The science and politics of comparing women and men. *American Psychologist, 50* 145–158.

Eagly, A. H., & Carli, L. (1981). Sex of researchers and sex-typed communications as determinants of sex differences in influence-ability: A meta-analysis of social influence studies. *Psychological Bulletin, 90,* 1–20.

Eagly, A. H., & Chaiken, S. (1998). Attitude structure and function. In D. T. Gilbert, S. T. Fiske, & G. Lindzey (Eds.), *The handbook of social psychology* (4th ed.). New York: McGraw Hill. 269–322.

Eagly, A. H., & Crowley, M. (1986). Gender and helping: A meta-analytic review of the social psychological literature. *Psychological Bulletin, 100,* 283–308.

Eagly, A. H., & Johnson, B. T. (1990). Gender and leadership style: A meta-analysis. *Psychological Bulletin, 108,* 309–330.

Eagly, A. H., & Steffen, V. J. (1986). Gender and aggressive behavior: A meta-analytic review of the social psycholgical literature. *Psychological Bulletin, 100,* 309–330.

Eagly, A. H., & Wood, W. (1999). The origins of sex differences in human behavior: Evolved dispositions versus social roles. *American Psychologist, 54,* 408–423.

Eagly, A. H., Karau, S. J., & Makhijani, M. G. (1995). Gender and the effectiveness of leaders: A meta-analysis. *Psychological Bulletin, 1,* 125–145.

Eagly, A. H., Makhijani, M. G., & Klonsky, B. G. (1992). Gender and the evaluation of leaders: A meta-analysis. *Psychological Bulletin, 1,* 3–22.

Eakin, E. (2000, January 15). Bigotry as mental illness or just another norm. *New York Times*, p. A21.

Eals, M., & Silverman, I. (1994). The hunter-gatherer theory of spatial sex differences: Proximate factors mediating the female advantage on recall of object arrays. *Ethology and Sociobiology, 15,* 95–105.

Earnest, C., & Angst, J. (1983). *Birth order: Its influence on personality.* Berlin: Springer-Verlag.

Eaves, L. J., Eysenck, H. J., & Martin, N. G. (1989). *Genes, culture and personality: An empirical approach.* London: Academic Press.

Ebbinghaus, H. (1885/1964). *Memory: A contribution to experimental psychology.* New York: Dover.

Eberman, C., & McKelvie, S. J. (2002). Vividness of visual imagery and source memory for audio and text. *Applied Cognitive Psychology, 16,* 87–95

Ebstein, R. P., Benjamin, J., & Belmaker, R. H. (2000). Genetics of personality dimensions. *Current Opinion in Psychiatry, 13,* 617–622.

Ebstein, R. P., Novick, O., Umansky, R., Priel, B., Osher,Y., Blaine, D., Bennett, E. R., Nemanoc, L., Katz, M., & Belmaker, R. H. (1996). Dopamine D4 receptor (D4DR) exon III polymorphism associated with the human personality trait of Novelty Seeking. *Nature Genetics, 12,* 78–80.

The Economist world atlas & almanac (1989). New York: Prentice Hall.

Edelman, G. M., & Tononi, G. (2000). *A universe of consciousness: How matter becomes imagination.* New York: Basic Books.

Eden, D. (1990). Pygmalion without interpersonal contrast effects: Whole groups gain from raising manager expectations. *Journal of Applied Psychology, 75,* 394–398.

Eder, R. A. (1989). The emergent personologist: The structure and content of 3-, 5-, and 7-year-olds' concepts of themselves and other persons. *Child Development, 60,* 1218–1228.

Edgerton, R. B., & Cohen, A. (1994). Culture and schizophrenia: The DOSMD challenge. *British Journal of Psychiatry, 164,* 222–231.

Edwards, E., Kornrich, W., Houtten, P. V., & Henn, F. A. (1992). Presynaptic serotonin mechanisms in rats subjected to inescapable shock. *Neuropharmacology, 31,* 323–330

Effa-Heap, G. (1996). The influence of media pornography on adolescents. *IFE Psychologia: An International Journal, 4,* 80–90

Egbert, L. D., Battit, G. E., Welch, C. E., & Barlett, M. K. (1964). Reduction of postoperative pain by encouragement and instruction of patients. *New England Journal of Medicine, 270,* 825–827.

Ehlers, A., Mayou, R. A., & Bryant, B. (1998). Psychological predictors of chronic posttraumatic stress disorder after motor vehicle accidents. *Journal of Abnormal Psychology, 107,* 508–519.

Eich, E. (1989). Theoretical issues in state dependent memory. In H. L. Roediger, III, & F. I. M. Craik (Eds.), *Varieties of memory and consciousness: Essays in honour of Endel Tulving* (pp. 331–354). Hillsdale, NJ: Erlbaum.

Eich, E. (1995). Searching for mood dependent memory. *Psychological Science, 6,* 67–75.

Eimas, P. D., & Corbit, J. D. (1973). Selective adaptation of linguistic feature detectors. *Cognitive Psychology, 4,* 99–109.

Einstein, A. (1945). A testimonial from Professor Einstein (Appendix II). In J. Hadamard, *An essay on the psychology of invention in the mathematical field* (pp. 142–143). Princeton, NJ: Princeton University Press.

Eisenberg, N., Miller, P. A., Schaller, M., Fabes, R. A., Fultz, J., Shell, R., & Shea, C. L. (1989). The role of sympathy and altruistic personality traits in helping: A reexamination. *Journal of Personality, 57,* 41–67.

Eisenberger, R. (1998). Reward, intrinsic interest, and creativity: New findings. *American Psychologist, 53,* 676–679.

Eisenberger, R., & Cameron, J. (1996). Detrimental effects of reward: Reality or myth? *American Psychologist, 51,* 1153–1166.

Eisenberger, R., Armeli, S., & Pretz, J. (1998). Can the promise of reward increase creativity? *Journal of Personality and Social Psychology, 74,* 704–714.

Ekman, P. (1980). Biological and cultural contributions to body and facial movement in the expression of emotion. In A. O. Rorty (Ed.), *Explaining emotions.* Berkeley, CA: University of California Press.

Ekman, P. (1984). Expression and the nature of emotion. In K. R. Scherer & P. Ekman (Eds.), *Approaches to emotion* (pp. 319–343). Hillsdale, NJ: Erlbaum.

Ekman, P. (1985). *Telling lies: Clues to deceit in the marketplace, marriage, and politics.* New York: Norton.

Ekman, P. (1992). Facial expressions of emotion: New findings, new questions. *Psychological Science, 3,* 34–38.

Ekman, P. (1993). Facial expression and emotion. *American Psychologist, 48,* 384–392.

Ekman, P., & Davidson, R. J. (1993). Voluntary smiling changes regional brain activity. *Psychological Science, 4,* 342–345.

Ekman, P., & Davidson, R. J. (1994). *The nature of emotion: Fundamental questions.* Cambridge, MA: MIT Press.

Ekman, P., and Friesen, W. (1971). Constants across cultures in the face and emotion. *Journal of Personality & Social Psychology, 17,* 124–129.

Ekman, P., & Friesen, W. V. (1975). *Unmasking the face.* Englewood Cliffs, NJ: Prentice-Hall.

Ekman, P., Davidson, R. J., & Friesen, W. V. (1990). The Duchenne smile: Emotional expression and brain psychology II. *Journal of Personality & Social Psychology, 58,* 342–353.

Ekman, P., O'Sullivan, M., & Frank, M. G. (1999). A few can catch a liar. *Psychological Science, 10,* 263–266.

El-Islam, M. F. (1991). Transcultural aspects of schizophrenia and ICD-10. *Psychiatria Danubina, 3,* 485–494.

Elber, T., Pantev, C., Wienbruch, C., Rockstroh, B., & Taub, E. (1995). Increased cortical representation of the fingers of the left hand in string players. *Science, 270,* 305–307.

Eley, T. C., Deater-Deckard, K., Fombone, E., Fulker, D. W., & Plomin, R. (1998). An adoption study of depressive symptoms in middle childhood. *Journal of Child Psychology & Psychiatry & Allied Disciplines, 39,* 337–345.

Elfenbein, H. A., & Ambady, N. (2002). On the universality and cultural specificity of emotion recognition: A meta-analysis. *Psychological Bulletin, 128,* 203–235.

Eliez, S., & Reiss, A. L. (2000). Genetics of childhood disorders: XI. Fragile X syndrome. *Journal of the American Academy of Child & Adolescent Psychiatry, 39,* 264–266.

Elkin, I. (1994). The NIMH treatment of depression colarborative research program: Where we began and where we are. In A. E. Bergin & S. L. Garfield (Eds.), *Handbook of psychotherapy and behavior change, 4th edition* (pp. 114–142). New York: John Wiley & Sons.

Elkin, I., Gibbons, R., Shea, M. T., Sotsky, S. M., Watkins, J. T., Pilkonis, P. A., & Hedeker, D. (1995). Initial severity and differential treatment outcome in the National Institute of Mental Health Treatment of Depression Collaborative Research Program., 63 841–847.

Elkind, D. (1967). Egocentrism in adolescence. *Child Development, 38,* 1025–1034.

Elkind, D., & Bowen, R. (1979). Imaginary audience behavior in children and adolescence. *Developmental Psychology, 15,* 33–44.

Elkins, I. J., McGue, M., & Iacono, W. G. (1997). Genetic and environmental influences on parent-son relationships: Evidence for increasing genetic influence during adolescence. *Developmental Psychology, 33,* 351–363.

Elliott, D., Huizinga, D., & Ageton, S. S. (1985). *Multiple problem youth: Delinquency, substance use, and mental health problems.* New York: Springer-Verlag.

Elliot, R., & Dolan, R. J. (1998). Neural resonse during preference and memory judgements for subliminally presented stimuli: a functional neuroimaging study. *Journal of Neuroscience. 18,* 4697–4704.

Ellis, A. (1994a). The treatment of borderline personalities with rational emotive behavioar therapy. *Journal of Rational-Emotive & Cognitive Behavior Therapy, 12,* 101–119.

Ellis, A. (1994b). Rational emotive behavior therapy approaches to obsessive-compulsive disorder (OCD). *Journal of Rational-Emotive & Cognitive Behavior Therapy, 12,* 121–141.

Ellis, A. W., & Young, A. W. (1987). *Human cognitive neuropsychology.* Hillsdale, NJ: Lawrence Erlbaum.

Ellis, G. J., & Peterson, L. R. (1992). Socialization values and parental control techniques: A cross-cultural analysis of child-rearing. *Journal of Comparative Family Studies, 23,* 39–54.

Ellis, H. C. (1973). Stimulus encoding processes in human learning and memory. In G. H. Bower (Ed.), *The psychology of learning and motivation* (Vol. 7, pp. 124–182). New York: Academic Press.

Ellis, H. C., & Hunt, R. R. (1993). *Fundamentals of cognitive psychology* (5th ed.). Dubuque, IA: Brown Communications.

Ellis, L., & Blanchard, R. (2001). Birth order, sibling sex ratio, and maternal miscarriages in homosexual and heterosexual men and women. *Personality & Individual Differences, 30,* 543–552.

Elman, J. L., Bates, E. A., Johnson, M. H., Karmiloff-Smith, A., et al. (1996). *Rethinking innateness: A connectionist perspective on development.* Cambridge: MIT Press.

Emerson, M. O., Kimbro, R. T., & Yancey, G. (2002). Contact theory extended: The effects of prior racial contact on current social ties. *Social Science Quarterly, 83,* 745–761.

Emmelkamp, P. M. G. (1994). Behavior therapy with adults. In A. E. Bergin & S. L. Garfield (Eds.), *Handbook of psychotherapy and behavior change* (4th edition) (pp. 379–427). New York: John Wiley & Sons.

Emmelkamp, P. M. G., Bruynzeel, M., Drost, L., & Van Der Mast, C. A. P. G. (2001). Virtual reality treatment in acrophobia: A comparison with exposure in vivo. *CyberPsychology & Behavior, 4,* 335–339.

Emmelkamp, P. M. G., Krijn, M., Hulsbosch, A. M., de Vries, S., Schuemie, M. J., & van der Mast, C. A. P. G. (2002). Virtual reality treatment versus exposure in vivo: A comparative evaluation in acrophobia. *Behaviour Research & Therapy, 40,* 509–516.

Emmorey, K. (1993). Processing a dynamic visual-spatial language: Psycholinguistic studies of American Sign Language. *Journal of Psycholinguistic Research, 22,* 153–187.

Endicott, J., Spitzer, R. L., Fleiss, J. L., & Cohen, J. (1976). The Global Assessment Scale: A procedure for measuring overall severity of psychiatric disturbance. *Archives of General Psychiatry, 33,* 766–771.

Engel, S. A., Glover, G. H., & Wandell, B. A. (1997). Retinotopic organization in human visual cortex and the spatial precision of functional MRI. *Cerebral Cortex, 7,* 181–192.

Engen, T. (1991). *Odor sensation and memory.* New York: Praeger.

Entwisle, D. R. (1972). To dispel fantasies about fantasy-based measures of achievement motivation. *Psychological Bulletin, 77,* 377–391.

Epps, J., & Kendall, P. C. (1995). Hostile attributional bias in adults. *Cognitive Therapy and Research, 19,* 159–178.

Epstein, C. M., Figiel, G. S., McDonald, W. M., Amazon-Leece, J., & Figiel, L. (1998). Rapid rate transcranial magnetic stimulation in young and middle-aged refractory depressed patients. *Psychiatric Annals, 28,* 36–39.

Epstein, H. T. (1980). EEG developmental stages. *Developmental Psychobiology, 13,* 629–631.

Epstein, W., & Franklin, S. (1965). Some conditions of the effect of relative size on perceived distance. *American Journal of Psychology, 78,* 466–470.

Erdelyi, M. H. (1984). The recovery of unconcious (inaccessible) memories: Laboratory studies of hypermnesia. In G. H. Bower (Ed.), *The psychology of learning and motivation: Advances in research and theory* (Vol. 18, pp. 95–127). New York: Academic Press.

Ericsson, K. A., & Charness, N. (1994). Expert performance. *American Psychologist, 49,* 725–747.

Ericsson, K. A., Krampe, R. Th., & Tesch-Ràmer, C. (1993). The role of deliberate practice in the acquisition of expert performance. *Psychological Review, 100,* 363–406.

Eriksen, C. W., & Murphy, T. D. (1987). Movement of attentional focus across the visual field: A critical look at the evidence. *Perception and Psychophysics, 42,* 299–305.

Eriksen, C. W., & St. James, J. D. (1986). Visual attention within and around the field of focal attention: A zoom lens model. *Perception and Psychophysics, 40,* 225–240.

Eriksen, C. W., & Yeh, Y. (1985). Allocation of attention in the visual field. *Journal of Experimental Psychology: Human Perception and Performance, 11,* 583–597.

Erikson, D. H., Beiser, M., & Iacono, W. G. (1998). Social support predicts 5-year outcome in first-episode schizophrenia. *Journal of Abnormal Psychology, 107,* 681–685.

Erikson, E. H. (1950). *Childhood and society.* New York: Norton.

Ernst, C., & Angst, J. (1983). *Birth order: Its influence on personality.* Berlin: Springer-Verlag.

Eskenazi, B. (1993). Caffeine during pregnancy: Grounds for concern? *Journal of the American Medical Association, 270,* 2973–2974.

Eskenazi, B., Stapleton, A. L., Kharrazi, M., & Chee, W. Y. (1999). Associations between maternal decaffeinated and caffeinated coffee consumption and fetal growth and gestational duration. *Epidemiology, 10,* 242–249.

Esser, J. K. (1998). Alive and well after 25 years: A review of groupthink research. *Organizational Behavior & Human Decision Processes, 73,* 116–141.

Esser, J. K., & Lindoerfer, J. S. (1989). Groupthink and the space shuttle Challenger accident: Toward a quantitative case analysis. *Journal of Behavioral Decision Making, 2,* 167–177.

Esses, V., & Zanna, M. P. (1995). Mood and the expression of ethnic stereotypes. *Journal of Personality & Social Psychology, 69,* 1052–1068.

Esterling, B. A., L'Abate, L., Murray, E. J., & Pennebaker, J. W. (1999). Empirical foundations for writing in prevention and psychotherapy: Mental and phsycial health outcomes. *Clinical Psychology Review, 19,* 79–96.

Estes, W. (1976). The cognitive side of probability learning. *Psychological Review, 83,* 37–64.

Etcoff, N. L., Ekman, P., Magee, J. J., & Frank, M. G. (2000). Lie detection and language comprehension. *Nature, 405,* 139.

Evans, G. W., Bullinger, M., & Hygge, S. (1998). Chronic noise exposure and physiological response: A prospective study of children living under environmental stress. *Psychological Science, 9,* 75–77.

Exner, J. E., Jr. (1986). *The Rorschach: A comprehensive system* (Volume 1, 2nd ed.). New York: Wiley: Interscience.

Eyferth, K. (1961). Ein Vergleich der Beurteilung projektiver Tests durch verschiedene Berteiler [A comparison of judging projective tests by different judges]. *Zeitschrift fuer Experimentelle und Angewandte Psychologie, 8,* 329–338.

Eysenck, H. J. (1967). *The biological basis of personality.* Springfield, IL: Charles C. Thomas, Publishers.

Eysenck, H. J. (1977). *Crime and personality,* St. Albans, England: Paladin Frogmore.

Eysenck, H. J. (1979). The conditioning model of neurosis. *Behavioral and Brain Sciences, 2,* 155–199.

Eysenck, H. J. (1990a). Genetic and environmental contributions to individual differences: The three major dimensions of personality. *Journal of Personality, 58,* 245–261.

Eysenck, H. J. (1990b). Biological dimensions of personality. In L. A. Pervin (Ed.), *Handbook of personality: Theory and research* (pp. 244–276). New York: Guilford.

Eysenck, H. J. (1992). Four ways five factors are *not* basic. *Personality and Individual Differences, 13,* 667–673.

Eysenck, H. J. (1993). The structure of phenotypic personality traits: Comment. *American Psychologist, 48,* 1299–1300.

Eysenck, H. J. (1995). *Genius: The natural history of creativity.* Cambridge, England: Cambridge University Press.

Eysenck, H. J., & Gudjonsson, G. (1989). *The causes and cures of criminality.* New York: Plenum Press.

Eysenck, S. B. G., & Eysenck, H. J. (1967). Salivary response to lemon juice as a measure of introversion. *Perceptional and motor skills, 24,* 1047–1053.

Fabbro, F. (2001). The bilingual brain: Bilingual aphasia. *Brain & Language, 79,* 201–210.

Faber, A., & Mazlish, E. (1987). *Siblings without rivalry.* New York: Norton.

Faber, S. (1981). *Identical twins reared apart.* London: Blackwell.

Fairburn, C. G., Cooper, Z., Doll, H. A., Welch, S. L. (1999). Risk factors for anorexia nervosa: Three integrated case-control comparisons. *Archives of General Psychiatry, 56,* 468–476.

Fairburn, C. G., Doll, H. A., Welch, S. L., Hay, P. J., Davies, B. A., & O'Connor, M. E. (1998). Risk factors for binge eating disorder: A community-based, case-control study. *Archives of General Psychiatry, 55,* 425–432.

Fairburn, C. G., Hay, P. J., & Welch, S. L. (1993). Binge eating and bulimia nervosa: Distribution and determinants. In C. G. Fairburn & G. T. Wilson (Eds.), *Binge eating: Nature, assessment, and treatment* (pp. 123–143). New York: Guilford Press.

Fantino, M., & Cabanac, M. (1980). Body weight regulation with a proportional hoarding response in the rat. *Physiology & Behavior, 24,* 939–942.

Farah, M. J., Soso, M. J., & Dasheiff, R. M. (1992). Visual angle of the mind's eye before and after unilateral occipital lobectomy. *Journal of Experimental Psychology: Human Perception and Performance, 18,* 241–246.

Farde, L., & Gustavsson, E. (1997). D2 dopamine receptors and personality traits *Nature, 385,* 590.

Farhi, P. (1996, February 26). Study finds real harm in TV violence. *Washington Post,* A1.

Farrar, W. T., IV, Van Orden, G. C., & Hamouz, V. (2001). When SOFA primes TOUCH: Interdependence of spelling, sound, and meaning in "semantically mediated" phonological priming. *Memory & Cognition, 29,* 530–539.

Farroni, T., Csibra, G., Simion, F., & Johnson, M. H. (2002). Eye contact detection in humans from birth. *Proceedings of the National Academy of Sciences USA, 99,* 9602–9605.

Farthing, G. (1992) *The psychology of consciousness.* Englewood Cliffs, NJ: Prentice-Hall.

Fast, K., & Fujiwara, E. (2001). Isolated retrograde amnesia. *Neurocase, 7,* 269–272.

Fasko, D., Jr. (2001). An analysis of multiple intelligences theory and its use with the gifted and talented. *Roeper Review, 23,* 126–130.

Fatt, I., & Weissman, B. A. (1992). *Physiology of the eye: An introduction to the vegetative functions* (2nd ed.). Boston: Butterworth-Heinemann.

Fava, G. A. Rafanelli, C., Grandi, S., Conti, S., & Belluardo, P. (1998a). Prevention of recurrent depression with cognitive behavioral therapy: Preliminary findings. *Archives of General Psychiatry, 55,* 816–820.

Fava, G. A., Rafanelli, C., Grandi, S., Canestrari, R., & Morphy, M. A. (1998b). Six-year outcome for cognitive behavioral treatmetn of residual symptoms in major depression. *American Journal of Psychiatry, 155,* 1443–1445.

Fawzy, F. I., Fawzy, M. O. Hyun, C. S., Elashoff, R., et al. (1993). Malignant melanoma: effects of an early structured psychiatric intervention, coping, and affective state on recurrence and survival six years later. *Archives of General Psychiatry, 50,* 681–689.

Fawzy, F. I., Kemeny, M. E., Fawzy, N. W., Elashoff, R., Morton, D., Cousins, N., Fahey, J. L. (1990). A structured psychiatric intervention for cancer patients: II. Changes over time in immunological measures. *Archives of General Psychiatry, 47,* 729–735.

Fay, R. E., Turner, C. F., Klassen, A. D., & Gagnon, J. H. (1989). Prevalence and patterns of same-gender sexual contact among men. *Science, 243,* 338–348.

Fazio, R. H., & Olson, M. A. (2003). Implicit measures in social cognition research: Their meaning and use. *Annual Review of Psychology, 54,* 297–327.

Fazio, R. H., Chen, J., McDonel, E. C., & Sherman, S. J. (1982). Attitude accessibility and the strength of the object-evaluation association. *Journal of Experimental Psychology, 18,* 339–357.

Fazio, R. H., Jackson, J. R., Dunton, B. C., & Williams, C. J. (1995). Variability in automatic activation as an unobstrusive measure of racial attitudes: A bona fide pipeline? *Journal of Personality and Social Psychology, 69,* 1013–1027.

Feather, N. T. (1996). Social comparisons across nations: Variables relating to the subjective evaluation of national achievement and to personal and collective. *Australian Journal of Psychology, 48,* 53–63.

Feingold, A. (1990). Gender differences in effects of physical attractiveness on romantic attraction: A comparison across five research paradigms. *Journal of Personality and Social Psychology, 59,* 981–993.

Feingold, A. (1992). In A. Manstead & M. Hewstone (Eds.). *The Blackwell encyclopedia of social psychology* (p. 313). New York: McGraw-Hill.

Feingold, A. (1994). Gender differences in personality: A meta-analysis. *Psychological Bulletin, 116,* 429–456.

Feldman, D. H., & Goldsmith, L. T. (1991). *Nature's gambit: Child prodigies and the development of human potential.* New York: Teachers College Press.

Feldman, R. S., Coats, E. J., & Spielman, D. A. (1996). Television exposure and children's decoding of nonverbal behavior. *Journal of Applied Social Psychology, 26,* 1718–1733.

Fell, J., Klaver, P., Elger, C. E., & Guillén, F. (2002). Suppression of EEG Gamma activity may cause the attentional blink. *Consciousness and Cognition, 11,* 114–122.

Felleman, D. J., & Van Essen, D. C. (1991). Distributed hierarchical processing in the primate cerebral cortex. *Cerebral Cortex, 1,* 1–47.

Fenton, W., & McGlashan, T. (1991). Natural history of schizophrenia subtypes: I. Longitudinal study of paranoid, hebephrenic, and undifferentiated schizophrenia. *Archives of General Psychiatry, 48,* 969–977.

Ferguson, N. B., & Keesey, R. E. (1975). Effect of a quinine-adulterated diet upon body weight maintenance in male rats with ventromedial hypothalamic lesions. *Journal of Comparative & Physiological Psychology, 89,* 478–488.

Ferketich, A. K., Schwartzbaum, J. A., Frid, D. J., & Moeschberger, M. L. (2000). Depression as an antecedent to heart disease among women and men in the NHANES I study. National Health and Nutrition Examination Survey. *Archives Internal Medicine, 160,* 1261–1268.

Fernald, A., Taeschner, T., Dunn, J., Papousek, M., Boysson-Bardies, B., & Fukui, I. (1989). A cross-language study of prosodic modifications in mothers' and fathers' speech to infants. *Child Development, 64,* 637–656.

Ferveur, J.-F., Stoertkuhl, K. F., Stocker, R. F., & Greenspan, R. J. (1995). Genetic feminization of brain structures and changed sexual orientation in male Drosophila. *Science, 267,* 902–905.

Feske, U., & Chambless, D. L. (1995). Cognitive behavioral versus exposure only treatment for social phobia: A meta-analysis. Behavior Therapy, 26, 695–720.

Festinger, L. (1950). Informed social comjmunicano., Psychological Review, 57, 271–282.

Festinger, L., & Carlsmith, J. M. (1959). Cognitive consequences of forced compliance. Journal of Abnormal and Social Psychology, 58, 203–210.

Ficca, G., Lombardo, P., Rossi, L., & Salzarulo, P. (2000). Morning recall of verbal material depends on prior sleep organization. Behavioural Brain Research, 112, 159–163.

Ficker, J. H. I., Wiest, G. H., Lehnert, G., Meyer, M., & Hahn, E. G. (1999). Are snoring medical students at risk of failing their exams? Sleep, 22, 205–209.

Field, A. E., Camargo, C. A., Jr., Taylor, B., Berkey, C. S., Colditz, G. A. (1999). Relation of peer and media influences to the development of purging behaviors among preadolescent and adolescent girls. Archives of Pediatric Adolescent Medicine, 153, 1184–1189.

Field, T., Schanberg, S., Scarfidi, F., Bauer, C., Vega-Lahr, N., Garcia, R., Nystrom, J., & Kuhn, C. (1986). Tactile/kinesthetic stimulation effects on preterm neonates. Pediatrics, 77, 654–658.

Field, T. M. (1998). Touch therapy effects on development. International Journal of Behavioral Development, 22, 779–797.

Field, T. M., Woodson, R., Greenberg, R., & Cohen, D. (1982). Discrimination and imitation of facial expressions by neonates. Science, 218, 179–181.

Figiel, G. S., Epstein, C., McDonald, W. M., Amazon-Leece, J., Figiel, L., Saldivia, A., & Glover, S. (1998). The use of rapid-rate transcranial magnetic stimulation (rTMS) in refractory depressed patients. Journal of Neuropsychiatry & Clinical Neurosciences, 10, 20–25.

File, S. E., & Bond, J. A. (1979). Impaired performance and sedation after a single dose of lorazepam. Psychopharmacologia, 61: 309–312.).

Finch, A. E., Lambert, M. J., & Brown, G., (2000). Attacking anxiety: A naturalistic study of a multimedia self-help program. Journal of Clinical Psychology, 56, 11–21.

Findley, M. J., & Cooper, H. M. (1983). Locus of control and academic achievement: A literature review. Journal of Personality and Social Psychology, 44, 49–427.

Finke, R. A. (1996). Imagery, creativity, and emergent structure. Consciousness & Cognition, 5, 381–393.

Finke, R. A., & Slayton, K. (1988). Explorations of creative visual synthesis in mental imagery. Memory & Cognition, 16, 252–257.

Finke, R. A., Ward, T. B., & Smith, S. M. (1992). Creative cognition: Theory, research, and applications. Cambridge, MA: MIT Press.

Finkel, D., Pedersen, N. L., McGue, M., & McClearn, G. E. (1995). Heritability of cognitive abilities in adult twins: Comparison of Minnesota and Swedish data. Behavioral Genetics, 25, 421–432.

Finlay, F. O., Jones, R., & Coleman, J. (2002). Is puberty getting earlier? The views of doctors and teachers. Child: Care, Health & Development, 28, 205–209.

Finn, J., & Banach, M. (2000). Victimization online: The down side of seeking services for women on the Internet. CyberPsychology & Behavior, 3, 243–254.

Fiorentine, R. (1999). After drug treatment: Are 12-step programs effective in maintaining abstinence? American Journal of Drug and Alcohol Abuse, 25, 93–116.

Fischer, C., Hatzidimitriou, G., Wlos, J., Katz, J., & Ricaurte, G. (1995). Reorganization of ascending 5-HT axon projections in animals previously exposed to recreational drug 3,4-methelenedioxymetham-phetamine (MDMA, "Ecstasy"). Journal of Neuroscience, 15, 5476–5485.

Fisher, H., Tillfors, M., Furmark, T., & Fredrikson, M. (2001). Dispositional pessimism and amygdala activity: A PET study in healthy volunteers. Neuroreport, 12, 1635–1638.

Fisher, P. J., Turic, D., Williams, N. M., McGuffin, P., Asherson, P., Ball, D., Craig, I., Eley, T., Hill, L., Chorney, K., Chorney, M. J., Benbow, C. P., Lubinski, D., Plomin, R., & Owen, M. J. (1999) DNA pooling identifies QTLs on Chromosome 4 for general cognitive ability in children. Human Molecular Genetics, 8, 915–922.

Fisher, R. P., & Craik, F. I. M. (1977). The interaction between encoding and retrieval operations in cued recall. Journal of Experimental Psychology: Human learning and Perception, 3, 153–171.

Fisher, R. P., & Geiselman, R. E. (1992). Memory enhancing techniques for investigative interviewing: The cognitive interview. Springfield: Charles C. Thomas.

Fisher, R. P., Geiselman, R. E., & Amador, M. (1989). Field test of the cognitive interview: Enhancing the recollection of actual victims and witnesses of crime. Journal of Applied Psychology, 74, 722–727.

Fiske, S. (1998). Stereotyping, prejudice, and discrimination. In D. T. Gilbert, S. T. Fiske, & G. Lindzey (Eds.), The handbook of social psychology (4th ed.). New York: McGraw Hill. 357–411.

Fiske, S. T. (2002). What we know about bias and intergroup conflict, the problem of the century. Current Directions in Psychological Science, 11, 123–128.

Fitton, A., & Heel, R. C. (1990). Clozapine: A review of its pharacological properties and therapeutic use schizophrenia. Drugs, 40, 722–747.

Flavell, J. H. (1999). Cognitive development: Children's knowledge about the mind. Annual Review of Psychology, 50, 21–45.

Fletcher, A. C., Elder, G. H. Jr., & Mekos, D. (2000). Parental influences on adolescent involvement in community activities. Journal of Research on Adolescence, 10, 29–48.

Fleury, C., Neverova, M., Collins, S., Raimbault, S., Champign, O., Levi-Meyrueis, C., Bouillaud, F., Seldin, M. F., Surwit, R. S., Ricquier, D., & Warden, C. H. (1977). Uncoupling protein-2: A novel candidate thermogenic protein linked to obesity and insulin resistance. Nature Genetics, 15, 269–272.

Flexser, A., & Tulving, E. (1978) Retrieved independence in recognition and recall. Psychological Review, 85, 153–171.

Floersch, J., Longhofer, J., & Latta, K. (1997). Writing Amish culture into genes: biological reductionism in a study of manic depression. Culture, Medicine and Psychiatry, 21, 137–159.

Flor, H., Elbert, T., Knecht, S., Weinbrunch, C., Pantev, C., Birbaumer, N., Labig, W., & Taub, E. (1995). Phantom-limb pain as a perceptual correlate of cortical reorganization following arm amputation. Nature, 375, 482–484.

Floyd, R. L., Rimer, B. K., Giovino, G. A., Mullen, P. D., & Sullivan, S. E. (1993). A review of smoking in pregnancy: Effects on pregnancy outcomes and cessation efforts. Annual Review of Public Health, 14, 379–411.

Flynn, J. R. (1980). Race, IQ and Jensen. London: Routledge.

Flynn, J. R. (1984). The mean IQ of Americans: Massive gains 1932 to 1978. Psychological Bulletin, 95, 29–51.

Flynn, J. R. (1991). Asian Americans: Achievement beyond IQ. Hillsdale, NJ: Erlbaum.

Flynn, J. R. (1999a). Massive IQ gains in fourteen nations: What IQ tests really measure. Psychological Bulletin, 101, 171–191.

Flynn, J. R. (1999b). Searching for justice: The discovery of IQ gains over time. American Psychologist, 54, 5–20.

Flynn, J. R. (1999c). IQ trends over time: Intelligence, race and meritocracy. In S. Durlauf, K. A. Arrow & S. Bowles (Eds.), Meritocracy and inequality (pp. 35–60). Princeton, NJ: Princeton University Press.

Flynn, J. R. (in press). IQ trends over time: Intelligence, race and meritocracy. In S. Durlauf, K. Arrow, & S. Bowles (Eds.), Meritocracy and inequality. Princeton, NJ: Princeton University Press.

Foa, E. B., Steketee, G., & Olasov-Rothbaum, B. O. (1989). Behavioral/cognitive conceptualization of post-traumatic stress disorder. Behavior Therapy, 20, 155–176.

Fodor, J. A. (1968). Psychological explanation: An introduction to the philosophy of psychology. New York: Random House.

Fodor, J. A. (1983). The modularity of mind. Cambridge, MA: MIT Press.

Fodor, J. A. (2000). Why we are so good at catching cheaters. Cognition, 75, 29–32.

Fodor, J. A., Bever, T. G., & Garrett, M. F. (1974). The psychology of language: An introduction to psycholinguistics and generative grammar. New York: McGraw-Hill.

Fombonne, E. (1999). The epidemiology of autism: A review. Psychological Medicine, 29, 769–786.

Fones, C. S. L., Manfro, G. G., & Pollack, M. H. (1998). Social phobia: An update. Harvard Review of Psychiatry, 5, 247–259.

Forbes, E. J., & Pekala, R. J. (1993). Psychophysiological effects of several stress management techniques. Psychological Reports, 72, 19–27.

Ford, C. S., & Beach, F. (1951). Patterns of sexual behavior. New York: Harper & Row.

Ford, K., & Norris, A. E. (1997). Effects of interviewer age on reporting of sexual and reproductive behavior of Hispanic and African American youth. Hispanic Journal of Behavioral Sciences, 19, 369–376.

Ford, R. P., Schluter, P. J., Mitchell, E. A., Taylor, B. J., Scragg, R., & Stewart, A. W. (1998). Heavy caffeine intake in pregnancy and sudden infant death syndrome. New Zealand Cot Death Study Group. Archives of Disease in Childhood, 78, 9–13

Foreman, J. (1997, January 1). To drift off, work out: Exercise found to enhance sleep. Boston Globe, A1.

Forest, K. B. (1995). The role of critical life events in predicting world views: Linking two social psychologies. Journal of Social Behavior and Personality, 10, 331–348.

Forgas, J. P. (1998). On being happy and mistaken: Mood effects on the fundamental attribution error. Journal of Personality and Social Psychology, 75, 318–331.

Forgas, J. P., Levinger, G., & Moylan, S. (1994). Feeling good and feeling close: Mood effects on the perception of intimate relationships. Personal Relationships, 2, 165–184.

Forge, K. L., & Phemister, S. (1987). The erfect of prosocial cartoons on preschool children. Child Study Journal, 17, 83–88.

Forgione A. G. (1988). Hypnosis in the treatment of dental fear and phobia. Dental Clinics of North America, 32, 745–761.

Forsyth, D. R., Heiney, M. W., & Wright, S. S. (1998). Biases in appraisals of women leaders. Group Dynamics, 1, 98–103.

Foulke, E. (1991). Braile. In M. A. Heller & W. Schiff (Eds.), The psychology of touch (pp. 219–233). Hillsdale, NJ: Erlbaum.

Fouts, G., & Burggraf, K. (2000). Television situation comedies: Female weight, male negative comments, and audience reactions. Sex Roles, 42, 925–932.

Fouts, R., & Mills, S. (1997). Next of kin. New York: William Morrow.

Fowles, D. C., & Kochanska, G. (2000). Temperament as a moderator of pathways to conscience in children: The contribution of electrodermal activity. Psychophysiology, 37, 788–795.

Fox, C. H. (1994). Cocaine use in pregnancy. Journal of the American Board of Family Practice, 7, 225–228.

Fox, P. T., Ingham, R. J., Ingham, J. C., Hirsch, T. B., Downs, J. H., Martin, C., Jerabek, P., Glass, T., & Lancaster, J. L. (1996). A PET study of the neural systems of stuttering. Nature, 382, 158–162.

Fox, P. T., Mintun, M. A., Raichle, M. E., Miezin, F. M., Allman, J. M., & Van Essen, D. C. (1986). Mapping human visual cortex with positron emission tomography. Nature, 323, 806–809.

Fox, S., & Spector, P. E. (2000). Relations of emotional intelligence, practical intelligence, general intelligence, and trait affectivity with interview outcomes: It's not all just 'G'. Journal of Organizational Behavior, 21, 203–220.

Fox, W. M. (1982). Why we should abandon Maslow's Need Hierarchy Theory. Journal of Humanistic Education and Development, 21, 29–32.

Fozard, J. (1990). Vision and hearing in aging. In J. E. Birren & K. W. Schaie (Eds.), Handbook of the psychology of aging (3rd ed., pp. 150–170). San Diego: Academic Press.

Frances, A. (1998). Problems in defining clinical significance in epidemiological Studies. *Arch Gen Psychiatry, 55,* 119.

Francis, J. R., & Aronson, H. (1990). Communicative efficacy of psychotherapy research. *Journal of Consulting and Clinical Psychology, 58,* 368–370.

Francis, M. E., & Pennebaker, J. W. (1992). Putting stress into words: The impact of writing on physiological, absentee, and self-reported emotional well-being measures. *American Journal of Health Promotion, 6,* 280–286.

Franklin, M. E., Abramowitz, J. S., Bux, D. A. Jr., Zoellner, L. A., & Feeny, N. C. (2002). Cognitive-behavioral therapy with and without medicaiton in the treatment of obsessive-compulsive disorder. *Professional Psychology: Research & Practice, 33,* 162–168.

Fraser, J. S. (1996). All that glitters is not always gold: Medical offset effects and managed behavioral health care. *Professional Psychology: Research and Practice, 27,* 335–344.

Fraser, J. S. (1998). People who live in glass houses . . . : A response to the critique of the article "all that glitters is not always gold." *Professional Psyhology: Research and Practice, 29,* 624–627.

Frasure-Smith, N., Lesperance, F., Juneau, M., Talajic, M., & Bourassa, M. G. (1999). Gender, depression, and one-year prognosis after myocardial infarction. *Psychosomatic Medicine, 61,* 26–37.

Fredrickson, B. L. (2001). The role of postive emotions in positive psychology: The broaden-and-build theory of positive emotions. *American Psychologist, 56,* 218–226.

Freedman, J. L., & Fraser, S. C. (1966). Compliance without pressure: The foot-in-the-door technique. *Journal of Personality and Social Psychology, 4,* 195–202.

Freedman, M. S., Lucas, R. J., Soni, B., von Schantz, M., Muñoz, M., David-Gray, Z., & Foster, R. (1999). Regulation of mammalian circadian behavior by non-rod, non-cone, ocular photoreceptors. *Science, 284,* 502–504.

Freeman, D. (1983). *Margaret Mead and Samoa: The making and unmaking of an anthropological myth.* Cambridge, MA: Harvard University Press.

Freeman, H. (1994). Schizophrenia and city residence. *British Journal of Psychiatry, 164* (Suppl. 23), 39–50.

Freeman, J. H., Jr., & Nicholson, D. A. (2001). Ontogenetic changes in the neural mechanisms of eyeblink conditioning. *Integrative Physiological & Behavioral Science, 36,* 15–35.

Freeman, L. J., Templer, D. I., & Hill, C. (1999). The relationship between adult happiness and self-appraised childhood happiness and events. *Journal of Genetic Psychology, 160,* 46–54.

Freeman, W. J. (1991). The psychology of perception. *Scientific American, 264,* 78–85.

Freese, J., Powell, B., & Steelman, L. C. (1999). Rebel without a cause or effect: Birth order and social attitudes. *American Sociological Review, 64,* 207–231.

Fresko, B. (1997). Attitudinal change among university student tutors. *Journal of Applied Social Psychology, 27,* 1277–1301.

Freud, A. (1958). Adolescence. *Psychoanalytic Study of the Child, 15,* 255–278.

Freud, S. (1900/1958). *The interpretation of dreams.* New York: Basic Books.

Freud, S. (1910). The origin & development of psychoanalysis. *American Journal of Psychology, 21,* 181–218.

Freud, S. (1927). *The ego and the id.* London: Hogarth Press.

Freud, S. (1933/1965). *New introductory lectures on psychoanalysis.* New York: Norton.

Freud, S. (1937/1964). Analysis terminable and interminable. In J. Strachey (Ed. and Trans.), *The standard edition of the complete psychological works of Sigmund Freud* (Vol. 23, pp. 209–253).

Freud, S. (1938). *The basic writings of Sigmund Freud.* New York: Modern Library (Random House).

Fridlund, A. J. (1994). *Human facial expression: An evolutionary view.* San Diego, CA: Academic Press.

Fried, P. A., & Makin, J. E. (1987). Neonatal behavioral correlates of prenatal exposure to marijuana, cigarettes, and alcohol in a low risk population. *Neurobehavioral Toxicology and Teratology, 9,* 1–7.

Fried, P. A., & Watkinson, B. (2000). Visuoperceptual functioning differs in 9- to 12-year-olds prenatally exposed to cigarettes and marihuana. *Neurotoxicology & Teratology, 22,* 11–20.

Friede, M., Henneicke von Zepelin, H.-H., & Freudenstein, J. (2001). Differential therapy of mild to moderate depressive episodes (ICD-10 F 32.0; F 32.1) with St. John's wort. *Pharmacopsychiatry, 34,* S38–S41.

Friedler, G. (1996). Paternal exposures: Impact on reproductive and developmental outcome: An overview. *Pharmacology, Biochemistry & Behavior, 55,* 691–700.

Friedman, M. I. (1991). Metabolic control of calorie intake. In M. T. Friedman, M. G. Tordoff, & M. R. Kare (Eds.), *Chemical senses.* New York: Marcel Dekker.

Friedman, M., & Rosenman, R. (1974). *Type A behavior and your heart.* New York: Knopf.

Friedman, M., Thoresen, C., & Gill, J. (1986a). Alteration of Type A behavior and its effect on cardiac recurrence in post-myocardial infarction patients: Summary results of the recurrent coronary prevention project. *American Heart Journal, 112,* 653–665

Friedman, M. I., Tordoff, M. G., & Ramirez, I. (1986b). Integrated metabolic control of food intake. *Brain Research Bulletin, 17,* 855–859.

Frischholz, E. J. (1985). The relationship among dissocation, hypnosis, and child abuse in the dvelopment of multiple personality. In R. P. Kluft (Ed.), *Childhood antecedencts of multiples personality* (pp. 99–120). Washington, DC: American Psychiatric Press.

Frye, D., Zelazo, P. D., & Burack, J. A. (1998). Cognitive complexity and control: I. Theory of mind in typical and atypical development. *Current Directions in Psychological Science, 7,* 116–121.

Fryers, T. (1993). Epidemiological thinking in mental retardation: Issues in taxonomy and population frequency. In N. W. Bray (Ed.), *International review of research in mental retardation* (Vol. 19). Novato, Calif: Academic Therapy Publications.

Fuller, R. K., Branchey, L., Brightwell, D. R., Derman, R. M., Emrick, C. D., Iber, F. L., James, K. E., Lacoursiere, R. B., Lee, K. K., Lowenstaum, I., Maany, I., Neiderhiser, D., Nocks, J. J., & Shaw, S. (1986). Disulfiram treatment of alcoholism: A Veterans Administration cooperative study. Journal of the American Medical Association 256(11):1449–1455.

Fuller, S. R., & Aldag, R. J. (1998). Organizational Tonypandy: Lessons from a quarter century of groupthink phenomenon. *Organizational Behavior & Human Decision Processes, 73,* 163–184.

Fulton, S., Woodside, B., & Shizgal, P. (2000). Modulation of brain reward circuitry by leptin. *Science, 287,* 125–128.

Funder, D. C. (2001). *The personality puzzle* (2nd ed.). New York: Norton.

Funder, D. C., & Colvin, C. R. (1991). Explorations in behavioral consistency: Properties of persons, situations, and behaviors. *Journal of Personality and Social Psychology, 60,* 773–794.

Fung, H. H., Carstensen, L. L., & Lang, F. R. (2001). Age-related patterns in social networks among European Americans and African Americans: Implications for socioemotional selectivity across the life span. *International Journal of Aging & Human Development, 52,* 185–206.

Fung, H. H., Carstensen, L. L., & Lutz, A. M. (1999). Influence of time on social preferences: Implications for life-span development. *Psychology & Aging, 14,* 595–604.

Funk, S. C., & Houston, B. K. (1987). A critical analysis of the hardiness sale's validity and utility. *Journal of Personality and Social Psychology, 53,* 572–578.

Funtowicz, M. N., & Widiger, T. A. (1999). Sex bias in the diagnosis of personality disorders: An evaluation of the *DSM–IV* criteria. *Journal of Abnormal Psychology, 108,* 195–201.

Furnham, A., Shahidi, S., & Baluch, B. (2002). Sex and culture differences in perceptions of estimated multiple intelligence for self and family: A British-Iranian comparison. *Journal of Cross-Cultural Psychology, 33,* 270–285.

Fuster, J. M. (1997). Network memory. *Trends in Neuroscience, 20,* 451–459.

Futterman, A. D., Kemeny, M. E., Shapiro, D., Polonsky, W., & Fahey, J. L. (1992). Immunological variability associated with experimentally-induced positive and negative affective states. *Psychological Medicine, 22,* 231–238.

Gabbard, G. O. (1990). *Psychodynamic psychiatry in clinical practice.* Washington, DC: American Psychiatric Press.

Gabrieli, J. D. E. (1996). Memory systems analyses of mnemonic disorders in aging and age-related diseases. *Proceedings of the National Academy of Sciences, USA, 93,* 13534–13540.

Gabrieli, J. D. E., Desmond, J. E., Demb, J. B. Wagner, A. D., Stone, M. V., Vaidya, C. J., & Glover, G. H. (1996). Functional magnetic resonance imaging of semantic memory processes in the frontal lobes. *Psychological Science, 7,* 278–283.

Gabrieli, J. D. E., Fleischman, D. A., Keane, M. M., Reminger, S. L., & Morrell, F. (1995). Double dissociation between memory systems underlying explicit and implicit memory in the human brain. *American Psychological Society, 6,* 76–82.

Gagliese, L., & Katz, J. (2000). Medically unexplained pain is not caused by psychopathology. *Pain Research & Management, 5,* 251–257.

Galanski, E. (2001). The "imaginary audience" and the "personal fable" in relation to risk behavior and risk perception during adolescence. *Psychology: The Journal of the Hellenic Psychological Society, 8,* 411–430.

Galdzicki, Z., Siarey, R., Pearce, R., Stoll, J., & Rapoport, S. I. (2001). On the cause of mental retardation in Down syndrome: Extrapolation from full and segmental tirsomy 16 mouse models. *Brain Research Reviews, 35,* 115–145.

Gallaher, P. E. (1992). Individual differences in nonverbal behavior. Dimensions of style. *Journal of Personality and Social Psychology, 63,* 133–145.

Gallers, J., Foy, D. W., Donahoe, C. P., & Goldfarb, J. (1988). Post-traumatic stress disorder in Vietnam combat veterans: Effects of traumatic violence exposure with military adjustment. *Journal of Traumatic Stress, 1,* 181–192.

Gallistel, C. R. (1983). Self-stimulation. In J. A. Deutsch (Ed.), *The physiological basis of memory* (pp. 73–77). New York: Academic Press.

Gallo, L. C., & Matthews, K. A. (2003). Understanding the association between socioeconomic status and physical health: Do negative emotions play a role? *Psychological Bulletin, 129,* 10–51.

Gandour, J., & Baum, S. R. (2001). Production of stress retraction by left- and right-hemisphere-damaged patients. *Brain & Language, 79,* 482–494.

Gangestad, S. W. (1993). Sexual selection and physical attraiveness: Implications fo rmating dynamics. *Human Nature, 4,* 205–235.

Gangestad, S. W., & Snyder, M. (2000). Self-monitoring: Appraisal and reappraisal. *Psychological Bulletin, 126,* 530–555.

Gangestad, S. W,, Thornhill, R., & Garver, C. E. (2002). Changes in women's sexual interests and their partners' mate-retention tactics across the menstrual cycle: Evidence for shifting conflicts of interest. *Proceedings of the Royal Society of London: B, Biological Sciences, 269,* 975–982.

Garb, H. N. (1997). Race bias, social class bias, and gender bias in clinical judgment. *Clinical Psychology: Science & Practice, 4,* 99–120.

Garcia, J., & Koelling, R. (1966). Realtion of cue to consequence in avoidance learning. *Psychonomic Science, 4,* 123–124.

Garcia, J., Ervin, F. R., & Koelling, R. A. (1966). Learning with prolonged delay of reinforcement. *Psychonomic Science, 5,* 121–122.

Garcia-Arraras, J. E., & Pappenheimer, J. R. (1983). Site of action of sleep-inducing muramyl peptide isolated from human urine: Microinjection studies in rabbit brains. *Journal of Neurophysiology*, 49, 528–533.

Garden, S., Cornoldi, C., & Logie, R. H. (2002). Visuo-spatial working memory in navigation. *Applied Cognitive Psychology*, 16, 35–50.

Gardner, H. (1975). *The shattered mind: The person after brain damage.* New York: Knopf.

Gardner, H. (1985). *The mind's new science: A history of the cognitive revolution.* New York: Basic Books.

Gardner, H. (1993a). *Creating minds: An anatomy of creativity as seen through the lives of Freud, Einstein, Picasso, Stravinsky, Eliot, Graham, and Gandhi.* New York: Basic Books.

Gardner, H. (1993b). *Frames of mind: The theory of multiple intelligences.* New York: Basic Books. (Original work published 1983.)

Gardner, H. (1993c). *Multiple intelligences: The theory in practice.* New York: Basic Books.

Gardner, H. (1995, November). Reflections on multiple intelligences: Myths and messages. *Phi Delta Kappan*, pp. 200–209.

Gardner, H. (1999). *Intelligence reframed: Multiple intelligences for the 21st century.* New York: Basic Books.

Gardner, H. (in press). Three distinct meanings of intelligence. In R. Sternberg, J. Lautrey, & T. Lubart (Eds.), *Models of intelligence for the new millennium.* Washington, DC: American Psychological Association.

Gardner, H., Kornhaber, M. L., & Wake, W. K. (1996). *Intelligence: Multiple perspectives.* Ft. Worth, TX: Harcourt Brace.

Gardner, R. A., & Gardner, B. T. (1969). Teaching sign language to a chimpanzee. *Science*, 165, 664–672.

Garfield, M. J., Taylor, N. J., Dennis, A. R., & Satzinger, J. W. (2001). Research report: Modifying paradigms — Individual differences, creativity techniques, and exposure to ideas in group idea generation. *Information Systems Research*, 12, 322–333.

Garfield, S. L. (1994). Research on client variables in psychotherapy. In A. E. Bergin & S. L. Garfield (Eds.), *Handbook of psychotherapy and behavior change* (4th edition, pp. 190–228). New York: John Wiley & Sons.

Garfield, S. L., & Bergin, A. E. (1994). Introduction and historical overview. In A. E. Bergin & S. L. Garfield (Eds.), *Handbook of psychotherapy and behavior change* (4th edition, pp. 3–18). New York: John Wiley & Sons.

Garfinkel, P. E., Goldbloom, D., David, R., Olmsted, M. P., Garner, D. M., & Halmi, K. A. (1992). Body dissatisfaction in Bulimia Nervosa: Relationship to weight and shape concerns and psychological functioning. *International Journal of Eating Disorders*, 11, 151–161.

Garner, D. M. (1997). Psycho educational Principles in Treatment. In D. M. Garner & P. E. Garfinkel (Eds.), *Handbook of treatment for eating disorders* (2nd edition). New York: Guilford Press.

Garrard, P., Lambon R. M. A., Hodges, J. R., & Patterson, K. (2001). Prototypicality, distinctiveness, and intercorrelation: Analyses of the semantic attributes of living and nonliving concepts. *Cognitive Neuropsychology*, 18, 125–174.

Garrett, M., Bever, T., & Fodor, J. (1966). The active use of grammar in speech perception. *Perception & Psychophysics*, 1, 30–32.

Garrigue, S., Bordier, P., Jais, P., Shah D. C., Hocini M., Raherison C., Tunon De Lara, M., Haïssaguerre, M., & Clementy, J. (2002). Benefit of atrial pacing in sleep apnea syndrome. *New England Journal of Medicine*, 346, 404–412.

Garris, P. A., Kilpatrick, M., Bunin, M. A., Michael, D., Walker, Q. D., & Wightman, R. M. (1999). Dissociation of dopamine release in the nucleus accumbens from intracranial self-stimulation. *Nature*, 398, 67–69.

Garrison, M., & Bly, M. A. (1997). *Human relations: Productive approaches to the workplace.* Boston: Allyn & Bacon.

Garry, M., & Polaschek, D. L. L. (2000). Imagination and memory. *Current Directions in Psychological Science*, 9, 6–10.

Garvey, C. (1974). Requests and responses in children's speech. *Journal of Child Language*, 2, 41–60.

Gaster, B., & Holroyd, J. (2000). St. John's Wort for depression: A systematic review. *Archives of Internal Medicine*, 160, 152–156.

Gater, R., Tansella, M., Korten, A., Tiemens, B. G., Mavreas, V. G., & Olatawura, M. O. (1998). Report from the World Health Organization Collaborative Study on Psychological Problems in General Health Care. *Archives of General Psychiatry*, 55, 405–413.

Gauthier, I., Tarr, M. J., Anderson, A. W., Skudlarski, P., & Gore, J. C. (1997). Expertise training with novel objects can recruit the fusiform face area. *Society of Neuroscience Abstracts*, 23, 868.5.

Gazzaniga, M. S. (1995). Consciousness and the cerebral hemispheres. In M. S. Gazzaniga (Ed.), *The cognitive neurosciences* (pp. 1391–1400). Cambridge, MA: The MIT Press.

Gazzaniga, M. S., & LeDoux, J. E. (1979). *The integrated mind.* New York: Plenum.

Geary, D. C. (1996). Sexual selection and sex differences in mathematical abilities. *Behavioral and Brain Sciences*, 19, 229–284.

Geary, N., & Smith, G. P. (1985). Pimozide decreases the positive reinforcing effects of sham fed sucrose in the rat. *Pharmacology, Biochemistry, & Behavior*, 22, 787–790.

Geddes, J. R., & Lawrie, S. M. (1995). Obstetric complications and schizophrenia: a meta-analysis. *British Journal of Psychiatry*, 67, 786–793.

Gehring, W. J., & Willoughby, A. R. (2002). The medial frontal cortex and the rapid processing of monetary gains and losses. *Science*, 295, 2279–2282.

Geinisman, Y. (2000). Structural synaptic modifications associated with hippocampal LTP and behavioral learning. *Cerebral Cortex*, 10, 952–962.

Geiselman, R. E., Fisher, R. P., MacKinnon, D. P., & Holland, H. L. (1985). Eyewitness memory enhancement in the police interview. *Cognitive Journal of Applied Psychology*, 70, 401–412.

Gelfand, S. A. (1981). *Hearing.* New York: MarcelDekker.

Gelman, R. (1972). Logical capacity of very young children: Number invariance rules. *Child Development*, 43, 75–90.

General Accounting Office of the United States (GAO) (1998). *Alzheimer's Disease: Estimates of Prevalence in the United States.* GAO/HEHS-98-16. United States General Accounting Office: Washington, D.C.

Gentner, D., & Bowdle, B. F. (2001). Convention, form, and figurative language processing. *Metaphor & Symbol*, 16, 223–247.

Gentner, D., & Gunn, V. (2001). Structural alignment facilitates the noticing of differences. *Memory & Cognition*, 29, 565–577.

George, M. S., Lisanby, S. H., & Sackheim, H. A. (1999). Transcranial Magnetic Stimuluation: Applications in neuropsychiatry. *Archives in General Psychiatry*, 56, 300–311.

Gerhardstein, P., Adler, S. A., & Rovee-Collier, C. (2000). A dissociation in infants' memory for stimulus size: Evidence for the early development of multiple memory systems. *Developmental Psychobiology*, 36, 123–135.

Gerlai, R. (1996). Gene-targeting studies of mammalian behavior: Is it the mutation of the background genotype? *Trends in Neuroscience*, 19, 177–181.

German, D. C., & Bowden, D. M. (1974). Catecholamine systems as the neural substrate for intracranial self-stimulation: A hypothesis. *Brain Research*, 73, 381–419.

Gerrard, M., Gibbons, F. X., Reis-Bergan, M., & Russell, D. W. (2000). Self-esteem, self-serving cognitions, and health risk behavior. *Journal of Personality*, 68, 1177–1201.

Gershberg, F. B., & Shimamura, A. P. (1995). Impaired use of organizational strategies in free recall following frontal lobe damage. *Neuropsychologia*, 33, 1305–1333.

Gerstmann, J. (1942). Problem of imperception of disease and of impaired body territories with organic lesions. *Archives of Neurology and Psychiatry*, 48, 890–913.

Gerteis, J., & Savage, M. (1998). The salience of class in Britain and America: A comparative analysis. *British Journal of Sociology*, 49, 252–274.

Gesell, A., & Thompson, H. (1938). *The psychology of early growth including norms of infant behavior and a method of genetic analysis.* New York: Macmillan.

Getter, L. (1999, March 1). Cancer risk from air pollution still high, study says. *Los Angeles Times*, p. 0.

Gibbons, F. X. & Gerrard, M. (1995). Predicting young adults' health-risk behavior. *Journal of Personality and Social Psychology*, 69, 505–517.

Gibbs, R. W., Jr., & O'Brien, J. E. (1990). Idioms and mental imagery: The metaphorical motivation for idiomatic meaning. *Cognition*, 36, 35–68.

Gibson, E. J. (1969). *Principles of perceptual learning and development.* New York: Appleton-Century-Crofts.

Gibson, J. J. (1966). *The senses considered as perceptual systems.* Boston: Houghton Mifflin.

Gibson, J. J., & Walk, R. D. (1960). The "visual cliff." *Scientific American*, 202, 64–71.

Gibson, J. T. (1991). Training people to inflict pain: State terror and social learning. *Journal of Humanistic Psychology*, 31, 72–87.

Gick, M. L., & Holyoak, K. J. (1980). Analogical problem solving. *Cognitive Psychology*, 12, 306–355.

Gick, M. L., & Holyoak, K. J. (1983). Schema induction and analogical transfer. *Cognitive Psychology*, 15, 1–38.

Gidron, Y., Davidson, K., & Bata, I. (1999). The short-term effects of a hostility-reduction intervention on male coronary heart disease patients. *Health Psychology*, 18, 416–420.

Gigerenzer, G. (1994). Why the distinction between single-event probabilities and frequencies is relevant for psychology and vice versa. In G. Wright & P. Ayton (Eds.), *Subjective probability* (pp. 129–162). New York: Wiley.

Gigerenzer, G. (1996). On narrow norms and vague heuristics: A reply to Kahneman & Tversky (1996). *Psychological Review*, 103, 592–596.

Gigerenzer, G. (2002). *Calculated risks: How to know when numbers deceive you.* New York: Simon & Schuster.

Gigerenzer, G., & Goldstein, D. G. (1996). Reasoning the fast and frugal way: Models of bounded rationality. *Psychological Review*, 103, 650–669.

Gigerenzer, G., & Hug, K. (1992). Domain-specific reasoning: Social contracts, cheating, and perspective change. *Cognition*, 43, 127–171.

Gigerenzer, G., Hell, W., & Blank, H. (1988). Presentation and content: The use of base rates as a continuous variable. *Journal of Experimental Psychology: Human Perception and Performance*, 14, 513–525.

Gilbert, D. T. (1991). How mental systems believe. *American Psychologist*, 46, 107–119.

Gilbert, D. T. (1995). Attribution and interpersonal perception. In A. Tesser (Ed.), *Advanced social psychology* (pp. 99–147). New York: McGraw-Hill.

Gilbert, D. T. (2002). Are psychology's tribes ready to form a nation? *Trends in Cognitive Sciences*, 6, 3.

Gilbert, D. T., & Hixon, J. G. (1991). The trouble of thinking: Activation and application of stereotypic beliefs. *Journal of Personality and Social Psychology*, 60, 509–517.

Gilbert, D. T., & Malone, P. S. (1995). The correspondence bias. *Psychological Bulletin*, 117, 21–38.

Gilbert, S. (2002, June 25). When brain trauma is at the other end of the thrill ride. *New York Times*, D5.

Gilger, J. W. (1995). Behavioral genetics: Concepts for research and practice in language development and disorders. *Journal of Speech and Hearing Research, 38,* 1126–1142.

Gilligan, C. (1982). *In a different voice.* Cambridge, MA: Harvard University Press.

Gilmore, J. H., Sikich, L., & Lieberman, J. A. (1997). Neuroimaging, neurodevelopment, and schizophrenia. *Child & Adolescent Psychiatric Clinics of North America, 6*(2), 325–341.

Gladis, M. M. Gosch, E. A., Dishuk, N. M., & Crits-Christoph, P. (1999). Quality of life: Expanding the scope of clinical significance. *Journal of Consulting and Clinical Psychology, 67,* 320–331.

Gladwell, M. (1998, February 2). The pima paradox. *New Yorker,* pp. 44–57.

Glass, D., & Singer, J. (1972). *Urban stress: Experiments on noise and social stressors.* New York: Academic Press.

Glass, R. M. (2001). Electroconvulsive therapy: Time to bring it out of the shadows. *Journal of the American Medical Association, 285,* np.

Glater, J. D. (2001). Seasoning compensation stew: Varying the recipe helps TV operation solve morale problem. *The New York Times,* March 7, Business p. 1.

Glennon, F., & Joseph, S. (1993). Just world belief, self-esteem, and attitudes towards homosexuals with AIDS. *Psychological Reports, 72,* 584–586.

Glick, J. (1968). Cognitive style among the Kpelle of Liberia. Paper presented at the meeting on Cross-Cultural Cognitive Studies, American Educational Research Association, Chicago.

Glisky, E. L., Polster, M. R., & Routhieaux, B. C. (1995). Double dissociation between item and source memory. *Neuropsychology, 9,* 229–235.

Gloaguen, V., Cottraux, J., Cucherat, M., & Blackburn, I. (1998). A meta-analysis of the effects of cognitive therapy in depressed patients. *Journal of Affective Disorders, 49,* 59–72.

Glucksberg, S., Newsome, M. R., & Goldvarg, Y. (2001). Inhibition of the literal: Filtering metaphor-irrelevant information during metaphor comprehension. *Metaphor & Symbol, 16,* 277–293.

Glutting, J. J., Oh, H-J., Ward, T., & Ward, S. (2000). Possible criterion-related bias of the WISC-III with a referral sample. *Journal of Psychoeducational Assessment, 18,* 17–26.

Glynn, S. M. (1990). Token economy approaches for psychiatric patients: Progress and pitfalls over 25 years. *Behavior Modification, 14,* 383–407.

Godden, D. R., & Baddeley, A. D. (1975). Context-dependent memory in two natural environments: On land and underwater. *British Journal of Psychology, 66,* 325–331.

Godemann, F., Ahrens, B., Behrens, S., Berthold, R., Gandor, C., Lampe, F., & Linden, M. (2001). Classic conditioning and dysfunctional cognitions in patients with panic disorder and agoraphobia treated with an implantable cardioverter/defibrillator. *Psychosomatic Medicine, 63,* 231–238.

Goedde, H. W., & Agarwal, D. P. (1987). Aldehyde hydrogenase polymorphism: Molecular basis and phenotypic relationship to alcohol sensitivity. *Alcohol & Alcoholism* (Suppl. 1), 47–54.

Goetestam, K. G., & Berntzen, D. (1997). Use of the modelling effect in one-session exposure. *Scandinavian Journal of Behaviour Therapy, 26,* 97–101.

Goethals, G. R., & Zanna, M. P. (1979). The role of social comparison in choice shifts. *Journal of Personality and Social Psychology, 37,* 1469–1185.

Goethals, G. R., Cooper, J., & Naficy, A. (1979). Role of foreseen, foreseeable, and unforeseeable behavioral consequences in the arousal of cognitive dissonance. *Journal of Personality and Social Psychology, 37,* 1179–1185.

Goldberg, L. R. (1981). Language and individual differences: The search for universals in personality lexicons. In L. Wheeler (Ed.), *Review of personality and social psychology* (Vol. 2, pp. 141–165). Beverly Hills, CA: Sage.

Goldberg, P. (1968). Are women prejudiced against women? *Transaction, 5,* 28–30.

Goldenberg, J., Mazursky, D., & Solomon, S. (1999). Essays on science and society: Creative sparks. *Science, 285,* 1495–1496.

Goldin-Meadow, S., & Mylander, C. (1998). Spontaneous sign systems created by deaf children in two cultures. *Nature, 391,* 279–281.

Goldin-Meadow, S., Nusbaum, H., Kelly, S. D., & Wagner, S. (2001). Explaining math: Gesturing lightens the load. *Psychological Science, 12,* 516–522.

Golding, J. M., Sanchez, R. P., & Sego, S. A. (1996). Do you believe in repressed memories? *Professional Psychology Research and Practice, 27,* 429–237.

Goldman, W. P., Wolters, N. C. W., & Winograd, E. (1992). A demonstration of incubation in anagram problem solving. *Bulletin of the Psychonomic Society, 30,* 36–38.

Goldman-Rakic, P. S. (1987). Development of cortical circuitry and cognitive function. *Child Development, 58,* 601–622.

Goldstein, A. (1994). *Addiction: From biology to drug policy.* New York: Freeman.

Goldstein, D. G., & Gigerenzer, G. (2002). Models of ecological rationality: The recognition heuristic. *Psychological Review, 109,* 75–90.

Goldstein, D. S. (1995). *Stress, catecholamines, and cardiovascular disease.* New York: Oxford University Press.

Goldstein, J. M., Goodman, J. M., Seidman, L. J., Kennedy, D. N., Makris, N., Lee, H., Tourville, J., Caviness, V. S., Jr., Faraone, S. V., & Tsuang, M. T. (1999). Cortical abnormalities in schizophrenia identified by structural magnetic resonance imaging. *Archives of General Psychiatry, 56,* 537–547.

Goldstein, M. D., & Strube, M. J. (1994). Independence revisited: The relation between positive and negative affect in a naturalistic setting. *Personality & Social Psychology Bulletin, 20,* 57–64.

Goldstein, M. J. (1992). Psychosocial strategies for maximizing the effects of psychotropic medications for schizophrenia and mood disorder. *Psychopharmacology Bulletin, 28,* 237–240.

Goleman, D. (1995). *Emotional intelligence.* New York: Bantam Books.

Golombok, S., & Tasker, F. (1996). Do parents influence the sexual orientation of their children? Findings from a longitudinal study of lesbian families. *Developmental Psychology, 32,* 3–11.

Gontkovsky, S. T. (1998). Huntington's disease: A neuropsychological overview. *Journal of Cognitive Rehabilitation, 16,* 6–9.

Goodale, M. A., & Milner, A. D. (1992). Separate visual pathways for perception and action. *Trends in Neurosciences, 15,* 20–25.

Goode, E. (1999). *New clues to why we dream. New York Times.* Thursday, November 2, 1999, p. D1.

Goodfellow, P. N., & Lovell-Badge, R. (1993). SRY and sex determination in mammals. *Annual Review of Genetics, 27,* 71–92.

Goodglass, H. (1976). Agrammatism. In H. Whitaker & H. A. Whitaker (Eds.), *Studies of neurolinguistics.* New York: Academic Press.

Goodie, A. S., & Fantino, E. (1996). Learning to commit or avoid the base-rate error. *Nature, 380,* 247–249.

Goodman, N. (1983). *Fact, fiction, and forecast* (4th edition). Cambridge: Harvard University Press.

Goodman, R. (1988). Are complications of pregnancy and birth causes of schizphrenia? *Developmental Medical Child Neurology, 30,* 391–395.

Goodwin, F. K., & Ghaemi, S. N. (1998). Understanding manic–depressive illness. *Archives of General Psychiatry, 55,* 23–25.

Goodwin, F. K., & Jamison, K. R. (1990). *Manic-depressive illness.* New York: Oxford University Press.

Gopnik, A. (1996). The post-Piaget era. *Psychological Science, 7,* 221–225.

Gopnik, M. (1990). Dysphasia in an extended family. *Nature, 344,* 715.

Gopnik, M. (1997). Language deficits and genetic factors. *Trends in Cognitive Sciences, 1,* 5–9.

Gopnik, M. (1999). Familial language impairment: More English evidence. *Folia Phoniatrica et Logopaedica, 51,* 5–19.

Gopnik, M., & Crago, M. (1991). Familial aggregation of a developmental language disorder. *Cognition, 39,* 1–50.

Gorcynski, R. Cited in Dienstfrey, H. (1991). *Where the mind meets the body.* New York: HarperCollins.

Gorman, J. M., & Kent, J. M. (1999). SSRIs and SNRIs: Broad spectrum of efficacy beyond major depression. *Journal of Clinical Psychiatry, 60*(Suppl. 4) 33–39.

Gorman, J. M., Liebowitz, M. R., Fyer, A. J., &Stein, J. (1989). A neuroanatomical hypothesis for panic disorder. *American Journal of Psychiatry, 146,* 148–161.

Gortner, E. T., Gollan, J. K., Dobson, K. S., & Jacobson, N. S. (1998). Cognitive-behavioral treatment for depression: Relapse prevention. *Journal of Consulting and Clinical Psychology, 66,* 377–384.

Gotlib, I. H., & Robinson, L. A. (1982). Responses to depressed individuals: Discrepancies between self-report and observer rated behavior. *Journal of Abnormal Psychology, 91,* 231–240.

Gottesman, I. I. (1991). *Schizophrenia genesis: The origins of madness.* New York: Freeman.

Gottesman, I. I., & Moldin, S. O. (1998). Genotypes, Genes, Genesis, and pathogenesis in schizophrenia. In M. F. Lenzenweger & R. H. Dworkin (Eds.), *Origins and development of schizophrenia: Advances in experimental psychopathology.* Washington, DC: American Psychological Association. pp. 5–26.

Gottesman, I. I., Goldsmith, H. H., & Carey, G.. (1997). A developmental and a genetic perspective on aggression. In N. L. Segal, G. E. Weisfeld, C. C. Weisfeld (Eds.), *Uniting psychology and biology: Integrative perspectives on human development.* (pp. 107–130). Washington, DC, USA: American Psychological Association.

Gottfredson, L. (1997). Why "g" matters: The complexity of everyday life. *Intelligence, 24,* 79–132.

Gottfredson, M. R., & Hirschi, T. (1990). *A general theory of crime.* Stanford, CA: Stanford University Press.

Gottlieb, G. (1998). Normally occurring environmental and behavioral influences on gene activity: From central dogma to probabilistic epigenesis. *Psychological Review, 105,* 792–802.

Gould, E., Tanapat, P., Hastings, N. B., & Shors, T. J. (1999). Neurogenesis in adulthood: A possible role in learning. *Trends in Cognitive Sciences, 3,* 186–192.

Gould, J. L. (1998). Sensory bases of navigation. *Current Biology, 8,* R731–R738.

Gould, R. (1978). *Transformations.* New York: Simon & Schuster.

Gould, R. A., & Clum, G. A. (1993). A meta-analysis of self-help treatment approaches. *Clinical Psychology Review, 13,* 169–186.

Gould, R. A., Buckminster, S., Pollack, M. H., Otto, M. W., & Yap, L. (1997). Cognitive-behavioral and pharmacological treatment for social phobia: A meta-analysis. *Clinical Psychology: Science & Practice, 4,* 291–306.

Gould, R. A., Mueser, K. T., Bolton, E., Mays, V., & Goff, D. (2001). Cognitive therapy for psychosis in schizophrenia: An effect size analysis. *Schizophrenia Research, 48,* 335–342.

Gould, R. A., Otto, M. W., & Pollack, M. H. (1995). A meta-analysis of treatment outcome for panic disorder. *Clinical Psychology Review, 15,* 819–844.

Gould, S. J., & Lewontin, R. C. (1979). The spandrels of San Marco and the Panglossian paradigm: A critique of the adaptationist programme. *Proceedings of the Royal Society of London, Series B, 205,* 581–598.

Gouldner, A. W. (1960). The norm of reciprocity: A preliminary statement. *American Sociological Review, 25,* 161–179.

Graf, P., & Mandler, G. (1984). Activation makes words more accessible, but not necessarily more retrievable. *Journal of Verbal Learning and Verbal Behavior, 23,* 553–568.

Grafen, A. (2002). A state-free optimization model for sequences of behaviour. *Animal Behaviour, 63,* 183–191.

Graham, S., Hudley, C., & Williams, E. (1992). Attributional and emotional determinants of aggression among African American and Latino early adolescents. *Developmental Psychology, 31,* 274–284.

Grammer, K. (1990). Strangers meet: Laughter and nonverbal signs of interest in opposite-sex encounters. *Journal of Nonverbal Behavior, 14,* 209–236.

Grammer, K., & Thornhill, R. (1994). Human (*Homo sapiens*) facial attractiveness and sexual selection: The role of symmetry and averageness. *Journal of Comparative Psychology, 108,* 233–242.

Grant, B. F., & Dawson, D. A. (1997). Age at onset of alcohol use and its association with DSM–IV alcohol abuse and dependence: Results from the National Longitudinal Alcohol Epidemiologic Survey. *Journal of Substance Abuse, 9,* 103–110.

Grant, I., Marcotte, T. D., Heaton, R. K., & HNRC Group, San Diego, CA, USA. (1999). Neurocognitive complications of HIV disease. *Psychological Science, 10,* 191–195.

Gratton, G., & Fabiani, M. (2001a). The event-related optical signal: A new tool for studying brain function. *International Journal of Psychophysiology, 42,* 109–121.

Gratton, G., & Fabiani, M. (2001b). Shedding light on brain function: The event-related optical signal. *Trends in Cognitive Sciences, 5,* 357–363.

Graves, L., Pack, A., & Abel, T. (2001). Sleep and memory: A molecular perspective. *Trends in Neurosciences, 24,* 237–243.

Gray, J. A. (1987). Perspectives on anxiety and impulsiveness: A commentary. *Journal of Research in Personality, 21,* 493–509.

Gray, J. A. (1994). The neuropsychology of anxiety and schizophrenia. In M. S. Gazzaniga (Ed.), *The cognitive neurosciences* (pp. 1165–1176). Cambridge, MA: MIT Press.

Gray, J. R. (1999). A bias toward short-term thinking in threat-related negative emotional states. *Personality and Social Psychology Bulletin, 25,* 65–75.

Gray, J. R. (2001). Emotional modulation of cognitive control: Approach-withdrawal states double-dissociate spatial from verbal two-back task performance. *Journal of Experimental Psychology: General, 130,* 436–452.

Gray, J. R., Braver, T. S., & Raichle, M. E. (2002). Integration of emotion and cognition in the lateral prefrontal cortex. *Proceedings of the National Academy of Sciences USA, 99,* 4115–4120.

Gray, P. B., Kahlenberg, S. M., Barrett, E. S., Lipson, S. F., & Ellison, P. T. (2002). Marriage and fatherhood are associated with lower testosterone in males. *Evolution & Human Behavior, 23,* 193–201.

Grayson, B. and Stein, M. I. (1981) Attracting assault: Victims' nonverbal cues. *Journal of Communication 31,* 68–75.

Graziano, W. G., Jensen-Campbell, L. A., & Sullivan-Logan, G. M. (1998). Temperament, activity, and expectations for later personality development, *Journal of Persoanlity and Social Psychology, 74,* 1266–1277.

Green, D. E., Walkey, F. H., & Taylor, A. J. W. (1991). The three-factor structure of the Maslach Burnout Inventory: A multicultural, multinational confirmatory study. *Journal of Social Behavior & Personality, 6,* 453–472.

Green, D. M. (1976). *An introduction to hearing.* Hillsdale, NJ: Erlbaum.

Green, D. M., & Swets, J. A. (1966). *Signal detection theory and psychophysics.* New York: Wiley.

Green, J. P. (1999). Hypnosis, context effects, and the recall of early autobiographical memories. *International Journal of Clinical and Experimental Hypnosis, 47,* 284–300.

Green, J. P., & Lynn, S. J. (August, 2001). Hypnotic context and the recall of news events. Paper presented at the meeting of the American Psychological Association, San Francisco.

Green, J. P., Lynn, S. J., & Malinoski, P. (1998). Hypnotic pseudomemories, prehypnotic warnings, and the malleability of suggested memories. *Applied Cognitive Psychology, 12,* 431–444.

Green, M. W., Elliman, N. A., & Rogers, P. J. (1995). Lack of effect of short-term fasting on cognitive function. *Journal of Psychiatric Research, 29,* 245–253.

Green, M. W., Elliman, N. A., & Rogers, P. J. (1997). The effects of food deprivation and incentive motivation on blood glucose levels and cognitive function. *Psychopharmacology, 134,* 88–94.

Greenberg, B. D., Altemus, M., & Murphy, D. L. (1997). The role of neurotransmitters and neurohormones in obsessive-compulsive disorder. *International Review of Psychiatry, 9,* 31–44.

Greenberg, J. R., & Mitchell, S. A. (1983). *Object relations in psychoanalytic theory.* Cambridge, MA: Harvard University Press.

Greenberg, R. P., & Fisher, S. (1989). Examining antidepressant effectiveness: Findings, ambiguities and some vexing puzzles. In S. Fisher & R. P. Greenberg (Eds.), *The limits of biological treatments for psychological distress* (pp. 1–37). Hillsdale, NJ: Erlbaum.

Greene, W., Conron, D., Schalch, S., & Schreiner, B. (1970). Psychological correlates of growth hormone and adrenal secretory responses of patients undergoing cardiac catheterization. *Psychosomatic Medicine, 32,* 599–614.

Greenfield, P. (1992, June). *Notes and references for developmental psychology.* Conference on Making Basic Texts in Psychology More Culture-Inclusive and Culture-Sensitive, Western Washington University, Bellingham, WA.

Greenfield, P. M., & Savage-Rumbaugh, S. (1990). Grammatical combination in *Pan paniscus*: Processes of learning and invention in the evolution and development of language. In S. Parker & K. Gibson (Eds.), *"Language" and intelligence in monkeys and apes: Comparative developmental perspectives* (pp. 540–578). New York: Cambridge University Press.

Greenglass, E. R., Burke, R. J., & Konarski, R. (1998). Components of burnout, resources, and gender-related differences. *Journal of Applied Social Psychology, 28,* 1088–1106.

Greeno, J. G. (1989). A perspective on thinking. *American Psychologist, 44,* 134–141.

Greenough, W. T., & Black, J. E. (1992). Induction of brain structure by experience. In M. R. Gunnar & C. A. Nelson (Eds.), *Minnesota symposium on child psychology: Vol. 24. Developmental behavior neuroscience* (pp. 155–200). Hillsdale, NJ: Erlbaum.

Greenough, W. T., & Chang, F.-L. F. (1985). Synaptic structural correlates of information storage in mammalian nervous systems. In C. W. Cotman (Ed.), *Synaptic plasticity* (pp. 335–372). New York: Gilford.

Greenough, W. T., Black, J. E., & Wallace, C. S. (1987). Experience and brain development. *Child Development, 58,* 539–559.

Greenough, W. T., Larson, J. R., & Withers, G. S. (1985). Effect of unilateral and bilateral training in a reaching task on dendritic branching of neurons in the rat motor-sensory forelimb cortex. *Behavioral Neural Biology, 44,* 301–314.

Greenwald, A. G., & Banaji, M. R. (1995). Implicit social cognition: Attitudes, self-esteem, and stereotypes. *Psychological Review, 102,* 4–27.

Greenwald, A. G., Draine, S. C., Abrams, R. L. (1996). Three cogntive markers of unconscious semantic activation. *Science, 273,* 1699–1702.

Greenwald, A. G., McGhee, D. E., & Schwartz, J. L. K. (1998). Measuring individual differences in implicit cognition: The Implicit Association Test. *Journal of Personality and Social Psychology, 74,* 1464–1480.

Greenwald, A. G., Spangenberg, E. R., Pratkanis, A. R., & Eskenazi, J. (1991). Double-blind tests of subliminal self-help audiotapes. *Psychological Science, 2,* 119–122.

Gregg, V. R., Winer, G. A., Cottrell, J. E., Hedman, K. E., & Fournier, J. S. (2001). The persistence of a misconception about vision after educational interventions. *Psychonomic Bulletin and Review, 8,* 622–626.

Gregerson, M. B., Roberts, I. M., & Amiri, M. M. (1996). Absorption and imagery locate immune response in the body. *Biofeedback and Self-regulation, 21,* 149–165.

Gregory, G. D., & Munch, J. M. (1997). Cultural values in international advertising: An examination of familial norms and roles in Mexico. *Psychology & Marketing, 14,* 99–119.

Gregory, R. L. (1961). The brain as an engineering problem. In W. H. Thorpe & O. L. Zangwill (Eds.), *Current problems in animal behaviour.* Cambridge: Cambridge University Press.

Gregory, R. L. (1974). *Concepts and mechanisms of perception.* New York: Scribner.

Grèzes, J., & Decety, J. (2001). Functional anatomy of execution, mental simulation, observation, and verb generation of actions: A meta-analysis. *Human Brain Mapping, 12,* 1–19.

Grice, H. P. (1975). Logic and conversation. In P. Cole & J. L. Morgan (Ed.), *Syntax and semantics: Vol. 3, Speech acts* (pp. 41–58). New York: Seminar Press.

Grice, J. W., & Seely, E. (2000). The evolution of sex differences in jealousy: Failure to replicate previous results. *Journal of Research in Personality, 34,* 348–356.

Griggs, R. A., & Cox, J. R. (1982). The elusive thematic-materials effect in Wason's selection task. *British Journal of Psychology, 73,* 407–420.

Grill-Spector, K., Kushnir, T., Hendler, T., Edelman, S., Itzchak, Y., & Malach, R. (1998). A sequence of object-processing stages revealed by fMRI in the human occipital lobe. *Human Brain Mapping, 6,* 316–328.

Grillo, C., La Mantia, I., Triolo, C., Scollo, A., La Boria, A., Intelisano, G., & Caruso, S. (2001). Rhinomanometric and olfactometric variations throughout the menstrual cycle. *Annals of Otology, Rhinology & Laryngology, 110,* 785–789.

Grilly, D. (1994). *Drugs and human behavior,* 2nd edition. Boston: Allyn and Bacon.

Grimes, K., & Walker, E. F. (1994). Childhood emotional expressions, educational attainments, and age at onset of illness in schizophrenia. *Journal of Abnormal Psychology, 103,* 784–790.

Grimshaw, G. M., Adelstein, A., Bryden, M. P., & MacKinnon, G. E. (1998). First-language acquisition in adolescence: Evidence for a critical period for verbal language development. *Brain & Language, 63,* 237–255.

Grisaru, N., Amir, M., Cohen, H., & Kaplan, Z. (1998). Effect of transcranial magnetic stimulation in posttraumatic stress disorder: A preliminary study. *Biological Psychiatry, 44,* 52–55.

Grisaru, N., Chudakov, B., Yaroslavsky, Y., & Belmaker, R. H. (1998). Transcranial magnetic stimulation in mania: A controlled study. *American Journal of Psychiatry, 155,* 1608–1610.

Grissmer, D. W., Kirby, S. N., Bevends, M., & Williamson, S. (1994). *Student achievement and the changing American family.* Santa Monica, CA: RAND.

Grodzinsky, Y. (1986). Language deficits and the theory of syntax. *Brain and Language, 27,* 135–159.

Groome, L. J., Swiber, M. J., Bentz, L. S., Holland, S. B., et al. (1995). Maternal anxiety during pregnancy: Effect on fetal behavior at 38 to 40 weeks of gestation. *Journal of Developmental & Behavioral Pediatrics, 16,* 391–396.

Gross, J., & Levenson, R. W. (1997). Hiding feelings: The acute effects of inhibiting negative and positive emotion. *Journal of Abnormal Psychology, 106,* 95–103.

Gross, J. J., Carstensen, L. L., Pasupathi, M., Tsai, J., Goetestam Skorpen, C., & Hsu, A. Y. C. (1997). Emotion and aging: Experience, expression, and control. *Psychology & Aging, 12,* 590–599.

Grossarth-Maticek, R., Eysenck, H. J., Boyle, G. J., Heeb, J., Costa, C. D., & Diel, I. J. (2000). Interaction of psychosocial and physical risk factors in the causation of mammary cancer, and its prevention through psychological methods of treatment. *Journal of Clinical Psychology, 56,* 33–50.

Grossberg, S., Mingolla, E., & Ross, W. D. (1997). Visual brain and visual perception: How does the cortex do perceptual grouping? *Trends in Neuroscience, 20,* 106–111.

Grossman, R. P., & Till, B. D. (1998). The persistence of classically conditioned brand attitudes. *Journal of Advertising, 27,* 23–31.

Guadagno, R. W., Asher, T., Demaine, L. H., & Cialdini, R. B. (2001). When saying yes leads to saying no: Preference for consistency and the reverse foot-in-the-door effect. *Personality & Social Psychology Bulletin, 27,* 859–867.

Gudjonsson, G. H. (1991). Suggestibility and compliance among alleged false confessors and resisters in criminal trials. *Medicine, Science, and the Law, 31,* 147–151.

Guerin, B. (1993). *Social facilitation.* Paris: Cambridge University Press.

Guice, J. (1999, November). Sociologists go to work in high technology. *Footnotes,* p. 8.

Guilford, J. P. (1967). *The nature of human intelligence.* New York: McGraw-Hill.

Guilford, J. P. (1979). Some incubated thoughts on incubation. *Journal of Creative Behavior, 13,* 1–8.

Guilleminault, C., Raynal, D., Takahashi, S., Carskadon, M., & Dement, W. (1976). Evaluation of short-term and long-term treatment of the narcolepsy syndrome with clomipramine hydrochloride. *Acta Neurologica Scandinavica, 54,* 71–87.

Guillery, B., Desgranges, B., Katis, S., de la Sayette, V., Viader, F., & Eustache, F. (2001). Semantic acquisition without memories: Evidence from transient global amnesia. *Neuroreport, 12,* 3865–3869.

Guldner, G. T., & Swensen, C. H. (1995). Time spent together and relationship quality: Long-distance relationships as a test case. *Journal of Social and Personal Relationships, 12,* 313–320.

Gulick, W. L., Gescheider, G. A., & Frisina, R. D. (1989). *Hearing: Physiological acoustics, neural coding, and psychoacoustics.* New York: Oxford University Press.

Gulya, M., Rossi-George, A., Hartshorn, K., Vieira, A., Rovee Collier, C., Johnson, M. K., & Chalfonte, B. L. (2002). The development of explicit memory for basic perceptual features. *Journal of Experimental Child Psychology, 81,* 276–297.

Gunewardene, A., Huon, G. F., & Zheng, R. (2001). Exposure to westernization and dieting: A cross-cultural study. *International Journal of Eating Disorders, 29,* 289–293.

Gur, R. C., Turetsky, B. I., Matsui, M., Yan, M., Bilker, W., Hughett, P., & Gur, R. E. (1999). Sex differences in brain gray and white matter in healthy young adults: Correlations with cognitive performance. *Journal of Neuroscience, 19,* 4065–4072.

Gureje, O., Mavreas, V., Vazquez-Barquero, J. L., & Janca, A. (1997). Problems related to alcohol use: A cross-cultural perspective. *Culture, Medicine, and Psychiatry, 21,* 199–211.

Gustavson, C. R., Garcia, J., Hankins, W. G., & Rusiniak, K. W. (1974). Coyote predation control by aversive conditioning, *Science, 184,* 581–583.

Gustavson, C. R., Kelly, D. J., & Sweeney, M. (1976). Prey-lithium aversions I: Coyotes and wolves. *Behavioral Biology, 17,* 61–72.

Guthrie, G. M., Guthrie, H. A., Fernandez, T. L., & Esterea, N. O. (1982). Cultural influences and reinforcement stratefies. *Behavior Therapy, 13,* 624–637.

Glutting, J. J., Oh, H.-J., Ward, T., & Ward, S. (2000). Possible criterion-related bias of the WISC-III with a referral sample. *Journal of Psychoeducational Assessment, 18,* 17–26.

Guttmann, C. R. G., Jolesz, F. A., Kikinis, R., Killiany, R. J., Moss, M. B., Sandor, T., & Albert, M. S. (1998). White matter changes with normal aging, *Neurology, 50,* 972–978.

Gyulai, L., Abass, A., Broich, K., & Reilley, J. (1997). I-123 lofetamine single-photon computer emission tomography in rapid cycling bipolar disorder: A clinical study. *Biological Psychiatry, 41,* 152–161.

Haaga, D. A., & Davison, G. C. (1989). Slow progress in rational-emotive therapy outcome research: Etiology and treatment. *Cognitive Therapy & Research, 13,* 493–450.

Haapasalo, J., & Pokela, E. (1999). Child-rearing and child abuse antecedents of criminality. *Aggression & Violent Behavior, 4,* 107–127.

Haberlandt, K. (1997). *Cognitive psychology* (2nd ed.). Needham Heights, MA: Allyn & Bacon.

Hackenberg, T. D., & Hineline, P. N. (1990). Discrimination, symbolic behavior, and the origins of awareness. Unpublished manuscript, Temple University, Philadelphia.

Hacker, A. (1992). *Two nations: Black and white, separate, hostile, unequal.* New York: Scribner's.

Hacking, I. (1995). *Rewriting the soul: Multiple personality and the sciences of memory.* Princeton, NJ: Princeton University Press.

Hadamard, J. (1945). *An essay on the psychology of invention in the mathematical field.* Princeton, NJ: Princeton University Press.

Haddad, A., & Newby, R. (1999, May–June). Members comment on ASA's publication on affirmative action. *Footnotes,* p. 9.

Hahn, R. A. (1997). The nocebo phenomenon: Scope and foundations. In A. Harrington (Ed.). *The placebo effect: An interdisciplinary exploration.* Cambridge, MA: Harvard University Press.

Haier, R. J., Siegel, B. V., Nuechterlein, K. H., Hazlett, E., Wu, J. C., Paek, J., Browning, H. L., & Buchsbaum, M. S. (1988). Cortical glucose metabolic rate correlates of abstract reasoning and attention studied with positron emission tomography. *Intelligence, 12,* 199–217.

Haier, R. J., Siegel, B., Tang, C., Abel, L., & Buchsbaum, M. S. (1992). Intelligence and changes in regional cerebral glucose metabolic rate following learning. *Intelligence 16,* 415–426.

Haier, R. J., et al. (1984) Evoked potential augmenting-reducing and personality differences. *Personality & Indiv. Differences 5,* 293–301.

Hakuta, K., Bialystok, E., and Wiley, E. (2003). Critical evidence: A test of the critical-period hypothesis for second-language learning. *Psychological Science, 14,* 31–38.

Hall, C. S. (1984). "A ubiquitous sex difference in dreams." revisited. *Journal of Personality and Social Psychology, 46,* 1109–1117.

Hall, D. T., & Nougaim, K. E. (1968). An examination of Maslow's need hierarchy in an organizational setting. *Organizational Behavior and Human Performance, 3,* 12–35.

Hall, G. S. (1904). *Adolescence: Its psychology and its relation to physiology, anthropology, sociology, sex, crime, religion, and education* (Vols. I & II). Englewood Cliffs, NJ: Prentice-Hall.

Hall, J., Parkinson, J. A., Connor, T. M., Dickinson, A., & Everitt, B. J. (2001). Involvement of the central nucleus of the amygdala and nucleus accumbens core in mediating Pavlovian influences on instrumental behaviour. *European Journal of Neuroscience, 13,* 1984–1992.

Hall, J. A. (1978). Gender effects in decoding nonverbal cues. *Psychological Bulletin, 85,* 845–875.

Hall, J. A. (1987). On explaining gender differences: The case of nonverbal communication. In P. Shaver & C. Hendrick (Eds.). *Sex and gender.* Newbury Park, Calif.: Sage.

Hall, J. F. (1984). Backward conditioning in Pavlovian type studies: Reevaluation and present status. *Pavlovian Journal of Biological Science, 19,* 163–168.

Hall, J. F. (1989). *Learning and memory* (2nd. ed.). Massachusetts: Allyn & Bacon.

Halle, M. (1990). Phonology. In D. N. Osherson, & H. Lasnik (Ed.), *An invitation to cognitive science: Vol. 1, Language* (pp. 43–68). Cambridge, MA: MIT Press.

Hallstrom, T., & Samuelsson, S. (1990). Changes in women's sexual desire in middle life: The longitudinal study of women in Gothenburg. *Archives of Sexual Behavior, 19,* 259–268.

Halmi, K. (1995). Basic Biological overview of eating disorders. In F. E. Bloom & D. J. Kupfer (Eds.), *Psychopharmacology: The fourth generation of progress.* New York: Raven Press, Ltd.

Halmi, K. (1996). The psychobiology of eating behavior in anorexia nervosa. *Psychiatry Research, 62,* 23–29.

Halpern, A. R. (1988). Mental scanning in auditory imagery for songs. *Journal of Experimental Psychology: Learning, Memory and Cognition, 14,* 434–443.

Halpern, A. R., & Zatorre, R. J. (1999). When that tune runs through your head: A PET investigation of auditory imagery for familiar melodies. *Cerebral Cortex, 9,* 697–704.

Halpern, D. F. (1992). *Sex differences in cognitive ability.* Hillsdale, NJ: Erlbaum.

Halpern, D. F. (1997). Sex differences in intelligence: Implications for education. *American Psychologist, 52,* 1091–1102.

Hamann, S., & Mao, H. (2002). Positive and negative emotional verbal stimuli elicit activity in the left amygdala. *Neuroreport: For Rapid Communication of Neuroscience Research, 13,* 15–19.

Hamann, S. B., Stefanacci, L., Squire, L. R., Adolphs, R., Tranel, D., Damasio, H., & Damasio, A. (1996). Recognizing facial emotion. *Nature, 379,* 497.

Hamer, D. H., Hu, S., Magnuson, V. L., Hu, N., & Pattatucci, A. M. (1993). A linkage between DNA markers on the X chromosome and male sexual orientation. *Science, 261,* 321–327.

Hamilton, D. L., & Sherman, S. J. (1989). Illusory correlations: Implications for stereotype theory and research. In D. Bar-Tal, C. F. Graumann, A. W. Kruglanski, & W. Stroebe (Eds.), *Stereotyping and prejudice: Changing conceptions* (pp. 59–82). New York: Springer-Verlag.

Hamilton, G. V. (1978). Obedience and responsibility: A jury simulation. *Journal of Personality and Social Psychology, 36,* 126–146.

Hamilton, J. A., Haier, R. J., & Buchsbaum, M. S. (1984). Intrinsic enjoyment and boredom coping scales: Validation with personality, evoked potential and attention measures. *Personality and Individual Differences, 5,* 183–193.

Hamilton, M. (1967). Development of a rating scale for primary depressive illness. *British Journal of Social & Clinical Psychology, 6,* 278–296.

Hamilton, M. E., Voris, J. C., Sebastian, P. S., Singha, A. K., Krejci, L. P., Elder, I. R., Allen, J. E., Beitz, J. E., Covington, K. R., Newton, A. E., Price, L. T., Tillman, E., & Hernandez, L. L. (1998). Money as a tool to extinguish conditioned responses to cocaine in addicts. *Journal of Clinical Psychology, 54,* 211–218.

Hamilton, R. F. (1996). *The social construction of reality.* New Haven, CT: Yale University Press.

Hamilton, V. L., Hoffman, W. S., Broman, C. L., & Rauma, D. (1993). Unemployment, distress, and coping: A panel study of autoworkers. *Journal of Personality and Social Psychology, 65,* 234–247.

Hampson, E. (1990). Estrogen-related variations in human spatial and articulatory motor skills. *Psychoneuroendocrinology, 15,* 97–111.

Hampson, E., & Kimura, D. (1988). Reciprocal effects of hormonal fluctuations on human motor and perceptual-spatial skills. *Behavioral Neuroscience, 102,* 456–459.

Han, S., & Humphreys, G. W. (2002). Segmentation and selection contribute to local processing in hierarchical analysis. *Quarterly Journal of Experimental Psychology: Human Experimental Psychology, 55A,* 5–21.

Hansen, W. B., Graham, J. W., Wolkenstein, B. H., Lundy, B. Z., Pearson, J., Flay, B. R., & Johnson, C. A. (1988). Differential impact of three alcohol prevetion curricula on hypothesized mediating variables. *Journal of Drug Educaiton, 18,* 143–153.

Hanson, K. A., & Gidycz, C. A. (1993). Evaluation of a sexual assault prevention program. *Journal of Consulting & Clinical Psychology, 61,* 1046–1052.

Hapidou, E. G., & De Catanzaro, D. (1988). Sensitivity to cold pressor pain in dysmenorrheic and non-dysmenorrheic women as a function of menstrual cycle phase. *Pain, 34,* 277–283.

Haqq, C. M., King, C-Y., Ukiyama, E., Falsafi, S., Haqq, T. N., Donahoe, P. K., & Weiss, M. A. (1994). Molecular basis of mammalian sexual determination: Activation of mullerian inhibiting substance gene expression by SRY. *Science, 266,* 1494–1500.

Haracz, J. L., Minor, T. R., Wilkins, J. N., & Zimmermann, E. G. (1988). Learned helplessness: An experimental model of the DST in rats. *Biological Psychiatry, 23,* 388–396.

Harada, S. (1989). Polymorphism of aldehyde dehydrogenase and its application to alcoholism. *Electrophoresis 10* (8–9), Aug–Sep, pp. 652–655.

Haraldsson, E., & Gissurarson, L. R. (1987). Does geomagnetic activity affect extrasensory perception? *Personality and Individual Differences, 8,* 745–747.

Haraldsson, E., & Houtkooper, J. M. (1992). Effects of perceptual defensiveness, personality and belief on extrasensory perception tasks. *Personality and Individual Differences, 13,* 1085–1096.

Hardy, J. D., & Smith, T. W. (1988). Cynical hostility and vulnerability to disease: Social support, life stress, and physiological response to conflict. *Health Psychology, 7,* 447–459.

Hare, R. D. (1993). *Without conscience: The disturbing world of the psychopaths among us.* New York: Pocket Books.

Hariri, A. R., Mattay, V. S., Tessitore, A., Kolachana, B., Fera, F., Goldman, D., Egan, M. F., & Weinberger, D. R. (2002). Serotonin transporter genetic variation and the response of the human amygdala. *Science, 297,* 400–403.

Harkins, S., & Szymanski, K. (1989). Social loafing and group evaluation. *Journal of Personality and Social Psychology, 56,* 934–941.

Harkins, S. G., & Petty, R. E. (1982). Effects of task difficulty and task uniqueness on social loafing. *Journal of Personality & Social Psychology, 43,* 1214–1229.

Harman, D. (1956). Aging: A theory based on free radical and radiation chemistry. *Journal of Gerontology, 11,* 298–300.

Harris, C. R. (2000). Psychophysiological responses to imagined infidelity: The specific innate modular view of jealousy reconsidered. *Journal of Personality & Social Psychology, 78,* 1082–1091.

Harris, C. R. (2002). Sexual and romantic jealousy in heterosexual and homosexual adults. *Psychological Science, 13,* 7–12.

Harris, H. (1976). The false controversy: Clitoral vs. vaginal orgasm. *Psychotherapy: Theory, Research, and Practice, 13,* 99–103.

Harris, J. R. (1995). Where is the child's environment? A group socialization theory of development. *Psychological Review, 102,* 458–489.

Harris, J. R. (1998). *The nurture assumption: Why children turn out the way they do.* New York: The Free Press.

Harris, P. L. (1995). From simulation to folk psychology. In M. Davies & T. Stone (Eds.), *Folk psychology: The case for development* (pp. 207–221). Cambridge, England: Blackwell.

Harris, R. J., Schoen, L. M., & Hensley, D. L. (1992). A cross-cultural study of story memory. *Journal of Cross-Cultural Psychology, 23,* 133–147.

Hart, A. J., Whalen, P. J., Shin, L. M., McInerney, S. C., Fischer, H., & Rauch, S. L. (2000). Differential response in the human amygdala to racial outgroup vs. ingroup face stimuli. *Neuroreport, 11,* 2351–2355.

Hart, J., Berndt, R. S., & Caramazza, A. (1985). Category-specific naming deficit following cerebral infarction. *Nature, 316,* 439–440.

Hartman, B. J. (1982). An exploratory study of the effects of disco music on the auditory and vestibular systems. *Journal of Auditory Research, 22,* 271–274.

Hartshorne, H., & May, M. A. (1928). *Studies in deceit.* New York: Macmillan.

Hartung, C. M., & Widiger, T. A. (1998). Gender differences in the diagnosis of mental disorders: Conclusions and controversies of the DSM–IV. *Psychological Bulletin, 123,* 260–278.

Hasegawa, I., Fukushima, T., Ihara, T., & Miyashita, Y. (1998). Callosal window between prefrontal cortices: Cognitive interaction to retrieve long-term memory. *Science, 281,* 814–818.

Hasher, L., & Zacks, R. T. (1979). Automatic and effortful processes in memory. *Journal of Experimental Psychology: General, 108,* 356–388.

Hasher, L., & Zacks, R. T. (1984). Automatic processing of fundamental information. The case of frequency of occurence. *American Psychologist, 39,* 1327–1388.

Hastorf, A. H. & Cantril, H. (1954). They saw a game; a case study. *Journal of Abnormal and Social Psychology, 49,* 129–134.

Hatano, G., & Osawa, K. (1983). Digit memory of grand experts in abacus-derived mental calculation. *Cognition, 15,* 95–110.

Hatfield, E., & Sprecher, S. (1986). Men's and women's preferences in marital partners in the United States, Russia, and Japan. *Journal of Cross-Cultural Psychology. 26,* 728–750.

Hatfield, E., Brinton, C., & Cornelius, J. (1989). Passionate love and anxiety in young adolescents. *Motivation and Emotion, 13,* 271–289.

Haug, H. (1987). Brain sizes, surfaces, and neuronal sizes of the cortex cerebri: A stereological investigation of man and his variability and a comparison with some mammals (primates, whales, marsupials, insectivores, and one elephant). *American Journal of Anatomy, 180,* 126–42.

Haug, H., Barmwater, U., Eggers, R., Fischer, D., Kuhl, S., & Sass, N. L. (1983). Anatomical changes in the aging brain: Morphometric analysis of the human prosencephalon. In J. Cervos-Navarro & H. I. Sarkander (Eds.), *Aging: Vol. 21. Brain aging: Neuropathology and neuropharmacology* (pp. 1–22). New York: Raven Press.

Haugtvedt, C. P., & Petty, R. E. (1992). Personality and persuasion: need for cognition moderates the ersistence and resisance of attitude chagnes. *Journal of Personality and Social Psychology, 63,* 308–319.

Hauri, P. (1970). Evening activity, sleep mentation, and subjective sleep quality. *Journal of Abnormal Psychology, 76,* 270–275.

Hauser, M. (1996). *The evolution of communication.* Cambridge, MA: MIT Press.

Hausmann, M., Slabbekoorn, D., Van Goozen, S. H. M., Cohen-Kettenis, P. T., & Guenteurkuen, O. (2000). Sex hormones affect spatial abilities during the menstrual cycle. *Behavioral Neuroscience, 114,* 1245–1250.

Havinghurst, R. (1953). *Human development and education.* New York: Longmans, Green.

Hawkins, J. R. (1994). Sex determination. *Human Molecular Genetics, 3,* 1463–1467.

Haxby, J. V., Gobbini, M. I., Furey, M. L., Ishai, A., Schouten, J. L., & Pietrini, P. (2001). Distributed and overlapping representations of faces and objects in ventral temporal cortex. *Science, 293,* 2425–2430.

Haxby, J. V., Grady, C. L., Horowitz, B., Ungerleider, L. G., Mischkin, M., Carson, R. E., Hercovitch, P., Schapiro, M. B., & Rapoport, S. I. (1991). Dissociation of object and spatial visual processing pathways in human extrastriate cortex. *Proceedings of the National Academy of Sciences, USA, 88,* 1621–1625.

Haxby, J. V., Horowitz, B., Ungerleider, L. G., Maisog, J. M., Pietrini, P., & Grady, C. L. (1994). The functional organization of human extrastriate cortex: A PET-rCBF study of selective attention to faces and locations. *Journal of Neuroscience, 14,* 6336–6353.

Hayes, A. F., & Dunning, D. (1998). Construal Processes and Trait Ambiguity: Implications for Self-Peer Agreement in Personality Judgment. *Journal of Personality and Social Psychology, 72,* 664–677.

Hayflick, L. (1965). The limited in vitro lifetime of human diploid cell strains. *Experimental Cell Research, 37,* 614–636.

Haynor, A. L., & Varacalli, J. A. (1993). Sociology's fall from grace: The six deadly sins of a discipline at the crossroads. *Quarterly Journal of Ideology: A Critique of Conventional Wisdom, 16* (1 & 2), p. 3–29.

Hazan, C., & Shaver, P. R. (1987). Romantic love conceptualized as an attachment process. *Journal of Personality and Social Psychology, 52,* 511–524.

Hazan, C., & Shaver, P. R. (1990). Love and work: An attachment-theoretical perspective. *Journal of Personality and Social Psychology, 59,* 270–280.

Healey, B., & Wearing, A. (1989). Personality, life events, and subjective well-being: Toward a dynamic equilibrium model. *Journal of Personality and Social Psychology, 57,* 731–739.

Hearth, A. H. (1991, September 22). Two 'maiden ladies' with century-old stories to tell. *New York Times.*

Hearts and minds. (1997). *Harvard Mental Health Letter, 14*(1), 1–4.

Heath, A. C., & Martin, N. G. (1990) Psychoticism as a Dimension of Personality: A multivariate genetic test of Eysenck and Eysenck's Psychoticism construct. *Journal of Personality and Social Psychology, 58,* 11–121.

Heath, A. C., Cloninger, C. R., & Martin, N. G. (1994). Testing a model for the genetic structure of personality: A comparison of the personality systems of Cloninger and Eysenck. *Journal of Personality and Social Psychology, 66,* 762–775.

Heath, A. C., Neale, M. C., Kessler, R. C., Eaves, L. H., & Kendler, K. S. (1992). Evidence for genetic influences on personality from self-reports and informant ratings. *Journal of Personality and Social Psychology, 63,* 85–96.

Hébert, S., & Peretz, I. (1997). Recognition of music in long-term memory: Are melodic and temporal patterns equal partners? *Memory & Cognition, 25,* 518–533.

Hecker, M., Chesney, M. N., Black, G., & Frautsch, N. (1988). Coronary-prone behaviors in the Western Collaborative Group Study. *Psychosomatic Medicine, 50,* 153–164.

Hedges, C. (1997, November 26). Bosnia's factions push their versions of war into the history books. *International Herald Tribune,* 5.

Heider, K. G. (1976). Dani sexuality: A low energy system. *Man, 11,* 188–201.

Heimberg, R. G., Liebowitz, M. R., Hope, D. A., Schneier, F. R., Holt, C. S., Welkowitz, L. A., Juster, H. R., Campeas, R., Bruch, M. A., Cloitre, M., Fallon, B., & Klein, D. F. (1998). Cognitive behavioral group therapy vs phenelzine therapy for social phobia: 12-week outcome. *Archives of General Psychiatry, 55,* 1133–1141.

Heinssen, R. K., Perkins, D. O., Appelbaum, P. S., & Fenton, W. S. (2001). Informed consent in early psychosis research: NIMH workshop, November 15, 2000. *Schizophrenia Bulletin, 27,* 571–584.

Heiss, W. D., Pawlik, G., Herholz, K., Wagner, R., & Weinhard, K. (1985). Regional cerebral glucose metabolism in man during wakefulness, sleep, and dreaming. *Brain Research, 327,* 362–366.

Heit, G., Smith, M. E., & Halgren, E. (1988). Neural encoding of individual words and faces by the human hippocampus and amygdala. *Nature, 333,* 773–775.

Hekkanen, S. T., & McEvoy, C. (2002). False memories and source-monitoring problems: Criterion differences. *Applied Cognitive Psychology, 16,* 73–85.

Held, J. D., Alderton, D. L., Foley, P. P., & Segall, D. O. (1993). Arithmetic reasoning gender differences: Explanations found in the Armed Services Vocational Aptitude Battery. *Learning and Individual Differences, 5,* 171–186.

Hellige, J. B. (1993). *Hemispheric asymmetry: What's right and what's left.* Cambridge, MA: Harvard University Press.

Hellige, J. B., & Michimata, C. (1989). Categorization versus distance: Hemispheric differences for processing spatial information. *Memory & Cognition, 17,* 770–776.

Hellige, J. B., & Sergent, J. (1986). Role of task factors in visual field asymmetries. *Brain and Cognition, 5,* 200–222.

Hellström, K., & Öst, L.-G. (1995). One-session therapist directed exposure vs. two forms of manual directed self-exposure in the treatment of spider phobia. *Behaviour Research and Therapy, 33,* 959–965.

Helms, J. E. (1996). The triple quandary of race, culture, and social class in standardized cognitive ability testing. In D. P. Flanaghan, J. L. Genshaft, & P. L. Harrison (Eds.), *Contemporary intellectual assessment: Theories, test and issues* (pp. 517–532). New York: Builford Press.

Helms, J. E., & Cook, D. A. (1999). *Using race and culture in counseling and psychotherapy: Theory and process.* Needham Heights, MA: Allyn & Bacon.

Helson, H. (1964). *Adaptation-level theory: An experimental and systematic approach to behavior.* New York: Harper & Row.

Henderlong, J., & Lepper, M. R. (2002). The effects of praise on children's intrinsic motivation: A review and synthesis. *Psychological Bulletin, 128,* 774–795.

Hendricks, J., & Hendricks, C. D. (1986). *Aging in mass society: Myth and realities.* Boston: Little, Brown.

Heng, M. A. (2000). Scrutinizing common sense: The role of practical intelligence in intellectual giftedness. *Gifted Child Quarterly, 44,* 171–182.

Henley, N. M. (1977). *Body politics: Power, sex, and non-verbal communication.* Englewood Cliffs, NJ: Prentice-Hall.

Hennessey, B. A., & Amabile, T. M. (1998). Reward, Intrinsic Motivation, and Creativity. *American Psychologist, 53,* 674–675.

Henry, B., Caspi, A., Moffitt, T. E., & Silva, P. A. (1996). Temperamental and familial predictors of violent and nonviolent criminal convictions: Age 3 to Age 18. *Developmental Psychology, 32,* 614–623.

Henry, J. P. (1977). *Stress, health, and the environment.* New York: Springer-Verlag.

Henry, W. P., Strupp, H. H., Schacht, T. E., & Gaston, L. (1994). Psychodynamic approaches. In A. E. Bergin & S. L. Garfield (Eds.), *Handbook of psychotherapy and behavior change,* (4th ed., pp. 467–508). New York: John Wiley & Sons.

Hensel, H. (1982). *Thermal sensations and thermoreceptors in man.* Springfield, IL: Thomas.

Henslin, J. M. (1999). *Sociology: A down-to-earth approach* (4th ed.). Needham Heights, MA: Allyn & Bacon.

Henson, R., Shallice, T., & Dolan, R. (2000). Neuroimaging evidence for dissociable forms of repetition priming. *Science, 287,* 1269–1272.

Hepworth, S. L., Rovet, J. F., & Taylor, Margot J. (2001). Neurophysiological correlates of verbal and nonverbal short-term memory in children: Repetition of words and faces. *Psychophysiology, 38,* 594–600.

Herbert, T. B., & Cohen, S. (1993). Depression and immunity: A meta-analytic review. *Psychological Bulletin, 113,* 472–486.

Herbst, J. H., McCrae, R. R., Costa, P. T., Jr., Feaganes, J. R., & Siegler, I. C. (2000). Self-perceptions of stability and change in personality at midlife: The UNC Alumni Heart Study. *Assessment, 7,* 379–388.

Herman-Giddens, M. E., Slora, E. J., Wasserman, R. C., Bourdony, C. J., Bhapkar, M. V., Koch, G. G., & Hasemeier, C. M. (1997). Secondary sexual characteristics and menses in young girls seen in office practice: A study from the Pediatric Research in Office Settings network. *Pediatrics, 99,* 505–512.

Herman-Giddens M. E., Wang, L., & Koch, G. (2001). Secondary sexual characteristics in boys: Estimates from the National Health and Nutrition Examination Survey III, 1988–1994. *Achives of Pediatric Adolescent Medicine, 155,* 1022–1028.

Hermann, J. A., deMontes, A. I., Dominguez, B., Montes, F., & Hopkins, B. L. (1973). Effects of bonuses for punctuality on the tardiness of industrial workers. *Journal of Applied Behavior Analysis, 4,* 267–272.

Hermelin, B. (2001). *Bright splinters of the mind: A personal story of research with autistic savants.* London: Jessica Kingsley Publishers.

Herrera, H. (1983). *Frida: Biography of Frida Kahlo.* New York: Harper and Row.

Herrnstein, R. J. (1963). *IQ in the meritocracy.* Boston: Little, Brown.

Herrnstein, R. J. (1990). Behavior, reinforcement and utility. *Psychological Science, 1,* 217–224.

Herrnstein, R. J., & Loveland, D. H. (1964), Complex visual concept in the pigeon. *Science, 146,* 549–551.

Herrnstein, R. J., & Murray, C. (1994). *The bell curve: Intelligence and class structure in American life.* New York: Free Press.

Hershberger, S. L., Lichtenstein, P., & Knox, S. S. (1994). Genetic and environmental influences on perceptions of organizational climate. *Joiurnal of Applied Psychology, 79,* 24–33.

Hershman, D. J., & Lieb, J. (1988). *The key to genius/manic-depression and the creative life.* New York: Prometheus Books.

Hershman, D. J., & Lieb, J. (1998). *Manic depression and creativity.* New York: Prometheus Books.

Hertenstein, M. J., & Campos, J. J. (2001). Emotion regulation via maternal touch. *Infancy, 2,* 549–566.

Hertzog, C., & Schaie, K. W. (1988). Stability and change in adult intelligence: 2. Simultaneous analysis of longitudinal means and covariance structures. *Psychology and Aging, 3,* 122–130.

Herz, R. S., & Cahill, E. D. (1997). Differential use of sensory information in sexual behavior as a function of gender. *Human Nature, 8,* 275–286.

Herz, R. S., & Inzlicht, M. (2002). Sex differences in response to physical and social factors involved in human mate selection: The importance of smell for women. *Evolution & Human Behavior, 23,* 359–364.

Herzog, T. A., Abrams, D. B., Emmons, K. M., Linnan, L. A., & Shadel, W. G. (1999). Do Processes of Change Predict Smoking Stage Movements? A Prospective Analysis of the Transtheoretical Model. *Health Psychology, 18,* 369–375.

Hess, E. E. (1975). The role of pupil size in communication. *Scientific American, 233,* 110–119.

Hierholzer, R., Munson, J., Peabody, C., & Rosenberg, J. (1992). Clinical presentation of PTSD in World War II combat veterans. *Hospital and Community Psychiatry, 43,* 816–820.

Higginbotham, H. N., West, S., & Forsyth, D. (1988). *Psychotherapy and behavior change: Social, cultural and methodological perspectives.* New York: Pergamon.

Higgens, S. T., & Morris, E. K. (1984). Generality of free-operant avoidance conditioning to human behavior. *Psychological Bulletin, 96,* 247–272.

Higgins, E. T. (1996). Knowledge activation: Accessibility, applicability, and salience. In E. T. Higgins & A. Kruglanski (Eds.), *Social psychology: Handbook of basic principles* (pp. 133–168). New York: Guilford.

Hilgard, E. R. (1965). *Hypnotic susceptibility.* New York: Harcourt, Brace & World.

Hilgard, E. R. (1979). Consciousness and control: Lessons from hypnosis. *Australian Journal of Clinical & Experimental Hypnosis, 7,* 103–115.

Hilgard, E. R. (1992). Dissociation and theories of hypnosis. In E. Fromm and M. R. Nash (Eds.). *Contemporary hypnosis research* (pp. 69–101). New York: Guilford Press.

Hilgard, E. R., & Hilgard, J. R. (1999). *Hypnosis in the relief of pain.* New York: Brunnel/Mazel.

Hilgard, E. R., Hilgard, J. R., Macdonald, J., Morgan, A. H., & Johnson, L. S. (1978). Covert pain in hypnotic analgesia: Its reality as tested by the real-simulator design. *Journal of Abnormal Psychology, 87,* 239–246.

Hill, J. O., & Peters, J. C. (1998). Environmental contributions to the obesity epidemic. *Science, 280,* 1371–1374.

Hill, L., Chorney, M. J., Jubinski, D., Thompson, L. A., & Plomin, R. (2002). A quantitative trait locus not associated with cognitive ability in children: A failure to replicate. *Psychological Science, 13,* 561–562.

Hill, L., Craig, I. W., Asherson, P., Ball, D., Eley, T., Ninomiya, T., Fisher, P. J. Turic, D., McGuffin, P., Owen, M. J., Chorney, K., Chorney, M. J., Benbow, C. P., Lubinski, D., Thompson, L. A., & Plomin, R. (1999). DNA pooling and dense marker maps: A systematic search for genes for cognitive ability. *Neuroreport, 10,* 843–848.

Hillis, A. E., Wityk, R. J., Tuffiash, E., Beauchamp, N. J., Jacobs, M. A., Barker, P. B., & Selnes, O. A. (2001). Hypoperfusion of Wernicke's area predicts severity of semantic deficit in acute stroke. *Annals of Neurology, 50,* 561–566.

Hines, M., & Kaufman, F. R. (1994). Androgen and the development of human sex-typical behavior: Rough-and-tumble play and sex of preferred playmates in children with congenital adrenal hyperplasia (CAH). *Child Development, 65,* 1042–1053.

Hinton, D., Um, K., & Ba, P. (2001). Kyol goeu ('wind overload') Part I: A cultural syndrome of orthostatic panic among Khmer refugees. *Transcultural Psychiatry, 38,* 403–432.

Hirsch, J. (1971). Behavior-genetic analysis and its biosocial consequences. In R. Cancro (Ed.), *Intelligence: Genetic and environmental influences* (pp. 88–106). New York: Grune & Stratton.

Hirsch, J. (1997). The triumph of wishful thinking over genetic irrelevance. *Cahiers de Psychologie Cognitive/Current Psychology of Cognition, 16,* 711–720.

Hirschfeld, R. M. A. (1997). Long-term drug treatment of unipolar depression. *International Clinical Psychopharmacology, 11,* 211–217.

Hobson, J. A. (1995). *Sleep.* New York: Scientific American Library.

Hobson, J. A. (1996, February). How the brain goes out of its mind. *Harvard Mental Health Newsletter, 3.*

Hobson, J. A., & McCarley, R. W. (1977). The brain as a dream state generator: An activation-synthesis hypothesis of the dream process. *American Journal of Psychiatry, 134,* 1335–1348.

Hobson, J. A., Pace-Schott, E., & Stickgold, R. (2000). Dreaming and the brain: Toward a cognitive neuroscience of conscious states. *Behavioral and Brain Sciences, 23.*

Hochman, D. W. (2000). Optical monitoring of neuronal activity: Brain-mapping on a shoestring. *Brain & Cognition, 42,* 56–59.

Hochschild, A. (1989). *The second shift: Working parents and the revolution at home.* New York: Viking.

Hockemeyer, J., & Smyth, J. (2002). Evaluating the feasibility and efficacy of the self-administered manual-based stress management intervention for individuals with asthma: Results from a controlled study. *Behavioral Medicine, 27,* 161–172.

Hoeks, J. C., Vonk, W., & Schriefers, H. (2002). Processing coordinated structures in context: The effect of topic-structure on ambiguity resolution. *Journal of Memory & Language, 46,* 99–119.

Hoeksema-van Orden, C. Y. D., Gaillard, A. W. K., & Buunk, B. P. (1998). Social loafing under fatigue. *Journal of Personality and Social Psychology, 75,* 1179–1190.

Hoffart, A. (1998). Cognitive and guided mastery therapy of agoraphobia: Long-term outcome and mechanisms of change. *Cognitive Therapy and Research, 22,* 195–207.

Hoffman, D. D., & Richards, W. A. (1984). Parts of recognition. *Cognition, 18,* 65–96.

Hoffman, L. W. (1991). The influence of the family environment on personality: Accounting for sibling differerences. *Psychological Bulletin, 110,* 187–203.

Hoffman, M. L. (2000). *Empathy and moral development: Implications for caring and justice.* New York: Cambridge University Press.

Hoffman, R E., Hawkins, K. A., Gueorguieva, R., Boutros, N. N., Rachid, F., Carroll, K., & Krystal, J. H. (2003). Transcranial magnetic stimulation of left temporal cortex and medication-resistent auditory hallucinations. *Archives of General Psychiatry, 60,* 49–56.

Hoffrage, U., Gigerenzer, G., Krauss, S., & Martignon, L. (2002). Representation facilitates reasoning: What natural frequencies are and what they are not. *Cognition, 84,* 343–352.

Hogan, J., & Hogan, R. T. (1993). Ambiguities of conscientiousness. Presented at 10th Annual Meeting of Society Industrial and Organizational Psychology, Orlando, FL.

Hohlstein, L. A., Smith, G. T., & Atlas, J. G. (1998). An application of expectancy theory to eating disorders: Development and validation of measures of eating and dieting expectancies. *Psychological Assessment, 10,* 49–58.

Hohman, G. W. (1966). Some effects of spinal cord lesions on experienced emotional feelings. *Psychophysiology, 3,* 143–156.

Holahan, C. K., Holahan, C. J., & Belk, S. S. (1984). Adjustment in aging: The roles of life stress, hassles, and self-efficacy. *Health Psychology, 3,* 3315–328.

Holcombe, A. O., & Cavanagh, P. (2001). Early binding of feature pairs for visual perception. *Nature Neuroscience, 4,* 127–128.

Holden, C. (1980). Identical twins reared apart. *Science, 207,* 1323–1328.

Holland, A. J., Sicotte, N., & Treasure, J. (1988). Anorexia nervosa: Evidence for a genetic basis. *Journal of Psychosomatic Research, 32,* 561–571.

Hollerman, J. R., & Schultz, W. (1998). Dopamine neurons report an error in the temporal prediction of reward during learning. *Nature Neuroscience, 1,* 304–309.

Hollerman, J. R., Tremblay, L., & Schultz, W. (1998). Influence of reward expectation on behavior-related neuronal activity in primate striatum. *Journal of Neurophysiology, 80,* 947–963.

Hollis, K. L. (1997). Compenorary reserch on pavlovian conditioning: A 'new' functional analysis. *American Psychologist, 52,* 956–965.

Hollon, S. D., & Beck, A. T. (1994). Cognitive and cognitive-behavioral therapies. In A. E. Bergin & S. L. Garfield (Eds.), *Handbook of psychotherapy and behavior change* (4th ed., pp. 428–466). New York: John Wiley & Sons.

Holmes, D. S. (1984). Meditation and somatic arousal reduction. A review of the experimental evidence. *American Psychologist, 39,* 1–10.

Holmes, N. (1984). *Designer's guide to creating charts & diagrams.* New York: W. H. Freeman.

Holmes, T. H., & Rahe, R. H. (1967). The social readjustment rating scale. *Journal of Psychosomatic Research, 11,* 213–218.

Holyoak, K. J., & Thagard, P. (1997). The analogical mind. *American Psychologist, 52,* 35–44.

Holzman, P. S., Chen, Y., Nakayama, K., Levy, D. L., & Matthysse, S. (1998). How are deficits in motion perception related to eye-tracking dysfunction in schizophrenia? In M. F. Lenzenweger & R. H. Dworkin (Eds.), *Origins and development of schizophrenia: Advances in experimental psychopathology* (pp. 161–184). Washington, DC: American Psychological Association.

Holzman, P. S., Kringlen, E., Matthysse, S., Flanagan, S. D., Lipton, R. B., Cramer, S., Levin, S., Lange, K., & Levy, D. L. (1988). A single dominant gene can account for eye tracking dysfunctions and schizophrenia in offspring of discordant twins. *Archives of General Psychiatry, 45,* 641–647.

Honeybourne, C., Matchett, G., & Davey, G. C. (1993). Expectancy models of laboratory preparedness effects: A UCS-expectancy bias in phylogenetic and ontogenetic fear-relevant stimuli. *Behavior Therapy, 24,* 253–264.

Honeycutt, J. M., Cantrill, J. G., Kelly, P., & Lambkin, D. (1998). How do I love thee? Let me consider my options: Cognition, verbal strategies, and the escalation of intimacy. *Human Communication Research, 25,* 39–63.

Honig, A., Hofman, A., Rozendaal, N., & Dingemans, P. (1997). Psycho-education in bipolar disorder: Effect on expressed emotion. *Psychiatry Research, 72,* 17–22.

Honorton, C. (1997). The Ganzfeld novice: Four predictors of initial ESP performance. *Journal of Parapsychology, 61,* 143–158.

Hooley, J. M., & Licht, D. M. (1997). Expressed emotional and causal attributions in the spouses of depressed patients. *Journal of Abnormal Psychology, 106,* 298–306.

Hooper, F. H., Hooper, J. O., & Colbert, K. K. (1984) *Personality and memory correlates of intellectual functioning: Young adulthood to old age.* Basel, Switzerland: Karger.

Hopf, J.-M., & Mangun, G. R. (2000). Shifting visual attention in space: An electrophysiological analysis using high spatial resolution mapping. *Clinical Neurophysiology, 111,* 1241–1257.

Horesh, N., Amir, Marianne, Kedem, P., Goldberger, Y., & Kotler, M. (1997). Life events in childhood, adolescence and adulthood and the relationship to panic disorder. *Acta Psychiatrica Scandinavica, 96,* 373–378.

Horn, J. (1985). Remodeling old models of intelligence. In B. B. Wolman (Ed.), *Handbook of intelligence* (pp. 267–300). New York: Wiley.

Horn, J. (1989). Models of intelligence. In R. L. Linn (Ed.), *Intelligence: Measurement, theory, and public policy* (pp. 29–73). Urbana, IL: University of Illinois Press.

Horn, J., & Cattell, R. B. (1966). Refinement and test of the theory of fluid and crystallized general intelligences. *Journal of Educational Psychology, 57,* 253–270.

Horn, J. L. (1986). Intellectual ability concepts. In R. J. Sternberg (Ed.), *Advances in the psychology of human intelligence,* Vol. 3 (pp. 35–77). Hillsdale, NJ: Erlbaum.

Horn, J. L. (1994). Theory of fluid and crystallized intelligence. In R. J. Sternberg (Ed.), *The encyclopedia of human intelligence,* Vol. 1 (pp. 443–451). New York: Macmillan.

Horn, J. L., & Noll, J. (1994). A system for understanding cognitive capabilities: A theory and the evidence on which it is based. In D. K. Detterman (Ed.). *Current topics in human intelligence, Volume 4: Theories of intelligence.* Norwood, NJ: Ablex.

Horney, K. (1937). *Neurotic personality of our times.* New York: Norton.

Horowitz, J. L., & Newcomb, M. D. (2001). A multidimensional approach to homosexual identity. *Journal of Homosexuality, 42,* 1–19.

Horowitz, M. J. (1998). Personality disorder diagnoses. *American Journal of Psychiatry, 155,* 1464.

Hortacsu, N. (1997). Family- and couple-initiated marriages in Turkey. *Genetic, Social, and General Psychology Monographs, 123,* 325–342.

Horwath, E., & Weissman, M. M. (2000). The epidemiology and cross-national presentation of obsessive-compulsive disorder. *Psychiatric Clinics of North America, 23,* 493–507.

Horwitz, W. A., Kestenbaum, C., Person, E., & Jarvik, L. (1965). Identical twin—"idiot savants"—calendar calculators. *American Journal of Psychiatry, 121,* 1075–1079.

Hoshi, Y., Oda, I., Wada, Y., Ito, Y., Yamashita, Y., Oda, M., Ohta, K., Yamada, Y., and Tamura, M. (2000). Visuospatial imagery is a fruitful strategy for the digit span backward task: A study with near-infrared optical tomography. *Cognitive Brain Research, 9,* 339–342.

Hou, C., Miller, B. L., Cummings, J. L., Goldberg, M., Mychack, P., Bottino, V., & Benson, D. F. (2000). Artistic savants. *Neuropsychiatry, Neuropsychology, & Behavioral Neurology, 13,* 29–38.

House, J., Landis, K., & Umberson, D. (1988). Social relationships and health. *Science, 241,* 540–545.

House, R. J., & Podsakoff, P. M. (1994). Leadership effectiveness: Past perspectives and future directions for research. In J. Greenberg (Ed.), *Organizational behavior: The state of the science* (pp. 45–82). Hillsdale, NJ: Erlbaum.

Hovland, C. I., & Weiss, W. (1951). The influence of source credibility on communication effectiveness. *Public Opinion Quarterly, 15,* 635–650.

Howard, K. I., Kopta, S. M., Krause, M. S., & Orlinsky, D. E. (1986). The does-effect relationship in psychotherapy. *American Psychologist, 41,* 159–164.

Howard, R. W. (2001). Searching the real world for signs of rising population intelligence. *Personality & Individual Differences, 30,* 1039–1058.

Hsee, C. K., Elaine, H., Carlson, J. G., & Chemtob, C. (1990). The effect of power on susceptibility to emotional contagion. *Cognition & Emotion, 4*(4), 327–340.

Hsieh, L., Gandour, J., Wong, D., & Hutchins, G. D. (2001). Functional heterogeneity of inferior frontal gyrus is shaped by linguistic experience. *Brain & Language, 76,* 227–252.

Hu, W. (1990, Nov. 2–3). *The pragmatic motivation behind the use of the inverted sentence in the Beijing dialect.* Paper presented at Midwest Conference on Asian Affairs: Bloomington, Indiana.

Hu, W. (1995). Verbal semantics of presentative sentences. *Yuyan Yanjiu (Linguistic Studies), 29,* 100–112.

Hubacek, J. A., Pitha, J., Skodova, Z., Adamkova, V., Lanska, V., & Poledne, R. (2001). A possible role of apolipoprotein E polymorphism in predisposition to higher education. *Neuropsychobiology, 43,* 200–203.

Hubel, D. H., & Wiesel, T. N. (1962). Receptive fields, binocular interaction and functional architecture in the cat's visual cortex. *Journal of Physiology, 160,* 106–154.

Hubel, D. H., & Wiesel, T. N. (1965). Receptive fields of neurons in two nonstriate visual areas (18 and 19) of the cat. *Journal of Neurophysiology, 28,* 229–289.

Hubel, D. H., & Wiesel, T. N. (1974). Sequence regularity and orientation columns in the monkey striate cortex. *Journal of Comparative Neurology, 158,* 295–306.

Huddy, L., & Virtanen, S. (1995). Subgroup differentiation and subgroup bias among Latinos as a function of familiarity and positive distinctiveness. *Journal of Personality and Social Psychology, 68,* 97–108.

Hudspeth, A. J. (1983). The hair cells of the inner ear. *Scientific American, 248,* 54–64.

Huen, K. F., Leung, S. S., Lau, J. T., Cheung, A. Y., Leung, N. K., & Chiu, M. C. (1997). Secular trend in the sexual maturation of southern Chinese girls. *Acta Paediatrica, 86,* 1121–1124.

Huerta, P. T., Scearce, K. A., Farris, S. M., Empson, R. M., & Prusky, G. T. (1996). Preservation of spatial learning in fyn tryosine kinase knockout mice. *Neuroreport, 7,* 1685–1689.

Huesmann, L. R., & Eron, L. D. (1986). *Television and the aggressive child: A cross-national comparison.* Hillsdale, NJ: Erlbaum.

Huesmann, L. R., & Miller, L. S. (1994). Long-term effects of repeated exposure to media violence in childhood. In L. R. Huesmann (Ed.) et al. *Aggressive behavior: Current perspectives.* (pp. 153–186). New York, NY: Plenum Press.

Huff, D. (1954). *How to lie with statistics.* New York: Norton.

Hugdahl, K. (1995a). Classical conditioning and implicit learning: The right hemisphere hypothesis. In R. J. Davidson & K. Hugdahl (Eds.), *Brain asymmetry,* (pp. 235–267). Cambridge, MA: MIT Press.

Hugdahl, K. (1995b). *Psychophysiology: The mind-body perspective.* Cambridge, MA: Harvard University Press.

Hugdahl, K. (2001). *Psychophysiology: The mind-body perspective.* Cambridge, MA: Harvard University Press.

Hui, C. H., & Triandis, H. C. (1986). Individualism-collectivism: A study of cross-cultural researchers. *Journal of Corss-cultural psychology, 17,* 225–248.

Hull, J. G., Van Treuren, R. R., & Virnelli, S. (1987). Hardiness and health: A critique and alternative approach. *Journal of Personality & Social Psychology, 53,* 518–530.

Hultman, C. M., Wieselgren, I., & Oehman, A. (1997). Relationships between social support, social coping and life events in the relapse of schizophrenic patients. *Scandinavian Journal of Psychology, 38,* 3–13.

Hummel, J. E., & Biederman, I. (1992). Dynamic binding in a neural network for shape recognition. *Psychological Review, 99,* 480–517.

Hummel, J. E., & Holyoak, K. J. (1997). Distributed representations of structure: A theory of analogical access and mapping. *Psychological Review, 104,* 427–466.

Humphreys, G. W., Riddoch, M. J., & Price, C. J. (1997). Top-down processes in object identification: Evidence from experimental psychology, neuropsychology and functional anatomy. *Philosophical Transactions of the Royal Society, London, 352,* 1275–1282.

Hunt, E. (1995). *Will we be smart enough? A cognitive analysis of the coming workforce.* New York: Russell Sage.

Hunt, M. (1993). *The story of psychology.* New York: Doubleday.

Hunter, J. E. (1983). A casual analysis of cognitive ability, job knowledge, job performance, and supervisor ratings. In F. Landy, S. Zedeck, & J. Cleveland (Eds.), *Performance measurement and theory* (pp. 257–266). Hillsdale, NJ: Erlbaum.

Huppert, J. D., Bufka, L. F., Barlow, D. H., Gorman, J. M., Shear, M. K., & Woods, S. W. (2001). Therapists, therapist variables and cognitive-behavioral therapy outcome in a multicenter trial for panic disorder. *Journal of Consulting and Clinical Psychology, 69,* 747–755.

Hurvich, L. M., & Jameson, D. (1957). An opponent-process theory of color vision. *Psychological Review, 64,* 384–404.

Huttenlocher, J. (1968). Constructing spatial images: A strategy in reasoning. *Psychological Review, 75*(6), 550–560.

Huttenlocher, J., Higgins, E. T., Milligan, L., & Kaufman, B. (1970). The mystery of the "negative equative" construction. *Journal of Verbal Learning and Verbal Behavior, 9*, 334–341.

Huttenlocher, P. (2002). *Neural plasticity.* Cambridge, MA: Harvard University Press.

Huttenlocher, P. R. (1990). Morphometric study of human cerebral cortex development. *Neuropsychologia, 28*(6), 517–527.

Hyde, T. S., & Jenkins, J. J. (1973). Recall for words as a function of semantic, graphic, and syntactic orientation tasks. *Journal of Verbal Learning and Verbal Behavior, 12*, 471–480.

Hyman, A., Mentzer, T., & Calderone, L. (1979). The contribution of olfaction to taste discrimination. *Bulletin of Psychonomic Society, 13*, 359–362.

Hyman, I. E., & Billings, F. J. (1998). Individual differences and the creation of false childhood memories. *Memory, 6*, 1–20.

Hyman, I. E., & Pentland, J. (1996). The role of mental imagery in the creation of false childhood memories. *Journal of Memory and Language, 35*, 101–117.

Hyman, S. (1998). Personal communication.

Iacono, W. G., Moreau, M., Beiser, M., Fleming, J. A. E., & Lin, T. Y. (1992). Smooth-pursuit eye movement dysfunction and liability for schizophrenia: Implications for genetic modeling. *Journal of Abnormal Psychology, 101*, 104–116.

Iansek, R., & Porter, R. C. (1980). The monkey globus pallidus: Neuronal discharge properties in relation to movement. *Journal of Physiology, 301*, 439–455.

Iervolino, A. C., Pike, A., Manke, B., Reiss, D., Hetherington, E. M., & Plomin, R. (2002). Genetic and environmental influences in adolescent peer socialization: Evidence from two genetically sensitive designs. *Child Development, 73*, 162–174.

Imber, S. D., Pilkonis, P. A., Sotsky, S. M., Elkin, I., Watkins, J. T., Collins, J. F., Shea, M. T., & Leber, S. R. (1991). Mode-specific effects among three treatments for depression. *Journal of Consulting and Clinical Psychology, 58*, 352–359.

Ingledew, D. K., Hardy, L., & Cooper, C. L. (1997). Do resources bolster coping and does coping buffer stress? An organizational study with longitudinal aspect and control for negative affectivity. *Journal of Occupational Health Psychology, 2*, 118–133.

Inman, D. J., Silver, S. M., & Doghramji, K. (1990). Sleep disturbance in Post-Traumatic Stress Disorder: A comparison with non-PTSD insomnia. *Journal of Traumatic Stress, 3*, 429–437.

Insel, T. R. (1992). Toward a neuroanatomy of obsessive-compulsive disorder. *Archives of General Psychiatry, 49*, 739–744.

Insel, T. R. (2000). Toward a neurobiology of attachment. *Review of General Psychology, 4*, 176–185.

Intriligator, J., & Cavanagh, P. (2001). The spatial resolution of visual attention. *Cognitive Psychology, 43*, 171–216.

Inui, A. (1999). Feeding and body-weight regulation by hypothalamic neuropeptides—mediation of the actions of leptin. *Trends in Neurosciences, 22*, 62–67.

Ironson, G., Wynings, C., Schneiderman, N., Baum, A., Rodriguez, M., Greenwood, D., Benight, C., Antoni, M., LaPerriere, A., Huang, H., Klimas, N., & Fletcher, M. A. (1997). Posttraumatic stress symptoms, intrusive thoughts, loss, and immune function after Hurricane Andrew. *Psychosomatic Medicine, 59*, 128–141.

Irwin, M., Lacher, U., & Caldwell, C. (1992). Depression and reduced natural killer cytotoxicity: a longitudinal study of depressed patients and control subjects. *Psychological Medicine, 22*, 1045–50.

Isenberg, D. J. (1986). Group polarization: A critical review and meta-analysis. *Journal of Personality & Social Psychology, 50*, 1141–115?.

Iverson, J. M., & Goldin-Meadow, S. (1998). Why people gesture when they speak. *Nature, 396*, 228.

Iverson, J. M., & Goldin-Meadow, S. (2001). The resilience of gesture in talk: Gesture in blind speakers and listeners. *Developmental Science, 4*, 416–422.

Ivry, R. B., & Robertson, L. C. (1998). *The two sides of perception.* Cambridge, MA: The MIT Press.

Ivy, G., MacLeod, C., Petit, T., & Markus, E. (1992). A physiological framework for perceptual and cognitive changes in aging. In F. I. M. Craik & T. A. Salthouse (Eds.), *The handbook of aging and cognition* (pp. 273–314). Hillsdale, NJ: Erlbaum.

Iyengar, S. S., & Lepper, M. R. (2000). When choice is demotivating: Can one desire too much of a good thing? *Journal of Personality & Social Psychology, 79*, 995–1006.

Izard, C. E. (1971). *The face of emotion.* New York: Appleton-Century-Crofts.

Jacklin, C. N., & Reynolds, C. (1993). Gender and childhood socialization. In A. E. Beall & R. J. Sternberg (Eds.), *The psychology of gender* (pp. 197–214). New York: Guilford Press.

Jackson, D. C., Malmstadt, J. R., Larson, C. L., & Davidson, R. J. (2000). Suppression and enhancement of emotional responses to unpleasant pictures. *Psychophysiology, 37*, 515–522.

Jackson, N., & Butterfield, E. (1986). A conception of giftedness designed to promote research. In R. J. Sternberg & J. E. Davidson (Eds.), *Conceptions of giftedness* (pp. 151–181). New York: Cambridge University Press.

Jackson, P., & Delehanty, H. (1995). *Sacred hoops : Spiritual lessons of a hardwood warrior.* New York: Hyperion.

Jackson, S. E., Brett, J. F., Sessa, V. I., Cooper, D. M., Julin, J. A., & Peyronnin, K. (1991). Some differences make a difference: Indivdiual dissimilarity and group hetergeneity as correlates of recruitment, promotion, and turnover. *Journal of Applied Psychology, 76*, 675–689.

Jacobs, J. E., & Klaczynski, P. A. (2002). The development of judgment and decision making during childhood and adolescence. *Current Directions in Psychological Science, 11*, 145–149.

Jacobs, N., Van Gestel, S., Derom, C., Thiery, E., Vernon, P., Derom, R., & Vlietinck, R. (2001). Heritability estimates of intelligence in twins: Effect of chorion type. *Behavior Genetics, 31*, 209–217.

Jacobs, R. C., & Campbell, D. T. (1961). The perpetuation of an arbitrary tradition through several generations of a laboratory microculture. *Journal of Abnormal and Social Psychology, 62*, 649–648.

Jacobsen, A., & Gilchrist, A. (1988a). Hess and Pretori revisited: Resolution of some old contradictions. *Perception & Psychophysics, 43*, 7–14.

Jacobsen, A., & Gilchrist, A. (1988b). The ratio principle holds over a million-to-one range of illumination. *Perception & Psychophysics, 43*, 1–6.

Jacobsen, L. K., Southwick, S. M., & Kosten, T. R. (2001). Substance use disorders in patients with posttraumatic stress disorder: A review of the literature. *American Journal of Psychiatry, 158*, 1184–1190.

Jacobsen, P. B., Bovbjerg, D. H., Schwartz, M. D., & Andrykowski, M. A. (1994). Formation of food aversions in patients receiving repeated infusions of chemotherapy. *Behavior Research & Therapy, 38*, 739–748.

Jacobson, B. H., Aldana, S. G., Goetzel, R. Z., Vardell, K. D., et al (1996). The relationship between perceived stress and self-reported illness-related absenteeism. *American Journal of Health Promotion, 11*, 54–61.

Jacobson, E. (1925). Progressive relaxation. *American Journal of Psychology, 36*, 73–87.

Jacobson, N. S., & Christensen, A. (1996). Studying the effectiveness of psychotherapy: How well can clinical trials do the job? *American Psychologist, 51*, 1031–1039.

Jacobson, N. S., Dobson, K. S., Truax, P. A., Addis, M. E., Koerner, K., Gollan, J. K., Gortner, E., & Prince, S. E. (1996). A component analysis of cognitive-behavioral treatment for depression. *Journal of Consulting and Clinical Psychology, 64*, 295–304.

Jacoby, L. L., & Dallas, M. (1981). On the relationship between autobiographical memory and perceptual learning. *Journal of Experimental Psychology: General, 110*, 306–340.

Jadack, R. A., Hyde, J. S., Moore, C. F., & Keller, M. L. (1995). Moral reasoning about sexually transmitted diseases. *Child Development, 66*, 167–177.

Jaffee, S., Caspi, A., Moffitt, T. E., Belsky, J., & Silva, P. (2001). Why are children born to teen mothers at risk for adverse outcomes in young adulthood? Results from a 20-yr longitudinal study. *Development & Psychopathology, 13*, 377–397.

Jakobson, R., & Halle, M. (1956). *Fundamentals of language.* The Hague: Mouton.

James, L. E., Burke, D. M., Austin, A., & Hulme, E. (1998). Production and perception of "verbosity" in younger and older adults. *Psychology and Aging, 13*, 355–367.

James, W. (1884). What is emotion? *Mind, 9*, 188–205.

James, W. (1890/1950). *Principles of psychology.* New York: Dover.

Jameson, K. A., Highnote, S. M., & Wasserman, L. M. (2001). Richer color experience in observers with multiple photopigment opsin genes. *Psychonomic Bulletin & Review, 8*, 244–261.

Jamison, K. R. (1989). Mood disorders and patterns of creativity in British writers and artists. *Psychiatry, 52*, 125–134.

Jamison, K. R. (1993). *Touched with fire: Manic-depressive illness and the artistic temperament.* New York: Free Press.

Jamison, K. R. (1995). *An unquiet mind: A memoir of moods and madness.* New York: Vintage Books, p. 67.

Jamison, K. R., Gerner, R. H., Hammen, C., & Padesky, C. (1980). Clouds and silver linings: Positive experiences associated with primary affective disorders. *American Journal of Psychiatry, 137*, 198–202.

Jamner, L. D., & Leigh, H. (1999). Repressive/defensive coping, endogen fous opioids and health: How a life so perfect can make you sick. *Psychiatry Research, 85*, 17–31.

Jamner, L. D., Schwartz, G. E., & Leigh, H. (1988). The relationship between repressive and defensive coping styles and monocyte, eosinophile, and serum glucose levels: Support for the opioid peptide hypothesis of repression. *Psychosomatic Medicine, 50*, 567–575.

Jancke, L., & Steinmetz, H. (1994). Interhemispheric-transfer time and corpus callosum size. *Neuroreport, 5*, 2385–2388.

Jang, K. L. (1993). *A behavioral genetic analysis of personality, personality disorder, the environment, and the search for sources of nonshared environmental influences.* Unpublished doctoral dissertation, University of Western Ontario, London, Ontario.

Jang, K. L., Livesley, W. J., & Vernon, P. A. (1996). Heritability of the Big Five personality dimensions and their facets: A twin study. *Journal of Personality, 64*, 577–91.

Jang, K. L., McCrae, R. R., Angleitner, A., Riemann, R., & Livesley, W. J. (1998). Heritability of facet-level traits in a cross-cultural twin sample: Support for a hierarchical model of personality. *Journal of Personality and Social Psychology, 74*, 1556–1565.

Janicak, P. G., Dowd, S. M., Martis, B., Alam, D., Beedle, D., Krasuski, J., Strong, M. J., Sharma, R., Rosen, C., & Viana, M. (2002). Repetitive transcranial magnetic stimulation versus electroconvulsive therapy for major depression: Preliminary results of a randomized trial. *Biological Psychiatry, 51*, 659–667.

Janis, I. L. (1954). Personality correlates to susceptibility to persuasion. *Journal of Personality, 22*, 504–518.

Janis, I. L. (1972). *Victims of groupthink.* Boston: Houghton Mifflin.

Janis, I. L. (1982). *Victims of groupthink* (2nd ed.). Boston: Houghton Mifflin.

Janowiak, J. J. (1994). Meditation and college students' self-actualization and rated stress. *Psychological Reports, 75*, 1007–1010.

Janowsky, J. S., Oviatt, S. K., & Orwoll, E. S. (1994). Testosterone influences spatial cognitn in older men. *Behavioral Neuroscience, 108*, 325–332.

Jansen, B. R. J., & van der Maas, H. L. J. (2002). The development of children's rule use on the balance scale task. *Journal of Experimental Child Psychology, 81*, 383–416.

Jansma, L. L., Linz, D. G., Mulac, A., & Imrich, D. J. (1997). Men's interactions with women after viewing sexually explicit films: Does degradation make a difference? *Communication Monographs, 64*, 1–24

Jarvis, W. B. G., & Petty, R. E. (1996). The need to evaluate. *Journal of Personality and Social Psychology, 70*, 172–194.

Jeannerod, M. (1994). The representing brain: Neural correlates of motor intention and imagery. *Behavioral & Brain Sciences, 17*, 187–245.

Jeannerod, M. (1995). Mental imagery in the motor context. *Neuropsychologia, 33*, 1419–1432.

Jeannerod, M. (2001). Neural simulation of action: A unifying mechanism for motor cognition. *NeuroImage, 14*, 5110–5117.

Jeannerod, M., & Frak, V. (1999). Mental imaging of motor activity in humans. *Current Opinion in Neurobiology, 9*, 735–739.

Jenike, M. (1984). Obsessive-comulsive disorder: A question of a neurologic lesion. *Compr. Psychiatry, 25*, 298–304.

Jenike, M. A. (2000). An update on obsessive-compulsive disorder. *Bulletin of the Menninger Clinic, 65*, 4–25.

Jenkins, J. M., Rasbach, J., & O'Connor, T. G. (2003). The role of the shared family context in differential parenting. *Developmental Psychology, 39*, 99–113.

Jenkins-Hall, K., & Sacco, W. P. (1991). Effects of client race and depression on evaluations by white therapists. *Journal of Social Clinical Psychology, 10*, 322–333.

Jensen, A. R. (1969). How much can we boost IQ and scholastic achievement? *Harvard Educational Review, 39*, 1–123.

Jensen, A. R. (1980). *Bias in mental testing.* New York: Free Press.

Jensen, A. R. (1987). Psychometric g as a focus of concerted research effort. *Intelligence, 11*, 193–198.

Jensen, A. R. (1991). *General mental ability: From psychometrics to biology.* Paper presented at the Annual Meeting of the American Association for the Advancement of Science, Washington, DC.

Jensen, A. R. (1993). Why is reaction time correlated with psychometric g? *Current Directions in Psychological Science, 2*, 53–56.

Jensen, A. R. (1998). *The g factor: The science of mental ability.* Westport, CT: Praeger.

Jensen, J. P., Bergin, A. E., & Greaves, D. W. (1990). The meaning of eclecticism: New survey and analysis of commponents. *Professional Psychology: Research and Practice, 21*, 124–130.

Jevning, R., Wallace, R. K., & Beidebach, M. (1992). The physiology of Meditation: A review. A wadeful hypnometabolic integrated response. *Neuroscience and Biobehavioral Reviews, 16*, 415–424.

Ji, L-J, Nisbett, R. E., & Su, Y. (2001). Culture, change, and prediction. *Psychological Science, 12*, 450–456.

Johnson, J. A. (2000). Predicting observers' ratings of the Big Five from the CPI, HPI, and NEO-PI-R: A comparative validity study. *European Journal of Personality, 4*, 1–19.

Johnson, J. A., Germer, C. K., Efran, J. S., & Overton, W. F. (1988). Personality as the basis of theoretical predilections. *Journal of Personality and Social Psychology, 55*, 824–835.

Johnson, J. D., Noel, N. E., & Sutter, J. (2000). Alcohol and male sexual aggression: A cognitive disruption analysis. *Journal of Applied Social Psychology.*

Johnson, K. E., & Eilers, A. T. (1998). Effects of knowledge and development on subordinate level categorization. *Cognitive Development, 13*, 515–545.

Johnson, L. S., & Wright, D. G. (1975). Self-hypnosis versus heterohypnosis: Experiential and behavioral comparisons. *Journal of Abnormal Psychology, 85*, 523–526.

Johnson, M. H. (2001). Functional brain development in humans. *Nature Reviews Neuroscience, 2*, 475–483.

Johnson, M. K., & Raye, C. L. (1981). Reality monitoring. *Psychological Review, 88*, 67–85.

Johnson, M. K., Hashtroudi, S., & Lindsy, D. S. (1993). Source monitoring. *Psychological Bulletin, 114*, 3–28.

Johnson, M. K., Nolde, S. F., Mather, M., Kounios, J., Schacter, D. L., & Curran, T. (1997). The similarity of brain activity associated with true and false recognition memory depends on test format. *Psychological Science, 8*, 250–257.

Johnson, M. R., & Lydiard, B. (1995). Personality disorders in social phobia. *Psychiatric Annals, 25*, 554–563.

Johnson, S. (2000). The recognition of mentalistic agents in infancy. *Trends in Cognitive Sciences, 4*, 22–28.

Johnson, S. C., & Carey, S. (1998). Knowledge enrichment and conceptual change in folkbiology: Evidence from Williams syndrome. *Cognitive Psychology, 37*, 156–200.

Johnson, S. D., & Bechler, C. (1998). Examining the relationship between listening effectiveness and leadership emergence: Perceptions, behaviors, and recall. *Small Group Research, 29*, 452–471.

Johnson, S. L., & Miller, I. (1997). Negative life events and time to recovery from episodes of bipolar disorder. *Journal of Abnormal Psychology, 106*, 449–457.

Johnson, S. M., & Roberts, J. E. (1995). Life events and bipolar disorder: Implications from biological theories. *Psychological Bulletin, 117*, 434–449.

Johnson-Laird, P. N. (1983). *Mental models.* Cambridge, MA: Harvard University Press.

Johnson-Laird, P. N. (1995). Mental models, deductive reasoning, and the brain. In M. S. Gazzaniga (Ed.), *The cognitive neurosciences* (pp. 999–1008). Cambridge, MIT Press.

Johnson-Laird, P. N. (2001). Mental models and deduction. *Trends in Cognitive Science, 5*, 434–443.

Johnson-Laird, P. N., & Oatley, K. (1989). The language of emotions: An analysis of a semantic field. *Cognition and Emotion, 3*, 81–123.

Johnson-Laird, P. N., and Oatley, K. (1992). Basic emotions, rationality and folk theory. *Cognition and Emotion, 6*, 201–223.

Johnston, L. C., & Macrae, C. N. (1994). Changing socical stereotypes: The case of the information seeker. *European Journal of Social Psychology, 24*, 581–592.

Johnston, L. D., O'Malley, P. M., & Bachman, J. G. (1994). *National survey results on drug use from the Monitoring the Future study, 1975–1993* (NIH Publication No. 94–3810). Washington, DC: U.S. Government Printing Office.

Johnstone, E. C. (1998). Predictive symptomatology, course, and outcome in first-episode schizophrenia. *International Clinical Psychopharmacology, 13*, S97–S99

Joiner, T. E. (1994). Contagious depression: Existence, specificity to depressed symptoms, and the role of reassurance seeking. *Journal of Personality and Social Psychology, 67*, 287–296.

Jolicoeur, P. (1998). Modulation of the attentional blink by on-line response selection: Evidence from speeded and unspeeded Task 1 decisions. *Memory & Cognition, 26*, 1014–1032.

Jones, C. J., & Meredith, W. (1996). Patterns of personality change across the life span. *Psychology and Aging, 11*, 57–65.

Jones, D., & Hill, K. (1993). Criteria of facial attractiveness in five populations. *Human Nature, 4*, 271–296.

Jones, M. C. (1924a). The elimination of children's fears. *Journal of Experimental Psychology, 7*, 383–390.

Jones, M. C. (1924b). A laboratory study of fear: The case of Peter. *Journal of Genetic Psychology, 31*, 308–315.

Jones, M. K., & Menzies, R. G. (1995). The etiology of fear of spiders. *Anxiety, Stress & Coping: An International Journal, 8*, 227–234.

Jones, N. A., Field, T., & Davalos, M. (1998). Massage therapy attenuates right frontal EEG asymmetry in one-month-old infants of depressed mothers. *Infant Behavior & Development, 21*, 527–530.

Jones, T. A., & Greenough, W. T. (1996). Ultrastructural evidence for increased contact between astrocytes and synapses in rats reared in a complex environment. *Neurobiology of Learning and Memory, 65*, 48–56.

Jonides, J., Schumacher, E. H., Smith, E. E., Koeppe, R. A., Awh, E., Reuter Lorenz, P. A., Marshuetz, C., & Willis, C. R. (1998). The role of parietal cortex in verbal working memory. *Journal of Neuroscience, 18*, 5026–5034.

Jonides, J., Schumacher, E. H., Smith, E. E., Lauber, E. J., Awh, E., Minoshima, S., & Koeppe, R. A. (1997). Verbal working memory load affects regional brain activation as measured by PET. *Journal of Cognitive Neuroscience, 9*, 462–475.

Jonides, J., Smith, E. E., Koeppe, R. A., Awh, E., Minoshima, S., Mintin, M. A. (1993) Spatial working memory in humans as revealed by PET. *Nature, 363*, 623–625.

Joseph, J. (2001). Separated twins and the genetics of personality differences: A critique. *American Journal of Psychology, 114*, 1–30.

Joseph, S., Williams, R., & Yule, W. (1995). Psychosocial perspectives on post-traumatic stress disorder. *Clinical Psychology Review, 15*, 515–544.

Judd, C. M., Ryan, C. S., & Parke, B. (1991). Accuracy in the judgment of in-group and out-group variability. *Journal of Personality and Social Psychology, 61*, 366–379.

Judd, L. L., Akiskal, H. S., Maser, J. D., Zeller, P. J., Endicott, J., Coryell, W., Paulus, M. P., Kunovac, J. L., Leon, A. C., Mueller, T. I., Rice, J. A., & Keller, M. B. (1998). A prospective 12–year study of subsyndromal and syndromal depressive: Symptoms in unipolar major depressive disorders. *Archives of General Psychiatry, 55*, 694–700.

Judge, T. A., Erez, A., Bono, J. E., & Thoresen, C. J. (2002). Are measures of self-esteem, neuroticism, locus of control, and generalized self-efficacy indicators of a common core construct? *Journal of Personality and Social Psychology, 83*, 693–710.

Jusczyk, P. W. (1995). Language acquisition: Speech sounds and phonological development. In J. L. Miller & P. D. Eimas (Eds.), *Handbook of perception and cognition: Vol. 11. Speech, language, and communication* (pp. 263–301). Orlando, FL: Academic Press.

Kaas, J. H. (1995). The reorganization of sensory and motor maps in adult mammals. In M. S. Gazzaniga (Ed.), *The cognitive neurosciences* (pp. 51–71). Cambridge, MA: MIT Press.

Kabat-Zinn, J., Wheeler, E., Light, T., Skillings, A., Scharf, M. J., Copley, T. G., Hosmer, D., & Bernhard, J. D. (1998). Influence of a mindfulness meditation-based stress reduction intervention on rates of skin clearing in patients with moderate to severe psoriasis undergoing phototherapy (UVB) and photochemotherapy (PUVA). *Psychosomatic Medicine, 60*, 625–632.

Kac, G., Auxiliadora de Santa Cruz Coel, & Velasquez-Melendez, G. (2000). Secular trend in age at menarche for women born between 1920 and 1979 in Rio de Janeiro, Brazil. *Annals of Human Biology, 27*, 423–428.

Kaeufeler, R., Meier, B., & Brattstroem, A. (2001). Efficacy and tolerability of Ze 117 St. John's wort extract in comparison with placebo, imipramine, and fluoxetine for the treatment of mild to moderate depression according to ICD-10: An overview. *Pharmacopsychiatry, 34*, S49–S50.

Kagan, J. (1989a). Temperamental contributions to social behavior. *American Psychologist, 44*, 668–674.

Kagan, J. (1989). *Unstable ideas: Temperament, cognition, and self.* Cambridge, MA: Cambridge University Press.

Kagan, J. (1992). Behavior, biology, and the meanings of temperamental constructs. *Pediatrics, 90*, 510–513.

Kagan, J. (1994). On the nature of emotion. *Monographs of the Society for Research in Child Development, 59*, 7–24, 250–283.

Kagan, J. (1996). Three pleasing ideas. *American Psychologist, 51(9)*, 901–908.

Kagan, R. M., & Reid, W. J. (1986). Critical factors in the adoption of emotionally disturbed youths. *Child Welfare, 65*, 63–73.

Kagan, J., & Snidman, N. (1991). Temperamental factors in human development. *American Psychologist, 46*, 856–862.

Kagan, J., Kearsley, R. B., & Zelazo, P. R. (1978). *Infancy: Its place in human development*. Cambridge, MA: Harvard University Press.

Kagan, J., Reznick, J. S., & Snidman, N. (1988). Biological bases of childhood shyness. *Science, 240*, 167–171.

Kagan, J., Snidman, N., & Arcus, D. (1998). Childhood derivatives of high and low reactivity in infancy. *Child Development, 69*, 1483–1493.

Kagan, J., Snidman, N., & Arcus, D., & Reznick, J. S. (1994). *Galen's prophecy: Temperament in human nature*. New York: Basic Books.

Kahn, P. H., Jr. (1992). Children's obligatory and discretionary moral judgments. *Child Development, 63*, 416–430.

Kahneman, D., & Knetsch, J. (1993). *Strong influences and shallow inferences: An analysis of some anchoring effects*. Unpublished manuscript, University of California, Berkeley.

Kahneman, D., & Tversky, A. (1979). Prospect theory: An analysis of decision under risk. *Econometrica, 47*, 263–291.

Kahneman, D., & Tversky, A. (1984). Choices, values, and frames. *American Psychologist, 39*, 341–350.

Kahneman, D., & Tversky, A. (1996). On the reality of cognitive illusions: A reply to Gigerenzer's critique. *Psychological Review, 103*, 582–591.

Kahneman, D., Fredrickson, B. L., Schreiber, C. A., & Redelmeier, D. A. (1993). When more pain is preferred to less: Adding a better end. *Psychological Science, 4*, 401–405.

Kail, R. (1988). Developmental functions speeds of cognitive processes. *Journal of Experimental Child Psychology, 45*, 339–364.

Kail, R. (1991). Processing time declines exponentially during childhood and adolescence. *Developmental Psychology, 27*, 259–266.

Kalimo, R., Tenkanen, L., Haermae, M., Poppius, E., & Heinsalmi, P. (2000). Job stress and sleep disorders: Findings from the Helsinki Heart Study. *Stress Medicine, 16*, 65–75.

Kalish, R. A., & Reynolds, D. K. (1977). The role of age in death attitudes. *Death Education, 1*, 205–230.

Kalivas, P. W., & Nakamura, M. (1999). Neural systems for behavioral activation and reward. *Current Opinion in Neurobiology, 9*, 223–227.

Kameda, T., & Sugimori, S. (1993). Psychological entrapment in group decision making: An assigned decision rule and a groupthink phenomenon. *Journal of Personality and Social Psychology, 65*, 282–292.

Kamin, L. (1969). Predictability, surprise, attention and conditioning. In B. A. Campbell and R. M. Church (Eds.), *Punishment and aversive behavior*. New York: Appleton-Century-Crofts.

Kamins, M. L., & Dweck, C. S. (1999). Person versus process praise and criticism: Implications for contingent self-worth and coping. *Developmental Psychology, 35*, 835–847.

Kampe, K. K. W., Frith, C. D., Dolan, R. J., & Frith, U. (2002). Reward value of attractiveness and gaze: Correction. *Nature, 416*, 602.

Kane, H., & Oakland, T. D. (2000). Secular declines in Spearman's g: Some evidence from the United States. *Journal of Genetic Psychology, 161*, 337–345.

Kaniasty, K., & Norris, F. H. (1992). Social support and victims of crime: Matching event, support, and outcome. *American Journal of Community Psychology, 20*, 211–241.

Kaniasty, K. Z., Norris, F. H., & Murrell, S. A. (1990). Received and perceived social support following natural disaster. *Journal of Applied Psychology, 20*, 85–114.

Kanner, A. D., Coyne, J. C., Schaefer, C., & Lazarus, R. S. (1981). Comparison of two modes of stress management: Daily hassles and uplifts versus major life events. *Journal of Behavioral Medicine, 4*, 1–39.

Kanwisher, N. (1991). Repetition blindness and illusory conjunctions: Errors in binding visual types with visual tokens. *Journal of Experimental Psychology: Human Perception and Performance, 17*, 404–421.

Kanwisher, N. G. (1987). Repetition blindness: Type recognition without token individuation. *Cognition, 27*, 117–143.

Kaplan, F. (1997, January 19). Looks count. *Boston Sunday Globe*, E1.

Kaplan, H. S. (1979). *Disorders of sexual desire*. New York: Brunner/Mazel

Kaplan, H. S. (1981). *The new sex therapy: Active treatment of sexual dysfunctions*. New York: Brunner/Mazel.

Kaplan, M. F. (1987). The influencing process in group decision making. In C. Hendrick (Ed.), *Review of personality and social psychology* (Vol. 8, pp. 189–212). Newbury Park, CA: Sage.

Kaplan, P., Wang, P. P., & Francke, U. (2001). Williams (Williams Beuren) syndrome: A distinct neurobehavioral disorder. *Journal of Child Neurology, 16*, 177–190.

Kaplowitz, P. B., Slora, E. J., Wasserman, R. C., Pedlow, S. E., & Herman-Giddens, M. E. (2001). Earlier onset of puberty in girls: Relation to increased body mass index and race. *Pediatrics, 108*, 347–353.

Karacan, I., Goodenough, D. R., Shapiro, A., & Starker, S. (1966). Erection cycle during sleep in relatin to dream anxiety. *Archives of General Psychiatry, 15*, 183–189.

Karama, S., Lecours, A. R., Leroux, J-M., Bourgouin, P., Beaudoin, G., Joubert, S., & Beauregard, M. (2002). Areas of brain activation in males and females during viewing of erotic film excerpts. *Human Brain Mapping, 16*, 1–13.

Karasek, R. A. (1979). Job demands, job decision latitude, and mental strain: Implications for job redesign. *Administration Science Quarterly, 24*, 285–307.

Karasek, R. A., Baker, D., Marxer, F., Ahlbom, A. & Theorell, T. (1981). Job decision latitude, job demands, and cardiovascular disease: A prospective study of Swedish men. *American Journal of Public Health, 71*, 694–705.

Karau, S. J., & Williams, K. D. (1993). Social loafing: A meta-analytic review and theoretical integration. *Journal of Personality and Social Psychology, 65*, 681–706.

Karayiorgou, M., Altemus, M., Galke, B. L., Goldman, D., Murphy, D. L., Ott, J., & Gogos, J. A. (1997). Genotype determining low catechol-O-methyltransferase activity as a risk factor for obsessive-compulsive disorder. *Proceedings of the National Academy of Sciences, 94*, 4572–4575.

Karkowski, L. M., & Kendler, K. S. (1997). An examination of the genetic relationship between bipolar and unipolar illness in an epidemiological sample. *Psychiatric Genetics, 7*, 159–163.

Karni, A., & Bertini, G. (1997). Learning perceptual skills: Behavioral probes into adult cortical plasticity. *Current Opinion in Neurobiology, 7*, 530–535.

Karni, A., & Sagi, D. (1993). The time course of learning a visual skill. *Nature, 365*, 250–252.

Karni, A., Tanne, D., Rubenstein, B. S., Askenasi, J. J. M., & Sagi, D. (1994). Dependence on REM sleep of overnight improvement of a perceptual skill. *Science, 265*, 679–682.

Karon, B. J. (2000). The clinical interpretation of the Thematic Apperception Test, Rorschach, and other clinical data: A reexamination of statistical versus clinical prediction. *Professional Psychology: Research and Practice, 31*, 230–233.

Karpinski, A., & Hilton, J. L. (2001). Attitudes and the Implicit Association Test. *Journal of Personality & Social Psychology, 81*, 774–788.

Karpov, Y. V., & Haywood, H. C. (1998). Two ways to elaborate Vygotsky's concept of mediation. *American Psychologist, 53*, 27–36.

Karuza, J., & Carey, T. O. (1984). Relevance preference and adaptiveness of behavioral blame for observers of rape victims. *Journal of Personality, 52* 249–262.

Kasper, S., & Resinger, E. (2001). Panic disorder: The place of benzodiazpines and selective serotonin reuptake inhibitors. *European Neuropsychopharmacology, 11*, 307–321.

Kass, S. (1999). Breast cancer intervention group aids physical healing, research find. *APA Monitor*, October, p. 7.

Kassin, S. M. (1997). The psychology of confession evidence. *American Psychologist, 52*, 221–233.

Kassin, S. M., & Kiechel, K. L. (1996). The social psychology of false confessions: Compliance, internatlization, and confabulation. *Psychological Science, 7*, 125–128.

Kassin, S. M., & Wrightsman, L. S. (1981). Coerced confessions, judicial instruction, and mock juror verdicts. *Journal of Applied Social Psychology, 11*, 489–506.

Katchadourian, H. (1977). *The biology of adolescence*. San Francisco: Freeman.

Katigbak, M. S., Church, A. T., & Akamine, T. X. (1996). Cross-cultural generalizability of personality dimensions: Relating indigenous and imported dimensions in two cultures. *Journal of Personality and Social Psychology, 70*, 99–114.

Katigbak, M. S., Church, A. T., Guanzon-Lapena, M., Angleles, C., Annadaisy, J., & del Pilar, G. H. (2002). Are indigenous personality dimensions culture specific? Philippine inventories and the five-factor model. *Journal of Personality & Social Psychology, 82*, 89–101.

Katona, I., Rancz, E. A., Acsady, L., Ledent, C., Mackie, K., Hajos, N., & Freund, T. F. (2001). Distribution of CB1 cannabinoid receptors in the amygdala and their role in the control of GABAergic transmission. *Journal of Neuroscience, 21*, 9506–9518.

Katona, I., Sperlagh, B., Magloczky, Z., Santha, E., Kofalvi, A., Czirjak, S., Mackie, K., Vizi, E. S., & Freund, T. F. (2000). GABAergic interneurons are the targets of cannabinoid actions in the human hippocampus. *Neuroscience, 100*, 797–804.

Katz, J., Beach, S. R. H., & Joiner, T. E. (1999). Contagious depression in dating couples. *Journal of Social & Clinical Psychology, 18*(1), 1–13.

Kaufman, L., & Kaufman, J. H. (2000). Explaining the moon illusion. *Proceedings of the National Academy of Sciences, USA, 97*, 500–505.

Kaufman, L., & Rock, I. (1962). The moon illusion, I. *Science, 136*, 953–961.

Kaufman, M. H. (1997). The teratogenic effects of alcohol following exposure during pregnancy, and its influence on the chromosome constitution of the pre-ovulatory egg. *Alcohol & Alcoholism, 32*, 113–128.

Kaufmann, G. (1990). Imagery effects on problem solving. In P. J. Hampson, D. E. Marks, & J. T. E. Richardson (Eds.), *Imagery: Current developments* (pp. 169–197). London and New York: Routledge.

Kavanagh, D. J. (1992). Recent developments in expressed emotion in schizophrenia. *British Journal of Psychiatry, 148*, 601–620.

Kawakami & Dovidio, J. F. (2001). The reliability of implicit stereotyping. *Personality & Social Psychology Bulletin, 27*, 212–225.

Kawakami, K., Young, H., & Dovidio, J. F. (2002). Automatic stereotyping: Category, trait, and behavioral activations. *Personality & Social Psychology Bulletin, 28*, 3–15.

Kay, D. A., & Anglin, J. M. (1982). Overextension and underextension in the child's expressive and receptive speech. *Journal of Child Language, 9*, 83–98.

Kaye, W. H. (1995). Neurotransmitters and anorexia nervosa. In K. D. Brownell & C. G. Fairburn (Eds.), *Eating disorders and obesity: A comprehensive handbook* (pp. 255–260). New York: Guilford Press.

Kazdin, A. E. (1994). Methodology, design, and evaluation in psychotherapy research. In A. E. Bergin & S. L. Garfield (Eds.), *Handbook of psychotherapy and behavior change* (4th ed., pp. 19–71). New York: John Wiley & Sons.

Keane, R. M., Kolb, L. C., Kaloupek, D. G., Orr, S. P., Blanchard, E. B., Thomas, R. G., Hsieh, F. Y., & Lavori, P. W. (1998). Utility of psychophysiology measurement in the diagnosis of posttraumatic stress disorder: Results from a department of Veteran's Affairs cooperative study. *Journal of Consulting and Clinical Psychology*, 914–923.

Keane, T. M., & Barlow, D. H. (2002). Posttraumatic stress disorder. In D. H. Barlow (Ed.). *Anxiety and its disorders* (2nd edition, pp. 418–453). NY: Guilford.

Keane, T. M., Zimering, R. T., & Caddell, J. M. (1985). A behavioral formulation of post-traumatic stress disorder in Vietnam veterans. *The Behavior Therapist, 8*, 9–12.

Keefe, R. S. E., Silva, S. G., Perkins, D. O., & Lieberman, J. A. (1999). The effects of atypical antipsychotic drugs on neurocognitive impairment in schizophrenia: A review and meta-analysis. *Schizophrenia Bulletin, 25,* 201–222.

Keenan, J. P., Nelson, A., O'Connor, M., & Pascual-Leone, A. (2001). Self-recognition and the right hemisphere. *Nature, 409,* 305.

Keeton, W. T., Larkin, T. S., & Windsor, D. M. (1974). Normal fluctuations in the earth's magnetic field influence pigeon orientation. *Journal of Comparative Physiology, 95,* 95–103.

Keil, F. C. (1989a). *Concepts, kind, and cognitive development.* Cambridge, MA: MIT Press.

Keil, F. C. (1989b). The origins of an autonomous biology. In M. R. Gunnar & M. Marstsos (Eds.), *The Minnesota symposium on child psychology: Vol. 25. Modularity and constraints in language and cognition* (pp. 103–137). Hillsdale, NJ: Erlbaum.

Keil, F. C., & Silberstein, C. S. (1996). Schooling and the acquisition of theoretical knowledge. In D. R. Olson & N. Torrance (Eds.), *Handbook of education and human development: New models of learning, teaching and schooling.* Cambridge, MA: Blackwell.

Keith, P. M., & Schafer, R. B. (1991). *Relationships and well-being over the life stages.* New York: Praeger.

Keitner, G. I., Solomon, D. A., Ryan, C. E., Miller, I. W., & Mallinger, A. (1996). Prodromal and residual symptoms in bipolar I disorder. *Comprehensive Psychiatry, 37,* 362–367.

Kelleher, R. T. (1956). Intermittant reinforcement in chimpanzees. *Science, 124,* 679–680.

Kelleher, R. T. (1957). Conditioned reinforcement in chimpanzees. *Journal of Comparative and Physiological Psychology, 49,* 571–575.

Kelleher, R. T. (1958). Fixed-ratio schedules of conditioned reinforcement with cimpanzees. *Journal of the Experimental Analysis of Behavior, 1,* 281–289.

Keller, A., Ford, L. H., & Meacham, J. A. (1978). Dimensions of self-concept in preschool children. *Developmental Psychology, 14,* 483–489.

Kelley, H. H. (1972). Attribution in social interaction. In E. E. Jones , D. E. Kanouse, H. H. Kelley, R. E. Nisbett, S. Vahns, & B. Weiner (Eds.), *Attribution: Perceiving the causes of behavior.* Morristown, NJ: General Learning Press.

Kelley, H. H. (1979). *Personal relationships: Their structures and processes.* Hillsdale, NJ: Erlbaum.

Kelley, H. H., & Michela, J. L. (1980). Attribution theory and research. *Annual Review of Psychology, 31,* 57–501.

Kelley, T. (1998, October 1). To surf, perchance to dream. *New York Times,* E1, E5.

Kelley, W. M., Miezin, F. M., McDermott, K. B., Buckner, R. L., Raichle, M. E., Cohen, N. J., Ollinger, J. M., Akbudak, E., Conturo, T. E., Znyder, A. Z., & Petersen, S. E. (1998). Hemispheric specialization in human dorsal frontal cortex and medial temporal lobe for verbal and nonverbal memory encoding. *Neuron, 20,* 927–936.

Kelling, G. L., & Coles, C. M. (1996). *Fixing broken windows: Restoring order and reducing crime in our communities.* New York: Touchstone.

Kellogg, Ronald T. (2001). Presentation modality and mode of recall in verbal false memory. *Journal of Experimental Psychology: Learning, Memory, & Cognition, 27,* 913–919.

Kellogg, W. N., & Kellogg, L. A. (1933). *The ape and the child.* New York: McGraw-Hill.

Kelman, H. (1997). Group processes in the resolution of international conflicts. *American Psychologist, 52,* 212–220.

Kelsey, B. L. (1998). The dynamics of multicultural groups: Ethnicity as a determinant of leadership. *Small Group Research, 29,* 602–623.

Kelsey, J. E., & Baker, M. D. (1983). Ventromedial septal lesions in rats reduce the effects of inescapable shock on escape performance and analgesia. *Behavioral Neuroscience, 97,* 945–961.

Kemp, D. T. (1978). Stimulated acoustic emissions from within the human auditory system. *Journal of the Acoustical Society of America, 64,* 1386–1391.

Kemp, D. T. (1979). Evidence of mechanical nonlinearity and frequency selective wave amplification in the cochlea. *Archives of Otology, Rhinology, and Laryngology, 224,* 37–45.

Kempermann, G., & Gage, F. H. (1999). Experienced-dependent regulation of adult hippocampal neurogenesis: Effects of long-term stimulation and stimulus withdrawal. *Hippocampus, 9,* 321–332.

Kempermann, G., Kuhn, H. G., & Gage, F. H. (1998). Experience-induced neurogenesis in the senescent dentate gyrus. *Journal of Neuroscience, 18,* 3206–3212.

Kendler, K. S., & Diehl, S. R. (1993). The genetics of schizophrenia: A current genetic-epidemiologic perspective. *Schizophrenia Bulletin, 19,* 87–112.

Kendler, K. S., & Gardner, C. O. (1998). Boundaries of major depression: An evaluation of DSM–IV criteria *American Journal of Psychiatry, 155,* 172–177.

Kendler, K. S., Gardner, C. O., & Prescott, C. A. (1999). Clinical characteristics of major depression that predict risk of depression in relatives. *Archives of General Psychiatry, 56,* 322–327.

Kendler, K. S., Jacobsen, K. C., Myers, J., & Prescott, C. A. (2002). Sex differences in genetic and environmental risk factors for irrational fears and phobias. *Psychological Medicine, 32,* 209–217.

Kendler, K. S., MacLean, C., Neale, M., Kessler, R. C., Heath, A. C., & Eaves, L. J. (1991). The genetic epidemiology of bulimia nervosa. *American Journal of Psychiatry, 148,* 1627–1637.

Kendler, K. S., Myers, J., & Prescott, C. A., & Neale, M. C. (2001). The genetic epidemiology of irrational fears and phobias in men. *Archives of General Psychiatry, 58,* 257–265.

Kendler, K. S., Neale, M. C., Kessler, R. C., Heath, A. C., & Eaves, L. J. (1992). The genetic epidemiology of phobias in women: The interrelationship of agoraphobia, social phobia, situational phobia and simple phobia. *Archives of General Psychiatry, 49,* 273–281.

Kendler, K. S., Neale, M. C., Kessler, R. C., Heath, A. C., & Eaves, L. J. (1993). A twin study of recent life events and difficulties. *Archives of General Psychiatry, 50,* 789–796.

Kennedy, M. M. (1979). *The mystery of hypnosis.* New York: Contemporary Perspectives.

Kennedy, S. H., Javanmard, M., Franco, J., & Vaccarino, F. J. (1997). A review of functional neuroimaging in mood disorders: Positron Emission Tomography and depression. *Canadian Journal of Psychiatry, 42,* 467–475.

Kenny, D. A., & LaVoie, L. (1982). Reciprocity of attraction: A confirmed hypothesis. *Social Psychology Quarterly, 45,* 54–58.

Kenrick, D. T., & Funder, D. C. (1988). Profiting from the controversy: Lessons from the person-situation debate. *American Psychologist, 43,* 23–34.

Kenrick, D. T., & Stringfeld, D. O. (1980). Personality traits and the eye of the beholder: Crossing some traditional philosophical boundaries in search for consistency in all the people. *Psychological Review, 87,* 88–104.

Kerr, M., Lambert, W. W., Stattin, H., & Klackenberg-Larsson, I. (1994). Stability of inhibition in a Swedish longitudinal sample. *Child Development, 65,* 138–146.

Kerr, N. L., & Kaufman-Gilliland, C. M. (1997). " . . . and besides, I probably couldn't have made a difference anyway": Justification of social dilemma defection via perceived self-inefficacy. *Journal of Experimental Social Psychology, 33,* 211–230.

Kertesz, A. (1981). Anatomy of jargon. In J. Brown (Ed.), *Jargonaphasia* (pp. 63–112). New York: Academic Press.

Keshavan, M. S., Anderson, S., & Pettigrew, J. W. (1994). Is schizophrenia due to excessive synaptic pruning in the prefrontal cortex? The Feinberg hypothesis revisited. *Journal of Psychiatry Research, 28,* 239–265.

Kessler, R. C., & Frank, R. G. (1997). The impact of psychiatric disorders on work loss days. *Psychological Medicine, 27,* 861–873.

Kessler, R. C., Kendler, K. S., Heath, A., Neale, M. C., & Eaves, L. J. (1992). Social support, depressed mood, and the adjustment to stress: A genetic epidemiologic investigation. *Journal of Personality and Social Psychology, 62,* 257–272.

Kessler, R. C., McGonagle, K. A., Zhao, S., Nelson, C. B., Hughes, M., Eshelman, S., Whittchen, H. N., & Dendler, K. S. (1994). Lifetime and 12-month prevalence of DSM–III–R psychiatric disorders in the United States: Results from the National Comorbidity Study. *Archives of General Psychiatry, 51,* 8–19.

Kessler, R. C., Rubinow, D. R., Holmes, C., Abelson, J. M., & Zhao, S. (1997). The epidemiology of DSM–III-R bipolar I disorder in a general population. *Psychological Medicine, 27,* 1079–1089.

Kessler, R. C., Stang, P. E., Wittchen, H., Ustun, T., Bedirhan, R., Burne, P. P., & Walters, E. E. (1998). Lifetime panic-depression comorbidity in the National Comorbidity Survey. *Archives of General Psychiatry, 55,* 801–808.

Kessler, R. C., Stein, M. B., & Berglund, P. (1998). Social phobia subtypes in the National Comorbidity Survey. *American Journal of Psychiatry, 155,* 613–619.

Kety, S. (1974). Biochemical and neurochemical effects of electroconvulsive shock. In M. Fink, S. Kety, J. McGaugh, & T. A. Williams (Eds.), *Psychobiology of convulsive therapy* (pp. 285–294). Washington, DC: Winston.

Kety, S. S. (1974). From rationalization to reason. *American Journal of Psychiatry, 131,* 957–963.

Keverne, E. B. (1997). Genomic imprinting in the brain: Commentary. *Current Opinion in Neurobiology, 7,* 463–468.

Keys, A., Brozek, J., Henschel, A., Mickelsen, O., & Taylor, H. L. (1950). *The biology of human starvation.* Minneapolis: University of Minnesota Press.

Kidd, K. K. (1993). Associations of disease with genetic markers: Déjà vu all over again. *Neuropsychiatric Genetics, 48,* 71–73.

Kiecolt-Glaser, J. K., & Glaser, R. (2002). Depression and immune function: Central pathways to morbidity and mortality. *Journal of Psychosomatic Research, 53,* 873–876.

Kiecolt-Glaser, J. K., & Newton, T. L. (2001). Marriage and health: His and hers. *Psychological Bulletin, 127,* 472–503.

Kiecolt-Glaser, J., Garner, W., Speicher, C., Penn, G., & Glaser, R. (1984). Psychosocial modifiers of immuno-competence in medical students. *Psychosomatic Medicine, 46,* 7–14.

Kiecolt-Glaser, J., Glaser, R., Strain, E., Stout, J., Tarr, K., Holliday, J., & Speicher, C. (1986). Modulation of cellular immunity in medical students. *Journal of Behavioral Medicine, 9,* 5–?.

Kiecolt-Glaser, J. K., Kennedy, S., Malkoff, S., Fisher, L., Speicher, C., & Glaser, R. (1988). Marital discord and immunity in males. *Psychosomatic Medicine, 50,* 213–229.

Kiecolt-Glaser, J. K., Marucha, P. T., Atkinson, C., & Glaser, R. (2001). Hypnosis as a modulator of cellular immune dysregulation during acute stress. *Journal of Consulting and Clinical Psychology, 69,* 674–682.

Kiecolt-Glaser, J. K., Marucha, P. T., Malarky, W. B., Mercado, A. M., & Glaser, R. (1995). Slowing of wound healing by psychological stress. *The Lancet, 346,* 1194–1196.

Kiecolt-Glaser, J. K., Page, G. G., Marucha, P. T., MacCallum, R. C., & Glaser, R. (1998). Psychological influences on surgical recovery perspectives from psychoneuroimmunology. *American Psychologist, 53,* 1209–1218.

Kiepenheuer, J. (1982). The effect of magnetic anomalies on the homing behavior of pigeons: An attempt to analyze the possible factors involved. In F. Papi & H. G. Wallraff (Eds.), *Animal navigation* (pp. 120–128). Berlin: Springer-Verlag.

Kiepenheuer, J. (1986). A further analysis of the orientation behavior of homing pigeons released within magnetic anomalies. In G. Maret, N. Boccara, & J. Kiepenheuer (Eds.), *Biophysical effects of steady magnetic fields* (pp. 148–153). Berlin: Springer-Verlag.

Kiesler, C. A., & Kiesler, S. B. (1969). *Conformity*. Reading, MA: Addison-Wesley.

Kihlstrom, J. F. (1985). Hypnosis. *Annual Review of Psychology, 36*, 385–418.

Kihlstrom, J. F. (1987). The cognitive unconscious. *Science, 273*, 1445–1452.

Kilham, W., & Mann, L. (1974). Level of destructive obedience as a function of transmitter and executant roles in the Milgram obedience paradigm. *Journal of Personality and Social Psychology, 29*, 696–702.

Killen, J. D., Hayward, C., Wilson, D. M., Haydel, K. F., Robinson, T. N., Taylor, C. B., Hammer, L. D., & Varady, A. (1996). Predicting onset drinking in a community sample of adolescents: The role of expectancy and temperament. *Addictive Behaviors, 21*, 473–480.

Kim, J., Lim, J., & Bhargava, M. (1998). The role of affect in attitude formation: A classical conditioning. *Journal of the Academy of Marketing Science, 26*, 143–152.

Kim, K. H. S., Relkin, N. R., Lee, K., & Hirsch, J. (1997). Distinct cortical areas associated with native and second languages. *Nature, 388*, 171–174.

Kim, M., & Kim, H. (1997). Communication goals: Individual differences between Korean and American speakers. *Personality & Individual Differences, 23*, 509–517.

Kimble, G. A. (1981). Biological and cognitive constraints of learning. In L. T. Benjamin, Jr. (Ed.), *The G. Stanley Hall Lecture Series* (Vol. 1). Washington, DC: American Psychological Association.

Kimmel, M. S., & Linders, A, (1996). Does censorship make a difference? An aggregate empirical analysis of pornography and rape. *Journal of Psychology & Human Sexuality, 8*, 1–20.

Kimura, D. (1994). Body asymmetry and intellectual pattern. *Personality and Individual Differences, 17*, 53–60.

King, A. C., Oman, R. F., Brassington, G. S., Bliwise, D. L., & Haskell, W. L. (1997). Moderate-intensity exercise and self-rated quality of sleep in older adults: A randomized controlled trial. *Journal of the American Medical Association, 277*, 32–37.

King, D. W., King, L. A., Foy, D. W., Keane, T. M., & Fairbank, J. A. (1999). Posttraumatic stress disorder in a national sample of female and male Vietnam veterans: Risk factors, war-zone stressors, and resilience-recovery variables. *Journal of Abnormal Psychology, 108*, 164–170.

King, L. A., King, D. W., Fairbank, J. A., Keane, T. M., & Adams, G. A. (1998). Resilience-recovery factors in post-traumatic stress disorder among female and male Vietnam veterans: Hardiness, postwar social support, and additional stressful life events. *Journal of Personality and Social Psychology, 74*, 420–434.

King, M. L., Jr. (1963, August 28). I have a dream. Speech delivered at the Lincoln Memorial, Washington, DC.

King, S. A., Engi, S., & Poulos, S. T. (1998). Using the internet to assist family therapy. *British Journal of Guidance and Counselling, 26*, 43–52.

Kintsch, W. (1998). *Comprehension: A paradigm for cognition*. New York: Cambridge University Press.

Kipnis, D. (1993). Unanticipated consequences of using behavior technology. *Leadership Quarterly, 4*, 149–171.

Kirby, K. C., Marlowe, D. B., Festinger, D. S., Lamb, R. J., & Platt, J. J. (1998). Schedule of voucher delivery influences initiation of cocaine abstinence. *Journal of Consulting and Clinical Psychology, 66*, 761–767.

Kirby, K. N. (1994). Probabilities and utilities of fictional outcomes in Wason's four-card selection task. *Cognition, 51*, 1–28.

Kirkness, E. F., & Durcan, M. J. (1992). Genomic imprinting: Parental origin effects on gene expression. *Alcohol Health & Research World, 16*(4), 312–316.

Kirkpatrick, L. A., & Locke, E. A. (1991). Leadership: Do traits matter? *Academy of Management Executive, 5*, 48–60.

Kirsch, I. (1999). Clinical hypnosis as a nondeceptive placebo. In I. Kirsch, A. Capafons, E. Cardeña-Buelna, & S. Amigó, *Clinical hypnosis and self-regulation: Cognitive-behavioral perspectives* (pp. 211–225). Washington, D.C.: American Psychological Association.

Kirsch, I., & Council, J. R. (1992). Situational and personality correlates of hypnotic responsiveness. In E. Fromm and M. R. Nash (Eds.). *Contemporary hypnosis research* (pp. 267–291). New York: Guilford.

Kirsch, I., & Lynn, S. J. (1999). Automaticity in clinical psychology. *American Psychologist, 54*, 504–515.

Kirsch, I., & Sapirstein, G. (1998). Listening to Prozac but hearing placebo: A meta-analysis of antidepressant medication. *Prevention & Treatment, 1*, Article 0002a.

Kirsch, I., Moore, T. J., Scoboria, A., & Nicholls, S. S. (2002a). The emperor's new drugs: An analysis of antidepressant medication data submitted to the U.S. Food and Drug Administration. *Prevention and Treatment, 5*, np.

Kirsch, I., Scoboria, A., & Moore, T. J. (2002b). Antidepressants and placebos: Secrets, revelations, and unanswered questions. *Prevention & Treatment, 5*, np.

Kirschvink, J. L., Walker, M. M., & Diebel, C. E. (2001). Magnetite-based magnetoreception. *Current Opinion in Neurobiology, 11*, 462–467.

Kisilevsky, B. S., & Low, J. A. (1998). Human fetal behavior: 100 years of study. *Developmental Review, 18*, 1–29.

Kitayama, S., Markus, H. R., Matsumoto, H., & Norasakkunkit, V. (1997). Individual and collective processes in the construction of the self: Self-enhancement in the United States and self-criticism in Japan. *Journal of Personality & Social Psychology, 72*, 1245–1267.

Kitchener, R. F. (1996). The nature of the social for Piaget and Vygotsky. *Human Development, 39*, 243–249.

Kitzmann, K. M. (2000). Effects of marital conflict on subsequent triadic family interactions and parenting. *Developmental Psychology, 36*, 3–13.

Kivlighan, D. M., Jr., Multon, K. D., & Patton, M. J. (2000). Insight and symptom reduction in time-limited psychoanalytic counseling. *Journal of Counseling Psychology, 47*, 50–58.

Kleemeier, R. W. (1962). Intellectual changes in the senium. *Proceedings of the American Statistical Association, 1*, 290–295.

Klein, D. F. (1993). False suffocation alarms, spontaneous panics, and related conditions: An integrative hypothesis. *Archives of General Psychiatry, 50*, 306–317.

Klein, E., Kreinin, I., Chistyakov, A., Koren, D., Mecz, L., Marmur, S., Ben-Shachar, D., & Feinsod, M. (1999). Therapeutic efficacy of right prefrontal slow repetitive transcranial magnetic stimulation in major depression: A double-blind controlled study. *Archives of General Psychiatry, 56*, 315–320.

Kleinke, C. L., & Taylor, C. (1991). Evaluation of opposite-sex person as a function of gazing, smiling, and forward lean. *Journal of Social Psychology, 131*, 451–453.

Kleinknecht, R. A., & Lenz, J. (1989). Blood/injury fear, fainting and avoidance of medical treatment: A family correspondence study. *Behaviour Research and Therapy, 27*, 537–547.

Kleinman, A. (1978). Clinical relevance of anthropological and cross-cultural research: Concepts and strategies. *American Journal of Psychiatry, 135*, 427–431.

Klima, E. S., & Bellugi, U. (1979). *The signs of language*. Cambridge, MA: Harvard University Press.

Klinkenborg, V. (1997, January 5). Awakening to sleep. *Sunday New York Times Magazine*, 26.

Klinteberg, B., Andersson, T., Magnusson, D., & Stattin, H. (1993). Hyperactive behavior in childhood as related to subsequent alcohol problems and violent offending: A longitudinal study of male subjects. *Personality and Individual Differences, 15*, 381–388.

Klosko, J. S., Barlow, D. H., Tassinari, R., & Cerny, J. A. (1990). A comparison of alprazolam and behavior therapy in treatment of panic disorder. *Journal of Consulting and Clinical Psychology, 58*, 77–84.

Knapp, S., & VandeCreek, L. (1996). Risk management for psychologists: Treating patients who recover lost memories of childhood abuse. *Professional Psychology Research and Practice, 27*, 452–459.

Knauth, P. (1997). Changing schedules: Shiftwork. *Chronobiology International, 14*, 159–171.

Knobloch, H., & Pasamanick, B. (Eds.). (1974). *Gessell and Amatruda's developmental diagnosis*. Hagerstown, MD: Harper & Row.

Knutson, B., Adams, C. M., Fong, G. W., & Hommer, D. (2001). Anticipation of increasing monetary reward selectively recruits nucleus accumbens. *Journal of Neuroscience, 21*, RC159.

Kobasa, S. C. (1979). Stressful life events, personality and health: An inquiry into hardiness. *Journal of Personality and Social Psychology, 37* 1–11.

Kobasa, S. C., Maddit, S. R., & Kuhn, S. (1982). Hardiness and health: A prospective study. *Journal of Personality and Social Psychology, 42*, 168–177.

Kochanska, G. (1997). Multiple pathways to conscience for children with different temperaments: From toddlerhood to age 5. *Development Psychology, 33*, 228–240.

Kochanska, G., DeVet, K., Goldman, M., Murray, K., & Putman, S. P. (1994). Maternal reports of conscience development and temperament in young children. *Child Development, 65*, 852–868.

Kochanska, G., Gross, J. N., Lin, M-H., & Nichols, K. E. (2002). Guilt in young children: Development, determinants, and relations with a broader system of standards. *Child Development, 73*, 461–482.

Koestler, A. (1964). *The act of creation*. New York: Macmillan.

Koffka, K. (1935). *Principles of Gestalt psychology*. New York: Harcourt Brace.

Koga, H., Yuzuriha, T., Yao, H., Endo, K., Hiejima, S., Takashima, Y., Sadanaga, F., Matsumoto, T., Uchino, A., Ogomori, K., Ichimiya, A., Uchimura, H., & Tashiro, N. (2002). Quantitative MRI findings and cognitive impairment among community dwelling elderly subjects. *Journal of Neurology, Neurosurgery & Psychiatry, 72*, 737–741.

Kohlberg, L. (1969). Stage and sequence: The cognitive-developmental approach to socialization. In D. S. Goslin (Ed.), *Handbook of socialization theory and research* (pp. 347–480). Chicago: Rand McNally.

Kohlberg, L. (1981). *Essays on moral development. Vol. 1. The philosophy of moral development: Moral stages and the idea of justice*. San Francisco: Harper & Row.

Kohler, P. F., Rivera, V. J., Eckert, E. D., Bouchard, T. J., Jr., & Heston, L. L. (1985). Genetic regulation of immunoglobulin and specific antibody levels in twins reared apart. *Journal of Clinical Investigation, 75*, 883–888.

Kohler, S., Kapur, S., Moscovitch, M., Winocur, G., & Houle, S. (1995). Dissociation of pathways for object and spatial vision: A PET study in humans. *Neuroreport, 6*, 1865–1868.

Köhler, W. (1925/1956). *The mentality of apes*. New York: Vintage.

Kohn, M. L., & Schooler, C. (1973). Occupational experience and psychological functioning: An assessment of reciprocal effects. *American Sociological Review, 38*, 97–118.

Kohut, H. (1977). *The restoration of self*. New York: International Universities Press.

Kolata, G. (1997, January 14). Which comes first: Depression or heart disease? *New York Times*, C1.

Kolata, G., & Peterson, I. (2001, July 21). New photo method may aid witnesses in saying, "It's him." *New York Times*, A1, A13.

Kolb, F. C., & Braun, J. (1995). Blindsight in normal observers. *Nature, 377*, 336–338.

Komarova, N., & Hauser, M. (2001). Building the tower of babble. *Trends in Cognitive Sciences, 5*, 412–413.

Kondo, T., Zakany, J., Innis, J. W., & Duboule, D. (1997). Of fingers, toes and penises. *Nature, 390*, 185–198.

Konishi, M. (1993). Listening with two ears. *Scientific American, 268*, 66–73.

Konishi, S., Nakajima, K., Uchida, I., Kikyo, H., Kameyama, M., & Miyashita, Y. (1999). Common inhibitory mechanism in huma inferior prefrontal cortex revealed by event-related functional MRI. *Brain, 122,* 981–991.

Koob, G. F. (1999). Drug reward and addiction. In M. J. Zigmond, F. E. Bloom, S. C. Landis, J. L. Roberts, & L. R. Squire (Eds.). *Fundamental neuroscience* (pp. 1261–1279). San Diego: Academic Press.

Koob, G. F., & Bloom, F. E. (1988). Cellular and molecular mechanisms of drug dependence. *Science, 242,* 715–723.

Kosslyn, S. M. (1975). On retrieving information from visual images. In R. Schank & B. Nash-Webber (Eds.), *Theoretical issues in natural language processing.* Arlington, VA: Association for Computational Linguistics.

Kosslyn, S. M. (1976). Can imagery be distinguished from other forms of internal representation? Evidence from studies of information retrieval times. *Memory and Cognition, 4,* 291–297.

Kosslyn, S. M. (1978). Measuring the visual angle of the mind's eye. *Cognitive Psychology, 10,* 356–389.

Kosslyn, S. M. (1980). *Image and mind.* Cambridge, MA.: Harvard University Press.

Kosslyn, S. M. (1987). Seeing and imagining in the cerebral hemispheres: A computational approach. *Psychological Review, 94,* 148–175.

Kosslyn, S. M. (1992). Cognitive neuroscience and the human self. In A. Harrington (Ed.), *So human a brain.* New York: Pergamon.

Kosslyn, S. M. (1994a). *Elements of graph design.* New York: Freeman.

Kosslyn, S. M. (1994b). *Image and brain: The resolution of the imagery debate.* Cambridge, MA: MIT Press.

Kosslyn, S. M., & Intriligator, J. M. (1992). Is cognitive neuropsychology plausible? The perils of sitting on a one-legged stool. *Journal of Cognitive Neuroscience, 4,* 96–106. (Translated into Italian and reprinted in *Sistemi Intelligenti, 6,* 181–205, 1994)

Kosslyn, S. M., & Koenig, O. (1995). *Wet mind: The new cognitive neuroscience.* New York: Free Press.

Kosslyn, S. M., Alpert, N. M., Thompson, W. L., Maljkovic, V., Weise, S. B., Chabris, C. F., Hamilton, S. E., & Buonano, F. S. (1993). Visual mental imagery activates topographically organized visual cortex: PET investigations. *Journal of Cognitive Neuroscience, 5,* 263–287.

Kosslyn, S. M., Ball, T. M., & Reiser, B. J. (1978). Visual images preserve metric spatial information: Evidence from studies of image scanning. *Journal of Experimental Psychology: Human Perception and Performance, 4,* 47–60.

Kosslyn, S. M., Daly, P. F., McPeek, R. M., Alpert, N. M., Kennedy, D. N., & Caviness, V. S. (1993). Using locations to store shape: An indirect effect of a lesion. *Cerebral Cortex, 3,* 567–582.

Kosslyn, S. M., Digirolamo, G. J., Thompson, W. L., & Alpert, N. M. (1998). Mental rotation of objects versus hands: Neural mechanisms revealed by positron emission tomography. *Psychophysiology, 35,* 151–161.

Kosslyn, S. M., Ganis, G., & Thompson, W. L. (2001). Neural foundations of imagery. *Nature Reviews Neuroscience, 2,* 635–642.

Kosslyn, S. M., Koenig, O., Barrett, A., Cave, C. B., Tang, J., & Gabrieli, J. D. E. (1989). Evidence for two types of spatial representations: Hemispheric specialization for categorical and coordinate relations. *Journal of Experimental Psychology: Human Perception and Performance, 15,* 723–735.

Kosslyn, S. M., Pascual-Leone, A., Felician, O., Camposano, S., Keenan, J. P., Thompson, W. L., Ganis, G., Sukel, K. E., & Alpert, N. M. (1999). The role of area 17 in visual imagery: Convergent evidence from PET and rTMS. *Science, 284,* 167–170.

Kosslyn, S. M., Segar, C., Pani, J., & Hillger, L. A. (1990). When is imagery used in everyday life? A diary study. *Journal of Mental Imagery. 14,* 131–152.

Kosslyn, S. M., Thompson, W. L., & Alpert, N. M. (1997). Neural systems shared by visual imagery and visual perception: A positron emission tomography study. *NeuroImage, 6,* 320–334.

Kosslyn, S. M., Thompson, W. L., Costantini-Ferrando, M. F., Alpert, N. M., & Spiegel, D. (2000). Hypnotic visual illusion alters brain color processing. *American Journal of Psychiatry.*

Kosslyn, S. M., Thompson, W. L., Kim, I. J., & Alpert, N. M. (1995). Topographical representations of mental images in primary visual cortex. *Nature, 378,* 496–498.

Kosslyn, S. M., Thompson, W. L., Kim, I. J., Rauch, S. L., & Alpert, N. M. (1996). Individual differences in cerebral blood flow in area 17 predict the time to evaluate visualized letters. *Journal of Cognitive Neuroscience, 8,* 78–82.

Koutstaal, W., & Schacter, D. L. (1997). Inaccuracy and inaccessibility in memory retrieval: Contributions from cognitive psychology and cognitive neuropsychology. In P. S. Appelbaum, L. Uyehara, & M. Elin (Eds.), *Trauma and memory: Clinical and legal controversies* (pp. 93–137). New York: Oxford University Press.

Kovacs, I. (1996). Gestalten of today: Early processing of visual contours and surfaces. *Behavioural Brain Research, 82,* 1–11.

Kovacs, I., & Julesz, B. (1993). A closed curve is much more than an incomplete one: Effect of closure in figure-ground segmentation. *Proceedings of the National Academy of Sciences, USA, 90,* 7495–7497.

Kowalski, U., Waltschko, R., & Fuller, E. (1998). Normal fluctuations of the geomagnetic field may affect initial orientation of pigeons. *Journal of Comparative Physiology, 163,* 593–600.

Kozak, M. J., Liebowitz, M. R., & Foa, E. B. (2000). Cognitive behavior therapy and pharmacotherapy for obsessive-compulsive disorder: The NIMH-sponsored collaborative study. In W. K. Goodman, M. V. Rudorfer & J. D. Masur (Eds.). *Obsessive-compulsive disorder: Contemporary issues in treatment* (pp. 501–530). Mahwah, NJ: Erlbaum.

Kozhevnikov, M., Hegarty, M., & Mayer, R. (1998, August). Visual/spatial abilities in problem solving in physics. *Proceedings of the Thinking with Diagrams 98 Conference,* The University of Wales, Aberystwyth.

Kraepelin, E. (1921). Ueber Entwurtzelung [Depression]. *Zietschrift fuer die Gasamte Neurologie und Psychiatrie, 63,* 1–8.

Krafft, K. C., & Berk, L. E. (1998). Private speech in two preschools: Significance of open-ended activities and make-believe play for verbal self-regulation. *Early Childhood Research Quarterly, 13,* 637–658.

Kramer, M. S., Cutler, N., Feighner, J., Shrivastava, R., Carman, J., Sramek, J. J., et al. (1998). Distinct mechanism for antidepressant activity by blockade of central substance P receptors. *Science, 281,* 1640–1645.

Kranzler, J. H., & Jensen, A. R. (1989). Inspection time and intelligence: A meta-analysis. *Intelligence, 13,* 329–347.

Kraut, R., Patterson, M., Lundmark, V., Kiesler, S., Mukophadhyay, T., & Scherlis, W. (1998). Internet paradox: A social technology that reduces social involvement and psychological well-being? *American Psychologist, 53,* 1017–1031.

Kreitzer, A. C., & Regehr, W. G. (2001a). Retrograde inhibition of presynaptic calcium influx by endogenous cannabinoids at excitatory synapses onto Purkinje cells. *Neuron, 29,* 717–727.

Kreitzer, A. C., and Regehr, W. G. (2001b).Cerebellar depolarization-induced suppression of inhibition is mediated by endogenous cannabinoids. *Journal of Neuroscience, 21,* RC174.

Kreitzer, A. C., Carter, A. G., & Regehr, W. G. (2002). Inhibition of interneuron firing extends the spread of endocannabinoid signaling in the cerebellum. *Neuron, 34,* 787–796.

Kring, A. M., & Gordon, A. H. (1998). Sex differences in emotion: Expression, experience, and physiology. *Journal of Personality & Social Psychology, 74,* 686–703.

Kringelbach, M. L., Araujo, I., & Rolls, E. T. (2001). Face expression as a reinforcer activates the orbitofrontal cortex in an emotion-related reversal task. *Neuroimage 13(6),* S433.

Kroon, M. B. R., van Kreveld, D., & Rabbie, J. M. (1992). Group versus individual decision making: Effects of accountability on gender and groupthink. *Small Group Research, 23,* 427–458.

Krueger, J. (1996). Personal beliefs and cultural stereotypes about racial characteristics. *Journal of Personality and Social Psychology, 71,* 536–548.

Krueger, L. E. (1992). The word-superiority effect and phonological recoding. *Memory & Cognition, 20,* 685–694.

Krug, R., Pietrowsky, R., Fehm, H. L., & Born, J. (1994). Selective influence of menstrual cycle on perception of stimuli with reproductive significance. *Psychosomatic Medicine, 56,* 410–417.

Kruglanski, A. W., & Webster, D. M. (1996). Motivated closing of the mind: "Seizing" and "freezing." *Psychological Review, 103,* 263–283.

Krumhansl, C. L., (1991). Music perception: Tonal structures in perception and memory. *Annual Review of Psychology, 42,* 277–303.

Krumhansl, C. L. (2000). Rhythm and pitch in music cognition. *Psychological Bulletin, 126,* 159–179.

Krupnick, J. L., Sotsky, S. M., Simmens, S., Moyer, J., Elkin, I., Watkins, J., & Paulinis, P. A. (1996). The role of the therapeutic alliance in psychotherapy and pharmacotherapy outcome: Findings in the National Institute of Mental Health Treatment of Depression Collaborative Research Program. *Journal of Consulting & Clinical Psychology, 64,* 532–539.

Kübler-Ross, E. (1969). *On death and dying.* New York: Macmillan.

Kubzansky, L. D., & Kawachi, I. (2000). Going to the heart of the matter: Do negative emotions cause coronary heart disease? *Journal of Psychosomatic Research, 48,* 323–337.

Kubzansky, L. D., Kawachi, I., Weiss, S. T., & Sparrow, D. (1998). Anxiety and coronary heart disease: A synthesis of epidemiological, psychological, and experimental evidence. *Annals of Behavioral Medicine, 20,* 47–58.

Kubzansky, L. D., Sparrow, D., Vokonas, P., & Kawachi, I. (2001). Is the glass half empty or half full? A prospective study of optimism and coronary heart disease in the normative aging study. *Psychosomatic Medicine, 63,* 910–916.

Kuhl, P. K. (1989). On babies, birds, modules, and mechanisms: A comparative approach to the acquisition of vocal communication. In R. J. Dooling & S. H. Husle (Eds.), *The comparative psychology of audition: Perceiving complex sounds* (pp. 379–419). Hillsdale, NJ: Erlbaum.

Kuhl, P. K., Williams, K. A., Lacerda, F., Stevens, K. N., et al. (1992). Linguistic experience alters phonetic perception in infants by 6 months of age. *Science, 255,* 606–608.

Kuipers, E., Fowler, D., Garety, P. Chisholm, D., Freeman, D., Dunn, G., Bebbington, P., & Hadley, C. (1998). London-East Anglia randomised controlled trial of cognitive-behavioural therapy for psychosis. III: Followup and economic evaluation at 18 months. *British Journal of Psychiatry, 173,* 61–68.

Kuipers, L. D., Garety, P., Fowler, D., Dunne, G., Bebbington, P., Freeman, D., & Hadley, C. (1997). London-East Anglia randomised controlled trial of cognitive-behavioural therapy for psychosis. I: Effects of the treatment phase. *British Journal of Psychiatry, 171,* 319–327.

Kulhara, P., & Chakrabarti, S. (2001). Culture and schizophrenia and other psychotic disorders. *Psychiatric Clinics of North America, 24,* 449–464.

Kunda, Z., & Oleson, K. C. (1995). Maintaining stereotypes in the face of disconfirmation: Constructing grounds for subtyping deviants. *Journal of Personality and Social Psychology, 68,* 565–579.

Kuntze, M. F., Stoermer, R., Mager, R., Roessler, A., Mueller-Spahn, F., & Bullinger, A. H. (2001). Immersive virtual environments in cue exposure. *CyberPsychology & Behavior, 4,* 497–501.

Kunz, G., Beil, D., Deiniger, H., Einspanier, A., Mall, G., & Leyendecker, G. (1997). The uterine peristaltic pump. Normal and impeded sperm transport within the female genital tract. *Advances in Experimental Medicine and Biology, 424*, 267–277.

Kurihara, T., Kato, M., Reverger, R., & Yagi, G. (2000). Outcome of schizophrenia in a non-industrial society: Comparative study between Bali and Tokyo. *Acta Psychiatrica Scandinavica, 101*, 148–152.

Kushner, M., Riggs, D., Foa, E., & Miller, S. (1992). Perceived controllability and the development of posttraumatic stress disorder (PTSD) in crime victims. *Behaviour Research and Therapy, 31*, 105–110.

Kushnir, T., Malkinson, R., & Ribak, J. (1998). Rational thinking and stress management in health workers: A psychoeducational program. *International Journal of Stress Management, 5*, 169–178.

Kutchinsky, B. (1991). Pornography and rape: Theory and practice? Evidence from crime data in four countries where pornography is easily available. *International Journal of Law & Psychiatry, 14*, 47–64.

Kvale, G., & Hugdahl, K. (1994). Cardiovascular conditioning and anticipatory nausea and vomiting in cancer patients. *Behavioral Medicine, 20*, 78–83.

Labrell, F., Pecheux, M.-G., & Le Metayer, F. (2002). Effect of parental input and effect of children's competence on the recall of object in preschool children. *Cahiers de Psychologie Cognitive/Current Psychology of Cognition, 21*, 91–111.

Lachman, H. M., Papolos, D. F., Boyle, A., Sheftel, G., Juthani, M., Edwards, E., & Henn, F. A. (1993). Alterations in glucocorticoid inducible RNAs in the limbic system of learned helpless rats. *Brain Research. 609*, 110–116.

Lachman, M. E., & Weaver, S. L. (1998). The sense of control as a moderator of social class differences in health and well-being. *Journal of Personality and Social Psychology, 74*, 763–773.

Lacks, P., & Morin, C. M. (1992). Recent advances in the assessment and treatment of insomnia. *Journal of Consulting & Clinical Psychology, 60*, 586–594.

Laeng, B., Shah, J., & Kosslyn, S. M. (1999). Identifying objects in conventional and contorted poses: Contributions of hemisphere-specific mechanisms. *Cognition, 70*, 53–85.

Lafuente, M. J., Grifol, R., Segarra, J., Soriano, J., Gorba, M. A., & Montesinos, A. (1997). Effects of the Firstart method of prenatal stimulation on psychomotor development: The first six months. *Pre- & Peri-Natal Psychology Journal, 11*, 151–162.

Lai, C. S. L., Fisher, S. E., Hurst, J. A., Vargha-Khadem, F., & Monaco, A. P. (2001). A forkhead-domain gene is mutated in a severe speech and language disorder. *Nature, 413*, 519–523.

Laird, J. D. (1974). Self-attribution of emotion: The effects of expressive behavior on the quality of emotional experience. *Journal of Personality & Social Psychology, 29*, 475–486.

Laird, J. D. (1984). The real role of facial response in the experience of emotion: A reply to Tourangeau and Ellsworth, and others. *Journal of Personality & Social Psychology, 47*, 909–917.

Laird, J. D., Alibozak, T., Davainis, D., Deignan, K., Fontanella, K., Hong, J., Levy, B., & Pacheco, C. (1994). Individual differences in the effects of spontaneous mimicry on emotional contagion. *Motivation and Emotion, 18*, 231–247.

Lakey, B., & Dickenson, L. G. (1994). Antecedents of perceived support: Is perceived family environment generalized to new social relationships? *Cognitive Therapy and Research, 18*, 39–53.

Lakey, B., & Heller, K. (1988). Social support form a friend, perceived support, and social problem solving. *American journal of Community Psychology, 16*, 811–824.

Lakey, B., & Lutz, C. J. (1996). Social support and preventative and therapeutic interventions. In G. R. Pierce, B. R. Sarason, & I. G. Sarason (Eds.), *Handbook of social support and the family*. New York: Plenum Press.

Lakey, B., Moineau, S., & Drew, J. B. (1992). Perceived social support and individual differences in the interpretation and recall of support behavior. *Journal of Social and Clinical Psychology, 11*, 336–348.

Lakey, B., Ross, L. T., Butler, C., & Bentley, K. (1996). Making social support judgments: The role of similarity and conscientiousness. *Journal of Social and Clinical Psychology, 15*, 283–304.

Lalumiere, M. L., & Quinsey, L. (1998). Pavlovian conditioning of sexual interests in human males. *Archives of Sexual Behavior, 27*, 241–252.

Lam, A. G., & Sue, S. (2001). Client diversity. *Psychotherapy: Theory, Research, Practice, Training, 38*, 479–486.

Lam, R. W., Bartley, S., Yatham, L. N., Tam, E. M., & Zis, A. P. (1999). Clinical predictors of short-term outcome in electroconvulsive therapy. *Canadian Journal of Psychiatry, 44*, 158–163.

Lambert, A. J. (1995). Stereotypes and social judgment: The consequences of group variability. *Journal of Personality and Social Psychology, 68*, 388–403.

Lambert, M. J. (1983). Introduction to assessment of psychotherapy outcome: Historical perspective and current issues. In M. J. Lambert, E. R. Christensen, & S. S. De-Julio (Eds.), *The assessment of psychotherapy outcome* (pp. 3–32). New York: Wiley-Interscience.

Lambert, M. J. (1999). Are differential treatment effects inflated by researcher therapy allegiance? Could Clever Hans count? *Clinical Psychology: Science & Practice, 6*, 127–130.

Lambert, M. J., & Bergin, A. E. (1994). The effectiveness of psychotherapy. In A. E. Bergin & S. L. Garfield (Eds.), *Handbook of psychotherapy and behavior change* (4th ed., pp. 143–189). New York: John Wiley & Sons.

Lamm, C., Windischberger, C., Leodolter, U., Moser, E., & Bauer, H. (2001). Evidence for premotor cortex activity during dynamic visuospatial imagery from single-trial functional magnetic resonance imaging and event-related slow cortical potentials. *NeuroImage, 14*, 268–283.

Lamme, V. A. F., Super, H., Landman, R., Roelfsema, P. R., & Spekreijse, H. (2000). The role of primary visual cortex (V1) in visual awareness. *Vision Research, 40*, 1507–1521.

Land, E. H. (1959). Experiments in color vision. *Scientific American, 200*, 84–99.

Land, E. H. (1977). The retinex theory of color vision. *Scientific American, 237*, 108–128.

Land, E. H. (1983). Recent advances in retinex theory and some implications for cortical computations: Color vision and the natural image. *Proceedings of the National Academy of Sciences, USA, 80*, 5163–5169.

Landauer, T., & Whiting, J. (1964). Infantile stimulation and adult stature of human males. *American Anthropologist, 66*, 1007–1028.

Lane, H. (1976). *The wild boy of Aveyron*. Cambridge, MA: Harvard University Press.

Lane, R. D., Reiman, E. M., Bradley, M. M., Lang, P. J., Ahern, G. L., Davidson, R. J., and Schwartz, G. E. (1997). Neuroanatomical correlates of pleasant and unpleasant emotion. *Neuropsychologia, 35*, 1437–1444.

Lang, E. V., Benotsch, E. G., Fick, L. J., Lutgendorf, S. K., Berbaum, M. L., Berbaum, K. S., Logan, H., & Spiegal, D. (2000). Adjunctive non-pharmacological analgesia for invasive medical procedures: A randomised trial. *The Lancet, 355*, 1486–90.

Lang, F. R., & Carstensen, L. L. (2002). Time counts: Future time perspective, goals, and social relationships. *Psychology & Aging, 17*, 125–139.

Lang, P. J. (1994). The varieties of emotional experience: A meditation on the James-Lange theory. *Psychological Review: Special Issue: The Centennial Issue of the Psychological Review, 101*, 211–221.

Lang, P. J. (1995). The emotion probe: Studies of motivation and attention. *American Psychologist, 50*, 372–385.

Lang, P. J., Bradley, M. M., Cuthbert, B. N. (1990). Emotion, attention, and the startle reflex. *Psychological Review, 97*, 377–395.

Lange, A., van de Ven, J.-P., Schrieken, B., & Emmelkamp, P. M. G. (2001). Interapy. Treatment of posttraumatic stress through the Internet: A controlled trial. *Journal of Behavior Therapy & Experimental Psychiatry, 32*, 73–90.

Lange, C. (1887). *Uber gemuthsbewegungen*. Leipzig: Theodor Thomas.

Langer, E. J., & Rodin, J. (1976). The effects of choice and enhanced personal responsibility for the aged: A field experiment in an institutional setting. *Journal of Personality & Social Psychology, 34*, 191–198.

Langevin, R., Lang, R. A., Wright, P., Handy, L., Frenzel, R. R., & Black, E. L. (1988). Pornography and sexual offences. *Annals of Sex Research, 1*, 335–362.

Lansford, J. E., Sherman, A. M., & Antonucci, T. C. (1998). Satisfaction with social networks: An examination of socioemotional selectivity theory across cohorts. *Psychology & Aging, 13*, 544–552.

La Piere, R. T. (1934). Attitude and actions. *Social Forces, 13*, 230–237.

Lapsley, D. K. (1990). Egocentrism theory and the "new look" at the imaginary audience and personal fable in adolescence. In R. M. Lerner, A. C. Petersen, & J. Brooks-Gunn (Eds.), *The encyclopedia of adolescence* (pp. 281– 286). New York: Garland.

Lapsley, D. K., Jackson, S., Rice, K., & Shadid, G. (1988). Self-monitoring and the "new look" at the imaginary audience and personal fable: An ego-developmental analysis. *Journal of Adolescent Research, 3*, 17–31.

Lapsley, D. K., Milstead, M., Quintana, S. M., Flannery, D., & Buss, R. (1986). Adolescent egocentrism and formal operations: Tests of a theoretical assumption. *Developmental Psychology, 22*, 800–807.

Larimer, M. E., Irvine, D. L., Kilmer, J. R., & Marlatt, G. A. (1997). College drinking and the Greek system: Examining the role of perceived norms for high-risk behavior. *Journal of College Student Development, 38*, 587–598.

Larkin, T., & Keeton, W. T. (1976). Bar magnets mask the effect of normal magnetic disturbances on pigeon orientation. *Journal of Comparative Physiology, 110*, 227–231.

LaRossa, M. M. (2000). Developmental milestones. http://www.emory.edu/Peds/neonatology/mileston.htm.

Larson, J. A. (1932). *Lying and its detection: A study of deception and deception tests*. Chicago, IL: University of Chicago Press.

Larson, R., & Richards, M. H. (1994). *Divergent realities: The emotional lives of mothers, fathers, and adolescents*. New York: Basic Books.

Larson, S. A., Lakin, K. C., Anderson, L., Kwak, N., Lee, J., & Anderson, D. (2001). Prevalence of mental retardation and developmental disabilities: Estimates from the 1994/1995 National Health Interview Survey Disability Supplements. *American Journal on Mental Retardation, 106*, 231–252.

Laruelle, M., Ai-Dargham, A., Casanova, M., Toti, R., Weinberger, D., & Kleinman, J. (1993). Selective abnormalities of prefrontal serotonergic receptors in schizophrenia. *Archives of General Psychiatry, 50*, 810–818.

Lassiter, G. D., Apple, K. J., & Slaw, R. D. (1996). Need for cognition and thought-induced attitude polarization: Another look. *Journal of Social Behavior & Personality, 11*, 647–665.

Latané, B., & Darley, J. M. (1968). Group inhibition of bystander intervention. *Journal of Personality and Social Psychology, 10*, 215–221.

Latané, B., & Darley, J. M. (1970). *The unresponsive bystander: Why doesn't he help?* New York: Appletone-Crofts.

Latané, B., Williams, K., & Harkins, S. (1979). Many hands make light the work: The causes and consequences of social loafing. *Journal of Personality and Social Psychology, 37*, 822–832.

Laursen, B., Coy, K. C., & Collins, W. A. (1998). Reconsidering changes in parent-child conflict across adolescence: A meta-analysis. *Child Development, 69*, 817–832.

Lautrey, J., & Caroff, X. (1996). Variability and cognitive development. *Polish Quarterly of Developmental Psychology, 2*, 71–89.

Lavergne, G. M. (1997). *A sniper in the tower: The Charles Whitman murders*. Denton, TX: University of North Texas Press.

Lawless, H. T. (1984). Oral chemical irritation: Psychophysical properties. *Chemical Senses, 9*, 143–155.

Lazarus, R. S. (1984). On the primacy of cognition. *American Psychologist, 39*, 124–129.

Lazarus, R. S., & Folkman, S. (1984). *Stress, appraisal, and coping*. New York: Springer.

Lazev, A. B., Herzog, T. A., & Brandon, T. H. (1999). Classical conditioning of environmental cues to cigarette smoking. *Experimental and Clinical Psychopharmacology, 7*, 56–63.

Leary, W. (1997, December 18). Responses of alcoholics to therapists seem similar. *New York Times*, A17.

Leask, M. J. M. (1977). A physicochemical mechanism for magnetic field detection by migrating birds and homing pigeons. *Nature, 267*, 144–145.

Leavitt, F. (1997). False attribution of suggestibility to explain recovered memory of childhood sexual abuse following extended amnesia. *Child Abuse & Neglect, 21*, 265–272.

LeBihan, D., Jezzard, P., Turner, R., Cuenod, C. A., Pannier, L., & Prinster, A. (1993). Practical problems and limitations in using z-maps for processing of brain function MR images. *Abstracts of the 12th Meeting of the Society of Magnetic Resonance in Medicine, 1*, 11.

Leccese, A. P. (1991). *Drugs and society: Behavioral medicines and abusable drugs*. Englewood Cliffs, NJ: Prentice-Hall, Inc.

LeDoux, J. E. (1994). Emotion, memory, and the brain. *Scientific American, 270*, 50–57.

LeDoux, J. E. (1995). Emotion: Clues from the brain. *Annual Review of Psychology, 46*, 209–235.

LeDoux, J. E. (1996). *The emotional brain: The mysterious underpinnings of emotional life*. New York: Simon & Schuster.

LeDoux, J. E., Ruggiero, D. A., & Reis, D. J. (1985). Projections to the subcortical forebrain from anatomically defined regions of the medial geniculate body in the rat. *Journal of Comparative Neurology, 242*, 182–213.

LeDoux, J. E., Wilson, D. H., & Gazzaniga, M. S. (1977). A divided mind: Observations on the conscious properties of the separated hemispheres. *Annals of Neurology, 2*, 417–421.

Lee, A. M., & Lee, S. (1996). Disordered eating and its psychosocial correlates among Chinese adolescent females in Hong Kong. *International Journal of Eating Disorders, 20*, 177–183.

Lee, E. S. (1951). Negro intelligence and selective migration: A Philadelphia test of the Klineberg hypothesis. *American Sociological Review, 16*, 227–233.

Lee, S. (1996). Clinical lessons from the cross-cultural study of anorexia nervosa. *Eating Disorders Review, 7*(3), 1

Lee, S., & Lee, A. M. (2000). Disordered eating in three communities of China: A comparative study of female high school students in Hong Kong, Shenzhen, and rural Hunan. *International Journal of Eating Disorders, 27*, 317–327.

Lee, S., & Tedeschi, J. T. (1996). Effects of norms and norm-violations on inhibition and instigation of aggression. *Aggressive Behavior, 22*, 17–25,

Leedy, C., & Dubeck, L. (1971). Physiological changes during tournament chess. *Chess Life and Review*, 708.

Leffler, A., Gillespie, D. L., & Conaty, J. C. (1982). The effects of status differentiation on non-verbal behavior. *Social Psychology Quarterly, 45*, 153–151.

Lehman, A. F., & Steinwachs, D. M. (1998). Translating research into practice: The Schizophrenia Patients Outcome Research Team (PORT) Treatment Recommendations. *Schizophrenia Bulletin, 24*, 1–10.

Lehman, D. R., & Nisbett, R. E. (1990). A longitudinal study of the effects of undergraduate training on reasoning. *Developmental Psychology, 26*, 952–960.

Lehrl, S., & Fischer, B. (1990) A basic information psychological parameter (BIP) for the reconstruction of concepts of intelligence. *European Journal of Personality, 4*, 259–286.

Leibowitz, H. W. (1971). Sensory, learned and cognitive mechanisms of size perception. *Annals of the New York Academy of Sciences, 188*, 47–62.

Leitenberg, H., Rosen, J. C., Gross, J., Nudelman, S., & Vara, L. (1988). Exposure plus response-prevention treatment of bulimia nervosa. *Journal of Consulting and Clinical Psychology, 56*, 535–541.

Lemme, B. H. (1995). *Development in adulthood*. Needham Heights, MA: Allyn & Bacon.

Lennenberg, E. H. (1967). *Biological foundations of language*. New York: Wiley.

Lennon, R., & Eisenberg, N. (1987). Gender and age differences in empathy and sympathy. In N. Eisenberg & J. Strayer (Eds.), *Empathy and its development* (pp. 195–217). New York: Cambridge University Press.

Lensvelt-Mulders, G., & Hettema, J. (2001a). Analysis of genetic influences on the consistency and variability of the Big Five across different stressful situations. *European Journal of Personality, 15*, 355–371.

Lensvelt-Mulders, G., & Hettema, J. (2001b). Genetic analysis of autonomic reactivity to psychologically stressful situations. *Biological Psychology, 58*, 25–40.

Leo, R. A. (1992). From coercion to deception: The changing nature of police interrogation in America. *Crime, Law, and Social Change, 18*, 35–39.

Leone, C., & Ensley, E. (1986). Self-generated attitude change: A person by situation analysis of attitude polarization and attenuation. *Journal of Research in Personality, 20*, 434–446.

Leopold, D. A., & Logothetis, N. K. (1996). Activity changes in early visual cortex reflect monkeys' percepts during binocular rivalry. *Nature, 379*, 549–553.

Lepper, M. R., Greene, D., & Nisbett, R. E. (1973). Undermining children's intrinsic interest with extrinsic reward: A test of the "overjustification" hypothesis. *Journal of Personality and Social Psychology, 28*, 129–137.

Leproult, R., Copinschi, G., Buxton, O., & Van Cauter, E. (1997). Sleep loss results in an elevation of cortisol levels the next evening. *Sleep, 20*, 865–870.

Leproult, R., Van Reeth, O., Byrne, M. M., Sturis, J., & Van Cauter, E. (1997). Sleepiness, performance, and neuroendocrine function during sleep deprivation: Effects of exposure to bright light or exercise. *Journal of Biological Rhythms, 12*, 245–258.

Lerner, M. J. (1980). *The belief in a just world: A fundamental illusion*. New York: Plenum Press.

Lesch, K-P., Bengel, D., Heils, A., Sabol, S. Z., Greenberg, B. D., Petri, S., Benjamin, J., Müller, D. H., Hamer, D. H., & Murphy, D. L. (1996). Association of anxiety-related traits with a polymorphism in the serotonin transporter gene regulatory region. *Science, 274*, 1527–1531.

Leserman, J., Stuart, E. M., Mamish, M. E., & Benson, H. (1989). The efficacy of the relaxation response in preparing for cardiac surgery. *Behavioral Medicine, 15*, 111–117.

Leshner, A. I., & Segal, M. (1979). Fornix transection blocks "learned helplessness" in rats. *Behavioral & Neural Biology, 26*, 497–501.

Leslie, A. (1994) TOMM, ToBy, and agency: Core architecture and domain specificity. In L. A. Hirschfeld & S. A. Gelman (Eds.). *Mapping the mind: Domain specificity in cognition and culture*. (pp. 119–148). New York: Cambridge University Press.

Leslie, A. (1999). The innate capacity to acquire a 'theory of mind': Synchronic or diachronic modularity? *Mind & Language, 17*, 141–155 (1999)

Lester, B. M. (2000). Prenatal cocaine exposure and child outcome: A model for the study of the infant at risk. *Israel Journal of Psychiatry & Related Sciences, 37*, 223–235.

Lester, B. M., LaGasse, L. L., & Seifer, R. (1998). Cocaine exposure and children: The meaning of subtle effects. *Science, 282*, 633–634.

Leuchter, A. F., Cook, I. A., Witte, E. A., Morgan, M., & Abrams, M. (2002). Changes in brain function of depressed subjects during treatment with placebo. *American Journal of Psychiatry, 159*, 122–129.

LeVay, S. (1991). A difference in hypothalamic structure between heterosexual and homosexual men. *Science, 253*, 1034–1037.

LeVay, S., & Hamer, D. (1994). Evidence for a biological influence in male homosexuality. *Scientific American, 270*, 44–49.

Levenson, R. W. (1992). Autonomic nervous system differences among emotions. *Psychological Science, 3*, 23–27.

Levenson, R. W, Ekman, P., and Friesen, W. V. (1990). Voluntary facial action generates emotion-specific autonomic nervous system activity. *Psychophysiology, 27*, 363–384.

Leventhal, G. S., Singer, R., & Jones, S. (1965). The effects of fear and specificity of recommendation upon attitudes and behavior. *Journal of Personality and Social Psychology, 2*, 20–29.

Levie, W. H., & Lentz, R. (1982). Effects of text illustrations: A review of research. *Educational Communication and Technology Journal, 30*, 195–232.

Levin, J. R., Anglin, G. J., & Carney, R. N. (1987). On empirically validating functions of pictures in prose. In D. M. Willows & H. A. Houghton (Eds.), *The psychology of illustration: I. Basic research* (pp. 51–85). New York: Springer-Verlag.

Levin, R. J. (1994). Human male sexuality: Appetite and arousal, desire and drive. In C. R. Legg & D. Booth (Eds.), *Appetite: Neural and behavioral bases*. (pp. 127–164). New York: Oxford University Press.

Levin, R. S. (1980). The physiology of sexual function in women. *Clinics in Obstetrics and Gynaecology, 7*, 213–252.

Levine, A. S., & Billington, C. J. (1997). Why do we eat? A neural systems approach. *Annual Review of Nutrition, 17*, 597–619.

Levine, D. N. (1982). Visual agnosia in monkey and man. In D. J. Ingle, M. A. Goodale, & R. J. W. Mansfield (Eds.), *Analysis of visual behavior* (pp. 629–670). Cambridge: MIT Press.

Levine, J. A., Eberhardt, N. L., & Jensen, M. D. (1999). The role of nonexercise activity thermogenesis in resistance to fat gain in humans. *Science, 283*, 212–214.

Levine, J. M., & Moreland, R. L. (1998). Small groups. In D. T. Gilbert, S. T. Fiske, & G. Lindzey (Eds.), *The handbook of social psychology* (4th ed., pp. 415–469). New York: McGraw Hill..

Levine, L., Prohaska, V., Burgess, S. L., Rice, J. A., & Laulhere, T. M. (2001). Remembering past emotions: The role of current appraisals. *Cognition & Emotion, 15*, 393–417.

Levine, R. L., & Bluni, T. D. (1994). Magnetic field effects on spatial discrimination learning in mice. *Physiology and Behavior, 55*, 465–467.

Levine, R. L., & Stadtman, E. R. (1992). Oxidation of proteins during aging. *Generations, 16*(4), 39–42.

Levinson, D. J. (1977). The mid-life transition: A period in adult psychosocial development. *Psychiatry: Journal for the Study of Interpersonal Processes, 40*, 99–112.

Levinson, D. J. (1978). Eras: The anatomy of the life cycle. *Psychiatric Opinion, 15*, 10–11, 39–48.

Levinson, D. J. (1986). A conception of adult development. *American Psychologist, 41*, 3–13.

Levinson, D. J. (1990). A theory of life structure development in adulthood. In C. N. Alexander & E. J. Langer (Eds.), *Higher stages of human development: Perspectives on adult growth* (pp. 35–53). New York: Oxford University Press.

Levinson, D. J., & Levinson, J. D. (1997). *The seasons of a woman's life*. New York: Ballantine.

Levinson, D., Darrow, C., Klein, E. Levinson, M., & Braxton, M. (1978). *The seasons of a man's life*. New York: Ballantine.

Levitas, A. (2000). Fragile X syndrome. *Journal of the American Academy of Child and Adolescent Psychiatry, 39*, 398–399.

Levitt, A. G., & Wang, Q. (1991). Evidence for language-specific rhythmic influences in the reduplicative babbling of French- and English-learning infants. *Language and Speech, 34*, 235–249.

Levitt, M. J., Weber, R. A., & Guacci, N. (1993). Convoys of social support: An intergenerational analysis. *Psychology and Aging, 8*, 323–326.

Levy, B., Ashman, O., & Dror, I. (1999–2000). To be or not to be: The effects of aging stereotypes on the will to live. *Omega: Journal of Death & Dying, 40*, 409–420.

Levy, S. M., Herberman, R. B., Lippman, M. N., & d'Angelo, T. (1987). Correlation of stress factors with sustained depression of natural killer cell activity and predicted prognosis in patients with breast cancer. *Journal of Clinical Oncology, 5*, 348–353.

Levy, S. M., Herberman, R. B., Maluish, A. M., Schlien, B., & Lippman, M. (1985). Prognostic risk assessment in primary breast cancer by behavioral and immunological parameters. *Health Psychology, 4*, 99–113.

Levy, S. M., Lee, J., Bagley, C., & Lippman, M. (1988). Survival hazards analysis in first year recurrent breast cancer patients: Seven-year follow-up. *Psychosomatic Medicine, 50*, 520–528.

Lewin, K., Lippitt, R., & White, R. K. (1939). Patterns of aggressive behavior in experimentally created "social climates." *Journal of Social Psychology, 10*, 271–299.

Lewinsohn, P. M., Mischel, W., Chaplin, W., & Barton, R. (1980). Social competence and depression: The role of illustory self-perceptions. *Journal of Abnormal Psychology, 89*, 203–212.

Lewinsohn, P. M., Rohde, P., Seeley, J. R., & Fischer, S. A. (1993). Age-cohort changes in the lifetime occurrence of depression and other mental disorders. *Journal of Abnormal Psychology, 102*, 110–120.

Lewis, B., & Thompson, L. A. (1992). A study of developmental speech and language disorders in twins. *Journal of Speech and Hearing Research, 35*, 1086–1094.

Lewis, D. O., Yeager, C. A., Swica, Y., Pincus, J. H., & Lewis, M. (1997). Objective documentation of child abuse and dissociation in 12 murderers with dissociative identity disorder. *American Journal of Psychiatry, 154*, 1703–1710.

Lewis, F. M., & Daltroy, L. H. (1990). How causal explanations influence health behavior: Attribution theory. In K. Glanz, F. M. Lewis, & B. K. Rimer (Eds.), *Health education and health behavior: Theory, research, and practice* (pp. 92–114). San Francisco, CA: Jossey-Bass.

Lewis, M., & Brooks-Gunn, J. (1979). *Social cognition and the acquisition of self*. New York: Plenum.

Lewontin, R. C. (1976a). Further remarks on race and the genetics of intelligence. In N. J. Block & G. Dworkin (Eds.), *The IQ controversy* (pp. 107–112). New York: Pantheon Books.

Lewontin, R. C. (1976b). Race and intelligence. In N. J. Block & G. Dworkin (Eds.), *The IQ controversy* (pp. 78–92). New York: Pantheon Books.

Li, D., Chokka, P., & Tibbo, P. (2001). Toward an integrative understanding of social phobia. *Journal of Psychiatry & Neuroscience, 26*, 190–202.

Li, S-C, Lindenberger, U., & Sikström, S. (2001). Aging cognition: From neuromodulation to representation. *Trends in Cognitive Science, 5*, 479–486.

Li, N. P., Bailey, J. M., Kenrick, D. T., & Linsenmeier, J. A. W. (2002). The necessities and luxuries of mate preferences: Testing the tradeoffs. *Journal of Personality & Social Psychology, 82*, 947–955.

Liben, L. S., Susman, E. J., Finkelstein, J. W., Chinchilli, V. M., Kunselman, S., Schwab, J., Semon Dubas, J., Demers, L. M., Lookingbill, G., D'Arcangelo, M. R., Krogh, H. R., & Kulin, H. E. (2002). The effects of sex steroids on spatial performance: A review and an experimental clinical investigation. *Developmental Psychology, 38*, 236–253.

Liddell, C. (1997). Every picture tells a story—or does it? Young South African children interpreting pictures. *Journal of Cross-Cultural Psychology, 28*, 266–282.

Lieberman, M. D., Ochsner, K. N., Gilbert, D. T., & Schacter, D. L. (2001). Attitude change in amnesia and under cognitive load. *Psychological Science, 12*, 135–140.

Lifton, P. D. (1985). Individual differences in moral development: The relation of sex, gender, and personality to morality. *Journal of Personality, 53*, 306–334.

Light, L. (1991). Memory and aging: Four hypotheses in search of data. *Annual Review of Psychology, 42*, 333–376.

Lijam, N., Paylor, R., McDonald, M. P., Crawley, J. N., Deng, C. X., Herrup, K., Stevens, K. E., Maccaferri, G., McBain, C. J., Sussman, D. J., & Wynshaw-Boris, A. (1997). Social interaction and sensorimotor gating abnormalities in mice lacking Dvl1. *Cell, 90*, 895–905.

Lilenfeld, L. R., Kaye, W. H., Greeno, C. G., Merikangas, K. R., Plotnicov, K., Pollice, C., Raol, R., Strober, M., Bulik, C. M., & Nagy, L. (1998). A controlled family study of anorexia nervosa and bulimia nervosa: Psychiatric disorders in first-degree relatives and effects of proband comorbidity. *Archives of General Psychiatry, 55*, 603–610.

Lilienfeld, S. O., Lynn, S. J., Kirsch, I., Chaves, J. F., Sarbin, T. R., Ganaway, G. K., & Powell, R. A. (1999). Dissociative identity disorder and the sociocognitive model: Recalling the lessons of the past. *Psychological Bulletin, 125*, 507–523.

Lilienfeld, S. O., Wood, J. M., & Garb, H. N. (2000). The scientific status of projective techniques. *Psychological Science in the Public Interest, 1*, 27–66.

Lillard, A. S. (1999). Developing a cultural theory of mind: The CIAO approach. *Current Directions in Psychological Science, 8*, 57–61.

Lin, E. L., & Murphy, G. L. (2001). Thematic relations in adults' concepts. *Journal of Experimental Psychology: General, 130*, 3–28.

Lindblom, K. (2001). Cooperating with Grice: A cross-disciplinary metaperspective on uses of Grice's cooperative principle. *Journal of Pragmatics, 33*, 1601–1623.

Lindemann, E. (1991). The symptomatology and management of acute grief. *American Journal of Psychiatry, 144*, 141–148.

Lindley, R. H., Wilson, S. M., Smith, W. R., & Bathurst, K., (1995). Reaction time (RT) and IQ: Shape of the task complexity function. *Personality and Individual Differences, 18*, 339–345.

Lindsay, D. S., & Johnson, M. K. (1989). The eyewitness suggestibility effect and memory for source. *Memory & Cognition, 17*, 349–358.

Lindsay, P. H., & Norman, D. A. (1977). *Human information processing: An introduction to psychology* (2nd ed.). New York: Academic Press.

Lindsay, R. C., & Wells, G. L. (1985). Improving eyewitness identifications from lineups: Simultaneous versus sequential lineup presentation. *Journal of Applied Psychology, 70*, 556–564.

Lindstrom, T. C. (2002). "It ain't necessarily so" . . . Challenging mainstream thinking about bereavement. *Family & Community Health, 25*, 11–21.

Linehan, M. M. (1993). *Skills training manual for treating borderline personality disorder*. New York: Guilford.

Linner, B. (1972). *Sex and society in Sweden*. New York: Harper Colophon Books.

Linnoila, M., Virkkunen, M., Scheinin, M., Nuutila, A., Romin, R., & Goodwin, F. K. (1983). Low cerebrospinal fluid 5-hydroxindoleacetic acid concentration differentiates impulsive from non-impulsive violent behavior. *Life Sciences, 33*, 2609–2614.

Linville, P. W., & Fischer, G. W. (1993). Exemplar and abstraction models of perceived group variability and stereotypicality. *Social Cognition, 11*, 92–125.

Lipkus, I. M., & Siegler, I. C. (1993). The belief in a just world and perceptions of discrimination. *Journal of Psychology, 127*, 465–474.

Lipkus, I. M., Dalbert, C., & Siegler, I. C. (1996). The importance of distinguishing the belief in a just world for self versus for others: Implications for Psychological Well-being. *Personality and Social Psychology Bulletin, 22*, 666–677.

Lipsey, M. W., & Wilson, D. B. (1993). The efficacy of psychological, educational, and behavioral treatment: Confirmation from meta-analysis. *American Psychologist, 48*, 1181–1209.

Litt, M. D., Kleppinger, A., & Judge, J. O. (2002). Initiation and maintenance of exercise behavior in older women: Predictors from the social learning model. *Journal of Behavioral Medicine, 25*, 83–97.

Liu, D., Diorio, J., Tannenbaum, B., Caldji, C., Francis, D., Freedman, A., Sharma, S., Pearson, D., Plotsky, P. M., & Meaney, M. J. (1997). Maternal care, hippocampal glucocorticoid receptors, and hypothalamic-pituitary-adrenal responses to stress. *Science, 277*, 1659–1662.

Liu, J. H., & Latané, B. (1998). Extremitization of attitudes: Does thought- and discussion-induced polarization cumulate? *Basic & Applied Social Psychology, 20*, 103–110.

Liu, J. H., Campbell, S. M., & Condie, H. (1995). Ethnocentrism in dating preferences for an American sample: The ingroup bias in social context. *European Journal of Social Psychology, 25*, 95–115.

Livesley, W. J. (1998). Suggestions for a framework for an empirically based classification of personality disorder. *Canadian Journal of Psychiatry 43*, 137–147.

Livingstone, M. S., & Hubel, D. H. (1984). Anatomy and physiology of a color system in the primate visual cortex. *Journal of Neuroscience, 4*, 309–356.

Llinas, R. R., Ribary, U., Joliot, M., & Wang, X.-J. (1994). Content and context in temporal thalamocortical binding. In G. Buzsaki, R. R. Llinas, & W. Singer (Eds.), *Temporal coding in the brain*. Berlin: Springer Verlag.

Lobaugh, N. J., Cole, S., & Rovet, J. F. (1998). Visual search for features and conjunctions in development. *Canadian Journal of Experimental Psychology, 52*, 201–212.

Locke, S. E., Kraus, L., Leserman, J., Hurst, M. W., Heisel, J. S., & Williams, R. M. (1984). Life change stress, psychiatric symptoms, and natural killer-cell activity. *Psychosomatic Medicine, 46*, 441–453.

Loehlin, J. C. (1989). Partitioning environmental and genetic contributions to behavioral development. *American Psychologist, 44*, 1285–1292.

Loehlin, J. C. (1992). *Genes and environment in personality development*. Newbury Park, CA: Sage.

Loehlin, J. C. (1997). A test of J. R. Harris' theory of peer influences on personality. *Journal of Personality and Social Psychology, 72*, 1197–1201.

Loehlin, J. C., Horn, J. M., & Willerman, L. (1981). Personality resemblance in adoptive families. *Behavior Genetics, 11*, 309–330.

Loehlin, J. C., Willerman, L., & Horn, J. M. (1985). Personality resemblances in adoptive families when the children are late-adolescent or adult. *Journal of Personality and Social Psychology, 48*, 376–392.

Loehlin, J. C., Willerman, L., & Horn, J. M. (1987). Personality resemblance in adoptive families: A 10-year follow-up. *Journal of Personality and Social Psychology, 53*, 961–969.

Loewenstein, R. J. (1994). Diagnosis, epidemiology, clinical course, treatment, and cost effectiveness of treatment for dissociative disorders and MPD: Report submitted to the Clinton Administration Task Force on Health Care Financing Reform. *Dissociation: Progress in the Dissociative Disorders, 7*, 3–11.

Loftus, E. F. (1993). The reality of repressed memories. *American Psychologist, 48*, 518–537.

Loftus, E. F., & Hoffman, H. G. (1989). Misinformation and memory: The creation of new memories. *Journal of Experimental Psychology: General, 118*, 100–114.

Loftus, E. F., & Palmer, J. C. (1974). Reconstruction of automobile destruction: An example of the interaction between language and memory. *Journal of Verbal Learning and Verbal Behavior, 13*, 585–589.

Mather, M., Henkel, L. A., & Johnson, M. K. (1997). Evaluating characteristics of false memories: Remember/know judgments and memory characteristics questionnaire compares. *Memory & Cognition, 25,* 826–837.

Matsumae, M., Kikinis, R., Mórocz, I. A., Lorenzo, A. V., Sándor, T., Albert, M. S., Black, P. M., & Jolesz, F. A. (1996). Age-related changes in intracranial compartment volumes in normal adults assessed by magnetic resonance imaging. *Journal of Neurosurgery, 84,* 982–992.

Matt, G. E., Navarro, A. M. (1997). What meta-analyses have and have not taught us about psychotherapy effects: A review and future directions. *Clinical Psychology Review, 17,* 1–32.

Matthews, B. A., & Norris, F. H. (2002). When is believing "seeing"? Hostile attribution bias as a function of self-reported aggression. *Journal of Applied Social Psychology, 32,* 1–32.

Matthews, B. A., Shimoff, E., Catania, A. C., & Sagvolden, T. (1977). Uninstructed human responding: Sensitivity to ratio and interval contingencies. *Journal of the Experimental Analysis of Behavior, 27,* 453–467.

Matthews, G., & Amelang, M. (1993). Extraversion, arousal theory and performance: A study of individual differences in the EEG. *Personality and Individual Differences, 14,* 347–363.

Matthews, G., & Gilliland, K. (1999). The personality theories of H. J. Eysenck and J. A. Gray: A comparative review. *Personality and Individual Differences, 26,* 583–626.

Mauro, R. (1988). Opponent processes in human emotions? An experimental investigation of hedonic contrast and affective interactions. *Motivation & Emotion, 12,* 333–351.

Mayer, J. D., & Salovey, P. (1997). What is emotional intelligence? In P. Salovey & D. J. Sluyter (Eds.), *Emotional development and emotional intelligence.* New York: Basic Books.

Mayer, R. E. (1997). *Thinking, problem solving, cognition.* New York: Freeman.

Mayes, A. R., & Downes, J. J. (Eds.). (1997). *Theories of organic amnesia.* Hove, England: Psychology Press/Erlbaum (UK) Taylor & Francis.

Maynard, R. A. (Ed.). (1996). *Kids having kids: A Robin Hood Foundation special report on the costs of adolescent childbearing.* New York: Robin Hood Foundation.

Maznevski, M. L. (1994). Understanding our differences: Performance in decision—making groups with diverse members. *Human Relations, 47,* 531–552.

McAdams, D. (2001). Generativity: The new definition of success. *Spirituality & Health Magazine,* Fall.

McAdams, D. P., & de St. Aubin, E. (1992). A theory of generativity and its assessment through self-report, behavioral acts, and narrative themes in autobiography. *Journal of Personality & Social Psychology, 62,* 1003–1015.

McAdams, D. P., Reynolds, J., Lewis, M., Patten, A. H., & Bowman, P. J. (2001). When bad things turn good and good things turn bad: Sequences of redemption and contamination in life narrative and their relation to psychosocial adaptation in midlife adults and in students. *Personality & Social Psychology Bulletin, 27,* 474–485.

McAdams, D. P., de St. Aubin, E., & Logan, R. L. (1993). Generativity among young, midlife, and older adults. *Psychology & Aging, 8,* 221–230.

McArdle, J. J., Ferrer-Caja, E., Hamagami, F., & Woodcock, R. W. (2002). Comparative longitudinal structural analyses of the growth and decline of multiple intellectual abilities over the life span. *Developmental Psychology, 38,* 115–142.

McBride, J. (1999). *Steven Spielberg: A biography.* New York: Da Capo.

McCarlet, R. W., & Hobson, J. A. (1977). The neurobiological origins of psychoanalytic dream theory. *American Journal of Psychiatry, 134,* 1211–1221.

McCarley, R. W., & Hobson, J. A. (1975). Neuronal excitability modulation over the sleep cycle: A structural and mathematical model. *Science, 189,* 58–60.

McCartney, K., Harris, M. J., & Bernieri, F. (1990). Growing up and growing apart: A developmental meta-analysis of twin studies. *Psychological Bulletin, 107,* 226–237.

McCauley, C. R., Jussim, L. J., & Lee, Y. (1995). Stereotype accuracy: Toward appreciating group differences. In Y. Lee, L. J. Jussim, & C. R. McCauley (Eds.), *Stereotype accuracy: Toward appreciating group differences* (pp. 293–312). Washington DC: American Psychological Association.

McClearn, G. E., Johansson, B., Berg, S., Pedersen, N. L., Ahern, F., Petrill, S. A., & Plomin, R. (1997). Substantial genetic influence on cognitive abilities in twins 80 or more years old. *Science, 276,* 1560–1563.

McClelland, D. C., & Atkinson, J. W. (1953). *The achievement motive.* New York: Appleton-Century-Crofts.

McClelland, D. C., Koestner, R., & Weinbereger, J. (1989). How do self-attributed and implicit motives differ? *Psychological Review, 96,* 690–702.

McClelland, J. L., & Rumelhart, D. E. (1981). An interactive activation model of context effects in letter perception: Part 1. An account of basic findings. *Psychological Review, 88,* 375–407.

McClelland, J. L., & Rumelhart, D. E. (1986). *Parallel distributed processing: Explorations in the microstructure of cognition.* Cambridge: MIT Press.

McClintock, M. K. (1971). Menstrual synchrony and suppression. *Nature, 229,* 244–245.

McClintock, M. K., & Herdt, G. (1996). Rethinking puberty: The development of sexual attraction. *Current Directions in Psychological Science, 5,* 178–183.

McCloskey, M., Caramazza, A., & Green, B. (1980). Curvilinear motion in the absence of external forces: Naive beliefs about motion of objects. *Science, 210,* 1139–1141.

McCloskey, M., & Zaragoza, M. (1985). Misleading postevent information and memory for events: Arguments and evidence against memory impairment hypotheses. *Journal of Experimental Psychology: General, 114,* 1–16.

McClure, E. B. (2000). A meta-analytic review of sex differences in facial expression processing and their development in infants, children, and adolescents. *Psychological Bulletin, 126,* 424–453.

McConnell, A. R., & Leibold, J. M. (2001). Relating among the Implicit Association Test, discriminatory behavior, and explicit measures in racial attitudes. *Journal of Experimental Social Psychology, 37,* 435–442.

McCornack, S. A., & Parks, M. R. (1990). What women know that men don't: Sex differences in determining the truth behind deceptive messages. *Journal of Social and Personal Relationships, 7,* 107–118.

McCoy, N. L., & Pitino, L. (2002). Pheromonal influences on sociosexual behavior in young women. *Physiology and Behavior, 75,* 367–75.

McCrae, R. H., & Costa, P. T., Jr. (1984). *Emerging lives, enduring dispositions: Personality in adulthood.* Boston: Little, Brown.

McCrae, R. H., & Costa, P. T., Jr. (1987). Validation of the five-factor model of personality across instruments and observers. *Journal of Personality and Social Psychology, 52,* 81–90.

McCrae, R. H., & Costa, P. T., Jr. (1989a). Reinterpreting the Myers-Briggs type indicator from the perspective of the five-factor model of personality. *Journal of Personality, 57,* 17–40.

McCrae, R. H., & Costa, P. T., Jr. (1989b). Different points of view: Self-reports and ratings in the assessment of personality. In J. P. Forgas & J. M. Innes (Eds.), *Recent advance in social psychology: An international perspective* (pp. 429–439). Amsterdam: Elsevier North-Holland.

McCrae, R. H., & Costa, P. T., Jr. (1997). Personality trait structure as a human universal. *American Psychologist, 52,* 509–516.

McCrae, R. H., Costa, P. T., Jr., DelPilar, G. H. Rolland, J. P., & Parker, W. D. (1998). Cross-cultural assessment of the five-factor model: The revised NEO personality inventory. *Journal of Cross-Cultural Psychology, 29,* 171–188.

McCrae, R. H., Stone, S. V., Fagan, P. J., & Costa, Jr., P. T. (1998). Identifying causes of disagreement between self-reports and spouse ratings of personality. *Journal of Personality, 66,* 285–313.

McDaniel, M. A., & Einstein, G. O. (1986). Bizarre imagery as an effective memory aid: The importance of distinctiveness. *Journal of Experimental Psychology: Learning, Memory, & Cognition, 12,* 54–65.

McDaniel, M. A., Einstein, G. O., DeLosh, E. L., & May, C. P. (1995). The bizarreness effect: It's not surprising, it's complex. *Journal of Experimental Psychology: Learning, Memory, & Cognition, 21,* 422–435.

McDermott, K. B., & Roediger, H. L., III. (1998). Attempting to avoid illusory memories: Robust false recognition of associates persists under conditions of explicit warnings and immediate testing. *Journal of Memory and Language, 39,* 508–520.

McDougall, W. (1908/1960). *Introduction to social psychology.* New York: Barnes & Noble.

McEwen, B. S. (1997). Possible mechanisms for atrophy of the human hippocampus. *Molecular Psychiatry, 2,* 255–262.

McEwen, B. S., & Schmeck, H. M., Jr. (1994). *The hostage brain.* New York: Rockefeller University Press.

McEwen, B. S., Biron, C. A., Brunson, K. W., Bulloch, K., Chambers, W. H., Dhabhar, F. S., Goldfarb, R. H., Kitson, R. P., Miller, A. H., Spencer, R. L., & Weiss, J. M. (1997). The role of adrenocorticoids as modulators of immune function in health and disease: Neural, endocrine and immune interactions. *Brain Research Review, 23,* 79–133.

McFadden, D. (1982). *Tinnitus: Facts, theories and treatments.* Washington, DC: National Academy Press.

McFadden, D., & Pasanen, E. G. (1999). Spontaneous otoacoustic emissions in heterosexuals, homosexuals, and bisexuals. *Journal of the Acoustical Society of America, 105,* 2403–2413.

McFadden, D., & Plattsmier, H. S. (1983). Aspirin can potentiate the temporary hearing loss induced by intense sounds. *Hearing Research, 9,* 295–316.

McFadyen, R. G. (1998). Attitudes toward the unemployed. *Human Relations, 51,* 179–199.

McGaugh, J. L., & Herz, M. J. (1972). *Memory consolidation.* San Francisco, CA: Albion.

McGoldrick, M., Giordano, J., Pearce, J. K. (Eds.) (1996). *Ethnicity and family therapy* (2nd ed.). New York: Guilford Press.

McGorry, P. D., & Edwards, J. (1998). The feasibility and effectiveness of early intervention in psychotic disorders: The Australian experience. *International Clinical Psychopharmacology, 13*(Suppl 1), S47–S52.

McGraw, K., Hoffman, R. I., Harker, C., & Herman, J. H. (1999). The development of circadian rhythms in a human infant. *Sleep, 22,* 303–310.

McGraw, M. B. (1943). *The neuromuscular maturation of the human infant.* New York: Columbia University Press.

McGue, M., & Lykken, D. T. (1992). Genetic influence on the risk of divorce. *Psychological Science, 3,* 368–373.

McGue, M., Bouchard, T. J., Jr., Iacono, W. G., & Lykken, D. T. (1993). Behavioral genetics of cognitive ability: A life-span perspective. In R. Plomin & G. E. McClearn (Eds.). *Nature, nurture & psychology* (pp. 59–76). Washington, DC, USA: American Psychological Association.

McGuffin, P., & Gottesman, I. I. (1985). Genetic influences on normal and abnormal development. In M. Rutter & L. Hersov (Eds.), *Child and adolescent psychiatry: Modern approaches.* (2nd edition, pp. 17–33). Oxford: Blackwell Scientific.

McGuffin, P., Katz, R., Aldrich, J., & Bebbington, P. (1988). The Camberwell Collaborative Depression Study. II. Investigation of family members. *British Journal of Psychiatry, 152,* 766–774.

McGuffin, P., Katz, R., & Rutherford, J. (1991). Nature, nurture, and depression: A twin study. *Psychological Medicine, 21,* 329–335.

McHale, S. M., Crouter, A. C., McGuire, S. A., & Updegraff, K. A. (1995). Congruence between mothers' and fathers' differential treatment of siblings: Links with family relations and children's well-being. *Child Development, 66,* 116–128.

McHugh, T. J., Blum, K. I., Tsien, J., Tonegawa, S., & Wilson, M. (1996). Impaired hippocampal representation of space in CA1-specific NMDAR1 knockout mice. *Cell, 87,* 1339–1349.

McIntosh, W. D., Martin, L. L., & Jones, J. B., III (1997). Goal beliefs, life events, and the malleability of people's judgments of their happiness. *Journal of Social Behavior & Personality, 12,* 567–575.

McKay, P. F., Doverspike, D., Bowen-Hilton, D., & Martin, Q. D. (2002). Stereotype threat effects on the Raven Advanced Progressive Matrices scores of African-Americans. *Journal of Applied Social Psychology, 32,* 767–787.

McKellar, P. (1965). The investigation of mental images. In S. A. Bartnet & A. McLaren (Eds.), *Penguin science survey B (biological sciences)* (pp. 79–94). New York: Penguin Books.

McKelvie, S. J. (2000). Quantifying the availability heuristic with famous names. *North American Journal of Psychology, 2,* 347–356.

McKenna, R. J. (1972). Some effects of anxiety level and food cues on the eating behavior of obese and normal subjects: A comparison of the Schachterian and psychosomatic conceptions. *Journal of Personality and Social Psychology, 22,* 311–319.

McKnight, J., & Malcolm, J. (2000). Is male homosexuality maternally linked? *Psychology, Evolution & Gender, 2,* 229–239.

McKoon, G., Ratcliff, R., & Dell, G. S. (1986). A critical evaluation of the semantic-episodic distinction. *Journal of Experimental Psychology: Learning, Memory, and Cognition, 12,* 295–306.

McLaughlin, S., & Margolskee, R. F. (1994). The sense of taste. *American Scientist, 82,* 538–545.

McLean, A. A. (1980). *Work stress.* Reading, MA: Addison-Wesley.

McLean, D. E., Hatfield-Timajchy, K., Wingo, P. A., & Floyd, R. L. (1993). Psychosocial measurement: Implications of the study of preterm delivery in black women. *American Journal of Preventive Medicine, 9,* 39–81.

McLeod, P. L., & Lobel, S. A. (1992). The effects of ethinic diversity on idea generation in small groups. *Academy of Management Best Paper Proceedings, 22,* 227–231.

McMillen, D. L., & Austin, J. B. (1971). Effect of positivev feedback on complaince following transgression. *Psychonomic Science, 24,* 59–61.

McNeil, T. F., Cantor-Graae, E., & Weinberger, D. R. (2000). Relationship of obstetric complications and differences in size of brain structures in monozygotic twin pairs discordant for schizophrenia. *American Journal of Psychiatry, 157,* 203–212.

McNicol, D. (1972). *A primer of signal detection theory.* London: Allen & Unwin.

McRoberts, C., Burlingame, G. M., & Hoag, M. J. (1998). Comparative efficacy of individual and group psychotherapy: A meta-analytic perspective. *Group Dynamics, 2,* 101–117.

Mead, M. (1928). *Coming of age in Samoa.* New York: Morrow.

Mealey, L., Bridgestock, R., & Townsend, G. C. (1999). Symmetry and perceived facial attractiveness: A monozygotic co-twin comparison. *Journal of Personality and Social Psychology, 76,* 151–158.

Meaney, M. J., Mitchell, J. B., Aitken, D. H., Bhatnagar, S., Bodnoff, S. R., Iny, L. J., & Sarrieau, A. (1991). The effects of neonatal handling on the development of the adrenocortical response to stress: Implications for neuropathology and cognitive deficits in later life. *Psychoneuroendocrinology, 16,* 85–103.

Medin, D. L., & Schaffer, M. M. (1978). A context theory of classification learning. *Psychological Review, 85,* 207–238.

Medin, D. L., Lynch, E. B., & Solomon, K. O. (2000). Are there kinds of concepts? In S. T. Fiske, D. L. Schacter, & C. Zahn-Waxler (Eds.), *Annual Review of Psychology, 51,* 121–147.

Mednick, S. (1962). The associative basis of the creative process. *Psychological Review, 69,* 220–232.

Mednick, S. A., Gabrielli, W. F., & Hutchings, B. (1984). Genetic factors in criminal behavior: Evidence from an adoption cohort. *Science, 224,* 891–893.

Mednick, S. A., Watson, J. B., Huttunen, M., Cannon, T. D., Katila, H., Machon, R., Mednick, B., Hollister, M., Parnas, J., Schulsinger, F., Sajaniemi, N., Voldsgaard, P., Pyhala, R., Gutkind, D., & Wang, X. (1998). A two-hit workikng model of the etiology of schizophrenia. In M. F. Lenzenweger & R. H. Dworkin (Eds.), *Origins and development of schizophrenia: Advances in experimental psychopathology.* Washington, DC: American Psychological Association. pp. 27–66.

Meehl, P. (1960). The cognitive activity of the clinician. *American Psychologist, 15,* 19–27.

Mehl, L. E. (1994). Hypnosis and conversion of the breech to the vertex position. *Archives of Family Medicine, 3,* 881–887l.

Mehler, J., Jusczyk, P. W., Lambertz, G., Halsted, N., Bertoncini, J., & Amiel-Tison, C. (1988). A precursor of language acquisition in young infants. *Cognition, 29,* 143–178.

Melchert, T. P. (1996). Childhood memory and a history of different forms of abuse. *Professional Psychology Research and Practice, 27,* 438–446.

Melding, P. S. (1995). How do older people respond to chronic pain? A review of coping with pain and illness in elders. *Pain Review, 2,* 65–75.

Mellet, E., Petit, L., Mazoyer, B., Denis, M., & Tzourio, N. (1998). Reopening the mental imagery debate: Lessons from functional neuroanatomy. *NeuroImage, 8,* 129–139.

Mellet, E., Tzourio, N., Denis, M., & Mazoyer, B. (1998). Cortical anatomy of mental imagery of concrete nouns based on their dictionary definition. *Neuroreport, 9,* 803–808.

Mello, C., Nottebohm, F., & Clayton, D. (1995). Repeated exposure to one song leads to a rapid and persistent decline in an immediate early gene's response to that song in zebra finch telencephalon. *Journal of Neuroscience, 15,* 6919–6925.

Mello, C. V., Vicario, D. S., & Clayton, D. F. (1992). Song presentation induces gene expression in the songbird forebrain. *Proceedings of the National Academy of Science, USA, 89,* 6818–6822.

Melson, G. F., Windecker-Nelson, E., & Schwarz, R. (1998). Support and stress in mothers and fathers of young children. *Early Education & Development, 9,* 261–281.

Meltzoff, A. N., & Moore, M. K. (1977). Imitation of facial and manual gestures by human neonates. *Science, 198,* 75–78.

Melzack, R., & Wall, P. D. (1982). *The challenge of pain.* New York: Basic Books.

Menard, M. T., Kosslyn, S. M., Thompson, W. T., Alpert, N. M., & Rauch, S. L. (1996). Encoding words and pictures: A positron emission tomography study. *Neuropsychologia, 34,* 185–194.

Menyuk, P., Liebergott, J. W., & Schultz, M. C. (1995). *Early language development in full-term and premature infants.* Hillsdale, NJ: Erlbaum.

Menzies, R. G., & Clarke, J. C. (1993). The etiology of childhood water phobia. *Behaviour Research & Therapy, 31,* 499–501.

Menzies, R. G., & Clarke, J. C. (1995a). The etiology of acrophobia and its relationship to severity and individual response patterns. *Behaviour Research & Therapy, 33,* 795–803.

Menzies R. G., & Clarke, J. C. (1995b). The etiology of phobias: A nonassociative account. *Clinical Psychology Review, 15,* 23–48.

Mercer, R. T., Nichols, E. G., & Doyle, G. C. (1989). *Transitions in a woman's life: Major life events in developmental context.* New York: Springer.

Meredith, L. S., Wells, K. B., Kaplan, S. H., & Mazel, R. M. (1996). Counseling typically provided for depression. Role of clinican specialty and payment system. *Arch Gen Psychiatry, 53,* 905–12.

Merrick, E. N. (1995). Adolescent childbearing as career "choice": Perspective from an ecological context. *Journal of Counseling & Development, 73,* 288–295.

Merzenich, M. M., Jenkins, W. M., Johnston, P., Shreiner, C., Miller, S. L., & Tallal, P. (1996). Temporal processing deficits of language-learning impaired children ameliorated by training. *Science, 271,* 77–81.

Merzenich, M. M., Kaas, J. H., Wall, J. T., Sur, M., Nelson, R. J., & Felleman, D. J. (1983). Progression of change following median nerve section in the cortical representation of the hand in areas 3b and 1 in adult owl and squirrel monkeys. *Neuroscience, 10(3),* 639–665.

Merzenich, M. M., Kaas, J. H., Wall, J., Nelson, R. J., & Sur, M. (1983). Topographic reorganization of somatosensory cortical areas 3b and 1 in adult monkeys following restricted deafferentation. *Neuroscience, 8,* 33–55.

Messinger, S. M. (1998). Pleasure and complexity: Berlyne revisited. *Journal of Psychology, 132,* 558–560.

Meston, C. M., & Frohlich, P. F. (2000). The neurobiology of sexual function. *Archives of General Psychiatry, 57,* 1012–1030.

Metalsky, G. I., Joiner, T. E., Hardin, T. S., Abramson, L. Y. (1993). Depressive reactions to failure in a naturalistic setting: A test of the hopelessness and self-esteem theories of depression. *Journal of Abnormal Psychology, 103,* 101–109.

Metcalfe, J. (1986). Premonitions of insight predict impending error. *Journal of Experimental Psychology: Learning, Memory, and Cognition, 12,* 623–634.

Metcalfe, J., & Wiebe, D. (1987). Intuition in insight and non-insight problem solving. *Memory and Cognition, 15,* 238–246.

Meunier, M., Hadfield, W., Bachevalier, J., & Murray, E. A. (1996). Effects of rhinal cortex lesions combined with hippocampectomy on visual recognition memory in rhesus monkeys. *Journal of Neurophysiology, 75,* 1190–1205.

Meyer, D. E., & Schvaneveldt, R. W. (1971). Facilitation in recognizing pairs of words: Evidence of a dependence between retrieval operations. *Journal of Experimental Psychology, 90,* 227–234.

Meyer, G. J., & Archer, R. P. (2001). The hard science of Rorschach research: What do we know and where do we go? *Psychological Assessment, 13,* 486–502.

Meyer, S-L., Murphy, C. M., Cascardi, M., & Birns, B. (1991). Gender and relationships: Beyond the peer group. *American Psychologist, 46,* 537.

Meyers, A. W., Stunkard, A. J., & Coll, M. (1980). Food accessibility and food choice: A test of Schachter's externality hypothesis. *Archives of General Psychiatry, 37,* 1133–1135.

Miscallef, J., and Blin, O. (2001). Neurobiology and clinical pharmacology of obsessive-compulsive disorder. *Clinical Neuropharmacology, 24,* 191–207.

Micheli, R. (1985, June). Water babies. *Parents, 60(6),* 8–13.

Michener, W., & Rozin, P. (1994). Pharmacological versus sensory factors in the satiation of chocolate craving. *Physiology & Behavior, 56,* 419–422.

Mickelson, K. D., Kessler, R. C., & Shaver, P. R. (1997). Adult attachment in a nationally representative sample. *Journal of Personality & Social Psychology, 73,* 1092–1106.

Mignot, E. (2001). A commentary on the neurobiology of the hypocretin/orexin system. *Neuropsychopharmacology, 25,* S5-S13.

Miklowitz, D. J., Goldstein, M. J., Nuechterlein, K. H., Snyder, K. S., & Mintz, J. (1988). Family factors and the course of bipolar affective disorder. *Archives of General Psychiatry, 45,* 225–231.

Mikulincer, M. (1994). *Human learned helplessness: A coping perspective.* New York: Plenum.

Mikulincer, M., & Horesh, N. (1999). Adult attachment style and the perception of others: The role of projective mechanisms. *Journal of Personality and Social Psychology, 76,* 1022–1034.

Miles, L. E. M., Raynal, D. M., & Wilson, M. A. (1977). Blind man living in normal society has circadian rhythms of 24.9 hours. *Science, 198,* 421–423.

Miles, W. F. S. (1993). Hausa dreams. *Anthropologica, 35,* 105–116.

Milgram, S. (1963). Behavioral study of obedience. *Journal of Abnormal and Social Psychology, 67,* 371–378.

Milgram, S. (1965). Some conditions of obedience and disobedience to authority. *Human Relations, 18,* 57–76.

Milgram, S. (1974). *Obedience to authority: An experimental view.* New York: Harper & Row.

Miller, A. G., Collins, B. E., Brief, D. E. (1995). Perspectives on obedience to authority: The legacy of the Milgram experiments. *Journal of Social Issues, 51,* 1–19.

Miller, D. D., Andreasen, N. C., O'Leary, D. S., Watkins, G. L., Ponto, L. L. B., & Hichwa, R. D. (2001). Comparison of the effects of risperidone and haloperidol on regional cerebral blood flow in schizophrenia. *Biological Psychiatry, 49,* 704–715.

Miller, E. M. (1992). On the correlation of myopia and intelligence. *Genetic, Social and General Psychology Monographs 118,* 361–383.

Miller, G. A. (1956). The magical number seven, plus or minus two: Some limits on our capacity for processing information. *Psychological Review, 63,* 81–97.

Miller, G. E., & Cohen, S. (2001). Psychological interventions and the immune system: A meta-analytic review and critique. *Health Psychology, 20,* 47–63.

Miller, G. E., Dopp, J. M., Stevens, S. Y., & Fahey, J. L. (1999). Psychosocial predictors of natural killer cell mobilzation during marital conflict. *Health Psychology, 18,* 262–271.

Miller, I. W., Keitner, G. E., Whisman, M. A., Ryan, C. E., Epstein, N. B., & Bishop, D. S. (1992). Depressed patients with dysfunctional families: Description and course of illness. *Journal of Abnormal Psychology, 101,* 637–646.

Miller, J. M., Boudreaux, M. C., & Regan, F. A. (1995). A case-control study of cocaine use in pregnancy. *American Journal of Obstetrics and Gynecology, 172,* 180–185.

Miller, L. C., Putcha-Bhagavatula, A., & Pedersen, W. C. (2002). Men's and women's mating preferences: Distinct evolutionary mechanisms? *Current Directions in Psychological Science, 11,* 88–93.

Miller, L. K. (1999). The Savant Syndrome: Intellectual impairment and exceptional skill. *Psychological Bulletin, 125,* 31–46.

Miller, M. G., & Ross, M. (1975). Self-serving biases in attribution of causality: Fact or fiction? *Psychological Bulletin, 82,* 313–325.

Miller, N., Maruayama, G., Beaber, R. J., & Valone, K. (1976). Speed of speech and persuasion. *Journal of Personality and Social Psychology, 34,* 615–624.

Miller, N. E. (1959). Liberalization of basic S-R concepts: Extensions to conflict behavior, motivation, and social learning. In S. Koch (Ed.), *Psychology: A study of science: Vol. 2.* New York: McGraw-Hill.

Miller, T. Q., Smith, T. W., Turner, C. W., Guijarro, M. L., & Hallet, A. J. (1996). A meta-analytic review of research on hostility and physical health. *Psychological Bulletin, 119,* 322–348.

Miller, W. B., Pasta, D. J., MacMurray, J., Chiu, C., Wu, H., & Comings, D. E. (1999). Dopamine receptor genes are associated with age at first sexual intercourse. *Journal of Biosocial Science, 31,* 43–54.

Millet, B., Leclaire, M., Bourdel, M. C., Loo, H., Tezcan, E., & Kuloglu, M. (2000). Comparison of sociodemographic, clinical and phenomenological characteristics of Turkish and French patients suffering from obsessive-compulsive disorder. *Canadian Journal of Psychiatry, 45,*848.

Millon, T. (1975). Reflections on Rosenhan's "On being sane in insane places." *Journal of Abnormal Psychology, 84,* 456–461.

Mills, D. L., Coffey-Corina, S., & Neville, H. J. (1997). Language comprehension and cerebral specialization from 13 to 20 months. *Developmental Neuropsychology, 13,* 397–445.

Milner, A. D., & Goodale, M. A. (1995). *The visual brain in action.* Oxford University Press.

Milner, B., Corkin, S., & Teuber, H. L. (1968). Further analysis of the hippocampal amnesic syndrome: 14-year followup study of H. M. *Neuropsychologia, 6,* 215–234.

Milton, J., & Weisman, R. (1999a). Does psi exist? Lack of replication of an anomalous process of information transfer. *Psychological Bulletin, 125,* 387–391.

Milton, J., & Weisman, R. (1999b). A meta-analysis of mass-media tests of extrasensory perception. *British Journal of Psychology, 90,* 235–240.

Minckler, T. M., & Boyd, E. (1968). Physical growth. In J. Minckler (Ed.), *Pathology of the nervous system* (Vol. 1, pp. 98–122). New York: McGraw-Hill.

Mineka, S., Davison, M., Cook, M., & Keir, R. (1984). Observational conditioning of snake fear in Rhesus monkeys. *Journal of Abnormal Psychology, 93,* 355–372.

Minton, H. L. (1988). Charting life history: Lewis M. Terman's study of the gifted. In J. G. Morawski (Ed.). *The rise of experimentation in American psychology* (pp. 138–162). New Haven, CT: Yale University Press.

Minuchin, S. (1974). *Families and family therapy.* Cambridge, MA: Harvard University Press.

Minuchin, S., & Fishman, H. C. (1981). *Family therapy techniques.* Cambridge, MA: Harvard University Press.

Mirsky, A. F., & Quinn, O. W. (1988). The Genain quadruplets. *Schizophrenia Bulletin, 14,* 595–612.

Mischel, W. (1984). Convergences and challenges in the search for consistency. *American Psychologist, 39,* 351–364.

Mischel, W., & Peake, P. K. (1982). Beyond déjà vu in the search for cross-situational consistency. *Psychological Review, 90,* 394–402.

Mischel, W., Shoda, Y., & Rodriguez, M. L. (1989). Delay of gratification in children. *Science, 244,* 933–938.

Mishkin, M. (1982). A memory system in the monkey. *Philosophical Transactions of the Royal Society of London Series B, 298,* 85–95.

Mishkin, M., & Appenzeller, T. (1987). The anatomy of memory. *Scientific American, 256,* 80–89.

Mishkin, M., Ungerleider, L. G., & Macko, K. A. (1983). Object vision and spatial vision: Two cortical pathways. *Trends in Neurosciences, 6,* 414–417.

Miyazaki, K. (1993). Absolute pitch as an inability: Identification of musical intervals in a tonal context. *Music Perception, 11,* 55–71.

Modell, J. (1996). Family niche and intellectual bent. [Review of *Born to Rebel* by Frank J. Sulloway]. *Science, 275,* 624.

Modell, J., Mountz, J., Curtis, G., & Greden, J. (1989). Neurophysiologic dysfunction in basal ganglia/limbic striatal and thalamocortical circuits as a pathogenetic mechanisms of obsessive-compulsive disorder. *Journal of Neuropsychiatry, 1,* 27–36.

Mogilner, A., Grossman, J. A., Ribary, U., Joliot, M., Volkman, J., Rapaport, D., Beasley, R. W., & Llinas, R. R. (1993). Somatosensory cortical plasticity in adult humans revealed by magnetoencephalography. *Proceedings of the National Academy of Sciences, USA, 90(8),* 3593–3597.

Mojtabai, R., Nicholson, R. A., & Carpenter, B. N. (1998). Role of psychosocial treatments in management of schizophrenia: A meta-analytic review of controlled outcome studies. *Schizophrenia Bulletin, 24,* 569–587.

Money, J. (1975). Ablatio penis: normal male infant sex-reassigned as a girl. *Archives of Sexual Behavior, 4,* 65–71.

Monk, T. H., Buysse, D. J., Reynolds, C. F., Berga, S. L., Jarrett, D. B., Begley, A. E., & Kupfer, D. J. (1997). Circadian rhythms in human performance and mood under constant conditions. *Journal of Sleep Research, 6,* 9–18.

Monroe, S. M., & Depue, R. A. (1991). Life stress and depression. In J. Becker & A. Kleinman (Eds.), *Psychosocial aspects of depression* (pp. 101–130). Hillsdale, NJ: Erlbaum.

Monteith, M. J. (1996). Affective reactions to prejudice-related discrepant responses: The impact of standard salience. *Personality and Social Psychology Bulletin, 22,* 48–59.

Montgomery, G. H., & Bovbjerg, D. H. (1997). The development of aniticpatory nausea in patients receving adjuvant chemotherapy for breast cancer. *Physiology & Behavior, 5,* 737–741.

Montgomery, G. H., & Sheehan, J. (1998). Surreptitious observation of responses to hypnotically suggested hallucinations: A test of the compliance hypothesis. *International Journal of Clinical & Experimental Hypnosis, 46,* 191–203.

Monthly Vital Statistics Reports. (2000). 48(11), July 24. Death and death rates for the 10 leading causes of death specified in age groups, by race and sex: United States, 1998: Table 8, p. 26; http://www.cdc.gov/nchs/fastats/suicide.htm

Montreys, C. R., & Borod, J. C. (1998). A preliminary evaluation of emotional experience and expression following unilateral braiin damage. *International Journal of Neuroscience, 96,* 269–283.

Moody, D. B., Stebbins, W. C., & May, B. J. (1990). Auditory perception of communication signals by Japanese monkeys. In W. C. Stebbins & M. A. Berkley (Eds.), *Comparative perception: Complex signals* (pp. 311–343). New York: Wiley.

Moore, B. C. J. (1982). *Introduction to the psychology of hearing* (2nd ed.). New York: Academic Press.

Moore, K. L., & Persaud, T. V. N. (1993). *Before we are born* (4th ed.). Philadelphia: Saunders.

Moore-Ede, M. (1982). *The clocks that time us: Physiology of the circadian timing system.* Cambridge, MA: Harvard University Press.

Mooren, J. H., & Van Krogten, I. A. (1993). Contributions to the history of psychology: CXII. Magda B. Arnold revisited: 1991. *Psychological Reports, 72,* 67–84.

Moorhead, G., Ference, R., & Neck, C. P. (1991). Group decision fiascoes continue: Space shuttle Challenger and a revised groupthink framework. *Human Relations, 44,* 539–550.

Moran, P. (1999). The epidemiology of antisocial personality disorder. *Social Psychiatry & Psychiatric Epidemiology, 34,* 231–242.

Moreland, R. L., & Zajonc, R. B. (1982). Exposure effects in person perception: Familiarity, similarity, and attraction. *Journal of Experimental Social Psychology, 18,* 395–415.

Moreland, R. L., Argote, L., & Krishnan, R. (1996). Socially shared cognition at work: Transactive memory and group performance. In J. L. Nye & M. Bower (Eds.), *What so social about social cognition? Social cognition in small groups* (pp. 57–84). Newbury Park, CA: Sage.

Morf, C. C., & Rhodewalt, F. (2001). Unraveling the paradoxes of narcissism: A dynamic self-regulatory processing model. *Psychological Inquiry, 12,* 177–196.

Morgan, A. H. (1973). The heritability of hypnotic susceptibility in twins. *Journal of Abnormal Psychology, 82,* 55–61.

Morgan, J. L., & Demuth, K. D. (1996). *Signal to syntax: Bootstrapping from speech to grammar in early acquisition.* Hillsdale, NJ: Erlbaum.

Morgan, M. J., McFie, L., Fleetwood, L. H., & Robinson, J. A. (2002). Ecstasy (MDMA): Are the psychological problems associated with its use reversed by prolonged abstinence? *Psychopharmacology, 159,* 294–303.

Morgane, P. J., Austin-LaFrance, R., Bronzino, J., Tonkiss, J., Diaz-Cintra, S., Cintra, L., Kemper, T., & Galler, J. R. (1993). Prenatal malnutrition and development of the brain. *Neuroscience and Biobehavioral Reviews, 17,* 91–128.

Mori, H., Kamada, M., Maegawa, M., Yamamoto, S., Aono, T., Futaki, S., Yano, M., Kido, H., & Koide, S. S. (1998). Enzymatic activation of immunoglobulin binding factor in female reproductive tract. *Biochemical and Biophysical Research Communications, 246,* 409–413.

Morin, R. (1997, November 6). Skewering the perpetrators of science's most improbable research. *International Herald Tribune*, Thursday, Nov. 6, 1977, p. 1.

Morris, C. D., Bransford, J. D., & Franks, J. J. (1977). Levels of processing versus transfer-appropriate processing. *Journal of Verbal Learning and Verbal Behavior, 16*, 519–533.

Morris, J. S., Oehman, A., & Dolan, R. J. (1998). Conscious and unconscious emotional learning in the human amygdala. *Nature, 393*, 460–470.

Morris, M. W., & Peng, K. (1994). Culture and cause: American and Chinese attributions for social and physical events. *Journal of Personality and Social Psychology, 67*, 949–971.

Morris, R. (1984). Developments of a water-maze procedure for studying spatial learning in the rat. *Journal of Neuroscience Methods, 11*, 47–60.

Morris, S. (1979) *The Book of Strange Facts and Useless Information*. Garden City, NY: Doubleday.

Morris, W., & Miller, R. (1975). The effects of consensus-breaking and consensus preempting partner onreduction in conformity. *Journal of Experimental Social Psychology, 11*, 215–23.

Morris, W. N., Worchel, S., Bois, J. L., Pearson, J. A., Rountree, C. A., Samaha, G. M., Wachtler, J., & Wright, S. I. (1976). Collective coping with stress: Group reactions to fear, anxiety, and ambiguity. *Journal of Personality and Social Psychology, 33*, 674–679.

Morrison, E. W., & Bies, R. J. (1991). Impression management in the feedback-seeking process: A literature review and research agenda. *Academy of Management Review, 16*, 322–341.

Morse, D. R., Martin, J. S., Furst, M. L., & Dubin, L. L. (1977). A physiological and subjective evaluation of meditation, hypnosis, and relaxation. *Psychosomatic Medicine, 39*, 304–324.

Mortensen, P. B., Pedersen, C. B., Westergaard, T., Wohlfahrt, J., Ewald, H., Mors, O., Andersen, P. K., & Melbye, M. (1999). Effects of family history and place and season of birth on the risk of schizophrenia. *New England Journal of Medicine, 340*, 603–608.

Moscovitch, M., & Craik, F. I. M. (1976). Depth of processing, retrieval cues, and uniqueness of encoding as factors in recall. *Journal of Verbal Learning and Verbal Behavior, 15*, 447–458.

Moser, M., Lehofer, M., Hoehn-Saric, R., McLeod, D. R., Hildebrandt, G., Steinbrenner, B., Voica, M., Liebmann, P., & Zapotoczky, H. (1998). Increased heart rate in depressed subjects in spite of unchanged autonomic balance. *Journal of Affective Disorders, 48*, 115–124.

Moskowitz, D. S. (1993). Dominance and friendliness: On the interaction of gender and situation. *Journal of Personality, 61*, 387–409.

Mowrer, O. H. (1939). A stimulus-response analysis of anxiety and its role as a reinforcing agent. *Psychological Review, 46*, 553–565.

Mrazek, P., & Haggerty, R. (1994). *Reducing risks for mental disorders: Frontiers for preventive intervention research*. Washington, DC: National Academy Press.

Muczyk, J. P., & Reimann, B. C. (1987). The case for directive leadership. *Academy of Management Review, 12*, 647–687.

Muehlenhard, C. L., & Linton, M. A. (1987). Date rape and sexual aggression in dating situations: Incidence and risk factors. *Journal of Counseling Psychology, 34*, 186–196.

Mueser, K. T., Goodman, L. B., Trumbetta, S. L., Rosenberg, S. D., Osher, F. C., Vidaver, R., Auciello, P., & Foy, D. W. (1998). Trauma and posttraumatic stress disorder in severe mental illness. *Journal of Consulting & Clinical Psychology, 66*, 493–499.

Mullen, B., & Johnson, C. (1990). Distinctiveness-based illusory correlations and stereotyping: A meta-analytic integration. *British Journal of Social Psychology, 29*, 11–28.

Mullen, B., Anthony, T., Salas, E., & Driskell, J. E. (1994). Group cohesiveness and quality of decision making: An integration of tests of the groupthink hypothesis. *Small Group Research, 25*, 189–204.

Mullen, B., Symons, C., Hu, L., & Salas, E. (1989). Group size, leadership, behavior, and subordinate satisfaction. *Journal of General Psyuchology, 116*, 155–170.

Mulvany, F., O'Callaghan, E., Takei, N., Byrne, M., Fearson, P., & Larkin, C. (2001). Effect of social class at birth on risk and presentation of schizophrenia: Case control study. *British Medical Journal, 323*, 1398–1401.

Mumford, M. D. (2001). Something old, something new: Revisiting Guilford's conception of creative problem solving. *Creativity Research Journal, 13*, 267–276.

Münte, T. F., Altenmüller, E., & Jäncke, L. (2002). The musician's brain as a model of neuroplasticity. *Nature Reviews Neuroscience, 3*, 473–478.

Murphy, C. (1986). Taste and smell in the elderly. In H. L. Meiselman & R. S. Rivlin (Eds.), *Clinical measurement of taste and smell* (pp. 343–371). New York: Macmillan.

Murphy, C. (1995). Age-associated differences in memory for odors. In F. R. Schab & R. G. Crowder (Eds.), *Memory for odors* (pp. 109–131). Mahwah, NJ: Erlbaum.

Murphy, L. J., & Mitchell, D. L. (1998). When writing helps to heal: e-mail as therapy. *British Journal of Guidance and Counseling, 26*, 21–32.

Murray, C. J. L., and Lopez, A. D. (Eds.). (1996). *The global burden of disease. A comprehensive assessment of mortality and disability from diseases, injuries, and risk factors in 1990 and projected to 2020*. Cambridge, MA: Harvard School of Public Health.

Murray, E. A. (1996). What have ablation studies told us about the neural substrates of stimulus memory? *Seminars in Neuroscience, 8*, 13–22.

Murray, E. J., Lamnin, A., & Carver, C. (1989). Emotional expression in written essays and psychotherapy. *Journal of Social and Clinical Psychology, 8*, 414–429.

Murray, I. R., Arnott, J. L., & Rohwer, E. A. (1996). Emotional stress in synthetic speech: Progress and future directions. *Speech Communication, 20*, 85–91.

Murray, S. L., Holmes, J. G., & Griffin, D. W. (1996a). The benefits of positive illusions: Idealization and the construction of satisfaction in close relationships. *Journal of Peresonaltiy and Social Psychology, 70*, 78–98.

Murzynski, J. & Degelman, D. (1996). Body language of women and judgments of vulnerability to sexual assault. *Journal of Applied Social Psychology 26*, 1617–1626.

Myers, C. E., McGlinchey-Berroth, R., Warren, S., Monti, L., Brawn, C. M., & Gluck, M. A. (2000). Latent learning in medial temporal amnesia: Evidence for disrupted representational but preserved attentional processes. *Neuropsychology, 14*, 3–15.

Myers, D. G. (1993). *The pursuit of happiness: Discovering the pathway to fulfillment, well-being, and enduring personal joy*. New York: Avon Books.

Myers, D. G. (2000). The funds, friends, and faith of happy people. *American Psychologist, 55*, 56–67.

Myers, M. B., & McCaulley, M. H. (1985). *Manual: A guide to the development and the use of the Myers-Briggs Type Indicator*. Palo Alto, CA: Consulting Psychologists Press.

Nadeau, S. N. (2001). Phonology: A review and proposals from a connectionist perspective. *Brain & Language, 79*, 511–579.

Nadel, L., & Moscovitch, M. (1997). Memory consolidation, retrograde amnesia and the hippocampal complex. *Current Opinion in Neurobiology, 7*, 217–227.

Nader, K., Bechara, A., & van der Kooy, D. (1997). Neurobiological constraints on behavioral models of motivation. *Annual Review of Psychology, 48*, 85–114.

Nagahama, Y., Okada, T., Katsumi, Y., Hayashi, T., Yamauchi, H., Oyanagi, C., Konishi, J., Fukuyama, H., & Shibasaki, H. (2001). Dissociable mechanisms of attentional control within the human prefrontal cortex. *Cerebral Cortex, 11*, 85–92.

Nagel, E. (1979). *The structure of science: Problems in the logic of scientific explanation* (2nd ed.). Indianapolis: Hackett.

Naito, T., & Lipsitt, L. P. (1969). Two attempts to condition eyelid responses in human infants. *Journal of Experimental Child Psychology, 8*, 263–270.

Nakai, Y., Fujita, T., Kuboki, T., Nozoe, S., Kubo, C., Yoshimasa, Y., Inaba, Y., Suematsu, H., & Nakao, K. (2001). Nationwide survey of eating disorders in Japan. *Seishin Igaku (Clinical Psychiatry), 43*, 1373–1378.

Nakamura, J., & Csikszentmihalyi, M. (2001). Catalytic creativity: The case of Linus Pauling. *American Psychologist, 56*, 337–341.

Nakayama, K., & Mackeben, M. (1989). Sustained and transient components of focal visual attention. *Vision Research, 29*, 1631–1647.

Nakayama, K., He, Z. J., & Shimojo, S. (1995). Visual surface representation: A critical link between lower-level and higher-level vision. In S. M. Kosslyn & D. N. Osherson (Eds.), *Visual cognition: An invitation to cognitive science, Vol. 2* (2nd ed., pp. 1–70). Cambridge, MA: MIT Press.

Nasby, W., Hayden, B., & DePaulo, B. M. (1979). Attributional bias among aggressive boys to interpret unambiguous social stimuli as displays of hostility. *Journal of Abnormal Psychology 89*, 459–468.

Nathans, J. (1994). In the eye of the beholder: Visual pigments and inherited variations in human vision. *Cell, 78*, 357–360.

Nathawat, S. S., Singh, R., & Singh, B. (1997). The effect of need for achievement on attributional style. *Journal of Social Psychology, 137*, 55–62.

National Alliance for Caregiving, and the American Association of Retired Persons. (1997). *Family Caregiving in the U.S.: Findings from a National Study*.

National Center on Addiction and Substance Abuse at Columbia University. (1994). *Cost of substance abuse to America's health care system; Report 2: Medicare Hospital Costs*.

National Institute on Alcohol Abuse and Alcoholism (2001). http://www.niaaa.nih.gov/databases/brfss01.txt.

National Institute on Drug Abuse (1998). Slide Teaching Packet I, For Health Practitioners, Teachers and Neuroscientists. Section III: Introduction to Drugs of Abuse: Cocaine, Opiates (Heroin) and Marijuana (THC).

National Institute on Drug Abuse. (1997). Monitoring the Future Study: Drug use among high school Seniors. *http://www.whitehousedrugpolicy.gov/drugfact/factsheet/druguse.html*.

National Institute on Drug Abuse, (2003). InfoFax: Drug Addiction treatment methods. http://www.drugabuse.gov/infofax/treatmeth.html.

National Opinion Research Center. (1994). *General social surveys, 1972–1994: Cumulative codebook*. Chicago: Author, pp. 881–889.

National Sleep Foundation. (2002). *2002 "Sleep in America" Poll*. www.sleepfoundation.org/2002poll.html.

Natsoulas, T. (2001). On the intrinsic nature of states of consciousness: Attempted inroads from the first-person perspective. *Journal of Mind & Behavior, 22*, 219–248.

Nauta, M. C. E. & Vorst, H. C. M. (1994). A meta-analysis on the treatment of obsessive-compulsive disorder: A comparison of antidepressants, behavior, and cognitive therapy. *Clinical Psychology Review, 14*, 359–381.

Neel, R. G., Tzeng, O. C., & Baysal, C. (1986). Need achievement in a cross-cultural contact study. *International Review of Applied Psychology, 35*, 225–229.

Neeper, S. A., Gómez-Pinilla, F., Choi, J., & Cotman C. (1995). Exercise and brain neurotropins. *Nature, 373*, 109.

Neeper, S. A., Gómez-Pinilla, F., Choi, J., & Cotman C. W. (1996). Physical activity increases mRNA for brain-derived neurotrophic factor and nerve growth factor in rat brain. *Brain Research, 726*, 49–56.

Neimeyer, G. J., MacNair, R., Metzler, A. E., & Courchaine, K. (1991). Changing personal beliefs: Effects of forewarning, argument quality, prior bias, and personal exploration. *Journal of Social & Clinical Psychology, 10*, 1–20.

Neisser, U. (1967). *Cognitive psychology*. New York: Appleton-Century-Crofts.

Neisser, U. (1982). *Memory observed: Remembering in natural contexts.* San Francisco: Freeman.

Neisser, U., & Harsch, N. (1992). Phantom flashbulbs: False recollections of hearing news about *Challenger.* In E. Winograd & U. Neisser (Eds.), *Affect and accuracy in recall: Studies of "flashbulb memories"* (pp. 9–31). Cambridge, UK: Cambridge University Press.

Neisser, U., Boodoo, G., Bouchard, T. J., Jr., Boykin, A. W., Brody, N., Ceci, S. J., Halpern, D. F., Loehlin, J. C., Perloff, R., Sternberg, R. J., & Urbina, S. (1996). Intelligence: Knowns and unknowns. *American Psychologist, 51,* 77–101.

Neitz, M., & Neitz, J. (1995). Numbers and ratios of visual pigment genes for normal red-green color vision. *Science, 267,* 1013–1016.

Neitz, J., Neitz, M., & Jacobs, G. H. (1993). More than three different cone pigments among people with normal color vision. *Vision Research, 33,* 117–122.

Neitz, J., Neitz, M., & Kainz, P. M. (1996). Visual pigment gene structure and the severity of color vision defects. *Science, 274,* 801–804.

Nelson, C. A. (1999). Human plasticity and human development. *Current Directions in Psychological Science, 8,* 42–45.

Nelson, C. B., Heath, A. C., & Kessler, R. C. (1998). Temporal progression of alcohol dependence symptoms in the U.S. household population: results from the National Comorbidity Survey. *Journal of Consulting & Clinical Psychology, 66, 3,* 474–483.

Nelson, K. (1981). Individual differences in language development: Implications for development and language. *Developmental Psychology, 17,* 170–187.

Nelson, K. E. (1989). Strategies for first language teaching. In M. L. Rice & R. L. Schiefelbusch (Eds.), *The teachability of language* (pp. 263–310). Baltimore: Paul H. Brookes.

Nelson, M. D., Saykin, A. J., Flashman, L. A., & Riordan, H. J. (1998). Hippocampal volume reduction in schizophrenia as assessed by magnetic resonance imaging: A meta-analytic study (1998). *Archives of General Psychiatry, 55,* 433–440.

Nemec, P., Altmann, J., Marhold, S., Burda, H., & Oelschläger, H. H. A. (2001). Neuroanatomy of magnetoreception: The superior colliculus involved in magnetic orientation in a mammal. *Science, 294,* 366–368.

Nemeroff, C., & Rozin, P. (1989). "You are what you eat": Applying the demand-free "impressions" technique to an unacknowledged belief. *Ethos, 17,* 50–69.

Nemeroff, C. J., Stein, R., Diehl, N. S., & Smilach, K. M. (1994). From the Cleavers to the Clintons, Role choices and body orientation as reflected in magazine article content. *International Journal of Eating Disorders, 16,* 167–176.

Nemeth, P. (1979). *An investigation into the relationship between humor and anxiety.* Unpublished doctoral dissertation. University of Maryland, College Park.

Nestler, E. J. (1997). Schizophrenia: An emerging pathophysiology. *Nature, 385,* 578–579.

Nettelbeck, T. (1987). Inspection time and intelligence. In P. A. Vernon (Ed.), *Speed of information processing and intelligence.* Norwood, NJ: Ablex.

Neubauer, A. C., Spinath, F. M., Riemann, R., Borkenau, P., & Angleitner, A. (2000). Genetic and environmental influences on two measures of speed of information processing and their relation to psychometric intelligence: Evidence from the German Observational Study of Adult Twins. *Intelligence, 28,* 267–289.

Neuman, J. H., & Baron, R. A. (1998). Workplace violence and workplace aggtression: Evbidence concerning specific forms, potential causes, and preferred targets. *Journal of Management, 3,* 391–419.

Neumann, C., & Walker, E. F. (1996). Childhood neuromotor soft signs, behavior problems, and adult psychopathology. In: T. Ollendick & R. Prinz (Eds.), *Advances in Clinical Child Psychology.* New York: Plenum Press.

Nevid, J., Rathus, S., & Rubenstein, H. (1998). *Health in the new millennium.* New York: Worth.

Neville, H. J. (1988). Cerebral organization for spatial attention. In J. Stiles-Davis, M. Kritchevsky, & U. Bellugi (Eds.), *Spatial cognition. Brain bases and development.* Hillsdale, NJ: Erlbaum.

Neville, H. J. (1990). Intermodal competition and compensation in development. *Annals of the New York Academy of Sciences, 608,* 71–91.

Neville, H. J., & Lawson, D. (1987). Attention to central and peripheral visual space in movement detection tasks: An event-related and behavioral study: II. Congenitally deaf adults. *Brain Research, 405,* 268–283.

Neville, H. J., Schmidt, A., & Kutas, M. (1983). Altered visual-evoked potentials in congenitally deaf adults. *Brain Research, 266,* 127–132.

Newcombe, N. S., Drummney, A. B., Fox, N. A., Lie, E, & Ottinger-Alberts, W. (2000). Remembering early childhood: How much, how, and why (or why not). *Current Directions in Psychological Science, 9,* 55–58.

Newcomer, J. W., Selke, G., Melson, A. K., Hershey, T., Craft, S., Richards, K., & Alderson, A. L. (1999). Decreased memory performance in healthy humans induced by stress-level cortisol treatment. *Archives of General Psychiatry, 56,* 527–533.

Newell, A. (1990). *Unified theories of cognition.* Cambridge, MA: Harvard University Press.

Newell, A., & Simon, H. A. (1972). *Human problem solving.* Englewood Cliffs, NJ: Prentice-Hall.

Newman, E. A., & Zahs, K. R. (1998). Modulation of neuronal activity by glial cells in the retina. *Journal of Neuroscience, 18,* 4022–4028.

Newman, J., Rosenbach, J. H., Burns, K. L., Latimer, B. C. Matocha, H. R. & Vogt, E. R. (1995). An experimental test of "The Mozart effect": Does Listening to his music improve spatial ability? *Perceptual and Motor Skills, 81,* 1379–1387.

Newman, L. S., Duff, K. J., & Baumeister, R. F. (1997). A new look at defensive projection: Thought suppression, accessibility, and biased person perception. *Journal of Personality and Social Psychology, 72,* 980–1001.

Newman, M. G., Kenardy, J., Herman, S., & Taylor, C. B. (1997). Comparison of palmtop-computer-assisted brief cognitive-behavioral treatment to cognitive-behavioral treatment for panic disorder. *Journal of Consulting and Clinical Psychology, 65,* 178–183.

Newsome, G. L., III (2000). A review of some promising approaches to understanding and improving thinking skills. *Journal of Research & Development in Education, 33,* 199–222.

Newton, P. M. (1970). Recalled dream content and the maintenance of body image. *Journal of Abnormal Psychology, 76,* 134–139.

Nezu, A. M., Nezu, C. M., & Blissett, S. E. (1988). Sense of humor as a moderator of the relationship between stressful events and psychological distress: A prospective study. *Journal of Personality and Social Psychology, 54,* 520–525.

NICHD Early Child Care Research Network. (1997). The effects of infant child care on infant-mother attachment security: Results of the NICHD study of early child care. *Child Development, 68,* 860–879.

NICHD Early Child Care Research Network. (1999). Child care and mother–child interaction in the first 3 years of life. *Developmental Psychology, 35,* 1309–1413.

Nichelli, P., Grafman, J., Pietrini, P., Alway, D., Carton, J. J., & Miletich, R. (1994). Brain activity in chess playing. *Nature, 369,* 191.

Nichols, R. C. (1978). Twin studies of ability, personality, and interests. *Homo, 29,* 158–173.

Nickerson, R. S., & Adams, M. J. (1979). Long-term memory for a common object. *Cognitive Psychology, 11,* 287–307.

Nigg, J. T., & Goldsmith, H. H. (1994). Genetics of personality disorders: Perspectives from personality and psychopathology research. *Psychological Bulletin, 115,* 346–380.

NIH Technology Assessment Panel. (1996). Integration of behavioral and relaxation approaches into the treatment of chronic pain and insomnia. *Journal of the American Medical Association, 276,* 313–318.

Nikelly, A. G. (1988). Does *DSM-III-R* diagnose depression in non-Western patients? *International Journal of Social Psychiatry, 34,* 316–320.

Niles, S. (1998). Achievement goals and means: A cultural comparison. *Journal of Cross-Cultural Psychology, 29,* 656–667.

Nilsson, L., & Hamberger, L. (1990). *A child is born.* New York: Delacorte.

Nilsson, T., Ericsson, M., Poston, W. S. C., Linder, J., Goodrick, G. K., & Foreyt, J. P. (1998). Is the assessment of coping capacity useful in the treatment of obesity? *Eating Disorders: The Journal of Treatment & Prevention, 6,* 241–251.

Nisbett, R. E. (1972). Hunger, obesity, and the ventromedial hypothalamus. *Psychological Review, 79,* 433–453.

Nisbett, R. E. (1996). Race, genetics, and IQ. In C. Jencks & M. Phillips (Eds.), *The black-white test score gap* (pp. 86–102). Washington, DC: Brookings Institution.

Nisbett, R. E., & Cohen, D. (1996). *Culture of honor: The psychology of violence in the South.* Boulder, CO: Westview.

Nisbett, R. E., & Kanouse, D. E. (1969). Obesity, food deprivation, and supermarket shopping behavior. *Journal of Personality & Social Psychology, 12,* 389–294.

Nodelmann, P. (1988). *Words about pictures.* Athens: University of Georgia Press.

Nolan, S. A., & Mineka, S. (1997, November). Verbal, nonverbal, and gender-related factors in the interpersonal consequences of depression and anxiety. Presented at the annual meeting of the Association for the Advancement of Behavior Therapy, Miami Beach, FL.

Nolde, S. F., Johnson, M. K., & Raye, C. L. (1998). The role of prefrontal cortex during tests of episodic memory. *Trends in Cognitive Sciences, 2,* 399–406.

Nolen-Hoeksema, S. (1987). Sex differences in unipolar depression: Evidence and theory. *Psychological Bulletin, 101,* 259–282.

Nolen-Hoeksema, S., & Davis, C. G. (1999). "Thanks for sharing that": Ruminators and their social support networks. *Journal of Personality and Social Psychology, 77,* 801–814.

Nolen-Hoeksema, S., & Morrow, J. (1993). Effects of rumination and distraction on naturally occurring depressed mood. *Cognition & Emotion, 7,* 561–570.

Norman, D. (1988). *The psychology of everyday things.* New York: Basic Books.

Norman, G. R., Brooks, L. R., Colle, C. L., & Hatala, R. M. (1999). The benefit of diagnostic hypotheses in clinical reasoning: Experimental study of an instructional intervention for forward and backward reasoning. *Cognition & Instruction, 17,* 433–448.

Norman, K. A., & Schacter, D. L. (1997). False recognition in younger and older adults: Exploring the characteristics of illusory memories. *Memory & Cognition, 25,* 838–848.

Northcraft, G. B., & Neale, M. A. (1987). Experts, amateurs, and real estate: An anchoring-and-adjustment perspective on property pricing decisions. *Organizational Behavior & Human Decision Processes, 39,* 84–97.

Nosek, B. A., Banaji, M. R., & Greenwald, A. G. (2002). Harvesting implicit group attitudes and beliefs from a demonstration web site. *Group Dynamics: Theory, Research, & Practice, 6,* 101–115.

Nowakowski, R. S. (1987). Basic concepts of CNS development. *Child Development, 58,* 568–595.

Nozick, R. (in preparation). *The structure of the objective world.* Cambridge, MA: Harvard University Press.

Nurmi, J. E., & Salmela-Aro, K. (1997). Social strategies and loneliness: A prospective study. *Person. Individ. Diff., 23,* 205–215.

Nurnberger, J. I., & Hingtgen, J. N. (1973). Is symptom substitution an important issue in behavior therapy? *Biological Psychiatry, 7,* 221–236.

Nyberg, L., Cabeza, R., & Tulving, E. (1996). PET studies of encoding and retrieval: The HERA model. *Psychonomic Bulletin & Review, 3,* 134–148.

Nyberg, L., McIntosh, A. R., Houle, S., Nilsson, L. G., & Tulving, E. (1996). Activation of medial temporal structures during episodic memory retrieval. *Nature, 380*, 715–717.

Nye, R. D. (1992). *Three psychologies: Perspectives from Freud, Skinner, and Rogers.* California: Brooks-Cole.

Nyklicek, I., Vingerhoets, A. J. J. M., Van Heck, G. L., & Van Limpt, M. C. A. M. (1998). Defensive coping in relation to casual blood pressure and self-reported daily hassles and life events. *Journal of Behavioral Medicine, 21*, 145–161.

Oaksford, M., & Chater, N. (1994). A rational analysis of the selection task as optimal data selection. *Psychological Review, 101*, 608–631.

Ochsner, K. N., & Lieberman, M. D. (2001). The emergence of social cognitive neuroscience. *American Psychologist, 56*, 717–734.

O'Connor, D. B., & Shimizu, M. (2002). Sense of personal control, stress and coping style: A cross-cultural study. *Stress & Health: Journal of the International Society for the Investigation of Stress, 18*, 173–183.

O'Connor, W. E., Morrison, T. G., McLeod, L. D., & Anderson, D. (1996). A meta-analytic review of the relationship between gender and belief in a just world. *Journal of Social Behavior and Personality, 11*, 141–148.

Oden, M. H. (1968). The fulfillment of promise: Forty-year follow-up of the Terman gifted group. *Genetic Psychology Monographs, 77*, 3–93.

O'Doherty, J., Kringelbach, M. L., Rolls, E. T., Hornak, J., & Andrews, C. (2001). Abstract reward and punishment representations in the human orbitofrontal cortex. *Nature Neuroscience, 4*, 95–102.

Oei, T. P. S., & Yeoh, A. E. O. (1999). Pre-existing antidepressant medication and the outcome of group cognitive-behavioural therapy. *Australian & New Zealand Journal of Psychiatry, 33*, 70–76.

Ogden, J. A. (1988). Language and memory functions after long recovery periods in left-hemispherectomized subjects. *Neuropsychologia, 26*, 645–659.

Öhman, A. (2002). Automaticity and the amygdala: Nonconscious responses to emotional faces. *Current Directions in Psychological Science, 11*, 62–66.

Ohman, A., Fredrikson, M., Hugdahl, K., & Rimmo, P.-A. (1976). The premise of equipotentiality in human classical conditioning: Conditioned electrodermal responses to potentially phobic stimuli. *Journal of Experimental Psychology: General, 105*, 313–337.

Ohzawa, I., DeAngelis, G. C., & Freeman, R. D. (1990). Stereoscopic depth discrimination in the visual cortex: Neurons ideally suited as disparity detectors. *Science, 249*, 1037–1041.

Ojemann, G. A. (1983). Brain organization for language from the perspective of electrical stimulation mapping. *Behavioral and Brain Sciences, 6*, 189–230.

Ojemann, G. A., Ojemann, J., Lettich, E., & Berger, M. (1989). Cortical language localization in left, dominant hemisphere. *Journal of Neurosurgery, 71*, 316–326.

Okonkwo, R. U. N. (1997). Moral development and culture in Kohlberg's theory: A Nigerian (Igbo) evidence. *IFE Psychologia: An International Journal, 5*, 117–128.

Okubo, M., & Michimata, C. (2002). Hemispheric processing of categorical and coordinate relations in the absence of low spatial frequencies. *Journal of Cognitive Neuroscience, 14*, 291–297.

Okubo, Y., Suhara, T., & Suzuki, K., Kobayashi, K., Inoue, O., Teraski, O., Someya, Y., Sassa, T., Sudo, Y., Matsushima, E., Iyo, M., Tateno, Y., & Toru, M. (1997). Decreased prefrontal dopamine D1 receptors in schizophrenia revealed by PET. *Nature, 385*, 634–636.

Olczak, P. V., Kaplan, M. F., & Penrod, S. (1991). Attorneys' lay psychology and its effectiveness in selecting jurors: Three empirical studies. *Journal of Social Behavior and Personality, 6*, 431–452.

Olds, J., & Milner, P. (1954). Positive reinforcement produced by electrical stimulation of septal area and other regions of rat brain. *Journal of Comparative & Physiological Psychology, 47*, 419–427.

Olson, I. R., & Chun, M. M. (2002). Perceptual constraints on implicit learning of spatial context. *Visual Cognition, 9*, 273–302.

Olson, J. M., Vernon, P. A., Harris, J. A., & Jang, K. L. (2001). The heritability of attitudes: A study of twins. *Journal of Personality & Social Psychology, 80*, 845–860.

Olton, R. M. (1979). Experimental studies of incubation: Searching for the elusive. *Journal of Creative Behavior, 13*, 9–22.

Oppenheim, J. S., Skerry, J. E., Tramo, M. J., & Gazzaniga, M. S. (1989). Magnetic resonance imaging morphology of the corpus callosum in monozygotic twins. *Annals of Neurology, 26*, 100–104.

O'Regan, J. K. (1992). Solving the "real" mysteries of visual perception: The world as an outside memory. *Canadian Journal of Psychology, 46*, 461–488.

Organ, D. W., & Ryan, K. (1995). A meta-analytic review of attitudinal and dispositional predictors of organizational citizenship behavior. *Personnel Psychology, 48*, 775–802.

Orive, R. (1988). Social projection and social comparison of opinions. *Journal of Personality and Social Psychology, 54*, 953–964.

Orlans, H. (1999, May–June). Members comment on ASA's publication on affirmative action. *Footnotes*, p. 8.

Ornish, D., Scherwitz, L. W., Billings, J. H., Gould, K. L., Merritt, T. A., Sparler, S., Armstrong, W. T., Ports, T. A., Kirkeeide, R. L., Hogeboom, C., & Brand, R. J. (1998). Intensive lifestyle changes for reversal of coronary heart disease. *Journal of the American Medical Association, 280*, 2001–2007.

Ornstein, R. (1986). *Multimind: A new way of looking at human behavior.* Boston: Houghton Mifflin.

Orth-Gomér, K., Wamala, S. P., Horsten, M., Schenck-Gustafsso, K., Schneiderman, N., & Mittleman, M. A. (2000). Marital stress worsens prognosis in women with coronary heart disease: The Stockholm female coronary risk study. *Journal of the American Medical Association, 284*, 3008–3014.

Osborn, A. F. (1953). *Applied imagination.* New York: Scribner's.

Osherson, D., Perani, D., Cappa, S., Schnur, T., Grassi, F., & Fazio, F. (1998). Distinct brain loci in deductive versus probabilistic reasoning. *Neuropsychologia, 36*, 369–376.

Osherson, D. N., & Markman, E. M. (1975). Language and the ability to evaluate contradictions and tautologies. *Cognition, 2*, 213–226.

Öst, L.-G., Alm, T., Brandberg, M. & Breitholtz, E. (2001). One vs. five sessions of exposure and five sessions of cognitive therapy in the treatment of claustrophobia. *Behaviour Research and Therapy, 39*, 167–183.

Öst, L.-G., Brandberg, M., & Alm, T. (1997). One vs. five sessions of exposure in the treatment of flying phobia. *Behaviour Research and Therapy, 35*, 987–996.

Ostatnikova, D., Laznibatova, J., Putz, Z., Mataseje, A., Dohnanyiova, M., & Pastor, K. (2000). Salivary testosterone levels in intellectually gifted and non-intellectually gifted preadolescents: An exploratory study. *High Ability Studies, 11*, 41–54.

Ostatnikova, D., Laznibatova, J., Putz, Z., Mataseje, A., Dohnanyiova, M., & Pastor, K. (2002). Biological aspects of intellectual giftedness. *Studia Psychologica, 44*, 3–13.

O'Sullivan, C. S., & Durso, F. T. (1984). Effects of schema-incongruent information on memory for stereotypical attributes. *Journal of Personality and Social Psychology, 47*, 55–70.

Otte, C., Kellner, M., Arlt, J., Jahn, H., Holsboer, F., & Wiedemann, K. (2002). Prolactic but not ACTH increases during sodium lactate-induced panic attacks. *Psychiatry Research, 109*, 201–205.

Otto, M. W., Gould, R. A., & Pollack, M. H. (1994). Cognitive-behavioral treatment of panic disorder: Considerations for the treatment of patients over the long term. *Psychiatric Annals, 24*, 307–315.

Overmier, J. B. (2002). On learned helplessness. *Integrative Physiological & Behavioral Science, 37*, 4–8.

Overmeier, J. B., & Seligman, M. E. P. (1967). Effects of inescapable shock upon subsequent escape and avoidance responding. *Journal of Comparative and Physiological Psychology, 63*, 28–33.

Owens, L., Shute, R., & Slee, P. (2000). "I'm in and you're out . . . " Explanations for teenage girls' indirect aggression. *Psychology, Evolution & Gender, 2*, 19–46.

Oyserman, D., Coon, H. M., & Kemmelmeier, M. (2002). Rethinking individualism and collectivism: Evaluation of theoretical assumptions and meta-analyses. *Psychological Bulletin, 128*, 3–72.

Ozer, D. J., & Reise, S. P. (1994). Personality assessment. *Annual Review of Psychology, 45*, 357–88.

Ozer, D. J., Best, S. R., Lipsey, T. L., & Weiss, D. S. (2003). Predictors of posttraumatic stress disorder and symptoms in adults: A meta-analysis. *Psychological Bulletin, 129*, 52–73.

Pacak, K., & Palkovits, M. (2001). Stressor specificity of central neuroendocrine responses: Implications for stress-related disorders. *Endocrine Review, 22*, 502–548.

Páez, D., Velasco, C., & González, J. L. (1999). Expressive writing and the role of alexythimia as a dispositional deficit in self-disclosure and psychological health. *Journal of Personality and Social Psychology, 77*, 630–641.

Pagano, R. R., Rose, R. M., Stivers, R. M., & Warrenburg, S. (1976). Sleep during transcendental meditation. *Science, 191*, 308–309.

Page, D. C., Mosher, R., Simpson, E. M., Fisher, E. M. C., Mardon, G., Pollack, J., McGillivray, B., de la Chapelle, A., & Brown, L. G. (1987). The sex-determining region of the human Y chromosome encodes a finger protein. *Cell, 51*, 1091–1104.

Page, S. (1990). The turnaround on pornography research: Some implications for psychology and women. *Canadian Psychology, 31*, 359–367.

Pagnoni, G., Zink, C. F., Montague, P. R., & Berns, G. S. (2002). Activity in human ventral striatum locked to errors of reward prediction. *Nature Neuroscience, 5*, 97–98.

Paivio, A. (1971). *Imagery and verbal processes.* New York: Holt, Rinehart & Winston.

Palace, E. M. (1999). Response expectancy and sexual dysfunction. In I. Kirsch (Ed.), *How expectancies shape experience* (pp. 173–196). Washington, DC: American Psychological Association.

Palmer, S. E. (1975). The effects of contextual scenes on the identification of objects. *Memory & Cognition, 3*, 519–526.

Palmer, S. E. (1992a). Modern theories of Gestalt perception. In G. W. Humphreys (Ed.), *Understanding vision: An interdisciplinary perspective* (pp. 39–70). Oxford: Blackwell.

Palmer, S. E. (1992b). Common region: A new principle of perceptual grouping. *Cognitive Psychology, 24*, 436–447.

Panksepp, J. (1998). *Affective neuroscience: The foundations of human and animal emotions.* New York: Oxford University Press.

Papi, F., Meschini, E., & Baldaccini, N. E. (1983). Homing behavior of pigeons released after having been placed in an alternating magnetic field. *Comparative Biochemistry & Physiology, 76A*, 673–682.

Papolos, D. F., Yu, Y-M., Rosenbaum, E., & Lachman, H. M. (1996). Modulation of learned helplessness by 5-hydroxytrptamine-2A receptor antisense oligodeoxynucleotides. *Psychiatry Research, 63*, 197–203.

Papp, L. A., Klein, D. F., & Gorman, J. M. (1993). Carbon dioxide hypersensitivity, hyperventilation, and panic disorder. *American Journal of Psychiatry, 150*, 1149–1157.

Papp, L. A., Martinez, J. M., Klein, D. F., Coplan, J. D., Norman, R. G., Cole, R., de Jesus, M. J., Ross, D., Goetz, R., & Gorman, J. M. (1997). Respiratory psychophysiology of panic disorder: Three respiratory challenges in 98 subjects. *American Journal of Psychiatry, 154*, 1557–1565.

Paradis M. (1990). Language lateralization in bilinguals: Enough already! *Brain and Language, 39*, 576–586.

Paradis M. (1992). The Loch Ness monster approach to bilingual language lateralization: A response to Berquier and Ashton. *Brain and Language, 43*, 534–537.

Paradis, M. (2001). The need for awareness of aphasia symptoms in different languages. *Journal of Neurolinguistics, 14*, 85–91.

Paradis M., & Goldblum, M. C. (1989). Selective crossed aphasia in a trilingual aphasic patient followed by reciprocal antagonism. *Brain and Language, 36*, 62–75.

Park, S., & Holzman, P. S. (1992). Schizophrenics show spatial working memory deficits. *Archives of General Psychiatry, 49*, 975–982.

Park, S., & Holzman, P. S. (1993). Associatoin of working memory deficit and eye tracking dysfunction in schizophrenia. *Schizophrenia Research, 11*, 55–61.

Park, S., Holzman, P. S., & Goldman-Rakic, P. (1995). Spatial working memory deficits in the relatives of schizophrenics. *Archives of General Psychiatry, 52*, 821–828.

Parker, A., & Gellatly, A. (1997). Movable cues: A practical method for reducing context-dependent forgetting. *Applied Cognitive Psychology, 11*, 163–173.

Parker, J., Cheah, Y.-C., & Roy, K. (2001). Do the Chinese somatize depression? A cross-cultural study. *Social Psychiatry & Psychiatric Epidemiology, 36*, 287–293.

Parkin, A. J. (1987). *Memory and amnesia: An introduction.* Oxford, England: Basil Blackwell.

Parkin, A. J., & Walter, B. M. (1992). Recollective experience, normal aging, and frontal dysfunction. *Psychology and Aging, 7*, 290–298.

Parks, M. R., & Eggert, L. L. (1991). The role of social context in the dynamics of personal relationships. In W. H. Jones & D. Perlman (Eds.), *Advances in personal relationships* (Vol. 2, pp. 1–34). London: Jessica Kingsley.

Parks, M. R., & Roberts, L. D. (1998). "Making MOOsic": The development of personal relationships on line and a comparison to their off-line counterparts. *Journal of Social & Personal Relationships, 15*, 517–537.

Parsons, L. M. (1987). Imagined spatial transformation of one's body. *Journal of Experimental Psychology: General, 116*, 172–191.

Parsons, L. M. (1994). Temporal and kinematic properties of motor behavior reflected in mentally simulated action. *Journal of Experimental Psychology: Human Perception & Performance, 20*, 709–730.

Parsons, L. M., & Fox, P. T. (1998). The neural basis of implicit movements used in recognising hand shape. *Cognitive Neuropsychology, 15*, 583–615.

Pascalis, O., de Haan, M., Nelson, C. A., & de Schonen, S. (1998). Long-term recognition memory for faces assessed by visual paired comparison in 3- and 6-month-old infants. *Journal of Experimental Psychology: Learning, Memory, & Cognition, 24*, 249–260.

Pascual-Leone, A., Grafman, J., Cohen, L. G., Roth, B. J., & Hallett, M. (1997). Transcranial magnetic stimulation. A new tool for the study of higher cognitive functions in humans. In J. Grafman & F. Boller (Eds.), *Handbook of neuropsychology* (Vol. 11). Amsterdam: Elsevier B.V.

Pascual-Leone, A., Tormos, J. M., Keenan, J., Tarazona, F., Cañete, C., & Catalá, M. D. (1998). Study and modulation of human cortical excitability with transcranial magnetic stimulation. *Journal of Clinical Neurophysiology, 15*, 333–343.

Pascual-Leone, J. (1970). A mathematical model for the transition rule in Piaget's developmental stages. *Acta Psychologia, 32*, 301–345.

Patel, V., Abas, M., Broadhead, J., Todd, C., & Reeler, A. (2001). Depression in developing countries: Lessons from Zimbabwe. *British Medical Journal, 322*,482–484.

Patterson, G. R. (1986). Performance models for antisocial boys. *American Psychologist, 41*, 432–444.

Patterson, G. R., DeBaryshe, B. D., & Ramsey, E. (1989). A developmental perspective on antisocial behavior. *American Psychologist, 44*, 329–335.

Patterson, R., & Martin, W. L. (1992). Human stereopsis. *Human Factors, 34*, 669–692.

Patterson, T. L., Semple, S. J., Shaw, W. S., Yu, E., He, Y., Zhang, M. Y., Wu, W., & Grant, I. (1998). The cultural context of caregiving: A comparison of Alzheimer's caregivers in Shanghai, China and San Diego, California. *Psychological Medicine, 28*, 1071–1084.

Paulesu, E., Frith, C. D., & Frackowiak, R. S. J. (1993). The neural correlates of verbal component of working memory. *Nature, 362*, 342–345.

Paulesu, E., Harrison. J., Baron-Cohen, S., Watson, J. D. G., Goldstein, L., Heather, J., Frackowaik, R. S. J., & Frith, C. D. (1995). The physiology of coloured hearing: A PET activation study of colour-word synaesthesia. *Brain, 118*, 661–676.

Paulhus, D. L., & Bruce, M. N. (1992). The effect of acquaintanceship on the validity of personality impressions: a longitudinal study. *Journal of Personality and Social Psychology, 63*, 816–824.

Paunonen, S. V. (1998). Hierarchical organization of personality and prediction of behavior. *Journal of Personality and Social Psychology, 74*, 538–556.

Paunonen, S. V., & Ashton, M. C. (1998). The structured assessment of personality across cultures. *Journal of Cross-Cultural Psychology, 29*, 150–170.

Paunonen, S. V., Zeidner, M., Engvik, H. A., Oosterveld, P., & Maliphant, R. (2000). The nonverbal assessment of personality in five cultures. *Journal of Cross-Cultural Psychology, 31*, 220–239.

Paus, T. (1996). Location and function of the human frontal eye-field: A selective review. *Neuropsychologia, 34*, 475–483.

Pavlov, I. P. (1927). *Condtioned reflexes* (G. V. Anrep, Trans.). London: Oxford University Press.

Payne, B. K. (2001). Prejudice and perception: The role of automatic and controlled processes in misperceiving a weapon. *Journal of Personality & Social Psychology, 81*, 181–192.

Payne, B. R., & Lomber, S. G. (2001). Reconstructing functional systems after lesions of cerebral cortex. *Nature Reviews Neuroscience, 2*, 911–919.

Payne, D. G. (1987). Hypermnesia and reminiscence in recall: A historical and empirical review. *Psychological Bulletin, 101*, 5–27.

Payne, D. L. (1992). *Pragmatics of word order flexibility.* Amsterdam: John Benjamins Publishing Co.

Pearson, S. E., & Pollack, R. H. (1997). Female response to sexually explicit films. *Journal of Psychology & Human Sexuality, 9*, 73–88.

Pecher, D. (2001). Perception is a two-way junction: Feedback semantics in word recognition. *Psychonomic Bulletin & Review, 8*, 545–551.

Pedersen, W. C., Miller, L. C., Putcha-Bhagavatula, A. D., & Yang, Y. (2002). Evolved sex differences in the number of partners desired? The long and short of it. *Psychological Science, 13*, 157–161.

Pederson, N. L., Plomin, R., McClearn, G. E., & Friberg, L. (1988) Neuroticism, extraversion and related traits in adult twins reared apart and reared together. *Journal of Personality and Social Psychology, 55*, 950–957.

Peltonen, L. (1995). Schizophrenia: All out for chromosome six. *Nature, 378*, 665–666.

Penfield, W. (1955). The permanent record of the stream of consciousness. *Acta Psychologica, 11*, 47–69.

Penfield, W., & Perot, P. (1963). The brain's record of auditory and visual experience. *Brain, 86*, 595–696.

Penfield, W., & Rasmussen, T. (1950). *The cerebral cortex of man: A clinical study of localization of function.* New York: Macmillan.

Pengilly, J. W., & Dowd, E. T. (1997). Hardiness and social support as moderator of stress in college students. Paper presented at the 1997 annual convention of the Association for the Advancement of Behavior Therapy, Miami Beach, FL.

Pengilly, J. W., & Dowd, E. T. (2000). Hardiness and social support as moderators of stress. *Journal of Clinical Psychology, 56*, 813–820.

Pennebaker, J. W. (1989). Confession, inhibition and disease. In L. Berkowitz (Ed.), *Advances in experimental social psychology* (Vol. 22, pp. 211–244). New York: Academic Press.

Pennebaker, J. W. (1993). Social mechanisms of constraint. In D. M. Wegner & J. W. Pennebaker (Eds.), *Handbook of mental control* (pp. 200–219). Englewood Cliffs, NJ: Prentice Hall.

Pennebaker, J. W., & Francis, M. E. (1996). Cognitive, emotional, and language processes in disclosure. *Cognition & Emotion, 10*, 601–626.

Pennebaker, J. W., Colder, M., & Sharp, L. K. (1990). Accelerating the coping process. *Journal of Personality and Social Psychology, 58*, 528–537.

Pennebaker, J. W., Kiecolt-Glaser, J. K., & Glaser, R. (1988). Disclosures of trauma and immune function: health implications for psychotherapy. *Journal and Consulting and Clinical Psychology, 56*, 239–245.

Penton-Voak, I. S., & Perrett, D. I. (2000). Female preference for male faces changes cyclically: Further evidence. *Evolution & Human Behavior, 21*, 39–48.

Perdue, C. W., Dovidio, J. F., Gurtman, M. B., & Tyler, R. B. (1990). Us and them: Social categorization and the process of intergroup bias. *Journal of Personality and Social Psychology, 59*, 475–486.

Perera, S., Sabin, E., Nelson, P., & Lowe, D. (1998). Increases in salivary lysozyme and IgA concentrations and secretory rates independent of salivary flow rates following viewing of a humorous videotape. *International Journal of Behavioral Medicine, 5*, 118–128.

Perez Y Perez, R., & Sharples, M. (2001). MEXICA: A computer model of a cognitive account of creative writing. *Journal of Experimental & Theoretical Artificial Intelligence, 13*, 119–139.

Perkins, D. N., & Grotzer, T. A. (1997). Teaching intelligence. *American Psychologist, 52*, 1125–1133.

Perkins, H. W., & Berkowitz, A. D. (1986). Perceiving the community norms of alchol use among students.: Some research implications for campus alcohol education programming. *International Journal of the Addictions, 21*, 961–976.

Perkins, H. W., & Wechsler, H. (1996). Variation in perceived college drinking norms and its impact on alcohol abuse: A nationwide study. *Journal of Drug Issues, 26*, 961–974.

Perlmutter, M. (1988). Cognitive potential throughout life. In J. E. Birren & V. L. Bengtson (Eds.), *Emergent theories of aging* (pp. 247–267). New York: Springer.

Perrett, D. I., Lee, K. J, Penton-Voak, I., Rowland, D., Yoshikawa, S., Burt, D. M., Henzi, S. P., Castles, D. L., & Akamatsu, S. (1998). Effects of sexual dimorphism on facial attractiveness. *Nature, 394*, 884–887.

Perrett, D. I., Smith, P. A. J., Potter, D. D., Mistlin, A. J., Head, A. S., Milner, A. D., & Jeeves, M. A. (1985). Visual cells in the temporal cortex sensitive to face view and gaze direction. *Proceedings of the Royal Society of London, Series B: Biological Sciences, 223*, 293–317.

Perry, B. D., Pollard, R. A., Blakley, T. L., Baker, W. L., & Vigilante, D. (1995). Childhood trauma, the neurobiology of adaptation, and "use-dependent" development of the brain: How "states" become "traits." *Infant Mental Health Journal, 16*, 271–291.

Perugini, E. M., Kirsch, I, Allen, S. T., Coldwell, E., Meredith, J., Montgomery, G. H., & Sheehan, J. (1998). Surreptitious observation of responses to hypnotically suggested hallucinations: A test of the compliance hypothesis. *International Journal of Clinicacl and Experimental Hypnosis, 46*, 191–203.

Petersen, A. C., Compas, B. E., Brooks-Gunn, J., Stemmler, M., Ey, S., & Grant, K. E. (1993). Depression in adolescence. *American Psychologist, 48*, 155–168.

Petersen, R. C. (1977). Marihuana research findings: 1976: Summary. *NIDA Research Monograph, Jul (14)*, 1–37.

Petersen, R. C. (1979). Importance of inhalation patterns in determining effects of marihuana use. *Lancet, 31*, 727–728.

Peterson, C. (2000). The future of optimism. *American Psychologist, 55*, 44–55.

Peterson, C., & Seligman, M. E. (1984). Causal explanations as a risk factor for depression: Theory and evidence. *Psychological Review, 91*, 347–374.

Petitto, L. A., & Marentette, P. F. (1991). Babbling in the manual mode: Evidence for the ontogeny of language. *Science, 251*, 1493–1496.

Petrides, K. V., & Furnham, A. (2000). Gender differences in measured and self-estimated trait emotional intelligence. *Sex Roles, 42*, 449–461.

Petrides, M., Alivisatos, B., Meyer, E., & Evans, A. C. (1993). Functional activation of the human frontal cortex during the performance of verbal working memory tasks. *Proceedings of the National Academy of Sciences, USA, 90*, 878–882.

Petrie, K. J., Booth, R. J., & Pennebaker, J. W. (1998). The immunological effects of thought suppression. *Journal of Personality and Social Psychology, 75*, 1264–1272.

Petrie, K. J., Booth, R. J., Pennebaker, J. W., Davison, K. P., & Thomas, M. G. (1995). Disclosure of trauma and Iimmune response to a hepatitis B vaccination program. *Journal of Consulting and Clinical Psychology, 63*, 787–792.

Petrill, S. A., Ball, D., Eley, T., Hill, L., Plomin, R., McClearn, G. E., Smith, D. L., Chorney, K., Chorney, M., Hershz, M. S., Detterman, D. K., Thompson, L. A., Benbow, C., Lubinski, D., Daniels, J., Owen, M. J., & McGuffin, P. (1997a). Failure to replicate a QTL association between a DNA marker identified by EST00083 and IQ. *Intelligence, 25*, 179–184.

Petrill, S. A., Plomin, R., Berg, S., Johansson, B., Pedersen, N. L., Ahern, F., & McClearn, G. E. (1998). The genetic and environmental relationship between general and specific cognitive abilities in twins age 80 and older. *Psychological Science, 9*, 183–189.

Petrill, S. A., Plomin, R., McClearn, G. E., Smith, D. L., Vignetti, S., Chorney, M. J., Chorney, K., Thompson, L. A., Detterman, D. K., Benbow, C., Lubinski, D., Daniels, J., Owen, M., & McGuffin, P. (1997). No association between general cognitive ability and the A1 allele of the D2 dopamine receptor gene. *Behavior Genetics, 27*, 29–31.

Petrill, S. A., Thompson, L. A., & Detterman, D. K. (1995). The genetic and environmental variance underlying elementary cognitive tasks. *Behavior Genetics, 25*, 199–209.

Petrovic, P., Kalso, E., Petersson, K. M., & Ingvar, M. (2002). Placebo and opioid analgesia—imaging a shared neuronal network. *Science, 295*, 1737–1740.

Pettigrew, T. F. (1969). Racially separate or together? *Journal of Social Issues, 24*, 43–69.

Pettigrew, T. F. (1981). Extending the stereotype concept. In D. L. Hamilton (Ed.), *Cognitive processes in stereotyping and intergroup behavior* (pp. 303–331). Hillsdale, NJ: Erlbaum.

Pettigrew, T. F., & Meertens, R. W. (1995). Subtle and blatant prejudice in western Europe. *European Journal of Social Psychology, 25*, 57–75.

Petty, F., Kramer, G., Wilson, L., & Jordan, S. (1994). In vivo serotonin release and learned helplessness. *Psychiatry Research, 52*, 285–293.

Petty, R. E., & Cacioppo, J. T. (1981). *Attitudes and persuasion: Classic and contemporary approaches.* Dubuque, IA: Wm. C. Brown.

Petty, R. E., & Cacioppo, J. T. (1986). The elaboration likelihood model of persuasion. In L. Berkowitz (Ed.), *Advances in experimental social psychology, 19*, (pp. 123–205). New York: Academic Press.

Petty, R. E., & Krosnick, J. A. (1996). *Attitude strength: Anetecedents and consequences.* Hillsdale, NJ: Erlbaum.

Petty, R. E., & Wegener, D. T. (1998). Attitude Change: multiple roles for persuasion variables. In D. T. Gilbert, S. T. Fiske, & G. Lindzey (Eds.), *The handbook of social psychology* (4th ed.). New York: McGraw Hill. 323–390.

Pezdek, K., Finger, K., & Hodge, D. (1997). Planting false childhood memories: The role of event plausibility. *Psychological Science, 8*, 437–441.

Pfaffmann, C. (1978). The vertebrate phylogeny, neural code, and integrative processes of taste. In E. C. Carterette & M. P. Friedman (Eds.), *Handbook of perception* (pp. 51–123). New York: Academic Press.

Phan, K. L., Wager, T., Taylor, S. F., & Liberzon, I. (2002). Functional neuroanatomy of emotion: A meta-analysis of emotion activation studies in PET and fMRI. *NeuroImage, 16*, 331–348.

Phelps, E. A., O'Connor, K. J., Cunningham, W. A., Funayama, E. S., Gatenby, J. C., Gore, J. C., & Banaji, M. R. (2000). Performance on indirect measures of race evaluation predicts amygdala activation. *Journal of Cognitive Neuroscience, 12*, 729–738.

Phelps, J. A., Davis, J. O., & Schartz, K. M. (1997). Nature, nurture, and twin research strategies. *Current Directions in Psychological Science, 6*, 117–121.

Phillips, C., Pellathy, T., Marantz, A., Yellin, E., Wexler, K., Poeppel, D., McGinnis, M., & Roberts, T. (2000). Auditory cortex accesses phonological categories: An MEG mismatch study. *Journal of Cognitive Neuroscience, 12*, 1038–1055.

Phillips, D. P., & Smith, D. G. (1990). Postponement of death until symbolically meaningful occasions. *Journal of the American Medical Association, 263*, 1947–1951.

Phillips, D. P., Van Voorhees, C. A., & Ruth, T. E. (1992). The birthday: Lifeline or deadline? *Psychosomatic Medicine, 54*, 532–542.

Phillips, J. B. (1986a). Two magnetoreception pathways in a migratory salamander. *Science, 233*, 765–767.

Phillips, J. B. (1986b). Magnetic compass orientation in the Eastern red-spotted newt (*Notophthalmus viridescens*). *Journal of Comparative Physiology, 158*, 103–109.

Phillips, J. B. (1996). Magnetic navigation. *Journal of Theoretical Biology, 180*, 309–319.

Phillips, K., & Matheny, A. P., Jr. (1995). Quantitative genetic analysis of injury liability in infants and toddlers. *American Journal of Medical Genetics (Neuropsychiatric Genetics), 60*, 64–71.

Phillips, S. D., & Imhoff, A. R. (1997). Women and career development: A decade of research. *Annual Review of Psychology, 48*, 31–59.

Piaget, J. (1954). *The construction of reality in the child.* New York: Free Press.

Piaget, J. (1962). *Play, dreams, and imitation in childhood.* New York: W. W. Norton.

Piaget, J. (1969). *The mechanisms of perception.* (G. N. Seagrim, Trans.). New York: Basic Books.

Piazza, C. C., Hanley, G. P., Fisher, W. W., Ruyter, J. M., & Gulotta, C. S. (1998). On the establishing and reinforcing effects of termination of demands for destructive behavior maintained by positive and negative reinforcement. *Research in Developmental Disabilities, 19*, 395–407.

Pickles, J. O. (1988). *An introduction to the physiology of hearing* (2nd ed.). London: Academic Press.

Pierce, C. A. (1992). *The effects of physical attractiveness and height on dating choice: A meta-analysis.* Unpublished masters thesis, University at Albany, State University of New York, Albany, NY.

Pietromonaco, P. R., Manis, J., & Frohardt-Lane, K. (1986). Psychological consequences of multiple social roles. *Psychology of Women Quarterly, 10*, 373–381.

Pine, D. S., Cohen, P., & Brook, J. (2001). Adolescent fears as predictors of depression. *Biological Psychiatry, 50*, 721–724.

Pinel, J. P. J. (1993). *Biopsychology* (2nd ed.). Boston: Allyn & Bacon.

Pinhey, T. K., Rubinstein, D. H., & Colfax, R. S. (1997). Overweight and happiness: The reflected self-appraisal hypothesis reconsidered. *Social Science Quarterly, 78*, 747–755.

Pinker, S. (1994). *The language instinct: How the mind creates language.* New York: Morrow.

Pinker, S. (1997). *How the mind works.* New York: Norton.

Pinker, S. (1999). *Words and rules: The ingredients of language.* New York: Basic Books, Inc.

Pinkerman, J. E., Haynes, J. P., & Keiser, T. (1993). Characteristics of psychological practice in juvenile court clinics. *American Journal of Forensic Psychology, 11*, 3–12.

Pirke, K. M. (1995). Physiology of bulimia nervosa. In K. D. Brownell & C. G. Fairburn (Eds.), *Eating disorders and obesity: A comprehensive handbook.* New York: Guilford Press, 261–265.

Pitman, D. L., Natelson, B. H., Ottenmiller, J. E., McCarty, R., Pritzel, T., & Tapp, W. N. (1995). Effects of exposure to stressors of varying predictability on adrenal function in rats. *Behavioral Neuroscience, 109*, 767–776.

Plaks, J. E., Stroessner, S. J., Dweck, C. S., & Sherman, J. W. (2001). Person theories and attention allocation: Preferences for stereotypic versus counterstereotypic information. *Journal of Personality and Social Psychology, 80*, 876–893.

Plato. (1956). Meno (Menon). In R. H. D. Rouse (Trans.), *Great dialogues of Plato.* New York: New American Library.

Platt, L. A., & Persico, V. R., Jr. (Eds.) (1992). *Grief in cross-cultural perspective: A casebook.* New York: Garland.

Plaut, D. C., McClelland, J. L., Seidenberg, M. S., & Patterson, K. E. (1996). Understanding normal and impaired word reading: Computational principles in quasi-regular domains. *Psychological Review, 103*, 56–115.

Plehn, K., & Peterson, R. A. (2002). Anxiety sensitivity as a predictor of the development of panic symptoms, panic attacks, and panic disorder: A prospective study. *Journal of Anxiety Disorders, 16*, 455–474.

Ploghaus, A., Tracey, I., Gati, J. S., Clare, S., Menon, R. S., Matthews, P. M., & Rawlins, J. N. P. (1999). Dissociating pain from its anticipation in the human brain. *Science, 284*, 1979–1981.

Plomin, R. (1988). The nature and nurture of cognitive abilities. In R. J. Sternberg (Ed.), *Advances in the psychology of human intelligence* (Vol. 4, pp. 1–33). Hillsdale, NJ: Erlbaum.

Plomin, R. (1990). *Nature and nurture : An introduction to human behavioral genetics.* Pacific Grove, CA: Brooks/Cole.

Plomin, R. (1995). Genetics and children's experiences in the family. *Journal of Child Psychology and Psychiatry, 36*, 33–68.

Plomin, R. (2001). Genetic factors contributing to learning and language delays and disabilities. *Child & Adolescent Psychiatric Clinics of North America, 10*, 259–277.

Plomin, R., & Bergeman, C. S. (1991). The nature of nurture: Genetic influences on "environmental" measures. *Behavioral and Brain Sciences, 14*, 373–427.

Plomin, R., & DeFries, J. C. (1998). The genetics of cognitive abilities and disabilities: Investigations of specific cognitive skills can help clarify how genes shape the components of intellect. *Scientific American, 278*, 40–47.

Plomin, R., & Foch, T. T. (1980). A twin study of objectrively assessed personality in childhood. *Journal of Personality and Social Psychology, 39*, 680–688.

Plomin, R., & Kosslyn, S. M. (2001). Genes, brain and cognition. *Nature Neuroscience, 4*, 1153–1155.

Plomin, R., Chipuer, H. M., & Loehlin, J. C. (1990). Behavioral genetics and personality. In L. A. Pervin (Ed.), *Handbook of personality: Theory and research* (pp. 225–243). New York: Guilford.

Plomin, R., Corley, R., Caspi, A., Fulker, D. W., & DeFries, J. (1998). Adoption results for self-reported personality: Evidence for nonadditive genetic effects? *Journal of Personality and Social Psychology 75*, 211–218.

Plomin, R., Corley, R., DeFries, J. C., & Fulker, D. W. (1990). Individual Differences in television viewing in early childhood: Nature as well as nurture. *Psychological Science, 1*, 371–377.

Plomin, R., DeFries, J. C., & Loehlin, J. C. (1977). Genotype-environment interaction and correlation in the analysis of human behavior. *Psychological Bulletin, 84*, 309–322.

Plomin, R., DeFries, J. C., McClearn, G. E., & Rutter, M. (1997). *Behavioral genetics* (3rd ed.). New York: Freeman.

Plomin, R. Lichtenstein, P., Pedersen, N. L., McClearn, G. E., & Nesselroade, J. R. (1990b). Genetic influence on life events during the last half of the life span. *Psychology and Aging, 5,* 25–30.

Plomin, R., Pedersen, N. L., Lichtenstein, P., & McClearn, G. E. (1994). Variability and stability in cognitive abilities are largely genetic later in life. *Behavior Genetics, 24*(3), 207–215.

Plomin, R., Scheier, M. F., Bergeman, C. S., Pederson, N. L., Nesselroade, J. R., & McClearn, G. E. (1992). Optimism, pessimism and mental health: A twin/adoption analysis. *Personality and Individual Differences, 13,* 921–930.

Plotkin, H. (1994). *The nature of knowledge: Concerning adaptations, instinct and the evolution of intelligence.* New York: Allen Lane/Viking Penguin.

Plotkin, H. (1997). *Evolution in mind: An introduction to evolutionary psychology.* Cambridge, MA: Harvard University Press.

Plucker, J. A. (1998). Beware of simple conclusions: The case for content generality of creativity. *Creativity Research Journal, 11,* 179–182.

Plucker, J. A. (1999a). Is the proof in the pudding? Reanalyses of Torrance's (1958 to present) longitudinal data. *Creativity Research Journal, 12,* 103–114.

Plucker, J. A. (1999b). Reanalyses of student responses to creativity checklists: Evidence of content generality. *Journal of Creative Behavior, 33,* 126–137.

Poizner, H., & Kegl, J. (1992). Neural basis of language and motor behavior: Perspectives from American Sign Language. *Aphasiology, 6,* 219–256.

Poizner, H., Klima, E. S., & Bellugi, U. (1987). *What the hands reveal about the brain.* Cambridge, MA: MIT Press.

Poldrack, R. A., Clark, J., Paré-Blagoev, E. J., Shohamy, D., Creso Moyano, J., Myers, C., & Gluck, M. A. (2001). Interactive memory systems in the human brain. *Nature, 414,* 546–550.

Poldrack, R. A., Temple, E., Protopapas, A., Nagarajan, S., Tallal, P., Merzenich, M., & Gabrieli, J. D. E. (2001). Relations between the neural bases of dynamic auditory processing and phonological processing: Evidence from fMRI. *Journal of Cognitive Neuroscience, 13,* 687–697.

Polivy, J., & Herman, C. P. (1993). Etiology of binge eating: Psychological mechanisms. In C. G. Fairburn & G. T. Wilson (Eds.), *Binge eating: Nature, assessment, and treatment* (pp. 173–205). New York: Guilford Press.

Pollack, H. A. (2001). Sudden infant death syndrome, maternal smoking during pregnancy, and the cost-effectiveness of smoking cessation intervention. *American Journal of Public Health, 91,* 432–436.

Pollard, C. A., Pollard, H. J., & Corn, K. J. (1989). Panic onset and major events in the lives of agoraphobics: A test of contiguity. *Journal of Abnormal Psychology, 98,* 318–321.

Pollock, V. E., Briere, J., Schneider, L., Knop, J., Mednick, S. A., & Goodwin, D. H. (1990). Childhood antecedents of antisocial behavior: Parental alcoholism and physical abusiveness. *American Journal of Psychiatry, 147,* 1290–1293.

Ponomarenko, V. V., & Kamyshev, N. G. (1997). Genetic aspects of the mechanisms of learning. *Neuroscience and Behavioral Physiology, 27,* 245–249.

Pope, K. S. (1996). Memory, abuse, and science: Questioning claims about the false memory syndrome epidemic. *American Psychologist, 51,* 957–974.

Porter, D., & Neuringer, A. (1984). Music discriminations by pigeons. *Journal of Experimental Psychology: Animal Behavior Processes, 10,* 138–148.

Porter, R. H. (1991). Human reproduction and the mother-infant relationship: The role of odors. In T. V. Getchell, R. L. Doty, L. M. Bartoshuk, & J. B. Snow, Jr. (Eds.), *Smell and taste in health and disease* (pp. 429–442). New York: Raven.

Porter, R. H., Cernoch, J. M., & Balogh, R. D. (1985). Odor signatures and kin recognition. *Physiology & Behavior, 24,* 445–448.

Porter, R. H., Cernoch, J. M., & McLaughlin, F. J. (1983). Maternal recognition of neonates through olfactory cues. *Physiology & Behavior, 30,* 151–154.

Porter, R. H., Makin, J. W., Davis, L. B., & Christensen, K. M. (1992). An assessment of the salient olfactory environment of formula-fed infants. *Physiology & Behavior, 50,* 907–911.

Posthuma, D., Neale, M. C., Boomsma, D. I., & de Geus, E. J. C. (2001). Are smarter brains running faster? Heritability of alpha peak frequency, IQ, and their interrelation. *Behavior Genetics, 31,* 567–579.

Posner, M. I., & Raichle, M. (1994). *Images of mind.* New York: Freeman.

Posner, M. I., DiGirolamo, G. J., & Fernandez-Duque, D. (1997). Brain mechanisms of cognitive skills. *Consciousness and Cognition, 6,* 267–290.

Post, R. M. (1992). Transdirection of psychosocial stress into the neurobiology of recurrent affective disorder. *American Journal of Psychiatry, 149,* 999–1010.

Postmes, T., & Spears, R. (1998). Deindividuation and antinormative behavior: A meta-analysis. *Psychological Bulletin, 123,* 238–259.

Postmes, T., Spears, R., & Cihangir, S. (2001). Quality of decision making and group norms. *Journal of Personality & Social Psychology, 80,* 918–930.

Poston, W. S. C., Ericsson, M., Linder, J., Nilsson, T., Goodrick, G. K., & Foreyt, J. P. (1999). Personality and the prediction of weight loss and relapse in the treatment of obesity. *International Journal of Eating Disorders, 25,* 301–309.

Poulton, R., & Menzies, R. G. (2002). Non-associative fear acquisition: A review of the evidence from retrospective and longitudinal research. *Behaviour Research & Therapy, 40,* 1227–1249.

Poulton, R., Menzies, R. G., Craske, M. G., Langley, J. D., & Silva, P. A. (1999). Water trauma and swimming experiences up to age 9 and fear of water at age 18: A longitudinal study. *Behaviour Research & Therapy, 37,* 39–48.

Powell, M. C., & Fazio, R. H. (1984). Attitude accessibility as a function of repeated attitudinal expression. *Personality and Social Psychology Bulletin, 10,* 139–148.

Powers, P. C., & Green, R. G. (1972). Effects of the behavior and perceived arousal of a model on instrumental aggression. *Journal of Personality and Social Psychology, 23,* 175–184.

Prabhakaran, V., Smith, J. A. L., Desmond, J. E., Glover, G. H., & Gabrieli, J. E. (1997). Neural substrates of fluid reasoning: An fMRI study of the neocortical activation during performance of the Raven's Progressive Matrices Test. *Cognitive Psychology, 33,* 43–63.

Practice Directorate (1998). *How to find help through psychotherapy.* Washington DC: American Psychological Association.

Prapavessis, H., & Carron, A. V. (1997). Sacrifice, cohesion, and conformity to norms in sport teams. *Group Dynamics: Theory, Research, and Practice, 1,* 231–240.

Prasada, S. (2000). Acquiring generic knowledge. *Trends in Cognitive Science, 4,* 66–72.

Prather, D. C. (1973). Prompted mental practice as a flight simulator. *Journal of Applied Psychology, 57,* 353–355.

Prechtl, H. F. R., & Beintema, D. (1965). *The neurological examination of the full-term newborn infant.* London: Heinemann.

Prescott, C. A., Johnson, R. C., & McArdle, J. J. (1991). Genetic contributions to television viewing. *Psychological Science, 2,* 430–431.

Pressley, M., Brown, R. El-Dinary, P. B., & Allferbach, P. (1995). The comprehension instruction that students need: Instruction fostering constructively responsive reading. *Learning Disabilities Research & Practice, 10,* 215–224.

Pressman, E. K., DiPietro, J. A., Costigan, K. A., Shupe, A. K., & Johnson, T. R. B. (1998). Fetal neurobehavioral development: Associations with socioeconomic class and fetal sex. *Developmental Psychobiology, 33,* 79–91.

Prickett, T., Gada-Jain, N., & Bernieri, F. J. (in preparation). First impression formation in a job interview: The first 20 seconds. Cited in Ambady (2000); cited in Gladwell, M. (2000); *The New Yorker* (May 29, 2000); The New-Boy network: What do job interviews really tell us? www.gladwell.com/pdf/newboy.pdf

Prien, R. F., & Kocsis, J. H. (1995). Long term treatment of mood disorders. In F. E. Bloom & D. J. Kupfer (Eds.), *Psychopharmacology: The fourth generation of progress* (pp. 1067–1080). New York: Raven Press.

Priester, J. R., & Petty, R. E. (1995). Source attributions and persuaion: Perceived honesty as a determinant of message scrutiny. *Personality and Social Psychology Bulletin, 21,* 637–654.

Privette, G., & Landsman, T. (1983). Factor analysis of peak performance: The full use of potential. *Journal of Personality and Social Psychology, 44,* 195–200.

Prochaska, J. O., & Norcross, J. C. (2001). Stages of change. *Psychotherapy: Theory, Research, Practice, Training, 38,* 443–448.

Prochaska, J. O., Norcross, J. C., & DiClemente, C. C. (1994). *Changing for good.* New York: William Morrow & Co.

Prochaska, J. O., Velicer, W. F., Rossi, J. S., Goldstein, M. G., Marcus, B. H., Rakowski, W., Fiore, C., Harlow, L. L., Redding, C. A., Rosenbloom, D., & Rossi, S. R. (1994). Stages of change and decisional balance for 12 problem behaviors. *Health Psychology, 13,* 39–46.

Proctor, R. W., & Van Zandt, T. (1994). *Human factors in simple and complex systems.* Boston: Allyn & Bacon.

Project MATCH Research Group National Institute on Alcohol Abuse and Alcoholism Bethesda, MD (1997). Project MATCH secondary a priori hypotheses. *Addiction, 92,* 1671–169.

Project on the Status and Education of Women (1987). Association of American Colleges, 1818 R St. NW, Washington, DC 20009, 202/387-1300.

Proksch, J., & Bavelier, D. (2002). Changes in the spatial distributions of visual attention after early deafness. *Journal of Cognitive Neuroscience, 14,* 687–701.

Przybyla, D. P., & Byrne, D. (1984). The mediating role of cognitive processes in self-reported sexual arousal. *Journal of Research in Personality, 18,* 54–63.

Pujol, R., Lavigne-Rebillard, M., & Uziel, A. (1990). Physiological correlates of development of the human cochlea. *Seminars in Perinatology, 14,* 275–280.

Puka, B. (Ed.) (1994). *Kohlberg's original study of moral development.* New York: Garland.

Putnam, F. W. (1989). *Diagnosis and treatment of Multiple Personality Disorder.* New York: Guilford Press.

Putnam, F. W., Helmers, K., Horowitz, L. A., & Trickett, P. K. (1995). Hypnotizability and dissociativity in sexually abused girls. *Child Abuse and Neglect, 19,* 645–655.

Putnam, H. (1973). Reductionism and the nature of psychology. *Cognition, 2,* 131–146.

Quadrel, M. J., Fischhoff, B., & Davis, W. (1993). Adolescent (in)vulnerabilty. *American Psychologist, 48,* 102–116.

Quay, H. C. (1965). Psychopathic personality as pathological stimulus-seeking. *American Journal of Psychiatry, 122,* 180–183.

Quinn, J. G. (1991). Encoding and maintenance of information in visual working memory. In R. H. Logie & M. Denis (Eds.), *Mental images in human cognition.* (pp. 95–104). Amsterdam: North-Holland.

Quinn, P. C., Bhatt, R. S., Brush, D., Grimes, A., & Sharpnack, H. (2002). Development of form similarity as a Gestalt grouping principle in infancy. *Psychological Science, 13,* 320–328.

Raag, T., & Rackliff, C. L. (1998). Preschoolers' awareness of social expectations of gender: Relationships to toy choices. *Sex Roles, 38,* 685–700.

Rabin, M. D., & Cain, W. S. (1986). Determinants of measured olfactory sensitivity. *Perception & Psychophysics, 39,* 281–286.

Rabinowitz, F. E., Sutton, L., Schutter, T., Brow, A., Krizo, C., Larsen, J., Styn, J., Welander, A., Wilson, D., & Wright, S. (1997). Helpfulness to lost tourists. *Journal of Social Psychology, 137,* 502–509.

Rachman, S. (1997). A cognitive theory of obsessions. *Behaviour Research & Therapy, 35,* 793–802.

Radvansky, G. A. (1999). Aging, memory, and comprehension. *Current Directions in Psychological Science, 8,* 49–53.

Raemae, P., Sala, J. B., Gillen, J. S., Pekar, J. J., & Courtney, S. M. (2001). Dissociation of the neural systems for working memory maintenance of verbal and nonspatial visual information. *Cognitive, Affective & Behavioral Neuroscience, 1*, 161–171.

Räikkönen, K., Matthews, K. A., Flory, J. D., & Owens, J. F. (1999). Effects of hostility on ambulatory blood pressure and mood during daily living in healthy adults. *Health Psychology, 18*, 44–53.

Raine, A., Reynolds, C., Venables, P. H., & Mednick, S. A. (2002). Stimulation seeking and intelligence: A prospective longitudinal study. *Journal of Personality & Social Psychology, 82*, 663–674.

Raine, A., Venables, P. H., & Wiliams, M. (1990). Relationships between central and autonomic measures of arousal at age 15 years and criminality at age 24 years. *Archives of General Psychiatry, 47*, 1003–1007.

Rainville, P., Duncan, G. H., Price, D. D., Carrier, B., & Bushnell, M. C. (1997). Pain affect encoded in human anterior cingulate but not somatosensory cortex. *Science, 277*, 968–971.

Rajaram, S., Srinivas, K., & Roediger, H. L., III. (1998). A transfer-appropriate processing account of context effects in word fragment completion. *Journal of Experimental Psychology: Learning, Memory, & Cognition, 24*, 993–1004.

Rakic, P. (1975). Timing of major ontogenetic events in the visual cortex of the rhesus monkey. In N. Buchwald & M. Brazier (Eds.), *Brain mechanisms in mental retardation* (pp. 3–40). New York: Academic Press.

Rakic, P., Bourgeois, J-P., & Goldman-Rakic, P. S. (1994). Synaptic development of the cerebral cortex: Implications for learning, memory, and mental illness. In J. van Pelt, M. A. Corner, H. B. M. Uylings, & F. H. Lopes da Silva (Eds.), *Progress in brain research: Vol. 102. The self-organizing brain: From growth cones to functional networks* (pp. 227–243). Amsterdam: Elsevier.

Ramachandran, V. S. (1993). Behavioral and magnetoencephalographic correlates of plasticity in the adult human brain. *Proceedings of the National Academy of Sciences, 90*, 10413–10420.

Ramachandran, V. S., Rogers-Ramachandran, D., & Cobb, S. (1995). Touching the phantom limb. *Nature, 377*, 489–490.

Ramachandran, V. S., Rogers-Ramachandran, D., & Stewart, M. (1992). Perceptual correlates of massive cortical reorganization. *Science, 258*, 1159–1160.

Ramey, C. T., & Ramey, S. L. (1998). Early intervention and early experience. *American Psychologist, 53*(2), 109–120.

Ramirez, M., III. (1999). *Multicultural Psychotherapy: An approach to invidividual and cultural differences* (2nd edition). Needham Heights, MA: Allyn & Bacon.

Ranieri, D. J., & Zeiss, A. M. (1984). Induction of depressed mood: A test of opponent-process theory. *Journal of Personality & Social Psychology, 47*, 1413–1422.

Rankinen, T., Pérusse, L., Weisnagel, S. J., Snyder, E. E. Chagnon, Y. C., & Bouchard, C. (2002). The human obesity gene map: The 2001 update. *Obesity Research, 10*, 196–243.

Rao, S. C., Rainer, G., & Miller, E. K. (1997). Integration of what and where in the primate prefrontal cortex. *Science, 276*, 821–834.

Rapee, R. M., & Heimberg, R. G. (1997). A cognitive-behavioral model of anxiety in social phobia. *Behaviour Research & Therapy, 35*, 741–756.

Ratliff-Schaub, K., Hunt, C. E., Crowell, D., Golub, H., Smok-Pearsall, S., Palmer, P., Schafer, S., Bak, S., Cantey-Kiser, J., & O'Bell, R. (2001). Relationship between infant sleep position and motor development in preterm infants. *Journal of Developmental & Behavioral Pediatrics, 22*, 293–299.

Ratner, R. K., & Miller, D. T. (2001). The norm of self-interest and its effects on social action. *Journal of Personality & Social Psychology, 81*, 5–16.

Rauch, S. L., Jenike, M. A., Alpert, N. M., Baer, L., Breiter, H. C. R., Savage, C. R., & Fischman, A. J. (1994). Regional cerebral blood flow measured during symptom provocation in obsessive-compulsive disorder using oxygen 15-labeled carbon dioxide and poitron emission tomography. *Archives of General Psychiatry, 51*, 62–70.

Rauch, S. L., van der Kolk, B. A., Risler, R. E., Alpert, N. M., Orr, S. P., Savage, C. R., Fischman, A. J., Jenike, M. A., & Pitman, R. K. (1996). A symptom provocation study of posttraumatic stress disorder using positron emission tomography and script-driven imagery. *Archives of General Psychiatry, 53*, 380–387.

Raudenbush, S. W. (1984). Magnitude of teacher expectancy effects on pupil IQ as a function of the credibility of expectancy induction: A synthesis of findings from 18 experiments. *Journal of Educational Psychology, 76*, 85–97.

Rauscher, F. H. (1999). Prelude or requiem for the "Mozart effect"? *Nature, 400*, 827–828.

Rauscher, F. H., Shaw, G. L., & Ky, K. N. (1993). Music and spatial task performance. *Nature, 365*, 611.

Raven, B. (1998). Groupthink, Bay of Pigs, and Watergate reconsidered. *Organizational Behavior & Human Decision Processes, 73*, 352–361.

Raven, J. C. (1965). *Advanced progressive matrices: Sets I and II*. London: Lewis.

Raven, J. C. (1976). *Standard progressive matrices: Sets A, B, C, D & E*. Oxford: Oxford Psychologists Press.

Ravussin, E., & Bouchard, C. (2000). Human genomics and obesity: Finding appropriate target drugs. *European Journal of Pharmacology, 410*, 131–145.

Ray, J., & Sapolsky, R. (1992). Styles of male social behavior and their endocrine correlates among high-ranking wild baboons. *American Journal of Primatology, 28*, 231–250.

Ray, W. J., Sabsevitz, D., DePascalis, V., Quigley, K., Aikens, D., & Tubbs, M. (2000). Cardiovascular reactivity during hypnosis and hypnotic susceptibility: Three studies of heart rate variability. *International Journal of Clinical & Experimental Hypnosis, 48*, 22–31.

Raymond, J. E., Shapiro, K. L., & Arnell, K. M. (1992). Temporary suppression of visual processing in an RSVP task: An attentional blink? *Journal of Experimental Psychology: Human Perception and Performance, 18*, 849–860.

Razran, G. H. S. (1940). Conditioned response changes in rating and appraising sociopolitical solutions. *Psychological Bulletin, 37*, 481.

Rechtschaffen, A., Gilliland, M. A., Bergmann, B. M., & Winter, J. B. (1983). Physiological correlates of prolonged sleep deprivation in rats. *Science, 221*: 182–4.

Rector, N. A., & Beck, A. T. (2001). Cognitive behavioral therapy for schizophrenia: An empirical review. *Journal of Nervous & Mental Disease, 189*, 278–287.

Redd, W. H., Dadds, M. R., Futterman, A. D., Taylor, K. L., & Bovbjerg, D. J. (1993). Nausea induced by mental images of chemotherapy. *Cancer, 72*, 629–636.

Redelmeier, D. A., & Kahneman, D. (1996). Patients' memories of painful medical treatments: Real-time and retrospective evaluations of two minimally invasive procedures. *Pain, 66*, 3–8.

Reed, T. E., & Jenson, A. R. (1990). Choice reaction time and visual pathway nerve conduction velocity both correlate with intelligence but appear not to correlate with each other: Implications for information processing. *Intelligence, 17*, 191–203.

Reese, H. W., Lee, L.-J., Cohen, S. H., & Puckett, J. M., Jr. (2001). Effects of intellectual variables, age, and gender on divergent thinking in adulthood. *International Journal of Behavioral Development, 25*, 491–500.

Regan, D. T., & Fazio, R. H. (1977). On the consistency between attitudes and behavior: Look to the method of attitude formation. *Journal of Experimental Psychology, 13*, 38–45.

Regan, P. C. (1996). Rhythms of desire: The association between menstrual cycle phases and female sexual desire. *Canadian Journal of Human Sexuality, 5*, 145–156.

Regier D. A., & Kaelber, C. T. (1995). The Epidemiologic Catchment Area (ECA) program: studying the prevalence and incidence of psychopathology. In: M. T. Tsuang, M. Tohen, G. E. P. Zahner (Eds.), *Textbook in psychiatric epidemiology* (pp. 133–157). New York: John Wiley & Sons Inc.

Regier, D. A., Narrow, W. E., Rae, D. S., Manderscheid, R. W., Locke, B. Z., & Goodwin, F. K. (1993). The de facto US mental and addictive disorders service system. Epidemiologic Catchment Area prospective 1-year prevalence rates of disorders and services. *Archives of General Psychiatry, 50*, 85–94.

Reicher, G. M. (1969). Perceptual recognition as a function of meaningfulness of stimulus material. *Journal of Experimental Psychology, 81*, 275–280.

Reid, J. E. (1947). A revised questioning technique in lie-detection tests. *Journal of Criminal Law & Criminology, 37*, 542–547.

Reid, R. C. (1999). Vision. In M. J. Zigmond, F. E. Bloom, S. C. Landis, J. L. Roberts, & L. R. Squire (Eds.), *Fundamental neuroscience* (pp. 821–851). New York: Academic Press.

Reifman, A., & Windle, M. (1995). Adolescent suicidal behaviors as a function of depression, hopelessness, alcohol use, and social support: A longitudinal investigation. *American Journal of Community Psychology, 23*, 329–354.

Reiman, E. M., Lane, R. D., Ahern, G. L., Schwartz, G. E., Davidson, R. J., Friston, K. J., Yun, L-S., & Chen, K. (1997). Neuroanatomical correlates of externally and internally generated human emotion. *American Journal of Psychiatry, 154*, 918–925.

Reinberg, A., Vieux, N., Andlauer, P., & Smolensky, M. (1983). Tolerance to shift work" A chronobiological approach. In J. Mendlewicz & H. M. van Praag (Eds.), *Biological rhythms and behavior advances in biological psychiatry* (Vol. 2, pp. 20–34). Basel, Switzerland: S. Karger.

Reinisch, J. M., & Sanders, S. A. (1992). Prenatal hormonal contributions to sex differences in human cognitive and personality development. In A. A. Gerall, H. Moltz, & I. I. Ward (Eds.), *Sexual differentiation: Vol. II. Handbook of behavioral neurobiology* (pp. 221–243). New York: Plenum.

Reis, H. T., & Shaver, P. (1988). Intimacy as an interpersonal process. In S. W. Duck (Ed.), *Handbook of basic principles* (pp. 367–389). Chichester, England: Wiley.

Rende, R., & Plomin, R. (1992). Diathesis-stress models of psychopathology: A quantitative genetic perspective. *Applied & Preventative Psychology. 1*, 177–182.

Rensink, R. A., O'Regan, J. K., & Clark, J. J. (1997). To see or not to see: The need for attention to perceive changes in scenes. *Psychological Science, 8*, 368–373.

Repetti, R. L. (1993). Short-term effects of occupational stressors on daily mood and health complaints. *Health Psychology, 12*, 125–131.

Rescorla, R. A. (1966). Predictability and number of pairings in Pavlovian fear conditiong. *Psychonomic Science, 4*, 383–385.

Rescorla, R. A. (1967). Pavlovian conditioning and its proper control procedures. *Psychological Review, 74*, 71–80.

Resnick, H. S., Kilpatrick, D. G., Dansky, B. S., Saunders, B., & Best, C. L. (1993). Prevalence of civilian trauma and posttraumatic stress disorder in a representative national sample of women. *Journal of Consulting and Clinical Psychology, 61*, 984–991.

Rest, J. R. (1979). *Development in judging moral issues*. Minneapolis: University of Minnesota Press.

Rest, J. R. (1986). *Moral development: Advances in research and theory*. New York: Praeger.

Retsinas, J. (1988). A theoretical reassessment of the applicability of Kübler-Ross's stages of dying. *Death Studies, 12*, 207–216.

Reynolds, C. F., III, Frank, E., Perel, J. M., Imber, S. D., Cornes, C., Miller, M. D., Mazumdar, S., Houck, P. R., Dew, M. A., Stack, J. A., Pollock, B. G., & Kupfer, D. J. (1999). Nortriptyline and interpersonal psychotherapy as maintenance therapies for recurrent major depression: A randomized controlled trial in patients older than 59 years. *Journal of the American Medical Association, 281,*:39–45.

Reynolds, S., Stiles, W. B., Barkham, M., Shapiro, D. A., Hardy, G. E., & Rees, A. (1996). Acceleration of changes in session impact during contrasting time-limited psychotherapies. *Journal of Consulting & Clinical Psychology, 64,* 577–586.

Reznick, J. S., & Goldfield, B. A. (1992). Rapid change in lexical development in comprehension and production. *Developmental Psychology, 28,* 406–413.

Rhine, J. B. (1934). *Extra-sensory perception.* Boston: Boston Society for Psychic Research.

Rhine, L. E. (1967). *ESP in life and lab: Tracing hidden channels.* New York: Macmillan.

Rhodewalt, F., & Davison, J., Jr. (1983). Reactance and the coronary-prone behavior pattern: The role of self-attribution in response to reduced behavioral freedom. *Journal of Personality and Social Psychology, 44,* 220–228.

Rhodes, G., Halberstadt, J., & Brajkovich, G. (2001). Generalization of mere exposure effects to averaged composite faces. *Socia Cognition, 19,* 57–70.

Rice, G., Anderson, C., Risch, N., & Ebers, G. (1999). Male homosexuality: Absence of linkage to microsatellite markers at Xq28. *Science, 284,* 665–667.

Rice, M. E., & Grusec, J. E. (1975). Saying and doing: Effects on observer performance. *Journal of Personality and Social Psychology, 32,* 584–593.

Rich, A. N., & Mattingley, J. B. (2002). Anomalous perception in synaesthesia: A cognitive neuroscience perspective. *Nature Reviews Neuroscience, 3,* 43–52.

Richards, J. C., Edgar, L. V., & Gibbons, P. (1996). Cardiac acuity in panic disorder. *Cognitive Therapy and Research, 20,* 361–376.

Richardson, A. (1994). *Individual differences in imaging: Their measurement, origins, and consequences.* Amityville, NY: Baywood.

Richert, E. S. (1997). Excellence with equity in identification and programming. In N. Colangelo & G. A. Davis (Eds.), *Handbook of gifted education* (2nd ed., pp. 75–88). Boston: Allyn & Bacon.

Ridgeway, C. L. (1991). The social construction of status calue: Gender and other nominal characteristics. *Social Forces, 70,* 367–386.

Rijsdijk, F. V., & Boomsma, D. I. (1997). Genetic meditation of the correlation between peripheral nerve conduction velocity and IQ. *Behavior Genetics, 27,* 87–98.

Rilling, J. K., Gutman, D. A., Zeh, T. R., Pagnoni, G., Berns, G. S., & Kilts, C. D. (2002). A neural basis for social cooperation. *Neuron, 35,* 395–405.

Riordan-Eva, P. (1992). Blindness. In D. Vaugh, T. Ashbury, & P. Riordan-Eva (Eds.), *General opthalmology* (pp. 404–409). Norwalk, CT: Appleton & Lange.

Rips, L. (2001). Necessity and natural categories. *Psychological Bulletin, 127,* 827–852.

Rips, L. J., & Marcus, S. L. (1977). Supposition and the analysis of conditional sentences. In M. A. Just & P. A. Carpenter (Eds.), *Cognitive processes in comprehension* (pp. 185–220). Hillsdale, NJ: Erlbaum.

Rips, L. J., Shoben, E. J., & Smith, E. E. (1973). Semantic distance and the verification of semantic relations. *Journal of Verbal Learning and Verbal Behavior, 12,* 1–20.

Rivas-Vazques, R. A. (2001). Antidepressants as first-line agents in the current pharmacotherapy of anxiety disorders. *Professional Psychology: Research and Practice, 32,* 101–104.

Rivera, G., & Colle, M.-P.(1994). *Frida's fiesta's: Recipes and reminiscences of life with Frida Kahlo.* Translation by Krabbenhoft, K. New York: Clarkson N. Potter, Inc.

Rivera-Arzola, M., & Ramos-Grenier, J. (1997). Anger, ataques de nervios, and la mujer puertorriquena: Sociocultural considerations and treatment implications. In J. G. Garcia & M. C. Zea (Eds.), *Psychological interventions and research with Latino populations.* Boston, MA: Allyn & Bacon, Inc.

Robbins, T. W., & Everitt, B. J. (1998). Motivation and reward. In M. J. Zigmond, F. E. Bloom, S. C. Landis, J. L. Roberts, and L. R. Squire (Eds.), *Fundamental neuroscience.* New York: Academic Press, pp. 1245–1260.

Robbins, T. W., & Everitt, B. J. (1999b). Interaction of the dopaminergic system with mechanisms of associative learning and cognition: Implications for drug abuse. *Psychological Science, 10,* 199–202.

Roberts, A. H., Kewman, D. G., Mercier, L., & Hovell, M. (1993). The power of nonspecific effects in healing: implications for psychosocial and biological treatments. *Clinical Psychology Review, 13,* 375–391.

Roberts, B. W., & DelVecchio, W. F. (2000). The rank-order consistency of personality traits from childhood to old age: A quantitative review of longitudinal studies. *Psychological Bulletin, 126,* 3–25.

Roberts, B. W., Caspi, A., & Moffitt, T. E. (2001). The kids are alright: Growth and stability in personality development from adolescence to adulthood. *Journal of Personality & Social Psychology, 81,* 670–683.

Roberts, P., & Newton, P. M. (1987). Levinsonian studies of women's adult development. *Psychology and Aging, 2,* 154–163.

Robertson, L. C., & Delis, D. C. (1986). "Part-whole" processing in unilateral brain damaged patients: Dysfunction of hierarchical organization. *Neuropsychologia, 24,* 363–370.

Robertson, L. C., Lamb, M. R., & Knight, R. T. (1988). Effects of lesions of temporal-parietal junction on perceptual and attentional processing in humans. *Journal of Neuroscience, 8(10),* 3757–3769.

Robins, L. N., & Regier, D. A. (1991). *Psychiatric disorders in America: The epidemiological catchment area study.* New York: The Free Press.

Robinson, J. L., Kagan, J., Reznick, J. S., & Corley, R. (1992). The heritability of inhibited and uninhibited behavior: A twin study. *Developmental Psychology, 28,* 1030–1037.

Robinson, Linda C. (2000). Interpersonal relationship quality in young adulthood: A gender analysis. *Adolescence, 35,* 775–784.

Robinson, N. M., Abbott, R. D., Berninger, V. W., & Busse, J. (1996). The structure of abilities in math-precocious young children: Gender similarities and differences. *Journal of Educational Psychology, 88,* 341–352.

Robinson, N. M., Zigler, Z., & Gallagher, J. J. (2000). Two tails of the normal curve: Similarities and differences in the study of mental retardation and giftedness. *American Psychologist, 55,* 1413–1424.

Robinson, S. J., & Manning, J. T. (2000). The ratio of the 2nd to 4th digit length and male homosexuality. *Evolution and Human Behaviour, 21,* 333–345.

Robinson, T. E., & Berridge, K. C. (2001). Incentive-sensitization and addiction. *Addiction, 96,* 103–114.

Robinson, T. N., Wilde, M. L., Navracruz, L. C., Haydel, K. F., & Varady, A. (2001). Effects of reducing children's television and video game use on aggressive behavior: A randomized controlled trial. *Archives of Pediatric Adolescent Medicine, 155,* 17–23.

Robinson, V. (1977a). *Humor and the health professions.* Thorofare, NJ: Slack.

Robinson, V. (1977b). Humor in nursing. In C. Carlson & B. Blackwell (Eds.), *Behavioral concepts and nursing interventions.* Philadelphia: Lippincott.

Robinson-Whelen, S., Kim, C., MacCallum, R. C., & Kiecolt-Glaser, J. K. (1998). Distinguishing optimism from pessimism in older adults: Is it more important to be optimistic or not to be pessimistic? *Journal of Personality and Social Psychology, 73,* 1345–1353.

Rochat, P., & Hespos, S. J. (1997). Differential rooting response by neonates: Evidence for an early sense of self. *Early Development & Parenting, 6,* 105–112.

Rock, I. (1983). *The logic of perception.* Cambridge, MA: MIT Press.

Rock, I., & Ebenholtz, S. (1959). The relational determination of perceived size. *Psychological Review, 66,* 387–401.

Rodda, G. H. (1984). The orientation and navigation of juvenile alligators: Evidence of magnetic sensitivity. *Journal of Comparative Physiology, 154,* 649–658.

Rodier, P. (1980). Chronology of neuron development. *Developmental Medicine and Child Neurology, 22,* 525–545.

Rodin, J. (1981). Current status of the internal/external hypothesis for obesity: What went wrong? *American Psychologist, 36,* 361–372.

Rodin, J., & Langer, E. J. (1977). Long-term effects of a control-relevant intervention with the institutionalized aged. *Journal of Personality & Social Psychology, 35,* 897–902.

Rodriguez, V., Valdes-Sosa, M., & Freiwald, W. (2002). Dividing attention between form and motion during transparent surface perception. *Cognitive Brain Research, 13,* 187–193.

Roe, A. W., Pallas, S. L., Hahm, J. O., & Sur, M. (1990). A map of visual space induced in primary auditory cortex. *Science, 250,* 818–820.

Roediger, H. L., III (1980). Memory metaphors in cognitive psychology. *Memory & Cognition, 8,* 231–246.

Roediger, H. L., III, & McDermott, K. B. (1993). Implicit memory in normal human subjects. In F. Bohler & J. Grafman (Eds.), *Handbook of neuropsychology* (Vol. 8, pp. 63–131). Amsterdam: Elsevier.

Roediger, H. L., III, & McDermott, K. B. (1995). Creating false memories: Remembering words not presented in lists. *Journal of Experimental Psychology: Learning, Memory, and Cognition, 21,* 803–814.

Roediger, H. L., III, & Thorpe, L. A. (1978). The role of recall time in producing hypermnesia. *Memory & Cognition, 6,* 296–305.

Roediger, H. L., III, Meade, M. L., & Bergman, E. T. (2001). Social contagion of memory. *Psychonomic Bulletin & Review, 8,* 365–371.

Roggman, L. A., Langlois, J. H., Hubbs-Tait, L., & Rieser-Danner, L. A. (1994). Infant day-care, attachment, and the "file drawer problem." *Child Development, 65,* 1429–1443.

Rojas, I. G., Padgett, D. A., Sheridan, J. F., & Marucha, P. T. (2002). Stress-induced susceptibility to bacterial infection during cutaneous wound healing. *Brain, Behavior and Immunity, 16,* 74–84.

Roland, P. E., & Seitz, R. J. (1989). Mapping of learning and memory functions in the human brain. In D. Ottoson (Ed.), *Visualization of brain functions.* London: Stockton Press, pp. 141–151.

Roll, S., McClelland, G., Abel, T. (1996). Differences in susceptibility to influence in Mexican American and Anglo females. *Hispanic Journal of Behavioral Sciences, 18,* 13–20.

Rollman, G. B. (1987). The detectability, discriminability, and perceived magnitude of painful electrical shock. *Perception & Psychophysics, 42,* 257–268.

Rollman, G. B. (1991). Pain responsiveness. In M. A. Heller & W. Schiff (Eds.), *The psychology of touch* (pp. 91–114). Hillsdale, NJ: Erlbaum.

Rollman, G. B., & Harris, G. (1987). The detectability, discriminability, and perceived magnitude of painful electrical shock. *Perception & Psychophysics, 42,* 257–268.

Rolls, B. J., Rolls, E. T., Rowe, E. A., & Sweeney, K. (1981a). Sensory specific satiety in man. *Physiology & Behavior, 27,* 137–142.

Rolls, B. J., Rowe, E. A., Rolls, E. T., Kingston, B., Megson, A., & Gunary, R. (1981b). Variety in a meal enhances food intake in man. *Physiology & Behavior, 26,* 215–221.

Rolls, E. T. (1992). Neurophysiology and functions of the primate amygdala. In J. P. Aggleton (Ed.), *The amygdala: Neurobiological aspects of emotion, memory, and mental dysfunction* (pp. 143–165). New York: Wiley-Liss.

Rolls, E. T., & Cooper, S. J. (1974). Connection between the prefrontal cortex and pontine brain-stimulation reward sites in the rat. *Experimental Neurology, 42,* 687–699.

Romach, M. K., & Sellers, E. M. (1991). Management of the alcohol withdrawal syndrome. *Annual Review of Medicine, 42,* 323–340.

Romani, G. L., Williamson, S. J., & Kaufman, L. (1982). Tonotopic organization of the human auditory cortex. *Science, 216*, 1339–1340.

Romero, A. A., Agnew, C. R., & Insko, C. A. (1996). The cognitive mediation hypothesis revisited: An empirical response to methodological and theoretical criticism. *Personality & Social Psychology Bulletin, 22*, 651–665.

Romero, L., & Sapolsky, R. (1996). Patterns of ACTH secretagog secretion in response to psychological stimuli. *Journal of Neuroendocrinology, 8*, 243–258.

Rosch, E. (1973). Natural categories. *Cognitive Psychology, 4*, 328–350.

Rosch, E. (1975). The nature of mental codes for color categories. *Journal of Experimental Psychology: Human Perception and Performance, 1*, 303–322.

Rosch, E. (1978). Principles of categorization. In E. Rosch, & B. B. Lloyd (Ed.), *Cognition and categorization* (pp. 27–48). Hillsdale, NJ: Erlbaum.

Rosch, E., Mervis, C. B., Gray, W. D., Johnson, D. M., & Boyes-Braem, P. (1976). Basic objects in natural categories. *Cognitive Psychology, 8*, 382–439.

Rosen, A. C., Rao, S. M., Caffarra, P., Scaglioni, A., Bobholz, J. A., Woodley, S. J., Hammeke, T. A., Cunningham, J. M., Prieto, T. E., & Binder, J. R. (1999). Neural basis of endogenous and exogenous spatial orienting: A functional MRI study. *Journal of Cognitive Neuroscience, 11*, 135–152.

Rosen, C. M. (1987). The eerie world of reunited twins. *Discover, 8*, 36–46.

Rosenbaum, M., & Leibel, R. L. (1999). The role of leptin in human physiology. *New England Journal of Medicine, 341*, 913–915.

Rosenbaum, M. E. (1986). The repulsion hypothesis: On the nondevelopment of relationships. *Journal of Personality and Social Psychology, 51*, 1156–1166.

Rosenberg, M. (1979). *Conceiving the self.* New York: Basic Books.

Rosenfarb, I. S., Goldstein, M. J., Mintz, J., & Nuechterlein, K. H. (1995). Expressed emotion and subclinical observable within transactions between schizophrenia patients and their family members. *Journal of Abnormal Psychology, 104*, 259–267.

Rosenhan, D. L. (1973). On being sane in insane places. *Science, 179*, 250–258.

Rosenheim, M. K., & Testa, M. F. (Eds.) (1992). *Early parenthood and coming of age in the 1990s.* New Brunswick, NJ: Rutgers University Press.

Rosenthal, A. M. (1964). *Thiry-eight witnesses.* New York: McGraw-Hill.

Rosenthal, D. (1963). *The Genain quadruplets.* New York: Basic Books.

Rosenthal, R. (1976). *Experimenter effects in behavioral research.* New York: Irvington.

Rosenthal, R. (1986). Meta-analytic procedure and the nature of replication: The Ganzfeld debate. *Journal of Parapsychology, 50*, 316–336.

Rosenthal, R. (1991). *Meta-analytic procedures for social research.* Beverly Hills, CA: Sage.

Rosenthal, R. (1993) Interpersonl expectations: Some antecedents and some consequences. In P. D. Blanck (Ed.), *Interpersonal expectations: Theory, research, and applications* (pp. 3–24). Cambridge: Cambridge University Press.

Rosenthal, R. (1994). Interpersonal expectancy effects: A 30-year perspective. *Current Directions in Psychological Sciences, 3*, 176–179.

Rosenthal, R., & Jacobson, L. (1968). *Pygmalion in the classroom.* New York: Holt, Rinehart & Winston.

Roskill, M. (1963). *The letters of Vincent van Gogh.* London: William Collins.

Ross, C. A. (1991). Epidemiology of multiple personality disorder and dissociation. *Psychiatric Clinics of North America, 14*, 503–517.

Ross, C. A., Miller, S. D., Bjornson, L., Reagor, P., & Fraser, G. A. (1991). Abuse histories in 102 cases of multiple personality disorder. *Canadian Journal of Psychiatry, 36*, 97–101.

Ross, C. E. (1995). Reconceptualizing marital status as a continuum of social attachment. *Journal of Marriage & the Family, 57*, 129–140.

Ross, H. E., & Ross, G. M. (1976). Did Ptolemy understand the moon illusion? *Perception, 5*, 377–385.

Ross, L., Greene, D., & House, P. (1977). The false consensus effect: An egocentric bias in social perception and attribution processes. *Journal of Experimental Social Psychology, 13*, 279–301.

Rossi, E. L., & Cheek, D. B. (1988). *Mind-body therapy,* New York: Norton.

Rothbaum, B. O., Hodges, L., Anderson, P. L., Price, L., & Smith, S. (2002). Twelve-month follow-up of virtual reality and standard exposure therapies for the fear of flying. *Journal of Consulting & Clinical Psychology, 70*, 428–432.

Rothbaum, B. O., Hodges, L., Smith, S., Lee, J. H., & Price, L. (2001). A controlled study of virtual reality exposure therapy for the fear of flying. *Journal of Consulting & Clinical Psychology, 68*, 1020–1026.

Rothman, A. J., Salovey, P., Antone, C., Keough, K., & Martin, C. (1993). The influence of message framing on intentions to perform health behaviors. *Journal of Experimental Social Psychology, 29*, 408–433

Rotter, J. B. (1966). Generalized expectancies for internal versus extrnal control of reinforcement. *Psychological Monographs, 80* (1, Whole No. 609).

Rouhana, N. N., & Bar-Tal, D. (1998). Psychological dynamics of intractable ethnonational conflicts: The Israeli-Palestinian case. *American Psychologist, 53*, 761–770.

Rouillon, F. (1997). Epidemiology of panic disorder. *Human Psychopharmacology Clinical & Experimental, 12*(Suppl. 1), S7–S12.

Roux, A. V. D., Merkin, S. S., Arnett, D., Chambless, L. D., Massing, M., Nieto, F. J., Sorlie, P., Szklo, M., Tyroler, H. A., & Watson, R. L. (2001). Neighborhood of residence and incidence of coronary heart disease. *New England Journal of Medicine, 345*, 99–106.

Rovee-Collier, C. (1997). Dissociations in infant memory: Rethinking the development of implicit and explicit memory. *Psychological Review, 104*, 467–498.

Rowatt, W. C., Cunningham, M. R., & Druen, P. B. (1998). Deception to get a date. *Personality and Social Psychology Bulletin, 24*, 1228–1242.

Rowe, J. W., & Kahn, R. L. (1998). *Successful aging.* New York: Pantheon.

Roy, R., Benenson, J. F., & Lilly, F. (2000). Beyond intimacy: Conceptualizing sex differences in same-sex relationships. *Journal of Psychology, 134*, 93–101.

Roysamb, E., Harris, J. R., Magnus, P., Vitterso, J., & Tambs, K. (2002). Subjective well-being: Sex-specific effects of genetic and environmental factors. *Personality & Individual Differences, 32*, 211–223.

Rozin, P. (1982). "Taste-smell confusions" and the duality of the olfactory sense. *Perception and Psychophysics, 31*, 397–401.

Rozin, P. (1990). Getting to like the burn of chili pepper: Biological, psychological and cultural perspectives. In B. G. Green, J. R. Mason, & M. R. Kare (Eds.), *Chemical senses: Volume 2, Irritation* (pp. 231–269). New York: Marcel Dekker.

Rozin, P., & Fallon, A. (1986). The acquisition of likes and dislikes for foods. In National Research Council et al., *What is America eating?: Proceedings of a symposium.* Washington, DC: National Academy Press.

Rozin, P., & Jonides, J. (1977). Mass reaction time: Measurement of the speed of the nerve impulse and the duration of mental processes in class. *Teaching of Psychology, 4*, 91–94.

Rozin, P., Ashmore, M., & Markwith, M. (1996). Lay American conceptions of nutrition: Dose insensitivity, categorical thinking, contagion, and the monotonic mind. *Health Psychology, 15*, 438–447.

Rozin, P., Dow, S., Moscovitch, M., & Rajaram, S. (1998). What causes humans to begin and end a meal? A role for memory for what has been eaten, as evidenced by a study of multiple meal eating in amnesic patients. *Psychological Science, 9*, 392–396.

Rozin, P., Levine, E., & Stoess, C. (1991). Chocolate craving and linking. *Appetite, 17*, 199–212

Rozin, P., Lowery, L., & Ebert, R. (1994). Varieties of disgust faces and the structure of disgust. *Journal of Personality & Social Psychology, 66*, 870–881.

Rozin, P., Lowery, L., Imada, S., & Haidt, J. (1999). The CAD triad hypothesis: A mapping between three moral emotions (contempt, anger, disgust) and three moral codes (community, autonomy, divinity). *Journal of Personality & Social Psychology, 76*, 574–586.

Rozin, P., Millman, L., & Nemeroff, C. (1986). Operation of the laws of sympathetic magic in disgust and other domains. *Journal of Personality & Social Psychology, 50*, 703–712.

Rubin, L. J. (1996). Childhood sexual abuse: False accusations of "False memory"? *Professional Psychology Research and Practice, 27*, 447–451.

Rubin, Z. (1970). Measurement of romantic love. *Journal of Personality and Social Psychology, 16*, 265–273.

Rumelhart, D. E. (1975). Notes on schema for stories. In D. G. Bobrow & A. M. Collins (Eds.), *Representations and understanding: Studies in cognitive science* (pp. 211–236). New York: Academic Press.

Rumelhart, D. E., & McClelland, J. L. (1986). *Parallel distributed processing: Explorations in the microstructure of cognition: Volume 1, Foundations* (2nd ed.), Cambridge, MA: MIT Press.

Runco, M. A., & Albert, R. S. (1986). The threshold theory regarding creativity and intelligence: An empirical test with gifted and nongifted children. *Creative Child & Adult Quarterly, 11*, 212–218.

Rupniak, N. M. (2002). Elucidating the antidepressant actions of substance P (NK1 receptor) antagonists. *Current Opinion in Investigational Drugs 2002 Feb. 3(2)*, 257–261.

Rush, A. N., Robinette, B. L., & Stanton, M. E. (2001). Ontogenetic differences in the effects of unpaired stimulus preexposure on eyeblink conditioning in the rat. *Developmental Psychobiology, 39*, 8–18.

Rushton, J. P. (1975). Generosity in children: Immediate and long-term effects of modeling, preaching, and moral judgement. *Journal of Personality and Social Psychology, 31*, 459–466.

Rushton, J. P. (1980). *Altruism, socializaion and society.* Englewood Cliffs, NJ: Prentice Hall.

Rushton, J. P. (1995). *Race, evolution and behavior: A life-history perspective.* New Brunswick, NJ: Transaction.

Rushton, J. P., & Ankney, C. D. (1996). Brain size and cognitive ability: Correlations with age, sex, social class, and race. *Psychonomic Bulletin & Review, 3*, 21–36.

Rushton, J. P., Jackson, D. N., & Paunonen, S. V. (1981). Personality: Nomothetic or idiographic? A response to Kenrick and Stringfield. *Psychological Review, 88*, 582–589.

Russell, M. J. (1976). Human olfactory communication. *Nature, 260*, 520–522.

Russell, M. J., Switz, D. M., & Thompson, K. (1980). Olfactory influences on the human menstrual cycle. *Pharmacology, Biochemistry, & Behavior, 13*, 737–8.

Russo, J. E., & Schoemaker, P. J. H. (1989). *Decision traps.* New York: Doubleday.

Russo, J. E., & Schoemaker, P. J. H. (2002). *Winning decisions: Getting it right the first time.* New York: Doubleday.

Rustemli, A., Mertan, B., & Ciftci, O. (2000). In-group favoritism among native and immigrant Turkish cypriots: Trait evaluations of in-group and out-group targets. *Journal of Social Psychology, 140*, 26–34.

Rutter, M. (2002). Nature, nurture, and development: From evangelism through science toward policy and practice. *Child Development, 73*, 1–21.

Ruzyla-Smith, P, Barabasz, A., Barabasz, M., & Warner, D. (1995) Effects of hypnosis on the immune response: B cells, T cells, helper and suppressor cells. *American Journal of Clinical Hypnosis, 38*, 72–79.

Ryan, R. M., & Deci, E. L. (2000). Self-determination theory and the facilitation of intrinsic motivation, social development, and well-being. *American Psychologist, 55*, 68–78.

Rymer, R. (1993). *Genie: An abused child's flight from silence.* NY: HarperCollins.

Ryner, L. C., Goodwin, S. F., Castrillon, D. H., Anand, A., Villella, A., Baker, B. S., Hall, J. C., Taylor, B. J., & Wasserman, S. A. (1996). Control of male sexual behavior and sexual orientation in Drosophila by the fruitless gene. *Cell, 87,* 1079–1089.

Ryska, T. A. (1998). Cognitive-behavioral strategies and precompetitive anxiety among recreational athletes. *Psychological Record, 48,* 697–708.

Sabourin, M. E., Cutcomb, S. D., Crawford, H. J., & Pribram, K. (1990–1991). EEG correlates of hypnotic susceptibility and hypnotic trance: Spectral analysis and coherence. *International Journal of Psychophysiology, 10,* 125–142.

Sachdev, I., & Bourhis, R. Y. (1991). Power and status differentials in minority and majority relations. *European Journal of Social Psychology, 21,* 1–24.

Sachs, J. S. (1967). Recognition memory for syntactic and semantic aspects of connected discourse. *Perception and Psychophysics, 2,* 437–442.

Sackeim, H. A., Devanand, D. P., & Nobler, M. S. (1995). Electroconvulsive therapy. In F. E. Bloom & D. J. Kupfer (Eds.), *Psychopharmacology: The fourth generation of progress.* New York: Raven Press. pp. 1123–1141.

Sackeim, H. A., Haskett, R. F., Mulsant, B. H., Thase, M. E., Mann, J. J., Pettinati, H. M., Greenberg, R. M., Crowe, R. R., Cooper, T. B., & Prudic, J. (2001). Continuation pharmacotherapy in the prevention of relapse following electroconvulsive therapy: A randomized controlled trial. *Journal of the American Medical Association, 285,* 1299–1307.

Sackett, P. R. (1994). Integrity testing for personnel selection. *Current Directions in Psychological Science, 3,* 73–76.

Sackett, P. R., Schmitt, N., Ellingson, J. E., & Kabin, M. B. (2001). High-stakes testing in employment, credentialing, and higher education: Prospects in a post-affirmative-action world. *American Psychologist, 56,* 302–318.

Sacks, O. (1995). *An anthropologist on Mars: Seven paradoxical tales.* New York: Knopf.

Sadato, N., Pascual-Leone, A., Grafman, J., Ibanez, V., Deiber, M. P., Dold, G., & Hallett, M. (1996). Activation of the primary visual cortex by Braille reading in blind subjects. *Nature, 380,* 526–528.

Sadler, T. W. (1995). *Langman's medical embryology* (7th ed.). Baltimore: Williams & Wilkins.

Sadowski, C. J., & Guelgoez, S. (1996). Elaborative processing mediates the relationship between need for cognition and academic performance. *Journal of Psychology, 130,* 303–307.

Saffran, E. M., & Schwartz, M. F. Of Cabbages and things: Semantic memory from a neuropsychological perspective—a tutorial review. In D. Meyer & S. Cornblum (Eds.), *International symposium on attention and performance performance* XV (pp. 507–536). Cambridge, MA: MIT Press.

Saffran, J. R. (2001). Words in a sea of sounds: The output of infant statistical learning. *Cognition, 81,* 149–169.

Saffran, J. R., Aslin, R. N., & Newport, E. L. (1996). Statistical learning by 8-month-old infants. *Science, 274,* 1926–1928.

Saffran, J. R., & Griepentrog, G. J. (2001). Absolute pitch in infant auditory learning: Evidence for developmental reorganization. *Developmental Psychology, 37,* 74–85.

Saggino, A. (2000). The Big Three or the Big Five? A replication study. *Personality & Individual Differences, 28,* 879–886.

Sagie, A., Elizur, S., & Hirotsugu, Y. (1996). The structure and strength of achievement motivation: A cross-cultural comparison. *Journal of Organization Behavior, 17,* 431–444.

Sakai, N., Kobayakawa, T., Gotow, N., Saito, S., & Imada, S. (2001). Enhancement of sweetness ratings of aspartame by a vanilla odor presented either by orthonasal or retronasal routes. *Perceptual & Motor Skills, 92,* 1002–1008.

Saldana, H. N., & Rosenblum, L. D. (1993). Visual influences on auditory pluck and bow judgments. *Perception & Psychophysics, 54,* 406–416.

Salkovskis, P. M. (1985). Obsessional-compulsive problems: A cognitive-behavioral analysis. *Behaviour Research and Therapy, 23,* 571–583.

Sallis, J., Johnson, C., Treverow, T., Kaplan, R., & Hovell, M. (1987). The relationship between cynical hostility and blood pressure reactivity. *Journal of Psychosomatic Research, 31,* 111–116.

Salmon, C. A. (1998). The evocative nature of kin terminology in political rhetoric. *Politics and the Life Sciences 17,* 51–57.

Salmon, C. A. (1999). On the impact of sex and birth order on contact with kin. *Human Nature, 10,* 183–197.

Salmon, C. A., & Daly, M. (1998). Birth order and familial sentiment: middleborns are different. *Evolution and Behavior, 19,* 299–312.

Salmon, D. P., & Butters, N. (1995). Neurobiology of skill and habit learning. *Current Opinion in Neurobiology, 5,* 184–190.

Salovey, P., & Mayer, J. D. (1990). Emotional intelligence. *Imagination, Cognition, and Personality, 9,* 185–211.

Salthouse, T. A. (1984). Effects of age and skill in typing. *Journal of Experimental Psychology: General, 113,* 345–371.

Salthouse, T. A. (1985). Speed of behavior and its implications for cognition. In J. E. Birren & K. W. Schaie (Eds.), *Handbook of the psychology of aging* (2nd ed., pp. 400–426). New York: Van Nostrand Reinhold.

Salthouse, T. A. (1991a). Cognitive facets of aging well. *Generations, 15*(1), 35–38.

Salthouse, T. A. (1991b). *Theoretical perspectives on cognitive aging.* Hillsdale, NJ: Erlbaum.

Salthouse, T. A. (1996). The processing-speed theory of adult age differences in cognition. *Psychological Review, 103,* 403–428.

Salthouse, T. A., & Somberg, B. L. (1982). Skilled performance: Effects of adult age and experience on elementary processes. *Journal of Experimental Psychology: General, 111,* 176–207.

Sameroff, A. J., & Haith, M. M. (Eds.) (1996). *The five to seven year shift: The age of reason and responsibility.* Chicago, IL: University of Chicago Press.

Samoluk, S. B., & Stewart, S. H. (1998). Anxiety sensitivity and situation-specific drinking. *Journal of Anxiety Disorders, 12,* 407–419.

Sampaio, E., Maris, S., & Bach-y-Rita, P. (2001). Brain plasticity: 'Visual' acuity of blind persons via the tongue. *Brain Research, 908,* 204–207.

Sanbonmatsu, D. M., & Fazio, R. H. (1990). The role of attitudes in memory-based decision making. *Journal of Personality and Social Psychology, 59,* 614–622.

Sand, G., & Miyazaki, A. D. (2000). The impact of social support on salesperson burnout and burnout components. *Psychology & Marketing, 17,* 13–26.

Sandvik, E., Diener, E., & Larsen, R. J. (1985). The opponent process theory and affective reactions. *Motivation & Emotion, 9,* 407–418.

Sanna, L. J. (1996). Defensive pessimism, optimism, and simulating alternatives: Some ups and downs of prefactual and counterfactual thinking. *Journal of Personality and Social Psychology, 71,* 1020–1036.

Sanudo-Pena, M., Tsou, K., Romero, J., Mackie, K., & Walker, J. M. (2000). Role of the superior colliculus in the motor effects of cannabinoids and dopamine. *Brain Research, 853,* 207–214.

Sapolsky, R. M. (1992). *Stress, the aging brain, and the mechanisms of neuron death.* Cambridge, MA: MIT Press.

Sapolsky, R. M. (1996). Why stress is bad for your brain. *Science, 273,* 749–750.

Sapolsky, R. M. (1997). *Why zebras don't get ulcers.* New York: Freeman.

Sapp, D. D. (1992). The point of creative frustration and the creative process: A new look at an old model. *The Journal of Creative Behavior, 26,* 21–28.

Sarbin, T. R. (1995). On the belief that one body may be host to two or more personalities. *International Journal of Clinical & Experimental Hypnosis, 43,* 163–183.

Sarbin, T. R., & Coe, W. C. (1972). *Hypnosis: A social psychological analysis of influence communication.* New York: Holt, Rinehart, & Winston.

Sargent, J. D., Beach, M. L., Dalton, M. A., Mott, L. A., Tickle, J. J., Ahrens, M. B., & Heatherton, T. L. (2001). Effect of seeing tobacco use in films on trying smoking among adolescents: Cross sectional study. *British Medical Journal, 323,* 1394–1397.

Sargent, P. A., Sharpley, A. L., Williams, C., Goodall, E. M., & Cowen, P. J. (1997). 5-HT-sub(2C) receptor activation decreases appetite and body weight in obese subjects. *Psychopharmacology, 133,* 309–312.

Satcher, D. (1999). *Mental health: A report of the Surgeon General.* Washington, DC: Department of Health and Human Services.

Saudino, K. J., Gagne, J. R., Grant, J., Ibatoulina, A., Marytuina, T., Ravich-Scherbo, I., & Whitfield, K. (1999). Genetic and environmental influences on personality in adult Russian twins. *International Journal of Behavioral Development, 23,* 375–389.

Saudino, K. J., Pedersen, N. L., Lichtenstein, P., McClearn, G. E., & Plomin, R. (1997). Can personality explain genetic influences on life events? *Journal of Personality and Social Psychology, 72,* 196–206.

Savage-Rumbaugh, S., McDonald, K., Sevcik, R. A., Hopkins, W. D., & Rubert, E. (1986). Spontaneous symbol acquisition and communicative use by pygmy chimpanzees (Pan paniscus). *Journal of Experimental Psychology: General, 112,* 211–235.

Savazzi, S., & Marzi, C. A. (2002). Speeding up reaction time with invisible stimuli. *Current Biology, 12,* 403–407.

Saxe, G. B. (1988). Candy selling and math learning. *Educational Research. 17,* 14–21.

Saxena, S., & Rauch, S. L., (2000). Functional neuroimaging and the neuroanatomy of obsessive-compulsive disorder. *Psychiatric Clinics of North America, 23,* 563–586.

Scarmeas, N., Levy, G., Tang, M. -X., Manly, J., & Stern, Y. (2001). Influence of leisure activity on the incidence of Alzheimer's disease. *Neurology, 57,* 2236–2242.

Scarr, S. (1976). An evolutionary perspective on infant intelligence: Species patterns and individual variations. In M. Lewis (Ed.), *Origins of intelligence* (pp. 165–197). New York: Plenum.

Scarr, S. (1987). Personality and experience: Individual encounters with the world. In J. Aronoff, A. I. Rabin, and R. A. Zucker (Eds.), *The mergence of personality* (pp. 49–78). New York: Springer.

Scarr, S. (1997). Why child care has little impact on most children's development. *Current Directions in Psychological Science, 6*(5), 143–148.

Scarr, S. (1998). American child care today. *American Psychologist, 53*(2), 95–108.

Scarr, S., & McCartney, K. (1983). How people make their own environments: A theory of genotype-environment effects. *Child Development, 54,* 424–435.

Scarr, S., & Weinberg, R. A. (1983). The Minnesota Adoption Studies: Genetic differences and malleability. *Child Development, 54,* 260–267.

Schab, F. R. (Ed.), (1995). *Memory and odors.* Mahwah, NJ: Erlbaum.

Schacter, D. L. (1987). Implicit memory: History and current status. *Journal of Experimental Psychology: Learning, Memory, and Cognition, 13,* 501–518.

Schacter, D. L. (1996). *Searching for memory: The brain, the mind, and the past.* New York: Basic Books.

Schacter, D. L. (1999). The seven sins of memory: Insights from psychology and cognitive neuroscience. *American Psychologist, 54,* 182–203.

Schacter, D. L., & Badgaiyan, R. D. (2001). Neuroimaging of priming: New perspectives on implicit and explicit memory. *Current Directions in Psychological Science, 10,* 1–4.

Schacter, D. L., & Wagner, A. D. (1999). Medial temporal lobe activations in fMRI and PET studies of episodic encoding and retrieval. *Hippocampus, 9,* 7–24.

Schacter, D. L., Cendan, D. L., Dodson, C. S., & Clifford, E. R. (2001). Retrieval conditions and false recognition: Testing the distinctiveness heuristic. *Psychonomic Bulletin & Review, 8,* 827–833.

Schacter, D. L., Kaszniak, A. K., Kihlstrom, J. F., & Valdiserri, M. (1991). The relation between source memory and aging. *Psychology and Aging, 6,* 559–568.

Schacter, D. L., Koutstaal, W., & Norman, K. A. (1997). False memories and aging. *Trends in Cognitive Sciences, 1,* 229–236.

Schacter, D. L., Osowiecki, D., Kaszniak, A. W., Kihlstrom, J. F., & Valdiserri, M. (1994). Source memory: Extending the boundaries of age-related deficits. *Psychology and Aging, 9,* 81–89.

Schacter, D. L., Reiman, E., Curran, T., Yun, L. S., Bandy, D., McDermott, K. B., & Roediger, H. L., III (1996). Neuroanatomical correlates of veridical and illusory recognition memory: Evidence from positron emission tomography. *Neuron, 2,* 267–274.

Schachter, S. (1968). Obesity and eating. *Science, 16,* 751–756.

Schachter, S. (1971). Some extraordinary facts about obese humans and rats. *American Psychologist, 26,* 129–144.

Schachter, S., & Gross, L. P. (1968). Manipulated time and eating behavior. *Journal of Personality & Social Psychology, 10,* 98–106.

Schachter, S., & Latané, B. (1964). Crime, cognition, and the autonomic nervous system. In D. Levine (Ed.), *Nebraska Symposium on Motivation* (Vol. 12, pp. 221–273). Lincoln: University of Nebraska Press.

Schachter, S., & Singer, J. (1962). Cognitive, social and physiological determinants of emotional state. *Psychological Review, 69,* 379–399.

Schaefer, S. M., Jackson, D. C., Davidson, R. J., Aguirre, G. K., Kimberg, D. Y., & Thompson-Schill, S. L. (2002). Modulation of amygdalar activity by the conscious regulation of negative emotion. *Journal of Cognitive Neuroscience, 14,* 913–921.

Schaffner, K. F. (1967). Approaches to reduction. *Philosophy of Science, 34,* 137–147.

Schaie, K. W. (1983). The Seattle longitudinal study: A twenty-one-year exploration of psychometric intelligence in adulthood. In K. W. Schaie (Ed.), *Longitudinal studies of adult psychological development* (pp. 64–135). New York: Guilford.

Schaie, K. W. (1989). Individual differences in rate of cognitive change in adulthood. In V. L. Bengtson & K. W. Schaie (Eds.), *The course of later life: Research and reflections* (pp. 65–85). New York: Springer.

Schaie, K. W. (1990a). Intellectual development in adulthood. In J. E. Birren & K. W. Schaie (Eds.), *Handbook of the psychology of aging* (3rd ed., pp. 291–309). San Diego, CA: Academic Press.

Schaie, K. W. (1990b). The optimization of cognitive functioning in old age: Predictions based on cohort-sequential and longitudinal data. In P. B. Baltes & M. M. Baltes (Eds.), *Successful aging: Perspectives from the behavioral sciences* (pp. 94–117). Cambridge, England: Cambridge University Press.

Schaie, K. W., & Willis, S. L. (1993). Age difference patterns of psychometric intelligence in adulthood: Generalizability within and across ability domains. *Psychology and Aging, 8,* 44–55.

Schaller, M. (1994). The role of statistical reasoning in the formation, preservation and prevention of group stereotypes. *British Journal of Social Psychology, 33,* 47–61.

Schaller, M., Asp, C. H., Rosell, M. C., & Heim, S. J. (1996). Training in statistical reasoning inhibits the formation of erroneous group stereotypes. *Personality and Social Psychology Bulletin, 22,* 829–844.

Schank, R. C., & Abelson, R. P. (1977). *Scripts, plans, goals, and understanding.* Hillsdale, NJ: Erlbaum.

Scharf, B., & Houtsma, A. J. M. (1986). Audition II. In K. R. Boff, L. Kaufman, & J. P. Thomas (Eds.), *Handbook of perception and human performance* (pp. 15.1–15.60). New York: Wiley.

Scheflin, A., & Brown, D. (1996). Repressed memory or dissociative amnesia: What science says. *Journal of Psychiatry and Law, 24,* 143–188.

Scheier, M. F., & Carver, C. S. (1985). Optimism, coping, and health: Assessment and implications of generalized outcome expectancies. *Health Psychology, 4,* 219–247.

Scheier, M. F., & Carver, C. S. (1993). On the power of positive thinking: The benefits of being optimistic. *Current Directions in Psychology Science, 2,* 26–30.

Scheier, M. F., Matthews, K. A., Owens, J. F., Magovern, G. J., Lefebvre, R. C., Abbott, R. A., & Carver, C. S. (1989). Dispositional optimism and recovery from coronary artery bypass surgery: The beneficial effects on physical and psychological well-being. *Journal of Personality and Social Psychology, 57,* 1024–1040.

Scheier, M. F., Matthews, K. A., Owens, J. F., Schulz, R., Bridges, M. W., Magovern, G. J., & Carver, C. S. (1999). Optimism and rehospitalization after coronary artery bypass graft surgery. *Archives of Internal Medicine, 159,* 829–835.

Schellenberg, E. G., & Trehub, S. E. (1996). Natural musical intervals: Evidence from infant listeners. *Psychological Science, 7,* 272–277.

Schiavi, R. C., White, D., Mandeli, J., & Levine, A. C.(1997). Effect of testosterone administration on sexual behavior and mood in men with erectile dysfunction. *Archives of Sexual Behavior, 26,* 231–241

Schiffman, S. S. (1992). Aging and the sense of smell: Potential benefits of fragrance enhancement. In S. Van Toller & G. H. Dodd (Eds.). *Fragrance: The psychology and biology of perfume.* (pp. 51–62). London: Elsevier.

Schiffman, S. S., Graham, B. G., Sattely-Miller, E. A., & Warwick, Z. S. (1999). Orosensory perception of dietary fat. *Current Directions in Psychological Science, 7,* 137–143.

Schilder, P. (1938). Psychoanalytic remarks on Alice in Wonderland and Lewis Carroll. *Journal of Nervous & Mental Disease, 87,* 159–168.

Schizophrenia: Two roads to schizophrenia. (1996, September). *Harvard Mental Health Letter,* 1.

Schlaug, G., Jancke, L., Huang, Y., & Steinmetz, H. (1995). In vivo evidence of structural brain asymmetry in musicians. *Science, 267,* 699–701.

Schlegel, A., & Barry, H., III. (1991). *Adolescence: An anthropological inquiry.* New York: Free Press.

Schlenker, B. R. (1980). *Impression management: The self-concept, social identity, and interpersonal relations.* Belmont, CA: Brooks/Cole.

Schmidt, N. B., Lerew, D. R., & Jackson, R. J. (1997). The role of anxiety sensitivity in the pathogenesis of panic: Prospective evaluation of spontaneous panic attacks during acute stress. *Journal of Abnormal Psychology, 106,* 355–364.

Schmidt, N. B., Lerew, D. R., & Jackson, R. J. (1999). Prospective evaluation of anxiety sensitivity in the pathogenesis of panic: Replication and extension. *Journal of Abnormal Psychology, 108,* 532–537.

Schmidt, S. R. (2002). Outstanding memories: The positive and negative effects of nudes on memory. *Journal of Experimental Psychology: Learning, Memory, & Cognition, 28,* 353–361.

Schmitt, B. H., Gilovich, T., Goore, N., & Joseph, L. (1986). Mere presence and social facilitation: One more time. *Journal of Experimental Social Psychology, 22,* 242–248.

Schmolck, H., Buffalo, E. A., & Squire, L. R. (2000). Memory distortions develop over time: Recollections from the O. J. Simpson trial verdict after 15 and 32 months. *Psychological Science, 11,* 39–45.

Schneider, B. S., Goldstein, H. W., & Smith, D. B. (1996). The ASA framework: an update. *Personality Psychology, 48,* 747–773.

Schneider, B., Smith, D. B., Taylor, S., & Fleenor, J. (1998). Personality and organizations: A test of the homogeneity of personality hypothesis. *Journal of Applied Psychology, 83,* 462–470.

Schneider, L. H., Davis, J. D., Watson, C. A., & Smith, G. P. (1990). Similar effect of raclopride and reduced sucrose concentration on the microstructure of sucrose sham feeding. *European Journal of Pharmacology, 186,* 61–70.

Schneider, M., & Koch, M. (2002). The cannabinoid agonist WIN 55, 212-2 reduces sensorimotor gating and recognition memory in rats. *Behavioural Pharmacology, 13,* 29–37.

Schofield, P. E., Pattison, P. E., Hill, D. J., & Borland, R. (2001). The influence of group identification on the adoption of peer group smoking norms. *Psychology & Health, 16,* 1–16.

Scholnick, E. K. (1995, Fall). Knowing and constructing plans. *SRCD Newsletter,* pp. 1–2, 17.

Schrof, J. M., & Schultz, S. (1999). Melencholy nation. *U.S. News and World Report.* March 8, 126(9), p. 56–63.

Schul, R., Slotnick, B. M., & Dudai, Y. (1996). Flavor and the frontal cortex. *Behavioral Neuroscience, 110,* 760–765.

Schulberg, H. C., Magruder, K. M., & deGruy, F. (1996). Major depression in primary medical care practice: Research trends and future priorities. *General Hospital Psychiatry, 18,* 395–406.

Schulenberg, J., Wadsworth, K. N., O'Malley, P. M., Bachman, J. G., & Johnston, L. D. (1996). Adolescent risk factors for binge drinking during the transition to young adulthood: Variable- and pattern-centered approaches to change. *Developmental Psychology, 32,* 659–674.

Schultz, W. (1997). Dopamine neurons and their role in reward mechanisms. *Current Opinion in Neurobiology, 7,* 191–197.

Schultz, W., Dayan, P., & Montague, P. R. (1997). A neural substrate of prediction and reward. *Science, 275,* 1593–1599.

Schultz, W., Tremblay, W., & Hollerman, J. R. (2000). Reward processing in primate orbitofrontal cortex and basal ganglia. *Cerebral Cortex, 10,* 272–283.

Schwartz, B. (1984). *Psychology of learning and behavior* (2nd ed.) New York: Norton.

Schwartz, C. E., Snidman, N., & Kagan, J. (1996). Early childhood temperament as a determinant of externalizing behavior in adolescence. *Development & Psychopathology, 8,* 527–537.

Schwartz, D. L., & Black, T. (1999). Inferences through imagined actions: Knowing by simulated doing. *Journal of Experimental Psychology: Learning, Memory & Cognition, 25,* 116–136.

Schwartz, J. E., Neale, J., Marco, C., Shiffman, S. S., & Stone, A. A. (1999). Does trait coping exist? A momentary assessment approach to the evaluation of traits. *Journal of Personality and Social Psychology, 77,* 360–369.

Schwartz, J. M., Stoessel, P. W., Baxter, L. R., Martin, K. M., Phelps, M. E. (1996). Systematic changes in cerebral glucose metabolic rate after successful behavior modification treatment of obsessive-compulsive disorder. *Archives of General Psychiatry, 53,* 109–113.

Schwartz, N., & Bless, H. (1992). Constructing reality and its alternatives: An inclusion/exclusion model of assimilation and contrast effects in social judgment. In L. L. Martin & A. Tesser (Eds.), *The construction of social judgments* (pp. 217–245). Hillsdale, NJ: Erlbaum.

Schwartz, T. (1999, January 10). The test under stress. *New York Times Magazine,* pp. 30–63.

Schwartzwald, J., Amir, Y., & Crain, R. L. (1992). Long-term effects of school desegregation experiences on interpersonal relations in the Israeli defense forces. *Personality and Social Psychology Bulletin, 18,* 357–368.

Schwarz, N. (1999). Self-reports: How the questions shape the answers. *American Psychologist, 54,* 93–105.

Schyns, P. (1998). Crossnational differences in happiness: Economic and cultural factors explored. *Social Indicators Research, 43,* 3–26.

Sclafani, A. & Aravich, P. F. (1983). Macronutrient self-selection in three forms of hypothalamic obesity. *American Journal of Physiology, 244,* R686–R694.

Sclafani, A., Aravich, P. F., & Xenakis, S. (1983). Macronutrient preferences in hypothalamic hyperphagic rats. *Nutrition & Behavior, 1,* 233–251.

Scogin, F., Bynum, J., Stephens, G., & Calhoon, S. (1990). Efficacy of self-administered treatment programs: Meta-analytic review. *Professional Psychology: Research & Practice, 21,* 42–47.

Scott, B., & Melin, L. (1998). Psychometric properties and standardised data for questionnaires measuring negative affect, dispositional style and daily hassles: A nationwide sample. *Scandinavian Journal of Psychology*, 39, 301–307.

Scott, S. K., Young, A. W., Calder, A. J., Hellawell, D. J., Aggleton, J. P. & Johnson, M., (1997) Impaired auditory recognition of fear and anger following bilateral amygdala lesions. *Nature*, 385, 254–257.

Scott, T. R., & Plata-Salaman, C. R. (1991). Coding of taste quality. In T. V. Getchell, R. L. Doty, L. M. Bartoshuk, & J. B. Snow, Jr. (Eds.), *Smell and taste in health and disease* (pp. 345–368). New York: Raven.

Searle, J. R. (2000). Consciousness. *Annual Review of Neuroscience*, 23, 557–578.

Sears, R., Maccoby, E., & Levin, H. (1957). *Patterns of child rearing*. New York: Harper & Row.

Seay, B., Alexander, B. K., & Harlow, H. F. (1964). Maternal behavior of socially deprived rhesus monkeys. *Journal of Abnormal and Social Psychology*, 69, 345–354.

Sedikides, C., Gaertner, L., & Toguchi, Y. (2003). Pancultural self-enhancement. *Journal of Personality & Social Psychology*, 84, 60–79.

Seeman, R. E., Berkman, L. F., Blazer, D., & Rowe, J. W. (1994). Social ties and support and neuroendocrine function: The MacArthur studies of successful aging. *Annals of Behavioral Medicine*, 16, 95–106.

Segal, N. L. (1999). *Entwined lives: Twins and what they tell us about human behavior*. New York: Dutton/Penguin Books.

Segal, Z. V., Gemar, M., & Williams, S. (1999). Differential cognitive response to a mood challenge following successful cognitive therapy or pharmacotherapy for unipolar depression. *Journal of Abnormal Psychology*, 108, 3–10.

Seger, C. A., Desmond, J. E., Glover, G. H., & Gabrieli, J. D. E. (2000). Functional magnetic resonance imaging evidence for right-hemisphere involvement in processing unusual semantic relationships. *Neuropsychology*, 14, 361–369.

Segerstrom, S. C., Taylor, S. E., Kemeny, M. E., & Fahey, J. L. (1998). Optimism is associated with mood, coping, and immune change in response to stress. *Journal of Personality and Social Psychology*, 74, 1646–1655.

Segerstrom, S. C., Taylor, S. E., Kemeny, M. E., Reed, G. M., & Visscher, B. R. (1996). Causal attributions predict rate of immune decline in HIV-seropositive gay men. *Health Psychology*, 15, 485–493.

Segrin, C., & Abramson, L. Y. (1994). Negative reactions to depressive behaviors: A communication theory analysis. *Journal of Abnormal Psychology*, 103, 655–668.

Segrin, C., Dillard, J. P. (1992). The interactional theory of depression: A meta-analysis of the research literature. *Journal of Social & Clinical Psychology*, 11(1), 43–70.

Seith, R. (2000). Back sleeping may delay infant crawling. CWK Network, http://www.kidsmd.com/Tipsheets/21_may2301/crawling.html

Sekine, Y., Iyo, M., Ouchi, Y., Matsunaga, T., Tsukada, H., Okada, H., Yoshikawa, E., Futatsubashi, M., Takei, N., & Mori, N. (2001). Methamphetamine-related psychiatric symptoms and reduced brain dopamine transporters studied with PET. *American Journal of Psychiatry*, 158, 1206–1214.

Seligman, C., Fazio, R. H., & Zanna, M. P. (1980). Effects of salience of extrinsic rewards on liking and loving. *Journal of Personality and Social Psychology*, 38, 453–460.

Seligman, M. E. P. (1971). Phobias and preparedness. *Behavior Therapy*, 2, 307–320.

Seligman, M. E. P. (1995). The effectiveness of psychotherapy: The Consumer Reports study. *American Psychologist*, 50, 965–974.

Seltzer, J., & Numeroff, R. E. (1988). Supervisory leadership and subordinate burnout. *Academy of Management Journal*, 31, 439–446.

Selye, H. (1976). *The stress of life*. New York: McGraw Hill.

Semenov, L. A., Chernova, N. D., & Bondarko, V. M. (2000). Measurement of visual acuity and crowding effect in 3–9-year-old children. *Human Physiology*, 26, 16–20.

Sensky, T., Turkington, D., Kingdon, D., Scott, J. L., Scott, J., Siddle, R., O'Carroll, M., & Barnes, T. R. E. (2000). A randomized controlled trial of cognitive-behavioral therapy for persistent symptoms in schizophrenia resistant to medication. *Archives of General Psychiatry*, 57, 165–172.

Seppa, N. (1996). What qualities make a good president? *APA Monitor*, 27 (11), p. 1.

Sereny, G., Sharma, V., Holt, J., and Gordis, E. (1986). Mandatory supervised Antabuse therapy in an outpatient alcoholism program: A pilot study. *Alcoholism* (NY), 10, 290–292.

Sergent, J., & Hellige, J. B. (1986). Role of input factors in visual-field asymmetries. *Brain and Cognition*, 5, 174–199.

Serpell, R. (1979). How specific are perceptual skills? A cross-cultural study of pattern reproduction. *British Journal of Psychology*, 70, 365–380.

Seta, J. J., & Seta, C. E. (1992). Increments and decrements in mean arterial pressure as a function of audience composition: An averaging and summation analysis. *Personality and Social Psychology Bulletin*, 18, 173–181.

Setliff, A. E., & Marrnurek, H. H. C. (2002). The mood regulatory function of autobiographical recall is moderated by self-esteem. *Personality and Individual Differences*, 32, 761–771.

Settersten, R. A., Jr. (1998). A time to leave home and a time never to return? Age constraints on the living arrangements of young adults. *Social Forces*, 76, 1373–1400.

Seuling, B. (1975). *You can't eat peanuts in church and other little-known laws*. New York: Doubleday.

Seuling, B. (1976). *The loudest screen kiss and other little-known facts about the movies*. New York: Doubleday.

Seuling, B. (1978). *The last cow on the White House lawn and other little-known facts about the Presidency*. New York: Doubleday.

Seuling, B. (1982). *You can't show kids in underwear and other little-known fact about television*. New York: Doubleday and Co., Inc.

Seuling, B. (1986). *You can't sneeze with your eyes open and other freaky facts about the human body*. New York: Ballantine Books.

Seuling, B. (1988). *It is illegal to quack like a duck and other freaky laws*. New York: Dutton.

Seuling, B. (1991). *The man in the moon is upside down in Argentina and other freaky facts about geography*. New York: Ballantine Books.

Shadish, W. R., Matt, G. E., Navarro, A. M., Siegle, G., Crits-Cristophe, P., Hazelrigg, M. D., Jorm, A. F., Lyons, L. C., Nietzel, M. T., Robinson, L., Prout, H. T., Smith, M. L., Svartberg, M., & Weiss, B. (1997). Evidence that therapy works in clincally representative conditions. *Journal of Consulting & Clinical Psychology*, 65, 355–365.

Shafir, E., & Tversky, A. (1995). Decision making. In E. E. Smith & D. N. Osherson (Eds.), *An invitation to cognitive science: Thinking* (pp. 77–100). Cambridge, MA: MIT Press.

Shafran, R., Thordarson, D. S., & Rachman, S. (1996). Thought-action fusion in obsessive compulsive disorder. *Journal of Anxiety Disorders*, 10, 379–391.

Shalev, A. Y., Peri, T., Brandes, D., Freedman, S., Orr, S. P., & Pitman, R. K. (2000). Auditory startle response in trauma survivors with posttraumatic stress disorder: A prospective study. *American Journal of Psychiatry*, 157, 255–261.

Shalev, A. Y., Sahar, T., Freedman, S., Peri, T., Glick, N., Brandes, D., Orr, S. P., & Pitman, R. K. (1998). A prospective study of heart rate response following trauma and the subsequent development of posttraumatic stress disorder. *Archives of General Psychiatry*, 55, 553–559.

Shallenberger, R. S. (1993). *Taste chemistry*. New York: Blackie Academic.

Shallice, T. (Vol. Ed.). (1988). *From neuropsychology to mental structure* (2nd ed.). Cambridge: Cambridge University Press.

Shallice, T., & Warrington, E. K. (1980). Single and multiple component central dyslexic syndromes. In M. Coltheart, K. E. Patterson, & J. C. Marshall (Eds.), *Deep dyslexia* (pp. 119–145). London: Routledge.

Shallice, T., Fletcher, P., Frith, C. D., Grasby, P., Frackowiak, R. S. J., & Dolan, R. J. (1994). Brain regions associated with acquisition and retrieval of verbal episodic memory. *Nature*, 368, 633–635.

Shanab, M. E., & Yahya, K. A. (1977). A behavioral study of obedience in children. *Journal of Personality and Social Psychology*, 35, 530–536.

Shapira, B., Tubi, N., Drexler, H., Lidsky, D., Calev, A., & Lerer, B. (1998). Cost and benefit in the choice of ECT schedule: Twice versus three times weekly ECT. *British Journal of Psychiatry*, 172, 44–48.

Shapiro, A. K. (1964). Factors cfontributing to the placebo effect: Their significance for psychotherapy. *American Journal of Psychotherapy*, 18, 73–88.

Shapiro, A. K., & Morris, L. A. (1978). The placebo effect in medical and psychological therapies. In S. L. Garfield & A. E. Bergin (Eds.), *Handbook of psychotherapy and behavior change: An empirical analysis* (2nd ed.). New York: Wiley.

Shapiro, D. A., & Shapiro, D. (1982). Meta-analysis of comparative therapy outcome studies: A replication and refinement. *Psychological Bulletin*, 92, 581–604.

Shapiro, D. H. (1982). Overview: Clinical and physiological comparison of meditation with other self-control strategies. *American Journal of Psychiatry*, 139, 267–274.

Shapiro, D. H. Jr., Schwartz, C. E., & Astin, J. A. (1996). Controlling ourselves, controlling our world: Psychology's role in understandinf positive and negative consequences of seeking and gaining control. *American Psychologist*, 51, 1213–1230.

Shapley, R., Kaplan, E., & Purpura, K. (1993). Contrast sensitivity and light adaptation in photoreceptors or in the retinal network. In R. Shapley & D. M.-K. Lam (Eds.), *Contrast sensitivity: Proceedings of the Retina Research Foundation Symposia* (pp. 103–116). Cambridge, MA: MIT Press.

Sharfstein, S. S., Muszynski, S., & Myers, E. S. (1984) *Health insurance and psychiatric care: Update and apraisal*. Washinton, DC: American Psychiatric Press.

Shaver, P. R., & Hazan, C. (1994). A. L. Weber & J. H. Harvey (Eds.), Attachment. In *Perspectives on close relationships*. Boston: Allyn & Bacon.

Shaw, J. B., & Riskind, J. H. (1981 or 1983). Predicting job stress using data from the position analysis questionnaire. *Journal of Applied Psychology*, 68, 253–261.

Shaw, P. J., Bergmann, B. M., & Rechtschaffen, A. (1998). Effects of paradoxical sleep deprivation on thermoregulation in the rat. *Sleep*, 21, p. 7–17.

Shaywitz, B. A., Shaywitz, S. E., Pugh, K. R., Constable, R. T., Skudlarski, P., Fulbright, R. K., Bronen, R. A., Fletcher, J. M., Shankweller, D. P., Katz, L., & Gore, J. C. (1995). Sex differences in the functional organization of the brain for language. *Nature*, 373, 607–611.

Shea, J. D., Burton, R., & Girgis, A. (1993). Negative affect, absorption, and immunity. *Physiological Behavior*, 53, 449–457.

Shea, M. T., Elikin, I., Imber, S. D., Sotsky, S. M., Watkins, J. T., Collins, J. F., Pilkonis, P. A., Beckham, E., Glass, D. R., Dolan, R. T., & Parloff, M. B. (1992). Course of depressive symptoms over follow-up: Findings from the National Institute of Mental Health Treatment of Depression Collaborative Research Program. *Archives of General Psychiatry*, 49, 782–787.

Sheehan, P. W. (1988). Memory distortion in hypnosis. *International Journal of Clinical Experimental Hypnosis*, 36, 296–311.

Sheen, M., Kemp, S., & Rubin, D. (2001). Twins dispute memory ownership: A new false memory phenomenon. *Memory & Cognition*, 29, 779–788.

Shekelle, R., Raynor, W., Ostfeltd, A., Garron, D., Bieliauskas, L., Liu, S., Maliza, C., & Paul, O. (1981). Psychological depression and 17-year risk of death from cancer. *Psychosomatic Medicine*, 43, 177–?

Shekim, W. O., Bylund, D. B., Frankel, F., Alexson, J., Jones S. B., Blue, L. D., Kirby, J., & Corchoran, C. (1989). Platelet MAO activity and personality variations in normals. *Psychiatry Research*, 27, 81–88.

Sheldon, K. M., Ryan, R., & Reis, H. T. (1996). What makes for a good day? Competence and autonomy in the day and in the person. *Personality & Social Psychology Bulletin*, 22, 1270–1279.

Shelton, J. R., & Caramazza, A. (1999). Deficits in lexical and semantic processing: Implications for models of normal language. *Psychonomic Bulletin & Review, 6*, 5–27.

Shepard, R. N. (1967). Recognition memory for words, sentences and pictures. *Journal of Verbal learning and Verbal Behavior, 6*, 156–163.

Shepard, R. N., & Cooper, L. A. (1982). *Mental images and their transformations.* Cambridge, MA: MIT Press/Bradford Books.

Shepard, R. N., & Metzler, J. (1971). Mental rotation of three-dimensional objects. *Science, 171*, 701–703.

Shepherd, G. M. (1999). Information processing in dendrites. In M. J. Zigmond, F. E. Bloom, S. C. Landis, J. L. Roberts, & L. R. Squire (Eds.), *Fundamental neuroscience* (pp. 363–388). New York: Academic Press.

Shepherd, M. D., Schoenberg, M., Slavich, S., Wituk, S., Warren, M., & Meissen, G. (1999). Continuum of professional involvement in self-help groups. *Journal of Community Psychology, 27,* 39–53.

Sherif, M. (1966). *Group conflict and co-operation: Tgheir social psychology.* London: Routledge & Kegen Paul.

Sherif, M., & Sherif, C. W. (1953). *Groups in harmony and tension: An integration of studies on intergroup relations.* New York: Octagon.

Sherif, M., Harvey, O. J., White, B. J., Hood, W. R., & Sherif, C. W. (1961). *Intergroup conflict and cooperation: The robber's cave experiment.* Norman, OK: The University Book Exchange.

Sherman, J. J. (1998). Effects of psychotherapeutic treatments for PTSD: A meta-analysis of controlled clinical trials. *Journal of Traumatic Stress, 11*, 413–435.

Sherman, S. S. (1980). On the self-erasing nature of errors of prediction. *Journal of Personality and Social Psychology, 16*, 388–403.

Shibahara, H., Shigeta, M., Toji, H., & Koyama, K. (1995). Sperm immobilizing antibodies interfere with sperm migration from the uterine cavity through the fallopian tubes. *American Journal of Reproductive Immunology, 34*, 120–124.

Shidara, M., & Richmond, B. J. (2002). Anterior cingulate: Single neuronal signals related to degree of reward expectancy. *Science, 296*, 1709–1711.

Shields, S. A. (1987). Women, men, and the dilemma of emotion. In P. Shaver & C. Hendrick (Eds.), *Sex and gender* (pp. 229–250). Newbury Park, Calif.: Sage.

Shiffrin, R. M. (1999). 30 years of memory. In C. Izawa (Ed.), *On human memory: Evolution, progress, and reflections on the 30th anniversary of the Atkinson-Shiffrin model* (pp. 17–33). Hillsdale, NJ: Erlbaum.

Shin, L. M., Kosslyn, S. M., McNally, R. J., Alpert, N. M., Thompson, W. L., Raush, S. L., Macklin, M. L., & Pitman, R. K. (1997). Visual imagery and perception in posttraumatic stress disorder: A positron emission tomographic investigation. *Archives of General Psychiatry, 54*, 233–241.

Shioiri, S., Cavanagh, P., Miyamoto, T., & Yaguchi, H. (2000). Tracking the apparent location of targets in interpolated motion. *Vision Research, 40*, 1365–1376.

Shiraishi, T., Oomura, Y., Sasaki, K., & Wayner, M. J. (2000). Effects of leptin and orexin-A on food intake and feeding related hypothalamic neurons. *Physiology & Behavior, 71*, 251–261.

Shortridge, J. R. (1993). The Great Plains. In M. K. Cayton, E. J. Gorn, & P. W. Williams (Eds.), *Encyclopedia of American Social History* (Vol. 2, pp. 1001–1015). New York: Scribner.

Shouksmith, G., & Taylor, J. E. (1997). The interaction of culture with general job stressors in air traffic controllers. *International Journal of Aviation Psychology, 7*, 343–352.

Shulman, S., Elicker, J., & Sroufe, L. A. (1994). Stages of friendship growth in preadolescence as related to attachment history. *Journal of Social & Personal Relationships, 11*, 341–361.

Shweder, R. A., Much, N. C., Mahapatra, M. & Park, L. (1997). The "big three" of morality (autonomy, community, divinity) and the "big three" explanations of suffering. In A. M. Brandt & P. Rozin (Eds.), *Morality and health* (pp. 119–169). New York: Routledge.

Siegel, J. L., & Longo, D. L. (1981). The control of chemotherapy induced emesis. *Annals of Internal Medicine, 95*, 352–359.

Siegel, M., Brisman, J., & Weinshel, M. (1988). *Surviving an eating disorder: Strategies for family and friends.* New York: Harper and Row.

Siegel, S. (1988). State dependent learning and morphine tolerance. *Behavioral Neuroscience, 102*, 228–232.

Siegel, S., Baptista, M. A. S., Kim, J. A., McDonald, R. V., & Weise-Kelly, L. (2000). Pavlovian psychopharmacology: The associative basis of tolerance. *Experimental & Clinical Psychopharmacology, 8*, 276–293.

Siegel, S., Hinson, R. E., Krank, M. D., & McCully, J. (1982). Heroin "overdoes" death: Contribution of drug-associated environmental cues. *Science, 216*, 436–437.

Siegler, R. S. (1989). Mechanisms of cognitive development. *Annual Review of Psychology, 40*, 353–379.

Siegler, R. S. (1996). *Emerging minds. The process of change in children's thinking.* New York: Oxford University Press.

Siegler, R. S., & Svetina, M. (2002). A microgenetic/cross-sectional study of matrix completion: Comparing short-term and long-term change. *Child Development, 73*, 793–809.

Sifneos, P. E. (1992). *Short-term anxiety-provoking psychotherapy: A treatment manual.* New York: Basicbooks, Inc.

Silverman, L. (1976). Psychoanalytic theory: The reports of my death are greatly exaggerated. *American Psychologist, 31*, 621–637.

Silverman, L. K. (1993a). Counseling families. In L. K. Silverman (Ed.), *Counseling the gifted and talented* (pp. 43–89). Denver: Love.

Silverman, L. K. (1993b). A developmental model for counseling the gifted. In L. K. Silverman (Ed.), *Counseling the gifted and talented* (pp. 51–78). Denver: Love.

Silvia, P. J. (2002). Self-awareness and emotional intensity. *Cognition & Emotion, 16*, 195–216.

Simcock, G., & Hayne, H. (2002). Breaking the barrier? Children fail to translate their preverbal memories into language. *Psychological Science, 13*, 225–231.

Simmons, J. A., & Chen, L. (1989). The acoustic basis for target discrimination by FM echolocating bats. *Journal of the Acoustical Society of America, 86*, 1333–1350.

Simon, H. A., & Chase, W. G. (1973). Skill in chess. *American Scientist, 61*, 394–403.

Simon, L., Greenberg, J., & Brehm, J. (1995). Trivialization: The forgotten mode of dissonance reduction. *Journal of Personality and Social Psychology, 68*, 247–260.

Simons, D. J. (1999). Current approaches to change blindness. *Visual Cognition, 7*, 1–15.

Simons, D. J., & Levin, D. T. (1997). Change blindness. *Trends in Cognitive Sciences, 1*, 261–267.

Simonton, D. K. (1984). *Genius, creativity, and leadership: Historiometric inquiries.* Cambridge, MA: Harvard University Press.

Simonton, D. K. (1988). Creativity, leadership, and chance. In R. J. Sternberg (Ed.), *The nature of creativity* (pp. 386–436). New York: Cambridge University Press.

Simonton, D. K. (1990). Political pathology and societal creativity. *Creativity Research Journal, 3*, 85–99.

Simonton, D. K. (1994). *Greatness: Who makes history and why.* New York: Guilford.

Simonton, D. K. (1995). Foresight in insight? A Darwinian answer. In R. J. Sternberg & J. E. Davidson (Eds.), *The nature of insight* (pp. 465–494). Cambridge, MA: MIT Press.

Simonton, D. K. (1997). Creative productivity: A predictive and explanatory model of career trajectories and landmarks. *Psychological Review, 104*, 66–89.

Simpson, M. (1996). Suicide and religion. *American Sociological Review, 63*, pp. 895–896.

Singer, L. T., Arendt, R., Minnes, S., Farkas, K., Salvator, A., Kirchner, H. L., & Kliegman, R. (2002b) Cognitive and motor outcomes of cocaine-exposed infants. *JAMA: Journal of the American Medical Association, 287*, 1952–1960.

Singer, L. T., Salvator, A., Arendt, R., Minnes, S., Farkas, K., & Kliegman, R. (2002a). Effects of cocaine/polydrug exposure and maternal psychological distress on infant birth outcomes. *Neurotoxicology & Teratology, 24*, 127–135.

Singer, W. (1998). Consciousness and the structure of neuronal representation. *Philosophical Transactions of the Royal Society B, 353*, 1829–1840.

Singh, D., Meyer, W., Zambarano, R. J., & Hurlbert, D. F. (1998). Frequency and timing of coital orgasm in women desirous of becoming pregnant. *Archives of Sexual Behavior, 27*, 15–29.

Singh, V. N. (1995). Human uterine amylase in relation to infertility. *Hormone and Metabolic Research, 27*, 35–36.

Sinha, B. K., Willson, L. R., & Watson, D. C. (2000). Stress and coping among students in India and Canada. *Canadian Journal of Behavioral Sciences, 32*, 218–225.

Siomi, M. C., Zhang, Y., Siomi, H., & Dreyfuss, G. (1996). Specific sequences in the fragile X syndrome protein FMR1 and the FXR proteins mediate their binding to 60S ribosomal subunits and the interactions among them. *Molecular and Cellular Biology, 16*, 3825–3832.

Sireteanu, R. (2000). Texture segmentation, "pop-out," and feature binding in infants and children. In C. Rovee-Collier & L. P. Lipsitt (Eds.), *Progress in infancy research* (Vol. 1, pp. 183–249). Mahwah, NJ: Erlbaum.

Skinner, B. F. (1938). *The behavior of organisms: An experimental analysis.* New York: Appleton-Century.

Skinner, B. F. (1953). *Science and human behavior.* New York: MacMillan.

Skinner, B. F. (1956). A case history in scientific method. *American Psychologist, 11*, 221–233.

Skinner, B. F. (1961, November). Teaching Machines. *Scientific American*, 91–102.

Skinner, B. F. (1983). Can the experimental analysis of behavior rescue psychology? *Behavior Analyst, 6*, 9–17.

Skinner, B. F. (1989). Teaching machines. *Science, 243*, 1535.

Skuder, P., Plomin, R., McClearn, G. E., Smith, D. L., Vignetti, S., Chorney, M. J., Chorney, K., Kasarda, S., Thompson, L. A., Detterman, D., Petrill, S. A., Daniels, J., Owen, M. J., & McGuffin, P. (1995). A polymorphism in mitochondrial DNA associated with IQ? *Intelligence, 21*, 1–11.

Skvoretz, J. (1988). Models of participation in status-differentiated groups,. *Social Psychology Quarterly, 51*, 43–57.

Slater, A., Brown, E., & Badenoch, M. (1997). Intermodal perception at birth: Newborn infants' memory for arbitrary auditory-visual pairings. *Early Development & Parenting, 6*, 99–104.

Sleek, S. (1997, November). Online therapy services raise ethical questions. *APA Monitor*, p. 1, 38.

Slep, A. M. S., & O'Leary, S. G. (1998). The effects of maternal attributions on parenting: An experimental analysis. *Journal of Family Psychology, 12*, 234–243.

Slimp, J. C., Hart, B. L., & Goy, R. W. (1978). Heterosexual, autosexual and social behavior of adult male rhesus monkeys with medial preoptic-anterior hypothalamic lesions. *Brain Research, 142*, 105–122.

Slob, A. K., Bax, C. M., Hop, W. C. J., Rowland, D. L., & van der Werff ten Bosch, J. J. (1996). Sexual arousability and the menstrual cycle. *Psychoneuroendocrinology, 21*, 545–558.

Slotnick, S. D., Moo, L. R., Tesoro, M. A., & Hart, J. (2001). Hemispheric asymmetry in categorical versus coordinate spatial processing revealed by temporary cortical deactivation. *Journal of Cognitive Neuroscience, 13*, 1088–1096.

Small, B. J., & Bäckman, L. (2000). Time to death and cognitive performance. *Current Directions in Psychological Science, 6*, 168–172.

Small, D. M., Zatorre, R. J., Dagher, A., Evans, A. C., & Jones-Gotman, M. (2001). Changes in brain activity related to eating chocolate: From pleasure to aversion. *Brain, 124,* 1720–1733.

Smeets, M. A. M., Smit, F., Panhuysen, G. E. M., & Ingleby, J. D. (1997). The influence of methodological differences on the outcome of body size estimation studies in anorexia nervosa. *British Journal of Clinical Psychology, 36,* 263–277.

Smith, D. (1982). Trends in counseling and psychotherapy. *American Psychologist, 37,* 802–809.

Smith, D. E., Roberts, J., Gage, F. H., & Tuszynski, M. H. (1999). Age-associated neuronal atrophy occurs in the primate brain and is reversible by growth factor gene therapy. *Proceedings of the National Academy of Sciences U.S.A., 96,* 10893–10898.

Smith, D. V., & Frank, M. E. (1993). Sensory coding by peripheral taste fibers. In S. A. Simon & S. D. Roper (Eds.), *Mechanisms of taste transduction* (pp. 295–338). Boca Raton, FL: CRC Press.

Smith, E. E. (1988). Concepts and thought. In R. J. Sternberg & E. E. Smith (Eds.), *The psychology of human thought* (pp. 19–49). New York: Cambridge University Press.

Smith, E. E. (2000). Neural bases of human working memory. *Current Directions in Psychological Science, 9,* 45–49.

Smith, E. E., & Jonides, J. (1997). Working memory: A view from neuroimaging. *Cognitive Psychology, 33,* 5–42.

Smith, E. E., & Jonides, J. (1999). Storage and executive processes in the frontal lobes. *Science, 283,* 1657–1661.

Smith, E. E., & Medin, D. L. (1981). *Categories and concepts.* Cambridge, MA: Harvard University Press.

Smith, E. E., Jonides, J., & Koeppe, R. A. (1996). Dissociating verbal and spatial working memory using PET. *Cerebral Cortex, 6,* 11–20.

Smith, E. E., Patalano, A. L., & Jonides, J. (1998). Alternative strategies of categorization. *Cognition, 65,* 167–196.

Smith, E. R. (1998). Mental Representation and memory. In D. T. Gilbert, S. T. Fiske, & G. Lindzey (Eds.), *The handbook of social psychology* (4th ed.) (Vol. 1, pp. 391–445). New York: McGraw Hill.

Smith, G. E. (1996). Framing in advertising and the moderating impact of consumer education. *Journal of Advertising Research. 36,* 49–64.

Smith, J. T., Barabasz, A., & Barabasz, M. (1996) Comparison of hypnosis and distraction in severely ill children undergoing painful medical procedures. *Journal of Counseling Psychology, 43,* 187–195.

Smith, M. E. (1993). Television violence and behavior: a research summary. ERIC Digest. Syracuse, NY: Educational Resources Information Center Clearinghouse on Information and Technology. ED 366 329.

Smith, M. L., & Glass, G. V. (1977). Meta-analysis of psychotherapy outcome studies. *American Psychologist, 32,* 752–760.

Smith, R. E., Leffingwell, T. R., & Ptacek, J. T. (1999). Can people remember how they coped? Factors associated with discordance between same-day and retrospective reports. *Journal of Personality and Social Psychology, 76,* 1050–1061.

Smith, S. M. (1988). In G. M. Davies, & D. M. Thompson (Eds.), *Memory in context: Context in memory* (pp. 13–34). Chichester, UK: Wiley.

Smith, S. M., & Blankenship, S. E. (1989). Incubation effects. *Bulletin of the Psychonomic Society, 27,* 311–314.

Smith, S. M., & Blankenship, S. E. (1991). Incubation and the persistence of fixation in problem solving. *American Journal of Psychology, 104,* 61–87.

Smith, S. M., & Levin, I. P. (1996). Need for cognition and choice framing effects. *Journal of Behavioral Decision Making, 9,* 283–290.

Smith, S. M., & Shaffer, D. R. (1991). Celerity and cajolery: Rapid speech may promote or inhibit persuasion through its impact on message elaboration. *Personality and Social Psychology Bulletin, 17,* 663–669.

Smith, S. M., & Vela, E. (2001). Environmental context-dependent memory: A review and meta-analysis. *Psychonomic Bulletin & Review, 8,* 203–220.

Smith, T. W., & Ruiz, J. M. (2002). Psychosocial influences on the development and course of coronary heart disease: Current status and implications for research and practice. *Journal of Consulting & Clinical Psychology, 70,* 548–568.

Smolucha, F. C. (1992). A reconstruction of Vygotsky's theory of creativity. *Creativity Research Journal, 5,* 49–67.

Smyth, J. M., Stone, A. A., Hurewitz, A., & Kaell, A. (1999). Effects of writing about stressful experiences on symptom reduction in patietns with asthma or rheumatoid arthritis. *Journal of the American Medical Association, 281,* 1304–1329.

Snidman, N., Kagan, J, Riordan, L., & Shannon, D. C. (1995). Cardiac function and behavioral reactivity during infancy. *Psychophysiology, 32,* 199–207.

Snodgrass, S. E. (1985). Women's intuition: The effect of subordinate roel on interpersonal sensitivity. *Journal of Personality and Social Psychology, 49,* 146–155.

Snow, C. E. (1991). The language of the mother–child relationship. In M. Woodhead & R. Carr (Eds.), *Becoming a person* (pp. 195–210). London: Routledge.

Snow, C. E. (1999). Social perspectives on the emergence of language. In B. MacWhinney (Ed.), *The emergence of language* (pp. 257–276). Mahwah, NJ: Erlbaum.

Snow, C. E. (2002). Second language learners' contributions to our understanding of languages of the brain. In A. M. Galaburda, S. M. Kosslyn, & Y. Christen (Eds.), *Languages of the brain.* (pp. 151–165) Cambridge, MA: Harvard University Press.

Snow, R., & Yalow, R. (1982). Education and intelligence. In R. J. Sternberg (Ed.), *Handbook of human intelligence* (pp. 493–585). New York: Cambridge University Press.

Snowdon, D. A., Greiner, L. H., & Markesbery, W. R. (2000). Linguistic ability in early life and the neuropathology of Alzheimer's disease and cerebrovascular disease: Findings from the Nun Study. *Annals of the New York Academy of Sciences, 903,* 34–38.

Snyder, C. R., & Larson, G. R. (1972). A further look at student acceptance of general personality interpretations. *Journal of Consulting and Clinical Psychology, 38,* 384–388.

Snyder, L. H., Batista, A. P., & Andersen, R. A. (2000). Intention-related activity in the posterior parietal cortex: A review. *Vision Research, 40,* 1433–1441.

Snyder, M. (1974). Self-monitoring of expressive behavior. *Journal of Personality and Social Psychology, 30,* 526–537.

Snyder, M. (1984). When belief creates reality. In L. Berkowitz (Ed.), *Advances in experimental social psychology* (Vol. 25, pp. 67–114). San Diego, CA: Academic Press.

Snyder, M. (1992). Motivational foundations of behavioral confirmation. In M. P. Zanna (Ed.), *Advances in experimental social psychology* (Vol. 18, pp. 248–306). New York: Academic Press.

Snyder, M., & Ickes, W. (1985). Personality and social behavior. In G. Lindzey & E. Aronson (Eds.), *Handbook of social psychology* (3rd ed.) (Vol. 2, pp. 883–947). New York: Random House.

Snyder, M., Tanke, E. D., & Berscheid, E. (1977). Social perception and interpersonal behavior: On the self-fulfilling nature of social stereotypes. *Journal of Personality and Social Psychology, 35,* 656–666.

Snyderman, M., & Herrnstein, R. J. (1983). Intelligence tests and the Immigration Act of 1924. *American Psychologist, 38,* 986–995.

Sohal, R. S., & Weindruch, R. (1996). Oxidative stress, caloric restriction, and aging. *Science, 273,* 59–63.

Soli, S. D. (1994). Hearing aids: Today and tomorrow. *Echoes: The newsletter of the Acoustical Society of America, 4,* 1–5.

Solms, M. (1997). *The neuropsychology of dreams: A clinico-anatomical study.* Mahwah, NJ: Erlbaum.

Solomon, D. A., Keller, M. B., Leon, A. C., Mueller, T. I., Lavori, P. W., Shea, M. T., Coryell, W., Warshaw, M., Turvey, C., Maser, J. D., & Endicott, J. (2000). Multiple recurrences of major depressive disorder. *American Journal of Psychiatry, 157,* 229–233.

Solomon, R. L. (1980). The opponent-process theory of acquired motivation: The costs of pleasure and the benefits of pain. *American Psychologist, 35,* 691 712.

Solomon, R. L., & Corbit, J. D. (1973). An opponent-process theory of motivation: II. Cigarette addiction. *Journal of Abnormal Psychology, 81,* 158–171.

Solomon, R. L., & Corbit, J. D. (1974a). An opponent-process theory of motivation: I. Temporal dynamics of affect. *Psychological Review, 78,* 3–43.

Solomon, R. L., & Corbit, J. D. (1974b). An opponent-process theory of motivation: I. Temporal dynamics of affect. *Psychological Review, 81,* 119–145.

Sommer, F. G., & Ling, D. (1970). Auditory testing of newborns using eyeblink conditioning. *Journal of Auditory Research, 10,* 292–295.

Sommers, E. K., & Check, J. V. (1987). An empirical investigation of the role of pornography in the verbal and physical abuse of women. *Violence & Victims, 2,* 189–209.

Soper, B., Milford, G. E., & Rosenthal, G. T. (1995). Belief when evidence does not support the theory. *Psychology & Marketing, 12,* 415–422.

Sosik, J. J., Kahai, S. S., & Avolio, B. J. (1999). Transformational leadership and dimensions of creativity: Motivating idea generation in computer-mediated groups. *Creativity Research Journal, 11,* 111–121.

Sowell, E. R., Thompson, P. M., Holmes, C. J., Jernigan, T. L., & Toga, A. W. (1999). In vivo evidence for post-adolescent brain maturation in frontal and striatal regions. *Nature Neuroscience, 2,* 859–61.

Spain, J. A., Eaton, L. G., & Funder, D. C. (2000). Perspectives on personality: The relative accuracy of self versus others for the prediction of emotion and behavior. *Journal of Personality, 68,* 837–867.

Spangler, D. L., Simons, A. D., Monroe, S. M., & Thase, M. E. (1997). Relationships between cognitive constructs and cognitive diathesis-stress match. *Journal of Abnormal Psychology, 106,* 395–403.

Spangler, W. D. (1992). Validity of questionnaire and TAT measures of need for achievement: Two meta-analyses. *Psychological Bulletin, 112,* 140–154.

Spanos, N. P. (1994). Multiple identity enactments and multiple personality disorder: A sociocognitive perspective. *Psychological Bulletin, 116,* 143–165.

Spearman, C. (1927). *The abilities of man.* New York: Macmillan.

Speed, A., & Gangestad, S. (1997). Romantic popularity and mate preferences: A peer-nomination study. *Personality & Social Psychology Bulletin, 23,* 928–935.

Speisman, J. C., Lazarus, R. S., Mordkoff, A., & Davison, L. (1964). Experimental reduction of stress based on ego-defense theory. *Journal of Abnormal and Social Psychology, 68,* 367–380.

Spelke, E. S. (1991). Physical knowledge in infancy: Reflections on Piaget's theory. In S. Carey & R. Gelman (Eds.), *The epigenesis of mind: Essays on biology and cognition* (pp. 133–169). Hillsdale, NJ: Erlbaum.

Spelke, E. S., Breinlinger, K., Jacobson, K., & Phillips, A. (1993). Gestalt relations and object perception: A developmental study. *Perception, 22,* 1483–1501.

Spelke, E. S., Breinlinger, K., Macomber, J., & Jacobson, K. (1992). Origins of knowledge. *Psychological Review, 99,* 605–632.

Spence, M. J., & DeCasper, A. J. (1987). Prenatal experience with low-frequency maternal voice sounds influences neonatal perception of maternal voice samples. *Infant Behavior and Development, 10,* 133–142.

Spencer, W. D., & Raz, N. (1995). Differential age effects on memory for content and context: A meta-analysis. *Psychology and Aging, 10,* 527–539.

Sperber, D., Cara, F., & Girotto, V. (1995). Relevance theory explains the selection task. *Cognition, 57,* 31–95.

Sperling, G. (1960). The information available in brief visual presentations. *Psychological Monographs, 74*, 1–29.

Sperling, R. (2001). The volumes of memory. *Journal of Neurology, Neurosurgery & Psychiatry, 71*, 5–6.

Spiegel, D. (1993). Social support: how friends, family and groups can help. In D. Goleman and J. Gurin (Eds.), *Mind body medicine*. New York: Consumer Reports Books.

Spiegel, D (1994). *Living beyond limits: new hope and help for facing life-threatening illness*. New York: Ballantine/Fawcett.

Spiegel, D. (1997). Psychosocial aspects of breast cancer treatment. *Seminars in Oncology, 24*, S1-36–S1-47.

Spiegel, D. (1999). Personal communication.

Spiegel, D., & Cardeña, E. (1991). Disintegrated experience: The dissociated disorders revisited. *Journal of Abnormal Psychology, 100*, 366–378.

Spiegel, D., & King, R. (1992). Hypnotizability and CSF HVA levels among psychiatric patients. *Biological Psychiatry, 31*, 95–98.

Spiegel, D., Bierre, P., & Rootenberg, J. (1989). Hypnotic alteration of somatosensory perception. *American Journal of Psychiatry, 146*, 749–754.

Spiegel, D., Bloom, J., & Kraemer, H. (1989). Effect of psychosocial treatment on survival of patients with metastatic breast cancer. *The Lancet, 2*, 888–891.

Spiegel, D., Cutcomb, S., Ren, C., & Pribram, K. (1985). Hypnotic hallucination alters evoked potentials. *Journal of Abnormal Psychology, 94*, 249–255.

Spiegel, D., Sephton, S., Terr, A., & Stites, D. (1998). Effects of psychosocial treatment in prolonging cancer survival may be mediated by neuroimmune pathways. In S. McCann, J. Lipton, E. Sternberg, et al. (Eds.), *Neuroimmunomodulation: Molecular aspects, integrative systems, and clinical advances* (pp. 674–683). New York: New York Academy of Sciences.

Spiers, H. J., Maguire, E. A., & Burgess, N. (2001). Hippocampal amnesia. *Neurocase, 7*, 357–382.

Spitzer, H., Desimone, R., & Moran, J. (1988). Increased attention enhances both behavioral and neuronal performance. *Science, 240*, 338–340.

Spitzer, R. L. (1975). On pseudoscience in science, logic in remission, and psychiatric diagnosis: A critique of Rosenhan's "On being sane in insane places." *Journal of Abnormal Psychology, 84*, 442–452.

Sprecher, S. (1989). The importance of males and females of physical attractiveness, earning potential and expressiveness in initial attraction. *Sex Roles, 21*, 591–607.

Sprecher, S. (1998). The effect of exchange orientation on close relationships. *Social Psychology Quarterly, 61*, 220–231.

Sprecher, S. (1999). "I love you more today than yesterday": Romantic partners' perceptions of changes in love and related affect over time. *Journal of Personality and Social Psychology, 76*, 46–53.

Sprecher, S., Aron, A., Hatfield, E., Cortese, A., Potapova, E., & Levitskaya, A. (1994). Love: American style, Russian style and Japanese style. *Personal Relationships, 1*, 349–369.

Sprecher, S., Sullivan, Q., & Hatfield, E. (1994). Mate selection preferences: Gender differences examined in a national sample. *Journal of Personality and Social Psychology, 66*, 1074–1080.

Springer, S. P., & Deutsch, G. (1994). *Left brain, right brain*. New York: Freeman.

Springer, S. P., & Deutsch, G. (1998). *Left brain, right brain: Perspectives from cognitive neuroscience* (5th ed.). New York: W. H. Freeman.

Sprock, J., & Yoder, C. Y. (1997). Women and depression: An update on the report of the APA Task Force. *Sex Roles, 36*, 269–303.

Spyraki, C., Fibiger, H. C., & Phillips, A. G. (1982). Dopaminergic substrates of amphetamine-induced place preference conditioning. *Brain Research, 253* (1-sup-2), 185–193.

Squire, L. R. (1987). *Memory and the brain*. New York: Oxford University Press.

Squire, L. R. (1992). Memory and the hippocampus: A synthesis from findings with rats, monkeys, and humans. *Psychological Review, 99*, 195–231.

Squire, L. R., & Kandel, E. R. (1999). *Memory: From mind and molecules*. New York: Scientific American Library/Scientific American Books.

Squire, L. R., Ojemann, J. G., Miezin, F. M., Petersen, S. E., Videen, T. O., & Raichle, M. E. (1992). Activation of the hippocampus in normal humans: A functional anatomical study of memory. *Proceedings of the National Academy of Sciences, USA, 89*, 1837–1841.

Sroufe, L. A., & Fleeson, J. (1986). Attachment and the construction of relationships. In W. W. Hartup and Z. Rubin (Eds.), *Relationships and development* (pp. 51–71). Hillsdale, NJ: Erlbaum.

Stack, S., & Eshleman, J. R. (1998). Marital status and happiness. *Journal of Marriage and the Family, 60*, 527–536.

Stager, C. L., & Werker, J. F. (1997). Infants listen for more phonetic detail in speech perception than in word-learning tasks. *Nature, 388*, 381–382.

Stalder, D. R., & Baron, R. S. (1998). Attributional complexity as a moderator of dissonance-produced attitude change. *Journal of Personality and Social Psychology, 75*, 449–455.

Stallone, D. D., & Stunkard, A. J. (1994). Obesity. In A. Frazer & P. B. Molinoff (Eds.), *Biological bases of brain function and disease* (pp. 385–403). New York: Raven Press.

Stanbury, J. B. (1992). Iodine and human development. *Medical Anthropology, 13*, 413–423.

Stanley, M. A., & Turner, S. M. (1995). Current status of pharmacological and behavioral treatment of obsessive-compulsive disorder. *Behavior Therapy, 25*, 153–186.

Stanley, M. A., Beck, J. G., Averill, P. M., & Balwin, L. E., Deagle, R. A., III, & Stadler, J. G. (1996). Patterns of change during cognitive behavioral treatment for panic disorder. *Journal of Nervous & Mental Disease, 184*, 567–572.

Stanton, M. D. (1981). Strategic approaches to family therapy. In A. S. Gurman & D. P. Kniskern (Eds.), *Handbook of family therapy*. (pp. 361–402). New York: Brunner/Mazel.

Starker, S. (1988). Psychologists and self-help books: Attitudes and prescriptive practices of clinicians. *American Journal of Psychotherapy, 42*, 448–455.

Stayman, D. M., & Kardes, F. R. (1992). Spontaneous inference processes in advertising: Effects of need for cognition and self-monitoring on inference generation and utilization. *Journal of Consumer Psychology, 1*, 125–142.

Steblay, N. M., & Bothwell, R. K. (1994). Evidence for hypnotically refreshed testimony: The view from the laboratory. *Law & Human Behavior, 18*, 635–651.

Steblay, N., Dysart, J., Fulero, S., & Lindsay, R. C. L. (2001). Eyewitness accuracy rates in sequential and simultaneous lineup presentations: A meta-analytic comparison. *Law & Human Behavior, 25*, 459–473.

Steele, C., & Josephs, R. A. (1990). Alcohol myopia: Its prized and dangerous effects. *American Psychologist, 45*, 921–933.

Steele, C. M. (1997). A threat in the air: How stereotypes shape intellectual identity and performance. *American Psychologist, 52*, 613–629.

Steele, C. M., & Aronson, J. (1995). Stereotype threat and the intellectual test performance of African Americans. *Journal of Personality & Social Personality, 69*, 797–811.

Steele, C. M., & Southwick, L. (1985). Alcohol and social behavior I: The psychology of drunken excess. *Journal of Personality and Social Psychology, 48*, 18–34.

Steele, C. M., Critchlow, B., & Liu, T. J. (1985). Alcohol and social behavior II: The helpful drunkard. *Journal of Personality and Social Psychology, 48*, 35–46.

Steele, K. M., Ball, T. N., & Runk, R. (1997). Listening to Mozart does not enhance backwards digit span performance. *Perceptual and Motor Skills, 84*, 1179–1184.

Steele, K. M., Bella, S. D., Peretz, I., Dunlop, T., Dawe, L. A., Humphrey, G. K., Shannon, R. A., Kirby, J. L., Jr., & Olmstead, C. G. (1999). Prelude or requiem for the "Mozart effect"? *Nature, 400*, 827–828.

Steele, R. L. (1992). Dying, death, and bereavement among the Maya Indians of Mesoamerica: A study in antropological psychology. In L. A. Platt & V. R. Persico, Jr. (Eds.), *Grief in cross-cultural perspective: A casebook* (pp. 399–424). New York: Garland.

Steinberg, M. (1994). Systematizing dissociation: Symptomatology and diagnostic assessment. In D. Spiegel (Ed.), *Dissociation: Culture, mind, and body* (pp. 59–90). Washington, DC: American Psychiatric Press.

Steketee, G., & White, K. (1990). When once is not enough: Help for obsessive-compulsives. Oakland, CA: New Harbinger Publications, Inc.

Stelmack, R. M. (1990). Biological bases of extraversion: Psychophysiological evidence. *Journal of Personality, 58*, 293–311.

Stephan, W. G., Stephan, C. W., & de Vargas, M. C. (1996). Emotional expression in Costa Rica and the United States. *Journal of Cross-Cultural Psychology, 27*, 147–160.

Stephens, T. A., & Burroughs, W. A. (1978). An application of operant conditioning to absenteeism in a hospital setting. *Journal of Applied Pychilogy, 63*, 518–521.

Steptoe, A., Lipsey, Z., & Wardle, J. (1998). Stress, hassles and variations in alcohol consumption, food choice and physical exercise: A diary study. *British Journal of Health Psychology, 3*, 51–63.

Sterling-Smith, R. S. (1976). A special study of drivers most responsible in fatal accidents. Summary for Management Report, Contract DOT HS 310-3-595. Washington, DC: Department of Transportation.

Stern, K., & McClintock, M. K. (1998). Regulation of ovulation by human pheromones. *Nature, 392*, 177–179.

Stern, P. C., & Carstensen, L. L. (Eds.) (2000). *The aging mind: Opportunities in cognitive research*. Washington, D.C.: National Academy Press.

Stern, Y. (2002). What is cognitive reserve? Theory and research application of the reserve concept. *Journal of the International Neuropsychological Society, 8*, 448–460.

Sternbach, R. A. (1978). Psychological dimensions and perceptual analyses, including pathologies of pain. In E. C. Carterette & M. P. Friedman (Eds.), *Handbook of perception* (pp. 231–261). New York: Academic Press.

Sternberg, R. J. (1985). *Beyond IQ: A triarchic theory of human intelligence*. Cambridge: Cambridge University Press.

Sternberg, R. J. (1986a). A triangular theory of love. *Psychological Review, 93*, 119–135.

Sternberg, R. J. (1986b). *What is intelligence?* Norwood, NJ: Ablex.

Sternberg, R. J. (1988a). *The triangle of love*. New York: Basic Books.

Sternberg, R. J. (1988b). *The triarchic mind: A new theory of human intelligence*. New York: Viking.

Sternberg, R. J. (1990). *Metaphors of mind: Conceptions of the nature of intelligence*. New York: Cambridge University Press.

Sternberg, R. J. (1997). Educating intelligence: Infusing the triarchic theory into school instruction. In R. J. Sternberg & E. L. Grigorenko (Eds.), *Intelligence, heredity, and environment* (pp. 343–362). New York: Cambridge University Press.

Sternberg, R. J. (2000). (Ed.), *Handbook of intelligence*. New York: Cambridge University Press.

Sternberg, R. J. (2001). Teaching psychology students that creativity is a decision. *The General Psychologist, 36*, 8–11.

Sternberg, R. J., & Detterman, D. K. (Eds.). (1986). *What is intelligence? Contemporary viewpoints on its nature and definition*. Norwood, NJ: Ablex.

Sternberg, R. J., & Wagner, R. K. (1993). The g-ocentric view of intelligence and job performance is wrong. *Current Directions in Psychological Science, 2*, 1–5.

Thelen, E., & Ulrich, B. D. (1991). Hidden skills: A dynamic systems analysis of treadmill stepping during the first year. *Monographs of the Society for Research in Child Development, 56* (1, Serial No. 223).

Theorell, T., & Karasek, R. A. (1996). Current issues relating to psychosocial job strain and cardiovascular disease research. *Journal of Occupational Health Psychology, 1,* 9–26.

Thibaut, J. W., & Kelley, H. H. (1959). *The social psychology of groups.* New York: Wiley.

Thomas, A., & Chess, S. (1996). *Temperament: Theory and practice.* New York: Brunner/Mazel.

Thompson, J. K. (1990). *Body image disturbance: Assessment and treatment.* New York: Pergamon Press.

Thompson, P. M., Cannon, T. D., Narr, K. L., van Erp, T., Poutanen, V. P., Huttunen, M, Lonnqvist, J., Standertskjold-Nordenstam, C. G., Kaprio, J., Khaledy, M., Dail, R., Zoumalan, C. I., & Toga, A. W. (2001). Genetic influences on brain structure. *Nature Neuroscience, 12,* 1253–1258.

Thompson, P. M., Giedd, J. N., Woods, R. P., MacDonald, D., Evans, A. C., & Toga, A. W. (2000). Growth patterns in the developing brain detected by using continuum mechanical tensor maps. *Nature, 404,* 190–193.

Thompson, R. F. (1993). *The brain, a neuroscience primer* (2nd ed.). New York: Freeman.

Thompson, R. F., and Krupa, D. J. (1994). Organization of memory traces in the mammalian brain. *Annual Review of Neuroscience, 17,* 519–549.

Thompson, W. L., & Kosslyn, S. M. (2000). Neural systems activated during visual mental imagery: A review and meta-analyses. In A. W. Toga & J. C. Mazziotta (Eds.), *Brain mapping: The systems.* San Diego, CA: Academic Press.

Thorn, B. L., & Gilbert, L. A. (1998). Antecedents of work and family role expectations of college men. *Journal of Family Psychology, 12,* 259–267.

Thorndike, E. L. (1927). The law of effect. *American Journal of Psychology, 39,* 212–222.

Thorndike, E. L. (1933). A proof of the law of effect. *Science, 77,* 173–175.

Thorndike, E. L. (1949). The law of effect. in E. L. Thorndike, *Selected writings from a connectionist's psychology* (pp. 13–26). New York: Appleton-Century-Crofts. (Original work published 1933).

Thorndike, R. L., Hagen, E. P., & Sattler, J. M. (1986). *Stanford-Binet Intelligence Scale* (4th ed.). Itasca, IL: Riverside.

Thornhill, R., & Gangestad, S. W. (1993). Human facial beauty: Averageness, symmetry, and parasite resistance. *Human Nature, 4,* 237–269.

Thurlow, W. R. (1971). Audition. In J. W. Kling & L. A. Riggs (Eds.), *Woodworth and Schlosberg's experimental psychology* (pp. 223–271). New York: Holt, Rinehart & Winston.

Thurstone, L. L. (1938). *Primary mental abilities.* Chicago: University of Chicago Press.

Thurstone, L. L., & Thurstone, T. G. (1941). *Factorial studies of intelligence.* Chicago: University of Chicago Press.

Tidwell, M. O., Reis, H. T., Shaver, P. R. (1996). Attachment, attractiveness, and social interaction: A diary study. *Journal of Personality & Social Psychology, 71,* 729–745.

Tiernari, P. (1991). Interaction between genetic vulnerability and family environment: The Finnish adoptive family study of schizophrenia. *Acta Psychiatrica Scandinavica, 84,* 460–465.

Till, B. D., & Priluck, R. L. (2000). Stimulus generalization in classical conditioning: An initial investigation and extension. *Psychology & Marketing, 17,* 55–72.

Timmerman, I. G. H., Emmelkamp, P. M. G., & Sanderman, R. (1998). The effects of a stress-management training program in individuals at risk in the community at large. *Behaviour Research & Therapy, 36,* 863–875.

Tingey, H., Kiger, G., & Riley, P. J. (1996). Juggling multiple roles: Perceptions of working mothers. *Social Science Journal, 33,* 183–191.

Tinker, J. E., & Tucker, J. A. (1997). Motivations for weight loss and behavior change strategies associated with natural recovery from obesity. *Psychology of Addictive Behaviors, 11,* 98–106.

Tinney, W. J., Jr. (1999, May–June). Members comment on ASA's publication on affirmative action. *Footnotes,* pp. 8–9.

Tkachuk, G. A. (1999). Exercise therapy for patients with psychiatric disorders: Research and clinical implications. *Professional Psychology: Research and Practice, 30,* 275–282.

Tohen, M., & Grundy, S. (1999). Management of acute mania. *Journal of Clinical Psychology, 60*(Supplement 5), 31–34.

Tolman, E. C. and Honzik, C. H. (1930a). "Insight" in rats. *University of California Publications in Psychology, 4,* 215–232.

Tolman, E. C., & Honzik, C. H. (1930b). Degrees of hunger, reward and non-reward, and maze learning in rats. *University of California Publications in Psychology, 4,* 241–256.

Tolman, E. C., & Honzik, C. H. (1930c). Introduction and removal of reward, and maze performance in rats. *Univeristy of California Publications in Psychology, 4,* 257–275.

Tom, G., & Rucker, M. (1975). Fat, full, and happy: Effects of food deprivation, external cues, and obesity on preference ratings, consumption, and buying intentions. *Journal of Personality & Social Psychology, 32,* 761–766.

Tomkins, S. S. (1962). *Affect, imagery, consciousness, Vol I. The positive affects.* New York: Springer-Verlag.

Tootell, R. B. H., Hadjikhani, N. K., Vanduffel, W., Lui, A. K., Medola, J. D., Sereno, M. I., & Dale, A. M. (1998). Functional analysis of primary visual cortex (V1) in humans. *Proceedings of the National Academy of Sciences, USA, 95,* 811–817.

Tootell, R. B. H., Mendola, J. D., Hadjikhani, N. K., Ledden, P. J., Liu, A. K., Reppas, J. B., Serano, M. I., & Dale, A. M. (1997). Functional analysis of V3A and related areas in human visual cortex. *The Journal of Neuroscience, 17,* 7060–7078.

Tootell, R. B., Silverman, M. S., Switkes, E., & de Valois, R. L. (1982). Deoxyglucose analysis of retinotopic organization in primate striate cortex. *Science, 218,* 902–904.

Torgersen, S. G. (1983). Genetic factors in anxiety disorders. *Archives of General Psychiatry, 40,* 1085–1089.

Torrance, E. P. (1980). Creativity and style of learning and thinking characteristics of adaptors and innovators. *Creative Child and Adult Quarterly, 5,* 80–85.

Torrey, E. F. (1988). *Nowhere to go: The tragic odyssey of the homeless mentally ill.* New York: Harper & Row.

Torrey, E. F., Miller, J., Rawlings, R., & Yolken, R. H. (1997). Seasonality of births in schizophrenia and bipolar disorder: A review of the literature. *Schizophrenia Research, 28,* 1–38.

Trafimow, D., & Finlay, K. (1996). The importance of subjective norms for a minority of people: Between-subjects and with-subjects analyses. *Personality and Social Psychology Bulletin, 22,* 820–828.

Tramo, M. J., Loftus, W. C, Stukel, T. A., Green, R. L., Weaver, J. B., & Gazzaniga, M. S. (1998). Brain size, head size, and intelligence quotient in monozygotic twins. *Neurology, 50,* 1246–1252.

Tramo, M. J., Loftus, W. C., Thoman, C. E., Green, R. L., Mott, L. A., & Gazzaniga, M. S. (1995). Surface area of human cerebral cortex and its gross morphological subdivisions: In vivo measurements in monozygotic twins suggest differential hemisphere effects of genetic factors. *Journal of Cognitive Neuroscience, 7,* 292–301.

Treisman, A. M. (1964a). Monitoring and storage of irrelevant messages in selective attention. *Journal of Verbal Learning and Verbal Behavior, 3,* 449–459.

Treisman, A. M. (1964b). Selective attention in man. *British Medical Bulletin, 20,* 12–16.

Treisman, A. M., & Gormican, S. (1988). Feature analysis in early vision: Evidence from search asymmetries. *Psychological Review, 95,* 15–48.

Treisman, A. M., & Schmidt, H. (1982). Illusory conjunctions in the perception of objects. *Cognitive Psychology, 14,* 107–141.

Treisman, A. M., & Souther, J. (1985). Search asymmetry: A diagnostic for preattentive processing of separable features. *Journal of Experimental Psychology: General, 114,* 285–310.

Trevethan, S. D., & Walker, L. J. (1989). Hypothetical versus real-life moral reasoning among psychopathic and delinquent youth. *Development and Psychopathology, 1,* 91–103.

Triandis, H. C., Bontempo, R. Villareal, M. J., Asai, M., & Lucca, N. (1988). Individualism and collectivism: Cross-cultural perspectives on self-ingroup relationships. *Journal of Prsonality and Social Psychology, 54,* 323–338.

Triandis, H. C., McCusker, C., & Hui, C. H. (1990). Multimethod probes of individualism and collectivism. *Journal of Personality and Social Psychology, 59,* 1006–1020.

Trimpop, R., & Kirkcaldy, B. (1997). Personality predictors of driving accidents. *Personality & Individual Differences, 23,* 147–152.

Trivedi, N., & Sabini, J. (1998). Volunteer bias, sexuality, and personality. *Archives of Sexual Behavior, 27,* 181–195.

Trivers, R. (1972). Parental investment and sexual selection. In B. Campbell (Ed.), *Sexual selection and the descent of man, 1871–1971* (pp. 136–179). Chicago: Aldine.

Trivers, R. (1985). *Social evolution.* Menlo Park, CA: Benjamin/Cummings.

True, W. R., Rice, J., Eisen, S. A., Heath, A. C., Phil, D., Goldberg, J., Lyons, M., & Nowak, J. (1993). A twin study of genetic and environmental contributions to liability for posttraumatic stress symptoms, *Archives of General Psychiatry, 50,* 257–264.

Truscott, S. D., & Frank, A. J. (2001). Does the Flynn effect affect IQ scores of students classified as LD? *Journal of School Psychology, 39,* 319–334.

Tsai, S-J., Yu, Y. W.-Y., Lin, C-H., Chen, T-J., Chen, S-P., & Hong, C-J. (2002). Dopamine D2 receptor and N-methyl-D-aspartate receptor 2B subunit genetic variants and intelligence. *Neuropsychobiology, 45,* 128–130.

Tsai, J. L., Levenson, R. W., & Carstensen, L. L. (2000). Autonomic, subjective, and expressive responses to emotional films in older and younger Chinese Americans and European Americans. *Psychology & Aging, 15,* 684–693.

Tsang, J. (2002). Moral rationalization and the integration of situational factors and psychological processes in immoral behavior. *Review of General Psychology, 6,* 25–50.

Tsien, J. Z., Chen, D. F., Gerber, D., Tom, C., Mercer, E. H., Anderson, D. J., Mayford, M., Kandel, E. R., & Tonegawa, S. (1996). Subregion- and cell type-restricted gene knockout in mouse brain. *Cell, 87,* 1317–1326.

Tsuang, M. T., Lyons, M. J., Eisen, S. A., True, W. T., Goldberg, J., & Henderson, W. (1992). A twin study of drug exposure and intitiation of use. *Behavior Genetics, 22,* 756 (abstract).

Tucker, G. J. (1998). Putting DSM–IV in perspective. *Am J Psychiatry 155:2,* February 1998, pp. 159–161

Tuller, D. (2002). A quiet revolution for those prone to nodding off. *New York Times,* Jan. 8.

Tulving, E. (1972). Episodic and semantic memory. In E. Tulving & W. Donaldson (Eds.), *Organization and memory* (pp. 381–403). New York: Academic Press.

Tulving, E. (1983). *Elements of episodic memory.* New York: Oxford University Press.

Tulving, E. (1985). How many memory systems are there? *American Psychologist, 40,* 395–398.

Tulving, E., & Markowitsch, H. J. (1997). Memory beyond the hippocampus. *Current Opinion in Neurobiology, 7,* 209–216.

Tulving, E., & Thomson, D. M. (1973). Encoding specificity and retrieval processes in episodic memory. *Psychological Review, 80,* 359–380.

Tulving, E., Kapur, S., Craik, F. I. M., Moscovitch, M., & Houle, S. (1994). Hemispheric encoding/retrieval asymmetry in episodic memory: Positron emission tomography findings. *Proceedings of the National Academy of Science, USA, 91,* 2016–2020.

Tulving, E., Schacter, D. L., & Stark, H. (1982). Priming effects in word-fragment completion are independent of recognition memory. *Journal of Experimental Psychology: Learning, Memory, and Cognition, 8,* 336–342.

Turkheimer, E., & Waldron, M. (2000). Nonshared environment: A theoretical, methodological, and quantitative review. *Psychological Bulletin, 126,* 78–108.

Turner, A. M., & Greenough, W. T. (1985). Differential rearing effects on rat visual cortex synapses. I. Synaptic and neuronal density and synapses per neuron. *Brain Research, 329,* 195–203.

Tversky, A., & Kahneman, D. (1974). Judgment under uncertainty: Heuristics and biases. *Science, 185,* 1124–1131.

Tversky, A., & Kahneman, D. (1992). Advances in prospect theory: Cumulative representation of uncertainty. *Journal of Risk and Uncertainty, 5,* 297–323.

Twenge, J. M. (2000). The age of anxiety? Birth cohort change in anxiety and neuroticism, 1952–1993. *Journal of Personality and Social Psychology, 79,* 1007–1021.

Twisk, J. W. R., Snel, J., Kemper, H. C. G., & van Mechelen, W. (1999). Changes in daily hassles and life events and the relationship with coronary heart disease risk factors: A 2-year longitudinal study in 27–29-yr-old males and females. *Journal of Psychosomatic Research, 46,* 229–240.

Tykocinksi, O., Higgens, E. T., & Chaiken, S. (1994). Message framing, self-discrepancies, and yielding to persuasive messages: The motivational significance of psychological situations. *Personality & Social Psychology Bulletin, 20,* 107–115.

Tyrka, A. R., Waldron, I., Graber, J. A., & Brooks-Gunn, J. (2002). Prospective predictors of the onset of anorexic and bulimic syndromes. *International Journal of Eating Disorders, 32,* 282–290.

Tzeng, O. C., Ware, R., & Chen, J. (1989). Measurement and utility of continuous unipolar ratings for the Myers-Briggs Type Indicator. *Journal of Personality, 53,* 727–738.

Tzschentke, T. M., & Schmidt, W. J. (2000). Functional relationship among medial prefrontal cortex, nucleus accumbens, and ventral tegmental area in locomotion and reward. *Critical Reviews in Neurobiology, 14,* 131–142.

Ubell, E. (1995). New devices can help you hear. *Parade Magazine,* Jan. 15, pp. 14–15.

Udwin, O., & Yule, W. (1990). Expressive language of children with Williams syndrome. *American Journal of Medical Genetics Supplement, 6,* 108–114.

Udwin, O., & Yule, W. (1991). A cognitive and behavioral phenotype in Williams syndrome. *Journal of Clinical and Experimental Neuropsychology, 13,* 232–244.

Ullian, E. M., Sapperstein, S. K., Christoherson, K. S., & Barres, B. A. (2001). Control of synapse number by glia. *Science, 291,* 657–661.

Ullman, M. T. (2001). The neural basis of lexicon and grammar in first and second language: The declarative/procedural model. *Bilingualism: Language & Cognition, 4,* 105–122.

Ullman, S. (1996). *High-level vision.* Cambridge: MIT Press.

Ulrich, R. (1984). View through a window may influence recovery from surgery. *Science, 224,* 420.

Ulrich, R. E., Stachnik, T. J., & Stainton, N. R. (1963). Student acceptance of generalized personality interpretations. *Psychological Reports, 13,* 831–834.

Ungerleider, L. G. (1995). Functional brain imaging studies of cortical mechanisms for memory. *Science, 270,* 769–775.

Ungerleider, L. G., & Mishkin, M. (1982). Two cortical visual systems. In D. J. Ingle, M. A. Goodale, & R. J. W. Mansfield (Eds.), *Analysis of visual behavior* (pp. 549–586). Cambridge, MA: MIT Press.

Ungerleider, L. G., & Haxby, J. V. (1994). "What" and "where" in the human brain. *Current Opinion in Neurology, 4,* 157–165.

United Nations. (1991). *The world's women 1970–1990: Trends and statistics.* New York: United Nations.

Ursin, H., Baade, E., & Levine, S. (1978). *Psychobiology of stress.* San Diego: Academic Press.

U.S. Office of Technology Assessment. (1991). *Adolescent health: Vol. 3, Crosscutting issues in the delivery of health and related services.* (Publication No. OTA-H-467). Washington, DC: U.S. Congress.

Vaillancourt, M. (1996). Campaigns try to soften image. *The Boston Globe.* Monday, October 7, 1996, p. B1.

Vaillant, G. (1977). *Adaptation to life.* Boston: Little, Brown.

Vajk, F. C., Craighead, W. E., Craighead, L. W., & Holley, C. (1997). Risk of major depression as a function of response styles to depressed mood. Poster presented at the annual meeting of the Association for the Advancement of Behavior Therapy, November, Miami Beach, FL.

Valenstein, E. T. (1973). *Brain control.* New York: Wiley.

Valins, S. (1966). Cognitive effects of false heart-rate feedback. *Journal of Personality & Social Psychology, 4,* 400–408.

van Balkom, A. J. L. M., van Oppen, P., Vermeulen, A. W. A., Nauta, N. C. E., Vorst, H. C. M., & van Dyck, R. (1994). A meta-analysis on the treatment of obsessive-compulsive disorder: A comparison of antidepressants, behaviour and cognitive therapy. *Clinical Psychology Review, 14,* 359–381.

Van Cauter, E., & Turek, F. W. (in press). Roles of sleep-wake and dark-light cycles in the control of endocrine, metabolic, cardiovascular and cognitive function. In B. S. McEwen, Ed.). *Coping with the environment: Handbook of Physiology Series. Part. 2: Environmental regulation of states and functions of the organism.*

van den Heuval, O. A., van de Wetering, B. J., Veltman, D. J., & Pauls, D. L. (2000). Genetic studies of panic disorder: A review. *Journal of Clinical Psychiatry, 61,* 756–766.

Vandello, J. A., & Cohen, D. (1999). Patterns of individualism and collectivism across the United States. *Journal of Personality and Social Psychology, 77,* 279–292.

Van der Hart, O. (1990). "Is multiple personality disorder really rare in Japan?": Commentary. *Dissociation: Progress in the Dissociative Disorders, 3,* 66–67.

Vanderlinden, J., Grave, R. D., Vandereycken, W., & Noorduin, C. (2001). Which factors do provoke binge-eating? An exploratory study in female students. *Eating Behaviors, 2,* 79–83.

Van Essen, D. C. (1997). A tension-based theory of morphogenesis and compact wiring in the central nervous system. *Nature, 385,* 313–318.

Van Goozen, S. H. M, Cohen-Kettenis, P. T., Gooren, J. J. G., Frijda, N. H., & Van De Poll, N. E. (1995). Gender differences in behaviour: Activating effects of cross-sex hormones. *Psychoneuroendocrinology, 20,* 343–363.

Van Goozen, S. H., Wiegant, V. M., Endert, E., Helmond, F. A., & Van de Poll, N. E. (1997). Psychoendocrinological assessment of the menstrual cycle: The relationship between hormones, sexuality, and mood. *Archives of Sexual Behavior, 26,* 359–382.

van Honk, J., Tuiten, A., Hermans, E., Putnam, P., Koppeschaar, H., Thijssen, J., Verbaten, R., & van Doornen, L. (2001). A single administration of testosterone induces cardiac accelerative responses to angry faces in healthy young women. *Behavioral Neuroscience, 115,* 238–242.

van Honk, J., Tuiten, A., van den Hout, M., Koppeschaar, H., Thijssen, J., de Haan, E., & Verbaten, R. (2000). Conscious and preconscious selective attention to social threat: Different neuroendocrine response patterns. *Psychoneuroendocrinology, 25,* 577–591.

Vanni, S., Revonsuo, A., Saarinen, J., & Hari, R. (1996). Visual awareness of objects correlates with activity of right occipital cortex. *Neuroreport, 8,* 183–186.

van Praag, H., Kempermann, G., & Gage, F. H. (1999). Running increases cell proliferation and neurogenesis in the adult mouse dentate gyrus. *Nature Neuroscience, 2,* 266–270.

van Reekum, R., Black, S. E., Conn, D., & Clarke, D. (1997). Cognition-enhancing drugs in dementia: A guide to the near future. *Canadian Journal of Psychiatry, 42,* suppl 1, 35S–50S.

Varela, F., & Shear, J. (Eds.) (1999). *The view from within: First-person methodologies.* London, UK: Imprint Academic.

Vargha-Khadem, F., Isaacs, E. B., Papaleloudi, H., Polkey, C. E., & Wilson, J. (1991). Development of language in 6 hemispherectomized patients. *Brain, 114,* 473–495.

Vargha-Khadem, F., Watkins, K., Alcock, K., Fletcher, P., & Passingham, R. (1995). Praxic and nonverbal cognitive deficits in a large family with a genetically transmitted speech and language disorder. *Proceedings of the National Academy of Sciences, USA, 92,* 930–933.

Varma, A. (2000). Impact of watching international television programs on adolescents in India. *Journal of Comparative Family Studies, 31,* 117–126.

Vartanian, L. R. (2001). Adolescents' reactions to hypothetical peer group conversations: Evidence for an imaginary audience? *Adolescence, 36,* 347–380.

Vasterling, J., Jenkins, R. A., Tope, D. M., & Burish, T. G. (1993). Cognitive distraction and relaxation training for the control of side effects due to cancer chemotherapy. *Journal of Behavioral Medicine, 16,* 65–80.

Vaughan, S. C. (1997). *The talking cure: The science behind psychotherapy.* New York: Putnam & Sons.

Vaughn, C., & Leff, J. (1976). Measurement of expressed emotion in the families of psychiatric patients. *British Journal of Social and Clinical Psychology, 15,* 1069–1177.

Vehmanen, L., Kaprio, J., & Loennqvist, J. (1995). Twin studies on concordance for bipolar disorder. *Psychiatria Fennica, 26,* 107–116.

Velakoulis, D., Pantelis, C., McGorry, P. D., Dudgeon, P., Brewer, W., Cook, M., Desmond, P., Bridle, N., Tierney, P., Murrie, V., Singh, B., & Copolov, D. (1999). Hippocampal volume in first-episode psychoses and chronic schizophrenia: A high-resolution magnetic resonance imaging study. *Archives of General Psychiatry, 56,* 133–140.

Ventura, J., Nuechterlein, K. H., Lukoff, D., & Hardesty, J. P. (1989). A prospective study of stressful life events and schizophrenic relapse. *Journal of Abnormal Psychology, 98,* 407–411.

Verfaellie, M., Keane, M. M., & Cook, S. P. (2001). The role of explicit memory processes in cross-modal priming: An investigation of stem completion priming in amnesia. *Cognitive, Affective & Behavioral Neuroscience, 1,* 222–228.

Verhaeghen, P., Marcoen, A., & Goosens, L. (1992). Improving memory performance in the aged through mnemonic training: A meta-analytic study. *Psychology and Aging, 7,* 242–251.

Vermetten, E., & Brenner, J. D. (2002). Circuits and systems in stress. I. Preclinical studies. *Depression & Anxiety, 15,* 126–147.

Vernon, P. A., Jang, K. L., Harris, J. A., & McCarthy, J. M. (1997). Environmental predictors of personality differences: A twin and sibling study. *Journal of Personality and Social Psychology, 72,* 177–183.

Verstraten, F. A. J., Cavanagh, P., & Labianca, A. T. (2000). Limits of attentive tracking reveal temporal properties of attention. *Vision Research, 40,* 3651–3664.

Verwey, W. B., & Zaidel, D. M. (2000). Predicting drowsiness accidents from personal attributes, eye blinks and ongoing driving behaviour. *Personality & Individual Differences, 28,* 123–142.

Vickers, K. S., & Vogeltanz, N. D. (2000). Dispositional optimism as a predictor of depressive symptoms over time. *Personality and Individual Differences, 28,* 259–272.

Vieilledent, S., Kosslyn, S. M., Berthoz, A., & Giraudo, M. D. (in press). Does mental simulation of following a path improve navigation performance without vision? *Behavioral Brain Review*.

Viereck, G. S. (1929, October 26). What life means to Einstein: An interview by George Sylvester Viereck. *The Saturday Evening Post*.

Vieweg, R., & Shawcross, C. R. (1998). A trial to determine any difference between two and three times a week ECT in the rate of recovery from depression. *Journal of Mental Health (UK)*, 7, 403–409.

Villarreal, D. M., Do, V., Haddad, E., & Derrick, B. E. (2002). NMDA receptor antagonists sustain LTP and spatial memory: Active processes mediate LTP decay. *Nature Neuroscience*, 5, 48–52.

Villringer, A., & Chance, B. (1997). Non-invasive optical spectroscopy and imaging of human brain function. *Trends in Neurosciences*, 20, 435–442.

Vinar, O. (2001). Neurobiology of drug dependence. *Homeostasis in Health & Disease*, 41, 20–34.

Vincent, K. R. (1991). Black/White IQ differences: Does age make the difference? *Journal of Clinical Psychology*, 47, 266–270.

Viney, W. (1993). *A history of psychology: Ideas and context*. Needham Heights, MA: Allyn & Bacon.

Vogel, G. (1996). School achievement: Asia and Europe top in the world, but reasons are hard to find. *Science*, 274, 1296.

Vogel, G. (1997). Cocaine wreaks subtle damage on developing brains. *Science*, 278, 38–39.

Volkmar, F. R., Klin, A., Siegel, B., et al. (1994). Field trial for autistic disorder in DSM-IV. *American Journal of Psychiatry*, 151, 1361–1367.

Volkow, N. D., Chang, L., Wang, G., Fowler, J. S., Franceschi, D., Sedler, M. J., Gatley, S. J., Hitzemann, R., Ding, Y. S., Wong, C., & Logan, J. (2001). Higher cortical and lower subcortical metabolism in detoxified methamphetamine abusers. *American Journal of Psychiatry*, 158, 383–389.

von der Heydt, R., & Peterhans, E. (1989). Mechanisms of contour perception in monkey visual cortex. I. Lines of pattern discontinuity. *Journal of Neuroscience*, 9, 1731–1748.

von der Heydt, R., Peterhans, E., & Baumgartner, G. (1984). Illusory contours and cortical neuron responses. *Science*, 224, 1260–1262.

von der Malsburg, C. (2002). How are neural signals related to each other and to the world? *Journal of Consciousness Studies*, 9, 47–60.

Vonk, R., & van Knippenberg, A. (1995). Processing attitude statements from in-group and out-group members: Effects of within-group and within-person inconsistencies on reading times. *Journal of Personality and Social Psychology*, 68, 215–227.

von Zerssen, D., Leon, C. A. Moller, H., Wittchen, H., Pfister, H., & Sartorius, N. (1990). Care strategies for schizophrenic patients in a transcultural comparison. *Comprehensive Psychiatry*, 31, 398–408.

Voth, H. M., & Orth, M. H. (1973). *Psychotherapy and the role of the environment*. New York: Behavioral Press.

Voudouris, N. J., Peck, C. L., & Coleman, G. (1985). Conditioned placebo responses. *Journal of Personality and Social Psychology*, 48, 47–53.

Vrana, S. R. & Lang, P. J. (1990). Fear imagery and the startle-probe reflex. *Journal of Abnormal Psychology*, 99, 181–189.

Vrana, S. R., Spence, E. L., & Lang, P. J. (1988). The startle probe response: A new measure of emotion? *Journal of Abnormal Psychology*, 97, 487–491.

Vranas, P. B. M. (2000). Gigerenzer's normative critique of Kahneman and Tversky. *Cognition*, 76, 179–193.

Vrij, A., & Mann, S. (2001). Telling and detecting lies in a high-stake situation: The case of a convicted murderer. *Applied Cognitive Psychology*, 15, 187–203.

Vrugt, A., & Luyerink, M. (2000). The contribution of bodily posture to gender stereotypical impressions. *Social Behavior & Personality*, 28, 91–104.

Vuilleumier, P., & Sagiv, N. (2001). Two eyes make a pair: Facial organization and perceptual learning reduce visual extinction. *Neuropsychologia*, 39, 1144–1149.

Vurpillot, E. (1968). The development of scanning strategies and their relation to visual differentiation. *Journal of Experimental Child Psychology*, 6, 632–650.

Vygotsky, L. S. (1962). On inner speech. In E. Hanfman & G. Vakar (Eds. and Trans.), *Thought and language* (pp. 130–138). Cambridge, MA: MIT Press.

Vygotsky, L. S. (1978). *Mind in society: The development of higher mental processes*. Cambridge, MA: Harvard University Press. (Original works published 1930, 1933, and 1935)

Vygotsky, L. S. (1986). (A. Kozulin, Trans.). *Thought and language*. Cambridge, MA: MIT Press (originally published 1934).

Vygotsky, L. S. (1988). On inner speech. In M. B. Franklin & S. S. Barten (Eds.), *Child language: A reader* (pp. 181–187). New York: Oxford University Press.

Waddell, C. (1998). Creativity and mental illness: Is there a link? *Canadian Journal of Psychiatry*, 43, 166–172.

Wade, N. (2002, June 18). A genomic treasure hunt may be striking gold. *The New York Times*, D1–D4.

Wade, T., Martin, N. G., & Tiggemann, M. (1998). Genetic and environmental risk factors for the weight and shape concerns characteristic of bulimia nervosa. *Psychological Medicine*, 28, 761–771.

Wagner, A. D., Schacter, D. L., Rotte, M., Koutstaal, W., Maril, A., Dale, A. M., Rose, B. R., & Buckner, R. L. (1998). Building memories: Remembering and forgetting of verbal experiences as predicted by brain activity. *Science*, 281, 1188–1191.

Wagner, J. A. (1995). Studies of individualism-collectivism: Effects on cooperation in groups. *Academy of Management Review*, 38, 152–172.

Wagner, R. K. (1997). Intelligence, training, and employment. *American Psychologist*, 52, 1059–1069.

Wagner, R. K., & Sternberg, R. J. (1986). Tacit knowledge and intelligence in the everyday world. In R. J. Sternberg & R. W. Wagner (Eds.), *Practical intelligence: Nature and origins of competence in the everyday world*. Cambridge, England: Cambridge University Press.

Wagstaff, G. F. (1999). Hypnosis and forensic psychology. In Kirsch, I. Capafons, A., Cardeña-Buelna E., & Amigó, S. *Clinical hypnosis and self-regulation: Cognitive-behavioral perspectives* (pp. 277–308). Washington, D.C.: American Psychological Association.

Wahba, M. A., & Bridwell, L. G. (1976). Maslow reconsidered: A review of research on the need hierarchy theory. *Organizational Behavior & Human Decision Processes*, 15, 212–240.

Wahlbeck, K., Forsén, T., Osmond, C., Barker, D. J. P., & Eriksson, J. G. (2001). Association of schizophrenia with low maternal body mass index, small size at birth, and thinness during childhood. *Archives of General Psychiatry*, 58, 48–52.

Walach, H., & Maidhof, C. (1999). Is the placebo effect dependent on time? A meta-analysis. In I. Kirsch (Ed.), *How expectancies shape experience* (1st ed., pp. 321–332). Washington, DC: American Psychological Association.

Waldron, V. R., Lavitt, M., & Kelley, D. (2000). The nature and prevention of harm in technology-mediated self-help settings: Three exemplars. *Journal of Technology in Human Services*, 17, 267–293.

Walker, E. F., & Diforio, D. (1997). Schizophrenia: A neural diathesis-stress model. *Psychological Review*, 104, 667–685.

Walker, E. F., Grimes, K. E., Davis, D., & Smith, A. (1993). Childhood precursors of schizophrenia: Facial expressions of emotion. *American Journal of Psychiatry*, 150, 1654–1660.

Walker, E. F., Logan, C. B., & Walder, D. (1999). Indicators of neurdevelopmental abnormality in schizotypcal personality disorder. *Psychiatric Annals*, 29, 132–136.

Walker, E. F., Savoie, T., Davis, D. (1994). Neuromotor precursors of schizophrenia. *Schizophrenia Bulletin*, 148, 661–666.

Walker, I., & Crogan, M. (1998). Academic performance, prejudice, and the Jigsaw classroom: New pieces of the puzzle. *Journal of Community & Applied Social Psychology*, 8, 381–393.

Walker, L. J. (1995). Sexism in Kohlberg's moral psychology? In W. M. Kurtines & J. L. Gewirtz (Eds.), *Moral development: An introduction* (pp. 83–107). Boston: Allyn & Bacon.

Walker, L. J., & Taylor, J. H. (1991). Stage transitions in moral reasoning: A longitudinal study of developmental processes. *Developmental Psychology*, 27, 330–337.

Wall, P. (2000). *Pain: The science of suffering*. New York: Columbia University Press.

Wallace, R. K. (1970). Physiological effects of transcendental meditation. *Science*, 167, 1751–1754.

Wallace, R. K., Benson, H., & Wilson, A. F. (1971). A wakeful hypometabolic physiologic state. *American Journal of Physiology*, 221, 795–799.

Wallas, G. (1926). *The art of thought*. New York: Harcourt, Brace.

Waller, N. G., & Shaver, P. R. (1994). The importance of non-genetic influences on romantic love styles: A twin family study. *Psychological Science*, 5, 268–274.

Waller, N. G., Kojetin, B. A., Bouchard, T. J., Jr, Lykken, D. T., & Tellegen, A. (1990). Genetic and environmental influences on religious interests, attitudes, and values: A study of twins reared apart and together. *Psychological Science*, 1, 138–142.

Wallis, G., & Bülthoff, H. (1999). Learning to recognize objects. *Trends in Cognitive Sciences*, 3, 22–30.

Walsh, B. T. (1993). Binge eating in bulimia nervosa. In C. G. Fairburn & G. T. Wilson (Eds.), *Binge eating: Nature, assessment, and treatment* (pp. 37–49). New York: Guilford Press.

Walsh, V., & Cowey, A. (1998). Magnetic stimulation studies of visual cognition. *Trends in Cognitive Sciences*, 2, 103–111.

Walsh, V., & Pascual-Leone, A. (in press). *Transcranial magnetic stimulation: A neurochronometrics of mind*. Cambridge, MA: MIT Press.

Walster, E., Walster, G. W., & Berscheid, E. (1978). *Equity: Theory and research*. Needham Heights, MA: Allyn & Bacon.

Walters, E. E., Neale, M. C., Eaves, L. H., Health, A., Kessler, R. C., & Kendler, K. S. (1992). Bulimia nervosa and major depression: A study of common genetic and environmental factors. *Psychological Medicine*, 22, 617–622.

Walters, J., & Gardner, H. (1985). The development and education of intelligences. In F. Link (Ed.), *Essays on the intellect* (pp. 1–21). Washington, DC: Curriculum Development Association/Association for Supervision and Curriculum Development.

Wandell, B. A. (1995). *Foundations of vision*. Sunderland, MA: Sinauer.

Wang, A. Y., & Hguyen, H. T. (1995). Passionate love and anxiety: A cross-generational study. *The Journal of Social Psychology*, 135, 459–470.

Wang, A. Y., & Newline, M. H. (2000). Characteristics of students who enroll and succeed in psychology web-based classes. *Journal of Educational Psychology*, 92, 137–143.

Wang, G., Tanaka, K., & Tanifuji, M. (1996). Optical imaging of functional organization in the monkey inferotemporal cortex. *Science*, 272, 1665–1668.

Wang, T., Hartzell, D. L., Rose, B. S., Flatt, W. P., Hulsey, M. G., Menon, N. K., Makula, R. A., & Baile, C. A. (1999). Metabolic responses to intracerebroventricular leptin and restricted feeding. *Physiology & Behavior*, 65, 839–848.

Wang, X., Merzenich, M. M., Sameshima, K., & Jenkins, W. (1995). Remodelling of hand representation in adult cortex determined by timing of tactile stimulation. *Nature*, 378, 71–75.

Wanska, S. K., & Bedrosian, J. L. (1995). Conversational structure and topic performance in mother–child interaction. *Journal of Speech and Hearing Research*, 28, 579–584.

Wanska, S. K., & Bedrosian, J. L. (1996). Topic and communicative intent in mother–child discourse. *Journal of Child Language*, 13, 523–535.

Ward, C. (Ed.) (1989). *Altered states of consciousness and mental health: A cross-cultural perspective*. Newbury Park, CA: Sage.

Ward, C. (1994). Culture and altered states of consciousness. In W. J. Lonner & R. S. Malpass (Eds.). *Psychology and culture*. Boston: Allyn & Bacon.

Ward, T. B. (2001). Creative cognition, conceptual combination, and the creative writing of Stephen R. Donaldson. *American Psychologist*, 56, 350–354.

Wark, G. R., & Krebs, D. L. (1996). Gender and dilemma differences in real-life moral judgment. *Developmental Psychology*, 32, 220–230.

Warren, R. M., & Warren, R. P. (1970). Auditory illusions and confusions. *Scientific American*, 223, 30–36.

Warrington, E. K., & McCarthy, R. (1987). Categories of knowledge: Further fractionation and an attempted integration. *Brain*, 110, 1273–1296.

Warrington, E. K., & McCarthy, R. A. (1988). The fractionation of retrograde amnesia. *Brain and Cognition*, 7, 184–200.

Warrington, E. K., & Shallice, T. (1984). Category-specific semantic impairments. *Brain*, 107, 829–854.

Washburne, C. (1956). Alcohol, self and the group. *Quarterly Journal of Studies on Alcohol*, 17, 108–123.

Wason, P. C., & Johnson-Laird, P. N. (1972). *Psychology of reasoning: Structure and content*. Cambridge, MA: Harvard University Press.

Wasserman, E. A. Comparative cognition: Toward a general understanding of cognition in behavior. *Psychological Science*, 4, 156–161.

Watson, D., & Hubbard, B. (1996). Adaptation style and dispositional structure: Coping in the context of the five-factor model. *Journal of Personality*, 64, 737–774.

Watson, J., & Raynor, R. (1920). Conditioned emotional reactions. *Journal of Experimental Psychology*, 3, 1–14.

Watson, J. B. (1913). Psychology as a behaviorist views it. *Psychological Review*, 20, 158–177.

Watson, M., Greer, S., Rowden, L., Gorman, C., Robertson, B., Bliss, J. M., & Tunmore, R. (1991). Realtionships between emotional control, adjustment to cancer, and depression and anxiety in breast cancer patients. *Psychological Medicine*, 21, 51–57.

Watt, C. A., & Morris, R. L. (1995). The relationship among performance on a prototype indicator of perceptual defence/vigilance, personality, and extrasensory perception. *Personality and Individual Differences*, 19, 635–648.

Watts, A. G. (2000). Understanding the neural control of ingestive behaviors: Helping to separate cause from effect with dehydration-associated anorexia. *Hormones and Behavior*, 37, 261–283.

Waugh, N. C., & Norman, D. A. (1965). Primary memory. *Psychological Review*, 72, 89–104.

Waxman, S. R. (1992). Linguistic and conceptual organization. *Lingua*, 92, 229–257.

Wayne, S. J., & Ferris, G. R. (1990). Influence tactics and exchange quality in supervisor-subordinate interactions: A laboratory experiment and field study. *Journal of Applied Psychology*, 75, 487–499.

Webb, S. J., & Nelson, C. A. (2001). Perceptual priming for upright and inverted faces in infants and adults. *Journal of Experimental Child Psychology*, 79, 1–22.

Webb, W. B. (1982). Some theories about sleep and their clinical implications. *Psychiatric Annals*, 11, 415–422.

Webb, W. B., & Cartwright, R. D. (1978). Sleep and dreams. *Annual Review of Psychology*, 29, 223–252.

Webster, M. J., Bachevalier, J., & Ungerleider, L. G. (in press). Development and plasticity of visual memory circuits. In B. Julesz & I. Kovacs (Eds.), *Maturational windows and cortical plasticity in human development: Is there reason for an optimistic view?* Reading, MA: Addison-Wesley.

Wechsler, D. (1958). *The measurement and appraisal of adult intelligence* (5th ed.). Baltimore: Williams & Wilkins.

Wechsler, H., Dowdall, G. W., Maenner, G., Gledhill-Hoyt, J., & Lee, H. (1998). Changes in binge drinking and related problems among American college students between 1993 and 1997. *Journal of American College Health*, 47, 57–68.

Wechsler, H., Fulop, M., Padilla, A., Lee, H., & Patrick, K. (1997). Binge drinking among college students: A comparison of California with other states. *Journal of American College Health*, 45, 273–277.

Weerasinghe, J., & Tepperman, L. (1994). Suicide and happiness: Seven tests of the connection. *Social Indicators Research*, 32, 199–233.

Wegner, D. M., & Gold, D. B. (1995). Fanning old flames: Emotional and cognitive effects of suppressing thoughts of a past relationship. *Journal of Personality and Social Psychology*, 68, 782–792.

Wegner, D. M., & Zanakos, S. (1994). Chronic thought suppression. *Journal of Personality*, 62, 615–640.

Wegner, D. M., Erber, R., & Raymond, P. (1991). Transactive memory in close relationships. *Journal of Personality and Social Psychology*, 61, 923–929.

Wegner, D. M., Schneider, D. J., Carter, S. R., & White, T. L. (1987). Paradoxical effects of thought suppression. *Journal of Personality & Social Psychology*, 53, 5–13.

Wehr, T. A., Turner, E. H., Shimada, J. M., Clark, C. H., Barker, C., & Liebenluft, E. (1998). Treatment of a rapidly cycling bipolar patient by using extended bedrest and darkness to stabilize the timing and duration of sleep. *Biological Psychiatry*, 43, 822–828.

Weinberg, R. A. (1989). Intelligence and IQ: Landmark issues and great debates. *American Psychologist*, 44, 98–104.

Weinberger D. R. (1987). Implications of normal brain development for the pathogenesis of schizophrenia. Arch Gen Psychiatry. 1987; 44:660–669.

Weinberger, D. R., & Lipska, B. K. (1995). Cortical maldevelopment, anti-psychotic drugs, and schiophrenia: a search for common ground. *Schizophrenia Research*, 16, 87–110.

Weiner, B. (1980). A cognitive (attribution) emotion-action model of motivated behavior: An analysis of judgments of help-giving. *Journal of Personality and Social Psychology*, 39, 186–200.

Weiner, B., & Kukla, A. (1970). An attributional analysis of achievement motivation. *Journal of Personality & Social Psychology*, 15, 1–20.

Weingarten, H. P., Chang, P., & McDonald, T. J. (1985). Comparison of the metabolic and behavioral disturbances following paraventricular- and ventromedial-hypothalamic lesions. *Brain Research Bulletin*, 14, 551–559.

Weinstein, N. D. (1984). Why it won't happen to me: Perceptions of risk factors and susceptibility. *Health Psychology*, 3, 431–457.

Weinstein, N. D. (1993a). Optimisitic biases about perosnal risks. *Science*, 155, 1232–1233.

Weinstein, N. D. (1993b). Testing four competing theories of health-protective behavior. *Health Psychology*, 12, 324–333.

Weinstein, N. D. (2000). Perceived probability, perceived severity, and health-protective behavior. *Health Psychology*, 19, 65–74.

Weinstein, S. (1968). Intensive and extensive aspects of tactile sensitivity as a function of body part, sex, and laterality. In D. R. Kenshalo (Ed.), *The skin senses* (pp. 195–218). Springfield, IL: Thomas.

Weinstock, M. (1997). Does prenatal stress impair coping and regulation of hypothalamic-pituitary-adrenal axis? *Neuroscience & Biobehavioral Reviews*, 21, 1–10.

Weisberg, R. W. (1994). Genius and madness?: A quasi-experimental test of the hypothesis that manic-depression increases creativity. *Psychological Science*, 5, 361–367.

Weisberg, R. W., & Alba, J. W. (1981). An examination of the alleged role of "fixation" in the solution of several "insight" problems. *Journal of Experimental Psychology: General*, 110, 169–192.

Weiskrantz, L. (1986). *Blindsight: A case study and implications*. New York: Oxford University Press.

Weisman, A. D., & Hackett, T. P. (1961). Predilection to death: Death and dying as a psychiatric problem. *Psychosomatic Medicine*, 23, 232–256.

Weiss, R. L., & Heyman, R. E. (1990). Observation of marital interaction. In F. D. Fincham & T. N. Bradbury (Eds.), *The psychology of marriage: Basic issues and applications* (pp. 87–117). New York: Guilford.

Weiss, R. S. (1986). Continuities and transformations in social relationships from childhood to adulthood. In W. W. Hartup and Z. Rubin (Eds.), *Relationships and development* (pp. 95–110). Hillsdale, NJ: Erlbaum.

Weiss, V. (1995) The advent of a molecular genetics of general intelligence. *Intelligence*, 20, 115–124.

Weissman, D. E., Griffie, J., Gordon, D. B., & Dahl, J. L. (1997). A role model program to promote institutional changes for management of acute and cancer pain. *Journal of Pain & Symptom Management*, 14, 274–279.

Weissman, M. M., Bland, R. C., Canino, G. J., Greenwald, S., Hwu, H., Lee, C. K., Newman, S., Oakley-Brown, M. A., Rubio-Stipec, M., Wickramartne, P., Wittchen, H. U., & Yeh, E. K. (1994). The cross national epidemiology of obsessive compulsive disorder: The Cross National Collaborative Group. *Journal of Clinical Psychiatry*, 55(3, Suppl.), 5–10.

Weissman, M. M., Bruce, M. L., Leaf, P. J., Florio, L., & Holzer, C. (1991). Affective disorders. In L. N. Robins & D. A. Regier (Eds.), *Psychiatric disorders in America* (pp. 53–80). New York: The Free Press.

Wellen, J. M., Hogg, M. A., & Terry, D. J. (1998). Group norms and attitude-behavior consistency: The role of group salience and mood. *Group Dynamics: Theory, Research, and Practice*, 2, 48–56.

Wellman, H. M. (1990). *The child's theory of mind*. Cambridge, MA: Bradford/MIT Press.

Wells, G. L., Malpass, R. S., Lindsay, R. C. L., Fisher, R. P., Turtle, J. W., & Fulero, S. M. (2000). From the lab to the police station: A successful application of eyewitness research. *American Psychologist*, 55, 581–598.

Wender, P. H., Kety, S. S., Rosenthal, D., Schulsinger, F., Ortmann, J., & Luhde, I. (1986). Psychiatric disorders in the biological and adoptive families of adopted individuals with affective disorders. *Archives of General Psychiatry*, 43, 923–929.

Werner, C., Brown, B., & Altman, I. (1997). Environmental psychology. In J. W. Berry, M. H. Segall, & C. Kagitcibasi (Eds.), *Cross-cultural psychology*, Vol. 3: *Social behavior and applications*. 255–290

Wertheimer, M. (1923). Untersuchungen zur Lehre von der Gestalt, II. (Translated as Laws of organization in perceptual forms.). In W. D. Ellis (Ed.), *A source book of Gestalt psychology* (pp. 71–88). London: Routledge & Kegan Paul.

Werthemimer, M. (1912/1938). Uber das Denken des Naturvolker. In W. D. Ellis (Trans.), *A source book of Gestalt psychology* (pp. 265–273). New York: Harcourt Brace.

Westen, D. (1998). The scientific legacy of Sigmund Freud. Toward a psychodynamically informed psychological science. *Psychological Bulletin*, 124, 333–371.

Westen, D. (1999). The scientific status of unconscious processes: Is Freud really dead? *Journal of the American Psychoanalytic Association*, 47, Supplement, 1–45.

Westman, M., & Eden, D. (1997). Effects of a respite from work on burnout: Vacation relief and fade-out. *Journal of Applied Psychology*, 82, 516–527.

Wetzstein, C. (2002, June 7). U.S. Teens' birthrate lowest in 6 decades. *The Washington Times*.

Whalen, P. J., Rauch, S. L., Etcoff, N. L., McInerney, S. C., Lee, M. B., & Jenike, M. A. (1998). Masked presentations of emotional facial expressions modulate amygdala activity without explicit knowledge. *Journal of Neuroscience*, 18, 411–418.

Wheeler, L., & Kim, Y. (1997). What is beautiful is culturally good: The physical attractiveness stereotype has different content in collectivistic cultures. *Personality and Social Psychology Bulletin, 23,* 795–800.

Wheeler, M. D. (1991). Physical changes of puberty. *Endocrinology and Metabolism Clinics of North America, 20,* 1–14.

Whiskey, E., Werneke, U., & Taylor, D. (2001). A systematic review and meta-analysis of Hypericum perforatum in depression: A comprehensive clinical review. *International Clinical Psychopharmacology, 16,* 239–252.

White, A., & Hardy, L. (1995). Use of different imagery perspectives on the learning and performance of different motor skills. *British Journal of Psychology, 86*(2), 169–180.

White, J. M., & Ryan, C. F. (1996). Pharmacological properties of ketamine. *Drug & Alcohol Review, 15,* 145–155.

White, S. H. (1965). Evidence for a hierarchical arrangement of learning processes. In L. P. Lipsitt & C. C. Spiker (Eds.), *Advances in child development and behavior* (Vol. 2, pp.187–220). New York: Academic Press.

White, T. G. (1982). Naming practices, typicality, & underextension in child language. *Journal of Experimental Child Psychology, 33,* 324–346.

Whitehouse, W. G., Dinges, D. F., Orne, E. C., Keller, S. E., Bates, B. L., Bauer, N. K., Morahan, P., Haupt, B. A., Carlin, M. M., Bloom, P. B., Zaugg, L., & Orne, M. T. (1996). Psychosocial and immune effects of self-hypnosis training for stress management throughout the first semester of medical school. *Psychosomatic Medicine, 58,* 249–263.

Whiting, J. W. M., Burbank, V. K., & Ratner, M. S. (1986). The duration of maidenhood across cultures. In J. B. Lancaster & B. Hamburg (Eds.), *School-age pregnancy and parenthood: Biosocial dimensions* (pp. 273–302). New York: Aldine De Gruyter.

Whittal, M. L., Agras, W. S., & Gould, R. A. (1999). Bulimia nervosa: A meta-analysis of psychosocial and pharmacological treatments. *Behavior Therapy, 30,* 117–135.

Whorf, B. (1956). *Language, thought, and reality.* Cambridge, MA: MIT Press.

Whyte, G. (1998). Recasting Janis's groupthink model: The key role of collective efficacy in decision fiascoes. *Organizational Behavior & Human Decision Processes, 73,* 185–209.

Wickramasekera, I., Davies, T. E., & Davies, S. M. (1996). Applied psychophysiology: A bridge between the biomedical model and the biopsychosocial model in family medicine. *Professional Psychology: Research & Practice, 27,* 221–233.

Wiebe, D. J., & McCallum, D. M. (1986). Health practices and hardiness as mediators in the stressllness relationship. *Health Psychology, 5,* 425–438.

Wiedemann, G., Pauli, P., Dengler, W., Lutzenberger, W., Birbaumer, N., & Buchkremer, G. (1999). Frontal brain asymmetry as a biological substrate of emotions in patients with panic disorders. *Archives of General Psychiatry, 56,* 78–84.

Wiggins, J. S. (1992). Have model, will travel. *Journal of Personality, 60,* 527–532.

Wiggins, J. S., & Pincus, A. L. (1992). Conceptions of personality disorders and dimensions of personality. *Psychological Assessment: Journal of Consulting and Clinical Psychology, 1,* 305–316.

Wilder, D. A., Simon, A. F., & Faith, M. (1996). Enhancing the impact of counterstereotypic information: Dispositional attributions for deviance. *Journal of Personality and Social Psychology, 71* 276–287.

Wildman, D. E., Grossman, L. I., and Goodman, M. (2002). Functional DNA in humans and chimpanzees shows they are more similar to each other than either is to other apes. In M. Goodman & A. S. Moffat (Eds.), *Probing human origins,* (pp. 1–10). Cambridge, MA: American Academy of Arts and Sciences.

Wilkins, L. & Richter, C. P. (1940). A great craving for salt by a child with corticoadrenal insufficiency. *Journal of the American Medical Association, 114,* 866–868.

Wilkinson, D. J. C., Thompson, J. M., Lambert, G. W., Jennings, G. L., Schwarz, R. G., Jefferys, D., Turner, A. G., & Esler, M. D. (1998). Sympathetic activity in patients with panic disorder at rest, under laboratory mental stress, and during panic attacks. *Archives of General Psychiatry, 55,* 511–520.

Willer, J. C., Le, B. D., & De, B. T. (1990). Diffuse noxious inhibitory controls in man: Involvement of an opioidergic link. *European Journal of Pharmacology, 182,* 347–355.

Williams, J. E., Paton, C. C., I. C., Eigenbrodt, M. L., Nieto, F. J., & Tyroler, H. A. (2000). Anger proneness predicts coronary heart disease risk: Prospective analysis from the atherosclerosis risk in communities (ARIC) study. *Circulation, 101,* 2034–2039.

Williams, J. M. G., Healy, H., Eade, J., Windle, G., Cowen, P. J., Green, M. W., & Durlach, P. (2002). Mood, eating behaviour and attention. *Psychological Medicine, 32,* 469–481.

Williams, K. D., & Karau, S. J. (1991). Social loafing and social compensation: The effects of expectations of coworker performance. *Journal of Personality and Social Psychology, 61,* 570–581.

Williams, L. M. (1994). Recall of childhood trauma: A prospective study of women's memories of child sexual abuse. *Journal of Consulting and Clinical Psychology, 62,* 1167–1176.

Williams, R., Barefoot, J., Califf, R., Haney, T., Saunders, E., Pryor, D., Hlatky, M., Siefler, I., & Mark, D. (1992). Prognostic importance of social and economic resources among patients with angiographically documented coronary artery disease. *Journal of the American Medical Association, 267,* 520–?.

Williams, S., & Luthans, F. (1992). The impact of choice of rewards and feedback on task performance. *Journal of Organizational Behavior, 13,* 653–666.

Williams, S. M., Sanderson, G. F., Share, D. L., & Silva, P. A. (1988). Refractive error, IQ and reading ability: A longitudinal study from age seven to 11. *Developmental Medicine & Child Neurology, 30,* 735–742.

Williams, T. J., Pepitone, M. E., Christensen, S. E., Cooke, B. M., Huberman, A. D., Breedlove, N. J., Breedlove, T. J., Jordan, C. I., & Breedlove, S. M. (2000). Finger length patterns and human sexual orientation. *Nature, 404,* 455–456.

Williams, W. (1998). Are we raising smarter kids today? School-and-home-related influences on IQ. In U. Neisser (Ed.), *The rising curve: Long-terms gains in IQ and related measures* (pp. 125–154). Washington, DC: American Psychological Association.

Wilson, C. S. (2002). Reasons for eating: Personal experiences in nutrition and anthropology. *Appetite, 38,* 63–67.

Wilson, D. K., Kaplan, R. M., Schneiderman, L. (1987). Framing of decisions and selections of alternatives in health care. *J. Social Behaviour, 2,* 51–59.

Wilson, J. Q., & Kelling, G. L. (1982). Broken windows, *The Atlantic Monthly,* March,*249* (3), 29–38.

Wilson, R. I., & Nicoll, R. A. (2001). Endogenous cannabinoids mediate retrograde signalling at hippocampal synapses. *Nature, 410,* 588–592.

Wilson, R. I., & Nicoll, R. A. (2002). Endocannabinoid signaling in the brain. *Science, 296,* 678–682.

Wilson, R. I., Kunos, G., & Nicoll, R. A. (2001). Presynaptic specificity of endocannabinoid signaling in the hippocampus. *Neuron, 31,* 453–462.

Wilson, T. D., Houston, C. E., Etling, K. M., & Brekke, N. (1996). A new look at anchoring effects: Basic anchoring and its antecedents. *Journal of Experimental Psychology: General, 125,* 387–402.

Wilson, T. L., & Brown, T. L. (1997). Reexamination of the effect of Mozart's music on spatial-task performance. *Journal of Psychology, 131,* 365–370.

Wiltschko, W., Munro, U., Beason, R., Ford, H., & Wiltschko, R. (1994). A magnetic pulse leads to a temporary deflection in the orientation of migratory birds. *Experientia, 50,* 697–700.

Winderickx, J., Battisti, L., Hibiya, Y., Motulsky, A. G., & Deeb, S. S. (1993). Haplotype diversity in the human red and green opsin genes: Evidence for frequent sequence exchange in exon 3. *Human Molecular Genetics, 2,* 1413.

Winderickx, J., Lindsey, D. T., Sanocki, E., Teller, D. Y., Motulsky, A. G., & Deeb, S. S. (1992). Polymorphism in red photopigment underlies variation in colour matching. *Nature, 356,* 431–433.

Winer, G. A., & Cottrell, J. E. (1996). Does anything leave the eye when we see? Extramission beliefs of children and adults. *Current Directions in Psychological Science, 5,* 137–142.

Winer, G. A., Cottrell, J. E., Gregg, V., Fournier, J. S., & Bica, L. A. (2002). Fundamentally misunderstanding visual perception: Adults' belief in visual emissions. *American Psychologist, 57,* 417–424.

Winer, G. A., Cottrell, J. E., Karefilaki, K. D., & Gregg, V. R. (1996). Images, words and questions: Variables that influence beliefs about vision in children and adults. *Journal of Experimental Child Psychology, 63,* 499–525.

Winick, C., & Evans, J. T. (1996). The relationship between nonenforcement of state pornography laws and rates of sex crime arrests. *Archives of Sexual Behavior, 25,* 439–453.

Winner, E. (1996). *Gifted children: Myths and realities.* New York: Basic Books.

Winner, E. (1997). Exceptionally high intelligence and schooling. *American Psychologist, 52,* 1070–1081.

Winner, E. (2000). The origins and ends of giftedness. *American Psychologist, 55,* 159–169.

Winner, E. (2000). Giftedness: Current theory and research. *Current Directions in Psychological Science, 9,* 153–156.

Winnicott, D. W. (1958). *Collected papers. through paediatrics to psycho-analysis.* London: Tavistock Publications; New York: Basic Books, 1958; London: Hogarth Press and the Inst. of Psa, 1975; London: Inst of Psa and Karnac Books, 1992. Brunner/Mazel, 1992.

Winter, A. (1998). *Mesmerized: Powers of mind in Victorian Britain.* Chicago: University of Chicago Press.

Winzelberg, A. (1997). The analysis of an electronic support group for individuals with eating disorders. *Computers in Human Behavior, 13,* 393–407.

Winzelberg, A., & Humphreys, K. (1999). Should patients' religiosity influence clinicians' referral to 12-step self-help groups? Evidence from a study of 3,018 male substance abuse patients. *Journal of Consulting and Clinical Psychology, 67,* 790–794.

Wise, P. M., Krajnak, K. M., & Kashon, M. L. (1996). Menopause: The aging of multiple pacemakers. *Science, 273,* 67–70.

Wise, R. A. (1982). Neuroleptics and operant behavior: The anhedonia hypothesis. *Behavioral & Brain Sciences, 5,* 39–87.

Wise, R. A. (1996). Addictive drugs and brain stimulation reward. *Annual Review of Neuroscience, 19,* 319–340.

Wisniewski, H. M., & Terry, R. D. (1976). Neuropathology of the aging brain. In R. D. Terry & S. Gershod (Eds.), *Neurobiology of aging* (pp. 65–78). New York: Raven.

Witelson, S. F., Kigar, D. L., & Harvey, T. (1999). The exceptional brain of Albert Einstein. *Lancet, 353,* 2149–2153.

Witt, S. D. (1997). Parental influence on children's socialization to gender roles. *Adolescence, 32,* 253–259.

Wixted, J. T., & Ebbesen, E. B. (1991). On the form of forgetting. *Psychological Science, 2,* 409–415.

Wixted, J. T., & Ebbesen, E. B. (1997). Genuine power curves in forgetting: A quantitative analysis of individual subject forgetting functions. *Memory & Cognition, 25,* 731–739.

Woelk, H. (2000). Comparison of St. John's wort and imipramine for treating depression: Randomised controlled trial. *British Medical Journal, 321,* 536–539.

Wojciulik, E., Kanwisher, N., & Driver, J. (1998). Covert visual attention modulates face-specific activity in the human fusiform gyrus: An fMRI study. *Journal of Neurophysiology*, 79, 1574–1578.

Wolf, A., & Thatcher, R. (1990). Cortical reorganization in deaf children. *Journal of Clinical and Experimental Neuropsychology*, 12, 209–221.

Wolf, N. (1991). *The beauty myth*. New York: Anchor Books, Doubleday.

Wolf, O. T., Preut, R., Hellhammer, D. H., Kudielka, B. M., Schuermeyer, T. H., & Kirschbaum, C. (2000). Testosterone and cognitive in elderly men: A single testoterone injection blocks the practice effect in verbal fluency, but has no effect on spatial or verbal memory. *Biological Psychiatry*, 47, 650–654.

Wolfe, B. E., & Maser, J. D. (Eds.). (1994). *Treatment of panic disorder: A consensus development conference*. Washington, DC: American Psychiatric Press, Inc.

Wolpe, J. (1958). *Psychotherapy by reciprocal inhibition*. Stanford: Stanford University Press.

Wolpe, J. (1973). *The practice of behavior therapy* (2nd ed.). New York: Pergamon.

Wolpe, J. (1982). *The practice of behavior therapy*. New York: Pergamon.

Wolpe, J. (1997). Thirty years of behavior therapy. *Behavior Therapy*, 28, 633–635.

Wolpe, J., & Rachman, S. (1960). Psychoanalytic evidence: A critique of Freud's case of little Hans. *Journal of Nervous and Mental Diseases*, 130, 198–220.

Wood, J. M., Lilienfeld, S. O., Nezworski, M. T., & Garb, H. N. (2001). Coming to grips with negative evidence for the comprehensive system for the Rorschach: A comment on Gacono, Loving, and Bodholdt; Ganellen; and Bornstein. *Journal of Personality Assessment*, 77, 48–70.

Wood, J. M., Nezworski, M. T., Garb, H. N., & Lilienfeld, S. O. (2001). Problems with the norms of the comprehensive system for the Rorschach: Methodological and conceptual considerations. *Clinical Psychology: Science & Practice*, 8, 397–402.

Wood, P. (1963). Dreaming and social isolation. *Dissertation Abstracts, Vol. 23*, 4749–4750.(9609).

Woods, S. C., & Stricker, E. M. (1999). Food intake and metabolism. In M. J. Zigmond, F. E. Bloom, S. C. Landis, J. L. Roberts, & L. R. Squire (Eds.), *Fundamental Neuroscience* (pp. 1111–1126). San Diego: Academic Press.

Woods, S. C., Schwartz, M. W., Baskin, D. G., & Seeley, R. J. (2000). Food intake and the regulation of body weight. *Annual Review of Psychology*, 51, 255–277.

Woodward, A. L. (1998). Infants selectively encode the goal object of an actor's reach. *Cognition*, 69, 1–34.

Woolfolk, R. L., Parrish, M. W., & Murphy, S. M. (1985). The effects of positive and negative imagery on motor skill performance. *Cognitive Therapy and Research*, 9, 335–341.

World Health Organization. (1948). *Charter*. Geneva, Switzerland: United Nations.

Worthington, T. S. (1979). The use in court of hypnotically enhanced testimony. *International Journal of Clinical & Experimental Hypnosis*, 27, 402–416.

Wortman, C. B., & Silver, R. C. (1989). The myths of coping with loss. *Journal of Consulting & Clinical Psychology*, 57, 349–357.

Wright, R. (1998, August 24). Viewpoint: The power of their peers. *Time*, 67.

Wu, J., Kramer, G. L., Kram, M., Steciuk, M., Crawford, I. L., & Petty, F. (1999). Serotonin and learned helplessness: A regional study of 5-HT-sub(1A), 5-HT-sub(2A) receptors and the serotonin transport site in rat brain. *Journal of Psychiatric Research*, 33, 17–22.

Wurtzel, E. (1995). *Prozac nation: A memoir*. New York: Riverhead Books.

Wyatt, R. J., Damiani, L. M., & Henter, I. D. (1998). First-episode schizophrenia: Early intervention and medication discontinuation in the context of course and treatment. *British Journal of Psychiatry*, 172, 77–83.

Wyatt, R. J., Green, M. F., & Tuma, A. H. (1997). Long-term morbidity associated with delayed treatment of first admission schizophrenic patients: A re-analysis of the Camarillo state hospital data. *Psychological Medicine*, 27, 261–268.

Wyer, N. A., Sherman, J. W., & Stroessner, S. J. (2000). The roles of motivation and ability in controlling the consequences of stereotype suppression. *Personality & Social Psychology Bulletin*, 26, 13–25.

Wynn, V. E., & Logie, R. H. (1998). The veracity of long-term memories—Did Bartlett get it right? *Applied Cognitive Psychology*, 12, 1–20.

Wyvell, C. L., & Berridge, K. C. (2000). Intra-accumbens amphetamine increases the conditioned incentive salience of sucrose reward: Enhancement of reward "wanting" without enhanced "liking" or response reinforcement. *Journal of Neuroscience*, 20, 8122–8130.

Xerri, C., Merzenich, M. M., Jenkins, W., & Santucci, S. (1999). Representational plasticity in cortical area 3b paralleling tactual motor skill acquisition in adult monkeys. *Cerebral Cortex*, 9, 264–276.

Yagueez, L., Nagel, D., Hoffman, H., Canavan, A., Wist, E., & Hoemberg, V. (1998). A mental route to motor learning: Improving trajectoral kinematics through imagery training. *Behavioral and Brain Research*, 90, 95–106.

Yamadori, A. (1997). Body awareness and its disorders. In M. Ito & Y. Miyashita (Eds.), *Cognition, computation, and consciousness* (pp. 169–176). Oxford, England: Oxford University Press.

Yang, K., & Bond, M. H. (1990). Exploring implicit personliaty theories with indigenous or imported constructs: The Chinese case. *Journal of Personality and Social Psychology*, 58, 1087–1095.

Yates, A. (1996). Eating disorders in women athletes. *Eating Disorders Review*, 7(4), p. 1.

Yazigi, R. A., Odem, R. R., & Polakoski, K. L. (1991). Demonstration of specific binding of cocaine to human spermatozoa. *Journal of the American Medical Association*, 266, 1956–1959.

Yehuda, R., McFarlane, A. C., & Shalev, A. Y. (1998). Predicting the development of posttraumatic stress disorder from the acute response to a traumatic event. *Biological Psychiatry*, 44, 1305–1313.

Yen, S., Robins, C. J., & Lin, N. (2000). A cross-cultural comparison of depressive symptom manifestation in China and the United States. *Journal of Consulting and Clinical Psychology*, 68, 993–999.

Yeomans, M. R., & Gray, R. W. (1997). Effects of naltrexone on food intake and changes in subjective appetite during eating: evidence for opioid involvement in the appetizer effect. *Physiology & Behavior*, 62, 15–21.

Yeshurun, Y., & Carrasco, M. (1998). Attention improves or impairs visual performance by enhancing spatial resolution. *Nature*, 396, 72–75.

Yeshurun, Y., & Carrasco, M. (1999). Spatial attention improves performance in spatial resolution tasks. *Vision Research*, 39, 293–306.

Yin, J. C. P., Del Vecchio, M., Zhou, H., & Tully, T. (1995). CREB as a memory modulator: Induced expression of a dCREB2 activator isoform enhances long-term memory in Drosophila. *Cell*, 81, 107–115.

Yokosuka, M., Xu, B., Pu, S., Kalra, P. S., & Kalra, S. P. (1998). Neural substrates for leptin and neuropeptide Y (NPY) interaction: Hypothalamic sites associated with inhibition of NPY-induced food intake. *Physiology & Behavior*, 64, 331–338.

Yost, W. A., & Dye, R. H. (1991). Properties of sound localization by humans. In R. A. Altschuler, R. P. Bobbin, B. M. Clopton, & D. W. Hoffman (Eds.), *Neurobiology of hearing: The central auditory system* (pp. 389–410). New York: Raven.

Young, A. W., Hellawell, D. J., Van De Wal, C., & Johnson, M. (1996). Facial expression processing after amygdalotomy. *Neuropsychologia*, 34, 31–39.

Young, F. A. (1981). Primate myopia. *American Journal of Optometry and Physiological Optics*, 58, 560–566.

Young, L. R., Oman, C. M., Merfeld, D., Watt, D., Roy, S., DeLuca, C., Balkwill, D., Christie, J., Groleau, N., Jackson, D. K., Law, G., Modestino, S., & Mayer, W. (1993). Spatial orientation and posture during and following weightlessness: Human experiments on Spacelab Life Sciences 1. *Journal of Vestibular Research: Equilibrium & Orientation*, 3, 231–239.

Zaccaro, S. J., Foti, R. J., & Kenny, D. A. (1991). Self-monitoring and trait-based variance in leadership: An investigation of leader flexibility across multiple group situations. *Journal of Applied Psychology*, 76, 308–315.

Zacks, J., & Tversky, B. (1999). Bars and lines: A study of graphic communication. *Memory & Cognition*, 27, 1073–1079.

Zaharia, M. D., Kulczycki, J., Shanks, N., Meaney, M. J., & Anisman, H. (1996). The effects of early postnatal stimulation on Morris water-maze acquisition in adult mice: Genetic and maternal factors. *Psychopharmacology*, 128, 227–239.

Zajonc, R. (1970). Brainwash: Familiarity breeds comfort. *Psychology Today*, 3, 32–35, 60–64.

Zajonc, R. B. (1968). Attitudinal effects of mere exposure. *Journal of Personality & Social Psychology*, 9(2, Pt. 2), 1–27.

Zajonc, R. B. (2001). Mere exposure: A gateway to the subliminal. *Current Directions in Psychological Science*, 10, 224–228.

Zakowski, S., Hall, M. H., & Baum, A. (1992). Stress, stress management, and the immune system. *Applied and Preventative Psychology*, 1, 1–13.

Zalla, T., Koechlin, E., Pietrini, P., Basso, G., Aquino, P., Sirigu, A., & Grafman, J. (2000). Differential amygdala responses to winning and losing: A functional magnetic resonance imaging study in humans. *European Journal of Neuroscience*, 12, 1764–1770.

Zamora, M. (1990). *Frida Kahlo: The brush of anguish*. San Francisco, CA: Chronicle Books.

Zane, N. W. S., Sue, S., Hu, L., & Kwon, J. H. (1991). Asian-American assertion: A social learning anyalysis of cultural differences. *Journal of Counseling Psychology*, 38, 63–70.

Zaragoza, M. S., Payment, K. E., Ackil, J. K., Drivdahl, S. B., & Beck, M. (2001). Interviewing witnesses: Forced confabulation and confirmatory feedback increase false memories. *Psychological Science*, 12, 473–477.

Zatorre, R. J., & Halpern, A. R. (1993). Effect of unilateral temporal-lobe excision on perception and imagery of songs. *Neuropsychologia*, 31, 221–232.

Zawadzki, B., Strelau, J., Oniszczenko, W., Riemann, R., & Angleitner, A. (2001). Genetic and environmental influences on temperament. *European Psychologist*, 6, 272–286.

Zebrowitz, L. A., Andreoletti, C., Collins, M. A., Lee, S. Y., & Blumenthal, J. (1998). Bright, bad, babyfaced boys: Appearance stereotypes do not always yield self-fulfilling prophecy effects. *Journal of Personality & Social Psychology*, 75, 1300–1320.

Zeki, S. M. (1978). Functional specialisation in the visual cortex of the rhesus monkey. *Nature*, 274, 423–428.

Zeki, S. M. (1993). *Vision of the brain*. London: Blackwell.

Zelazo, P. R., Zelazo, N. A., & Kolb, S. (1972). "Walking" in the new-born. *Science*, 177, 1058–1059.

Zenger, T. R., & Lawrence, B. S. (1989). Organizational demography: The differential effect of age and tenure distributions on technical communication. *Academy of Management Journal*, 32, 353–376.

Zentner, M. R., & Kagan, J. (1996). Perception of music by infants. *Nature*, 383, 29.

Zentner, M. R., & Kagan, J. (1998). Infants' perception of consonance and dissonance in music. *Infant Behavior & Development*, 21, 483–492.

Zhang, Q., & Zhu, Y. (2001). The relationship between individual differences in working memory and linear reasoning. *Journal of Psychology in Chinese Societies*, 2, 261–282.

Zhdanova, I., & Wurtman, R. (June, 1996). "How does melatonin affect sleep? *Harvard Mental Health Newsletter*, p. 8

Zhou, J-N., Hofman, M. A., Gooren, L. J. G., & Swaab, D. F. (1995). A sex difference in the human brain and its relation to transsexuality. *Nature, 378*, 68–70.

Zhu, H., Guo, Q., & Mattson, M. P. (1999). Dietary restriction protects hippocampal neurons against the death-promoting action of a presenilin-1 mutation. *Brain Research, 842*, 224–229.

Zhukov, D. A., & Vinogradova, E. P. (1998). Agonistic behavior during stress prevents the development of learned helplessness in rats. *Neuroscience & Behavioral Physiology, 28*, 206–210.

Zihl, J., von Cramon, D., & Mai, N. (1983). Selective disturbance of movement vision after bilateral brain damage. *Brain, 106*, 313–340.

Zimmer, E. Z., Fifter, W. P., Young-Ihl, K., Rey, H. R., Chao, C. R., & Myers, M. M. (1993). Response of the premature fetus to stimulation by speech sounds. *Early Human Development, 33*, 207–215.

Zimmerman, M. A., Salem, D. A., & Maton, K. I. (1995). Family structure and psychosocial correlates among urban African-American adolescent males. *Child Development, 66*, 1598–1613.

Zlotnick, C. (1999). Antisocial personality disorder, affect dysregulation and childhood abuse among incarcerated women. *Journal of Personality Disorders, 13*, 90–95.

Zoccolillo, M., Price, R., Ji, T., & Hwu, H. (1999). Antisocial personality disorder: Comparisons of prevalence, symptoms, and correlates in four countries. In P. Cohen, C. Slomkowski et al. (Eds.). *Historical and geographical influences on psychopathology.* (pp. 249–277). Mahwah, NJ: Erlbaum.

Zola, S. M., Squire, L. R., Teng, E., Stefanacci, L., Buffalo, E. A., & Clark, R. E. (2000). Impaired recognition memory in monkeys after damage limited to the hippocampal region. *Journal of Neuroscience, 20*, 451–463.

Zornberg, G. L., Buka, S. L., & Tsuang, M. T. (2000). Hypoxic-ischemia-related fetal/neonatal complications and risk of schizophrenia and other nonaffective psychoses: A 19-year longitudinal study. *American Journal of Psychiatry 157*, 196–202.

Zuckerman, M. (1979). *Sensation seeking: Beyond the optimal level of arousal.* Hillsdale, NJ: Erlbaum.

Zuckerman, M. (1991). *Psychobiology of personality.* Cambridge: Cambridge University Press.

Zuckerman, M. (1995). Good and bad humors: Biochemical bases of personality and its disorders. *Psychological Science, 6*, 325–332.

Zuckerman, M., DePaulo, B. M., & Rosenthal, R. (1981). Verbal and nonverbal communication of deception. In L. Berkowitz (Ed.), *Advances in experimental social psychology* (Vol. 14, pp. 1–59). New York: Academic Press.

Zuckerman, M., Kuhlman, D. M., & Camac, C. (1988). What lies beyond E and N? Factor analyses of scales believed to measure basic dimensions of personaity. *Journal of Personality and Social Psychology, 54*, 96–107.

Zurek, P. M. (1981). Spontaneous narrowband acoustic signal emitted by human ears. *Journal of Acoustical Society of America, 69*, 514–523.

Zurek, P. M. (1985). Acoustic emissions from the ear: A summary of results from humans and animals. *Journal of the Acoustical Society of America, 78*, 340–344.

Zurif, E. B. (1995). Brain regions of relevance to syntactic processing. In L. Gleitman and M. Lieberman (Eds.), *An invitation to cognitive science* (2nd ed., Vol. 1). Cambridge, MA: MIT Press.

Zurif, E. B. (2000). Syntactic and semantic composition. *Brain and Language, 71*, 261–263.

Zurif, E. B., Caramazza, A., & Myerson, R. (1972). Grammatical judgments of agrammatic aphasics. *Neuropsychologia, 10*, 405–417.

Zwicker, E., & Schloth, E. (1984). Interrelation of different oto-acoustic emissions. *Journal of Acoustical Society of America, 75*, 1148–1154.

Glossary

Absolute pitch: The ability to identify a particular note by itself, not simply in relation to other notes.

Absolute threshold: The smallest amount of a stimulus needed in order to detect that the stimulus is present.

Absorption: The capacity to concentrate totally on external material.

Academic psychologist: The type of psychologist who focuses on conducting research and teaching.

Accommodation: In Piaget's theory, the process that results in schemas' changing as necessary to cope with a broader range of situations. Occurs when muscles adjust the shape of the lens so that it focuses light on the retina from objects at different distances.

Acquisition: The technical name given to the initial learning of the conditioned response (CR).

Action potential: The shifting change in charge that moves down the axon.

Activation–synthesis hypothesis: The theory that dreams arise from random bursts of nerve cell activity, which may affect brain cells involved in hearing and seeing; the brain attempts to make sense of this hodgepodge of stimuli, resulting in the experience of dreams.

Active interaction: Occurs when people choose, partly based on genetic tendencies, to put themselves in specific situations and to avoid others.

Activity: A temperament dimension characterized by the general expenditure of energy; activity has two components—vigor (intensity of the activities) and tempo (speed of the activities).

Acute stressor: A stressor of short-term duration.

Adaptation: A characteristic that increases "fitness" for an environment.

Adolescence: The period between the onset of puberty and, roughly, the end of the teenage years.

Adoption study: A study in which characteristics of children adopted at birth are compared to those of their adoptive parents or siblings versus their biological parents or siblings (often twins). These studies often focus on comparisons of twins who were raised in the same versus different households.

Affirming the consequent: A reasoning error that occurs because of the assumption that if a result is present, a specific cause must also be present.

Afterimage: The image left behind by a previous perception.

Aggression: Behavior that is intended to harm another living being who does not wish to be harmed.

Agonist: A chemical that mimics the effects of a neurotransmitter (sometimes by preventing reuptake).

Agoraphobia: A condition in which people fear or avoid places that might be difficult to leave should panic symptoms occur.

Alarm phase: The first phase of the GAS, in which a stressor is perceived and a fight-or-flight response is activated.

Alcohol myopia: The disproportionate influence of immediate experience on behavior and emotion due to the effects of alcohol use.

Algorithm: A set of steps that, if followed methodically, will guarantee the solution to a problem.

All-or-none law: States that if the neuron is sufficiently stimulated, it fires, sending the action potential all the way down the axon and releasing chemicals from the terminal buttons; either the action potential occurs or it doesn't.

Altered state of consciousness (ASC): State of awareness that is other than the normal waking state.

Altruism: The motivation to increase another person's welfare.

Amnesia: A loss of memory over an entire time span, resulting from brain damage caused by accident, infection, or stroke.

Amphetamines: Synthetic stimulants.

Amplitude: The height of the peaks in a light wave.

Amygdala: A subcortical structure that plays a special role in fear and is involved in other sorts of emotions, such as anger.

Androgens: Male hormones, which cause many male characteristics such as beard growth and a low voice.

Anorexia nervosa: An eating disorder characterized by the refusal to maintain even a low normal weight, and an intense fear of gaining weight.

Antagonist: A chemical that blocks the effect of a neurotransmitter (sometimes by blocking a receptor or enhancing the reuptake mechanism).

Anterograde amnesia: Amnesia that leaves consolidated memories intact but prevents new learning.

Antipsychotic medication: Medication that reduces psychotic symptoms.

Antisocial personality disorder (ASPD): A long-standing pattern of disregard for others to the point of violating other people's rights.

Anxiety disorder: A category of disorders whose hallmark is intense and pervasive anxiety and fear, or extreme attempts to avoid these feelings.

Aphasia: A disruption of language caused by brain damage.

Applied psychologist: The type of psychologist who studies how to improve products and procedures and conducts research to help solve specific practical problems.

Approach–approach conflict: The predicament that occurs when competing alternatives are equally positive.

Approach–avoidance conflict: The predicament that occurs when a course of action has both positive and negative aspects.

Archetype: A Jungian concept of symbols that represent basic aspects of the world.

Artificial intelligence (AI): The field devoted to building smart machines.

Assimilation: In Piaget's theory, the process that allows use of existing schemas to take in new sets of stimuli and respond accordingly.

Atherosclerosis: A medical condition characterized by plaque buildup in the arteries.

Attachment: An emotional bond that leads us to want to be with someone and to miss him or her when we are separated.

Attention: The act of focusing on particular information, which allows it to be processed more fully than what is not attended to.

Attentional blink: A rebound period in which a person cannot pay attention to one thing after having just paid attention to another.

Attitude: An overall evaluation about some aspect of the world.

Attribution: An explanation for the cause of an event or behavior.

Attributional bias: A cognitive shortcut for determining attribution that generally occurs outside our awareness.

Attributional style: A person's characteristic way of explaining life events.

Autism: A condition of intense self-involvement to the exclusion of external reality; about three quarters of autistic people are mentally retarded.

Autonomic nervous system (ANS): Controls the smooth muscles in the body, some glandular functions, and many of the body's "self-regulating" activities, such as digestion and circulation.

Availability heuristic: The heuristic that the easier events or objects are to bring to mind, the more likely, common, or frequent they are judged to be.

Avoidance–avoidance conflict: The predicament that occurs when competing alternatives are equally unpleasant.

Avoidance learning: In classical conditioning, learning that occurs when a CS is paired with an unpleasant US that leads the organism to try to avoid the CS.

Axon: The sending end of the neuron; the long cable extending from the cell body.

Basal ganglia: Subcortical structures that play a role in planning and producing movement.

Base-rate rule: The rule stating that if something is sampled at random, the chances of obtaining a particular type are directly proportional to its percentage in the set from which the sample is taken.

Basic emotion: An innate emotion that is shared by all humans, such as surprise, happiness, anger, fear, disgust, and sadness.

Basic level: A level of specificity, which is usually the most likely to be applied to an object.

B cell: A type of white blood cell that matures in the bone marrow.

Behavior: The outwardly observable acts of an individual, alone or in a group.

Behavior modification: A category of therapeutic techniques for changing behavior based on operant conditioning principles. A technique that brings about therapeutic change in behavior through the use of secondary reinforcers.

Behavior therapy: A type of therapy, based on well-researched principles of learning, that focuses on changing observable, measurable behaviors.

Behavioral genetics: The field in which researchers attempt to determine how much of the differences among people are due to their genes and how much to the environment.

Behaviorism: The school of psychology that focuses on how a specific stimulus (object, person, or event) evokes a specific response (behavior in reaction to the stimulus).

Belief in a just world: An attributional bias that assumes people get what they deserve.

Benzodiazepine: A type of antianxiety medication that affects the target symptoms within 36 hours and does not need to be taken for more than a week to be effective.

Bereavement: The experience of missing a loved one and longing for his or her company.

Bias: An investigator's previous beliefs or expectations alter how a study is set up or conducted, leading it to come out a certain way. In signal detection theory, a person's willingness to report noticing a stimulus.

Bibliotherapy: The use of self-help books and tapes for therapeutic purposes.

"Big Five": The five superfactors of personality—extraversion, neuroticism, agreeableness, conscientiousness, and openness—determined by factor analysis.

Binocular cues: Cues to the distance of an object that arise from both eyes working together.

Biological preparedness: A built-in readiness for certain conditioned stimuli to elicit certain conditioned responses so that less learning is necessary to produce conditioning.

Bipolar disorder: A mood disorder marked by one or more episodes of either mania or hypomania.

Bisexual: A person who is sexually attracted to members of both sexes.

Blackout: A period of time for which an alcoholic has no memory of events that transpired while intoxicated.

Bottom-up processing: Processing that is initiated by stimulus input.

Brain circuit: A set of neurons that affect one another.

Brainstem: The set of neural structures at the base of the brain, including the medulla and pons.

Breadth of processing: Processing that organizes and integrates information into previously stored information, often by making associations.

Broca's aphasia: Problems with producing language following brain damage (typically to the left frontal lobe).

Bulimia nervosa: An eating disorder characterized by recurrent episodes of binge eating, followed by some attempt to prevent weight gain.

Burnout: A work-related state characterized by chronic stress, accompanied by physical and mental exhaustion and a sense of low accomplishment.

Bystander effect: The decrease in offers of assistance that occurs as the number of bystanders increases.

Case study: A scientific study that focuses on a single instance of a situation, examining it in detail.

Castration anxiety: A boy's anxiety-laden fear that, as punishment for loving mother and hating father, his father will cut off his penis (the primary zone of pleasure).

Categorical perception: Identifying sounds as belonging to distinct categories that correspond to the basic units of speech.

Category: A grouping in which the members are specific cases of a more general type.

Cell body: The middle part of a cell, which contains the nucleus.

Cell membrane: The skin of a cell.

Central executive: The set of processes that operates on information in one or another STM; part of working memory.

Central nervous system (CNS): The spinal cord and the brain.

Central tendency: The clustering of the most characteristic values, or scores, for a particular group.

Cerebellum: A large structure at the base of the brain that is concerned in part with physical coordination, estimating time, and paying attention.

Cerebral cortex: The convoluted pinkish-gray surface of the brain, where most mental processes take place.

Cerebral hemisphere: A left or right half-brain, roughly half a sphere in shape.

Chemical senses: Taste and smell, which rely on sensing the presence of specific chemicals.

Child-directed speech (CDS): Speech to babies that relies on short sentences with clear pauses, careful enunciation, exaggerated intonation, and a high-pitched voice; also known as *motherese.*

Chronic stressor: A stressor of long-term duration.

Chunk: A unit of information, such as a digit, letter, or word.

Circadian rhythms: The body's daily fluctuations in response to the dark and light cycle, which affects blood pressure, pulse rate, body temperature, blood sugar level, hormone levels, and metabolism.

Classical conditioning: A type of learning that occurs when a neutral stimulus becomes paired (associated) with a stimulus that causes a reflexive behavior and, in time, is sufficient to produce that behavior.

Client-centered therapy: A type of insight-oriented therapy that focuses on people's potential for growth and the importance of an empathic therapist.

Clinical psychologist: The type of psychologist who provides psychotherapy and is trained to administer and interpret psychological tests.

Cocktail party phenomenon: The effect of not being aware of other people's conversations until your name is mentioned, and then suddenly hearing it.

Code: A type of mental representation, an internal "re-presentation" of a stimulus or event (such as words or images).

Cognitive dissonance: The uncomfortable state that arises because of a discrepancy between an attitude and behavior or between two attitudes.

Cognitive distortion: Irrational thoughts that arise from a systematic bias in the way a person thinks about reality.

Cognitive engineering: The field devoted to using facts and theories about human information processing to guide the design of products and devices.

Cognitive learning: The acquisition of information that often is not immediately acted on but is stored for later use.

Cognitive neuroscience: A blending of cognitive psychology and neuroscience (the study of the brain) that aims to specify how the brain stores and processes information.

Cognitive psychology: The approach in psychology that attempts to characterize how information is stored and operated on internally.

Cognitive restructuring: The process of helping clients shift their thinking away from the focus on automatic, dysfunctional thoughts to more realistic ones.

Cognitive therapy: Therapy that focuses on the client's thoughts rather than his or her feelings or behaviors.

Cohort: A group of people who were born at about the same time and thus move through life together and share many experiences.

Collectivist culture: A culture that emphasizes the rights and responsibilities of the group over those of the individual.

Color blindness: An inability, either acquired (by brain damage) or inherited, to perceive hue.

Color constancy: Seeing objects as having the same color in different viewing situations.

Common factor: In psychotherapy, a curative factor of therapy common to all types of treatment.

Compassionate love: A type of love marked by very close friendship, mutual caring, liking, respect, and attraction.

Complex inheritance: The joint action of combinations of genes working together.

Compliance: A change in behavior prompted by a direct request rather than social norms.

Compulsion: A repetitive behavior or mental act that an individual feels compelled to perform in response to an obsession.

Computer-assisted tomography (CT, formerly **CAT):** A neuroimaging technique that produces a three-dimensional image of brain structure using X rays.

Concentrative meditation: A form of meditation in which the meditator restricts attention and concentrates on one stimulus while disregarding everything else.

Concept: An unambiguous, sometimes abstract, internal representation that defines a grouping of a set of objects (including living things) or events (including relationships).

Concrete operation: In Piaget's theory, a (reversible) manipulation of the mental representation of perceived events and actions that corresponds to the actual physical manipulation.

Conditioned emotional response (CER): An emotional response elicited by a previously neutral stimulus.

Conditioned response (CR): A response that depends, or is conditional, on pairings of the conditioned stimulus with an unconditioned stimulus; once learned, the conditioned response occurs when the CS is presented alone.

Conditioned stimulus (CS): An originally neutral stimulus that acquires significance through the "conditioning" of repeated pairings with an unconditioned stimulus (US).

Conduction deafness: A type of deafness caused by a physical impairment of the external or middle ear.

Cones: Retinal cells that respond most strongly to one of three wavelengths and that play a key role in producing color vision.

Confirmation bias: A tendency to seek information that will confirm a rule, and not to seek information that is inconsistent with the rule.

Conformity: A change of beliefs or actions in order to follow a group's norms.

Confound (or **confounding variable**): An independent variable that varies along with the ones of interest, and could be the actual basis for what you are measuring.

Consciousness: A person's awareness of his or her own existence, sensations, and cognitions.

Conservation: The Piagetian principle that certain properties of objects remain the same even when their appearance changes, provided that nothing is added or removed.

Consolidation: The process of converting information stored dynamically in long-term memory into a structural change in the brain.

Continuous reinforcement: Reinforcement given for each desired response.

Contrapreparedness: A built-in disinclination (or even an inability) for certain conditioned stimuli to elicit particular conditioned responses.

Control condition: Like a control group, but administered to the same participants who receive the experimental condition.

Control group: A group that is treated exactly the same way as the experimental group, except for the one aspect of the situation being studied—the independent variable. The control group holds constant—"controls"—all of the variables in the experimental group except the one of interest.

Coping: Taking a course of action regarding the stressor, its effects, or the person's reaction to it.

Cornea: The transparent covering over the eye, which serves partly to focus the light onto the back of the eye.

Corpus callosum: The huge band of nerve fibers that connects the two halves of the brain.

Correlation: An index of how closely interrelated two sets of measured variables are, which ranges from −1 to +1. The higher the correlation (in either direction), the better you can predict the value of one type of measurement when given the value of the other.

Cortisol: A hormone produced by the outer layer of the adrenal glands that helps the body cope with the extra energy demands of stress by breaking down and converting protein and fat to sugar.

Counseling psychologist: The type of psychologist who is trained to help people with issues that naturally arise during the course of life.

Crack: Cocaine in crystalline form, usually smoked in a pipe (free-basing) or rolled into a cigarette.

Creativity: The ability to produce something original of high quality or to devise effective new ways of solving a problem.

Critical period: A narrow window of time when certain types of learning are possible.

Cross-sectional study: A study in which different groups of people are tested, with each group at a different age.

Crystallized intelligence: According to Cattell and Horn, the kind of intelligence that relies on knowing facts and having the ability to use and combine them.

Cues: Stimuli that trigger or enhance remembering; reminders.

Curative factor: A therapy-related factor that helps make clients better.

Cybertherapy: Therapy over the Internet.

Dark adaptation: The process whereby exposure to darkness causes the eyes to become more sensitive, allowing for better vision in the dark.

Data: Objective observations.

Debriefing: An interview after a study to ensure that the participant has no negative reactions as a result of participation and understands why the study was conducted.

Decay: The fading away of memories with time because the relevant connections between neurons are lost.

Deductive reasoning: Reasoning that applies the rules of logic to a set of assumptions (stated as premises) to discover whether certain conclusions follow from those assumptions; deduction goes from the general to the particular.

Defense mechanism: An unconscious psychological means by which a person tries to prevent unacceptable thoughts or urges from reaching conscious awareness.

Deindividuation: The loss of sense of self that occurs when people are in a group but are anonymous.

Delayed reinforcement: Reinforcement given some period of time after the desired behavior is exhibited.

Deliberate practice: Practice that is motivated by the goal of improving performance, usually by targeting specific areas of weakness and working to improve them.

Delusions: Entrenched false beliefs that are often bizarre.

Dendrite: The twiggy part of a neuron that receives messages from the axons of other neurons.

Deoxyribonucleic acid, or **DNA:** The molecule that contains genes.

Dependent variable: The aspect of the situation that is measured as an independent variable is changed. The value of the dependent variable *depends* on the independent variable.

Depressant: A class of substances, including barbiturates, alcohol, and antianxiety drugs, that depress the central nervous system, decreasing the user's behavioral activity and level of awareness; also called *sedative–hypnotic drugs.*

Deprived reward: Reward that occurs when a biological need is filled.

Depth of processing: The number and complexity of the operations involved in processing information, expressed in a continuum from shallow to deep.

Descriptive statistics: Concise ways of summarizing properties of sets of numbers.

Diathesis–stress model: A way of understanding the development of a psychological disorder, in which a predisposition to a given disorder (diathesis) and specific factors (stress) combine to trigger the onset of the disorder.

Dichotic listening: A procedure in which participants hear stimuli presented separately to the two ears (through headphones) and are instructed to listen only to sounds presented to one ear.

Diffusion of responsibility: The diminished sense of responsibility to help that each person feels as the number of bystanders grows.

Discrimination: The ability to distinguish between the desired response and a similar but undesirable one.

Discriminative stimulus: The cue that tells the organism whether a specific response will lead to the expected reinforcement.

Disinhibition: The inhibition of inhibitory neurons, which make other neurons (the ones that are usually inhibited) more likely to fire and usually occurs as a result of depressant use.

Display rule: A culture-specific rule that indicates when, to whom, and how strongly certain emotions can be shown.

Dissociative amnesia: An inability to remember important personal information, often experienced as memory "gaps."

Dissociative disorder: A category of disorders involving a disruption in the usually integrated functions of consciousness, memory, or identity.

Dissociative fugue: An abrupt, unexpected departure from home or work, combined with an inability to remember some or all of the past.

Dissociative identity disorder (DID): A disorder in which a person has two or more distinct personalities that take control of the individual's behavior.

Divided attention: The process of shifting focus back and forth between different stimuli or tasks.

Dizygotic: From different eggs and sharing only as many genes as any pair of brothers or sisters—on average, half.

Door-in-the-face technique: A compliance technique in which someone makes a very large request; when it is denied, as expected, a second, smaller request (the desired one) is made.

Double-blind design: The participant is "blind" to (unaware of) the predictions of the study (and so cannot consciously or unconsciously produce the predicted results), and the experimenter is "blind" to the condition assigned to the participant (and so experimenter expectancy effects cannot produce the predicted results).

Double pain: The sensation that occurs when an injury first causes a sharp pain, and later a dull pain; the two kinds of pain arise from different fibers sending their messages at different speeds.

Down syndrome: A type of retardation that results from the creation of an extra chromosome during conception; it is genetic but not inherited.

Dream analysis: A technique used in psychoanalysis and psychodynamic therapy in which the therapist examines the content of dreams to gain access to the unconscious.

Drive: An internal imbalance that motivates animals (including humans) to reach a particular goal that will reduce the imbalance.

Dysthymia: A mood disorder similar to major depressive disorder, but less intense and longer lasting.

Eating disorder: A category of disorders involving a severe disturbance in eating behavior.

Effect: The difference in the dependent variable that is due to the changes in the independent variable.

Ego: A psychic structure, proposed by Freud, developed in childhood, that tries to balance the competing demands of the id, superego, and reality.

Egocentrism: In Piaget's theory, the inability to take another person's point of view.

Elaborative encoding: Encoding that involves great breadth of processing.

Electroconvulsive therapy (ECT): A controlled brain seizure, used to treat people with certain psychological disorders such as psychotic depression or those for whom medication has not been effective or recommended.

Electroencephalogram: A recording from the scalp of electrical activity over time, which produces a tracing of pulses at different frequencies.

Electroencephalograph (EEG): A machine that records electrical current produced by the brain.

Embryo: A developing baby from the point where the major axis of the body is present until all major structures are present, spanning from about 2 weeks to 8 weeks after conception.

Emotion: A positive or negative reaction to a perceived or remembered object, event, or circumstance, accompanied by a subjective feeling.

Emotional intelligence (EI): The ability to understand and regulate emotions effectively.

Emotionality: A temperament dimension characterized by an inclination to become aroused in situations in which the predominant emotions are distress, fear, and anger.

Emotion-focused coping: Coping focused on changing the person's emotional response to the stressor.

Empiricism (approach to language): The approach that views language as entirely the result of learning.

Enacted social support: The specific supportive behaviors provided by others.

Encoding: The process of organizing and transforming incoming information so that it can be entered into memory, either to be stored or to be compared with previously stored information.

Encoding failure: A failure to process to-be-remembered information well enough to begin consolidation.

Endogenous cannabinoids: Neuromodulators released by the receiving neuron that then influence the activity of the sending neuron; the cannabinoid receptors are also activated by chemicals in marijuana.

Endorphins: Painkilling chemicals produced naturally in the brain.

Episodic memories: Memories of events that are associated with a particular context—a time, place, and circumstance.

Estrogen: The hormone that causes breasts to develop and is involved in the menstrual cycle.

Estrogens: Female hormones, which cause many female characteristics such as breast development and the bone structure of the female pelvis.

Evocative (or reactive) interaction: Occurs when genetically influenced characteristics draw out behaviors from other people.

Evolution: Gene-based changes in the characteristics of members of a species over successive generations.

Evolutionary psychology: The approach in psychology that assumes that certain cognitive strategies and goals are so important that natural selection has built them into our brains.

Exhaustion phase: The final stage of the GAS, in which the continued stress response itself becomes damaging to the body.

Expectancies: Expectations that have a powerful influence on thoughts, feelings, and behavior, and in turn on personality.

Experimenter expectancy effects: Effects that occur when an investigator's expectations lead him or her (consciously or unconsciously) to treat participants in a way that encourages them to produce the expected results.

Explicit (or declarative) memories: Memories that can be retrieved at will and represented in STM; verbal and visual memories are explicit if the words or images can be called to mind.

Exposure: A theraputic technique based on classical conditioning that rests on the principle of habituation.

External attribution: An explanation of behavior that focuses on the situation; also called *situational attribution.*

Extinction: In classical conditioning, the process by which a CR comes to be eliminated through repeated presentations of the CS without the presence of the US. In operant conditioning, the fading out of a response following an initial burst of a behavior after the withdrawal of reinforcement.

Extrasensory perception (ESP): The ability to perceive and know things without using the ordinary senses.

Facial feedback hypothesis: The idea that emotions arise partly as a result of the position of facial muscles.

Factor analysis: A statistical method that uncovers the particular attributes (factors) that make scores more or less similar; the more similar the scores, the more strongly implicated are shared underlying factors.

False memories: Memories of events or situations that did not, in fact, occur.

Family therapy: A therapy modality in which a family (or certain members of a family) is treated.

Fetal alcohol syndrome: A type of retardation caused by excessive drinking of alcohol by the mother during pregnancy.

Fetus: A developing baby during the final phase of development in the womb, from about age 8 weeks until birth.

Figure: In perception, a set of characteristics (such as shape, color, texture) that corresponds to an object.

Fixed interval schedule: Reinforcement schedule in which reinforcement is given for a response emitted after a fixed interval of time.

Fixed ratio schedule: Reinforcement schedule in which reinforcement is given after a fixed ratio of responses.

Flashback: An hallucination that recurs without the use of a drug.

Flashbulb memory: An unusually vivid and accurate memory of a dramatic event.

Flow: The experience of complete absorption in and merging smoothly into an activity and losing track of time.

Fluid intelligence: According to Cattell and Horn, the kind of intelligence that underlies the creation of novel solutions to problems.

Flynn effect: Increases in IQ in the population with the passage of time.

Food aversion (taste aversion): A classically conditioned avoidance of a certain food or taste.

Foot-in-the-door technique: A technique that achieves compliance by beginning with an insignificant request, which is then followed by a larger request.

Forebrain: The cortex, thalamus, limbic system, and basal ganglia.

Forgetting curve: A graphic representation of the rate at which information is forgotten over time: Recent events are recalled better than more distant ones, but most forgetting occurs soon after learning.

Formal operation: In Piaget's theory, a mental act that can be performed (and reversed) even with abstract concepts.

Fovea: The small, central region of the retina with the highest density of cones and the highest resolution.

Fragile X syndrome: A type of retardation that affects the X chromosome; it is both genetic and inherited.

Free association: A technique used in psychoanalysis and psychodynamic therapies in which the patient says whatever comes to mind and the train of thoughts reveals the patient's issues and ways of dealing with them.

Frequency: The rate at which light waves move past a given point.

Frequency theory: The theory that higher frequencies produce higher rates of neural firing.

Frontal lobe: The brain lobe located behind the forehead; the seat of planning, memory search, motor control, and reasoning, as well as numerous other functions.

Functionalism: The school of psychology that sought to understand the ways that the mind helps individuals *function,* or adapt to the world.

Functional fixedness: When solving a problem, getting stuck on one interpretation of an object or one part of the situation.

Functional magnetic resonance imaging (fMRI): A type of MRI that usually detects the amount of oxygen being brought to a particular place in the brain.

Fundamental attribution error: The strong tendency to interpret other people's behavior as due to internal (dispositional) causes rather than external (situational) ones.

g: "General factor," a single intelligence that underlies the positive correlations among different tests of intelligence.

Gate control of pain: The top-down inhibition of interneurons that regulate the input of pain signals to the brain.

Gender identity: A person's belief that he or she is male or is female.

Gender roles: The culturally determined appropriate behaviors of males versus females.

Gene: A stretch of DNA that produces a specific protein, which in turn forms the building blocks of our bodies (including our brains) or drives the processes that allow us to live.

General adaptation syndrome (GAS): The technical name for the three phases of the body's response to stress.

Generalization: The ability to generalize both to similar stimuli and from a learned response to a similar response.

Generalized anxiety disorder: A disorder whose hallmark is excessive anxiety and worry that is not consistently related to a specific object or situation.

Generalized reality orientation fading: A tuning out of external reality during hypnosis.

Genotype: The genetic code carried by the organism.

Gestalt laws of organization: A set of rules describing the circumstances under which marks will be grouped into perceptual units, such as proximity, good continuation, similarity, closure, and good form.

Gestalt psychology: An approach to understanding mental processes that focuses on the idea that the whole is more than the sum of its parts.

Gifted: People who have IQs of at least 135, but more commonly between 150 and 180.

Glial cell: A cell that fills the gaps between neurons, influences the communication among them, and generally helps in the care and feeding of neurons.

Glove anesthesia: Hypnotically induced anesthesia of the hand.

Glucocorticoids: A type of hormone that is released when the stress response is triggered. Glucocorticoids have anti-inflammatory properties.

Grammar: The rules that determine how words can be organized into acceptable sentences in a language.

Grief: The emotion of distress that follows the loss of a loved one.

Ground: In perception, the background, which must be distinguished in order to pick out figures.

Group: A social entity characterized by regular interaction among members, emotional connection, a common frame of reference, and interdependence.

Group polarization: The tendency of group members' opinions to become more extreme (in the same direction as their initial opinions) after group discussion.

Group therapy: A therapy modality in which a number of clients with compatible needs meet together with one or two therapists.

Groupthink: The tendency of people who try to solve problems together to accept one another's information and ideas without subjecting them to critical analysis.

Gyrus: A bulge between sulci in the cerebral cortex.

Habit: A well-learned response that is carried out automatically (without conscious thought) when the appropriate stimulus is present.

Habituation: The learning that occurs when repeated exposure to a stimulus decreases an organism's responsiveness to the stimulus.

Hair cells: The cells with stiff hairs along the basilar membrane of the inner ear that, when moved, produce nerve impulses that are sent to the brain; these cells are the auditory equivalent of rods and cones.

Hallucinations: Mental images so vivid that they seem real.

Hallucinogen: A substance that induces hallucinations.

Hardy personality: The constellation of personality traits associated with health; these include commitment to themselves, a sense of control over what happens to them, and viewing stressors as a challenge.

Health psychology: The area of psychology concerned with the promotion of health and prevention and treatment of illness as it relates to psychological factors.

Heritability: The degree to which variability in a characteristic is due to genetics.

Heterosexual: A person who is sexually attracted to members of the opposite sex.

Heuristic: A rule of thumb that does not guarantee the correct answer to a problem but offers a likely shortcut to it.

Hidden observer: A part of the self that experiences (and can record) what the part of the self responding to hypnotic trance does not consciously experience.

High expressed emotion: An emotional style in families that are critical, hostile, and overinvolved.

Hindbrain: The medulla, pons, cerebellum, and parts of the reticular formation.

Hippocampus: A subcortical structure that plays a key role in allowing new information to be stored in the brain's memory banks.

Homeostasis: The process of maintaining a steady state, a constant level of a bodily substance or condition.

Homosexual: A person who is sexually attracted to members of the same sex.

Hormone: A chemical produced by glands that can act as a neuromodulator.

Hostile attribution bias: The propensity to misread the intentions of others as negative.

Hostility: The personality trait associated with heart disease, characterized by mistrust, an expectation of harm and provocation by others, and a cynical attitude.

Humanistic psychology: The school of psychology that assumes people have positive values, free will, and deep inner creativity, the combination of which leads them to choose life-fulfilling paths to personal growth.

Hypermnesia: Memory that improves over time without feedback, particularly with repeated attempts to recall.

Hypnogogic sleep: Occurs in the first minutes of sleep and can include the experience of gentle falling or floating, or "seeing" flashing lights and geometric patterns.

Hypnosis: A state of mind characterized by a focused awareness on vivid, imagined experiences and decreased awareness of the external environment.

Hypnotic induction: The procedure used to attain a hypnotic trance state.

Hypomania: A mood state similar to mania, but less severe, with fewer and less intrusive symptoms.

Hypothalamus: A brain structure that sits under the thalamus and plays a central role in controlling eating and drinking, and in regulating the body's temperature, blood pressure, and heart rate.

Hypothesis: A tentative idea that might explain a set of observations.

Id: A psychic structure, proposed by Freud, that exists at birth and houses sexual and aggressive drives and physical needs.

Immediate reinforcement: Reinforcement given immediately after the desired behavior is exhibited.

Implicit (or nondeclarative) memories: Memories that cannot be voluntarily called to mind, but nevertheless influence behavior or thinking.

Implicit motive: A need or want that unconsciously directs behavior.

Impression formation: The process of developing impressions of others.

Impression management: A person's efforts to control the type of impression he or she creates.

Impulsivity: A temperament dimension characterized by the propensity to respond to stimuli immediately, without reflection or concern for consequences.

Incentive: A stimulus that draws animals (including humans) toward a particular goal, in anticipation of a reward.

Incidental learning: Learning that occurs without intention.

Incongruence: According to client-centered therapy, a mismatch between a person's *real self* and his or her *ideal self*.

Incubation: Improved thinking following a period of not consciously working on solving a problem or performing a task.

Independent variable: The aspect of the situation that is intentionally varied while another aspect is measured.

Individualist culture: A culture that emphasizes the rights and responsibilities of the individual over those of the group.

Individual therapy: A therapy modality in which an individual client is treated by a single therapist.

Inductive reasoning: Reasoning that uses examples to figure out a rule; induction goes from the particular (examples) to the general (a rule).

Inferential statistics: The results of tests that reveal whether differences or patterns in measurements reflect true differences or patterns versus just chance variations.

Inferiority complex: The experience that occurs when inferiority feelings are so strong that they hamper striving for superiority.

Informed consent: The requirement that a potential participant in a study be told what he or she will be asked to do and possible risks and benefits of the study before agreeing to take part.

Ingroup: An individual's own group.

Inhibitory conflict: A response that is both strongly instigated and inhibited.

Insight: A new way to look at a problem that implies the solution.

Insight learning: Learning that occurs when a person or animal suddenly grasps what something means and incorporates that new knowledge into old knowledge.

Insight-oriented therapy: Therapy that aims to remove distressing symptoms by leading people to understand their causes through deeply felt personal insights.

Insomnia: Repeated difficulty falling asleep, difficulty staying asleep, or waking up too early.

Instinct: An inherited tendency to produce organized and unalterable responses to particular stimuli.

Insulin: A hormone that stimulates the storage of food molecules in the form of fat.

Intelligence: The ability to solve problems well and to understand and learn complex material.

Intelligence quotient (IQ): A score on an intelligence test, originally based on comparing mental age to chronological age but later based on norms.

Intentional learning: Learning that occurs as a result of trying to learn.

Interactionism: A view of personality in which both traits and situations are believed to affect thoughts, feelings, and behavior.

Interference: The disruption of the ability to remember one piece of information by the presence of other information.

Internal attribution: An explanation of someone's behavior that focuses on the person's beliefs, goals, or other dispositions; also called *dispositional attribution*.

Internal conflict: The emotional predicament experienced when making difficult choices.

Interneuron: A neuron that is connected to other neurons, not to sense organs or muscles.

Interpretation: A technique used in psychoanalysis and psychodynamic therapies in which the therapist deciphers the patient's words and behaviors, assigning unconscious motivations to them.

Interval schedule: Partial reinforcement schedule based on time.

Introspection: The process of "looking within."

Ion: An atom that has a positive or negative charge.

Iris: The circular muscle that adjusts the size of the pupil.

Islands of excellence: Areas in which retarded people perform remarkably well.

Just-noticeable difference (JND): The size of the difference in a stimulus property needed for the observer to notice that a change has occurred.

Kinesthetic sense: The sense that registers the movement and position of the limbs.

Knockin mice: Mice in which a new sequence of genetic code is added or is substituted for one already there.

Knockout mice: Mice in which part of the genetic code has been snipped away, deleting all (or crucial parts) of a gene so that it is disabled.

Language acquisition device (LAD): An innate mechanism, hypothesized by Chomsky, that contains the grammatical rules common to all languages and allows language acquisition.

Language comprehension: The ability to understand the message conveyed by words, phrases, and sentences.

Language production: The ability to speak or otherwise use words, phrases, and sentences to convey information.

Latent content: The symbolic content and meaning of a dream.

Latent learning: Learning that occurs without behavioral signs.

Law of Effect: Actions that subsequently lead to a "satisfying state of affairs" are more likely to be repeated.

Learned helplessness: The condition that occurs after an animal has an aversive experience in which nothing it does can affect what happens to it, and so it simply gives up and stops trying to change the situation or to escape.

Learning: A relatively permanent change in behavior that results from experience.

Lesion: A region of impaired tissue.

Level of the brain: Events that involve the structure and properties of the organ itself—brain cells and their connections, the chemical soup in which they exist, and the genes.

Level of the group: Events that involve relationships between people (e.g., love, competition, cooperation), relationships among groups, and culture. Events at the level of the group are one aspect of the environment; the other aspect is the physical environment itself (the time, temperature, and other physical stimuli).

Level of the person: Events that involve the nature of beliefs, desires, and feelings—the *content* of the mind, not just its internal mechanics.

Limbic system: A set of brain areas, including the hippocampus, amygdala, and other areas, that have long been thought of as being involved in fighting, fleeing, feeding, and sex.

Linguistic relativity hypothesis: The idea that perceptions and thoughts are shaped by language, and thus people who speak different languages think differently.

Lobes: The four major parts of each cerebral hemisphere—occipital, temporal, parietal, and frontal.

Locus of control: The source perceived to be the center of control over life's events.

Logic: The process of applying the principles of correct reasoning to reach a decision or evaluate the truth of a claim.

Longitudinal study: A study in which the same people are tested repeatedly, at different ages.

Long-term memory (LTM): A memory store that holds a huge amount of information for a long time (from hours to years).

Long-term potentiation (LTP): A receiving neuron's increased sensitivity to input from a sending neuron, resulting from previous activation.

Loudness: The strength of a sound; pressure waves with greater amplitude produce the experience of louder sound.

Lowball technique: A compliance technique that consists of getting someone to make an agreement and then increasing the cost of that agreement.

Magnetic resonance imaging (MRI): A technique that uses magnetic properties of atoms to take sharp pictures of the structure of the brain.

Major depressive disorder (MDD): A disorder characterized by at least 2 weeks of depressed mood or loss of interest in nearly all activities, along with sleep or eating disturbances, loss of energy, and feelings of hopelessness.

Manic episode: A period of at least 1 week during which an abnormally elevated, expansive, or irritable mood persists.

Manifest content: The obvious, memorable content of a dream.

Maturation: The developmental process that produces genetically programmed changes with increased age.

Mean: The arithmetic average.

Median: The score that is the midpoint of the values for the group; half the values fall above the median, and half fall below the median.

Meditation: An altered state of consciousness characterized by a sense of deep relaxation and loss of self-awareness.

Medulla: The lowest part of the lower brainstem, which plays a central role in automatic control of breathing, swallowing, and blood circulation.

Memory store: A set of neurons that serves to retain information over time.

Mendelian inheritance: The transmission of characteristics by individual elements of inheritance (genes), each acting separately.

Meninges: The covering of the brain.

Mental images: Internal representations like those that arise during perception, but based on stored information rather than on immediate sensory input.

Mentally retarded: People who have an IQ of 70 or less and significant limitations in at least two aspects of everyday life since childhood.

Mental model: An image or description of a specific situation used to reason about abstract entities.

Mental processes: What the brain does when a person stores, recalls, or uses information, or has specific feelings.

Mental set: A fixed way of viewing the kind of solution you seek.

Mere exposure effect: Simply becoming familiar with something can change your attitude toward it—generally, in a favorable way.

Meta-analysis: A statistical technique that allows researchers to combine results from different studies, which can determine whether a relationship exists among variables that transcends any one study.

Metabolism: The sum of the chemical events in each of the body's cells, events that convert food molecules to the energy needed for the cells to function.

Microelectrode: A tiny probe inserted into the brain to record the electrical activity of individual cells.

Microenvironment: The environment created by a person's own presence, which depends partly on appearance and behavior.

Midbrain: Brainstem structures that connect the forebrain and hindbrain, including parts of the reticular formation.

Mindfulness meditation: A combination of concentrative and opening-up meditation in which the meditator focuses on whatever is most prominent at the moment; also known as *awareness meditation*.

Minnesota Multiphasic Personality Inventory-2 (MMPI-2): A personality inventory primarily used to assess psychopathology.

Misattribution of arousal: The failure to interpret signs of bodily arousal correctly, which leads to the experience of emotions that ordinarily would not arise in that particular situation.

Mnemonic devices: Strategies that improve memory, typically by using effective organization and integration.

Modality: A form of therapy.

Modality-specific memory stores: Memory stores that retain input from a single sense, such as vision or audition, or from a specific processing system, such as language.

Mode: The value that appears most frequently in the set of data.

Monoamine oxidase inhibitor (MAOI): A type of antidepressant medication that requires strict adherence to a diet free of tyramine-based foods.

Monocular static cues: Information that specifies the distance of an object that can be picked up with one eye without movement of the object or eye.

Monozygotic: From the same egg and having identical genes.

Mood disorder: A category of disorders marked by persistent or episodic disturbances in emotion that interfere with normal functioning in at least one realm of life.

Moral dilemmas: Situations in which there are moral pros and cons for each of a set of possible actions.

Morpheme: The smallest unit of meaning in a language.

Motion cues: Information that specifies the distance of an object on the basis of its movement.

Motivation: The requirements and desires that lead animals (including humans) to behave in a particular way at a particular time and place.

Motor neuron: A neuron that sends signals to muscles to control movement.

Motor strip: The gyrus, located immediately in front of the central sulcus, that controls fine movements and is organized by body part; also called *primary motor cortex.*

Mutation: A physical change of a gene.

Myelin: A fatty substance that helps impulses travel down the axon more efficiently.

Narcolepsy: Sudden attacks of extreme drowsiness.

Narcotic analgesic: A class of strongly addictive drugs, such as heroin, that relieves pain.

Nativism (approach to language): The approach that views crucial aspects of language as innate.

Natural killer (NK) cell: A type of T cell that destroys damaged or altered cells, such as precancerous cells.

Natural selection: Changes in the frequency of genes in a population that arise because genes allow an organism to have more offspring that survive.

Need: A condition that arises from the lack of a requirement; needs give rise to drives.

Need for achievement (nAch): The need to reach goals that require skilled performance or competence to be accomplished.

Negative punishment: Occurs when a behavior leads to the removal of a pleasant event or circumstance, thereby decreasing the likelihood of a recurrence of the behavior.

Negative reinforcement: Occurs when an unpleasant event or circumstance is removed following a desired behavior, thereby increasing the likelihood of a recurrence of the behavior.

Negative symptom: A diminution or loss of normal functions, such as a restriction in speech.

Nerve deafness: A type of deafness that typically occurs when the hair cells are destroyed by loud sounds.

Neural network: A computer program whose units interact via connections that imitate (roughly) the way the brain works.

Neuroendocrine system: The system, regulated by the CNS, that makes hormones that affect many bodily functions; also provides the CNS with information.

Neuroimaging: Brain scanning techniques that produce a picture of the structure or functioning of neurons.

Neuromodulator: A chemical that alters the effects of neurotransmitters.

Neuron: A cell that receives signals from other neurons or sense organs, processes these signals, and sends the signals to other neurons, muscles, or bodily organs; the basic unit of the nervous system.

Neurosis: An abnormal behavior pattern relating to a conflict between the ego and either the id or the superego.

Neurotransmitter: A chemical that sends signals from the terminal buttons on one neuron to the dendrites or cell body of another.

Nightmare: A dream with strong negative emotion.

Night terrors: Vivid and frightening experiences while sleeping; the sleeper may appear to be awake during the experience but has no memory of it the following day.

Nocebo effect: A variation of the placebo effect in which the subject expects a negative outcome instead of a positive outcome.

Nondeprived reward: Reward that occurs even when a requirement is not being met.

Nonverbal communication: Facial expressions and body language that allow others to infer an individual's internal mental state.

Norm: A shared belief that is enforced through a group's use of penalties.

Normal consciousness: State of awareness that occurs during the usual waking state; also called *waking consciousness*.

Normal distribution: The familiar bell-shaped curve, in which most values fall in the midrange of the scale and scores are increasingly less frequent as they taper off symmetrically toward the extremes.

Norming: The process of setting the mean score and standard deviation of a test, based on results from a standardized sample.

Obedience: Compliance with an order.

Object permanence: The understanding that objects (including people) continue to exist even when they cannot be immediately perceived.

Observational learning: Learning that occurs through watching others, not through reinforcement.

Obsession: A recurrent and persistent thought, impulse, or image that feels intrusive and inappropriate, and is difficult to suppress or ignore.

Obsessive-compulsive disorder (OCD): A disorder marked by the presence of obsessions, and sometimes compulsions.

Occipital lobe: The brain lobe at the back of the head; concerned entirely with different aspects of vision.

Opening-up meditation: A form of meditation in which the meditator focuses on a stimulus but also broadens that focus to encompass the whole of his or her surroundings.

Operant conditioning: The process by which a behavior becomes associated with its consequences.

Operational definition: A definition of a variable that specifies how it is measured or manipulated.

Opiate: A narcotic, such as morphine, derived from the opium poppy.

Opponent cells: Cells that pit the colors in a pair, most notably blue/yellow or red/green, against each other.

Opponent process theory of color vision: The theory that if a color is present, it causes cells that register it to inhibit the perception of the complementary color (such as red versus green).

Optic nerve: The large bundle of nerve fibers carrying impulses from the retina into the brain.

Outcome research: Research that asks whether, after psychotherapy, the client is feeling better, functioning better, living more independently, has fewer symptoms.

Outgroup: A group different than an individual's own.

Overextension: An overly broad use of a word to refer to a new object or situation.

Overregularization error: A speaking error that occurs because the child applies a rule even to cases that are exceptions to the rule.

Panic attack: An episode of intense fear or discomfort accompanied by physical and psychological symptoms such as palpitations, breathing difficulties, chest pain, fear of impending doom or doing something uncontrollable, and a sense of unreality.

Panic disorder: A disorder whose hallmark is panic attacks.

Paradoxical cold: Occurs when stimulation of nerves by something hot produces the sensation of cold.

Paradoxical intention: A systems therapy technique that encourages a behavior that seems contradictory to the desired goal.

Parasympathetic nervous system: Part of the ANS that is "next to" the sympathetic system and that tends to counteract its effects.

Parietal lobe: The brain lobe at the top, center/rear of the head, involved in registering spatial location, attention, and motor control.

Partial reinforcement: Reinforcement given only intermittently.

Passionate love: An intense feeling that involves sexual attraction, a desire for mutual love and physical closeness, arousal, and a fear that the relationship will end.

Passive interaction: Occurs when genetically shaped tendencies of parents or siblings produce an environment that is passively received by the child.

Perceived social support: The subjective sense that support is available should it be needed.

Percentile rank: The percentage of data that have values at or below a particular value.

Perception: The act of organizing and interpreting sensory input as signaling a particular object or event.

Perceptual constancy: The perception of characteristics that occurs when an object or quality (such as shape or color) looks the same even though the sensory information striking the eyes changes.

Perceptual set: The sum of your assumptions and beliefs that lead you to expect to perceive certain objects or characteristics in particular contexts.

Peripheral nervous system (PNS): The autonomic nervous system and the skeletal system.

Personality: A consistent set of behavioral characteristics that people display over time and across situations, and that distinguish individuals from each other.

Personality disorder: A category of disorders where relatively stable personality traits are inflexible and maladaptive, causing distress or difficulty with daily functioning.

Personality inventory: A pencil-and-paper method for assessing personality that requires the test-taker to read statements and indicate whether each is true or false about themselves.

Personality trait: A relatively consistent characteristic exhibited in different situations.

Persuasion: Attempts to change people's attitudes.

Phenotype: The observable structure or behavior of an organism.

Pheromones: Chemicals that function like hormones but are released outside the body (in urine and sweat).

Phobia: A fear and avoidance of an object or situation extreme enough to interfere with everyday life. An irrational fear of a specific object or situation.

Phoneme: The basic building block of speech sounds.

Phonology: The structure of the sounds that can be used to produce words in a language.

Pitch: How high or low a sound seems; higher frequencies of pressure waves produce the experience of higher pitches.

Pituitary gland: The master gland that regulates other glands but is itself controlled by the brain, primarily via connections from the hypothalamus.

Placebo: A medically inactive substance that is presented as though it has medicinal effects.

Place theory: The theory that different frequencies activate different places along the basilar membrane.

Plasticity: The brain's ability to be molded by experience.

Polygraph: A machine that monitors the activity of the sympathetic and parasympathetic nervous systems, particularly changes in skin conductance, breathing, and heart rate. These machines are used in attempts to detect lying.

Pons: A bridge between the brainstem and the cerebellum that plays a role in functions ranging from sleep to control of facial muscles.

Pop-out: Occurs when a stimulus is sufficiently different from the ones around it that it is immediately evident.

Population: The entire set of relevant people or animals.

Positive punishment: Occurs when a behavior leads to an undesired consequence, thereby decreasing the likelihood of a recurrence of that behavior.

Positive reinforcement: Occurs when a desired reinforcer is presented after a behavior, thereby increasing the likelihood of a recurrence of that behavior.

Positive symptom: An excess or distortion of normal functions, such as a hallucination.

Positron emission tomography (PET): A neuroimaging technique that uses small amounts of radiation to track blood or energy consumption in the brain.

Posthypnotic suggestion: A suggestion regarding a change in perception, mood, or behavior that will occur *after* leaving the hypnotic state.

Posttraumatic stress disorder (PTSD): A disorder experienced by some people after a traumatic event, whose symptoms include an unwanted re-experiencing of the trauma, avoidance of anything associated with the trauma, and heightened arousal.

Pragmatics: The way that language conveys meaning indirectly, by implying rather than asserting.

Prediction: An expectation about specific events that should occur in particular circumstances if the theory or hypothesis is correct.

Prejudice: An attitude (generally negative) toward members of a group.

Primacy effect: Increased memory for the first few stimuli in a set.

Primary mental abilities: According to Thurstone, seven fundamental abilities that are not outgrowths of other abilities.

Primary reinforcer: An event or object that is inherently reinforcing, such as food, water, or relief from pain.

Priming: The result of having just performed a task that facilitates repeating the same or an associated task.

Private speech: The use of language in planning or in prompting oneself to behave in specific ways.

Proactive interference: Interference that occurs when previous knowledge makes it difficult to learn something new.

Problem: An obstacle that must be overcome to reach a goal.

Problem-focused coping: Coping focused on changing the environment itself, or how the person interacts with the environment.

Prodigies: People who early in life demonstrate immense talent in a particular domain, such as music or mathematics, but who are normal in other domains.

Progressive muscle relaxation: A relaxation technique whereby the person relaxes muscles sequentially from one end of the body to the other.

Projective test: A method used to assess personality and psychopathology that involves asking the test-taker to make sense of an ambiguous stimulus.

Propositional representation: A mental sentence that expresses the unambiguous meaning of an assertion.

Prosocial behavior: Acting to benefit others.

Prototype: A representation of the most typical example of a category.

Pruning: A process whereby certain connections among neurons are eliminated.

Pseudopsychology: Theories or statements that at first glance look like psychology, but are in fact superstition or unsupported opinion pretending to be science.

Psychiatric nurse: A nurse who holds a master's degree in nursing as well as a certificate of clinical specialization in psychiatric nursing (M.S.N., C.S.), and who provides psychotherapy and works with medical doctors to monitor and administer medications.

Psychiatrist: A physician who focuses on mental disorders; unlike psychologists, psychiatrists can prescribe drugs, but they are not trained to administer and interpret psychological tests, nor are they trained to interpret and understand psychological research.

Psychoanalysis: An intensive form of therapy, originally developed by Freud, based on the idea that people's psychological difficulties are caused by conflicts among the id, ego, and superego.

Psychodynamic theory: A theory of how thoughts and feelings affect behavior; refers to the continual push-and-pull interaction among conscious and unconscious forces.

Psychodynamic therapy: A less intensive form of psychoanalysis.

Psychoeducation: The process of educating clients about therapy and research findings pertaining to their disorders or problems.

Psychological determinism: The view that all behavior, no matter how mundane or insignificant, has a psychological cause.

Psychological disorder: The presence of a constellation of cognitive, emotional, and behavioral symptoms that create significant distress or impair work, school, family, relationships, or daily living.

Psychology: The science of mental processes and behavior.

Psychopharmacology: The use of medication to treat psychological disorders and problems.

Psychophysics: The study of the relation between physical events and the corresponding experience of those events.

Psychosexual stages: Freud's developmental stages based on erogenous zones; the specific needs of each stage must be met for its successful resolution.

Psychosis: An obvious impairment in the ability to perceive and comprehend events accurately, and a gross disorganization of behavior.

Psychosocial development: The effects of maturation and learning on personality and relationships.

Psychotherapy: The process of helping clients learn to change so they can cope with troublesome thoughts, feelings, and behaviors.

Psychotherapy integration: The use of techniques from different theoretical orientations with an overarching theory of how the integrated techniques will be used to achieve the goals of treatment.

Puberty: The time when hormones cause the sex organs to mature and secondary sexual characteristics appear, such as breasts for women and a beard for men.

Pupil: The opening in the eye through which light passes.

Random assignment: Participants are assigned randomly, that is, by chance, to the experimental and the control groups, so that no biases can sneak into the composition of the groups.

Range: The difference obtained when you subtract the smallest score from the largest, the simplest measure of variability.

Ratio schedule: Partial reinforcement schedule based on a specified number of emitted responses.

Raven's Progressive Matrices: A nonverbal test that assesses fluid intelligence and g.

Raw data: Individual measurements, taken directly from the phenomenon.

Reaction range: The range of possible reactions to environmental events that is set by the genes.

Reality monitoring: An ongoing awareness of perceptual and other properties that distinguish real from imagined stimuli.

Recall: The act of intentionally bringing explicit information to awareness, which requires transferring the information from LTM to STM.

Recategorization: A means of reducing prejudice by shifting the categories of "us" and "them" so that the two groups are no longer distinct entities.

Recency effect: Increased memory for the last few stimuli in a set.

Receptor: A site on the dendrite or cell body where a messenger molecule attaches itself; like a lock that is opened by one key, a receptor receives only one type of neurotransmitter or neuromodulator.

Reciprocal determinism: The interactive relationship between the environment, cognitive/ personal factors, and behavior.

Recognition: The act of encoding an input and matching it to a stored representation.

Reflex: An automatic response to an event.

Reframing: A therapy technique in which the therapist offers a new way of conceptualizing, or "framing," the problem.

Rehearsal: The process of repeating information over and over to retain it in STM.

Reinforcement: The process by which consequences lead to an increase in the likelihood that the response will occur again.

Reinforcer: An object or event that comes after a response that changes the likelihood of its recurrence.

Reliability. Data are reliable if the same results are obtained when the measurements are repeated.

REM rebound: The higher percentage of REM sleep following a night's sleep deprived of REM.

REM sleep: Stage of sleep characterized by rapid eye movements and marked brain activity.

Repetition blindness: The inability to see the second occurrence of a stimulus that appears twice in succession.

Repetition priming: Priming that makes the same information more easily accessed in the future.

Replication: Collecting the same observations or measurements and finding the same results as were found previously.

Representation problem: The challenge of how best to formulate the nature of a problem.

Representativeness heuristic: The heuristic that the more similar something is to a prototype stored in memory, the more likely it is to belong to the prototype's category.

Repressed memories: Real memories that have been pushed out of consciousness because they are emotionally threatening.

Repression: A defense mechanism that occurs when the unconscious prevents threatening thoughts, impulses, and memories from entering consciousness.

Resistance: A reluctance or refusal to cooperate with the therapist, which can range from unconscious forgetting to outright refusal to comply with a therapist's request.

Resistance phase: The second phase of the GAS, in which the body mobilizes its resources to attain equilibrium, despite the continued presence of the stressor; also called the *adaptation phase*.

Response bias: A tendency to respond in a particular way regardless of respondents' actual knowledge or beliefs.

Response contingency: The relationship that occurs when a consequence is dependent on the organism's emitting the desired behavior.

Resting potential: The negative charge within a neuron when it is at rest.

Reticular formation: Two-part structure in the brainstem; the "ascending" part plays a key role in keeping a person awake and alert; the "descending" part is important in producing autonomic nervous system reactions.

Retina: A sheet of tissue at the back of the eye containing cells that convert light to neural impulses.

Retinal disparity (also called *binocular disparity*): The difference between the images striking the retinas of the two eyes.

Retrieval: The process of accessing information stored in memory.

Retroactive interference: Interference that occurs when new learning impairs memory for something learned earlier.

Retrograde amnesia: Amnesia that disrupts previous memories.

Reuptake: The process by which surplus neurotransmitter is reabsorbed back into the sending neuron so that the neuron can effectively fire again.

Rods: Retinal cells that are very sensitive to light but register only shades of gray.

Role: The behaviors that a member in a given position in a group is expected to perform.

Rorschach test: A projective test consisting of a set of inkblots that people are asked to "interpret."

s: "Specific factors," or aspects of performance that are particular to a given kind of processing—and distinct from *g*.

Sample: A group from which one obtains measures or observations that is drawn from a larger population.

Sampling bias: A bias that occurs when the participants or items are not chosen at random, but instead are chosen so that one attribute is over- or underrepresented.

Sampling error: Non-random sampling from a population, which produces differences that arise from the luck of the draw, not because two samples are in fact representative of different populations.

Schema: A collection of concepts that specify necessary and optional aspects of a particular situation. In Piaget's theory, a mental structure that organizes perceptual input and connects it with the appropriate responses.

Schizophrenia: A psychotic disorder in which the patient's affect, behavior, and thoughts are profoundly altered.

Scientific method: The scientific method involves specifying a problem, systematically observing events, forming a hypothesis of the relation between variables, collecting new observations to test the hypothesis, using such evidence to formulate and support a theory, and finally testing the theory.

Secondary reinforcer: An event or object that is reinforcing but that does not inherently satisfy a physical need, such as attention, praise, money, good grades, or a promotion.

Selective attention: The process of picking out a particular quality, object, or event for relatively detailed analysis.

Selective serotonin reuptake inhibitor (SSRI): A type of antidepressant medication that affects only *selective* serotonin receptors, with relatively few side effects. A chemical that blocks the reuptake of the neurotransmitter serotonin.

Self-actualization: An innate motivation to attain the highest possible emotional and intellectual potential.

Self-concept: The beliefs, desires, values, and attributes that define a person to himself or herself.

Self-efficacy: The sense of being able to follow through and produce the specific behaviors one would like to perform.

Self-help group: A group whose members focus on a specific disorder or event and do not usually have a clinically trained leader; also called a *support group*.

Self-monitoring techniques: Behavioral techniques that help the client identify the antecedents, consequences, and patterns of a targeted behavior.

Self-perception theory: The theory that people come to understand themselves by making inferences from their behavior and the events surrounding their behavior, much like those they would make about another person's behavior.

Self-serving bias: A person's inclination to attribute his or her own failures to external causes and successes to internal causes, but to attribute other people's failures to internal causes and their successes to external causes.

Semantic memories: Memories of the meanings of words, concepts, and general facts about the world.

Semantics: The meaning of a word or sentence.

Sensation: The awareness of properties of an object or event that occurs when a type of receptor (such as those at the back of the eye, in the ear, on the skin) is stimulated.

Sensitive period: A window of time when a particular type of learning is *easiest*, but not the only time it can occur.

Sensitivity: In signal detection theory, the threshold level for distinguishing between a stimulus and noise; the lower the threshold, the greater the sensitivity.

Sensory memory (SM): The "lowest" level of memory, which holds a large amount of perceptual input for a very brief time, typically less than 1 second.

Sensory neuron: A neuron that responds to input from sense organs.

Separation anxiety: Fear of being away from the primary caregiver.

Serotonin/norepinephrine reuptake inhibitor (SNRI): A newer type of antidepressant that affects both serotonin and noradrenergic neurotransmitter systems.

Set point: The particular body weight that is easiest for an animal (including a human) to maintain.

Sexual response cycle (SRC): The stages the body passes through during sexual activity, now characterized as including sexual attraction, desire, excitement, and performance (which includes full arousal, orgasm, and resolution).

Shape constancy: Seeing objects as having the same shape even when the image on the retina changes.

Shaping: The gradual process of reinforcing an organism for behavior that gets closer to the desired behavior.

Short-term memory (STM): A memory store that holds relatively little information (typically 5 to 9 items) for a few seconds (but perhaps as long as 30 seconds); people are conscious only of the current contents of STM.

Signal detection theory: A theory explaining why people detect signals, which are always embedded in noise, in some situations but not in others.

Situationism: A view of personality that regards behavior as mostly a function of the situation, not of internal traits.

Size constancy: Seeing an object as being the same size when viewed at different distances.

Skeletal system: Consists of nerves that are attached to striated muscles and bones.

Sleep: The naturally recurrent experience during which normal consciousness is suspended.

Sleep apnea: Difficulty breathing accompanied by loud snoring during sleep.

Sociability: A temperament dimension characterized by a preference to be in other people's company rather than alone.

Social causation: The chronic psychological and social stresses of living in an urban environment that may lead to an increase in the rate of schizophrenia (especially among the poor).

Social cognition: The area of social psychology that focuses on how people perceive their social worlds, and how they attend to, store, remember, and use information about other people and the social world.

Social cognitive neuroscience: The field that attempts to understand social cognition not only by specifying the cognitive mechanisms that underlie it, but also by discovering how those mechanisms are rooted in the brain.

Social desirability: A bias in responding to questions such that people try to make themselves "look good" even if it means giving untrue answers.

Social exchange theory: A theory that proposes that individuals act to maximize the gains and minimize the losses in their relationships.

Social facilitation: The increase in performance that can occur simply by being part of a group or in the presence of other people.

Social loafing: The tendency to work less hard when responsibility for an outcome is spread over the group's members.

Social phobia: A type of phobia involving fear of public humiliation or embarrassment and the ensuing avoidance of situations likely to arouse this fear.

Social psychology: The field of psychology pertaining to how people think about other people and interact in relationships and groups.

Social selection: The tendency of the mentally disabled to drift to the lower economic classes; also called *social drift*.

Social support: The help and support gained through interacting with others.

Social worker: A mental health professional who helps families (and individuals) with psychotherapy and helps clients use the social service systems in their communities.

Sociocognitive theory: The view that a person in a trance voluntarily enacts the role of a hypnotized person as he or she understands it, which leads to behaviors and experiences believed to be produced by hypnosis.

Somasthetic senses: Senses that have to do with perceiving the body and its position in space—specifically, kinesthetic sense, vestibular sense, touch, temperature sensitivity, pain sense, and possibly magnetic sense.

Somatosensory strip: The gyrus, located immediately behind the central sulcus, that registers sensation on the body and is organized by body part.

Source amnesia: A failure to remember the source of information.

Specific factor: In psychotherapy, a curative factor related to the specific type of therapy being employed.

Specific language impairment: A specific problem in understanding grammar and complex words that is not related to more general cognitive deficits.

Specific phobia: A type of phobia involving persistent and excessive or unreasonable fear triggered by a specific object or situation, along with attempts to avoid the feared stimulus.

Speech segmentation problem: The problem of organizing a continuous stream of speech into separate parts that correspond to individual words.

Spinal cord: The flexible rope of nerves that runs inside the backbone, or spinal column.

Split-brain patient: A person whose corpus callosum has been severed for medical reasons, so that neuronal impulses no longer pass from one hemisphere to the other.

Spontaneous recovery: In classical conditioning, the process by which the CS will again elicit the CR after extinction has occurred. In operant conditioning, the process by which an old response reappears if there is a break after extinction.

Standard deviation: A kind of "average variability" in a set of measurements, based on squaring differences of each score and the mean and then taking the mean of those squared differences.

Standardized sample: A random selection of people, drawn from a carefully defined population.

State-dependent retrieval: Recall that is better if it occurs in the same psychological state that was present when the information was first encoded.

Statistical significance: The measured relationship is not simply due to chance.

Statistics: Numbers that summarize or indicate differences or patterns of differences in measurements.

Status hierarchy: The positioning of roles that reflect who has power over whom.

Stereopsis: The process that registers depth on the basis of retinal disparity.

Stereotype: A belief (or set of beliefs) about people in a particular social category.

Stimulant: A class of substances that excite the central nervous system, leading to increases in behavioral activity and heightened arousal.

Stimulus control: A behavior therapy technique that involves controlling the exposure to a stimulus that elicits a conditioned response, so as to decrease or increase the frequency of the response.

Stimulus discrimination: The ability to distinguish among similar conditioned stimuli and to respond only to actual conditioned stimuli.

Stimulus generalization: A tendency for the CR to be elicited by neutral stimuli that are like, but not identical to, the CS; in other words, the response generalizes to similar stimuli.

St. John's wort: An herbal remedy for mild to moderate depression.

Storage: The process of retaining information in memory.

Strategy: An approach to solving a problem, determined by the type of representation used and the processing steps to be tried.

Stress: The general term describing the psychological and bodily response to a stimulus that alters a person's state of equilibrium.

Stressor: A stimulus that throws the body's equilibrium out of balance.

Stress response: The bodily changes that occur to help people cope with a stressor; also called the *fight-or-flight response.*

Stroke: A result of the failure of blood (with its life-giving nutrients and oxygen) to reach part of the brain, causing neurons in that area to die.

Structuralism: The school of psychology that sought to identify the basic elements of experience and to describe the rules and circumstances under which these elements combine to form mental *structures.*

Subcortical structure: An organ that contains gray matter, located under the cerebral cortex.

Substance abuse: Drug or alcohol use that leads to legal difficulties, causes distress or trouble functioning in major areas of life, or occurs in dangerous situations.

Substance dependence: Chronic substance abuse that is characterized by seven symptoms, the two most important being tolerance and withdrawal.

Successive approximations: The series of smaller behaviors involved in shaping a complex behavior.

Sulcus: A crease in the cerebral cortex.

Superego: A psychic structure, proposed by Freud, that is formed during early childhood and houses the sense of right and wrong, based on the internalization of parental and cultural morality.

Suprachiasmatic nucleus (SCN): A small part of the hypothalamus just above the optic chiasm that registers changes in light, which lead to production of hormones that regulate various bodily functions.

Survey: A set of questions, typically about beliefs, attitudes, preferences, or activities.

Sympathetic nervous system: Part of the ANS that readies an animal to fight or to flee by speeding up the heart, increasing breathing rate to deliver more oxygen, dilating the pupils, producing sweat, increasing salivation, inhibiting activity in the stomach, and relaxing the bladder.

Synapse: The place where an axon of one neuron meets the membrane (on a dendrite or cell body) of another neuron.

Synaptic cleft: The gap between the axon of one neuron and the membrane of another, across which communication occurs.

Syntax: The internal grammatical structure of a sentence, determined by how words that belong to different parts of speech are organized into acceptable arrangements.

Systematic desensitization: A behavior therapy technique that teaches people to be relaxed in the presence of a feared object or situation.

Systems therapy: A type of therapy that views a client's symptoms as occurring in a larger context, or system (the family and subculture), in which a change in one part of the system affects the rest of the system.

Tardive dyskinesia: An irreversible movement disorder in which the person involuntarily smacks his or her lips, displays facial grimaces, and exhibits other symptoms; caused by traditional antipsychotic medication.

Taste buds: Microscopic structures on the bumps on the tongue surface, at the back of the throat, and inside the cheeks; the four types of taste buds are sensitive to sweet, sour, salty, and bitter tastes.

T cell: A type of white blood cell that matures in the thymus.

Technical eclecticism: The use of specific techniques that may benefit a particular client, without regard for an overarching theory.

Telegraphic speech: Speech that packs much information into few words typically omitting words such as "the," "a," and "of."

Temperament: Innate inclinations to engage in a certain style of behavior.

Temporal lobe: The brain lobe under the temples, in front of the ears, where sideburns begin to grow down; among its many functions are visual memory and hearing.

Teratogen: Any chemical, virus, or type of radiation that can cause damage to the zygote, embryo, or fetus.

Terminal button: A structure at the end of axons that, when the neuron is triggered, releases chemicals into the space between neurons.

Test bias: Test design features that lead a particular group to perform well or poorly and that thus invalidate the test.

Testosterone: The hormone that causes males to develop facial hair and other sex characteristics and to build up muscle volume.

Texture gradients: Progressive changes in texture that signal distance.

Thalamus: A subcortical region that receives inputs from sensory and motor systems and plays a crucial role in attention; often thought of as a switching center.

Theory: An interlocking set of concepts or principles that explain a set of observations.

Theory of causal attribution: Rules for deciding whether to attribute a given behavior to a person's enduring traits or to the situation.

Theory of mind: A theory of other people's mental states (their beliefs, desires, and feelings) that allows prediction of what other people can understand and how they will react in a given situation.

Theory of multiple intelligences: Gardner's theory of eight distinct types of intelligence, which can vary separately for a given individual.

Thought suppression: The coping strategy that involves purposefully trying not to think about something emotionally arousing or distressing.

Threshold: The point at which stimulation is strong enough to be noticed.

Tinnitus: A form of hearing impairment signaled by a constant ringing or noise in the ears.

Token economy: A treatment program that uses secondary reinforcers (tokens) to bring about behavior modification.

Tolerance: The condition of requiring more of a substance to achieve the same effect (or the usual amount providing a diminished response).

Tonotopic organization: The use of distance along a strip of cortex to represent differences in pitch.

Top-down processing: Processing that is guided by knowledge, expectation, or belief.

Trace conditioning: A type of forward classical conditioning where the presentation of the conditioned stimulus (CS) ends before the presentation of the unconditioned stimulus (US) begins.

Trance logic: An uncritical acceptance of incongruous, illogical events during a hypnotic trance.

Trance state: A hypnotically induced altered state of consciousness in which awareness of the external environment is diminished.

Trance theory: The view that a person in a trance experiences an altered, dissociated state of consciousness characterized by increasing susceptibility and responsiveness to suggestions.

Transcranial magnetic stimulation (TMS): A technique where the brain is stimulated from outside by putting a wire coil on a person's head and delivering a magnetic pulse. The magnetic fields are so strong that they make neurons under the coil fire.

Transduction: The process whereby physical energy is converted by a sensory neuron into neural impulses.

Transfer appropriate processing: Memory retrieval will be better if the same type of processing is used to retrieve material as was used when it was originally studied.

Transference: The process by which patients may relate to their therapists as they did to some important person in their lives.

Triangular model of love: A theory of love marked by the dimensions of (1) passion (including sexual desire), (2) intimacy (closeness), and (3) commitment.

Trichromatic theory of color vision: The theory that color vision arises from the combinations of neural impulses from three different kinds of sensors, each of which responds maximally to a different wavelength.

Tricyclic antidepressant (TCA): A common set of antidepressant medications named for the three rings in the chemical compound.

Twin study: A study that compares identical and fraternal twins to determine the relative contribution of genes to variability in a behavior or characteristic.

Typicality: The degree to which an entity is representative of its category.

Unconditional positive regard: Acceptance without any conditions.

Unconditioned response (UR): The reflexive response elicited by a particular stimulus.

Unconditioned stimulus (US): A stimulus that elicits an automatic response (UR), without requiring prior learning.

Unconscious: Outside conscious awareness and not able to be brought to consciousness at will.

Underextension: An overly narrow use of a word to refer to an object or situation.

Validation: A therapy technique in which the therapist conveys his or her understanding of the client's feelings and wishes.

Validity: A measure is valid if it does in fact measure what it is supposed to measure.

Variable: An aspect of a situation that can vary, or change—specifically, a characteristic of a substance, quantity, or entity that is measurable.

Variable interval schedule: Reinforcement schedule in which reinforcement is given for a response emitted after a variable interval of time.

Variable ratio schedule: Reinforcement schedule in which reinforcement is given after a variable ratio of responses.

Ventricle: A hollow area in the center of the brain that stores fluid.

Vestibular sense: The sense that provides information about the body's orientation relative to gravity.

Want: A condition that arises when you have an unmet goal that will not fill a requirement; wants turn goals into incentives.

Wavelength: The time between the arrival of peaks of a light wave; shorter wavelengths correspond to higher frequencies.

Weber's law: The rule that a constant percentage of a magnitude change is necessary to detect a difference.

Wechsler Adult Intelligence Scale (WAIS): The most widely used intelligence test; consists of both verbal and performance subtests.

Wernicke's aphasia: Problems with comprehending language following brain damage (typically to the left posterior temporal lobe).

Withdrawal symptoms: The onset of uncomfortable or life-threatening effects when the use of a substance is stopped.

Working memory (WM): The system that includes specialized STMs and the "central executive" processes that operate on them.

Zygote: A fertilized ovum (egg).

Name Index

DiClemente, C. C., 549, 550
DiDomenico, L., 612
Diebel, C. E., 165
Diedrich, O., 450
Diehl, M., 382
Diehl, N. S., 612
Diehl, S. R., 601
Diel, I. J., 547
Diener, E., 393, 400, 441, 701
Dienstfrey, H., 227
Diforio, D., 603, 604
DiGirolamo, G. J., 323, 334
DiGiuseppe, 544
Digman, J. M., 442
Diguer, L., 654
Dijk, D. J., 177, 183
DiLalla, L. F., 490
Dill, P. L., 537
Dillard, J. P., 589
Dillbeck, M. C., 196
Dille, B., 468
Dimberg, U., 589
Ding, Y. S., 205
Dingemans, P., 588
Dinges, D., 178
Dion, K., 151
Diorio, J., 490, 491
DiPietro, J. A., 485, 486–87
Dishuk, N. M., 661
Dittmann-Kohli, F., 522
Dittrich, W. H., 403
Dixon, R. A., 522
Do, V., 265
Dobbin, J. P., 540, 556
Dobson, K. S., 662
Dobson, M., 283
Dobson, R., 680
Docter, R. F., 431
Dodge, K., 544
Dodge, K. A., 558
Dodson, C. S., 284
Doghramji, K., 178
Doheny, M., 67
Dohnanyiova, M., 378
Dohrenwend, B. P., 604
Dohrmann, R. J., 241
Dolan, B., 613
Dolan, R., 263
Dolan, R. J., 260, 262, 338, 410
Dolan, R. T., 657
Dolata, D., 644
Dolberg, O. T., 645
Doll, H. A., 612
Domar, A. D., 196
Dominguez, B., 235
Donaldson, D. W., 288
Donaldson, S. O., 702
Donatelli, J. A., 602
Donlan, C., 317
Dostrovsky, J. O., 94, 492
Doty, R. L., 160, 520
Double, D., 578
Doverspike, D., 362
Dovidio, J. F., 683, 685, 687
Dowd, E. T., 561, 563
Dowd, S. M., 645
Dowdall, G. W., 200
Dowling, J. E., 73, 79, 128
Downes, J. J., 287
Downey, G., 588
Downing, J. W., 676
Draine, J., 649
Draycott, S. G., 443
Drayna, D., 158
Drew, J. B., 564
Drexler, H., 644
Dreyfuss, G., 377
Driessens, C., 602
Driskell, J., 67

Driskell, J. E., 710
Drivdahl, S. B., 281
Dronkers, N., 309
Drost, L., 628
Druckman, D., 67, 194
Druckman, J. N., 339
Druen, P. B., 696
Drummey, A. B., 287, 497
Drummond, S. P. A., 179
Druss, B. G., 581
Dube, E. M., 516
Dubin, L. L., 196
Duboule, D., 429
Dubrovsky, V. J., 703
Duclaux, R., 418
Duclos, S. E., 396
Dudai, Y., 162
Duff, K. J., 464
Duffy, F. H., 288
Duffy, J. F., 183
Duman, R. S., 586
Duncan, G. H., 164
Duncan, H. F., 139
Duncan, J., 365
Duncan, R. M., 504
Duncan, S. C., 249
Duncker, K., 328, 329, 331
Dunlop, T., 361
Dunn, F. A., 129, 182
Dunn, G., 659
Dunn, J., 309, 471–72
Dunn, V., 602
Dunn, V. J., 702–3
Dunne, G., 659
Dunnett, S. B., 417
Dunster, K. R., 486
Dunton, B. C., 684
Dupuy, B., 316
Durcan, M. J., 484
Durkin, K., 497
Durlach, P., 422
Durso, F. T., 683
Durston, S., 602
Dusek, D., 207
Dweck, C. S., 465, 683
Dye, D. A., 442, 443
Dye, R. H., 156
Dykens, E. M., 484
Dysart, J., 275

Eacott, M. J., 287
Eade, J., 422
Eagly, A. H., 473, 558, 674, 675, 699, 705
Eakin, E., 574
Eals, M., 373
Earle, T. L., 541, 566
Eaton, L. G., 445
Eaton, W. W., 661
Eaves, L., 455, 593
Eaves, L. H., 452
Eaves, L. J., 452, 611
Ebbesen, E. B., 284
Ebbinghaus, H., 257, 284
Eber, H. W., 446
Eberhardt, N. L., 421
Eberman, C., 283
Ebers, G., 429
Ebert, R., 391
Ebstein, R. P., 447
Eccles, J., 515, 516
Eckert, E. D., 547
Edelman, G. M., 173
Edelman, S., 134
Eden, D., 375, 543
Eder, R. A., 507
Edgar, L. V., 591
Edgerton, R. B., 604
Edwards, E., 416
Edwards, J., 652
Effa-Heap, G., 426

Egan, M. F., 399
Egbert, L. D., 563
Ehlers, A., 597
Eich, E., 278
Eicher, S., 515
Eigenbrodt, M. L., 429, 543
Eilers, A. T., 311
Eimas, P. D., 156
Einspanier, A., 483
Einstein, A., 89, 318
Einstein, G. O., 292
Eisele, J., 314
Eisen, S. A., 455, 597, 598
Eisenberg, N., 410, 472, 712
Eisenberger, R., 410
Eisenstein, E., 565
Ejnell, H., 37
Ekman, P., 35, 307, 314, 391, 392–93, 396, 397, 402, 406, 432, 476, 589
Ekselius, L., 649
Elaine, H., 589
Elashoff, R., 565
Elber, T., 105, 363
Elder, G. H., Jr., 248
Elder, I. R., 222
El-Dinary, P. B., 270
Eley, T. C., 365, 585
Elfenbein, H. A., 391, 403
Elger, C. E., 150
Elicker, J., 506
Eliez, S., 377
Elikin, I., 657
El-Islam, M. F., 604
Elizur, S., 414
Elkin, I., 11, 656, 657
Elkind, D., 514
Ellgring, H., 418
Ellingson, J. E., 372
Elliot, A. J., 685
Elliott, D., 617
Ellis, 710
Ellis, A., 630, 632
Ellis, A. W., 93
Ellis, H. C., 320, 335
Ellis, L., 429
Ellis, R., 284
Ellison, P. T., 404, 425
Elman, J. L., 309
Elsayed-Elkhouly, S. M., 474
Emens, J. S., 183
Emerson, M. O., 689
Emery, G., 590, 632
Emmelkamp, P. M. G., 565, 625, 628, 651
Emmons, K. M., 551
Emmons, R. A., 393
Emmorey, K., 315
Empson, R. M., 265
Emrick, C. D., 226
Emslie, H., 365
Endert, E., 425
Endicott, J., 581
Engel, S. A., 134
Engle, D., 663
Engvik, H. A., 474
Ensley, E., 413
Entwisle, D. R., 446
Epel, E. S., 543
Epstein, C. M., 183, 645
Epstein, H. T., 503
Epstein, N. B., 587
Erdelyi, M. H., 278
Erez, A., 467
Erhardt, J., 602
Ericsson, K. A., 271, 333, 334
Ericsson, M., 420
Erikson, D. H., 604
Erikson, E. H., 522, 523
Eriksson, J. G., 602
Ernst, C., 469

Eron, L. D., 249
Ervin, F. R., 226
Eshelman, S., 573, 583
Eshleman, J. R., 401
Eskenazi, B., 486
Eskenazi, J., 157
Esler, M. D., 591
Esterea, N. O., 235
Esterling, B. A., 640
Estes, W., 341
Etcoff, N. L., 307, 398, 399, 410
Eustache, F., 263
Evans, A. C., 418, 504
Evans, F. W., 542
Evans, G. W., 542
Evans, N., 683, 685
Everitt, B., 410, 411, 412
Everitt, B. J., 95, 97, 242
Ewald, H., 604
Exner, J. E., Jr., 447
Ey, S., 515
Eyferth, K., 373
Eysenck, H. J., 364, 381, 443, 449, 450, 451, 452, 455, 456, 457, 547
Eysenck, S. B. G., 450

Fabbro, F., 316
Faber, S., 403
Fabes, R. A., 712
Fabiani, M., 104
Fadil, C., 507
Fahey, J. L., 556, 562, 565
Fairbank, J. A., 598, 651
Fairburn, C. G., 612, 702–3
Faita, F., 147
Faith, M., 684
Falkowski, W., 226
Fallon, A., 419
Fallon, B., 659
Fallon, J., 273, 586
Fantino, E., 341
Fantino, M., 422
Far, J. M., 702
Faraday, M. M., 302
Faraone, S. V., 593, 602
Farhi, P., 248
Farkas, K., 486
Farrar, W. T., IV, 302
Farris, S. M., 265
Farroni, T., 494
Farthing, G., 179
Fasko, D., Jr., 356
Fasotti, L., 396
Fast, K., 287
Fatt, I., 127
Faulhaber, H. D., 562
Fava, G. A., 658
Favagehi, M., 546
Fawcett, J. W., 109
Fawzy, F. I., 565
Fawzy, N. W., 565
Fay, R. E., 428
Fazio, F., 338
Fazio, R. H., 675–76, 677, 684, 698
Feather, N. T., 687
Federmeier, K. D., 144
Feeny, N. C., 657
Fehm, H. L., 425
Feighner, J., 586, 643
Feingold, A., 472, 672, 699
Feinsod, M., 645
Feinstein, J. A., 413
Feisthauer, J., 418
Feldman, D. H., 379
Feldman, R. S., 403
Felician, O., 105, 323
Fell, J., 150

Felleman, D. J., 110, 148, 152
Fenson, J., 314
Fera, F., 399
Ferguson, N. B., 417
Ferketich, A. K., 548
Fernald, A., 309
Fernandez, E., 544
Fernandez, T. L., 235
Fernandez-Duque, D., 334
Ferng, H. K., 653
Ferrer-Caja, E., 521
Ferris, C. D., 78
Ferris, G. R., 671
Ferveur, J.-F., 108
Feske, U., 662
Festinger, L., 677, 678, 679, 681, 704
Fibiger, H. C., 240
Ficca, G., 36
Fichtenholtz, H., 265
Fick, L. J., 194
Ficker, J. H. I., 186
Field, A. E., 612
Field, T., 490, 491
Field, T. M., 491, 501
Fifer, W. P., 485
Fifter, W. P., 485
Figiel, G. S., 183, 645
Figiel, L., 183, 645
Fillenbaum, S., 143
Finch, A. E., 649
Finger, K., 281
Finke, R. A., 380, 382
Finkel, D., 521
Finkelstein, J. W., 374
Finlay, F. O., 512
Finlay, K., 704
Finn, J., 649
Fiore, C., 550, 551
Fiorentine, R., 649
Fischer, B., 364
Fischer, C., 205
Fischer, G. W., 686
Fischer, H., 682
Fischer, S. A., 583
Fischhoff, B., 514
Fischl, B., 141
Fischman, A. J., 595, 597
Fisher, L., 564
Fisher, P. J., 365
Fisher, R. P., 270, 275, 293, 294
Fisher, S., 646
Fisher, S. E., 317
Fisher, W. W., 231
Fishman, H. C., 648
Fiske, S. T., 412, 686, 688
Fitton, A., 421
Flatt, W. P., 421
Flaum, M., 602
Flavell, J. H., 501
Flay, B. R., 702
Fleeson, J., 506
Fleetwood, L. H., 265
Fleischman, D. A., 263
Fletcher, A. C., 248
Fletcher, J. M., 302, 374
Fletcher, M. A., 546
Fletcher, P., 260, 262, 318
Fleury, C., 421
Flexser, A., 277
Flier, J. S., 421
Florio, L., 583
Flory, J. D., 544
Floyd, R. L., 486, 487
Flynn, J. R., 352, 359, 360, 372
Foa, E. B., 598, 658
Foch, T. T., 452
Fodor, J. A., 6, 339

Graves, L., 36
Gray, J. A., 450
Gray, J. R., 342, 404
Gray, P. B., 404, 425
Gray, R. W., 416, 418
Gray, W. D., 325
Grayson, B., 404
Graziano, W. G., 456
Greaves, D. W., 649
Greden, J., 589, 595
Green, B. G., 162
Green, B. L., 410
Green, D. E., 542
Green, D. M., 125, 153
Green, J. P., 190, 192, 294
Green, M. F., 642
Green, M. W., 422
Greenberg, B. D., 447, 595, 642
Greenberg, J., 679
Greenberg, J. P., 71
Greenberg, J. R., 636
Greenberg, R., 501
Greenberg, R. L., 590
Greenberg, R. M., 644
Greenberg, R. P., 646
Greene, D., 284, 410, 693
Greenfield, P. M., 316, 374
Greenhouse, J. B., 658
Greeno, C. G., 611
Greenough, W. T., 110
Greenspan, R. J., 108
Greenwald, A. G., 157, 676, 684
Greenwald, M. K., 272
Greenwald, S., 596
Greenwood, D., 546
Greer, S., 547
Greeson, J. M., 182
Gregg, V. R., 126
Gregory, R. L., 167
Gregory, S. W., Jr., 359
Greiner, L. H., 287
Greve, D. N., 141
Grèzes, J., 67, 323
Grice, H. P., 306
Grice, J. W., 427
Grieder, T., 586
Griepentrog, G. J., 495
Griffie, J., 652
Griffin, D., 341
Griffith, J., 193
Griffiths, G. O., 164
Grifol, R., 487
Griggs, R. A., 338
Grigorenko, E. L., 357
Grillo, C., 159
Grill-Spector, K., 134
Grilly, D., 200
Grimes, A., 495
Grimes, K., 603
Grimes, K. E., 603
Grimshaw, G. M., 313, 314
Grisaru, N., 645
Grissmer, D. W., 372
Grochocinski, V., 658
Grodzinsky, Y., 304
Groleau, N., 42
Gross, J., 273, 450, 556
Gross, J. N., 510
Gross, P. H., 672
Grossarth-Maticek, R., 547
Grossberg, S., 135
Grossman, J. A., 110
Grossman, L. I., 109
Grossman, M., 264
Grossman, R. P., 223
Grotpeter, J. K., 559
Grotzer, T. A., 361
Grove, W., 602
Gruenewald, T. L., 537

Grundy, S., 659
Grunhaus, L., 645
Grusec, J. E., 246
Guadagno, R. W., 706
Guanzon-Lapena, M., 474
Gudjonsson, G., 451
Guelgoez, S., 413
Guenteurkuen, O., 374
Guerin, B., 711
Guijarro, M. L., 543
Guilford, J. P., 332, 354, 357, 380, 381
Guilleminault, C., 185
Guillén, F., 150
Guillery, B., 263
Gulick, W. L., 156
Gulotta, C. S., 231
Gulya, M., 496
Gunary, R., 418
Gunewardene, A., 613
Gunn, 331
Guo, Q., 109
Gur, R. C., 193, 374
Gur, R. E., 193, 374
Gureje, O., 203
Gurtman, M. B., 687
Gurung, R. A. R., 537
Gustavsson, J. P., 637
Guthrie, G. M., 235
Guthrie, H. A., 235
Gutkind, D., 602
Gutman, D. A., 712
Guttmann, C. R. G., 519
Guze, B. H., 653
Gyulai, L., 586

Haaga, D. A., 632
Haaga, D. A. F., 547
Haapasalo, J., 234
Hacker, A., 60
Hackett, R., 50
Hackett, T., 193
Hackett, T. P., 567
Hackmann, A., 661
Haddad, E., 265
Haddock, G., 659
Hadjikhani, N. K., 140
Hadley, C., 659
Hadley, S. W., 650
Haeffner, L. S., 512
Haellstroem, T., 37
Haermae, M., 542
Hagen, E. P., 372
Haggerty, R., 652
Hahn, E. G., 186
Hahn, R. A., 567
Haier, R. J., 173, 273, 374, 450, 586
Haïssaguerre, M., 187
Hajos, N., 79
Hakuta, K., 317
Halberstadt, J., 696
Halford, J. C. G., 420
Halgren, E., 101
Hall, C. S., 108, 216
Hall, D. T., 414
Hall, G. S., 515
Hall, J., 97, 410, 411, 412
Hall, J. A., 403, 472
Hall, J. C., 108
Hall, M. H., 565
Hall, N. E., 314
Hall, W. G., 418
Halle, M., 301
Hallet, A. J., 543
Hallett, M., 105
Halmi, K., 612
Halperin, G., 654
Halpern, A. R., 158, 259

Halpern, D. F., 302, 359, 360, 363, 367, 370, 371, 372, 373
Hamagami, F., 521
Hamann, S. B., 399
Hamberger, L., 485
Hamburg, P., 612
Hamer, D. H., 428, 429, 447
Hamilton, D. L., 686
Hamilton, M. E., 222
Hamilton, S. E., 323
Hamilton, V. L., 543
Hammeke, T. A., 146
Hammen, C., 381
Hammer, L. D., 466
Hamouz, V., 302
Hampson, E., 374
Han, S., 147
Haney, T., 563
Hanifin, J. P., 182
Hanley, G. P., 231
Hansen, D., 487
Hansen, W. B., 702
Hanson, K., 703
Hanson, K. A., 404
Hanson, M. A., 445
Hapidou, E. G., 164
Haraldsson, E., 165
Hardesty, J. P., 603
Hardin, C. D., 685
Harding, B., 422
Hardy, G. E., 650, 662
Hardy, J. D., 544
Hardy, L., 67, 554
Hare, R. D., 616
Hari, R., 173
Hariri, A. R., 399
Harker, C., 182
Harkins, S., 711
Harkins, S. G., 711
Harlow, L. L., 550, 551
Harman, D., 518
Harmon-Jones, E., 677
Harrington, H., 451
Harris, C. R., 44, 427
Harris, G., 164
Harris, H., 461
Harris, J. A., 455, 472
Harris, J. R., 412, 455, 470, 471–72, 502
Harris, M., 596
Harris, M. J., 369
Harris, R. J., 271
Harrison, K., 604
Harsch, N., 273
Hart, A. J., 682
Hart, B. L., 428
Hart, J., 43, 144
Hartman, B. J., 154
Hartshorn, K., 496
Hartshorne, H., 440
Hartung, C. M., 588
Hartzell, D. L., 421
Harvey, O. J., 687
Harvey, T., 89, 363
Hasegawa, I., 259
Hasemeier, C. M., 512
Hasher, L., 274, 341, 521
Hashtroudi, S., 283
Haskell, W. L., 186
Haskett, R. F., 644
Hastie, 710
Hastings, N. B., 110, 485
Hastorf, A. H., 674
Hatala, R. M., 330
Hatano, G., 271
Hatfield, E., 696, 697, 699
Hatfield-Timajchy, K., 487
Hatzidimitriou, G., 205
Haug, H., 363
Hauri, P., 180

Hauser, M., 305, 488
Hausmann, M., 374
Havinghurst, R., 523
Hawk, L. W., 399
Hawkins, J. R., 483
Haxby, J. V., 141, 326
Hayashi, T., 147
Haydel, K. F., 248, 466
Hayden, B., 558
Hayflick, L., 518
Hayne, H., 496
Haynes, J. P., 447
Hayward, C., 466
Haywood, H. C., 504
Hazan, C., 464, 697, 698
He, Y., 567
He, Z. J., 123, 134
Healy, H., 422
Hearth, A. H., 669
Heath, A. C., 203, 452, 454, 455, 593, 597, 611
Heath, T. B., 413
Heatherton, T. L., 248
Heaton, R. K., 486
Hecker, M., 543
Hedeker, D., 656, 657
Hedge, J. W., 445
Hedges, C., 689
Hedman, K. E., 126
Hedner, J., 37
Heeb, J., 547
Heel, R. C., 421
Heider, K. G., 430
Heijnen, C. J., 540
Heimberg, R. G., 594, 659
Heindel, W. C., 263
Heinsalmi, P., 542
Heinssen, 600
Heisel, J. S., 546
Heit, C., 101
Hekkanen, S. T., 281
Held, J. D., 373
Hell, W., 340
Hellawell, D. J., 399
Heller, K., 564
Hellhammer, D. H., 374
Hellige, J. B., 93, 144
Hellström, K., 650
Helmers, K., 609
Helmond, F. A., 425
Helms, J. E., 664
Helson, H., 409
Henderlong, J., 410
Henderson, A. K., 512
Henderson, W. G., 455, 598
Hendler, T., 134
Hendricks, B., 713
Heng, M. A., 357
Heninger, G. R., 586
Henkel, L. A., 284
Henley, N. M., 473
Henley, T. B., 537
Henn, F. A., 416
Henry, B., 451
Henry, J. P., 536
Henry, W. P., 662
Henschel, A., 422
Hensel, H., 164
Hensley, D. L., 271
Henslin, J. M., 7
Henson, R., 263
Henzi, S. P., 150, 696
Hepworth, S. L., 497
Herbener, E. S., 697
Herberman, R. B., 546, 562
Herbert, T. B., 545, 547
Hercovitch, P., 141
Herman, C. P., 613, 614
Herman, J. H., 182
Herman, S., 651
Herman-Giddens, M. E., 512

Hermann, J. A., 235
Hermans, E., 425
Hermelin, B., 376
Hernandez, L. L., 222
Hérot, C., 593
Herrera, H., 123, 129, 137, 157
Herrnstein, R. J., 16, 352, 370, 372
Herrup, K., 108
Hershey, T., 537
Hershlag, N., 503
Hershman, D. J., 381
Hershz, M. S., 365
Hertenstein, M. J., 491, 492
Hertzberg, V. S., 512
Hertzog, C., 521
Herz, 279
Herz, M. J., 269
Herz, R. S., 426, 696
Herzog, H., 365
Herzog, T. A., 222, 551
Hesketh, L. J., 377
Hespos, S. J., 507
Heston, L. L., 547
Hetherington, E. M., 472
Hetta, J., 37
Hettema, J., 455
Hichwa, R. D., 305
Hicks, J. L., 284
Hierholzer, R., 597
Higgenbotham, H. N., 664
Higgens, S. T., 239
Higgins, E. T., 338
Highnote, S. M., 131
Hildebrandt, G., 548
Hilgard, E. R., 188, 192, 194
Hilgard, J. R., 192, 194
Hill, D. J., 704
Hill, J. O., 422
Hill, K., 696
Hill, L., 365
Hillger, L. A., 320
Hillis, A. E., 304
Hillis, S. L., 196
Hilsenroth, M. J., 578
Hilton, J. L., 677
Hilton, S. C., 485
Hines, M., 508
Hinton, D., 592
Hirotsugu, Y., 414
Hirsch, J., 316, 371
Hirschfeld, R. M. A., 658
Hirschi, T., 515
Hirshfeld-Becker, D. R., 593
Hitzemann, R., 205
Hixon, J. G., 683
Hlatky, M., 563
Hobson, J. A., 36, 174, 176, 177, 179, 180, 181, 182, 186, 208
Hochman, D. W., 104
Hochschild, A., 566
Hocini, M., 187
Hockemeyer, J., 565
Hodge, D., 281
Hodges, J. R., 325, 399
Hodges, L., 628
Hodgson, A. B., 649, 663
Hodgson, D. M., 485
Hoehn-Saric, R., 548
Hoek, S. W., 602
Hoeks, J. C., 303
Hoeksema-van Orden, C. Y. D., 711
Hoffart, A., 661
Hoffman, 645
Hoffman, D. D., 141
Hoffman, L. W., 456, 471
Hoffman, M. L., 510
Hoffman, R. I., 182

Macomber, J., 501
MacPhillamy, D. J., 587
McQuirk, B., 715
Macrae, C. N., 683, 693
Maddit, S. R., 561
Madison, L. S., 377
Maegawa, M., 483
Maenner, G., 200
Magee, J. J., 307
Mager, R., 222
Magloczky, Z., 79
Magnus, P., 455
Magnuson, V. L., 429
Magnusson, D., 451
Magovern, G. J., 561
Magruder, K. M., 660
Maguire, E. A., 105, 262, 287
Maher, B. A., 600
Mai, N., 140
Maidhof, C., 646
Maier, S. F., 416
Maiolino, L., 159
Maisog, J. M., 141
Makin, J. E., 486
Makin, J. W., 488
Makris, N., 602
Makula, R. A., 421
Malach, R., 134
Malan, D. H., 636
Malarky, W. B., 178, 546
Malcolm, 429
Malik, 651
Malina, R. M., 513
Malinoski, P., 294
Maliphant, R., 474
Maljkovic, V., 323
Malkoff, S., 564
Malkoff-Schwartz, S., 588
Mall, G., 483
Mallinger, A., 585
Malmstadt, J. R., 404
Malone, B. E., 314
Malpass, R. S., 275
Maluish, A. M., 546, 562
Mamish, M. E., 196
Mandeli, J., 425
Manderino, J. V., 196
Manderscheid, R. W., 573
Mandler, G., 256
Manfred, M., 90
Manfro, G. G., 592, 593
Mangan, B., 172
Mangun, G. R., 146
Manichaikul, A., 158
Manis, J., 566
Manke, B., 472
Manly, J., 522
Mann, J. J., 644
Mann, L., 708
Mann, S., 406
Mann, T., 613, 703
Manning, B. H., 79
Manning, J. T., 429
Manning-Ryan, B., 427
Mansour, C. S., 374
Manstead, A. S. R., 693
Mantzoros, C. S., 421
Manuck, S. B., 545
Mao, H., 399
Maquet, P., 36
Marantz, A., 302
Marcel, A. J., 148
Marchetti, C., 264
Marco, C., 563
Marcotle, T. D., 486
Marcus, B. H., 550, 551
Marcus, G. F., 311
Marcus, M., 512
Marentette, P. F., 310
Margolskee, R. F., 161
Marhold, S., 165

Marica, James E., 515
Maril, A., 262, 269
Marinova-Todd, S., 317
Maris, S., 162
Mark, D., 563, 565
Markesbery, W. R., 287
Markey, E., 99
Markham, R., 283, 403
Markman, A. B., 677
Marks, I., 628, 662
Marks, I. M., 218
Marks, L. E., 520
Markson, L., 310
Markus, E., 520
Markus, H. R., 475, 507
Markwith, M., 419
Marley, C., 609
Marmot, M. G., 542, 567
Marmur, S., 645
Marmurek, H. H. C., 279
Marr, D., 6, 123, 134
Marsh, R. L., 284
Marshall, D., 317
Marshall, D. H., 497
Marshall, D. S., 430
Marshall, T. R., 490
Martignon, L., 341
Martin, A., 269, 326
Martin, D. C., 377, 378, 486
Martin, J. S., 196
Martin, K. C., 285
Martin, K. M., 490, 653
Martin, L., 455
Martin, L. L., 396
Martin, N. G., 364, 452, 454, 455, 611
Martin, Q. D., 362
Martin, R. A., 540, 556, 557
Martin, T., 472
Martin, W. L., 137
Martindale, C., 379, 381
Martinez, A., 659
Martinez, J. M., 591
Martino, G., 307
Martis, B., 645
Maruayama, G., 680
Marucha, P. T., 178, 546, 565
Marxer, F., 542
Marytuina, T., 452, 454
Marzi, C. A., 147
Masataka, N., 309
Maser, J. D., 581, 661
Maslach, C., 705
Maslow, A. H., 16, 413, 414, 464, 465
Mason, S. T., 240
Massing, M., 543
Masters, W. H., 423–24, 431, 461
Masuzaki, H., 421
Matar, M. A., 546
Mataraze, A., 378
Matarazzo, J. D., 348
Mataseje, A., 378
Matheny, A. P., Jr., 455
Mather, M., 283, 284
Matocha, H. R., 361
Matsui, M., 374
Matsumoto, H., 475
Matsushima, E., 602
Matt, G. E., 661
Mattay, V. S., 399
Matthews, B. A., 239
Matthews, G., 449, 450
Matthews, K. A., 543, 544, 561
Matthews, P. M., 164, 305
Mattingley, J. B., 142
Mattson, M. P., 109
Matus-Amat, P., 416
Mauss, A. L., 702
Mavreas, V., 203

Mavreas, V. G., 583
May, B. J., 156
May, C., 521
May, C. P., 292
May, M. A., 440
Mayer, J. D., 358
Mayer, R. E., 333
Mayer, W., 42
Mayes, A. R., 287
Mayford, M., 266
Maynard, R. A., 517
Mayou, R. A., 597
Mays, V., 659
Mazel, R. M., 660
Maznevski, M. L., 711
Mazoyer, B., 259, 323
Mazumdar, S., 658
Mazursky, D., 383, 384
Mazziota, J. C., 653
Meacham, J. A., 507
Meade, M. L., 281
Mealey, L., 699
Meaney, M. J., 490, 491
Mecz, L., 645
Medin, D. L., 325
Mednick, B., 602
Mednick, S., 381
Mednick, S. A., 367, 602, 617
Meehl, P., 577
Meertens, R. W., 684
Megson, A., 418
Mehl, L. E., 193
Mehta, B., 226
Meissen, G., 648–49
Mekos, D., 248
Melbye, M., 604
Melchert, T. P., 288
Melding, P. S., 518
Melin, J., 155
Melin, L., 566
Mellet, E., 259, 323
Mello, C. V., 110
Melson, A. K., 537
Meltzoff, A. N., 67, 501
Melzack, R., 164
Menchon, J. M., 645
Mendola, J. D., 140, 141
Meng, I. D., 79
Menlove, F. L., 246
Mennella, R., 370
Menon, N. K., 421
Menon, R. S., 164
Mentzer, T., 162
Menuik, P., 310
Menzies, R. G., 594
Merali, Z., 490
Mercado, A. M., 178, 546
Mercer, E. H., 266
Mercier, L., 566
Meredith, L. S., 660
Meredity, K., 663
Merfeld, D., 42
Merikangas, K. R., 611
Merin, N. M., 79
Merkin, S. S., 543
Merrick, E. N., 517
Merritt, T. A., 548
Merry, W., 663
Mertan, B., 686
Mervis, C. B., 325
Merzenich, M. M., 110, 302, 312
Messinger, S. M., 409
Messner, C., 677
Meston, C. M., 425
Metcalfe, J., 332
Metsahonkala, L., 399
Meulemans, T., 36
Meyer, B. A., 561
Meyer, D. E., 308
Meyer, G. J., 447

Meyer, J. M., 455, 598
Meyer, M., 186
Meyers, R., 226
Meyers, R. J., 226
Mezack, M., 468
Michael, D., 411
Michel, C., 155
Michela, J. L., 691
Michelow, D., 93, 307
Michimata, C., 93, 144
Mickelsen, O., 422
Mickelson, K. D., 697
Mico, J. A., 490
Miezin, F. M., 262, 263, 269
Mignot, E., 185
Miklowitz, D. J., 588
Mikulincer, M., 415, 464
Milberg, S. J., 413
Miles, L. E. M., 183
Miletich, R., 335
Milford, G. E., 414, 465
Milgram, S., 707–9, 716
Miller, A. G., 709
Miller, A. H., 545
Miller, B. L., 376
Miller, D. G., 281
Miller, D. T., 702
Miller, E. K., 141
Miller, E. M., 42
Miller, G. A., 256
Miller, G. E., 565
Miller, H. L., 586
Miller, I., 588
Miller, I. W., 585, 587
Miller, J. A., 702
Miller, J. M., 486
Miller, L. C., 427
Miller, L. K., 376
Miller, M. D., 658
Miller, M. G., 693
Miller, N., 559, 680
Miller, N. E., 539
Miller, P. A., 712
Miller, R., 704
Miller, S., 598
Miller, S. D., 608
Miller, S. L., 312
Miller, T. Q., 543
Miller, W. B., 427, 544
Millet, B., 596
Milligan, L., 338
Millon, T., 577
Mills, D., 376
Mills, D. L., 310
Mills, S., 316
Milne, A. B., 683
Milner, A. D., 140
Milner, B., 96
Milner, P., 95, 411
Milstein, V., 609
Milton, J., 166
Milun, R., 474
Mineka, S., 588, 591, 594
Mingolla, E., 135
Minnes, S., 486
Minor, L. L., 379
Minors, D. S., 183
Minton, H. L., 384
Mintz, J., 586, 588
Minuchin, S., 648
Miodownik, J., 546
Mirsky, A. F., 605, 606
Miscallef, J., 595
Mischel, W., 235, 440
Mischkin, M., 141
Mishkin, M., 140, 240, 262
Mitchell, D. L., 651
Mitchell, J. B., 490
Mitchell, J. F., 183
Mitchell, S. A., 636
Mitchison, F., 181, 208

Mitler, M. M., 174
Mittleman, M. A., 564
Miyamoto, T., 140
Miyashita, Y., 259, 330
Miyazaki, A. D., 543
Miyazaki, K., 158
Modell, J., 469, 595
Modestino, S., 42
Moeschberger, M. L., 548
Moeschler, J. B., 377
Moffitt, T. E., 441, 451, 517
Mogilner, A., 110
Mohr, D., 663
Moineau, S., 564
Mojtabai, R., 659
Moldin, S. O., 602
Moller, H., 604
Monaco, A. P., 317
Money, J., 507
Monk, T. H., 178
Monroe, S. M., 587
Montague, P. R., 97, 411
Monteith, M. J., 687
Montes, F., 235
Montesinos, A., 487
Monthly Vital Statistics
  Reports, 583
Monti, L., 244
Moo, L. R., 144
Moody, D. B., 156
Moore, B. C. J., 156
Moore, C. F., 509
Moore, M. K., 501
Moore, T. J., 646
Moore-Ede, M., 184
Mora, F., 418
Moran, A., 67
Moran, P., 616
Mordkoff, A., 537
Moreland, R. L., 696, 700, 710, 711
Morf, C. C., 559
Morgan, A. H., 192
Morgan, D., 403
Morgan, J. L., 42
Morgan, M., 646
Morgan, M. J., 265
Morgane, P. J., 486
Morgenthaler, J., 519
Mori, H., 483
Morin, C. M., 186
Morphy, M. A., 658
Morrell, F., 263
Morris, C. D., 270
Morris, E. K., 239
Morris, J., 659
Morris, L. A., 566
Morris, L. W., 520
Morris, M. W., 694
Morris, R., 265, 314
Morris, R. G., 520
Morris, R. L., 166
Morris, S., 294
Morris, W., 704
Morris, W. N., 704
Morrison, D. F., 519
Morrison, E. W., 671
Morrow, J., 587, 588
Morrow, J. E., 154
Mors, O., 604
Morse, D. R., 196
Mortensen, P. B., 604
Morton, D., 565
Morton, N. M., 421
Moscovitch, M., 141, 269, 270
Moser, E., 323
Moser, M., 548
Moskowitz, D. S., 473
Moss, L., 507
Moss, M. B., 519, 520

Seckl, J. R., 421
Sedikides, C., 475
Sedler, M. J., 205
Seeley, J., 652
Seeley, J. R., 583
Seeley, R. J., 418
Seely, E., 427
Seeman, R. E., 563
Seeman, T., 543, 566
Segal, N. L., 366, 453, 456
Segal, Z. V., 656
Segall, D. O., 373
Segar, C., 320
Segarra, J., 487
Seger, C. A., 380
Segerstrom, S. C., 562, 691
Sego, S. A., 288
Segrin, C., 586, 589
Seidenberg, M. S., 309
Seidman, L. J., 602
Seifer, R., 486
Seise, J., 677
Seith, R., 492
Seitz, R. J., 365
Seldin, M. F., 421
Seligman, C., 698
Seligman, D. A., 654
Seligman, M. E. P., 218, 415,
    587, 651, 660
Selin, C. E., 653
Selke, G., 537
Selkirk, L., 302
Sellers, E. M., 203
Selnes, O. A., 304
Seltzer, J., 542
Selye, H., 535, 536–37
Semenov, L. A., 496
Semmelroth, J., 427
Semon Dubas, J., 374
Semple, S. J., 567
Sensky, T., 659
Serano, M. I., 140
Sereny, G., 226
Sergent, J., 93
Serpell, R., 372
Serra, A., 159
Sessa, V. I., 711
Seta, C. E., 711
Seta, J. J., 711
Sethna, B. N., 703
Setliff, A. E., 279
Seuling, B., 132, 133, 140,
    157, 162, 180, 186, 226,
    248, 314, 364, 438
Sevcik, R. A., 316
Sexter, M., 396
Shadel, W. G., 551
Shadid, G., 514
Shadmehr, R., 269
Shafran, R., 596
Shah, D. C., 187
Shah, J., 143
Shah, R., 110
Shahidi, S., 357
Shalev, A. Y., 546, 597
Shallenberger, R. S., 162
Shallice, T., 260, 263, 326
Shaman, P., 520
Shanab, M. E., 708
Shanahan, T. L., 183
Shanks, N., 490
Shankweller, D. P., 302, 374
Shannon, D. C., 457, 490
Shannon, R. A., 361
Shapira, B., 644
Shapiro, A., 176
Shapiro, A. K., 566
Shapiro, C. M., 426
Shapiro, D., 556, 660
Shapiro, D. A., 650, 651, 660,
    662

Shapiro, D. H., 196
Shapiro, D. H., Jr., 538, 539
Shapiro, K. L., 148, 150
Share, D. L., 42
Sharma, R., 645
Sharma, S., 490, 491
Sharma, V., 226
Sharp, D. W., 280
Sharp, L. K., 555, 640
Sharples, M., 384
Sharpley, A. L., 421
Sharpnack, H., 495
Shaver, P. R., 464, 697, 698
Shaw, B. F., 632
Shaw, G. L., 361
Shaw, P. J., 179
Shaw, S., 226
Shaw, W. S., 567
Shawcross, C. R., 644
Shaywitz, B. A., 302, 374
Shaywitz, S. E., 302, 374
Shea, C. L., 712
Shea, J. D., 562
Shea, M. T., 581, 656, 657
Shear, J., 172
Shear, M. K., 651
Sheehan, P. W., 294
Sheen, M., 281
Sheftel, G., 416
Shekim, W. O., 451
Sheldon, K. M., 412
Shell, P., 364
Shell, R., 712
Shelton, J. R., 303
Shelton, R. C., 577, 592
Shepard, R. N., 257
Shepherd, G. M., 76
Shepherd, M. D., 648–49
Shepperd, J. A., 439
Sheridan, J. F., 546
Sheridan, K., 357
Sherif, C. W., 687
Sherif, M., 687
Sherman, J. J., 662
Sherman, J. W., 683
Sherman, S. J., 676, 686
Sherrill, J. T., 588
Sherwood, A., 565
Shevrin, H., 222
Shibahara, H., 483
Shibasaki, H., 147
Shidara, M., 410
Shields, S. A., 472
Shiffman, S. S., 563
Shiffrar, M. M., 136
Shiffrin, R. M., 254
Shigeta, M., 483
Shih, J. B., 400, 401
Shimada, J. M., 588
Shimamura, A. P., 279
Shimizu, M., 567
Shimoff, E., 239
Shimojo, S., 123, 134
Shin, L. M., 597, 682
Shin, R. K., 264
Shinyama, H., 421
Shioiri, S., 140
Shipherd, J. C., 591
Shiraishi, T., 417
Shizgal, P., 421
Shoben, E. J., 325
Shoda, Y., 235
Shohamy, D., 262
Shors, T. J., 110, 485
Shortridge, J. R., 476
Shouksmith, G., 542
Shrager, J., 503
Shreiner, C., 312
Shrivastava, R., 586, 643
Shrout, P. E., 604

Shulman, G. L., 142, 143,
    146
Shulman, S., 506
Shupe, A. K., 486–87
Shute, R., 516
Sian, T., 662
Siarey, R., 377
Sicotte, N., 611
Siddle, R., 659
Siefler, I., 563
Siegel, B., 377
Siegel, J. L., 227
Siegel, L., 588
Siegel, M., 610, 611, 613
Siegel, S., 222
Siegler, I. C., 519, 694
Siegler, R. S., 503
Sifneos, P. E., 636
Sigel, J. J., 464
Sigmundson, H. K., 508
Sikich, L., 602
Siksorski, L., 520
Sikström, S., 519, 520, 593
Silberstein, C. S., 501
Silva, E. J., 183
Silva, P., 517
Silva, P. A., 42, 451, 594
Silva, S. G., 642
Silver, R. C., 544
Silver, S. M., 178
Silverman, I., 373
Silverman, L., 464
Silverman, L. K., 379
Silverman, M. S., 134, 135
Silvia, P. J., 173
Simcock, G., 496
Simion, F., 494
Simmens, S., 11, 657
Simmons, J. A., 156
Simon, A. F., 684
Simon, H. A., 17, 333, 348,
    349
Simon, L., 679
Simons, D. J., 149
Simonton, D. K., 379, 381,
    382
Simpson, C. D., 201
Simpson, T. L., 307
Singer, B., 654
Singer, J., 397, 542
Singer, L. T., 486
Singer, R., 680
Singer, W., 172
Singh, B., 413
Singh, R., 413
Singh, V. N., 483
Singha, A. K., 222
Sinha, 567
Siomi, H., 377
Siomi, M. C., 377
Sireteanu, R., 496
Sirigu, A., 399
Sisson, R. W., 226
Sitskoorn, M. M., 602
Sjoelund, B. H., 164
Skakkebaek, N. E., 512
Skala, J. A., 548
Skillings, A., 196
Skinner, B. F., 15, 229, 240
Skodol, A. E., 604
Skodova, Z., 266
Skolnick, B., 193
Skuder, P., 365
Skudlarski, P., 302, 374
Skvoretz, J., 703
Slabbekoorn, D., 374
Slater, A., 488
Slavich, S., 648–49
Slaw, R. D., 413
Slayton, K., 380
Slee, P., 516

Sleek, S., 656
Slep, A. M. S., 691
Slimp, J. C., 428
Slob, A. K., 425
Sloman, S. A., 339
Slora, E. J., 512
Slotnick, B. M., 162
Slotnick, S. D., 144
Slyman, D., 591
Small, B. J., 519
Small, D. M., 418
Smania, N., 90
Smart, L., 559, 560
Smeets, M. A. M., 610
Smilach, K. M., 612
Smit, F., 610
Smith, A., 603
Smith, A. J., 587
Smith, C., 36
Smith, D., 649
Smith, D. E., 520
Smith, D. G., 545
Smith, D. L., 365
Smith, D. M., 673
Smith, D. V., 161
Smith, E. E., 263, 264, 278,
    325, 563
Smith, E. R., 683
Smith, G. A., 364
Smith, G. E., 327
Smith, G. P., 411
Smith, G. T., 231
Smith, J. A. L., 365
Smith, M. E., 101, 249
Smith, M. L., 660
Smith, P. B., 705–6
Smith, R. E., 563
Smith, S., 628
Smith, S. M., 278, 329, 332,
    380, 382, 413
Smith, T. W., 543, 544
Smith, W. R., 364
Smok-Pearsall, S., 492
Smolensky, M., 184
Smolucha, F. C., 504
Smyth, J., 555, 565
Snel, J., 540
Snidman, N., 421, 457, 490,
    593
Snieder, H., 158
Snodgrass, S. E., 473
Snow, C., 317
Snow, C. E., 42, 317
Snow, J. B., Jr., 160
Snow, R., 352
Snowdon, D. A., 287
Snyder, C. R., 439
Snyder, E. E., 420
Snyder, K. S., 588
Snyder, L. H., 146
Snyder, M., 673, 677, 688
Snyder, S. H., 78
Snyderman, M., 370
Sohal, R. S., 109
Soli, S. D., 154
Solms, M., 181, 208
Solomon, D. A., 581, 585
Solomon, K. O., 315, 325
Solomon, P., 649
Solomon, R. L., 393
Solomon, S., 383, 384
Someya, Y., 602
Sommer, F. G., 488
Sommerfield, C., 663
Song, E. J., 182
Song, S., 155
Soni, B., 129
Soper, B., 414, 465
Sorell, G. T., 509
Soriano, J., 487
Sorlie, P., 543

Sotsky, S. M., 11, 656, 657
Souther, J., 146
Southwick, L., 201
Southwick, S. M., 267, 598
Souza, L., 512
Sowell, E. R., 514
Spain, J. A., 445
Spangenberg, E. R., 157
Spangler, D., 613, 614
Spangler, W. D., 413
Spanos, N. P., 192, 609
Spanoudis, G., 504
Sparler, S., 548
Sparrow, D., 548
Spearman, C., 353, 354, 355,
    358
Spears, R., 701, 710
Spector, P. E., 359
Spector, T., 158
Spector, T. D., 164
Speed, A., 699
Speicher, C., 564, 565
Speisman, J. C., 537
Spelke, E., 331
Spelke, E. S., 495, 501
Spence, E. L., 398
Spencer, R. L., 545
Spencer, W. D., 520
Sperber, D., 339
Sperlagh, B., 79
Sperling, G., 255
Sperling, R., 262
Spiegel, D., 190, 193, 194,
    552
Spielman, D. A., 403
Spiers, H. J., 262, 287
Spinath, F. M., 364
Spitzberg, B. H., 695
Spitzer, R. L., 577
Sprecher, S., 696, 697, 698,
    699, 700
Springer, S. P., 93, 374
Sprock, J., 588
Spyraki, C., 240
Squire, L. R., 96, 259, 262,
    263, 273, 286, 399
Sramek, J. J., 586, 643
Srinivas, K., 270
Sroufe, L. A., 506
Stachnik, T. J., 439
Stack, J. A., 658
Stack, S., 401
Stadtman, E. R., 518
Stager, C. L., 310
Staib, L. H., 586
Stainton, N. R., 439
Stallone, D. D., 422
Standertskjold-Nordenstam,
    C. G., 113, 366
Stanescu, R., 331
Stanfield, B. B., 109
Stanley, M. A., 628
Stansfelt, S. A., 542
Stanton, M. D., 648
Stanton, M. E., 488
Stapleton, A. L., 486
Stark, A. C., 702
Starker, S., 176, 649
Starkes, J. L., 147
Staska, M., 309
Stattin, H., 451, 490
Stayman, D. M., 413
Stebbins, W. C., 156
Steblay, N., 192, 275
Steciuk, M., 416
Steele, C. M., 201, 202, 353,
    361, 362
Steele, K. M., 361
Steelman, L. C., 469
Stefanacci, L., 262, 399
Steffen, V. J., 558

Subject Index

Note: Page numbers followed by *f* indicate figures; page numbers followed by *t* indicate tables; **boldface** type indicates key terms and the page numbers where they are defined.

Client-centered therapy, 16–17, 465–466, 638–641, 640t, 662
Clinical neuropsychologists, 22, 25t
Clinical practice, ethics in, 28
Clinical psychologist, 21–22, 25t
Clinical psychology, 21–23
Clinton, Hillary, 466
Close Encounters of the Third Kind (film), 481
Closure, law of, 135
Cobain, Kurt, 381
Cocaine, 199t, 204–205, 486
Cochlea, 153, 153f
Cocktail party phenomenon, **157**
Code, 269–270
Cognition(s)
 attitudes and, 674–675
 conditioned stimulus and, 220–221
 creative, 380, 380f
 emotion and, 404
 need for (NC), 413
 prejudice and, 684–686
 social. *See* **Social cognition**
Cognitive appraisal, 538
Cognitive apprenticeship, 361
Cognitive-behavior therapy (CBT), 633, 634t, 662–663
 for anxiety disorders, 658–659
 computer-assisted, 651
 for depression, 658
 plus medication, 657–658, 659
 supplemental use of, 658
 in TDCRP assessment, 655–657
Cognitive component of attitude, 674
Cognitive development
 in adolescence, 513–515
 in adulthood, 519, 520–522, 527–529
 in infancy and childhood, 497–504, 498t
 information processing approach to, 502–504
 Piaget's theory of, 497–500, 498t
 sociocultural theory of, 504
 wave model of, 503
Cognitive dissonance, 677–680, 678f, 682, 687, 712, 716
Cognitive distortions, 514, 587, **630**, **631t**
Cognitive engineering, 336
Cognitive illusion, 340
Cognitive interpretation of emotions, 397f, 397–398
Cognitive learning, 243–244
Cognitive neuroscience, 18, 20t
 social, 681–682
Cognitive psychologist, 23, 25t
Cognitive psychology, 17–18, 20t
Cognitive restructuring, 632, 662
Cognitive revolution, 17–18, 20t, 629
Cognitive shortcuts, 683, 688, 693–694
Cognitive taste aversion, 419
Cognitive theory, 394f, 395, 399
 of personality, 466–468
Cognitive therapy, 622–623, 629–633, **630**, 634t, 661
 disorders best treated by, 662–663
 techniques, 631–633
 theory, 630
Cohesiveness, group
 conformity and, 704
 decision making and, 710
Cohort, 522
Collective unconscious, 463
Collectivist culture, 414
 conformity and, 705
 personality differences in individualist vs., 474–476
 recovery rate of schizophrenia in, 604
 self-concept in, 507
Colombine High School killings (1999), 559
Colonoscopy, judging pain of, 343
Color blindness, **132**
Color constancy, 137
Color mixing, 130–131
Color Purple, The (film), 482

Color vision, 129–132
Columbus, Christopher, 126
Commitment
 hardy personality and, 561
 in triangular model of love, 697
Commitment/consistency principle of compliance, 706
Common factors, **661**
Common fate, law of, 13
Communication, 314–316. *See also* Language
 nonverbal, 314, 403–404
Communication disorders, 317
Community mental health centers/hospitals, 652
Comoros, possession trance in, 197
Comparison level, 700
Compassionate love, 697
Compensation, social, 711
Competition, prejudice and, 687
Complex behaviors, learning, 237–238
Complex inheritance, **107**
Compliance, 706–707
Comprehension
 ambiguity and, 308–309
 language, 301, 304
Compulsions, 594–595
Computer(s)
 artificial intelligence and, 334–335
 cognitive revolution and, 17
 creative solutions from, 383–384, 384f
Computer-assisted tomography (CT, formerly CAT), 102
Computer-assisted treatment, 651
Computer games, social roles in, 473
Concentrative meditation, 195
Concepts, 324–327
 in brain, 326
 child's conceptions of world, 500–502
 organization of, 325–326
 prototypes, 324–325
Concrete operations, **500**
Concrete operations period, 498t, 500
Conditioned emotional response (CER), **217**–218, 450, 625
Conditioned response (CR), 214, 215, 215f, 216, 217f, 219, 594
Conditioned stimulus (CS), 214, 215, 215f, 216–217, 217f, 218, 219, 594
 cognition and, 220–221
 CS_1 and CS_2, 200, 220f
Conditioning. *See* **Classical conditioning; Operant conditioning**
Conditions of worth, 465–466
Conduction deafness, 154, **155**
Cones (eye), **128**, 128f, 129, 131
Confidence interval, 54
Confidentiality, states' laws of, 28
Confirmation bias, 338, **339**
Conflict
 adolescent-parent, 515–516
 in helping situations, alcohol's effect on, 201
 inhibitory, 201
 internal, 539–540
 realistic conflict theory, 687
 between stereotype and actual behavior, 683–684
Conformity, 703–706, 705f
Confound (or confounding variables), 39, 39f
Conscience, 510
Conscientiousness (dependability), 439, 440, 442t, 443
Conscious, the, 458, 458f
Consciousness, 170–209, **172**
 altered states of. *See* **Altered states of consciousness (ASC)**
 Freud on, 458
 functionalist view of, 12
 hypnosis and, 188–194
 meditation and, 186, 194–196
 normal, 173
 short-term memory as contents of, 256–257
 sleep and, 174–187
 stream of, 172

structuralist view of, 10
 substance use and abuse and, 173, 197–208, 266
 theories of function of, 172–173
Consciousness raising, 550
Conscious prejudice, 684
Consensus, causal attribution and, 692
Consequences, 625
Conservation, 499–500, 499f
Consistency
 causal attribution and, 692
 of personality traits, 438–441
Consolidation, **270**
Constancy
 perceptual, 136–137
 size, 60, 60f, 137
Construct validity, 45t
Consumer Reports study of mental health treatments (1994), 659–661, 660t
Contact hypothesis, 689
Contagion, social, 282
Contemplation stage of change, 549, 550f, 551
Content validity, 45t
Contexts, power of, 576
Contingency, response, 230, 628
Continuity, law of, 135
Continuous Positive Airway Pressure (CPAP), 186
Continuous reinforcement, **238**
Contrapreparedness, **218**
Control
 demand-control model, 542
 eating disorders and, 612–613
 hardy personality and, 561
 locus of, 466–467, 468
 perceived, 538–539, 547
 social, 474–475
 stimulus, 628
Control beliefs, 631t
Control condition, **40**
Control group, 39
Control question technique (CQT), 405
Control sequence, 267
Conventional level of moral development, 509
Convergent thinking, creativity and, 380–381
Cooke, Alistair, 293–294
Coordinate spatial relations, 144
Coping, 538, 552–568
 approaches and tactics for, 553t, 553–561
 gender and culture and, 566–567
 genes and, 562–563
 mind-body interventions, 565–566
 personality and, 561–563
 social support and, 563–564
Cornea, 126, 127, 127f
Corpus callosum, 86, 87f, 94f
 cut, in split-brain patients, 91–93
Correlation, 41, 440
 as example of inferential statistics, 56
 illusory, 686
 strength of, 41f
Correlational research, 40–42
Correlation coefficient, 41
Cortisol, 98, 187, 421, 490, 566, 602
 fight-or-flight response and, 267–268
 general adaptation syndrome and, 536, 537
 heightened susceptibility to stress and, 604–605
 prenatal development and, 487
 sleep deprivation and, 178
Counseling psychologist, 22, 25t
Counseling psychology, 21–23
Countering, 551
Counter-irritant, 164
Counting compulsion, 595
Couric, Katie, 680
Coyne, James, 588
Crack, **204**
Cramming, 273
Cranial nerves, 82
Cranium, 82
Creative cognition, 380, 380f
Creative intelligence, 357

Glucose, 417
Glutamate, 78t, 266
Goethe, Wilhelm von, 515
Good form, law of, 135
Gore, Albert, 48, 676, 677f
Gourmand syndrome, 417
Grain of mental space, 322
Grammar, 311–312
  critical period for acquiring, 314
  of second language, learning, 317
Grant, Ulysses S., 226
Graph design, 62
Graphs, lying with, 59–61
Gray matter, 86, 367
Grief, 526–527
Ground, 134, 135
Group(s), 700–701
  between-group vs. within-group differences,
    370–371
  decision making in, 709–711
  going along with, 703–709
  norms in, 701–703, 702t
  performance in, 709–711
  roles and status in, 703
  self-help, 648–649
  social loafing in, 711
Group, level of the, 5, 7, 9. *See also* Levels of
    analysis
  cults at, 716
  eating disorders at, 613
  happiness at, 401
  mood disorders at, 587–588
  obsessive-compulsive disorder at, 596
  panic disorders at, 592
  phobias at, 594
  posttraumatic stress disorder at, 598
  psychological disorders and factors at, 576–577
  schizophrenia at, 603–604
  shyness at, 457
Group differences in intelligence, 370–375
Group identity, prosocial behavior and, 712
Group polarization, 710
Group therapy, 647
Groupthink, 710
Guilt
  initiative vs., 523t
  polygraph detection of, 405–406
  superego and, 459
Guilty actions test, 405
Guilty knowledge test (GKT), 405
Gyrus (gyri), 86, 87

Habit (procedural memories), 262–263
  basal ganglia and formation of, 97
Habit Response level of Eysenck's pyramid, 449, 449f
Habituation, **213**
Habituation technique (looking time technique),
    493–494, 494f
Hair cells, 153, 153f
Haldol, 641
Hall, G. Stanley, 515
Hallucinations, 178, 206, 207, **574, 599t, 600**
Hallucinogens, 206–207
  biological actions and effects, 199t
Halo effect, 672
Hangover, 203
Happiness, 400–401
Happy expectations, 409–410
Hardy personality, **561**
Harlow, Harry, 505
Harm avoidance (personality dimension), 447–448
Harris, Eric, 559
Harris, Judith, 470–472
Hassles, 540–541
Having Our Say (Delany, Delany, & Hearth), 669
Headache, hypnosis to treat, 194
Head Start, Project, 360
Healing profession, psychology as, 21–23
Health
  cognitive dissonance to increase behaviors
    promoting, 680

emotional disclosure and, 554–555, 556
perception of control and, 539
stress and, 545–552
Health-impairing behaviors, 548–551
  changing, 549–551
Health insurance, 650, 665
Health psychology, 534. *See also* **Stress**
Hearing, 151–159
  aging and, 519
  auditory perception, 155–158
  auditory sensation, 151–155
  without awareness, 157
  in infancy and childhood, 495
  of newborn, 488
  phonology and, 302
Heart disease
  culture and, 567
  hostility and development of, 543–544
  social support and, 563
  stress and, 547–548
Heat, aggression and, 557
Heavens' Gate cult, 715, 716
Helping behavior, 712–715
  bystander intervention, 713–715, 714f, 715f
  prosocial behavior, 712–713
Helping situations, alcohol's effect on conflict in,
    201
Helplessness
  behavior disengagement and, 554
  learned, 414, 415f, 415–416, 538, 587
Hemispheric specialization, 93
Hering, Ewald, 131
Heritability, 112–113, 371. *See also* **Gene(s)**
  of IQ, 366, 367–370
  Minnesota Study of Twins Reared Apart
    (MISTRA), 453–454, 456
  of personality, 107, 452–456, 455f
Heroin, 199t, 206, 486
Hertz (Hz), 152
Heterogeneous group, decision making in, 710–711
Heterozygous genes, 107, 107f
Heuristic, 330, 331f, 339–341
  availability, 341, 343
  representativeness, 340–341
Hidden observer, **192**
Hierarchical organization, 292
  memory and, 272f
Hierarchy
  of needs, Maslow's, 413f, 413–414, 464
  status, 703
High expressed emotion, 603–604, 606
Hiking monk problem, 329f
Hindbrain, 94f, **97**
Hippocampus, 95f, 96, 109, 520
  amnesia and damage to, 287
  latent learning and, 244
  learning and, 240
  memory and, 263, 283
  mood disorders and, 586
  stress and size of, 267
Hispanics, IQ scores of, 371–373
Histrionic personality disorder, 615t
HIV, 486, 548–549
Homelessness, fundamental attribution error about,
    693
Homeostasis, **408**
Homosexuality
  in adolescence, 516
  removal from *DSM*, 574
Homozygous genes, 107, 107f
Honesty, trait of, 440
Honor in American South, 701
Hormones, 98–99
  in adolescence, 516
  female vs. male, perception of beauty and,
    150–151
  hypothalamus and, 95
  sex, 373–374, 508, 512–513
  stress, 487, 602–603
Horney, Karen, 463

Hostile attribution bias, **558**
Hostility, 543–544, 630
How to Lie with Statistics (Huff), 58
Hue, 130
Hull, Clark L., 15
Human factors psychologist, 23, 24, 25t
Human Genome Project, 108
Humanistic psychology, 16–17, 20t
  on personality, 464–466
Humanistic therapy, 638–640, 640t
Human research participants, ethical treatment
  of, 27
Humor
  comprehension of, 307
  as coping strategy, 556–557
"Humors" (body's four fluids), 575
Hunch, having a, 341–342
Hung, Samo, 243
Hunger, 416–422
Hurricane Andrew (1992), 546
5-Hydroxytryptamine (5HT, serotonin), 78t. *See
  also* Serotonin
Hyman, Steven, 110
Hypercolumn, 134
Hypermetropia (farsightedness), 133, 134f
Hypermnesia, **279**
Hypnic jerk, 175
Hypnogogic sleep, 174–175
Hypnosis, 188–194
  alterations in perception, mood, memory, and
    behavior, 189f
  individual differences in, 189–190, 190f
  memory and, 190–192, 294
  pain control through, 164
  as possession trance, 197
  practical applications of, 193–194
  sociocognitive theory of, 192–193
  for stress management, 565
  trance theory of, 192
Hypnotic induction, **188**
Hypocretin (orexin), 185
Hypomania, **585**
Hypothalamus, 95–96, 98f
  eating behavior and, 417, 418
  suprachiasmatic nucleus of, 182, 187
Hypothesis, 35, 65
  formation of, 35–36
  testing, 36

I Am Jackie Chan (Chan & Yang), 211
Iconic memory, 256
Id, 458f, 459, 635
Ideal self, 638
Identical twins, 113, 368f, 453–454, 454f, 456
Identification
  of sound, 156–158
  visual, 140–151
Identity
  dissociative identity disorder, 608–609
  gender, 507–508
  group, prosocial behavior and, 712
  in infancy and childhood, 506–507
  role confusion vs., 523t
  social identity theory, 686
Identity alteration, 607
Identity confusion, 607
Illusion(s)
  cognitive, 340
  of outgroup homogeneity, 686
  visual, 110f
Illusory correlation, 686
Images, imagery
  auditory, 158, 320
  interactive, 290
  manipulating objects in, 322f
  mental, 253, 320–323, 321f
Imaginal exposure, 627, 662
Imaginary audience, 514
Imitation, 501
  learning by, 67–68
Immediate reinforcement, **235**

Immigration Act of 1924, 370
Immune system
    conditioning, 226–227
    humor's effect on, 557
    positive effects of emotional expression on, 555, 556
    social support and functioning of, 563–564
    stress and, 545–546
Implanting memories, 281–282
Implicit Association Test (IAT), 676–677, 677f
Implicit attitudes, 676–677
Implicit motives, **410**
Implicit (nondeclarative) memories, 261–263, 342, 496
Impression formation, 671–674
    first impressions, 696
Impressionists, 123
Impression management, **671**
Imprinting, genomic (gametic), 484
Impulses, neural, 74–76
Impulsivity, **452**
Incentives, 409–410
Incidental learning, **273**
Income, IQ scores and, 372
Incongruence, 638, 639
Incubation, **332**
Independence, 705
Independent variable, 38–39
    relationship between dependent variable and, 38f
Indicated preventive interventions, 652
Individualist culture, 414
    conformity and, 705
    personality differences in collectivist vs., 474–476
    self-concept in, 507
Individuality, sex differences in, 472
Individual therapy, 646
Inductive reasoning, 338–**339**
Industrial/organizational (I/O) psychologist, 25, 25t
Industry vs. inferiority, 523t
Infancy and childhood, development in, 491–511
    cognitive development, 497–504, 498t
    gender role development, 510–511
    memory development, 496–497
    moral development, 508–510
    newborn, 488–491
    perceptual development, 492–496
    physical and motor development, 491–492, 493t
    social and emotional development, 504–511
Infantile amnesia, 287
Infants
    Maasai, survival during drought, 8–9
    premature, 490, 492
    sleep of, 176
Inferences of research report, 64–65
Inferential statistics, 55–58
    correlation, 56
    meta-analysis, 44t, 57–58
    samples and populations, 56–57
Inferiority, industry vs., 523t
Inferiority complex, **463**
Informational social influence, 704
Information processing, 17
    neural development and, 502–504
Information processing. See **Learning**; Memory(ies)
Informed consent, 27
Informed perception, 142–143
Ingroup, 686, 687
Ingroup differentiation, 686
Inheritance. See also **Gene**(s)
    complex, 107
    Mendelian, 106
Inhibitory conflict, **201**
Inhibitory neurotransmitters/neuromodulators, 79
Initialisms, 292
Initiative vs. guilt, 523t
Inkblots, Rorschach, 446, 446f
Inner ear, 153f
Inner speech (private speech), 504
Innovations in psychotherapy, 649–651
Insight, 332–333
Insight learning, 244–245

Insight-oriented therapies, 635–641, 655, 661–662
    disorders best treated by, 661–662
    humanistic therapy, 638–640, 640t
    psychodynamic therapy, 635–638, 640t
Insomnia, 184t, **185**–186
Instincts, 407–408
Instinct theory, 407
Institutional Review Board (IRB), 27
Insulin, **418**
Insurance company, therapist referrals from, 665
Integrity, ethical principle of, 29t
Integrity vs. despair, 523, 523t
Intellectualization, 462t
Intelligence, 346–387, 348. See also Cognitive development
    in adulthood, 354–355, 521–522, 527–528
    artificial (AI), 334–335
    brain size and, 363
    creativity and, 347, 379–384
    crystallized, 354–355, 521
    diversity in, 375–384
    emotional (EI), 358–359
    environment and, 359–361, 367–371, 372
    existential, 356
    fluid, 354–355, 359, 360f, 521
    genes and, 365–370
    of the gifted, 378–379
    group differences in, 370–375
    machinery of, 362–365
    measuring, 348–353
    mental retardation, 376–378, 378t, 486
    multiple intelligences, theory of, 355–357
    views on nature of, 358t
    working memory and, 364–365
Intelligence enhancement programs, 360–361
Intelligence quotient (IQ), 348–354
    achievement and, 352–353, 384–385
    amount of gray matter and, 367
    analytic intelligence measured by, 357
    brief history of intelligence testing, 348–349
    Flynn effect and, 359–360
    genes and, 366, 366f
    heritability of, 366, 367–370
    of mentally retarded, 376
    race differences in, 371–373
    scoring IQ tests, 349–352
    sex differences in, 373–374
    speed of mental processes and, 364
    temperament and, 367
    uses for results of, 353
    within-group vs. between-group differences in, 370
Intentional learning, 273
Interaction
    active, 111–112
    evocative, 111
    mother-infant, 491
    passive, 111
Interactional theory of depression, 588
Interactionism, 441–442
Interactive images, 290
Interference, **286**
Intermittent reinforcement, 16
Internal attributions (dispositional attributions), 691–693, 692t
Internal conflict, 539–540
Internals, 466, 468
International Space Station (ISS), 33–34, 37, 50, 66–67
Internet
    repeated contact through, 696
    self-help on, 649
    therapy over, 651
Interneurons, 73, 83
Interpersonal intelligence, 356
Interpersonal therapy (IPT), 655–657, 661
Interpretation, **637**
Interruptions, as stressor, 540–541
Interval schedules, 238–239
Interviews, structured, 444

Intimacy
    isolation vs., 522, 523t
    lasting love and, 698
    stages of, 698
    in triangular model of love, 697
Intrapersonal intelligence, 356
Intrinsic motivation, 410
Introduction to research paper, writing, 65
Introspection, **11**
Introvert, 450
Intuition, 342
Inuit of northern Canada, 319
Inventory, personality, 444–446
In vivo exposure, 627
Ions, 74
    action potential and, 75, 75f
IQ. See **Intelligence quotient (IQ)**
Iris, 126, 127, 127f
Irving, Amy, 482
Islands of excellence, **376**
Isolation, intimacy vs., 522, 523t

Jackson, Phil, 196
James, Nanny, 669
James, William, 12, 20t, 394
James-Lange theory, 394, 394f, 396, 399
Jamison, Kay Redfield, 585
Japanese culture
    emotional expression and, 402
    heart disease and, 567
    personality and, 476–477
Jet lag, recovery from, 187
"Jigsaw classroom," 690f, 690–691
Jim Crow laws, 669, 703
Job, as source of stress, 542
Job performance, IQ and, 352
Jordan, David Starr, 286
Jordan, Michael, 682
Jung, Carl, 462–463
Jury selection, stereotypes and, 683
Justice, ethical principle of, 29t
Justification, prosocial behavior and, 713
Just-noticeable difference (JND), **125**

Kahlo, Frida, 121–122, 123, 129, 151, 155, 156–157, 159
Kahlo, Guillermo, 123
Kaliai tribe in Papua New Guinea, 527
Kasparov, Garry, 334, 335, 342
K-complex, 175
Kelley, Harold, 692–693
Kennedy, John F., 274, 363
Ketamine ("Special K"), 206, 207
Khmer refugees, *kyol goeu* and panic attacks among, 592
Kinesthetic sense, **163**
King, Martin Luther, Jr., 274
Kinsey, Alfred, 423
Klebold, Dylan, 559
Knockin mice, **109**
Knockout mice, 108–109, 266–267
Knowledge
    distinguishing experts from nonexperts, 333–334
    of language, 302
Kohlberg, Lawrence, 508–509
Köhler, Wolfgang, 245
Kpelle tribe in rural western Africa, 280
Kulpe, Oswald, 11
Kyol goeu (wind overload), 592

Labels, power of, 576
Lange, Carl, 394
Language, 300–318. See also Thinking
    bilingualism, 316–317
    body, 403–404
    critical period for learning, 312–314
    development of, 309–314
    foundations of, 309
    grammar, 311–312, 314, 317
    hemispheric specialization and, 93
    memory and, 320

Psychoeducation, **633**
Psychokinesis, 165
Psychological determinism, **458**
Psychological disorders, 570–621, **573**. *See also*
    Treatment
    anxiety disorders, 589–598
    categorizing, 577–578, 579t
    creativity and, 381–382
    defining abnormality, 573–574
    diagnosis, cautionary note about, 618
    dissociative disorders, 607–609
    eating disorders, 21–22, 609–614
    explaining abnormality, 574–577
    mood disorders, 580–589
    personality disorders, 614–617
    schizophrenia, 29, 599–606
Psychological state, as retrieval cue, 279
Psychologists, types of, 21–25, 25f, 25t
Psychology, **4**
    academic, 23–24
    applied, 24–25
    behaviorism and, 15–16, 20t
    clinical and counseling, 21–23
    cognitive revolution and, 17–18, 20t, 629
    ethics and, 26–29
    evolutionary, 18–19, 20, 20t, 407–408
    evolution of, 9–19, 20
    functionalism and, 12, 20t
    Gestalt, 12–14, 20t
    humanistic, 16–17, 20t, 464–466
    levels of analysis in, 5–9, 6f
    psychodynamic theory and, 14–15, 20t, 420
    roots of, 10
    structuralism and, 10–11, 20t
Psychometric approaches, 353–354
Psychoneuroimmunology, 545
Psychopharmacology, 641–643, 644t
    psychotherapy vs., 658–659
Psychophysics, 124–125
Psychosexual stages, 459–462
Psychosis, **574**
    amphetamine, 205
Psychosocial development, 522–525, 523t
Psychotherapist. *See Therapist*
Psychotherapy, **22**. *See also Treatment*
Psychotherapy by Reciprocal Inhibition (Wolpe),
    625
Psychotherapy integration, 649–650
Psychoticism, 443, 451
Puberty, 512–513, 516
Puerto Rican women, *ataque de nervios* among, 664
Punishment, 232f, 233–234
    effective use of, 233
    facial expression as, 242
    introverts and, 450
    negative, 233
    positive, 233
Pupil, 126, 127, 127f
Purging, 611, 613–614
Purging type bulimia, 611
Puzzle box, Thorndike's, 229, 229f
p value, 56, 64

QALMRI method, 62–65
Quantitative data, 35
Quartiles, 55
Quasi-experimental design, 40, 44t
Question(s)
    addressed by research report, 63
    control question technique (CQT), 405
    about psychotherapy research, 654t, 655–657

Race differences in IQ, 371–373
Racial attitudes, 676–677, 682
    bias in diagnosis and treatment, 577
Racial stereotypes, 361–362, 685
Radiation
    electromagnetic, 126, 127f
    prenatal exposure to, 486
Rain Man (movie), 376
Random assignment, 40, 655

Range, **54**
    of reaction, 370
    using inappropriately large, to minimize differ-
        ence, 60, 60f
Rape, 560
    date, 202–203
    posttraumatic stress disorder after, 596
    punishing rapists, 694
Rapid eye movement (REM), 175–176
    REM sleep, 175–176, 177f, 179, 181, 182, 185
Rational-emotive therapy (RET), 630, 631–632
Rationalization, 462t
Ratio schedules, 238, 239–240
Raven's Progressive Matrices, **359, 360f, 365**
Raw data, **52**
Reactance, as obstacle to persuasion, 681
Reaction formation, 462t
Reaction range, **370**
Reactive interaction, **111**
Reagan, Ronald, 33
Realistic conflict theory, 687
Reality monitoring, **284**
Reality principle, 459
Real self, 638
Reasoning
    in adolescence, 513–514
    deductive, 337–338
    emotion and, 342
    frontal lobes and, 90
    inductive, 338–339
    mental model and, 338f
    moral, 510
Rebound effect, 556
Recall, 276, 520
Recategorization, 689–690
Recency effect, 258, 259
Receptors, 79–80
    olfactory, 159–160
Reciprocal determinism, 467–468, 467f
Reciprocity, lasting love and, 698
Reciprocity principle, 706, 707
Recognition, **276**
    of basic emotions, 392f
    explicit memory tapped by, 496
    of others' emotions, 359
    of sound, 156–158
    visual, 140–151
Redundant signal effect, 147
Referral agencies, finding therapist through, 664
Reflex(es), 83, 83f
    emotional, 398
    of newborn, 488–489, 489t
Reframing, **648**
Rehearsal, **257**
Reinforcement, 16, **229**–230, 231–233
    continuous, 238
    delayed, 235
    drives and, 408
    expectations of, 409–410
    facial expressions as, 242
    immediate, 235
    intermittent, 16
    negative, 231, 232f
    partial, 238
    positive, 231, 234
    self-regulation and, 467
    shaping as gradual, 237–238
Reinforcement schedules, 238–240, 239f
Reinforcer(s), **230**
    primary, 234
    secondary, 234–235, 634–635
Relational aggression, 559
Relationships, 695–700
    adult, 525–526
    handling, 359
    liking, 695–696
    loving, 696–698
    mating preferences, 698–700
    patient-therapist, 637
    peer, 470–472, 516
Relative standing, 55

Relaxation, 662
    meditation vs., 196
    progressive muscle, 186, 191, 625–626
    for stress management, 565
Relevant/irrelevant technique (RIT), 405
Reliability, **45**
    of IQ tests, 352
    of projective tests, 446–447
Religion, sex and emotional involvement and, 21
Remembering, act of, 254, 275–280
Remeron, 642
REM rebound, 177–178
REM sleep, 175–176, 177f, 179, 181, 182, 185
Repeated contact, development of liking and, 696
Repetition blindness, 149, 150
Repetition priming, 263–264
Replication, 35, 45
Representation problem, 328–330
Representativeness heuristic, **340**–341
Repressed memories, 288–289
Repression, 462, 462t
Repressors, 562
Research, 32–69
    academic psychology and, 23–24
    with animals, 27–28
    being critical consumer of, 44–49
    correlational, 40–42
    descriptive, 42–44
    ethics in, 26–28
    experimental, 38–40, 51
    outcome, 654–657
    with people, 27
    QALMRI method of reading, 62–65
    questions about psychotherapy, 654t, 655–657
    scientific method, 34–44
    split-brain, 90–93, 92f
    statistics and, 50–61
    writing your own papers, 65
Resistance, 637–638
Resistance phase (adaptation phase), **536**, 536f
Resistant attachment, 505–506
Respect for people's rights and dignity, ethical
    principle of, 29t
Response(s), 15–16
    conditioned (CR), 214, 215, 215f, 216, 217f, 219,
        594
    conditioned emotional (CER), 217–218, 450,
        625
    stress, 535–537, 536f
    unconditioned (UR), 214, 215, 215f, 216, 217f,
        221
Response bias, 47
Response contingency, 230, 628
Response prevention, exposure with, 628, 657, 661,
    662
Responsibility
    diffusion of, 715
    ethical principle of, 29t
Resting potential, 74
Restorative theory of sleep, 179
Restricting type anorexia nervosa, 611
Results section of research report, 64, 65
Retardation, mental, 376–378, 378t, 486
Reticular activating system (RAS), 97
Reticular formation, 94f, 97
Retina, 126, 127, 127f
Retinal disparity (binocular disparity), 137
Retinopic mapping in brain, 135
RET (rational-emotive therapy), 630, 631–632
Retrieval, 254, 292–294
    cues, 278–279
    state-dependent, 279
Retroactive interference, 286
Retrograde amnesia, 287
Reuptake, 80
Reward
    dependence on, 447–448
    deprived, 411–412
    expectations of, 409–410
    extraverts and, 450
    nondeprived, 411–412

Variable(s), **35**
  confounding, 39, 39f
  dependent, 38f, 38–39, 51
  independent, 38f, 38–39
Variable interval schedule, 239, 239f
Variable ratio schedules, 239–240, 239f
Venting in writing, 554–555, 556
Ventricles, 86, 602
Verbal subtests, Wechsler, 349, 350t
Vestibular sense, **163**
Victim, blaming the, 694
Victimization, body language and sexual, 403–404
Victorian age, fainting spells among stylish women in, 39f
Vigilance, 146
Vigor of activity, 452
Violence. *See also* Aggression
  by fans at European soccer matches, 701
  mass murder, 578–580
  on television, 248–249
  workplace, 543, 560
Virtual reality exposure, 627, 628
Virus as teratogen, 486
Visible spectrum, 127f
Vision, 123–151
  aging and, 519
  color, 129–132
  in infancy and childhood, 493–495
  of newborn, 488
  night, 128
  occipital lobes and, 88
  problems, 132–133, 134f
  shattered, 88f
  visual perception, 134–151
  visual sensation, 123–134
Visual cliff, 493
Visual illusions, 110f
Visual memories, 260
Visual mental images, 320–323, 321f
Visual pathways, 140f
Visual perception, 134–151
  attention and, 145–147
  distance perception, 137–139
  informed perception, 142–143
  perceptual constancy, 136–137
  perceptual organization, 134–136
  recognition and identification, 140–151
  seeing without awareness, 148–150
  spatial relations, 143–145
Visual sensation, 123–134
Visuospatial sketchpad, 265
Voluntary muscles, 84

von Helmholz, Hermann, 130
von Restorf effect, 274–275
Voodoo death, 567
Vygotsky, Lev S., 504, 514

Walker, Wesley, 139
Wallace, Alfred Russel, 114
Want, 410–414, 412f
Washing compulsion, 594
Washington, George, 186
Washington, Martha, 186
Watson, John B., 15, 20t, 319
Wavelength, **126**
Wave model of cognitive development, 503
Web, cyberstudents taking courses on the, 468
Weber, Ernst, 125
Weber's law, **125**
Wechsler, David, 349
Wechsler Adult Intelligence Scale (WAIS), 349
  subtests, 349, 350t
  WAIS-III, 365
  WAIS-III scores, 351f
Wechsler Intelligence Scale for Children (WISC), 349
Weight. *See also* **Eating disorders**
  dieting and, 422
  obesity and, 420–422
  set point, 419–420
Wernicke, Carl, 303
Wernicke's aphasia, 302, 303–304
Wernicke's area, 303–304, 304f
  bilingualism and activation of, 316
Wertheimer, Max, 13, 20t
Westerners, expression of emotion among, 402
"What" pathway, 140–143
"Where" pathway, 143–145
White Americans, IQ scores of, 371–373
White blood cells, 545
White matter, 86
Whitman, Charles, 578–580
Who Am I? (movie), 211
Wild Boy of Aveyron, 312–313
Wilder, Thornton, 560
Williams syndrome, 376
Wisdom, 521
Wisdom of the Body, The (Cannon), 408
Wish fulfillment, 180
Withdrawal emotions, 393
Withdrawal reflex, 489t
Withdrawal symptoms, **199**
  barbiturate, 204
  hangover due to alcohol withdrawal, 203

Within-group vs. between-group differences, 370–371
Witnesses, improving memory retrieval of, 293–294
Wolpe, Joseph, 625
Womb, fetal development in, 485
Women. *See also* Sex differences
  color vision in, 131
  economic power and changing mating preferences of, 699
  Freud on personality development of, 461
  menopause in, 518
  multiple roles, stress of, 566
  as primary caretakers of children, 473
  "tend and befriend" response to stressors, 537
Woods, Tiger, 3, 5, 11, 16
Words, 319–320
  learning, in childhood, 310–311, 311f
  putting thoughts into, 319
Work as source of stress, 541–543
Working in groups, 709–711
Working memory, 264–266, **265**, 265f, 269
  aging and, 503–504, 520
  intelligence and, 364–365
Workplace violence, 543, 560
Work spaces, stress and arrangement of, 541f, 541–542
Wounds, stress and healing of, 545–546
Writing
  expressive, 554–555, 556, 640–641
  research papers, 65
Wundt, Wilhelm, 10–11, 20t
Wurtzel, Elizabeth, 581–582

Xanax, 643
X chromosome, 483

Yates, Andrea, 574
Y chromosome, 483
Yerkes-Dodson law, 409
Young, Cy, 382
Young, Thomas, 130
Y (vertical) axis, shortened to exaggerate difference, 59, 59f

Zeigebers, 187
Zellweger, Renee, 607
Zoloft, 642
Zygote, 483–484, 484f

Credits

Chapter Opener Photo Credits

Chapter 1, p. 2: *Matisse's Model.* 1991. Faith Ringgold. Acrylic on canvas with fabric borders. 73 ½ × 79 ½. From the series: The French Collection #5. Faith Ringgold © 1991. Baltimore Museum of Art, Baltimore, Maryland.

Chapter 2, p. 32: *Reservoir.* 1961. Robert Rauschenberg. Oil, wood, graphite, fabric, metal, and rubber on canvas. 85 ½ × 62 ½ × 14 ¾ in. © Robert Rauschenberg/Licensed by VAGA, New York, NY. Copyright Smithsonian American Art Museum, Washington, DC/Art Resource, NY.

Chapter 3, p. 70: *Clouds (Wolken).* 1982. Gerhard Richter. Oil on canvas; two parts, overall, 6'7" × 8'6 ⅞". Acquired through the James Thrall Soby Bequest and purchase (GR 514-1). Location: The Museum of Modern Art, New York, NY. © Digital image © The Museum of Modern Art/Licensed by SCALA/Art Resource, NY. Reproduced courtesy of the artist and Marian Goodman Gallery, New York.

Chapter 4, p. 120: *Sea in the Evening Light.* [*Meer im Abendlicht*] Emil Nolde. Watercolor on Japanese Paper. 17.5 × 22.9 cm. Signed lower right "Nolde." Nolde-Stiftung Seebull. © Nolde-Stiftung Seebull.

Chapter 5, p. 170: *Landscape from a Dream.* 1936–1938. Paul Nash. Oil on canvas, 26 ¾ × 40 in. © Tate, London 2003/Art Resource, NY.

Chapter 6, p. 210: *The Meal, or The Bananas.* 1891. Paul Gauguin. Oil on paper mounted on canvas. Inv. RF 1954-27. Photo: H. Lewandowski. Musée d'Orsay, Paris, France. Copyright Réunion des Musées Nationaux/Art Resource, NY.

Chapter 7, p. 252: *Souvenirs.* 1976. Marc Chagall. © 2003 Artists Rights Society (ARS) New York/ADAGP, Paris. Private collection. © Scala/Art Resource, NY.

Chapter 8, p. 298: *In the North the African American had more educational opportunities.* Panel 58 from The Migration Series. (1940–41; text and title revised by the artist, 1993.) Jacob Lawrence. Tempera on gesso on composition board, 12 × 18". Gift of Mrs. David M. Levy. Location: Museum of Modern Art, New York, NY. © Digital Image © The Museum of Modern Art/Licensed by SCALA/Art Resource, NY. Artwork copyright 2003 Gwendolyn Knight Lawrence, courtesy of the Jacob and Gwendolyn Lawrence Foundation.

Chapter 9, p. 346: *Portrait of Marie-Thérèse,* January 6, 1937. Pablo Picasso. Oil on canvas, 100 × 81 cm. © 2003 Estate of Pablo Picasso/Artists Rights Society (ARS) New York. © Réunion des Musées Nationaux/Art Resource, NY. Photo: J. G. Berizzi. Musée Picasso, Paris, France.

Chapter 10, p. 388: *Two Nudes (Lovers).* About 1912–13. Oskar Kokoschka, Austrian, 1886-1980. Oil on canvas. 163.2 × 97.5 cm (64 ¼ × 38 3/8 in.) Museum of Fine Arts, Boston. Bequest of Mrs. Sarah Reed Platt. 1973.196. © 2003 Museum of Fine Arts, Boston. © 2003 Artists Rights Society (ARS) New York/ProLitteris, Zurich.

Chapter 11, p. 436: *The Modern Idol.* Peter Blake. © 2003 Artists Rights Society (ARS), New York/DACS, London. Copyright Victoria & Albert Museum, London/Art Resource, NY.

Chapter 12, p. 480: *Summer, New England.* 1912. Maurice Prendergast (1859–1924). Oil on canvas, 19 ¼ × 27 ½ in. © Smithsonian American Art Museum, Washington, DC/Art Resource, NY.

Chapter 13, p. 532: *Ashes.* 1894. Edvard Munch. Oil on canvas, 47 ½ × 55 ½ in. (12.1 × 14.1 cm). Location: National Gallery, Oslo, Norway. © 2003 The Munch Museum/The Munch-Ellingsen Group/Artists Rights Society (ARS) New York. Copyright Scala/Art Resource, NY.

Chapter 14, p. 570: *Melancholy.* Edvard Munch. Location: National Gallery, Oslo, Norway. © 2003 The Munch Museum/The Munch-Ellingsen Group/Artists Rights Society (ARS) New York.

Chapter 15, p. 622: *Variation.* 1916–17. Alexei von Jawlensky. Oil on canvas, 37 × 26 cm. © 2003 Artists Rights Society (ARS), New York/ VG Bild-Kunst, Bonn. Copyright Visual Arts Library/Art Resource, NY.

Chapter 16, p. 668: *Groovin High.* 1986. Faith Ringgold. Acrylic on canvas with fabric borders. 42 × 56. Faith Ringgold © 1986. Spellman College Museum of Fine Art, Atlanta.

Text and Illustration Credits

Table 1.3, p. 29: Direct quotes with portions abridged; a complete description can be found at http://www.apa.org/ethics/code.html. Copyright © 2002 by the American Psychological Association. Adapted with permission.

Figure 2.3, p. 41: From *Introduction to the Practice of Statistics* by David S. Moore and George P. McCabe. © 1989, 1993, 1999 by W. H. Freeman and Company. Used with permission.

Figure 3.1, p. 73: Figure from Dowling, J. E. (1992). *Neurons and Networks: An Introduction to Neuroscience.* Reprinted by permission of Cajal Institute, CSIC, Madrid, Spain.

Figure 3.6, p. 80: Adapted from *Psychology: Themes and Variations* (with Infotrac), 5th edition, by Weiten. © 2001. Reprinted with permission from Wadsworth, a division of Thomson Learning: www.thomsonrights.com. Fax: 800 730-2215.

Figure 3.13, p. 89: From Bisiach et al., "Brain and conscious representations of outside reality," *Neuropsychologica,* Vol. 19. Copyright 1981, with permission from Elsevier Science.

Figure 3.15, p. 92: From Gazzaniga, M. S., and LeDoux, J. E., *The Integrated Mind.* New York: Plenum Press, 1978. Reprinted with permission.

Figure 3.21, p.107: Adapted from *Introduction to Psychology,* 3rd edition, by Kalat. © 1993. Reprinted with permission from Wadsworth, a division of Thomson Learning: www.thomsonrights.com. Fax: 800 730–2215.

Figure 4.3, p. 127: From Dowling, J. E., and Boycott, B. B., "Organization of the primate retina: Electron microscopy" (1966). *Proceedings of the Royal Society* (London), B166, 80–111, Figure 7. Reprinted by permission.

Figure 4.18, p. 148: From *Psychology* by Peter Gray. © 1991, 1994, 2002 by Worth Publishers. Used with permission.

Figure 5.2, p. 176: From *Sleep* by J. Allan Hobson. Copyright 1989 by J. Allan Hobson, M.D. Reprinted by permission of Henry Holt and Company, LLC.

Figure 5.3, p.177: Reprinted with permission from H. P. Roffwarg, J. N. Muzio, and W. C. Dement, "Ontogenic development of human sleep-dream cycle," *Science, 152,* 604–619. Copyright 1966 American Association for the Advancement of Science.

Table 5.2, p. 198: Reprinted with permission from the *Diagnostic and Statistical Manual of Mental Disorders,* Fifth Edition. Copyright © 2000 American Psychiatric Association.

Figure 6.3 (Delayed, Trace, and Simultaneous), p. 216: From *Psychology: Themes and Variations* (with Infotrac), 5th edition, by Weiten. © 2001. Reprinted with permission from Wadsworth, a division of Thomson Learning: www.thomsonrights.com. Fax: 800 730-2215.

Figure 6.3 (Backward), p. 216: From *Psychology,* 3/e, by Kassin, Saul, © 2000. Adapted by permission of Pearson Education, Inc., Upper Saddle River, NJ.

Figure 6.13, p. 239: Figure from "Teaching machines" by B. F. Skinner, *Scientific American,* 1961. Reprinted by permission of the estate of Mary E. and Dan Todd.

Figure 7.4, p. 259: Figure adapted by Glanzer, M., and Cunitz, A. R., "Two storage mechanisms in free recall," *Journal of Verbal Learning and Verbal Behavior, 5,* 351–360, 1996. Reprinted by permission of the author.

Figure 7.5, p. 261: From Peter H. Lindsay and Donald A. Norman, *Human Information Processing: An Introduction to Psychology,* 2/e. Academic Press, 1977. Reprinted by permission of Donald A. Norman.

Figure 7.6, p. 264: Reprinted with permission from L. R. Squire and S. Zola-Morgan, "The medical temporal lobe memory system," in *Science,* 253, 1380–1386. Copyright 1992 American Association for the Advancement of Science.

Figure 7.7, p. 265: From *Working Memory* by Alan Baddeley, Clarendon Press (1986). Reprinted by permission of Oxford University Press.

Figure 7.9, p. 272: From G. H. Bower et al., "Hierarchical retrieval schemes in recall of categorized word lists," *Journal of Verbal Learning and Behavior,* Vol. 8, 323–343. Copyright 1969, with permission from Elsevier Science.

Figure 8.3, p. 311: Figure from Reznick, J. S., and Goldfield, B. A., "Rapid change in lexical development in comprehension and production," *Developmental Psychology,* 28, 406–413. Copyright © 1992 by the American Psychological Association. Reprinted with permission.

Figure 8.4, p. 321: From Kosslyn, S. M., Ball, T. M., and Reiser, B. J., "Visual images preserved metric spatial information: Evidence from studies of image scanning," *Journal of Experimental Psychology: Human Perception and Performance, 4,* 47–60. Copyright © 1978 by the American Psychological Association. Reprinted with permission.

Figure 8.5, p. 322: Reprinted with permission from R. N. Shephard and J. Metzler, "Mental rotation of three-dimensional objects," *Science, 171,* 701–703. Copyright 1971 American Association for the Advancement of Science.

Figure 8.10, p. 330: From *Cognition: Exploring the Science of the Mind* by Daniel Reisberg. Copyright © 1997 by W. W. Norton & Company, Inc. Used by permission of W. W. Norton & Company, Inc.

Figure 8.13, p. 338: From P. N. Johnson-Laird, "Mental models and deduction," *Trends in Cognitive Sciences,* Vol. 5, 434–443. Copyright 2001, with permission from Elsevier Science.

Figure 9.2, p. 360: From V. Prabhakaran et al., "Neural substrates of fluid reasoning: An fMRI study of the neocortical activation during performance of the Raven's Progressive Matrices Test," *Cognitive Psychology,* Vol. 33, 43–63. Copyright 1997, with permission from Elsevier Science.

Figure 9.3, p. 366: Adapted from *Behavioral Genetics* by R. Plomin, J. C. DeFries, G. E. McClearn, and M. Rutter. © 1980, 1990, 1997, 2001 by Worth Publishers. Used with permission.

Figure 9.6, p. 380: From Finke, R. A., and Slayton, K. (1988), "Explorations of creative visual synthesis in mental imagery," *Memory and Cognition, 16,* 252–257. Reprinted by permission.

Figure 10.2, p. 394: From Lester A. Lefton, *Psychology,* 7/e. Published by Allyn and Bacon, Boston, MA. © 2000 by Pearson Education. Reprinted by permission of the publisher.

Figure 10.9, p. 426: Figure from Cooper, M. L., Shapiro, C. M., and Powers, A. M., "Motivations for sex and risky behavior among adolescents and young adults: A functional perspective," *Journal of Personality and Social Psychology, 75,* 1528–1558. Copyright © 1998 by the American Psychological Association. Reprinted with permission.

Figure 10.10, p. 430: From "Human male sexuality: Appetite, arousal, desire and drive" by R. J. Levin, in *Appetite: Neural and Behavioral Bases* edited by Charles R. Legg and David Booth (1994). Reprinted by permission of Oxford University Press.

Figure 11.1, p. 345: Adapted from Cattell, Eber, and Tatsuoka. Copyright © 1970 by the Institute for Personality and Ability Testing, Inc. Reproduced by permission. "16PF" is a trademark belonging to IPAT, Inc.

Figure 11.3, p. 449: From Eysenck, *The Biological Basis of Personality,* 1967. Courtesy of Charles C. Thomas, Publisher, Ltd., Springfield, Illinois.

Figure 11.5, p. 458: From Lester A. Lefton, *Psychology,* 8/e. Published by Allyn and Bacon, Boston, MA. © 2003 by Pearson Education. Reprinted by permission of the publisher.

Figure 11.7, p. 476: Figure from Vandello, J. A., and Cohen, D. (1999), "Patterns of individualism and collectivism across the United States," *Journal of Personality and Social Psychology, 77,* 279–292. Copyright © 1999 by the American Psychological Association. Reprinted with permission.

Figure 12.4, p. 501: Figure from Baillargeon, Renee (1994), "How do infants learn about the physical world?" *Current Directions in Psychological Science,* 3(5), 133–140. Reprinted by permission of Blackwell Publishers.

Figure 13.1, p. 536: From Selye, Hans (1978). *The Stress of Life,* Second Edition. Copyright 1976. Reprinted by permission of The McGraw-Hill Companies.

Figure 13.4, p. 550: Figure from *Changing for Good* by James O. Prochaska, John C. Norcross, and Carlo C. Diclemente. Copyright © 1994 by James O. Prochaska, John C. Norcross, and Carlo C. Diclemente. Reprinted with permission of HarperCollins Publishers, Inc.

Table 14.1, p. 579; Table 14.2, p. 581; Table 14.4, p. 585; Table 14.5, p. 593; Table 14.7, p. 601; Table 14.8, p. 615: Reprinted with permission from the *Diagnostic and Statistical Manual of Mental Disorders*, Fifth Edition. Copyright 2000 American Psychiatric Association.

Figure 14.3, p. 610: From Thompson, J. K. (1990). *Body Image Disturbance: Assessment and Treatment.* Copyright 1990 by Pergamon Press. Reprinted by permission of The McGraw-Hill Companies.

Figure 15.4, p. 648: Adapted and reprinted by permission of the publisher from *Families and Family Therapy* by Salvador Minuchin, pp. 53, 61, Cambridge, Mass.: Harvard University Press, Copyright © 1974 by the President and Fellows of Harvard College.

Figure 16.6, p. 697: Sternberg's triangular Theory of Love. Reprinted by permission of Robert Sternberg.

Table 16.2, p. 702: Reprinted from Perkins and Berkowitz, "Perceiving the community norms of alcohol use among students," *International Journal of the Addictions, 21*, Sept/Oct 1986, pp. 961–974, by courtesy of Marcel Dekker, Inc.

Photo Credits

Chapter 1 **3:** © Monika Graff/The Image Works; **5 (left):** © Roger Tully/Getty Images/Stone; **5 (center):** © David Young-Wolff/PhotoEdit; **5 (right):** © Royalty Free/CORBIS; **9:** © H. Gans/The Image Works; **10:** Archives of the History of American Psychology; **11:** Archives of the History of American Psychology; **12:** ©2000 North Wind Picture Archives; **13:** © Kelly-Mooney Photography/CORBIS; **14:** © Mary Evans/Sigmund Freud Copyrights; **15:** THE FAR SIDE © 1986 FARWORKS, INC. Used by permission. All rights Reserved.;**17:** © Bettmann/CORBIS; **19 left:** AP/Wide World; **19 right:** © Louise Gubb/The Image Works; **21:** Courtesy of Wellesley College; **22:** © Bob Daemmrich/The Image Works; **23:** © Brian Smith/Stock Boston, LLC.; **24:** © Bob Daemmrich/The Image Works; **28:** © 1996 Jane Tyska/Stock Boston, LLC.

Chapter 2 **33:** Courtesy of NASA; **39:** © Mary Evans Picture Library; **42 (top):** © Terje Rakke/Getty Images/The Image Bank; **42 (bottom):** © Dennis MacDonald/PhotoEdit; **43:** © Cindy Charles/PhotoEdit; **47 (left):** © Bettmann/CORBIS; **47 (right):** © Chris McPherson/Getty Images/Stone: **49:** DILBERT reprinted by permission of United Features Syndicate, Inc.; **51:** DILBERT reprinted by permission of United Features Syndicate, Inc.; **53:** © PBNJ Productions/CORBIS; **54:** AP/Wide World Photos; **67:** Courtesy of NASA.

Chapter 3 **71:** © John Ficara/Woodfin Camp & Associates; **81:** © Ron Sachs/CORBIS Sygma; **86:** © A. Glaublerman/Photo Researchers, Inc.; **90:** Damasio H, Grabowski T, Frank R, Galaburda AM, Damasio AR: The return of Phineas Gage: Clues about the brain from a famous patient. *Science, 264*:1102–1105, 1994. Department of Neurology and Image Analysis Facility, University of Iowa.; **101:** © Will and Deni McIntyre/Science Source/Photo Researchers, Inc.; **102 (left):** © Susie Levines/Photo Researchers, Inc.; **102 (right):** © Scott Camazine/Photo Researchers, Inc.; **103 (left):** © Will and Deni McIntyre/Photo Researchers, Inc.; **103 (right):** Courtesy of Marcus E. Raichle, M. D. Washington University School of Medicine; **111:** © David Madison/Getty Images/Stone; **112:** © PhotoDisc/Getty Images; **115 (left):** AP/Wide World Photos; **115 (right):** © Bob Daemmrich/Stock Boston, LLC.

Chapter 4 **121:** © The Kobal Collection/MiraMax/Dimension Films/Peter Sorel; **122:** The Art Archive/Museum of Modern Art Mexico/Dagli Orti ; **123:** © Burstein Collection/CORBIS; **126:** © North Wind Pictures Archives; **127:** © S. R. Maglione/Photo Researchers, Inc.; **132:** © Robert Harbison; **134:** All artwork by Bev Doolittle has been reproduced with the permission of The Greenwich Workshop, Inc. For information on limited edition fine art prints contact The Greenwich Workshop, Inc. One Greenwich Place, Shelton, CT 06484.; **135:** Reprinted with permission from Tootell, RBH, Silverman, MS, Switkes, E, and DeValors, RL 1982. Deoxyglucose analysis of retinotopic organization in primate striate cortex. *Science*, Vol. 218, 26, November 1982. p. 902. © 1982 American Association for the Advancement of Science.; **135:** M. C. Escher. Dutch. 1898–1972. Sky and Water 1. M. C. Escher Heirs. Cordon Art, Baarn, Holland.; **138:** © Bill Lyons/Getty Agency; **139:** © Baron Wolman/Woodfin Camp & Associates; **141 (left):** © CORBIS Sygma; **141 (right):** © CORBIS Sygma; **149:** Corel, Courtesy of Ron Rensink/Rensink, O'Regan, and Clark, 1997. *Psychology Science.* Vol 8., No. 5, September 1997; 151: Perrett, D. I., et al, (1998). *Nature*, Vol. 394, August 27, 1998. p. 885. "Effects of Sexual Dimorphism on Facial Attractiveness," 884–887; **154:** © Mark Richards/PhotoEdit; **156:** © Jack K. Clark/The Image Works: **163:** © Addison Geary/Stock Boston, LLC.

Chapter 5 **171:** National Archives and Records Administration; **173:** © Dr. Neal Scolding/Photo Researchers, Inc.; **175:** © Michael Heron/Woodfin Camp & Associates; **177:** DENNIS THE MENACE® used by permission of Hank Ketcham and © by North America Syndicate.; **178:** © Mark Richards/PhotoEdit; **181:** © Jeremy Horner/CORBIS; **183:** © David Lees/CORBIS; **185:** © Mary Evans Picture Library; **186:** © Jon Feingersh/CORBIS; **188:** © Mary Evans Picture Library; **194:** © Bettmann/Corbis; **195:** © Robert Fried/Stock Boston, LLC.; **196:** © Reuters/Gary Hershorn/Getty Images; **200:** © Roy McMahon/CORBIS; **203:** © Robert Frerck/Woodfin Camp & Associates; **206:** © Mary Evans Picture Library; **207:** AP/Wide World Photos.

Chapter 6 **211:** © Kobal Collection/Dreamsworks/Kraychyk, George; **212:** © Kobal Collection /Dreamworks /Kraychyk, George; **223:** © Barbara Alper/PhotoEdit; **234:** "Illustrations" by Kimberley Ann Coe, from SIBLINGS WITHOUT RIVALRY: HOW TO HELP YOUR CHILDREN LIVE TOGETHER SO YOU CAN TOO by Adele Faber and Elaine Mazlish; **235:** © Dennis MacDonald/PhotoEdit; **236:** AP/Wide World Photos; **240:** © Bonnie Kamin/PhotoEdit; **245 (top):** © CORBIS; **245 (bottom):** DILBERT reprinted by permission of United Features Syndicate, Inc.; **248:** © James A. Sugar/CORBIS; **249:** © Rick Kopstein.

Chapter 7 **253:** © PhotoDisc/Getty Images; **256:** © Alex Hermant/Getty Images; **262 (left):** © David Young Wolff/PhotoEdit; **262 (right):** © Marko Haggerty/Getty Images/The Image Bank; **264:** Reprinted with permission from Smith, E. E., & Jonides, J., Storage and executive processes in the frontal lobes," *Science*, Vol. 283, 12 March 1999. pp. 1657–1661. © 1999 American Association for the Advancement of Science.; **273 (top):** © Bob Daemmrich/Stock Boston, LLC.; **273 (bottom):** AP/Wide World Photos; **274:** AP/Wide World Photos; **279:** © Ian O'Leary/Getty Images/Stone; **280:** © Michael Newman/PhotoEdit; **282:** © Tony Hopewell/Getty Images/Taxi; **283:** DILBERT reprinted by permission of United Features Syndicate, Inc.; **284:** © David Butow/CORBIS SABA; **287 (top):** © The Everett Collection; **287 (bottom):** © Paul Conklin/PhotoEdit; **291:** © PhotoDisc/Getty Images; **293:** © Tony Freeman/PhotoEdit.

Chapter 8 **299:** Albert Einstein™ Licensed by The Hebrew University of Jerusalem, Represented by The Roger Richman Agency, Inc. www.albert-einstein.net. Photo courtesy of the Archives, California Institute of Technology; **300:** © Topham/The Image Works; **302:** © Paul Barton/CORBIS; **303:** Cantalupo, C., and Hopikins, W. D., "Asymmetric Broca's areas in great apes. A region of the ape brain is uncannily similar to one linked with speech in humans." Reprinted by permission from *Nature, 414:* 505, (2001) MacMilliam Publishers Ltd.; **307:** © Catherine Karnow/Woodfin Camp & Associates; **310:** © Michael Newman/PhotoEdit; **312:** © Will Hart/PhotoEdit; **315 (top):** © Frank Siteman/PhotoEdit; **315 (bottom):** Courtesy of Language Research Center Staff/GSU; **319:** © Corbis; **331 (left):** © Jose Luis Pelaez, Inc./CORBIS; **331 (right):** © Myrleen F. Cate/PhotoEdit; **331 (bottom left):** © Lou Dematteis/The Image Works; **335:** AP/Wide World Photos; **339:** © Barbara Stitzer/PhotoEdit; **340:** © Kelly-Mooney Photography/Corbis; **341:** © Ellen Senisi/The Image Works; **342:** © Bettmann/CORBIS.

Chapter 9 **347:** © Eyewire/Getty Images; **349:** © Bob Daemmrich Photography; **352:** © Owen Franken/CORBIS; **354:** © 1994 David J. Sams/Stock Boston, LLC.; **355 (left):** © Jose L. Pelaez/CORBIS; **355 (right):** © Lawrence Migdale/Stock Boston, LLC.; **356:** © Tony Freeman/PhotoEdit; **357:** © Michael Newman/PhotoEdit; **361:** © Paula Lerner/Woodfin Camp & Associates: **369 (top left):** © Cleo Photography/PhotoEdit: **369 (top right):** © Robert Ginn/PhotoEdit; **370:** © Michael S. Yamashita/CORBIS; **373:** © Material World/Kirk McCoy; **374:** © T. Zuidema/The Image Works; **377:**Reprinted with permission from Streissguth, A. P., Landesman-Dwyer, S., Martin, J. C., & Smith, D. W. (1980). "Teratogenic effects of alcohol in humans and laboratory animals." *Science, 209* (18): 353–362. © 1980 American Association for the Advancement of Science; **381:** © Sandra Kimball Photography; **382:** AP/Wide World Photos; **383:** © Carol Ann DeSimine for Creative Competitions, Inc.

Chapter 10 **389:** © Paul Edmonson/Getty Images/Stone; **392:** Reprinted by permission of the Human Interaction Laboratory/Japanese and Caucasian Facial Expressions of Emotion, Matsimoto & Ekman, 1988; **396:** © Roger Ressmeyer/CORBIS; **399:** Whalen, P. J. et al., "Masked presentations of emotional facial expressions, modulate amygdala activity without explicit knowledge." *J. Neurosci. 18*: 411–418. Used with Permission; **401:** © Ariel Skelley/CORBIS; **403:** © Dwayne Newton/PhotoEdit; **405:** © Mark C. Burnett/Photo Researchers, Inc.; **407 (left):** © Doug Martin/Stock Boston, LLC.; **407 (center):** © Syracuse Newspapers/Steve Ruark/The Image Works; **407 (right):** AP/Wide World Photos; **410:** © George Shelley/CORBIS; **412:** © M. Granitsas/The Image Works; **417:** © Nathan Benn/Woodfin Camp & Associates; **419:** © Reuters NewMedia Inc./CORBIS; **420:** © Bob Daemmrich/Stock Boston, LLC.; **421:** AP/Wide World Photos; **427:** © David Young-Wolff/PhotoEdit; **431:** © Hans Pfletschinger/Peter Arnold, Inc.

Chapter 11 **437:** © Frank Siteman/PhotoEdit; **438:** © The Everett Collection; **440 (left):** © David Young-Wolff/PhotoEdit; **440 (right):** © David Young-Wolff/PhotoEdit; **441:** © Mike Yamashita/Woodfin Camp & Associates; **447:** © Lew Merrim/Photo Researchers, Inc.; **450:** © Lori Cain/Reuters/Archive Photos/Getty Images; **451:** © Robert Aschenbrenner/Stock Boston, LLC.; **452:** © Bob Sacha Photography; **456 (left):** © Jose Carrillo/Stock Boston, LLC.; **456 (right):** © Bill Bachmann/Stock Boston, LLC.; **460:** © Tosca Radigonda/Getty Images/The Image Bank; **465:** © Cindy Charles/PhotoEdit; **466:** AP/Wide World Photos; **471:** © Michael Newman/PhotoEdit; **473:** © Spencer Grant/PhotoEdit; **475:** © Joe Cavanaugh/DDB Stock Photo.

Chapter 12 **481:** © The Everett Collection; **483:** © Dr. Yorgos Nikas/Science Photo Library/Photo Resources, Inc.; **485:** © Petit Format/Nestle/Photo Researchers, Inc.; **487:** © Michael Krasowitz/Getty Images/Taxi; **489 (top):** © 1998 Laura Dwight; **489 (middle):** © Paul Conklin/PhotoEdit; **489 (bottom):** © E. Crews/The Image Works; **490:** © John Ficara/Woodfin Camp & Associates; **493:** © Mark Richards/PhotoEdit; **497:** © Bill Anderson/PhotoResearchers, Inc.; **499:** © Michael Newman/PhotoEdit; **501:** Reprinted with permission from A. N. Meltzoff & M. K. Moore, 1977, "Imitation of facial and manual gestures by human neonates." *Science, 198*, p. 75 © 1977 American Association for the Advancement of Science; **504:** © Nik Wheeler/CORBIS; **505:** Harlow Primate Laboratory; **506:** © Mark Wexler/Woodfin Camp Associates, Inc; **507:** © Michael Newman/PhotoEdit; **511:** © Kit Walling/Folio, Inc.; **513:** © Bob Daemmrich/Stock Boston, LLC.; **514:** © James Darell/Getty Images/Stone; **518:** © Steven Peters/Getty Images/Stone; **519:** © Tom Prettyman/PhotoEdit; **523:** © Timothy Greenfield-Sanders/CORBIS Outline; **524:** AP/Wide World Photos; **525:** © Photonews/Getty Images; **528:** © David Young-Wolff/PhotoEdit.

Chapter 13 **533:** © Bob Daemmrich/Stock Boston, LLC.; **537:** © B. Stitzer/PhotoEdit; **539:** © B. Deconinck/The Image Works; **540:** © Fridman Paulo/CORBIS SYGMA; **541 (left):** © Bill Horsman/Stock Boston, LLC.; **541 (right):** © Paul Gish; **542:** © Reuters/Kimimasa Mayama/Getty Images; **545:** © Meckes/Ottawa/Photo Researchers, Inc.; **546:** AP/Wide World Photos; **551:** © Nik Kleinberg/Stock Boston, LLC.; **555:** © Mark Romanelli/Getty Images/The Image Bank; **556:** © Reuters NewMedia Inc./CORBIS; **557:** AP/Wide World Photos; **559:** © Patrick Davidson/Rocky Mountain News/CORBIS Sygma; **559 (inset left):** © Reuters/Ho/Getty Images; **559 (inset right):** © Reuters/Ho/Getty Images; **561:** © Nancy Richmond/The Image Works; **564:** © Network Productions/The Image Works; **565:** © Bob Collins/The Image Works.

Chapter 14 **571:** © Archivo Iconografico, S. A./CORBIS; **573:** © Musée d'Orsay, Paris France, © Erich Lessing/Art Resource, NY; **574 (left):** © Fred Prouser/Reuters/ **574 (right):** © Michael Crabtree/Reuters; **581:** Painting by Kate Monson, Courtesy of Sistare; **587:** © Richard Pasley/Stock Boston, LLC.; **588:** © 2002 Bill Truslow Photography, Inc.; **590:** © The Everett Collection; **594:** © Margaret Ross/Stock Boston, LLC.; **596:** © Culver Pictures, Inc.; **602:** National Institute of Mental Health; **605:** Edna Morlock; **607:** © The Everett Collection; **608:** © Dale St. Hilaire; **612 (left):** © The Everett Collection; **612 (right):** © Chet Gordon/The Image Works; **616:** © Reuters/Ho/Getty Images.

Chapter 15 **623:** Freud Museum, London; **628 (top left):** © Bob Mahoney/The Image Works; **628 (top right):** © Bob Mahoney/The Image Works; **628 (bottom):** © Vincent DeWitt/Stock Boston, LLC.; **636 (left):** © Rhoda Sidney/Stock Boston, LLC.; **636 (right):** © Stone/Getty Images; **639:** © R. Lord/The Image Works; **643:** © Michael P. Gadomski/Photo Researchers, Inc.; **645:** © Julian Keenan; **647:** © Bob Daemmrich/Stock Boston, LLC.; **649:** © Dion Oqust/The Image Works; **651:** © David Young-Wolff/PhotoEdit; **652:** © Wendy Ashton/Getty Images/Taxi; **659:** © David Young-Wolff/PhotoEdit; **663:** © Chuck Fishman/Woodfin Camp & Associates.

Chapter 16 **669:** © Marianne Barcellona; **671 (top):** © Bob Daemmrich/The Image Works; **671 (bottom):** © PhotoDisc/Getty Images; **679:** DILBERT reprinted by permission of United Features Syndicate, Inc.; **680:** © Mario Tama/Getty Images; **681:** © Jeff Greenberg/Photo Researchers, Inc.; **683:** © John Neubauer/PhotoEdit; **685:** Payne, B. K. (2001) "Prejudice and perception: The role of automatic and controlled processes in misperceiving a weapon." *Journal of Personality and Social Psychology, 81*, 181–192. Used with Permission; **686 (left):** © Michael Newman/PhotoEdit; **686 (right):** © Stephen Simpson/Getty Images/Taxi; **689:** © Culver Pictures, Inc.; **693:** © David Frazier/Stock Boston, LLC.; **696:** © Photodisc/Getty Images; **699 (top):** © Jason Laure/ Woodfin Camp & Associates; **699 (bottom):** Kunsthistorisches Museum, Gemaeldegalerie, Vienna, Austria © Erich Lessing/Art Resource, NY; **700:** © David Wells/The Image Works; **701:** © Reuters/Yannis Behrakis/Getty Images; **703:** © Burbank/The Image Works; **707:** © Rhoda Sidney/The Image Works; **708 (top, bottom):** From the film *Obedience* copyright 1965 by Stanley Milgram and distributed by Penn State Media Sales; **711:** © James Nubile/The Image Works; **712:** © Shannon Stapleton/Reuters.

PRACTICE TESTS

Prepared by Stephen M. Kosslyn and Robin S. Rosenberg

CHAPTER 1 Psychology: Yesterday and Today

The Science of Psychology:
Getting to Know You

1. According to your textbook's authors, psychology
   a. cannot be defined in one simple sentence.
   b. is at work often in one's daily life, except when a person is asleep or daydreaming.
   c. seeks to describe, explain, predict, and control mental processes and behavior.
   d. relies most heavily on opinions, intuitions, and guesses.

2. Which of the following is true of the concept of levels of analysis?
   a. It is a thread that ties together the topics in your textbook.
   b. It has long held a central role in science in general and the field of psychology in particular.
   c. It allows you to see how theories and discoveries are interconnected.
   d. All of the above statements are true.

3. At the level of the person, what do psychologists focus on?
   a. The activity of the brain and the structure and properties of the organ itself
   b. The internal mechanics of mental processes, but not their content
   c. The ways collections of people shape individual mental processes and behavior
   d. None of the above

4. Events at the three levels of analysis
   a. are constantly changing and interacting.
   b. rarely occur in a specific physical context.
   c. can occur at the same time but cannot interact.
   d. should not be related to the physical world that surrounds us.

5. Among the Masai, the infants who were most likely to survive the drought were the ones who were
   a. cared for by an extended family.
   b. small in size.
   c. cooperative and calm.
   d. testy and demanding.

Psychology Then and Now:
The Evolution of a Science

6. Margaret Floy Washburn was
   a. a 17th-century English philosopher.
   b. a physiologist who focused attention on the distinction between mind and body.
   c. the first person to receive a Ph.D. in psychology from Harvard.
   d. Edward Titchener's first graduate student to receive a Ph.D.

7. The earliest scientific psychologists
   a. were most interested in why we behave as we do.
   b. focused their effort on understanding events at what we now think of as the level of the group.
   c. studied the operation of perception, memory, and problem solving.
   d. set up the first psychology laboratory in 1621 in Paris, France.

8. The term *psychodynamic theory*
   a. refers to the continual push-and-pull interaction among conscious and unconscious forces.
   b. was coined by Wilhelm Wundt.
   c. takes its name from the German word for "whole."
   d. refers to a school of psychology that sought to understand the ways that the mind helps individuals adapt to the world.

9. The behaviorists' emphasis on controlled, objective observation
   a. led to their extensive study of hidden mental processes.
   b. has had a deep and lasting impact on psychology.
   c. adversely affected psychotherapy and education.
   d. decreased the level of rigor used in studies of mental processes.

10. Self-actualization is a goal of _____ psychology.
   d. no type of
   b. all types of
   c. Gestalt
   d. humanistic

The Psychological Way:
What Today's Psychologists Do

11. A clinical neuropsychologist
   a. is a special type of psychiatrist.
   b. specializes in helping people with issues that naturally arise during the course of life.
   c. must earn both an M.S.W and an M.S.N.
   d. works specifically with tests designed to diagnose the effects of brain damage.

12. A personality psychologist studies
    a. how people think and feel about themselves and other people, and how groups function.
    b. how thinking, feeling, and behaving change with age and experience.
    c. individual differences in preferences and inclinations.
    d. thinking, memory, and related topics.

13. Industrial/organizational psychologists
    a. are the most common type of psychologist.
    b. apply psychology to improve cognitive, emotional, and social development of schoolchildren.
    c. focus on using psychology in the workplace.
    d. specialize in treating people with eating disorders.

14. The mere-exposure effect
    a. demonstrates that most results from psychological research are obvious.
    b. demonstrates that an event in the brain can affect an event at the level of the group.
    c. is just a laboratory curiosity.
    d. shows that familiarity breeds contempt.

15. Which of the following is *not* typically a function of an academic psychologist?
    a. Teaching
    b. Research
    c. Holding office hours
    d. All of the above are typically functions of academic psychologists.

Ethics: Doing It Right

16. Informed consent
    a. means that people must be told about the possible benefits of the research study after they participate, particularly if the study is one in which the pain outweighs the gain.
    b. is no longer included in most research studies.
    c. is especially important to obtain from animals.
    d. requires that a person be told what he or she will be asked to do and possible risks and benefits of a study before agreeing to take part in the study.

17. In which instance does a researcher at a hospital who plans to do a study not need to seek approval from the Institutional Review Board?
    a. The study's funds come from the U.S. government.
    b. The researcher is a psychiatrist.
    c. The study will use animals.
    d. None of the above statements are true.

18. Which of the following statements about debriefing is *true*?
    a. Debriefing is not allowed in California, Connecticut, Massachusetts, or Illinois.
    b. It is approved only when the participants will not be harmed.
    c. Debriefing is an interview after a study to ensure that a participant has no negative reactions as a result of participation and understands why the study was conducted.
    d. All of the above statements are true.

19. What spurred the development of codes of professional ethics?
    a. The cognitive revolution
    b. The 2002 study of suicidal teens in New York
    c. Nuremberg trials after World War II
    d. New brain-scanning technologies

20. Researchers have found that people with schizophrenia benefit greatly if they
    a. receive psychodynamic therapy.
    b. are medicated as soon as possible after the onset of the disease.
    c. receive treatment that causes them to become irritable around their families.
    d. are not medicated when they are placed into a group home.

The Scientific Method: Designed to Be Valid

1. Properly collected data
   a. can be replicated.
   b. cannot be replicated.
   c. cannot establish facts.
   d. must be numerical.

2. Which of the following is not part of the scientific method?
   a. Forming a hypothesis of the relation between variables
   b. Systematically observing events
   c. Relying on impressions or interpretations
   d. Testing the theory

3. What events do scientists study?
   a. Events that are themselves directly observable
   b. Events that can only be inferred
   c. Neither (a) nor (b)
   d. Both (a) and (b)

4. An operational definition
   a. is an expectation about specific events that should occur in particular circumstances if the theory or hypothesis is correct.
   b. specifies a variable by indicating how it is measured or manipulated.
   c. consists of an interlocking set of concepts or principles that explain a set of observations.
   d. focuses on possible relationships among variables.

5. How are hypotheses and theories related to each other?
   a. They are the same thing.
   b. Hypotheses produce predictions whereas theories report conclusions.
   c. Hypotheses are tested in studies; the results of these studies are then woven together into theories.
   d. Hypotheses may be either correct or incorrect; theories are always correct.

The Psychologist's Toolbox: Techniques of Scientific Research

6. In a quasi-experimental research design,
   a. participants are assigned randomly to different groups.
   b. conclusions can be as strong as those from genuine experiments.
   c. researchers should control for as many variables as they can to make the groups as similar as possible.
   d. you can be certain exactly what differences among groups are responsible for the observed results.

7. Suppose that someone tells you two variables have a strong positive relationship. As such, the correlation between these two variables is most likely to be
   a. near zero.
   b. near –0.3.
   c. near +20.
   d. near +0.9.

8. If a theory defines *fatigue* in terms of lack of alertness, but a study designed to test the theory measures fatigue with items that assess boredom, then _____ is likely threatened.
   a. reliability
   b. construct validity
   c. random assignment
   d. sampling bias

9. Experimenter expectancy effects
   a. cannot occur if a participant is "blind" to the predictions of a study.
   b. occur only in quasi-experiments.
   c. do not occur in double-blind experiments.
   d. result when an experimenter's conscious expectations cause him or her to mistreat participants.

10. Which of the following is not a potential difficulty associated with the use of surveys?
    a. What people say and what they do may be different.
    b. Not everyone who is asked to fill out a survey does so.
    c. People may not be truthful in their answers, especially with sensitive material.
    d. All of the above are potential difficulties associated with the use of surveys.

Statistics: Measuring Reality

11. Descriptive statistics
    a. are limited to figures and tables.
    b. indicate which differences or patterns in the data are worthy of attention.
    c. are concise ways of summarizing properties of sets of numbers.
    d. are one of four major types of statistics.

12. Which of the following statements is *not* true?
    a. The mean is the measure of central tendency that is most sensitive to extreme values or scores.
    b. The mode can be any value, from the highest to the lowest.
    c. If all participants score 10 on a particular scale, the mean, median, and mode are identical.
    d. If all participants score 10 on a particular scale, these data follow a normal distribution.

13. The margin of error, usually called a confidence interval,
    a. specifies the range of values within which the mode is likely to fall.
    b. is the difference obtained when you subtract the smallest score from the largest.
    c. specifies the range of values within which the mean is likely to fall.
    d. is the average of the deviation scores.

14. Statistical significance
    a. means that results are important.
    b. expresses the probability that a value (such as the size of a correlation) is true.
    c. is expressed in terms of the probability that a value could be due to chance.
    d. cannot occur unless there is substantial sampling error.

15. Because our visual system does not register height and width separately but rather simultaneously,
    a. graphs cannot be constructed to deceive.
    b. changing the width of a bar in a graph along with the height gives a much smaller impression of amount than is conveyed by changing height alone.
    c. data should always be transformed before they are plotted.
    d. changing the width of a bar in a graph along with the height gives a much larger impression of amount than is conveyed by changing height alone.

How to Think About Research Studies

16. Which of the following is true of the QALMRI method?
    a. The *I* represents the general idea behind the study—the way the study will distinguish among alternatives.
    b. The *M* represents the motivation behind the study, why it is important, and why anyone should care about the results.
    c. The *A* stands for "alternatives"; a good report describes at least two possible answers to the question and explains why both are plausible.
    d. All of the theories are required to make the same prediction.

17. When you write a research paper
    a. include more material in the Introduction than you need to put your question in context.
    b. keep the reader in suspense in the Results section: present the results that speak to the primary question at the very end.
    c. always put yourself in the place of the intelligent reader.
    d. be sure to include enough detail about materials and apparatus in the Introduction to allow another researcher to repeat exactly what you did.

18. Which of the following statements describes the QALMRI method?
    a. It helps you focus on the "big picture."
    b. It is a vehicle for understanding the meaning of a research study and for reporting your own research.
    c. It helps you become clear about what question is being asked, how the researchers have tried to answer it, and whether the results really do support the preferred answer (the hypothesis).
    d. All of the above statements are true.

19. The Method section of a research report
    a. describes the outcome of a study in detail.
    b. present the inferences the authors want to draw from their results.
    c. includes parts about participants, materials, apparatus, and procedure.
    d. should end with a clear statement of the logic of the study, the basic idea underlying what was done.

20. If a study is well designed,
    a. there should be many confounds in the study.
    b. it will yield results that are always consistent with previous studies on the same topic.
    c. the results can always be generalized to different populations and topics.
    d. the results should allow you to eliminate at least one of the alternatives.

CHAPTER 3 The Biology of Mind and Behavior

Brain Circuits: Making Connections

1. The human brain contains
   a. on average about 100 million glial cells.
   b. two types of neurons.
   c. on average about 100 billion neurons.
   d. mostly motor neurons.

2. Neurons
   a. may have many sending ends.
   b. may have many receiving ends.
   c. contain a part in the middle called a cell membrane.
   d. usually communicate via electrical impulses.

3. Substances that act as neuromodulators in the brain
   a. include nitric oxide and carbon monoxide.
   b. do not alter the effects of the neurotransmitters.
   c. play the same role as sound waves.
   d. are all released at terminal buttons.

4. Dopamine
   a. is a transmitter at the neuromuscular juncture that causes muscles to contract.
   b. excess is implicated in depression.
   c. is no longer considered an important neurotransmitter.
   d. plays a key role in the areas of the brain that are involved in planning movements.

5. An agonist is a chemical that
   a. facilitates the reuptake of the neurotransmitter serotonin specifically.
   b. mimics the effects of a neurotransmitter (sometimes by preventing reuptake).
   c. blocks the effect of a neurotransmitter (sometimes by blocking a receptor or enhancing the reuptake mechanism).
   d. is a type of terminal button.

The Nervous System: An Orchestra With Many Members

6. The spinal cord
   a. is simply a set of cables that relays commands and information between brain and body.
   b. can itself initiate some aspects of our behavior, such as reflexes.
   c. is a part of the peripheral nervous system.
   d. sends and receives information from the six cranial nerves.

7. The sympathetic nervous system
   a. always works against the parasympathetic nervous system.
   b. is unable to ready an animal to cope with an emergency.
   c. tends to slow things down.
   d. tends to affect all the organs at the same time.

8. The two halves of the brain are connected by
   a. meninges.
   b. sulci.
   c. the cerebral cortex.
   d. the corpus callosum.

9. The human brain is divided into _____ major lobes that usually function in _____.
   a. four; isolation
   b. four; in concert with each other
   c. five; isolation to carry out the same function
   d. none of the above

10. The left brain
    a. is best characterized as intuitive and perceptual.
    b. is better than the right brain at some types of perception (such as determining whether one object is above or below another).
    c. is better than the right at some aspects of language (such as making the pitch of the voice rise at the end of a question).
    d. is better than the right at understanding humor.

Probing the Brain

11. Natural experiments
    a. are usually very neat and thus affect one specific area.
    b. most often occur in younger people who have led healthy lives.
    c. are a type of lesioning study in which specific parts of the brain are removed.
    d. were the first evidence that different parts of the brain do different things.

12. Computer-assisted tomography
    a. gives an image that reflects the brain in action.
    b. suffers from the limitation that the electrical current is distorted when it passes through the skull.
    c. uses a series of X rays to build up a three-dimensional image of brain structure, slice by slice.
    d. relies on tiny probes that can be placed in individual cells in the brain.

13. Which of the following is true of functional magnetic imaging?
    a. It requires the introduction of radioactivity into the brain.
    b. It can build an image of events that occur in only a few seconds.
    c. It reveals structure by detecting the amount of iron being brought to a particular place in the brain.
    d. All of the above statements are true.

14. Study of the human brain has shown that
    a. areas that are used often actually grow larger.
    b. areas that are used often grow smaller, probably because of the formation of additional connections among neurons.
    c. part of the motor strip in the left half of the brain controls the fingers of the left hand.
    d. the brain is sometimes completely "off."

15. _____ show that when people look at words, some neurons respond to specific words but not others.
    a. Transcranial magnetic stimulation studies
    b. EEGs
    c. Single-cell recordings
    d. No studies

Genes, Brain, and Environment: The Brain in the World

16. In general, when a characteristic varies continuously, it reflects
    a. complex inheritance.
    b. the effects of individual elements of inheritance.
    c. Mendelian inheritance.
    d. a lack of deoxyribonucleic acid.

17. Homozygous genes
    a. are a type of allele.
    b. indicate a person's phenotype.
    c. are the same on both chromosomes of the pair.
    d. are different on both chromosomes of the pair.

18. Glutamate
    a. is one of the least common neurotransmitters in the brain.
    b. is toxic to neurons if too much of it is present.
    c. causes excitotoxic injury if not enough is present.
    d. is a type of knockout mice.

19. Genes
    a. are best characterized as blueprints for the body that fix our characteristics forevermore.
    b. program the structure of the brain in advance but do not interact with the environment.
    c. are constantly being turned on and off.
    d. and environment can really be considered as separate factors.

20. Heritability
    a. refers to the amount of a characteristic or trait that is inherited.
    b. is the contribution of genes across different environments.
    c. cannot be overshadowed by environmental factors.
    d. indicates how much of the variability in a characteristic or trait in a population is due to genetics.

Vision

1. Weber's law
   a. states that a constant percentage of a magnitude change is necessary to detect a difference.
   b. is rarely accurate, except for very small magnitude of stimuli.
   c. is the smallest amount of a stimulus needed in order to notice that the stimulus is present at all.
   d. is the study of the relation between physical events and the corresponding experience of those events.

2. In signal detection research, a miss occurs when a person
   a. makes an error.
   b. does not report the presence of a signal when a signal is not present.
   c. makes a false alarm.
   d. does not report the presence of a signal when a signal is present.

3. In the eye, a circular muscle called the _____ surrounds the _____.
   a. fovea; retina
   b. pupil; cornea
   c. iris; pupil
   d. lens; optic nerve

4. Which of the following statements is *true*?
   a. Cones allow us to see with less light, but not in color.
   b. People with hypermetropia have acquired color blindness.
   c. Some neurons in the visual areas of the brain have been found to respond best with relatively little retinal disparity.
   d. The "where" pathway in the brain going down to the temporal lobes is concerned with spatial properties (such as an object's location).

5. Top-down processing
   a. cannot occur at the same time as bottom-up processing.
   b. is initiated by the stimulus.
   c. occurs when the superior colliculus acts like a reflex, shifting attention automatically to an event.
   d. is guided by knowledge, expectation, or belief.

Hearing

6. About 40% of normal people emit a detectable soft humming sound from their ears that
   a. plays an important role in hearing.
   b. is like the natural sonar used by whales.
   c. is probably caused by feedback from the brain to the ear.
   d. is never loud enough to enable other people to hear it.

7. The middle ear contains
   a. the pinna and the cochlea.
   b. rods and cones that function the same way they do in vision.
   c. frequency theory.
   d. the smallest bones in the human body.

8. Nerve deafness
   a. affects all frequencies.
   b. typically occurs when the hair cells are destroyed by loud sounds.
   c. requires that people inherit a particular mutated gene.
   d. often results from drugs, such as aspirin, that can temporarily enhance a person's hearing.

9. Which of the following statements is *not* true?
   a. As in vision, we use many different cues to assess where an object is.
   b. Some cues to assess where an object is depend on only one ear, not two.
   c. The sound wave reaches the two ears at the same time.
   d. We hear speech sounds as distinct categories.

10. People with absolute pitch
    a. have an unusually small planum temporale.
    b. can identify a particular note by itself, not simply in relation to other notes.
    c. tend to be identical twins or fraternal twins who live in the same culture.
    d. are the only ones who hear notes an octave apart as more similar than consecutive notes.

Sensing and Perceiving in Other Ways

11. In general,
    a. men are better than women at detecting many types of odors.
    b. most people are remarkably good at identifying odors, even though they often think that they are bad at it.
    c. younger adults are not as good at detecting odors as are middle-aged adults (between 40 and 50 years old).
    d. women who do not take birth control pills are particularly sensitive to smell when they are ovulating.

12. Taste buds
    a. occur on the back of the throat.
    b. die and are replaced, on average, every 30 days.
    c. are less numerous in humans than in chickens.
    d. are less sensitive in children than in adults.

13. Somasthetic senses
    a. include taste and smell.
    b. are a collection of eleven senses.
    c. have to do with perceiving the body and its position in space.
    d. were described by Aristotle more than 4,000 years ago.

14. Pain

    a. involves strictly bottom-up processing.

    b. is no longer considered crucial to survival.

    c. may be treated with drugs that bind to the same receptors that accept endorphins.

    d. activates the same areas of the brain as does the anticipation of feeling pain.

15. Extrasensory perception

    a. explains how many birds migrate long distances each year.

    b. is also sometimes called anomalous cognition or psi.

    c. has a stronger magnetic field than that commonly used in magnetic resonance imaging machines.

    d. is reduced by a counter-irritant.

CHAPTER 5 Consciousness

To Sleep, Perchance to Dream

1. Consciousness
   a. requires attention.
   b. apparently does not arise from activity in those parts of the brain that first register perceptual information.
   c. is just about neurons and thus does not involve subjective experience.
   d. cannot be examined using sophisticated types of introspection to study the nature of experience itself.

2. Sleep
   a. is a single state.
   b. consists of several types, which occur in seven stages during the night.
   c. includes an initial stage, lasting approximately 5 minutes, that is sometimes described as hypogogic sleep.
   d. has five phases, each of which results in brain waves with the same amplitude (the height of the wave) and frequency (how often they occur).

3. Adults
   a. sleep longer than infants.
   b. have a lower percentage of REM sleep than infants.
   c. in their 40s have an increase in the amount of time spent in deep, slow-wave sleep.
   d. have less frequent Stage 4 sleep as they move from middle age to older adulthood.

4. Sleep deprivation
   a. can lead to decreases in the next day's level of cortisol.
   b. affects performance but not mood.
   c. can lead to increases in the next day's level of cortisol.
   d. increases immune system functioning.

5. Dreams
   a. take place only during REM sleep.
   b. tend to be less memorable if they occur during REM sleep than if they occur during NREM stages.
   c. are recalled by 16% of people on average who are awakened during REM sleep.
   d. may reflect the short-term lack of particular stimuli.

Hypnosis and Meditation

6. Generalized reality orientation fading
   a. is a suggestion regarding a change in perception, mood, or behavior that will occur after leaving the hypnotic state.
   b. studies have indicated that about 90% of people in the U.S. population are highly hypnotizable.
   c. is one of six hallmarks of a trance state.
   d. describes a tuning out of external reality during hypnosis.

7. Hypnotic ability
   a. peaks before adolescence across cultures.
   b. peaks before adolescence in Western cultures.
   c. increases during the middle adulthood years in Western cultures.
   d. is required to be able to go into a trance state; high motivation is not enough.

8. According to _____ theory, a person in a trance _____ enacts the role of a hypnotized person as he or she understands it.
   a. trance; voluntarily
   b. hidden observer; voluntarily
   c. trance; involuntarily
   d. sociocognitive; voluntarily

9. Hypnosis
   a. causes neurological changes during a hypnotic trance, most of which cannot be explained as arising from the actions that people perform in hypnosis.
   b. improves athletic ability by increasing anxiety.
   c. can help decrease anxiety and thereby increase the athlete's focus.
   d. cannot override the actual perceptual input.

10. Which statement describes awareness meditation?
    a. It is also known as mindfulness meditation.
    b. It is a combination of concentrative meditation and opening-up meditation.
    c. It is a technique in which you try to maintain a "floating" state of consciousness, one that allows you to focus on whatever is most prominent at the moment.
    d. All of the above statements are true.

Drugs and Alcohol

11. If a person needs more of a substance to achieve the same effect (or the usual amount of the substance provides a diminished response), then that person
    a. will cost society $67 billion per year.
    b. does not yet have substance dependence.
    c. has the seven signs of substance abuse.
    d. has developed tolerance to the substance.

12. Alcohol
    a. is classified as a depressant.
    b. stimulates the central nervous system through its inhibitory effect on excitatory neurotransmitters.
    c. changes the structure of the membrane of the neuron but does not alter neural transmission.
    d. at low doses causes a sense of increased awareness and a diminished sense of heat.

13. Benzodiazepines are
    a. a type of stimulant.
    b. more habit-forming than are barbiturates.
    c. sometimes prescribed because they can reduce symptoms of anxiety.
    d. drugs that block reuptake of some norepinephrine and dopamine at the synaptic cleft.

14. LSD

    a. research supports the subjective experience of increased creativity.

    b. is a narcotic analgesic.

    c. alters the functioning of serotonin.

    d. can result in withdrawal symptoms, but not tolerance or flashbacks.

15. Tetrahydrocannabinol

    a. is the inactive ingredient in marijuana.

    b. is chemically similar to some naturally occurring neurotransmitters in the body, such as anandamide.

    c. induces anesthesia, stimulation of the cardiovascular and respiratory systems, and hallucinogens at low doses.

    d. occurs as well in several stimulants, including cocaine and heroin.

CHAPTER 6 Learning

Classical Conditioning

1. Trace conditioning is a type of
   a. backward pairing.
   b. acquisition.
   c. forward conditioning.
   d. unconditioned stimulus.

2. The case of "Little Albert" best illustrates
   a. the rigorous ethical principles that have consistently governed psychological research.
   b. the concept of contrapreparedness.
   c. that strong conditioning most often occurs when there is a long interval between CS and US pairings.
   d. how classical conditioning can produce a straightforward conditioned emotional response of fear.

3. When a conditioned response has been extinguished and the CS is presented again,
   a. the CS will not elicit the CR.
   b. the CS will again elicit the CR, although sometimes not as strongly as before extinction.
   c. the CS will undergo a process called spontaneous recovery.
   d. the connection between the CS and US will completely vanish.

4. Which of the following statements is *not* true?
   a. The central nucleus of the amygdala leads to the behaviors that express conditioned fear.
   b. A mental image of an object—what you see in your "mind's eye" when you visualize something—can play a role in classical conditioning, either as a CS or a US.
   c. Backward conditioning takes place only if the pairing of the CS and US provides useful information about the likelihood of occurrence of the UR.
   d. All of the above statements are true.

5. Classically conditioned taste aversion
   a. is the mechanism behind the use of Antabuse to treat alcoholism.
   b. is a conditioned immune response that occurs in animals but not humans.
   c. demonstrates that the US needs to come immediately after the CS.
   d. is not properly regarded as a form of classical conditioning.

Operant Conditioning

6. The Law of Effect
   a. lies at the heart of classical conditioning.
   b. was developed by B. F. Skinner.
   c. states that actions that subsequently lead to a "satisfying state of affairs" are more likely to be repeated.
   d. is a type of learning in which a new stimulus will elicit the conditioned response if it is paired with the original conditioned stimulus.

7. Positive punishment
   a. is the same thing as negative reinforcement.
   b. occurs when a behavior leads to the removal of a pleasant event or circumstance, thereby decreasing the likelihood of a recurrence of a behavior.
   c. is exemplified by the example in your textbook in which moving a limb led to a whack of the cane for Jackie Chan.
   d. occurs when a behavior leads to an undesired consequence, thereby increasing the likelihood of a recurrence of that behavior.

8. Events or objects that are inherently reinforcing
   a. are called primary reinforcers.
   b. include food and praise.
   c. are used extensively in the technique called behavior modification.
   d. generally are not instinctually satisfying.

9. Shaping
   a. must not be done in phases.
   b. is used when the desired response is one that the organism would emit in the normal course of events.
   c. enables many complex behaviors to be learned all at one time.
   d. is the method that helps train dolphins to do high jumps.

10. Operant conditioning and classical conditioning
    a. both have limitless possible responses.
    b. use different neural systems.
    c. clearly draw on the same mechanisms.
    d. rely heavily on the cerebellum.

Cognitive and Social Learning

11. Cognitive learning
    a. is also called insight modeling.
    b. relies crucially on how information is stored in memory.
    c. always occurs without behavioral signs.
    d. never occurs without behavioral signs.

12. Bandura's study on observational learning showed that
    a. watching aggression by a live person has less of an impact than does watching a video of a person exhibiting the same behaviors.
    b. positive, nonviolent television programs can counterintuitively decrease helpful behaviors.
    c. children who observed the adult ignoring the Bobo doll were even less aggressive towards it than were children in the control group.
    d. learning from models is the best way to acquire a first second language.

13. Observational learning
    a. occurs infrequently in everyday life.
    b. is more effective when the model is a regular person, like you, and not an expert.
    c. occurs through watching others, not through reinforcement.
    d. is likely to produce desired learning but is very unlikely to produced undesired learning.

14. What have studies of television shows found?
- **a.** No harm comes to the victim in almost half of the violent interactions.
- **b.** Significantly more negative comments are made about and to overweight women as compared to underweight women.
- **c.** Some violence occurs in 57% of programs.
- **d.** All of the above statements are true.

15. Adolescents who have a _____ relationship with their _____ are likely to model use (or nonuse) of cigarettes.
- **a.** positive; fathers
- **b.** negative; fathers
- **c.** positive; mothers
- **d.** negative; mothers

CHAPTER 7   Memory: Living With Yesterday

Storing Information: Time and Space Are of the Essence

1. Research has shown that
   a. information about how to play the guitar is stored in the hands.
   b. information cannot flow to long-term memory without passing through short-term memory.
   c. rehearsal—repeating items over and over—does not help memorization if people think about the information.
   d. all memories are stored in the brain.

2. Short-term memory is known to
   a. be able to hold about 9 plus-or-minus 3 "chunks" at once.
   b. hold a large amount of perceptual input for a very brief time, typically less than 1 second.
   c. happen automatically, without effort.
   d. hold the only information of which you are conscious.

3. Reducing the presentation time
   a. affects only the primacy effect, and not the recency effect.
   b. affects both the primacy effect and the recency effect.
   c. does not affect either the primacy effect or the recency effect.
   d. affects only the recency effect, and not the primacy effect.

4. Implicit memories
   a. are of four major types.
   b. include procedural memories.
   c. cannot be acquired by animals.
   d. can be voluntarily recalled.

5. The articulatory loop
   a. holds visual and spatial information.
   b. is best characterized as a type of priming.
   c. is a short-term memory store that holds verbally produced sounds.
   d. has been compared to a pad with patterns drawn in fading ink.

Encoding and Retrieving Information From Memory

6. Memories
   a. are initially stored in long-term memory in a dynamic form.
   b. are stored as a structure through the process called *transfer appropriate processing.*
   c. depend on continuing neural activity when stored in a structural form.
   d. for older events are affected by electroconvulsive therapy.

7. A good way to learn material for an exam is generally to
   a. rely on massed practice.
   b. avoid elaborative encoding of the material.
   c. rely on distributed practice.
   d. attempt to achieve the von Restorf effect while studying.

8. Recognition is
   a. more difficult when the choices are dissimilar.
   b. the intentional bringing to mind of explicit information.
   c. less difficult than recall, all else being equal.
   d. generally not dependent on activating collections of fragments stored in long-term memory.

9. If you are in a happy mood at the time you learn something, you may remember it better when you are feeling happy than when you are feeling sad. This effect of mood
   a. is called state-independent retrieval.
   b. has been shown consistently to be a very powerful retrieval cue.
   c. can be overshadowed by other factors, such as how well the information is organized.
   d. does not appear to be a very powerful retrieval cue, unlike that of your psychological state.

10. Emotional stimuli
    a. tend to be remembered better by men than by women.
    b. cause less noradrenaline to be produced, which in turn causes enhanced memory encoding.
    c. cannot undergo the process of consolidation.
    d. are better remembered than neutral stimuli.

Fact, Fiction, and Forgetting: When Memory Goes Wrong

11. False memories
    a. cannot persist for 2 months.
    b. can occur even when participants are told to make up information about an event they viewed.
    c. do not reflect how willing people are to agree that they had encountered a previous stimulus.
    d. of words activate brain areas in the temporal and parietal lobes but not the hippocampus.

12. Apparently, the construction of memory
    a. activates the representations of the perceptual qualities of stored words.
    b. does not depend upon a kind of "social contagion," where one person's recounting memories can lead to another adopting them.
    c. results in false memories and real memories that do not differ in any aspect studied so far.
    d. does not activate the representations of the perceptual qualities of stored words.

13. People who experience vivid images, relative to those who do not,
    a. are less likely to confuse having read a description of an event with having seen it.
    b. are more likely to confuse having read a description of an event with having seen it.
    c. cannot use the cue of a "missing perception" nearly as well.
    d. are far more likely to engage in reality monitoring, which is the process of imagining stimuli.

15. Which of the following describes a neural network?
    a. It imitates (roughly) the way the brain works.
    b. It can recognize objects remarkably well but cannot generalize to novel examples of a familiar category.
    c. It is the term used to describe the field devoted to building smart machines.
    d. None of the above statements are true.

Logic, Reasoning, and Decision Making

16. Someone who makes the error of affirming the consequent
    a. applies the rules of logic to a set of assumptions to discover whether certain conclusions follow from those assumptions.
    b. tends to seek information that will confirm a rule.
    c. applies the principles of correct reasoning to reach a decision or evaluate the truth of a claim.
    d. makes the assumption that if a result is present, a specific cause must also be present.

17. What has research shown about logic and reason?
    a. Humans are not entirely logical.
    b. People often rely on sets of heuristics to reason.
    c. Much reasoning involves a combination of deductive and inductive processes.
    d. All of the above statements are true.

18. Suppose that more than half of the people at the meeting speak French, and more than half of the people at the meeting speak English. Does it follow that more than half of the people speak both French and English?
    a. Yes.
    b. There is not enough information given to answer the question.
    c. It is important to consider how many speak Spanish.
    d. No.

19. Which of the following is true about framing decisions?
    a. People tend to frame losses as more important than gains.
    b. People tend to frame gains as more important than losses.
    c. People tend to frame gains and losses as equally important.
    d. None of the above statements are true.

20. Suppose you have budgeted time to work on a paper and then run out of hours way too soon. You may have fallen victim to
    a. confirmation bias.
    b. the base-rate rule.
    c. the planning fallacy.
    d. deductive reasoning.

Is There More Than One Way to Be Smart?

1. The original test from which modern IQ tests derive
   a. was developed by Lewis Terman and his colleagues at Stanford University.
   b. was developed in 1942.
   c. had a more specific and general purpose than the modern tests.
   d. included verbal subtests and performance subtests.

2. According to William Stern's intelligence quotient, what is the mental age of a 10-year-old child whose intelligence quotient is 110?
   a. 15
   b. 9
   c. It is impossible to determine based on the information given.
   d. None of the above answers are true.

3. On the WASI-III IQ test, about _____ of all people have IQs from 85 to 115 points.
   a. half
   b. two thirds
   c. one third
   d. one quarter

4. IQ
   a. underpredicts job success among Japanese and Chinese Americans.
   b. is highly correlated with job performance; over 90% of the variation in levels of job success can be predicted by IQ.
   c. is more important in predicting job success for workers who are experienced, relative to those who have little experience on the job.
   d. tests do not produce any useful information.

5. According to Louis L. Thurstone, intelligence consists of
   a. fluid intelligence and crystallized intelligence.
   b. eight basic forms of intelligence, such as musical intelligence.
   c. a single underlying intellectual capacity.
   d. seven separate primary mental abilities.

What Makes Us Smart: Nature and Nurture

6. What has analysis of Albert Einstein's brain revealed?
   a. His brain had an unusually large number of glial cells in the top portions of the right parietal lobe.
   b. He had an especially large Sylvian fissure.
   c. His parietal lobes were about 15% wider than normal.
   d. All of the above statements are true.

7. People with high IQs
   a. are characterized by a brain that itself "runs faster."
   b. are faster at all steps in processing information.
   c. process information more effectively.
   d. require more exposure time to a stimulus in order to judge accurately which of two lines is longer.

8. Heritability estimates of IQ
   a. indicate that about one third of the variation in IQ can be attributed to inherited characteristics.
   b. have revealed that only two genes contribute to intelligence.
   c. explain how much of your personal intelligence is the result of your genes versus environmental factors
   d. are usually around .50.

9. The correlations on which heritability scores are based may _____ the role of genes and _____ the role of the environment, even when the correlations are drawn from adoption studies.
   a. underestimate; overestimate
   b. overestimate; underestimate
   c. ignore; reduce
   d. reduce; amplify

10. Which of the following statements is *not* true?
    a. The race difference in IQ is present on both the verbal and general information parts of the IQ test, as well as the performance parts.
    b. Although some findings may suggest very small sex differences in IQ, these effects are not always found.
    c. Some groups may be more vulnerable than others to the effects of stereotype threat when they take IQ tests.
    d. Women who receive massive doses of testosterone for 3 months have an increase in verbal abilities.

Diversity in Intelligence

11. Mental retardation
    a. affects about 100 times less people than does total blindness.
    b. appears to be on the decline.
    c. is traditionally considered to be an IQ score of 50 or lower.
    d. is traditionally considered to be an IQ score more than three standard deviations below the mean.

12. Down syndrome
    a. is more likely to occur in younger mothers.
    b. is the least common type of mental retardation.
    c. occurs in about 1 in 1,000 births.
    d. is caused by a repetition of a small bit of DNA on the X chromosome.

13. Girls who are gifted
    a. tend to have higher amounts of testosterone than nongifted girls.
    b. tend to have lower amounts of testosterone than nongifted girls.
    c. must have an IQ score of at least 180.
    d. have half the rate of emotional and social problems as nongifted girls.

14. Which of the following is true about creativity?
   a. It relies on a two-stage process.
   b. It can occur consciously or unconsciously.
   c. It often involves an interplay between two types of thinking, convergent and divergent.
   d. All of the above statements are true.

15. Research findings suggest that
   a. relying on a group discussion to find creative solutions may be a bad idea.
   b. people may actually produce more ideas in groups than when they work alone.
   c. differences in creativity are strongly related to genetic differences.
   d. creative people tend to have low self-esteem.

CHAPTER 10 Emotion and Motivation: Feeling and Striving

Emotion: I Feel, Therefore I Am

1. There is widespread agreement that
   a. basic emotions are "simple."
   b. perception of basic emotions is entirely innate.
   c. humans have a set of built-in emotions that express the most basic types of reactions.
   d. members of a minority group never recognize emotions on faces of members of the majority group as well as they recognize emotions of faces of their own group.

2. Researchers studying what happens in the brain when people experience emotion have found
   a. that clinically depressed patients have relatively diminished activity in the left frontal lobe.
   b. that people who normally have more activation in the right frontal lobe tend to have a rosier outlook on life than do people who have more activation in the left frontal lobe.
   c. no support for the notion that positive and negative emotions are independent.
   d. that there are separate systems in the brain for three general types of human emotions.

3. According to the Cannon-Bard theory of emotion,
   a. an emotion arises when you interpret the situation as a whole—your bodily state in the context of everything that surrounds it.
   b. you feel emotions after your body reacts.
   c. bodily arousal and the experience of emotion arise in tandem.
   d. fear relies on activation of the amygdala.

4. There is evidence that
   a. "put on a happy face" is just a good lyric.
   b. bodily factors are not enough to explain the range of feelings we have.
   c. smiles, frowns, and glowers are the only causes of our emotional experiences.
   d. cognitive interpretations that affect how we feel must be conscious.

5. Fear
   a. is one of the emotions scientists understand the least.
   b. does not cause changes in the brain.
   c. interacts with mental processes.
   d. cannot be experienced in patients with damaged amygdalae.

Motivation and Reward: Feeling Good

6. Which of the following is *true* about evolutionary theories of motivation?
   a. They have offered an alternative to instinct theory.
   b. They propose that goals that motivate us and general cognitive strategies for achieving goals are inborn.
   c. They are notoriously difficult to test.
   d. All of the above statements are true.

7. Homeostasis is a useful concept for understanding
   a. thirst, hunger, and certain other drives (such as for salt).
   b. why people select certain activities and situations and reject others.
   c. motivations for sex.
   d. motivations for any money-making activity.

8. Investigating dopamine as it relates to rewards, researchers have found that
   a. brain areas that rely on dopamine are activated more strongly by an attractive face when the eyes are averted than when the eyes look right at you.
   b. brain areas that rely on dopamine are not activated when humans expect rewards.
   c. blocking dopamine can disrupt both unconditioned and conditioned positive reinforcement.
   d. needs and wants rely on the same brain system.

9. According to Maslow's hierarchy of needs,
   a. needs lower in the pyramid must be met before needs higher in the pyramid become the focus of concern.
   b. needs higher in the pyramid must be met before needs lower in the pyramid become the focus of concern.
   c. higher-level needs are considered more essential to life.
   d. during crises (such as loss of a home by fire), lower-level needs are put on hold.

10. Achievement motivation
    a. seems unaffected by culture.
    b. tends to be higher in members of collectivist cultures, such as that of the United States.
    c. tends to be higher in members of individualist cultures, such as that of China.
    d. may vary for subgroups within a culture.

Hunger and Eating: Not Just About Fueling the Body

11. Lesions to the lateral hypothalamus
    a. enhance animals' interest in eating.
    b. do not affect animals' interest in eating.
    c. suppress animals' interest in eating but do not affect interest in drinking.
    d. suppress animals' interest in eating, drinking, sex, and caring for their young.

12. We, and other animals, have
    a. centers in the hypothalamus that say "eat" or "don't eat."
    b. some neurons that act like buttons or switches in eating behavior.
    c. some neurons that signal when nutrient levels are low.
    d. a feeling of fullness only after food is digested.

13. Someone who has gourmand syndrome
    a. never reports being hungry.
    b. overeats carbohydrates.
    c. is obsessed with fine food.
    d. invariably overeats.

14. Appetite
    a. is just about the brain.
    b. depends on events at the different levels of analysis, as well as their interactions.
    c. during the later phases of eating is driven by opioids in the brain, chemicals that cause you to feel full.
    d. is governed by one brain area.

15. There is good reason to believe that
    a. the personality characteristics of obese people make them slaves to food.
    b. variations in weight may be as much as 20% heritable.
    c. at least some forms of obesity have a genetic basis.
    d. obese people do not have the same "will power" to resist eating junk food as nonobese people.

Sex: Not Just About Having Babies

16. Men and women
    a. both pass through seven stages during sexual activity.
    b. are similar in their bodily reactions to sex.
    c. generally provide interview data about sex that are free of response bias.
    d. both have a refractory period following orgasm.

17. Women
    a. are less likely to be interested in men who are not their partners when they are ovulating.
    b. prefer "ruggedly handsome" male faces more when they are ovulating than when they are not ovulating.
    c. have the type of hormone called *estrogens,* but not the type of hormone called *androgens.*
    d. have the type of hormone called *androgens,* but not the type of hormone called *estrogens.*

18. Studying testosterone level, researchers have found that
    a. the more hours a man spent with his wife on his last day off work, the higher his testosterone level.
    b. single men have higher levels of testosterone than do married men throughout the day.
    c. testosterone level affects the amount of sexual satisfaction, the rigidity of the penis during sex, and mood.
    d. testosterone decreases more sharply over the course of the day for married men than for single men.

19. Research into sexual orientation has revealed that
    a. many bisexual men tend to become more homo-sexually oriented over time.
    b. a small part of the hypothalamus is typically larger in homosexual men than in heterosexual men.
    c. a small part of the hypothalamus is typically smaller in men than in women.
    d. there is no role for the environment in homosexuality.

20. The drug Viagra
    a. causes an erection.
    b. is a cure for impotence.
    c. increases the flow of blood to the penis.
    d. does not have an effect on a woman's clitoris.

CHAPTER 11   Personality: Vive la Différence!

What Is Personality?

1. What have researchers found in their studies of traits?
   a. Some traits are just irrelevant for some of us—they aren't important in our lives.
   b. Everyone is consistent on some traits.
   c. People are not equally consistent on all traits.
   d. All of the above statements are true.

2. Raymond Cattell proposed _____ personality factors; Hans Eysenck proposed _____.
   a. 5; 3
   b. 16; 5
   c. 5; 16
   d. 16; 3

3. Which of the following is *true?*
   a. The more narrowly a trait is defined, the better it predicts behavior.
   b. The more narrowly a trait is defined, the more circumstances there are to which it can be applied.
   c. The more narrowly a trait is defined, the less it predicts behavior.
   d. None of the above statements are true.

4. The response style called acquiescence
   a. refers to answering questions in a way that you think makes you "look good."
   b. can be reduced by wording half the items negatively.
   c. constitutes one of the Big Five superfactors.
   d. can be reduced by wording all the items positively.

5. The Rorschach test
   a. has been judged to have very high validity and reliability, as well as truly representative norms.
   b. was developed in the 1930s by Henry Murray.
   c. has ten cards, each with a different inkblot.
   d. is a type of Minnesota Multiphasic Personality Inventory-2 (MMPI-2).

The Brain: The Personality Organ

6. Eysenck proposed a hierarchy of personality, at the base of which
   a. are sets of stimulus–response associations.
   b. is the Habit Response level.
   c. are automatic responses such as shyness when meeting new people.
   d. are the three superfactors of extraversion, neuroticism, and psychoticism.

7. Relative to introverts, extraverts are
   a. more arousable.
   b. less sensitive to reward.
   c. more easily conditioned by punishment.
   d. more easily conditioned by reward.

8. Sensation seeking is
   a. the pursuit of novelty, often in high-stimulation situations.
   b. associated with higher levels of the chemical monoamine oxide (MAO), at least in males.
   c. associated with higher levels of the chemical monoamine oxide (MAO), at least in females.
   d. one of Eysenck's superfactors.

9. According to Buss and Plomin, the dimension of temperament they call *activity*
   a. is similar to the Big Five superfactor of neuroticism.
   b. has two components: vigor and tempo.
   c. refers to the propensity to respond to stimuli immediately.
   d. is the preference to be in the company of other people rather than alone.

10. Researchers studying heritability of personality traits have found that
    a. the amount of time you spend watching television is explicitly coded in your genes.
    b. within a superfactor, heritability of traits is variable.
    c. twins reared apart are generally more similar than twins reared together.
    d. all traits are equally heritable.

The Person: Beliefs and Behaviors

11. According to Freud, the preconscious
    a. houses the thoughts, feelings, and motivations that you cannot bring into consciousness but which nevertheless influence you.
    b. is available for inspection and provides normal awareness.
    c. holds subjective material that can easily be brought into conscious awareness but of which you are not aware most of the time.
    d. includes thoughts, feelings, and motivations of which you are aware.

12. The superego, according to Freud,
    a. exists from birth.
    b. is a physical structure.
    c. can cause feelings of guilt.
    d. houses the aggressive drive.

13. Someone who is characterized by cruelty, destructive acts, emotional outbursts, and a disregard for conventional rules has, according to Freudian theory
    a. an oral–aggressive personality style
    b. an oral–receptive personality style.
    c. an anal–retentive personality style.
    d. an anal–expulsive personality style.

14. A number of Freud's followers modified his theory of personality. Which theorist believed that the source of all motivation is a striving for superiority?
    a. Carl Jung
    b. Alfred Alder
    c. Karen Horney
    d. None of the above

15. Abraham Maslow and Carl Rogers both
    a. viewed humans as possessing a need for self-actualization.
    b. viewed the satisfaction of lower- to higher-order needs as the driving force behind personality.
    c. thought that we have a basic need for conditional positive regard.
    d. emphasized the importance of life revolving around meeting conditions of worth in order to meet one's full human potential.

The World: Social Influences on Personality

16. Frank Sulloway used meta-analyses to support his proposal that at least one aspect of personality, _____ (one of the Big Five superfactors), is shaped by birth order.
    a. openness to experience
    b. psychoticism
    c. activity
    d. vigor

17. Compared to first- and last-borns, middle-borns are
    a. less likely to define themselves by their last names.
    b. closer to their families.
    c. more likely to ask for parental help in an emergency.
    d. more likely to visit their parents.

18. A study of families with both biological and adoptive children (so that the first biological child may not have the "firstborn" position) revealed that the only trait common among those in the firstborn position was
    a. self-consciousness.
    b. adventuresomeness.
    c. conscientiousness.
    d. tender-mindedness.

19. Which of the following is a flaw with Harris' (1995) assumption that parents have minimal influence on childhood development?
    a. The same event in a family has different meaning for each of its members, based on age and cognitive ability.
    b. Parents, and the family in general, can play a role in the way people feel about themselves, which in turn affects the child's thoughts, feelings, and behaviors.
    c. If families had no effect on children's personalities, then birth order effects would not exist.
    d. All of the above statements are true.

20. In general,
    a. women tend to score higher than men on traits reflecting autonomy.
    b. men tend to score higher than women on traits reflecting neuroticism.
    c. personality differences between females and males are not very great.
    d. women tend to score lower than men on traits reflecting social connectedness.

CHAPTER 12   Psychology Over the Life Span: Growing Up, Growing Older, Growing Wiser

In the Beginning: From Conception to Birth

1. For each of us, life began with a meeting of two cells, a sperm and an egg; these specialized cells are
   a. gametes.
   b. zygotes.
   c. each the size of a pin prick.
   d. each supercells.

2. A deletion of part of chromosome 15
   a. leads to Angelman's syndrome if it is inherited from the mother.
   b. leads to Angelman's syndrome if it is inherited from the father.
   c. leads to Prader-Willi syndrome if it is inherited from the mother.
   d. does not affect behavior.

3. Studying the fetus, researchers have found that
   a. the fetus floats peacefully asleep in the womb at all times.
   b. as the fetus develops, the heart rate slows down (but becomes more variable).
   c. there are no sex differences in behavior in the womb.
   d. the fetus is sensitive to sound, but not to light, after 45 weeks of gestation.

4. Threats to healthy prenatal development include which of the following?
   a. Stressors in the mother's life
   b. Excessive amounts of caffeine (three cups of coffee a day, according to one study)
   c. Ionizing radiation
   d. All of the above

5. Babies are born
   a. with a relatively insensitive sense of smell.
   b. with a very narrow range of reflexes.
   c. sensitive to the range of frequencies of women's voices.
   d. without an ability to put visual and auditory stimuli together.

Infancy and Childhood: Taking Off

6. The typical age for the developmental motor milestones of sitting upright and crawling is
   a. 2–5 months.
   b. 6–9 months.
   c. 10–12 months.
   d. 12–18 months.

7. Infants
   a. are born with perfect vision and can thus see well.
   b. who are 6 months old want to crawl over the "deep end" in the visual cliff experiment.
   c. who are 2 months old have faster heart rates on the deep side of the visual cliff.
   d. have an increase in visual acuity as they age, in part because of developments in the eye, particularly in the lens and the retina.

8. For the most part,
   a. memory does improve from early childhood to adulthood.
   b. 3-month-old infants cannot store information both implicitly and explicitly.
   c. visual perception, compared with auditory perception, appears to be more fully developed at an earlier age.
   d. newborns do not notice if you make direct eye contact with them.

9. According to Piaget's periods of cognitive development, during the _____ period the child acts on the world as perceived and is not capable of thinking about objects in their absence.
   a. formal operations
   b. concrete operations
   c. preoperational
   d. sensorimotor

10. Infants who have a secure attachment
    a. do not use the mother as a base of operations but rather stay close to her and become angry when she leaves during the Strange Situation.
    b. tend to have worse social skills when later studied at age 11 than children who were not securely attached as infants.
    c. constitute about 5–10% of American babies.
    d. tend to have closer friendships when later studied at age 11 than children who were not securely attached as infants.

Adolescence: Between Two Worlds

11. In recent years, the age of puberty has
    a. declined for girls but not for boys.
    b. declined for boys but not for girls.
    c. declined for both boys and girls.
    d. not changed for either girls or boys.

12. During infancy and childhood,
    a. the body grows from the trunk inward.
    b. the lower arms grow before the upper arms.
    c. rapid growth of the hands, feet, and legs is followed by growth of the torso.
    d. the upper arms grow before the lower arms, which in turn grown before the hands.

13. By age 11,
    a. girls have stopped growing or have begun to grow more slowly.
    b. girls typically are taller and heavier than boys.
    c. boys typically are taller, but not heavier, than girls.
    d. boys' heights and weights have taken off.

14. The imaginary audience, a belief sometimes held by adolescents, is
    a. a story in which they are the star, and as the star they have extraordinary abilities and privileges.
    b. the period of formal operations.
    c. a belief in which they view themselves as actors and everyone else as an audience.
    d. the tendency to underestimate the amount of risk they would face in various circumstances.

15. Which is a normal tendency for adolescents?
    a. To have conflicts with their parents
    b. To have extreme mood swings
    c. To be prone to taking risks
    d. All of the above

Adulthood and Aging: The Continuously Changing Self

16. Studying how cognitive abilities change with age, researchers have found that
    a. aging in itself causes neurons to die.
    b. aging impairs communication among neurons.
    c. many healthy people exhibit terminal decline by age 40.
    d. by age 45, people perform most cognitive tasks more slowly than do younger people.

17. In old age,
    a. the frontal lobes become proportionally larger than other brain areas.
    b. the frontal lobes become proportionally smaller than other brain areas.
    c. semantic memory is severely adversely affected.
    d. the storing of new episodic memories is severely adversely affected.

18. According to Erik Erikson, during old age, the major issue to be resolved, called _____, is to be able to reflect back on life and feel that it was worthwhile, thereby avoiding feelings of despair and fear of death.
    a. *industry versus inferiority*
    b. *industry versus despair*
    c. *integrity versus despair*
    d. *integrity versus initiative*

19. Evidence indicates that
    a. personality changes substantially during adulthood.
    b. with age, people are less able to regulate their emotions.
    c. personality does not change substantially during adulthood.
    d. in general, as people age they interact with more people, but these interactions tend to be less intimate.

20. The cerebral reserve hypothesis states that
    a. education either strengthens the brain itself or helps people develop multiple strategies.
    b. older people come to focus on the limited time they had left, which in turn changes their motivations.
    c. people in the United States go through the grieving process in four stages.
    d. cultural differences do not influence the ways in which people view and react to death.

CHAPTER 13 Stress, Health, and Coping

What Is Stress?

1. According to Hans Selye, the overall stress response
   a. is called the *stressor.*
   b. has four distinct phases.
   c. includes a second phase in which the continued stress response itself becomes damaging to the body.
   d. is called the *general adaptation syndrome.*

2. When you perceive a threat,
   a. your brain responds to it by activating the parasympathetic nervous system.
   b. your brain responds to it by inhibiting the sympathetic nervous system.
   c. neurotransmitters and hormonal secretions cause breathing to increase.
   d. neurotransmitters and hormonal secretions cause blood pressure to decrease.

3. When the stress response is triggered, cortisol is released, which does what in the short run?
   a. Increases the production of energy from glucose
   b. Has an anti-inflammatory effect
   c. Helps restore the body's equilibrium after physical injury
   d. All of the above

4. Relative to traditional students, nontraditional students
   a. are more likely to enjoy doing homework.
   b. are less likely to enjoy going to classes.
   c. tend to worry more about how they are doing academically.
   d. are more affected by social activities.

5. Those who report more daily hassles, relative to those who report fewer daily hassles,
   a. tend to have lower cholesterol levels.
   b. tend to have higher cholesterol levels.
   c. are less likely to have suppressed immune systems.
   d. report fewer psychological symptoms, but the same number of physical symptoms.

Stress, Disease, and Health

6. The natural killer (NK) cell
   a. matures in the bone marrow.
   b. is a type of B cell.
   c. matures in the thymus.
   d. is formed by glucocorticoids.

7. Trauma survivors who go on to develop PTSD
   a. tend to have higher heart rates immediately after the trauma.
   b. tend to have lower heart rates immediately after the trauma.
   c. tend to be generally autonomically less reactive.
   d. cannot be distinguished from trauma survivors who do not go on to develop PTSD on any measure.

8. Studying depression and heart disease, researchers have found that
   a. those who are depressed tend to have low blood pressure.
   b. depressed people tend to have a slower heartbeat even when at rest.
   c. when the depression is treated, heart rate and blood pressure decrease.
   d. when the depression is treated, heart rate and blood pressure increase.

9. Countering is
   a. focused awareness and emotion direction towards change.
   b. taking stock, both emotionally and intellectually, and addressing the question of whether engaging in the problematic behavior is what you really want to be doing.
   c. the substitution of healthier behaviors for the problem behaviors.
   d. becoming aware of both the problem and the ways you avoid addressing it.

10. During the _____ stage of changing a problematic behavior, the person acknowledges that there is a problem and may even think about doing something about it, but real action is seen as far in the future.
    a. preparation
    b. contemplation
    c. precontemplation
    d. maintenance

Strategies for Coping

11. Problem-focused coping strategies
    a. are more common when people believe that their actions can affect the stressor.
    b. tend to be used by people with a low score on the Big Five personality factor conscientiousness.
    c. usually decrease arousal.
    d. change a person's emotional response to the stressor.

12. During the coping strategy of behavioral disengagement, a person
    a. seeks concrete advice, assistance, or information, and thinks about how to manage the stressor.
    b. focuses on and talks about positive feelings.
    c. focuses on and talks about distressing feelings.
    d. reduces efforts to deal actively with the stressor (as occurs with learned helplessness).

13. Which of the following is *true* regarding the attempt to suppress thoughts that are emotionally charged (either positive or negative)?
    a. It has been associated with changes in the sympathetic nervous system.
    b. It decreases the intensity of the thoughts.
    c. It is called the *rebound effect.*
    d. All of the above statements are true.

14. Studying aggression, researchers have found that
   a. aggression is more likely to be perpetrated by people who feel bad about themselves.
   b. most aggressors are people who have high self-esteem.
   c. relational aggression is instigated more by males than by females.
   d. females are more likely than males to be aggressive in response to criticism of their intellectual abilities.

15. Asking people how they did or would cope in certain stressful situations
   a. has revealed that optimism has a heritability of 75%.
   b. has indicated that repressors, relative to sensitizers, are more likely to have lower blood pressure.
   c. does not necessarily lead to an accurate picture of their actual coping behavior.
   d. shows that genetics alone, regardless of an individual's unique life experiences, influence 18 of 19 coping strategies.

CHAPTER 14   Psychological Disorders

Identifying Psychological Disorders: What's Abnormal?

1. Psychological disorders
   a. worldwide rank second among diseases that lead to death and disability.
   b. are experienced by 48% of Americans in any given year.
   c. rarely affect people's relationships or their functioning on the job.
   d. always cause observable distress.

2. What have researchers found about the determination of abnormality of behaviors?
   a. What is considered deviant changes from generation to generation.
   b. To be considered "disordered," it is not enough for a behavior or set of behaviors to be deviant from the mainstream culture.
   c. What is considered deviant can differ across cultures.
   d. All of the above statements are true.

3. What is a predisposition to a state or condition called?
   a. Psychosis
   b. Diathesis
   c. Delusion
   d. Hallucination

4. Axis IV of the *DSM* identifies
   a. personality disorders and mental retardation.
   b. psychosocial and environmental problems.
   c. any general medical conditions that might be relevant to a diagnosis on Axis I or II.
   d. the patient's highest level of functioning in major areas of life within the past year.

5. Somatoform disorders, according to the current edition of the *DSM*,
   a. focus on disorders of consciousness and cognition.
   b. include disorders related to sleep.
   c. are disorders in which the person intentionally fabricates symptoms of a medical or psychological disorder, but not for external gain.
   d. are disorders in which physical/medical complaints have no known medical origin (or the symptoms are not proportional to a medical condition).

Mood Disorders

6. To be diagnosed with major depressive disorder, a person must
   a. report daily insomnia or hypersomnia (sleeping a lot).
   b. have daily fatigue, or loss or energy.
   c. experience at least 2 weeks of depressed mood or loss or interest in nearly all activities.
   d. suffer daily psychomotor retardation (physical sluggishness).

7. Major depressive disorder
   a. is the second most common psychological disorder in the United States.
   b. is found among all cultural and ethnic groups.
   c. occurs far more often in women than in men in developing countries.
   d. is decreasing in the United States.

8. Studying bipolar disorder, researchers have found that
   a. there is evidence that the amygdala is enlarged.
   b. there is evidence that the amygdala is substantially reduced.
   c. neurotransmitters are not implicated in the condition.
   d. if an identical twin has bipolar disorder, the co-twin has a 20% chance of developing bipolar disorder.

9. Aaron Beck's "negative triad of depression" includes
   a. change in the activity of serotonin, norepinephrine, and substance P.
   b. change in the activity of the amygdala, the frontal lobes, and the hippocampus.
   c. a negative view of the world, a negative view of the self, and a negative view of the future.
   d. events at the level of the brain, an external attributional style, and a surfeit of positive reinforcement.

10. The course of bipolar disorder is affected by events at the level of the group, including
    a. disturbances in the functioning of serotonin.
    b. a person's characteristic way of explaining life events.
    c. living with critical families.
    d. errors in logic that maintain an outlook on life that perpetuates depressed feelings and behaviors.

Anxiety Disorders

11. Studying events at the level of the brain as they relate to panic attacks, researchers have found
    a. that a biological vulnerability for panic is apparently not inherited.
    b. that panic attacks may arise from a hyposensitivity involving the locus coeruleus.
    c. unusually strong activation in the left frontal lobe relative to the right when people with panic attacks see potentially panic-inducing stimuli.
    d. that changes in carbon dioxide levels can elicit panic.

12. Those with high anxiety sensitivity
    a. are at a lower risk of experiencing spontaneous panic attacks.
    b. do not believe that autonomic arousal can have harmful consequences.
    c. cannot develop panic disorder.
    d. are at a higher risk of experiencing spontaneous panic attacks.

13. Those who have experienced *kyol goeu*
    a. cannot experience panic attacks.
    b. are more likely to be sensitive to signs of autonomic arousal in their bodies.
    c. are less likely to have negative beliefs about what signs of autonomic arousal mean.
    d. always faint when sitting down.

14. During the compulsive behavior called ordering, a person might
    a. wash their hands repeatedly until they are raw.
    b. check again and again that the stove is turned off.
    c. put objects in precise symmetry.
    d. count to 100 after each obsessive thought.

15. Symptoms of PTSD
    a. always appear immediately after the traumatic event.
    b. can persist for months or even years.
    c. include repetitive behaviors or mental acts that a person feels driven to perform in response to an obsession.
    d. cannot occur as a consequence of a natural disaster.

Schizophrenia

16. Negative symptoms of schizophrenia
    a. include hallucinations and disorganized behavior.
    b. involve an excess or distortion of normal functions.
    c. include flat affect and avolition.
    d. do not affect behavior or social interactions.

17. A person who has a delusion of reference might believe that
    a. others are out to "get" him or her.
    b. his or her feelings, behaviors, or thoughts are controlled by others.
    c. normal events have special meaning directed toward him or her.
    d. he or she is an important person.

18. The schizophrenia subtype of _____ is characterized by bizarre, immobile, or relentless motor behaviors.
    a. disorganized
    b. catatonic
    c. undifferentiated
    d. paranoid

19. Someone with schizophrenia is more likely than others to have
    a. reduced ventricle size.
    b. enhanced frontal lobe functioning.
    c. abnormally high numbers of dopamine receptors in their frontal lobes.
    d. brain abnormalities even before psychotic symptoms appear.

20. People who develop schizophrenia, relative to people who not develop the disorder,
    a. experience more life stressors.
    b. have lower baseline levels of cortisol.
    c. are more likely to have suffered prenatal and birth complications.
    d. All of the above statements are true.

Other Axis I Disorders: Dissociative and Eating Disorders

21. Derealization is
    a. the experience of observing oneself as if from the outside.
    b. the sense that familiar objects have changed or seem "unreal."
    c. the adoption of a new identity.
    d. necessarily a sign of pathology.

22. What occurs during dissociative fugues?
    a. People usually create new identities for themselves.
    b. People are able to remember all of the past.
    c. People have obvious signs of a disorder.
    d. None of the above statements are true.

23. Dissociative identity disorder is
    a. the least controversial dissociative disorder.
    b. estimated to affect 1% of the American population.
    c. now called *multiple personality disorder.*
    d. a subtype of PTSD.

24. The classic restricting type of anorexia nervosa
    a. is characterized by the use of laxatives to get rid of unwanted calories.
    b. does not occur in Chinese women or North American women.
    c. is characterized by achieving weight loss primarily by undereating, without purging.
    d. involves achieving weight loss by periodically engaging in binge eating.

25. Genetic factors
    a. do not play a role in eating disorders.
    b. are implicated in both anorexia nervosa and bulimia nervosa.
    c. are much more important in bulimia nervosa than in anorexia nervosa.
    d. have not yet been studied with respect to their potential contribution to eating disorders.

Personality Disorders

26. _____ personality disorder is characterized by a pattern of detachment from social relationships and a narrow range of displayed emotion.
    a. Histrionic
    b. Borderline
    c. Schizoid
    d. Schizotypal

27. Personality disorders
    a. are often classified on Axis I.
    b. can be so subtle that they are unnoticeable in a brief encounter.
    c. are no longer considered disorders in the current *DSM.*
    d. rarely cause distress or difficulty with daily functioning.

28. Avoidant personality disorder is a pattern of
    a. instability in relationships, self-image, and feelings, and pronounced impulsivity.
    b. extreme discomfort in close relationships, odd or quirky behavior, and cognitive or perceptual distortions.
    c. preoccupation with perfectionism, orderliness, and control.
    d. social discomfort, feelings of inadequacy, and hypersensitivity to negative evaluation.

29. Antisocial personality disorder occurs
    a. in 90% of prisoners.
    b. in 10 to 20% of Americans.
    c. twelve times less frequently in women than in men.
    d. three times more frequently in men than in women.

30. People with antisocial personality disorder
    a. are characterized by physiological overresponsiveness.
    b. have difficulty modulating their anger.
    c. rarely abuse alcohol or drugs.
    d. tend to have had a surprisingly excellent attachment to their primary caretaker.

31. What have researchers found in their studies of antisocial personality disorder?
    a. The disorder runs in families.
    b. The environment matters only if a child's biological parents were criminals.
    c. As children, people with antisocial personality disorder often experienced or witnessed abuse, deviant behavior, or a lack of concern for others by peers, parents, or others.
    d. All of the above statements are true.

A Cautionary Note About Diagnosis

32. According to your textbook's authors, which psychological disorder may van Gogh have had?
    a. Major depressive disorder
    b. Bipolar disorder
    c. Schizophrenia
    d. All of the above disorders are possibilities.

33. Ruling out medical illnesses
    a. does not constitute part of making a proper diagnosis of a psychological disorder.
    b. should be done several years after a psychological disorder is diagnosed.
    c. invariably decreases the accuracy of the psychological diagnosis assigned.
    d. is essential to do to enable the mental health clinician or researcher to have confidence in a diagnosis of a psychological disorder.

34. Which of the following is evidence consistent with the hypothesis that van Gogh had a form of epilepsy?
    a. He had delirium tremens.
    b. He may have suffered symptoms of alcohol withdrawal.
    c. Before epileptic seizures, victims are sometimes overcome with religious feeling and delusions.
    d. There is no such evidence; researchers have ruled out the possibility that van Gogh had a form of epilepsy.

35. Which of the following statements is *true* according to your textbook's authors?
    a. Researchers now know with certainty the specific psychological disorder from which van Gogh suffered.
    b. No mental health clinician can really know with certainty from what, if any, specific disorder van Gogh suffered.
    c. Van Gogh did not have attacks during lengthy periods of sobriety.
    d. None of the above statements are true.

CHAPTER 15 Treatment

Behavior and Cognitive Therapy

1. The behavior therapist is interested in the ABCs of the behavior, in which the "A" refers to
   a. actions.
   b. alternatives.
   c. antecedents.
   d. acquisition.

2. Applied to the anxiety disorders, the behavioral technique called *in vivo* exposure
   a. relies on operant conditioning principles.
   b. involves imaging a feared stimulus.
   c. rests on the principle of habituation.
   d. is considered a type of rational-emotive therapy.

3. According to Albert Ellis, self-downing
   a. is defined as being unkind to or critical of others for performing poorly.
   b. does not interfere with healthy functioning.
   c. constitutes rational, logical thinking.
   d. is defined as being critical of oneself for performing poorly or being rejected.

4. Someone who magnifies the negative aspects of something while filtering out the positive is engaging in the common cognitive distortion known as
   a. *control beliefs of catastrophic exaggeration.*
   b. *mental filter.*
   c. *dichotomous thinking and mind reading.*
   d. *low frustration tolerance.*

5. Behavioral, cognitive, and cognitive–behavior therapies all
   a. focus on maladaptive behaviors.
   b. use relaxation techniques, as well as role playing.
   c. focus on symptom relief as a goal in and of itself.
   d. rely on token economies to mold social behavior.

Insight-Oriented Therapies

6. Psychodynamic therapy differs from psychoanalysis in that psychodynamic therapy
   a. is more intense.
   b. is less common today.
   c. has an increased emphasis on sexual drives.
   d. has a decreased emphasis on aggressive drives.

7. How can the goal of psychodynamic therapy be described?
   a. It differs from that of psychoanalysis.
   b. The goal is to have the patient act on unconscious impulses.
   c. The goal is to bring conscious impulses and conflicts into awareness.
   d. None of the above statements are true.

8. Psychodynamic therapists rely on interpretation, a technique in which
   a. the therapist deciphers the patient's words and behaviors, assigning unconscious motivations to them.
   b. the patient refuses to cooperate with the therapist and instead engages in behaviors such as the outright refusal to comply with a therapist's request.
   c. the patient says whatever comes to mind, and the train of thoughts reveals the patient's issues and ways of dealing with them.
   d. the therapist examines the content of dreams to gain access to the conscious.

9. The client-centered therapist strives to
   a. offer analyses to the client.
   b. continually show the client that he or she is inherently worthy as a human being.
   c. provide conditional positive regard, as well as accurate criticisms of the client's behavior.
   d. parrot the clients' words and phrases inaccurately.

10. Psychodynamic and client-centered therapies have in common
    a. the goal of unblocking the person's potential for growth by decreasing incongruence.
    b. a focus on unconscious conflict.
    c. their use of insight.
    d. the techniques of transference and genuineness toward the person.

Biomedical Therapies

11. Neuroleptic medication
    a. cures schizophrenia.
    b. treats tardive dyskinesia.
    c. has an effect on the positive symptoms of schizophrenia.
    d. increases the amount of free serotonin and dopamine available in the brain.

12. Tricyclic antidepressants (TCAs)
    a. are the only effective antidepressant medications readily available.
    b. include monoamine oxidase inhibitors.
    c. include the drug tyramine.
    d. can take weeks to work.

13. St. John's Wort
    a. is a type of serotonin/norepinephrine reuptake inhibitor (SNRI).
    b. can be effective in treating mild to moderately severe depression.
    c. stabilizes mood better than does lithium.
    d. blocks substance P, thereby altering norepinephrine and serotonin.

14. Benzodiazepines
    a. may cause kidney or gastrointestinal problems as well as dry mouth.
    b. take 10 days or more to build up to an effective level.
    c. are potentially lethal when taken with alcohol.
    d. cannot cause dependence.

15. Electroconvulsive therapy
    a. is not a recommended treatment for schizophrenia.
    b. is particularly helpful in treating psychotic depression and manic episodes of bipolar disorder.
    c. causes an uncontrolled brain seizure through the use of an electromagnetic coil placed on the scalp.
    d. in recent years has been more frequently administered to those in publicly funded hospitals than to affluent patients.

Other Forms of Treatment

16. Therapists conducting family therapy
    a. most commonly use a psychodynamic theoretical orientation.
    b. consider the client the "patient" that is to be treated.
    c. refer to the system (the couple, the family) as the "identified patient."
    d. often define "family" as those who think of themselves or function as a family.

17. The technique referred to as *paradoxical intention*
    a. is unrelated to the technique called *prescribing the symptom.*
    b. involves the therapist conveying his or her understanding of clients' feelings and wishes.
    c. encourages a behavior that seems contradictory to the desired goal.
    d. occurs when the therapist offers a new way of conceptualizing the problem.

18. Self-help groups
    a. that use the 12-step approach include the National Depressive and Manic Depressive Association.
    b. do not benefit those who are not religious.
    c. do not usually have a clinically trained leader.
    d. problematically increase feelings of isolation and shame.

19. Therapists who practice technical eclecticism
    a. use specific techniques that may benefit a particular client, without regard for an overarching theory.
    b. use techniques from different theoretical orientations with an overarching theory of how the integrated techniques will be used to achieve the goals of treatment.
    c. usually identify their work as exclusively psychodynamic or behavioral.
    d. rarely incorporate new techniques based on research findings.

20. Which of the following is true of research studies using manual-based treatment?
    a. They often include people whose symptoms do not meet the exact criteria for a disorder.
    b. They often exclude people who may simultaneously have more than one diagnosis.
    c. They often include people who may simultaneously have more than one diagnosis.
    d. None of the above statements are true.

Which Therapy Works Best?

21. The allegiance effect
    a. is a type of outcome research.
    b. states that patients who believe in the therapy that they receive tend to fare better.
    c. states that researchers of a particular orientation tend to find evidence supporting that orientation.
    d. is one of more than 400 types of psychotherapy currently available, most of which rest on well constructed and replicated research.

22. In the Treatment of Depression Collaborative Research Program (TDCRP),
    a. those who were more depressed were put into the medication group.
    b. inclusion was restricted to those who met the exact criteria for major depressive disorder, without any other disorder.
    c. all therapists provided unstandardized forms of treatment.
    d. self-defined CBT therapists focused on relationship issues, and self-defined IPT therapists gave concrete suggestions.

23. Studying the treatment of anxiety disorders, researchers have found that
    a. CBT provides less long-term relief of symptoms than medication.
    b. in the treatment of panic disorder, CBT does a better job of preventing symptom relapse.
    c. in the treatment of OCD, exposure with response prevention is not nearly as helpful as medication.
    d. in the treatment of social phobias, the effects of MAOIs continue after treatment ends, in contrast to CBT.

24. Several caveats are in order when interpreting the results of the *Consumer Reports* survey, including that
    a. very few respondents had schizophrenia.
    b. many respondents had bipolar disorder.
    c. the results were based on controlled studies.
    d. the results were based on methodologically rigorous studies.

25. Difficulties that surround the evaluation of the effectiveness of psychodynamic therapies include that
    a. there is a wealth of research to evaluate.
    b. insight is not objectively measurable, at least not yet.
    c. psychodynamic therapists have proved the accuracy of their interpretations.
    d. these therapies work best with patients who cannot articulate their feelings.

Social Cognition: Thinking About People

1. *Other-enhancement strategies* refers to
   a. the process of developing impressions of others.
   b. a person's efforts to control the type of impression he or she creates.
   c. making yourself look good, perhaps by appearing particularly well groomed or knowledgeable about particular topics.
   d. eliciting a positive mood or reaction from another person by asking for advice or being particularly attentive.

2. Research using the Implicit Association Test (IAT) has revealed that
   a. the IAT assesses deep, unconscious attitudes.
   b. although some studies have found IAT scores to predict relevant behaviors, others do not.
   c. even when people are motivated to reduce a negative attitude, they cannot compensate for their biases when taking the IAT.
   d. implicit associations are not readily shifted.

3. Cognitive dissonance
   a. reduces arousal.
   b. occurs with every inconsistency and may or may not reduce arousal, depending on the circumstances.
   c. results when two behaviors are inconsistent.
   d. results when two attitudes are inconsistent.

4. Studying persuasion, researchers have found that
   a. the mere exposure effect can change attitudes through the central route.
   b. fast speakers are generally more persuasive than slow speakers.
   c. people who are perceived as honest surprisingly are not perceived as more persuasive.
   d. if you are not paying full attention to an attempt at persuasion, you are more likely to be persuaded by a rational argument than by a simplistic argument.

5. If a researcher gives you two sets of stimuli that you like almost to the same degree and requires you to choose which one you like better,
   a. you will engage in reactance.
   b. you will later report that you like the two sets equally.
   c. you will later report that you like the one you chose even more than you did at the outset.
   d. you will later report that you like the one you did not choose much more than the one you did choose.

6. Which of the following is true about stereotypes?
   a. They can be useful shortcuts.
   b. They are often incorrect.
   c. They represent a type of schema.
   d. All of the above are true.

Social Behavior: Interacting With People

7. Findings of what constitutes attractiveness
   a. are consistent across cultures.
   b. indicate that people prefer men's faces that are "masculinized."
   c. suggest that women prefer men with a small chin.
   d. suggest that men prefer women without prominent cheekbones.

8. Those who have an anxious–ambivalent attachment style
   a. are not worried about the possibility of the loss of a relationship.
   b. structure their daily lives so as to avoid closeness.
   c. want but simultaneously fear a relationship.
   d. constitute about 45% of Americans.

9. Social exchange theory proposes that
   a. characteristics associated with reproduction are particularly likely to have been shaped by natural selection.
   b. individuals act to maximize the gains and minimize the losses in their relationships.
   c. love relationships are in part genetically determined.
   d. what is deemed an attractive body type changes with time.

10. Someone who is using the door-in-the-face technique might
    a. first make an insignificant request, and if compliance occurs, follow up with a larger request.
    b. first get someone to make an agreement and then increase the cost of that agreement.
    c. begin by making a very large request and then when it is denied, as expected, make a smaller request.
    d. begin by making a polite request, then follow up with an order.

11. Participants acting as teachers in Milgram's studies were less likely to obey when
    a. the experimenter gave face-to-face instructions, rather than telephoning his commands.
    b. a college student, rather than an older, white-coated experimenter, gave the order.
    c. they were female, compared to male.
    d. they did not see the learners while they were being shocked.

12. Social compensation usually occurs when
    a. a sense of importance and responsibility is instilled in each person.
    b. group members know that individual as well as group performance will be evaluated.
    c. some members of the group see the task to be done as important but don't expect that other members will pull their weight.
    d. responsibility for an outcome is spread among members of the group and diversity brings decreased innovation and flexibility.

13. What is the usual practice at the conclusion of a study that uses deception today?
  a. Investigators are sometimes encouraged to explain to participants the nature of the study, but not the reasons for deception.
  b. Participants are always required to explain to investigators their thoughts about the nature of the study.
  c. Investigators are prohibited from explaining to participants the nature of the study.
  d. None of the above statements are true.

14. Milgram
  a. expected participants to be willing to shock learners at higher "voltage" levels.
  b. continued to perform variants of his study after he knew the results of his first study.
  c. expected to cause psychological distress.
  d. did not continue to perform variants of his study after he knew the results of his first study.

15. Today, what is required for deception to be permitted in research?
  a. The participants will not be harmed.
  b. Important knowledge will be gained.
  c. The deception is minimal.
  d. All of the above are required to receive approval for a study that uses deception.

ANSWERS

Psychology: Yesterday and Today

1. c	6. d	11. d	16. d
2. d	7. c	12. c	17. d
3. d	8. a	13. c	18. c
4. a	9. b	14. b	19. c
5. d	10. d	15. d	20. b

The Research Process: How We Find Things Out

1. a	6. c	11. c	16. c
2. c	7. d	12. d	17. c
3. d	8. b	13. c	18. d
4. b	9. c	14. c	19. c
5. c	10. d	15. d	20. d

The Biology of Mind and Behavior

1. c	6. b	11. d	16. a
2. b	7. d	12. c	17. c
3. a	8. d	13. b	18. b
4. d	9. b	14. a	19. c
5. b	10. b	15. c	20. d

Sensation and Perception: How the World Enters the Mind

1. a	5. d	9. c	13. c
2. d	6. c	10. b	14. c
3. c	7. d	11. d	15. b
4. c	8. b	12. a	

Consciousness

1. b	5. d	9. c	13. c
2. c	6. d	10. d	14. c
3. d	7. b	11. d	15. b
4. c	8. d	12. a	

Learning

1. c	5. a	9. d	13. c
2. d	6. c	10. b	14. d
3. b	7. c	11. b	15. c
4. c	8. a	12. c	

Memory: Living With Yesterday

1. d	6. a	11. b	16. c
2. d	7. c	12. a	17. a
3. a	8. c	13. b	18. a
4. b	9. c	14. d	19. d
5. c	10. d	15. c	20. c

Language and Thinking

1. b	6. b	11. d	16. d
2. c	7. c	12. b	17. d
3. c	8. b	13. a	18. d
4. a	9. d	14. b	19. a
5. b	10. d	15. a	20. c

Types of Intelligence: What Does It Mean to be Smart?

1. c	5. d	9. b	13. a
2. d	6. c	10. d	14. d
3. b	7. c	11. b	15. a
4. a	8. d	12. c	

Emotion and Motivation: Feeling and Striving

1. c	6. d	11. d	16. b
2. a	7. b	12. c	17. b
3. c	8. c	13. c	18. d
4. b	9. a	14. b	19. a
5. c	10. d	15. c	20. c

Personality: Vive la Différence!

1. d	6. a	11. c	16. a
2. d	7. d	12. c	17. a
3. a	8. a	13. d	18. c
4. b	9. b	14. b	19. d
5. c	10. b	15. d	20. c

Psychology Over the Life Span: Growing Up, Growing Older, Growing Wiser

1. a	6. b	11. c	16. b
2. a	7. d	12. d	17. b
3. b	8. a	13. b	18. c
4. d	9. d	14. c	19. c
5. c	10. d	15. d	20. a

Stress, Health, and Coping

1. d	5. b	9. c	13. a
2. c	6. c	10. b	14. b
3. d	7. a	11. a	15. c
4. a	8. c	12. d	

Psychological Disorders

1. a	10. c	19. d	28. d
2. d	11. d	20. c	29. d
3. b	12. d	21. b	30. b
4. b	13. b	22. d	31. d
5. d	14. c	23. b	32. d
6. c	15. b	24. c	33. d
7. b	16. c	25. b	34. c
8. a	17. c	26. c	35. b
9. c	18. b	27. b	

Treatment					Social Psychology			
1. c	8. a	15. b	22. b		1. d	5. c	9. b	13. d
2. c	9. b	16. d	23. b		2. b	6. d	10. c	14. b
3. d	10. c	17. c	24. a		3. d	7. a	11. b	15. d
4. b	11. c	18. c	25. b		4. b	8. c	12. c	
5. c	12. d	19. a						
6. d	13. b	20. b						
7. d	14. c	21. c						